EYEWITNESS TRAVEL

GREAT BRITAIN

MAIN CONTRIBUTOR: MICHAEL LEAPMAN

2007

DK

LONDON, NEW YORK,
MELBOURNE, MUNICH AND DELHI
www.dk.com

ART EDITOR Stephen Bere
PROJECT EDITOR Marian Broderick
EDITORS Carey Combe, Sara Harper, Elaine Harries,
Kim Inglis, Ella Milroy, Andrew Szudek, Nia Williams
US EDITOR Mary Sutherland
DESIGNERS Susan Blackburn, Elly King,
Colin Loughrey, Andy Wilkinson

CONTRIBUTORS
Josie Barnard, Christopher Catling,
Juliet Clough, Lindsay Hunt, Polly Phillimore,
Martin Symington, Roger Thomas

MAPS
Jane Hanson, Phil Rose, Jennifer Skelley (Lovell Johns Ltd)
Gary Bowes (Era-Maptec Ltd)

PHOTOGRAPHERS
Joe Cornish, Paul Harris, Rob Reichenfeld, Kim Sayer

ILLUSTRATORS
Richard Draper, Jared Gilby (Kevin Jones Assocs), Paul Guest,
Roger Hutchins, Chris Orr & Assocs, Maltings Partnership,
Ann Winterbotham, John Woodcock

Reproduced by Colourscan (Singapore)
Printed and bound by South China Printing Co. Ltd., China

First American edition 1995
07 08 09 10 9 8 7 6 5 4 3 2 1
Published in the United States by DK Publishing, Inc.,
375 Hudson Street, New York, NY 10014

**Reprinted with revisions 1996, 1997, 1999, 2000, 2001,
2002, 2003, 2004, 2005, 2006, 2007**

Copyright © 1995, 2007 Dorling Kindersley Limited, London

Published in Great Britain by Dorling Kindersley Limited.

ISSN 1542-1554
ISBN 978-07566-1542-0

THROUGHOUT THIS BOOK, FLOORS ARE REFERRED TO IN ACCORDANCE
WITH EUROPEAN USAGE, I.E., THE "FIRST FLOOR" IS ONE FLIGHT UP.

Front cover main image: Merton College, Oxford

CONTENTS

HOW TO USE
THIS GUIDE **6**

A 14th-century illustration
of two knights jousting

INTRODUCING
GREAT BRITAIN

Beefeater at the Tower of London

LONDON

Eilean Donan Castle on Loch Duich in the Scottish Highlands

Jacobean "Old House" in Hereford

HOW TO USE THIS GUIDE

This guide helps you to get the most from your holidays in Great Britain. It provides both detailed practical information and expert recommendations. *Introducing Great Britain* maps the country and sets it in its historical and cultural context. The six regional chapters, plus *London*, describe important sights, using maps, pictures and illustrations. Features cover topics from houses and famous gardens to sport. Hotel, restaurant, and pub recommendations can be found in *Travellers' Needs*. The *Survival Guide* has practical information on everything from transport to personal safety.

LONDON

The centre of London has been divided into four sightseeing areas. Each has its own chapter, which opens with a list of the sights described. The last section, *Further Afield*, covers the most attractive suburbs. All sights are numbered and plotted on an area map. The information for each sight follows the map's numerical order, making sights easy to locate within the chapter.

Sights at a Glance lists the chapter's sights by category: Historic Streets and Buildings; Museums and Galleries; Churches and Cathedrals; Shops; Parks and Gardens.

All pages relating to London have red thumb tabs.

A locator map shows where you are in relation to other areas of the city centre.

1 Area Map
For easy reference, the sights are numbered and located on a map. Sights in the city centre are also marked on the Street Finder *on pages 127–47.*

2 Street-by-Street Map
This gives a bird's-eye view of the key areas in each chapter.

Stars indicate the sights that no visitor should miss.

A suggested route for a walk is shown in red.

3 Detailed information
The sights in London are described individually. Addresses, telephone numbers, opening hours, admission charges, tours and wheelchair access are also provided, as well as public transport links.

1 Introduction
The landscape, history and character of each region is outlined here, showing how the area has developed over the centuries and what it has to offer the visitor today.

GREAT BRITAIN AREA BY AREA
Apart from London, Great Britain has been divided into 14 regions, each of which has a separate chapter. The most interesting towns and places to visit have been numbered on a *Regional Map*.

Each area of Great Britain can be identified quickly by its colour coding, shown on the inside front cover.

2 Regional Map
This shows the main road network and gives an illustrated overview of the whole region. All entries are numbered and there are also useful tips on getting around the region by car, train and other forms of transport.

3 Detailed information
All the important sights, towns and other places to visit are described individually. They are listed in order, following the numbering on the Regional Map. Within each entry, there is detailed information on important buildings and other sights.

Story boxes explore related topics.

For all the top sights, a Visitors' Checklist provides the practical information you need to plan your visit.

4 The top sights
These are given one or more full pages. Three-dimensional illustrations reveal the interiors of historic buildings. Interesting town and city centres are given street-by-street maps, featuring individual sights.

INTRODUCING
GREAT BRITAIN

DISCOVERING GREAT BRITAIN

Each one of Great Britain's counties, that have grown out of kingdoms, principalities, shires, fiefs, boroughs, and parishes, has its own special flavour. This derives from Britain's landscape, its resources and its history, all of which have shaped its peoples, too.

Queen's Life Guard on Parade

There has always been something of a divide between the industrial North and the wealthier South. Regional pride is very strong. Vernacular architecture marks each region, and there is a rich variety of scenery to be found in every corner of this green and bounteous island.

A view of Big Ben and The British Airways London Eye

LONDON

- A ride on the British Airways London Eye
- Majestic parks
- World-class museums

Britain's capital can be enjoyed in all weathers. So many buildings, from **Big Ben** (see p77) to the **Tower of London** (see pp118–19), are emblematic of the city. To get an overview take a bus, riverboat or the **British**

Airways London Eye (seep81); visit the West End for the most exciting shops, or stroll through its lovely parks. The **National Gallery** (see p82–3) is one of the finest art museums in the world, the **British Museum** (see pp106–7) and **Victoria & Albert Museum** (see pp98–9) are storehouses of treasures while **Tate Modern** (see p121) has set a standard for contemporary art.

THE DOWNS AND CHANNEL COAST

- Great days out from London
- Fairytale castles
- Brighton's brilliant sea front

This is "The Garden of England", green and rural, with rolling Downs. Many places in this corner of the country are accessible on a day trip from London; **Hampton Court** (see p173) and **Leeds Castle** (see p189) are favourite excursions. Many estates have connections with great

figures from history: Winston Churchill's **Chartwell** (see p188), Queen Victoria's **Osborne** (see p168) on the Isle of Wight and J.M.W. Turner's **Petworth** (see p172), an antiques-hunters' paradise. Ancient cathedrals rise from **Chichester** (see pp171), **Winchester** (see pp170–1) and **Canterbury** (see pp186–7), which has many tales to tell. Breezy resorts dot the coast. The liveliest is **Brighton** (see pp174–9), known as "London-on-Sea", with its famous Lanes, Palace Pier and seafront promenade.

Punting on the River Cam past King's College Chapel, Cambridge

EAST ANGLIA

- A punt in Cambridge
- Magnificent Ely Cathedral
- A day at the races

This part of the country grew wealthy on the wool trade and its merchants built fabulous half-timbered houses and pretty towns such as **Lavenham** (see p206). In the charming university town of Cambridge (see p210–15) try

The promenade and Palace Pier, Brighton, Sussex

◁ *Salisbury Cathedral: from the meadows by John Constable (1776–1837)*

punting on the Backs with the students or, for a less vigourous outing, admire **King's College Chapel** *(see p212–13)*. For another cultural high, visit **Ely Cathedral** *(see pp194–5)*. Spend a day at the races at **Newmarket** *(see p207)*, or visit **Aldeburgh** *(see pp202–203)* during its prestigious annual music festival. The ports on the lovely coast provide seafood for your table.

THAMES VALLEY

- **Attractive riverside pubs**
- **Oxford's dreaming spires**
- **Imposing Blenheim Palace**

The River Thames has long been a pleasure ground. The riverside, from London's outer suburbs to **Windsor** *(see pp235–7)*, **Oxford** *(see pp222–7)* and beyond, has many appealing waterside pubs and restaurants located in attractive towns. Boats can be hired, and the annual rowing regatta at **Henley-on-Thames** *(see p63 and p66)* is the height of the summer season. No wonder that the song of Britain's most exclusive private school, Eton *(see p235)*, which is located by the river, is *The Eton Boating Song*. **Windsor Castle** *(see pp236–7)* is undoubtedly a main draw, easily reached in a day trip from London, as are the beautiful colleges of **Oxford University** *(see pp226–7)*. Not far away are other historic places to visit, including the Churchill family home at **Blenheim Palace** *(see*

Stonehenge, Wiltshire, Great Britain's famous prehistoric monument

pp228–9), the Duke of Bedford's **Woburn Abbey** *(see p230)* and **Stowe** *(see p230)*, which has one of the most magnificent gardens in England.

WESSEX

- **Mysterious Stonehenge**
- **Cheddar cheese and Taunton Cider**
- **Fine architecture in Bath and Salisbury**

The former kingdom of the West Saxons echoes with history and legends. Here are some of the most important Neolithic sites in the country, including the mysterious and magnificent **Stonehenge** *(see pp262–3)*. This is the country of good living, with Cheddar cheese from around the Cheddar Gorge, and Somerset cider. The Georgian spa town of **Bath** *(see pp258–61)* makes an excellent centre to explore the region. There are two coasts – in the north on the Bristol Channel and in the south on the English channel where **Poole** *(see pp270–1)* is a great yachting centre. Bath, **Wells** *(see pp252–3)* and **Salisbury** *(see pp264–5)* all have outstanding cathedrals. There are wild animals at **Longleat** *(see p266)*, wild landscapes on **Exmoor National Park** *(see pp250–1)*, while the **Glastonbury** *(see pp253)* music festival attracts fans in their thousands.

DEVON AND CORNWALL

- **Surfing fit for champions**
- **Seafood and cream teas**
- **Fabulous gardens**

Britain's best beaches are in the West Country, some of which have high cliffs and waves worthy of champion surfers. Its fishing villages have long attracted artists, in particular St Ives, where the **Tate St Ives** gallery *(see p277)* can be visited. Seafood is plentiful, and rich pasture-lands brings dairy ice-cream and cream teas. Seafaring is a way of life, as the **National Maritime Museum Cornwall** *(see pp280–1)* in Falmouth attests. **Bodmin Moor** *(see pp284–5)* and **Dartmoor** *(see p81)* present an untamed wilderness but some fine gardens are here, too, including the **Eden Project** *(see pp282–3)*.

A view of Blenheim Palace, Woodstock, Oxfordshire

Eden Project, Cornwall, a garden for the 21st century

THE HEART OF ENGLAND

- Shakespeare's birthplace
- Typically English Cotswold villages
- Half-timbered border towns

There is a great mix of attractions in this region where the Industrial Revolution began *(see pp314–15)*. The most popular sites are **Warwick Castle** *(see pp322–3)* and Shakespeare's birthplace in **Stratford-upon-Avon** *(see pp324–5)*. Cotswold villages built of golden limestone are quintessentially English. Other lovely rural spots include the Malvern Hills and the Wye Vallley. Attractive architecture distinguishes the half-timbered Welsh border towns including the city of **Chester** *(see pp310–11)*.

Anne Hathaway's cottage, Stratford-upon-Avon, Warwickshire

EAST MIDLANDS

- Chatsworth, a fine country house
- Great walking in the Peak District
- Buxton spa and opera house

One of the most impressive country houses, **Chatsworth** *(see pp334–5)*, is a high spot of this region. It sits at the edge of the **Peak District** *(see pp338–9)*, a popular area for walking. There are several attractive towns such as **Buxton** *(see p334)*, a spa town with an opera house while **Lincoln** *(see pp340–1)* has medieval buildings and a fine cathedral.

Mist on Rydal Water, Lake District, Cumbria

LANCASHIRE AND THE LAKES

- England at its most picturesque
- Liverpool, maritime city of Empire
- Manchester, capital of the North

The **Lake District** *(see pp352–68)* is where walking as an activity rather than a chore began, and you will see why when you encounter the stunning scenery of fells and lakes. Serious walkers put on their waterproofs and boots, while Sunday strollers hire row boats, or look in at Dove Cottage, where the poets William and Dorothy Wordsworth lived. To the south is **Liverpool** *(see pp354–5)*, a Unesco World Heritage city, with wonderful architecture and great art galleries. **Blackpool** *(see p371)* is the main resort, know for its illuminations. Inland is **Manchester** *(see pp372–5)* England's second largest city.

YORKSHIRE AND THE HUMBER REGION

- Haunting abbey ruins
- The Brontë sisters' dramatic moors
- The ancient city of York

Yorkshire is known for its striking moors, which the literary Brontë sisters of **Haworth** *(see p412)* knew so well. It is also known for its great abbeys, such as **Fountains** *(see pp390–1)*, **Rievaulx** *(see p393)* and **Whitby** *(see p396)*, which were reduced to haunting ruins after the English church broke from Rome. **York Minster** *(see pp406–407)* remains the most important church in the north and the ancient town is worth exploring. Sculptures by Henry Moore grace **Yorkshire Sculpture Park** *(see p413)*.

Whitby harbour and St Mary's Church, Yorkshire

NORTHUMBRIA

- The trail of Celtic Christianity
- Life as it was lived, in Beamish Open Air Museum
- Hadrian's Wall from coast to coast

A boat trip to the **Farne Islands** *(see p418)* off Lindisfarne is the starting point to unravelling early Celtic Christianity, a journey that can be followed as far as **Durham Cathedral** *(see pp428–9)*. The **Beamish Open Air Museum** *(see pp424–5)*, which re-creates life in the northeast in the 19th century, makes a great family day out. Castles on Northumberland's coast were built to withstand Viking attack, but it is **Hadrian's Wall** *(see pp422–3)*, erected by the Romans to keep out the Scots, that is particularly impressive.

NORTH WALES

- **Wild Snowdonia National Park**
- **Narrow-gauge railways**
- **Stunning medieval castles**

This is the part of Wales, where Welsh is commonly spoken, and the annual Eisteddfod literary festival is held. Its wildness is captured around Snowdon, the highest mountain in England and Wales. The centre for exploring **Snowdonia National Park** *(see pp450–1)* is Llanberis from where a narrow-gauge railway runs to the top. Another former slate-quarry railway takes passengers up from the coast at Porthmadog near **Portmeirion** *(see p454–5)*. Medieval castles keep watch at **Harlech** *(see p454)*, **Caernarfon** *(see p444)* and **Conwy** *(see p438 and p447)*.

SOUTH AND MID WALES

- **Pony trekking in the hills**
- **Scenic coastal walks**
- **Hay-on-Wye literary festival**

This is a region to tour by car, to go walking or pony trekking, across mountains like the **Brecon Beacons** *(see pp468–9)*. The roads are emptier than England's and the valleys are green and lush. The coast has some delightful ports and long-established resorts. The most attractive are around the **Gower Peninsula** *(see p466)*

Cliffs of the Pembrokeshire Coast National Park, South Wales

and in Pembrokeshire in the south west where there is the diminutive **St David's Cathedral** *(see pp464–5)*. Wales is known for its male voice choirs – as well as its men of letters – Hay-on-Wye *(see p461)* hosts an annual literary festival.

SCOTTISH LOWLANDS

- **Glasgow, dynamic city of art**
- **Medieval Edinburgh and its Georgian New Town**
- **Magnificent abbeys and castles**

The capital of **Edinburgh** *(see pp504–11)* and **Glasgow** *(see pp516–21)* are Scotland's dazzling cities, both full of interest and worth several

days' exploration. Charles Rennie Mackintosh left his Art Nouveau mark on Glasgow, while thousands of hopeful performers attempt to find fame in Edinburgh each August at the famous festival. The capital's high points are **Edinburgh Castle** *(see pp506–7)*, keeper of the Scottish Crown jewels and the **Palace of Holyroodhouse** *(see p510)*, the Queen's official Scottish residence. Castles abound in the Lowlands, notably the Renaissance gem **Stirling** *(see pp497–8)*.

SCOTTISH HIGHLANDS AND ISLANDS

- **Mountain climbing and skiing**
- **The castles of Royal Deeside**
- **Remote, idyllic hills**

This is as wild as Britain gets: mountainous, heather-clad and dramatically remote, drifting into offshore islands. You may well see eagles and stags, while on the west coast seals swoop in on the beautiful shores. **Aberdeen** *(see pp538–40)* is the starting point for a tour of the castles of **Royal Deeside** *(see p540–1)*. Climb mountains, go skiing in Aviemore in the **Cairngorms** *(see pp544–5)*, follow the whisky trails and take a ferry to the Western Isles.

A view of Edinburgh Castle, Scotland

Putting Great Britain on the Map

Lying in northwestern Europe, Great Britain is bounded by the Atlantic Ocean, the North Sea and the English Channel. The island's landscape and climate are varied, and it is this variety that even today affects the pattern of settlement. The remote shores of the West Country peninsula and the inhospitable mountains of Scotland and Wales are less populated than the relatively flat and fertile Midlands and Southeast, where the vast majority of the country's 58 million people live. Due to this population density, the south is today the most built-up part of the country.

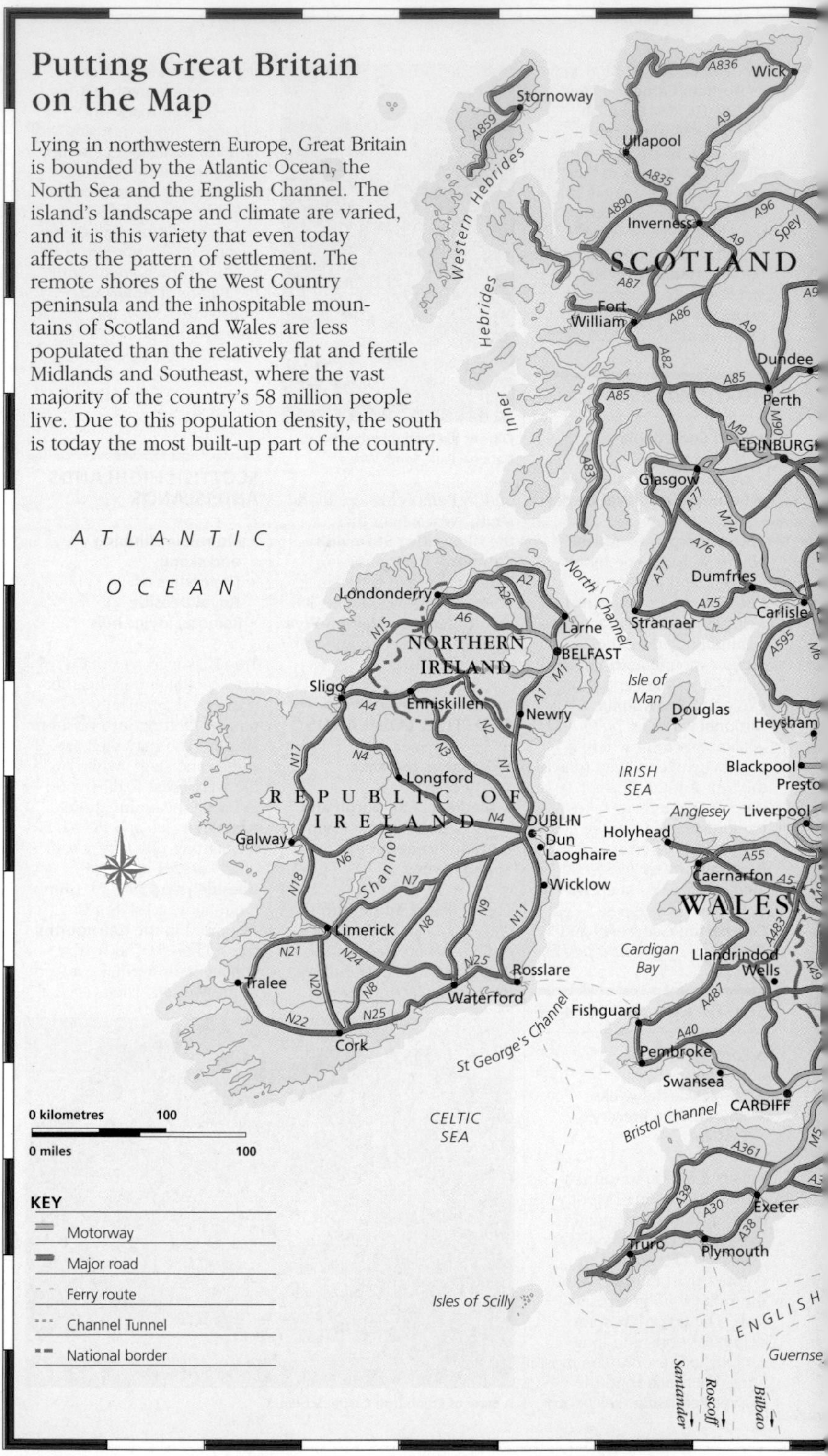

SCOTLAND

Wick
Stornoway
Ullapool
Inverness
A836
A859
A9
A835
A890
A96
Spey
Fort William
A87
A86
A9
Dundee
A82
A85
Perth
A85
EDINBURGH
Glasgow
A77
M74
M90
A76
Dumfries
A77
A75
Carlisle
Stranraer
A595
M6

Western Hebrides

Hebrides

Inner

ATLANTIC
OCEAN

Londonderry
A2
A26
NORTHERN IRELAND
N15
A6
Larne
BELFAST
Sligo
Enniskillen
A4
A1 M1
Newry
N2
North Channel

Isle of Man
Douglas
Heysham

REPUBLIC OF IRELAND
N17
N4
Longford
N3
N1
N4
DUBLIN
Dun Laoghaire
Galway
N6
Wicklow
N18
Shannon
N7
N9
N11
Limerick
N8
N21
N24
N25
Rosslare
Tralee
N20
N8
Waterford
N22
N25
Cork

IRISH SEA

Blackpool
Preston
Liverpool
Anglesey
Holyhead
A55
Caernarfon A5

WALES

Cardigan Bay
Llandrindod Wells
A487
A40
Pembroke
Swansea
CARDIFF
A361
M5
Bristol Channel

St George's Channel
Fishguard

CELTIC SEA

Isles of Scilly

Truro
A39
A30
A38
Exeter
Plymouth

ENGLISH

Santander
Roscoff
Bilbao
Guernsey

| 0 kilometres | 100 |
| 0 miles | 100 |

KEY

=== Motorway

── Major road

- - - Ferry route

···· Channel Tunnel

-- National border

Unst

*Shetland
Islands*

Mainland *Yell*

Foula

Westray *Sanday*

Mainland *Stronsay*

Stromness

Hoy *Kirkwall* *Orkney
Islands*

A836

Wick

A9

Europe

*Great Britain is situated in the northwest
corner of Europe. Its nearest neighbours
are Ireland to the west, and the Netherlands,
Belgium and France across the Channel.
Denmark, Norway and Sweden are also
easily accessible.*

EUROPE

NORWAY FINLAND

SWEDEN ESTONIA

DENMARK RUSSIAN
FED.

LATVIA

LITHUANIA

RUSSIAN
FED. BELORUSSIA

NETHERLANDS POLAND

London GERMANY

BELGIUM LUXEMBOURG UKRAINE

CZECH
REPUBLIC SLOVAKIA

FRANCE AUSTRIA HUNGARY

SWITZERLAND SLOVENIA ROMANIA

CROATIA

ITALY BOSNIA AND
HERZEGOVINA SERBIA AND
MONTENEGRO BULGARIA

MACEDONIA

ALBANIA GREECE

SPAIN

PORTUGAL

ALGERIA TUNISIA

Shetland and Orkney Islands

*These islands form the northern-
most part of Great Britain, with the
Shetlands lying six degrees south
of the Arctic Circle. There are
transport links to the mainland.*

*Shetland
Islands* *Lerwick*

*Fair
Isle*

Aberdeen

Shetland and Orkney Islands

N O R T H

S E A

*Göteborg
Esbjerg
Hamburg*

Aberdeen

A1

A696

Newcastle
upon Tyne

A69

Sunderland

A66 A1(M)

Swale

A165

A1(M) Leeds York

Bradford M62 Kingston upon Hull

A165

M62 Huddersfield

M180

Manchester Grimsby

Sheffield

A6 A16

Stoke-
on-Trent M1

ENGLAND

Derby Nottingham

A47 Norwich

Peterborough

A11

A14 A12

Birmingham A1(M) M11

Warwick Northampton Cambridge

M40 A14 Ipswich

Stratford-upon- M11 Felixstowe

Avon Harlow Harwich

Gloucester A12

M5

Oxford A1(M)

Bristol Windsor M2

Bath M3 LONDON Ramsgate

M25 Canterbury

Salisbury M23 Dover

A303 A36 Folkestone

Southampton Brighton Newhaven

Bournemouth Portsmouth

Isle of
Wight

CHANNEL

Cherbourg

St Malo

Jersey

N13

N175 Caen

N158

N138 A13

A13

Dieppe

N27 Amiens

D901

N1

Le N15

Havre Rouen

N14 A1

F R A N C E

A26

A4

Reims

PARIS

A4

Groningen A7

A31

A7 A28

A31 N37

N E T H E R L A N D S Zwolle

AMSTERDAM A6

A1

The Utrecht A50

Hague Arnhem A31

A15 A12

Rotterdam A3

A59 A57 Duisburg

Eindhoven A67 Essen

A58 A61

Zeebrugge A2

Ostend N9 A14 Antwerp Cologne

Dunkirk BRUSSELS A3 Aachen A4

Calais A10

Boulogne A25 Lille A16 **B E L G I U M** Liege

A26 A2 A15

G E R M A N Y

A26

A1

LUXEMBOURG

LUXEMBOURG A4

A1

Metz

A31

Strait of Dover

Regional Great Britain: London, the South, the Midlands and Wales

Great Britain has airline connections with most cities in the world. London is the main transport hub with three major international airports, including Heathrow, the world's busiest. Southern England, Britain's most populous area, is divided, within this book, into four regions – Southeast England, the West Country, Wales and the Midlands – with a separate chapter for London. Road and rail links to the North and Scotland (*see pp18–19*) are plentiful, as are links between all main towns.

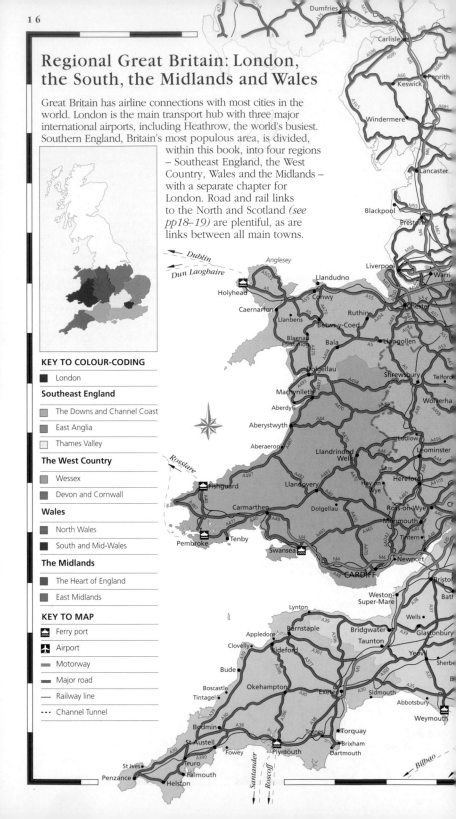

KEY TO COLOUR-CODING

- London

Southeast England
- The Downs and Channel Coast
- East Anglia
- Thames Valley

The West Country
- Wessex
- Devon and Cornwall

Wales
- North Wales
- South and Mid-Wales

The Midlands
- The Heart of England
- East Midlands

KEY TO MAP
- Ferry port
- Airport
- Motorway
- Major road
- Railway line
- Channel Tunnel

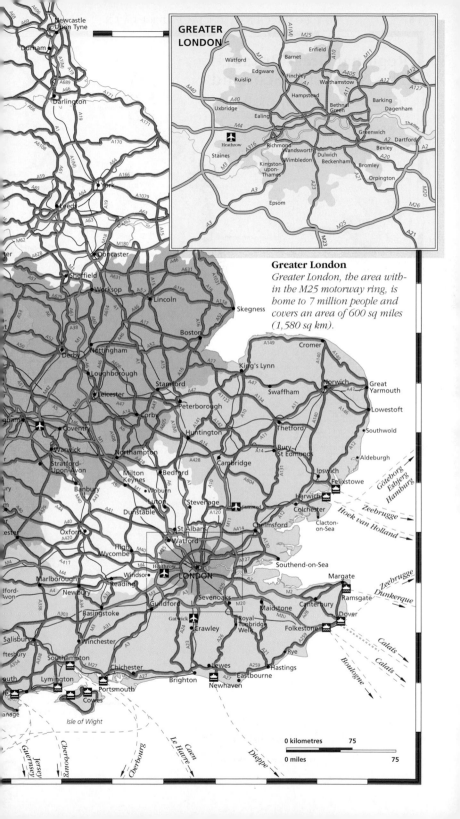

Watford
Enfield
Barnet
Edgware
Finchley
Ruislip
Walthamstow
Hampstead
Uxbridge
Bethnal
Green
Barking
Ealing
Dagenham
Thames
Heathrow
Greenwich
Dartford
Richmond
Wandsworth
Bexley
Staines
Dulwich
Beckenham
Kingston-
upon-
Thames
Wimbledon
Bromley
Orpington
Epsom

Greater London

*Greater London, the area with-
in the M25 motorway ring, is
home to 7 million people and
covers an area of 600 sq miles
(1,580 sq km).*

Newcastle
Upon Tyne
Durham
Darlington
York
Leeds
Doncaster
Sheffield
Worksop
Lincoln
Skegness
Boston
Derby
Nottingham
Loughborough
Stamford
King's Lynn
Cromer
Norwich
Great
Yarmouth
Leicester
Peterborough
Swaffham
Lowestoft
Corby
Thetford
Southwold
Coventry
Huntington
Bury
St Edmunds
Aldeburgh
Warwick
Northampton
Cambridge
Ipswich
Felixstowe
Stratford-
Upon-Avon
Milton
Keynes
Bedford
Harwich
Göteborg
Esbjerg
Hamburg
Banbury
Woburn
Colchester
Zeebrugge
Luton
Stevenage
Clacton-
on-Sea
Hoek van Holland
Dunstable
Chelmsford
Oxford
St Albans
High
Wycombe
Watford
Marlborough
Windsor
Heathrow
Southend-on-Sea
Margate
Newbury
Reading
LONDON
Zeebrugge
Dunkerque
Basingstoke
Guildford
Sevenoaks
Maidstone
Canterbury
Ramsgate
Dover
Gatwick
Crawley
Royal
Tunbridge
Wells
Folkestone
Calais
Salisbury
Winchester
Rye
Calais
Shaftesbury
Southampton
Chichester
Lewes
Hastings
Boulogne
Lymington
Portsmouth
Brighton
Newhaven
Eastbourne
Cowes
Isle of Wight

Jersey
Guernsey
Cherbourg
Cherbourg
Le Havre
Caen
Dieppe

0 kilometres 75

0 miles 75

Regional Great Britain: The North and Scotland

This part of Great Britain is divided into two sections in this book. Although it is far less populated than the southern sector of the country, there are good road and rail connections, and ferry services link the islands with the mainland.

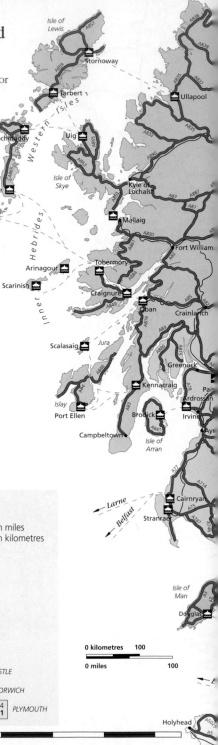

KEY TO COLOUR-CODING

The North Country

- Lancashire and the Lakes
- Yorkshire and Humber Region
- Northumbria

Scotland

- The Lowlands
- The Highlands and Islands

MILEAGE CHART

LONDON

10 = Distance in miles
10 = Distance in kilometres

111 **179**	*BIRMINGHAM*									
150 **241**	102 **164**	*CARDIFF*								
74 **119**	185 **298**	228 **367**	*DOVER*							
372 **599**	290 **466**	373 **600**	442 **711**	*EDINBURGH*						
389 **626**	292 **470**	374 **602**	466 **750**	45 **72**	*GLASGOW*					
529 **851**	448 **721**	530 **853**	600 **966**	158 **254**	167 **269**	*INVERNESS*				
184 **296**	81 **130**	173 **278**	257 **414**	213 **343**	214 **344**	371 **597**	*MANCHESTER*			
274 **441**	204 **328**	301 **484**	343 **552**	107 **172**	145 **233**	265 **426**	131 **211**	*NEWCASTLE*		
112 **180**	161 **259**	235 **378**	167 **269**	360 **579**	383 **616**	517 **832**	185 **298**	260 **418**	*NORWICH*	
212 **341**	206 **332**	152 **261**	287 **462**	427 **784**	426 **785**	545 **1038**	250 **451**	427 **655**	324 **521**	*PLYMOUTH*

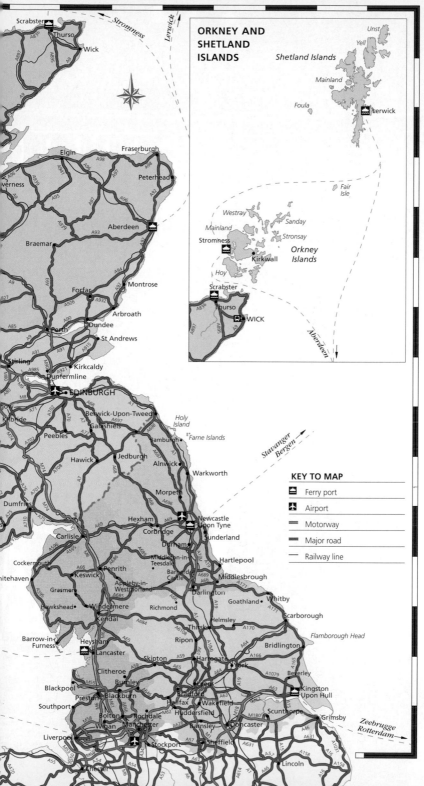

ORKNEY AND SHETLAND ISLANDS

Shetland Islands

Unst
Yell
Mainland
Foula
Lerwick

Fair Isle

Westray
Mainland
Stromness
Kirkwall
Sanday
Stronsay
Orkney Islands
Hoy

Scrabster
Thurso
WICK

Aberdeen

Scrabster
Thurso
Wick

Stromness
Lerwick

Elgin
Fraserburgh
Peterhead
Inverness
Aberdeen
Braemar
Forfar
Montrose
Arbroath
Dundee
St Andrews
Perth
Stirling
Kirkcaldy
Dunfermline
EDINBURGH
Berwick-Upon-Tweed
Galashiels
Peebles
Holy Island
Hawick
Jedburgh
Bamburgh
Farne Islands
Alnwick
Warkworth
Morpeth
Dumfries
Hexham
Newcastle Upon Tyne
Carlisle
Corbridge
Sunderland
Durham
Hartlepool
Middleton-in-Teesdale
Cockermouth
Keswick
Penrith
Appleby-in-Westmorland
Barnard Castle
Middlesbrough
Grasmere
Darlington
Goathland
Whitby
Hawkshead
Windermere
Richmond
Kendal
Scarborough
Helmsley
Barrow-in-Furness
Heysham
Thirsk
Ripon
Flamborough Head
Lancaster
Skipton
Harrogate
Bridlington
Clitheroe
York
Beverley
Blackpool
Burnley
Leeds
Kingston Upon Hull
Southport
Preston
Blackburn
Bradford
Halifax
Wakefield
Bolton
Rochdale
Huddersfield
Scunthorpe
Grimsby
Wigan
Manchester
Barnsley
Doncaster
Liverpool
Stockport
Sheffield
Lincoln
Chester

Stromness
Lerwick

Stavanger
Bergen

Zeebrugge
Rotterdam

KEY TO MAP

- Ferry port
- Airport
- Motorway
- Major road
- Railway line

A PORTRAIT OF GREAT BRITAIN

*B**ritain has been assiduous in preserving its traditions, but offers the visitor much more than stately castles and pretty villages. A diversity of landscape, culture, literature, art and architecture, as well as its unique heritage, results in a nation balancing the needs of the present with those of its past.***

Britain's character has been shaped by its geographical position as an island. Never successfully invaded since 1066, its people have developed their own distinctive traditions. The Roman invasion of AD 43 lasted 350 years but Roman culture and language were quickly overlain with those of the northern European settlers who followed. Ties with Europe were loosened further in the 16th century when the Catholic church was replaced by a less dogmatic established church.

Although today a member of the European Union, Britain continues to delight in its non-conformity, even in superficial ways such as driving on the left-hand side of the road instead of the right. The opening of the rail tunnel to France is a topographical adjustment that does not necessarily mark a change in national attitude.

The British heritage is seen in its ancient castles, cathedrals and stately homes with their gardens and Classical parklands. Age-old customs are renewed each year, from royal ceremonies to Morris dancers performing on village greens.

For a small island, Great Britain encompasses a surprising variety in its regions, whose inhabitants maintain distinct identities. Scotland and Wales are separate countries from England with their own legislative assemblies.

Tudor rose

Walking along the east bank of the River Avon, Bath

◁ Punting, a popular pastime on the River Cam, Cambridge

Widecombe-in-the-Moor, a Devon village clustered round a church and set in hills

They have different customs, traditions, and, in the case of Scotland, different legal and educational systems. The Welsh and Scots Gaelic languages survive and are sustained by their own radio and television networks. In northern and West Country areas, English itself is spoken in a rich variety of dialects and accents, and these areas maintain their own regional arts, crafts, architecture and food.

Scottish coat of arms at Edinburgh Castle

The landscape is varied, too, from the craggy mountains of Wales, Scotland and the north, through the flat expanses of the Midlands and eastern England to the soft, rolling hills of the south and west. The long, broad beaches of East Anglia contrast with the picturesque rocky inlets along much of the west coast.

Lake and gardens at Petworth House, Sussex

Despite the spread of towns and cities over the last two centuries, rural Britain still flourishes. Nearly three-quarters of Britain's land is used for agriculture. The main commercial crops are wheat, barley, sugar beet and potatoes, though what catches the eye in early summer are the fields of bright yellow rape or slate-blue flax.

The countryside is dotted with farms and charming villages, with picturesque cottages and lovingly tended gardens – a British passion. A typical village is built around an ancient church and a small, friendly pub. Here the pace of life slows. To drink a pint of ale in a cosy, village inn and relax before a fire is a time-honoured British custom. Strangers will be welcomed cordially, though perhaps with caution; for even if strict formality is a thing of the past, the British have a tendency to be reserved.

In the 19th and early 20th centuries, trade with the extensive British Empire, fuelled by abundant coal supplies, spurred manufacturing and created wealth. Thousands of people moved from the countryside to towns and cities near mines, mills and factories. By 1850 Britain was the world's strongest industrial nation. Now many of these old industrial centres have declined, and today manufacturing employs only 22 per cent of the labour force, while 66 per cent work in the growing service sector. These service industries are located mainly in the southeast, close to London, where modern office buildings bear witness to comparative prosperity.

Crowds at Petticoat Lane market in London's East End

is a multi-cultural society that can boast a wide range of music, art, food and religions. However, prejudice does exist and in some inner-city areas where poorer members of different communities live, racial tensions can occasionally arise. Even though discrimination in housing and employment on the grounds of race is against the law, it does occur in places.

SOCIETY AND POLITICS

British cities are melting-pots for people not just from different parts of the country but also from overseas. Irish immigration has long ensured a flow of labour into the country, and since the 1950s hundreds of thousands have come from former colonies in Africa, Asia and the Caribbean, many of which are now members of the Commonwealth. Nearly five per cent of Britain's 58 million inhabitants are from nonwhite ethnic groups – and about half of these were born in Britain. The result

Britain's class structure still intrigues and bewilders many visitors, based as it is on a subtle mixture of heredity and wealth. Even though many of the great inherited fortunes no longer exist, some old landed families still live on their

Bosses in Norwich Cathedral cloisters

large estates, and many now open them to the public. Class divisions are further entrenched by the education system. While more than 90 per cent of children are educated free by the state, richer parents often opt for private schooling, and the products of these private schools are disproportionately represented in the higher echelons of government and business.

The monarchy's position highlights the dilemma of a people seeking to preserve its most potent symbol of national unity in an age that is suspicious of inherited privilege. Without real political power, though still head of the Church of England, the Queen and her family are subject to increasing public scrutiny. Following a spate of personal scandals, some citizens advocate the abolition of the monarchy.

Democracy has deep foundations in Britain: there was even a parliament of sorts in London in the 13th century.

Priest in the Close at Winchester Cathedral

Yet with the exception of the 17th-century Civil War, power has passed gradually from the Crown to the people's elected representatives. A series of Reform Acts between 1832 and 1884 gave the vote to all male citizens, though women were not enfranchised on an equal basis until 1928. Margaret Thatcher – Britain's first woman Prime Minister – held office for 12 years from 1979. During the 20th

Afternoon tea on the back lawn at the Thornbury Castle Hotel, Avon

century, the Labour (left wing) and Conservative (right wing) parties have, during their periods in office, favoured a mix of public and private ownership for industry and ample funding for the state health and welfare systems.

The position of Ireland has been an intractable political issue since the 17th century. Part of the United Kingdom for 800 years, but divided in 1921, it has seen conflict between Catholics and Protestants for many years. The Good Friday Peace Agreement of 1998 was a huge step forward but the path to lasting peace is a rocky one.

CULTURE AND THE ARTS

Britain has a famous theatrical tradition stretching back to the 16th century and William Shakespeare. His plays

The House of Lords, in Parliament

have been performed on stage almost continuously since he wrote them and the works of 17th- and 18th-century writers are also frequently revived. Contemporary British playwrights such as Tom Stoppard, Alan Ayckbourn and David Hare draw on this long tradition with their vivid language and by using comedy to illustrate serious themes. British actors such as Vanessa Redgrave, Ian McKellen, Ralph Fiennes and Anthony Hopkins have international reputations.

While London is the focal point of British theatre, fine drama is to be seen in many other parts of the country. The Edinburgh Festival and its Fringe are the high point of Great Britain's cultural calendar with theatre and music to suit all tastes. Other music festivals are held across the country, chiefly in summer, while there are annual

Schoolboys at Eton, the famous public school

festivals of literature at Hay-on-Wye and Cheltenham. Poetry has had an enthusiastic following since Chaucer wrote the *Canterbury Tales* in the 14th century: poems from all eras can even be read on the London Underground, where they are interspersed with the advertisements in the carriages and on the station platforms.

In the visual arts, Britain has a strong tradition in portraiture, caricature, landscape and watercolour. In modern times David Hockney and Lucian Freud, and sculptors Henry Moore and Barbara Hepworth, have enjoyed worldwide recognition. Architects including

Christopher Wren, Inigo Jones, John Nash and Robert Adam all created styles that define British cities; and today, Norman Foster and Richard Rogers carry the standard for Post-Modernism. Britain is becoming famous for its

Reading the newspaper in Kensington Gardens

innovative fashion designers, many of whom now show their spring and autumn collections in Paris.

The British are avid newspaper readers. There are 11 national newspapers published from London on weekdays: the standard of the serious newspapers is very high; for example, *The Times* is read the world over because of its reputation for strong intentional reporting. Most popular, however, are the tabloids packed with gossip, crime and sport, which account for some 80 per cent of the total.

Naomi Campbell, a British supermodel

The indigenous film industry, although squeezed by Hollywood, produces a few international hits such as *The Full Monty* and *Notting Hill*. British television is famous for the quality of its news, current affairs and drama programmes. The publicly funded British Broadcasting Corporation (BBC), which controls five national radio networks and two terrestrial television channels, as well as additional radio stations and television channels via digital technology, is widely admired.

The British are great sports fans, and soccer, rugby, cricket and golf are popular. An instantly recognizable English image is that of the cricket match on a village green. Nationwide, fishing is the most popular sporting pastime, and

the British make good use of their national parks as keen walkers.

British food used to be derided for a lack of imagination. The cuisine relied on a limited range of quality ingredients, plainly prepared. But recent influences from abroad have introduced a wider range of ingredients and more adventurous techniques. Typical English food – plain home cooking and regional dishes – can still be found but they are being supplemented by a tastier modern British cuisine.

In this, as in other respects, the British are doing what they have done for centuries: accommodating their own traditions to influences from other cultures, while leaving the essential elements of their national life and character intact.

Whitby harbour and St Mary's Church, Yorkshire

Gardens Through the Ages

Styles of gardening in Britain have expanded alongside architecture and other evolving fashions. The Elizabethan knot garden became more elaborate and formal in Jacobean times, when the range of plants greatly increased. The 18th century brought a taste for large-scale "natural" landscapes with lakes, woods and pastures, creating the most distinctively English style to have emerged. In the 19th century, fierce debate raged between supporters of natural and formal gardens, developing into the eclecticism of the 20th century when "garden rooms" in differing styles became popular.

Monumental column

A grotto and cascade brought romance and mystery.

Capability Brown (1715–83) *was Britain's most influential garden designer, favouring the move away from formal gardens to man-made pastoral settings.*

Blackthorn

Classical temples were a much appreciated feature in 18th-century gardens and were often exact replicas of buildings that the designers had seen in Greece.

Elaborate parterres *were a feature of aristocratic gardens of the 17th century, when the fashion spread from Europe. This is the Privy Garden at Hampton Court Palace, restored in 1995 to its design under William III.*

IDEAL LANDSCAPE GARDEN

Classical Greece and Rome inspired the grand gardens of the early 18th century, such as Stourhead and Stowe. Informal clumps of trees played a critical part in the serene, manicured landscapes.

Maple

Winding paths were carefully planned to allow changing vistas to open out as visitors strolled around the garden.

DESIGN AND FORMALITY

A flower garden is a work of artifice, an attempt to tame nature rather than to copy it. Growing plants in rows or regular patterns, interspersed with statues and ornaments, imposes a sense of order. Designs change to reflect the fashion of the time and the introduction of new plants.

Medieval gardens usually had a herber (a turfed sitting area) and a vine arbour. A good reconstruction is Queen Eleanor's Garden, Winchester.

Tudor gardens featured edged borders and sometimes mazes. The Tudor House Garden, Southampton, also has beehives and heraldic statues.

Herbaceous borders, *full of lush plants, are the glory of the summer garden. Gertrude Jekyll (1843–1932), was high priestess of the mixed border, with her eye for seductive colour combinations.*

Cedar of Lebanon   Yew

Rhododendron

The Palladian bridge was a favourite feature, often decorative rather than practical.

Knot Gardens *were in vogue in the 1500s. Intersecting lines of lavender or box were filled with flowers, herbs or vegetables, as in this restoration at Pitmedden in Scotland.*

VISITORS' CHECKLIST

The "yellow book", Gardens of England and Wales, the annual guide to the National Gardens Scheme, lists gardens open to the public.

DEVELOPMENT OF THE MODERN PANSY

All garden plants derive from wild flowers, bred over the years to produce qualities that appeal to gardeners. The story of the pansy, one of our most popular flowers, is typical.

The wild pansy (Viola tricolor) native to Britain is commonly known as heartsease. It is a small-flowered annual which can vary considerably in colour.

The mountain pansy (Viola lutea) is a perennial. The first cultivated varieties resulted from crossing it with heartsease in the early 19th century.

The Show Pansy was bred by florists after the blotch appeared as a chance seedling in 1840. It was round in form with a small, symmetrical blotch.

The Fancy Pansy, developed in the 1860s, was much larger. The blotch covered all three lower petals save for a thin margin of colour.

Modern hybrids of pansies, violas and violettas, developed by selective breeding, are varied and versatile in a wide range of vibrant new colours.

17th-century gardening was more elaborate. Water gardens like those at Blenheim were often combined with parterres of exotic foreign plants.

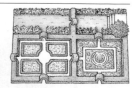

Victorian gardens, their formal beds a mass of colour, were a reaction to the landscapes of Capability Brown. Alton Towers has a good example.

20th-century gardens mix historic and modern styles, as at Hidcote Manor, Gloucestershire. Growing wild flowers is becoming a popular choice.

Stately Homes

The grand country house reached its zenith in the 18th and 19th centuries, when the old landed families and the new captains of industry enjoyed their wealth, looked after by a retinue of servants. The earliest stately homes date from the 14th century, when defence was paramount. By the 16th century, when the opulent taste of the European Renaissance spread to England, houses became centres of pleasure and showplaces for fine art *(see pp302–03)*. The Georgians favoured chaste Classical architecture with rich interiors, the Victorians flamboyant Gothic. Due to 20th-century social change many stately homes have been opened to the public, some administered by the National Trust.

Adam sketch (c.1760) for ornate panel

The saloon, a domed rotunda based on the Pantheon in Rome, was designed to display the Curzon family's Classical sculpture collection to 18th-century society.

The Drawing Room, the main room for entertaining, contains the most important pictures and some exquisite plasterwork.

The Marble Hall *is where balls and other social functions took place among Corinthian columns of pink alabaster.*

The Family Wing is a self-contained "pavilion" of private living quarters; the servants lived in rooms above the kitchen. The Curzon family still live here.

The Music Room is decorated with musical themes. Music was the main entertainment on social occasions.

TIMELINE OF ARCHITECTS

1650

Colen Campbell (1676–1729) designed Burlington House *(see p81)*

Sir John Vanbrugh *(see p398)* was helped by **Nicholas Hawksmoor** (1661–1736) on Blenheim Palace *(see pp228–29)*

William Kent (1685–1748) built Holkham Hall *(see p197)* in the Palladian style

Castle Howard (1702) by Sir John Vanbrugh

Robert Adam (1728–92), who often worked with his brother James (1730–94) was as famous for decorative details as for buildings

John Carr (1723–1807) designed the Palladian Harewood House *(see p410)*

1750

Henry Holland (1745–1806) designed the Neo-Classical south range of Woburn Abbey *(see p230)*

Adam fireplace, Kedleston Hall, adorned with Classical motifs

NATIONAL TRUST

National Trust oak leaf design

At the end of the 19th century, there were real fears that burgeoning factories, mines, roads and houses would obliterate much of Britain's historic landscape and finest buildings. In 1895 a group that included the social refomer Octavia Hill formed the National Trust, to preserve the nation's valuable heritage. The first building acquired by the trust was the medieval Clergy House at Alfriston in Sussex, in 1896 (see p180). Today the National Trust is a charity that runs many historic houses and gardens, and vast stretches of countryside and coastline (see p671). It is supported by more than two million members nationwide.

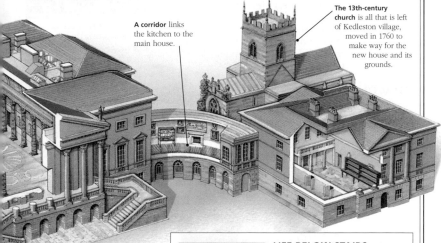

A corridor links the kitchen to the main house.

The 13th-century church is all that is left of Kedleston village, moved in 1760 to make way for the new house and its grounds.

KEDLESTON HALL

This Derbyshire mansion (see p336) is an early work of the influential Georgian architect Robert Adam, who was a pioneer of the Neo-Classical style derived from ancient Greece and Rome. It was built for the Curzon family in the 1760s.

Life Below Stairs by Charles Hunt (c.1890)

LIFE BELOW STAIRS

A large community of resident staff was essential to run a country house smoothly. The butler was in overall charge, ensuring that meals were served on time. The housekeeper supervised uniformed maids who made sure the place was clean. The cook ran the kitchen, using fresh produce from the estate. Ladies' maids and valets acted as personal servants.

1800	1850	

Dining Room, Cragside, Northumberland

Norman Shaw (1831–1912) was an exponent of Victorian Gothic, as in Cragside (above), and a pioneer of the Arts and Crafts movement (see p328)

Philip Webb (1831–1915) was a leading architect of the influential Arts and Crafts movement (see p328), whose buildings favoured the simpler forms of an "Old English" style, instead of flamboyant Victorian Gothic

Sir Edwin Lutyens (1869–1944) designed the elaborate Castle Drogo in Devon (see p295), one of the last grand country houses

Standen, West Sussex (1891–94) by Philip Webb

Heraldry and the Aristocracy

The British aristocracy has evolved over 900 years from the feudal obligations of noblemen to the Norman kings, who conferred privileges of rank and land in return for armed support. Subscquent monarchs bestowed titles and property on their supporters, establishing new aristocratic dynasties. The title of "earl" dates from the 11th century; that of "duke" from the 14th century. Soon the nobility began to choose their own symbols, partly to identify a knight concealed by his armour: these were often painted on the knight's coat (hence the term "coat of arms") and also copied onto his shield.

Order of the Garter medal

The College of Arms, London: housing records of all coats of arms and devising new ones

ROYAL COAT OF ARMS

The most familiar British coat of arms is the sovereign's. It appears on the royal standard, or flag, as well as on official documents and on shops that enjoy royal patronage. Over nearly 900 years, various monarchs have made modifications. The quartered shield in the middle displays the arms of England (twice), Scotland and Ireland. Surrounding it are other traditional images including the lion and unicorn, topped by the crown and the royal helm (helmet).

Edward III *(1327–77) was the founder of the chivalric Order of the Garter. The garter, bearing the motto,* Honi soit qui mal y pense *(evil be to him who thinks of evil), goes round the central shield.*

The lion is the most common beast in heraldry.

The red lion is the symbol of Scotland.

The unicorn is a mythical beast, generally regarded as a Scottish royal beast in heraldry.

Henry II *(1154–89) formalized his coat of arms to include three lions. This was developed by his son Richard I to become the "Gules three lions passant guardant or" seen on today's arms.*

The royal helm with gold protective bars was introduced to the arms by Elizabeth I (1558–1603).

Dieu et mon droit (God and my right) has been the royal motto since the reign of Henry V (1413–22).

Henry VII *(1485–1509) devised the Tudor rose, joining the white and red roses of York and Lancaster.*

ADMIRAL LORD NELSON

When people are ennobled they may choose their own coat of arms if they do not already have one. Britain's naval hero (1758–1805) was made Baron Nelson of the Nile in 1798 and a viscount in 1801. His arms relate to his life and career at sea; but some symbols were added after his death.

A seaman supports the shield.

The motto means "Let him wear the palm (or laurel) who deserves it".

A tropical scene shows the Battle of the Nile (1798).

The San Joseph was a Spanish man o'war that Nelson daringly captured.

TRACING YOUR ANCESTRY

Records of births, deaths and marriages in England and Wales since 1837 are at the **Family Records Centre**, 1 Myddelton St, London (020-8392 5300), and in Scotland at **New Register House**, 3 West Register St, Edinburgh EH1 3YT (0131 314 4433). For help in tracing family history, consult **Society of Genealogists**, 14 Charterhouse Bldgs, London EC1 (020-7251 8799).

Inherited titles

usually pass to the eldest son or the closest male relative, but some titles may go to women if there is no male heir.

The Duke of Edinburgh (born 1921), husband of the Queen, is one of several dukes who are members of the Royal Family.

The Marquess of Salisbury (1830–1903), Prime Minister three times between 1885 and 1902, was descended from the Elizabethan statesman Robert Cecil.

Earl Mountbatten of Burma (1900–79) was ennobled in 1947 for diplomatic and military services.

Viscount Montgomery (1887–1976) was raised to the peerage for his military leadership in World War II.

Lord Byron (1788–1824), the Romantic poet, was the 6th Baron Byron: the 1st Baron was an MP ennobled by Charles I in 1625.

PEERS OF THE REALM

There are nearly 1,200 peers of the realm. In 1999 the process began to abolish the hereditary system in favour of life peerages which expire on the death of the recipient *(see left and below)*. Ninety-two hereditary peers are entitled to sit in the House of Lords, including the Lords Spiritual – archbishops and senior bishops of the Church of England – and the Law Lords. In 1958 the Queen expanded the list of life peerages to honour people who had performed notable public service. From 1999 the system of "peoples peerages" began to replace inherited honours.

KEY TO THE PEERS

☐	25 dukes
☐	35 marquesses
☐	175 earls and countesses
☐	98 viscounts
☐	800+ barons and baronesses

THE QUEEN'S HONOURS LIST

Twice a year several hundred men and women nominated by the Prime Minister and political leaders for outstanding public service receive honours from the Queen. Some are made dames or knights, a few receive the prestigious OM (Order of Merit), but far more receive lesser honours such as OBEs or MBEs (Orders or Members of the British Empire).

Mother Theresa *received the OM in 1983 for her work in India.*

Terence Conran, *founder of Habitat, was knighted for services to industry.*

The Beatles *were given MBEs in 1965. Paul McCartney was knighted in 1997.*

Rural Architecture

For many, the essence of British life is found in villages. Their scale and serenity nurture a way of life envied by those who live in towns and cities. The pattern of British villages dates back some 1,500 years, when the Saxons cleared forests and established settlements, usually centred around a green or pond. Most of today's English villages existed at the time of the *Domesday Book* in 1086, though few actual buildings survive from then. The settlements evolved organically around a church or manor; the cottages and gardens were created from local materials. Today, a typical village will contain structures of various dates, from the Middle Ages onward. The church is usually the oldest, followed perhaps by a tithe barn, manor house and cottages.

Abbotsbury, in Dorset – a typical village built up around a church

A steep-pitched roof covers the whole house.

Timbers are of Wealden oak.

Eaves are supported by curved braces.

Wealden Hall House *in Sussex is a medieval timber-framed house, of a type found in southeast England. It has a tall central open hall flanked by bays of two floors and the upper floor is "jettied", overhanging the ground floor.*

A tiled roof keeps the grain dry.

The entrance is big enough for ox-wagons.

Holes let in air – and birds.

Walls and doors are weatherboarded.

The medieval tithe barn *stored produce for the clergy – each farmer was required to donate one tenth (tithe) of his annual harvest. The enormous roofs may be supported by crucks, large curved timbers extending from the low walls.*

THE PARISH CHURCH

The church is the focal point of the village and, traditionally, of village life. Its tall spire could be seen – and its bells heard – by travellers from a distance. The church is also a chronicle of local history: a large church in a tiny village indicates a once-prosperous settlement. A typical church contains architectural features from many centuries, occasionally as far back as Saxon times. These may include medieval brasses, wall paintings, misericords *(see p341)*, and Tudor and Stuart carvings. Many sell informative guide books inside.

Slender spire from the Georgian era

West elevation

Pinnacled towers dating from the 15th century are situated at the west end.

Bells summon the congregation.

Norman arches are rounded.

Buttresses support old walls.

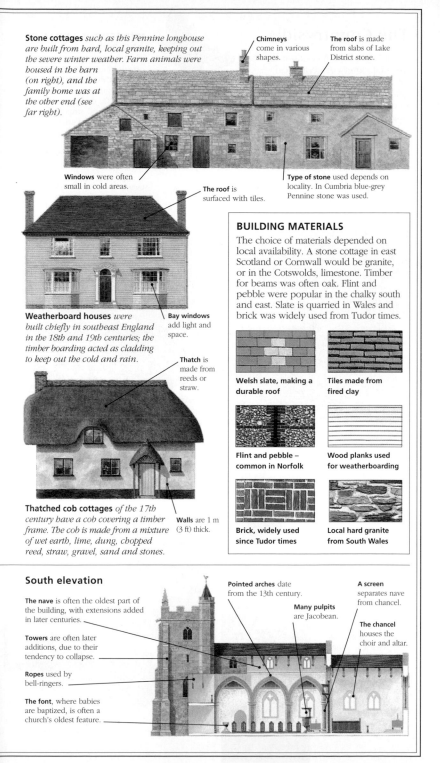

Stone cottages *such as this Pennine longhouse are built from hard, local granite, keeping out the severe winter weather. Farm animals were housed in the barn (on right), and the family home was at the other end (see far right).*

Chimneys come in various shapes.

The roof is made from slabs of Lake District stone.

Windows were often small in cold areas.

The roof is surfaced with tiles.

Type of stone used depends on locality. In Cumbria blue-grey Pennine stone was used.

Weatherboard houses *were built chiefly in southeast England in the 18th and 19th centuries; the timber boarding acted as cladding to keep out the cold and rain.*

Bay windows add light and space.

Thatch is made from reeds or straw.

Thatched cob cottages *of the 17th century have a cob covering a timber frame. The cob is made from a mixture of wet earth, lime, dung, chopped reed, straw, gravel, sand and stones.*

Walls are 1 m (3 ft) thick.

BUILDING MATERIALS

The choice of materials depended on local availability. A stone cottage in east Scotland or Cornwall would be granite, or in the Cotswolds, limestone. Timber for beams was often oak. Flint and pebble were popular in the chalky south and east. Slate is quarried in Wales and brick was widely used from Tudor times.

Welsh slate, making a durable roof

Tiles made from fired clay

Flint and pebble – common in Norfolk

Wood planks used for weatherboarding

Brick, widely used since Tudor times

Local hard granite from South Wales

South elevation

The nave is often the oldest part of the building, with extensions added in later centuries.

Towers are often later additions, due to their tendency to collapse.

Ropes used by bell-ringers.

The font, where babies are baptized, is often a church's oldest feature.

Pointed arches date from the 13th century.

Many pulpits are Jacobean.

A screen separates nave from chancel.

The chancel houses the choir and altar.

The Countryside

Common Blue butterfly

For its size, Britain contains an unusual variety of geological and climatic conditions that have shaped diverse landscapes, from treeless windswept moorland to boggy marshes and small hedged cattle pastures. Each terrain nurtures its typical wildlife and displays its own charm through the seasons. With the reduction in farming and the creation of footpaths and nature reserves, the countryside is becoming more of a leisure resource.

INDIGENOUS ANIMALS AND BIRDS

There are no large or dangerous wild animals in Britain but a wealth of small mammals, rodents and insects inhabit the countryside, and the rivers and streams are home to many varieties of fish. For bird-watchers there is a great range of songbirds, birds of prey and seabirds.

Livestock graze on low pastures.

Trees provide shelter and protection for wildlife.

Higher land is uncultivated.

Bushes and trees grow between rocks.

Streams flow over a stony bed from mountain springs.

The highest ground is often covered in snow until spring.

WOODED DOWNLAND

Chalk downland, seen here at Ditchling Beacon on the Downs *(see p181)*, has soil of low fertility and is grazed by sheep. However crops are sometimes grown on the lower slopes. Distinctive wild flowers and butterflies thrive here, while beech and yew predominate in the woods.

Spear thistle *has pink heads in summer that attract several species of butterfly.*

WILD HILLSIDE

Large tracts of Britain's uplands remain wild terrain, unsuitable for crops or forestry. Purple heather is tough enough to survive in moorland, the haunt of deer and game birds. The highest craggy uplands, such as the Cairngorms *(see p544–45)* in Scotland, pictured here, are the habitat of birds of prey, such as the golden eagle.

Ling, *a low-growing heather with tiny pink bell-flowers, adds splashes of colour to peaty moors and uplands.*

The dog rose *is one of Britain's best-loved wild flowers; its pink single flower is widely seen in hedgerows.*

Hogweed *has robust stems and leaves with large clusters of white flowers.*

Meadow cranesbill *is a wild geranium with distinctive purple flowers.*

Tormentil *has small yellow flowers. It prefers moist, acid soil and is found near water on heaths and moors in summer.*

Swallows, *swifts and house martins are all summer visitors.*

Kestrels *are small falcons that prey on mammals such as voles.*

Rabbits *are often spotted feeding at the edge of fields or near woods.*

Robins, *common in gardens and hedgerows, have distinctive red breast feathers.*

Foxes, *little bigger than domestic cats, live in hideaways in woods, near farmland.*

Cereal crops ripen in small fields.

Hedgerows provide refuge for wildlife.

Small mixed woods break up the field pattern.

Sheep graze on salty marshes.

Culverts drain water from the field.

Reed beds edge the water.

TRADITIONAL FIELDS

The patchwork fields here in the Cotswolds *(see p304)* reflect generations of small-scale farming. A typical farm would produce silage, hay and cereal crops, and keep a few dairy cows and sheep in enclosed pastures. The tree-dotted hedgerows mark boundaries that may be centuries old.

MARSHLAND

Flat and low-lying wetlands, criss-crossed with dykes and drainage canals, provide the scenery of Romney Marsh *(see also p182)* as well as much of East Anglia. Some areas have rich, peaty soil for crops, or salty marshland for sheep, but there are extensive uncultivated sections, where reed beds shelter wildlife.

The oxeye daisy *is a larger relative of the common white daisy, found in grassland from spring to late summer.*

Sea lavender *is a saltmarsh plant that is tolerant of saline soils. It flowers in late summer.*

Orchids *are among the rarer wild flowers. This species is the Common Spotted Orchid.*

Cowslips *belong to the primrose family. In spring they are often found in the grass on open meadowlands.*

Poppies *glow brilliant red in cornfields.*

Buttercups *are among the most common wild flowers. They brighten meadows in summer.*

Walkers' Britain

Walkers of all levels of ability and enthusiasm are well served in Britain. There is an unrivalled network of long-distance paths through some spectacular scenery, which can be tackled in stages with overnight stays en route, or dipped into for a single day's walking. For shorter walks, Britain is dotted with signposts showing public footpaths across common or private land. You will find books of walk routes in local shops and a large map will keep you on track. Choose river routes for easy walking or take to the hills for a greater challenge.

Walker resting on Scafell Pike, Lake District

The West Highland Way is an arduous 95 mile (153 km) route from Milngavie, near Glasgow, to north of Fort William, across mountainous terrain with fine lochs and moorland scenery *(see p494)*.

Fort William

Glasgow

The Pennine Way *was Britain's first designated long-distance path. The 268 mile (431 km) route from Edale in Derbyshire to Kirk Yetholm on the Scottish border is a challenging upland hike, with long, lonely stretches of moorland. It is only for experienced hill walkers.*

St Bees Head

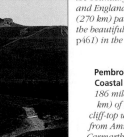

Offa's Dyke Footpath *follows the boundary between Wales and England. The 168 mile (270 km) path goes through the beautiful Wye Valley (see p461) in the Welsh borders.*

Dales Way runs from Ilkley in West Yorkshire to Bowness-on-Windermere in the Lake District, 81 miles (130 km) of delightful flat riverside walking and valley scenery.

Prestaty

Pembrokeshire Coastal path *is 186 miles (299 km) of rugged cliff-top walking from Amroth on Carmarthen Bay to the west tip of Wales at Cardigan.*

St Dogmaels

Amroth

Minehead

ORDNANCE SURVEY MAPS

The best maps for walkers are published by the Ordnance Survey, the official mapping agency (08456 050505). Out of a wide range of maps the most useful are the *Explorer* series, which include the more popular regions and cover a large area, on a scale of 1:25,000, and the *Landranger* series, on a scale of 1:50,000.

The Southwest Coastal Path offers varied scenery from Minehead on the north Somerset coast to Poole in Dorset, via Devon and Cornwall – in all a marathon 630 mile (1,014 km) round trip.

SIGNPOSTS

Long-distance paths are well signposted, some of them with an acorn symbol (or with a thistle in Scotland). Many shorter routes are marked with coloured arrows by local authorities or hiking groups. Local councils generally mark public footpaths with yellow arrows. Public bridleways, marked by blue arrows, are paths that can be used by both walkers and horse riders – remember, horses churn up mud. Signs appear on posts, trees and stiles.

The Coast to Coast Walk *crosses the Lake District, Yorkshire Dales and North York Moors, on a 190 mile (306 km) route. This demanding walk covers a spectacular range of North Country landscapes. All cross-country routes are best walked from west to east to take advantage of the prevailing wind.*

rk Yetholm

Windermere

Ilkley

Robin Hood's Bay

Edale

The Ridgeway *is a fairly easy path that follows an ancient track once used by cattle drovers. Starting near Avebury (see p263) it covers 85 miles (137 km) to Ivinghoe Beacon.*

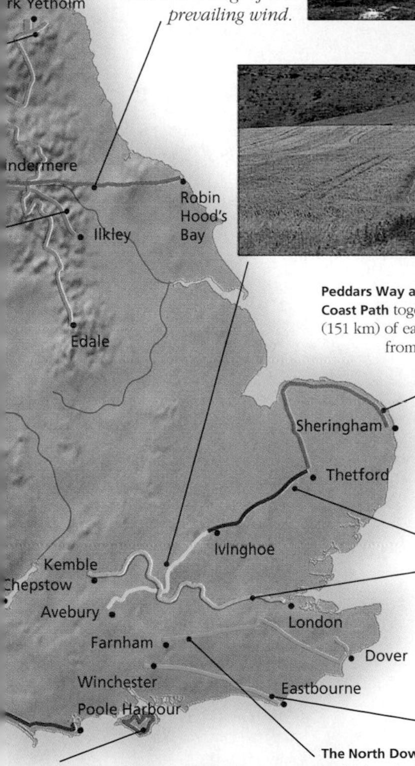

Peddars Way and the Norfolk Coast Path together make 94 miles (151 km) of easy lowland walking, from Thetford, north to the coast then east to Cromer.

Sheringham

Thetford

Icknield Way, the most ancient prehistoric road in Britain, is 105 miles (168 km) long and links the Ridgeway to Peddars Way.

Ivinghoe

Kemble

Chepstow

Avebury

Farnham

Winchester

Poole Harbour

London

Dover

Eastbourne

The Thames Path follows the river for 213 miles (341 km) from central London to Kemble, its source in Gloucestershire.

The Isle of Wight Coastal Path circles the entire island on an easy 65 mile (105 km) footpath.

The North Downs Way is an ancient route through 141 miles (227 km) of low-lying hills from Farnham in Surrey to Dover or Folkestone in Kent.

The South Downs Way *is a 101 mile (162 km) walk from Eastbourne on the south coast to Winchester (see p170–71). It can be completed in a week.*

THE HISTORY OF GREAT BRITAIN

Britain began to assume a cohesive character as early as the 7th century, with the Anglo-Saxon tribes absorbing Celtic and Roman influences and finally achieving supremacy. They suffered repeated Viking incursions and were overcome by the Normans at the Battle of Hastings in 1066. Over centuries, the disparate cultures of the Normans and Anglo-Saxons combined to form the English nation, a process nurtured by Britain's position as an island. The next 400 years saw English kings involved in military expeditions to Europe, but their control over these areas was gradually wrested from them. As a result they extended their domain over Scotland and Wales. The Tudor monarchs consolidated this control and laid the foundations for Britain's future commercial success. Henry VIII recognized the vital importance of sea power and under his daughter, Elizabeth I, English sailors ranged far across the world, often coming into

Medieval knights, masters of the arts of war

conflict with the Spanish. The total defeat of the Spanish Armada in 1588 confirmed Britain's position as a major maritime power. The Stuart period saw a number of internal struggles, most importantly the Civil War in 1641. But by the time of the Act of the Union in 1707 the whole island was united and the foundations for representative government had been laid. The combination of this internal security with continuing maritime strength allowed Britain to seek wealth overseas. By the end of the Napoleonic Wars in 1815, Britain was the leading trading nation in the world. The opportunities offered by industrialization were seized, and by the late 19th century, a colossal empire had been established across the globe. Challenged by Europe and the rise of the US, and drained by its leading role in two world wars, Britain's influence waned after 1945. By the 1970s almost all the colonies had become independent Commonwealth nations.

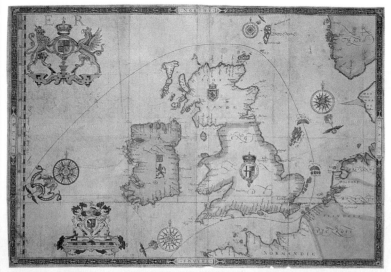

Contemporary map showing the defeat of the Armada (1588), making Britain into a world power

◁ Henry VIII, founder of the British navy, seen here with his children Edward and Mary

Kings and Queens

All English monarchs since the Norman Conquest in 1066 have been descendants of William the Conqueror. Scottish rulers, until James VI and the Union of Crowns in 1603 *(see pp482–3)*, have been more diverse. When the Crown passes to someone other than the monarch's eldest son, the name of the ruling family usually changes. The rules of succession have been precisely laid down and strongly favour men over women, but Britain has still had six queens since 1553. In Norman times the monarchy enjoyed absolute power, but today the position is largely symbolic.

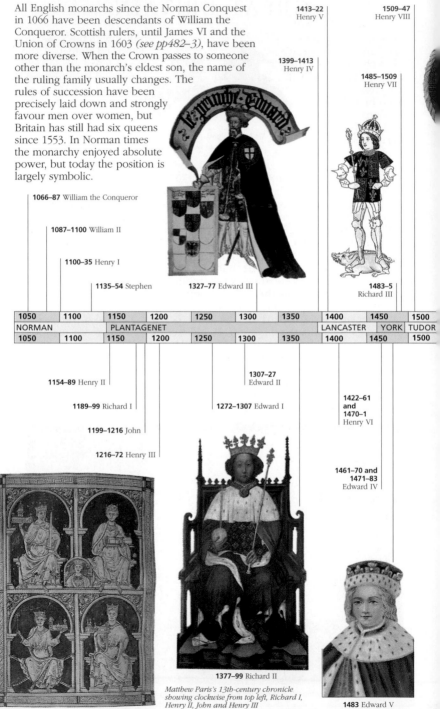

1413–22 Henry V

1509–47 Henry VIII

1399–1413 Henry IV

1485–1509 Henry VII

1066–87 William the Conqueror

1087–1100 William II

1100–35 Henry I

1135–54 Stephen

1327–77 Edward III

1483–5 Richard III

1050	1100	1150	1200	1250	1300	1350	1400	1450	1500
NORMAN		PLANTAGENET					LANCASTER	YORK	TUDOR
1050	1100	1150	1200	1250	1300	1350	1400	1450	1500

1154–89 Henry II

1189–99 Richard I

1199–1216 John

1216–72 Henry III

1307–27 Edward II

1272–1307 Edward I

1422–61 and 1470–1 Henry VI

1461–70 and 1471–83 Edward IV

1377–99 Richard II

Matthew Paris's 13th-century chronicle showing clockwise from top left, Richard I, Henry II, John and Henry III

1483 Edward V

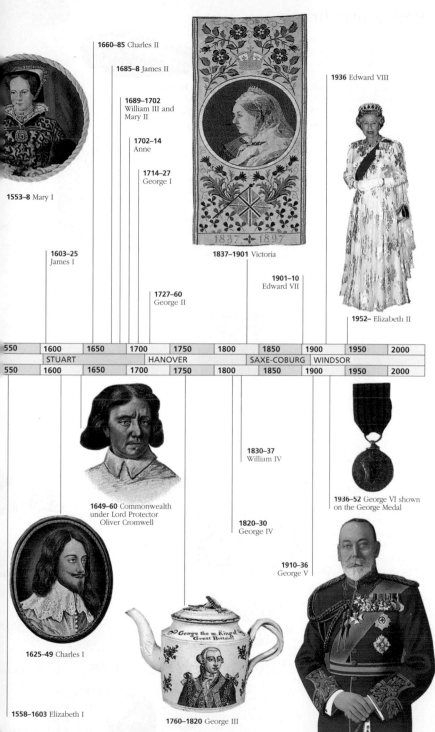

1660–85 Charles II

1685–8 James II

1689–1702 William III and Mary II

1702–14 Anne

1714–27 George I

1936 Edward VIII

1553–8 Mary I

1603–25 James I

1837–1901 Victoria

1901–10 Edward VII

1727–60 George II

1952– Elizabeth II

550	1600	1650	1700	1750	1800	1850	1900	1950	2000
	STUART			HANOVER		SAXE-COBURG	WINDSOR		
550	1600	1650	1700	1750	1800	1850	1900	1950	2000

1830–37 William IV

1936–52 George VI shown on the George Medal

1649–60 Commonwealth under Lord Protector Oliver Cromwell

1820–30 George IV

1910–36 George V

1625–49 Charles I

1558–1603 Elizabeth I

1760–1820 George III

547–53 Edward VI

Prehistoric Britain

Britain was part of the European landmass until the end of the last Ice Age, around 6000 BC, when the English Channel was formed by melting ice. The earliest inhabitants lived in limestone caves: settlements and farming skills developed gradually through the Stone Age. The magnificent wooden and stone henges and circles are masterworks from around 3000 BC, but their significance is a mystery. Flint mines and ancient pathways are evidence of early trading and many burial mounds (barrows) survive from the Stone and Bronze Ages.

Axe Heads
Stone axes, like this one found at Stonehenge, were used by Neolithic men.

Cup and ring marks were carved on standing stones, such as this one at Ballymeanoch.

MAPPING THE PAST

Monuments from the Neolithic (New Stone), Bronze and Iron Ages, together with artifacts found from these periods, provide a wealth of information about Britain's early settlers, before written history began with the Romans.

Neolithic Tools
Antlers and bones were made into Neolithic leather-working tools. These were found at Avebury (see p263).

Pottery Beaker
The Beaker People, who came from Europe in the early Bronze Age, take their name from these drinking cups often found in their graves.

Gold Breast Plate
Made by Wessex goldsmiths, its spectacular pattern suggests it belonged to an important chieftain.

Pentre Ifan, an impressive Neolithic burial chamber in South Wales, was once covered with a huge earth mound.

Mold Cape
Gold was mined in Wales and Cornwall in the Bronze Age. This intricately worked warrior's cape was buried in a grave at Mold, Clwyd.

This gold cup, found in a Cornish barrow, is evidence of the wealth of Bronze Age tribes.

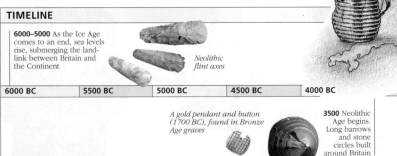

TIMELINE

6000–5000 As the Ice Age comes to an end, sea levels rise, submerging the land-link between Britain and the Continent

Neolithic flint axes

6000 BC	5500 BC	5000 BC	4500 BC	4000 BC

A gold pendant and button (1700 BC), found in Bronze Age graves

3500 Neolithic Age begins. Long barrows and stone circles built around Britain

Skara Brae is a Neolithic village of about 2500 BC *(see p529).*

Iron Age Brochs, round towers with thick stone walls, are found only in Scotland.

Maiden Castle
An impressive Iron Age hill fort in Dorset, its concentric lines of ramparts and ditches follow the contours of the hill top (see p269).

Iron Age Axe
The technique of smelting iron came to Britain around 700 BC, brought from Europe by the Celts.

Castlerigg Stone Circle is one of Britain's earliest Neolithic monuments *(see p361).*

Uffington White Horse
Thought to be 3,000 years old, the shape has to be "scoured" to keep grass at bay (see p221).

A chalk figure, thought to be a fertility goddess, was found at Grimes Graves *(see p194).*

This bronze Celtic helmet (50 BC) was found in the River Thames, London.

Stonehenge was begun around 3,500 years ago *(see pp262 63).*

WHERE TO SEE PREHISTORIC BRITAIN

Wiltshire, with Stonehenge *(p262)* and Avebury *(p263)*, has the best group of Neolithic monuments, and the Uffington White Horse is nearby *(p221)*. The Scottish islands have many early sites and the British Museum *(pp106–7)* houses a huge collection of artefacts.

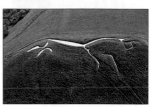

A circular bank *with over 180 stones encloses the Neolithic site at Avebury* (see p263).

Snettisham Torc
A torc was a neck ring worn by Celtic men. This one, found in Norfolk, dates from 50 BC and is made from silver and gold.

000 BC	2500 BC	2000 BC	1500 BC	1000 BC	500 BC
2500 Temples, or henges, are built of wood or stone	**1650–1200** Wessex is at the hub of trading routes between Europe and the mines of Cornwall, Wales and Ireland		**1000** First farmsteads are settled	**550–350** Migration of Celtic people from southern Europe	**500** Iron Age begins. Hill forts are built
	2100–1650 The Bronze Age reaches Britain. Immigration of the Beaker People, who make bronze implements and build ritual temples	*Chieftain's bronze sceptre (1700 BC)*	**1200** Small, self-sufficient villages start to appear		**150** Tribes from Gaul begin to migrate to Britain

Roman Britain

Throughout the 350-year Roman occupation, Britain was ruled as a colony. After the defeat of rebellious local tribes, such as Boadicea's Iceni, the Romans remained an unassimilated occupying power. Their legacy is in military and civil construction: forts, walls, towns and public buildings. Their long, straight roads, built for easy movement of troops, are still a feature of the landscape.

Roman jasper seal

Cavalry Sports Helmet
Found in Lancashire, it was used in tournaments by horsemen. Cavalry races and other sports were held in amphitheatres near towns.

Silver Jug
This 3rd-century jug, the earliest known silver item with Christian symbols, was excavated near Peterborough.

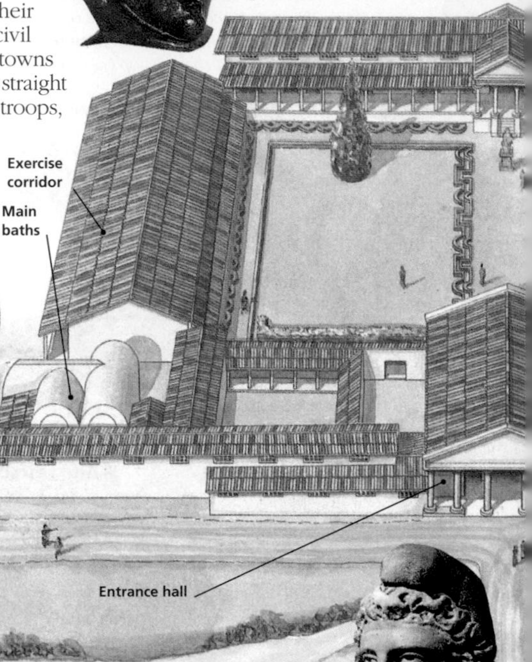

Exercise corridor

Main baths

Entrance hall

Fishbourne Palace was built at the site of a natural harbour and ships could moor here.

Hadrian's Wall
Started in 120 as a defence against the Scots; it marked the northern frontier of the Roman Empire and was guarded by 17 forts housing over 18,500 foot-soldiers and cavalry.

Mithras
This head of the god Mithras was found on the London site of a temple devoted to the cult of Mithraism. The sect demanded of its Roman followers loyalty and discipline.

TIMELINE

54 BC Julius Caesar lands in Britain but withdraws

Julius Caesar (c.102–44 BC)

AD 61 Boadicea rebels against Romans and burns their towns, including St Albans and Colchester, but is defeated (*see p195*)

AD 70 Romans conquer Wales and the North

Boadicea (1st century), Queen of the Iceni

140–143 Romans occupy southern Scotland and build Antonine Wall to mark the frontier

55 BC	AD 1	AD 50		150

AD 43 Claudius invades; Britain becomes part of the Roman Empire

AD 78–84 Agricola advances into Scotland, then retreats

120 Emperor Hadrian builds a wall on the border with Scotland

Flavian Mosaic
Roman floors of the 1st century used patterns in black and white stone. More mosaics survive at Fishbourne than at any other British site.

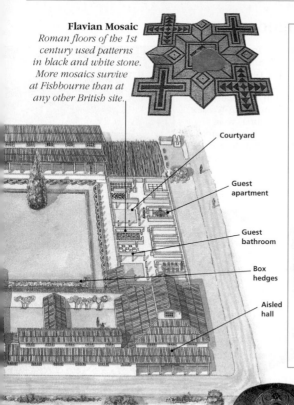

Courtyard

Guest apartment

Guest bathroom

Box hedges

Aisled hall

WHERE TO SEE ROMAN BRITAIN

Many of Britain's main towns and cities were established by the Romans and have Roman remains, including York *(see pp404–09)*, Chester *(see pp310–11)*, St Albans *(see p232)*, Colchester *(see p205)*, Bath *(see pp258–61)*, Lincoln *(see pp340–41)* and London *(see pp70–155)*. Several Roman villas were built in southern England, favoured for its mild climate and proximity to Europe.

The Roman baths in Bath
(see pp258–61), known as Aquae Sulis, were built between the 1st and 4th centuries around a natural hot spring.

Battersea Shield
Found in the Thames near Battersea, the shield bears Celtic symbols and was probably made at about the time of the first Roman invasion. Archaeologists suspect it may have been lost by a warrior while crossing the river, or offered as a sacrifice to one of the many river gods. It is now at the British Museum (see pp106–7).

FISHBOURNE PALACE

Built during the 1st century for Togidubnus, a pro-Roman governor, the palace (here reconstructed) had sophisticated functions such as under-floor heating and indoor plumbing for baths *(see p171)*.

Chi-Rho Symbol
This early Christian symbol is from a 3rd-century fresco at Lullingstone Roman villa in Kent.

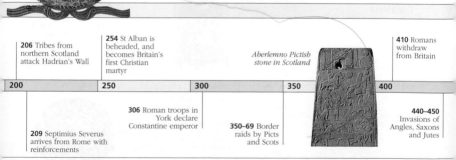

206 Tribes from northern Scotland attack Hadrian's Wall

254 St Alban is beheaded, and becomes Britain's first Christian martyr

Aberlemno Pictish stone in Scotland

410 Romans withdraw from Britain

200   250   300   350   400

306 Roman troops in York declare Constantine emperor

350–69 Border raids by Picts and Scots

440–450 Invasions of Angles, Saxons and Jutes

209 Septimius Severus arrives from Rome with reinforcements

Anglo-Saxon Kingdoms

**King Canute
(1016–35)**

By the mid-5th century, Angles and Saxons from Germany had started to raid the eastern shores of Britain. Increasingly they decided to settle, and within 100 years Saxon kingdoms, including Wessex, Mercia and Northumbria, were established over the entire country. Viking raids throughout the 8th and 9th centuries were largely contained, but in 1066, the last invasion of England saw William the Conqueror from Normandy defeat the Anglo-Saxon King Harold at the Battle of Hastings. William then went on to assume control of the whole country.

Viking Axe
The principal weapons of the Viking warriors were spear, axe and sword. They were skilled metal-workers with an eye for decoration, as seen in this axe-head from a Copenhagen museum.

Vikings on a Raiding Expedition
Scandinavian boat-building skills were in advance of anything known in Britain. People were terrified by these large, fast boats with their intimidating figureheads, which sailed up the Thames and along the coasts.

ANGLO-SAXON CALENDAR
These scenes from a chronicle of seasons, made just before the Norman invasion, show life in late Anglo-Saxon Britain. At first people lived in small farming communities, but by the 7th century towns began to spring up and trade increased. Saxon kings were supported by nobles but most of the population were free peasants.

TIMELINE

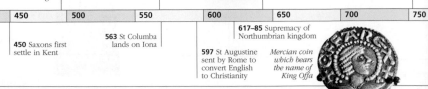

c.470–495 Saxons and Angles settle in Essex, Sussex and East Anglia	**c.556** Saxons move across Britain and set up seven kingdoms	*St Augustine (d.604)* **635** St Aidan establishes a monastery on Lindisfarne	**730–821** Supremacy of Mercia, whose king, Offa (d.796), builds a dyke along the Mercia–Wales border

450	500	550	600	650	700	750

450 Saxons first settle in Kent

563 St Columba lands on Iona

597 St Augustine sent by Rome to convert English to Christianity

617–85 Supremacy of Northumbrian kingdom

Mercian coin which bears the name of King Offa

Ox-drawn plough for tilling

Minstrels entertaining at a feast

Hawks, used to kill game

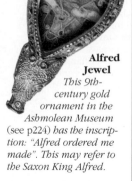

Alfred Jewel
This 9th-century gold ornament in the Ashmolean Museum (see p224) *has the inscription: "Alfred ordered me made". This may refer to the Saxon King Alfred.*

WHERE TO SEE ANGLO-SAXON BRITAIN

The best collection of Saxon artefacts is from a burial ship unearthed at Sutton Hoo in Suffolk in 1938 and now on display at the British Museum *(see pp106–7).* There are fine Saxon churches at Bradwell in Essex and Bosham in Sussex *(see p171).* In York the Viking town of Jorvik has been excavated *(see p408)* and actual relics are shown alongside models of people and dwellings.

The Saxon church *of St Laurence* (see p255) *was built in the late 8th century.*

Edward the Confessor
In 1042, Edward – known as "the Confessor" because of his piety – became king. He died in 1066 and William of Normandy claimed the throne.

Harold's Death
This 14th-century illustration depicts the victorious William of Normandy after King Harold was killed with an arrow in his eye. The Battle of Hastings (see p181) was the last invasion of Britain.

Legend of King Arthur
Arthur is thought to have been a chieftain who fought the Saxons in the early 6th century. Legends of his knights' exploits appeared in 1155 (see p285).

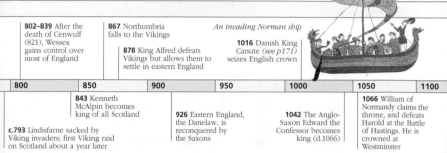

802–839 After the death of Cenwulf (821), Wessex gains control over most of England

867 Northumbria falls to the Vikings

878 King Alfred defeats Vikings but allows them to settle in eastern England

An invading Norman ship

1016 Danish King Canute *(see p171)* seizes English crown

| 800 | 850 | 900 | 950 | 1000 | 1050 | 1100 |

843 Kenneth McAlpin becomes king of all Scotland

c.793 Lindisfarne sacked by Viking invaders; first Viking raid on Scotland about a year later

926 Eastern England, the Danelaw, is reconquered by the Saxons

1042 The Anglo-Saxon Edward the Confessor becomes king (d.1066)

1066 William of Normandy claims the throne, and defeats Harold at the Battle of Hastings. He is crowned at Westminster

The Middle Ages

Noblemen stag hunting

Remains of Norman castles on English hill tops bear testimony to the military might used by the invaders to sustain their conquest – although Wales and Scotland resisted for centuries. The Normans operated a feudal system, creating an aristocracy that treated native Anglo-Saxons as serfs. The ruling class spoke French until the 13th century, when it mixed with the Old English used by the peasants. The medieval church's power is shown in the cathedrals that grace British cities today.

Magna Carta
To protect themselves and the church from arbitrary taxation, the powerful English barons compelled King John to sign a "great charter" in 1215 (see p235). This laid the foundations for an independent legal system.

Craft Skills
An illustration from a 14th-century manuscript depicts a weaver and a copper-beater – two of the trades that created a wealthy class of artisans.

Becket is received into heaven.

Henry II's knights murder Becket in Canterbury Cathedral.

MURDER OF THOMAS BECKET

The struggle between church and king for ultimate control of the country was brought to a head by the murder of Becket, the Archbishop of Canterbury. After Becket's canonization in 1173, Canterbury became a major centre of pilgrimage.

Ecclesiastical Art
Nearly all medieval art had religious themes, such as this window at Canterbury Cathedral (see pp186–7) depicting Jeroboam.

Black Death
A plague swept Britain and Europe several times in the 14th century, killing millions of people. This illustration, in a religious tract, produced around 100 years later, represents death taking its heavy toll.

TIMELINE

1071 Hereward the Wake, leader of the Anglo-Saxon resistance, defeated at Ely

1154 Henry II, the first Plantagenet king, demolishes castles, and exacts money from barons instead of military service

1170 Archbishop of Canterbury, Thomas à Becket, is murdered by four knights after quarrelling with Henry II

1100	1150	1200	1250

1086 The *Domesday Book*, a survey of every manor in England, is compiled for tax purposes

Domesday Book

1215 Barons compel King John to sign the *Magna Carta*

1256 First Parliament to include ordinary citizens

Battle of Agincourt

In 1415, Henry V took an army to France to claim its throne. This 15th-century chronicle depicts Henry beating the French army at Agincourt.

This casket (1190), in a private collection, is said to have contained Becket's remains.

Becket takes his place in Heaven after his canonization.

Two clergymen look on in horror at Becket's murder.

Richard III

Richard, shown in this 16th-century painting, became king during the Wars of the Roses: a bitter struggle for power between two factions of the royal family – the houses of York and Lancaster.

John Wycliffe (1329–84)

This painting by Ford Madox Brown (1821–93) shows Wycliffe with the Bible he translated into English to make it accessible to everyone.

WHERE TO SEE MEDIEVAL BRITAIN

The university cities of Oxford (pp222–27) and Cambridge (pp210–15) contain the largest concentrations of Gothic buildings. Magnificent cathedrals rise high above many historic cities, among them Lincoln (pp340–41) and York (pp404–09). Both cities still retain at least part of their ancient street pattern. Military architecture is best seen in Wales (pp438–9) with the formidable border castles of Edward I.

All Souls College in Oxford (see p226), which only takes graduates, is a superb blend of medieval and later architecture.

Castle Life

Every section of a castle was allotted to a baron whose soldiers helped defend it. This 14th-century illustration shows the coats of arms (see p30) of the barons for each area

1282–3 Edward I conquers Wales

1314 Scots defeat English at the Battle of Bannockburn (see p482)

1348 Europe's population halved by Black Death

1387 Chaucer starts writing the *Canterbury Tales* (see p186)

1485 Battle of Bosworth ends Wars of the Roses

Geoffrey Chaucer (c.1345–1400)

1300   **1350**   **1400**   **1450**

1296 Edward I invades Scotland but Scots resist stoutly

Edward I (1239–1307)

1381 Peasants' revolt after the imposition of a poll tax on everyone in the country over 14

1415 English victory at Agincourt

1453 End of Hundred Years' War against France

Tudor Renaissance

Hawking, a popular pastime

After years of debilitating civil war, the Tudor monarchs established peace and national self-confidence, reflected in the split from the church of Rome – due to Henry VIII's divorce from Catherine of Aragon – and the consequent closure of the monasteries. Henry's daughter, Mary I, tried to re-establish Catholicism but under her half-sister, Elizabeth I, the Protestant church secured its position. Overseas exploration began, provoking clashes with other European powers seeking to exploit the New World. The Renaissance in arts and learning spread from Europe to Britain, with playwright William Shakespeare adding his own unique contribution.

Curtains behind the queen are open to reveal scenes of the great English victory over the Spanish Armada in 1588.

Sea Power
Henry VIII laid the foundations of the powerful English navy. In 1545, his flagship, the Mary Rose *(see p169), sank before his eyes in Portsmouth harbour on its way to do battle with the French.*

Theatre
Some of Shakespeare's plays were first seen in purpose-built theatres such as the Globe (see p120) in south London.

The globe signifies that the queen reigns supreme far and wide.

Monasteries
With Henry VIII's split from Rome, England's religious houses, like Fountains Abbey (see pp390–91), were dissolved. Henry stole their riches and used them to finance his foreign policy.

TIMELINE

1497 John Colet denounces the corruption of the clergy, supported by Erasmus and Sir Thomas More

1533–4 Henry VIII divorces Catherine of Aragon and is excommunicated by the Pope. He forms the Church of England

1542–1567 Mary, Queen of Scots rules Scotland

1490   **1510**   **1530**

1497 John Cabot *(see p256)* makes his first voyage to North America

1513 English defeat Scots at Flodden *(see p482)*

Henry VIII (1491–1547)

1535 Act of Union with Wales

1536–40 Dissolution of the Monasteries

1549 First Book of Common Prayer introduced

Mary, Queen of Scots
As great-granddaughter of Henry VII, she laid claim to the English throne in 1559. But in 1567, Elizabeth I had her imprisoned for 20 years until her execution for treason in 1587.

Jewels symbolize triumph.

WHERE TO SEE TUDOR BRITAIN

Hampton Court Palace (p173) has been altered over the centuries but remains a Tudor showpiece. Part of Elizabeth I's former home at Hatfield (p231) still survives. In Kent, Leeds Castle, Knole (pp188–9) and Hever Castle (p189) all have connections with Tudor royalty. Burghley House (pp342–3) and Hardwick Hall (p302), both Midlands mansions, retain their 16th-century character.

This astronomical clock *at Hampton Court (see p173), with its intriguing zodiac symbols, was installed in 1540 by Henry VIII.*

Protestant Martyrs
Catholic Mary I reigned from 1553 to 1558. Protestants who opposed her rule were burned, such as these six churchmen at Canterbury in 1555.

DEFEAT OF THE ARMADA
Spain was England's main rival for supremacy on the seas, and in 1588 Philip II sent 100 powerfully armed galleons towards England, bent on invasion. The English fleet – under Lord Howard, Francis Drake, John Hawkins and Martin Frobisher – sailed from Plymouth and destroyed the Spanish navy in a famous victory. This commemorative portrait of Elizabeth I by George Gower (d.1596) celebrates the triumph.

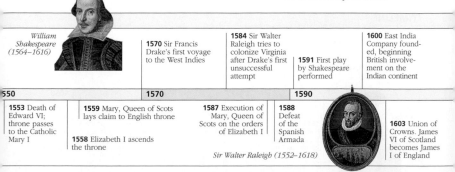

William Shakespeare (1564–1616)

1570 Sir Francis Drake's first voyage to the West Indies

1584 Sir Walter Raleigh tries to colonize Virginia after Drake's first unsuccessful attempt

1591 First play by Shakespeare performed

1600 East India Company founded, beginning British involvement on the Indian continent

550   1570   1590

1553 Death of Edward VI; throne passes to the Catholic Mary I

1559 Mary, Queen of Scots lays claim to English throne

1558 Elizabeth I ascends the throne

1587 Execution of Mary, Queen of Scots on the orders of Elizabeth I

1588 Defeat of the Spanish Armada

Sir Walter Raleigh (1552–1618)

1603 Union of Crowns. James VI of Scotland becomes James I of England

Stuart Britain

The end of Elizabeth I's reign signalled the start of internal turmoil. The throne passed to James I, whose belief that kings ruled by divine right provoked clashes with Parliament. Under his son, Charles I, the conflict escalated into Civil War that ended with his execution. In 1660 Charles II regained the throne, but after his death James II was ousted for Catholic leanings. Protestantism was reaffirmed with the reign of William and Mary, who suppressed the Catholic Jacobites (*see p483*).

A 17th-century barber's bowl

Science
Sir Isaac Newton (1642–1727) invented this reflecting telescope, laying the foundation for a greater understanding of the universe, including the law of gravity.

Charles I stayed silent at his trial.

Oliver Cromwell
A strict Protestant and a passionate champion of the rights of Parliament, he led the victorious Parliamentary forces in the Civil War. He became Lord Protector of the Commonwealth from 1653 to 1658.

On the way to his death, the king wore two shirts for warmth, so onlookers should not think he was shivering with fright.

Theatre
After the Restoration in 1660, when Parliament restored the monarchy, theatre thrived. Plays were performed on temporary outdoor stages.

EXECUTION OF CHARLES I
Cromwell was convinced there would be no peace until the king was dead. At his trial for treason, Charles refused to recognize the authority of the court and offered no defence. He faced his death with dignity on 30 January 1649, the only English king to be executed. His death was followed by a republic known as the Commonwealth.

TIMELINE

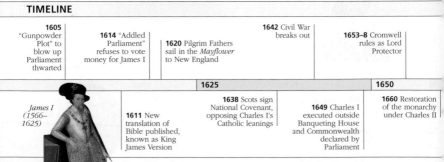

1605 "Gunpowder Plot" to blow up Parliament thwarted

1614 "Addled Parliament" refuses to vote money for James I

1620 Pilgrim Fathers sail in the *Mayflower* to New England

1642 Civil War breaks out

1653–8 Cromwell rules as Lord Protector

1625

1650

James I (1566–1625)

1611 New translation of Bible published, known as King James Version

1638 Scots sign National Covenant, opposing Charles I's Catholic leanings

1649 Charles I executed outside Banqueting House and Commonwealth declared by Parliament

1660 Restoration of the monarchy under Charles II

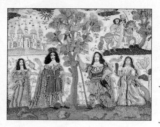

Restoration of the Monarchy
This silk embroidery celebrates the fact that Charles II escaped his father's fate by hiding in an oak tree. There was joy at his return from exile in France.

WHERE TO SEE STUART BRITAIN

The best work of the two leading architects of the time, Inigo Jones and Christopher Wren, is in London, and includes St Paul's Cathedral *(pp114–15)*. In the southeast two classic Jacobean mansions are Audley End *(p208)* and Hatfield House *(p231)*. The Palace of Holyrood *(p510)*, in Edinburgh, is another example.

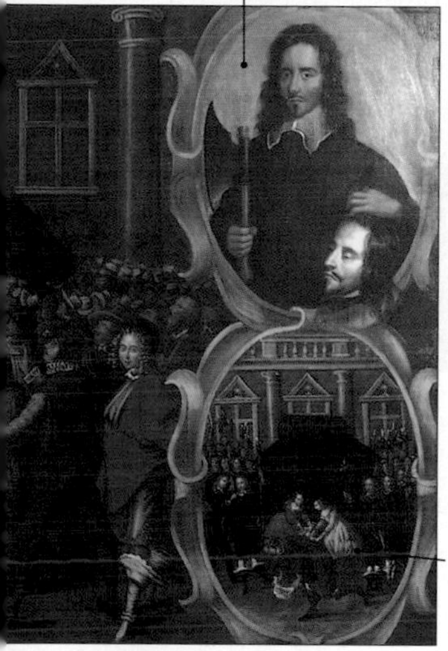

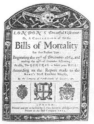

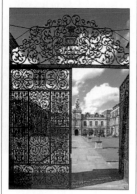

Hatfield House (p231) *is a splendid Jacobean mansion.*

The headless body kneels by the block.

The axeman holds the severed head of Charles I.

Onlookers soaked up the king's blood with their handkerchiefs to have a memento.

Plague
Bills of mortality showed the weekly deaths as bubonic plague swept London in 1665. Up to 100,000 Londoners died.

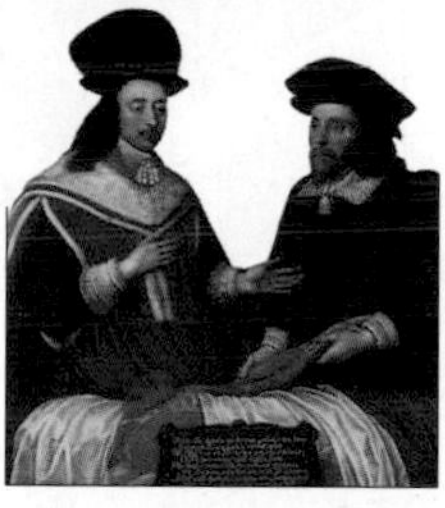

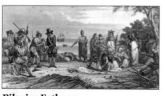

Pilgrim Fathers
In 1620 a group of Puritans sailed to America. They forged good relations with the native Indians; here they are shown being visited by the chief of the Pokanokets.

Anatomy
By dissecting corpses, physicians began to gain an understanding of the working of the human body – a crucial step towards modern surgery and medicine.

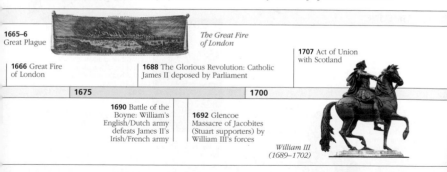

1665–6 Great Plague

The Great Fire of London

1666 Great Fire of London

1688 The Glorious Revolution: Catholic James II deposed by Parliament

1707 Act of Union with Scotland

1675

1700

1690 Battle of the Boyne: William's English/Dutch army defeats James II's Irish/French army

1692 Glencoe Massacre of Jacobites (Stuart supporters) by William III's forces

William III (1689–1702)

Georgian Britain

The 18th century saw Britain, now recovered from the trauma of its Civil War, develop as a commercial and industrial powerhouse. London became a centre of banking, and a mercantile and professional class grew up. Continuing supremacy at sea laid the foundations of an empire; steam engines, canals and railways heralded the Industrial Revolution. Growing confidence was reflected in stately architecture and elegant fashions but, as cities became more crowded, conditions for the underclass grew worse.

Actress Sarah Siddons (1785), Gainsborough

Slate became the preferred tile for Georgian buildings. Roofs became less steep to achieve an Italian look.

A row of sash windows is one of the most characteristic features of a Georgian house.

Battle of Bunker Hill
In 1775 American colonists rebelled against British rule. The British won this early battle in Massachusetts, but in 1783 Britain recognized the United States of America.

Oak was used in the best dwellings for doors and stairs, but pine was standard in most houses.

The saloon was covered in wallpaper, a cheaper alternative to hanging walls with tapestries or fabrics.

The drawing room was richly ornamented and used for entertaining visitors.

The dining room was used for all family meals.

Watt's Steam Engine
The Scottish engineer James Watt (1736–1819) patented his engine in 1769 and then developed it for locomotion.

Lord Horatio Nelson
Nelson (see p31) became a hero after his death at the Battle of Trafalgar fighting the French.

Steps led to the servants' entrance in the basement.

TIMELINE

1720 "South Sea Bubble" bursts: many speculators ruined in securities fraud

1746 Bonnie Prince Charlie *(see p535),* Jacobite claimant to throne, defeated at the Battle of Culloden

| 1715 | 1730 | 1745 | 1760 |

1714 George, Elector of Hanover, succeeds Queen Anne, ending the Stuart dynasty and giving Britain a German-speaking monarch

1721 Robert Walpole (1646–1745) becomes the first Prime Minister

George I (1660–1727)

Satirical engraving about the South Sea Bubble, 1720

1757 Britain's first canal completed

Canal Barge *(1827)*
Canals were a cheap way to carry the new industrial goods but were gradually superseded by railways during the 19th century.

The attics were where children and servants slept.

WHERE TO SEE GEORGIAN BRITAIN

Bath *(see pp258–61)* and Edinburgh *(see pp504–11)* are two of Britain's best-preserved Georgian towns. The Building of Bath Museum in Bath *(see p261)* has a real Georgian flavour and Brighton's Royal Pavilion *(see pp178–9)* is a Regency extravaganza by John Nash.

Charlotte Square (see p504) *in Edinburgh has fine examples of Georgian architecture.*

The master bedroom often had a mahogany four-poster bed.

Chippendale Armchair *(1760)*
Thomas Chippendale (1718–79) designed elegant furniture in a style still popular today.

Furniture was often carved, depicting animal heads and legs.

GEORGIAN TOWN HOUSE

Tall, terraced dwellings were built to house wealthy families. The main architects of the time were Robert Adam *(see p28)* and John Nash *(see p105)*.

The servants lived and worked in the basement during the day.

Kitchen

Hogarth's Gin Lane
Conditions in London's slums shocked William Hogarth (1697–1764), who made prints like this to urge social reform.

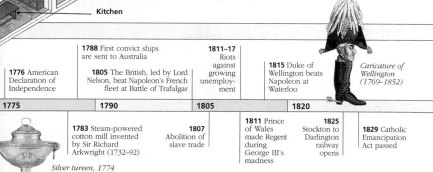

1776 American Declaration of Independence

1788 First convict ships are sent to Australia

1805 The British, led by Lord Nelson, beat Napoleon's French fleet at Battle of Trafalgar

1811–17 Riots against growing unemployment

1815 Duke of Wellington beats Napoleon at Waterloo

Caricature of Wellington (1769–1852)

1775   **1790**   **1805**   **1820**

1783 Steam-powered cotton mill invented by Sir Richard Arkwright (1732–92)

1807 Abolition of slave trade

1811 Prince of Wales made Regent during George III's madness

1825 Stockton to Darlington railway opens

1829 Catholic Emancipation Act passed

Silver tureen, 1774

Victorian Britain

When Victoria became Queen in 1837, she was only 18. Britain was in the throes of its transformation from an agricultural country to the world's most powerful industrial nation. The growth of the Empire fuelled the country's confidence and opened up markets for Britain's manufactured goods. The accelerating growth of cities created problems of health and housing and a powerful Labour movement began to emerge. But by the end of Victoria's long and popular reign in 1901, conditions had begun to improve as more people got the vote and universal education was introduced.

Florence Nightingale *(1820–1910)*
Known as the Lady with the Lamp, she nursed soldiers in the Crimean War and pioneered many improvements in army medical care.

Victoria and Disraeli, 1887

Glass walls and ceiling

Prefabricated girders

Newcastle Slum *(1880)*
Rows of cheap houses were built for an influx of workers to the major industrial cities. The awful conditions spread disease and social discontent.

UNITED SOCIETY OF BOILERMAKERS AND IRON AND STEEL SHIPBUILDERS

LONDON DISTRICT COMMITTEE

Union Banner
Trade unions were set up to protect industrial workers against unscrupulous employers.

As well as silk textiles exhibits included carriages, engines, jewels, glass, plants, cutlery and sculptures.

Ophelia by Sir John Everett Millais *(1829–96)*
The Pre-Raphaelite painters chose Romantic themes, reflecting a desire to escape industrial Britain.

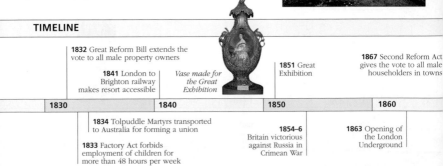

TIMELINE

1832 Great Reform Bill extends the vote to all male property owners

1841 London to Brighton railway makes resort accessible

Vase made for the Great Exhibition

1851 Great Exhibition

1867 Second Reform Act gives the vote to all male householders in towns

1830	1840	1850	1860

1834 Tolpuddle Martyrs transported to Australia for forming a union

1833 Factory Act forbids employment of children for more than 48 hours per week

1854–6 Britain victorious against Russia in Crimean War

1863 Opening of the London Underground

Triumph of Steam and Electricity
This picture from the Illustrated London News *(1897) sums up the feeling of optimism engendered by industrial advances.*

Elm trees were incorporated into the building along with sparrows, and sparrow hawks to control them.

WHERE TO SEE VICTORIAN BRITAIN
The industrial cities of the Midlands and the North are built around grandiose civic, commercial and industrial buildings. Notable Victorian monuments include the Manchester Museum of Science and Industry *(p373)* and, in London, the vast Victoria and Albert Museum *(see pp98–9)*.

The Rotunda, Manchester *is a stately Victorian building.*

GREAT EXHIBITION OF 1851
The brainchild of Prince Albert, Victoria's consort, the exhibition celebrated industry, technology and the expanding British Empire. It was the biggest of its kind held up till then. Between May and October, six million people visited Joseph Paxton's lavish crystal palace, in London's Hyde Park. Nearly 14,000 exhibitors brought 100,000 exhibits from all over the world. In 1852 it was moved to south London where it burned down in 1936.

Cycling Craze
The bicycle, invented in 1865, became immensely popular with young people, as illustrated by this photograph of 1898.

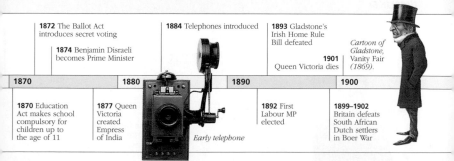

1872 The Ballot Act introduces secret voting

1874 Benjamin Disraeli becomes Prime Minister

1884 Telephones introduced

1893 Gladstone's Irish Home Rule Bill defeated

Cartoon of Gladstone, Vanity Fair *(1869).*

1901 Queen Victoria dies

| 1870 | 1880 | 1890 | 1900 |

1870 Education Act makes school compulsory for children up to the age of 11

1877 Queen Victoria created Empress of India

Early telephone

1892 First Labour MP elected

1899–1902 Britain defeats South African Dutch settlers in Boer War

Britain from 1900 to 1950

When Queen Victoria's reign ended in 1901, British society threw off many of its 19th-century inhibitions, and an era of gaiety and excitement began. This was interrupted by World War I. The economic troubles that ensued, which culminated in the Depression of the 1930s, brought misery to millions. In 1939 the ambitions of Germany provoked World War II. After emerging victorious from this conflict, Britain embarked on an ambitious programme of social, educational and health reform.

Playwright Noel Coward

Welwyn Garden City was based on the Utopian ideals of Sir Ebenezer Howard (1850–1928), founder of the garden city movement.

Suffragettes
Women marched and chained themselves to railings in their effort to get the vote; many went to prison. Women over 30 won the vote in 1919.

The Roaring Twenties
Young flappers discarded the rigid social codes of their parents and instead discovered jazz, cocktails and the Charleston.

NEW TOWNS

A string of new towns was created on the outskirts of London, planned to give residents greenery and fresh air. Welwyn Garden City was originally founded in 1919 as a self-contained community, but fast rail links turned it into a base for London commuters.

World War I
British troops in Europe dug into deep trenches protected by barbed wire and machine guns, only metres from the enemy, in a war of attrition that cost the lives of 17 million.

Wireless
Invented by Guglielmo Marconi, radios brought news and entertainment into homes for the first time.

TIMELINE

1903 Suffragette movement founded

1911 MPs are given a salary for the first time, allowing working men to be elected

1914–18 World War I

1924 First Labour government

| 1905 | 1910 | 1915 | 1920 |

Henry Asquith (1852–1928), Prime Minister

1908 Asquith's Liberal government introduces old age pensions

1918 Vote given to all women over 30

1922 First national radio service begins

Marching for Jobs
These men were among thousands who marched for their jobs after being put out of work in the 1920s. The stock market crash of 1929 and the ensuing Depression caused even more unemployment.

Garden cities all had trees, ponds and open spaces.

World War II
German night-time air raids targeted transport, military and industrial sites and cities, such as Sheffield, in what was known as the "Blitz".

Modern Homes
Labour-saving devices, such as the vacuum cleaner, invented by William Hoover in 1908, were very popular. This was due to the virtual disappearance of domestic servants, as women took jobs outside the home.

Cheap housing and the promise of a cleaner environment attracted many people to these new cities.

Family Motoring
By the middle of the century, more families could afford to buy mass-produced automobiles, like the 1950s Hillman Minx pictured in this advertisement.

| 1926 General Strike | 1936 Abdication of Edward VIII | 1944 Education Act: school leaving age raised to 15; grants provided for university students | 1948 National Health Service introduced |
| | | | 1947 Independence for India and Pakistan |

Edward VIII (1894–1972) and Wallis Simpson (1896–1986)

| 925 | 1930 | 1935 | 1940 | 1945 |

| 1929 Stock market crashes | 1936 First scheduled television service begins | 1939–45 Winston Churchill leads Britain to victory in World War II | 1945 Majority Labour government; nationalization of railways, road haulage, civil aviation, Bank of England, gas, electricity and steel |
| 1928 Votes for all men and women over 21 | | *Food ration book* | |

Britain Today

With the deprivations of war receding, Britain entered the Swinging Sixties, an explosion of youth culture characterized by the mini-skirt and the emergence of pop groups. The Age of Empire came to an end as most colonies gained independence by the 1970s – although Britain went to war again in 1982 when Argentina sought to annex the tiny Falkland Islands.

People were on the move; immigration from the former colonies enriched British culture – though it also gave rise to social problems – and increasing prosperity allowed millions of people to travel abroad. Britain joined the European Community in 1973, and forged a more tangible link when the Channel Tunnel opened in 1994.

Designer Vivienne Westwood and Naomi Campbell

1960s The mini-skirt takes British fashion to new heights of daring – and Flower Power arrives from California

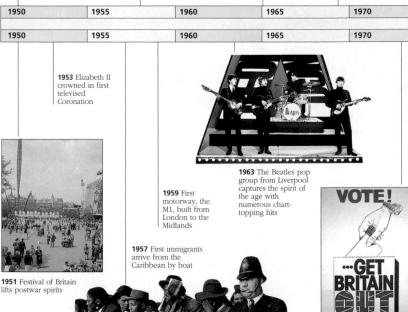

1951 Winston Churchill comes back as Prime Minister as Conservatives win general election

1958 Campaign for Nuclear Disarmament launched, reflecting young people's fear of global annihilation

1965 Death penalty is abolished

1950	1955	1960	1965	1970

1950	1955	1960	1965	1970

1953 Elizabeth II crowned in first televised Coronation

1963 The Beatles pop group from Liverpool captures the spirit of the age with numerous chart-topping hits

1959 First motorway, the M1, built from London to the Midlands

1957 First immigrants arrive from the Caribbean by boat

1951 Festival of Britain lifts postwar spirits

VOTE!

...GET BRITAIN OUT

1973 After years of negotiation, Britain joins the European Community

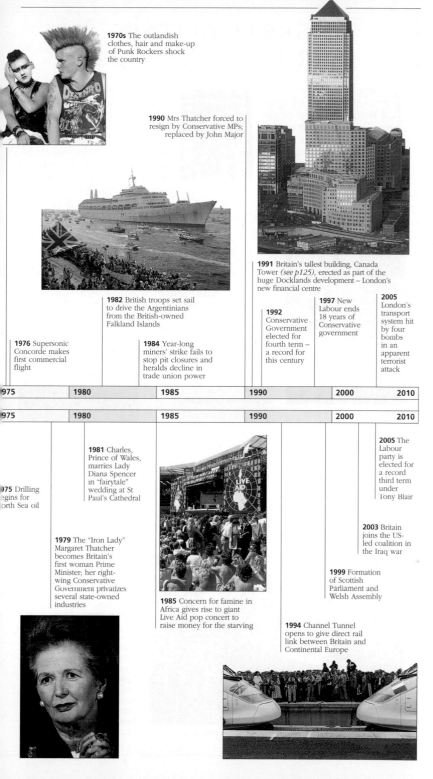

1970s The outlandish clothes, hair and make-up of Punk Rockers shock the country

1990 Mrs Thatcher forced to resign by Conservative MPs; replaced by John Major

1991 Britain's tallest building, Canada Tower (see p125), erected as part of the huge Docklands development – London's new financial centre

1982 British troops set sail to drive the Argentinians from the British-owned Falkland Islands

1992 Conservative Government elected for fourth term – a record for this century

1997 New Labour ends 18 years of Conservative government

2005 London's transport system hit by four bombs in an apparent terrorist attack

1976 Supersonic Concorde makes first commercial flight

1984 Year-long miners' strike fails to stop pit closures and heralds decline in trade union power

975   1980   1985   1990   2000   2010

975   1980   1985   1990   2000   2010

1981 Charles, Prince of Wales, marries Lady Diana Spencer in "fairytale" wedding at St Paul's Cathedral

2005 The Labour party is elected for a record third term under Tony Blair

975 Drilling egins for orth Sea oil

1979 The "Iron Lady" Margaret Thatcher becomes Britain's first woman Prime Minister; her right-wing Conservative Government privatizes several state-owned industries

2003 Britain joins the US-led coalition in the Iraq war

1999 Formation of Scottish Parliament and Welsh Assembly

1985 Concern for famine in Africa gives rise to giant Live Aid pop concert to raise money for the starving

1994 Channel Tunnel opens to give direct rail link between Britain and Continental Europe

GREAT BRITAIN
THROUGH THE YEAR

Every British season has its particular charms. Most major sights are open all year round, but many secondary attractions may be closed in winter. The weather is changeable in all seasons and the visitor is as likely to experience a crisp, sunny February day as to be caught in a cold, heavy shower in July. Long periods of

Film festival sign

adverse weather and extremes of temperature are rare. Spring is characterized by daffodils and bluebells, summer by roses and autumn by the vivid colours of changing leaves. In wintertime, country vistas are visible through the bare branches of the trees. Annual events and ceremonies, many stemming from age-old traditions, reflect the attributes of the seasons.

Bluebells in spring in Angrove woodland, Wiltshire

SPRING

As the days get longer and warmer, the countryside starts to come alive. At Easter many stately homes and gardens open their gates to visitors for the first time, and during the week before Whit

Sunday, or Whitsun (the seventh Sunday after Easter), the Chelsea Flower Show takes place. This is the focal point of the gardening year and spurs on the nation's gardeners to prepare their summer displays. Outside the capital, many music and arts festivals mark the middle months of the year.

MARCH

Ideal Home Exhibition *(second week),* Earl's Court, London. New products and ideas for the home.
Crufts Dog Show, National Exhibition Centre, Birmingham.
International Book Fair *(third week),* Olympia, London.
St Patrick's Day *(17 March).* Musical events in major cities celebrate the feast day of Ireland's patron saint.

APRIL

Maundy Thursday (Thursday before Easter), the Queen gives money to pensioners.
St George's Day *(23 April),* English patron saint's day.
Antiques for Everyone *(last week),* National Exhibition Centre, Birmingham.

Water garden exhibited at the Chelsea Flower Show

MAY

Furry Dancing Festival *(8 May),* Helston, Cornwall. Spring celebration *(see p280).*
Well-dressing festivals *(Ascension Day),* Tissington, Derbyshire *(see p337).*
Chelsea Flower Show *(May),* Royal Hospital, London.
Brighton Festival *(last three weeks).* Performing arts.
Glyndebourne Festival Opera Season *(mid-May–end Aug),* near Lewes, East Sussex. Opera productions.
International Highland Games *(last weekend),* Blair Atholl, Scotland.

Yeomen of the Guard conducting the Maundy money ceremony

SUMMER

Life moves outdoors in the summer months. Cafés and restaurants place tables on the pavements and pub customers take their drinks outside. The Queen holds garden parties for privileged guests at Buckingham Palace while, more modestly, village fêtes – a combination of a carnival and street party – are organized. Beaches and swimming pools become crowded and office workers picnic in city parks at lunch. The rose, England's national flower, bursts into bloom in millions of gardens. Cultural treats include open-air theatre performances, outdoor concerts, the Proms in London, the National Eisteddfod in Wales, Glyndebourne's opera festival, and Edinburgh's festival of the performing arts.

Deck chair at Brighton

JUNE

Royal Academy Summer Exhibitions *(Jun–Aug)*. Large and varied London show of new work by many artists.
Bath International Festival *(late May–early Jun)*, various venues. Arts events.
Beaumaris Festival *(27 May–4 Jun)*, various venues. Concerts, craft fairs plus fringe activities.
Trooping the Colour *(Sat closest to 10 Jun)*, Whitehall,

Assessment of sheep at the Royal Welsh Show, Builth Wells

London. The Queen's official birthday parade.
Glastonbury Festival *(late June)*, Somerset.
Aldeburgh Festival *(second and third weeks)*, Suffolk. Arts festival with concerts and opera.
Royal Highland Show *(third week)*, Ingliston, near Edinburgh. Scotland's agricultural show.
Leeds Castle *(last week)*. Open-air concerts.
Glasgow International Jazz Festival *(last weekend)*. Various venues.

JULY

Royal Show *(first week)*, near Kenilworth, Warwickshire. National agricultural show.
International Eisteddfod *(first week)*, Llangollen, North Wales. International music and dance competition *(see p450)*.
Hampton Court Flower Show *(early July)*, Hampton Court Palace, Surrey.
Summer Music Festival *(third weekend)*, Stourhead, Wiltshire.
International Henley Royal Regatta *(first week)*, Henley-on-Thames. Rowing regatta on the Thames.
Cambridge Folk Festival *(last weekend)*. Music festival with top international artists.
Royal Welsh Show *(last weekend)*, Builth Wells, Wales. Agricultural show.
International Festival of Folk Arts *(late Jul–early Aug)*, Sidmouth, Devon *(see p289)*.

Glastonbury music festival, a major event attracting thousands of people

AUGUST

Royal National Eisteddfod *(early in month)*. Traditional arts competitions, in Welsh *(see p435)*. Various locations.

Reveller in bright costume at the Notting Hill Carnival

Henry Wood Promenade Concerts *(mid-Jul–mid-Sep)*, Royal Albert Hall, London. Famous concert series popularly known as the Proms.
Edinburgh International Festival *(mid-Aug–mid-Sep)*. The largest festival of theatre, dance and music in the world *(see p481)*.
Edinburgh Festival Fringe. Alongside the festival, there are 400 shows a day.
Brecon Jazz *(mid-Aug)*, jazz festival in Brecon, Wales.
Beatles Festival *(last weekend)*, Liverpool. Music and entertainment related to the Fab Four *(see p377)*.
Notting Hill Carnival *(last weekend)*, London. West Indian street carnival with floats, bands and stalls.

Boxes of apples from the autumn harvest

AUTUMN

After the heady escapism of summer, the start of the new season is marked by the various party political conferences held in October and the royal opening of Parliament. All over the country on 5 November, bonfires are lit and fireworks let off to celebrate the foiling of an attempt to blow up the Houses of Parliament by Guy Fawkes and his co-conspirators in 1605. Cornfields become golden, trees turn fiery yellow through to russet and orchards

are heavy with apples and other autumn fruits. In churches throughout the country, thanksgiving festivals mark the harvest. The shops stock up for the run-up to Christmas, their busiest time of the year.

SEPTEMBER

Blackpool Illuminations *(beg Sep–end Oct).* A 5 mile (8 km) spectacle of lighting along Blackpool's seafront.
Royal Highland Gathering *(first Sat),* Braemar, Scotland. Kilted clansmen from all over the country toss cabers, shot putt, dance and play the bagpipes. The royal family usually attends.
International Sheepdog Trials *(14–16 Sep),* all over Britain, with venues changing from year to year.

Shot putting at Braemar

Great Autumn Flower Show *(third weekend),* Harrogate, N Yorks. Displays by nurserymen and national flower organizations.
Oyster Festival *(Sat at beginning of oyster season),* Colchester. Lunch hosted by the mayor to celebrate the beginning of the much awaited oyster season.

OCTOBER

Harvest Festivals *(whole month),* all over Britain especially in farming areas.
Horse of the Year Show *(6–10 Oct),* NEC, Birmingham.
Nottingham Goose Fair *(second weekend).* One of Britain's oldest traditional fairs now has a funfair.
Canterbury Festival *(second and third weeks).* Music, drama and the arts.
Aldeburgh Britten Festival *(third weekend).* Concerts with music by Britten *(see p201)* and other composers.

Procession leading to the state opening of Parliament

NOVEMBER

Opening of Parliament *(Oct or Nov).* The Queen goes from Buckingham Palace to Westminster in a state coach, to open the new parliamentary session.
London Film Festival *(end Oct–beg Nov).* Forum for new films, various venues.
Lord Mayor's Procession and Show *(second Sat).* Parade in the City, London.
Remembrance Day *(second Sun).* Services and parades at the Cenotaph in Whitehall, London, and all over Britain.
RAC London to Brighton Veteran Car Rally *(first Sun).* A 7am start from Hyde Park, London to Brighton, East Sussex.
Guy Fawkes Night *(5 Nov),* fireworks and bonfires all over the country.
Regent Street Christmas Lights *(mid-Nov),* London.

Fireworks over Edinburgh on Guy Fawkes Night

Winter landscape in the Scottish Highlands, near Glencoe

WINTER

Brightly coloured fairy
lights and Christmas trees
decorate Britain's principal
shopping streets as shoppers
rush to buy their seasonal
gifts. Carol services are held
in churches across the
country, and pantomime, a
traditional entertainment for
children deriving from the
Victorian music hall, fills
theatres in major towns.

Brightly lit Christmas tree at the
centre of Trafalgar Square

Many offices close between
Christmas and the New Year.
Shops reopen for the January
sales on 27 December – a
paradise for bargain-hunters.

DECEMBER

Christmas Tree *(first Thu)*,
Trafalgar Square, London.
The tree is donated by the
people of Norway and is lit
by the Mayor of Oslo; this is
followed by carol singing.
Carol concerts *(whole
month)*, all over Britain.
Grand Christmas Parade
(beg Dec), London. Parade
with floats to celebrate
myth of Santa Claus.
Midnight Mass *(24 Dec)*,
in churches everywhere
around Britain.
**Allendale Tarbaal
Festival** *(31 Dec)*,
Northumberland.
Parade by villagers with burning tar barrels on their heads
to celebrate the New Year.

Sprig of holly

PUBLIC HOLIDAYS

New Year's Day (1 Jan).
2 Jan (Scotland only).
Easter weekend (March or
April). In England it begins
on **Good Friday** and ends
on **Easter Monday**; in
Scotland there is no Easter
Monday holiday.
May Day (usually first Mon
in May).
Late Spring Bank Holiday
(last Mon in May).
Bank Holiday (first Mon in
August, Scotland only).
August Bank Holiday (last
Mon in August, except
Scotland).
**Christmas and Boxing
Day** (25– 26 December).

JANUARY

Hogmanay and **New Year**
(31 Dec,1 Jan), Scottish celebrations. **Burns Night** *(25
Jan)*. Scots everywhere
celebrate poet
Robert Burns' birth
with poetry, feast-
ing and drinking.

FEBRUARY

**Chinese New
Year** *(late Jan or
early Feb)*. Lion dances, fire-
crackers and processions in
Chinatown, London.

Morris dancing on May Day in
Midhurst, Sussex

The Sporting Year

Many of the world's major competitive sports, including soccer, cricket and tennis, were invented in Britain. Originally devised as recreation for the wealthy, they have since entered the arena of mass entertainment. Some, however, such as the Royal Ascot race meeting and Wimbledon tennis tournament, are still valued as much for their social prestige as for the sport itself. Other delightful sporting events in Britain take place at a local level: village cricket, point-to-point racing and the Highland Games are all popular amateur events.

Kelly Holmes

Royal Ascot *is the four-day social highlight of the horse racing year. The high class of the thoroughbreds is matched by the high style of the fashions, with royalty attending.*

Oxford and Cambridge Boat Race, *first held in 1829 at Henley, has become a national event, with the two university eights now battling it out between Putney and Mortlake on the Thames.*

The FA Cup Final *is the apex of the football season.*

Derby Day horse races, Epsom

January	February	March	April	May	June

Cheltenham Gold Cup steeplechase *(see p328)*

Grand National steeple-chase, Aintree *(see p376),* **Liverpool**

Rugby League Cup Final, Wembley

Embassy World Snooker Championships, Sheffield

Wimbledon Lawn Tennis Tournament *is the world's most prestigious lawn tennis championship.*

Henley Royal Regatta *(see p234) is an international rowing event on the Thames (first held in 1839). It is also a glamorous social occasion.*

Six Nations Rugby Union *is an annual contest between England, France, Italy, Ireland (left), Scotland (right) and Wales. This league-based competition runs through winter ending in March.*

London Marathon *attracts thousands of long-distance runners, from the world's best to fancy-dressed fund raisers.*

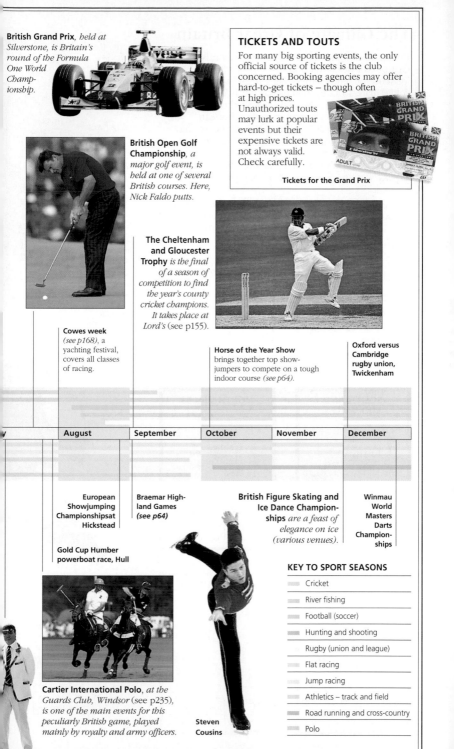

British Grand Prix, *held at Silverstone, is Britain's round of the Formula One World Championship.*

TICKETS AND TOUTS

For many big sporting events, the only official source of tickets is the club concerned. Booking agencies may offer hard-to-get tickets – though often at high prices. Unauthorized touts may lurk at popular events but their expensive tickets are not always valid. Check carefully.

Tickets for the Grand Prix

British Open Golf Championship, *a major golf event, is held at one of several British courses. Here, Nick Faldo putts.*

The Cheltenham and Gloucester Trophy *is the final of a season of competition to find the year's county cricket champions. It takes place at Lord's (see p155).*

Cowes week *(see p168),* a yachting festival, covers all classes of racing.

Horse of the Year Show brings together top show-jumpers to compete on a tough indoor course *(see p64).*

Oxford versus Cambridge rugby union, Twickenham

	August	September	October	November	December

European Showjumping Championshipsat Hickstead

Braemar High-land Games *(see p64)*

British Figure Skating and Ice Dance Champion-ships *are a feast of elegance on ice (various venues).*

Winmau World Masters Darts Champion-ships

Gold Cup Humber powerboat race, Hull

KEY TO SPORT SEASONS

	Cricket
	River fishing
	Football (soccer)
	Hunting and shooting
	Rugby (union and league)
	Flat racing
	Jump racing
	Athletics – track and field
	Road running and cross-country
	Polo

Cartier International Polo, *at the Guards Club, Windsor (see p235), is one of the main events for this peculiarly British game, played mainly by royalty and army officers.*

Steven Cousins

The Climate of Great Britain

Britain has a temperate climate. No region is far from the sea, which exerts a moderating influence on temperatures. Seldom are winter nights colder than -15°C, even in the far north, or summer days warmer than 30°C in the south and west: a much narrower range than in most European countries. Despite Britain's reputation, the average annual rainfall is quite low – 108 cm (42 inches) – and heavy rain is rare. The Atlantic coast is warmed by the Gulf Stream, making the west slightly warmer, though wetter, than the east.

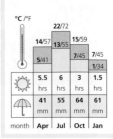

LANCASHIRE AND THE LAKES

°C /°F

	Apr	Jul	Oct	Jan
max	12/54	19/66	14/57	6/43
		13/55	8/46	
min	5/41			2/36
☼	5.5 hrs	6 hrs	3 hrs	1.5 hrs
☂	53 mm	85 mm	104 mm	90 mm
month	Apr	Jul	Oct	Jan

THE HEART OF ENGLAND

°C /°F

	Apr	Jul	Oct	Jan
max	12/54	20/68	13/55	6/43
		13/55	8/46	
min	5/41			2/36
☼	4.5 hrs	5.5 hrs	3 hrs	1.5 hrs
☂	53 mm	69 mm	69 mm	74 mm
month	Apr	Jul	Oct	Jan

- Average monthly maximum temperature
- Average monthly minimum temperature
- Average daily hours of sunshine
- Average monthly rainfall

SOUTH AND MID-WALES

°C /°F

	Apr	Jul	Oct	Jan
max	13/55	20/68	14/57	7/45
		13/55	8/46	
min	5/41			2/36
☼	5.5 hrs	6 hrs	3.5 hrs	1.5 hrs
☂	65 mm	89 mm	109 mm	108 mm
month	Apr	Jul	Oct	Jan

NORTH WALES

°C /°F

	Apr	Jul	Oct	Jan
max	11/52	17/63	14/57	6/43
		11/52	8/46	
min	5/41			1/34
☼	3 hrs	3.5 hrs	2.5 hrs	1.5 hrs
☂	144 mm	206 mm	261 mm	252 mm
month	Apr	Jul	Oct	Jan

DEVON AND CORNWALL

°C /°F

	Apr	Jul	Oct	Jan
max	13/55	19/66	15/59	8/46
		13/55	9/48	
min	6/43			4/39
☼	6 hrs	6.5 hrs	3.5 hrs	2 hrs
☂	53 mm	70 mm	91 mm	99 mm
month	Apr	Jul	Oct	Jan

WEST COUNTRY

°C /°F

	Apr	Jul	Oct	Jan
max	14/57	21/70	15/59	7/45
		14/57	9/48	
min	6/43			2/36
☼	5.5 hrs	6.5 hrs	3.5 hrs	2 hrs
☂	49 mm	65 mm	85 mm	74 mm
month	Apr	Jul	Oct	Jan

THAMES VALLEY

°C /°F

	Apr	Jul	Oct	Jan
max	14/57	22/72	15/59	7/45
		13/55	7/45	
min	5/41			1/34
☼	5.5 hrs	6 hrs	3 hrs	1.5 hrs
☂	41 mm	55 mm	64 mm	61 mm
month	Apr	Jul	Oct	Jan

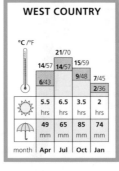

Wi[ck]

Inverness

The Highlands and Islands

EDINBURG[H]
Glasgow

The Lowlands

Lancashire and the Lakes

Liverpo[ol]

North Wales
Caernarfon

South and Mid-Wales

CARDIFF

Br[istol]
West Coun[try]

Exeter

Devon and Cornwall

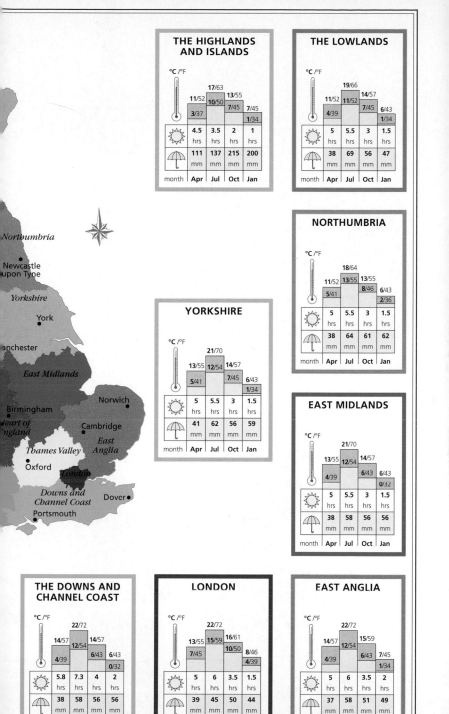

THE HIGHLANDS AND ISLANDS

°C /°F

	Apr	Jul	Oct	Jan
high °C/°F	11/52	17/63	13/55	7/45
		10/50	7/45	
low °C/°F	3/37			1/34
☀	4.5 hrs	3.5 hrs	2 hrs	1 hrs
☂	111 mm	137 mm	215 mm	200 mm
month	Apr	Jul	Oct	Jan

THE LOWLANDS

°C /°F

	Apr	Jul	Oct	Jan
	11/52	19/66	14/57	
		11/52	7/45	6/43
	4/39			1/34
☀	5 hrs	5.5 hrs	3 hrs	1.5 hrs
☂	38 mm	69 mm	56 mm	47 mm
month	Apr	Jul	Oct	Jan

NORTHUMBRIA

°C /°F

	Apr	Jul	Oct	Jan
	11/52	18/64	13/55	
		13/55	8/46	6/43
	5/41			2/36
☀	5 hrs	5.5 hrs	3 hrs	1.5 hrs
☂	38 mm	64 mm	61 mm	62 mm
month	Apr	Jul	Oct	Jan

YORKSHIRE

°C /°F

	Apr	Jul	Oct	Jan
	13/55	21/70	14/57	
		12/54	7/45	6/43
	5/41			1/34
☀	5 hrs	5.5 hrs	3 hrs	1.5 hrs
☂	41 mm	62 mm	56 mm	59 mm
month	Apr	Jul	Oct	Jan

EAST MIDLANDS

°C /°F

	Apr	Jul	Oct	Jan
	13/55	21/70	14/57	
		12/54	6/43	6/43
	4/39			0/32
☀	5 hrs	5.5 hrs	3 hrs	1.5 hrs
☂	38 mm	58 mm	56 mm	56 mm
month	Apr	Jul	Oct	Jan

THE DOWNS AND CHANNEL COAST

°C /°F

	Apr	Jul	Oct	Jan
	14/57	22/72	14/57	
		12/54	6/43	6/43
	4/39			0/32
☀	5.8 hrs	7.3 hrs	4 hrs	2 hrs
☂	38 mm	58 mm	56 mm	56 mm
month	Apr	Jul	Oct	Jan

LONDON

°C /°F

	Apr	Jul	Oct	Jan
	13/55	22/72	16/61	
		15/59	10/50	8/46
	7/45			4/39
☀	5 hrs	6 hrs	3.5 hrs	1.5 hrs
☂	39 mm	45 mm	50 mm	44 mm
month	Apr	Jul	Oct	Jan

EAST ANGLIA

°C /°F

	Apr	Jul	Oct	Jan
	14/57	22/72	15/59	
		12/54	6/43	7/45
	4/39			1/34
☀	5 hrs	6 hrs	3.5 hrs	2 hrs
☂	37 mm	58 mm	51 mm	49 mm
month	Apr	Jul	Oct	Jan

Northumbria
Newcastle upon Tyne
Yorkshire
York
Manchester
East Midlands
Norwich
Birmingham
Heart of England
Cambridge
East Anglia
Thames Valley
Oxford
London
Downs and Channel Coast
Dover
Portsmouth

LONDON

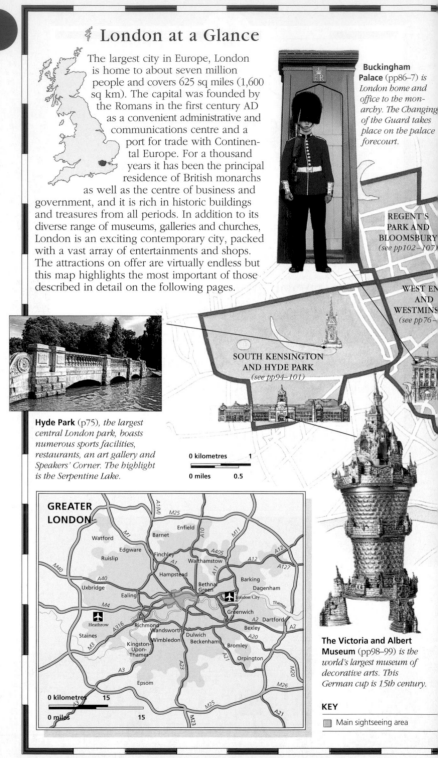

London at a Glance

The largest city in Europe, London is home to about seven million people and covers 625 sq miles (1,600 sq km). The capital was founded by the Romans in the first century AD as a convenient administrative and communications centre and a port for trade with Continental Europe. For a thousand years it has been the principal residence of British monarchs as well as the centre of business and government, and it is rich in historic buildings and treasures from all periods. In addition to its diverse range of museums, galleries and churches, London is an exciting contemporary city, packed with a vast array of entertainments and shops. The attractions on offer are virtually endless but this map highlights the most important of those described in detail on the following pages.

Buckingham Palace (pp86–7) *is London home and office to the monarchy. The Changing of the Guard takes place on the palace forecourt.*

REGENT'S PARK AND BLOOMSBURY
(see pp102–107)

WEST END AND WESTMINS
(see pp76–

SOUTH KENSINGTON AND HYDE PARK
(see pp94–101)

Hyde Park (p75), *the largest central London park, boasts numerous sports facilities, restaurants, an art gallery and Speakers' Corner. The highlight is the Serpentine Lake.*

0 kilometres 1

0 miles 0.5

GREATER LONDON

Watford
M25
A1(M)
M1
Barnet
Enfield
A10
M11
Edgware
Finchley
A1
Walthamstow
A405
A12
A127
Ruislip
A40
Hampstead
A1
Barking
Dagenham
Uxbridge
Ealing
M4
London City
Thames
Heathrow
A316
Richmond
Wandsworth
Greenwich
A2
Dartford
A2
Staines
Kingston-Upon-Thames
Wimbledon
Dulwich
Beckenham
Bexley
A20
M3
A3
A23
Bromley
Orpington
M20
Epsom
M26
M25
M23
A21

The Victoria and Albert Museum (pp98–99) *is the world's largest museum of decorative arts. This German cup is 15th century.*

0 kilometres 15

0 miles 15

KEY

☐ Main sightseeing area

◁ **Nelson's Column (1843) and the National Gallery, Trafalgar Square**

The British Museum's (pp106–7) *vast collection of antiquities from all over the world includes this Portland Vase from the 1st century BC.*

The National Gallery's (pp82–3) *world-famous collection of paintings includes works such as* Christ Mocked *(c.1495) by Hieronymus Bosch.*

THAMES

THE CITY AND SOUTHWARK *(see pp108–121)*

St Paul's (pp114–15) *huge dome is the cathedral's most distinctive feature. Three galleries around the dome give spectacular views of London.*

Westminster Abbey (pp92–3) *has glorious medieval archi- tecture and is crammed with impressive tombs and monu- ments to some of Britain's greatest public figures.*

Tate Britain (p91) *displays an outstanding collec- tion of British art ranging from stylized Elizabethan portraiture, such as* The Cholmondeley Sisters, *to cutting edge installation and film.*

The Tower of London (pp118–19) *is most famous as the prison where enemies of the Crown were executed. The Tower houses the Crown Jewels, including the Imperial State Crown.*

London's Parks and Gardens

Camellia japonica

London has one of the world's greenest city centres, full of tree-filled squares and large expanses of grass, some of which have been public land since medieval times. From the elegant terraces of Regent's Park to the botanic gardens of Kew, every London park and garden has its own charm and character. Some are ancient crown or public land, while others were created from the grounds of private houses or disused land. Londoners make the most of these open spaces: for exercise, listening to music, or simply escaping the bustle of the city.

Holland Park (see pp122–23) *offers acres of peaceful woodland, an open-air theatre (see p153) and a café.*

Kew Gardens (see p126) *are the world's premiere botanic gardens. An amazing variety of plants from all over the world is complemented by an array of temples, monuments and a landscaped lake.*

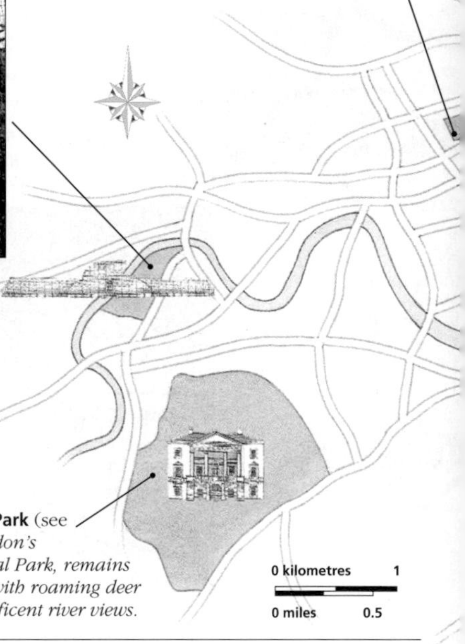

Richmond Park (see p126), *London's largest Royal Park, remains unspoiled with roaming deer and magnificent river views.*

0 kilometres   1

0 miles   0.5

SEASONAL BEST

As winter draws to a close, spectacular drifts of crocuses, daffodils and tulips are to be found peeping above the ground in Green Park and Kew. Easter weekend marks the start of outdoor events with funfairs on many commons and parks. During the summer months the parks are packed with picnickers and sunbathers and you can often catch a free open-air concert in St James's or Regent's parks. The energetic can play tennis in most

Winter in Kensington Gardens, adjoining Hyde Park

parks, swim in Hyde Park's Serpentine or the ponds on Hampstead Heath, or take rowing boats out on the lakes in Regent's and Battersea parks. Autumn brings a different atmosphere, and on 5 November firework displays and bonfires celebrate Guy Fawkes Night *(see p64).* Winter is a good time to visit the tropical glasshouses and the colourful outdoor winter garden at Kew. If the weather gets really cold, the Round Pond in Kensington Gardens may be fit for ice-skating.

Hampstead Heath *(see p124)* is a breezy open space embracing a variety of landscapes.

Regent's Park (see p103) *has a large boating lake, an open-air theatre* (see p153) *and London Zoo. Surrounded by Nash's graceful buildings, it is one of London's most civilized retreats.*

St James's Park, *in the heart of the city, is a popular escape for office workers. It is also a reserve for wildfowl.*

THAMES

Green Park, *with its shady trees and benches, offers a cool, restful spot in the heart of London.*

Battersea Park is a pleasant riverside site with a man-made boating lake.

Greenwich Park (see p125) *is dominated by the National Maritime Museum. There are fine views from the Old Royal Observatory on the hill top.*

Hyde Park and Kensington Gardens (see p101) *are both popular London retreats. There are sporting facilities, a lake and art gallery in Hyde Park. This plaque is from the ornate Italian Garden in Kensington Gardens.*

HISTORIC CEMETERIES

In the late 1830s, a ring of private cemeteries was established around London to ease the pressure on the monstrously overcrowded and unhealthy burial grounds of the inner city. Today the cemeteries, notably **Highgate** *(see p124)* and **Kensal Green**, are well worth visiting for their flamboyant Victorian monuments.

Kensal Green cemetery on the Harrow Road

WEST END AND WESTMINSTER

T he West End is the city's social and cultural centre and the London home of the royal family. Stretching from the edge of Hyde Park to Covent Garden, the district bustles all day and late into the night. Whether you're looking for art, history, street- or café-life, it is the most rewarding area in which to begin an exploration of the city.

Horse Guard on Whitehall

Westminster has been at the centre of political and religious power for a thousand years. In the 11th century, King Canute founded Westminster Palace and Edward the Confessor built Westminster Abbey, where all English monarchs have been crowned since 1066. As modern government developed, the great offices of state were established in the area.

SIGHTS AT A GLANCE

Historic Streets and Buildings
Banqueting House **18**
Buckingham Palace pp86–7 **13**
Cabinet War Rooms and Churchill Museum **16**
Downing Street **17**
Houses of Parliament pp90–91 **19**
Piccadilly Circus **8**
Ritz Hotel **10**
Royal Mews **15**
The Mall **12**
The Piazza and Central Market **1**

Museums and Galleries
London's Transport Museum **2**
National Gallery pp82–3 **6**
National Portrait Gallery **7**
Queen's Gallery **14**
Royal Academy **9**
Somerset House **4**
Tate Britain **21**
Theatre Museum **3**

Churches
Queen's Chapel **11**
Westminster Abbey pp92–3 **20**

Attractions
British Airways London Eye **5**

KEY

- ▮ Street-by-Street map *pp78–9*
- ▮ Street-by-Street map *pp84–5*
- ▮ Street-by-Street map *pp88–9*
- ⊖ Underground station
- ⇄ Railway station
- ▬ River boat pier

GETTING THERE
This area is the hub of the city's public transport system, served by virtually all tube lines and scores of buses (see *pp690–91*). The most convenient tube and railway station is Charing Cross.

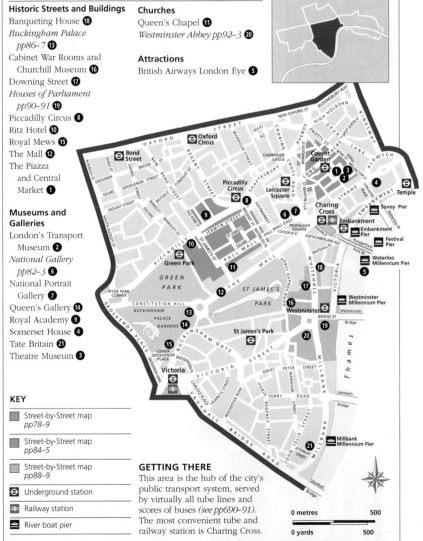

0 metres 500
0 yards 500

◁ **Big Ben and the Houses of Parliament**

Street-by-Street: Covent Garden

Until 1973, Covent Garden was an area of decaying streets and warehouses, which only came alive after dark when the fruit and vegetable market traders packed up for the day. Since then the Victorian market and elegant buildings nearby have been converted into stylish shops, restaurants, bars and cafés, creating an animated district which attracts a lively young crowd, night and day.

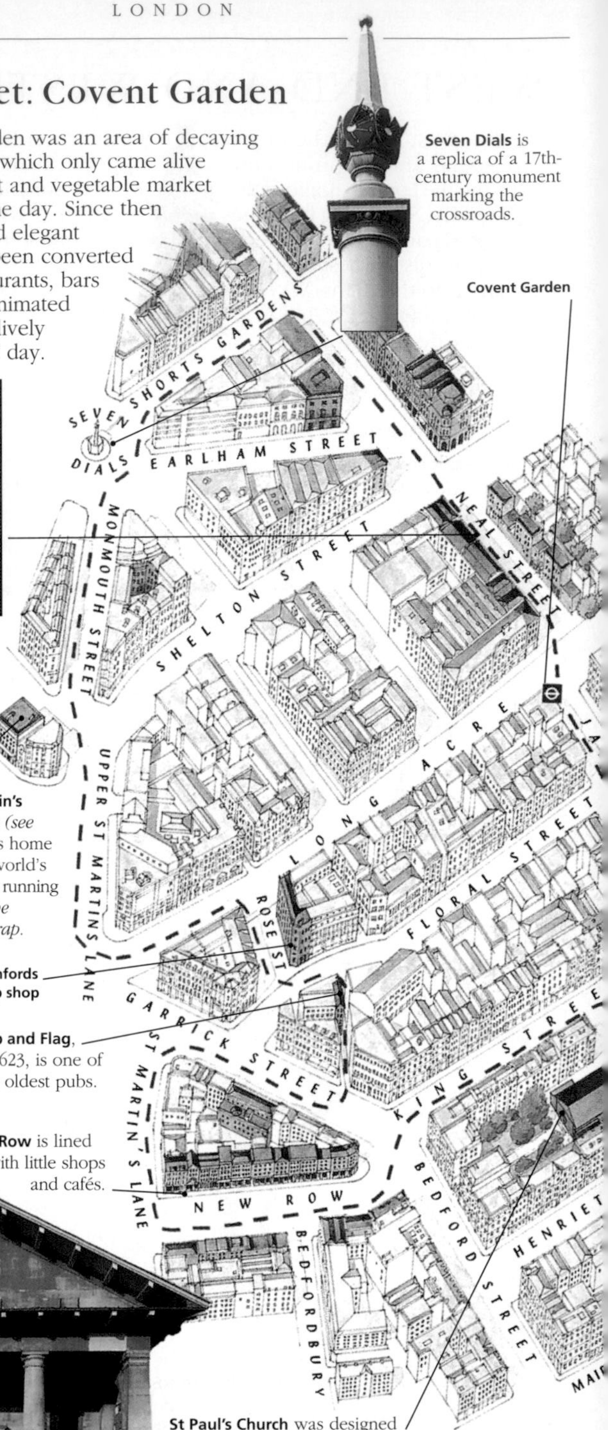

Seven Dials is a replica of a 17th-century monument marking the crossroads.

Covent Garden

Neal Street and Neal's Yard are lined with many specialist shops converted from former warehouses.

St Martin's Theatre *(see p153)* is home to the world's longest running play, *The Mousetrap.*

Stanfords map shop

The Lamb and Flag, built in 1623, is one of London's oldest pubs.

New Row is lined with little shops and cafés.

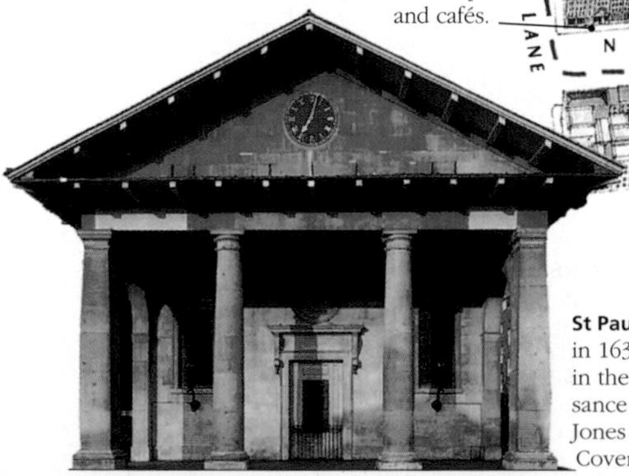

St Paul's Church was designed in 1633 by Inigo Jones *(see p53),* in the style of the Italian Renaissance architect, Andrea Palladio. Jones also designed the original Covent Garden Piazza.

Theatre Museum
This houses a collection of theatrical memorabilia ❸

The Royal Opera House
(*see p154*) is where many of the greatest opera singers and ballet dancers have performed.

LOCATOR MAP
See Street Finder map 11

KEY

– – –   Suggested route

0 metres	100
0 yards	100

London's Transport Museum
This museum's intriguing collection brings to life the history of the city's tubes, buses and trains. It also displays examples of 20th-century commercial art ❷

Jubilee Market

★ **Piazza and Central Market**
Shops and cafés fill the piazza and market ❶

STAR SIGHTS

★ Piazza and Central Market

The Piazza and Central Market ❶

Covent Garden WC2. **Map** 11 C2. ⊖ *Covent Garden.* ♿ *cobbled streets.* **Street performers in Piazza:** *10am–dusk daily.*

The 17th-century architect Inigo Jones (*see p53*) planned the Piazza in Covent Garden as an elegant residential square, modelled on the piazza in the Tuscan town of Livorno, which he had seen under construction during his travels in Italy. For a brief period, the Piazza became one of the most fashionable addresses in London, but it was superseded by the even grander St James's Square (*see p85*) which lies to the southwest.

Decline accelerated when a fruit and vegetable market developed. By the mid-18th century, the Piazza had become a haunt of prostitutes and most of its houses had turned into seedy lodgings, gambling dens, brothels and taverns.

A mid-18th-century view of Covent Garden's Piazza

Meanwhile the wholesale produce market became the largest in the country and in 1828 a market hall was erected to ease congestion. The market, however, soon outgrew its new home and despite the construction of new buildings, such as Floral and Jubilee halls, the congestion grew worse. In 1973 the market moved to a new site in south London, and over the next two decades Covent Garden was redeveloped. Today only St Paul's Church remains of Inigo Jones's buildings, and Covent Garden, with its many small shops, cafés, restaurants, market stalls and street entertainers, is one of central London's liveliest districts.

London's Transport Museum ➋

The Piazza, Covent Garden WC2.
Map 11 C2. **Tel** 020-7379 6344.
🔵 Covent Garden. ⬜ 10am–6pm
Sat–Thu, 11am–6pm Fri. ▨ ♿ ☎
phone in advance. 🔲 🖥
www.ltmuseum.co.uk

This collection of buses,
trams and underground trains
ranges from the earliest
horse-drawn omnibuses to
a present-day Hoppa bus.
Housed in the Victorian
Flower Market of Covent
Garden built in 1872, the
museum is particularly good
for children, who can sit in
the driver's seat of a bus or
an underground train, operate
signals and chat to an actor
playing a 19th-century tube-
tunnel miner.

London's bus and train
companies have long been
prolific patrons of artists, and
the museum holds a fine
collection of 19th- and 20th-
century commercial art. Copies
of some of the best posters
and works by distinguished
artists, such as Paul Nash and
Graham Sutherland, are on
sale at the museum shop.

METRO-LAND
PRICE TWO-PENCE

**Poster by Michael Reilly (1929),
London Transport Museum**

Theatre Museum ➌

Russell St WC2. **Map** 11 C2. **Tel** 020-
7943 4700. 🔵 Covent Garden. ⬜
10am–6pm Tue–Sun. ⚫ public hols.
🔲 ♿ **www**.theatremuseum.org

Children can be made up
with gruesome wounds in
this museum, and find out
how Cyrano de Bergerac's
nose was created for the film.
An exhibition reveals how a
theatre production is mounted,
from cast readings of the

author's original script, through
videoed rehearsals and back-
stage procedures, to the first
staged performance.

More conventionally, the
intriguing history of show
business is traced through a
collection of memorabilia –
playbills, programmes, props
and costumes.

Somerset House ➍

Strand WC2. **Map** 11 C2. **Tel** 020-
7845 4600. 🔵 Temple. ⬜10am–6pm
daily (last adm: 5.15pm). ⚫ 1 Jan,
24–26 Dec. **Ice rink** ⬜ two months in
winter. ▨ 🔲 **Courtauld Institute of
Art Gallery**. **Tel** 020-7848 2526. 🔲
🔲 **Gilbert Collection**. **Tel** 020-7240
9400. ◪ 🔲 🔲 **Hermitage Rooms**. **Tel**
020-7845 4630. ◪ 🔲 🔲 ▨ all
galleries. ♿ all galleries. **Admiralty
Restaurant**. **Tel** 020-7845 4646.
www.somerset-house.org.uk

Designed in 1770 by William
Chambers, Somerset House
is home to three great
collections of art, the
**Courtauld Institute of Art
Gallery**, the **Gilbert Collection**
and the **Hermitage Rooms**.

Somerset House: Strand façade

The courtyard forms an
attractive piazza (which
becomes an ice rink in winter),
and the riverside terrace has a
café. The Admiralty Restaurant
is highly regarded. Located in
Somerset House but famous in
its own right is the Courtauld
Institute of Art Gallery, which
includes important Impressionist and Post-Impressionist
works. The Gilbert Collection
is a major decorative arts
museum, with pieces dating
from the 16th century, including European silverware. The
Hermitage Rooms recreate, in
miniature, the splendour of
the Winter Palace which now

SOHO AND CHINATOWN

Soho has been renowned for pleasures of the table, the flesh
and the intellect ever since it was first developed in the late
17th century. At first a fashionable residential area, it declined
when high society shifted west to Mayfair and immigrants
from Europe moved into its narrow streets. Furniture-makers
and tailors set up shop here and were joined in the late 19th
century by pubs, nightclubs, restaurants and brothels. In
the 1960s, Hong Kong Chinese moved into the area around
Gerrard and Lisle streets and they
created an aromatic Chinatown, packed with many
restaurants and food
shops. Soho's raffish
reputation has long
attracted artists and
writers, ranging from
the 18th-century
essayist Thomas de
Quincey to poet Dylan
Thomas and painter
Francis Bacon. Although
strip joints and peep
shows remain, Soho has
enjoyed something of a
renaissance, and today is
full of stylish and lively
bars and restaurants.

**Lion dancer in
February's
Chinese
New Year
celebrations**

The opulent Palm Court of the Ritz Hotel

comprises the State Hermitage Museum, St Petersburg, and exhibitions are mounted from the museum's collections.

British Airways London Eye ⑤

Jubilee Gardens, South Bank, SE1. **Map** 12 D2. **Tel** 0870 5000 600 (information and 24-hr advance booking – recommended as tickets sell out days in advance). 🚇 Waterloo, Westminster. 🚌 11, 24, 211. 🕐 Oct–May: 10am–8pm daily; Jun–Sept: 10am–9pm daily. ● 25 Dec & early Jan (for maintenance). 🎟 Pick up tickets at County Hall (adjacent to Eye) at least 30 mins before boarding time. 🚻 🎁 🚻 www.londoneye.com

The British Airways London Eye is a 135-m (443-ft) observation wheel that was installed on the South Bank to mark the Millennium. Its enclosed passenger capsules offer a gentle, 30-minute ride as the wheel makes a full turn, with breathtaking views over London and for up to 42 km (26 miles) around. Towering over one of the world's most familiar river-scapes, it has understandably captured the hearts of Londoners and visitors alike, and is one of the city's most popular attractions. "Flights" on the wheel are on the hour and half-hour.

National Gallery ⑥

See pp82–3.

National Portrait Gallery ⑦

2 St Martin's Place WC2. **Map** 11 B3. **Tel** 020-7306 0055. 🚇 Charing Cross, Leicester Sq. 🕐 10am–6pm Sat–Wed, 10am–9pm Thu & Fri. ● 1 Jan, Good Fri, 24 & 25 Dec. ♿ 🔊 🚻 🚻 🎁 www.npg.org.uk

This museum celebrates Britain's history through portraits, photographs and sculptures; subjects range from Elizabeth I to David Beckham. The 20th-century section contains paintings and photographs of the royal family, politicians, rock stars, designers, artists and writers.

Piccadilly Circus ⑧

W1. **Map** 11 A3. 🚇 Piccadilly Circus.

Dominated by garish neon advertising hoardings, Piccadilly Circus is a hectic traffic junction surrounded by shopping malls. It began as an early 19th-century crossroads between Piccadilly and John Nash's *(see p105)* Regent Street. It was briefly an elegant space, edged by curving stucco façades, but by 1910 the first electric advert-isements had been installed. For years people have con-gregated at its centre, beneath the delicately poised figure of Eros, erected in 1892.

Royal Academy ⑨

Burlington House, Piccadilly W1. **Map** 10 F3. **Tel** 020-7300 8000. 🚇 Piccadilly Circus, Green Park. 🕐 10am–6pm Sat–Thu, 10am–10pm Fri. ● 24–25 Dec, Good Fri. 🎟 ♿ 🎟 by appointment. 🚻 🚻 🎁 www.royalacademy.org.uk

Founded in 1768, the Royal Academy is best known for its summer exhibition, which has been an annual event for over 200 years and comprises a rewarding mix of around 1,200 new works by established and unknown painters, sculptors and architects. During the rest of the year, the gallery shows prestigious touring exhibitions from around the world, and the courtyard in front of Burlington House, one of the West End's few surviving mansions from the early 18th century, is often filled with people waiting to get in. Quite apart from its aesthetic delights, the Royal Academy provides the weary traveller with a little lacuna of tranquillity. Its interior decoration inspires calm, and seems to be cut off from the stresses and strains of modern city life.

The Statue of Eros

Ritz Hotel ⑩

Piccadilly W1. **Map** 10 F3. **Tel** 020-7493 8181. 🚇 Green Park. ♿ See **Where to Stay** p540. www.theritzlondon.com

Cesar Ritz, the Swiss hotelier who inspired the word "ritzy", had virtually settled down to a quiet retirement by 1906 when this hotel was built and named after him. The colonnaded front of the château-style building was erected in 1906 to suggest just the merest whiff of Paris, where the grandest hotels were to be found at the turn of the century. It still maintains its Edwardian air of *fin de siècle* opulence and sophisticated grandeur, and is a popular venue for afternoon tea (reservations are required). A touch of *soigné* danger may be found in the casino.

National Gallery ❻

The National Gallery is London's leading art museum, with over 2,300 paintings, most on permanent display. It has flourished since 1824 when George IV persuaded the government to purchase 38 major paintings. These became the core of a national collection of European art that now ranges from Cimabue in the 13th century to 19th-century Impressionists. The gallery's particular strengths are in Dutch, Italian Renaissance and 17th-century Spanish painting. To the left of the main gallery lies the Sainsbury Wing, financed by the grocery family and completed in 1991. It houses the Early Renaissance collection.

The Adoration of the Kings *(1564)*
This realistic work is by Flemish artist Pieter Brueghel the Elder (1520–1569).

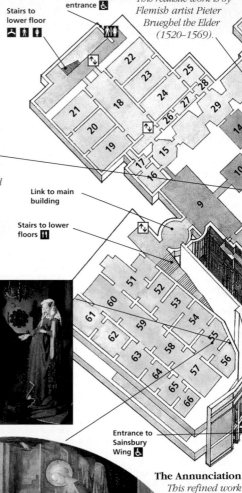

Education Centre entrance ♿

Stairs to lower floor

Link to main building

Stairs to lower floors ⏻

Entrance to Sainsbury Wing ♿

The Ambassadors
The strange shape in the foreground of this Hans Holbein portrait (1533) is a foreshortened skull, a symbol of mortality.

KEY TO FLOORPLAN

☐	Painting 1250–1500
☐	Painting 1500–1600
☐	Painting 1600–1700
☐	Painting 1700–1900
☐	Special exhibitions
☐	Non-exhibition space

Arnolfini Portrait
Jan van Eyck (1389–1441), one of the pioneers of oil painting, shows his mastery of colour, texture, and minute detail in this portrait of 1434.

The Annunciation
This refined work of the late 1450s, by Fra Filippo Lippi, forms part of the gallery's exceptional Italian Renaissance collection.

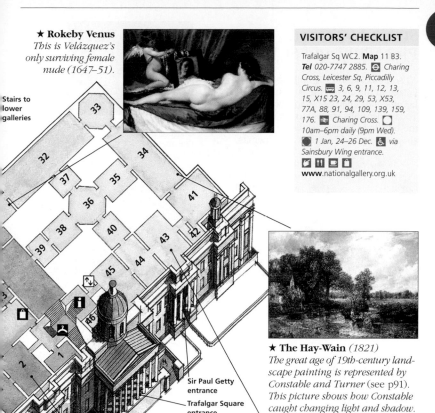

★ **Rokeby Venus**
This is Velázquez's only surviving female nude (1647–51).

Stairs to lower galleries

VISITORS' CHECKLIST

Trafalgar Sq WC2. **Map** 11 B3. **Tel** 020-7747 2885. 🚇 Charing Cross, Leicester Sq, Piccadilly Circus. 🚌 3, 6, 9, 11, 12, 13, 15, X15 23, 24, 29, 53, X53, 77A, 88, 91, 94, 109, 139, 159, 176. 🚆 Charing Cross. 🕐 10am–6pm daily (9pm Wed). ⬤ 1 Jan, 24–26 Dec. ♿ via Sainsbury Wing entrance.
🎫 🚻 🖥 📷 🍴
www.nationalgallery.org.uk

★ **The Hay-Wain** *(1821)*
The great age of 19th-century land-scape painting is represented by Constable and Turner (see p91). This picture shows how Constable caught changing light and shadow.

Sir Paul Getty entrance

Trafalgar Square entrance

The Neo-Classical façade is made of Portland stone.

GALLERY GUIDE

Most of the collection is housed on the first floor. The paintings hang chronologically, with the earliest works, notably the Italian Renaissance collection (1250–1500), in the Sainsbury Wing. Lesser paintings of all periods are displayed on the lower floor of the main building. The better of the two restaurants is on the first floor in the Sainsbury Wing.

★ **The Leonardo Cartoon** *(c.1499–1500)*
The genius of Leonardo da Vinci glows through this picture of the Virgin and Child, St Anne and John the Baptist.

STAR PAINTINGS

★ Cartoon by Leonardo da Vinci

★ Rokeby Venus by Diego Velázquez

★ The Hay-Wain by John Constable

At the Theatre *(1876–7)*
Renoir was one of the greatest painters to be influenced by the Impressionist movement. The theatre was a popular subject among artists of the time.

Street-by-Street: Piccadilly and St James's

As soon as Henry VIII built St James's Palace in the 1530s, the surrounding area became the centre of fashionable court life. Today Piccadilly forms a contrast between the bustling commercial district full of shopping arcades, eateries and cinemas, with St James's, to the south, which is still the domain of the wealthy and the influential.

St James's Church was designed by Sir Christopher Wren in 1684.

★ **Royal Academy**
The permanent art collection here includes this Michelangelo relief of the Madonna and Child (1505) ❾

Fortnum & Mason
(see p148) was founded in 1707.

The Ritz
César Ritz founded one of London's most famous hotels in 1906 ❿

Burlington Arcade, an opulent covered walk, has fine shops and beadles on patrol.

St James's Palace
was built on the site of a leper hospital.

To the Mall and Buckingham Palace
(see pp86–7)

Spencer House, recently restored to its 18th-century splendour, contains fine period furniture and paintings. This Palladian palace was completed in 1766 for the 1st Earl Spencer, an ancestor of the late Princess of Wales.

STAR SIGHTS

★ Piccadilly Circus

★ Royal Academy

For hotels and restaurants in this region see pp556–560 and pp608–616

★ **Piccadilly Circus**
The crowds and dazzling neon lights make this the West End's focal point ❽

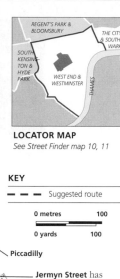

LOCATOR MAP
See Street Finder map 10, 11

KEY

— — — Suggested route

0 metres   100

0 yards   100

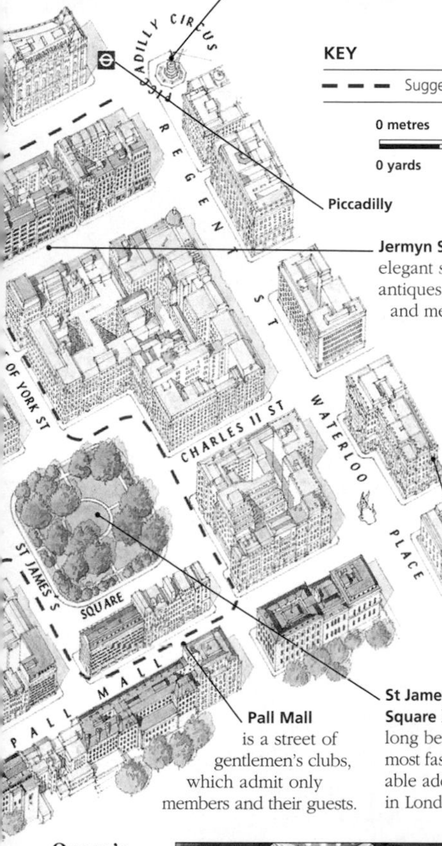

Piccadilly

Jermyn Street has elegant shops selling antiques, unusual gifts and men's clothing.

St James's Square has long been the most fashion-able address in London.

Pall Mall is a street of gentlemen's clubs, which admit only members and their guests.

Queen's Chapel
This was the first Classical church in England ❶❶

Royal Opera Arcade is lined with quality shops. Designed by John Nash, it was com-pleted in 1818.

Queen's Chapel ❶❶

Marlborough Rd SW1. **Map** 11 A4. *Tel* 020-7930 4832. ⊖ *Green Park.* ☐ *to the public Sun services (Easter–end Jul) and major Saints' Days only.* ♿

The sumptuous Queen's Chapel was designed by Inigo Jones for the Infanta of Spain, the intended bride of Charles I (*see pp52–3*). Work started in 1623 but ceased when the marriage negoti-ations were shelved. The chapel was finally completed in 1627 for Charles's eventual queen, Henrietta Maria. It was the first church in England to be built in a Classical style, with a coffered ceiling based on a reconstruction by Palladio of an ancient Roman temple.

Interior of Queen's Chapel

The Mall ❶❷

SW1 **Map** 11 A4 ⊖ *Charing Cross, Green Park.*

This broad triumphal approach from Trafalgar Square to Buckingham Palace was created by Aston Webb when he redesigned the front of the palace and the Victoria Monument in 1911. The spacious tree-lined avenue follows the course of an old path at the edge of St James's Park. The path was laid out in the reign of Charles II, when it became London's most fashionable and cosmo-politan promenade. The Mall is used for royal processions on special occasions. Flag-poles down both sides fly the national flags of foreign heads of state during official visits. The Mall is closed to traffic on Sundays.

Buckingham Palace ⑬

Queen Elizabeth II

Opened to visitors for the first time in 1993 to raise money for repairing fire damage to Windsor Castle *(see pp236–7)*, the Queen's official London home and office is an extremely popular attraction in August and September. John Nash *(see p105)* began converting the 18th-century Buckingham House into a palace for George IV in 1826 but was taken off the job in 1831 for overspending his budget. The first monarch to occupy the palace was Queen Victoria, just after she came to the throne in 1837. The tour takes visitors up the grand staircase and through the splendour of the State Rooms, but not into the royal family's private apartments.

Music Room
State guests are presented and royal babies christened in this room.

White Drawing Room
Green Drawing Room
Grand Staircase
Blue Drawing Room

State Dining Room

Queen's Gallery
Masterpieces from the Royal Collection, such as Vermeer's The Music Lesson *(c.1660), are displayed here in a series of changing exhibitions.*

Throne Room
The Queen carries out many formal ceremonial duties here, under the richly gilded ceiling.

View over the Mall
On special occasions the Royal Family wave to crowds from the balcony.

VISITORS' CHECKLIST

SW1. **Map** 10 F5. *Tel* 020-7766 7300. ⊖ *St James's Park, Victoria.* 🚍 *11, 16, 24, 25, 28, 36, 38, 52, 73, 135, C1.* 🚆 *Victoria.* **State Rooms** ⬤ *9:45am–6pm daily (last admission: 3:45pm). The ticket office is located in Ambassador's Court. Each ticket has a set entry time.* 📷 ♿ *phone first.* **Changing of the Guard**: *11:30am daily or alternate days. Subject to change without notice.* *Tel* 020-7321 2233. **www**.royal.gov.uk

The Royal Standard flies while the Queen is in residence.

The East Wing façade was added by Aston Webb in 1913.

The Changing of the Guard takes place on the palace forecourt.

THE CHANGING OF THE GUARD

Dressed in brilliant scarlet tunics and tall furry hats called bearskins, the palace guards stand in sentry boxes outside the Palace. Crowds gather to watch the colourful and musical military ceremony as the guards march from Wellington Barracks to Buckingham Palace, parading for half an hour while the palace keys are handed by the old guard to the new.

Queen's Gallery ⑭

Buckingham Palace Rd SW1. **Map** 10 F5. *Tel* 020-7766 7301. ⊖ *St James's Park, Victoria.* ⬤ *10am–5:30pm daily (last admission for exhibitions: 4:30pm).* ⬤ *25, 26 Dec.* 🎟 📷 **www**.royalcollection.org.uk

The Queen's art collection is one of the finest and most valuable in the world, rich in the works of old masters such as Rembrandt and Leonardo. The gallery hosts a rotating programme of exhibitions, enabling the year-round display of many masterpieces, drawings and decorative arts from the Queen's collection.

Detail: The Gold State Coach (1762), Royal Mews

Royal Mews ⑮

Buckingham Palace Rd SW1. **Map** 10 E5. *Tel* 020-7766 7302. ⊖ *Victoria.* ⬤ *Mar–Oct: 11am–4pm daily (advisable to check opening times on day of visit). Extended opening hrs may operate Aug–Sep.* 🎟 *open 9:30am–5pm daily all year (closed 25, 26 Dec).* 📷 ♿ **www**.royalcollection.org.uk

Lovers of horses and royal pomp should not miss this working stable and coach house. Designed by John Nash in 1825, it houses horses and state coaches used on official occasions. Among them is the glass coach used for royal weddings and foreign ambassadors. The star exhibit is the ornate gold state coach, built for George III in 1762, which was used by the Queen during the Golden Jubilee celebrations in 2002. The shop sells interesting merchandise.

Street-by-Street: Whitehall and Westminster

The broad avenues of Whitehall and Westminster are lined with imposing buildings that serve the historic seat of both government and the established church. On weekdays the streets are crowded with civil servants whose work is based here, while at weekends the area takes on a different atmosphere with a steady flow of tourists.

Downing Street
Sir Robert Walpole was the first Prime Minister to live here in 1732 ⑰

Cabinet War Rooms
Now open to the public, these were Winston Churchill's World War II headquarters ⑯

St Margaret's Church is a favourite venue for political and society weddings.

★ **Westminster Abbey**
The abbey is London's oldest and most important church ⑳

Central Hall (1911) is a florid example of the Beaux Arts style.

Richard I's Statue is an 1860 depiction of the king, killed in battle in 1199.

Dean's Yard is a secluded grassy square surrounded by picturesque buildings from different periods, many used by Westminster School.

The Burghers of Calais is a cast of Auguste Rodin's 1886 original in France.

To Trafalgar Square

Banqueting House
Inigo Jones designed this elegant building in 1622 ⑱

LOCATOR MAP
See Street Finder map 11

REGENT'S PARK & BLOOMSBURY

WEST END & WESTMINSTER

THE CITY & SOUTH-WARK

SOUTH KENSINGTON & HYDE PARK

THAMES

The Cenotaph (1920) is a war memorial by Sir Edwin Lutyens.

WHITEHALL

RICHMOND TERRACE

VICTORIA EMBANKMENT

STREET

Horse Guards is a parade ground protected by a guard, changed twice each day.

Westminster Pier is the main starting point for river trips *(pp74–5)*.

Westminster

★ Houses of Parliament
The seat of government is dominated by the clock tower, holding the 14-tonne bell Big Ben, hung in 1858. Its deep chimes are broadcast daily on BBC radio ⑲

KEY

– – – Suggested route

0 metres   100

0 yards   100

STAR SIGHTS

★ Westminster Abbey

★ Houses of Parliament

Cabinet War Rooms ⑯

Clive Steps, King Charles St SW1.
Map 11 B5. **Tel** 020-7930 6961.
⊖ Westminster. ⬚ 9:30am–6pm daily. ● 24–26 Dec. ⬚ ⬚ ⬚ ⬚ ⬚
www.iwm.org.uk

This warren of cellars below a government office building is where the War Cabinet – first under Neville Chamberlain, then Winston Churchill from 1940 – met during World War II when German bombs were falling on London. The rooms include living quarters for ministers and military leaders and a Cabinet Room, where strategic decisions were taken. They are laid out as they were when the war ended, complete with Churchill's desk, communications equipment, and maps for plotting battles and strategies. The Churchill Museum is a new addition, which records and illustrates Churchill's life and career.

Telephones in the Map Room, Cabinet War Rooms

Downing Street ⑰

SW1. **Map** 11 B4. ⊖ Westminster.
● to the public.

Number 10 Downing Street has been the official residence of the British Prime Minister since 1732. It contains a Cabinet Room in which government policy is decided, an impressive State Dining Room and a private apartment; outside is a well-protected garden.

Next door at No. 11 is the official residence of the Chancellor of the Exchequer, who is in charge of the nation's financial affairs. In 1989, iron gates were erected at the Whitehall end of Downing Street for security purposes.

Banqueting House ⑱

Whitehall SW1. **Map** 11 B4. *Tel 020-7839 8919.* 🚇 *Charing Cross.* ⬜ *10am–5pm Mon–Sat.* 🔴 *public hols & for functions.* 🔲 📷 ♿
www.hrp.org.uk

Completed by Inigo Jones *(see p53)* in 1622, this was the first building in central London to embody the Palladian style of Renaissance Italy. In 1629 Charles I commissioned Rubens to paint the ceiling with scenes exalting the reign of his father, James I. They symbolize the divine right of kings, disputed by the Parliamentarians, who executed Charles I outside the building in 1649 *(see pp52–3).*

Panels from the Rubens ceiling (1629–34), Banqueting House

Houses of Parliament ⑲

SW1. **Map** 11 C5. *Tel 020-7219 3000.* 🚇 *Westminster.* **Visitors' Galleries** ⬜ *2:30–10:30pm Mon; 11:30am–7:30pm Tue, Wed; 11:30am–6:30pm Thu; 9:30am–3pm sitting Fri. Queue or UK residents may apply in advance to local MP.* 🔴 *frequently for parliamentary recesses.* ♿ 📷 *call 0870-906 3773 or go to* www.keithprowse.com *to book tickets for tours.* 🔲
www.parliament.uk

There has been a Palace of Westminster here since the 11th century, though only Westminster Hall remains from that time. The present Neo-Gothic structure by Sir Charles Barry was built after the old palace was destroyed by fire in 1834. Since the 16th century it has housed the two Houses of Parliament, the Lords and the Commons. The House of Commons consists of elected Members of Parliament (MPs).

The party with most MPs forms the Government, and its leader becomes Prime Minister. The House of Lords comprises peers, law lords, bishops and archbishops.

Westminster Abbey ⑳

See pp92–3.

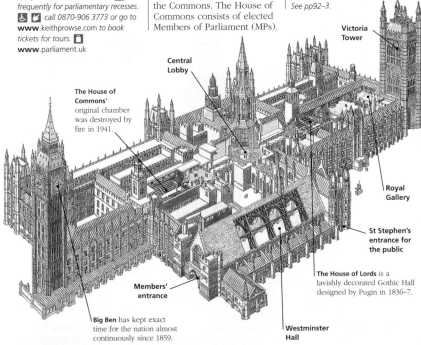

Victoria Tower

Central Lobby

The House of Commons' original chamber was destroyed by fire in 1941.

Royal Gallery

St Stephen's entrance for the public

The House of Lords is a lavishly decorated Gothic Hall designed by Pugin in 1836–7.

Members' entrance

Big Ben has kept exact time for the nation almost continuously since 1859.

Westminster Hall

Portico of Tate Britain

Tate Britain ㉑

Millbank SW1. **Map** 19 B2. **Tel** 020-7887 8000. 🚇 Pimlico. 🚌 77a, 88, C10. 🚆 Victoria, Vauxhall. 🚤 to Tate Modern every 40 mins. 🕙 10am–5:50pm daily. 🔴 24–26 Dec. 💷 for major exhibitions. 🚾 Atterbury St. 📷 🍴 🛗 🎁 www.tate.org.uk

Formerly the Tate Gallery, Tate Britain is the national gallery of British art, and includes works from the 16th to the 21st century. Displays draw on the enormous Tate Collection, which also includes the international modern art seen at Tate Modern (p121). A river boat, *Tate to Tate*, takes visitors between the two galleries. Located in the Clore Galleries is the Turner Bequest (see box).

The size of the collection necessitates some rotation of displays, which are organized in various imaginative and innovative ways. Major themes change on a three-yearly basis, solo artists' rooms and smaller themed rooms more frequently. Loan exhibitions are installed in the ground floor galleries and part of the main floor.

The section on the years 1500–1800 covers a period of dramatic change in British history, from the Tudors and Stuarts through to the age of Thomas Gainsborough. The section concludes with a series of changing displays about the poet and artist William Blake.

The years 1800 to 1900 saw dramatic expansion and change in the arts in Britain. This section shows the new themes that began to emerge. Included are the "Victorian Narrative" painters such as William Powell Frith, and the work of the Pre-Raphaelites, such as John Everett Millais and Dante Gabriel Rossetti.

Mr. and Mrs. Clark and Percy (1970–71) by **David Hockney**

Captain Thomas Lee (1594) by **Marcus Gheeraerts II**

The period 1900–1960 includes the work of Jacob Epstein, that of Wyndham Lewis and his Vorticist group, and the celebrated modernist works of Henry Moore, Barbara Hepworth, Ben Nicholson, Francis Bacon and Lucian Freud.

The Tate Collection is outstanding in its wealth of British art from 1960 to the present, and the displays in this section are changed on a regular basis. From the 1960s, Tate's funding for the purchase of works began to increase substantially, while artistic activity continued to pick up speed, encouraged by public spending. As a result, Tate Britain's collection is particularly rich in this period. Works range from the 1960s Pop artists David Hockney, Richard Hamilton and Peter Blake, through the works of Gilbert and George and the landscape artist Richard Long, to the 1980s paintings of Howard Hodgkin and R B Kitaj. The so-called Young British Artists (YBAs) of the 1990s are well represented by leading figures Damian Hirst, Tracey Emin and Sarah Lucas.

Recumbent Figure (1938) by **Henry Moore**

THE TURNER BEQUEST

The Turner Bequest comprises some 300 oil paintings and 20,000 watercolours and drawings, received by the nation from the great landscape painter J M W Turner some years after his death in 1851. Turner's will had specified that a gallery be built to house his pictures and this was finally done in 1987 with the opening of the Clore Galleries. Most of the oils are on view in the main galleries, and the water-colours are the subject of changing displays.

The Scarlet Sunset: A Town on a River (c.1830–40)

Westminster Abbey ⑳

Westminster Abbey has been the burial place of
Britain's monarchs since the 11th century and the
setting for many coronations and royal weddings. It
is one of the most beautiful buildings in London, with
an exceptionally diverse array of architectural styles,
ranging from the austere French Gothic of the nave to
the astonishing complexity of Henry VII's chapel. Half
national church, half national museum, the abbey aisles
and transepts are crammed with an extraordinary collection of tombs and monuments honouring some of Britain's
greatest public figures, ranging from politicians to poets.

North Entrance
*The mock-medieval
stonework is
Victorian.*

**Statesmen's
Aisle**

Flying buttresses help
redistribute the great
weight of the roof.

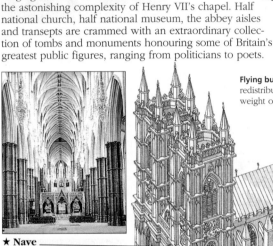

★ Nave
*At a height of 31 m
(102 ft), the nave is
the highest in England.
The ratio of height to
width is 3:1.*

CORONATION

The coronation ceremony
is over 1,000 years old
and since 1066, with the
crowning of William the
Conqueror on Christmas
Day, the abbey has been
its sumptuous setting.
The coronation of Queen
Elizabeth II, in 1953, was
the first to be televised.

Cloisters
*Built mainly in the 13th and
14th centuries, the cloisters
link the Abbey church with
the other buildings.*

STAR FEATURES

★ Nave

★ Henry VII Chapel

★ Chapter House

★ **Henry VII Chapel**
The chapel, built in 1503–19, has superb late Perpendicular vaulting and choir stalls dating from 1512.

Poets' Corner
A host of great poets are honoured here, including Shakespeare, Chaucer and T S Eliot.

The Sanctuary, built by Henry III, has been the scene of 38 coronations.

VISITORS' CHECKLIST

Broad Sanctuary SW1. **Map** 11 B5. **Tel** 020-7222 5152. 🚇 Westminster. 🚌 3, 11, 12, 24, 29, 53, 70, 77, 77a, 88, 109, 159, 170. 🚆 Victoria. ⛴ Westminster Pier. **Cloisters** ☐ 8am–6pm daily. **Abbey, including Royal Chapels, Poets' Corner, Choir, Statesmen's Aisle, Nave** ☐ 9:30am–3:45pm Mon, Tue, Thu, Fri, 9:30am–6pm Wed, 9:30am–1:45pm Sat (last adm: 12:45pm). 🎟 **Chapter House, Pyx Chamber & Museum** ☐ 10:30am–4pm daily. 🎟 **College Garden** ☐ Apr–Sep: 10am–6pm Tue–Thu; Oct–Mar: 10am–4pm Tue–Thu. **Evensong** 5pm Mon–Fri, 3pm Sat, Sun. **Concerts.** 🎵 🖥 www.westminster-abbey.org

The Museum has many of the abbey's treasures including wood, plaster and wax effigies of monarchs.

The Pyx Chamber is where the coinage was tested in medieval times.

★ **Chapter House**
A beautiful octagonal room, remarkable for its 13th-century tile floor. It is lit by six huge stained glass windows showing scenes from the abbey's history.

St Edward's Chapel
The shrine of Edward the Confessor is housed here, along with the tombs of many medieval monarchs.

HISTORICAL PLAN OF THE ABBEY

The first abbey church was established as early as the 10th century, but the present French-influenced Gothic structure was begun in 1245 at the behest of Henry III. Because of its unique role as the coronation church, the abbey escaped Henry VIII's onslaught on Britain's monastic buildings *(see pp50–51)*.

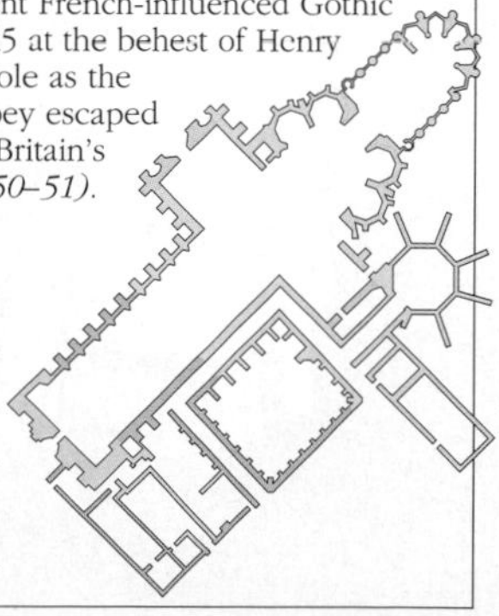

KEY

☐ Built between 1055–1350
☐ Added from 1350–1420
☐ Built between 1500–1512
☐ Towers completed 1745
☐ Restored after 1850

SOUTH KENSINGTON AND HYDE PARK

This exclusive district embraces one of London's largest parks and some of its finest museums, shops, restaurants and hotels. Until the mid-19th century it was a genteel, semi-rural backwater of large houses and private schools lying to the south of Kensington Palace. In 1851, the Great Exhibition, until then the largest arts and science event ever staged (*see pp56–7*), was held in Hyde Park, transforming the area into a celebration of Victorian learning and self-confidence.

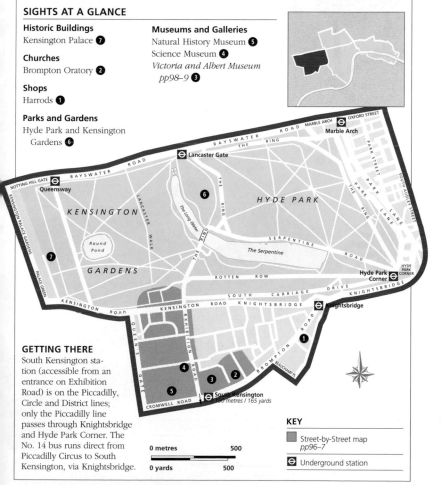

Peter Pan statue in Kensington Gardens

The brainchild of Queen Victoria's husband, Prince Albert, the exhibition was a massive success and the profits were used to buy 35 ha (87 acres) of land in South Kensington. Here, Prince Albert encouraged the construction of a concert hall, museums and colleges devoted to the applied arts and sciences; most of them survive. The neighbourhood soon became modish, full of flamboyant red-brick mansion blocks, garden squares and the elite shops still to be found in Knightsbridge.

SIGHTS AT A GLANCE

Historic Buildings
Kensington Palace ❼

Churches
Brompton Oratory ❷

Shops
Harrods ❶

Parks and Gardens
Hyde Park and Kensington Gardens ❻

Museums and Galleries
Natural History Museum ❺
Science Museum ❹
Victoria and Albert Museum pp98–9 ❸

GETTING THERE

South Kensington station (accessible from an entrance on Exhibition Road) is on the Piccadilly, Circle and District lines; only the Piccadilly line passes through Knightsbridge and Hyde Park Corner. The No. 14 bus runs direct from Piccadilly Circus to South Kensington, via Knightsbridge.

0 metres   500
0 yards   500

KEY

Street-by-Street map *pp96–7*

Underground station

◁ **Ennismore Mews in South Kensington, built 1843–6**

Street-by-Street: South Kensington

The numerous museums and colleges created in the wake of the Great Exhibition of 1851 *(see pp56–7)* continue to give this neighbourhood an air of leisured culture. Visited as much by Londoners as tourists, the museum area is liveliest on Sundays and on summer evenings during the Royal Albert Hall's famous season of classical "Prom" concerts *(see p154).*

The Royal Albert Hall opened in 1870 and was modelled on Roman amphitheatres.

The Memorial to the Great Exhibition is surmounted by a bronze statue of its instigator, Prince Albert.

The Royal College of Music, founded in 1882, exhibits historic musical instruments such as this harpsichord dating from 1531.

★ **Science Museum**
Visitors can experiment with over a thousand interactive displays ❹

★ **Natural History Museum**
The Creepy Crawlies exhibition has proved highly popular ❺

STAR SIGHTS

- ★ Science Museum
- ★ Natural History Museum
- ★ Victoria and Albert Museum

Entrance to South Kensington tube

KEY

– – – Suggested route

| 0 metres | 100 |
| 0 yards | 100 |

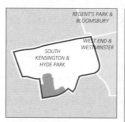

The Albert Memorial was built in memory of Queen Victoria's husband who died in 1861.

LOCATOR MAP
See Street Finder maps 8, 16, 17

★ **Victoria and Albert Museum**
The museum has a fine collection of applied arts and photography from around the world ❸

Brompton Oratory
This ornate Baroque church is famous for its splendid musical tradition ❷

Brompton Square (1821)

To Knightsbridge and Harrods

Harrods Food Hall

Harrods ❶

Knightsbridge SW1. **Map** 9 B5.
Tel 020-7730 1234. ⊖ *Knightsbridge.*
◯ 10am–7pm Mon–Sat. ♿ 🍴 📷
See **Shops and Markets** pp120–1.
www.harrods.com

In 1849 Henry Charles Harrod opened a small grocery shop on Brompton Road, which soon became famous for its impeccable service and quality. The store moved into these extravagant premises in Knightsbridge in 1905.

Brompton Oratory ❷

Brompton Rd SW7. **Map** 17 B1. *Tel* 020-7808 0900. ⊖ *South Kensington.* ◯ 6:30am–8pm daily. ♿ 📷
www.bromptonoratory.com

The Italianate Oratory is a lavish monument to the 19th-century English Catholic revival. It was established as a base for a community of priests by John Henry Newman (later Cardinal Newman), who introduced the Oratorian movement to England in 1848. The church was opened in 1884, and the dome and façade added in the 1890s.

The sumptuous interior holds many fine monuments. The 12 huge 17th-century statues of the apostles are from Siena Cathedral, the elaborate Baroque Lady Altar (1693) is from the Dominican church at Brescia, and the 18th-century altar in St Wilfred's Chapel is from Rochefort in Belgium.

Victoria and Albert Museum ❸

The Victoria and Albert Museum (the V&A) contains one of the world's widest collections of art and design, ranging from early Christian devotional objects and the mystical art of southeast Asia to cutting-edge furniture design. Originally founded in 1852 as the Museum of Manufactures to inspire students of design, it was renamed by Queen Victoria in 1899 in memory of Prince Albert. The museum is undergoing a dramatic redisplay of much of its collection, alongside a spectacular redesign of the garden, Sculpture galleries and main shop. To find out if a particular gallery will be open, phone 020 7942 2211.

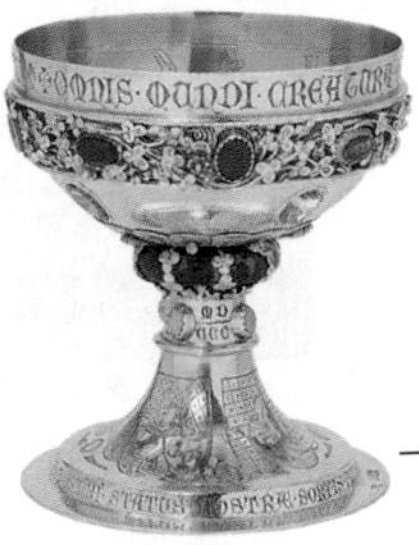

The Glass gallery, room 131

★ British Galleries

The Great Bed of Ware has been a tourist attraction since 1601, when Shakespeare sparked interest in it by making reference to it in Twelfth Night.

Silver galleries

Radiant pieces such as the Burgess Cup (Britain, 1863) fill these stunning galleries.

★ Fashion gallery

In this gallery, European clothing from the mid-1500s to the present day is displayed, such as these famous Vivienne Westwood shoes.

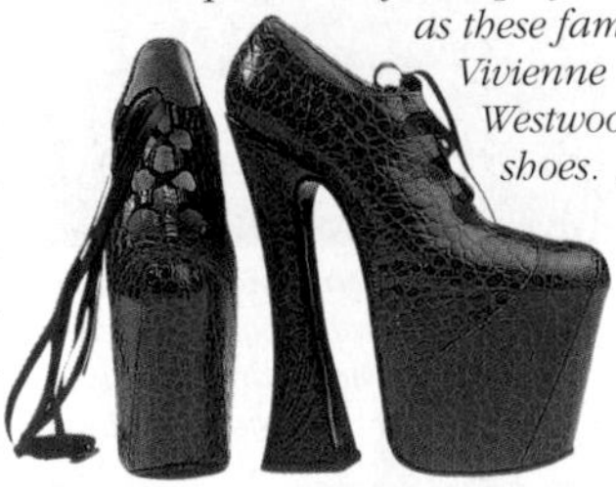

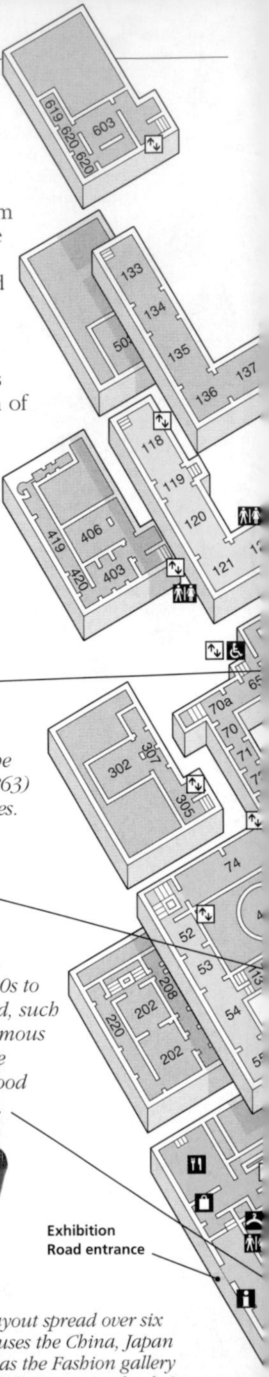

Exhibition Road entrance

KEY TO FLOORPLAN

- Level 0
- Level 1
- Level 2
- Level 3
- Level 4
- Henry Cole Wing
- Non-exhibition space

STAR EXHIBITS

- ★ British Galleries
- ★ Fashion gallery
- ★ Architecture gallery
- ★ South Asia gallery

GALLERY GUIDE

The V&A has a 7-mile (11-km) layout spread over six levels. The main floor, level 1, houses the China, Japan and South Asia galleries, as well as the Fashion gallery and the Cast Courts. The British Galleries are on levels 2 and 4. Level 3 contains the 20th Century galleries and displays of silver, ironwork, paintings and works of 20th-century design. The textile galleries are in the far north-eastern corner of this floor. The glass display is also on upper level 4. The Henry Cole Wing houses the Education Centre, RIBA Architecture Study Rooms and the Prints and Drawings Study Rooms.

★ Architecture gallery
Features highlights from the world class collection of drawings, models, photographs and architectural fragments of the V&A, such as this 1930s-style doll's house.

VISITORS' CHECKLIST

Cromwell Rd SW7. **Map** 17 A1.
Tel 020-7942 2000.
🚇 *South Kensington.* 🚌 14, 74, 414, C1. ⬭ 10am–5:45pm daily (10am–10pm Wed and last Fri of each month). ⬤ 24–26 Dec. ♿ 🎫 🍴 🛍 📷
www.vam.ac.uk

Sacred Silver and Stained Glass gallery
Illuminated European stained glass, such as Susannah and the Elders (c. 1520), is located in rooms 83 and 84.

China gallery
This magnificent ancestor portrait is among the many exquisite pieces on show in this gallery.

Aston Webb's façade (1909) is decorated with 32 sculptures of English craftsmen and designers.

★ South Asia gallery
Considered the greatest collection outside India, it includes Tippoo's Tiger (1795), a pump organ in the form of a man being mauled by a tiger.

Main entrance

Science Museum ❹

Exhibition Rd SW7. **Map** 16 F1. **Tel** *0870-870 4868.* ⊖ *South Kensington.* ☐ *10am–6pm daily.* ● *24–26 Dec.* 🎦 *for IMAX, special exhibitions and simulators only.* ♿ 📷 🖥 🔌 **www**.sciencemuseum.org.uk

Centuries of continuing scientific and technological development lie at the heart of the Science Museum's massive collections. The hardware displayed is magnificent: from steam engines to aeroengines; spacecraft to the very first mechanical computers. Equally important is the social

Newcomen's Steam Engine (1712), Science Museum

context of science – what discoveries and inventions mean for day-to-day life – and the process of discovery itself. There are many interactive and hands-on displays which are very popular with children.

The museum is spread over seven floors and includes the recent Wellcome Wing at the west end of the museum. The basement features the excellent hands-on galleries for children, including The Launch Pad and Garden. The Energy Hall dominates the ground floor, and is dedicated to steam power, with the still-operational Harle Syke Mill Engine of 1903. Here too are Space and Making the Modern World, a highlight of which is the display of the scarred Apollo 10 spacecraft, which carried three astronauts to the moon and back in May 1969. In Challenge of Materials, located on the first floor,

our expectations of materials are confounded with exhibits such as a bridge made of glass and a steel wedding dress.

The Flight gallery on the third floor is packed with early flying contraptions, fighter planes and aeroplanes. The fourth and fifth floors house the medical science galleries, where Science and the Art of Medicine has a 17th-century Italian vase for storing snake bite treatment.

The high-tech Wellcome Wing offers four floors of interactive technology, including 'Who Am I?', a fascinating exhibition exploring the science of you. With an IMAX 3D Cinema and the SimEx simulator ride, it is a breathtaking addition to the museum. The museum cafés and shop are particularly good.

Natural History Museum ❺

Cromwell Rd SW7. **Map** 16 F1. **Tel** *020-7942 5000.* ⊖ *South Kensington.* ☐ *10am–5:50pm Mon–Sat, 11am–5:50pm Sun & public hols.* ● *25, 26 Dec.* 🔌 ♿ 📷 🖥 **www**.nhm.ac.uk

This vast cathedral-like building is the most architecturally flamboyant of the South Kensington museums. Its richly sculpted stonework conceals an iron and steel frame; this building technique was revolutionary when the museum opened in 1881. The imaginative displays tackle fundamental issues such as the ecology and evolution of the planet, the origin of species and the development of human beings – all explained through a dynamic

Relief from a decorative panel in the Natural History Museum

combination of the latest technology, interactive techniques and traditional displays.

The museum is divided into three sections: the Blue Zone, Green Zone and Red Zone. In the Blue Zone, the Ecology exhibition begins its exploration of the complex web of the natural world through a replica of a moonlit rainforest buzzing with the sounds of insects. One of the most popular exhibits is the Dinosaur Gallery, which includes life-like animatronic models of dinosaurs. The Green Zone explores the history of Earth and its wealth of natural resources. The Spirit Collection, with over 22 million specimens, is housed in a new scientific research centre. Tours are available.

The Tuojiangasaurus skeleton (about 150 million years old), Natural History Museum

For hotels and restaurants in this region see pp556–560 and pp608–616

Statue of the young Queen Victoria outside Kensington Palace, sculpted by her daughter, Princess Louise

Hyde Park and Kensington Gardens ❻

W2. **Map** 9 B3. **Tel** 020-7298 2000.
Hyde Park 🚇 *Hyde Park Corner,
Knightsbridge, Lancaster Gate, Marble
Arch.* ⬜ *dawn–midnight daily.* ♿
Kensington Gardens. Tel 020-7298
2000. 🚇 *Queensway, Lancaster Gate.*
⬜ *dawn–dusk daily.* ♿ 🖥 *See also
pp74–5.* **Diana, Princess of Wales
Memorial Playground** 🚇 *Queensway, Bayswater.* ⬜ *10am–dusk daily.*
♿ 🖥 www.royalparks.org.uk

The ancient manor of Hyde
was part of the lands of
Westminster Abbey seized by
Henry VIII at the Dissolution
of the Monasteries in 1536
(see pp50–51). James I opened
the park to the public in the
early 17th century, and it was
soon one of the city's most
fashionable public spaces.
Unfortunately it also
became popular
with duellists and
highwaymen, and conse-
quently

William III had 300 lights
hung along Rotten Row, the
first street in England to be lit
up at night. In 1730, the
Westbourne River was
dammed by Queen Caroline
in order to create the
Serpentine, an artificial lake
that is today used for boating
and swimming, and Rotten
Row for horse riding. The
park is also a rallying point
for political demonstrations,
while at Speaker's Corner, in
the northeast, anyone has
had the right to address the
public since 1872. Sundays
are particularly lively, with
many budding orators
and a number of
eccentrics revealing
their plans for the
betterment of
mankind.
Adjoining Hyde
Park is Kensington
Gardens, the
former grounds of
Kensington
Palace. Three
great attractions
for children are
the innovative
Diana, Princess of Wales
Memorial Playground, the
bronze statue of J M Barrie's
fictional Peter Pan (1912), by
George Frampton, and the
Round Pond where people
sail model boats. Also worth
seeing is the dignified
Orangery (1704),
once used by
Queen Anne as a
"summer supper house" and
now a summer café.

**Detail of the Coalbrookdale
Gate, Kensington Gardens**

Kensington Palace ❼

Kensington Palace Gdns W8. **Map** 8
D4. **Tel** 0870-451 5170. 🚇 *High St
Ken, Queensway.* ⬜ *Nov–Feb: 10am–
5pm daily; Mar–Oct: 10am–6pm daily
(last adm: 1 hr before close).* ● *1 Jan,
24–26 Dec.* 🄯 🖼 ♿ *ground floor.*
🖥 www.historicroyalpalaces.org

Kensington Palace was the
principal residence of the
royal family from the 1690s
until 1760, when George III
moved to Buckingham
Palace. Over the years it
has seen a number of
important royal events.
In 1714 Queen Anne
died here from a fit of
apoplexy brought on
by over-eating and, in
June 1837, Princess
Victoria of Kent was
woken to be told
that her uncle
William IV had
died and she
was now queen
– the beginning
of her 64-year
reign. Half of the palace still
holds royal apartments, but the
other half is open to the public. Among the highlights are
the 18th-century state rooms
with ceilings and murals by
William Kent *(see p28).* After
the death of Princess Diana in
1997, the palace became a
focal point for mourners who
gathered in their thousands at
its gates and turned the area
into a field of bouquets.

REGENT'S PARK AND BLOOMSBURY

Ancient Greek vase, British Museum

Cream stuccoed terraces built by John Nash *(see p105)* fringe the southern edge of Regent's Park in London's highest concentration of quality Georgian housing. The park, named for the Prince Regent, was also designed by Nash, as the culmination of a triumphal route from the Prince's house in St James's *(see pp84–5)*. Today it is the busiest of the royal parks and boasts a zoo, an open air theatre, boating lake, rose garden, cafés and London's largest mosque. To the northeast is Camden Town *(see p124)* with its popular market, shops and cafés, reached by walking, or taking a boat, along the picturesque Regent's Canal.

Bloomsbury, an enclave of attractive garden squares and Georgian brick terraces, was one of the most fashionable areas of the city until the mid-19th century, when the arrival of large hospitals and railway stations persuaded many of the wealthier residents to move west to Mayfair, Knightsbridge and Kensington. Home to the British Museum since 1753 and the University of London since 1828, Bloomsbury has long been the domain of artists, writers and intellectuals, including the Bloomsbury Group *(see p163)*, George Bernard Shaw, Charles Dickens and Karl Marx. Traditionally a centre for the book trade, it remains a good place for literary browsing.

SIGHTS AT A GLANCE

Historic Streets
Bloomsbury ❺

Museums and Galleries
British Museum pp106–7 ❹

Madame Tussaud's and Tussaud's Auditorium ❶
Sherlock Holmes Museum ❷
Wallace Collection ❸

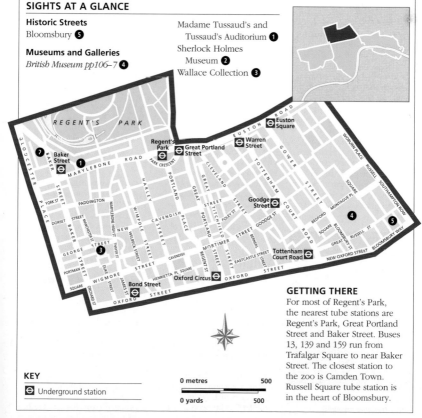

GETTING THERE

For most of Regent's Park, the nearest tube stations are Regent's Park, Great Portland Street and Baker Street. Buses 13, 139 and 159 run from Trafalgar Square to near Baker Street. The closest station to the zoo is Camden Town. Russell Square tube station is in the heart of Bloomsbury.

KEY

🚇 Underground station

0 metres   500
0 yards   500

◁ St Andrew's Place, Regent's Park

Madame Tussaud's and Tussaud's Auditorium ❶

Marylebone Rd NW1. **Map** 2 D5.
0870 400 3000. *Baker St.*
9:30am–5:30pm Mon–Fri, 9am–6pm Sat -Sun. *25 Dec.*
phone first.
www.madame-tussauds.com

Madame Tussaud began her wax-modelling career making death masks of victims of the French Revolution. She moved to England and in 1835 set up an exhibition of her work in Baker Street, near the present site. Traditional techniques are still used to create figures of royalty, politicians, actors, pop stars and sporting heroes. The main sections of the exhibition are: Blush, where

**Wax figure of
Elizabeth II**

visitors get to feel what it is like to be at a celebrity A-list party; Première Night, devoted to the giants of the entertainment world; and the World Stage, a collection of various royalty, statesmen, world leaders, writers and artists.

The Chamber of Horrors is the most renowned part of Madame Tussaud's for its recreations of murders and executions. In the Spirit of London finale, visitors travel in stylized taxi-cabs through

**Conan Doyle's fictional detective
Sherlock Holmes**

the city's history to "witness" events, from the Great Fire of 1666 to the Swinging 1960s. Next door, Tussaud's Auditorium, built in 1958, offers exciting virtual space travel and laser shows, such as "Journey to Infinity".

Sherlock Holmes Museum ❷

221b Baker St NW1. **Map** 1 C4.
Tel *020-7935 8866.* *Baker St.*
9:30am–6pm daily. *25 Dec.*
www.sherlock-holmes.co.uk

Sir Arthur Conan Doyle's fictional detective was supposed to live at 221b Baker Street, which did not exist. The museum, labelled 221b, actually stands between Nos. 237 and 239, and is the only surviving Victorian lodging house in the street. There is a reconstruction of Holmes's front room, and memorabilia from the stories decorate every room. Visitors can buy plaques, Holmes hats, Toby jugs and meerschaum pipes.

Wallace Collection ❸

Hertford House, Manchester Sq W1.
Map 10 D1. *020-7563 9500.*
Bond St, Baker St.
10am–5pm daily. *24–26 Dec, 1 Jan, Good Fri.* *phone first.*
www.wallace-collection.org

One of the world's finest private collections of European art, it has remained intact since 1897. The product of

passionate collecting by four generations of the Seymour-Conway family who were Marquesses of Hertford, it was bequeathed to the state on the condition that it would go on permanent public display with nothing added or taken away. Hertford House still retains the atmosphere of a grand 19th-century house, and the recent Centenary Project has created more gallery space and a stunning high-level glass roof for the central courtyard, which now contains a sculpture garden and an elegant restaurant.

The 3rd Marquess (1777–1842), a flamboyant London figure, used his Italian wife's fortune to buy works by Titian and Canaletto, along with numerous 17th-century Dutch paintings including works by Van Dyck. The collection's particular strength is 18th-century French painting, sculpture and decorative arts, acquired by the 4th Marquess (1800–70) and his natural son, Sir Richard Wallace (1818–90).

**A 16th-century Italian majolica
dish from the Wallace Collection**

The Marquess had a taste for lush romanticism, and notable among his acquisitions are Watteau's *Champs Elysées* (1716–17), Fragonard's *The Swing* (1766) and Boucher's *The Rising and Setting of the Sun* (1753).

Other highlights at the Wallace Collection include Rembrandt's *Titus, the Artist's Son* (1650s), Titian's *Perseus and Andromeda* (1554–6) and Hals's famous *Laughing Cavalier* (1624). There is also an important collection of Renaissance armour, and superb examples of Sèvres porcelain and Italian majolica.

**Wax model of Luciano Pavarotti
(1990), Madame Tussaud's**

John Nash's Regency London

Statue of John Nash (1752–1835)

John Nash, the son of a Lambeth millwright, was designing houses from the 1780s. However, it was not until the 1820s that he also became known as an inspired town planner, when his "royal route" was completed. This took George IV from his Pall Mall palace, through Piccadilly Circus and up the elegant sweep of Regent Street to Regent's Park, which Nash bordered with rows of beautiful Neo-Classical villas, such as Park Crescent and Cumberland Terrace. Though many of his plans were never completed, this map of 1851, which unusually places the south at the top, shows Nash's overall architectural impact on London. His other work included the revamping of Buckingham Palace *(see pp86–7)*, and the building of several theatres and churches.

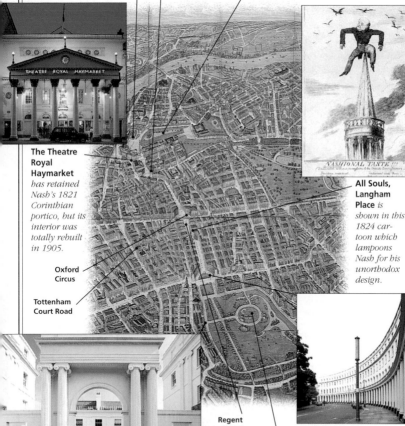

Pall Mall

Piccadilly Circus *(see p81)*

St James's Park *(see pp74–5)*

The Theatre Royal Haymarket *has retained Nash's 1821 Corinthian portico, but its interior was totally rebuilt in 1905.*

Oxford Circus

Tottenham Court Road

All Souls, Langham Place *is shown in this 1824 cartoon which lampoons Nash for his unorthodox design.*

Regent Street

Regent's Park *(see p103)*

Cumberland Terrace, *the longest and most ornate of the stuccoed terraces surrounding Regent's Park, was intended to face a royal palace, which was never built.*

Park Crescent *was designed by Nash to be the southern half of a circle, but the northern half was never built. The interiors were refurbished in the 1960s but the dramatic façade was kept intact.*

British Museum ❹

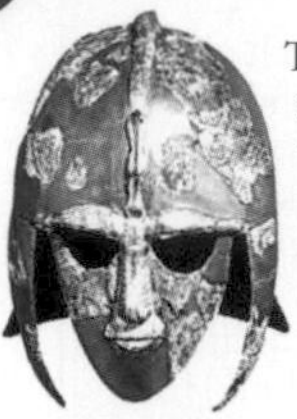

The oldest public museum in the world, the British Museum was established in 1753 to house the collections of the physician Sir Hans Sloane (1660–1753). Sloane's collection has been added to by gifts and purchases from all over the world, and the museum now contains objects spanning thousands of years. The main part of the building (1823–50) is by architect Robert Smirke, but the architectural highlight is the modern Great Court, with the Reading Room at its centre.

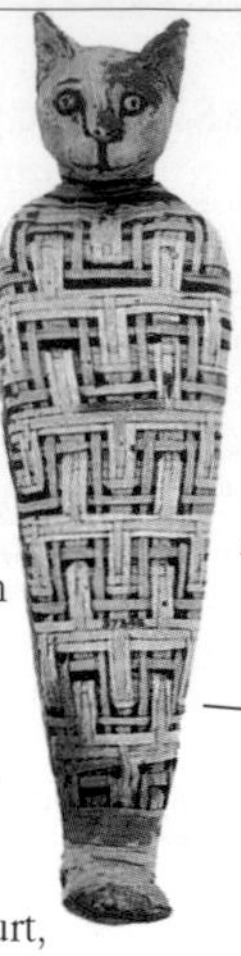

Helmet from Sutton Hoo ship burial

★ Egyptian Mummies
Animals such as this cat (30 BC) were preserved alongside humans by the ancient Egyptians.

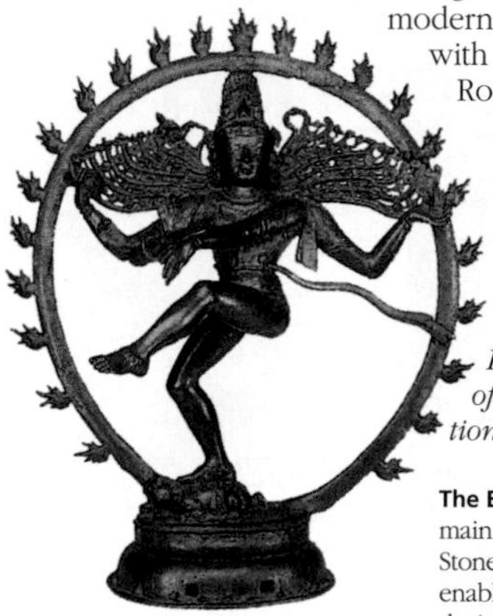

Upper floors

90
67
61
59
60

Montague Place entrance

34
33
2
24

Bronze Figure Shiva Nataraja
This statue of the Hindu God Shiva Nataraja (c.1100) from South India forms part of the fine collection of Oriental art.

The Egyptian Gallery on the main floor houses the Rosetta Stone, the inscription that enabled 19th-century scholars to decipher Egyptian hieroglyphs.

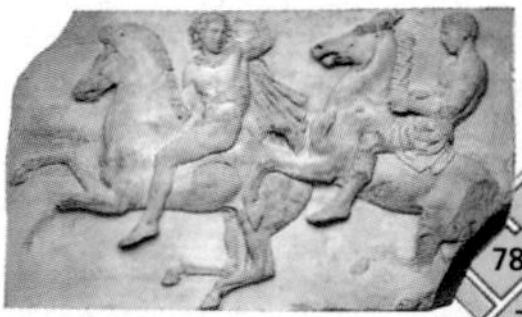

25
21
20
9
19
22
4
8

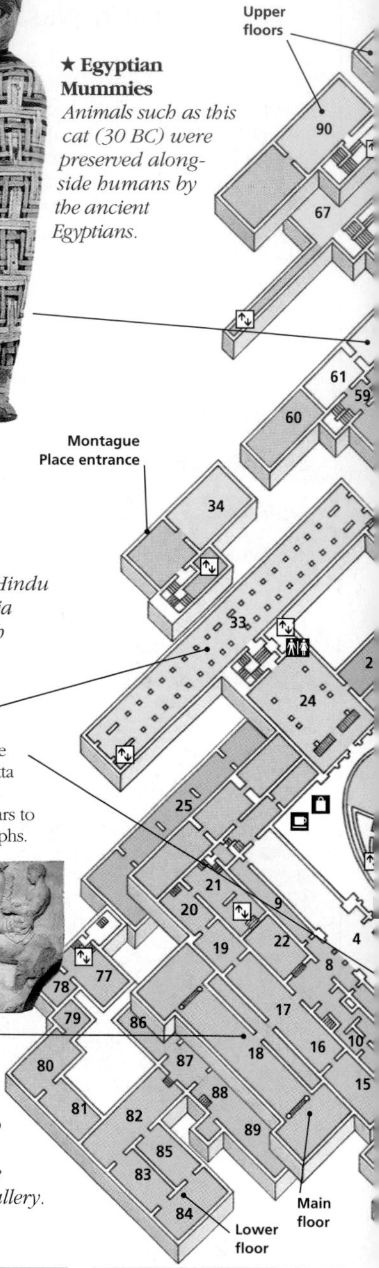

GALLERY GUIDE

The Greek and Roman, and Ancient Near Eastern collections are found on all three levels of the museum, predominantly on the west side. The African collection is located on the lower floor, while Asian exhibits are found on the main and upper floors on the north side of the museum. The Americas collection is located in the northeast corner off the main floor. Egyptian artifacts are found in the large gallery to the west of the Great Court and on the first floor.

78
77
79
86
17
80
87
18
16
10
81
82
88
15
85
89
83
84

★ Parthenon Sculptures
These reliefs from the Parthenon in Athens were brought to London by Lord Elgin around 1802 and are housed in a special gallery.

Main floor
Lower floor

STAR EXHIBITS

- ★ Egyptian Mummies
- ★ Parthenon Sculptures
- ★ Lindow Man

KEY TO FLOORPLAN

- ☐ Asian collection
- ☐ Enlightenment
- ☐ Coins, medals, prints and drawings
- ☐ Greek and Roman collections
- ☐ Egyptian collection
- ☐ Ancient Near Eastern collection
- ☐ Europe collection
- ☐ Temporary exhibitions
- ☐ Non-exhibition space
- ☐ World collection
- ☐ Special Exhibitions

First floor

The Great Court is London's largest covered square, with shops, cafés, a restaurant, display areas and educational facilities.

Mildenhall Treasure
The Great Dish was among the 34 pieces of 4th-century Roman silver tableware ploughed up in Suffolk in 1942.

Reading Room

Main entrance

★ **Lindow Man**
The skin on this 2,000-year-old human body was preserved by the acids of a peat-bog in Cheshire. He was probably killed in an elaborate ritual.

VISITORS' CHECKLIST

Great Russell St WC1. **Map** 3 B5.
Tel 020-7323 8000. ⊖ Holborn,
Russell Sq, Tottenham Court Rd.
🚌 7, 8, 10,14, 19, 24, 25, 29,
30, 38, 55, 134,188. 🚊 Euston,
King's Cross. ◻ 10am–5:30pm
daily (selected galleries until
8:30pm Thu & Fri). ◑ 1 Jan,
Good Fri, 24–26 Dec. 🎟 ♿
📷 🍴 🖥
www.thebritishmuseum.ac.uk

Private gardens of Bedford Square

Bloomsbury ⑤

WC1. **Map** 3 B4. ⊖ Russell Sq,
Tottenham Court Rd. **Charles Dickens
Museum** 48 Doughty St WC1. **Tel**
020-7405 2127. ◻ 10am–5pm Mon–
Sat, 11am–5pm Sun (last adm: 4:30pm).
📷 www.dickensmuseum.com

Home to numerous
writers and artists,
Bloomsbury is a traditional
centre of the book trade.
It is dominated by the
British Museum and the
University of London and
characterized by several fine
Georgian squares. These
include **Russell Square**, where
the poet T S Eliot (1888–1965)
worked for a publisher for 40
years; **Queen Square** which
contains a statue of Queen
Charlotte, wife of George III;
and **Bloomsbury
Square**, laid out in 1661.
A plaque here comme-
morates members of
the Bloomsbury
Group *(see p163)*.
One of London's
best-preserved
18th-century
oases is **Bed-
ford Square**.
Charles Dickens
(see p189) lived
at 48 Doughty
Street during a
brief but critical
stage in his car-
eer, and it was
here that
he wrote *Oliver Twist* and
Nicholas Nickleby, both
completed in 1839.

**Queen Charlotte
(1744–1818)**

His former home is now the
Charles Dickens Museum,
which has rooms laid out as
they were in Dickens's time,
with objects taken from his
other London homes and first
editions of many of his works.

THE CITY AND SOUTHWARK

Dominated today by glossy office blocks, the City is the oldest part of the capital. The Great Fire of 1666 obliterated four-fifths of its buildings. Sir Christopher Wren rebuilt much of it and many of his churches survived World War II (*see pp58–9*). Commerce has always been the City's lifeblood, and the power of its merchants and bankers secured it a degree of autonomy from state control. Humming with activity in business hours, it empties at night.

In the Middle Ages Southwark, on the south bank of the Thames, was a

Old bank sign on Lombard Street

refuge for pleasure-seekers, prostitutes, gamblers and criminals. Even after 1550, when the area fell under the jurisdiction of the City, its brothels and taverns thrived. There were also several bear-baiting arenas in which plays were staged until the building of theatres such as the Globe (1598), where many of Shakespeare's works were first performed. Relics of old Southwark are mostly on the waterfront, which has been imaginatively redeveloped and provided with a pleasant walkway.

SIGHTS AT A GLANCE

Historic Sights and Buildings
HMS Belfast ⑫
Lloyd's Building ⑦
Monument ⑧
The Old Operating Theatre ⑭
Temple ③
Tower Bridge ⑩
Tower of London pp118–19 ⑨

Pubs
George Inn ⑮

Museums and Galleries
Design Museum ⑪
London Dungeon ⑬
Museum of London ⑥
Shakespeare's Globe ⑱
Sir John Soane's Museum ④
Tate Modern ⑲

Markets
Borough Market ⑯

Churches and Cathedrals
St Bartholomew-the-Great ⑤
St Paul's Cathedral pp114–15 ②
St Stephen Walbrook ①
Southwark Cathedral ⑰

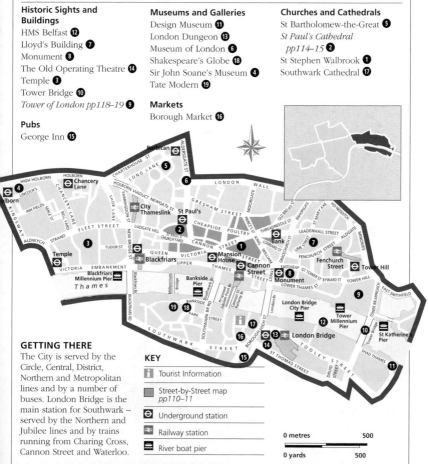

GETTING THERE

The City is served by the Circle, Central, District, Northern and Metropolitan lines and by a number of buses. London Bridge is the main station for Southwark – served by the Northern and Jubilee lines and by trains running from Charing Cross, Cannon Street and Waterloo.

KEY

ℹ️	Tourist Information
	Street-by-Street map pp110–11
⊖	Underground station
⇌	Railway station
⛴	River boat pier

0 metres 500
0 yards 500

◁ **St Paul's Cathedral in the heart of the City, with the NatWest Tower (1980) to the left**

Street-by-Street: The City

Detail: St Paul's Cathedral

This is the financial heart of London and has been ever since the Romans set up a trading post here 2,000 years ago. For years it was London's main residential area but today very few people live here. The City was severely bombed in World War II and the main clues to its past are streets named after vanished inns and markets. Its numerous churches, many built after the Great Fire of 1666 by the architect Sir Christopher Wren *(see p114),* are now dwarfed by lavish banks and post-modern developments.

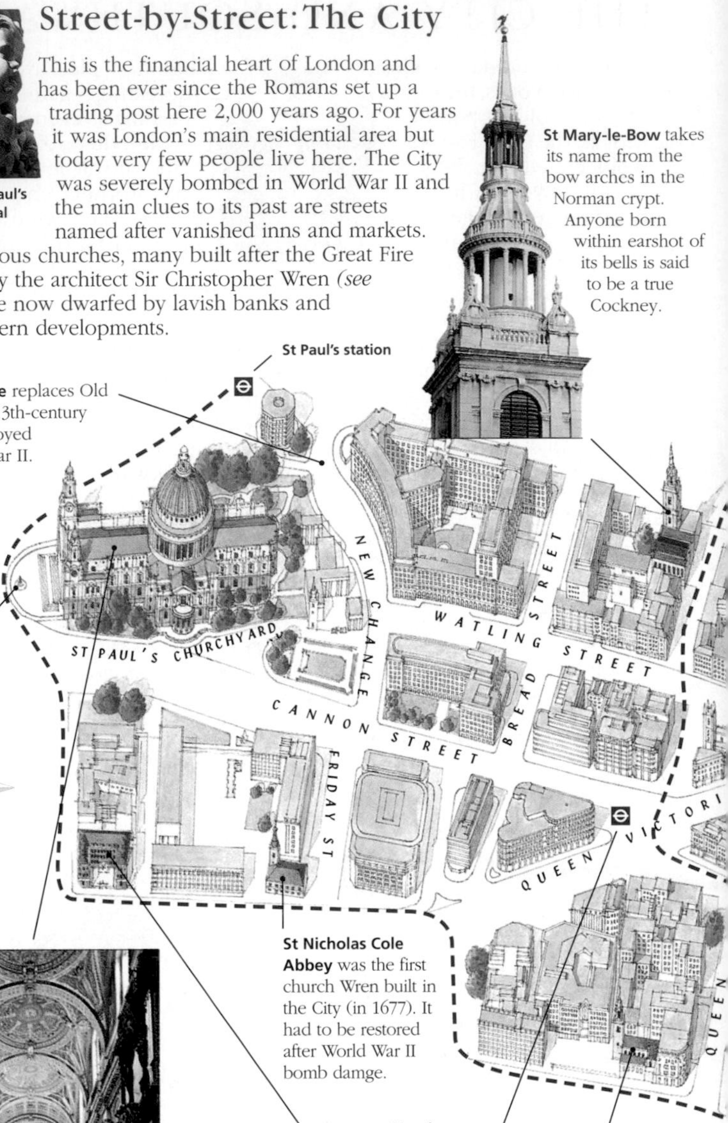

St Mary-le-Bow takes its name from the bow arches in the Norman crypt. Anyone born within earshot of its bells is said to be a true Cockney.

St Paul's station

New Change replaces Old Change, a 13th-century street destroyed in World War II.

Statue of Queen Anne

ST PAUL'S CHURCHYARD

NEW CHANGE

WATLING STREET

BREAD STREET

CANNON STREET

FRIDAY ST

QUEEN VICTORIA

QUEEN

St Nicholas Cole Abbey was the first church Wren built in the City (in 1677). It had to be restored after World War II bomb damge.

★ St Paul's Cathedral
Built after the Great Fire of 1666, Wren's masterpiece was funded by a tax on coal ➋

Mansion House station

St James Garlickhythe contains unusual sword rests and hat stands, beneath Wren's elegant spire of 1717.

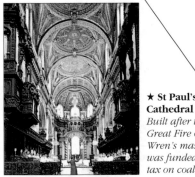

STAR SIGHTS

★ St Paul's Cathedral

★ St Stephen Walbrook

COLLEGE · OF · ARMS

The College of Arms is the official repository of the coats of arms and pedigrees of British families *(see p30).* It was rebuilt here, on its former site, in the 1670s after the Great Fire.

Mansion House (1753), designed by George Dance the Elder, is the official home of the Lord Mayor. The Palladian façade is a familiar City landmark.

The Temple of Mithras is an important Roman relic discovered during World War II.

LOCATOR MAP
See Street Finder map 13

Bank of England Museum

The Royal Exchange was founded in 1565 by Sir Thomas Gresham as a centre for commerce. The current building dates from 1844.

Bank station

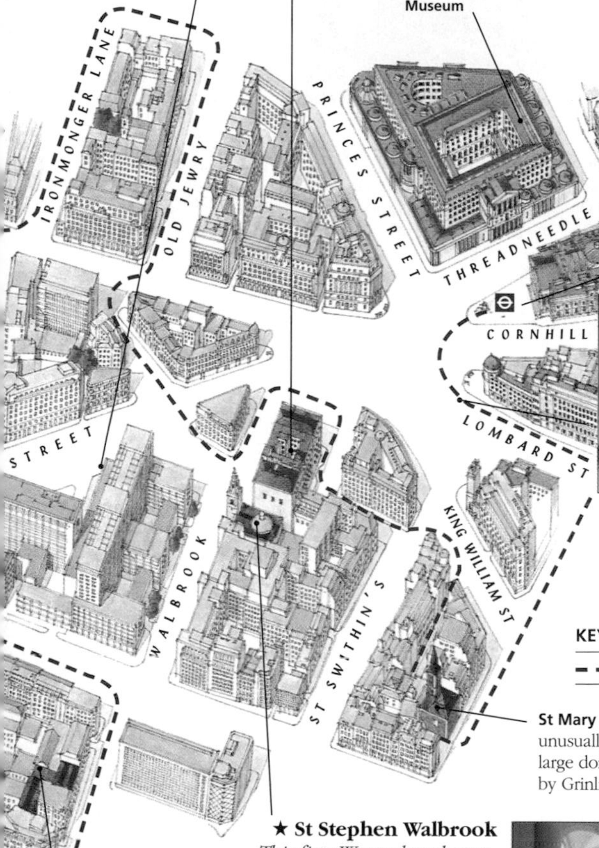

Lombard Street, named after bankers who came here from Lombardy in the 13th century, retains its traditional banking signs.

KEY

– – – Suggested route

St Mary Abchurch owes its unusually spacious feel to Wren's large dome. The altar carving is by Grinling Gibbons.

0 metres 100
0 yards 100

★ St Stephen Walbrook
This fine Wren church contains a striking white stone altar by Henry Moore ❶

Skinners' Hall is an 18th-century Italianate building constructed for the ancient guild that controlled trade in fur and leather.

St Stephen Walbrook ❶

39 Walbrook EC4. **Map** 13 B2. **Tel** 020-7626 8242. ⊖ *Bank, Cannon St.* ◯ *10am–4pm Mon–Thu, 10am–3pm Fri.* ◉ *public hols.* ⬛ *12:45am Thu.*

The Lord Mayor's parish church was built by Sir Christopher Wren in the 1670s and is among the finest of all his City churches. The bright, airy interior is flooded with light by a huge dome that appears to float above the eight columns and arches that support it. The dome, deep and coffered with ornate plasterwork, was a forerunner of St Paul's. Original fittings, such as the highly decorative font cover and pulpit canopy, contrast with the stark simplicity of Henry Moore's massive white stone altar (1987). The best time to see the church is during one of its free organ recitals from 12.30 to 1.30pm on Fridays.

St Paul's ❷

See pp116–17.

Effigies in Temple Church

Temple ❸

Inner Temple, King's Bench Walk EC4. **Tel** 020-7797 8250. **Map** 12 E2. ⊖ *Temple.* ◯ *12:30am–3pm Mon–Fri (grounds only).* ♿ **Middle Temple Hall**, Middle Temple Ln EC4. **Tel** 020-7427 4800. ◯ *10–11:30am, 3–4pm Mon–Fri.* ♿ **Temple Church. Tel** 020-7353 3470. ◯ *Wed–Fri; call for times and services.* ◉ *book ahead.*

A cluster of atmospheric squares form the Inner and Middle Temples, two of

London's four Inns of Court, where law students are trained. The name Temple derives from the medieval Knights Templar, a religious order which protected pilgrims to the Holy Land and was based here until 1312. Marble effigies of knights lie on the floor of the circular Temple Church, part of which dates from the 12th century. Middle Temple Hall has a fine Elizabethan interior.

St Bartholomew-the-Great ❺

West Smithfield EC1. **Map** 12 F1. **Tel** 020-7606 5171. ⊖ *Barbican, St Paul's.* ◯ *8:30am–5pm (4pm in winter) Tue–Fri, 10:30am–1:30pm Sat, 8:30am–8pm Sun.* ◉ *25, 26 Dec, 1 Jan.* ♿ ◉ *by appt.* **Concerts.** **www.**greatstbarts.com

The historic area of Smithfield has witnessed a number of bloody events over the years, among them the execution of rebel peasant leader Wat Tyler in 1381, and, in the reign of Mary I (1553–58), the burning of scores of Protestant martyrs.

Sir John Soane's Museum ❹

13 Lincoln's Inn Fields WC2. **Map** 12 D1. **Tel** 020-7405 2107. ⊖ *Holborn.* ◯ *10am–5pm Tue–Sat, 6–9pm 1st Tue of month.* ◉ *1 Jan, 24–26 Dec, Easter.* ♿ *ground floor only.* ◉ *Sat 2:30pm.* **www.**soane.org

One of the most eccentric museums in London, this house was left to the nation by Sir John Soane in 1837, with a stipulation that nothing should be changed. The son of a bricklayer, Soane became one of Britain's leading late Georgian architects developing a restrained Neo-Classical style of his own. After marrying the niece of a wealthy builder, whose fortune he inherited, he bought and re-constructed No. 12 Lincoln's Inn Fields. In 1813 he and his wife moved into No. 13 and in 1824 he rebuilt No. 14, adding a picture gallery and the mock medieval Monk's

Parlour. Today, true to Soane's wishes, the collections are much as he left them – an eclectic gathering of beautiful, instructional and often simply peculiar artifacts. There are casts, bronzes, vases, antique fragments, paintings and a selection of bizarre trivia which ranges from a giant fungus from Sumatra to a scold-bridle, a device designed to silence nagging wives. Highlights include the sarcophagus of Seti I, Soanes's own designs, including those for the Bank of England, models by leading Neo-Classical sculptors and the *Rake's Progress* series of paintings (1734) by William Hogarth, which Mrs Soane bought for £520.

The building itself is full of architectural surprises and illusions. In the main ground floor room, cunningly placed mirrors play tricks with light and space, while an atrium stretching from the basement to the glass-domed roof allows light on to every floor.

A glass dome lets light on to all the floors.

A vast sarcophagus (1300 BC) stands on the floor of the crypt.

Hidden in a quiet corner behind Smithfield meat market (central London's only surviving wholesale food market), this is one of London's oldest churches. It once formed part of a priory founded in 1123

St Bartholomew's gatehouse

by a monk, Rahere, whose tomb is here. He was Henry I's court jester until he dreamed that St Bartholomew had saved him from a winged monster.

The 13th-century arch, now topped by a Tudor gatehouse, used to be the entrance to the church until the old nave was pulled down during the Dissolution of the Monasteries (*see pp50–51*). The painter William Hogarth was baptized here in 1697. The church featured in the films *Four Weddings and a Funeral* and *Shakespeare in Love*.

Museum of London ⑥

London Wall EC2. **Map** 13 A1.
Tel 0870 444 3851. ⊖ Barbican, St Paul's. ◐ 10am–5:50pm Mon–Sat & public hols, noon–5:50pm Sun. ◉ 1 Jan, 24–26 Dec. ♿ ▢ ▢
www.museumoflondon.org.uk

This museum traces life in London from prehistoric times to the outbreak of World War I. Displays of archaeological finds and domestic objects alternate

Delft plate made in London 1600, Museum of London

with reconstructed street scenes and interiors. The World City galleries chart the birth of modern London from the French Revolution to World War I, and display Nelson's bejewelled sword.

The Roman London gallery has a brightly coloured 2nd-century fresco from a Southwark bath house, while the 17th-century section holds the shirt that Charles I wore on the scaffold (*see pp52–3*). Popular exhibits are the Lord Mayor's State Coach, built in 1757 and still used for the Lord Mayor's Show in November, and the working model of the Great Fire of 1666.

Every wall is covered and every room filled with artifacts from Soane's voluminous collection.

In the picture gallery, panels covered with paintings unfold to reveal more works of art hidden behind them.

The Monk's Parlour is full of grotesque Gothic casts.

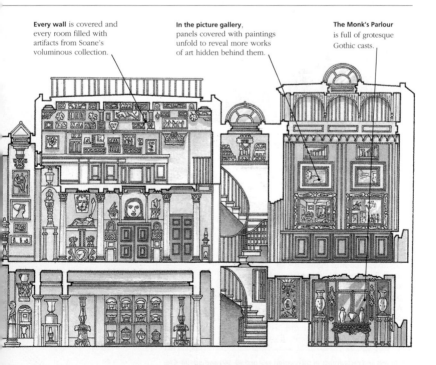

St Paul's Cathedral ❷

The Great Fire of London in 1666 left the medieval cathedral of St Paul's in ruins. Wren was commissioned to rebuild it, but his design for a church on a Greek Cross plan (where all four arms are equal) met with considerable resistance. The authorities insisted on a conventional Latin cross, with a long nave and short transepts, which was believed to focus the congregation's attention on the altar. Despite the compromises, Wren created a magnificent Baroque cathedral, which was built between 1675 and 1710 and has since formed the lavish setting for many state ceremonies.

★ Dome
At 111 m (360 ft), the elaborate dome is one of the highest in the world.

The balustrade along the top was added in 1718 against Wren's wishes.

★ West Front and Towers
Inspired by the Italian Baroque architect, Borromini, the towers were added by Wren in 1707.

The West Portico consists of two storeys of coupled Corinthian columns, topped by a pediment carved with reliefs showing the Conversion of St Paul.

The Nave
An imposing succession of massive arches and saucer domes open out into the vast space below the cathedral's main dome.

CHRISTOPHER WREN

Trained as a scientist, Sir Christopher Wren (1632–1723) began his impressive architectural career at the age of 31. He became a leading figure in the rebuilding of London after the Great Fire of 1666, building a total of 52 new churches. Although Wren never visited Italy, his work was influenced by Roman, Baroque and Renaissance architecture, as is apparent in his masterpiece, St Paul's Cathedral.

West Porch

Main entrance approached from Ludgate Hill

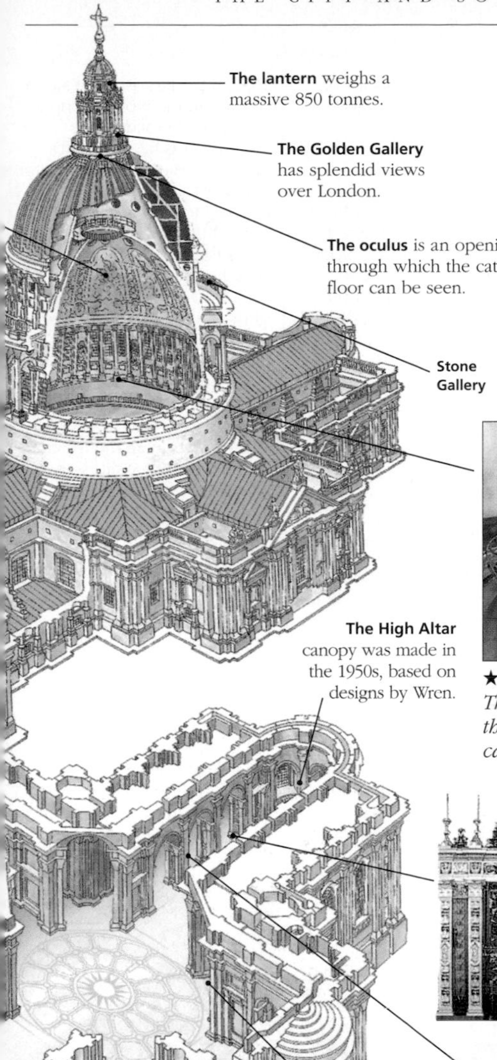

The lantern weighs a massive 850 tonnes.

The Golden Gallery has splendid views over London.

The oculus is an opening through which the cathedral floor can be seen.

Stone Gallery

VISITORS' CHECKLIST

Ludgate Hill EC4. **Map** 13 A2.
Tel 020-7236 4128.
🚇 St Paul's, Mansion House.
🚌 4, 11, 15, 17, 23, 25, 76, 172. 🚆 City Thameslink.
Cathedral ⬜ 8:30am–4pm Mon–Sat. **Galleries** ⬜ 9:30am–4pm. **Crypt & ambulatory** ⬜ 8:45am–4:15pm. ⬤ for sightseeing on Sun. 🎦 ✝ 11am Sun. ♿ 🎦 🍴 🛈 📷 📖
www.stpauls.co.uk

The High Altar canopy was made in the 1950s, based on designs by Wren.

★ Whispering Gallery
The dome's unusual acoustics mean that words whispered against the wall can be heard clearly on the opposite side.

Choir
Jean Tijou, a Huguenot refugee, created much of the fine wrought iron-work in Wren's time, including these choir screens.

Entrance to crypt, which has many memorials to the famous.

Entrance to Golden, Whispering and Stone galleries

The South Portico was inspired by the porch of Santa Maria della Pace in Rome. Wren absorbed the detail by studying a friend's collection of architectural engravings.

STAR SIGHTS

★ West Front and Towers

★ Dome

★ Whispering Gallery

Choir Stalls
The 17th-century choir stalls and organ case were made by Grinling Gibbons (1648–1721), a wood-carver from Rotterdam. He and his team of craftsmen worked on these intricate carvings for two years.

Richard Rogers's Lloyd's building

Lloyd's Building ❼

1 Lime St EC3. **Map** 13 C2. **Tel** 020-7327 1000. Monument, Bank, Aldgate. to the public.

Lloyd's was founded in the late 17th century and soon became the world's main insurers, issuing policies on everything from oil tankers to Betty Grable's legs. The present building, designed by Richard Rogers, dates from 1986 and is one of the most interesting modern buildings in London. Its exaggerated stainless-steel external piping and high-tech ducts echo Rogers' forceful Pompidou Centre in Paris. Lloyd's is well worth seeing floodlit at night.

Monument ❽

Monument St EC3. **Map** 13 C2. **Tel** 020-7626 2717. Monument. 9:30am–5pm daily. 1 Jan, 24–26 Dec. www.towerbridge.org.uk

This doric column, designed by Wren to commemorate the Great Fire of London that devastated the original walled city in September 1666, was, in 1681, the tallest isolated stone column in the world. Topped with a bronze flame, the Monument is 62 m (205 ft) high; the exact distance west to Pudding Lane, where the fire is believed to have started. Reliefs around the column's base show Charles II restoring the city after the tragedy.

The 311 tightly-spiralled steps lead to a tiny, claustro-phobia-inducing viewing platform. (In 1842, it was enclosed with an iron cage to prevent suicides.) The steep climb is well worth the effort as the views from the top are spectacular and visitors are rewarded with a certificate.

Tower of London ❾

See pp118–19.

Tower Bridge ❿

SE1. **Map** 14 D3. **Tel** 020-7403 3761. Tower Hill. **The Tower Bridge Exhibition** Apr–Sep: 10am–6:30pm daily; Oct–Mar: 9:30am–6pm daily (last adm: 5:30pm). 24 & 25 Dec. access lift. www.towerbridge.org.uk

This flamboyant piece of Victorian engineering, designed by Sir Horace Jones, was completed in 1894 and soon became a symbol of London. Its two Gothic towers contain the mechanism for raising the roadway to permit large ships to pass through. The towers are made of a supporting steel framework clad in stone, and are linked by two high level walkways which were closed between 1909 and 1982 due to their popularity with suicides and prostitutes. The bridge now houses The Tower Bridge Exhibition, with interactive displays bringing the bridge's history to life. There are fine river views from the walkways, and a look at the steam engine room that powered the lifting machinery until 1976, when the system was electrified.

Walkways, open to the public, give panoramic views over the Thames and London.

The roadway, when raised, creates a space 40 m (135 ft) high and 60 m (200 ft) wide, big enough for large cargo ships.

Engine room

Lifts and 300 steps lead to the top of the towers.

The Victorian winding machinery was originally powered by steam.

Entrance

South Bank

North Bank

Design Museum ⓫

Butlers Wharf, Shad Thames SE1.
Map 14 E4. *Tel* 0870-833 9955.
🚇 *Tower Hill, London Bridge.*
🕐 *10am–5:45pm daily (last adm:
5:15pm).* 🔴 *25 & 26 Dec.* 🅿️ ♿
🍴 **Blueprint Café** 020-7378 7031
for reservations. ♿ 🖥️ 📷
www.designmuseum.org

This museum was the first
in the world to be devoted
solely to modern and contemporary design when it was
founded in 1989. A frequently
changing programme of
exhibitions explores landmarks in modern design
history and the most exciting
innovations in contemporary
design set against the context
of social, cultural, economic
and technological changes.
The Design Museum embraces
every area of design, from
furniture and fashion, to
household products, cars,
graphics, websites and architecture in exhibitions and
new design commissions.
Each spring the museum
hosts Designer of the Year, a
national design prize, with an
exhibition at which the public
can vote for the winner.

The museum is arranged
over three floors, with major
exhibitions on the first floor.
There is a choice of smaller
displays on the second,
which also houses an
Interaction Space, where
visitors can play vintage video
games and learn about the
designers featured in the
museum in the Design at the
Design Museum online
research archive. The shop
and café are on the ground
floor. On the first floor is the
Blueprint Café restaurant,
which has stunning views of
the Thames (booking ahead
recommended).

Austin Mini in the Design Museum

**The now familiar sight of the naval
gunship HMS Belfast on the Thames**

HMS Belfast ⓬

Morgan's Lane, Tooley St SE1. **Map**
13 C3. 📞 020-7940 6300. 🚇
London Bridge, Tower Hill. 🕐
*Mar–Oct: 10am–6pm daily; Nov–Feb:
10am–5pm daily (last adm: 45 mins
before closing).* 🔴 *24–26 Dec.* 🅿️
♿ *limited.* 🖥️ 📷 **www**.iwm.org.uk

Originally launched in 1938
to serve in World War II,
the 11,500-ton battle ship
HMS *Belfast* was instrumental
in the destruction of the
German battle cruiser
Scharnhorst in the battle of
North Cape, and also played
an important role in the
Normandy Landings.

After the war, the battle
cruiser, designed for offensive
action and for supporting
amphibious operations, was
sent to work for the United
Nations in Korea. The ship
remained in service with the
British navy until 1965.

Since 1971, the cruiser has
been used as a floating naval
museum. Part of it has been
atmospherically recreated
to show what the ship was
like in 1943, when it partici-
pated in sinking the German
battle cruiser. Other displays
portray life on board during
World War II, and there are
also general exhibits which
relate to the history of the
Royal Navy.

As well as being a great
family day out, it is also
possible for children to
take part in the educational
activity weekends that take
place on board the ship.

London Dungeon ⓭

Tooley St SE1. **Map** 13 C3. 📞 020-
7403 7221. 🚇 *London Bridge.* 🕐
*Jul–Aug 9:30am–6pm; Sep & Oct
10am–5:30pm; Nov–Easter 10:30am–
5pm; Easter–Jun 10am–5:30pm; daily.*
🔴 *25 Dec.* 🅿️ ♿ 🖥️ 📷
www.thedungeons.com

In effect a much expanded
version of the chamber of
horrors at Madame Tussaud's
(see p104), this museum is
a great hit with children. It
illustrates the most bloodthirsty events in British history.
It is played strictly for terror,
and screams abound as Druids
perform a human sacrifice at
Stonehenge, Henry VIII's wife
Anne Boleyn is beheaded,
and a room full of people die
in agony during the Great
Plague. Other displays include
torture, murder and witchcraft.

19th-century surgical tools

The Old Operating Theatre ⓮

9a St Thomas St SE1. **Map** 13 B4. *Tel*
020-7188 2679. 🚇 *London Bridge.*
🕐 *10:30am–5pm daily.* 🔴 *15 Dec–
5 Jan.* 🅿️ 📷 **www**.thegarret.org.uk

St Thomas's Hospital stood
here from its foundation in
the 12th century until it was
moved west in 1862. At this
time most of its buildings
were demolished to make
way for the railway. The
women's operating theatre
(The Old Operating Theatre
Museum and Herb Garret)
survived only because it was
located away from the main
buildings, in a garret over the
hospital church. It lay, bricked
up and forgotten, until the
1950s. Britain's oldest operating theatre, dating back to
1822, it has now been fitted
out as it would have been in
the early 19th century.

Tower of London ❾

Soon after William the Conqueror became King in 1066, he built a fortress here to guard the entrance to London from the Thames Estuary. In 1097 the White Tower was completed in sturdy stone; other fine buildings have been added over the centuries. The Tower has served as a royal residence, armoury, treasury and most famously as a prison. Some were tortured here and among those who met their death were the "Princes in the Tower", the sons and heirs of Edward IV. Today the tower is a popular attraction, housing the Crown Jewels and other exhibits, such as the new displays in the Medieval Palace, which explore the story of royal residence in the Tower. The most celebrated residents are the seven ravens; legend has it that the kingdom will fall if they desert the tower.

Beauchamp Tower
Many high-ranking prisoners were held here, often with their own retinues of servants. The tower was built by Edward I around 1281.

"Beefeaters"
Thirty-six Yeoman Warders guard the Tower and live here. Their uniforms hark back to Tudor times.

Two 13th-century curtain walls protect the tower.

Tower Green was the execution site for favoured prisoners, away from crowds on Tower Hill, where many had to submit to public execution. Seven people died here, including two of Henry VIII's six wives, Anne Boleyn and Catherine Howard.

Queen's House
This Tudor building is the sovereign's official residence at the Tower.

Main entrance from Tower Hill

THE CROWN JEWELS

The world's best-known collection of precious objects, now displayed in a splendid exhibition room, includes the gorgeous regalia of crowns, sceptres, orbs and swords used at coronations and other state occasions. Most date from 1661, when Charles II commissioned replacements for regalia destroyed by Parliament after the execution of Charles I *(see pp52–3)*. Only a few older pieces survived, hidden by royalist clergymen until the Restoration – notably, Edward the Confessor's sapphire ring, now incorporated into the Imperial State Crown *(see p73)*. The crown was made for Queen Victoria in 1837 and has been used at every coronation since.

The Sovereign's Ring (1831)

The Sovereign's Orb (1661), a hollow gold sphere encrusted with jewels

★ **Jewel House**
Among the magnificent Crown Jewels is the Sceptre with the Cross (1660), which now contains the world's biggest diamond.

★ **White Tower**
When the tower was finished in 1097, it was the tallest building in London at 27 m (90 ft) high.

VISITORS' CHECKLIST

Tower Hill EC3. **Map** 14 D3. *Tel* 0870-756 7070 for advance booking. 🚇 Tower Hill; Tower Gateway (DLR). 🚌 RV1, 15, X15, 25, 42, 78, 100, D1, D9, D11. 🚆 Fenchurch Street. ⬜ Mar–Oct: 9am–6pm Tue–Sat, 10am–6pm Sun–Mon; Nov–Feb: 9am–5pm Tue–Sat, 10am–5pm Sun & Mon. ⬛ 1 Jan, 24–26 Dec. 🎫 ♿ limited, except Jewel House. ⬜
🎦 **Ceremony of the Keys**: 9:30pm daily (book in advance). www.hrp.org.uk

★ **Chapel of St John**
This austerely beautiful Romanesque chapel is a particularly fine example of Norman architecture.

Traitors' Gate
The infamous entrance was used for prisoners brought from trial in Westminster Hall.

THAMES

Bloody Tower
A new permanent display explores the mysterious disappearance of Edward IV's two sons, who were put here by their uncle, Richard of Gloucester (later Richard III), after their father died in 1483. The princes disappeared and Richard was crowned later that year. In 1674 the skeletons of two children were found nearby.

STAR SIGHTS

★ Jewel House

★ White Tower

★ Chapel of St John

The George Inn, now owned by the National Trust

George Inn ⑮

77 Borough High St SE1. **Map** 13 B4.
Tel *020-7407 2056.* ⊖ *London Bridge, Borough.* ◯ *11am–11pm Mon–Sat, noon–10:30pm Sun.* 🔢

Dating from the 17th century, this building is the only traditional galleried coaching inn left in London and is mentioned in Dickens's *Little Dorrit*. It was rebuilt after the Southwark fire of 1676 in a style that dates back to the Middle Ages. There were originally three wings around a courtyard, where plays were staged in the 17th century. In 1889 the north and east wings were demolished, so there is only one wing remaining.

The inn is still a restaurant and a popular pub with a well-worn, comfortable atmosphere, perfect on a cold, damp day. In the summer, the yard fills with picnic tables and patrons are occasionally entertained by actors and morris dancers. The house bitter is highly recommended.

Borough Market ⑯

8 Southwark St SE1. **Map** 13 B4.
⊖ *London Bridge.* **Retail market** ◯ *Fri noon–6pm, Sat 9am–4pm.*

Borough Market was until recently an exclusively wholesale fruit and vegetable market, which had its origins in medieval times, and moved to its current atmospheric position beneath the railway tracks in 1756. A popular and

fine food market has now become well established, selling gourmet foods from Britain and abroad, as well as quality fruit and vegetables, to locals and tourists alike.

Shakespeare window (1954), Southwark Cathedral

Southwark Cathedral ⑰

Montague Close SE1. **Map** 13 B3.
Tel *020 7367 6713.* ⊖ *London Bridge.* ◯ *8am–6pm daily.* 📷 🏠
www.
southwark.anglican.org/cathedral

Although some parts of this building date back to the 12th century, it was not until 1905 that it became a cathedral. Many original medieval features remain, notably the tomb of the poet John Gower (c.1325–1408), a contemporary of Chaucer *(see p172)*. There is a monument to Shakespeare, carved in 1912, and a memorial window *(above)* installed in 1954.

Shakespeare's Globe ⑱

New Globe Walk SE1. **Map** 13 A3.
Tel *020-7902 1400. Box office: 020-7401 9919.* ⊖ *Southwark, London Bridge.* **Exhibition** ◯ *May–Sep: 9am–5pm daily; Oct–Apr: 10am–5pm daily.* 📷 ♿ 🎥 *every 30 mins. (Rose Theatre tours for groups of 15 or more by appt only).* **Performances** *mid-May–Sep.* ♿ *limited.* 🔢 📷 🏠 **www.**shakespeares-globe.org

Opened in 1997, this circular building is a faithful reproduction of an Elizabethan theatre, close to the site of the original Globe where many of Shakespeare's plays were first performed. It was built using handmade bricks and oak laths, fastened with wooden pegs rather than metal screws, and has the first thatched roof allowed in London since the Great Fire of 1666. The theatre was erected thanks to a heroic campaign waged by the American actor and director Sam Wanamaker. Open to the elements (although the seats are protected), it operates only in the summer, and seeing a play here can be a thrilling experience, with top-quality acting under the artistic direction of Mark Rylance among others (any performances with him in the cast are well worth seeing).

Beneath the theatre, Shakespeare's Globe Exhibition is open all year and covers many aspects of Shakespeare's work and times. Groups of 15 or more may book to see the foundations of the nearby Rose Theatre.

Shakespeare's *Henry IV* (performed at the Globe Theatre around 1600)

Tate Modern ⑲

Holland St, SE1. **Map** 13 A3.
Tel 020-7887 8000. 🚇 *Blackfriars,
Southwark.* 🚤 *to Tate Britain every
40 mins.* 🚉 *Blackfriars* ◯
*10am–6pm Sun–Thu, 10am–10pm Fri
& Sat.* ● *24–26 Dec.* 🎫 *major
exhibitions.* ♿ 🍴 ▢ 📷
www.tate.org.uk

Looming over the southern
bank of the Thames, Tate
Modern occupies the converted
Bankside power station, a
dynamic space for one of the
world's premier collections of
contemporary art. Tate Modern
draws its main displays from
the expansive Tate Collection,
also shown at the other Tate
galleries: Tate St Ives *(p277),*
Tate Liverpool *(p377)* and Tate
Britain *(p91).* A river boat, *Tate
to Tate,* transports visitors
between Tate Modern and Tate
Britain. Tate Modern has just

**Death from Death Hope Life Fear
(1984) by Gilbert and George**

completed a major re-hang of
its collection in 2006, so
works and displays may change
from those described here.
The gallery's west entrance
leads straight into the massive
Turbine Hall. Each year an
artist is commissioned to
install in this space. Louise
Bourgeois was the first to
install here, creating three
giant towers and a gargantuan
spider, *Maman* (2000).
Recently, Olafur Eliasson's *The
Weather Project* lit the Turbine
Hall with a giant glowing sun.
An escalator whisks visitors
from the Turbine Hall, up to
level 3 where the main
galleries are located. In a break
with convention,
Tate Modern
organizes its
displays by
theme rather
than chronology
or school – a
practice that cuts across
movements and mixes up
media. Four themes based
on traditional genres reveal
how traditions have been
confronted, extended
or rejected by artists
throughout the 20th and
into the 21st centuries.
The new USB Openings:
Tate Modern Collection
features four wings, which
can be found on level 3
and level 5, each
focusing on a
specific period of
artistic innovation
in the 20th
century. These periods fall
into the categories of Cubism,
Futurism and Vorticism;
Surrealism and Surrealist
tendencies; Abstract

**Scrapheap Services (1995) by
Michael Landy**

Expressionism and European
Informal Art; and Minimalism.
At the centre
of each of
the four
exhibitions
is a focal
diplay, from
which all the
other displays rotate.
Over 40 per cent of the
work on display since
the re-hang has never
been on display at Tate
Modern before, and
includes work such as
the iconic painting
Whaam! by Roy
Lichtenstein as well as
other important
pieces by the likes of
Francis Picabia and
Anish Kapoor.
Tate Modern
Soft Drainpipe – Blue (Cool) presents a
(1967) by Claes Oldenburg dynamic
programme of
temporary exhibitions,
including three large-scale
shows per year. Major live
events will take place in May
2007 and 2008.

BANKSIDE POWER STATION

This forbidding fortress was designed in 1947 by Sir Giles
Gilbert Scott, the architect of Battersea Power Station, Waterloo
Bridge and London's famous red telephone boxes. The power
station is of a steel-framed brick skin construction, comprising
over 4.2 million bricks. The Turbine Hall was designed to
accommodate huge oil-burning generators and three vast oil
tanks are still in situ, buried under the ground just south of
the building. The tanks are to be employed in a future stage
of Tate Modern development. The power station itself was converted by Swiss architects Herzog and de Meuron who designed
the two-storey glass box, or lightbeam, which runs the length
of the building. This serves to flood the upper galleries with
light and also provides wonderful views of London.

The façade, chimney and light beam of Tate Modern

FURTHER AFIELD

Over the centuries London has steadily expanded to embrace the scores of villages that surrounded it, leaving the City as a reminder of London's original boundaries. Although now linked in an almost unbroken urban sprawl, many of these areas have maintained their old village atmosphere and character. Hampstead and Highgate are still distinct enclaves, as are artistic Chelsea and literary Islington. Greenwich, Chiswick and Richmond have retained features that hark back to the days when the Thames was an important artery for transport and commerce, while just to the east of the City the wide expanses of the former docks have, in the last 20 years, been imaginatively rebuilt as new commercial and residential areas.

SIGHTS AT A GLANCE

Camden and Islington **7**
Chelsea **1**
Chiswick **10**
East End and Docklands **8**

Greenwich **9**
Hampstead **4**
Hampstead Heath **5**
Highgate **6**

Holland Park **2**
Notting Hill and
  Portobello Road **3**
Richmond and Kew **11**

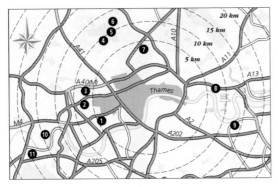

KEY

▦	Main sightseeing areas
◻	Greater London
◻	Parks
═	Motorway
▬	Major road
═	Minor road

10 miles = 15 km

Chelsea **1**

SW3.  *Sloane Square.* **Map** 17 B2.

Riverside Chelsea has been fashionable since Tudor times when Sir Thomas More, Henry VIII's Lord Chancellor

Statue of Sir Thomas More (1478–1535), Cheyne Walk

(see p50), lived here. The river views attracted artists and the arrival of the historian Thomas Carlyle and essayist Leigh Hunt in the 1830s began a literary connection. Blue plaques on the houses of **Cheyne Walk** celebrate former residents such as J M W Turner *(see p91)* and writers George Eliot, Henry James and T S Eliot.

  Chelsea's artistic tradition is maintained by its galleries and antique shops, many of them scattered among the clothes boutiques on **King's Road**. This begins at **Sloane Square**, named after the physician Sir Hans Sloane, who bought the manor of Chelsea in 1712. Sloane expanded the **Chelsea Physic Garden** (1673) along Swan Walk to cultivate plants and herbs.

  Wren's **Royal Hospital**, on Royal Hospital Road was built in 1692 as a retirement home for old soldiers and still houses 400 Chelsea Pensioners.

Arab Hall, Leighton House (1866)

Holland Park **2**

W8, W14.  *Holland Park.* **Map** 7 B5.

This small but delightful park is more intimate than the large royal parks such as Hyde Park *(see p101).* It was opened in 1952 on the grounds of **Holland House**, a centre of social and political intrigue in its 19th-century heyday.

  Around the park are some magnificent late Victorian

houses. **Linley Sambourne House** was built about 1870 and has received a much-needed facelift, though it remains much as Sambourne furnished it, in the Victorian manner, with china ornaments and heavy velvet drapes. He was a political cartoonist for the satirical magazine *Punch* and drawings cram the walls.

Leighton House, built for the Neo-Classical painter Lord Leighton in 1866, has been preserved as an extraordinary monument to the Victorian Aesthetic movement. The highlight is the Arab Hall, which was added in 1879 to house Leighton's stupendous collection of 13th- to 17th-century Islamic tiles. The best paintings include some by Leighton himself and by his contemporaries Edward Burne-Jones and John Millais.

🏛 **Linley Sambourne House**
18 Stafford Terrace W8. *Tel* 020-7602 3316. ⊖ *High St Ken.* ☐ *10am–5pm Mon–Fri.* 🎫 🎥 *mandatory; every hr Sat & Sun till 3:30pm.* ☐

🏛 **Leighton House**
12 Holland Park Rd W14. *Tel* 020-7602 3316. ⊖ *High St Kensington.* ☐ *11am–5:30pm Wed–Mon.* 🔴 *public hols.* 🎫 🎥 *Wed & Thu.* ☐

Notting Hill and Portobello Road ❸

W11. ⊖ *Notting Hill Gate.* **Map** 7 B2.

In the 1950s and 60s, Notting Hill became a centre for the Caribbean community and today it is a vibrant cosmopolitan part of London. It is also home to Europe's largest street carnival *(see p63)* which began in 1965 and takes over the entire area on the August bank holiday weekend, when costumed parades flood through the crowded streets.

Nearby, Portobello Road market *(see pp148–9)* has a bustling atmosphere with hundreds of stalls and shops selling a variety of collectables.

Hampstead ❹

NW3, N6. ⊖ *Hampstead.* 🚇 *Hampstead Heath.*

Positioned on a high ridge north of the metropolis, Hampstead has always remained aloof from London. Essentially a Georgian village with many perfectly maintained mansions and houses, it is one of London's most desirable residential areas, home to a community of artists and writers since Georgian times.

Situated in a quiet Hampstead street, **Keats House** (1816), is an evocative and memorable tribute to the life and work of the poet John Keats (1795–1821). Keats lived here for two years before his tragic death from consumption at the age of 25, and it was under a plum tree in the garden that he wrote his celebrated *Ode to a Nightingale*.

Georgian house, Hampstead

Mementoes of Keats and of Fanny Brawne, the neighbour to whom he was engaged, are on display.

The **Freud Museum**, which opened in 1986, is dedicated to the dramatic life of Sigmund Freud (1856–1939), the founder of psychoanalysis. At the age of 82, Freud fled from Nazi persecution in Vienna to this Hampstead house where he lived and worked for the last year of his life. His daughter Anna, pioneer of child psychoanalysis, continued to live here until her death in 1982. Inside, Freud's rich Viennese-style consulting rooms remain unaltered, and 1930s home movies show moments of Freud's life, including scenes of the Nazi attack on his home in Vienna.

🏛 **Keats House**
Keats Grove NW3. 🆔 020-7435 2062. ⊖ *Hampstead, Belsize Pk.* ☐ *1pm–5pm Tue–Sun.* 🌐 www.cityoflondon.gov.uk/keats

🏛 **Freud Museum**
20 Maresfield Gdns NW3. *Tel* 020-7435 2002. ⊖ *Finchley Rd.* ☐ *noon–5pm Wed–Sun.* 🎫 🔴 *limited.* 🌐 www.freud.org.uk

Antique shop on Portobello Road

View east across Hampstead Heath to Highgate

Hampstead Heath ❺

N6. 🔵 *Hampstead, Highgate.* 🚉 *Hampstead Heath.*

Separating the hill-top villages of Hampstead and Highgate, the open spaces of Hampstead Heath are a precious retreat from the city. There are meadows, lakes and ponds for bathing and fishing, and fine views over the capital from **Parliament Hill**, to the east.

Situated in landscaped grounds high on the edge of the Heath is the magnificent **Kenwood House**, where classical concerts *(see p154)* are held by the lake in summer. The house was remodelled by Robert Adam *(see p28)* in 1764 and most of his interiors have survived, the highlight of which is the library. The mansion is filled with Old Master paintings, such as works by Van Dyck, Vermeer, Turner *(see p91)* and Romney; the star attraction is Rembrandt's self-portrait of 1663.

🏠 **Kenwood House**
Hampstead Lane NW3. **Tel** 020-8348 1286. ⬜ *daily.* ♿ 🅿️ 🛗
www.english-heritage.org.uk

Handmade crafts and antiques, Camden Lock indoor market

Highgate ❻

N6. 🔵 *Highgate, Archway.*

A settlement since the Middle Ages, Highgate, like Hampstead, became a fashionable aristocratic retreat in the 16th century. Today, it still has an exclusive rural feel, aloof from the urban sprawl below, with a Georgian high street and many expensive houses.

Highgate Cemetery *(see p75)*, with its monuments and hidden overgrown corners, has an extraordinary, magical atmosphere. Tour guides (daily in summer, weekends in winter) tell of the many tales of intrigue, mystery and vandalism connected with the cemetery since it opened in 1839. In the eastern section is the tomb of Victorian novelist George Eliot (1819–80) and of the cemetery's most famous incumbent, Karl Marx (1818–83).

🏠 **Highgate Cemetery**
Swains Lane N6. **Tel** 020-8340 1834. 🔵 *Archway, Highgate.* ⬜ *daily.* 🔴 *during burials, 25–26 Dec.* 🏷️ 🎫
www.highgate-cemetery.org

Camden and Islington ❼

NW1, N1. **Camden** 🔵 *Camden Town, Chalk Farm.* **Islington** 🔵 *Angel, Highbury & Islington.*

Camden is a lively area packed with restaurants, shops and a busy **market** *(see p148–9)*. Thousands of people come here each weekend to browse among the wide variety of stalls or simply to soak up the atmosphere of the lively cobbled area around the canal, which is enhanced by the buskers and street performers.

Neighbouring Islington was once a fashionable spa but the rich moved out in the late 18th century and the area deteriorated rapidly. In the 20th century, writers such as Evelyn Waugh, George Orwell and Joe Orton lived here. In recent decades, Islington has been rediscovered and is again fashionable as one of the first areas in London to become "gentrified", with many professionals buying the old houses.

East End and Docklands **8**

E1, E2, E14. **East End** 🚇 *Aldgate East, Liverpool St, Bethnal Green.* **Docklands** 🚇 *Canary Wharf.*

In the Middle Ages the East End was full of craftsmen practising noxious trades such as brewing, bleaching and vinegar-making, which were banned within the City. The area has also been home to numerous immigrant communities since the 17th century, when French Huguenots, escaping religious persecution moved into Spitalfields, and made it a silk-weaving centre. Even after the decline of the silk industry, textiles and clothing continued to dominate, with Jewish tailors and furriers setting up workshops in the 1880s, and Bengali machinists sewing in cramped premises from the 1950s.

A good way to get a taste of the East End is to explore its Sunday street markets *(see p149)*, and sample freshly baked bagels and spicy Indian food. By way of contrast, anyone interested in contemporary architecture should visit the **Docklands**, an ambitious re-development of disused docks, dominated by the Canada Tower; at 250 m (800 ft) it is London's tallest building. Other attractions include the **Bethnal Green Museum of Childhood**, a delightful toy museum with lots of activities, and **Dennis Severs' House**, in which you are taken on a historic journey from the 17th to the 19th centuries.

Royal Naval College framing the Queen's House, Greenwich

🏛 **Bethnal Green Museum of Childhood**
Cambridge Heath Rd E2. *Tel* 020-8983 5200. 🕐 *10am–5:50pm Sat–Thu.* ● *1 Jan, 24–26 Dec.* ♿ 🖥 🎫
www.museumofchildhood.org.uk

🚻 **Dennis Severs' House**
18 Folgate St E1. *Tel* 020-7247 4013.
🕐 *1st Sun & Mon of month.* 📷
www.dennissevershouse.co.uk

Greenwich **9**

SE10. 🚉 *Greenwich, Maze Hill.* 🚇 *Cutty Sark (DLR).*

The world's time has been measured from the **Royal Observatory Greenwich** (now housing a museum) since 1884. The area is full of maritime and royal history, with Neo-Classical mansions, a park, many antique and book shops and various markets *(see pp148–9)*.

The **Queen's House**, designed by Inigo Jones for James I's wife, was completed in 1637 for Henrietta Maria, the queen of Charles I. It has now been restored to its original state. The highlights of the Queen's

Canada Tower, Canary Wharf

House include the perfectly cubic main hall and the unusual spiral "tulip staircase".

The adjoining **National Maritime Museum** has exhibits that range from primitive canoes, through Elizabethan galleons, to modern ships. Anyone interested in naval history should visit the **Old Royal Naval College**, which was designed by Christopher Wren *(see p114)* in two halves

An 18th-century compass, National Maritime Museum

so that the Queen's House kept its river view. It began as a royal palace, became a hospital in 1692, and in 1873 the Old Royal Naval College moved here. The Rococo chapel and the 18th-century *trompe l'oeil* Painted Hall are open to the public.

🏛 **Royal Observatory Greenwich**
Greenwich Park SE10. *Tel* 020-8312 6565. 🕐 *daily.* ● *24–26 Dec.* 🎫
www.rog.nmm.ac.uk

🏛 **Queen's House and National Maritime Museum**
Romney Rd SE10. *Tel* 020-8312 6565.
🕐 *daily.* ● *24–26 Dec.* 📷 ♿ *limited.* 🖥 🎫 www.nmm.ac.uk

🚻 **Old Royal Naval College**
King William Walk, Greenwich SE10.
Tel 020-8269 4791. 🕐
10am–5pm daily. ● *public hols.*

Chiswick ❿

W4. 🔵 *Chiswick.*

Chiswick is a pleasant sub-urb of London, with pubs, cottages and a variety of birdlife, such as herons, along the picturesque riverside. One of the main reasons for a visit is **Chiswick House**, a magnificent country villa inspired by the Renaissance architect Andrea Palladio. It was designed in the early 18th century by the 3rd Earl of Burlington as an annexe to his larger house (demol-ished in 1758), so that he could display his art collec-tion and entertain friends. The gardens are now fully restored.

🏛 **Chiswick House**
Burlington Lane W4. *Tel 020-8995 0508.* ☐ *Apr–Oct: Wed–Sun & bank hols.* 🎫 ♿ *call ahead.* ☐ 🗐
www.english-heritage.org.uk

Richmond and Kew ⓫

SW15. 🔵 🚆 *Richmond.*

The attractive village of Richmond took its name from a palace built by Henry VII (the former Earl of Richmond in Yorkshire) in 1500, the remains of which can be seen off the green. Nearby is the expansive **Richmond Park**, which was once Charles I's royal hunting ground. In summer, boats

Heron

sail down the Thames from Westminster Millennium Pier, making a pleasant day's excursion from central London.

The nobility continued to favour Richmond after royalty had left, and some of their mansions have survived. The Palladian villa, **Marble Hill House**, was built in 1724–9 for the mistress of George II and has been restored to its original appearance. On the opposite side of the Thames, the brooding **Ham House**, built in 1610, had its heyday later that century when it became the home of the Lauderdales. The Countess of Lauderdale inherited the house from her father, who had been Charles I's "whip-ping boy" – meaning that he was punished whenever the future king misbehaved. He was rewarded as an adult by being given a peerage and the lease of Ham estate.

A little further north along the Thames, **Syon House** has been inhabited by the Dukes and Earls of Northumberland for over 400 years. Numerous attractions here include a but-terfly house, a museum of historic cars and a spectacular conservatory built in 1830. The lavish Neo-Classical inter-iors of the house, created by Robert Adam in the 1760s *(see p28)*, remain the highlight.

Brewers Lane, Richmond

On the riverbank to the south, **Kew Gardens**, the most complete botanic gardens in the world, are flawlessly maintained, with examples of nearly every plant that can be grown in Britain. There are also conservatories where thousands of exotic tropical blooms are on display.

🏛 **Marble Hill House**
Richmond Rd, Twickenham.
Tel 020-8892 5115. ☐ *Apr–Oct: Sat & Sun.* ♿ *limited.* 🚻 ☐ 🗐
🏛 **Ham House**
Ham St, Richmond. *Tel 020-8940 1950.* ☐ *Apr–Oct: Sat–Wed.* 🎫 ♿
🏛 **Syon House**
London Rd, Brentford. *Tel 020-8560 0881.* **House** ☐ *mid-Mar–Oct: Wed, Thu, Sun.* **Gardens** ☐ *daily.* ☐ *Nov–mid-Mar.* 🎫 🚗 ♿ *gardens only.* ☐ 🗐 **www**.syonpark.co.uk
🍀 **Kew Gardens**
Royal Botanic Gdns, Kew Green, Richmond. *Tel 020-8332 5655.*
☐ *daily.* ● *25 Dec, 1 Jan.* 🎫 ♿
🚗 🚻 ☐ 🗐 **www**.kew.org

Chiswick House

LONDON STREET FINDER

The map references given with the sights, hotels, restaurants, shops and entertainment venues based in central London refer to the following four maps. All the main places of interest within the central area are marked on the maps in addition to useful practical information, such as tube, railway and coach stations. The key map below shows the area of London that is covered by the Street Finder. The four main city-centre areas (colour-coded in pink) are shown in more detail on the inside back cover.

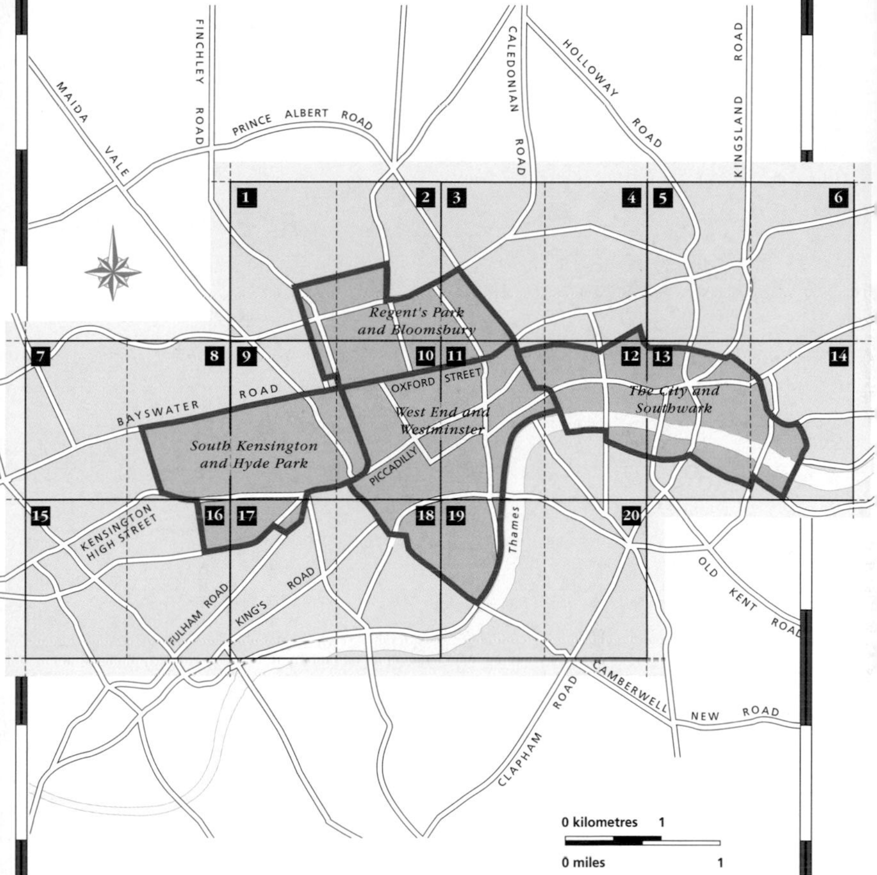

MAIDA VALE

FINCHLEY ROAD

PRINCE ALBERT ROAD

CALEDONIAN ROAD

HOLLOWAY ROAD

KINGSLAND ROAD

1 **2** **3** **4** **5** **6**

Regent's Park and Bloomsbury

7 **8** **9** **10** **11** **12** **13** **14**

OXFORD STREET

BAYSWATER ROAD

West End and Westminster

The City and Southwark

South Kensington and Hyde Park

PICCADILLY

15 **16** **17** **18** **19** **20**

KENSINGTON HIGH STREET

FULHAM ROAD

KING'S ROAD

Thames

OLD KENT ROAD

CLAPHAM ROAD

CAMBERWELL ROAD

NEW ROAD

0 kilometres 1

0 miles 1

KEY

■ Major sight	🛈 Tourist information	▬ Motorway
□ Other sight	✚ Hospital with casualty unit	Pedestrian street
□ Other building	🚓 Police station	«56 House number (main street)
Ⓔ Underground station	✝ Church	
🚆 British rail	✡ Synagogue	**SCALE OF MAP PAGES**
🚌 Bus stop	⊠ Post office	0 metres 200
River boat boarding point	═ Railway line	0 yards 200 1:11,000

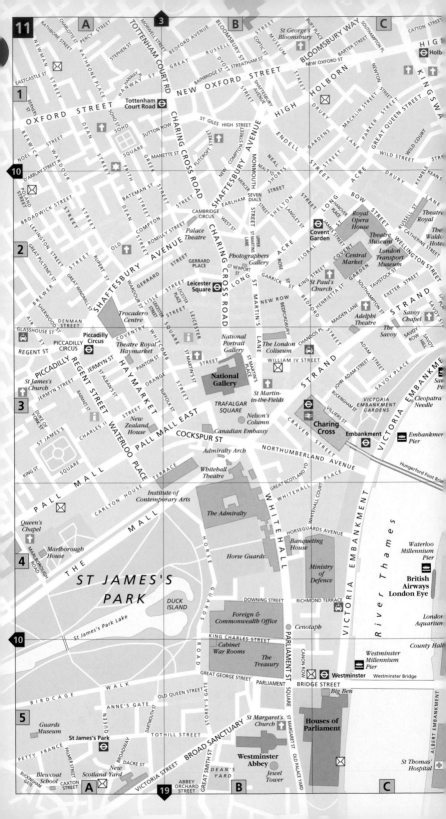

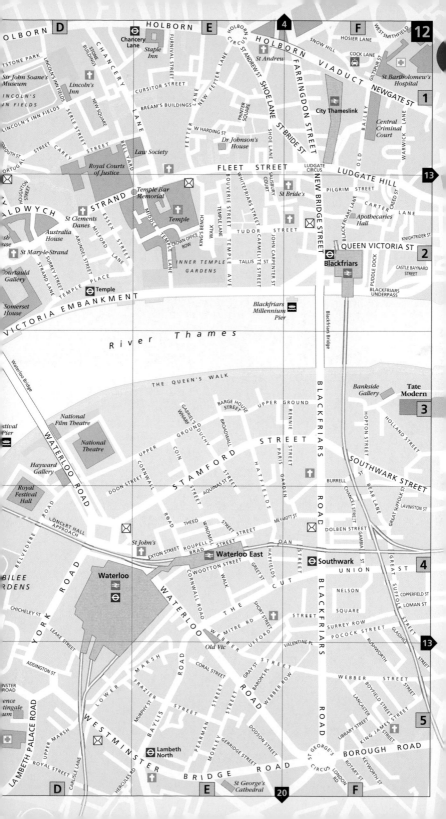

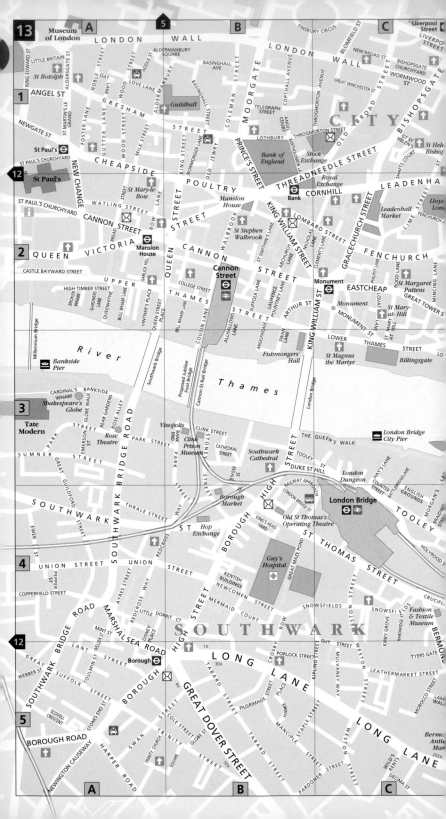

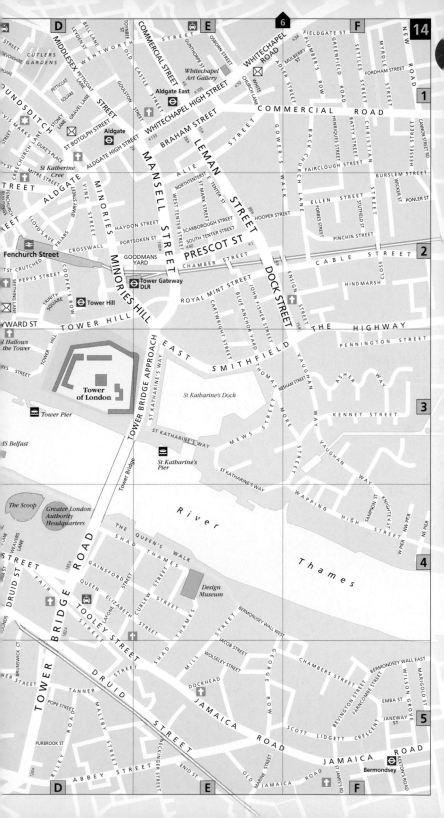

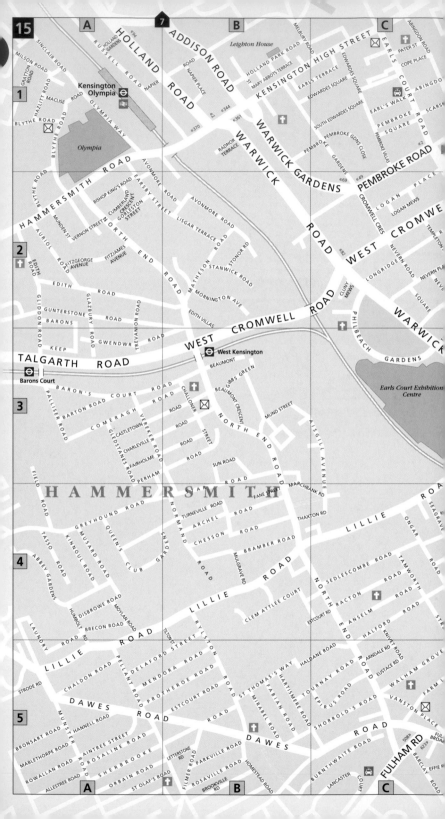

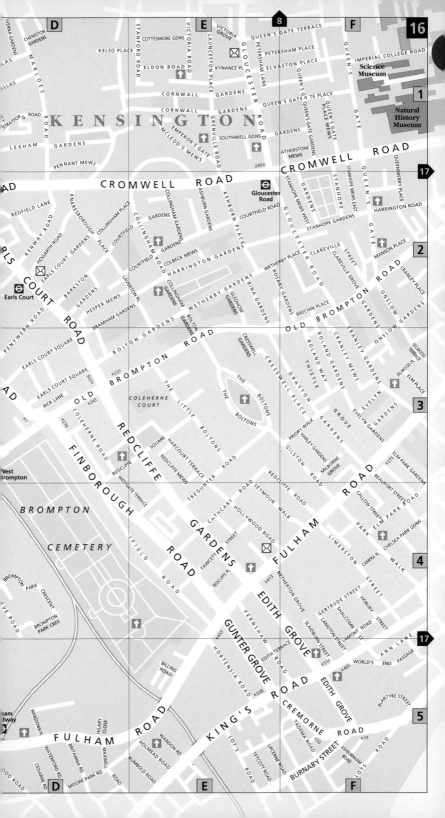

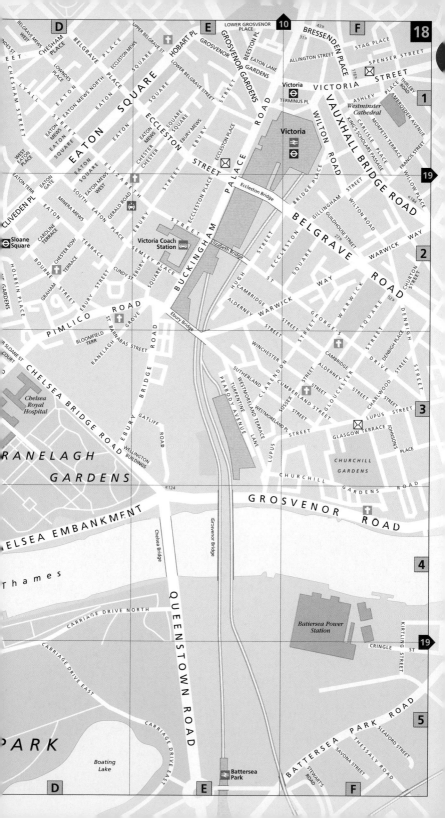

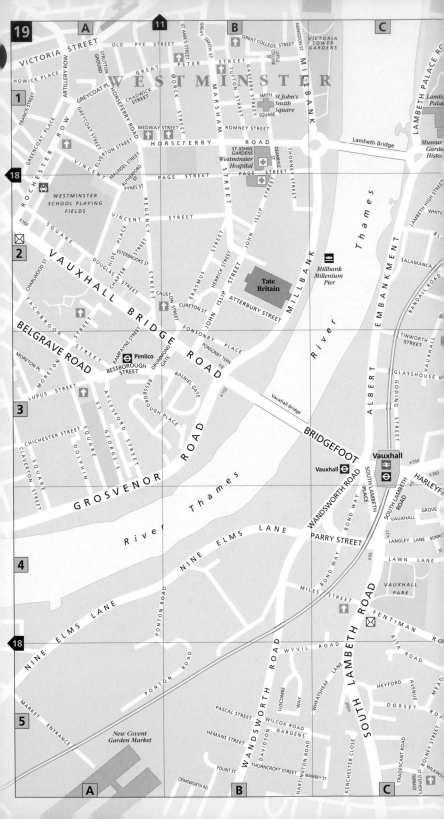

SHOPS AND MARKETS

London is one of the great shopping cities of Europe, with bustling, lively street markets, world-famous department stores and a wide variety of eclectic shops selling clothes, antiques, crafts and much more. The best shopping areas range from up-market districts such as Knightsbridge and Bond Street, which sell expensive

Bags from two famous London department stores

designer clothes, to the busy, chaotic stretch of Oxford Street. The vibrant markets of Covent Garden, Berwick Street and Brick Lane are also popular. The city is best known, however, for its huge range of clothes shops selling everything from traditional tweeds to the latest zany designs of the ever-changing high-street fashion trends.

WHEN TO SHOP

In central London, most shops stay open from 10am to about 5.30–6pm Monday to Saturday. Many department stores, however, have longer hours. The "late night" shopping until 7 or 8pm is on Thursday and Friday in Oxford Street and the rest of West End; and on Wednesday in Knightsbridge and Chelsea. Some shops in tourist areas, such as Covent Garden and the Trocadero, are open until 7pm or later every day, including Sunday. Some street markets and a number of other shops are usually open on Sundays as well.

TWICE-YEARLY SALES

The traditional sale season is from January to February and from June to July, when shops slash prices and sell off left-over stock. The department stores have some of the best reductions – queues for the famous Harrods sale start to form long before it opens.

SHOPPING AREAS

London's best shopping areas range from the up-market Knightsbridge, where porcelain, jewellery and couture come at the highest prices, to colourful markets, where getting the cheapest bargains is what it's all about.

The city beckons specialist shoppers with its treasures and collectibles crammed into inviting antiques shops, and streets full of antiquarian booksellers and art galleries.

BEST OF THE DEPARTMENT STORES

Harrods is the king of the city's department stores with over 300 departments and a staff of 5,000. The spectacular food hall with Edwardian tiles displays fish, cheese, fruit and vegetables. Other specialities include fashion, china and glass, kitchenware and electronics. Londoners also often head for the nearby **Harvey Nichols**, which stocks the best of everything. The clothing department is particularly strong, with an emphasis on talented British, European and American names. The food hall, opened in 1992, is one of London's most stylish.

Selfridges, on Oxford Street, has expanded its range in recent years. It has arguably the widest choice of labels, a great lingerie department and a section devoted to emerging

designers. It also has a food hall that features delicacies from all over the world.

Originally a drapery, **John Lewis**, to this date, has a good selection of fabrics and haberdashery. Its china, glass and household items make this store and its Sloane Square partner, **Peter Jones**, equally popular with Londoners.

Liberty, near Carnaby Street, has been famous ever since 1875 for its beautiful silks and other Oriental goods. Don't forget to check out the famous scarf department.

Fortnum and Mason's is best known for its ground-floor food department. It has everything from Fortnum's tins of biscuits and tea to cured meats and lovely wicker hampers. In fact, these exquisite delicacies are so engrossing that the upper floors filled with classic fashion and luxury items often remain free of crowds.

Harrods at night, illuminated by 11,500 lights

MARKETS

Whatever you're looking for, it's definitely worth visiting one of London's colourful markets. Many of them mix English traditions with those of more recent immigrants, creating an exotic atmosphere and a truly fascinating array of merchandise. At some, the seasoned hawkers have honed their sales patter to an entertaining art, which reaches fever pitch just before closing, when the plummeting prices at the end of the day are announced. Keep your wits about you, your hand on your purse and join in the fun.

Among the best of the West End markets are **Grays Antiques** and **Jubilee and Apple** markets in Covent Garden. Although it is somewhat touristy, **Piccadilly Crafts** is also very popular. In Soho, the spirited costermongers of **Berwick Street** peddle some of the cheapest and freshest fruit and vegetables in the area.

In the East End, **Petticoat Lane** is probably the most famous of London's street markets. Those in search of the latest street fashions make a beeline for **Old Spitalfields**, while **Brick Lane** is massively popular due

Bustling Petticoat Lane market, officially known as Middlesex Street

to its trendy location. Here you can find everything from shellfish to trainers. Nearby, **Columbia Road** is perfect for greenery and blossoms.

South of the river, **East Street** also has a flower market, but the majority of its traders sell clothes. **Bermondsey Market** is a gathering point for London's antiques traders. Collectors set off early to scrutinize the fine paintings and old jewellery. **Borough** *(see p120)* caters to the restaurant trade with it's fine food and farmer's market. **Brixton Market** stocks a superb

assortment of Afro-Caribbean foods, often to the pounding beat of reggae music.

In north London, **Camden Lock Market** offers a vibrant atmosphere and stalls selling everything from vintage clothes to lovely crafts. In nearby Islington, **Camden Passage** is a quiet cobbled street where charming cafés nestle among quaint antiques shops.

In Notting Hill, **Portobello Road** is actually a bunch of markets rolled into one, and an entire afternoon can be spent browsing there.

DIRECTORY

DEPARTMENT STORES

Fortnum & Mason
181 Piccadilly W1. **Map** 11
A3. **Tel** 020-7734 8040.

Harrods
87–135 Brompton Rd
SW1. **Map** 9 C5.
Tel 020-7730 1234.

Harvey Nichols
109–125 Knightsbridge
SW1. **Map** 9 C5.
Tel 020-7235 5000.

John Lewis
278–306 Oxford St W1.
Map 10 E1.
Tel 020-7629 7711.

Liberty
210–20 Regent St W1.
Map 10 F2.
Tel 020-7734 1234.

Peter Jones
Sloane Sq, SW1. **Map** 18
D2. **Tel** 020-7730 3434.

Selfridges
400 Oxford St W1. **Map**
10 D2. **Tel** 08708 377 377.

MARKETS

Bermondsey Market
Long Lane & Bermondsey
St SE1. **Map** 13 C5.
Open 5am–2pm Fri.

Berwick Street
Berwick St W1. **Map** 11
A2. *Open 9am–6pm
Mon–Sat.*

Borough
8 Southwark St SE1. **Map**
13 B4. *Open noon–6pm
Fri, 9am–4pm Sat.*

Brick Lane
Brick Lane E1. **Map** 6
E5. *Open dawn – 1pm
Sun.*

Brixton Market
Electric Ave SW9. ⊖
Brixton. *Open
8.30am–5.30pm daily.*

Camden Lock Market
Chalk Farm Rd NW1. ⊖
Camden Town, Chalk
Farm. *Open 9:30am
–5:30pm daily.*

Camden Passage
Camden Passage N1. **Map**
4 F1. *Open 10am–2pm
Wed, 10am–5pm Sat.*

Columbia Road
Columbia Rd E2. **Map** 6
D3. ⊖ Shoreditch, Old St.
Open 8am–2pm Sun.

East Street
East St SE17. ⊖ Elephant
& Castle. *Open 8–5pm
daily (8–2pm Thu & Sun).*

Grays Antiques
58 Davies St, Mayfair.
Map 10 E2. *Open 10am –
6pm Mon–Fri.*

Greenwich
College Approach SE10.
⊖ Greenwich. *Open
9am–6pm Sat & Sun.*

Jubilee and Apple
Covent Gdn Piazza WC2.
Map 11 C2. *Open
9am–5pm daily.*

Old Spitalfields
Commercial St E1. **Map** 6
D1. ⊖ Liverpool St. *Open
9:30am–5:30pm daily.*

Petticoat Lane
Middlesex St E1. **Map** 14
E2. *Open 9am–2pm Sun.*

Piccadilly Crafts
St James's Church,
Piccadilly W1. **Map** 11 A3.
Open 9am–6pm.

Portobello Road
Portobello Rd W10.
Map 7 C3. 1 Notting Hill
Gate. *Open daily (main
market Sat).*

Exclusive designer clothes on sale at Harrods, Knightsbridge

CLOTHES

British tailoring and fabrics are world renowned for their high quality. **Henry Poole & Co**, **H Huntsman & Sons** and **Gieves & Hawkes** are among the most highly respected tailors on Savile Row.

The past decade has seen the advent of a new generation of trend conscious tailors who specialize in modern cuts and fabrics. The line-up includes **Richard James** and **Ozwald Boateng**. Several stalwarts of classic British style have also recently reinvented themselves as fashion labels. **Burberry** is the best example, although it still does a brisk trade in its famous trenchcoats, and distinctive accessories. Designers **Margaret Howell** and **Nicole Farhi** create trendsetting versions of British country garments for men as well as women.

London designers are known for their eclectic, irreverent style. *Grande dames* of fashion, **Zandra Rhodes** and **Vivienne Westwood** have been on the scene since the 1970s. Many other British designers of international stature also have their flagship stores in the capital, including the popular **Stella McCartney**, **Alexander McQueen**, **Paul Smith** and **Matthew Williamson.** Designer clothes, however, are not just the preserve of the rich. If you want to flaunt a bit of British design, but can't afford the high prices, it's worth

visiting **Debenhams**, which has harnessed the talents of numerous leading designers. Cheaper versions of all the latest styles appear in the shops almost as soon as they have been sashayed down the catwalk. **Topshop** and **Oasis** have both won celebrity fans for their up-to-the-minute ensembles of hip and youthful fashions for women. The up-market chains, **Jigsaw** and **Whistles** are more expensive, with their emphasis on beautiful fabrics and shapes which, while stylish, don't copy the catwalk. Fashion conscious young men can turn to **Reiss** and **Ted Baker** for trendy clothing.

SHOES

Some of the most famous names in the footwear industry are based in Britain. If you can spare a few thousand pounds, you can have a pair custom-made by the Royal Family's shoemaker, **John Lobb**. Ready-made, traditional brogues and Oxfords are the mainstay of **Church's Shoes**. **Oliver Sweeney** gives classics a contemporary edge. **The British Boot Company** in Camden has the widest range of funky Dr Martens, appropriated by rock'n'rollers and the grunge set. **Jimmy Choo** and **Manolo Blahnik** are two all-time favourites of most fashionable women all over the world. Less expensive, yet good quality designs can be found in **Hobbs** or **Pied à Terre**, while **Faith** and **Office** turn out young, voguish styles.

GIFTS AND SOUVENIRS

London has no shortage of interesting gift and curio shops. **Contemporary Applied Arts** and the market in Covent Garden Piazza stock uniquely British pottery, knitwear and other crafts. To buy all your gifts under one roof, visit Liberty *(see p148)*, where all kinds of exquisite items can be found in every department.

Leading museums such as the Victoria and Albert *(see pp98–9)*, Natural History and Science Museums *(see p100)* sell unusual mementos as well.

BOOKS AND MAGAZINES

The bookshops in London rank among its most illustrious specialities. Charing Cross Road is a treasure trove for those hunting for antiquarian, second-hand as well as new volumes. It is the home of **Foyles**, famous for its massive stock. Large branches of chains such as **Waterstone's** and **Borders** co-exist with many specialist stores in this highly learned street.

Hatchards in Piccadilly is the city's oldest bookshop, and also one of its best, offering an extensive choice of titles.

Vintage Magazines in Soho, as its name suggests, stocks publications dating back to the early 1900s – collectors of back issues will be delighted.

Well-stocked bookshop on the legendary Charing Cross Road

ART AND ANTIQUES

Art and antiques shops abound in London. Whatever your tastes, you are bound to find something of beauty and value within your means.

Cork Street is the centre of Britain's contemporary art world. **Waddington Galleries** is the best known, while **Redfern Art Gallery** and **Flowers Central** exhibit unusual modern art.

Visit **Bond Street Antiques Centre** and Grays Antiques *(see p148)* for striking vintage jewellery and objets d'art.

The East End is a growing area for contemporary art. The cutting-edge **White Cube Gallery** is there, as is a cluster of galleries in the **Tea Building**.

For photography, visit the **Photographers' Gallery**, which has the largest collection of originals for sale in Britain. **Hamiltons Gallery** also hosts interesting exhibitions.

DIRECTORY

CLOTHES

Alexander McQueen
4–5 Old Bond St W1.
Map 10 F3.
Tel 020-7355 0088.

Burberry
21–23 New Bond St W1.
Map 10 F2.
Tel 020-7930 3343.
One of several branches.

Debenhams
334–348 Oxford St W1.
Map 10 E2.
Tel 020-7580 3000.

Gieves & Hawkes
1 Savile Row W1.
Map 10 F3.
Tel 020-7434 2001.

H Huntsman & Sons
11 Savile Row W1.
Map 10 F3.
Tel 020-7734 7441.

Henry Poole & Co
15 Savile Row W1.
Map 10 F3.
Tel 020-7734 5985.

Jigsaw
6 Duke of York Sq, Kings
Rd SW3. **Map** 17 C2.
Tel 020-7730 4404.

Margaret Howell
34 Wigmore St W1.
Map 10 E1.
Tel 020-7009 9009.

Matthew Williamson
28 Bruton St W1.
Map 10 E3.
Tel 020-7629 6200.

Nicole Farhi
158 New Bond St W1.
Map 10 E2.
Tel 020-7499 8368.

Oasis
12–14 Argyll St W1.
Map 10 F2.
Tel 020-7434 1799.

Ozwald Boateng
12A Savile Row & 9 Vigo
St W1. **Map** 10 F3.
Tel 020-7437 0620.

Paul Smith
Westbourne House
120 & 122 Kensington
Park Rd W11. **Map** 7 B2.
Tel 020-7727 3553.

Reiss
Kent House, 14–17
Market Place W1.
Map 10 F1.
Tel 020-7637 9113.
One of several branches.

Richard James
29 Savile Row W1.
Map 10 F2.
Tel 020-7434 0605.

Stella McCartney
30 Bruton St W1.
Map 10 E3.
Tel 020-7518 3100.

Ted Baker
9–10 Floral St WC2.
Map 11 C2.
Tel 020-7836 7808.
One of several branches.

Topshop
Oxford Circus W1.
Map 10 F1.
Tel 020-7636 7700.
One of several branches.

Vivienne Westwood
6 Davies St W1.
Map 10 E2.
Tel 020-7629 3757.

Whistles
12–14 St Christopher's
Pl W1. **Map** 10 D1.
Tel 020-7487 4484.
One of several branches.

Zandra Rhodes
79 Bermondsey St, SE1.
Map 11 C5.
Tel 020-7403 5333.

SHOES

The British Boot Company
5 Kentish Town Rd NW1.
Map 2 F1.
Tel 020-7485 8505.

Church's Shoes
201 Regent St W1.
Map 10 F2.
Tel 020-7734 2438.

Faith
192–194 Oxford St W1.
Map 10 F1.
Tel 020-7580 9561.

Hobbs
47–48 South Molton St
W1. **Map** 10 E2.
Tel 020-7629 0750.
One of several branches.

Jimmy Choo
169 Draycott Ave SW3.
Map 17 B2.
Tel 020-7584 6111.

John Lobb
9 St James's St SW1.
Map 10 F4.
Tel 020-7930 3664.

Manolo Blahnik
49–51 Old Church St,
Kings Road SW3.
Map 17 A4.
Tel 020-7352 3863.

Office
57 Neal St WC2.
Map 11 B1.
Tel 020-7379 1896.
One of several branches

Oliver Sweeney
29 King's Rd SW3.
Map 17 C2.
Tel 020-7730 3666.

Pied à Terre
179 South Molton St W1.
Map 10 E2.
Tel 020-7629 1362.

GIFTS AND SOUVENIRS

Contemporary Applied Arts
2 Percy St WC1.
Map 11 A1.
Tel 020-7436 2344.

BOOKS AND MAGAZINES

Borders
120 Charing Cross Rd
WC2. **Map** 11 B1.
Tel 020-7379 8877.
One of several branches.

Foyles
113–119 Charing Cross Rd
WC2. **Map** 11 B1.
Tel 020-7437 5660.

Hatchards
187 Piccadilly W1.
Map 10 F3.
Tel 020-7439 9921.

Waterstone's
19–23 Oxford St W1.
Map 11 A1.
Tel 020-7434 9759.
One of several branches.

Vintage Magazines
39–43 Brewer St W1.
Map 11 A2.
Tel 020-7439 8525.

ART AND ANTIQUES

Bond Street Antiques Centre
124 New Bond St W1.
Map 10 F3.
Tel 020-7351 5353.

Flowers Central
21 Cork St W1.
Map 10 F3.
Tel 020-7439 7766.

Hamiltons Gallery
13 Carlos Place London
W1. **Map** 10 E3.
Tel 020-7499 9493.

Photographers' Gallery
5 & 8 Great Newport St
WC2. **Map** 11 B2.
Tel 020-7031 1772.

Redfern Art Gallery
20 Cork St W1.
Map 10 F3.
Tel 020-7734 1732.

Tea Building
56 Shoreditch High St E1.
Map 6 D4.
Tel 020-7729 2973.

Waddington Galleries
11, 12, 34 Cork St W1.
Map 10 F3.
Tel 020-7437 8611.

White Cube Gallery
Hoxton Square N1.
Map 5 C3.
Tel 020-7930 5373.

ENTERTAINMENT IN LONDON

Many London cafés have free live music

London has the enormous variety of entertainment that only the great cities of the world can provide. The historical backdrop and the lively bustling atmosphere add to the excitement. Whether dancing the night away at a famous disco or making the most of London's varied arts scene, the visitor has a bewildering choice. A trip to London is not complete without a visit to the theatre which ranges from glamorous West End musicals to experimental Fringe plays. There is world-class ballet and opera in fabled venues such as Sadler's Wells and the Royal Opera House. The musical menu covers everything from classical, jazz and rock to rhythm and blues performed in atmospheric basement clubs, old converted cinemas and outdoor venues such as Wembley. Movie buffs can choose from hundreds of films each night. Sports fans can watch cricket at Lord's or participate in a host of activities from water sports to ice skating.

Time Out, published every Tuesday, is the most comprehensive guide to what is on in London, with detailed weekly listings and reviews. *The Evening Standard*, *The Guardian* (Saturday) and *The Independent* also have reviews and information on events. If you buy tickets from booking agencies rather than direct from box offices, do compare prices – and only buy from ticket touts if you are desperate.

WEST END AND NATIONAL THEATRES

Palace Theatre poster (1898)

The glamorous, glittering world of West End theatreland, emblazoned with the names of world-famous performers, offers an extraordinary range of entertainment.

West End theatres (see Directory for individual theatres) survive on their profits and rely on financial backers, known as "angels". Consequently, they tend to stage commercial productions with mass appeal: musicals, classics, comedies and plays by bankable contemporary playwrights.

The state-subsidized **National Theatre** is based in the South Bank Centre *(see p154)*. It has three auditoriums – the large, open-staged Olivier, the proscenium-arched Lyttelton, and the small studio space of the Cottesloe.

The **Royal Shakespeare Company** (RSC) regularly stages Shakespeare plays, but its repertoire includes Greek tragedies, Restoration comedies and modern works. Based at Stratford-upon-Avon *(see pp325–27)*, its major productions perform at London West End theatres. The RSC ticket hotline has information. **The Old Vic** has been rejuvenated recently under the artistic directorship of Kevin Spacey, whose exciting programme of drama attracts wide audiences.

Theatre tickets generally cost from £5 to £30 and can be bought direct from box offices, by telephone or post. The "tkts" discount theatre ticket booth in Leicester Square sells tickets for a wide range of shows on the day of performance. It is open Monday to Saturday (10am–7pm) for matinees and evening shows, and Sundays (noon–3pm) for matinees only (cash or credit card only).

OFF-WEST END AND FRINGE THEATRES

Off-West End theatre is a middle category bridging the gap between West End and Fringe theatre. It includes venues that, regardless of location, have a permanent management team and often provide the opportunity for established directors and actors to turn their hands to more adventurous works in a smaller, more intimate, environment. Fringe theatres, on the other hand, are normally venues hired out to visiting companies. Both offer a vast array of innovative productions, serving as an outlet for new, often experimental writing.

Venues (too numerous to list – see newspaper listings),

The Old Vic, the first home of the National Theatre from 1963

Open-air theatre at Regent's Park

range from tiny theatres or rooms above pubs such as the Gate, which produces neglected European classics, to theatres such as the Donmar Warehouse, which attracts major directors and actors.

OPEN-AIR THEATRE

In summer, a performance of one of Shakespeare's airier creations such as *A Midsummer Night's Dream*, takes on an atmosphere of enchantment among the green vistas of Regent's Park (0870-060 1811). Lavish summer opera productions are staged at Holland Park (020-7602 7856). Shakespeare's Globe (*see p120*) offers open-air theatrical performances in a beautifully recreated Elizabethan theatre.

CINEMAS

The West End abounds with multiplex cinema chains (MGM, Odeon, UCI) which show big budget Hollywood films, usually in advance of the rest of the country, although release dates tend to lag well behind the US and many other European countries.

The Odeon Marble Arch has the largest commercial screen in Europe, while the Odeon Leicester Square boasts London's biggest auditorium with almost 2,000 seats.

Londoners are well-informed cinema-goers and even the larger cinema chains include some low-budget and foreign films in their repertoire. The majority of foreign films are

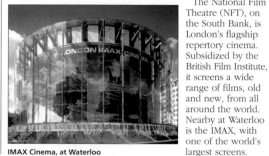
IMAX Cinema, at Waterloo

subtitled, rather than dubbed. A number of independent cinemas, such as the Other Cinema, the Renoir and Prince Charles in central London, and the Curzon in Mayfair, show foreign-language and art films.

The largest concentration of cinemas is in and around Leicester Square although there are local cinemas in most areas. Just off Leicester Square, the Prince Charles is the West End's cheapest cinema. Elsewhere in the area you can expect to pay as much as £10 for an evening screening – almost twice the price of the local cinemas. Monday and afternoon performances in the West End are often cheaper.

The National Film Theatre (NFT), on the South Bank, is London's flagship repertory cinema. Subsidized by the British Film Institute, it screens a wide range of films, old and new, from all around the world. Nearby at Waterloo is the IMAX, with one of the world's largest screens.

DIRECTORY

Adelphi
Strand. **Map** 11 C3.
Tel 0870 403 0303.

Albery
St Martin's Lane. **Map** 11 B2. *Tel* 0870-060 6621.

Aldwych
Aldwych. **Map** 11 C2. *Tel* 020-7379 3367.

Apollo
Shaftesbury Ave. **Map** 11 B2. *Tel* 020-7494 5050.

Cambridge
Earlham St. **Map** 11 B2. *Tel* 0870-264 3333.

Comedy
Panton St. **Map** 11 A3. *Tel* 0870-060 6622.

Criterion
Piccadilly Circus. **Map** 11 A3. *Tel* 020-7413 1437.

Dominion
Tottenham Court Rd. **Map** 11 A1. *Tel* 0870-607 7460.

Duchess
Catherine St. **Map** 11 C2. *Tel* 020-7494 5050.

Duke of York's
St Martin's Lane. **Map** 11 B2. *Tel* 0870-060 6623.

Fortune
Russell St. **Map** 11 C2. *Tel* 0870-060 6626.

Garrick
Charing Cross Rd. **Map** 11 B2. *Tel* 0870-264 3333.

Gielgud
Shaftesbury Ave. **Map** 11 B2. *Tel* 0870-264 3333.

Her Majesty's
Haymarket. **Map** 11 A3. *Tel* 0870-264 3333.

Lyceum
Wellington St. **Map** 11 C2. *Tel* 0870 243 9000.

Lyric
Shaftesbury Ave. **Map** 11 B2. *Tel* 0870-890 1107.

National
South Bank. **Map** 12 D3. *Tel* 020 7452 3000.

New London
Drury Lane. **Map** 11 C1. *Tel* 0870-264 3333.

The Old Vic
Waterloo Rd SE1. **Map** 12 E4. *Tel* 0870 060 6628.

Palace
Shaftesbury Ave. **Map** 11 B2. *Tel* 0870-264 3333.

Phoenix
Charing Cross Rd. **Map** 11 B2. *Tel* 0870-060 6629.

Piccadilly
Denman St. **Map** 11 A2. *Tel* 0870-060 6630.

Prince Edward
Old Compton St. **Map** 11 D5. *Tel* 0870 850 9191.

Prince of Wales
Coventry St. **Map** 11 A3. *Tel* 0870 850 0393.

Queen's
Shaftesbury Ave. **Map** 11 B2. *Tel* 020-7494 5050.

RSC *Tel* 0870 609 1110.

Shaftesbury
Shaftesbury Ave. **Map** 11 B2. *Tel* 020-7379 3345.

Strand Aldwych. **Map** 12 D2. *Tel* 0870-060 2335.

St Martin's
West St. **Map** 11 B2. *Tel* 0870 162 8787.

Theatre Royal:
–Drury Lane
Catherine St. **Map** 11 C2. *Tel* 0870-264 3333.

–Haymarket
Haymarket. **Map** 11 A3. *Tel* 0870-901 3356.

Vaudeville
Strand. **Map** 11 C3. *Tel* 020-7494 5050.

Wyndham's
Charing Cross Rd. **Map** 11 B2. *Tel* 0870 950 0920.

Royal Festival Hall, South Bank Centre

CLASSICAL MUSIC, OPERA AND DANCE

London is one of the world's great centres for classical music, with five symphony orchestras, internationally renowned chamber groups such as the Academy of St-Martin-in-the-Fields and the English Chamber Orchestra, as well as a number of contemporary groups. There are performances virtually every week by major international orchestras and artists, reaching a peak during the summer Proms season at the **Royal Albert Hall** *(see p63)*. The newly restored **Wigmore Hall** has excellent acoustics and is a fine setting for chamber music, as is the converted Baroque church (1728) of **St John's, Smith Square**.

Although televised and outdoor performances by major stars have greatly increased the popularity of opera, prices at the **Royal Opera House** are still aimed at corporate entertainment but the policy now is to keep a few cheaper seats. The refurbished building is elaborate and productions are often extremely lavish. English National Opera, based at the **London Coliseum**, has more adventurous productions, appealing to a younger audience (nearly all operas are sung in English). Tickets range from £5 to £200 and it is advisable to book in advance.

The Royal Opera House is also home to the Royal Ballet, and the London Coliseum to the English National Ballet, the two leading classical ballet companies in Britain. Visiting ballets also perform in both. There are numerous young contemporary dance companies, and **The Place** is a dedicated contemporary

dance theatre where many companies perform. Other major dance venues are **Sadler's Wells**, the **ICA**, the **Peacock Theatre** and the **Chisenhale Dance Space**.

The **Barbican Concert Hall** and **South Bank Centre** (comprising the Royal Festival Hall, Queen Elizabeth Hall and Purcell Room) host an impressive variety of events ranging from touring opera and classical music performances to free foyer concerts.

Elsewhere in London many outdoor musical events take place in summer *(see pp62–3)* at venues such as **Kenwood House**. Events to look out for are: the London Opera Festival (June) with singers from all over the world; the City of London Festival (July) which hosts a range of varied musical events; and contemporary dance festivals Spring Loaded (February–April) and Dance Umbrella (October) – see *Time Out* and newspaper listings.

Kenwood House on Hampstead Heath *(see p124)*

DIRECTORY

CLASSICAL MUSIC, OPERA AND DANCE

Barbican Concert Hall
Silk St EC2. **Map** 5 A5.
Tel 0845-120 7500.
www.barbican.org.uk

Chisenhale Dance Space
64–84 Chisenhale Rd E3.
🚇 *Bethnal Green, Mile End.* **Tel** 020-8981 6617.

ICA
The Mall SW1. **Map** 11 A4. **Tel** 020-7930 0493.
www.ica.org.uk

Kenwood House
Hampstead Lane NW3.
🚇 *Archway, then bus.*
Tel 020-8348 1286.

London Coliseum
St Martin's Lane WC2. **Map** 11 B3. **Tel** 020-7632 8300. www.eno.org

Peacock Theatre
Portugal St WC2. **Map** 12 D1. **Tel** 020-7863 8000.

The Place
17 Duke's Rd WC1. **Map** 3 B3. **Tel** 020-7387 0031.

Royal Albert Hall
Kensington Gore SW7.
Map 8 F5.
Tel 020-7589 8212.
www.royalalberthall.com

Royal Opera House
Floral St WC2. **Map** 11 C2. **Tel** 020-7304 4000.
www.royalopera.org

Sadler's Wells
Rosebery Ave EC1. 🚇 *Angel.* **Tel** 020-7863 8000.
www.sadlerswells.com

St John's, Smith Sq
Smith Sq SW1. **Map** 19 B1. **Tel** 020-7222 1061.
www.sjss.org.uk

South Bank Centre
SE1. **Map** 12 D3. **Tel** 020-7921 0600. www.southbanklondon.com

Wigmore Hall
Wigmore St W1. **Map** 10 D1. **Tel** 020-7935 2141.
www.wigmore-hall.org.uk

ROCK, POP, JAZZ AND CLUBS

100 Club
100 Oxford St W1. **Map** 10 F1. **Tel** 020-7636 0933.

Brixton Academy
211 Stockwell Rd SW9.
🚇 *Brixton.*
Tel 0870-771 2000.

Forum
9–17 Highgate Rd NW5.
🚇 *Kentish Town.*
Tel 0870-534 4444.

Fridge
Town Hall Parade, Brixton Hill SW2. 🚇 *Brixton.*
Tel 020-7326 5100.

The Hippodrome, Leicester Square

ROCK, POP, JAZZ AND CLUBS

An ordinary week night in London features scores of concerts, ranging from rock and pop, to jazz, Latin, world, folk and reggae. Artists guaranteed to fill thousands of seats play large venues such as **Wembley Arena** or the **Royal Albert Hall**. However, many major bands prefer to play the **Brixton Academy** and the **Forum**, both former cinemas.

The number of jazz venues has increased over the last few years. Best of the old crop is **Ronnie Scott's**, while of the newcomers the **100 Club**, **Jazz Café** and **Pizza on the Park** have good reputations.

London's club scene is one of the most innovative in Europe, particularly since 1990, when all-night clubbing (though not drinking) was legalized. It is dominated by big-name DJs, who host different nights in different clubs, and some of the best clubs are one-nighters (see *Time Out* and newspaper listings). The world-famous mainstream discos **Stringfellows** and the **Hippodrome** are glitzy, expensive and very much part of the tourist circuit. In contrast the New York-style **Ministry of Sound**, the camp cabaret of **Madame Jojo's**, the trendy Shoreditch clubs **333** and **Cargo**, and a host of other venues ensure that you will never be short of choice. Alternatives are the excellent laser and light shows at **Heaven**, the glamorous super-club **Pacha London**, or the ska, classic soul and R'n'B at the **Soho Lounge** on Thursdays. Heaven and the **Fridge** are among the most popular of London's gay clubs.

Opening times are usually 10pm–3am, but on weekends many clubs open until 6am.

SPORTS

An impressive variety of public sports facilities are to be found in London and they are generally inexpensive to use. Swimming pools, squash courts, gyms and sports centres, with an assortment of keep-fit classes, can be found in most districts, and tennis courts hired in most parks. Water sports, ice skating and golf are among the variety of activities on offer. Spectator sports range from football and rugby at various club grounds to cricket at **Lord's** or the **Oval**, and tennis at the **All England Lawn Tennis Club**, Wimbledon. Tickets for the most popular matches can often be hard to come by *(see p67)*. More traditional sports include polo at **Guards**, croquet at **Hurlingham** and medieval tennis at **Queen's Club Real Tennis**. See pages 662 to 665 for more information on sporting activities.

Ticket agency, Shaftesbury Avenue

Cargo
83 Rivington St EC2. ⊖
Old St. **Tel** *020-7739 3440.*

Heaven
Under the Arches, Villiers St WC2. **Map 11** C3.
Tel *020-7930 2020.*

Hippodrome
Cranbourne St WC2.
Map 11 B2.
Tel *020-7437 4311.*

Jazz Café
3–5 Parkway NW1.
⊖ *Camden Town.*
Tel *020-7916 6060.*

Madame Jojo's
8–10 Brewer St W1. **Map 11** A2. **Tel** *020-7734 3040.*

Ministry of Sound
103 Gaunt St SE1. ⊖
Elephant & Castle.
Tel *020-7378 6528.*

Pacha London
Terminus Place, SW1. **Map 18** F1. **Tel** *020-7833 3139.*
www.pachalondon.com

Pizza on the Park
11 Knightsbridge SW1.
Map 10 D5. **Tel** *020-7235 5550.* **www**.
pizzaonthepark.com

Ronnie Scott's
47 Frith St W1. **Map 11** A2.
Tel *020-7439 0747.*
www.ronniescotts.uk

Soho Lounge
69 Dean St W1. **Map 11** A2. **Tel** *020-7434 4480.*

Stringfellows
16–19 Upper St Martin's Lane WC2. **Map 11** B2.
Tel *020-7240 5534.*

333
333 Old St EC1.
Tel *020 7739 5949.*
www.333mother.com

SPORTS

All England Lawn Tennis Club
Church Rd, Wimbledon SW19. ⊖ *Southfields.*
Tel *020-8946 2244.*

Guards Polo Club
Windsor Great Park, Englefield Green, Egham, Surrey. 🚉 *Egham.*
Tel *01784 434212.*

Hurlingham Club
Ranelagh Gdns SW6.
Map 18 D3.
Tel *020-7736 8411.*

Lord's Cricket Ground
St John's Wood NW8.
⊖ *St John's Wood.*
Tel *020-7289 1611.*

Oval Cricket Ground
The Oval, Kennington SE11.
⊖ *Oval.*
Tel *020-7582 6660.*

Queen's Club Real Tennis
Palliser Rd W14.
⊖ *Barons Court.*
Tel *020-7385 3421.*

SOUTHEAST ENGLAND

Southeast England at a Glance

The old Saxon kingdoms covered the areas surrounding London, and today, while their accessibility to the capital makes them a magnet for commuters, each region retains a character and history of its own. The attractions include England's oldest universities, royal palaces, castles, stately homes and cathedrals, many of which played critical roles in the nation's early history. The landscape is soft, with the green and rounded hills of the south country levelling out to the flat fertile plains and fens of East Anglia, fringed by broad, sandy beaches.

Blenheim Palace (see pp228–9) *is a Baroque masterpiece. The Mermaid Fountain (1892) is part of the spectacular gardens.*

Bedfordshire

Hertfo

Buckinghamshire

THAMES VALLEY *(see pp216–37)*

Oxfordshire

Surrey

Oxford University's *buildings (see pp222–7) amount to a textbook of English architecture from the Middle Ages to the present. Christ Church College (1525) is the largest in the university.*

Hampshire

West Susse

Windsor Castle (see pp236–7) *is Britain's oldest royal residence. The Round Tower was built in the 11th century when the palace guarded the western approaches to London.*

Winchester Cathedral (see pp170–1) *was begun in 1097 on the ruins of a Saxon church. The city has been an important centre of Christianity since the 7th century. The cathedral's northwest door is built in a characteristic medieval style.*

Ely Cathedral's (see pp194–5) *south transept contains some of the finest stone carving in Britain. The octagonal corona was added in the 14th century when the Norman tower collapsed; the replacement tower dominates the surrounding flat fenland.*

Norfolk

mbridgeshire

EAST ANGLIA
(see pp190–215)

Suffolk

Cambridge University's (see pp210–15) *buildings are enhanced by the quiet college gardens, the Backs and the public commons. King's College Chapel is the outstanding example of late medieval architecture in the city.*

Essex

LONDON
e pp70–157)

Kent

THE DOWNS AND CHANNEL COAST
(see pp164–89)

East Sussex

Canterbury Cathedral (see pp186–7) *is the spiritual home of the Church of England. It contains some of the country's most exquisite medieval stained glass such as the nave's west window. It also has some well-preserved 12th-century wall paintings.*

Brighton's Royal Pavilion (see pp178–9) *was built for the Prince Regent and is one of the most lavish buildings in the land. Its design by John Nash (see p107) is based on Oriental themes and it has recently been restored to its original splendour.*

| 0 kilometres | 25 |
| 0 miles | 25 |

The Garden of England

With its fertile soil, mild climate and regular rainfall, the Kentish countryside has flourished as a fruit-growing region ever since its first orchards were planted by the Romans. There has been a recent boom in wine-making, as the vine-covered hillsides around Lamberhurst show, and several vineyards may be visited. The orchards are dazzling in the blossom season, and in the autumn the branches sag with ripening fruit – a familiar sight which inspired William Cobbett (1762–1835) to describe the area as "the very finest as to fertility and diminutive beauty in the whole world". Near Faversham, the fruit research station of Brogdale is open to the public, offering orchard walks, tastings and informative displays.

White wine from the southeast

HOPS AND HOPPING

Hop-picking, a family affair

Oast houses, topped with distinctive angled cowls, are a common feature of the Kentish landscape, and many have now been turned into houses. They were original

SEASONAL FRUIT

This timeline shows the major crops in each month of the farming year. The first blossoms may appear when the fields are still dusted with snow. As the petals fall, fruit appears among the leaves. After ripening in the summer sun, the fruit is harvested in the autumn.

Peach blossom *is usually to be found on south-facing walls, as its fruit requires warm conditions.*

Orchards *are used to grow plums, pears and apples. The latter (blossoming above) remain Kent's most important orchard crop.*

Raspberries *are a luscious soft fruit. Many growers allow you to pick your own from the fields, and then pay by weight.*

MARCH	APRIL	MAY	JUNE	JU

Sour cherry blossom *is the earliest flower. Its fruit is used for cooking.*

Pear blossom *has creamy white flowers which appear two or three weeks before apple blossom.*

Cherry plum blossom *is one of the most beautiful blossoms; the plum is grown more for its flowers than its fruit.*

Srawberries *are Britain's favourite and earliest soft fruit. New strains allow them to be picked all summer.*

Gooseberries *are not always sweet enough to eat raw, though all types are superb in pies and other desserts.*

uilt to dry hops, an ingredient
 brewing beer *(see pp604–5)*.
any are still used for that, for
though imports have reduced
omestic hop-growing, more
an four million tonnes are
roduced in Britain annually,
ostly in Kent.

In summer, the fruiting plants
an be seen climbing the rect-
gular wire frames in fields by
e roadside. Until the middle of
e 20th century thousands of
milies from London's East End
ould move to the Kentish hop
elds every autumn for working
olidays harvesting the crop and
mping in barns. That tradition
as faded, because now the
ops are picked by machine.

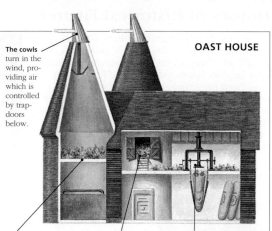

OAST HOUSE

The cowls turn in the wind, providing air which is controlled by trap-doors below.

Hops are dried above a fan which blows hot air from the underlying radiators.

After drying, the hops are cooled and stored.

A press packs the hops into bags, ready for the breweries.

Cherries *are the sweetest of Kent's fruit: two popular varieties are Stella (top) and Duke.*

Plums *are often served stewed, in pies, or dried into prunes. The Victoria plum (left) is the classic English dessert plum and is eaten raw. The Purple plum is also popular.*

Greengages *are green plums. They have a distinctive taste and can be made into jam.*

Bramley Seedling *is one of the best cooking apples, but it is not sweet enough to eat raw.*

Pears, *such as the William (left), should be eaten at the height of ripeness. The Conference keeps better.*

AUGUST	SEPTEMBER	OCTOBER	NOVEMBER

urrants *are among the most assertively flavoured fruit and are used in desserts and jams.*

Peaches, *grown in China 4,000 years ago, came to England in the 19th century.*

Dessert apples, *such as Cox's Orange Pippin (right), are some of England's best-loved fruits. The newer Discovery is easier to grow.*

The Kentish cob, *a variety of hazelnut, is undergoing a revival, having been eclipsed by European imports. Unlike many nuts, it is best picked fresh from the tree.*

Vineyards *are now a familiar sight in Kent (as well as Sussex and Hampshire). Most of the wine produced, such as Lamberhurst, is white.*

Houses of Historical Figures

Visiting the homes of artists, writers, politicians and royalty is a rewarding way of gaining an insight into their private lives. Southeast England, near London, boasts many historic houses that have been preserved as they were when their illustrious occupants were alive. All these houses, from large mansions such as Lord Mountbatten's Broadlands to the more modest dwellings, like Jane Austen's House, contain exhibits relating to the life of the famous people who lived there.

Florence Nightingale
(1820–1910), the "Lady with the Lamp", was a nurse during the Crimean War (see p56). She stayed at Claydon with her sister, Lady Verney.

Nancy Astor *(1879–1964) was the first woman to sit in Parliament in 1919. She lived at Cliveden until her death and made it famous for political hospitality.*

The Duke of Wellington *(1769–1852) was given this house by the nation in 1817, in gratitude for leading the British to victory at Waterloo (see p55).*

Claydon House, Winslow, nr Milton Keynes

THAMES VALLEY
(see pp216–17)

Cliveden House, nr Maidenhead

Stratfield Saye, Basingstoke, nr Windsor

Jane Austen *(1775–1817) wrote three of her novels, including* Emma, *and revised the others at this house where she lived for eight years until shortly before her death (see p172).*

Broadlands, nr Southampton

Jane Austen's House, Chawton, nr Winchester

Lord Mountbatten (1900–79), a British naval commander and statesman, was the last Viceroy of India in 1947. He lived here all his married life and remodelled the original house considerably.

Osborne House, Isle of Wight

Queen Victoria (1819–1901) and her husband, Prince Albert, built Osborne House *(see p168)* in 1855 as a seaside retreat for their family because they never truly warmed to the Royal Pavilion in Brighton.

BLOOMSBURY GROUP

A circle of avant-garde artists, designers and writers, many of them friends as students, began to meet at a house in Bloomsbury, London, in 1904 and soon gained a reputation for their Bohemian lifestyle. When Duncan Grant and Vanessa Bell moved to Charleston in 1916 *(see p180)*, it became a Sussex outpost of the celebrated group. Many of the prominent figures associated with the circle, such as Virginia Woolf, EM Forster, Vita Sackville-West and JM Keynes paid visits here. The Bloomsbury Group was also known for the Omega Workshops, which made innovative ceramics, furniture and textiles.

Vanessa Bell at Charleston by Duncan Grant (1885–1978)

Gainsborough's House, Sudbury, nr Ipswich

EAST ANGLIA
(see pp190–215)

Thomas Gainsborough *(1727–88), one of Britain's greatest painters, was born in this house (see p194). He was best known for his portraits, such as this one of* Mr and Mrs Andrews.

Charles Darwin *(1809–82), who developed the theory that man and apes have a common ancestor, wrote his most famous book,* On the Origin of Species, *at the house where he lived.*

Down House, Downe, nr Sevenoaks

THE DOWNS AND CHANNEL COAST
(see pp164–89)

Bleak House, Broadstairs, nr Margate

Charles Dickens *(1812–70), the prolific and popular Victorian novelist (see p189), had many connections with Kent. He took holidays at Bleak House, later named after his famous novel.*

Chartwell, Westerham, nr Sevenoaks

Batemans, Burwash, nr Hastings

Winston Churchill (1874–1965), Britain's inspirational Prime Minister in World War II *(see p189)*, lived here for 40 years until his death. He relaxed by rebuilding parts of the house.

Rudyard Kipling *(1865–1936), the poet and novelist, was born in India, but lived here for 34 years until his death. His most famous works include* Kim, *the two* Jungle Books *and the* Just So Stories.

Charleston, Lewes

Vanessa Bell (1879–1961), artist and member of the Bloomsbury Group, lived here until her death in 1961. The 18th-century farmhouse reflects her decorative ideas and is filled with murals, paintings and painted furniture *(see p180)*.

THE DOWNS AND CHANNEL COAST

HAMPSHIRE · SURREY · EAST SUSSEX · WEST SUSSEX · KENT

W*hen settlers, invaders and missionaries came from Europe, the southeast coast was their first landfall. The wooded chalk ridges and lower-lying weald beyond them made an ideal base for settlement and proved to be productive farmland.*

The Romans were the first to build major fortifications along the Channel Coast to discourage potential attackers from the European mainland. The remains of many of these can be seen today, and some, like Portchester Castle just outside Portsmouth, were incorporated into more substantial defences in later centuries. There also exists substantial evidence of Roman domestic buildings, such as Fishbourne Palace, in coastal areas and further inland.

The magnificence of cathedrals such as Canterbury and Winchester bear witness to their role as important bases of the medieval church, then nearly as powerful as the state. Many Kent and Sussex ports grew prosperous on trade with the Continent – as did the hundreds of smugglers who operated from them. From Tudor times on, monarchs, noblemen and courtiers acquired estates and built manor houses in the countryside between London and the coast, appreciating the area's moderate climate and proximity to the capital. Many of these survive and are popular attractions for visitors. Today the southeast corner of England is its most prosperous and populous region. Parts of Surrey and Kent, up to 20 miles (32 km) from the capital, are known as the Stockbroker Belt: the area has many large, luxurious villas belonging to wealthy people prominent in business and the professions, attracted by the same virtues that appealed to the Tudor gentry.

The fertile area of Kent has long been known as the Garden of England, and despite the incursion of bricks and mortar, it is still a leading area for growing fruit *(see pp160–1)*, being in a prime position for the metropolitan market nearby.

Aerial view of the medieval and moated Leeds Castle

◁ **A lush covering of bluebells in the deciduous woodlands of Kent**

Exploring the Downs and Channel Coast

The North and South Downs, separated by the lower-lying Weald are ideal walking country as well as being the site of many stately homes. From Tudor times, wealthy, London-based merchants and courtiers built their country residences in Kent, a day's ride from the capital, and many are open to the public. On the coast are the remains of sturdy

View of Brighton Pier from the promenade

castles put up to deter invaders from across the Channel. Today, though, the seashore is largely devoted to pleasure. Some of Britain's earliest beach resorts were developed along this coast, and sea bathing is said to have been invented in Brighton.

Oast houses at Chiddingstone near Royal Tunbridge Wells

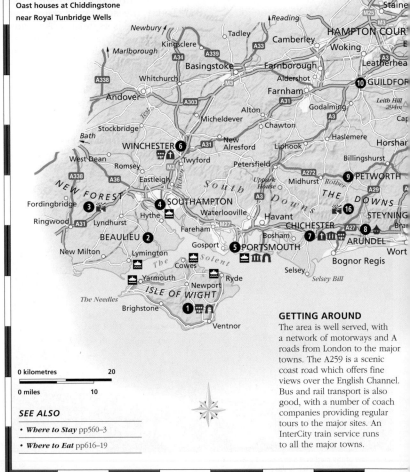

GETTING AROUND

The area is well served, with a network of motorways and A roads from London to the major towns. The A259 is a scenic coast road which offers fine views over the English Channel. Bus and rail transport is also good, with a number of coach companies providing regular tours to the major sites. An InterCity train service runs to all the major towns.

0 kilometres   20

0 miles   10

SEE ALSO

For additional map symbols see back flap

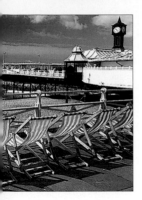

SIGHTS AT A GLANCE

- Arundel 8
- Beaulieu 2
- Bodiam Castle 18
- *Brighton pp174–9* 13
- *Canterbury pp186–7* 23
- Chichester 7
- Dover 21
- The Downs 16
- Eastbourne 15
- Guildford 10
- *Hampton Court p173* 11
- Hastings 17
- Hever Castle 27
- Isle of Wight 1
- Knole 26
- Leeds Castle 24
- Lewes 14
- Margate 22
- Rochester 25
- New Forest 3
- Petworth House 9
- Portsmouth 5
- Romney Marsh 20
- Royal Tunbridge Wells 28
- *Rye pp184–5* 19
- Southampton 4
- Steyning 12
- *Winchester pp170–71* 6

KEY

- Motorway
- Major road
- Secondary road
- Minor road
- Scenic route
- Main railway
- Minor railway
- Summit

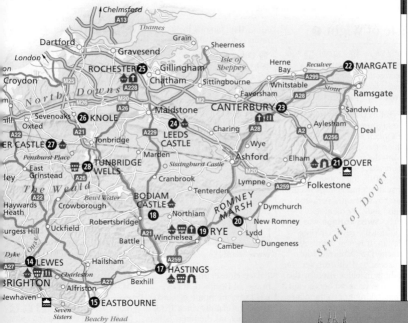

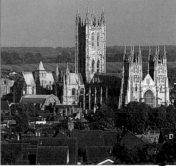

Canterbury Cathedral's spire, dominating the skyline

The Victorian Osborne House, Isle of Wight

Isle of Wight ❶

Isle of Wight. 🏛 *138,000.* 🚢 *from
Lymington, Southampton,
Portsmouth.* 🛈 *Westridge Centre,
Brading Road, Ryde (01983 813818).*
www.islandbreaks.co.uk

A visit to **Osborne House**,
the favoured seaside retreat
of Queen Victoria and Prince
Albert *(see p160)*, is alone
worth the ferry ride from the
mainland. Furnished much as
they left it, the house
provides a marvellous insight
into royal life and is dotted
with family mementoes.

The **Swiss Cottage** was
built for the royal children to
play in. It is now a museum
attached to Osborne House.
Adjacent to it you can see the
bathing machine used by the
queen to preserve her modesty
while taking her to the edge
of the sea *(see p369)*.

The other main sight on the
island is **Carisbrooke Castle**,
built in the 11th century. A
walk on its outer wall and the
climb to the top of its keep
provides spectacular views. It
was here that Charles I *(see
pp52–3)* was held prisoner in
1647; an attempt to escape
was foiled when he got stuck
between the bars of a window.

The island is a base for
ocean sailing, especially during
Cowes Week *(see p67)*. The
scenic highlight is the
Needles – three towers of
rock jutting out of the sea at
the island's western end. This
is only a short walk from

Alum Bay, famous for its
multi-coloured cliffs and sand.

🚪 **Osborne House**
(EH) East Cowes. **Tel** 01983 200022.
⭕ *Apr–Oct: daily; Nov–Mar: open
Wed–Sun for* 🚍 *only, phone for
details.* 🏛 🅿️ *limited.* 🍴 🛒 *(also
🛒 in Swiss Cottage Apr–Oct only)* 📷

🏰 **Carisbrooke Castle**
Newport. **Tel** 01983 522107.
⭕ *daily.* ⬤ *1 Jan, 24–26 Dec.* 🅿️
🛒 *limited.* 🎫 🛒 📷

Beaulieu ❷

Brockenhurst, Hampshire. **Tel** 01590
612345. 🚆 *Brockenhurst then taxi.*
⭕ *daily.* ⬤ *25 Dec.* 📷 🅿️ 🛒
🎫 *by arrangement.* 🛒
www.beaulieu.co.uk

Palace House, once the gatehouse of Beaulieu Abbey,
has been the home of Lord
Montagu's family since 1538. It
now contains the finest collection of vintage cars in the
country at the **National Motor
Museum**, along with boats
used in the James Bond films.

There is also an exhibition
of monastic life in the ruined

ancient **abbey**, founded in
1204 by King John *(see p48)*
for Cistercian monks. The
original refectory now serves
as the parish church.

Environs: Just south is the
maritime museum at **Buckler's
Hard**, telling the story of shipbuilding in the 18th century.
The yard employed 4,000
men at its peak but declined
when steel began to be used.

🏛 **Buckler's Hard**
Beaulieu. **Tel** 01590 614645.
⭕ *daily.* ⬤ *25 Dec.* 🅿️ 🛒 *limited.*

New Forest ❸

Hampshire. 🚆 *Brockenhurst.*
🚌 *Lymington then bus.* 🛈 *main car
park, Lyndhurst (023 8028 2269).*
www.thenewforest.co.uk

This unique expanse of heath
and woodland is, at 145 sq
miles (375 sq km), the largest
area of unenclosed land in
southern Britain.

William the Conqueror's
"new" forest, despite its name,
is one of the few primeval oak
woods in England. It was the
popular hunting ground of
Norman kings, and in 1100
William II was fatally wounded
here in a hunting accident.

Today it is enjoyed by up to
seven million visitors a year
who share it with the New Forest ponies, unique to the area,
and over 1,500 fallow deer.

Southampton ❹

Hampshire. 🏛 *220,000.* ✈️ 🚆 🚢
🚍 🛈 *9 Civic Centre Road (023 8083
3333).* **www**.southampton.gov.uk

For centuries this has been
a flourishing port. The
Mayflower sailed from here
to America in 1620 with the

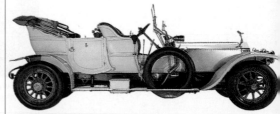

A 1909 Rolls-Royce Silver Ghost at Beaulieu's National Motor Museum

Pilgrim Fathers, as did the *Titanic* on its maiden and ultimately tragic voyage in 1912.

The **Maritime Museum** has exhibits about both these ships, along with displays on the huge romantic liners that sailed from the port in the first half of the 20th century.

There is a walk around the remains of the medieval city wall. At the head of the High Street stands the old city gate, **Bargate**, the most elaborate gate to survive in England. It still has its 13th-century drum towers and is decorated with intricate, 17th-century armorial carvings. **God's**

The luxurious liner the *Titanic*, which sank in 1912

House Tower Museum of Archaeology consists of a 13th-century gatehouse and 15th-century gallery and tower, and includes displays from the Roman to medieval periods.

🏛 **Maritime Museum**
Town Quay Rd. **Tel** 023 8022 3941.
◯ *Tue–Sun (closed 1–2pm).* ● *1 Jan, 25, 26 Dec, public hols.* ⬛ *limited.* ◻

🏛 **God's House Tower Museum**
Winkle St. **Tel** 023 8063 5904.
◯ *Tue–Sat (closed noon–1pm), 2–5pm Sun.* ⬛ *foyer & shop only.* ◻

Portsmouth ❺

Hampshire. 🏘 190,000. 🚉 🚌 ℹ
The Hard (023 9282 6722). ⬛ Thu–Sat. www.visitportsmouth.co.uk

Once a vital naval port, Portsmouth is today a quiet town but fascinating for those interested in English naval history. Under the banner of **Portsmouth Historic Dockyard**, the city's historic dockyard is the hub of Portsmouth's most important sights. Among these is the hull of the **Mary Rose**, the favourite of Henry VIII (*see p50*), which capsized on its maiden voyage as it left to fight the French in 1545. It was recovered from the sea bed in 1982 along with thousands of 16th-century objects now on display nearby, giving an absorbing insight into life at sea in Tudor times.

Alongside it is **HMS *Victory***, the English flagship on which Admiral Nelson was killed at Trafalgar (*see p31*) and now restored to its former glory. You can also visit the **Royal Naval Museum** which deals with naval history from the 16th century to the Falklands War, the 19th-century **HMS Warrior**, and galleries telling the story of Nelson.

Portsmouth's other military memorial is the **D-Day Museum**. This is centred on the *Overlord Embroidery*, a masterpiece of needlework commissioned in 1968 from the Royal School of Needlework, depicting the World War II Allied landing in Normandy in 1944.

The figurehead on the bow of HMS *Victory* at Portsmouth

Portchester Castle, on the north edge of the harbour, was fortified in the third century and is the best example of Roman sea defences in northern Europe. The Normans later used the Roman walls to enclose a castle – only the keep survives – and a church. Henry V used the castle as a garrison before the Battle of Agincourt (*see p49*). In the 18th–19th centuries it was a prisoner-of-war camp.

Among less warlike attractions is the **Charles Dickens Museum** (*see p189*), the house where the author was born in 1812.

The striking structure that is **Spinnaker Tower** adds an innovative touch to Portsmouth's skyline. Rising to 170 m (558 ft), the views over the harbour and beyond are quite magnificent.

🏛 **Portsmouth Historic Dockyard**
The Hard. **Tel** 023 9286 1512.
◯ *daily.* ● *25 Dec.* 📷 ⬛ 🍴 ◻

🏛 **D-Day Museum**
Clarence Esplanade. **Tel** 023 9282 7261. ◯ *daily.* ● *24–26 Dec.*
📷 ⬛ 🍴 ◻

♜ **Portchester Castle**
Castle St, Porchester. **Tel** 023 9237 8291. ◯ *daily.* ● *24–26 Dec, 1 Jan.* 📷 🎫 *by arrangement.*

🏛 **Charles Dickens Museum**
393 Old Commercial Rd. **Tel** 023 9282 7261. ◯ *Apr–Oct: daily, 7 Feb (Dickens's birthday).* 📷 ◻

❈ **Spinnaker Tower**
Gunwharf Quays. **Tel** 023 9285 7520. ◯ *Tue–Sun.* 📷 ◻

A wild pony and her foal roaming freely in the New Forest

Winchester **6**

Hampshire. 🏛 *36,000.* 🚉 🚌
🛈 *Guildhall, High St (01962
840500).* 🛒 *Wed–Sat.*
www.visitwinchester.co.uk

Capital of the ancient kingdom of Wessex, the city of
Winchester was also the headquarters of the Anglo-Saxon
kings until the Norman
Conquest *(see p47).*

William the Conqueror built
one of his first English castles
here. The only surviving part
of the castle is the **Great Hall**,
erected in 1235 to replace the
original. It is now home
to the legendary Round
Table. The story
behind the table is a
mix of history and
myth. King Arthur *(see
p285)* had it shaped so
no knight could claim
precedence. It was said
to have been built by the
wizard Merlin but was
actually made in the
13th century.

The **Westgate Museum** is
one of the two surviving 12th-
century gatehouses in the city
wall. The room (once a prison)
above the gate has a 16th-
century painted ceiling. It was
moved here from Winchester
College, England's oldest fee-
paying, or "public" school.
Winchester has been an

**The 13th-century Round Table,
Great Hall, Winchester**

ecclesiastical centre for many
centuries. **Wolvesey Castle**
(built around 1110) was the
home of the **cathedral's**
bishops after the Conquest.
The **Hospital of St Cross** is an
almshouse built in 1446.

Author Izaac Walton *(1593–1683) is
depicted in the stained glass Anglers'
Window made in 1914.*

STUDY TO BE QUIET

The Lady Chapel was
rebuilt by Elizabeth of York
(c.1500) after her son was
baptized in the cathedral.

**These magnificent
choir-stalls** (c.1308)
are England's
oldest.

The Perpendicular nave is the
highlight of the building.

**Jane Austen's
grave**

**Main
entrance**

**Visitors'
centre**

WINCHESTER
CATHEDRAL

The Close. **Tel** *01962 857200.*
⬜ *daily.* 📷 ♿ 🍴 🚻
www.winchester-cathedral.org.uk
The first church was built here in
648 but the present building was begun
in 1097. Originally a Benedictine monastery,
much of the Norman architecture remains despite
continual modifications until the early 16th century.

The
century
Tournai marble

Weary strangers may claim the "Wayfarer's Dole" a horn (cup) of ale and bread, given out since medieval times.

🏰 Great Hall & Visitor Centre
Castle Ave. **Tel** 01962 846476.
⭕ daily. ⚫ 25, 26 Dec. ♿

🏰 Westgate Museum
High St. **Tel** 01962 848269.
⭕ Feb, Mar: Tue–Sun; Apr–Oct: Mon–Sun. 📷

🏰 Hospital of St Cross
St Cross Rd. **Tel** 01962 851375.
⭕ Mon–Sat. ⚫ Good Fri, 25 Dec.
📷 ♿ www.stcrosshospital.co.uk

The Library
has over 4,000 books. This "B" from Psalm 1 is found in the Winchester Bible, an exquisite work of 12th-century illumination.

The Norman chapter house ceased to be used in 1580. Only the Norman arches survive.

Prior's Hall

The Close originally contained the domestic buildings for the monks of the Priory of St Swithun – the name before it became Winchester Cathedral. Most of the buildings, such as the refectory and cloisters, were destroyed during the Dissolution of the Monasteries *(see p50)*.

Chichester ⑦

West Sussex. 🏠 26,000. 🚊 🚌 ℹ️
29A South St (01243 775888). 🚫
Wed, Sat. **www**.visitsussex.org

This wonderfully preserved market town, with an elaborate early 16th-century market cross at its centre, is dominated by its **cathedral**, consecrated in 1108. The exterior is a lovely mix of greenish limestone and Caen stone and its graceful spire, said to be the only English cathedral spire visible from the sea, dominates the town. The cathedral still contains much of interest, including a unique detached bell tower dating from 1436.

There are two carved stone panels in the choir, dating from 1140. Modern works include paintings by Graham Sutherland (1903–80), and a stained-glass window by Marc Chagall (1887–1985).

Environs: Just west at Bosham is the Saxon **Holy Trinity Church**, thought to have been used by King Canute *(see p46)*. Myth has it that this was where Canute failed to stop the incoming tide and so proved to his courtiers that his powers had limits. The church appears in the *Bayeux Tapestry*, held in France, because Harold heard mass here in 1064 before he was shipwrecked off Normandy and then rescued by William the Conqueror *(see p47)*.

The refurbished **Fishbourne Roman Palace** *(see p45)*, between Bosham and Chichester, is the largest Roman villa in Britain. It covers 3 ha (7 acres) and was discovered in 1960 by a workman.

Chagall's stained glass window (1978), Chichester Cathedral

Constructed from AD 75, it was destroyed by fire in 285. The north wing has some of the finest mosaics in Britain, including one of Cupid.

To the north is the 18th-century **Goodwood House**. Its magnificent art collection features works by Canaletto (1697–1768) and Stubbs (1724–1806). This impressive house, home to the Earl of March, has a racecourse on the Downs.

🕍 Chichester Cathedral
West St. **Tel** 01243 782595.
⭕ daily. ⚫ during services. ♿ 📷

🏛 Fishbourne Roman Palace
Fishbourne. **Tel** 01243 785859. ⭕
Feb–mid-Dec: daily; mid-Dec–Jan (café closed): Sat, Sun. 📷 ♿ 📷
🚫 📷 www.sussexpast.co.uk

🏰 Goodwood House
Goodwood. **Tel** 01243 755048.
📷 01243 755040. ⭕ Apr–Sep: Sun–Mon (pm); Aug: Sun–Thu (pm).
⚫ special events. 📷 ♿ 🚫 📷

WILLIAM WALKER

At the beginning of the 20th century, the cathedral's east end seemed certain to collapse unless its foundations were underpinned. But because the water table lies only just below the surface, the work had to be done under water. From 1906 to 1911, Walker, a deep-sea diver, worked six hours a day laying sacks of cement beneath the unsteady walls, until the building was safe.

William Walker in his diving suit

The dominating position of Arundel Castle, West Sussex

Arundel Castle ⑧

Arundel, West Sussex. **Tel** 01903
882173. 🚉 Arundel. ◯ Apr–Oct:
Sun–Fri. ◯ Good Fri. 🎦 ✔ by
arrangement. 🍴 🖴 🏛
www.arundelcastle.org

Dominating the small riverside town below, this vast,
grey hill-top castle, surrounded
by castellated walls, was first
built by the Normans.

During the 16th century it
was acquired by the powerful
Dukes of Norfolk, the country's
senior Roman Catholic family,
whose descendants still live
here. They rebuilt it after the
original was virtually destroyed
by Parliamentarians in 1643
(see p52), and restored it
again in the 19th century.

In the castle grounds is the
parish church of **St Nicholas**.
The small Catholic Fitzalan
chapel (c.1380) was built into
its east end by the castle's
first owners, the Fitzalans,
and can only be entered from
the grounds.

Petworth House ⑨

(NT) Petworth, West Sussex.
Tel 01798 342207. 🚉 Pulborough
then bus. **House** ◯ Mar–Nov:
Sat–Wed. **Park** ◯ daily. 🎦 ♿
limited. 🍴 🏛
www.nationaltrust.org.uk/petworth

This late 17th-century house
was immortalized in a series
of famous views by the
painter J M W Turner (see
p91). Some of his best
paintings are on display here
and are part of Petworth's

outstanding art collection
which also includes works by
Titian (1488–1576), Van Dyck
(1599–1641) and Gainsborough
(see p163). Also extremely
well represented is ancient
Roman and Greek sculpture,
such as the 4th-century BC
Leconfield Aphrodite, widely
thought to be by Praxiteles.

The Carved Room is decor-
ated with intricately carved
wood panels of birds, flowers
and musical instruments, by
Grinling Gibbons (1648–1721).

The large deer park includes
some of the earliest work of
Capability Brown (see p26).

The Restoration clock on the
Tudor Guildhall, Guildford

Guildford ⑩

Surrey. 🏛 63,000. 🚉 🚌 🚊 🛈 14
Tunsgate (01483 444333). 🏪 Fri, Sat.
www.visitguildford.com

The county town of Surrey,
settled since Saxon times,
incorporates the remains of a
small refurbished Norman

castle. The attractive High
Street is lined with Tudor
buildings, such as the impressive **Guildhall**. But it is the
huge modern red-brick cathedral, completed in 1954, that
dominates the town's skyline.

Environs: Guildford stands on
the end of the North Downs,
a range of chalk hills which
are popular for walking (see
p37). The area also has two
famous beauty spots: **Leith
Hill** – the highest point in
southeast England – and **Box
Hill**. The view from the latter
is well worth the short, gentle
climb from West Humble.

Just to the south of the town
is the perfect red brickwork
of **Clandon Park**. This 18th-
century house has a sump-
tuous interior, especially the
Marble Hall – one of the
grandest English interiors of
the period. It has an intricate
Baroque ceiling, and the hall's
side lamps are supported by
black ivory forearms jutting
from the wall, which represent
the Park's West Indian servants.

Southwest is Chawton,
where **Jane Austen's House**
(see p162) is located. This
small red-brick house is where
she wrote most of her gentle,
witty comedies of middle-class
manners in Georgian England,
such as *Pride and Prejudice*.

🏛 **Clandon Park**
(NT) West Clandon, Surrey. **Tel** 01483
222482. ◯ Mar–Oct: Tue–Thu, Sun;
public hols. 🎦 ♿ limited. 🍴 🏛
🏛 **Jane Austen's House**
Alton, Hants. **Tel** 01420 83262. ◯
Dec–Feb: Sat & Sun; Mar–Nov: daily.
● 25 & 26 Dec. 🎦 ♿ limited. 🏛

Hampton Court ⑪

East Molesey, Surrey. 📞 0870-752 7777. 🚆 Hampton Court. ⭕ daily. ⬤ 24–26 Dec. 🈳 ♿ 🎥 🍴 🚻
www.hrp.org.uk

The powerful chief minister and Archbishop of York to Henry VIII *(see pp50–51)*, Cardinal Wolsey, leased a small manor house in 1514 and transformed it into a magnificent country residence. In 1528, to retain royal favour, Wolsey gave it to the king. After the royal takeover, Hampton Court was extended twice, first by Henry himself and in the 1690s by William and Mary, who used Christopher Wren *(see p114)* as the architect. From the outside the palace is a harmonious blend of Tudor and English Baroque; inside there is a striking contrast between Wren's Classical royal rooms,

Ceiling decoration, Hampton Court

which include the King's Apartments, and Tudor architecture, such as the Great Hall. Many of the state apartments are decorated with paintings and furnishings from the Royal Collection.

The Baroque gardens, with their radiating avenues of majestic limes, collections of rare plants and formal plant beds, have been painstakingly restored.

The Baroque maze *is one of the garden's most famous features; visitors often become lost in it.*

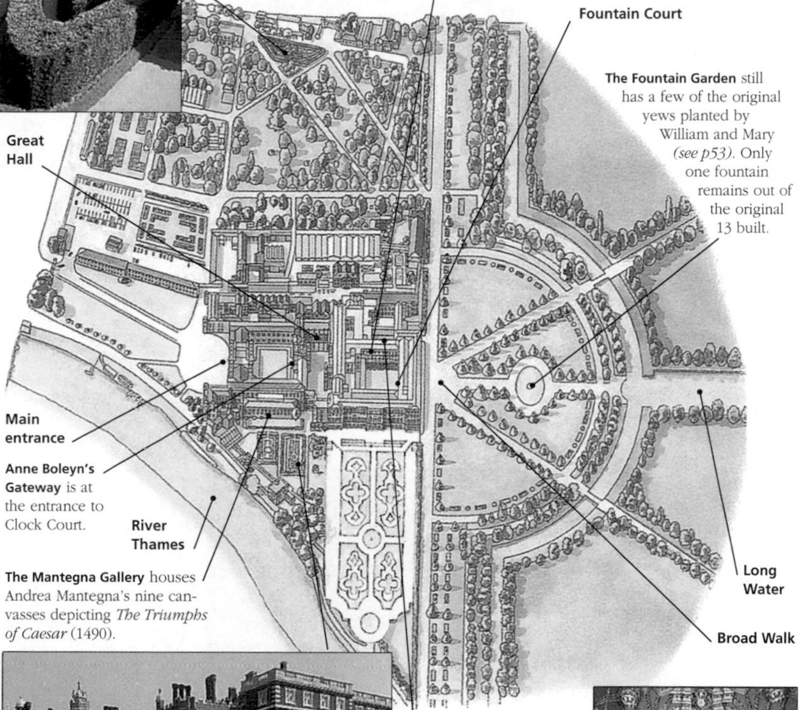

The Queen's Apartments, including the Presence Chamber and Bedchamber, are arranged around the the north and east sides of Fountain Court.

Fountain Court

The Fountain Garden still has a few of the original yews planted by William and Mary *(see p53)*. Only one fountain remains out of the original 13 built.

Great Hall

Main entrance

Anne Boleyn's Gateway is at the entrance to Clock Court.

River Thames

The Mantegna Gallery houses Andrea Mantegna's nine canvasses depicting *The Triumphs of Caesar* (1490).

Long Water

Broad Walk

The Pond Garden, *a sunken water garden, was part of Henry VIII's elaborate designs. The small pond in the middle contains a single-jet fountain.*

The Tudor Chapel Royal *was completed by Henry VIII. But the superb woodwork, including the massive reredos by Grinling Gibbons, all date from a major refurbishment by Queen Anne (c.1711).*

Steyning ⑫

West Sussex. 🏠 5,000 🚉 ℹ️ 9 The
Causeway, Horsham (01403 211661).

This lovely little town in the
lee of the Downs is packed
with timber-framed houses
from the Tudor period and
earlier, with some built of flint
and others in sandstone.

In Saxon times, Steyning was
an important port and shipbuilding centre on the River
Adur: King Ethelwulf, father
of King Alfred *(see p47)*, was
buried here in 858; his body
was later moved to Winchester.
The *Domesday Book (see p48)*
records that Steyning had 123
houses, making it one of the
largest towns in the south. The
12th-century church is spacious
and splendid, evidence of the
area's ancient prosperity: the
tower, of chequered stone and
flint, was added around 1600.

In the 14th century the river
silted up and changed course
away from the town, putting
an end to its days as a port.
Later it became an important
coaching stop on the south
coast road: the **Chequer Inn**
recalls this prosperous period,
with its unusual 18th-century
flint and stone façade.

Environs: The remains of a
Norman castle can be visited
at Bramber, east of Steyning.
This small, pretty village also
contains the timber-framed **St
Mary's House** (1470). It has
fine panelled rooms, including
the Elizabethan Painted Room,
and one of the oldest trees in
the country, a *Ginkgo biloba.*
Chanctonbury Ring and
Cissbury Ring, on the hills
west of Steyning, were Iron
Age forts and the latter has the
remains of a Neolithic flint
mine. Worthing is the resort
where Oscar Wilde (1854–
1900) wrote *The Importance
of Being Earnest.*

🏛 **St Mary's House**
Bramber. *Tel* 01903 816205. ◯
*Easter–Sep: Sun, Thu (pm), public
hols.* 🔲 🎨 🎥 🖥

Street-by-Street: Brighton ⑬

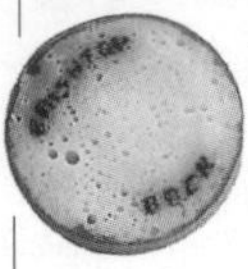

A stick of
Brighton rock

As the nearest south coast resort to London,
Brighton is perennially popular, but has
always been more refined than its boisterous
neighbours further east, such as Margate *(see
p183)* and Southend. The spirit of the Prince
Regent *(see p179)* lives on, not only in the
magnificence of his Royal Pavilion, but in
the town's reputation as a
venue for adulterous weekends in
discreet hotels. Brighton has
always attracted actors and
artists – Laurence Olivier
made his final home here.

Old Ship Hotel
*Built in 1559, it
was later bought by
Nicholas Tettersells,
with the money given
to him by Charles II as
a reward for taking him
to France during the
Civil War (see p52).*

★ **Brighton Pier**
*Built in 1899, this typical late-
Victorian pier now caters
for today's visitors
with amusement
arcades.*

KING'S ROAD

BLACK LION

GRAND JUNCTION ROAD

KEY
‒ ‒ ‒ Suggested route

STAR SIGHTS
★ Brighton Pier
★ Royal Pavilion

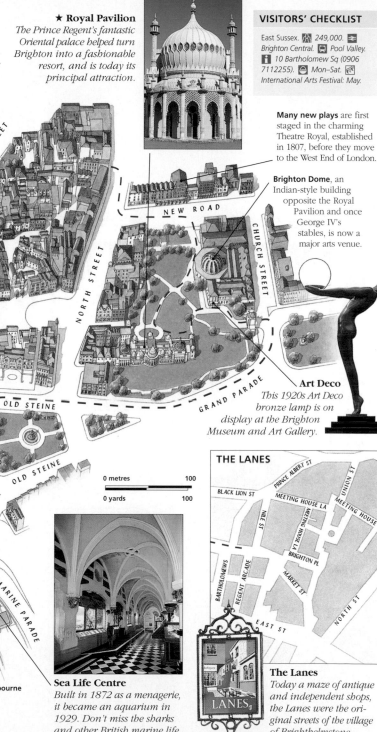

★ Royal Pavilion
The Prince Regent's fantastic Oriental palace helped turn Brighton into a fashionable resort, and is today its principal attraction.

VISITORS' CHECKLIST

East Sussex. 249,000.
Brighton Central. Pool Valley.
10 Bartholomew Sq (0906
7112255). Mon–Sat.
International Arts Festival: May.

Many new plays are first staged in the charming Theatre Royal, established in 1807, before they move to the West End of London.

Brighton Dome, an Indian-style building opposite the Royal Pavilion and once George IV's stables, is now a major arts venue.

Art Deco
This 1920s Art Deco bronze lamp is on display at the Brighton Museum and Art Gallery.

THE LANES

Sea Life Centre
Built in 1872 as a menagerie, it became an aquarium in 1929. Don't miss the sharks and other British marine life.

The Lanes
Today a maze of antique and independent shops, the Lanes were the original streets of the village of Brighthelmstone.

Eastbourne

Brighton: Royal Pavilion

As sea bathing became fashionable in the mid-18th century, Brighton was transformed into England's first seaside resort. Its gaiety soon appealed to the rakish Prince of Wales, who became George IV in 1820. When, in 1785, he secretly married Mrs Fitzherbert, it was here that they conducted their liaison. He moved to a farmhouse near the shore and had it enlarged by Henry Holland *(see p28)*. As his parties grew more lavish, George needed a suitably extravagant setting for them, and in 1815 he employed John Nash *(see p105)* to transform the house into a lavish Oriental palace. Completed in 1823, the exterior has remained largely unaltered. Queen Victoria sold the Pavilion to the town of Brighton in 1850.

Central Dome
Nash adopted what he called the Hindu Style, as in this delicate tracery on one of the imposing turban domes.

★ Banqueting Room
Fiery dragons feature in many of the interior schemes. This colourful one dominates the centre of the Banqueting Room's extraordinary ceiling, and has a huge crystal chandelier suspended from it.

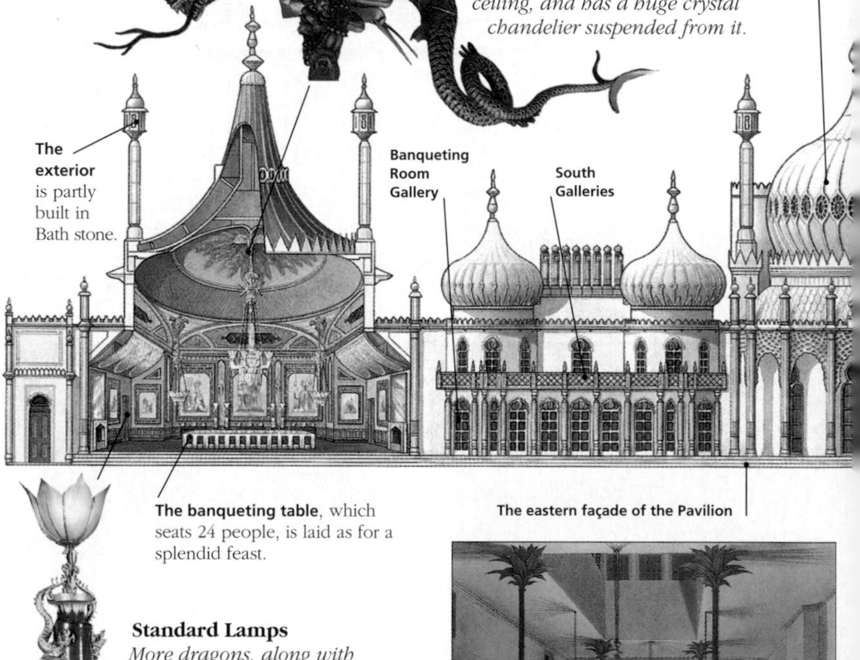

The exterior is partly built in Bath stone.

Banqueting Room Gallery

South Galleries

The banqueting table, which seats 24 people, is laid as for a splendid feast.

The eastern façade of the Pavilion

Standard Lamps
More dragons, along with dolphins and lotus flowers, figure on the Banqueting Room's eight original standard lamps, made of porcelain, ormolu and gilded wood.

STAR SIGHTS

★ Banqueting Room

★ Great Kitchen

★ Great Kitchen
The Prince's epic banquets required a kitchen of huge proportions. The vast ranges and long shelves of gleaming copper pans were used by famous chefs of the day.

◁ Front façade of George IV's extravagant Royal Pavilion, Brighton

Saloon
The gilded wall decorations were designed on Indian themes, but the Chinese wallpaper harks back to an earlier decorative scheme. The long couch mimics an Egyptian river boat.

VISITORS' CHECKLIST

Old Steine, Brighton. *Tel* 01273 290900. ○ Apr–Sep: 9:30am–5:45pm; Oct–Mar: 10am–5:15pm (last adm: 45 mins before closing); daily. ● 25, 26 Dec. limited.
www.royalpavilion.org.uk

Long Gallery
Mandarin figures, which can nod their heads, line the pink and blue walls of this 49 m (162 ft) gallery.

Queen Victoria's Bedroom
This reproduction four-poster is on display in the upper floor apartments that were used by Queen Victoria (see pp56–7).

The Music Room, with its crimson and gold murals, was where a 70-piece orchestra played to the Prince's guests.

The domes are made of cast iron.

Music Room Gallery

Yellow Bow Rooms

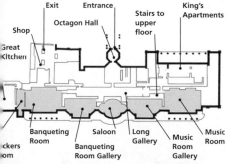

Exit · Entrance · Stairs to upper floor · King's Apartments

Shop · Octagon Hall

Great Kitchen

Banqueting Room · Saloon · Long Gallery · Music Room · Music Room Gallery

Banqueting Room Gallery

ckers om

PLAN OF THE ROYAL PAVILION
Both Holland and Nash made additions and changes to the original farmhouse. The upper floor contains bedrooms, such as the Yellow Bow Rooms, which George's brothers used. The shaded areas represent the artwork above.

PRINCE OF WALES AND MRS FITZHERBERT
The Prince of Wales was only 23 years old when he fell in love with Maria Fitzherbert, a 29-year-old Catholic widow, and secretly married her. They lived in the farmhouse together and were the toast of Brighton society until George's official marriage took place to Caroline of Brunswick in 1795. Mrs Fitzherbert moved into a small house nearby.

Upstairs interior of Anne of Cleves House, Lewes

Lewes ⑭

East Sussex. 🏘 16,000. 🚉 🚹 187
High St (01273 483448).
www.lewes.gov.uk

The ancient county town of
Sussex was a vital strategic site
for the Saxons, because of its
high vantage point looking
out over the coastline. William
the Conqueror built a wooden
castle here in 1067 but this
was soon replaced by a large
stone structure whose remains
can be visited today.

In 1264 it was the site of a
critical battle in which Simon
de Montfort and his barons
defeated Henry III, enabling
them to establish the first
English Parliament.

The Tudor **Anne of Cleves
House** is a museum of local
history, although Anne of
Cleves, Henry VIII's fourth
wife, never actually lived here.

On Guy Fawkes Night *(see
p64)* lighted tar barrels are
rolled to the river and effigies
of the pope are burned instead
of the customary Guy Fawkes.
This commemorates the town's
17 Protestant martyrs burnt at
the stake by Mary I *(see p51)*.

Environs: Nearby are the 16th-
century **Glynde Place**, a fine
courtyard house, and the charming **Charleston**, home to the
Bloomsbury Group *(see p163)*.

🏛 **Anne of Cleves House**
Lewes. **Tel** 01273 474610. ☐ Mar–
Oct: daily; Nov–Feb: Tue–Sat. 🎟 🚹

🏠 **Glynde Place**
Lewes. 🗓 01273 858224. ☐ May–
Aug: Wed, Sun & public hols. 🎟 🚻
🚹 www.glyndeplace.com

🏠 **Charleston**
Lewes. **Tel** 01323 811265. ☐ Apr–
Oct: Wed–Sun, Bank Hol Mon. 🎟
🚻 🚹 🚹 www.charleston.org.uk

Eastbourne ⑮

East Sussex. 🏘 93,000. 🚉 🚹 🚹
Cornfield Rd (01323 411400). 🚐
Tue, Sat. **www**.eastbourne.org

This Victorian seaside resort
is a popular place for
retirement, as well as a first-
rate centre for touring the
Downs. The South Downs
Way *(see p37)* begins at
Beachy Head, the spectacular
163 m (536 ft) chalk cliff just
on the outskirts of the town.
From here it is a bracing walk
to the cliff top at Birling Gap,
with views to the **Seven
Sisters**, the chalk hills that end
abruptly as they meet the sea.

Environs: To the west of Eastbourne is **Seven Sisters
Country Park**, a 285 ha (700
acre) area of chalk cliffs and
Downland marsh. The **Park
Visitor's Centre** contains
information on the local
area, history and geology.

Just north is the pretty
village of **Alfriston**, with an
ancient market cross and a
15th-century inn, **The Star**, in
its quaint main street. Near
the church is the 14th-century
Clergy House that, in 1896,
became the first National
Trust property *(see p29)*. To
the east is the huge prehistoric
chalk carving, the **Long Man
of Wilmington** *(see p221)*.

🚹 **Park Visitor's Centre**
Exceat, Seaford. **Tel** 01323 870280.
☐ Apr–Oct: daily; Nov–Mar: Sat,
Sun. 🚗 25 Dec. 🚹 🚻 🚻

🏠 **Clergy House**
(NT) Alfriston. **Tel** 01323 870001.
☐ Mar: Sat & Sun; Apr–Dec:
Sat–Mon, Wed & Thu. 🚹 🎟

The lighthouse (1902) at the foot of Beachy Head, Eastbourne

The meandering River Cuckmere flowing through the South Downs to the beach at Cuckmere Haven

The Downs ⑯

East Sussex. 🚇 🚉 Eastbourne.
ℹ Cornfield Rd, Eastbourne (0906 7112212). www.visiteastbourne.com

The North and South Downs are parallel chalk ridges that run from east to west all the way across Kent, Sussex and Surrey, separated by the lower-lying and fertile Kent and Sussex Weald.

The smooth Downland hills are covered with springy turf, kept short by grazing sheep, making an ideal surface for walkers. The hill above the precipitous **Devil's Dyke**, just north of Brighton, offers spectacular views for miles across the Downs. The legend is that the Devil cut the gorge to let in the sea and flood the countryside, but was foiled by divine intervention. The River Cuckmere runs through one of the most picturesque parts of the South Downs.

Located at the highest point of the Downs is **Uppark House**. This neat square building has been meticulously restored to its mid-18th-century appearance after a fire in 1989.

🏠 **Uppark House**
(NT) Petersfield, West Sussex.
Tel 01730 825857. ☐ Apr–Oct: Sun–Thu (pm). 🖼 ⚙ 🍴 🚻

Hastings ⑰

East Sussex. 🔼 83,000. 🚉 🚉
ℹ Queens Square , Priory Meadow (0845 2741001). www.visithastings.com

This fascinating seaside town was one of the first Cinque Ports (see p182) and is still a thriving fishing port. The town is characterized by the unique tall wooden "net shops" on the beach, where for hundreds of years fishermen have stored their nets. In the 19th century, the area to the west of the Old Town was built up as a seaside resort, which left the narrow, characterful streets of the old

The wooden net shops, on Hastings' shingle beach

fishermen's quarter intact. There are two cliff railways and smugglers' caves displaying where contraband used to be stored (see p280).

Environs: Seven miles (11 km) from Hastings is Battle. The centre square of this small town is dominated by the gatehouse of **Battle Abbey**. William the Conqueror built this on the site of his great victory, reputedly placing the high altar where Harold fell, But the abbey was destroyed in the Dissolution (see p50). There is an evocative walk around the actual battlefield.

🏛 **Battle Abbey (EH)**
High St, Battle. **Tel** 01424 773792.
☐ daily: Easter–Sep: 10am–6pm; Oct–Easter: 10am–4pm.
☐ 1 Jan, 24–26 Dec. 🖼 ⚙ 🚻

BATTLE OF HASTINGS

In 1066, William the Conqueror's (see p47) invading army from Normandy landed on the south coast, aiming to take Winchester and London. Hearing that King Harold and his army were camped just inland from Hastings, William confronted them. He won the battle after Harold was mortally wounded by an arrow in his eye. This last successful invasion of England is depicted on the *Bayeux Tapestry* in Normandy, France.

King Harold's death,
Bayeux Tapestry

The fairy-tale 14th-century Bodiam Castle surrounded by its moat

Bodiam Castle ⑱

(NT) Nr Robertsbridge, East Sussex.
Tel 01580 830436. ⮀ Robertsbridge then taxi. ◯ mid-Feb–Oct:
daily; Nov– mid-Feb: Sat–Sun. ●
24–26 Dec. ▨ & limited. ▯ ▯

Surrounded by its wide,
glistening moat, this late
14th-century castle is one of
the most romantic in England.
It was previously thought to
have been built as a defence
against French invasion, but is
now believed to have been
intended as a home for a
Sussex knight. The castle saw
action during the Civil War
(see p52), when it was
damaged in an assault by
Parliamentary soldiers. They
removed the roof to reduce
its use as a base for Charles
I's troops.

It has been uninhabited since,
but its grey stone has proved
indestructible. With the
exception of the roof, it was
restored in 1919 by Lord Curzon who gave it to the nation.

Environs: To the east is **Great
Dixter**, a 15th-century manor
house restored by Sir Edwin
Lutyens in 1910. The late
Christopher Lloyd created a
magnificent garden with an
Edwardian blend of terraces
and borders.

🏠 **Great Dixter**
Northiam, Rye. **Tel** 01797 252878.
◯ Apr–Oct: 2–5:30pm Tue–Sun &
public hols. ▨ ▯
www.greatdixter.co.uk

Rye ⑲

See pp184–5.

Romney Marsh ⑳

Kent. ⮀ Ashford. ◉ Ashford,
Hythe. ℹ Magpies Church Approach,
New Romney (01797 364044).

Until Roman times Romney
Marsh and its southern
neighbour Walland Marsh
were entirely covered by the
sea at high tide. The Romans
drained the Romney section,
and Walland Marsh was
gradually reclaimed during
the Middle Ages. Together they
formed a large area of fertile
land, particularly suitable for
the bulky Romney Marsh
sheep bred for the quality
and quantity of their wool.
   Dungeness, a desolate and
lonely spot at the southeastern
tip of the area, is dominated
by a lighthouse and two
nuclear power stations that

COASTAL DEFENCE AND
THE CINQUE PORTS

Before the Norman Conquest (see pp46–7),
national government was weak and, with
threats from Europe, it was important for
Saxon kings to keep on good terms with
the Channel ports. So, in return for keeping
the royal fleet supplied with ships and
men, five ports – Hastings, Romney, Hythe,
Sandwich and Dover – were granted the
right to levy taxes; others were added
later. "Cinque" came from the old French
word for five. The privileges were revoked
during the 17th century. In 1803, in
response to the growing threat from France,
74 fixed defences were built along the coast.
Only 24 of these Martello towers still exist.

The cliff-top position
of Dover Castle

A Martello tower,
built as part of the
Channel's defences

break up the skyline. It is also the southern terminus of the popular **Romney, Hythe and Dymchurch Light Railway** which was opened in 1927. During the summer this takes passengers 14 miles (23 km) up the coast to Hythe on trains a third the conventional size.

The northern edge of the marsh is crossed by the Royal Military Canal, built to serve both as a defence and supply line in 1804, when it was feared Napoleon was planning an invasion (*see p55*).

Dover ㉑

Kent. 🏛 *30,000.* 🚋 🚌 🚢 🛈 *Old Town Jail, Biggin St (01304 205108).* 🏪 *Sat.* **www**.whitecliffscountry.org.uk

Its proximity to the European mainland makes Dover, with its neighbour Folkestone (now the terminal for the Channel Tunnel, *see p680*), the leading port for cross-Channel travel. Its famous white cliffs exert a strong pull on returning travellers.

Dover's strategic position and large natural harbour mean the town has always had an important role to play in the nation's defences.

Built on the original site of an ancient Saxon fortification, **Dover Castle**, superbly positioned on top of the high cliffs, has helped defend the town from 1198, when Henry II first built the keep, right up to World War II, when it was used as the command post for the Dunkirk evacuation. Exhibits in the castle and in the labyrinth of tunnels beneath made by prisoners in the Napoleonic Wars (*see p55*) cover all these periods.

Environs: One of the most significant sites in England's early history is the ruin of **Richborough Roman Fort**. Now a large grassy site two miles (3 km) inland, this was where, in AD 43, Claudius's Roman invaders (*see p44*) made their first landing. For hundreds of years afterwards, Rutupiae, as it was known, was one of the most important ports of entry and military bases in the country.

⚓ **Dover Castle**
Castle Hill. *Tel 01304 211067.* ⭕ *Feb–Oct: daily; Nov–Jan: Thu–Mon.* ⬛ *1 Jan, 24–26 Dec.* 📷 🖥 🏠

⋔ **Richborough Roman Fort**
Richborough. *Tel 01304 612013.* ⭕ *Apr–Sep: daily.* 📷 ♿ 🏠

Margate ㉒

Kent. 🏛 *40,000.* 🚋 🚌 🛈 *12–13 The Parade (0870 2646111).* **www**.tourism.thanet.gov.uk

A boisterous seaside resort on the Isle of Thanet, Margate has long been a popular destination. Nowadays **The Turner Centre** (opening 2007) is the big draw, both architecturally and for its varied contemporary exhibitons.

Environs: Just south is a 19th-century gentleman's residence, **Quex House**, which has two unusual towers in its grounds. The adjoining museum has a fine collection of African and Oriental art, as well as unique dioramas of tropical wildlife. To the west is a Saxon church, built within the remains of the

Visitors relaxing on Margate's popular sandy beach

bleak Roman coastal fort of **Reculver**. Dramatic twin towers, known as the Two Sisters, were added to the church in the 12th century. The church now stands at the centre of a very pleasant, if rather windy, 37 ha (91 acre) camp site.

🏛 **The Turner Centre**
The Parade. *Tel 01843 294208.* ⭕ *from 2007, phone for details.* 📷 🖥 🏠

🏰 **Quex House**
Birchington. *Tel 01843 842168.* ⭕ *Apr–Oct: Tue–Thu, Sun & public hols (Museum only: Nov, Mar: Sun).* 📷 ♿ 📷 *for groups.* 🍴 🏠

⋔ **Reculver Fort**
Reculver. *Tel 01227 361911 (Herne Bay Tourist Information).* ⭕ *daily.*

A drainage dyke running through the fertile plains of Romney Marsh

Street-by-Street: Rye ⑲

The ancient and charming fortified town was added to the original Cinque ports *(see p182)* in the 12th–13th century. A huge storm in 1287 diverted the River Rother so that it met the sea at Rye, and for more than 300 years it was one of the most important Channel ports. However, in the 16th century the harbour began to silt up and the town is now 2 miles (3 km) inland. Rye was frequently attacked by the French, culminating in 1377 when it was burnt to the ground.

The Mermaid Inn sign

★ Mermaid Street
This delightful cobbled street, its huddled houses jutting out at unlikely angles, has hardly altered since it was rebuilt in the 14th century.

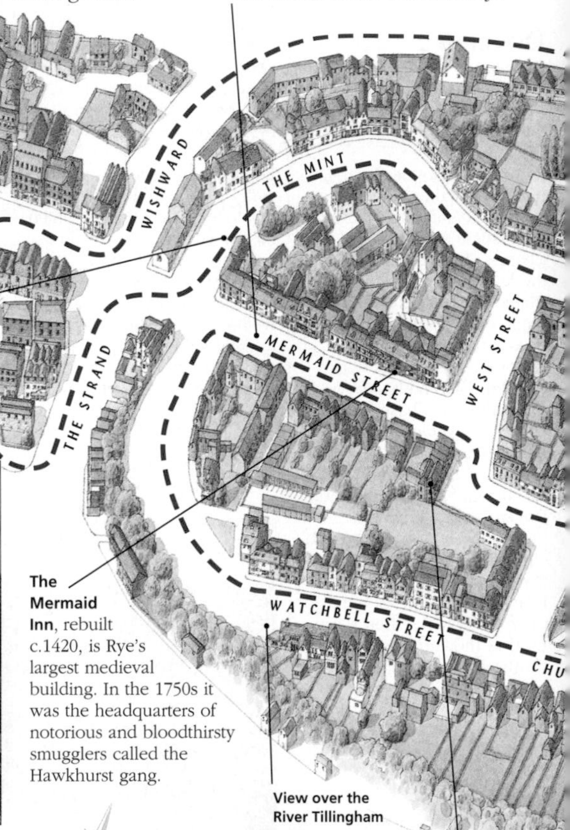

The Mint
Site of 12th-century Mint in the time of King Stephen.

The Mermaid Inn, rebuilt c.1420, is Rye's largest medieval building. In the 1750s it was the headquarters of notorious and bloodthirsty smugglers called the Hawkhurst gang.

View over the River Tillingham

Strand Quay
The brick and timber warehouses survive from the prosperous days when Rye was a thriving port.

STAR SIGHTS

★ Mermaid Street

★ Ypres Tower

Lamb House
This fine Georgian house was built in 1722. George I stayed here when stranded in a storm, and author Henry James (1843–1916) lived here.

St Mary's Church
The turret clock (1561) is claimed to be the oldest working clock in the country.

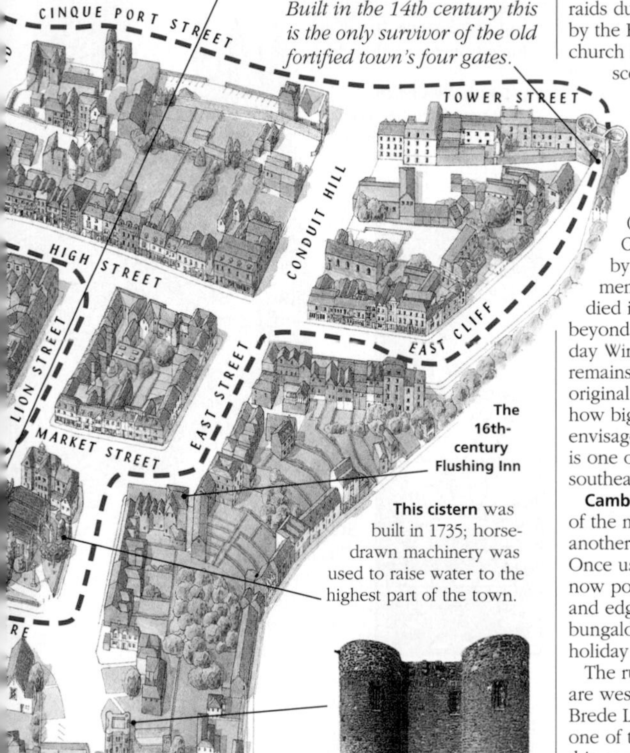

↑ Hastings and railway station

VISITORS' CHECKLIST

East Sussex. 🚶 4,500. 🚉 Station Approach. 🚌 Station Approach. 🛈 Strand Quay (01797 226696). 🏪 Wed, Thu. 🎭 Medieval Weekend: Jul or Aug; Rye Festival: Sep. **www**.visitrye.co.uk

Land Gate
Built in the 14th century this is the only survivor of the old fortified town's four gates.

CINQUE PORT STREET

TOWER STREET

CONDUIT HILL

HIGH STREET

LION STREET

EAST STREET

MARKET STREET

EAST CLIFF

RE

The 16th-century **Flushing Inn**

This cistern was built in 1735; horse-drawn machinery was used to raise water to the highest part of the town.

Gun Garden, Ypres Tower

KEY

\- - - Suggested route

| 0 metres | 50 |
| 0 yards | 50 |

★ Ypres Tower
Built as a castle in 1250, it was turned into a house in 1430. It is now used as the museum.

Environs: Just 2 miles (3 km) to the south of Rye is the small town of **Winchelsea**. At the behest of Edward I, it was moved to its present position in 1288, when most of the old town on lower land to the southeast, was drowned by the same storm that diverted the River Rother in 1287.

Winchelsea is probably Britain's first coherently planned medieval town. Although not all of it was built as originally planned, its rectangular grid survives today, as does the **Church of St Thomas Becket** (begun c.1300) at its centre. Several raids during the 14th century by the French damaged the church and burned down scores of houses. The church has three tombs, and there are also two well-preserved medieval tombs in the chantry. The three windows (1928–33) in the Lady Chapel were designed by Douglas Strachan as a memorial to those who died in World War I. Just beyond the edges of present-day Winchelsea are the remains of three of the original gates – showing just how big a town was first envisaged. The beach below is one of the finest on the southeast coast.

Camber Sands, to the east of the mouth of the Rother, is another excellent beach. Once used by fishermen it is now popular with swimmers and edged with seaside bungalows and a bustling holiday camp.

The ruins of **Camber Castle** are west of the sands, near Brede Lock, Rye. This was one of the forts built along this coast by Henry VIII when he feared an attack by the French. When the castle was built it was on the edge of the sea but it was abandoned in 1642 when it became stranded inland as the river silted up.

🏰 **Camber Castle**
(EH) Camber, Rye. **Tel** 01797 223862. ☐ Jul–Sep: Sat, Sun pm for 🅿 only.

**Jesus on Christ Church Gate,
Canterbury Cathedral**

Canterbury ㉓

Kent. 🏛 *50,000.* 🚆 🚌 ℹ️ *Sun
St, Buttermarket (01227 378100).* 🚌
Wed, Fri. **www**.canterbury.co.uk

Its position on the London to
Dover route meant Canter-
bury was an important Roman
town even before the arrival
of St Augustine in 597, sent by
the pope to convert the Anglo-
Saxons to Christianity. The
town rose in importance, soon
becoming the centre of the
Christian Church in England.

With the building of the
cathedral and the martyrdom
of Thomas Becket *(see p48),*
Canterbury's future as a
religious centre was assured.

Adjacent to the ruins of **St
Augustine's Abbey**, destroyed
in the Dissolution *(see p50),* is
St Martin's Church, the oldest
in England. This was where
St Augustine first worshipped
and it has impressive Norman
and Saxon work.

West Gate Museum, with
its round towers, is an imposing medieval gatehouse. It
was built in 1381 and
contains a display of arms
and armoury.

The Poor Priests' Hospital,
founded in the 12th century,
now houses the **Museum of
Canterbury**.

🏛 **West Gate Museum**
St Peter's St. **Tel** *01227 789576.*
⬜ *Mon–Sat.* ⬛ *24–28 Dec, 1 Jan,
Good Fri.* 📷 ⬜

🏛 **Museum of Canterbury**
Stour St. **Tel** *01227 475202.* ⬜ *Jun–
Sep: daily; Oct–May: Mon–Sat.* 📷 ⬜
www.canterbury-museum.co.uk

Canterbury Cathedral

To match Canterbury's growing ecclesiastical rank as
a major centre of Christianity, the first Norman archbishop, Lanfranc, ordered a new cathedral to be built on
the ruins of the Anglo-Saxon cathedral in 1070. It was
enlarged and rebuilt many times and as a result embraces
examples of all styles of medieval architecture. The most
poignant moment in its history came in 1170 when
Thomas Becket was murdered here *(see p48).* Four
years after his death a fire devastated the cathedral and
the Trinity Chapel was built to house Becket's remains.
The shrine quickly became an important
religious site and until the Dissolution
(see p50) the cathedral was
one of Christendom's chief
places of pilgrimage.

The nave at 60 m (188 ft)
makes Canterbury one of the
longest medieval churches.

The South West Porch
(1426) may have been built
to commemorate the victory
at Agincourt *(see p49).*

**Main
entrance**

★ **Medieval
Stained Glass**
*This depiction of the
1,000-year-old
Methuselah is a detail
from the southwest
transept window.*

GEOFFREY CHAUCER

Considered to be the first
great English poet, Geoffrey
Chaucer (c.1345–1400), a
customs official by profession,
wrote a rumbustious and witty
account of a group of pilgrims
travelling from London to Becket's
shrine in 1387 in the *Canterbury
Tales.* The pilgrims represent a
cross-section of 14th-century English
society and the tales remain one of
the greatest and most entertaining
works of early English literature.

**Wife of Bath,
Canterbury Tales**

Bell Harry Tower
The central tower, dominating the skyline, was built in 1498 to house a bell donated by Henry of Eastry 100 years before. The fan vaulting is a superb example of the late Perpendicular style.

VISITORS' CHECKLIST

11 The Precincts, Canterbury. **Tel** *01227 762862.* ☐ *Oct–May: 9am–4:30pm Mon–Sat, Jun–Sept: 9am–6pm Mon–Sat (contact advised).* ● *during services & concerts; 25 Dec.* 🎧 🚻 *8am daily; 11am Sun; 3:15pm Sat, Sun; 5:30pm Mon–Fri.* ♿ 🚻 **www**.canterbury-cathedral.org

★ Site of the Shrine of St Thomas Becket
This Victorian illustration (anon) portrays Becket's canonization. The Trinity Chapel was built to house his tomb which stood here until it was destroyed in 1538. The spot is now marked by a lighted candle.

★ Black Prince's Tomb
This copper effigy is on the tomb of Edward III's son, who died in 1376.

Great Cloister

Chapter House

The Great South Window has four stained glass panels (1958) by Erwin Bossanyi.

STAR FEATURES

★ Medieval Stained Glass

★ Site of the Shrine of St Thomas Becket

★ Black Prince's Tomb

St Augustine's Chair

The quire (choir), completed in 1184, is one of the longest in England.

Trinity Chapel

The circular Corona Chapel

The keep of Rochester Castle, dominating Rochester and the Medway Valley

Leeds Castle ㉔

Maidstone, Kent. *Tel 01622 765400.*
Bearsted then bus. *daily.*
for concerts & 25 Dec.
www.leeds-castle.com

Surrounded by a lake that
reflects the warm buff
stone of its crenellated turrets,
Leeds is often considered to
be the most beautiful castle in
England. Begun in the early
12th century, it has been
continuously inhabited and its
present appearance is a result
of centuries of rebuilding and
extensions, most recently in
the 1930s. Leeds has royal
connections going back to
1278, when it was given to
Edward I by a courtier
seeking favour.

Henry VIII loved the castle
and visited it often, escaping
from the plague in London.
It contains a life-sized bust of
Henry from the late 16th century. Leeds passed out of royal
ownership when Edward VI
gave it to Sir Anthony St Leger
in 1552 as a reward for helping to pacify the Irish.

Rochester ㉕

Kent. 145,000.
95 High Street (01634 843666).

Clustered at the mouth of
the River Medway are the
towns of Rochester, Chatham
and Gillingham, all rich in
naval history, but none more

so than Rochester, which
occupied a strategic site on
the London to Dover road.

England's tallest Norman
keep is at **Rochester Castle**,
worth climbing for the views
over the Medway. The town's
medieval history is still visible,
with the original city walls –
which followed the lines of the
Roman fortifications – on view
in the High Street, and some
well-preserved wall paintings
in the **cathedral**, built in 1088.

Environs: In Chatham, the
Historic Dockyard is now a
museum of shipbuilding and
nautical crafts. **Fort Amherst**
nearby was built in 1756 to
protect the dockyard and river
entrance from attack, and has
1,800 m (5,570 ft) of tunnels
to explore that were hewn by
Napoleonic prisoners of war.

♣ Rochester Castle
Castle Hill. *Tel 01634 402276.*
daily. *1 Jan, 24–26, 31 Dec.*
grounds only.

A gladiator,
Knole

🏛 Historic Dockyard
Dock Rd, Chatham. *Tel 01634
823800.* *mid-Feb–Oct: daily;
Nov: Sat, Sun.*
♭ Fort Amherst
Dock Rd, Chatham. *Tel 01634
847747.* *call for details.*

Knole ㉖

(NT) Sevenoaks, Kent. *Tel 01732
462100.* *Sevenoaks then taxi.*
House *Mar–Oct: Wed–Sun (pm),
Good Fri & public hols.* **Park**
daily. *limited.* *by
arrangement.*

This huge Tudor mansion
was built in the late 15th
century, and was seized by
Henry VIII from the Arch-
bishop of Canterbury at the
Dissolution *(see p50).* In 1566
Queen Elizabeth I gave it to
her cousin Thomas Sackville.
His descendants have lived
here ever since, including the
writer Vita Sackville-West,
(1892–1962). The house is
well known for its 17th-
century furniture,
such as the
elaborate bed
made for James II.
The 405-ha (1,000-acre) park
has deer and lovely walks.

Environs: A small manor
house, **Ightham Mote**, east of
Knole, is one of the finest
examples of English medieval
architecture. Its 14th-century
timber-and-stone building

encloses a central court and is encircled by a moat.

At **Sissinghurst Castle Garden** are gardens created by Vita Sackville-West and her husband Harold Nicolson in the 1930s.

🏰 **Ightham Mote**
(NT) Ivy Hatch, Sevenoaks. *Tel 01732 810378.* ◯ mid-Mar–Oct: Wed–Fri, Sun, Mon & public hols. 🖼 ♿ 🍴 📷

🌿 **Sissinghurst Castle Garden**
(NT) Cranbrook. *Tel 01580 710700.* ◯ Apr–Oct: 11am–6:30pm Mon, Tue, Fri; 10am–6:30pm Sat, Sun, Good Fri. 🖼 ♿ limited. 🍴 📷

Hever Castle ㉗

Edenbridge, Kent. *Tel 01732 865224.* ⇄ Edenbridge Town. ◯ Mar–Nov: daily; **Gardens** 11am–6pm; **Castle** noon–6pm. 🖼 ♿ limited. 🍴 📷 groups by arrangement. 📷 **www**.hever-castle.co.uk

This small, moated castle is famous as the 16th-century home of Anne Boleyn, the doomed wife of Henry VIII, executed for adultery. She lived here as a young woman and the king often visited her while staying at Leeds Castle. In 1903 Hever was bought by William Waldorf Astor, who undertook a restoration programme, building a Neo-Tudor village alongside it to accommodate guests and servants. The moat and gatehouse date from around 1270.

Environs: To the northwest of Hever is **Chartwell**, the family home of Sir Winston Churchill *(see p59).* It remains furnished as it was when he lived here. Some 140 of his paintings are on display.

🏰 **Chartwell**
(NT) Westerham, Kent. 📞 01732 868381. ◯ mid-Mar–Jun, Sep–Nov: 11am–5pm Wed–Sun & public hols; Jul–Aug: 11am–5pm Tue–Sun & public hols. 🖼 ♿ limited. 🍴 📷

The façade of Chartwell, Winston Churchill's home

Royal Tunbridge Wells ㉘

Kent. 🚶 55,000. ⇄ 🚌 📮 ℹ Old Fish Market, The Pantiles (0800 393686). 🚲 Wed. **www**.visittunbridgewells.com

Helped by royal patronage, the town became a popular spa in the 17th and 18th centuries after mineral springs were discovered in 1606. The Pantiles – the colonnaded and paved promenade – was laid out in the 1700s.

Environs: Nearby is a superb manor house, **Penshurst Place**. Built in the 1340s, it has an 18 m (60 ft) high Great Hall.

🏰 **Penshurst Place**
Tonbridge, Kent. *Tel 01892 870307.* ◯ Apr–Oct: daily; Mar: Sat, Sun: **House** noon–4pm; **Gardens** 10:30am–6pm; **Toy Museum** noon–5pm. 🖼 ♿ limited. 🍴 📷 📷

CHARLES DICKENS

Charles Dickens (1812–70), a popular writer in his own time, is still widely read today. He was born in Portsmouth but moved to Chatham aged five. As an adult, Dickens lived in London but kept up his Kent connections, taking holidays in Broadstairs, just south of Margate – where he wrote *David Copperfield* – and spending his last years at Gad's Hill, near Rochester. The town celebrates the famous connection with an annual Dickens festival.

An early 18th-century astrolabe to measure the stars, Hever Castle garden

EAST ANGLIA

NORFOLK · SUFFOLK · ESSEX · CAMBRIDGESHIRE

The bulge of land between the Thames Estuary and the Wash, flat but far from featureless, sits aside from the main north–south axis through Britain, and for that reason it has succeeded in maintaining and preserving its distinctive architecture, traditions and rural character in both cities and countryside.

East Anglia's name derives from the Angles, the people from northern Germany who settled here during the 5th and 6th centuries. East Anglians have long been a breed of plain-spoken and independent people. Two prominent East Anglians – Queen Boadicea in the 1st century and Oliver Cromwell in the 17th century – were famous for their stubbornness and their refusal to bow to constituted authority. During the Civil War, East Anglia was Cromwell's most reliable source of support. The hardy people who made a difficult living hunting and fishing in the swampy fens, which were drained in the 17th century, were called the Fen Tigers. After draining, the peaty soil proved ideal for arable farming, and today East Anglia grows about a third of Britain's vegetables. The rotation of crops, heralding Britain's agricultural revolution, was perfected in Norfolk in the 18th century. Many of the region's towns and cities grew prosperous on the agricultural wealth, including Norwich. The sea also plays a prominent role in East Anglian life. Coastal towns and villages support the many fishermen who use the North Sea, rich in herring in former days but now known mainly for flat fish.

In modern times, the area has become a centre of recreational sailing, both off the coast and on the inland waterway system known as the Norfolk Broads. East Anglia is also home to one of Britain's top universities: Cambridge.

Lavender fields in full bloom in July, Heacham, Norfolk

◁ Cley windmill overlooking the sea marshes on the north Norfolk coast

Exploring East Anglia

As you move away from London, you soon reach the countryside immortalized by the painter Constable *(see p204)* and in many ways unchanged since his day, scattered with churches, windmills and medieval agricultural barns. Nature lovers will find it fruitful territory, especially North Norfolk with its bird reserves and seal colonies. Boating enthusiasts, too, are well catered for in this, Britain's driest and sunniest region. The local architecture ranges from a mix of medieval to modern. The distinctive pink-washed cottages in Suffolk, flint cottages in

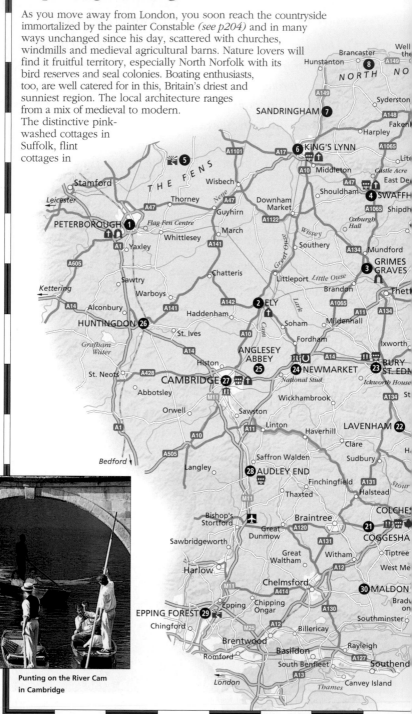

**Punting on the River Cam
in Cambridge**

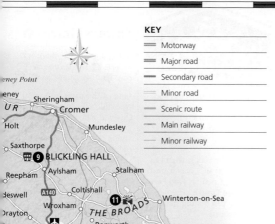

KEY

══	Motorway
═	Major road
▬	Secondary road
═	Minor road
▬	Scenic route
▬	Main railway
—	Minor railway

GETTING AROUND

The region's more isolated sights can be very difficult to reach by public transport and, for a few people, car rental may be a cheaper and more efficient method of travelling around. The M11 motorway runs from London to Cambridge. The coast road from Aldeburgh to King's Lynn takes you through some of the best countryside in the area. There are frequent mainline trains to Norwich, Ipswich and Cambridge although the local trains are more sporadic. There are international and domestic airports at Stansted (*see p682*) and Norwich.

SEE ALSO

• *Where to Stay* pp563–6

• *Where to Eat* pp619–21

Beach huts on Wells-next-the-Sea beach, north Norfolk

SIGHTS AT A GLANCE

0 kilometres 10

0 miles 10

Peterborough ●

Cambridgeshire. 🏛 156,000. ⚊
🚇 ℹ️ 3 Minster Precinct (01733
452336). ⚊ Tue–Sat.
www.visitpeterborough.com

Although one of the oldest
settlements in Britain,
Peterborough was designated
a New Town in 1967, and is
now a mixture of ancient
and modern.

The city centre is dominated
by the 12th-century **St Peter's
Cathedral** which gave the city
its name. The interior of this
classic Norman building, with
its vast yet simple nave, was
badly damaged by Cromwell's
troops *(see p52)*, but its unique
painted wooden ceiling (1220)
has survived intact. Catherine
of Aragon, the first wife of

Peterborough's coat of arms with
a Latin inscription: Upon this Rock

Henry VIII, is buried here,
although Cromwell's troops
also destroyed her tomb.

Environs: The oldest wheel in
Britain (1,300 BC) was found
preserved in peat at **Flag Fen
Bronze Age Centre**. The site
provides a fascinating glimpse
into prehistory.

**⋔ Flag Fen Bronze Age
Centre**
Droveway, Northey, Peterborough. **Tel**
01733 313414. ⚪ daily 10am–5pm.
🈲 ♿ 📷 💻 **www**.flagfen.com

Grimes Graves ●

(EH) Lynford, Norfolk. **Tel** 01842
810656. 🚇 Brandon then taxi. ⚪
daily. ⚫ 1 Jan, 24–26 Dec. 🈲 📷

One of the most important
Neolithic sites in England,
this was once an extensive
complex of flint mines – 433
shafts have been located –
dating from before 2000 BC.

Using antlers as pickaxes,
Stone Age miners hacked
through the soft chalk to
extract the hard flint below to
make axes, weapons and tools.
It is possible that the flint was
transported long distances
around England on the
prehistoric network of paths.
You can descend 9 m (30 ft)
by ladder into one of the
shafts and see the galleries

Ely ●

Cambridgeshire. 🏛 14,000.
🚇 ℹ️ 29 St Mary's St (01353
662062). ⚊ Thu (general),
Sat (craft & antiques).
www.eastcambs.gov.uk

Built on a chalk hill, this
small city is thought to be
named after the eels in the
nearby River Ouse. The hill
was once an inaccessible
island in the then marshy and
treacherous Fens *(see p196)*.
It was also the last stronghold
of Anglo-Saxon resistance,
under Hereward the Wake
(see p48), who hid in the
cathedral until the Normans
crossed the Fens in 1071.

Today this small prosperous
city, totally dominated by the
huge **cathedral**, is the market
centre for the rich agricultural
area surrounding it.

The lantern's glass
windows admit light
into the dome.

**This painted
wooden angel** *is
one of hundreds of
bosses that were
carved all over the
south and north
transepts in the 13th
and 14th centuries.*

**Stained glass
museum**

The tomb is that of
Alan de Walsingham,
designer of the
unique Octagon.

The Octagon,
*made of wood, was built
in 1322 when the Norman
tower collapsed. Its roof,
the lantern, took an extra
24 years to build and
weighs 200 tonnes.*

Octagon   Area of cutaway

ELY CATHEDRAL
Ely. **Tel** 01353 667735.
⚪ daily. ⚫ special events. 🈲 ♿ 📷 🍴 💻 📷
Begun in 1083, the cathedral took 268 years to
complete. It survived the Dissolution *(see p50)*
but was closed for 17 years by Cromwell *(see
p52)* who lived in Ely for a time.

where the flint was mined. During excavations, unusual chalk models of a fertility goddess *(see p43)* and a phallus were discovered.

Environs: Nearby, at the centre of the once fertile plain known as the Breckland, is the small market town of **Thetford**.

Once a prosperous trading town, its fortunes dipped in the 16th century, when its priory was destroyed *(see p50)* and the surrounding land deteriorated due to excessive sheep grazing. The area was later planted with pine trees. A mound in the city marks the site of a pre-Norman castle.

The revolutionary writer and philosopher Tom Paine, author of *The Rights of Man,* was born here in 1737.

The huge cathedral spire *dominates the flat Fens countryside surrounding Ely.*

Painted ceiling, 19th century

The Prior's Door (c.1150)

The south aisle has 12 classic Norman arches at its foot, with pointed Early English windows above.

Oxburgh Hall surrounded by its medieval moat

Swaffham ❹

Norfolk. 🏠 *6,700.* 🚉 ℹ️ *Market Place (01760 722255).* 🏪 *Sat.* **www.**aroundswaffham.co.uk

The best-preserved Georgian town in East Anglia and a fashionable resort during the Regency period, Swaffham is at its liveliest on Saturdays when a market is held in the square around the market cross of 1783. In the centre of the town is the 15th-century **Church of St Peter and St Paul**, with a small spire added in the 19th century. It has a magnificent Tudor north aisle, said to have been paid for by John Chapman, the Pedlar of Swaffham. He is depicted on the two-sided town sign near the market place. Myth has it that he went to London and met a stranger who told him of hidden treasure at Swaffham. He returned, dug it up and used it to embellish the church, where he is shown in a window.

Environs: Castle Acre, north of the town, has the remains of a massive Cluniac **priory**. Founded in 1090, its stunning Norman front still stands.

A short drive south is **Oxburgh Hall and Garden**, built by Sir Edmund Bedingfeld in 1482. The hall, entered through a huge 24 m (80 ft) fortified gatehouse, displays the velvet Oxburgh Hangings, embroidered by Mary, Queen of Scots *(see p511).*

🏛 Castle Acre Priory
(EH) Castle Acre. **Tel** *01760 755394.*
🕐 *Apr–Oct: daily; Nov–Mar: Wed–Sun.* ⬛ *24-26 Dec, 1 Jan.* 🎟️
♿ *limited.* 📷
🏛 Oxburgh Hall & Garden
(NT) Oxborough. **Tel** *01366 328258.*
🕐 *Mar–Nov: Sat–Wed (garden also Dec: Sat, Sun).* 🎟️ ♿ *limited.* 🍴📷

Swaffham town sign

BOADICEA AND THE ICENI

When the Romans invaded Britain, the Iceni, the main tribe in East Anglia, joined forces with them to defeat the Catuvellauni, a rival tribe. But the Romans then turned on the Iceni, torturing Queen Boadicea (or Boudicca). In AD 61, she led a revolt against Roman rule: her followers burned down London, Colchester and St Albans. The rebellion was put down and the queen took poison rather than submit. At Cockley Cley, near Swaffham, an Iceni camp has been excavated.

Illustration of Queen Boadicea leading her Iceni followers

A windmill on Wicken Fen

The Fens ⑤

Cambridgeshire/Norfolk. ⇌ *Ely.*
29 St Mary's St, Ely (01353 662062).
www.eastcambs.gov.uk

This is the open, flat, fertile
expanse that lies between
Lincoln, Cambridge, Bedford

and King's Lynn. Up until the
17th century it was a swamp,
and settlement was possible
only on "islands", such as Ely
(*see p194*), raised above their
low-lying surroundings.

Through the 17th century,
speculators, recognizing the
value of the peaty soil for farmland, brought in Dutch experts
to drain the fens. However,
as the peat dried it
contracted, and the
fens have slowly
been getting lower.
Powerful electric
pumps now keep
it drained.

Nine miles (14 km)
from Ely is Wicken
Fen, 243 ha (600
acres) of undrained
fen providing a
habitat for water
life, wildfowl and
wild flowers.

**Trinity Guildhall,
King's Lynn**

King's Lynn ⑥

Norfolk. 🏘 *42,000.* ⇌ 🚌
🛈 *Custom House, Purfleet Quay
(01553 763044).* 🛒 *Tue, Fri, Sat.*
www.west-norfolk.gov.uk

Formerly Bishop's Lynn, its
name was changed at the
Reformation (*see p50*) to
reflect the changing political
reality. In the Middle Ages
it was one of
England's most
prosperous ports,
shipping grain and
wool from the sur-
rounding countryside
to Europe. There are
still a few warehouses
and merchants'
houses by the River
Ouse surviving
from this period.
At the north end of
the town is **True's**

North Norfolk Coastal Tour ⑧

This tour takes you through some of the most
beautiful areas of East Anglia; nearly all of the
north Norfolk coast has been designated an Area of
Outstanding Natural Beauty. The sea has dictated the
character of the area. With continuing deposits of silt,
once busy ports are now far inland and the shingle
and sand banks that have been built up are home to
a huge variety of wildlife. Do bear in mind when
planning your journey that this popular route can get
congested during summer.

TIPS FOR DRIVERS

Tour length: 28 miles (45 km).
*Stopping-off points: Holkham
Hall makes a pleasant stop for a
picnic lunch. There are some good
pubs in Wells-next-the-Sea. (See
also pp684–5.)*

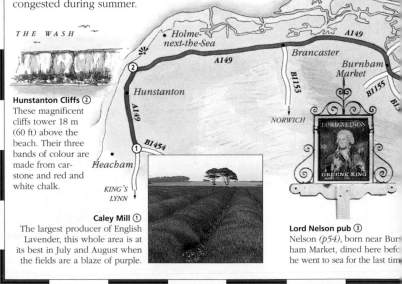

THE WASH

Holme-
next-the-Sea

A149

Brancaster

*Burnham
Market*

Hunstanton

B1153

NORWICH

A149

B1454

Heacham

*KING'S
LYNN*

Hunstanton Cliffs ②
These magnificent
cliffs tower 18 m
(60 ft) above the
beach. Their three
bands of colour are
made from car-
stone and red and
white chalk.

Caley Mill ①
The largest producer of English
Lavender, this whole area is at
its best in July and August when
the fields are a blaze of purple.

Lord Nelson pub ③
Nelson (*p54*), born near Burnham Market, dined here befo[re]
he went to sea for the last tim[e]

Yard, a relic of the old fishermen's quarter.

The **Trinity Guildhall**, located in the Saturday Market Place, dates back to the 15th century and was formerly a prison. The handsome **Customs House**, overlooking the river, was built in the 17th century as a merchant exchange. It is now a museum dedicated to the town's colourful maritime history. The Tourist Information Centre is also located here. **St Margaret's Church**, on the Market Place, dates back to 1101, and the interior includes a fine Elizabethan screen. In 1741 the tall spire on the southwest tower collapsed in a storm.

🏛 **Customs House**
Purfleet Quay. **Tel** 01553 763044.
◯ daily. ♿ ground floor.

Sandringham House, where the Royal Family spend every Christmas

Sandringham 🟡

Norfolk. **Tel** 01553 612908. 🚌 from King's Lynn. ◯ Easter–Oct: daily. 🔴 one wk Jul. 🏷 ♿ 🍴 🛍
www.sandringhamestate.co.uk

This sizeable Norfolk estate has been in royal hands since 1862 when it was bought by the Prince of Wales, who later became Edward VII. The 18th-century house was elaborately embellished and refurbished by the prince and now retains an appropriately Edwardian atmosphere.

The large stables are now a museum and contain several trophies that relate to hunting, shooting and horse racing – all favourite royal activities. A popular feature is a display of royal motor cars spanning nearly a century. In the park there are scenic nature trails.

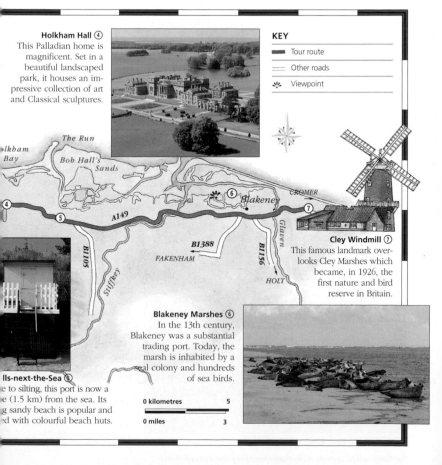

Holkham Hall ④
This Palladian home is magnificent. Set in a beautiful landscaped park, it houses an impressive collection of art and Classical sculptures.

KEY

━━ Tour route

═══ Other roads

🌟 Viewpoint

Cley Windmill ⑦
This famous landmark overlooks Cley Marshes which became, in 1926, the first nature and bird reserve in Britain.

Blakeney Marshes ⑥
In the 13th century, Blakeney was a substantial trading port. Today, the marsh is inhabited by a seal colony and hundreds of sea birds.

lls-next-the-Sea ⑤
e to silting, this port is now a
e (1.5 km) from the sea. Its
g sandy beach is popular and
d with colourful beach huts.

0 kilometres   5

0 miles   3

The symmetrical red-brick façade of the 17th-century Blickling Hall

Blickling Hall ⑨

(NT) Aylsham, Norfolk. **Tel** *01263 738 030*. ⿻ *Norwich, then bus.* **House** ○ *mid-Mar–Oct: 1–5pm Wed–Sun & public hols.* **Garden** ○ *Apr–Oct: 10:15am–5:15pm Wed–Sun & public hols; Nov–Mar: Thu–Sun.* **Park** ○ *daily.* 🌄 🚻 ❶ 🅿 *www.nationaltrust.org.uk*

Approached from the east, its symmetrical Jacobean front framed by trees and flanked by two yew hedges, Blickling Hall offers one of the most impressive vistas of any country house in the area.

Anne Boleyn, Henry VIII's tragic second queen, spent her childhood here, but very little of the original house remains. Most of the present structure dates from 1628, when it was home to James I's Chief Justice Sir Henry Hobart. Later in 1767 the 2nd Earl of Buckinghamshire, John Hobart, celebrated the Boleyn connection with reliefs in the Great Hall depicting Anne and her daughter, Elizabeth I. The Long Gallery is the most

spectacular room to survive from the 1620s. Its ceiling depicts symbolic representations of learning.

The Peter the Great Room marks the 2nd earl's service as ambassador to Russia and was built to display a huge spectacular tapestry (1764) of the tsar on horseback, a gift from, Catherine the Great. It also has portraits (1760) of the ambassador and his wife by Gainsborough *(see p163)*.

Norwich ⑩

See pp200–201.

The Broads ⑪

Norfolk. ⿻ *Hoveton, Wroxham.* 🚌 *Norwich, then bus.* ❶ *Station Rd, Hoveton (01603 782281) Apr–Oct.* *www.broads-authority.gov.uk*

These shallow lakes and waterways south and northeast of Norwich, joined by six rivers – the Bure, Thurne, Ant,

Yare, Waveney and Chet – were once thought to have been naturally formed, but in actual fact they are medieval peat diggings which flooded when the water level rose in the 13th century.

During summer the 125 miles (200 km) of open waterways, uninterrupted by locks, teem with thousands of boating enthusiasts, from devotees of pure sail to those who prefer motorboats. You can either hire a boat yourself or take one of the many trips on offer to view the plants and wildlife of the area. Look out for Britain's largest butterfly, the swallowtail. Wroxham, the unofficial capital of the Broads, is the starting point for many of these excursions.

The waterways support substantial beds of strong and durable reeds, much in demand for thatching *(see p33)*. They are cut in winter and carried to shore in the distinctive Broads punts.

For a more detailed look at the origins of the Broads and their varied wildlife, visit the **Norfolk Wildlife Trust** – a large thatched floating information centre on Ranworth Broad, with displays on all aspects of the area, and a bird-watching gallery.

In the centre of Ranworth is **St Helen's Church** which has a painted medieval screen, a well-preserved 14th-century illuminated manuscript and spectacular views over the entire area from its tower.

✕ Norfolk Wildlife Trust
Ranworth. **Tel** *01603 625540.* ○ *Apr–Oct: daily.* ♿ 🚻

Sailing boat, Wroxham Broad, Norfolk

Great Yarmouth ⑫

Norfolk. 🏘 90,000. ⌁ 🖂
🛈 Marine Parade (01493 846345).
🖂 Wed, Fri (summer), Sat.
www.great-yarmouth.co.uk

Herring fishing was once
the major industry of
this port, with 1,000 boats
engaged in it just before
World War I. Over-fishing led
to a depletion of stocks and,
for the port to survive, it
started to earn its living from
servicing container ships and
North Sea oil rigs.

It is also the most popular
seaside resort on the Norfolk
coast and has been since the
19th century, when Dickens
(see p189) gave it useful pub-
licity by setting part of his
novel *David Copperfield* here.

The **Elizabethan House
Museum** has a large, eclectic
display which illustrates the
social history of the area.

In the old part of the town,
around South Quay, are a
number of charming houses
including the 17th-century
Old Merchant's House. It
retains its original patterned
plaster ceilings as well as
examples of old ironwork

Fishing trawlers at Lowestoft's quays

and architectural fittings from
nearby houses, which were
destroyed during World War II.
The guided tour of the house
includes a visit to the adjoining
cloister of a 13th-century friary.

**🏛 Elizabethan House
Museum**
(NT) 4 South Quay. **Tel** 01493 855746.
◻ Apr–Oct: daily. 🔲 🔲
🚪 Old Merchant's House
(EH) South Quay. **Tel** 01493 857900.
◻ Apr–Oct: Thu–Tue. 🔲 🔲 🔲

Corn mill at Saxtead Green,
near Framlingham

Herringfleet Smock Mill,
near Lowestoft

WINDMILLS ON THE
FENS AND BROADS

The flat, open countryside
and the stiff breezes from the
North Sea made windmills
an obvious power source for
East Anglia well into the 20th
century, and today they are
an evocative and recurring
feature of the landscape. On
the Broads and Fens, some
were used for drainage,
while others, such as that at
Saxtead Green, ground corn.
On the boggy fens they were
not built on hard founda-
tions, so few survived, but
elsewhere, especially on
the Broads, many have
been restored to working
order. The seven-storey
Berney Arms Windmill is
the tallest on the Broads.
Thurne Dyke Drainage Mill
is the site of an exhibition
about the occasionally
idiosyncratic mills and their
more unusual mechanisms.

Lowestoft ⑬

Suffolk. 🏘 55,000. ⌁ 🖂
🛈 East Point Pavilion, Royal Plain
(01502 533600). 🖂 Tue, Fri, Sat.
www.visit-lowestoft.co.uk

The most easterly town in
Britain was long a rival to
Great Yarmouth, both as a
holiday resort and a fishing
port. Its fishing industry has
only just survived.

The coming of the railway
in the 1840s gave the town an
advantage over other resorts,
and the solid Victorian and
Edwardian boarding houses
are evidence of its popularity.

Lowestoft Museum, in a
17th-century house, has a good
display of the fine porcelain
made here in the 18th century,
as well as exhibits on local
archaeology and domestic life.

Environs: Somerleyton Hall
is built in Jacobean style on
the foundations of a smaller
mansion. Its gardens are a
real delight, and there is a
genuinely baffling yew
hedge maze.

🏛 Lowestoft Museum
Oulton Broad. **Tel** 01502 511457.
◻ May–Oct: 10:30am–5pm
Mon–Fri, 2–5pm Sat & Sun. 🔲 🔲
limited. 🔲 by arrangement.
🚪 Somerleyton Hall
On B1074. **Tel** 01502 511457. ◻
Easter Sun–Oct: Thu, Sun & public hols
(Jul–Aug: Tue–Thu, Sun & public hols).
🔲 🔲 🔲 🔲 by arrangement. 🔲
www.somerleyton.co.uk

Norwich ⑩

In the heart of the fertile East Anglian countryside, Norwich, one of the best-preserved cities in Britain, is steeped in a relaxed provincial atmosphere. The city was first fortified by the Saxons in the 9th century and still has the irregular street plan of that time. With the arrival of Flemish settlers in the early 12th century and the establishment of a textile industry, the town soon became a prosperous market and was the second city of England until the Industrial Revolution in the 19th century *(see pp56–7)*.

One of over a thousand carved bosses in the cathedral cloisters

The cobbled street, Elm Hill

Exploring Norwich

The oldest parts of the city are Elm Hill, one of the finest medieval streets in England, and Tombland, the old Saxon market place by the cathedral. Both have well-preserved medieval buildings, which are now incorporated into pleasant areas of small shops.

With a trading history spanning hundreds of years, the colourful market in the city centre is well worth a visit. A good walk meanders around the surviving sections of the 14th-century flint city wall.

🔒 Norwich Cathedral
The Close. **Tel** 01603 218321.
◻ *daily.* **Donations.** 🚻 🗂 🍴 📷
www.cathedral.org.uk
This magnificent building was founded in 1096 by Bishop Losinga and built with stone from Caen in France and Barnack.

The precinct originally included a monastery, and the surviving cloister is the most extensive in England. The thin cathedral spire was added in the 15th century, making it, at 96 m (315 ft), the second tallest in England after Salisbury *(see pp264–5)*. In the majestic

nave, soaring Norman pillars and arches support a 15th-century vaulted roof whose stone bosses, many of which illustrate well-known Bible stories, have recently been beautifully restored.

Easier to appreciate at close hand is the elaborate wood carving in the choir – the canopies over the stalls and the misericords beneath the seats, one showing a small boy being smacked. Not to be missed is the 14th-century Despenser Reredos in St Luke's Chapel. It was hidden for years under a carpenter's table to prevent its destruction by Puritans.

Two gates to the cathedral close survive: **St Ethelbert's,**

a 13th-century flint arch, and the **Erpingham Gate** at the west end, built by Sir Thomas Erpingham, who led the triumphant English archers at the Battle of Agincourt in 1415 *(see p49)*.

Beneath the east outer wall is the grave of Edith Cavell, the Norwich-born nurse who was arrested and executed in 1915 by the Germans for helping Allied soldiers escape from occupied Belgium.

🏛 Castle Museum
Castle Meadow. **Tel** 01603 493625.
◻ *daily (Sun pm only).* ● *1 Jan, 25 & 26 Dec.* 🚻 🖵 📷
www.museumsnorfolk.gov.uk
The brooding keep of this 12th-century castle has been a museum since 1894, when it ended 650 years of service as a prison. The most important Norman feature is a carved door that used to be the main entrance.

Exhibits include significant collections of archaeology,

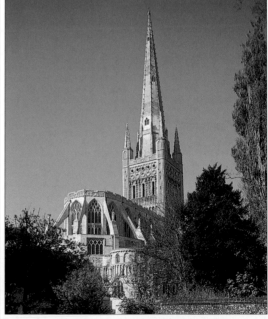

A view of Norwich Cathedral's spire and tower from the southeast

COLMAN'S MUSTARD

It was said of the Colmans that they made their fortune from what diners left on their plate. In 1814 Jeremiah Colman started milling mustard at Norwich because it was at the centre of a fertile plain where mustard was grown. Today at 15 Royal Arcade a shop sells mustard and related items, while a small museum illustrates the history of the company.

A 1950s advertisement for Colman's Mustard

VISITORS' CHECKLIST

Norfolk. 125,000. Thorpe Road. Surrey St. Millennium Plane (01603 727927). www.visitnorwich-area.co.uk

🏛 Strangers' Hall

Charing Cross. Wed, Sat for only. Tickets from Castle Museum (01603 667229).
This 14th-century merchant's house gives a glimpse into English domestic life through the ages. The costume display features a unique collection of underwear. The house was lived in by immigrant weavers – the "strangers". It has a fine 15th-century Great Hall.

natural history, fine art as well as the world's largest collection of ceramic teapots.

The art gallery is dominated by works from the Norwich School of painters. This group of early 19th century landscape artists painted directly from nature, getting away from the stylized studio landscapes that had been fashionable up to then. Chief among the group were John Crome (1768–1821), whom many compare with Constable (see p204), and John Sell Cotman (1782–1842), known for his watercolours. There are also regular exhibitions held here which are brought from the Tate Gallery in London.

🚪 Church of St Peter Mancroft

Market Place. **Tel** 01603 610443.
10am–4pm Mon–Sat; 10am–4pm Sat (summer), 10am–1pm (winter); Sun (services only). **Donations**. 🚹
This imposing Perpendicular church, built around 1455, so dominates the city centre that many visitors assume it is the cathedral. John Wesley (see p279) wrote of it, "I scarcely ever remember to have seen a more beautiful parish church".

The large windows make the church very light, and the dramatic east window still has most of its 15th-century glass. The roof is unusual in having wooden fan tracery – it is normally in stone – covering the hammerbeam construction. The famous peal of 13 bells rang out in 1588 to celebrate the defeat of the Spanish

Armada (see p51) and is still heard every Sunday.

Its name derives from the Latin *magna crofta* (great meadow) which described the area in pre-Norman times.

🏛 Bridewell Museum

Bridewell Alley. **Tel** 01603 629127.
Apr–Oct: Tue–Sat. 🖼 🚹
One of the oldest houses in Norwich, this 14th-century flint-faced building was for years used as a jail. It now houses an exhibition of local industries, with displays of old machines, advertisements and reconstructed shops.

🏛 Guildhall

Gaol Hill. 🖼
Above the city's ancient market place is the imposing 15th-century flint and stone Guildhall with its gable of checkered flushwork (now a café).

🏛 The Sainsbury Centre for Visual Arts

University of E Anglia (on B1108). **Tel** 01603 593199. Tue–Sun. 23 Dec–2 Jan. 🖼 🚹 by arrangement. 🖼 🚹 www.uea.ac.uk/scva
This important art gallery was built in 1978 to house the collection of Robert and Lisa Sainsbury given to the University of East Anglia in 1973.

The collection's strength is in its modern European paintings, including works by Modigliani, Picasso and Bacon, and in its sculptures by Giacometti and Moore. There are also displays of ethnographic art from Africa, the Pacific and the Americas.

The centre, designed by Lord Norman Foster, one of Britain's leading and most innovative architects, was among the first to display its steel structure openly.

***Back of the New Mills* (1814) by John Crome of the Norwich School**

Purple heather in flower on Dunwich Heath

Southwold ⓮

Suffolk. ⚏ 3,900. ⬚ ⓘ High Street
(01502 724729). ⬚ Mon, Thu.
www.visit-southwold.co.uk

This picture-postcard
seaside resort, with its
charming white-
washed villas
clustered around
small greens has,
largely by historical
accident, remained
unspoiled. The
railway line which
connected it with
London was closed
in 1929, which effect-
ively isolated this
Georgian town
from an influx of
day-trippers.
    That this was also
once a large port can
be judged from the size of
the 15th-century **St Edmund
King and Martyr Church**,
worth a visit for the 16th-
century painted screens. On

Jack o'the Clock,
Southwold

its tower is a small figure
dressed in the uniform of a
15th-century soldier and
known as Jack o'the Clock.
Southwold Museum tells the
story of the Battle of Sole Bay,
which was fought offshore
between the English and
Dutch navies in 1672.

Environs: The pretty
village of **Walberswick**
lies across the creek.
By road it is a long
detour and the only
alternatives are a
rowing-boat ferry
across the harbour
(summer only) or a
footbridge across the
river half a mile inland.
Further inland at
Blythburgh, the 15th-
century **Holy Trinity
Church** dominates the
surrounding land. In 1944 a
US bomber blew up over the
church, killing Joseph
Kennedy Jr, brother of the
future American president.

🏛 **Southwold Museum**
9–11 Victoria St. ◯ Easter–Oct:
2–4pm daily. ♿

Dunwich ⓯

Suffolk. ⚏ 1,400.

This tiny village is all that
remains of a "lost city" con-
signed to the sea by erosion.
In the 7th century Dunwich
was the seat of the powerful
East Anglian kings. In the 13th
century it was still the biggest
port in Suffolk and some 12
churches were built. But the
land was being eroded at
about a metre (3 ft) a year,
and the last original church
collapsed into the sea in 1919.
    Dunwich Heath, to the
south, runs down to a sandy
beach and is an important
nature reserve. **Minsmere
Reserve** has observation
hides for watching a huge
variety of birds.

⚒ **Dunwich Heath**
(NT) Nr Westleton. **Tel** 01728 648505.
◯ phone for details. ▣ ▯

⚒ **Minsmere Reserve**
Minsmere, Westleton. **Tel** 01728
648281. ◯ daily. ● 25, 26 Dec. ▨
♿ ▣ ▯ www.rspb.org.uk

Aldeburgh ⓰

Suffolk. ⚏ 3,840. ⬚ ⓘ High St
(01728 453637).
www.suffolkcoastal.gov.uk/leisure

Best known today for the
music festivals at Snape
Maltings just up the River
Alde, Aldeburgh has been a

Intricate carving on the exterior of the Tudor Moot Hall, Aldeburgh

port since Roman times (the Roman area is under water).

Erosion has resulted in the fine Tudor **Moot Hall**, once far inland, now being close to the beach and promenade. Its ground floor, originally the market, is now a museum. The large timbered court room above can only be reached by the original outside staircase.

The **church**, also Tudor, contains a large stained glass window placed in 1979 as a memorial to Benjamin Britten.

⊞ Moot Hall
Market Cross Pl *Tel* 01728 454666.
⬚ Apr, May: Sat, Sun (pm); Jun: daily (pm); Jul, Aug: daily. ▨ ▯

Framlingham Castle ⑰

(EH) Framlingham, Suffolk. *Tel* 01728 724189. ⬛ Wickham Market then taxi. ⬚ daily. ⬤ 24–26 Dec, 1 Jan. ▨ ▯ ▨

Perched on a hill, the small village of Framlingham has long been an important strategic site, even before the present castle was built in 1190 by the Earl of Norfolk.

Little of the castle from that period survives except the powerful curtain wall and its towers; walk round the top of it for fine views of the town.

Mary Tudor, daughter of Henry VIII, was staying here in 1553 when she heard she was to become queen.

Environs: To the southeast, on the coast, is the 27 m (90 ft) keep of **Orford Castle**, built for Henry II as a coastal defence at around the same time as Framlingham. It is an early example of an English castle with a 16-sided keep; earlier they were square and later round. A short climb to the top of the castle gives fantastic views.

⋔ Orford Castle
(EH) Orford. *Tel* 01394 450472. ⬚ Apr–Oct: daily; Nov–Mar: Thu–Mon. ⬤ 24–26 Dec, 1 Jan. ▨ ▯

ALDEBURGH MUSIC FESTIVAL

Composer Benjamin Britten (1913–76), born in Lowestoft, Suffolk, moved to Snape in 1937. In 1945 his opera *Peter Grimes* – inspired by the poet George Crabbe (1754–1832), once a curate at Aldeburgh – was performed in Snape. Since then the area has become the centre of musical activity. In 1948, Britten began the Aldeburgh Music Festival, held every June *(see p63)*. He acquired the Maltings at Snape and converted it into a music venue opened by the Queen in 1967. It has since become the focus of an annual series of East Anglian musical events in churches and halls throughout the entire region.

Benjamin Britten in Aldeburgh

Ipswich ⑱

Suffolk. ⬛ 120,000. ⬛ ▯ ▯ St Stephen's Lane (01473 258070). ⬚ Tue, Fri, Sat. ▨ IPART (music & arts): last wk Jun–1st wk Jul.
www.visit-ipswich.com

Suffolk's county town has a largely modern centre but several buildings remain from earlier times. It rose to prominence after the 13th century as a port for the rich Suffolk wool trade *(see p207)*. Later, with the Industrial Revolution, it began to export coal.

The **Ancient House** in Buttermarket has a superb example of pargeting – the ancient craft of ornamental façade plastering. The town's museum and art gallery, **Christchurch Mansion**, is a Tudor house from 1548, where Elizabeth I stayed in 1561. It also boasts the best collection of Constable's paintings out of London *(see p204)*, including four marvellous Suffolk landscapes, as well as paintings by Gainsborough *(see p163)*.

Ipswich Museum contains replicas of the Mildenhall and Sutton Hoo treasures, the originals being in the British Museum *(see pp106–7)*.

In the centre of the town is **St Margaret's**, a 15th-century church built in flint and stone with a double hammerbeam roof and 17th-century painted ceiling panels. **Wolsey's Gate**, a Tudor gateway of 1527, provides a link with Ipswich's most famous son, Cardinal Wolsey *(see p173)*. He started to build an ecclesiastical college in the town, but fell from royal favour before it was finished.

血 Christchurch Mansion
Christchurch Pk. *Tel* 01473 433554. ⬚ 10am–5pm Tue–Sat & public hols; 2:30–4:30pm Sun. ⬤ 1 Jan, Good Fri, 24–26 Dec. ▨ limited. ▨ by arrangement. ▯ ▯

血 Ipswich Museum
High St. *Tel* 01473 433550. ⬚ Tue–Sat. ▯ ▨

Pargeting on the Ancient House in Ipswich

Constable Walk ⑲

This walk in Constable country follows one of the most picturesque sections of the River Stour. The route taken would have been familiar to the landscape painter John Constable (1776–1837). Constable's father, a wealthy merchant, owned Flatford Mill, which was depicted in many of the artist's important paintings. Constable claimed to know and love "every stile and stump, and every lane" around East Bergholt.

The River Stour, used as a backdrop for Constable's *Boatbuilding* (1814)

↑ A12

TIPS FOR WALKERS

Starting point: *Park off Flatford Lane, East Bergholt (charge to park).* ℹ️ *01206 299460;* **(NT)** *Bridge Cottage (01206 298260).* ***Getting there:*** *A12 to East Bergholt, then follow signs to Flatford.* 🚉 *Manningtree is within walking distance of Flatford.* 🚌 *from Ipswich or Colchester.* ***Stopping-off point:*** *Dedham.* ***Length:*** *3 miles (5 km).* ***Difficulty:*** *Flat trail along riverside footpath with kissing gates.*

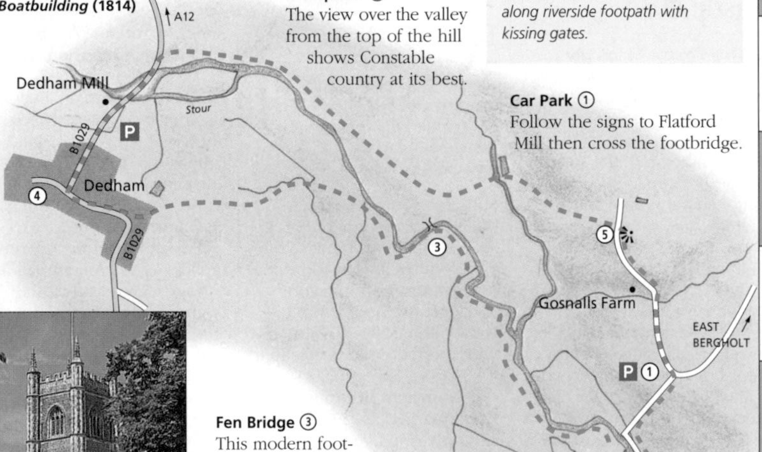

Viewpoint ⑤
The view over the valley from the top of the hill shows Constable country at its best.

Dedham Mill •

Stour

🅿️

Dedham

Car Park ①
Follow the signs to Flatford Mill then cross the footbridge.

③

⑤ 🚻

Gosnalls Farm

EAST BERGHOLT

🅿️ ①

Fen Bridge ③
This modern foot-bridge replaced one that Constable used as a focus for many of his paintings.

Ram Lock •

Flatford Mill •
②

Dedham Church ④
The tall church tower appears in many of Constable's pictures including the *View on the Stour near Dedham* (1822).

✴️

KEY

‐ ‐ Route

═══ B road

═══ Minor road

🔆 Viewpoint

🅿️ Parking

0 metres	500
0 yards	500

Willy Lott's Cottage ②
This cottage remains much the same as it did when featured in Constable's painting *The Hay-Wain (see p83).*

Colchester ⑳

Essex. 🚗 160,000. 🚉 🚌 ℹ️ *Queen St (01206 282920).* 🅿️ *Fri, Sat.* **www**.visitcolchester.com

The oldest recorded town in Britain, Colchester was the effective capital of south-east England when the Romans invaded in AD 43, and it was here that the first permanent Roman colony was established.

After Boadicea *(see p195)* burnt the town in AD 60, a 2 mile (3 km) wall was built, 3 m (10 ft) thick and 9 m (30 ft) high, to deter future attackers. You can still see these walls and the surviving Roman town gate, the largest in Britain.

During the Middle Ages Colchester developed into an important weaving centre. In the 16th century, a number of immigrant Flemish weavers settled in an area west of the castle, known as the **Dutch Quarter**, which still retains the original tall houses and steep, narrow streets.

Colchester was besieged for 11 weeks during the Civil War *(see p52)* before being captured by Cromwell's troops.

🏛 Tymperleys
Trinity St. **Tel** *01206 282943.* ⭕ *May–Oct: Tue–Sat.* ♿ 📷
www.colchestermuseums.org.uk
Clock-making was an important craft in Colchester, and it is celebrated in this restored half-timbered, 15th-century mansion, also worth visiting for its formal Tudor garden.

🏛 Hollytrees Museum
High St. **Tel** *01206 282947.* ⭕ *daily.* ⚫ *24–26 Dec, 1 Jan.* ♿ 📷
www.colchestermuseums.org.uk
This elegant Georgian townhouse was built in 1719. Now a charming museum of social history, you can experience the day-to-day lives of Colchester people and changing technology over 300 years.

🏛 Castle Museum
High St. **Tel** *01206 282939.* ⭕ *daily; 11am–5pm Sun.* ⚫ *24–27 Dec.* 📷 🎨 ♿ 📷
www.colchestermuseums.org.uk
This is the oldest and largest Norman keep still standing in England. Twice the size of the White Tower at the Tower of

The Norman keep of the Castle Museum, Colchester

London *(see pp118–19),* it was built in 1076 on the platform of a Roman temple dedicated to Claudius *(see p44),* using stones and tiles from other Roman buildings. The museum's displays relate the story of the town from prehistoric times to the Civil War. There is also a medieval prison.

🏰 Layer Marney Tower
Off B1022. **Tel** *01206 330784.* ⭕ *Apr–Sep: noon–5pm Sun–Thu.* 🎨 ♿ *limited.* 📷 *by arrangement.* 📷 📷
www.layermarneytower.co.uk
This remarkable Tudor gatehouse is the tallest in Britain: its pair of six-sided, eight-storey turrets reach to 24 m (80 ft). It was intended to be part of a larger complex but the designer, Sir Henry Marney, died before it was completed. The brickwork and terracotta ornamentation around the roof and windows are models of Tudor craftsmanship.

🌿 Beth Chatto Garden
Elmstead Market. **Tel** *01206 822007.* ⭕ *Mar–Oct: 9am–5pm Mon–Sat; Nov–Feb: 9am–4pm Mon–Fri.* ⚫ *24 Dec–6 Jan.* 📷 🎨
📷 **www**.bethchatto.co.uk
One of Britain's most eminent gardening writers began this experiment in the 1960s to test her belief that it is possible to create a garden in the most adverse conditions. The dry and windy slopes, boggy patches, gravel beds and wooded areas all support an array of plants best suited to that particular environment.

Coggeshall ㉑

Essex. 🚗 4,000. 🅿️ *Thu.* **www**.coggeshall-pc.gov.uk

This town has two of the most important medieval and Tudor buildings in the country. Dating from 1140, **Coggeshall Grange Barn** is the oldest surviving timber-framed barn in Europe. Inside is a display of historic farm wagons. The half-timbered merchant's house, **Paycocke's**, was built around 1500 and has a beautifully panelled interior. There is a display of Coggeshall lace.

🏰 Coggeshall Grange Barn
(NT) Grange Hill. 📷 *01376 562226.* ⭕ *Mar–Oct: Tue, Thu, Sun & public hols (pm).* ⚫ *Good Fri.* 🎨 ♿
🏰 Paycocke's
(NT) West St. **Tel** *01376 561305.* ⭕ *Apr–Oct: Tue, Thu, Sun & public hols (pm).* ⚫ *Good Fri.* 🎨 ♿

Beth Chatto Garden, Colchester, in full summer bloom

For hotels and restaurants in this region see pp563–566 and pp619–621

Lavenham ㉒

Suffolk. 👥 *1,800.* ℹ️ *Lady St (01787 248207).*

Often considered the most perfect of all English small towns, Lavenham is a treasure trove of beautiful timber-framed houses ranged along streets whose pattern is virtually unchanged from medieval times. For 150 years, between the 14th and 16th centuries, Lavenham was the prosperous centre of the Suffolk wool trade. It still has many outstanding and well-preserved buildings; indeed no less than 300 of the town's buildings are listed, including the magnificent **Little Hall**.

Environs: Gainsborough's House, Sudbury, is a museum on this painter *(see p163).*

🏛 **Little Hall** Market Place. *Tel 01787 247179.* ⏰ *Apr–Oct: Wed, Thu, Sat, Sun; public hols.* 📷

🏛 **Gainsborough's House** Sudbury. *Tel 01787 372958.* ⏰ *Mon–Sat.* ⚫ *24 Dec–1 Jan, Good Fri.* ♿ 📷 www.gainsborough.org

LITTLE HALL

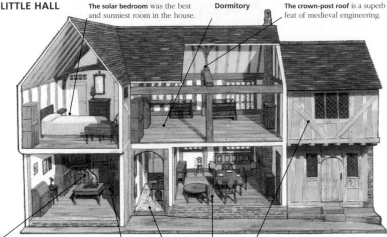

The solar bedroom was the best and sunniest room in the house.

Dormitory

The crown-post roof is a superb feat of medieval engineering.

Bronze of Egyptian Goddess Cat Bastet

Library

Entrance

Dining room

The herringbone-style timber on the exterior was used often in the 14th century.

Bury St Edmunds ㉓

Suffolk. 👥 *34,000.* 🚌 🚆 ℹ️ *Angel Hill (01284 764667).* 🛒 *Wed, Sat.* www.stedmundsbury.gov.uk

St Edmund was the last Saxon king of East Anglia, decapitated by Danish raiders in 870. Legend has it that a wolf picked up the severed head – an image that appears in a number of medieval carvings. Edmund was canonized in 900 and buried in Bury, where in 1014 King Canute *(see p171)* built an **abbey** in his honour, the wealthiest in England until its destruction in the Dissolution of the Monasteries *(see p351).* The abbey ruins now lie in the town centre.

Nearby are two large 15th-century churches, built when the wool trade made the town wealthy. **St James's** was designated a cathedral in 1914. The best features of **St Mary's** are the north porch and the hammerbeam roof over the nave. A stone slab in the north-east corner marks the tomb of Mary Tudor *(see pp50–51).*

Illustration of St Edmund

Just below the **market cross** in Cornhill – remodelled by Robert Adam *(see p28)* in 1714 – stands the large 12th-century **Moyse's Hall**, a merchant's house that serves as the local history museum, displaying archaeology from the area.

Environs: Three miles (5 km) southwest of Bury is the late 18th-century **Ickworth House**. This eccentric Neo-Classical mansion features an unusual rotunda with a

The 18th-century rotunda of Ickworth House, Bury St Edmunds

domed roof flanked by two huge wings. The art collection includes works by Reynolds and Titian. There are also fine displays of silver, porcelain and sculpture, for example, John Flaxman's (1755–1826) moving *The Fury of Athamas*. The house is set in a large park.

The stallion unit at the National Stud, Newmarket

🏛 Moyse's Hall

Cornhill. *Tel* 01284 706183. ⬤ daily.
⬤ 24–26 Dec, Good Fri. 🈯 ♿ 📷

🏛 Ickworth House (NT)

Horringer. *Tel* 01284 735270. ⬤
Mar–Oct: Fri–Tue. 🈯 ♿ 🍴 📷

Newmarket ㉔

Suffolk. 🧍 17,000. 🚆 🚌
🛈 Palace House, Palace St (01638 719215). 🛒 Tue, Sat.
www.forest-heath.gov.uk

A walk down the short main street tells you all you need to know about this busy and wealthy little town. The shops sell horse feed and all manner of riding accessories; the clothes on sale are tweeds, jodhpurs and the soft brown hats rarely worn by anyone except racehorse trainers.

Newmarket has been the headquarters of British horse racing since James I decided that its open heaths were ideal for testing the mettle of his fastest steeds against those of his friends. The first ever recorded horse race was held here in 1622. Charles II shared his grandfather's enthusiasm and after the Restoration *(see p53)* would move the whole court to Newmarket, every spring and summer, for the sport – he is the only British king to have ridden a winner.

A horse being exercised on Newmarket Heath

The modern racing industry began to take shape here in the late 18th century. There are now over 2,500 horses in training in and around the town, and two racecourses staging regular race meetings from around April to October *(see pp66–7)*. Training stables are occasionally open to the public but you can view the horses being exercised on the heath in the early morning. Tattersall's, the auction house for thoroughbreds, is in the centre of Newmarket.

The **National Stud** can also be visited. You will see the five or six stallions on stud, mares in foal and if you are lucky a newborn foal – most likely in April or May.

The **National Horseracing Museum** tells the history of the sport and contains many offbeat exhibits such as the skeleton of Eclipse, one of the greatest horses ever, unbeaten in 18 races and the ancestor of most of today's fastest performers. It also has a large display of sporting art.

🔘 National Stud

Newmarket. *Tel* 01638 663464 ⬤
Mar–Sep: daily. 🈯 ♿ 🎦 📺 📷
www.nationalstud.co.uk

🏛 National Horseracing Museum

99 High St, Newmarket. *Tel* 01638 667333. ⬤ Apr–Oct: daily. 🈯 ♿
🎦 📺 📷 **www**.nhrm.co.uk

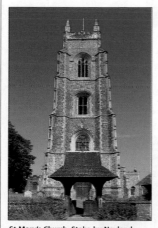

St Mary's Church, Stoke-by-Nayland, southeast of Bury St Edmunds

THE RISE AND FALL OF THE WOOL TRADE

Wool was a major English product from the 13th century and by 1310 some ten million fleeces were exported every year. The Black Death *(see p48)*, which swept Britain in 1348, perversely provided a boost for the industry: with labour in short supply, land could not be cultivated and was grassed over for sheep. Around 1350 Edward III decided it was time to establish a home-based cloth industry and encouraged Flemish weavers to come to Britain. Many settled in East Anglia, particularly Suffolk, and their skills helped establish a flourishing trade. This time of prosperity saw the construction of the sumptuous churches, such as the one at Stoke-by-Nayland, that we see today – East Anglia has more than 2,000 churches. The cloth trade here began to decline in the late 16th century with the development of water-powered looms. These were not suited to the area, which never regained its former wealth. Today's visitors are the beneficiaries of this decline, because the wool towns such as Lavenham and Bury St Edmunds never became rich enough to destroy their magnificent Tudor halls and houses and construct new buildings.

The façade of Anglesey Abbey

Anglesey Abbey 🔵

(NT) Lode, Cambridgeshire. *Tel*
01223 810080. ➡ *Cambridge then
bus.* **House** ◯ *Apr–Oct: Wed–Sun;*
Garden ◯ *Wed–Sun.* 🅿 ♿
limited. 🍴 📷

The original Abbey was built
in 1135 for an Augustinian
order. But only the crypt – also
known as the monks' parlour
– with its vaulted ceiling on
marble and stone pillars, survived the Dissolution *(see p50)*.

This was later incorporated
into a manor house whose
treasures include furniture
from many periods and a rare
seascape by Gainsborough
(see p206). The superb garden
was created in the 1930s by
Lord Fairhaven as an ambitious, Classical landscape of
trees, sculptures and borders.

Huntingdon 🔵

Cambridgeshire. 🏘 *18,000.* ➡ 🚌
ℹ *Princes St (01480 388588).* 🅿
Wed, Sat. **www**.huntsleisure.org

More than 300 years after
his death, Oliver Cromwell
(see p52) still dominates this
small town. Born here in 1599,
a record of his baptism can be
seen in the County Records
Office in Huntingdon. You can
see his name and traces of
ancient graffiti scrawled all
over it which says "England's
plague for five years".
Cromwell Museum, his
former school, traces his life
with pictures and mementos,
including his death mask.

Cromwell remains one of
the most disputed figures in
British history. An MP before
he was 30, he quickly became
embroiled in the disputes
between Charles I and Parliament over taxes and religion.
In the Civil War *(see p52)* he
proved an inspired general
and – after refusing the title
of king – was made Lord
Protector in 1653, four years
after the King was beheaded.
But just two years after his
death the monarchy was restored by popular demand,
and his body was taken out
of Westminster Abbey *(see
pp92–3)* to hang on gallows.

There is a 14th-century
bridge across the River Ouse
which links Huntingdon with
Godmanchester, the site of a
Roman settlement.

🏛 Cromwell Museum
Grammar School Walk. *Tel 01480
375830.* ◯ *Apr–Oct: Tue–Sun; Nov–
Mar: Tue–Sun (pm only except Sat).* ●
24–27 Dec, 1 Jan, some public hols. 📷

Cambridge 🔵

See pp210–15.

Audley End 🔵

(EH) Saffron Walden, Essex. *Tel 01799
522 399.* ➡ *Audley End then taxi.*
◯ *Apr–Sep (phone in advance for
details of opening hours & tours).*
🅿 ♿ *limited.* 🎥 🍴 🛍 📷
www.english-heritage.org.uk

This was the largest house
in England when built,
1603–1614, for Thomas
Howard, Lord Treasurer and
1st Earl of Suffolk. James I
joked that Howard's house
was too big for a king but not
for a Lord Treasurer. Charles
II, his grandson, disagreed and
bought it in 1667; but he and
his successors seldom went
there and in 1701 it was given
back to the Howards, who
demolished two thirds of it.

What remains is a Jacobean
mansion, retaining its original
hall and many fine plaster ceilings. Robert Adam *(see p28)*
remodelled some of the
interior in the 1760s and these
rooms have been restored to
his original designs. At the
same time, Capability Brown
(see p26) landscaped the
magnificent 18th-century park.

The Chapel *was completed
in 1772 to a Gothic design.
The furniture was made to
complement the wooden
pillars and vaulting which
are painted to imitate stone.*

Stained glass window,
installed in 1771, represents
the Last Supper.

Main entrance

The Great Hall,
*hung with family
portraits, is the highlight
of the house, with the
massive oak screen and
elaborate hammerbeam
roof surviving in their
Jacobean form.*

Epping Forest 🟔

Essex. 🚆 *Chingford.* 🚇 *Loughton, Theydon Bois.* 🛈 *High Beach, Loughton (020-8508 0028).*

As one of the large open spaces near London, the 2,400 ha (6,000 acre) forest is popular with walkers, just as, centuries ago, it was a favourite hunting ground for kings and courtiers – the word forest denoted an area for hunting.

Epping Forest contains oaks and beeches up to 400 years old

A depiction of the Battle of Maldon (991) on the *Maldon Embroidery*

Henry VIII had a lodge built in 1543 on the edge of the forest. His daughter Elizabeth I, also a keen hunter, often used the lodge and it soon became known as **Queen Elizabeth's Hunting Lodge**.

This three-storey timbered building has been fully renovated and now houses an exhibition explaining the lodge's history and other aspects of the forest's life.

The tracts of open land and woods interspersed with a number of lakes, make an ideal habitat for a variety of plant, bird and animal life: deer roam the northern part, many of a special dark strain introduced by James I. The Corporation of London bought the forest in the mid-19th century to ensure it remained open to the public.

🏛 Queen Elizabeth's Hunting Lodge
Rangers Rd, Chingford. **Tel** 020-8529 6681. ◻ *Wed–Sun (pm).* ● *24–26 Dec, 1 Jan.* ♿ *limited.* 📷 *by appointment.* 🛈 🖥

Maldon 🟤

Essex. 🏠 *21,000.* 🚆 *Chelmsford then bus.* 🛈 *Coach Lane (01621 856503).* 🛒 *Thu, Sat.* **www**.maldon.gov.uk

This delightful old town on the River Blackwater, its High Street lined with shops and inns from the 14th century on, was once an important harbour. One of its best-known industries is the production of Maldon sea salt, panned in the traditional way.

A fierce battle here in 991, when Viking invaders defeated the Saxon defenders, is told in *The Battle of Maldon,* one of the earliest known Saxon poems. The battle is also celebrated in the *Maldon Embroidery* on display in the **Maeldune Centre**. This 13 m (42 ft) long embroidery, made by locals, depicts the history of Maldon from 991 to 1991.

Environs: East of Maldon at Bradwell-on-Sea is the sturdy Saxon church of **St Peter's-on-the-Wall**, a simple stone building that stands isolated on the shore. It was built in 654, from the stones of a former Roman fort, by St Cedd, who used it as his cathedral. It was restored in the 1920s.

🏛 Maeldune Centre
High St. **Tel** 01621 851628. ◻ *Oct–Mar: Thu–Sat; Apr–Sep: Mon–Sat; pm only.* ● *24–26 Dec, 1 Jan.* 📷

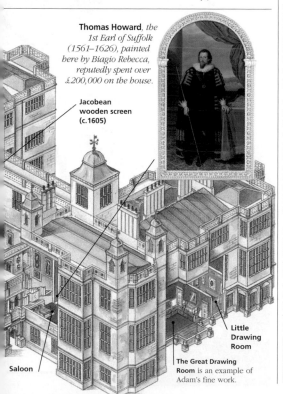

Thomas Howard, *the 1st Earl of Suffolk (1561–1626), painted here by Biagio Rebecca, reputedly spent over £200,000 on the house.*

Jacobean wooden screen (c.1605)

Little Drawing Room

The Great Drawing Room is an example of Adam's fine work.

Saloon

Street-by-Street: Cambridge ㉗

Carving, King's College Chapel

Cambridge has been an important town since Roman times as it was sited at the first navigable point on the River Cam. In the 11th century religious orders began to be established in the town and, in 1209, a group of religious scholars broke away from Oxford University *(see pp222–27)* after academic and religious disputes and came here. Student life dominates the city but it is also a thriving market centre serving a rich agricultural region.

Cyclists in Cambridge

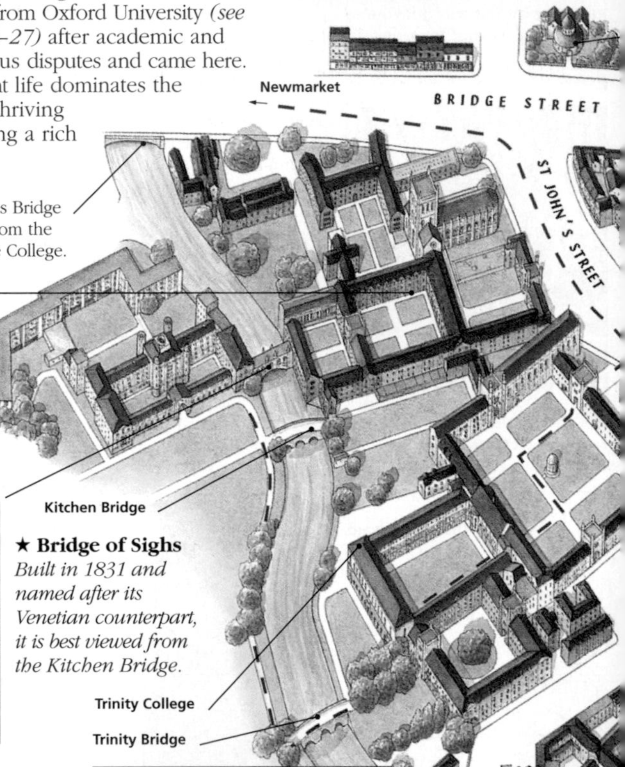

Newmarket

BRIDGE STREET

ST JOHN'S STREET

Magdalene Bridge carries Bridge Street across the Cam from the city centre to Magdalene College.

St John's College has superb Tudor and Jacobean architecture.

Kitchen Bridge

★ Bridge of Sighs
Built in 1831 and named after its Venetian counterpart, it is best viewed from the Kitchen Bridge.

Trinity College

Trinity Bridge

The Backs
This is the name given to the grassy strip lying between the backs of the big colleges and the banks of the Cam – a good spot to enjoy this classic view of King's College Chapel.

KEY

– – – Suggested route

STAR SIGHTS

★ Bridge of Sighs

★ King's College Chapel

Clare College

Clare Bridge

Grantchester

| 0 metres | 75 |
| 0 yards | 75 |

Round Church
The 12th-century Church of the Holy Sepulchre has one of the few round naves in the country. Its design is based on the Holy Sepulchre in Jerusalem.

Gonville and Caius
(pronounced "keys"), founded in 1348, is one of the oldest colleges.

Great St Mary's Church
This clock is over the west door of the university's official church. Its tower offers fine views.

VISITORS' CHECKLIST

Cambridgeshire. 120,000. Stansted. Cambridge. Station Rd. Drummer St. Wheeler St (0871 2268006). daily. Folk Festival: July; Strawberry Fair: June.
www.visitcambridge.org

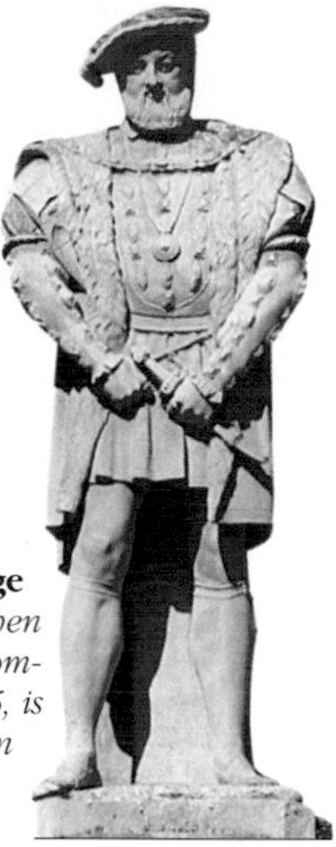

★ **King's College Chapel**
This late medieval masterpiece took 70 years to build (see pp212–13).

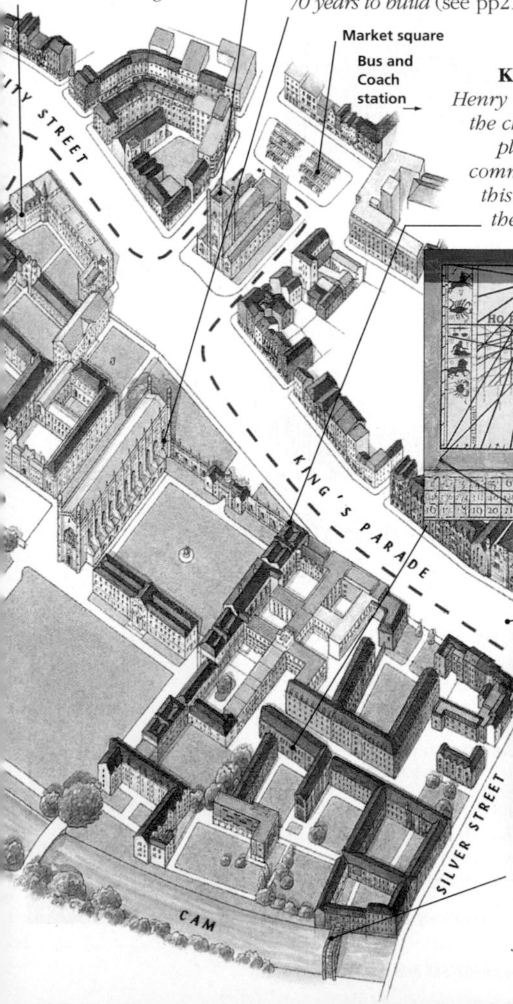

Market square

Bus and Coach station →

King's College
Henry VIII, king when the chapel was completed in 1515, is commemorated in this statue near the main gate.

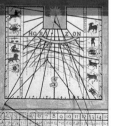

Queens' College
Its Tudor courts are among the university's finest. This 18th-century sundial is over the old chapel – now a reading room.

Corpus Christi College

To London and railway station

Mathematical Bridge
It is a myth that this bridge over the Cam at Queens' College was first built without nuts or bolts.

🏛 **Fitzwilliam Museum**
Trumpington St. **Tel** 01223 332900.
⬜ Tue–Sun; public hols. ● 24–27
Dec, 1 Jan, Good Fri. **Donation**. ♿
📷 by arrangement. ⬜ 📷
www.fitzmuseum.cam.ac.uk

One of Britain's oldest public
museums, this massive Classical building has works of
exceptional quality and rarity,
especially antiquities, ceramics,
paintings and manuscripts.

The core of the collection
was bequeathed in 1816 by
the 7th Viscount Fitzwilliam.
Other gifts have since greatly
added to the exhibits.

Works by Titian (1488–1576)
and the 17th-century Dutch
masters, including Hals, Cuyp
and Hobbema's *Wooded
Landscape* (1686), stand out
among the paintings. French
Impressionist gems include
Monet's *Le Printemps* (1866)
and Renoir's *La Place Clichy*
(1880), while Picasso's *Still
Life* (1923) is notable among
the modern works. Most of
the important British artists
are represented, from
Hogarth in the 18th century
through Constable in the 19th
to Ben Nicholson in the 20th.

The miniatures include the
earliest surviving depiction of
Henry VIII. In the same gallery
are some dazzling illuminated
manuscripts, notably the 15th-
century *Metz Pontifical*, a
French liturgical work.

The impressive Glaisher
collection of European
earthenware and stoneware
includes a unique display of
English delftware from the
16th and 17th centuries.

Handel's bookcase contains
folios of his work, and nearby
is Keats's original manuscript
for *Ode to a Nightingale* (1819).

Cambridge: King's College

**King's College
Coat of Arms**

Henry VI founded this college in
1441. Work on the chapel – one of
the most important examples of late
medieval English architecture – began
five years later, and took 70 years to
complete. Henry himself decided that
it should dominate the city and gave
specific instructions about its dimensions: 88 m (289 ft) long, 12 m (40 ft)
wide and 29 m (94 ft) high. The detailed design is
thought to have been by master stonemason Reginald
Ely, although it was altered in later years.

★ **Fan Vaulted Ceiling**
*This awe-inspiring ceiling,
supported by 22 buttresses,
was built by master stonemason John Wastell in 1515.*

The Fellows' Building was
designed in 1724 by James
Gibbs, as part of an
uncompleted design for
a Great Court.

Henry VI's statue
*This bronze statue of the college's
founder was erected in 1879.*

**Portrait of Richard James
(c.1740s) by William Hogarth**

KING'S COLLEGE CHOIR

When he founded the chapel,
Henry VI stipulated that a choir
of six lay clerks and 16 boy
choristers – educated at the
College school – should sing
daily at services. This still
happens in term time but today
the choir also gives concerts all
over the world. Its broadcast
service of carols has become a
much-loved Christmas tradition.

Choristers in King's College Chapel

Crown and Tudor Rose
This detail of Tudor heraldry on the west door of the Chapel reflects Henry VII's vision of English supremacy.

One of four octagonal turrets

Stained-Glass Windows
The 16th-century windows in the chapel all depict biblical scenes. This one shows Christ baptizing his followers.

VISITORS' CHECKLIST

King's Parade. **Tel** *01223 331212.*
☐ *Oct–Sep: daily (pm only on Sun during term time).*
● *for events ring first.* 📷
✝ *term-time: 5:30pm Mon–Sat, 10:30am & 3:30pm Sun* ♿ 📷
www.kings.cam.ac.uk

Organ
The massive 17th-century organ case above the screen is decorated with two angels playing trumpets.

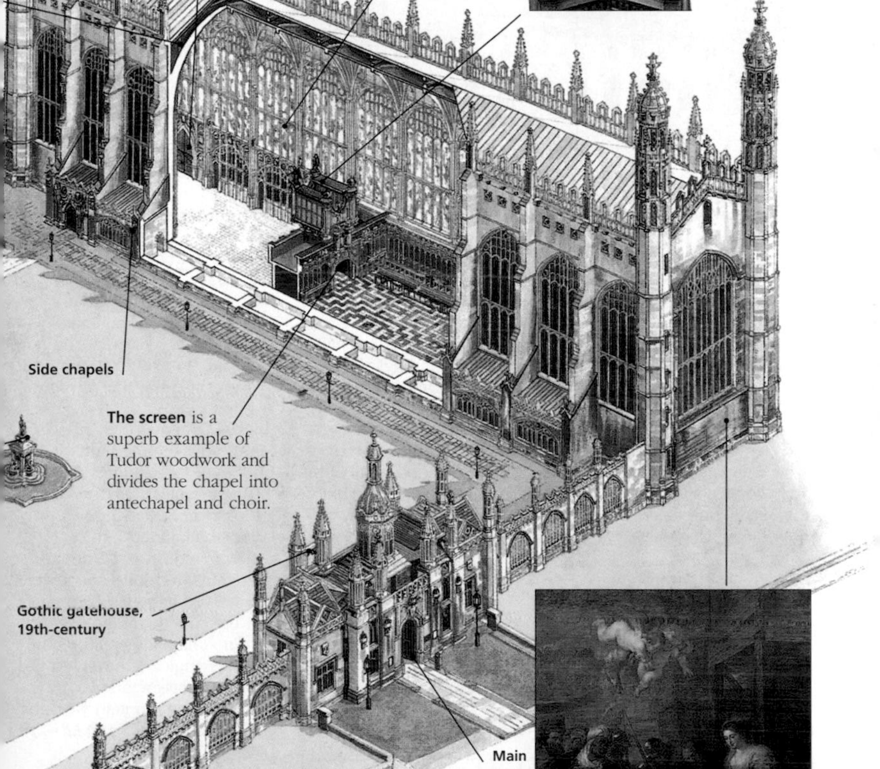

Side chapels

The screen is a superb example of Tudor woodwork and divides the chapel into antechapel and choir.

Gothic gatehouse, 19th-century

Main entrance

STAR SIGHTS

★ Fan Vaulted Ceiling

★ Altarpiece by Rubens

★ Altarpiece by Rubens
Painted in 1634 for the convent of the White Nuns in Belgium, The Adoration of the Magi *was privately donated to King's in 1961.*

Exploring Cambridge University

Cambridge University has 31 colleges *(see also pp210–11)*, the oldest being Peterhouse (1284) and the newest being Robinson (1979). Clustered around the city centre, many of the older colleges have peaceful gardens backing onto the River Cam, which are known as the "Backs". The layout of the older colleges, as at Oxford *(see pp226–7)*, derives from their early connections with religious institutions, although few escaped heavy-handed modification in the Victorian era. The college buildings are generally grouped around squares called courts and offer an unrivalled mix of over 600 years of architecture from the late medieval period through Wren's masterpieces and up to the present day.

The nave of the Wren Chapel at Pembroke College

The imposing façade of Emmanuel College

Emmanuel College

Built in 1677 on St Andrew's Street, Sir Christopher Wren's *(see p114)* chapel is the highlight of the college. Some of the intricate interior details, particularly the plaster ceiling and Amigoni's altar rails (1734), are superb. Founded in 1584, the college has a Puritan tradition. One notable graduate was the clergyman John Harvard, who emigrated to America in 1636 and left all his money to the Massachusetts college that now bears his name.

Senate House

King's Parade is the site of this Palladian building, which is used primarily for university ceremonies. It was designed by James Gibbs in 1722 as part of a grand square of university buildings – which was never completed.

Corpus Christi College

Just down from Senate House, this was founded in 1352 by the local trade guilds, anxious to ensure that education was not the sole prerogative of church and nobility. Its Old Court is remarkably well preserved and looks today much as it would have done when built in the 14th century.

The college is connected by a 15th-century gallery of red brick to St Bene't's Church (short for St Benedict's), whose large Saxon tower is the oldest structure in Cambridge.

King's College
See pp212–13.

Pembroke College

The college chapel was the first building completed by Wren *(see pp114–15)*. A formal classical design, it replaced a 14th-century chapel that was turned into a library. The college, just off Trumpington Street, also has fine gardens.

Jesus College

Although founded in 1497, some of its buildings on Jesus Lane are older, as the college took over St Radegond's nunnery, built in the 12th century. There are traces of Norman columns, windows and a well-preserved hammerbeam roof in the college dining hall.

The chapel keeps the core of the original church but the stained glass windows are modern and contain work by William Morris *(see pp220–21)*.

Queens' College

Built in 1446 on Queens' Land, the college was endowed in 1448 by Margaret of Anjou, queen of Henry VI, and again in 1465 by Elizabeth Woodville, queen of Edward IV, which explains the position of the apostrophe. Queens' has a

---

PUNTING ON THE CAM

Punting captures the essence of carefree college days: a student leaning on a long pole, lazily guiding the flat-bottomed river craft along, while others stretch out and relax. Punting is still popular both with students and visitors, who can hire punts from boatyards along the river – with a chauffeur if required. Punts do sometimes capsize, and novices should prepare for a dip.

Punting by the King's College "Backs"

marvellous collection of Tudor buildings, notably the half-timbered President's Gallery, built in the mid-16th century on top of the brick arches in the charming Cloister Court. The Principal Court is 15th century, as is Erasmus's Tower, named after the Dutch scholar.

Pepys Library in Magdalene College

The college has buildings on both sides of the Cam, linked by the bizarre Mathematical Bridge, built in 1749 to hold together without the use of nuts and bolts – although they have had to be used in subsequent repairs.

Magdalene College

Pronounced "maudlin" – as is the Oxford college *(see p226)* – the college, on Bridge Street, was established in 1482. The diarist Samuel Pepys (1633–1703) was a student here and left his large library to the college on his death. The 12 red-oak bookcases have over 3,000 books. Magdalene was the last all-male Cambridge college and it admitted women students only in 1987.

St John's College

Sited on St John's Street, the imposing turreted brick and stone gatehouse of 1514, with its colourful heraldic symbols, provides a fitting entrance to the second largest Cambridge college and its rich store of 16th- and 17th-century buildings. Its hall, most of it Elizabethan, has portraits of the college's famous alumni, such as the poet William Wordsworth *(see p366)* and the statesman Lord Palmerston. St John's spans the Cam and boasts two bridges, one built in 1712 and the other, the Bridge of Sighs, in 1831, based on its Venetian namesake.

Peterhouse

The first Cambridge college, on Trumpington Street, is also one of the smallest. The hall still has original features from 1286 but its best details are later – a Tudor fireplace which is backed with 19th-century tiles by William Morris *(see pp220–21)*. A gallery connects the college to the 12th century church of St Mary the Less, which used to be called St Peter's Church – hence the college's name.

William Morris tiles, Peterhouse

Trinity College

The largest college, situated on Trinity Street, was founded by Henry VIII in 1547 and has a massive court and hall. The entrance gate, with statues of Henry and James I (added later), was built in 1529 for King's Hall, an earlier college incorporated into Trinity. The Great Court features a late Elizabethan fountain – at one time the main water supply. The chapel, built in 1567, has life-size statues of college members, notably Roubiliac's statue of the scientist Isaac Newton (1755).

University Botanic Garden

A delightful place for a leisurely stroll, just off Trumpington Street, as well as an important academic resource, the garden has been on this site since 1846. It has a superb collection of trees and a sensational water garden. The winter garden is one of the finest in the country.

The Bridge of Sighs over the River Cam, linking the buildings of St John's College

THAMES VALLEY

BUCKINGHAMSHIRE · OXFORDSHIRE · BERKSHIRE
BEDFORDSHIRE · HERTFORDSHIRE

The mighty tidal river on which Britain's capital city was founded has modest origins, meandering from its source in the hills of Gloucestershire through the lush countryside towards London. Almost entirely agricultural land in the 19th century, the Thames Valley maintains its pastoral beauty despite the incursion of modern industry.

There are ancient royal connections with the area. Windsor Castle has been a residence of kings and queens for more than 900 years, and played a critical role in history in 1215, when King John set out from here to sign the *Magna Carta* at Runnymede on the River Thames. Further north, Queen Anne had Blenheim Palace built for her military commander, the 1st Duke of Marlborough. Elizabeth I spent part of her childhood at Hatfield House, and part of the Tudor palace still stands.

Several towns in this region, most notably Burford in Oxfordshire, developed as coach staging posts on the important trunk routes between London and the West Country. With the introduction of commuter transportation in the early 20th century, much of the area became an extension of suburbia and saw some imaginative experiments in Utopian town planning such as the garden city of Welwyn and the Quaker settlement at Jordans.

Oxford, the Thames Valley's principal city, owes its importance to the foundation of Britain's first university there in 1167; many of its colleges are gems of medieval architecture. In the 17th century, a number of battles during the Civil War *(see p52)* were fought around Oxford, which for a time was the headquarters of King Charles I, who was supported by the students. When the royalists were forced to flee Oxford, Cromwell made himself chancellor of the university.

Punting on the River Cherwell, Oxford

◁ **Medieval staircase in Christchurch College, Oxford**

Exploring the Thames Valley

The pleasant countryside of the Chiltern Hills and of the Thames Valley itself appealed to aristocrats who built stately homes close to London. Many of these are among the grandest in the country, including Hatfield House and Blenheim. Around these great houses grew picturesque villages, with half-timbered buildings and, as you move towards the Cotswolds, houses built in attractive buff-coloured stone. That the area has been inhabited for thousands of years is shown by the number of prehistoric remains, including the most remarkable chalk hillside figure, the White Horse of Uffington.

SIGHTS AT A GLANCE

A thatched cottage, Upper Swarford, Banbury

GETTING AROUND

As an important commuter belt, the Thames Valley is well served by public transport, as well as a good network of motorways and major roads into London. Mainline trains travel to all the major towns and there are many coach services that run from London to the major sights and attractions.

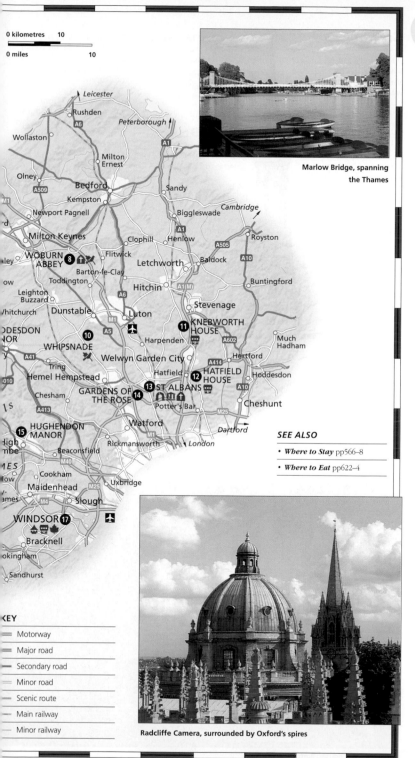

0 kilometres 10

0 miles 10

Leicester

Rushden
A6

Peterborough

Wollaston

Milton
Ernest

Olney
A509

Bedford

Sandy

Kempston

Cambridge

Newport Pagnell

Biggleswade

Milton Keynes

Clophill

Henlow

A1

Royston

WOBURN
ABBEY **8**

Flitwick

Letchworth

A505

A10

Barton-le-Clay

Baldock

Toddington

Hitchin
A1(M)

Buntingford

Leighton
Buzzard

A6

Dunstable

Luton

Stevenage

Whitchurch

M1

A5

KNEBWORTH
HOUSE **11**

DDESDON
OR

10

Harpenden

A602

Much
Hadham

WHIPSNADE

Welwyn Garden City

Hertford
A414

A41

Tring

Hatfield

HATFIELD
HOUSE **12**

Hoddesdon

Hemel Hempstead

Chesham

GARDENS OF
THE ROSE **14**

ST ALBANS **13**

A10

Cheshunt

010

Potter's Bar

M25

HUGHENDON
MANOR **15**

Watford

Dartford

igh
be

Beaconsfield

Rickmansworth

M1

London

ES
ow
/
ames

Cookham

M40

Maidenhead

Uxbridge

M25

M4

Slough

WINDSOR **17**

Bracknell

okingham

Sandhurst

Marlow Bridge, spanning
the Thames

SEE ALSO

- *Where to Stay* pp566–8
- *Where to Eat* pp622–4

Radcliffe Camera, surrounded by Oxford's spires

KEY

— Motorway

— Major road

— Secondary road

— Minor road

— Scenic route

— Main railway

— Minor railway

Great Tew ❶

Oxfordshire. 🚶 250. 🚈 Oxford or Banbury then taxi. ℹ️ Castle Quay Shopping Centre (01295 259855). **www**.visit-northoxfordshire.co.uk

This secluded village of ironstone was founded in the 1630s by Lord Falkland for estate workers. It was heavily restored between 1809 and 1811 in the Gothic style. Thatched cottages stand in gardens with clipped box hedges, and in the centre of the village is the 16th-century pub, the **Falkland Arms**, which retains its original period atmosphere.

Environs: Five miles (8 km) west are the **Rollright Stones**, three Bronze Age monuments. They comprise a stone circle of 77 stones, about 30 m (100 ft) in diameter, known as the King's Men; the remains of a burial chamber called the Whispering Knights; and the solitary King Stone.

Further north is **Banbury**, well known for its spicy flat cakes and its market cross, immortalized in the nursery rhyme, *Ride a Cock-horse to*

The 19th-century Banbury Cross

Banbury Cross. The original medieval cross was destroyed but it was replaced in 1859.

🏨 **Falkland Arms**
Great Tew. *Tel 01608 683653.*
⭕ daily. ● 25 Dec. 🍴

Burford ❷

Oxfordshire. 🚶 1,000. ℹ️ Sheep St (01993 823558).

A charming small town, Burford has hardly changed from Georgian times, when it was an important coach stop between Oxford and the West Country. Cotswold stone houses, inns and shops, many built in the 16th century, line its main street. **Tolsey Hall** is a Tudor house with an open ground floor where stalls are still set up. The house is located on the corner of Sheep Street, itself a reminder of the importance of the medieval wool trade *(see p207)*.

Environs: Just east of Burford is **Swinbrook**, whose church contains the Fettiplace Monuments, six carved figures from the Tudor and Stuart periods.

Two miles (3 km) beyond are the ruins of **Minster Lovell Hall**, a 15th-century manor house whose unusual dovecote survives intact.

Witney, further west, has a town hall dating from 1730. On its outskirts lies **Cogges Manor Farm**, a working farm and museum of rural life, restored to its Victorian state.

🏨 **Minster Lovell Hall**
Minster Lovell. ⭕ daily.

🏨 **Cogges Manor Farm**
Witney. *Tel 01993 772602.* ⭕ Easter–Oct: Tue–Sun (Sat & Sun pm) & public hols. 🎫 ♿ limited. 🍴 🚻

Kelmscott ❸

Oxfordshire. 🚶 100. ℹ️ 5 Market Place, Faringdon (01367 242191). **www**.faringdon.org

The imaginative designer and writer William Morris lived in this pretty Thameside village from 1871 until his death in 1896. He shared his house, the classic Elizabethan **Kelmscott Manor**, with fellow painter Dante Gabriel Rossetti (1828–82), who left after an affair with Morris's wife Jane – the model for many pre-Raphaelite paintings.

Morris and his followers in the Arts and Crafts movement were attracted by the

Cotswold stone houses, Burford, Oxfordshire

The formal entrance of the Elizabethan Kelmscott Manor

medieval feel of the village and several cottages were later built in Morris's memory.

Today Kelmscott Manor has works of art by members of the movement – including some William de Morgan tiles. Morris is buried in the village churchyard, with a tomb designed by Philip Webb.

Two miles (3 km) to the east is **Radcot Bridge**, thought to be the oldest bridge still standing over the Thames. Built in the 13th century from the local Taynton stone, it was a strategic river crossing, and in 1387 was damaged in a battle between Richard II and his barons.

🚃 Kelmscott Manor
Kelmscott. *Tel* 01367 252486. ⬤
Apr–Sep: Wed & some Sat; Gardens & shop: Thu 🈂 🚫 limited.
www.kelmscottmanor.co.uk

Vale of the White Horse ❹

Oxfordshire. 🚃 Didcot. 🛈 25 Bridge St, Abingdon (01235 522711); 19 Church St, Wantage (01235 760176). **www**.wantage.com

This lovely valley gets its name from the huge chalk horse, 100 m (350 ft) from nose to tail, carved into the hillside above Uffington. It is believed to be Britain's oldest hillside carving and has sparked many legends: some say it was cut by the Saxon leader Hengist (whose name means stallion in German), while others believe it is to do with Alfred the Great, thought to have been born nearby.

It is, however, a great deal older than either of these stories suggest, having been dated at around 1000 BC.

Nearby is the Celtic earth ramparts of the Iron Age hill fort, **Uffington Castle**. A mile (1.5 km) west along the Ridgeway, an ancient trade route, (*see p37*), is an even older monument, a large Stone Age burial mound which is known as **Wayland's Smithy**. This is immersed in legends that Sir Walter Scott (*see p512*) used in his novel *Kenilworth*.

The best view of the horse is to be had from Uffington village, which is also worth visiting for the **Tom Brown's School Museum**. This 17th-century school house contains exhibits devoted to the author Thomas Hughes (1822–96). Hughes set the early chapters of his Victorian novel, *Tom Brown's Schooldays*, here. The museum also contains material about excavations on White Horse Hill.

🏛 Tom Brown's School
Broad St, Uffington. 🛈 01367 820259. ⬤ Easter–Oct: Sat, Sun & public hols (pm). 🈂 🚫 limited. 🅿
www.uffington.net/museum

HILLSIDE CHALK FIGURES

It was the Celts who first saw the potential for creating large-scale artworks on the chalk hills of southern England. Horses – held in high regard by both the Celts and later the Saxons, and the objects of cult worship – were often a favourite subject, but people were also depicted, notably Cerne Abbas, Dorset (*see p269*) and the Long Man of Wilmington (*see p180*). The figures may have served as religious symbols or as landmarks by which tribes identified their territory. Many chalk figures have been obliterated, because without any attention they are quickly overrun by grass. Uffington is "scoured", to prevent encroachment by grass, a tradition once accompanied by a fair and other festivities. There was a second flush of hillside carving in the 18th century, especially in Wiltshire. In some cases – for instance at Bratton Castle near Westbury – an 18th-century carving has been superimposed on an ancient one.

Britain's oldest hillside carving, the White Horse of Uffington

Street-by-Street: Oxford ❺

Oxford has long been a strategic point on the western routes into London – its name describes its position as a convenient spot for crossing the river (a ford for oxen). The city's first scholars, who founded the university, came from France in 1167. The development of England's first university created the spectacular skyline of tall towers and "dreaming spires".

Old Ashmolean
Now the Museum of the History of Science, this resplendent building was designed in 1683 to show Elias Ashmole's collection of curiosities. The displays were moved in 1845.

The Ashmolean Museum displays one of Britain's foremost collections of fine art and antiquities.

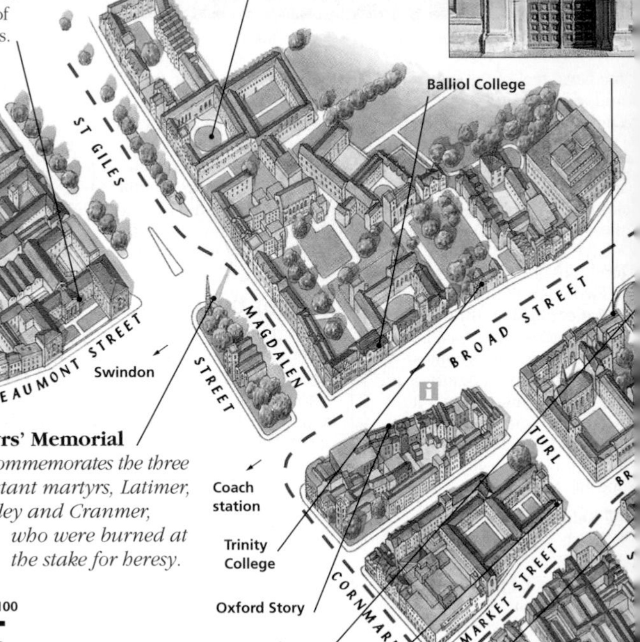

St John's College

Balliol College

ST GILES

BEAUMONT STREET

Swindon

MAGDALEN STREET

BROAD STREET

TURL

Martyrs' Memorial
This commemorates the three Protestant martyrs, Latimer, Ridley and Cranmer, who were burned at the stake for heresy.

Coach station

Trinity College

CORNMARKET STREET

MARKET STREET

0 metres	100
0 yards	100

KEY

– – – Suggested route

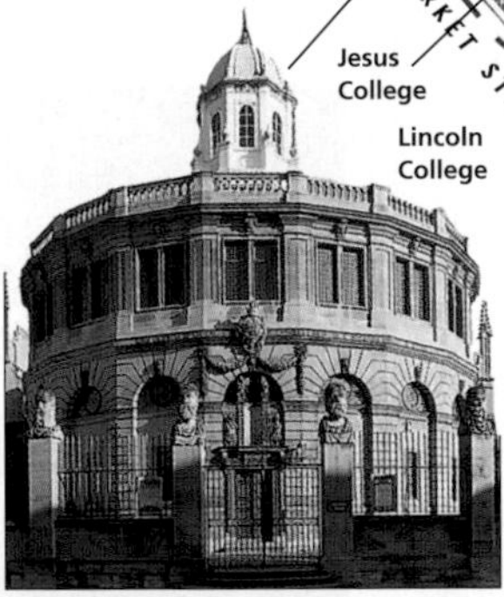

Oxford Story

Jesus College

Lincoln College

Covered market

Railway station

Lincoln College Library

PERCY BYSSHE SHELLEY

Shelley (1792–1822), one of the Romantic poets *(see p366)*, attended University College, Oxford, but was expelled after writing the revolutionary pamphlet *The Necessity of Atheism*. Despite that disgrace, the college has put up a marble memorial to him.

Museum of Oxford

Sheldonian Theatre
The first building designed by Wren (see p114) is the scene of Oxford University's traditional graduation ceremonies.

STAR SIGHTS

★ Radcliffe Camera

★ Christ Church

★ Radcliffe Camera
This Classical rotunda is Oxford's most distinctive building and is now a reading room of the Bodleian. It was one of the library's original buildings (see p227).

VISITORS' CHECKLIST

Oxfordshire. 134,248. Park End St. Gloucester Green. 15–16 Broad St (01865 726871). Wed, 1st Thu of mth (farmers' market), Thu (flea market). **www**.visitoxford.org

Bridge of Sighs
A copy of the steeply arched bridge in Venice, this picturesque landmark, built in 1914, joins the old and new buildings of Hertford College.

New College

St Mary the Virgin Church

Queen's College

All Souls College

→ London

University College

→ Botanic Garden and Magdalen College

Oriel College

Merton College

Corpus Christi College

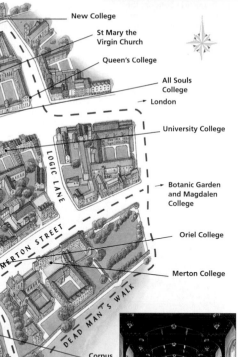

QUEEN'S LANE

HIGH STREET

ORIEL STREET

MAGPIE LANE

LOGIC LANE

MERTON STREET

BEAR LANE

DEAD MAN'S WALK

★ Christ Church
Students still eat at long tables in all the college halls. Senior academics sit at the high table and grace is always said in Latin.

Exploring Oxford

A bust on the Sheldonian Theatre

Oxford is more than just a university city; it has one of Britain's most important car factories in the suburb of Cowley. Despite this, Oxford is dominated by institutions related to its huge academic community: like Blackwell's bookshop which has over 20,000 titles in stock. The two rivers, the Cherwell and the Isis (the name given to the Thames as it flows through the city), provide lovely riverside walks, or you can hire a punt and spend an afternoon on the Cherwell.

🏛 Ashmolean Museum

Beaumont St. **Tel** 01865 278000.
⭕ Tue–Sun (Sun pm only) & public hols. ⬤ 1 Jan, Good Fri, 25–28 Dec.
♿ 🎧 Tue, Fri, Sat. ▯ ▮
www.ashmole.ox.ac.uk

One of the best museums in Britain outside London, the Ashmolean – the first purpose-built museum in England – opened in 1683, based on a display known as "The Ark" collected by the two John Tradescants, father and son.

On their many voyages to the Orient and the Americas they collected stuffed animals and tribal artifacts, the like of which had never before been displayed in England. The collection was acquired on their death by the antiquarian Elias Ashmole, who donated it to the university and had a building made for the exhibits on Broad Street – the Old Ashmolean, now the Museum of the History of Science.

During the 19th century part of the Tradescant collection was moved to the University Galleries, a magnificent Neo-Classical building of 1845. This greatly expanded museum is now known as the Ashmolean.

However, what is left of the original curio collection is overshadowed by the other exhibits in the museum, in particular the paintings and drawings. These include Bellini's *St Jerome Reading in a Landscape* (late 15th century); Raphael's *Heads of Two Apostles* (1519); Turner's *Venice: The Grand Canal* (1840); Rembrandt's *Saskia Asleep* (1635); Michelangelo's *Crucifixion* (1557), Picasso's *Blue Roofs* (1901) and a large group of Pre-Raphaelites, including Rossetti, Millais and Holman Hunt. There are also fine Greek and Roman carvings and a collection of stringed musical instruments.

Items of more local interest include a Rowlandson watercolour of Radcliffe Square in about 1790 and the Oxford Crown. This silver coin was minted here during the Civil War in 1644 *(see p52)* when Charles I was based in Oxford, and forms part of the second largest coin collection in Britain. Perhaps the single most important item is the gold enamelled ring known as the Alfred Jewel *(see p47)*, which is over 1,000 years old.

The entrance to the Ashmolean Museum

🌷 Botanic Garden

Rose Lane. **Tel** 01865 286690.
⭕ daily. ⬤ 25 Dec, Good Fri.
📷 Mar–Oct. **Donation** Nov–Feb.
♿ **www**.botanic-garden.ox.ac.uk

Britain's oldest botanic garden was founded in 1621 – one ancient yew tree survives from that period. The entrance gates were designed by Nicholas Stone in 1633 and paid for, like the garden itself, by the Earl of Danby. His statue adorns the gate, along with those of Charles I and II. This small garden is a delightful spot for a stroll, with an original walled garden, a more recent herbaceous border and rock garden, and a new insectivorous house.

The 17th-century Botanic Gardens

🏰 Carfax Tower

Carfax Sq. **Tel** 01865 792653. ⭕ daily. ⬤ 25 & 26 Dec, 1 Jan. 📷 ▮

The tower is all that remains of the 14th-century Church of St Martin, demolished in 1896 so that the adjoining road could be widened. Be there to watch the clock strike the quarter hours, and climb to the top for a panoramic view of the city. Carfax was the crossing point of the original north-to-south and east-to-west routes through Oxford and the word comes from the French *quatre voies*, or "four ways".

🎵 Holywell Music Room

Holywell St. ⭕ concerts only. 📷 ♿

This was the first building in Europe designed, in 1752, specifically for public musical performances. Previously, concerts had been held in private houses for invited guests only. Its two splendid chandeliers originally adorned Westminster Hall at the coronation of George IV in 1820, and were given by the king to Wadham College, of which the music room technically forms a part. The room is regularly used for contemporary and classical concerts.

🏛 Museum of Oxford

St Aldate. *Tel* 01865 252761. ☐ Tue–Sun. ● 25, 26 Dec, 1 Jan. 🈳 www.oxford.gov.uk/museum

A well-organized display in the Victorian town hall illustrates the long history of Oxford and its university. Exhibits include a Roman pottery kiln. The main features are a series of well-reconstructed rooms, including one from an Elizabethan inn and an 18th-century student's room.

🏛 Martyrs' Memorial

Magdalen St.

This commemorates the three Protestants burned at the stake on Broad Street – Bishops Latimer and Ridley in 1555, and Archbishop Cranmer in 1556. On the accession of Queen Mary in 1553 (see p51), they were committed to the Tower of London, then sent to Oxford to defend their views before the doctors of divinity who, after the hearing, condemned them as heretics.

The memorial was designed in 1843 by George Gilbert Scott and based on the Eleanor crosses erected in 12 English towns by Edward I (1239–1307) to honour his queen.

🏛 Oxford Story

6 Broad St. *Tel* 01865 728822. ☐ daily. ● 25 Dec. 🈳 🈳 🈳 limited.

This audio-visual account of the city's history has a train ride through exhibits which are brought to life with animated, life-size models of major historical characters.

🏛 St Mary the Virgin Church

High St. *Tel* 01865 279111. ☐ daily. ● Good Fri, 25, 26 Dec. 🈳 🈳 www.university-church.ox.ac.uk

This, the official church of the university, is said to be the most visited parish church in England. The oldest parts date from the early 13th century and include the tower, from the top of which you can enjoy a fine view. Its Convocation House, of the same date, served as the university's first library until the Bodleian was founded in 1488 (see p227). The church is where the three Oxford Martyrs were pronounced heretics in 1555. An architectural highlight of the church is the Baroque south porch.

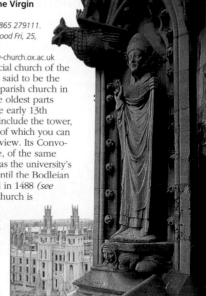

Thomas Cranmer statue, St Mary the Virgin Church

🏛 University Museum

Parks Rd. *Tel* 01865 272950. ☐ daily (pm). ● 24–26 Dec, Easter. 🈳 🈳 www.oum.ox.ac.uk

🏛 Pitt Rivers Museum

Parks Rd. *Tel* 01865 270927. ☐ daily (pm). ● 24–26 Dec, Easter. 🈳 🈳 www.prm.ox.ac.uk

Two of Oxford's most interesting museums adjoin each other. The first is a museum of natural history containing relics of dinosaurs as well as a stuffed dodo. This flightless bird has been extinct since the 17th century, but was immortalized by Lewis Carroll (an Oxford mathematics lecturer whose real name was Charles Dodgson) in his book *Alice in Wonderland (see p401)*. The exhibits are housed in a large Victorian building with cast-iron columns which support a glass roof leading to a cavernous interior. This leads into the Pitt Rivers Museum, which has one of the world's most extensive ethnographic collections – masks and totems from Africa and the Far East – and archaeological displays, including exhibits collected by the explorer Captain Cook.

🏛 Sheldonian Theatre

Broad St. *Tel* 01865 277299. ☐ call for details. ● Christmas period, Easter & public hols. 🈳 🈳 limited. www.sheldon.ox.ac.uk

Completed in 1669, this building was designed by Sir Christopher Wren (see p114). It was paid for by Gilbert Sheldon, the Archbishop of Canterbury, as a place to hold university degree ceremonies. The Classical design of the D-shaped building is based on the Theatre of Marcellus in Rome. The octagonal cupola – larger than the original – was built in 1838 and there is a very famous view from its huge Lantern. In the theatre the beautifully painted ceiling depicts the triumph of religion, art and science over envy, hatred and malice.

The impressive frontage of the University Museum and Pitt Rivers Museum

Exploring Oxford University

Many of the 36 colleges which go to make up the university were founded between the 13th and 16th centuries and cluster around the city centre. As scholarship was then the exclusive preserve of the church, the colleges were designed along the lines of monastic buildings but were often surrounded by beautiful gardens. Although most colleges have been altered over the years, many still incorporate a lot of their original features.

The spectacular view of All Souls College from St Mary's Church

All Souls College
Founded in 1438 on the High Street by Henry VI, the chapel on the college's north side has a classic hammerbeam roof, unusual misericords *(see p341)* on the choir stalls and 15th-century stained glass.

Christ Church College
The best way to view this, the largest of the Oxford colleges, is to approach through the meadows from St Aldate's. Christ Church dates from 1525 when Cardinal Wolsey founded it as an ecclesiastical college to train cardinals. The upper part of the tower in Tom Quad – a rectangular courtyard – was built by Wren *(see p114)* in 1682 and is the largest in the

city. When its bell, Great Tom, was hung in 1648, the college had 101 students, which is why the bell is rung 101 times at 9:05pm, to mark the curfew for students (which has not been enforced since 1963). The odd timing is because night falls here five minutes later than at Greenwich *(see p125)*. Christ Church has produced 16 British prime ministers in the last 200 years. Beside the main quad is the 12th-century Christ Church Cathedral, one of the smallest in England.

Lincoln College
One of the best-preserved of the medieval colleges, it was founded in 1427 on Turl Street, and the front quad and façade

are 15th century. The hall still has its original roof, including the gap where smoke used to escape. The Jacobean chapel is notable for its stained glass. John Wesley *(see p279)* was at college here and his rooms, now a chapel, can be visited.

Magdalen College
At the end of the High Street is perhaps the most typical and beautiful Oxford college. Its 15th-century quads in contrasting styles are set in a park by the Cherwell, crossed by Magdalen Bridge. Every May Day at 6am, the college choir sings from the top of Magdalen's bell tower (1508) – a 16th-century custom to mark the start of summer.

New College
One of the grandest colleges, it was founded by William of Wykeham in 1379 to educate clergy to replace those killed by the Black Death of 1348 *(see p49)*.

Magdalen Bridge spanning the River Cherwell

Its magnificent chapel on New College Lane, restored in the 19th century, has vigorous 14th-century misericords and El Greco's (1541–1614) famous painting of *St James*.

Queen's College
Most of the college buildings date from the 18th century and represent some of the finest work from that period in Oxford. Its superb library was built in 1695 by Henry Aldrich (1647–1710) The front screen with its bell-topped gatehouse is a feature of the High Street.

STUDENT LIFE
Students belong to individual colleges and usually live in them for the duration of their course. The university gives lectures, sets exams and awards degrees but much of the students' tuition and social life is based around their college. Many university traditions date back hundreds of years, like the graduation ceremonies at the Sheldonian which are still held in Latin.

Graduation at the Sheldonian *(see p224)*

For hotels and restaurants in this region see pp566–568 and pp622–624

Merton College seen from Christ Church Meadows

St John's College
The impressive frontage on St Giles dates from 1437, when it was founded for Cistercian scholars. The old library has lovely 17th-century bookcases and stained glass, while the Baylie Chapel has a display of 15th-century vestments.

Trinity College
The oldest part of the college on Broad Street, Durham Quad, is named after the earlier college of 1296 which was incorporated into Trinity in 1555. The late 17th-century chapel has a magnificent reredos and wooden screen.

Corpus Christi College
The whole of the charming front quad on Merton Street dates from 1517, when the college was founded. The quad's sundial, topped by a pelican – the college symbol – bears an early 17th-century calendar. The chapel has a rare 16th-century eagle lectern.

Merton College
Off Merton Street, this is the oldest college (1264) in Oxford. Much of its hall dates from then, including a sturdy decorated door. The chapel choir contains allegorical reliefs representing music, arithmetic, rhetoric and grammar. Merton's Mob Quad served as a model for the later colleges.

BODLEIAN LIBRARY
Founded in 1320, the library was expanded in 1426 by Humphrey, Duke of Gloucester (1391–1447) and brother of Henry V, when his collection of manuscripts would not fit into the old library. It was refounded in 1602 by Thomas Bodley, a wealthy scholar, who insisted on strict rules: the keeper was forbidden to marry. The library is one of the six copyright deposit libraries in the country – it is entitled to receive a copy of every book published in Britain.

The Radcliffe Camera (1748), a domed Baroque rotunda, was built by James Gibbs as a memorial to the physician Dr John Radcliffe (1650–1714).

Main entrance

This extension was built in 1630.

The Divinity School *(1488) has a unique vaulted ceiling with 455 carved bosses representing biblical scenes and both mythical and real beasts – one of the country's finest Gothic interiors.*

Duke Humphrey's Library *has ceiling panels that carry the university crest and Latin motto* Dominus Illuminatio Mea *– the Lord, my Light.*

Blenheim Palace 6

After John Churchill, the 1st Duke of Marlborough, defeated the French at the Battle of Blenheim in 1704, Queen Anne gave him the Manor of Woodstock and had this palatial house built for him in gratitude. Designed by both Nicholas Hawksmoor and Sir John Vanbrugh *(see p398)*, it is a Baroque masterpiece. It was also the birthplace of Britain's World War II leader, Winston Churchill, in 1874.

★ Long Library
This 55 m (183 ft) room was designed by Vanbrugh as a picture gallery. The portraits include that of Queen Anne by Sir Godfrey Kneller (1646–1723). The stucco on the ceiling is by Isaac Mansfield (1725).

Winston Churchill and his wife, Clementine

The Grand Bridge was begun in 1708. It has a 31 m (101 ft) main span and contains rooms within its structure.

Chapel
The marble monument to the 1st Duke of Marlborough and his family was sculpted by Michael Rysbrack in 1733.

STAR SIGHTS

★ Long Library
★ Saloon
★ Park and Gardens

Water Terraces
These magnificent gardens were laid out in the 1920s by French architect Achille Duchêne in 17th-century style, with detailed patterned beds and fountains.

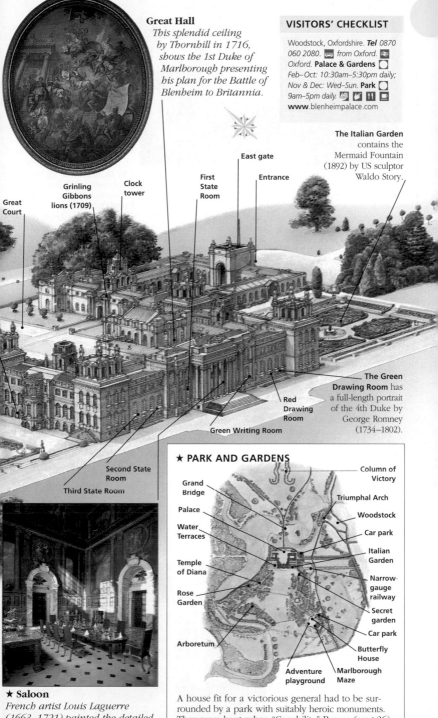

Great Hall
This splendid ceiling by Thornhill in 1716, shows the 1st Duke of Marlborough presenting his plan for the Battle of Blenheim to Britannia.

VISITORS' CHECKLIST

Woodstock, Oxfordshire. *Tel* 0870 060 2080. ⊞ from Oxford. ⊞ Oxford. **Palace & Gardens** ☐ Feb–Oct: 10:30am–5:30pm daily; Nov & Dec: Wed–Sun. **Park** ☐ 9am–5pm daily. ⬛ ▮ ▮ ▮ **www**.blenheimpalace.com

The Italian Garden contains the Mermaid Fountain (1892) by US sculptor Waldo Story.

East gate

First State Room

Entrance

Grinling Gibbons lions (1709)

Clock tower

Great Court

The Green Drawing Room has a full-length portrait of the 4th Duke by George Romney (1734–1802).

Red Drawing Room

Green Writing Room

Second State Room

Third State Room

★ PARK AND GARDENS

Column of Victory

Grand Bridge

Triumphal Arch

Palace

Woodstock

Water Terraces

Car park

Temple of Diana

Italian Garden

Rose Garden

Narrow-gauge railway

Secret garden

Car park

Arboretum

Butterfly House

Adventure playground

Marlborough Maze

A house fit for a victorious general had to be surrounded by a park with suitably heroic monuments. They were kept when "Capability" Brown *(see p26)* re-landscaped the park (1764–74) and created the lake.

★ Saloon
French artist Louis Laguerre (1663–1721) painted the detailed scenes on the walls and ceiling.

Canaletto's *Entrance to the Arsenal* (1730) hangs at Woburn Abbey

Stowe Gardens ❼

(NT) Buckingham, Buckinghamshire.
Tel 01280 822850. ☒ Milton Keynes
then bus. ☐ Mar–22 Dec: Wed–Sun,
public hols. **Stowe House** ☐ Access
may be restricted due to a 20-year
restoration project. 🖼 🚹 limited. ☐
🚹 www.nationaltrust/stowegardens

This is the most ambitious
and important landscaped
garden in Britain, as well as
being one of the finest examples of the 18th-century
passion for improving on
nature to make it conform to
fashionable notions of taste.
In the space of nearly 100
years the original garden, first
laid out around 1680, was
enlarged and transformed by
the addition of monuments,
Greek and Gothic temples,
grottoes, statues, ornamental
bridges, artificial lakes and
"natural" tree plantings.
Most of the leading designers
and architects of the period
contributed to the design,
including Sir John Vanbrugh,
James Gibbs and Capability
Brown *(see p26),* who was
head gardener at Stowe for 10
years, at the start of his career.
From 1593 to 1921 the huge
property was owned by the
Temple and Grenville families
– later the Dukes of Buckingham – until the large Palladian
house at its centre was sold
and converted into an elite
boys' school (tours can be
arranged in school holidays).
The family were soldiers
and politicians in the liberal
tradition, and many of the
buildings and sculptures in
the garden symbolize Utopian
ideals of democracy and freedom. There are temples of
British Worthies, of Ancient

Virtue and the Fane (temple)
of Pastoral Poetry. Some features deteriorated in the 19th
century and statues were sold.
But a major restoration programme has meant that statues
have been bought back and
copies made of others.

Woburn Abbey ❽

Woburn, Bedfordshire. *Tel* 01525
290666. ☒ Flitwick then taxi.
☐ Apr–Sep: daily; Jan–Mar, Oct: Sat,
Sun. **Grounds** ☐ daily. 🚹 🖼 🚹
ring first. 🏞 by arrangement. 🚹
www.woburnabbey.co.uk

The Dukes of Bedford have
lived here for over 350 years
and were among the first
owners of an English stately
home to open their house to
the public some 40 years ago.
The abbey was built in the
mid-18th century on the foundations of a large 12th-century
Cistercian monastery. Its mix
of styles range from Henry
Flitcroft and Henry Holland
(see p28). It is also popular for
its 142 ha (350 acre) safari
park and attractive deer park

with nine species including
the Manchurian Sika deer
from China.
Its magnificent state apartments house an important
private art collection with
works by Reynolds (1723–92)
and Canaletto (1697–1768).

Waddesdon Manor ❾

Nr Aylesbury, Buckinghamshire.
Tel 01296 653 203. ☒ Aylesbury
then taxi. **House** ☐ Apr–Oct:
11am–4pm Wed–Sun & bank hol
Mon; Christmas (phone for details).
Grounds ☐ Mar–23 Dec: 10am–
5pm Wed–Sun & bank hol Mon.
Bachelors' Wing ☐ Mar–Oct:
11am–4pm Wed–Fri. 🖼 🚹 ☐ 🚹
www.waddesdon.org.uk

Waddesdon Manor was
built between 1874–89
by Baron Ferdinand de
Rothschild and designed by
French architect Gabriel-
Hippolyte Destailleur. The
garden was originally laid
out by French landscape
gardener Elie Lainé.
Built in the style of a French
16th-century chateau, Waddesdon Manor houses one of
the world's finest collections
of French 18th-century decorative art. It also contains
renowned collections of
French furniture, Savonnierie
carpets, Sèvres porcelain and
17th-century paintings.
The garden is renowned for
its seasonal displays and over
the next five years, displays
are being designed by contemporary artists. Wine tasting
events are also hosted in the
comprehensive Wine Cellars.

The 17th-century Palladian bridge over the Octagon Lake in Stowe Park

Hatfield House, one of the largest Jacobean mansions in the country

Whipsnade Wild Animal Park ⑩

Nr Dunstable, Bedfordshire. **Tel** 01582 872171. 🚃 Hemel Hempsted then bus or Whipsnade (from Victoria Station, London) ◯ daily. 🎦 ♿ 🖥 www.whipsnade.co.uk

The rural branch of London Zoo, this was one of the first zoos to minimize the use of cages, confining animals safely but without constriction.

At 240 ha (600 acres), it is Europe's largest conservation park, with more than 2,500 species. You can drive through some areas or go by steam train. Also popular are the adventure playground and sea lions' underwater display.

Knebworth House ⑪

Knebworth, Hertfordshire. **Tel** 01438 812661. 🚃 Stevenage then taxi. ◯ Sat, Sun; two weeks at Easter: daily; Jul–Sep: daily. 🖥 🎦 ♿ limited. 🖼 www.knebworthhouse.com

A notable Tudor mansion, with a beautiful Jacobean banqueting hall, Knebworth was overlain with a 19th-century Victorian Gothic exterior by Lord Lytton, the head of the family. His eldest son, the 1st Earl of Lytton, was Viceroy of India, and exhibits illustrate the Delhi Durbar of 1877, when Queen Victoria became Empress of India.

A visit includes the house, gardens, park, and a dinosaur trail for children.

Hatfield House ⑫

Hatfield, Hertfordshire. **Tel** 01707 287010. 🚃 Hatfield. ◯ Easter Sat–Sep: daily. 🖥 🎦 ♿ 🖥 www.hatfield-house.co.uk

One of England's finest Jacobean houses, it was built between 1607 and 1611 for the powerful statesman Robert Cecil.

Its chief historical interest, though, lies in the surviving wing of the original Tudor Hatfield Palace, where Queen Elizabeth I *(see pp50–51)* spent much of her childhood. She held her first Council of State here when she was crowned in 1558. The palace was partly demolished in 1607 to make way for the new house, which contains mementoes of her life, including the *Rainbow* portrait painted around 1600 by Isaac Oliver. Visitors can attend medieval banquets in the old palace's Great Hall.

Originally laid out by Robert Cecil with help from John Tradescant, the gardens have been restored to reflect these Jacobean origins.

FAMOUS PURITANS

Three major figures connected with the 17th-century Puritan movement are celebrated in the Thames area. John Bunyan (1628–88), who wrote the allegorical tale *The Pilgrim's Progress*, was born at Elstow, near Bedford. A passionate Puritan orator, he was jailed for his beliefs for 17 years. The Bunyan Museum in Bedford is a former site of Puritan worship. William Penn (1644–1718), founder of Pennsylvania in the USA, lived, worshipped and is buried at Jordans, near Beaconsfield. A bit further north at Chalfont St Giles is the cottage where the poet John Milton (1608–74) stayed to escape London's plague. There he completed his greatest work, *Paradise Lost*. The house is now a museum based on his life and works.

18th-century engraving of John Bunyan

William Penn, founder of Pennsylvania

John Milton painted by Pieter van der Plas

St Albans ⑬

Today a thriving market town and a base for London commuters, St Albans was for centuries at the heart of some of the most stirring events in English history. A regional capital of ancient Britain, it became a major Roman settlement and then a key ecclesiastical centre – so important that during the Wars of the Roses *(see p49)*, two battles were fought for it. In 1455 the Yorkists drove King Henry VI from the town and six years later the Lancastrians retook it.

The martyr St Alban

Exploring St Albans

Part of the appeal of this ancient and fascinating town, little more than an hour's drive from London, is that its 2,000-year history can be traced vividly by visiting a few sites within easy walking distance of one another. There is a large car park within the walls of the Roman city of Verulamium, between the museum and St Michael's Church and across the road from the excavated theatre. From there it is a pleasant lakeside walk across the park, passing more Roman sites, Ye Olde Fighting Cocks inn, the massive cathedral and the historic High Street. Marking the centre of the town, the High Street is lined with several Tudor buildings and a clock tower dating from 1412, from which the curfew bell used to ring at 4am in the morning and 8:30pm at night.

⋔ Verulamium

Just outside the city centre are the walls of Verulamium, one of the first British cities the Romans established after their invasion of Britain in AD 43. Boadicea *(see p195)* razed it to the ground during her unsuccessful rebellion against the Romans in AD 62, but its position on Watling Street, an important trading route, meant that it was quickly rebuilt on an even larger scale and the city flourished until 410.

⛁ Verulamium Museum

St Michael's St. *Tel 01727 751810.*
◯ *daily.* ● *25 Dec–2 Jan.* 🖼 🖆 🚹
www.stalbansmuseum.org.uk
This excellent museum tells the story of the city, but its main attraction is its splendid collection of well-preserved Roman artefacts, notably some breathtaking mosaic floors, including one depicting the head of a sea god, and another of a scallop shell. Other finds included burial urns and lead coffins.

On the basis of excavated plaster fragments, a Roman room has been painstakingly recreated, its walls painted in startlingly bright colours and geometric patterns.

Between here and St Albans Cathedral are a bath house with a mosaic, remnants of the ancient city wall and one of the original gates.

⛪ Ye Olde Fighting Cocks

Abbey Mill Lane. *Tel 01727 869152.*
◯ *daily.* 🚹
Believed to be England's oldest surviving pub, Ye Olde Fighting Cocks is certainly, with its

One of the oldest surviving pubs in England

octagonal shape, one of the most unusual. It originated as the medieval dovecote of the old abbey and moved here after the Dissolution *(see p50).*

⋔ Roman Theatre

Bluehouse Hill. *Tel 01727 835035.*
◯ *daily.* ● *25, 26 Dec.* 🖼 🚹
www.romantheatre.co.uk
Just across the road from the museum are the foundations of the open-air theatre, first built around AD 140 but enlarged several times. It is one of only six known to have been built in Roman Britain. Alongside it are traces of a row of Roman shops and a house, from which many of the museum's treasures – such as a bronze statuette of Venus – were excavated in the 1930s.

⛪ St Michael's Church

St Michael's. *Tel 01727 835037.*
◯ *Apr–Sep: phone for details.* 🚹
This church was first founded during the Saxon reign and is built partly with bricks taken from Verulamium, which by then was in decline. Numerous additions have been made since then, including a truly splendid Jacobean pulpit.

The church contains an early 17th-century monument to the statesman and writer Sir Francis Bacon; his father owned nearby Gorhambury, a large Tudor house, now in ruins.

A scallop shell, one of the mosaic floors at the Verulamium Museum

St Albans Cathedral

Sumpter Yard. **Tel** 01727 860780.
daily. 11:30am & 2:30pm.
This outstanding example of
medieval architecture has
some classic features such as
the 13th- and 14th-century wall
paintings on the Norman piers.

It was begun in 793, when
King Offa of Mercia founded
the abbey in honour of St
Alban, Britain's first Christian
martyr, put to death by the
Romans in the third century
for sheltering a priest. The
oldest parts, which still stand,

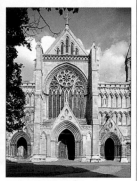

**The imposing west side of
St Albans Cathedral**

were first built in 1077 and
are easily recognizable as
Norman by the round-headed
arches and windows. They
form part of the 84 m (276 ft)
nave – the longest in England.

The pointed arches further
east are Early English (13th
century), while the decorated
work of the 14th century was
added when some of the
Norman arches collapsed.

East of the crossing is
what remains of St Alban's
shrine – a marble pedestal
made up of more than
2,000 tiny fragments. Next
to it is the tomb of Humphrey,
Duke of Gloucester *(see p227)*.

It was also here that the
cathedral that the English
barons drafted the *Magna
Carta* document *(see p48)*,
which King John was then
forced to sign.

The splendour of the Gardens of the Rose in June

Gardens of the Rose ⑭

Chiswell Green, Hertfordshire. **Tel**
01727 850461. St Albans then
bus. Jun–Sep: 9am–5pm Mon–Sat,
10am–6pm Sun & public hols.
www.rnrs.org

As well as being England's
national symbol, the rose
is the most popular flower
with British gardeners.

The 5 ha (12 acre) garden
of the Royal National Rose
Society, with over 30,000
plants and 1,700 varieties, is
at its peak in late June. The
gardens trace the history of
the flower as far back as the
white rose of York, the red
rose of Lancaster *(see p49)*
and the Rosa Mundi – named
by Henry II for his mistress
Fair Rosamond after she was
poisoned by Queen Eleanor

in 1177. During 2005–2006
the gardens were extensively
redeveloped by leading garden
designer Michael Balston.

Hughenden Manor ⑮

(NT) High Wycombe, Buckinghamshire.
Tel 01494 755565. High Wycombe
then bus. Mar: Sat, Sun; Apr–Nov:
Wed–Sun & public hols. Good Fri.
limited.

The Victorian statesman and
novelist Benjamin Disraeli,
Prime Minister from 1874 to
1880, lived here for 33 years
until his death. Originally a
Georgian villa, Disraeli adapted
it in 1862 to the Gothic style.
Furnished as it was in his day,
the house gives an idea of
the life of a wealthy Victorian
gentleman and shows some
portraits of his contemporaries.

GEORGE BERNARD SHAW

Although a controversial playwright and known
as a mischievous character, the Irish-born
George Bernard Shaw (1856–1950) was a man
of settled habits. He lived near St Albans in a
house at Ayot St Lawrence, now called Shaw's
Corner, for the last 44 years of his life,
working until his last weeks in a
summer-house at the bottom of his
large garden. His plays,
combining wit with a powerful
political and social message, still
seem fresh today. One of the most
enduring is *Pygmalion* (1913),
on which the musical *My Fair
Lady* is based. The house and
garden are now a museum
of his life and works.

Touring the Thames ⑯

The Thames between Pangbourne and Eton is leafy and romantic and best seen by boat. But if time is short, the road keeps close to its bank for much of the way. Swans glide gracefully below ancient bridges, voles dive into the water for cover, and elegant herons stand impassive at the river's edge. Huge beech trees overhang the banks which are lined with fine houses, their gardens sloping to the water. The tranquil scene has inspired painters and writers through the ages as well as operating, until recently, as an important transport link.

Hambledon Mill ⑥
The white weather-boarded mill, which was operational until 1955, is one of the largest on the Thames as well as one of the oldest in origin. There are traces of the original 16th-century mill.

Beale Park ①
The philanthropist Gilbert Beale (1868–1967) created a 10 ha (25 acre) park to preserve this beautiful stretch of river intact and breed endangered birds like owls, ornamental water fowl, pheasants and peacocks.

Henley ⑤
This lovely old river town boasts houses and churches dating from the 15th and 16th centuries and an important regatta, first held in 1829 (see p66).

Pangbourne ②
Kenneth Grahame (1859–1932), author of *The Wind in the Willows*, lived here. Pangbourne was used as the setting by artists Ernest Shepard in 1908 and Arthur Rackham in 1951 to illustrate the book.

Sonning Bridge ④
The 18th-century bridge is made up of 11 brick arches of varying width.

TIPS FOR DRIVERS

Tour length: 50 miles (75 km).
Stopping-off points: The picturesque town of Henley has a large number of riverside pubs which will make good stops for lunch. If you are boating you can often moor your boat alongside the river bank. (See also pp684–5.)

Whitchurch Mill ③
This charming village, linked to Pangbourne by a Victorian toll bridge, has a picturesque church and one of the many disused watermills that once harnessed the power of this stretch of river.

Cookham ⑦
This is famous as the home of Stanley Spencer (1891–1959), one of Britain's leading 20th-century artists. The former Methodist chapel, where Spencer worshipped as a child, has been converted into a gallery that contains some of his paintings and equipment. This work, entitled *Swan Upping* (1914–19), recalls a Thames custom.

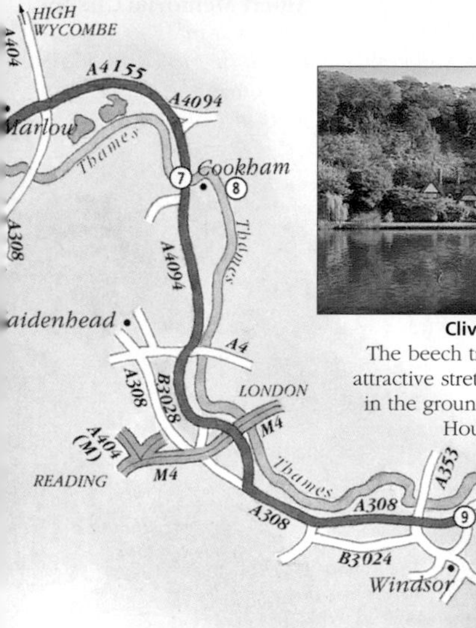

Cliveden Reach ⑧
The beech trees lining this attractive stretch of river are in the grounds of Cliveden House *(see p162)*.

Eton College ⑨
Founded by Henry VI in 1440, Eton is Britain's most famous public school. It has a superb Perpendicular chapel (1441) with a series of English wall paintings (1479–88).

KEY

- Tour route
- Other roads
- Viewpoint

0 kilometres 10
0 miles 5

Salter Bros hire boats, moored at Henley

BOATING TOURS

In summer, scheduled river services run between Henley, Windsor, Runnymede and Marlow. Several companies operate from towns along the route. You can hire boats by the hour or the day or, for a longer tour, you can rent cabin cruisers and sleep on board *(see also p689)*. Ring Salter Bros on 01753 865 832 for more information.

Windsor ⑰

Berkshire. 30,000. *HighSt (01753 743900).* **www**.windsor.gov.uk

The town of Windsor is dwarfed by the enormous **castle** *(see pp2 –7)* on the hill above – in fact its original purpose was to serve the castle's needs. The town is full of quaint Georgian shops, houses and inns. The most prominent building on the High Street is the **Guildhall** completed by Wren *(see p114)* in 1689, where Prince Charles and Camilla Parker-Bowles were married in 2005. The **Household Cavalry Museum** has a large collection of arms and uniforms.

The huge 1,940-ha (4,800-acre) **Windsor Great Park** stretches from the castle three miles (5 km) to Snow Hill, where there is a statue of George III.

Environs: Four miles (7 km) to the southeast is the level grassy meadow, **Runnymede**. This is one of England's most historic sites, where in 1215 King John was forced by his rebellious barons to sign the *Magna Carta (see p48)*, thereby limiting his royal powers. The dainty memorial pavilion at the top of the meadow was erected in 1957.

Household Cavalry Museum
St Leonard's Rd. ***Tel** 01753 755112.* *until Spring 2007.* **Donation**

King John signing the *Magna Carta*, Runnymede

Windsor Castle

Henry II rebuilt the castle

The oldest continuously inhabited royal residence in Britain, the castle, originally made of wood, was built by William the Conqueror in around 1080 to guard the western approaches to London. He chose the site as it was on high ground and just a day's journey from his base in the Tower of London. Successive monarchs have made alterations that render it a remarkable monument to royalty's changing tastes. King George V's affection for it was shown when he chose Windsor for his family surname in 1917. The castle is an official residence of the Queen and her family who stay here many weekends.

Albert Memorial Chapel
First built in 1240, it was rebuilt in 1485 and finally converted into a memorial for Prince Albert in 1863.

King Henry VIII Gate and main exit

★ St George's Chapel
The architectural highlight of the castle, it was built between 1475 and 1528 and is one of England's outstanding Perpendicular Gothic churches. Ten monarchs are buried here.

The Round Tower was first built in wood by William the Conqueror. In 1170 it was rebuilt in stone by Henry II *(see p48)*. It now houses the Royal Archives and Photographic Collection.

Statue of Charles II

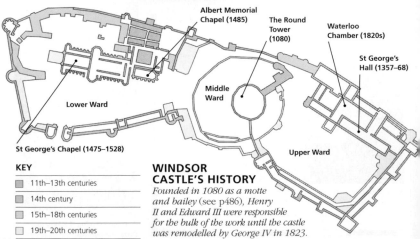

Albert Memorial Chapel (1485)

The Round Tower (1080)

Waterloo Chamber (1820s)

St George's Hall (1357–68)

Middle Ward

Lower Ward

St George's Chapel (1475–1528)

Upper Ward

KEY

▨	11th–13th centuries
▨	14th century
▨	15th–18th centuries
▨	19th–20th centuries

WINDSOR CASTLE'S HISTORY
Founded in 1080 as a motte and bailey (see p486), Henry II and Edward III were responsible for the bulk of the work until the castle was remodelled by George IV in 1823.

Drawings Gallery
This chalk etching of Christ by Michelangelo is part of the Royal Collection. Various pieces in the collection are on display here, including works by Holbein and Leonardo da Vinci among others.

VISITORS' CHECKLIST

Castle Hill. **Tel** 020-7766 7304.
☐ *Mar–Oct: 9:45am–5:15pm; Nov–Feb: 9:45am–4:15pm (last adm: 1 hr 15 mins before close).*
● *25 & 26 Dec, Good Fri.*
▨ ৬ ✝ *St Georges Chapel*
www.royalcollection.org.uk

The Audience Chamber is where the Queen greets her guests.

The Queen's Ballroom

Queen Mary's Dolls' House, designed by Sir Edwin Lutyens, was given to Queen Mary in 1924. The wine cellar contains genuine vintage wine.

Waterloo Chamber
This banqueting hall was created as part of Charles Long's brief for the remodelling of the castle in 1823.

Brunswick Tower

The East Terrace Garden was created by Sir Jeffry Wyatville for King George IV in the 1820s.

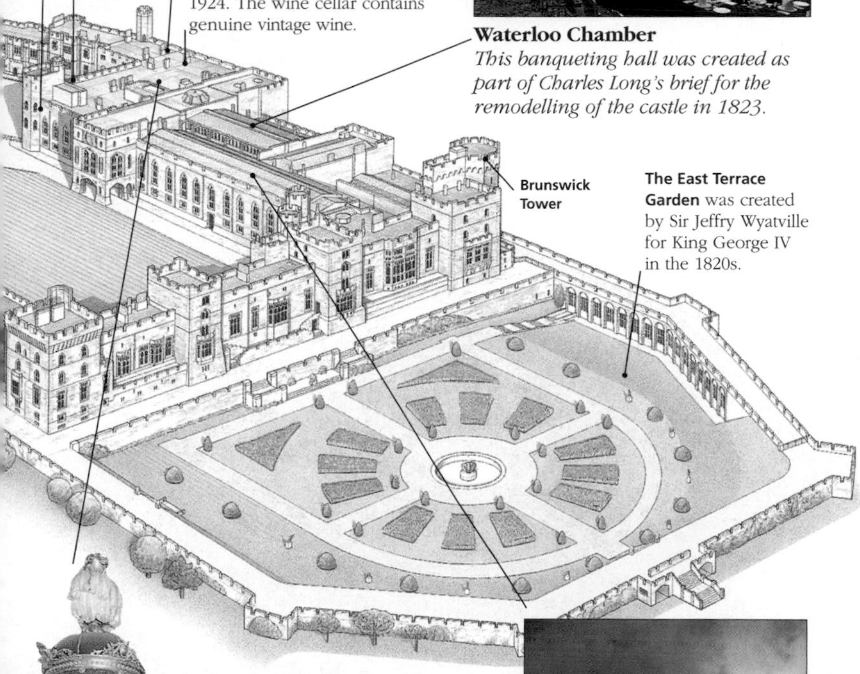

★ **State Apartments**
These rooms contain many treasures, such as this 18th-century bed in the King's State Bedchamber, hung in its present splendour for the visit in 1855 of Napoleon III.

STAR SIGHTS

★ St George's Chapel

★ State Apartments

The Fire of 1992
A devastating blaze began during maintenance work on the State Apartments. St George's Hall was destroyed but has been rebuilt.

THE WEST COUNTRY

The West Country at a Glance

The West Country forms a long penin-sula bounded by the Atlantic to the north and the English Channel to the south, tapering down to Land's End, mainland Britain's westernmost point. Whether exploring the great cities and cathedrals, experiencing the awesome solitude of the moors and their prehistoric monuments, or simply enjoying the miles of coastline and mild climate, this region has an en-during appeal for holiday-makers.

Wells (see pp252–3) *is a charming town nestling at the foot of the Mendip Hills. It is famous for its exquisite three-towered cathedral with an ornate west façade, featuring an array of statues. Alongside stand the moated Bishop's Palace and the 15th-century Vicar's Close.*

Exmoor's (see pp250–51) *heather-clad moors and wooded valleys, grazed by wild ponies and red deer, lead down to some of Devon and Somerset's most dramatic cliffs and coves.*

St Ives (see p277) *has a branch of the Tate Gallery that shows modern works by artists associated with the area. Patrick Heron's bold coloured glass (1993) is on per-manent display.*

Devon

DEVON AND CORNWALL
(see pp272–95)

Cornwall

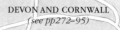

Dartmoor (see pp294–5) *is a wild-erness of great natural beauty covering an area of 365 sq miles (945 sq km). Stone clapper bridges, picturesque villages and weathered granite tors punctuate the landscape.*

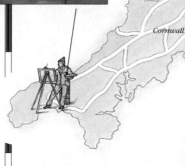

◁ **Stunning views of the Lizard Peninsula**

Bath (see pp258–9) is named after the Roman baths that stand at the heart of the old city next to the splendid medieval abbey. It is one of Britain's liveliest and most rewarding cities, full of elegant Georgian terraces, built in local honey-coloured limestone by the two John Woods (Elder and Younger).

Stonehenge (see pp262–3), the world-famous prehistoric monument, was built in several stages from 3000 BC. Moving and erecting its massive stones was an extraordinary feat for its time. It is likely that this magical stone circle was a place of worship to the sun.

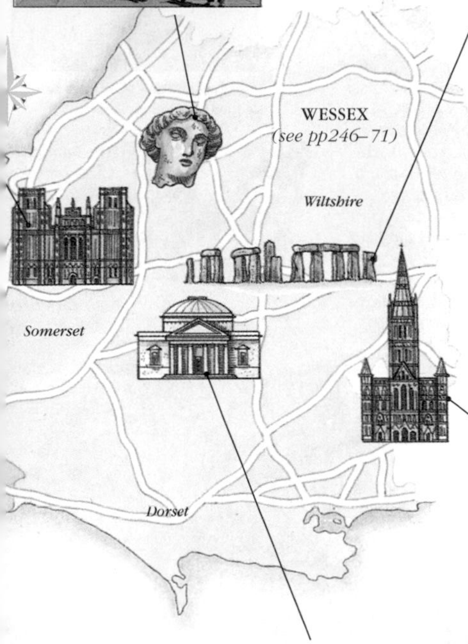

WESSEX
(see pp246–71)

Wiltshire

Somerset

Dorset

0 kilometres   25

0 miles   25

Salisbury's (see pp264–5) cathedral with its soaring spire was the inspiration for one of John Constable's best-loved paintings. The picturesque Cathedral Close has a number of fine medieval buildings.

Stourhead garden (see pp266–7) was inspired by the paintings of Claude and Poussin. Created in the 18th century, the garden is itself a work of art. Contrived vistas, light and shade and a mixture of landscape and gracious buildings, such as the Neo-Classical Pantheon at its centre, are vital to the overall effect.

Coastal Wildlife

The long and varied West Country coastline, ranging from the stark, granite cliffs of Land's End to the pebble-strewn stretch of Chesil Bank, is matched with an equally diverse range of wildlife. Beaches are scattered with colourful shells, while rock pools form miniature marine habitats teeming with life. Caves are used by larger creatures, such as grey seals, and cliffs provide nest sites for birds. In the spring and early summer, an astonishing range of plants grow on the foreshore and cliffs which can be seen at their best from the Southwest Coastal Path *(see p36)*. The plants in turn attract numerous moths and butterflies.

Cliff-tops of Land's End with safe ledges for nesting birds

Chesil Bank *is an unusual ridge of pebbles* (see p256) *stretching 18 miles (29 km) along the Dorset coast. The bank was created by storms and the pebbles increase in size from northwest to southeast due to varying strengths of coastal currents. The bank encloses a lagoon called the Fleet, habitat of the Abbotsbury swans, as well as a large number of wildfowl.*

The Painted Lady, *often see on cliff-top coastal plants, migrates to Brita in the spring.*

High tides wash u driftwood and sh

Cliff-top turf contains many species of wild flowers.

Thrift, *in hummocks of honey-scented flowers, is a familiar sight on cliff ledges in spring.*

Yellowhammers *are to be seen perched on cliff-top bushes.*

Marram grass roots help hold back sand against wind erosion.

Grey seals *come on land to give birth to their young. They can be spotted on remote beaches.*

A BEACHCOMBER'S GUIDE

The best time to observe the natural life of the s shore is when the tide begins to roll back, befo the scavenging seagulls pick up the stranded cr fish and sandhoppers, and the seaweed dries u Much plant and marine life can be found in the secure habitat provided by rock pools.

Durdle Door *was formed by waves continually eroding the weaker chalk layers of this cliff* (see p270) *in Dorset, leaving the stronger oolite to create a striking arch, known in geology as an eyelet.*

COLLECTING SHELLS

Most of the edible molluscs, such as scallops and cockles, are known as bivalves; others, such as whelks and limpets, are known as gastropods.

Great scallop

Common cockle

Common whelk

Common limpet

Seaweed, *such as bladder wrack, can resemble coral or lichen when in water.*

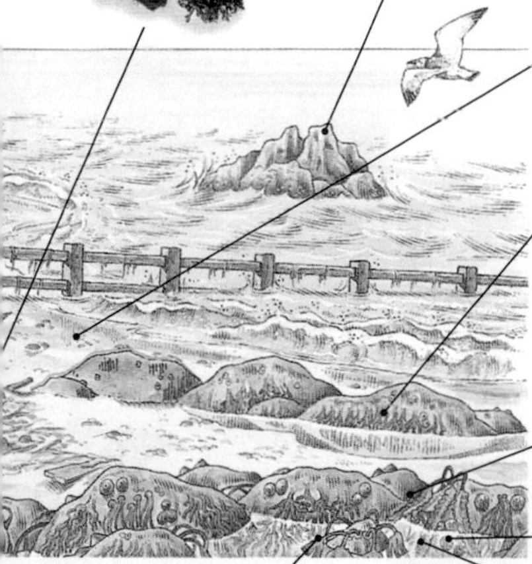

Rocks are colonized by clusters of barnacles, mussels and limpets.

Oystercatchers *have a distinctive orange beak. They hunt along the shore, feeding on all kinds of shellfish.*

Starfish *can be aggressive predators on shellfish. The light-sensitive tips of their tentacles help them to "see" the way.*

Mussels *are widespread and can be harvested for food.*

Rock pools teem with crabs, mussels, shrimps and plant life.

The Velvet Crab, *often found hiding in seaweed, is covered with fine downy hair all over its shell.*

Grey mullet, *when newly hatched, can often be seen in rock pools.*

West Country Gardens

Gardeners have long been attracted to the West Country. Its mild climate is perfect for growing tender and exotic plants, many of which were brought from Asia in the 19th century. As a result, the region has some of England's finest and most varied gardens, covering the whole sweep of garden styles and history *(see pp26–7)*, from the clipped formality of Elizabethan Montacute, to the colourful and crowded cottage-garden style of East Lambrook Manor.

Lanhydrock's (p284) *clipped yews and low box hedges frame a blaze of colourful annuals.*

Trewithen (p281) *is renowned for its rare camellias, rhododendrons and magnolias, grown from seed collected in Asia. The huge garden is at its most impressive in March and June.*

Cotehele *(p293)* has a lovely lush valley garden.

DEVON AND CORNWALL *(see pp272–*

Trelissick *(p281)* has memorable views over the Fal Estuary through shrub-filled woodland.

Glendurgan *(p281)* is a plant-lover's paradise set in a steep, sheltered valley.

Mount Edgcumbe *(p292)* preserves its 18th-century French, Italian and English gardens.

Trengwainton (p276) *has a fine stream garden, whose banks are crowded with moisture-loving plants, beneath a lush canopy of New Zealand tree ferns.*

Overbecks *(near Salcombe)* enjoys a spectacular site overlooking the Salcombe Estuary. There are secret gardens, terraces and rocky dells.

CREATIVE GARDENING

Gardens are not simply collections of plants; they rely for much of their appeal on man-made features. Whimsical topiary, ornate architecture, fanciful statuary and mazes help to create an atmosphere of adventure or pure escapism. The many gardens dotted around the West Country offer engaging examples of the vivid imagination of designers.

Mazes *were created in medieval monasteries to teach patience and persistence. This laurel maze at Glendurgan was planted in 1833.*

Fountains *and flamboyant statuary have adorned gardens since Roman times. Such eye-catching embellishments add poetic and Classical touches to the design of formal gardens, such as Mount Edgcumbe.*

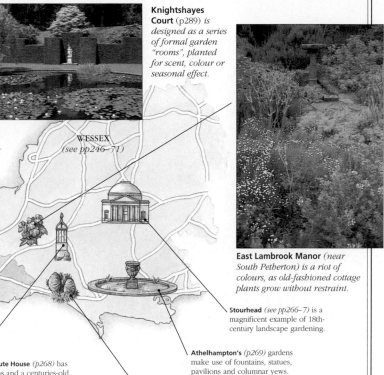

Knightshayes Court (p289) *is designed as a series of formal garden "rooms", planted for scent, colour or seasonal effect.*

WESSEX
(see pp246–71)

East Lambrook Manor *(near South Petherton) is a riot of colours, as old-fashioned cottage plants grow without restraint.*

Stourhead *(see pp266–7)* is a magnificent example of 18th-century landscape gardening.

Athelhampton's *(p269)* gardens make use of fountains, statues, pavilions and columnar yews.

Montacute House *(p268)* has pavilions and a centuries-old yew hedge, and is renowned for its collection of old roses.

0 kilometres   25

0 miles   25

Parnham *(near Beaminster), like many West Country gardens, has several parts devoted to different themes. Here conical yews complement the formality of the stone balustrade; elsewhere there are woodland, kitchen, shade and Mediterranean gardens.*

Many garden buildings *are linked by an element of fantasy; while country houses had to conform to everyday practicalities, the design of many smaller buildings gave more scope for imagination. This fanciful Elizabethan pavilion on the forecourt at Montacute House was first and foremost decorative, but sometimes served as a lodging house.*

Topiary *can be traced back to the Greeks. Since that time the sculpting of trees into unusual, often eccentric shapes has been developed over the centuries. The yew topiary of*

1920s Knightshayes features a fox being chased by a pack of hounds. The figures form a delightful conceit and come into their own in winter when little else is in leaf.

WESSEX

WILTSHIRE · SOMERSET · DORSET

T*he natural and diverse beauty of this predominantly rural region is characterized by rolling hills and charming villages. The area is enriched by a wealth of historical and architectural attractions, ranging from the prehistoric stone circle of Stonehenge to the Roman baths and magnificent Georgian townscape of Bath.*

Vast swathes of bare windswept downland give way to lush river valleys, and the contrast between the two may explain the origin in medieval times of the saying, "as different as chalk and cheese". The chalk and limestone hills provided pasture for sheep whose wool was exported to Europe or turned to cloth in mill towns such as Bradford-on-Avon. Meanwhile the rich cow-grazed pastures of the valleys produced the Cheddar cheese for which the region has become famous.

The area's potential for wealth was first exploited by prehistoric chieftains whose large, mysterious monuments, such as Stonehenge and Maiden Castle, are striking features of the landscape. From this same soil sprang King Arthur *(see p285)* and King Alfred the Great, about whom there are numerous fascinating legends. It was King Arthur who is thought to have led British resistance to the Saxon invasion in the 6th century. The Saxons finally emerged the victors and one of them, King Alfred, first united the West Country into one political unit, called the Kingdom of Wessex *(see p47)*.

Wilton House and Lacock Abbey, both former monasteries, were turned into splendid stately homes during the 16th century, due to the Dissolution of the Monasteries *(see pp50–51)*. Today, their previous wealth can be gauged by the size and grandeur of their storage barns.

Matching the many man-made splendours of the region, Wessex is rich in rare wildlife and plants.

Two visitors enjoying the Elizabethan gardens of Montacute House, Somerset

◁ Eighteenth-century cottages lining Gold Hill, Shaftesbury

Exploring Wessex

From the rolling chalk plains around Stonehenge
to the rocky cliffs of Cheddar Gorge and the
heather-covered uplands of Exmoor, Wessex is a
scenically varied microcosm of England.
Reflecting the underlying geology, each part of
Wessex contributes its own distinctive
architecture, with the Neo-Classically inspired
buildings of Bath giving way to the mellow brick
and timber of Salisbury and the thatched flint-and-
chalk cottages of the Dorset landscape.

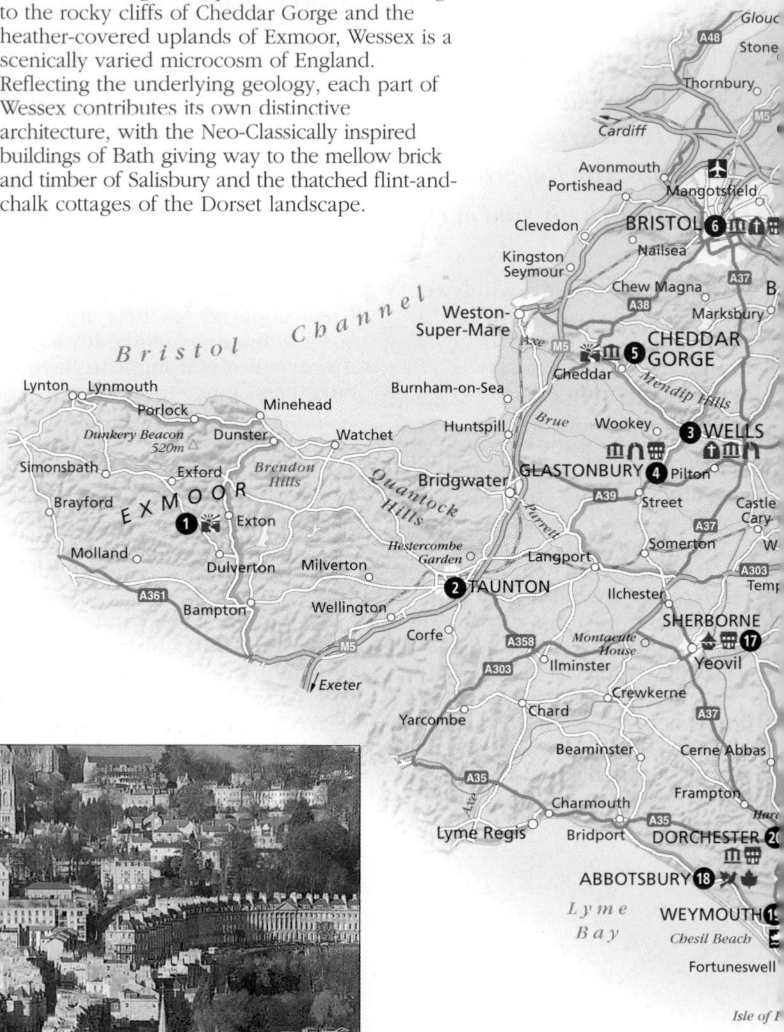

Glouc

A48   Stone

Cardiff   Thornbury

Avonmouth   M5

Portishead   Mangotsfield

Clevedon   **BRISTOL** 6

Kingston   Nailsea
Seymour

Chew Magna   B

A37

A38   Marksbury

Weston-   Axe   Cheddar   **CHEDDAR**
Super-Mare   M5   5 **GORGE**

Bristol Channel   Cheddar   *Mendip Hills*

Burnham-on-Sea   Wookey   3 **WELLS**

Lynton   Lynmouth   *Brue*   Huntspill

Porlock   Minehead   **GLASTONBURY** 4 Pilton

Dunkery Beacon   Dunster   Watchet   Street
520m   *Brendon*   Castle
Simonsbath   *Hills*   Bridgwater   A37   Cary

Exford   *Parrett*

Brayford   **E X M O O R**   1   Somerton   W

Exton   A303
Molland   *Hestercombe*   Langport   Temp
Dulverton   *Garden*

Milverton   2 **TAUNTON**   Ilchester   **SHERBORNE**

A361   Wellington   Montacute   17
Bampton   A358   *House*   **Yeovil**
Corfe   A303   Ilminster   A37

Exeter   Crewkerne

Yarcombe   Chard

A35   Beaminster   Cerne Abbas

Charmouth   Frampton

Lyme Regis   Bridport   A35   **DORCHESTER** 2

          ABBOTSBURY 18

L y m e   **WEYMOUTH** 1
B a y   *Chesil Beach*

          Fortuneswell

          Isle of F

KEY

═══	Motorway
▬▬▬	Major road
▬▬	Secondary road
───	Minor road
───	Scenice route
───	Main railway
──	Minor railway
△	Summit

Bath's abbey and Georgian townscape

Exmoor National Park

SEE ALSO

- **Where to Stay** pp568–71

- **Where to Eat** pp624–6

SIGHTS AT A GLANCE

**Huge sarsen stones of Stonehenge,
dating from around 3000 BC**

GETTING AROUND

Bath and Bristol are served by fast mainline trains, other major towns and seaside resorts by regional railways and long-distance bus services. Popular sights such as Stonehenge feature on many tour operators' bus excursions. The rural heart of Wessex, however, has little in the way of public transport and unless you have the time to walk the region's footpaths, you will need a car.

Exmoor National Park ❶

The majestic cliffs plunging into the Bristol Channel along Exmoor's northern coast are interrupted by lush, wooded valleys carrying rivers from the high moorland down to sheltered fishing coves. Inland, wild rolling hills are grazed by sturdy Exmoor ponies, horned sheep and the local

Curlew wild red deer. Buzzards are also a common sight wheeling over the bracken-clad terrain looking for prey. For walkers, Exmoor offers 1,000 km (620 miles) of wonderful public paths and varied, dramatic scenery, while the tamer perimeters of the National Park offer less energetic attractions – everything from traditional seaside entertainments to picturesque villages and ancient churches.

View east along the South West Coast Path

Combe Martin is a pretty setting for the Pack of Cards Inn *(see p286)*.

Parracombe Old Church has a Georgian interior with a complete set of wooden furnishing

Combe Martin

Parracombe

Lynton
Lynmouth

BARNSTAPLE

B3358

TIVERTON

Heddon's Mouth
The River Heddon passes through woodland and meadows down to this attractive point on the coast.

The Valley of Rocks
Sandstone outcrops, eroded into fantastical shapes, characterize this natural gorge.

KEY

🛈	Tourist information
▬	A road
▭	B road
▭	Minor road
‒ ‒	Coast path
☼	Viewpoint

Lynmouth
Above the charming fishing village of Lynmouth stands hill-top Lynton. The two villages are connected by a cliff railway (see p286).

Watersmeet

The East Lyn and Hoar Oak Water join together in a tumbling cascade at this spot in the middle of a beautifully wooded valley. There is also a tearoom with a pretty garden.

Culbone church, a mere 10.6 m (35 ft) in length, claims to be Britain's smallest parish church.

Malmsmead has a Natural History Centre illustrating local wildlife.

Oare's church commemorates the writer R D Blackmore, whose romantic novel *Lorna Doone* (1869) is set in the area.

VISITORS' CHECKLIST

Somerset/Devon. ✈ 🚂 *Tiverton then bus.* ℹ *Fore St, Dulverton (01398 323841).* **Natural History Centre**, *Malmsmead.* **Tel** *01643 707624.* ◻ *mid-May–Sep: 1:30–5pm Wed, Thu; Aug: Tue–Thu.* ♿ **Dunster Castle (NT)**, *Dunster.* **Tel** *01643 821314.* ◻ *Apr–Oct: Sat–Wed.* 📷 ♿ 🎁 **www**.nationaltrust.org.uk **National Park Centre Dulverton**, ◻ *Open all year* **Tel** *01398 23841* **www**.exmoor-nationalpark.gov.uk

Porlock

The flower-filled village of Porlock has retained its charm, with winding streets, thatched houses and a fascinating old church.

Selworthy is a picturesque village of thatched cottages.

Minehead is a major resort built around a pretty quay. A steam railway runs all the way from here to Bishop's Lydeard.

DUNKERY BEACON
520 m
1,704 ft

Culbone · Malmsmead
Oare
Porlock ℹ
A39
Selworthy
Minehead

Exe
B3223
ath
Exford
B3224

BRENDON HILLS

Dunster
A396 A39

B3190

TAUNTON

Barle
B3223
Exe
A396

B3224

TIVERTON

Dunster has an ancient castle and an unusual octagonal Yarn Market (1609) where local cloth was once sold.

Dane's Brook

WIMBLEBALL LAKE

Simonsbath is a good starting point for walkers. The Exmoor ponies found locally are thought to descend from prehistoric ancestors.

Dulverton ℹ
B3222

Barle

TIVERTON

Tarr Steps is an ancient "clapper" bridge built of stone slabs.

Dunkery Beacon

Rising to a height of 520 m (1,700 ft), this is the highest point on Exmoor.

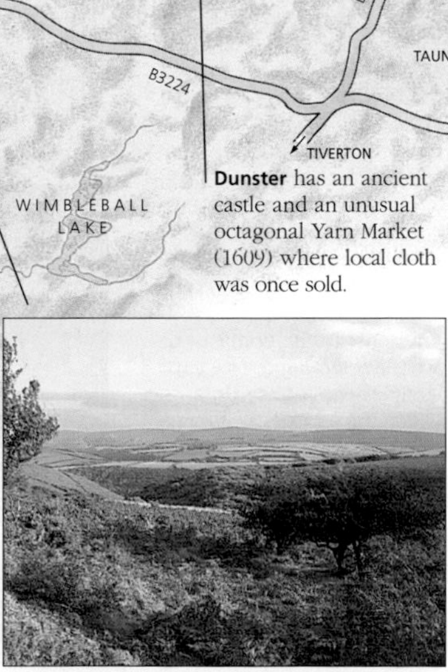

0 kilometres   5

0 miles   3

Taunton ❷

Somerset. 🏛 77,000. 🚉 🚌 ℹ️
Paul St (01823 336 344). 🛒 *Thu
(farmers'), Tue & Sat (livestock).*
www.heartofsomerset.com

Taunton lies at the heart of a
fertile region famous for its
apples and cider, but it was
the prosperous wool industry
that financed the massive
church of **St Mary Magdalene**
(1488–1514) with its glorious
tower. Taunton's **castle** was
the setting for the notorious
Bloody Assizes of 1685 when
"Hanging" Judge Jeffreys dispensed harsh retribution on
the Duke of Monmouth and
his followers for an uprising
against King James II. The

12th-century building now
houses the **Somerset County
Museum**. A star exhibit is the
Roman mosaic from a villa at
Low Ham, Somerset, showing
the story of Dido and Aeneas.

**Environs: Hestercombe
Garden** is one of Sir Edwin
Lutyens and Gertrude
Jekyll's great masterpieces.

🏛 **Somerset County
Museum**
Castle Green. **Tel** 01823
320201. 🕐 Tue–Sat, public
hols. 🚻 ground floor. 🛈
www.somersetgov.uk/museums

🌸 **Hestercombe Garden**
Cheddon Fitzpaine. **Tel** 01823
413923. 🕐 daily. 🚻 🛈
www.hestercombegardens.com

SOMERSET CIDER

Somerset is one of the few
English counties where
real farmhouse cider,
known as "scrumpy",
is still made using
the traditional
methods. Cider
once formed
part of the farm
labourer's wages
and local folk-
lore has it that
various unsav-
oury additives,
such as iron
nails, were added to give
strength. Cider-making can
be seen at **Sheppy's** farm,
on the A38 near Taunton.

**Scrumpy
cider**

Wells ❸

Somerset. 🏛 10,000. 🚌 ℹ️ *Market
Place (01749 672552).* 🛒 *Wed
(farmers'), Sat.* www.wells.gov.uk

Wells is named after St
Andrew's Well, the sacred
spring that bubbles up from
the ground near the 13th-
century **Bishop's
Palace**, residence
of the Bishop of
Bath and Wells. A
tranquil city, Wells
is famous for its
magnificent cathe-
dral which was
begun in the late
1100s. Penniless
Porch, where
beggars once
received alms,
leads from the
bustling market
place to the calm
of the cathedral
close. **Wells Museum** has
prehistoric finds from nearby
Wookey Hole and other caves.

Environs: To the northeast of
Wells lies the impressive cave
complex of **Wookey Hole**,
which has an extensive range
of popular amusements.

**Cathedral
clock
(1386–92)**

🏛 **Wells Museum**
8 Cathedral Green. **Tel** 01749 673477.
🕐 daily 🚻 🚻 limited. 🛈
🦇 **Wookey Hole**
Off A371. **Tel** 01749 672243. 🕐 daily.
🚻 🍴 🛈 www.wookey.co.uk

The West Front
*features 300 fine
medieval statues of
kings, knights and
saints – many of
them life-size.*

**The Vicars'
Close**, built in
the 14th century
for the Vicars'
Choir, is one
of the oldest
complete streets
in Europe.

The Chain Gate (1460)

Cloisters

**Path leading
round the moat**

This graceful flight of steps
*curves up to the octagonal
Chapter House which has delicate vaulting dating from 1306.
The 32 ribs springing from the
central column create a
beautiful palm-tree effect.*

Glastonbury Abbey, left in ruins in 1539 after the Dissolution

Bishops' tombs *circle the chancel. This sumptuous marble tomb, in the south aisle, is that of Bishop Lord Arthur Hervey, who was Bishop of Bath and Wells (1869–94).*

The palace moat *is home to swans which ring a bell by the gatehouse when they want to be fed. Feeding times are at 11am and 4pm.*

The Bishop's Palace (1230–40)

WELLS CATHEDRAL AND THE BISHOP'S PALACE

The Close. **Tel** *01749 674483.*
◯ *daily.* ♿ *limited.*
Bishop's Palace Tel *01749 678691.*
◯ *Apr–Oct: Tue– Fri, Sun & public hols (Aug: daily).* 🎫 ♿

Wells has maintained much of its medieval character with its cathedral, Bishop's Palace and other buildings around the close forming a harmonious group. The most striking features of the cathedral are the west front and the "scissor arches" installed in 1338 to support the tower.

13th-century ruins of the Great Hall

Glastonbury ➍

Somerset. 🏠 *9,000.* 🚌 🛈 *Tribunal, High St (01458 832954).* 🛒 *Tue.*
www.glastonbury.co.uk

Shrouded in Arthurian myth and rich in mystical association, the town of Glastonbury was once one of the most important destinations for pilgrims in England. Now thousands flock here for the annual rock festival *(see p63)* and for the summer solstice on Midsummer's Day (21 June).

Over the years history and legend have become intertwined, and the monks who founded **Glastonbury Abbey**, around 700, found it profitable to encourage the association between Glastonbury and the mythical "Blessed Isle" known as Avalon – alleged to be the last resting place of King Arthur and the Holy Grail *(see p285)*.

The great abbey was left in ruins after the Dissolution of the Monasteries *(see p50)*. Even so, some magnificent relics survive, including parts of the vast Norman abbey church, the unusual Abbot's Kitchen, with its octagonal roof, and the Victorian farmhouse, now the **Somerset Rural Life Museum**.

Growing in the abbey grounds is a cutting from the famous Glastonbury thorn which is said to have miraculously grown from the staff of St Joseph of Arimathea. According to myth, he was sent around AD 60 to convert England to Christianity. The English hawthorn flowers at Christmas as well as in May.

The **Lake Village Museum** has some interesting finds from the Iron Age settlements that once fringed the marshlands around **Glastonbury Tor**. Seen for miles around, the Tor is a hill crowned by the remains of a 14th-century church.

🏛 Somerset Rural Life Museum
Chilkwell St. **Tel** *01458 831197.* ◯
Apr–Oct: Tue–Sun; Nov–Apr: Tue–Sat & public hols. ⬤ *24–26 Dec, 1 Jan, Good Fri.* ♿ *limited.* 🚫 *closed winter.* 🚫
www.somerset.gov.uk/museums

🏛 Lake Village Museum
Tribunal, High St. **Tel** *01458 832954.*
◯ *daily.* ⬤ *25, 26 Dec.* 🎫

Cheddar Gorge ⑤

Described as a "deep frightful chasm" by novelist Daniel Defoe in 1724, Cheddar Gorge is a spectacular ravine cut through the Mendip plateau by fast-flowing streams during the glacial phases of the last Ice Age. Cheddar has given its name to a rich cheese which originates from here and is now produced worldwide. The caves in the gorge once provided the perfect environment of constant temperature and high humidity for storing and maturing the cheese.

VISITORS' CHECKLIST

On B3135, Somerset. ▌ 01934 744071. 🚌 from Wells. 🚻 🚹
🖥 www.somersetbythesea.co.uk
Cheddar Caves & Gorge
Tel 01934 742343. ◯ daily.
📷 ♿ limited. 🖥 🛒
www.cheddarcaves.co.uk
Cheddar Gorge Cheese Co.
Tel 01934 742810. ◯ daily.
♿ 🖥 🛒 www.cheddargorgecheeseco.co.uk

The Cheddar Gorge Cheese Company *is the only working Cheddar dairy in Cheddar. Visitors can see Cheddar being made, and taste and buy cheese in the new store.*

"Cheddar Man", *a 9,000-year-old skeleton, is on display at the Cheddar Caves and Gorge.*

The B3135 road winds round the base of the 3 mile (5 km) gorge.

A footpath follows the top of the gorge on its southern edge.

Gough's Cave is noted for its cathedral-like proportions.

Tourist information

The gorge *is a narrow, winding ravine with limestone rocks rising almost vertically on either side to a height of 120 m (400 ft).*

Cox's Cave contains unusually shaped stalactites and stalagmites.

Jacob's Ladder has 274 steps leading to the top of the gorge.

The rare Cheddar Pink *is among the astonishing range of plant and animal life harboured in the rocks.*

Lookout Tower has far-reaching views over the area to the south and west.

Bristol ❻

See pp256–7.

Bath ❼

See pp258–61.

Bradford-on-Avon ❽

Wiltshire. 🏛 *9,500.* 🚉 ℹ *St Margaret St (01225 865797).* 🛒 *Thu.*
www.bradfordonavon.co.uk

This lovely Cotswold-stone town with its steep flagged lanes is full of flamboyant houses built by wealthy wool and cloth merchants in the 17th and 18th centuries. One fine Georgian example is **Abbey House**, on Church Street. A little further along, **St Laurence Church** is a remarkably complete Saxon building founded in 705 *(see p47).* The

Typical Cotswold-stone architecture in Bradford-on-Avon

church was converted to a school and cottage in the 12th century and was rediscovered in the 19th century when a vicar recognized the characteristic cross-shaped roof.

At one end of the medieval **Town Bridge** is a small stone cell, built as a chapel in the 13th century but later used as a lock-up for 17th-century vagrants. A short walk away, near converted mill buildings and a stretch of the Kennet and Avon Canal, is the massive 14th-century **Tithe Barn** *(see p32).*

🏛 **Tithe Barn**
Pound Lane. ⭘ *daily.* ⬤ *25, 26 Dec.* ♿

Corsham ❾

Wiltshire. 🏛 *12,000.* ℹ *High St (01249 714660).*
www.northwilts.gov.uk

The streets of Corsham are lined with stately Georgian houses in Cotswold stone. **St Bartholomew's Church** has an elegant spire and a lovely carved alabaster tomb (1960) to the late Lady Methuen, whose family founded Methuen publishers. The family acquired **Corsham Court** in 1745 with its picture gallery and a remarkable collection of Flemish, Italian and English paintings, including works by Van Dyck, Lippi and Reynolds. Peacocks wander through the grounds, adding their colour and elegance to the façade of the Elizabethan mansion.

Peacock in grounds, Corsham Court

🏛 **Corsham Court**
off A4. *Tel 01249 701610.* ⭘ *mid-Mar– Sep: Tue–Sun (pm); Oct–mid-Mar: Sat, Sun (pm).* ⬤ *Dec.* 📷 ♿ *limited.*

Lacock ❿

Wiltshire. 🏛 *1,000.*

Maintained in its pristine state by the National Trust, with very few modern intrusions, Lacock is a picturesque and delightful village to explore. The meandering River Avon forms the boundary to the north side of the churchyard, while humorous stone figures look down from **St Cyriac Church**. Inside the 15th-century church is the splendid Renaissance-style tomb of Sir William Sharington (1495–1553). He acquired **Lacock Abbey** after the Dissolution of the Monasteries *(see p50),* but it was a later owner, John Ivory Talbot, who had the buildings remodelled in the Gothic

revival style, in vogue in the early 18th century.
The abbey is famous for the window (in the south gallery) from which his descendant William Henry Fox Talbot, an early pioneer of photography, took his first picture in 1835, and for the sheets of snowdrops which cover the abbey grounds in early spring. A 16th-century barn at the abbey gates has been converted to the **Fox Talbot Museum**, which has displays on his experiments.

Environs: Designed by Robert Adam *(see pp32–3)* in 1769, **Bowood House** includes the laboratory where Joseph Priestley discovered oxygen in 1774, and a rich collection of sculpture, costumes and paintings. Italianate gardens surround the house while the lake-filled grounds, landscaped by Capability Brown *(see p30),* contain a Doric temple, grotto, cascade and now a large adventure playground.

🔓 **Lacock Abbey**
(NT) Lacock. *Tel 01249 730227.* ⭘ *Mar–Oct: Wed–Mon (pm).* ⬤ *Good Fri.* 📷 ♿ *limited in house.*
www.nationaltrust.org.uk

🏛 **Fox Talbot Museum**
(NT) Lacock. *Tel 01249 730459.* ⭘ *Mar–Oct: daily.* ⬤ *Good Fri.* 📷 ♿

🏛 **Bowood House**
Derry Hill, nr Calne. *Tel 01249 812102.* ⭘ *Apr–Oct: daily.* 📷 ♿ 🍴 ⬛ 📷

William Henry Fox Talbot (1800–77)

Bristol ❻

It was in 1497 that John Cabot sailed from Bristol on his historic voyage to North America. The city, at the mouth of the Avon, became the main British port for transatlantic trade, pioneering the era of the ocean-going steam liner with the construction of SS *Great Britain*. The city flourished as a major trading centre, growing rich on the distribution of wine, tobacco and, in the 17th century, slaves.

King Brennus, St John's Gate

Because of its docks and aero-engine factories, Bristol was heavily bombed during World War II and the city centre bears witness to the ideas of post-war planners. The docks have been shifted to deeper waters at Avonmouth and the old dock area has been transformed, taking on new life characterized by waterside cafés, shops and art galleries.

Memorial to William Canynge the Younger (1400–74)

🔒 St Mary Redcliffe

Redcliffe Way. **Tel** 0117 9291487.
⬜ daily. ♿ 📷 by arrangement.
🖥 www.stmaryredcliffe.co.uk
This magnificent 14th-century church was claimed by Queen Elizabeth I to be "the fairest in England". The church owes much to the generosity of William Canynge the Elder and Younger, both famous mayors of Bristol. Inscriptions on the tombs of merchants and sailors tell of lives devoted to trade in Asia and the West Indies. Look out for the Bristol maze in the north aisle.

🏛 SS *Great Britain*

Gas Ferry Rd. 📷 0117 9260680.
⬜ daily. ⬛ 24, 25 Dec. 🔲 🎦 ♿
📷 by arrangement. 🖥
www.ss-great-britain.com
Designed by Isambard Kingdom Brunel, this is the world's first large iron passenger ship. Launched in 1843, she travelled 32 times round the world before she was abandoned in the Falkland Islands in 1886. The ship has recently been fully restored.

🚇 Georgian House

7 Great George St. **Tel** 0117 9211362.
⬜ Sat–Wed. www.bristol-city.gov.uk/museums
Life in a wealthy Bristol merchant's house of the 1790s is illustrated by furnishings in the elegant drawing room and the servants' area.

🏛 British Empire & Commonwealth Museum

Station Approach, Temple Meads. **Tel** 0117 9254980. ⬜ daily. ⬛ 25, 26 Dec. 🔲 🎦 ♿ 📷 🖥
www.empiremuseum.co.uk
This major new national museum is located in the 1841 railway terminus by Brunel, and presents the dramatic 500-year history of the British empire and the emergence of the modern Commonwealth, in over 20 themed galleries, special exhibitions, a library and archive.

Exploring Bristol

The oldest part of the city lies around Broad, King and Corn streets, known as the Old Quarter. The lively St Nicholas covered market, part of which occupies the **Corn Exchange**, was built by John Wood the Elder *(see p258)* in 1743. Outside are the famous Bristol Nails, four bronze 16th–17th-century pedestals which Bristol merchants used as tables when paying for goods – hence the expression "to pay on the nail". **St John's Gate**, at the head of Broad Street, has medieval statues of Bristol's two mythical founders, King Brennus and King Benilus. Between Lewins Mead and Colston Street, **Christmas Steps** is a steep lane lined with specialist shops and cafés. The **Chapel of the Three Kings** at the top was founded in 1504.

A group of buildings around the cobbled King Street include the 17th-century timber-framed **Llandoger Trow** inn. It is here that Daniel Defoe is said to have met Alexander

The Two Sisters (c.1889) by Renoir, City Museum and Art Gallery

Selkirk, whose true-life island exile served as the inspiration for Defoe's novel *Robinson Crusoe* (1719). Just up from here is the **Theatre Royal**, built in 1766, and home to the famous Bristol Old Vic.

Not far away, the renowned gallery the **Arnolfini**, on Narrow Quay, is a showcase for contemporary art, drama, dance and cinema.

On the Harbourside, **At-Bristol** combines the interactive science centre Explore, an IMAX cinema and the wildlife centre Wildwalk.

Not far from the Harbourside, elegant **Clifton** revels in ornate Regency crescents. The impressive **Clifton Suspension Bridge** by Brunel, completed in 1864, perfectly complements the drama of the steep Avon gorge. **Bristol Zoo Gardens**, houses over 400 exotic and endangered species set in stunning gardens.

The bow of SS *Great Britain*

Warehouses overlooking the Floating Harbour

🏛 Bristol Blue Glass Factory and Shop

Brislington. **Tel** 0117 972 0818.
◯ daily. www.brisol-glass.co,uk
The Bristol Blue Glass name is over 350 years old and represents the best tools, techniques and traditions from the past. Every piece of glass is free blown and hand-made, making each one unique and collectable. Glass blowing demonstrations take place at the visitor centre, where there is also a gallery shop.

🏛 City Museum and Art Gallery

Queen's Rd. **Tel** 0117 922 3571. ◯ daily. ● 24, 25 Dec. ♿ limited. 🖥 www.bristol-city.gov.uk/museums
Varied collections include Egyptology, dinosaur fossils, Roman tableware, the largest collection of Chinese glass outside China and a fine collection of European paintings including works by Renoir and Bellini. Bristol artists include Sir Thomas Lawrence and Francis Danby.

VISITORS' CHECKLIST

Bristol. 🏠 450,000. ✈ 7 miles (11 km) SW Bristol. 🚆 Temple Meads. 🚌 Marlborough St. 🛈 Wildwalk-At-Bristol (0906-711 2191). 🚢 daily. 🎪 Harbour Festival: Jul–Aug; Balloon Festival: Aug.
www.visitbristol.co.uk

✚ Bristol Cathedral

College Green. **Tel** 0117 9264879.
◯ daily. **Donation.** ♿ limited.
www.bristol-cathedral.co.uk
Bristol's cathedral, begun in 1140, took an unusually long time to build. Rapid progress was made between 1298 and 1330, when the inventive choir was rebuilt; the transepts and tower were finished in 1515, and another 350 years passed before the Victorian architect, G E Street, built the nave. Humorous medieval carving abounds – a snail crawling across the stone foliage in the Berkeley Chapel, musical monkeys in the Elder Lady Chapel, and a fine set of wooden misericords in the choir.

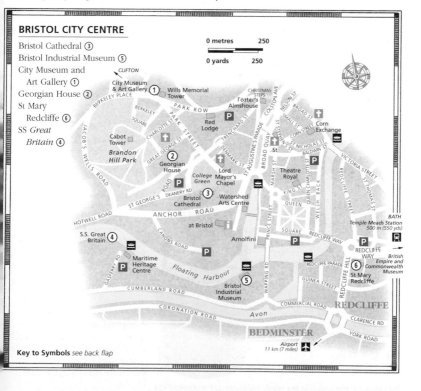

BRISTOL CITY CENTRE

Bristol Cathedral ③
Bristol Industrial Museum ⑤
City Museum and
  Art Gallery ①
Georgian House ②
St Mary
  Redcliffe ⑥
SS *Great
  Britain* ④

0 metres 250
0 yards 250

Key to Symbols see back flap

Street-by-Street: Bath ❼

Bath owes its magnificent Georgian town-scape to the bubbling pool of water at the heart of the Roman Baths. The Romans transformed Bath into England's first spa resort and it regained fame as a spa town in the 18th century. At this time the two John Woods (Elder and Younger), both architects, designed the city's Palladian-style buildings. Many houses bear plaques recording the numerous famous people who have resided here.

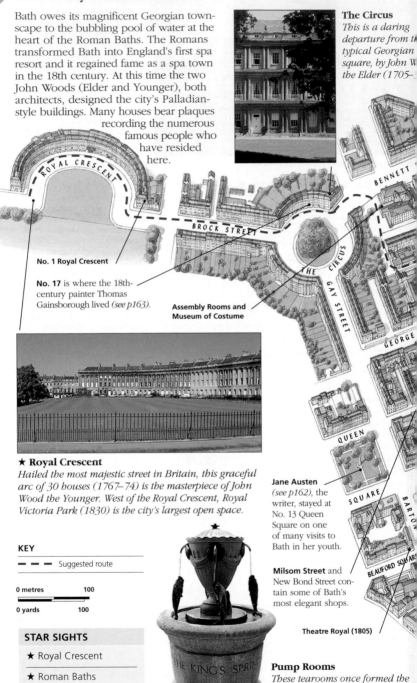

The Circus
This is a daring departure from the typical Georgian square, by John Wood the Elder (1705–

No. 1 Royal Crescent

No. 17 is where the 18th-century painter Thomas Gainsborough lived *(see p163)*.

Assembly Rooms and Museum of Costume

★ **Royal Crescent**
Hailed the most majestic street in Britain, this graceful arc of 30 houses (1767–74) is the masterpiece of John Wood the Younger. West of the Royal Crescent, Royal Victoria Park (1830) is the city's largest open space.

Jane Austen
(see p162), the writer, stayed at No. 13 Queen Square on one of many visits to Bath in her youth.

Milsom Street and New Bond Street contain some of Bath's most elegant shops.

Theatre Royal (1805)

KEY

– – – Suggested route

0 metres   100

0 yards   100

THE KING'S SPRING

STAR SIGHTS

★ Royal Crescent

★ Roman Baths

★ Bath Abbey

Pump Rooms
These tearooms once formed the social hub of the 18th-century spa community. They contain this decorative drinking fountain.

Pulteney Bridge
This charming bridge (1769–74), designed by Robert Adam, is lined with shops and links the centre with the magnificent Great Pulteney Street. Look out for a rare Victorian pillar box on the east bank.

The Building of Bath Museum

★ Roman Baths
Built in the 1st century, this bathing complex is one of Britain's greatest memorials to the Roman era.

★ Bath Abbey
The splendid abbey stands at the heart of the old city in the Abbey Church Yard, a paved courtyard enlivened by buskers. Its unique façade features stone angels climbing Jacob's Ladder to heaven.

Holburne Museum

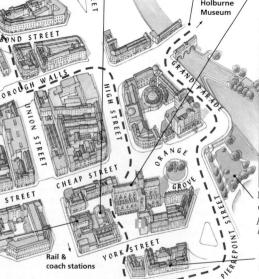

Parade Gardens
Courting couples came to this pretty riverside park for secret liaisons in the 18th century.

Sally Lunn's House (1482) is one of Bath's oldest houses.

Rail & coach stations

Exploring Bath

The beautiful and compact city of Bath is set among the rolling green hills of the Avon valley, and wherever you walk you will enjoy spendid views of the surrounding countryside. The traffic-free heart of this lively city is full of street musicians, museums, cafés and enticing shops, while the elegant honey-coloured Georgian houses, so characteristic of Bath, form an elegant backdrop to city life.

Piazza cellist

Bath Abbey, at the heart of the old city, begun in 1499

🛈 Bath Abbey
13 Kingston Bldgs, Abbey Churchyard.
Tel 01225 422462. ⬜ daily. 🔴 during services. **Donation.** &. 🖐
www.bathabbey.org

This splendid abbey was supposedly designed by divine agency. According to legend, God dictated the form of the church to Bishop Oliver King in a dream; this story has been immortalized in the wonderfully eccentric carvings on the west front. The bishop began work in 1499, rebuilding a church that had been founded in the 8th century. Memorials cover the walls and the varied Georgian inscriptions make fascinating reading. The spacious interior is remarkable for the fan vaulting of the nave, an addition made by Sir George Gilbert Scott in 1874.

🏛 Assembly Rooms and Museum of Costume
Bennett St. **Tel** 01225 477785.
⬜ daily. 🔴 25, 26 Dec. 🖐 for Museum of Costume. &. 🖐 🖐
www.museumofcostume.co.uk

The Assembly Rooms were built by Wood the Younger in 1769, as a meeting place for the fashionable elite and as an elegant backdrop for many glittering balls. Jane Austen's novel *Northanger Abbey* (1818) describes the atmosphere of gossip and flirtation here.

In the basements is a collection of costumes in period settings. The display illustrates fashions from the 16th century to the present day.

🏛 No. 1 Royal Crescent
Royal Crescent. **Tel** 01225 428 126. ⬜ Tue–Sun & public hols. 🔴 Dec, Jan, Good Fri. 🖐 🖐
www.bath-preservation-trust.org.uk

This museum lets you inside the first house of this beautiful Georgian crescent, giving a glimpse of what life was like for 18th-century aristocrats, such as the Duke of York, who probably lived here. It is furnished down to such details as the dog-powered spit used to roast meat in front of the fire.

🏛 Holburne Museum of Art
Great Pulteney St. **Tel** 01225 466669.
⬜ mid-Jan–mid-Dec: Tue–Sun. 🖐 &. limited. 🖐 🖐
www.bath.ac.uk/holburne

This historic building is named after William Holburne of Menstrie (1793–1874), whose collections form the nucleus of the display of fine and decorative arts. Paintings can be seen by British artists such as Gainsborough and Stubbs.

ROMAN BATHS MUSEUM
Entrance in Abbey Churchyard.
🖐 01225 477784. ⬜ daily. 🔴 25, 26 Dec. 🖐 &. limited.
www.romanbaths.co.uk

According to legend, Bath owes its origin to the Celtic King Bladud who discovered the curative properties of its natural hot springs in 860 BC. Cast out from his kingdom as a leper, Bladud cured himself by imitating his swine and rolling in the hot mud at Bath.

In the first century, the Romans built baths around the spring, and a temple dedicated to the goddess Sulis Minerva, who combined the attributes of the Celt water goddess Sulis and the Roman goddess Minerva. Among the Roman relics is a bronze head of the goddess.

Medieval monks of Bath Abbey also exploited the springs' properties, but it was when Queen Anne visited in 1702–3 that Bath reached its zenith as a fashionable watering place.

Gilded bronze head of Sulis Minerva

🏛 Building of Bath Museum

The Vineyards. *Tel* 01225 333895.
◻ Tue–Sun & public hols. ⬤ end-
Nov–mid-Feb. 🎫 ♿ limited. 📷
www.bath-preservation-trust.org.uk

This museum, housed in an old Methodist chapel, is an excellent starting point for exploring the city. It shows how, in the 18th century, Bath was transformed from a medieval wool town into one of Europe's most elegant spas. John Wood and his son designed the Classically inspired stone fronts of the Royal Crescent and the Circus, leaving individual property speculators to develop the houses behind. While the façades speak of harmony and order, the houses behind show the result of rampant individualism, with no two houses alike. The museum looks at every aspect of the buildings, from their construction to a new gallery of Georgian interiors.

🏛 American Museum

Claverton Manor, Claverton Down.
Tel 01225 460503. ◻ Aug:
daily (pm); Mar–Oct: Tue–Sun (pm)
& bank hols. 🎫 ♿ limited. 📺 📷
www.americanmuseum.org

Founded in 1961, this was the first American museum to be established in this country. Rooms in the 1820 manor house are decorated in many styles, from the rudimentary dwellings of the first settlers to opulent 19th-century homes. There are special sections on Shaker furniture, quilts and Native American art, and a replica of George Washington's Mount Vernon garden of 1785.

A 19th-century American Indian weathervane

---

e dome (1897) is based on St
ephen Walbrook church in London
e p112).

The Great Bath

The open-air Great Bath, which stands at the heart of the Roman spa complex, was not discovered until the 1870s. Leading off this magnificent pool were various bathing chambers which became increasingly sophisticated over the four centuries the Romans were here. The baths fell into ruin, but extensive excavations have revealed the remarkable skill of Roman engineering.

Around the edges of the bath are the bases of piers that once supported a barrel-vaulted roof.

York Street

A late 19th-century terrace bears statues of famous Romans such as Julius Caesar.

The sacred spring is enclosed by a resevoir now named the King's Bath.

The water flows from the spring into the corner of the bath at a constant temperature of 46° C (115° F).

The lead-lined bath, steps, column bases and paving stones around the edge all date from Roman times.

Stonehenge

Built in several stages from about 3000 BC, Stonehenge is Europe's most famous prehistoric monument. We can only guess at the rituals that took place here, but the alignment of the stones leaves little doubt that the circle is connected with the sun and the passing of the seasons, and that its builders possessed a sophisticated understanding of both arithmetic and astronomy. Despite popular belief, the circle was not built by the Druids, an Iron Age priestly cult that flourished in Britain from around 250 BC – more than 1,000 years after Stonehenge was completed.

Finds from a burial mound near Stonehenge (Devizes Museum)

Stonehenge as it is today

The Heel Stone casts a long shadow straight to the heart of the circle on Midsummer's day.

The Avenue forms a ceremonial approach to the site.

The Slaughter Stone, named by 17th-century antiquarians who believed Stonehenge to be a place of human sacrifice, was in fact one of a pair forming a doorway.

The Outer Bank, dug around 3000 BC, is the oldest part of Stonehenge.

BUILDING OF STONEHENGE

Stonehenge's monumental scale is more impressive given that the only tools available were made of stone, wood and bone. The labour involved in quarrying, transporting and erecting the huge stones was such that its builders must have been able to command immense resources and vast numbers of people. One method is explained below.

RECONSTRUCTION OF STONEHENGE

This illustration shows what Stonehenge probably looked like about 4,000 years ago.

A sarsen stone *was moved on rollers and levered into a pit.*

With levers *supported by timber packing, it was gradually raised.*

The stone *was then pulled upright by about 200 men hauling on ropes.*

The pit *round the* *was packed tightly stones and chalk.*

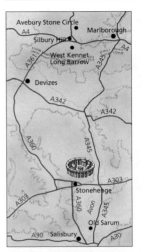

WILTSHIRE'S OTHER PREHISTORIC SITES

The open countryside of the Salisbury Plain made this area an important centre of prehistoric settlement, and today it is covered in many ancient remains. Ringing the horizon around Stonehenge are scores of circular barrows, or burial mounds, where members of the ruling class were honoured with burial close to the temple site. Ceremonial bronze weapons and other finds excavated around Stonehenge and the other local prehistoric sites can be seen in the museum at Salisbury (*see pp264–5*) and the main museum at Devizes.

Silbury Hill (NT) is Europe's largest prehistoric earthwork,

Silbury Hill

but despite extensive excavations its purpose remains a mystery. Built out of chalk blocks around 2750 BC, the hill covers 2 ha (5 acres) and rises to a height of 40 m (131 ft). Nearby **West Kennet Long Barrow** (NT) is the biggest

The **Sarsen Circle** was erected around 2300 BC and is capped by lintel stones held in place by mortice and tenon joints.

The **Bluestone Circle** was built around 2000 BC out of some 80 slabs quarried in south Wales. It was never completed.

Horseshoe of Bluestones

Horseshoe of Sarsen Trilothons

ternate ends *the lintel were ered up.*

The weight *of the lintel was suppor-ted by a timber platform.*

The lintel *was then levered sideways on to the uprights*

Sarsen stone forming part of the Avebury Stone Circle

Avebury ⑫

Wiltshire. 🏘 *600.* 🚆 *Swindon then bus.* ℹ *Green St (01672 539425).*

Built around 2500 BC, the **Avebury Stone Circle** (EH/NT) surrounds the village of Avebury and was probably once some form of religious centre. Although the stones used are smaller than those at Stonehenge, the circle itself is wider. Superstitious villagers smashed many of the stones in the 18th century, believing the circle to have been a place of pagan sacrifice.

The original form of the circle is best appreciated by a visit to the excellent **Alexander Keiller Museum** to the west of the site, which illustrates in detail the construction of the circle. There is also a fascinating exhibition entitled "6,000 Years of Mystery", which explains the changing landscape of Avebury.

St James's Church has a Norman font carved with sea monsters, and a rare 15th-century choir screen.

Environs: A few minutes' drive east, **Marlborough** is an attractive town with a long and broad High Street lined with colonnaded Georgian shops.

🏛 **Alexander Keiller Museum**
(NT) Off High St. **Tel** *01672 539250.*
⬜ *daily.* ⬤ *24–26 Dec.* 📷 ♿ 🚻
📚 🏪 www.nationaltrust.org.uk

chambered tomb in England, with numerous stone-lined "rooms" and a monumental entrance. Built as a communal cemetery around 3250 BC, it was in use for several centuries – old bodies were taken away to make room for newcomers.

Old Sarum is set within the massive ramparts of a 1st-century Romano-British hill fort. The Norman founders of Old Sarum built their own motte and bailey castle inside this ready-made fortification, and the remains of this survive along with the foundations of the huge cathedral of 1075. Above ground nothing remains of the town that once sat within the ramparts. The town's occupants moved to the fertile

river valley site that became Salisbury during the early 12th century *(see pp264–5)*.

🏛 **Old Sarum**
(EH) Castle Rd. **Tel** *01722 335398.* ⬜ *daily.* ⬤ *24–26 Dec, 1 Jan.* 📷 🏪

The chambered tomb of West Kennet Long Barrow (c.3250 BC)

Salisbury ⓭

The "new" city of Salisbury was founded in 1220, when the old hill-top settlement of Old Sarum *(see p263)* was abandoned, being too arid and windswept, in favour of a new site among the lush water meadows where the rivers Avon, Nadder and Bourne meet. Locally sourced Purbeck marble and Chilmark stone were used for the construction of a new cathedral which was built mostly in the early 13th century, over the remarkably short space of 38 years. Its magnificent landmark spire – the tallest in England – was an inspired afterthought added in 1280–1310.

The early 14th-century house of John A'Port, Queen's Street

Bishop's Walk and a sculpture by Elisabeth Frink (1930–93), Cathedral Close

Exploring Salisbury

The spacious and tranquil **Close**, with its schools, alms-houses and clergy housing, makes a fine setting for Salisbury's cathedral. Among the numerous elegant buildings here are the **Matrons' College**, built in 1682 as a home for widows and unmarried daughters of the clergy, and 13th-century **Malmesbury House** with its splendid early Georgian façade (1719), fronted by lovely wrought-iron gates. Other buildings of interest include the 13th-century **Medieval Hall**, the 13th-century **Wardrobe**, now a regimental museum, and the **Cathedral School**, housed in the 13th-century Bishop's Palace and famous for the quality of its choristers.

Beyond the walls of the Cathedral Close, Salisbury developed its chessboard layout, with areas devoted to different trades, perpetuated in street names such as Fish Row and Butcher Row. Leaving the Close through **High Street Gate**, you reach the busy High Street leading to the 13th-century **Church of St Thomas**, which has a lovely carved timber roof (1450), and a late 15th-century Doom painting, showing Christ seated in judgement and demons seizing the damned. Nearby in Silver Street, **Poultry Cross** was built in the 14th century as a covered poultry market. An intricate network of alleys

fans out from this point with a number of fine timber-framed houses. In the large bustling **Market Place** the **Guildhall** is an unusual cream stone building from 1787–95, used for civic functions. More attractive are the brick and tile-hung houses on the north side of the square, many with Georgian façades concealing medieval houses.

The Cloisters are the largest in England. They were added between 1263 and 1284 in the Decorated style.

The Chapter House has an original of the *Magna Carta*. Its walls have stone friezes of the Old Testament.

The Trinity Chapel contains the grave of St Osmund who was bishop of Old Sarum from 1078–1099.

Choir stalls

Bishop Audley's Chantry, a magnificent 16th-century monument to the bishop, is one of several small chapels clustered round the altar.

Street signs reflecting trades of 13th-century Salisbury

🏠 Mompesson House

(NT) The Close. *Tel* 01722 335659.
🕐 Apr–Oct: 11am–5pm Sat–Wed.
📷 👤 limited. 🚻

Built by a wealthy Wiltshire family in 1701, the handsomely furnished rooms of this house give an indication of life for the Close's inhabitants in the 18th century. The delightful garden, bounded by the north wall of the Close, has fine herbaceous borders.

The graceful spire soars to a height of 123 m (404 ft).

The West Front *is decorated by rows of lavish symbolic figures and saints in niches.*

A roof tour takes you up to an external gallery at the base of the spire with views of the town and Old Sarum.

North transept

SALISBURY CATHEDRAL
The Close. *Tel* 01722 555120. 🕐 daily. Donation. 👤 🚻
🌐 www.salisburycathedral.org.uk
The cathedral was mostly built between 1220 and 1258. It is a fine example of Early English Gothic architecture, typified by tall, sharply pointed lancet windows.

The clock dating from 1386 is the oldest working clock in Europe.

The nave is divided into ten bays by columns of polished Purbeck marble.

Numerous windows add to the airy and spacious atmosphere of the interior.

🏛 Salisbury and South Wiltshire Museum
The Close. *Tel* 01722 332151. 🕐
Mon–Sat (Jul–Aug: Sun pm). 📷 🚻
🌐 www.salisburymuseum.org.uk
In the medieval King's House, this museum has displays on early man, Stonehenge and nearby Old Sarum (*see p263*).

Environs: The town of Wilton is renowned for its carpet industry, founded by the 8th Earl of Pembroke using French Huguenot refugee weavers. The town's ornate **church** (1844) is a brilliant example of Neo-Romanesque architecture, incorporating genuine Roman columns, Flemish Renaissance woodwork, German and Dutch stained glass and Italian mosaics.

Wilton House has been home to the Earls of Pembroke since it was converted from a nunnery after the Dissolution (*see p50*). The house, largely rebuilt by Inigo Jones in the 17th century, includes one of the original Tudor towers, a fine collection of art and a landscaped park with a Palladian bridge (1737). The Single and Double Cube State Rooms have magnificently frescoed ceilings and gilded stucco work, and were designed to hang a series of family portraits by Van Dyck.

🏠 Wilton House
Wilton. *Tel* 01722 746729.
🕐 Easter–Sep: Sun–Fri. 📷 👤
🍴 🚻 🌐 www.wiltonhouse.co.uk

Double Cube room, designed by Inigo Jones in 1653

The Longleat Tree **tapestry (1980)**
depicting a 400-year history

Longleat House ⑭

Warminster, Wiltshire. **Tel** *01985*
844400. ⊠ *Warminster then taxi.*
House ◯ *daily.* ● *25 Dec.*
Safari Park ◯ *Feb–Nov: daily.*
🖼 🚻 🍴 🛍 📷
www.longleat.co.uk

The architectural historian
John Summerson coined the
term "prodigy house" to
describe the exuberance and
grandeur of Elizabethan
architecture that is so well
represented at Longleat. The
house was started in 1540,
when John Thynne bought
the ruins of a priory on the
site for £53. Over the
centuries subsequent owners
have added their own
touches. These include the
Breakfast Room and Lower
Dining Room (dating from
the 1870s), modelled on the
Venetian Ducal Palace, and
erotic murals painted by the
present owner, the 7th
Marquess of Bath. Today, the
Great Hall is the only
remaining room which
belongs to Thynne's time.

In 1949, the 6th Marquess
was the first landowner in
Britain to open his stately
home to the public, in order
to fund the maintenance and
preservation of the house and
its estate. Parts of the grounds,
landscaped by Capability
Brown *(see p26),* were turned
into an expansive safari park
in 1966, where lions, tigers
and other wild animals roam
freely. This, along with other
additions such as the world's
longest hedge maze, the
Adventure Castle and Blue
Peter Maze, and special
events, now draw even more
visitors than the house.

Stourhead ⑮

Stourhead is among the finest examples of 18th-century
landscape gardening in Britain *(see pp26–7).* The garden
was begun in the 1740s by Henry Hoare (1705–85),
who inherited the estate and transformed it into a breathtaking work of art. Hoare created the lake, surrounding
it with rare trees and plants, and Neo-
Classical Italianate temples, grottoes and
bridges. The Palladian-style house, built by
Colen Campbell *(see p28),* dates from 1724.

Pantheon
*Hercules is among the
statues of Roman gods
housed in the elegant
Pantheon (1753).*

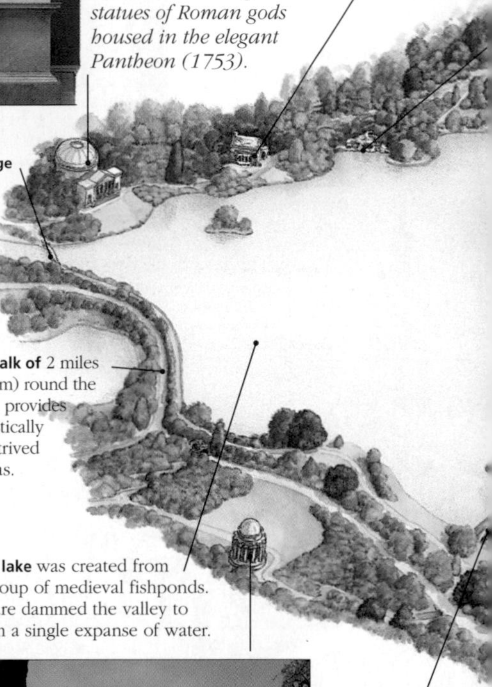

Gothic Cottage
(1806)

**Iron
Bridge**

A walk of 2 miles
(3 km) round the
lake provides
artistically
contrived
vistas.

The lake was created from
a group of medieval fishponds.
Hoare dammed the valley to
form a single expanse of water.

**Turf
Bridge**

**Temple of
Flora (1744)**

★ **Temple
of Apollo**
*The Classical
temples that dot the
garden were all
designed by
influential archi-
tect Henry Flitcroft
(1679–1769).*

Grotto
Tunnels lead to an artificial cave with a pool and a life-size statue of the guardian of the River Stour, sculpted by John Cheere in 1748.

VISITORS' CHECKLIST

(NT) Stourton, Wiltshire. **Tel** 01747 841152. 🚆 Gillingham (Dorset) then taxi. **House** 🕒 Apr–Oct: 11:30am–4:30pm Fri–Tue. **Gardens** 🕒 9am–7pm (or dusk if earlier) daily. 🅿️ 🦽 limited. 🎫 🍴 🛒 🎁 www. nationaltrust.org.uk/stourhead

★ Stourhead House
Reconstructed after a fire in 1902, the house contains fine Chippendale furniture. The art collection reflects Henry Hoare's Classical tastes and includes The Choice of Hercules (1637) *by Nicolas Poussin.*

Colourful shrubs around the house include fragrant rhododendrons in spring.

Stourton village was incorporated into Hoare's overall design. 🍴 🛒

Pelargonium House is a historical collection of over 100 species and cultivars.

The reception offers information to help you enjoy your visit.

Entrance and car park

St Peter's Church
The parish church contains monuments to the Hoare family. The medieval Bristol Cross, nearby, was brought from Bristol in 1765.

STAR SIGHTS

★ Temple of Apollo

★ Stourhead House

Shaftesbury ⑯

Dorset. 🏘 8,000. 🚉 🅿 **🛈** 8 Bell St
(01747 853514). 🅰 Thu.
www.shaftesburydorset.co.uk

Hilltop Shaftesbury, with its
cobbled streets and 18th-
century cottages is often used
as a setting for films to give a
flavour of Old England.
Picturesque **Gold Hill** is lined
on one side by a wall of the
demolished **abbey**, founded
by King Alfred in 888. Only
the excavated remains of the
abbey church survive, and
many masonry fragments are
found in the local museum.

**The Almshouse (1437) adjoining
the Abbey Church, Sherborne**

Sherborne ⑰

Dorset. 🏘 9,500. 🚉 🅿 **🛈** Digby
Rd (01935 815341). 🅰 Thu, Sat.
www.westdorset.com

Few other towns in Britain
have such a wealth of
unspoilt medieval buildings.
Edward VI *(see p41)* founded
the famous Sherborne School
in 1550, saving intact the
splendid **Abbey Church** and
other monastic buildings that
might otherwise have been
demolished in the Dissolution
(see p50). Remains of the Saxon
church can be seen in the
abbey's façade, but the most
striking feature is the 15th-
century fan-vaulted ceiling.

Sherborne Castle, built by
Sir Walter Raleigh *(see p51)* in
1594, is a wonderfully varied
building that anticipates the
flamboyant Jacobean style.
Raleigh also lived briefly in
the early 12th-century **Old
Castle**, which now stands
in ruins, demolished during
the Civil War *(see p52)*.

Environs: West of Sherborne,
past Yeovil, is the magnificent
Elizabethan **Montacute House**
(see p245), set in 120 ha (300
acres) of grounds. It is noted
for tapestries, and for the
Tudor and Jacobean portraits
in the vast Long Gallery.

🏛 **Sherborne Castle**
Off A30. **Tel** 01935 813182.
Castle ◻ Apr–Oct: Tue–Thu, Sat,
Sun & bank hols (pm). **Grounds** ◻
Apr–Oct: Thu–Tue. 🎫 🖵 🛈
www.sherbornecastle.com

🏛 **Old Castle**
(EH) Off A30. **Tel** 01935 812730.
◻ Easter–Oct: Tue–Sun. ● 25, 26
Dec, 1 Jan. 🎫 🔂 🛈

🏰 **Montacute House**
(NT) Montacute. **Tel** 01935 823289.
Grounds ◻ Apr–Nov: Wed–Mon.
🎫 🍴 🛈

Abbotsbury ⑱

Dorset. 🏘 400. **🛈** Bakehouse
Market St (01305 871130).
www.abbotsbury-tourism.co.uk

The name Abbotsbury recalls
the town's 11th-century
Benedictine abbey of which
little but the huge tithe barn,
built around 1400, remains.
　Nobody knows when the
Swannery here was founded,
but the earliest record dates
to 1393. Mute swans come to
nest in the breeding season,
attracted by the reed beds
along the Fleet, a brackish
lagoon protected from

The Swannery at Abbotsbury

the sea by a high ridge of
pebbles called **Chesil Bank**
(see p242). Its wild atmosphere
makes an appealing contrast
to the south coast resorts,
although strong currents make
swimming too dangerous.
**Abbotsbury Sub-Tropical
Gardens** are the frost-free
home to many new plants, discovered by botanists travelling
in South America and Asia.

🦢 **Swannery**
New Barn Rd. **Tel** 01305 871858. ◻
mid-Mar–Oct: daily. 🎫 🔂 🖵 🛈

🌿 **Abbotsbury Sub-Tropical
Gardens**
Off B3157. **Tel** 01305 871387. ◻
daily. ● 24 Dec–1 Jan. 🎫 🔂 🖵 🛈

Weymouth ⑲

Dorset. 🏘 62,000. 🚉 🅿 ⛴
🛈 King's Statue, The Esplanade
(01305 785747). 🅰 Thu.
www.weymouth.gov.uk

Weymouth's popularity as
one of Britain's earliest
seaside resorts began in 1789
when George III paid the first
of many summer visits here.
The king's bathing machine

Weymouth Quay, Dorset's south coast

For hotels and restaurants in this region see pp568–571 and pp624–626

can be seen in the old brewery complex, **Brewers' Quay**, and his statue is a prominent feature on the seafront. Here gracious Georgian terraces and hotels look across to the beautiful expanse of Weymouth Bay. Different in character is the old town around Custom House Quay with its fishing boats and old seamen's inns.

🏛 **Brewers' Quay**
Hope Sq. **Tel** 01305 777622. ☐ daily.
🌑 25 & 26 Dec, 2 wks in Jan. 🎟

A 55 m (180 ft) giant carved on the chalk hillside, Cerne Abbas (NT)

Dorchester ⑳

Dorset. 🏘 16,000. 🚊 🛈 Antelope Walk (01305 267992). 🖳 Wed.
www.westdorset.com

Dorchester, the county town of Dorset, is still recognizably the town in which Thomas Hardy based his novel *The Mayor of Casterbridge* (1886). Here, among the many 17th- and 18th-century houses lining the High Street, is the **Dorset County Museum**, where the original manuscript of the novel is displayed. Dorchester has the only example of a **Roman town house** in Britain. The remains reveal architectural details including a fine mosaic. There are also finds from Iron Age and Roman sites on the outskirts of the town. **Maumbury Rings** (Weymouth Avenue), is a Roman amphitheatre, originally a Neolithic henge. To the west, many Roman graves have been found below the Iron Age hill fort, **Poundbury Camp**.

Environs: Just southwest of Dorchester, **Maiden Castle** *(see p43)* is a massive monument dating from around 100 BC. In AD 43 it was the scene of a battle when the Romans fought the Iron Age people of southern England. To the north lies the charming village of **Cerne Abbas** with its magnificent medieval tithe barn and monastic buildings. The huge chalk figure of a giant on the hillside here is a fertility figure thought to represent either the Roman god Hercules or an Iron Age warrior.

East of Dorchester are the churches, thatched villages and rolling hills immortalized in Hardy's novels. Picturesque **Bere Regis** is the Kingsbere of *Tess of the D'Urbervilles*, where the tombs of the family whose name inspired the novel may be seen in the Saxon **church**. **Hardy's Cottage** is where the writer was born and **Max Gate** is the house he designed and lived in from 1885 until his death. His heart is buried with his family at **Stinsford** church – his body was given a public funeral at Westminster Abbey *(pp92–3)*.

Hardy's statue, Dorchester

There are beautiful gardens *(see p245)* and a magnificent medieval hall at 15th-century **Athelhampton House**.

🏛 **Dorset County Museum**
High West St. **Tel** 01305 262735. ☐ Nov–Apr: Mon–Sat; May–Oct: daily. 🌑 25, 26 Dec. 🎟 🚻 limited. 📷
www.dorsetcountymuseum.org

🏚 **Hardy's Cottage**
(NT) Higher Bockhampton. **Tel** 01305 262366. ☐ Apr–Oct: Sun–Thu. 🎟 🚻 🚻 garden only.

🏚 **Max Gate**
(NT) Alington Ave, Dorchester. **Tel** 01305 262538. ☐ Apr–Sep: Sun, Mon & Wed (pm). 🎟 🚻 📷

🏚 **Athelhampton House**
Athelhampton. **Tel** 01305 848363. ☐ Mar–Oct: Sun–Thu; Nov: Sun. 🎟 🚻 gardens only. 🎟 🍴 📷

THOMAS HARDY (1840–1928)

The vibrant, descriptive novels and poems of Thomas Hardy, one of England's best-loved writers, are set against the background of his native Dorset. The Wessex countryside provides a constant and familiar stage against which his characters enact their fate. Vivid accounts of rural life record a key moment in history, when mechanization was about to destroy ancient farming methods, just as the Industrial Revolution had done in the towns a century before *(see pp54–5)*. Hardy's powerfully visual style has made novels such as *Tess of the D'Urbervilles* (1891) popular with modern film-makers, and drawn literary pilgrims to the villages and landscapes that inspired his fiction.

Nastassja Kinski in Roman Polanski's film *Tess* (1979)

Corfe Castle ㉑

(NT) Dorset. *Tel* 01929 481294. ⊉
Wareham then bus. ◯ *daily.* ⬤ *25
& 26 Dec.* 🎟 ♿ *limited.* 📷
Mar–Oct; Nov–Feb by arrangement.
🖥 📷 www.nationaltrust.org.uk

The spectacular ruins of
Corfe Castle romantically
crown a jagged pinnacle of
rock above the charming unspoilt village that shares its
name. The castle has dominated the landscape since the
11th century, first as a royal
fortification, then as the dramatic ruins seen today. In
1635 the castle was purchased
by Sir John Bankes, whose
wife and her retainers – mostly
women – courageously held
out against 600 Parliamentary
troops, in a six-week siege
during the Civil War *(see
pp52–3).* The castle was
eventually taken through trea-
chery and in 1646 Parliament
voted to have it "slighted" –
deliberately blown up to
prevent it being used again.
From the ruins there are far-
reaching views over the Isle of
Purbeck and its coastline.

The ruins of Corfe Castle, dating mainly from Norman times

Isle of Purbeck ㉒

Dorset. ⊉ *Wareham.* 🚢 *Shell Bay,
Studland.* ℹ *Swanage (01929
422885).* www.swanage.gov.uk

The Isle of Purbeck, which
is in fact a peninsula, is the
source of the grey shelly
limestone, known as Purbeck
marble, from which the castle
and surrounding houses were
built. The geology changes to
the southwest at **Kimmeridge**,
where the muddy shale is rich
in fossils and recently

discovered oil reserves. The
Isle, a World Heritage site, is
fringed with unspoilt beaches.
Studland Bay (NT) – with its
white sand and its sand-dune
nature reserve, rich in birdlife
– has been rated one of
Britain's best beaches.
Sheltered **Lulworth Cove** is
almost encircled by white
cliffs, and there is a fine cliff-
top walk to Durdle Door *(see
p243),* a natural chalk arch.

The main resort in the area
is **Swanage**, the port where
Purbeck stone was trans-
ported by ship to London, to
be used for everything from
street paving to church building. Unwanted masonry from
demolished buildings was
shipped back and this is how
Swanage got its wonderfully
ornate **Town Hall** façade, designed by Wren around 1668.

Poole ㉓

Dorset. 🏃 *142,000.* ⊉ 🚉 🚌
ℹ *Poole Quay (01202 253253).*
www.pooletourism.com

Situated on one of the largest
natural harbours in the world,
Poole is an ancient, still thriving, seaport. The quay is lined
with old warehouses, modern
apartments and a marina,
overlooking a safe sheltered
bay. The **Waterfront
Museum**, partly housed in
15th-century cellars on the
quay, has undergone a major
refurbishment and will be
open in 2007.

Nearby **Brownsea Island**
(reached by boat from the
quay) is given over to a
woodland nature reserve with

Beach adjoining Lulworth Cove, Isle of Purbeck

a waterfowl and heron sanctuary. The fine views of the Dorset coast add to the appeal of the island.

🏛 Waterfront Museum
High St. **Tel** 01202 262600. ☐ daily. ● 25, 26 Dec, 1 Jan. ♿ www.poole.gov.uk

✈ Brownsea Island
(NT) Poole. **Tel** 01202 707744. ☐ Apr–Nov: daily (boat trips leave the quayside every 30 mins during the season). ▨ ♿ ✎ ▢ ▢

Boats in Poole harbour

Wimborne Minster ㉔

Dorset. 🏠 6,500. 🚍 ℹ 29 High St (01202 886116). 🛍 Fri–Sun. www.ruraldorset.com

The fine collegiate church of Wimborne's **Minster** was founded in 705 by Cuthburga, sister of King Ina of Wessex. It fell prey to marauding Danish raiders in the 10th century, and the imposing grey church we see today dates from the refounding by Edward the Confessor (see p47) in 1043. Stonemasons made use of the local Purbeck marble, carving beasts, biblical scenes, and a mass of zig-zag decoration.

The 16th-century **Priest's House Museum** has rooms furnished in the style of different periods and an enchanting hidden garden.

Environs: Designed for the Bankes family after the destruction of Corfe Castle, **Kingston Lacy** was acquired by the National Trust in 1981. The estate has always been farmed by traditional methods

and is astonishingly rich in wildlife, rare flowers and butterflies. This quiet, forgotten corner of Dorset is grazed by rare Red Devon cattle and can be explored using paths and "green lanes" that date back to Roman and Saxon times. The fine 17th-century house on the estate contains an outstanding collection of paintings, including works by Rubens, Velázquez and Titian.

🏛 Priest's House Museum
High St. **Tel** 01202 882533. ☐ Apr–Oct: Mon–Sat. ▨ ♿ limited. ▢ ▢

♛ Kingston Lacy
(NT) on B3082. **Tel** 01202 883402. **House** ☐ Apr–Oct: Wed–Sun. **Gardens** ☐ Apr–Oct: daily; Nov–Mar: Sat & Sun. ▨ ♿ gardens only. 🍴 ▢

Bournemouth ㉕

Dorset. 🏠 165,000. 🚶 � 🚍 ℹ Westover Rd (0906 8020234). www.bournemouth.co.uk

Bournemouth's popularity as one of England's favourite seaside resorts is due to an almost unbroken sweep of sandy beach, extending from the mouth of Poole Harbour to Hengistbury Head. Most of the seafront is built up, with many large seaside villas and exclusive hotels. To the west there are numerous clifftop parks and gardens, interrupted by beautiful wooded river ravines, known as "chines". The varied and colourful garden of **Compton Acres** was conceived as a museum of many different garden styles.

In central Bournemouth the amusement arcades, casinos, nightclubs and shops cater for the city's many visitors. During the summer, pop groups, TV comedians and the

A toy train on the popular seafront at Bournemouth

Marchesa Maria Grimaldi by Sir Peter Paul Rubens (1577–1640), Kingston Lacy

highly regarded Bournemouth Symphony Orchestra perform at various venues in the city. The **Russell-Cotes Art Gallery and Museum**, housed in a late Victorian villa, has an extensive collection with many fine Oriental and Victorian artefacts.

Environs: The magnificent **Christchurch Priory**, east of Bournemouth, is 95 m (310 ft) in length – the longest church in England. It was rebuilt between the 13th and 16th centuries and presents a sequence of different styles. The original nave, built around 1093, is an impressive example of Norman architecture, but the highlight is the intricate stone reredos which features a Tree of Jesse, tracing the lineage of Christ. Next to the Priory are the ruins of a Norman **castle**.

Between Bournemouth and Christchurch, **Hengistbury Head** is well worth climbing for grassland flowers, butterflies and sea views, while **Stanpit Marsh**, to the west of Bournemouth, is an excellent spot for viewing herons and other wading birds.

♣ Compton Acres
Canford Cliffs Rd. **Tel** 01202 700 778. ☐ daily. ▢ ▨ ♿ 🍴 www.comptonacres.co.uk

🏛 Russell-Cotes Art Gallery and Museum
Eastcliff. **Tel** 01202 451800. ☐ Tue–Sun. ♿ 🍴 ▢ www.russell-cotes.bournemouth.gov.uk

DEVON AND CORNWALL

DEVON · CORNWALL

*M*iles of magnificently varied coastline dominate this magical corner of Britain. Popular seaside resorts alternate with secluded coves and unspoilt fishing villages rich in maritime history. In contrast there are lush, exotic gardens and the wild terrain of the moorland interior, dotted with tors and historic remains.

Geographical neighbours, the counties of Devon and Cornwall are very different in character. Celtic Cornwall, with its numerous villages named after early Christian missionaries, is mostly stark and treeless at its centre. In many places it is still scarred by the remains of tin and copper mining that has played an important part in the economy for some 4,000 years. Yet this does not detract from the beauty and variety of the coastline dotted with lighthouses and tiny coves, and penetrated by deep tidal rivers.

Devon, by contrast, is a land of lush pasture divided into a patchwork of tiny fields and threaded with narrow lanes, whose banks support a mass of flowers from the first spring primroses to summer's colourful mixture of campion, foxglove, oxeye daisies and blue cornflowers. The leisurely pace of rural life here, and in Cornwall, contrasts with life in the bustling cities. Exeter with its magnificent cathedral, historic Plymouth, elegant Truro and Elizabethan Totnes are urban centres brimming with life and character.

The spectacular coastline and the mild climate of the region attract families, boating enthusiasts and surfers. For those in search of solitude, the Southwest Coastal Path provides access to the more tranquil areas. There are fishing villages and harbours whose heyday was in the buccaneering age of Drake and Raleigh *(see p51)*, and inland the wild moorland of Bodmin and Dartmoor, which provided inspiration for many romantic tales. Many of these are associated with King Arthur *(see p285)* who, according to legend, was born at Tintagel on Cornwall's dramatically contorted north coast.

Beach huts on the seafront at Paignton, near Torquay

◁ **Fishing boats in Port Isaac, on Cornwall's north coast**

Exploring Devon and Cornwall

Romantic Moorland dominates the inland parts of
Devon and Cornwall, ideal walking country with
few roads and magnificent views stretching for miles.
By contrast the extensive coastline is indented by
hundreds of sheltered river valleys, each one seem-
ingly isolated from the rest of the world – one reason
why Devon and Cornwall can absorb so many visitors
and yet still seem uncrowded. Wise tourists get to
know one small part of Devon or Cornwall intimately,
soaking up the atmosphere of the region, rather than
rushing to see everything in the space of a week.

KEY

═══	Motorway
──	Major road
──	Secondary road
═══	Minor road
──	Scenic route
──	Main railway
──	Minor railway
▲	Summit

SIGHTS AT A GLANCE

Appledore **16**
Barnstaple **17**
Bideford **15**
Bodmin **11**
Buckfastleigh **23**
Buckland Abbey **26**
Bude **13**
Burgh Island **24**
Clovelly **14**
Cotehele **27**
Dartmoor pp294–5 **29**
Dartmouth **21**
Eden Project pp282–3 **9**
Exeter **19**
Falmouth **6**
Fowey **10**
Helston and the
  Lizard Peninsula **5**
Lynton and Lynmouth **18**
Morwellham Quay **28**
Penzance **3**
Plymouth **25**
St Austell **8**
St Ives **2**
*St Michael's Mount
  pp278–9* **4**
Tintagel **12**
Torbay **20**
Totnes **22**
Truro **7**

Walks and Tours

Penwith Tour **1**

The dramatic cliffs of Land's End,
England's most westerly point

SEE ALSO

- *Where to Stay* pp571–5
- *Where to Eat* pp626–9

Sub-tropical gardens at Torquay, the popular seaside resort

18 LYNTON & LYNMOUTH
→ *Minehead*

Combe Martin
Parracombe
Arlington Court
Braunton
Brayford
Exmoor

STAPLE 17 🏛🏺
APPLEDORE
IDEFORD
South Molton
Molland
A361 Oakford Bampton
Taunton
Great Torrington A377
Chulmleigh
Witheridge
Tiverton
Yeovil
Lapford
Upottery
A386
Winkleigh
Bickleigh
M5
North Tawton
Crediton *Exe* *Killerton House* Talaton
Honiton
A30
A35
kehampton
Whiddon Down
Tedburn St Mary
Broad Clyst
Ottery St. Mary
Otter
Beer
High Willhays 621m
Teign
Dunsford
EXETER 19 ⛪🏛🏺
Topsham
Sidmouth
A386
Chagford
A38
Budleigh Salterton
DARTMOOR
Bovey Tracy
Chudleigh
Exmouth
Lyme Bay
Postbridge
Dawlish
Two Bridges
🎿 **29**
A380
ORWELLHAM QUAY
Ashburton
Newton Abbot
Babbacombe Bay
26 BUCKLAND ABBEY
Kingskerswell
EHELE
🏛🏺 **23**
Torquay
BUCKFASTLEIGH
🏛🏺 **22**
🏛 **20 TORBAY**
ash
Plympton A38
South Brent
TOTNES
Dart
Paignton
25 PLYMOUTH
🚢🏺🍴🏛
Modbury
DARTMOUTH 21
Brixham
Newton Ferrers
🏛 Stoke Fleming
Kingswear
24 BURGH ISLAND
Torcross
Salcombe
Start Point
Prawle Point

0 kilometres   15
0 miles   10

GETTING AROUND
Large numbers of drivers, many towing caravans (trailers), travel along the M5 motorway and A30 trunk road from mid-July to early September and travel can be slow, especially on Saturdays. Once in Devon and Cornwall, allow ample time if you are travelling by car along the region's narrow and high-banked lanes.

The regular train services, running from Paddington to Penzance, along Brunel's historic Great Western Railway, stop at most major towns. Aside from this, you are dependent on taxis or infrequent local buses.

Typical thatched, stone cottages, Buckland-in-the-Moor, Dartmoor

Penwith Tour ❶

This tour passes through a spectacular, remote Cornish landscape, dotted with relics of the tin mining industry, picturesque fishing villages and many prehistoric remains. The magnificent coastline varies between the gentle rolling moorland in the north and the rugged, windswept cliffs that characterize the dramatic south coast. The beauty of the area, combined with the clarity of light, has attracted artists since the late 19th century. Their work can be seen in Newlyn, St Ives and Penzance.

TIPS FOR DRIVERS

Tour length: 31 miles (50 km)
Stopping-off points: There are pubs and cafés in most villages. Sennen Cove makes a pleasant mid-way stop. (See also pp684–5.)

Zennor ①
The carved mermaid in the church recalls the legend of the mermaid who lured the local squire's son to her ocean lair.

Lanyon Quoit ②
One of many prehistoric monuments, this chambered tomb is visible on the left from the road to Madron.

Botallack Mine ⑧
Derelict enginehouses clinging to the cliffside are a vivid reminder of the region's former industry of tin-mining.

Trengwainton ③
These gardens are noted for their luxuriance (p244).

Land's End ⑦
England's most westerly point is noted for its dramatic and wild landscape. A local exhibition reveals its history, geology and wildlife.

Newlyn ④
Cornwall's largest fishing port gave its name to a school of artists founded in the 1880s (p278). Examples of their work can be seen in the art gallery here.

Merry Maidens ⑤
This Bronze Age stone circle is said to be 19 girls turned to stone for dancing on Sunday.

Minack Theatre ⑥
This Ancient Greek-style theatre (1923) overlooks a magical bay of Porthcurno. It forms a magnificent backdrop for productions in summer.

ST IVES

Morvah

B3306

B3306

B3318

St Just

A3071

Madron

PENZANCE

A30

B3306

A30

B3283

B3315

Sennen Cove

A30

B3315

B3283

Mousehole

Lamorna

B3315

Porthcurno

0 kilometres   3

0 miles   2

KEY

━━━ Tour route

═══ Other roads

☆ Viewpoint

St Ives ❷

Cornwall. 🏘 11,000. 🚉 🚌
ℹ Street-an-Pol (01736 796297).
www.go-cornwall.com

St Ives is renowned for the **Barbara Hepworth Museum and Sculpture Garden** and **Tate St Ives**, which together celebrate the work of a group of artists who set up a seaside art colony here from the 1920s. Tate St Ives, designed to frame a panoramic view of Porthmeor Beach, reminds visitors of the natural surroundings that inspired the art on display within. The Barbara Hepworth Museum presents the sculptor's work in the house and garden where she lived and worked for many years.

The town of St Ives remains a typical English seaside resort,

The Lower Terrace, Tate St Ives

surrounded by a crescent of golden sands. Popular taste rules in the many other art galleries tucked down winding alleys with names such as Teetotal Street, a legacy of

the town's Methodist heritage. Many galleries are converted cellars and lofts where fish were once salted and packed. In between are whitewashed cottages with tiny gardens brimming with marigolds, sunflowers and trailing lobelia, their vibrant colours made intense by the unusually clear light that first attracted artists to St Ives.

🏛 **Barbara Hepworth Museum and Sculpture Garden**
Barnoon Hill. **Tel** 01736 796226.
◐ Mar–Oct: daily; Nov–Feb: Tue–Sun. ● 24–26 Dec. ▨
🦽 by arrangement. ▣

🏛 **Tate St Ives**
Porthmeor Beach. **Tel** 01736 796226.
◐ Mar–Oct: daily; Nov–Feb: Tue–Sun.
● 24–26 Dec; occasionally for rehanging – phone to check. ▨ 🦽 🍴 ▣
www.tate.org.uk/stives

TWENTIETH-CENTURY ARTISTS OF ST IVES

Ben Nicholson and Barbara Hepworth formed the nucleus of a group of artists that made a major contribution to the development of abstract art in Europe. In the 1920s, St Ives together with Newlyn *(see p276)* became a place for aspiring artists. Among the prolific artists associated with the town are the potter Bernard Leach (1887–1979) and the painter Patrick Heron (1920–99), whose *Coloured Glass Window (see p240)* dominates the Tate St Ives entrance. Much of the art on display at Tate St Ives is abstract and illustrates new responses to the rugged Cornish landscape, the human figure and the ever-changing patterns of sunlight on sea.

Barbara Hepworth *(1903–75) was one of the foremost abstract sculptors of her time.* Madonna and Child *(1953) can be seen in the church of St Ia.*

John Wells' *(1907–2000) key interests are in light, curved forms and birds in flight, as revealed in* Aspiring Forms *(1950).*

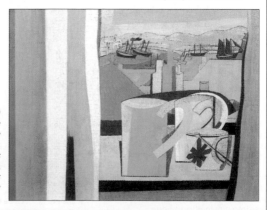

Ben Nicholson's *(1894–1982) work shows a change in style from simple scenes, such as the view from his window, to a preoccupation with shapes – as seen in this painting* St Ives, Cornwall *(1943–5). Later, his interest moved towards pure geometric blocks of colour.*

Penzance ❸

Cornwall. 🚊 15,000. 🚆 🚌 🛥
ℹ️ *Station Approach (01736 362207).*
www.visit-westcornwall.com

Penzance is a bustling resort with a climate so mild that palm trees and sub-tropical plants grow happily in the lush **Morrab Gardens**. The town commands fine views of St Michael's Mount and a great sweep of clean sandy beach.

The main road through the town is Market Jew Street, at the top of which stands the magnificent domed Market House (1837), fronted by a statue of Sir Humphrey Davy (1778–1829). Davy, who came from Penzance, invented the miner's safety lamp which detected lethal gases.

Chapel Street is lined with curious buildings, none more striking than the flamboyant **Egyptian House** (1835), with its richly painted façade and lotus bud decoration. Just as curious is **Admiral Benbow Inn** (1696) on the same street, which has a pirate perched on the roof looking out to sea. The town's **Museum and Art Gallery** has pictures by the Newlyn School of artists.

Environs: A short distance south of Penzance, **Newlyn** *(see p276)* is Cornwall's largest fishing port, which has given its name to the local school of artists founded by Stanhope Forbes (1857–1947). They painted outdoors, aiming to capture the fleeting impressions of wind, sun and sea. Continuing south, the coastal road ends at **Mousehole** (pronounced Mowzall), a pretty, popular village with a

The Egyptian House (1835)

tiny harbour, tiers of cottages and a maze of narrow alleys.

North of Penzance, overlooking the magical Cornish coast, **Chysauster** is a fine example of a Romano-British village. The site has remained almost undisturbed since it

St Michael's Mount ❹

(NT) Marazion, Cornwall. *Tel 01736 710507; tide and ferry information 01736 710265.* 🛥 *from Marazion (Apr–Oct) or on foot at low tide.* ⭘ *Apr–Oct: Sun–Fri; Nov–Mar guided tours only (book ahead).* 🎦 🍴 🛍
🏠 www.stmichaelsmount.co.uk

St Michael's Mount emerges dramatically from the waters of Mount Bay. According to ancient Roman historians, the mount was the island of Ictis, an important centre for the Cornish tin trade during the Iron Age. It is dedicated to the archangel St Michael who, according to legend, appeared here in 495.

When the Normans conquered England in 1066 *(see pp46–7)*, they were struck by the island's resemblance to their own Mont-St-Michel, whose Benedictine monks were invited to build a small abbey here. The abbey was absorbed into a fortress at the Dissolution *(see p351)*, when Henry VIII set up a chain of coastal defences to counter an expected attack from France.

In 1659 St Michael's Mount was purchased by Sir John St Aubyn, whose descendants subsequently turned the fortress into a magnificent house.

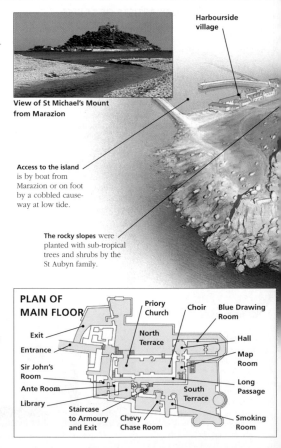

View of St Michael's Mount from Marazion

Harbourside village

Access to the island is by boat from Marazion or on foot by a cobbled causeway at low tide.

The rocky slopes were planted with sub-tropical trees and shrubs by the St Aubyn family.

PLAN OF MAIN FLOOR

Priory Church

Choir

Blue Drawing Room

Exit

North Terrace

Hall

Entrance

Map Room

Sir John's Room

Long Passage

Ante Room

South Terrace

Library

Smoking Room

Staircase to Armoury and Exit

Chevy Chase Room

was abandoned during the 3rd century.

From Penzance, regular boat and helicopter services depart for the **Isles of Scilly**, a beautiful archipelago forming part of the same granite mass as Land's End, Bodmin Moor and Dartmoor. Along with tourism, flower-growing forms the main source of income here.

🏛 Penlee House Gallery and Museum

Morrab Rd.
Tel 01736 363625. ◐ May–Sep: 10am–5pm Mon–Sat; Oct–Apr: 10:30am–4:30pm Mon–Sat.
◐ 25–26 Dec, 1 Jan. 🎫 📷 but free admission on Sat. ♿ 🔲
www.penleehouse.org.uk

🏠 Chysauster

(EH) Off B3311.
Tel 07831 757934.
◐ Apr–Oct: daily. 📷 🎫

THE GROWTH OF METHODISM

John Wesley (1703–91)

The hard-working and independent mining and fishing communities of the West Country had little time for the established church, but they were won over by the new Methodist religion, with its emphasis on hymn singing, open-air preaching and regular or "methodical" Bible reading. When John Wesley, the founder of Methodism, made the first of many visits to the area in 1743, sceptical Cornishmen pelted him with stones. His persistence, however, led to many conversions and by 1762 he was preaching to congregations of up to 30,000 people. Simple places of worship were built throughout the county; one favoured spot was the amphitheatre **Gwennap Pit**, at Busveal, south of Redruth. Methodist memorabilia can be seen in the Royal Cornwall Museum in Truro (see p281).

Castle entrance

The South Terrace forms the roof of the large Victorian wing. Beneath it there are five floors of private quarters.

The Blue Drawing Room *was formed from the Lady Chapel in the mid-18th century and is decorated in charming Rococo Gothic style. It contains fine plaster work, furniture and paintings by Gainsborough and Thomas Hudson.*

The Armoury displays sporting weapons and military trophies brought back by the St Aubyn family from various wars.

The Priory Church, *rebuilt in the late 14th century, forms the summit of the island. Beautiful rose windows are found at both ends.*

The Chevy Chase Room *takes its name from a plaster frieze (1641) representing hunting scenes.*

Pinnacles of serpentine rock at Kynance Cove (NT), Lizard Peninsula

Helston and the Lizard Peninsula ⑤

Cornwall. 🚉 from Penzance.
ℹ️ 79 Meneage St (01326 565431).
www.go-cornwall.com

The attractive town of Helston makes a good base for exploring the windswept coastline of the Lizard Peninsula. The town is famous for its Furry Dance which welcomes spring with dancing through the streets (see p62); the **Folk Museum** explains the history of this ancient custom. The Georgian houses and inns of Coinagehall Street are a reminder that Helston was once a thriving stannary town where tin ingots were brought for weighing and

stamping before being sold. Locally mined tin was brought down river to a harbour at the bottom of this street until access to the sea was blocked in the 13th century by a shingle bar that formed across the estuary. The bar created the freshwater lake, Loe Pool, and an attractive walk skirts its wooded shores. In 1880, Helston's trade was taken over by a new harbour created to the east on the River Helford, at Gweek. Today, Gweek is the home of the **National Seal Sanctuary**, where sick seals are nursed before being returned to the sea.

Cornwall's tin mining industry, from Roman to recent times, is covered at the **Poldark Mine** where underground tours show the working

conditions of 18th-century miners. Another major attraction is **Flambards Experience**, with its recreation of a Victorian village and of Britain during the Blitz.

Further south, huge satellite dishes rise from the heathland. The **Goonhilly Earth Station** visitors' centre here explores the world of satellite communications.

Local shops sell souvenirs carved from serpentine, a soft greenish stone which forms the unusual-shaped rocks that rise from the sandy beach at picturesque **Kynance Cove**.

🏛 **Folk Museum**
Market Place, Helston. **Tel** 01326 564027. ⬜ Mon–Sat ⬛ Christmas week. 🎟 ♿ limited. 📷
www.kerrierleisure.org.uk

🦭 **National Seal Sanctuary**
Gweek. **Tel** 01326 221361. ⬜ daily. ⬛ 25 Dec. 🎟 ♿ 📷 📷
www.sealsanctuary.co.uk

🏛 **Poldark Mine**
Wendron. **Tel** 01326 573173.
⬜ 2 wks at Easter, Jul & Aug: daily; Apr–Jun, Sep & Oct: Sun–Fri; Nov–Mar: tours only, by arrangement. 🎟 📷 📷 📷 **www**.poldark-mine.co.uk

🏛 **Flambards Experience**
Culdrose Manor, Helston. **Tel** 0845 6018684. ⬜ Easter–Aug: daily; Sep & Oct: Tue–Thu, Sat & Sun. ♿ 📷 📷 **www**.flambards.co.uk

🏛 **Goonhilly Earth Station**
Nr Helston, off B3293. **Tel** 0800 679 593. ⬜ Apr–Oct: daily; Oct–Dec: Tue–Sun. 🎟 ♿ 📷 📷 📷

CORNISH SMUGGLERS

In the days before income tax was invented, the main form of government income came from tax on imported luxury goods, such as brandy and perfume. Huge profits were to be made by evading these taxes, which were at their height during the Napoleonic Wars (1780–1815). Remote Cornwall, with its coves and rivers penetrating deep into the mainland, was prime smuggling territory; estimates put the number of people involved, including women and children, at 100,000. Some notorious families resorted to deliberate wrecking, setting up deceptive lights to lure vessels onto the sharp rocks, in the hope of plundering the wreckage.

Falmouth ⑥

Cornwall. 🏰 22,000. 🚉 🚌 ⛴
ℹ️ 28 Killigrew St (01326 312300).
www.go-cornwall.com

Falmouth stands at the point where seven rivers flow into a long stretch of water called the **Carrick Roads**. The drowned river valley is so deep that huge ocean-going ships can sail up almost as far as Truro. Numerous creeks are ideal for boating excursions to view the varied scenery and birdlife.

Falmouth has the third largest naturally deep harbour after Sydney and Rio de Janeiro, and it forms the most interesting part of this seaside resort. On the harbour waterfront stands the recently constructed **National Maritime Museum Cornwall**, part of a projected large new waterside complex, to include cafés, shops and restaurants. With an exterior that is oak-clad to reflect the history of wooden boat sheds in the area, the museum is dedicated to the great maritime tradition of Cornwall, and contains Britain's finest public collection of historic and contemporary small craft. The building is designed to bring to life the stories of boats, maritime themes and Cornwall's heritage, as well as the story of the people whose lives depended on the sea. It aims to be accessible to the whole family.

The many old houses on the harbour include the striking **Customs House** and the chimney alongside, known as the "King's Pipe" because it was used for burning contraband tobacco seized from smugglers in the 19th century. **Pendennis Castle** and St Mawes Castle opposite, were built by King Henry VIII.

Environs: To the south, **Glendurgan** *(see p244)* and **Trebah** gardens are both set in sheltered valleys leading down to delightful sandy coves on the Helford River.

Truro Cathedral, designed by J L Pearson and completed in 1910

🏛 **National Maritime Museum Cornwall**
Discovery Quay, Falmouth.
Tel 01326 313388. ⬜ *daily.*
🔴 25, 26 Dec. 🎫 ⬇ 🔲 📷
www.nmmc.co.uk

Ship's figure-head, Falmouth

⚓ **Pendennis Castle**
(EH) The Headland.
Tel 01326 316594. ⬜ *daily.*
🔴 24–26 Dec, 1 Jan. 🎫 ⬇
limited. 🎫 🔲 📷

🌺 **Glendurgan**
(NT) Mannan Smith.
Tel 01326 250906. ⬜ *mid-Feb–mid-Nov: Tue–Sat &*
public hols. 🔴 *Good Fri.* 🎫 🔲 📷
www.nationaltrust.org.uk

🌺 **Trebah**
Mawnan Smith. *Tel* 01326 250448.
⬜ *daily.* 📷 🎫 ⬇ 🔲
www.trebahgarden.co.uk

Truro ❼

Cornwall. 🏘 19,000. 🚋 🚌
ℹ Boscawen St (01872 274555).
🌾 Wed (cattle), Wed & Sat (farmers' market). www.truro.gov.uk

Once a market town and port, Truro is now the administrative capital of Cornwall. Truro's many gracious Georgian buildings reflect its prosperity during the tin mining boom of the 1800s. In 1876 the 16th-century parish church was rebuilt to create the first new **cathedral** to be built in England since Wren built St Paul's *(see pp114–15)* in the 17th century. With its central tower, lancet windows and spires, the cathedral is an exuberant building that looks more French than English.

Truro's cobbled streets and alleys lined with craft shops are also a delight to explore. The **Royal Cornwall Museum** provides an excellent introduction to the history of the county with displays on tin mining, Methodism *(see p279)*, and smuggling.

Environs: On the outskirts of the city lie **Trewithen** and **Trelissick** gardens *(see p244)*. The former has a rich collection of Asiatic plants.

🏛 **Royal Cornwall Museum**
River St. *Tel* 01872 272205. ⬜ *Mon–Sat.* 🔴 *public hols.* ⬇ 🔲 📷
www.royalcornwallmuseum.org.uk

🌺 **Trewithen**
Grampound Rd. *Tel* 01726 883647.
⬜ *Mar–Sep: Mon–Sat (Apr & May: daily).* 🎫 ⬇ 🎫 *by arrangement.* 🔲
🔲 www.trewithengardens.co.uk

🌺 **Trelissick**
(NT) Feock. *Tel* 01872 862090.
⬜ *mid-Feb–Dec: daily; Jan–mid-Feb: Thu–Sun.* 🎫 ⬇ 🍴 📷

The "Cornish Alps": china-clay spoil tips north of St Austell

St Austell ❽

Cornwall. 🏘 20,000. 🚋 🚌
ℹ Jet Service Station, Southbourne Rd (0845 094 0428). 🌾 Fri–Sun.
www.cornish-riviera.co.uk

The busy industrial town of St Austell is the capital of the local china-clay industry which rose to importance in the 18th century. Clay is still a vital factor here; until recently, China was the only other place where such quality and quantity of clay could be found. Spoil tips are a prominent feature; on a sunny day they look like snow-covered peaks, meriting the local name the "Cornish Alps".

Environs: The famous **Lost Gardens of Heligan** are an amazing restoration project to recreate the extraordinary gardens created by the Tremayne family from the 16th century to World War I. At the **Wheal Martyn China Clay Museum**, nature trails weave through clay works that operated from 1878 until the 1920s.

🌺 **Lost Gardens of Heligan**
Pentewan. *Tel* 01726 845100. ⬜ *daily.* 🔴 24 & 25 Dec. 🎫 ⬇ *limited.*
🍴 🔲 📷 www.heligan.com

🏛 **Wheal Martyn China Clay Museum**
Carthew. *Tel* 01726 850362. ⬜ *Mar–Oct: daily; Nov–Easter: Wed–Sun.* 🎫 ⬇ *limited.* 🔲 📷

Eden Project ❾

Built in a china clay pit that had reached the end of its useful life, the Eden Project is a global garden for the 21st century, and a dramatic setting in which to tell the fascinating story of mankind's dependence on plants. Two futuristic conservatories called Biomes have been designed to mimic the environments of warmer climes: one hot and humid, the other warm and dry. The outer Biome is planted with species that thrive in the Cornish climate. The Eden Project seeks to educate by telling the story of plants, people and places. The relationship between humans and nature is interpreted by storytellers and artists throughout the site.

④ Tropical South America
Some plants in this area reach enormous proportions. The leaves of the giant waterlily can be up to 2 m (6 ft) across.

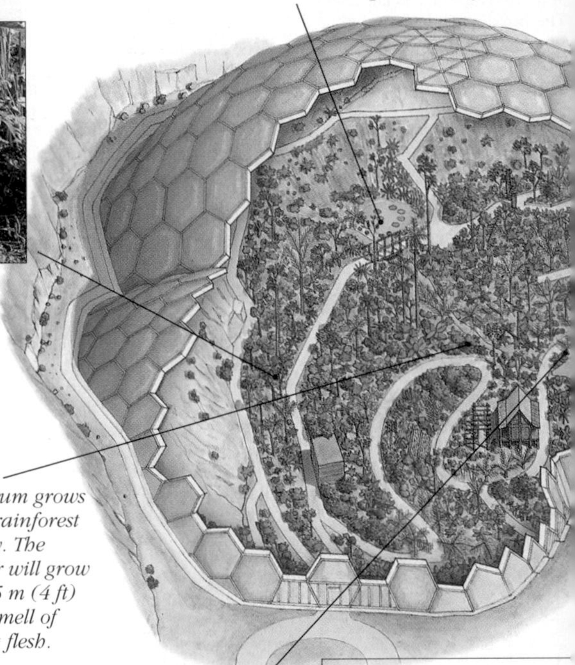

③ West Africa
Iboga is central to the African religion Bwiti. Highly hallucinogenic, it is an integral part of initiation ceremonies.

② Malaysia
The Titan arum grows within this rainforest display. The flower will grow to 1.5 m (4 ft) and smell of rotting flesh.

① Tropical Islands
Set apart from the rest of the world, these islands have many fascinating plants. The rare Madagascar Periwinkle (Catharanthus roseus) is thought to help cure leukemia.

THE SITE

Access to the outdoor and the covered Biomes is via the Visitor Centre.

Humid Tropics Biome
① Tropical Islands
② Malaysia
③ West Africa
④ Tropical South America
⑤ Crops & cultivation

Warm Temperate Biome
⑥ The Mediterranean
⑦ South Africa
⑧ California
⑨ Crops & cultivation

VISITORS' CHECKLIST

Bodelva, St Austell, Cornwall.
Tel 01726 811911. 🚂 St Austell.
🚌 dedicated bus service from St
Austell. ⬜ Apr–Oct: 10am–
6pm daily (last adm 5pm);
Nov–Mar: 10am–4:30pm daily
(last adm 3pm). ⬤ 24, 25 Dec.
🅿 ♿ 🍴 🛍 📷
www.edenproject.com

Building Eden
*Cornwall's declining china clay industry has left behind
many disused pits. The Eden Project makes ingenious use
of this industrial landscape. After partly infilling a pit,
the massive Biomes were nestled into its base and walls.*

⑤ Crops and cultivation
*The coffee plant (Coffea
arabica) is one of the many
plants on display that are
used in our everyday lives.*

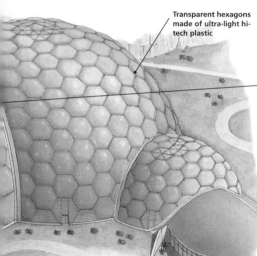

**Transparent hexagons
made of ultra-light hi-
tech plastic**

The entrance to both
the Humid Tropics
and Warm Temperate
Biomes is via the Link,
where two restaurants
are located.

...MID TROPICS BIOME
...vast conservatory houses a lush jungle of 8,000
... and plants. The dome is high enough to allow
...e rainforest trees to grow to their full height.

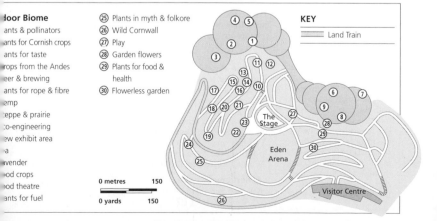

...door Biome
...ants & pollinators
...ants for Cornish crops
...ants for taste
...rops from the Andes
...eer & brewing
...ants for rope & fibre
...emp
...teppe & prairie
...o-engineering
...ew exhibit area
...a
...avender
...od crops
...od theatre
...ants for fuel

㉕ Plants in myth & folkore
㉖ Wild Cornwall
㉗ Play
㉘ Garden flowers
㉙ Plants for food &
  health
㉚ Flowerless garden

KEY

▨ Land Train

The Stage

Eden Arena

Visitor Centre

0 metres 150

0 yards 150

View of Polruan across the estuary from Fowey

Fowey 🔟

Cornwall. 🏠 *2,000.*
ℹ️ *5 South St (01726 833616).*
www.fowey.co.uk

Fowey (pronounced Foy), has been immortalized under the name of Troy Town in the humorous novels of Sir Arthur Quiller-Couch (1863–1944), who lived here in a house called **The Haven**. A resort favoured by many wealthy Londoners with a taste

DAPHNE DU MAURIER

The period romances of Daphne du Maurier (1907–89) are inextricably linked with the wild Cornish landscape where she grew up. *Jamaica Inn* established her reputation in 1936, and with the publication of *Rebecca* two years later she found herself one of the most popular authors of her day. *Rebecca* was made into a film directed by Alfred Hitchcock, starring Joan Fontaine and Lord Laurence Olivier.

for yachting and expensive seafood restaurants, Fowey is the most gentrified of the Cornish seaside towns. The picturesque charm of the flower-filled village is undeniable, with its tangle of tiny steep streets and its views across the estuary to Polruan. The church of **St Fimbarrus** marks the end of the ancient Saint's Way footpath from Padstow – a reminder of the Celtic missionaries who arrived on the shores of Cornwall to convert people to Christianity. Its flower-lined path leads to a majestic porch and carved tower. Inside there are some fine 17th-century memorials to the Rashleigh family whose seat, Menabilly, became Daphne du Maurier's home and featured as Manderley in *Rebecca* (1938).

Environs: For a closer look at the town of **Polruan** and the ceaseless activity of the harbour there is a number of river trips up the little creeks. At the estuary mouth are the twin towers from which chains were once hung to de-mast invading ships – an effective form of defence.

A fine stretch of coast leads further east to the picturesque fishing villages of **Polperro**, nestling in a narrow green ravine, and neighbouring **Looe**.

Upriver from Fowey is the tranquil town of **Lostwithiel**. Perched on a hill just to the north are the remains of the Norman **Restormel Castle**.

⚓ Restormel Castle
(EH) *Lostwithiel.* **Tel** *01208 872687.*
⭕ *Apr–Oct: daily.* ♿ 📷

Bodmin ⓫

Cornwall. 🚉 *Bodmin Parkway.*
🚌 *Bodmin.* ℹ️ *Mount Folly Sq,
Bodmin (01208 76616).*
www.bodminlive.com

Bodmin, Cornwall's ancient county town, lies on the sheltered western edge of the great expanse of moorland that shares its name. The history and archaeology of the town and moor is covered by **Bodmin Town Museum**, while **Bodmin Jail**, where public executions took place until 1909, has been turned into a gruesome tourist attraction. The churchyard is watered by the ever-gushing waters of a holy spring, and it was here that St Guron established a Christian cell in the 6th century. The **church** is dedicated to St Petroc, a Welsh missionary who founded a monastery here in the same period, as well as many others in the region. The monastery has disappeared, but the bones of St Petroc remain, housed in a splendid 12th-century ivory casket in the church.

Jamaica Inn,
Bodmin Moor

South of Bodmin is the **Lanhydrock** estate. Amid its extensive wooded acres and formal gardens *(see p244)* lies the massive house, rebuilt after a fire in 1881, but retaining some Jacobean features. The labyrinth of corridors and rooms illustrates life in a Victorian manor house and the fine 17th-century plaster ceiling in the Long Gallery depicts scenes from the Bible.

The desolate wilderness of Bodmin Moor is noted for its network of prehistoric field boundaries. The main attraction, however, is the 18th-century **Jamaica Inn**, made famous by Daphne du Maurier's tale of smuggling and romance. Today there is a restaurant and bar based on du Maurier's novel, and a small museum. A 30-minute walk from the Inn is **Dozmary Pool**, reputed to be bottomless until it dried up in 1976.

The ruins of Tintagel Castle on the north coast of Cornwall

According to legend, the dying King Arthur's sword Excalibur was thrown into the pool.

To the east is **Altarnun**. Its spacious 15th-century church of **St Nonna** is known as the "Cathedral of the Moor".

🏛 **Bodmin Town Museum**
Mt Folly Sq, Bodmin. **Tel** 01208 77067. ◻ Easter–Oct: Mon–Sat, Good Fri. ● public hols. ⬧ limited. ◻

🏯 **Bodmin Jail**
Berrycombe Rd, Bodmin. **Tel** 01208 76292. ◻ daily. ● 25 Dec. ◻ ◲ ◻

🏯 **Lanhydrock**
(NT) Bodmin. **Tel** 01208 265950. House ◻ Apr–Oct: Tue–Sun & public hols. **Gardens** ◻ daily. ◻ ◲ ⬧ ⬦

Tintagel ⑫

Cornwall. 🏯 1,700. ℹ 01840 779084. ☐ Thu (summer). **www**. visitboscastleandtintagel.com

The romantic and mysterious ruins of **Tintagel Castle**, built around 1240 by Earl Richard of Cornwall, sit high on a hill-top surrounded by slate cliffs. Access to the castle is via two steep staircases clinging to the cliffside where pink thrift and purple sea lavender abound.

The earl was persuaded to build in this isolated, wind-swept spot by the popular belief, derived from Geoffrey of Monmouth's fictitious *History of the Kings of Britain*, that this was the birthplace of the legendary King Arthur.

Large quantities of fine eastern Mediterranean pottery dating from around the 5th century have been discovered, indicating that the site was an important trading centre, long before the medieval castle was built. Whoever lived here, perhaps the ancient Kings of Cornwall, could evidently afford a luxurious lifestyle.

A clifftop path leads from the castle to Tintagel's **church**, which has Norman and Saxon masonry. In Tintagel village the **Old Post Office** is a rare example of a 14th-century restored and furnished Cornish manor house.

Environs: A short distance to the east, **Boscastle** is a pretty National Trust village. The River Valency runs down the middle of the main street to the fishing harbour, which is sheltered from the sea by high slate cliffs. Access from the harbour to the sea is via a channel cut through the rocks.

🏯 **Tintagel Castle**
Off High St. **Tel** 01840 770328. ◻ daily. ● 24–26 Dec, 1 Jan. ◲ **www**.english-heritage.org.uk/tintagel

🏯 **Old Post Office**
(NT) Fore St. **Tel** 01840 770024. ◻ Apr–Oct: daily. ◻ ◲

KING ARTHUR

Historians think the legendary figure of King Arthur has some basis in historical fact. He was probably a Romano-British chieftain or warrior who led British resistance to the Saxon invasion of the 6th century (*see pp46–7*). Geoffrey of Monmouth's *History of the Kings of Britain* (1139) introduced Arthur to literature with an account of the many legends connected with him – how he became king by removing the sword Excalibur from a stone, his final battle with the treacherous Mordred, and the story of the Knights of the Round Table (*see p170*). Other writers, such as Alfred, Lord Tennyson, took up these stories and elaborated on them.

King Arthur, from a 14th-century chronicle by Peter of Langtoft

Bude ⑬

Cornwall. 🏯 9,000. ℹ Crescent car park (01288 354240). ☐ Fri (summer). **www**.visitbude.co.uk

Wonderful beaches around this area make Bude a popular resort for families. The expanse of clean golden sand that attracts visitors today once made Bude a bustling port. Shelly, lime-rich sand was transported along a canal to inland farms where it was used to neutralize the acidic soil. The canal was abandoned in 1880 but a short stretch survives, providing a haven for birds such as kingfishers and herons.

Kingfisher

Clovelly ⑭

Devon. 🏠 *350. Tel 01237 431781.*
Town & Visitors' Centre ☐ *daily.*
⚫ *25 & 26 Dec.* 🦽 🔽 *Visitors'
Centre.* www.clovelly.co.uk

Clovelly has been a noted
beauty spot since the novelist
Charles Kingsley (1819–75)
wrote about it in his stirring
story of the Spanish Armada,
Westward Ho! (1855). The
whole village is privately
owned and has been turned
into a tourist attraction, with
little sign of the flourishing
fishing industry to which it
owed its birth. It is a charming,
picturesque village with
steep, traffic-free cobbled
streets rising up the cliff from
the harbourside, white-washed
houses and gardens brimming
with brightly coloured flowers.
There are superb views from
the lookout points and fine
coastal paths to explore from
the tiny quay.
   Hobby Drive is a scenic 3-
mile (5-km) approach on foot
to the village which runs
through woodland along the
coast. The road was con-
structed in 1811–29 to give

Bideford's medieval bridge, 203 m (666 ft) long with 24 arches

employment to local men who
had been made redundant at
the end of the Napoleonic
Wars *(see pp54–5).*

Bideford ⑮

Devon. 🏠 *14,000.* 🚊 ℹ️ *Victoria
Park (01237 477676).* 🛒 *Tue, Sat.*

Strung out along the boat-
filled estuary of the River
Torridge, Bideford grew and
thrived on importing tobacco
from the New World. Some
17th-century merchants'
houses survive in Bridgeland
Street, including the splendid
bay-windowed house at No. 28
(1693). Beyond is Mill Street,

leading to the parish church
and the fine medieval bridge.
The quay stretches from here
to a pleasant park and a
statue which commemorates
Charles Kingsley, whose novels
helped bring visitors to the
area in the 19th century.

Environs: To the west of
Bideford, the village **Westward
Ho!** was built in the late 19th
century and named after
Kingsley's popular novel. The
development failed and the
Victorian villas and hotels are
now part of a holiday resort.
Rudyard Kipling *(see p163)*
was at school here and the
hill to the south, known as
Kipling Tors, was the background for *Stalky & Co* (1899).
   Also to the west is **Hartland
Abbey**, built as a monastery
c.1157, now a family home.
Visitors can enjoy a museum,
art and antiques as well as
gardens and a woodland walk.
   Henry Williamson's *Tarka
the Otter* (1927) describes the
otters of the **Torridge Valley**
and naturalists are hoping to
reintroduce otters here. Part
of a Tarka Trail has been laid
out along the Torridge and
bicycles can be hired from the
old railway station. The trail
passes close to the magnificent **Rosemoor Garden**.
   Day trips run from either
Bideford or Ilfracombe (depending on the tide) to **Lundy**
island, which is abundant in
birds and wildlife.

🌺 **RHS Rosemoor Garden**
Great Torrington. *Tel 01805 624067.*
☐ *daily.* ⚫ *25 Dec.* 🦽 🔽 🍴 🏠
www.rhs.org.uk

🏛️ **Hartland Abbey** nr. Bideford.
Tel 01237 441264. ☐ *Apr–Oct:
2–5:30pm Tue (Jul–Aug only), Wed,
Thu, Sun, public hols.* 🦽 🖼️ 🏠
www.hartlandabbey.com

Fishing boats in Clovelly's harbour

Fishermen's cottages, Appledore

Appledore ⑯

Devon. 🏘 *3,000.* ℹ️ *Bideford (01237 477676).*

Appledore's remote position at the tip of the Torridge Estuary has helped to preserve its charms intact. Busy boatyards line the long riverside quay, which is also the departure point for fishing trips and ferries to the sandy beaches of Braunton Burrows on the opposite shore. Timeworn Regency houses line the main street which runs parallel to the quay, and behind is a network of narrow cobbled lanes with 18th-century fishermen's cottages. Several shops retain their original bow-windows and sell an assortment of crafts, antiques and souvenirs.

Uphill from the quay is the **North Devon Maritime Museum**, with an exhibition on the experiences of Devon emigrants in Australia and displays explaining the work of local shipyards. The tiny **Victorian Schoolroom** which is affiliated to the museum, shows various documentary videos on local trades such as fishing and shipbuilding.

🏛 **North Devon Maritime Museum**
Odun Rd. **Tel** *01237 474852.* ⬜ *May– Sep: daily; Apr, Oct: pm.* 🎫 ♿ *limited.*
🖥 www.devonheritage.com

Barnstaple ⑰

Devon. 🏘 *33,000.* 🚆 🚍 ℹ️ *The Square (01271 375000).* 🅿 *Mon–Sat.* www.staynorthdevon.co.uk

Although Barnstaple is an important distribution centre for the whole region, its town centre remains calm due to the exclusion of traffic. The massive glass-roofed **Pannier Market** (1855) has stalls of organic fruit and vegetables, honey and eggs, much of it produced by farmers' wives to supplement their income. Nearby is **St Peter's Church** with its twisted broach spire, said to have been caused by a lightning strike which warped the timbers in 1810.

On the Strand is a wonderful arcade topped with a statue of Queen Anne, now the **Heritage Centre**. This was built as an exchange where merchants traded the contents of their cargo boats moored on the River Taw alongside. Nearby is the 15th-century bridge and the **Museum of Barnstaple and North Devon**, where displays cover local history and the 700-year-old pottery industry, as well as local wildlife, such as the otters. The 180-mile (290 km) Tarka Trail circuits around Barnstaple; 35 miles (56 km) of it can be cycled.

Statue of Queen Anne (1708)

Environs: Just west of Barnstaple, **Braunton "Great Field"** covers over 120 ha (300 acres) and is a well-preserved relic of medieval open-field cultivation. Beyond lies **Braunton Burrows**, one of the most extensive wild-dune reserves in Britain. It is a must for plant enthusiasts who would like to spot sea kale, sea holly, sea lavender and horned poppies growing in their natural habitat. The sandy beaches and pounding waves at nearby Croyde and Woolacombe, are favourites among surfing enthusiasts, but there are also calmer areas of warm shallow water and rock pools.

Arlington Court, north of Barnstaple, has a collection of model ships, magnificent perennial borders and a lake. The stables house a collection of horse-drawn vehicles. Carriage rides are available.

🏛 **Museum of Barnstaple and North Devon**
The Square. **Tel** *01271 346747.* ⬜ *Mon–Sat.* ⬤ *24 Dec–1 Jan.* ♿ *limited.*
🖥 www.devonmuseums.net

🚇 **Arlington Court**
(NT) Arlington. **Tel** *01271 850296.* ⬜ *Easter–Oct: Sun–Fri.* 🎫 ♿ *limited.* 🖥 🅿

Barnstaple's Pannier Market

DEVONSHIRE CREAM TEAS

Devon people claim all other versions of a cream tea are inferior to their own. The essential ingredient is Devonshire clotted cream which comes from Jersey cattle fed on rich Devon pasture – anything else is second best, or so it is claimed. Spread thickly on freshly baked scones, with lashings of homemade strawberry jam, this makes a seductive, delicious, but fattening, tea-time treat.

A typical cream tea with scones, jam and clotted cream

The village of Lynmouth

Lynton and Lynmouth ⑱

Devon. 🏛 *2,000.* 🚉 ℹ *Town Hall, Lee Rd (0845 6603232).* See pp250–51. **www**.lyntourism.co.uk

Situated at the point where the East and West Lyn rivers meet the sea, Lynmouth is a picturesque, though rather commercialized, fishing village. The pedestrianized main street, lined with shops selling clotted cream and seaside souvenirs, runs parallel to the Lyn, now made into a canal with high embankments as a precaution against flash floods. One flood devastated the town at the height of the holiday season in 1952. The scars caused by the flood, which was fuelled by heavy rain on Exmoor, are now overgrown by trees in the pretty **Glen Lyn Gorge**, which leads north out of the village. Lynmouth's sister town, Lynton, is a mainly Victorian village perched on the clifftop 130 m (427 ft) above, giving lovely views across the Bristol Channel to the Welsh coast. It can be reached from the harbour front by a cliff railway, by road or by a steep path.

Environs: Lynmouth makes an excellent starting point for walks on Exmoor. There is a 2 mile (3 km) trail that leads southeast to tranquil **Watersmeet** *(see p251).* On the western edge of Exmoor, **Combe Martin** *(see p250)* lies in a sheltered valley. On the main street, lined with Victorian villas, is the 18th-century Pack of Cards Inn, built by a gambler with 52 windows, for each card in the pack.

Exeter ⑲

Exeter is Devon's capital, a bustling and lively city with a great deal of character, despite the World War II bombing that destroyed much of its city centre. Built high on a plateau above the River Exe, the city is encircled by substantial sections of Roman and medieval wall, and the street plan has not changed much since the Romans first laid out what is now the High Street. Elsewhere the Cathedral Close forms a pleasant green, and there are cobbled streets and narrow alleys which invite leisurely exploration. For shoppers there is a wide selection of big stores and smaller speciality shops.

Exploring Exeter

The intimate green and the close surrounding Exeter's distinctive cathedral were the setting for Anthony Trollope's novel *He Knew He Was Right* (1869). Full of festive crowds listening to buskers in the summer, the close presents an array of architectural styles. One of the finest buildings here is the Elizabethan **Mol's Coffee House**. Among the other historic buildings that survived World War II are the magnificent **Guildhall** (1330) on the High Street (one of Britain's oldest civic buildings), the opulent **Custom House** (1681) by the quay, and the elegant 18th-century **Rougement House** which stands near the remains of a Norman **castle** built by William the Conqueror *(see pp46–7).*

The port area has been transformed into a tourist attraction with its early 19th-century warehouses converted into craft shops, antique galleries and cafés. Boats can be hired for cruising down the short stretch of canal. The **Quay House Interpretation Centre**

The timber-framed Mol's Coffee House (1596), Cathedral Close

West front and south tower, Cathedral Church of St Peter

(open daily April–October; weekends November–March) has audio-visual and other displays on the history of Exeter.

🏛 Cathedral Church of St Peter

Cathedral Close. **Tel** *01392 255573.* ◯ *daily.* 🏛 ♿ 🚻
Exeter's cathedral is one of the most gloriously ornamented in Britain. Except for the two Norman towers, the cathedral is mainly 14th century and built in the style aptly known as Decorated because of the swirling geometric patterns of the stone work. The West Front, the largest single collection (66) of medieval figure sculptures in England, includes kings, apostles and prophets. Started in the 14th century, it was completed by 1450. Inside, the splendid Gothic vaulting sweeps from one end of the church to the other, impressive in its uniformity and punctuated by gaily painted ceiling bosses.

Among the tombs around the choir is that of Edward II's treasurer, Walter de Stapledon (1261–1326), who was murdered by a mob in London. Stapledon raised much of the money needed to fund the building of this cathedral.

Collection of shells and other objects in the library of A La Ronde

🏛 Underground Passages

Roman Gate Passage. **Tel** 01392 665 887. ● for refurbishment until Autumn 2007 – phone for details. 🅿 ♿

Under the city centre lie the remains of Exeter's medieval water-supply system. An excellent video and guided tour explain how the stone-lined tunnels were built in the 14th and 15th centuries on a slight gradient in order to bring in fresh water for townspeople from springs outside the town.

🏛 St Nicholas Priory

The Mint. **Tel** 01392 665858. ● for conservation work – phone for details .

Built in the 12th century, this building has retained many of its original features and rooms. These help visitors to trace its fascinating history from austere monastic beginnings, through its secular use as a Tudor residence for wealthy merchants, to its 20th-century incarnation as five separate business premises occupied by various tradesmen including a bootmaker and an upholsterer.

🏛 Royal Albert Memorial Museum and Art Gallery

Queen St. **Tel** 01392 665858. ◻ Mon–Sat. ● 24–26 Dec, 1 Jan, Good Fri, public hols. 🅿 ♿ 💻

This museum has a wonderfully varied collection, including Roman remains, a zoo of stuffed animals, West Country art and a particularly good ethnographic display. Highlights include displays on silverware, watches and clocks.

Environs: South of Exeter on the A376, the eccentric **A La Ronde** is a 16-sided house built in 1796 by two spinster cousins, who decorated the interior with shells, feathers and souvenirs gathered while on tour in Europe.

Further east, the unspoilt Regency town of **Sidmouth** lies in a sheltered bay. There is an eclectic array of architecture, the earliest buildings dating from the 1820s when Sidmouth became a popular summer resort. Thatched cottages stand opposite huge Edwardian villas, and elegant terraces line the seafront. In summer the town hosts the famous International Festival of Folk Arts (see p63).

19th-century head of an Oba, Royal Albert Museum

VISITORS' CHECKLIST

Devon. 🚶 111,000. ✈ 5 miles (8 km) east. 🚆 Exeter St David's, Bonhay Rd; Exeter Central, Queen St. 🚌 Paris St. 🛈 Paris St (01392 265700). 🛒 daily. **www.**heart-of-devon.com

North of Sidmouth lies the magnificent church at **Ottery St Mary**. Built in 1338–42 by Bishop Grandisson, the church is clearly a scaled-down version of Exeter Cathedral, which he also helped build. A memorial in the churchyard wall recalls the fact the poet Coleridge was born in the town in 1772.

Nearby **Honiton** is famous for its extraordinarily intricate and delicate lace, made here since Elizabethan times.

To the north of Exeter, **Killerton** is home to the National Trust's costume collection. Here, displays of bustles and corsets and vivid tableaux illustrate aristocratic fashions from the 18th century to the present day.

Further north near Tiverton, is **Knightshayes Court**, a Victorian Gothic mansion with fine gardens (see p245).

🏛 A La Ronde

(NT) Summer Lane, Exmouth. **Tel** 01395 265514. ◻ Apr–Oct: Sun–Thu. 💻 💻 🅿

🏛 Killerton

(NT) Broadclyst. **Tel** 01392 881345. **House** ◻ Apr–Oct: Wed–Mon. **Garden** ◻ daily. 💻 ♿ 💻 🅿

♣ Knightshayes Court

(NT) Bolham. **Tel** 01884 254665. ◻ Apr–Nov: Sat–Thu, Good Fri (gardens Apr–Nov daily). 💻 ♿ limited. 🍴 🅿

Mexican dancer at Sidmouth's International Festival of Folk Arts

Torbay ㉒

Torbay. 🚊 🚇 *Torquay, Paignton.* 🛈
*Vaughan Parade, Torquay (01803 297
428).* **www**.theenglishriviera.co.uk

The three seaside towns
of Torquay, Paignton and
Brixham form an almost continuous resort around the great
sweep of sandy beach and
blue waters of Torbay. Because
of its mild climate, extensive
semi-tropical gardens and
exuberant Victorian hotel architecture, this popular coastline
has been dubbed the English
Riviera. In its heyday, Torbay
was patronized by the wealthy,
especially during Victorian
times. Today, mass entertainment is the theme and there
are plenty of attractions, mostly
in and around Torquay.

Torre Abbey includes the
remains of a monastery founded in 1196. It is currently
undergoing an extensive £6.5
million restoration programme,
completely renovating the
abbey and gardens. Its grand
doors are due to open to the
public July in 2008. **Torquay**

Museum nearby covers natural history and archaeology,
including finds from **Kents
Cavern**, on the outskirts of
the town. This is one of
England's most important prehistoric sites and the spectacular caves include displays on
people and animals who lived
here up to 350,000 years ago.

The charming miniature
town of **Babbacombe Model
Village** is north of Torquay,
while a mile (1.5 km) inland
is the lovely village of
Cockington. Visitors travel by
horse-drawn carriage to the
preserved Tudor manor house,
church and thatched cottages.

In Paignton, the celebrated
Paignton Zoo teaches children about the planet's wildlife,
and from here you can take
the steam railway – an ideal
way to visit Dartmouth.

Continuing south from
Paignton, the pretty town of
Brixham was once England's
most prosperous fishing port.

🛈 **Torre Abbey**
King's Drive, Torquay. **Tel** 01803
293593. ● *until 2008.* 🅿 ▣

Bayards Cove, Dartmouth

🏛 **Torquay Museum**
Babbacombe Rd, Torquay. **Tel** 01803
293975. ◯ *daily (Nov–Easter: Mon–
Sat).* ● *Christmas wk.* 🅿 ♿ ▣
🏠 **www**.torquaymuseum.org

🦇 **Kents Cavern**
Ilsham Rd, Torquay. ☎ *01803 215136.*
◯ *daily.* ● *25 & 26 Dec.* 🅿 🎁 🍴
▣ **www**.kents-cavern.co.uk

🏛 **Babbacombe Model
Village**
Hampton Ave, Torquay. **Tel** 01803
315315. ◯ *daily.* 🅿 ♿ ▣

🐾 **Paignton Zoo**
Totnes Rd, Paignton. ☎ *01803 697
500.* ◯ *daily.* ● *25 Dec.* 🅿 ♿
🍴 🎁 **www**.paigntonzoo.org.uk

Dartmouth ㉑

Devon. 🏘 *5,500.* 🚊 🛈 *Mayors Ave
(01803 834224).* 🏪 *Tue–Fri am.*
www.discoverdartmouth.com

Sitting high on the hill
above the River Dart is the
Royal Naval College, where
British naval officers have
trained since 1905. Dartmouth
has always been an important
port and it was from here that
English fleets set sail to join
the Second and Third Cru-
sades. Some 18th-century
houses adorn the cobbled
quay of Bayards Cove, while
carved timber buildings line
the 17th-century Butterwalk,
home to **Dartmouth Museum**.
To the south is **Dartmouth
Castle** (1388).

🏛 **Dartmouth Museum**
Butterwalk. **Tel** 01803 832923.
◯ *Mon–Sat.* ● *25 & 26 Dec, 1 Jan.*
🅿 🎁 **www**.devonmuseums.net

⚓ **Dartmouth Castle**
(EH) Castle Rd. **Tel** 01803 833588.
◯ *daily (Nov–Easter: Sat & Sun).*
● *24–26 Dec, 1 Jan.* 🅿 ▣ 🅿

Torquay, on the "English Riviera"

Stained-glass window in Blessed Sacrament Chapel, Buckfast Abbey

Totnes ㉒

Devon. 🏘 *7,500.* ⊠ 🔲 ⊡
🏛 *Coronation Rd (01803 863168).*
🔲 *Tue am (May–Sep), Fri, Sat.*
www.totnesinfo.org.uk

Totnes sits at the highest
navigable point on the River
Dart with a Norman **castle**
perched high on the hill
above. Linking the two is the
steep High Street, lined with
bow-windowed Elizabethan
houses. Bridging the street is
the **Eastgate**, part of the medieval town wall. Life in the
town's heyday is explored in
the **Totnes Elizabethan
Museum**, which also has a
room devoted to the mathe-
matician Charles Babbage
(1791–1871), who is regarded
as the pioneer of
modern computers.
There is a **Guildhall**,
and a **church** with
a delicately carved
and gilded rood
screen. On
Tuesdays in the
summer, market
stallholders dress in
Elizabethan costume.

Environs: A few miles
north of Totnes, **Dar-
tington Hall** has 10
ha (25 acres) of lovely
gardens and a famous
music school where concerts
are held in the timbered 14th-
century Great Hall.

**Stallholders in
Totnes market**

♣ **Totnes Castle**
(EH) Castle St. **Tel** *01803 864406.*
🔲 *Apr–Oct: daily.* 🎫
🏛 **Totnes Elizabethan
Museum**
Fore St. **Tel** *01803 863821.* 🔲
Easter–Oct: Mon–Fri. 🎫 👢 *limited.*
🏛 **Guildhall**
Rampart Walk. **Tel** *01803 862147.*
🔲 *Apr–Oct: Mon–Wed.* 🎫
♣ **Dartington Hall Gardens**
Tel *01803 862367.* 🔲 *daily.*
www.dartingtonhalltrust.com

Buckfastleigh ㉓

Devon. 🏘 *3,300.* ⊠ 🏛 *Fore St
(01364 644522).*

This market town, situated
on the edge of Dartmoor *(see
pp294–5)*, is dominated by
Buckfast Abbey. The original
abbey, founded in
Norman times, fell
into ruin after the
Dissolution of the
Monasteries and
it was not until
1882 that
a small group
of French
Benedictine
monks set up a
new abbey here.
Work on the pres-
ent building was
financed by
donations and carried
out by the monks. The abbey
was completed in 1938 and
lies at the heart of a thriving

community. The fine mosaics
and modern stained-glass
window are also the work of
the monks.

Nearby is the **Buckfast
Butterfly Farm and Otter
Sanctuary**, and the **South
Devon Steam Railway** ter-
minus where steam trains leave
for Totnes.

🔒 **Buckfast Abbey**
Buckfastleigh. **Tel** *01364 645500.*
🔲 *daily.* 🌑 *25–27 Dec, Good Fri.*
👢 🚻 📷 **www**.buckfast.org.uk
🦋 **Buckfast Butterfly Farm
and Otter Sanctuary**
Buckfastleigh. **Tel** *01364 642916.*
🔲 *Easter–Nov: daily.* 📷 👢
www.ottersandbutterfliestrust.com

Burgh Island ㉔

Devon. ⊠ *Plymouth, then taxi.* 🏛
The Quay, Kingsbridge (01548 853195).
www.kingsbridgeinfo.co.uk

The short walk across the
sands at low tide from
Bigbury-on-Sea to Burgh Island
takes you back to the era of
the 1920s and 1930s. It was
here that the millionaire
Archibald Nettlefold built the
luxury **Burgh Island Hotel**
(see p567) in 1929. Created in
Art Deco style with a natural
rock sea-bathing pool, this
was the exclusive retreat of
figures such as the Duke of
Windsor and Noel Coward.
The restored hotel is worth a
visit for the photographs of its
heyday and the Art Deco
fittings. You can also explore
the island and **Pilchard Inn**
(1336), reputed to be haunted
by the ghost of a smuggler.

The Art Deco style bar in Burgh
Island Hotel

Plymouth ㉕

Plymouth. 250,000. *The Mayflower, The Barbican. (01752 304849).* daily. **www**.visitplymouth.co.uk

The tiny port from which Drake, Raleigh, the Pilgrim Fathers, Cook and Darwin all set sail on pioneering voyages has now grown to a substantial city, much of it boldly rebuilt after wartime bombing. Old Plymouth clusters around the **Hoe**, the famous patch of turf on which Sir Francis Drake is said to have calmly finished his game of bowls as the Spanish Armada approached the port in 1588 (*see pp50–51*). Today the Hoe is a pleasant park and parade ground surrounded by memorials to naval men, including Drake himself. Alongside is Charles II's **Royal Citadel**, built to guard the harbour in

Drake's coat of arms

the 1660s. A popular attraction is **Plymouth Dome**, a visitor centre which uses high-tech displays to explain Plymouth's past and present, including live satellite weather pictures and radar screens for monitoring ships. On the harbour is the **National Marine Aquarium**. Nearby is the **Mayflower Stone and Steps**, the spot where the Pilgrim Fathers set sail for the New World in England's third and successful attempt at colonization in 1620.

Environs: A boat tour of the harbour is the best way to see the dockyards where warships have been built since the Napoleonic Wars. There are also splendid views of various fine gardens, such as **Mount Edgcumbe Park** (*see p244*), scattered around the coastline. East of the city, the 18th-century **Saltram House** has two rooms by

Mid-18th-century carved wood chimneypiece, Saltram House

Adam (*see pp28–9*) and portraits by Reynolds, who was born in nearby Plympton.

🏰 **Royal Citadel**
(EH) The Hoe. **Tel** 0117 9750700. call for details. only.

🏛 **Plymouth Dome**
The Hoe. **Tel** 01752 603300. Apr–Oct: daily; Nov–Mar: Tue–Sat. **www**.plymouthdome.gov.uk

🐟 **National Marine Aquarium**
Rope Walk, Coxside. **Tel** 01752 600 301. daily. 25 Dec. **www**.national-aquarium.co.uk

🌸 **Mount Edgcumbe Park**
Cremyll, Torpoint. from Torpoint car park. **Tel** 01752 822236. **House** Apr–Sep: Sun–Thu. **Grounds** all year. **www**.mountedgcumbe.gov.uk

🏰 **Saltram House**
(NT) Plympton. **Tel** 01752 333500. **Gallery** Mar–Dec: Sat–Thu; Jan, Feb: Sat, Sun. **Gardens** all year. open all year.

Buckland Abbey ㉖

(NT) Yelverton, Devon. **Tel** 01822 853607. from Yelverton. Fri–Wed (Nov–Mar: Sat & Sun pm). Christmas–mid-Feb. **www**.nationaltrust.org.uk

Founded by the Cistercian monks in 1278, Buckland Abbey was converted to a house after the Dissolution of the Monasteries and became the home of Drake from 1581–96. Many of the monastic buildings survive in a garden setting, notably the 14th-century tithe barn (*see p28*). Drake's life is explained through paintings and memorabilia in the house.

View of Plymouth Harbour from the Hoe

Cotehele ㉗

(NT) St Dominick, Cornwall. **Tel** 01579 351346. Calstock. **House** Apr–Oct: Sat–Thu & Good Fri. **Grounds** daily. limited.

Magnificent woodland and lush river scenery make Cotehele (pronounced Coteal) one of the most delightful spots on the River Tamar and a rewarding day can be spent exploring the estate. Far from civilization, tucked into its wooded fold in the Cornish countryside, Cotehele has slumbered for 500 years. The main attraction is the house and valley garden at its centre. Built mainly between 1489 and 1520, it is a rare example of a medieval house, set around three courtyards with a magnificent open hall, kitchen, chapel and a warren of private parlours and chambers. The romance of the house is enhanced by colourful terraced gardens to the east, leading via a tunnel into a richly planted valley garden. The path through this garden passes a large domed medieval dovecote and descends to a quay, to which lime and coal were once shipped. There are fine views up and down the winding reed-fringed Tamar from Prospect Tower, and a gallery on the quayside specializes in local arts and crafts. The estate includes a village, a quay with a small maritime museum, working mill buildings, ancient lime kilns and workshops with 19th-century equipment.

Medieval dovecote in the gardens of Cotehele estate

Spanish Armada and British fleets in the English Channel, 1588

SIR FRANCIS DRAKE

Sir Francis Drake (c.1540–1596) was the first Englishman to circumnavigate the globe and he was knighted by Elizabeth I in 1580. Four years later he introduced tobacco and potatoes to England, after bringing home 190 colonists who had tried to establish a settlement in Virginia. To many, however, Drake was no more than an opportunistic rogue, renowned for his exploits as a "privateer", the polite name for a pirate. Catholic Spain was the bitter enemy and Drake further endeared himself to queen and people by his part in the victory over Philip II's Armada *(see pp50–51)*, defeated by bad weather and the buccaneering spirit of the English.

Morwellham Quay ㉘

Near Tavistock, Devon. **Tel** 01822 832766. Gunnislake. daily. 24–26 Dec, 1 Jan. limited. www.morwellham-quay.co.uk

Morwellham Quay was a neglected and overgrown industrial site until 1970, when members of a local trust began restoring the abandoned cottages, schoolhouse, farmyards, quay and copper mines to their original condition.

Today, Morwellham Quay is a thriving and rewarding industrial museum, where you can easily spend a whole day partaking in the typical activities of a Victorian village, from preparing the shire horses for a day's work, to riding a tramway deep into a copper mine in the hillside behind the village. The museum is brought to life by characters in costumes, some of whom give demonstrations throughout the day. You can watch, or lend a hand to the

Industrial relics at Morwellham Quay in the Tamar Valley

cooper while he builds a barrel, attend a lesson in the schoolroom, take part in Victorian playground games or dress up in 19th-century hooped skirts, bonnets, top hats or jackets. The staff, who convincingly play the part of villagers, lead you through their lives and impart a huge amount of information about the history of this small copper-mining community.

Dartmoor National Park ⊗

Buzzard

The high, open moorland of central Dartmoor provides the eerie background for Conan Doyle's thriller, *The Hound of the Baskervilles* (1902). Here at Princetown, surrounded by weathered outcrops of granite tors is one of Britain's most famous prisons. Also dotting the landscape are scores of prehistoric remains which have survived because of the durability of granite. Elsewhere the mood is very different. Streams tumble through wooded and boulder-strewn ravines forming cascades and waterfalls, and thatched cottages nestle in the sheltered valleys around the margins of the moor. Many establishments offer cream teas and warming fires to weary walkers.

Characteristic moorland, eastern Dartmoor

Okehampton has the Museum of Dartmoor Life and a ruined 14th-century castle.

Okehampton

LAUNCESTON A386

MELDON RESERVOIR

West Okement

High Willhays

621 m
2,038 ft

Lydford Gorge (NT) (open Apr–Oct) is a dramatic ravine, leading to a waterfall.

Lydford

MINISTRY OF DEFENCE FIRING RANGES

Postbrick

Walkham

The Ministry of Defence uses much of this area for training but access is available most days (0800 458 4868 to check).

A386

Two Bridges

Merrivale

Blackbrook

Tavistock

Princetown

Meavy

LISKEARD

High Moorland Visitor Centre

Brentor
This volcanic hill crowned by a tiny church (first built in 1130) is visible for miles.

KEY

ℹ️	Information centre
▬	A road
▭	B road
═	Minor road
✹	Viewpoint

Yelverton

BURRATOR RESERVOIR

0 kilometres 5

0 miles 5

PLYMOUTH Plym

PLYMOU

Ivy

Postbridge
Dartmoor's northern moor can be explored from the village of Postbridge. The gently rolling moorland is crossed by many dry-stone walls.

Dartmoor Ponies
These small, tough ponies have lived on the moor since at least the 10th century.

Grimspound is the impressive remains of a Bronze Age settlement.

Castle Drogo (NT) is a magnificent mock-castle built by the architect Sir Edwin Lutyens *(see p29)* in 1910–30.

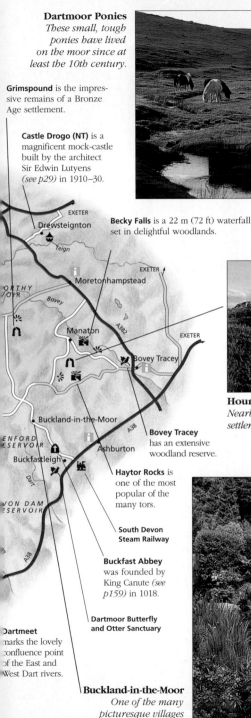

EXETER
Drewsteignton

Teign

Becky Falls is a 22 m (72 ft) waterfall set in delightful woodlands.

EXETER
Moretonhampstead

ORTHY OOR

Bovey

Manaton

A382

EXETER
Bovey Tracey

Buckland-in-the-Moor

ENFORD ESERVOIR
Buckfastleigh

A38
Ashburton

Bovey Tracey has an extensive woodland reserve.

Hound Tor
Nearby lie the remains of a Medieval settlement abandoned in the 14th century.

Dart

VON DAM ESERVOIR

A38

Haytor Rocks is one of the most popular of the many tors.

South Devon Steam Railway

Buckfast Abbey was founded by King Canute *(see p159)* in 1018.

Dartmoor Butterfly and Otter Sanctuary

Dartmeet marks the lovely confluence point of the East and West Dart rivers.

Buckland-in-the-Moor
One of the many picturesque villages on Dartmoor.

THE
MIDLANDS

The Midlands at a Glance

The Midlands is an area that embraces wonderful landscapes and massive industrial cities. Visitors come to discover the wild beauty of the rugged Peaks, cruise slowly along the Midlands canals on gaily painted narrowboats and explore varied and enchanting gardens. The area encompasses the full range of English architecture from mighty cathedrals and humble churches to charming spa towns, stately homes and country cottages. There are fascinating industrial museums, many in picturesque settings.

Tissington Trail (see p337) *combines a walk through scenic Peak District countryside with an entertaining insight into the ancient custom of well-dressing.*

Cheshire

Staffordsh

Shropshire

Ironbridge Gorge (see pp314–15) *was the birthplace of the Industrial Revolution (see pp348–9). Now a World Heritage Centre, the site is a reminder of the lovely countryside in which the original factories were located.*

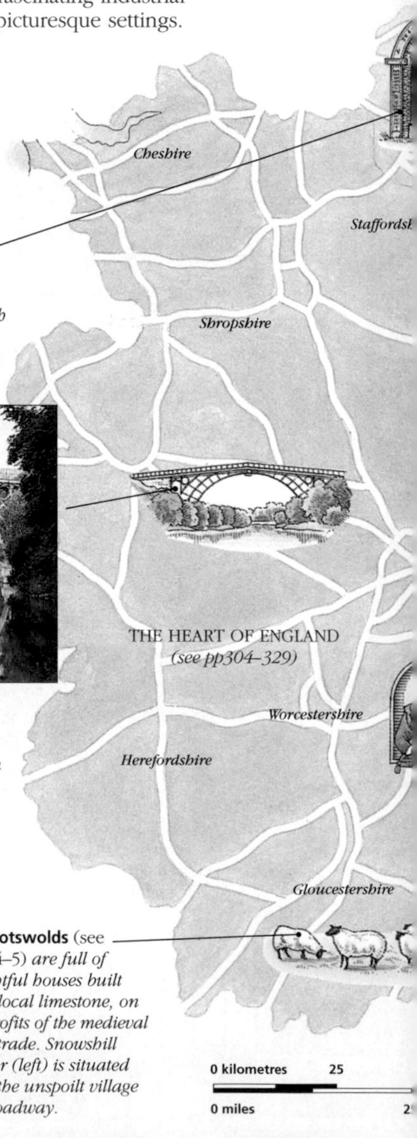

THE HEART OF ENGLAND
(see pp304–329)

Worcestershire

Herefordshire

Gloucestershire

The Cotswolds (see pp304–5) *are full of delightful houses built from local limestone, on the profits of the medieval wool trade. Snowshill Manor (left) is situated near the unspoilt village of Broadway.*

0 kilometres 25

0 miles 2

◁ The front of the half-timbered Lord Leycester Hospital, Warwick

Chatsworth House (see pp334–5), *a magnificent Baroque edifice, is famous for its gorgeous gardens. The "Conservative" Wall, a greenhouse for exotic plants, is pictured above.*

Lincoln Cathedral (see p341), *a vast, imposing building, dominates the ancient town. Inside are splendid misericords and the superb 13th-century Angel Choir, which has 30 carved angels.*

Nottinghamshire

Lincolnshire

Derbyshire

EAST MIDLANDS
(see pp330–343)

Leicestershire

Burghley House (see pp342–3) *is a dazzling landmark for miles around in the flat East Midlands landscape, with architectural motifs from the European Renaissance.*

rwickshire

Warwick Castle (see pp322–3) *is an intriguing mixture of medieval power base and country house, complete with massive towers, battlements, a dungeon and state apartments, such as the Queen Anne Bedroom.*

Northamptonshire

Stratford-upon-Avon (see pp324–7) *has many picturesque houses connected with William Shakespeare's life, some of which are open to visitors. These black and white timber-framed buildings, which abound in the Midlands, are a typical example of Tudor architecture (see pp302–3).*

Canals of the Midlands

One of England's first canals was built by the 3rd Duke of Bridgewater in 1761 to link the coal mine on his Worsley estate with Manchester's textile factories. This heralded the start of a canal-building boom and by 1805, a 3,000 mile (4,800 km) network of waterways had been dug across the country, linking into the natural river system. Canals provided the cheapest, fastest way of transporting goods, until competition began to arrive from the railways in the 1840s. Cargo transport ended in 1963 but today nearly 2,000 miles (3,200 km) of canals are still navigable, for travellers who wish to take a leisurely cruise on a narrowboat.

The Grand Union Canal *(pictured in 1931) is 300 miles (485 km) long and was dug in the 1790s to link London with the Midlands.*

Lock-keepers were provided with canalside houses.

Lockside inns cater for narrowboats.

The Farmer's Bridge *is a flight of 13 locks in Birmingham. Locks are used to raise or lower boats from one level of the canal to another. The steeper the gradient, the more locks are needed.*

Heavy V-shaped timber gates close off the lock.

Water pressing against the gate keeps it shut.

The towpath is where horses pulled the canal boats before engines were invented. They were changed periodically for fresh animals.

Narrowboats *have straight sides and flat bottoms and are pointed at both ends. Cargo space took up most of the boat, with a small cabin for the crew. Exteriors were brightly painted.*

MIDLANDS CANAL NETWORK

The industrial Midlands was the birthplace of the English canal system and still has the biggest concentration of navigable waterways.

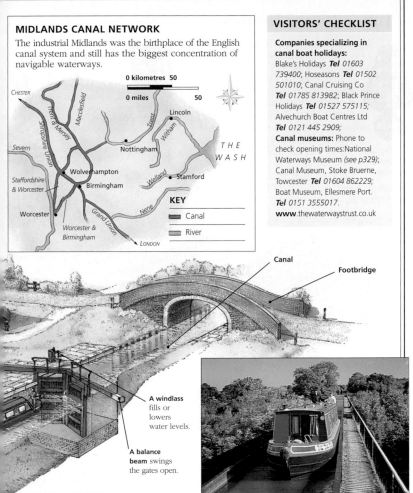

0 kilometres 50

0 miles 50

CHESTER

Macclesfield

Trent & Mersey

Shropshire Union

Severn

Lincoln

Trent

Witham

THE WASH

Nottingham

Staffordshire & Worcester

Wolverhampton

Birmingham

Welland

Stamford

Worcester

Grand Union

Nene

KEY

▬▬ Canal

▬▬ River

Worcester & Birmingham

LONDON

VISITORS' CHECKLIST

Companies specializing in canal boat holidays: Blake's Holidays **Tel** *01603 739400*; Hoseasons **Tel** *01502 501010*; Canal Cruising Co **Tel** *01785 813982*; Black Prince Holidays **Tel** *01527 575115*; Alvechurch Boat Centres Ltd **Tel** *0121 445 2909*;

Canal museums: Phone to check opening times:National Waterways Museum *(see p329)*; Canal Museum, Stoke Bruerne, Towcester **Tel** *01604 862229*; Boat Museum, Ellesmere Port. **Tel** *0151 3555017*. **www**.thewaterwaystrust.co.uk

Canal

Footbridge

A windlass fills or lowers water levels.

A balance beam swings the gates open.

CANAL LOCKS

Canals used tunnels, embankments and locks for the speedy transportation of goods across country. Locks were used to convey boats up or down hills.

The Edstone Aqueduct, *just north of Stratford-upon-Avon, carries the canal in a cast iron trough. This is supported on brick piers for 180 m (495 ft), over roads and a busy railway line.*

CANAL ART

Canal boat cabins are very small and every inch of space is utilized to make a comfortable home for the occupants. Interiors were enlivened with colourful paintings and attractive decorations.

Furniture was designed to be functional and to brighten up the cramped cabin.

Narrowboats are often decorated with ornamental brass.

Water cans were also painted. The most common designs were roses and castles, with local variations in style.

Tudor Manor Houses

Many striking manor houses were built in central England during the Tudor Age *(see pp50–51)*, a time of relative peace and prosperity. The abolition of the monasteries meant that vast estates were broken up and sold to secular landowners, who built houses to reflect their new status *(see p28)*. In the Midlands, wood was the main building material, and the gentry flaunted their wealth by using timber panelling for flamboyant decorative effect.

The Lucy family arms

The decorative moulding *on the south wing dates from the late 16th century. Ancient motifs, such as vines and trefoils, are combined with the latest imported Italian Renaissance styles.*

The rectangular moat *was for decoration rather than defence. It surrounds a recreated knot garden (see p26) that was laid out in 1972 using plants known to have been available in Tudor times.*

The Long Gallery *was the last part of the Hall to be built (c.1560–1562). It has original plasterwork portraying* Destiny *(left) and* Fortune.

Brickwork chimney

Jetties (overhanging upper stories)

TUDOR MANSIONS AND TUDOR REVIVAL

There are many sumptuously decorated Tudor mansions in the Midlands. In the 19th century Tudor Revival architecture became a very popular "Old English" style, intended to invoke family pride and values rooted in the past.

Hardwick Hall *in Derbyshire, whose huge kitchen is pictured, is one of the finest Tudor mansions in the country. These buildings are known as "prodigy" houses (see p342) due to their gigantic size.*

Charlecote Park, *Warwickshire, is a brick mansion built by Sir Thomas Lucy in 1551–59. It was heavily restored in Tudor style in the 19th century, but has a fine original gatehouse. According to legend, the young William Shakespeare (see pp324–7) was caught poaching deer in the park.*

The Parlour *was an informal reception room. Biblical scenes such as Susannah and the Elders (right) expressed religious faith and learning.*

Entrance

The Great Hall *(c.1504–1508) is the oldest part of the house, and in Tudor times was the most important. The open-plan hall was the main communal area for dining and entertainment.*

Wood panelling

Courtyard

LITTLE MORETON HALL

The Moreton family home *(see p311)* was built between 1504 and 1610, from a number of box-shapes, fitted together. Wood panelling and jetties displayed the family's wealth.

The patterned glazing *in the great bay window is typically 16th century: small pieces of locally made glass were cut into diamond shapes and held in place by lead glazing bars.*

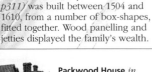

Packwood House *in Warwickshire is a timber-framed mid-Tudor house with extensive 17th-century additions. The unusual garden of clipped yew trees dates from the 17th century and is supposed to represent the Sermon on the Mount.*

Moseley Old Hall, *Staffordshire, has a red brick exterior concealing its early 17th-century timber frame. The King's Room is where Charles II hid after the Battle of Worcester (see pp52–3).*

Wightwick Manor, *West Midlands, was built in 1887–93. It is a fine example of Tudor Revival architecture and has superb late 19th-century furniture and decorations.*

Building with Cotswold Stone

The Cotswolds are a range of limestone hills running over 50 miles (80 km) in a north-easterly direction from Bath *(see pp258–61)*. The thin soils are difficult to plough but ideal for grazing sheep, and the wealth engendered by the medieval wool trade was poured into building majestic churches and opulent town houses. Stone quarried from these hills was used to build London's St Paul's Cathedral *(see pp114–15)*, as well as the villages, barns and manor houses that make the landscape so picturesque.

Dragon, Deerhurst Church

Arlington Row Cottages *in Bibury, a typical Cotswold village, were built in the 17th century for weavers whose looms were set up in the attics.*

Windows were taxed and glass expensive. Workers' cottages had only a few, not very large windows made of small panes of glass.

A drip mould keeps rain off the chimney.

The roof is steeply pitched to carry the weight of the tiles. These were made by master craftsmen who could split blocks of stone into sheets by using natural fault lines.

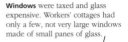

COTSWOLD STONE COTTAGE

The two-storey Arlington Row Cottages are asymmetrical and built of odd-shaped stones. Small windows and doorways make them quite dark inside.

Timber lintels and doors

Timber framing was cheaper than stone, and was used for the upper rooms in the roof.

VARIATIONS IN STONE

Cotswold stone is warmer-toned in the north, pearly in central areas and light grey in the south. The stone seems to glow with absorbed sunlight. It is a soft stone that is easily carved and can be used for many purposes, from buildings to bridges, headstones and gargoyles.

"Tiddles" *is a cat's gravestone in Fairford churchyard.*

Lower Slaughter *gets its name from the Anglo-Saxon word slough, or muddy place. It has a low stone bridge, over the River Eye.*

COTSWOLD STONE TOWNS AND VILLAGES

The villages and towns on this map are prime examples of places built almost entirely from stone. By the 12th century almost all of the villages in the area were established. Huge deposits of limestone resulted in a wealth of stone buildings. Masons worked from distinctive local designs that were handed down from generation to generation.

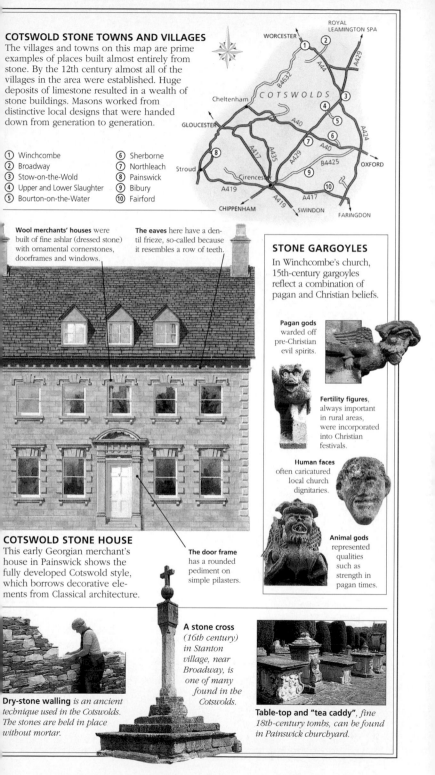

① Winchcombe
② Broadway
③ Stow-on-the-Wold
④ Upper and Lower Slaughter
⑤ Bourton-on-the-Water
⑥ Sherborne
⑦ Northleach
⑧ Painswick
⑨ Bibury
⑩ Fairford

Wool merchants' houses were built of fine ashlar (dressed stone) with ornamental cornerstones, doorframes and windows.

The eaves here have a dentil frieze, so-called because it resembles a row of teeth.

STONE GARGOYLES

In Winchcombe's church, 15th-century gargoyles reflect a combination of pagan and Christian beliefs.

Pagan gods warded off pre-Christian evil spirits.

Fertility figures, always important in rural areas, were incorporated into Christian festivals.

Human faces often caricatured local church dignitaries.

Animal gods represented qualities such as strength in pagan times.

COTSWOLD STONE HOUSE

This early Georgian merchant's house in Painswick shows the fully developed Cotswold style, which borrows decorative elements from Classical architecture.

The door frame has a rounded pediment on simple pilasters.

Dry-stone walling *is an ancient technique used in the Cotswolds. The stones are held in place without mortar.*

A stone cross *(16th century) in Stanton village, near Broadway, is one of many found in the Cotswolds.*

Table-top and "tea caddy", *fine 18th-century tombs, can be found in Painswick churchyard.*

The Cotswold Arm

Bar Snacks
Restaurant
Beer Garden
Morning Coffee

THE HEART OF ENGLAND

CHESHIRE · GLOUCESTERSHIRE · HEREFORDSHIRE
SHROPSHIRE · STAFFORDSHIRE · WARWICKSHIRE · WORCESTERSHIRE

B *ritain's great attraction is its variety, and nowhere is this more true than at the heart of the country, where the Cotswold hills, enfolding stone cottages and churches, give way to the flat, fertile plains of Warwickshire. Shakespeare country borders on the industrial heart of England, once known as the workshop of the world.*

Coventry, Birmingham, the Potteries and their hinterlands have been manufacturing iron, textiles and ceramics since the 18th century. In the 20th century these industries have declined, and a new type of museum has developed to commemorate the towns' industrial heyday and explain the manufacturing processes which were once taken for granted. Ironbridge Gorge and Quarry Bank Mill, Styal, where the factories are now living museums, are fascinating industrial sites and enjoy beautiful surroundings.

These landscapes may be appreciated from the deck of a narrowboat, making gentle progress along the Midlands canals, to the region on the border with Wales known as the Marches. Here the massive walls of Chester and the castles at Shrewsbury and Ludlow recall the Welsh locked in fierce battle with Norman barons and the Marcher Lords. The Marches are now full of rural communities served by the peaceful market towns of Leominster, Malvern, Ross-on-Wye and Hereford. The cities of Worcester and Gloucester both have modern shopping centres, yet their majestic cathedrals retain the tranquillity of an earlier age.

Cheltenham has Regency terraces, Cirencester a rich legacy of Roman art and Tewkesbury a solid Norman abbey. Finally, there is Stratford-upon-Avon, where William Shakespeare, the Elizabethan dramatist, lived and died.

BOWLS CLUB

Leisurely village pastimes, reminiscent of a more tranquil age

◁ Cotswold stone: an extremely popular building material in the Heart of England

Exploring the Heart of England

The heart of England, more than any other region, takes its character from the landscape. Picturesque houses, pubs and churches, made from timber and Cotswold stone, create a harmonic appearance that delights visitors and adds greatly to the pleasures of exploration. The area around Birmingham and Stoke-on-Trent, however – once the industrial hub of England – contrasts sharply. The bleak concrete skyline may not appeal, but the area has a fascinating history that is reflected in the self-confident Victorian art and architecture, and a series of award-winning industrial heritage museums.

Arlington Row: stone cottages in the Cotswold village of Bibury

SIGHTS AT A GLANCE

Birmingham ⑬
Cheltenham ⑳
Chester ❷
Chipping Campden ⑱
Cirencester ㉒
Coventry ⑭
Gloucester ㉑
Great Malvern ⑪
Hereford ❽
Ironbridge pp314–15 ❺
Ledbury ⑩
Leominster ❼
Ludlow ❻
Quarry Bank Mill, Styal ❶
Ross-on-Wye ❾
Shrewsbury ❹
Stoke-on-Trent ❸
Stratford-upon-Avon pp324–7 ⑰
Tewkesbury ⑲
Warwick pp321–3 ⑯
Worcester ⑫

Walks and Tours
Midlands Garden Tour ⑮

GETTING AROUND

The Heart of England is easily reached by train, with mainline rail services to Cheltenham, Worcester, Birmingham, and Coventry. The M5 and M6 motorways are the major road routes but are frequently congested. Long-distance buses provide regular shuttle services to Cheltenham and Birmingham. Travelling within the region is best done by car. Rural roads are delightfully empty, although major attractions, such as Stratford-upon-Avon, may be very crowded during the summer.

SEE ALSO

Warrin
Runcorn
Mersey M56
Ellesmere
Port
Dee
CHESTER ❷ Tarvin
A55
Aldford Bun
Bun
A41
▲Wrexham
Chirk Whitchur
A5 A495 Pree
Oswestry
West Felton
A483 Nesscliffe
Severn
Middletown
SHREWSBURY ❹
A458
Minsterley
A483 A49 V
Severn
Chirbury Church
Strettc
A489 *Long Mynd*
Lydham
Wenlock
Newcastle
Teme Stokesay Castle Craven A
A489
Knighton LUDLOW ❻
Wigmore Woo
Presteigne
LEOMINSTER ❼
Pembridge A49
Eardisley Hope under
Dinmore
Clifford
HEREFORD ❽
Kingstone A465
A49
Kilpeck
Abbey Dore
Abergavenny ROSS
Goodrich Ca
A
Monmouth
Chepstow

0 kilometres 10

0 miles 10

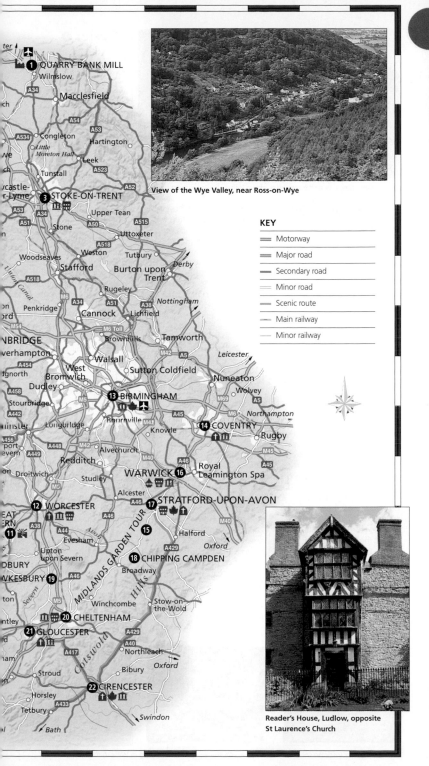

1 QUARRY BANK MILL
Wilmslow

Macclesheld

A34

A54
A534 Congleton
Hartington
Little
Moreton Hall
Leek
Tunstall
A523

castle-
r-Lyme **3 STOKE-ON-TRENT**
A52
Upper Tean
Stone A50 Uttoxeter
A515
A518
Weston Tutbury
Woodseaves
Stafford Burton upon
Trent
Derby
A518
Rugeley

Penkridge A34 A51 A38 Nottingham
Cannock Lichfield
M6 Toll
NBRIDGE Brownhills Tamworth
verhampton
A454 Walsall M42 A5 Leicester
gnorth West
Bromwich Sutton Coldfield
Dudley Nuneaton
A458 M69 Wolvey
Stourbridge A5
13 BIRMINGHAM M6 Northampton
A442
Longbridge M42 A45
Bournville Coventry **14**
port- A448 Knowle Rugby
evern A449 Alvechurch
Redditch M40 M45
Droitwich Studley A46
Royal
WARWICK 16 Leamington Spa
Alcester A46
12 WORCESTER **17 STRATFORD-UPON-AVON**
A46
A38 A44 Avon **15** Halford
11 Evesham Oxford
Upton A429
upon Severn **18 CHIPPING CAMPDEN**
Broadway
KESBURY 19 A46
Winchcombe Stow-on-
the-Wold
20 CHELTENHAM
ntley A429
21 GLOUCESTER
A417
Northleach
Bibury Oxford
Stroud
22 CIRENCESTER
Horsley A433
Tetbury Swindon
Bath

View of the Wye Valley, near Ross-on-Wye

KEY

▬	Motorway
▬	Major road
▬	Secondary road
▬	Minor road
▬	Scenic route
—	Main railway
—	Minor railway

**Reader's House, Ludlow, opposite
St Laurence's Church**

Quarry Bank Mill, a working reminder of the Industrial Revolution

Quarry Bank Mill, Styal ❶

(NT) Cheshire. **Tel** 01625 527468.
🚆 Manchester Airport, then bus.
⭕ Apr–Sep: daily; Oct–Mar: Tue–Sun
(& Mon in school hols). ⭘ 24 & 25
Dec. 📷 ♿ limited. 🍴 🏪
www.quarrybankmill.org.uk

The history of the Industrial Revolution *(see pp54–5)* is brought vividly to life at Quarry Bank Mill, an early factory now transformed into a museum. Here, mill master Samuel Greg first used the waters of the Bollin Valley in 1784 to power the water frame, a machine for spinning raw cotton fibres into thread. By the 1840s, the Greg cotton empire was one of the biggest in Britain, and the mill produced bolts of material to be exported all over the world.

Today the massive old mill buildings have been restored to house a living museum of the cotton industry. This dominated the Manchester area for nearly 200 years, but was finally destroyed by foreign competition. The entire process, from the spinning and weaving to the bleaching, printing and dyeing, is shown through a series of reconstructions, demonstrations and

hands-on displays. The weaving shed is full of clattering looms producing textiles. There are fascinating contraptions that demonstrate how water can be used to drive machinery, including an enormous wheel, 50 tons in weight and 7 m (24 ft) high, that is still used to power the looms.

The Greg family realized the importance of having a healthy, loyal and stable workforce. A social history exhibition explains how the mill workers were housed in the purpose-built village of Styal, in spacious cottages which had vegetable gardens and toilets. Details of their wages, working conditions and medical facilities are displayed on information boards.

There are guided tours of the nearby **Apprentice House**. Local orphans lived here, and were sent to work up to 12 hours a day at the mill when they were just six or seven years old. Visitors can try the beds in the house and even sample the medicine they were given. Quarry Bank Mill is surrounded by over 115 ha (284 acres) of woodland.

Chester ❷

Cheshire. 🏠 125,000. 🚆 🅿
ℹ️ Town Hall, Northgate St (01244
402111). ⭘ Mon–Sat.
www.chestertourism.com

First settled by the Romans *(see pp44–5)*, who established a camp in AD 79 to defend fertile land near the River Dee, the main streets of Chester are now lined with timber buildings. These are the **Chester Rows**, which, with their two tiers of shops and continuous upper gallery, anticipate today's multi-storey shops by several centuries.

Although their oriel windows and decorative timber-work are mostly 19th century, the Rows were first built in the 13th and 14th centuries, and the original structures can be seen in many places. The façade of the 16th-century **Bishop Lloyd's House** in Watergate Street is the most richly carved in Chester. The Rows are at their most varied and attractive where Eastgate Street meets Bridge Street. Here, views of the cathedral and the town walls give the impression of a perfectly preserved medieval city. This illusion is helped by the Town Crier, who calls the hour and announces news in summer from the Cross, a reconstruction of the 15th-century stone crucifix that was destroyed in the Civil War *(see pp52–3)*.

The **Grosvenor Museum**, south of the Cross, explains the town's history. To the north is the **cathedral**. The choir stalls have splendid misericords *(see p341)*, with

Chester's 1897 clocktower

Examples of the intricate carving on Bishop Lloyd's House, a Tudor building in Watergate Street, Chester

The Chester Rows, where shops line the first-floor galleries

scenes including a quarrelling couple. In sharp contrast are the delicate spire-lets on the stall canopies. The cathedral is surrounded on two sides by the **city walls**, originally Roman but rebuilt at intervals. The best stretch is from the cathedral to Eastgate, where a wrought-iron **clock** was erected in 1897. The route to Newgate leads to a **Roman amphitheatre** built in AD 100.

🏛 **Grosvenor Museum**
Grosvenor St. **Tel** 01244 402008.
☐ Mon–Sat, Sun pm. ● 25 & 26
Dec, 1 Jan, Good Fri. 🎫 🔊 limited.
www.chester.uk/museums

🏛 **Roman Amphitheatre**
Little St John St. **Tel** 01244 402009.
☐ daily.

Stoke-on-Trent ❸

Stoke-on-Trent. 🚶 252,000.
🚊 🚌 🛈 Bagnell St (01782
236000). 🛍 Mon–Sat.
www.visitstoke.co.uk

From the mid-18th century, Staffordshire became a leading centre for mass-produced ceramics. Its fame arose from the fine bone china and porcelain products of Wedgwood,

Minton, Doulton and Spode, but the Staffordshire potteries also make a wide range of utilitarian products such as baths, toilets and wall tiles.

In 1910 a group of six towns – Longton, Fenton, Hanley, Burslem, Tunstall and Stoke – merged to form the conurbation of Stoke-on-Trent, also known as the Potteries. Fans of the writer Arnold Bennett (1867–1931) may recognise this area as the "Five Towns",

a term he used in a series of novels about the region (Fenton was excluded).

The **Gladstone Pottery Museum** is a Victorian complex of workshops, kilns, galleries and an engine house. There are demonstrations of traditional pottery techniques. The **Potteries Museum and Art Gallery** in Hanley has historic and modern ceramics.

Josiah Wedgwood began his earthenware firm in 1769 and built a workers' village, Etruria. The last surviving steam-powered pottery mill is on display at the **Etruria Industrial Museum**.

Environs: About 10 miles (16 km) north of Stoke-on-Trent is **Little Moreton Hall** *(see p303)*, a Tudor manor house.

🏛 **Gladstone Pottery Museum**
Uttoxeter Rd, Longton. **Tel** 01782 319
232. ☐ daily. ● 24 Dec–2 Jan. 🎫 🔊
🔊 📷 **www**.stoke.gov.uk/gladstone

🏛 **Potteries Museum and Art Gallery** Bethesda St, Hanley.
Tel 01782 232323. ☐ daily.
● 25 Dec–1 Jan. 🔊 🖼 📷
www.stoke.gov.uk/museums

🏛 **Etruria Industrial Museum**
Lower Bedford St, Etruria. **Tel** 01782
233144. ☐ Jan–Mar: Mon–Wed;
Apr–Dec: Sat–Wed. ● 25 Dec–1
Jan. 🎫 🎫 by arrangement. 📷 📷

🏰 **Little Moreton Hall**
(NT) Congleton, off A34. **Tel** 01260
272018. ☐ Mar–Oct: Wed–Sun &
public hols; last week Nov–22 Dec:
Sat, Sun. 🎫 🎫 🔊 limited. 🍴 📷

STAFFORDSHIRE POTTERY

An abundance of water, marl, clay and easily mined coal to fire the kilns enabled Staffordshire to develop as a ceramics centre; and local supplies of iron, copper and lead were used for glazing. In the 18th century, pottery became widely accessible and affordable. English bone china, which used powdered animals' bones for strength and translucence, was shipped all over the world, and Josiah Wedgwood (1730–95) introduced simple, durable crockery – though his best known design is the blue jasperware decorated with white Classical themes. Coal-powered bottle kilns fired the clay until the 1950s Clean Air Acts put them out of business. They have been replaced by electric or gas-fired kilns.

Wedgwood candlesticks, 1785

Timber-framed, gabled mansions in Fish Street, Shrewsbury

Shrewsbury ❹

Shropshire. 🏘 96,000. 🚆 🚌
ℹ The Square (01743 281200).
🛒 Tue, Wed, Fri, Sat.
www.visitshrewsbury.com

Shrewsbury is almost an island, enclosed by a great loop of the River Severn. A gaunt **castle** of red sandstone, first built in 1083, guards the entrance to the town, standing on the only section of land not surrounded by the river. Such defences were necessary on the frontier between England and the wilder Marches of Wales, whose inhabitants fiercely defied Saxon and Norman invaders *(see pp46–7)*. The castle, rebuilt over the centuries, now houses the Shropshire Regimental Museum.

In AD 60 the Romans *(see pp44–5)* built the garrison town of Viroconium, modern Wroxeter, 5 miles (8 km) east of Shrewsbury. Finds from the excavations are displayed at **Shrewsbury Museum and Art Gallery**, including a decorated silver mirror from the 2nd century and other luxury goods imported by the Roman army.

The town's medieval wealth as a centre of the wool trade is evident in the many timber-framed buildings found along the High Street, Butcher Row,

Roman silver mirror in Rowley's House Museum

and Wyle Cop. Two of the grandest High Street houses, **Ireland's Mansions** and **Owen's Mansions**, are named after Robert Ireland and Richard Owen, the wealthy wool merchants who built them in 1575 and 1570 respectively. Similarly attractive buildings in Fish Street frame a view of the **Prince Rupert Hotel**, which was briefly the headquarters of Charles I's nephew, Rupert, in the English Civil War *(see pp52–3)*.

Outside the loop of the river, the **Abbey Church** survives from the medieval monastery. It has a number of interesting memorials, including one to Lieutenant WES Owen MC, better known as the war poet Wilfred Owen (1893–1918), who taught at the local Wyle Cop school and was killed in the last days of World War I.

Environs: To the south of Shrewsbury, the road to Ludlow passes through the landscapes celebrated in the 1896 poem by AE Housman (1859–1936), *A Shropshire Lad*. Highlights include the bleak moors of **Long Mynd**, with 15 prehistoric barrows, and **Wenlock Edge**, wonderful walking country with glorious, far-reaching views.

🏰 **Shrewsbury Castle**
Castle St. **Tel** *01743 361196.* ◯
Feb–Dec: Tue–Sat. ● *late Dec–mid-Feb.* ⬤ 🅿
🏛 **Shrewsbury Museum and Art Gallery**
Barker St. **Tel** *01743 361196.* ◯
Oct–May: Tue–Sat; Jun–Sep: daily. ●
2 wks over Christmas. ⬤ *limited.* 🅿
www.shrewsburymuseums.com

Ironbridge Gorge ❺

See pp314–15.

Ludlow ❻

Shropshire. 🏘 10,000. 🚆 ℹ
Castle St (01584 875053). 🛒 *Mon, Wed, Fri, Sat.* 🎭 *music & drama (end Jun).* www.ludlow.org.uk

Ludlow attracts large numbers of visitors to its splendid castle, but there is much else to see in this town, with its small shops and its lovely Georgian and half-timbered Tudor buildings. Ludlow is an important area of geological research and the **museum**, just off the town centre, has fossils of the oldest known animals and plants.

The ruined **castle** is sited on cliffs high above the River Teme. Built in 1086, it was damaged in the Civil War *(see pp52–3)* and abandoned in 1689. *Comus*, a court masque using music and drama, by John Milton (1608–74) was first performed here in 1634 in the Great Hall.

The 13th-century south tower and hall of Stokesay Castle, near Ludlow

Prince Arthur (1486–1502), elder brother of Henry VIII (see pp50–51), died at Ludlow Castle. His heart is buried in **St Laurence Church** at the other end of Castle Square, as are the ashes of the poet A E Housman. The east end of the church backs onto the **Bull Ring**, with its ornate timber buildings. Two inns vie for attention across the street: **The Bull**, with its Tudor back yard, and **The Feathers**, with its flamboyant façade, whose name recalls the feathers used in arrow-making, once a local industry.

Environs: About 5 miles (8 km) north of Ludlow, in a lovely setting, is **Stokesay Castle**, a fortified manor house with a colourful moated garden.

♣ **Ludlow Castle**
The Square. **Tel** 01584 873355. ◯ daily (Jan: Sat & Sun only). 🖼 ♿ 🚻 limited. **www**.ludlowcastle.com

🏛 **Ludlow Museum**
Castle St. **Tel** 01584 875384. ◯ Apr–Oct: Mon–Sat (Jun–Aug: daily). 🖼 ♿

♣ **Stokesay Castle**
Craven Arms, A49. **Tel** 01588 672544. ◯ Mar–Oct: Thu–Mon (Jun–Aug: daily); Nov–Feb: Fri–Sun. 🖼 🚻 🅿

Leominster ❼

Herefordshire. 👥 11,000. 🚇 🛈 Corn Sq (01568 616460). 🎪 Fri. **www**.visitorlinks.com

Farmers come to Leominster (pronounced "Lemster") from all over this rural region to buy supplies. There are two buildings of note in the town, which has been a wool-manufacturing centre for 700 years. In the town centre stands the magnificent **Grange Court**, carved with bold and bizarre figures in 1633. Nearby is the **priory**, whose imposing Norman portal is carved with an equally strange mixture of mythical birds and beasts. The lions, at least, can be explained: medieval monks believed the name of Leominster was derived from *monasterium leonis*, "the monastery of the lions". In fact, *leonis* probably comes from medieval, rather than

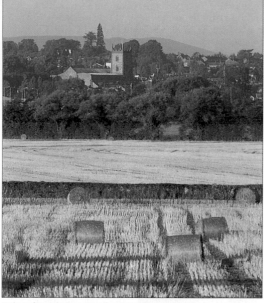

A view of Leominster, set on the River Lugg in rolling border country

Classical Latin, and it means "of the marshes". The aptness of this description can readily be seen in the green lanes around the town, following the lush river valleys.

Environs: South of the town, the magnificent gardens and parkland at **Hampton Court** have recently been restored and include island pavilions and a maze. To the west of the town, along the River Arrow, are the villages of **Eardisland** and **Pembridge**, with their well-kept gardens and timber-framed houses. **Berrington Hall**, 3 miles

Gatehouse of Stokesay Castle, near Ludlow

(5 km) north of Leominster, is a Neo-Classical house set in grounds by Capability Brown. Inside are beautifully pre-served ceiling decorations and period furniture.

To the northeast of Leo-minster is **Tenbury Wells**, which enjoyed brief popular-ity as a spa in the 19th century. The River Teme flows through it, full of minnows, trout and other fish and beloved of the composer Sir Edward Elgar (see p317), who came to seek inspiration on its banks. The river also feeds **Burford House Gardens**, on the western outskirts of Tenbury Wells, where the water is used to create streams, fountains and pools that are rich in unusual moisture-loving plants.

🌿 **Hampton Court Gardens**
nr Hope Under Dinmore. **Tel** 01568 797 777. ◯ Apr–21 Dec: 11am–5pm (to 4pm Nov–Dec) Tue–Sun. 🖼 ♿ 🍴 🚻 **www**.hamptoncourt.org.uk

🏰 **Berrington Hall**
Berrington. **Tel** 01568 615721. ◯ mid-Mar–Nov: Sat–Wed. 🖼 🍴 🚻

🌿 **Burford House Gardens**
Tenbury Wells. **Tel** 01584 810777. ◯ daily. ● 1 Jan, 25 & 26 Dec. 🖼 ♿ 🍴 🚻 **www**.burford.co.uk

Ironbridge Gorge ❺

Ironbridge Gorge was one of the most important centres of the Industrial Revolution *(see pp54–5)*. It was here, in 1709, Abraham Darby I (1678–1717) pioneered the use of inexpensive coke, rather than charcoal, to smelt iron ore. The use of iron in bridges, ships and buildings transformed Ironbridge Gorge into one of the world's great iron-making centres. Industrial decline in the 20th century led to the Gorge's decay, although today it has been restored as an exciting complex of industrial archaeology, with several museums strung along the wooded banks of the River Severn.

VISITORS' CHECKLIST

Shropshire. *2,900. Telford then bus (Telford Travelink 01952 200005).* ***Tel*** *01952 435900. Ironbridge town (01952 884391). mid-Apr–Oct: daily; Nov–mid-Apr: call for details. 1 Jan, 24, 25 Dec. Some sites closed Nov–Apr, call for details. most sites. by arrangement.* **www**.ironbridge.org.uk

Wrought-iron clock (1843) on the roof of the Museum of Iron

MUSEUM OF IRON

The history of iron and the men who made it is traced in this remarkable museum. Abraham Darby I's discovery of how to smelt iron ore with coke allowed the mass production of iron, paving the way for the rise of large-scale industry. His original blast furnace forms the museum's centrepiece.

One of the museum's themes is the history of the Darby dynasty, a Quaker family who had a great impact on the Coalbrookdale community. The social and working conditions faced by the labourers, who sometimes had to toil for 24 hours at a stretch, are also illustrated.

Ironbridge led the world in industrial innovation, producing the first iron wheels and cylinders for the first steam engine. A restored locomotive and cast-iron statues, many of them commissioned for the 1851 Great Exhibition *(see pp56–7)*, are among the many Coalbrookdale Company products on display.

One of the Darby family's homes in the nearby village of Coalbrookdale, **Rosehill House**, has been furnished in mid-Victorian style.

MUSEUM OF THE GORGE

This partly castellated, Victorian building was a warehouse for storing products from the ironworks before they were shipped down the River Severn. The warehouse is now home to the Museum of the Gorge, and has displays illustrating the history of the Severn and the development of the water industry.

Until the arrival of the railways in the mid-19th century, the Severn was the main form of transport and communication to and from the Gorge. Sometimes too shallow, at other times in flood, the river was not a particularly reliable means of transportation; by the 1890s river trading had stopped completely.

The highlight of the museum is a wonderful 12 m (40 ft) model of the Gorge as it would have appeared in 1796, complete with foundries, cargo boats and growing villages.

Europe **(1860), statue in the Museum of Iron**

JACKFIELD TILE MUSEUM

There have been potteries in this area since the 17th century, but it was not until the Victorian passion for decorative tiles that Jackfield became famous. There were two tile-making factories here – Maw and Craven Dunnill – that produced a tremendous variety of tiles from clay mined nearby.

Peacock Panel (1928), one of the tile museum's star attractions

Talented designers created an astonishing range of images. The newly refurbished Jackfield Tile Museum, in the old Craven Dunnill works, has a collection of the decorative floor and wall tiles that were produced here from the 1850s to the 1960s. Visitors can watch small-scale demonstrations of traditional methods of tile-making in the old factory buildings, including the kilns and the decoration workshops.

IRONBRIDGE GORGE SIGHTS

Blists Hill Victorian Town ⑥
Coalport China
   Museum ⑤
Iron Bridge ③
Jackfield Tile
   Museum ④
Museum of Iron ①
Museum of the Gorge ②

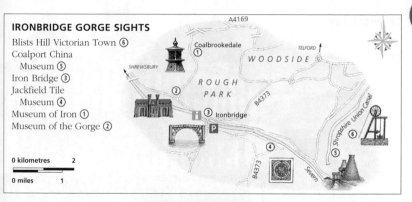

0 kilometres 2

0 miles 1

COALPORT CHINA MUSEUM

In the mid-19th century the Coalport Works was one of the largest porcelain manufacturers in Britain, and its name was synonymous with fine china. The Coalport Company still makes porcelain but has long since moved its operations to Stoke-on-Trent *(see p311)*. Today the china workshops have been converted into a museum, where visitors can watch demonstrations of the various stages of making porcelain, including the skills of pot-throwing, painting and gilding. There is a superb collection of 19th-century china housed in one of the museum's distinctive bottle-shaped kilns.

Coalport China Museum with its bottle-shaped kiln

Nearby is the **Tar Tunnel**, an important source of natural bitumen discovered 110 m (360 ft) underground in the 18th century. It once yielded 20,500 litres (4,500 gal) of tar every week; visitors can still explore part of the tunnel.

BLISTS HILL VICTORIAN TOWN

This enormous open-air museum recreates Victorian life in an Ironbridge Gorge town. A group of 19th-century buildings has been reconstructed on the 20 ha (50 acre) site of Blists Hill, an old coal mine that used to supply the ironworks in the Gorge. Here, people in period costume enact roles and perform tasks such as iron forging.

The site has period housing, a church and even a Victorian school. Visitors can change money into old coinage to buy items from the baker or even pay for a drink in the local pub.

The centrepiece of Blists Hill is a complete foundry that still produces wrought iron. One of the most spectacular sights is the Hay Inclined Plane, which was used to transport canal boats up and down a steep slope. Other attractions include steam engines, a saddlers, a doctors, a chemist, a candlemakers and a sweetshop.

THE IRON BRIDGE

Abraham Darby III (grandson of the first man to smelt iron with coke) cast the world's first iron bridge in 1779, revolutionizing building methods in the process. Spanning the Severn, the bridge is a monument to the ironmasters' skills. The toll-house on the south bank charts its construction.

Hereford **8**

Herefordshire. 👥 *50,000.* 🚊 🚌
🛈 *King St (01432 268430).*
📅 *Wed (cattle, general), Sat (general).*
www.visitherefordshire.gov.uk

Once the capital of the Saxon kingdom of West Mercia, Hereford is today an attractive town which serves the needs of a primarily rural community. A cattle market is held here every Wednesday, and local produce is sold at the covered market in the town centre. Almost opposite, the timber-framed **Old House** of 1621 is now a museum of local history.

In the **cathedral**, only a short stroll away, interesting features include the Lady Chapel, in richly ornamented Early English style, the *Mappa Mundi* (see below) and the Chained Library, whose 1,500 books are tethered by iron chains to bookcases as a precaution against theft. The story of these national treasures is told through models, original artifacts and interactive computer technology. The best place for an overall view of the cathedral is at the Bishop's Meadow, south of the centre, leading down to the banks of the Wye.

Hereford's many rewarding museums include the **City Museum and Art Gallery**, noted for its Roman mosaic and for watercolours by local artists, and the **Cider**

Hereford's 17th-century Old House, furnished in period style

Museum and King Offa Distillery. In the museum, visitors can discover the history of traditional cider making. The King Offa Distillery, which is open for visits and tastings, is the first distillery licensed to produce cider brandy for 200 years.

Environs: During the 12th century, Oliver de Merlemond made a pilgrimage from Hereford to Spain. Impressed by several churches he saw on the way, he brought French masons over to England and introduced their techniques to this area. One result was **Kilpeck Church**, 6 miles (10 km) southwest, covered in

Detail of figures on
Kilpeck Church

lustful figures showing their genitals, and tail-biting dragons. At **Abbey Dore**, 4 miles (6 km) west, the Cistercian abbey church is complemented by the serene riverside gardens of **Abbey Dore Court**.

🏛 **Old House**
High Town. **Tel** *01432 260694.*
◯ *Apr–Sep: Tue–Sun; Oct–Mar: Tue–Sat; public hols.* ● *25 & 26 Dec, 1 Jan, Good Fri.* ♿ *limited.* 📷
www.herefordshire.gov.uk/museums

🏛 **City Museum and Art Gallery**
Broad St. **Tel** *01432 260692.* ◯ *Apr–Sep: Tue–Sun; Oct–Mar: Tue–Sat, public hols.* ● *25 & 26 Dec, 1 Jan, Good Fri.* ♿
www.herefordshire.gov.uk

🏛 **Cider Museum and King Offa Distillery**
Ryelands St. **Tel** *01432 354207.*
◯ *Tue–Sat & public hols.*
● *25 & 26 Dec, 1 Jan.* 📷 ♿
limited. 🎦 *by arrangement.* 🅿
🛈 **www**.cidermuseum.co.uk

MEDIEVAL VIEW

Hereford Cathedral's most celebrated treasure is the *Mappa Mundi*, the Map of the World, drawn in 1290 by a clergyman, Richard of Haldingham. The world is depicted here on Biblical principles: Jerusalem is at the centre, the Garden of Eden figures prominently and monsters inhabit the margins of the world.

Central detail, *Mappa Mundi*

Ross-on-Wye **9**

Herefordshire. 👥 *10,000.* 🚌 🛈
Edde Cross St (01989 562768). 📅 *Thu, Sat; farmers' market 1st Fri of month.*
www.visitherefordshire.co.uk

The fine town of Ross sits on a cliff of red sandstone above the water meadows of the River Wye. There are wonderful views over the river from the cliff-top gardens,

The wooded Wye Valley near Ross

given to the town by a local benefactor, John Kyrle (1637–1724). Kyrle was lauded by the poet Alexander Pope (1688–1744) in his *Moral Essays on the Uses of Riches* (1732) for using his wealth in a practical way, and he came to be known as "The Man of Ross". There is a memorial to Kyrle in **St Mary's Church**.

Environs: From Hereford to Ross, the **Wye Valley Walk** follows 16 miles (26 km) of gentle countryside. From Ross it continues south for 33 miles (54 km), over rocky ground in deep, wooded ravines.

Goodrich Castle, 5 miles (8 km) south of Ross, is a 12th-century red sandstone fort on a rock above the river.

⚑ Goodrich Castle
(EH) Goodrich. *Tel* 01600 890538. ◻ daily (Nov–Mar: Thu–Mon). ◪ ▢ (Apr–Sep). **www**.english-heritage.org.uk

Ledbury ⑩

Herefordshire. 👥 *8,000.* ⊒ ▣ ℹ *The Homend (01531 636147).* **www**.visitherefordshire.co.uk

Ledbury's main street is lined with timbered houses, including the **Market Hall** which dates from 1655. Church Lane, a cobbled lane running up from the High Street, has lovely 16th-century buildings: the **Heritage Centre** and **Butcher Row House** are both now museums. **St Michael and All Angels Church** has a massive detached bell tower, ornate Early English decoration and interesting monuments.

Medieval tile from the Priory at Great Malvern

🏛 **Heritage Centre**
Church Lane. ◻ *Easter–Oct: daily.* ♿
🏛 **Butcher Row House**
Church Lane. ◻ *Easter–Oct: daily.*

Great Malvern and the Malverns ⑪

Worcestershire. 👥 *35,000.* ⊒ ▣ ℹ *21 Church St (01684 892289).* ◪ *Fri; farmers' market 3rd Sat of month.* **www**.malvernhills.gov.uk

The ancient granite rock of the Malvern Hills rises from the plain of the River Severn, its 9 miles (15 km) of glorious scenery visible from afar. Composer Sir Edward Elgar (1857–1934) wrote many of his greatest works here, including the oratorio *The Dream of Gerontius* (1900), inspired by what the diarist John Evelyn (1620–1706) described as "one of the goodliest views in England". Elgar's home was in **Little Malvern**, whose truncated Church of St Giles, set on a steep, wooded hill, lost its nave when the stone was stolen during the Dissolution (*see p339*). **Great Malvern**, capital of the hills, is graced with 19th-century buildings which look like Swiss sanitoria: patients would stay at institutions such as Doctor Gulley's Water Cure Establishment. The water gushing from the hillside at St Ann's Well, above the town, is bottled and sold throughout Britain. The town is home to the famous Morgan cars (contact 01684 573104 to arrange a factory visit).

Malvern's highlight is the **Priory**, with its 15th-century stained-glass windows and medieval misericords. The old monastic fishponds below the church form the lake of the **Winter Gardens**. Here the theatre hosts performances of Elgar's music and plays by George Bernard Shaw.

A view of the Malverns range, formed of hard Pre-Cambrian rock

Worcester ⑫

Worcestershire. 🏙 95,000. 🚆
🚗 ℹ High St (01905 722480).
🛍 Mon–Sat.
www.cityofworcester.gov.uk

Worcester is one of many
English cities whose character
has been transformed by
modern development. The
architectural highlight remains
the **cathedral**, off College
Yard, which suffered a collapsed tower in 1175 and a
disastrous fire in 1203, before
the present structure was
started in the 13th century.

The nave and central tower
were completed in the 1370s,
after building was severely
interrupted by the Black Death,
which decimated the labour
force *(see p48)*. The most
recent and ornate addition
was made in 1874, when Sir
George Gilbert Scott *(see p465)*
designed the High Gothic
choir, incorporating 14th-
century carved misericords.

There are many interesting
tombs, including King John's,

**Charles I holding a symbol of the
Church on Worcester's Guildhall**

a masterpiece of medieval
carving, in front of the altar.
Prince Arthur, Henry VIII's
brother *(see p313)*, who died
at the age of 15, is buried in
the chantry chapel south of
the altar. Underneath, the
huge Norman crypt survives
from the first cathedral (1084).

From the cathedral cloister,
a gate leads to College Green
and out into Edgar Street and

its Georgian houses. Here the
**Museum of Worcester
Porcelain** displays Royal
Worcester porcelain dating
back to 1751. On the High
Street, north of the cathedral,
the **Guildhall** of 1723 is
adorned with statues of Stuart
monarchs, reflecting the city's
Royalist allegiances. In Corn-
market is **Ye Olde King
Charles House**, in which
Prince Charles, later Charles
II, hid after the Battle of Wor-
cester in 1651 *(see pp52–3)*.

Some of Worcester's finest
timber buildings are found in
Friar Street: **Greyfriars**, built
around 1480, has been
restored in period style. The
Commandery was originally
an 11th-century hospital. It
was rebuilt in the 15th century
and used by Prince Charles as
a base during the Civil War.
Now a museum, it has a fine
hammerbeam roof.

Elgar's Birthplace was the
home of composer Sir Edward
Elgar *(see p318)* and contains
memorabilia of his life.

🏛 **Museum of Worcester
Porcelain**
Severn St. **Tel** 01905 746000 ⬜
daily. ⬛ 25 Dec. 📷 ♿ 🎁 🍽 🏪

♟ **Greyfriars**
(NT) Friar St. **Tel** 01905 23571. ⬜
Apr–Oct: Wed–Sat (public hols pm
only). 📷

🏛 **Commandery**
Sidbury. **Tel** 01905 361821.
⬜ daily (Sun: pm). ⬛ 25–26 Dec,
1 Jan. 📷 📷

🏛 **Elgar's Birthplace**
Lower Broadheath. **Tel** 01905
333224. ⬜ daily. ⬛ 24 Dec–mid-
Jan. 📷 📷 **www**.elgarmuseum.org

Birmingham ⑬

Birmingham. 🏙 1,000,000. ✈ 🚆
🚗 ℹ 0121 2025099. 🛍 Mon–Sat.
www.beinbirmingham.com

Brum, as it is affectionately
known to its inhabitants,
grew up as a major centre of
the Industrial Revolution in
the 19th century. A vast range
of manufacturing trades was
based in Birmingham and
was responsible for the rapid
development of grim factories
and cramped housing. Since
the clearance of several of

Worcester Cathedral, overlooking the River Severn

The Last of England, Ford Madox Brown, Birmingham Art Gallery

these areas after World War II, Birmingham has raised its cultural profile. The city succeeded in enticing Sir Simon Rattle to conduct the City of Birmingham Symphony Orchestra, and persuaded the former Royal Sadler's Wells Ballet (now the Birmingham Royal Ballet) to leave London for the more up-to-date facilities of Birmingham. The **National Exhibition Centre**, 8 miles (13 km) east of the centre, draws thousands of people to its conference, lecture and exhibition halls.

Set away from the massive Bullring shopping centre, Birmingham's 19th-century civic buildings are excellent examples of Neo-Classical architecture. Among them are the **City Museum and Art Gallery**, where the collection includes outstanding works by pre-Raphaelite artists such as Sir Edward Burne-Jones (1833–98), who was born in Birmingham, and Ford Madox Brown (1821–93). The museum also organizes some interesting temporary exhibitions of art, such as

works by J M W Turner (1775–1851).

Birmingham's extensive canal system is now used mainly for leisure boating *(see pp300–01)*, and several former warehouses have been converted into museums and galleries. **Thinktank – the Birmingham Museum of Science and Discovery** celebrates the city's contributions to the world of railway engines, aircraft, and the motor trade. The old jewellery quarter has practised its traditional crafts here since the 16th century.

Suburban Birmingham has many attractions, including the **Botanical Gardens** at Edgbaston, and **Cadbury World** at Bournville, where there is a visitor centre dedicated to chocolate (booking ahead is advisable). Bournville village was built in 1890 by the Cadbury brothers for their workers and is a pioneering example of a garden suburb.

🏛 **City Museum and Art Gallery**
Chamberlain Sq. **Tel** 0121 303 2834. ◯ daily (Sun: pm). ● 25 & 26 Dec. ⛾ ▢ ▯

🏛 **Thinktank**
Millennium Point. **Tel** 0121 202 222. ◯ daily. ● 24 26 Dec.

🌿 **Botanical Gardens**
Westbourne Rd, Edgbaston. **Tel** 0121 454 1860. ◯ daily. ● 25 Dec. ▯
🈂 ⛾ 🎦 by arrangement. ▮

🏛 **Cadbury World**
Linden Rd, Bournville. **Tel** 0121 4514159. ◯ 20 Jan–Oct: daily; Nov, Dec: call for details. ● first two weeks Jan. 🈂 ⛾

Coventry ⓮

Coventry. 🕮 300,000. 🚆 🔲 🛈
4 Priory Row (024 7622 7264). 🏠
Mon–Sat. **www**.visitcoventry.co.uk

As an armaments centre, Coventry was a prime target for German bombing raids in World War II, and in 1940 the **cathedral** in the city centre was hit. After the war the first totally modern cathedral by Sir Basil Spence (1907–76) was built alongside the ruins. It includes sculptures by

Epstein's *St Michael Subduing the Devil*, on Coventry Cathedral

Sir Jacob Epstein and a tapestry by Graham Sutherland.

The **Herbert Gallery and Museum** has displays on the 11th-century legend of Lady Godiva, who rode naked through the streets. The recently renovated **Museum of British Road Transport** has the largest collection of Britain's road transport in the world, including cars, cycles and models, and features the fastest car in the world as well as interactive displays.

🏛 **Herbert Gallery and Museum**
Jordan Well. **Tel** 024 7683 2381. ◯ daily (Sun: pm) 1 Jan. ▢ ▯

🏛 **Museum of British Road Transport**
Hales St. **Tel** 024 7623 4270. ◯ daily. ⛾ ▢ ▯
www.transport-museum.com

Stately civic office buildings in Victoria Square, Birmingham

Midlands Garden Tour ⑮

The charming Cotswold stone buildings perfectly complement the lush gardens for which the region is famous. This picturesque route from Warwick to Cheltenham is designed to show every type of garden, from tiny cottage plots, brimming with bell-shaped flowers and hollyhocks, to the deer-filled, landscaped parks of stately homes. The route follows the escarpment of the Cotswold Hills, taking in spectacular scenery and some of the prettiest Midlands villages on the way.

Plum tree in blossom

TIPS FOR DRIVERS

Tour length: 35 miles (50 km).
Stopping-off points: Hidcote Manor has excellent lunches and teas; there are refreshments at Kiftsgate Court and Sudeley Castle. Travellers will find a good choice in Broadway, from traditional pubs and tea shops to the de luxe Lygon Arms. (See also pp684–5.)

Cheltenham Imperial Gardens ⑨
These colourful public gardens on the Promenade were laid out in 1817–18 to encourage people to walk from the town to the spa (*see p328*).

Sudeley Castle ⑧
The restored castle is complemented by box hedges, topiary and an Elizabethan knot garden (*see p26*). Catherine Parr, Henry VIII's widow, died here in 1548.

Broadway ⑤
Wisteria and cordoned fruit trees cover 17th-century cottages, fronted by immaculate gardens.

Stanway House ⑦
This Jacobean manor has many lovely trees in its grounds and a pyramid above a cascade of water.

Snowshill Manor ⑥
This Cotswold stone manor contains an extraordinary collection, from bicycles to Japanese armour. There are walled gardens and terraces full of *objets d'art* such as the clock (left). The colour blue is a recurrent theme.

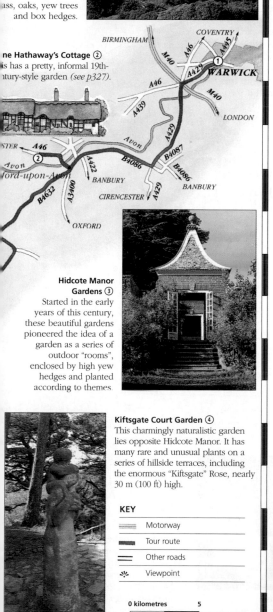

Warwick Castle ①
The castle's gardens
(see pp322–3) include
e Mound, planted in
medieval style, with
ass, oaks, yew trees
and box hedges.

ne Hathaway's Cottage ②
is has a pretty, informal 19th-
ntury-style garden (see p327).

Hidcote Manor Gardens ③
Started in the early
years of this century,
these beautiful gardens
pioneered the idea of a
garden as a series of
outdoor "rooms",
enclosed by high yew
hedges and planted
according to themes.

Kiftsgate Court Garden ④
This charmingly naturalistic garden
lies opposite Hidcote Manor. It has
many rare and unusual plants on a
series of hillside terraces, including
the enormous "Kiftsgate" Rose, nearly
30 m (100 ft) high.

KEY

▭▭▭	Motorway
▬▬▬	Tour route
═══	Other roads
☆	Viewpoint

0 kilometres 5

0 miles 5

Warwick ⑯

Warwickshire. 🏠 28,000. 🚉 🚌
ℹ The Courthouse, Jury St (01926
492212). 🛒 Sat.
www.warwick-uk.co.uk

Though Warwick suffered
a major fire in 1694, some
spectacular medieval buildings
survived. **St John's House
Museum** in St John's is a
charming Jacobean mansion
housing reconstructions of a
Victorian parlour, kitchen and
classroom. At the west end of
the High Street, a row of
medieval guild buildings were
transformed in 1571 by the Earl
of Leicester, who founded the
Lord Leycester Hospital as a
refuge for his old soldiers.

The arcaded **Market Hall**
(1670) is part of the Warwickshire Museum, renowned for
its unusual tapestry map of
the county, woven in 1558.

In Church Street, to the
south of St Mary's Church, is
the **Beauchamp Chapel**
(1443–64). It is a superb example of Perpendicular architecture and has tombs of the Earls
of Warwick. There is a view of
Warwick Castle (see pp322–
3) from St Mary's tower.

🏛 **St John's House Museum**
St John's. **Tel** 01926 412132.
◻ May–Sep: Tue–Sun; Oct–Apr:
Tue–Sat; bank hol Mon. 🚹 limited.
🏥 **Lord Leycester Hospital**
High St. **Tel** 01926 491422. ◻ Tue–
Sun & public hols. ● 25 Dec, Good
Fri. **Gardens** ◻ same as house but
Easter–Sep only. 🎫 🚌 🚹 limited. 🅿
🏛 **Market Hall** Market Place.
Tel 01926 412500. ◻ Mon–Sat
(May–Sep: daily). 🚹 limited. 🅿

The Lord Leycester Hospital,
now a home for ex-servicemen

Warwick Castle

Warwick's magnificent castle is a splendid medieval fortress which is also one of the country's finest stately homes. The original Norman castle was rebuilt in the 14th century, when huge outer walls and towers were added, mainly to display the power of the great feudal magnates, the Beauchamps and the Nevilles, the Earls of Warwick. The castle passed in 1604 to the Greville family who, in the 17th and 18th centuries, transformed it into a great country house. In 1978 the owners of Madame Tussaud's *(see p104)* bought the castle and set up tableaux of portraits to illustrate its history.

Neville family at prayer (c.1460)

The Ghost Tower is where the ghost of Sir Fulke Greville, murdered by a servant in 1628, is said to walk.

The Mound has remains of the motte and bailey castle *(see p486)* and the 1 century keep

Royal Weekend Party
The portrait of the valet is part of the award-winning exhibition of the Prince of Wales's visit in 1898.

★ Great Hall and State Rooms
Medieval apartments were transformed into the Great Hall and State Rooms. A mark of conspicuous wealth, they display a collection of family treasures from around the world.

The Mill and Engine House

Kingmaker Attraction
Dramatic displays recreate medieval life as "Warwick the Kingmaker", Richard Neville, prepared for battle in the Wars of the Roses .

View of Warwick Castle, south front, by Antonio Canaletto (1697–1768)

Ramparts and towers, of local grey sandstone, were added in the 14th century to fortify the castle.

Guy's Tower (1393) had lodgings for guests and members of the Earl of Warwick's retinue.

★ Death or Glory, the Armoury
The exhibits include Oliver Cromwell's helmet and a massive 14th-century two-handed sword.

Entrance

The underground dungeon

STAR SIGHTS

★ Great Hall and State Rooms

★ Death or Glory

Caesar's Tower

The Gatehouse is defended by portcullises and "murder holes" through which boiling pitch was dropped onto attackers beneath.

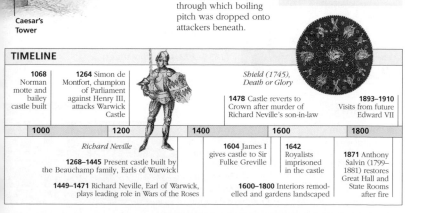

TIMELINE

Shield (1745), Death or Glory

Richard Neville

1068 Norman motte and bailey castle built	**1264** Simon de Montfort, champion of Parliament against Henry III, attacks Warwick Castle		**1478** Castle reverts to Crown after murder of Richard Neville's son-in-law		**1893–1910** Visits from future Edward VII
1000	**1200**	**1400**	**1600**		**1800**
	1268–1445 Present castle built by the Beauchamp family, Earls of Warwick	**1604** James I gives castle to Sir Fulke Greville	**1642** Royalists imprisoned in the castle	**1871** Anthony Salvin (1799–1881) restores Great Hall and State Rooms after fire	
	1449–1471 Richard Neville, Earl of Warwick, plays leading role in Wars of the Roses		**1600–1800** Interiors remodelled and gardens landscaped		

Street-by-Street: Stratford-upon-Avon ⑰

A 1930s jester

Situated on the west bank of the River Avon, in the heart of the Midlands, is one of the most famous towns in England. Stratford-upon-Avon dates back to at least Roman times but its appearance today is that of a small Tudor market town, with mellow, half-timbered architecture and tranquil walks beside the tree-fringed Avon. This image belies its popularity as the most visited tourist attraction outside London, with eager hordes flocking to see buildings connected to William Shakespeare or his descendants.

Bancroft Gardens
There is an attractive boat-filled canal basin here and a 15th-century causeway.

Tourist information

WATE

UNION STREET

BRIDGE STREET

HIGH STREET

★ Shakespeare's Birthplace
This building was almost entirely reconstructed in the 19th century, but in the style of the Tudor original.

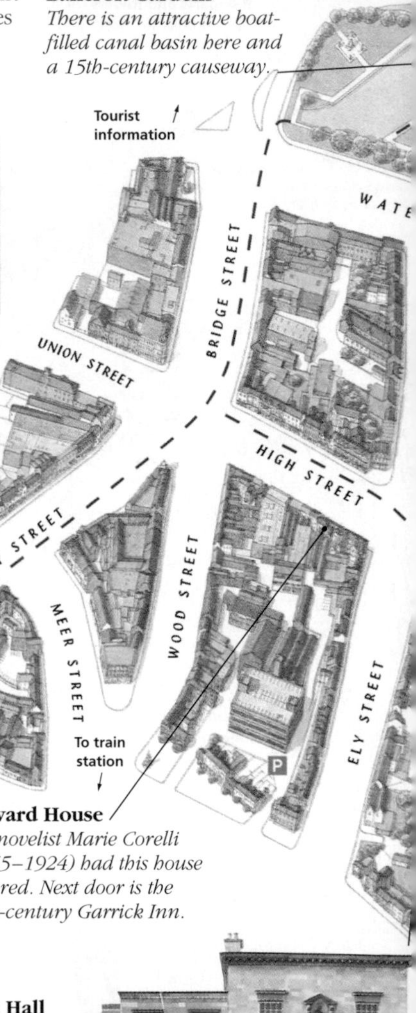

| 0 metres | 100 |
| 0 yards | 100 |

Shakespeare Centre

HENLEY STREET

MEER STREET

WOOD STREET

ELY STREET

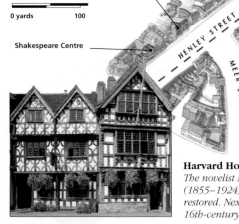

To train station

Harvard House
The novelist Marie Corelli (1855–1924) had this house restored. Next door is the 16th-century Garrick Inn.

STAR SIGHTS

★ Shakespeare's Birthplace

★ Hall's Croft

★ Holy Trinity Church

Town Hall
Built in 1767, there are traces of 18th-century graffiti on the front of the building saying God Save the King.

Royal Shakespeare Theatre and Swan Theatre
Closed for redevelopment from April 2007 to 2009, the RSC will instead perform at the Courtyard Theatre.

VISITORS' CHECKLIST

Warwickshire. ⌂ *22,000.*
✈ *20 miles (32 km) NW of Stratford-upon-Avon.* ⊟ *Alcester Rd.* ⊟ *Bridge St.*
ℹ *Bridge Foot **Tel** 0870 160 7930.* ⊟ *Fri.* ⊡ *Shakespeare's Birthday: Apr; Stratford Festival: Jul.* **www.**shakespeare-country.co.uk

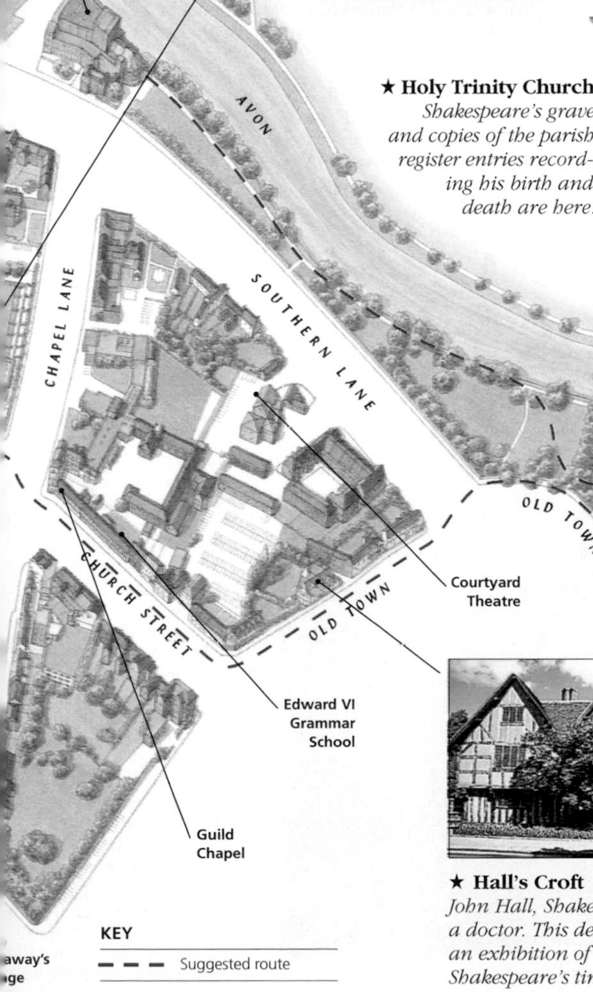

Nash's House
The foundations of New Place, where Shakespeare died, form the garden beside this house.

★ Holy Trinity Church
Shakespeare's grave and copies of the parish register entries recording his birth and death are here.

AVON

CHAPEL LANE

SOUTHERN LANE

OLD TOWN

OLD TOWN

CHURCH STREET

Courtyard Theatre

Edward VI Grammar School

Guild Chapel

KEY

- - - Suggested route

away's
ge

★ Hall's Croft
John Hall, Shakespeare's son-in-law, was a doctor. This delightful house includes an exhibition of medicine in Shakespeare's time.

Exploring Stratford-upon-Avon

Mosaic of Shakespeare on the beautiful Old Bank (1810)

William Shakespeare was born in Stratford-upon-Avon on St George's Day, 23 April 1564. Admirers of his work have been coming to the town since his death in 1616. In 1847 a public appeal successfully raised the money to buy the house in which he was born. As a result Stratford has become a literary shrine to Britain's greatest dramatist. It also has a thriving cultural reputation as the provincial home of the prestigious Royal Shakespeare Company, whose dramas are usually performed in Stratford before playing a second season in London (see pp152–3).

Anne Hathaway's Cottage, home of Shakespeare's wife

Around Stratford

The centre of Stratford-upon-Avon has many buildings that are connected with William Shakespeare and his descendants. On the High Street corner is the **Cage**, a 15th-century prison. It was converted into a house where Shakespeare's daughter Judith lived, and is now a shop. At the end of the High Street, the **Town Hall** has a statue of Shakespeare on the façade given by David Garrick (1717–79), the actor who in 1769 organized the first Shakespeare festival.

The High Street leads into Chapel Street where the half-timbered **Nash's House** is a museum of local history. It is also the site of **New Place**, where Shakespeare died in 1616, and which is now a herb and knot garden (see p26). In Church Street opposite, the **Guild Chapel** (1496) has a *Last Judgement* painting (c.1500) on the chancel wall. Shakespeare is thought to have attended the **Edward VI Grammar School** (above the former Guildhall) next door.

A left turn into Old Town leads to **Hall's Croft**, home of Shakespeare's daughter Susanna, which displays 16th- and 17th-century medical artefacts. An avenue of lime trees leads to **Holy Trinity Church**, where Shakespeare is buried. A walk along the river follows the Avon to **Bancroft Gardens**, which lies at the junction of the River Avon and the Stratford Canal.

⚜ Shakespeare's Birthplace

Henley St. **Tel** 01789 201823. ◯ daily. ⬤ 23–26 Dec. 🈸 ♿ limited. 🌐 www.shakespeare.org.uk

Bought for the nation in 1847, when it was a public house, Shakespeare's Birthplace was converted back to Elizabethan style. Objects associated with Shakespeare's father, John, a glovemaker and wool merchant, are on display. There is a birth room, in which Shakespeare was supposedly born, and another room has a window etched with visitors' autographs, including that of Sir Walter Scott (see p512).

Holy Trinity Church, seen across the River Avon

🏛 Harvard House

High St. **Tel** 01789 204016. ⬤ May–
Oct: Fri–Sun, bank hol Mon. 🗺 ♿
limited. **www**.shakespeare.org.uk

Built in 1596, this ornate
house was the home of
Katherine Rogers, whose son,
John Harvard, emigrated to
America and in 1638 left his
estate to a new college, later
renamed Harvard University.
The house contains a Museum
of British Pewter and displays
relating to John Harvard.

Environs: No tour of Stratford
would be complete without a
visit to **Anne Hathaway's
Cottage**. Before her marriage
to William Shakespeare she
lived at Shottery, 1 mile (1.5
km) west of Stratford. Despite
fire damage in 1969, the cottage is still impressive, with
some original 16th-century
furniture. The Hathaway descendants lived here until the
early 20th century *(see p321)*.

🏛 Anne Hathaway's Cottage

Cottage Lane. **Tel** 01789 292100.
⬤ daily. ⬤ 23–26 Dec. 🗺 🚻
www.shakespeare.org.uk

Kenneth Branagh in *Hamlet*

THE ROYAL SHAKESPEARE COMPANY

The Royal Shakespeare
Company is renowned for
its new interpretations of
Shakespeare's work. The
company performs at the
1932 Royal Shakespeare
Theatre, a windowless
brick building adjacent to
the Swan Theatre, built in
1986 to a design based on
an Elizabethan playhouse.
Next to it is a building
displaying sets, props and
costumes. The RSC also
performs at the 150-seat
theatre, known as the
Other Place, and in
London *(see pp152–3)*.

Grevel House, the oldest house in Chipping Campden

Chipping Campden ⑱

Gloucestershire. 🚉 2,500.
ℹ High St (01386 841206).
www.cotswold.gov.uk

This perfect Cotswold town
is kept in pristine condition
by the Campden Trust. Set up
in 1929, the Trust has kept
alive the traditional skills of
stonecarving and repair that
make Chipping Campden such
a unified picture of golden-
coloured and lichen-patched
stone. Visitors travelling from
the northwest along the B4035
first see a group of ruins: the
remains of **Campden Manor**,
begun around 1613 by Sir
Baptist Hicks, 1st Viscount
Campden. The manor was
burned by Royalist troops to
stop it being sequestered by
Parliament at the end of the
Civil War *(see pp52–3)*, but
the almshouses opposite the
gateway were spared. They
were designed in the form of
the letter "I" (which is Latin for
"J"), a symbol of the owner's
loyalty to King James I.

The town's **Church of St
James**, one of the finest in
the Cotswolds, was built in
the 15th century, financed by
merchants who bought wool
from Cotswold farmers and
exported it at a high profit.
Inside the church there are
many elaborate tombs, and a

magnificent brass dedicated
to William Grevel, describing
him as "the flower of the wool
merchants of England". He
built **Grevel House** (c.1380)
in the High Street, the oldest
in a fine row of buildings,
which is distinguished by a
double-storey bay window.

Viscount Campden donated
the **Market Hall** in 1627. His
contemporary, Robert Dover,
founded in 1612 the "Cotswold
Olimpicks", long before the
modern Olympic Games had
been established. The 1612
version included such painful
events as the shin-kicking contest. It still takes place on the
first Friday after each Spring
Bank Holiday, followed by a
torchlit procession into town
ready for the Scuttlebrook
Wake Fair on the next day.
The setting for the games is a
spectacular natural hollow on
Dover's Hill above the town,
worth climbing on a clear day
for the marvellous views over
the Vale of Evesham.

**The 17th-century Market Hall in
Chipping Campden**

Tewkesbury's abbey church overlooks the town, crowded onto the bank of the River Severn

Tewkesbury ⑲

Gloucestershire. 🏠 11,000.
🚻 Barton St (01684 295027).
🛒 Wed, Sat. **www**.
visitcotswoldsandsevernvale.gov.uk

This lovely town sits on the
confluence of the rivers
Severn and Avon. It has one of
England's finest Norman abbey
churches, **St Mary the Virgin**,
which locals saved during the
Dissolution of the Monasteries
(see p50) by paying Henry VIII
£453. Around the church, with
its bulky tower and Norman
façade, timbered
buildings are
crammed within
the bend of the
river. Warehouses
are a reminder of
past wealth, and
Borough Mill
on Quay Street,
the only mill
left harnessed
to the river's energy,
still grinds corn.

**Pump Room detail,
Cheltenham**

Environs: Boat trips run from
the river to **Twyning**'s riverside
pub, 6 miles (10 km) north.

Cheltenham ⑳

Gloucestershire. 🏠 107,000. 🚉 🚌
🚻 77 Promenade (01242 522878). 🛒
Sun; farmers' market 2nd & last Fri of
month. **www**.visitcheltenham.info

Cheltenham's reputation for
elegance was first gained in
the late 18th century, when
high society flocked to the spa

town to "take the waters",
following the example set by
George III (see pp54–5). Many
gracious terraced houses were
built, in a Neo-Classical style,
along broad avenues. These
survive around the Queen's
Hotel, near **Montpellier**, a
lovely Regency arcade lined
with craft and antique shops,
and in the **Promenade**, with
its smart department stores and
couturiers. A more modern
atmosphere prevails in the
newly built Regency Arcade,
where the star attraction is the
1987 **clock** by Kit Williams:
visit on the hour to
see fish blowing
bubbles over the
onlookers' heads.
The **Museum and
Art Gallery** is
worth a visit to
see its unusual
collection of
furniture and
other crafts
made by members of
the influential Arts
and Crafts Movement (see p29),
whose strict principles of utilitarian design were laid down
by William Morris (see p220).
The **Pitville Pump Room**
(1825–30), modelled on the
Greek Temple of Ilissos in
Athens, is frequently used for
performances during the
town's renowned annual
festivals of music (July) and
literature (October).
The event that really attracts
the crowds is the Cheltenham
Gold Cup – the premier event
of the National Hunt season –
held in March (see p66).

🏛 Museum and Art Gallery
Clarence St. **Tel** 01242 237431.
◻ Mon–Sat. ● 25 Dec, 1 Jan &
public hols. ♿ 📷 by
arrangement. ▢ 🖼 **www**.
cheltenham.artgallery.museum

🎹 Pitville Pump Room
Pitville Park. **Tel** 01242 523852.
◻ Wed–Mon. ● 25 & 26 Dec,
1 Jan, public hols & frequently for
functions: call to check. ♿

Fantasy clock, by Kit Williams,
in Cheltenham's Regency Arcade

Gloucester Cathedral's nave

Gloucester ㉑

Gloucestershire. 🏛 *110,000.* 🚃
🚉 🛈 *28 Southgate St (01452
396572).* 🛍 *Wed, Sat.*
www.gloucester.gov.uk/tourism

Gloucester has played a
prominent role in the history
of England. It was here that
William the Conqueror
ordered a vast survey of all the
land in his kingdom, that was
to be recorded in the *Domesday Book* of 1086 *(see p48).*

The city was popular with
the Norman monarchs and in
1216 Henry III was crowned
in its magnificent **cathedral**.
The solid, dignified nave was
begun in 1089. Edward II *(see
p439),* who was murdered in
1327 at Berkeley Castle, 14
miles (22 km) to the southwest, is buried in a tomb near
the high altar. Many pilgrims
came to honour Edward's
tomb, leaving behind generous donations, and Abbot
Thoky was able to begin
rebuilding in 1331. The result
was the wonderful east
window and the cloisters,
where the fan vault was
developed and then copied
in other churches all over
the country.

The impressive buildings
around the cathedral include
College Court, with its **House
of the Tailor of Gloucester**
museum, in the house that the
children's author Beatrix
Potter used as the setting *(see
p367)* for her illustrations of
that story. A museum complex
has been created in the
Gloucester Docks, part of
which is still a port, linked to
the Bristol Channel by the

Gloucester and Sharpness
Canal (opened in 1827). In
the old port, and housed in a
Victorian warehouse, the
National Waterways Museum
incorporates hands-on
displays to relate the history
of canals.

> 🏛 **House of the Tailor of
> Gloucester**
> College Court. **Tel** *01452 422856.*
> ⬜ *Mon–Sat.* ⬤ *public hols.*
> 🗐 🈁
>
> 🏛 **National Waterways
> Museum**
> Llanthony Warehouse, Gloucester
> Docks.
> **Tel** *01452 318054.* ⬜ *daily.* ⬤
> *25 Dec.* 🗐 🈁 ♿ 🖵 🖴
> **www**.nwm.org.uk

Cirencester ㉒

Gloucestershire. 🏛 *20,000.*
🚉 🛈 *Market Place (01285
654180).* 🛍 *Mon, Tue (cattle)
& Fri.*
www.cotswold.gov.uk

Known as the capital of the
Cotswolds, Cirencester has
as its focus a market place,
where there is a market every
Monday and Friday.
Overlooking the market is the
Church of St John Baptist,
whose "wineglass" pulpit
(1515) is one of the few pre-
Reformation pulpits to survive in England. To the west,
Cirencester Park was laid out
by the 1st Earl of Bathurst
from 1714, with help from
the poet Alexander Pope *(see
p317).* The mansion is

surrounded by a massive yew
hedge. Clustering round the
park entrance are the 17th-
and 18th-century wool merchants' houses of Cecily Hill,
built in grand Italianate style.
Much humbler Cotswold
houses are to be found in
Coxwell Street, and underlying
this is a Roman town,
evidence of which emerges
whenever the ground is dug.

The **Corinium Museum**,
since its renovation in 2004, is
a must-see site. It features
excavated objects in a series
of tableaux illustrating life in
a Roman household.

> 🌿 **Cirencester Park**
> Cirencester Park. **Tel** *01285
> 653135.* ⬜ *daily.* ♿
> **www**.cirencesterpark.co.uk
>
> 🏛 **Corinium Museum**
> Park St. **Tel** *01285 655611.*
> ⬜ *daily (Sun pm only).* ⬤ *25 &
> 26 Dec, 1 Jan.* 🈁 ♿ 🖵 🖴

**Cirencester's fine parish church,
one of the largest in England**

ART AND NATURE IN THE ROMAN WORLD

Cirencester was an important centre of mosaic production
in Roman days. Fine examples of the local style are shown
in the Corinium Museum and mosaics range from Classical
subjects, such as Orpheus taming lions and tigers with the
music of his lyre, to the naturalistic depiction of a hare. At

Chedworth Roman Villa, 8
miles (13 km) north, mosaics
are inspired by real life. In
the *Four Seasons* mosaic,
Winter shows a peasant,
dressed in a woollen hood
and a wind-blown cloak,
clutching a recently caught
hare in one hand and a
branch for fuel in the other.

Hare mosaic, Corinium Museum

EAST MIDLANDS

DERBYSHIRE · LEICESTERSHIRE · LINCOLNSHIRE
NORTHAMPTONSHIRE · NOTTINGHAMSHIRE

*hree very different kinds of landscape greet visitors to the East
Midlands. In the west, wild moors rise to the craggy heights of
the Peak District. These give way to the low-lying plain and
the massive industrial towns at the region's heart. In the east, hills
and limestone villages stretch to a long, flat seaboard.*

The East Midlands owes much of its
character to a conjunction of
the pastoral with the urban.
The spa resorts, historical
villages and stately homes
coexist within a landscape
shaped by industrialization.
Throughout the region there are
swathes of scenic countryside –
and grimy industrial cities.

The area has been settled since
prehistoric times. The Romans
mined lead and salt, and they
built a large network of roads and
fortresses. Anglo-Saxon and Viking
influence is found in many of the
place names. During the Middle Ages
profits from the wool industry enabled
the development of towns such as
Lincoln, which still has many fine old
buildings. The East Midlands was the
scene of ferocious battles during the

Wars of the Roses and the Civil War,
and insurgents in the Jacobite
Rebellion reached as far as Derby.

In the west of the region is the Peak
District, Britain's first national park.
Created in 1951, it draws crowds in
search of the wild beauty of the
heather-covered moors, or the
wooded dales of the River Dove.
The peaks are very popular
with rock climbers and hikers.

The eastern edge of the
Peaks descends through stone-walled
meadows to sheltered valleys. The
Roman spa of Buxton adds a final note
of elegance before the flatlands of
Derbyshire, Leicestershire and Nottinghamshire are reached. An area of coal
mines and factories since the late 18th
century, the landscape is set to be
transformed over the next century into
a new national forest.

Well-dressing dance, an ancient custom at Stoney Middleton in the Peak District

◁ **West front of Chatsworth House, a superb Baroque stately home in the Peak District**

Exploring the East Midlands

The East Midlands is a popular tourist destination,
easily accessible by road, but best explored on foot.
Numerous well-marked trails pass through the Peak
District National Park. There are superb country
houses at Chatsworth and Burghley and the
impressive historic towns of Lincoln and
Stamford to discover.

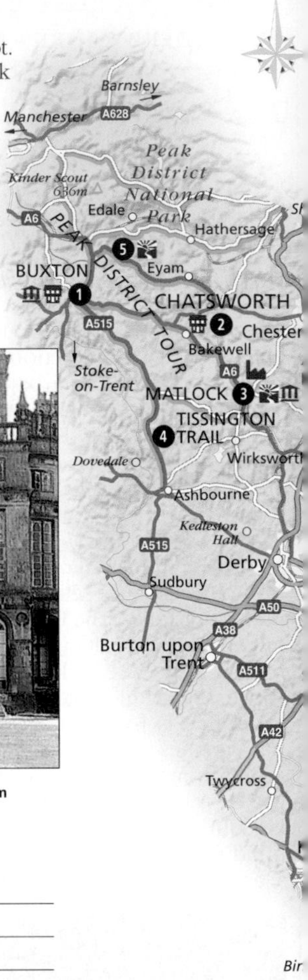

SIGHTS AT A GLANCE

Burghley pp342–3 **8**
Buxton **1**
Chatsworth pp334–5 **2**
Lincoln pp340–41 **7**
Matlock Bath **3**
Northampton **10**
Nottingham **6**
Stamford **9**

Walks and Tours

Peak District Tour **5**
Tissington Trail **4**

GETTING AROUND

The M6, M1 and A1 are the
principal road routes to the
East Midlands, but they are
subject to frequent delays
because of the volume of traffic
they carry. It can be faster and
more interesting to find cross-
country routes to the region,
for example through the
attractive countryside and
villages around Stamford and
Northampton. Roads in the
Peak District become very
congested during the summer
and an early start to the day is
advisable. Lincoln and
Stamford are well served by
fast mainline trains from
London. Rail services in the
Peak District are far more
limited, but local lines run as
far as Matlock and Buxton.

KEY

▬▬	Motorway
▬▬	Major road
—	Secondary road
▭▭	Minor road
—	Scenic route
▬▬	Main railway
—	Minor railway
△	Summit

**View of Burghley House from
the north courtyard**

SEE ALSO

- *Where to Stay* pp578–80

- *Where to Eat* pp632–4

Peak District countryside seen from the Tissington Trail

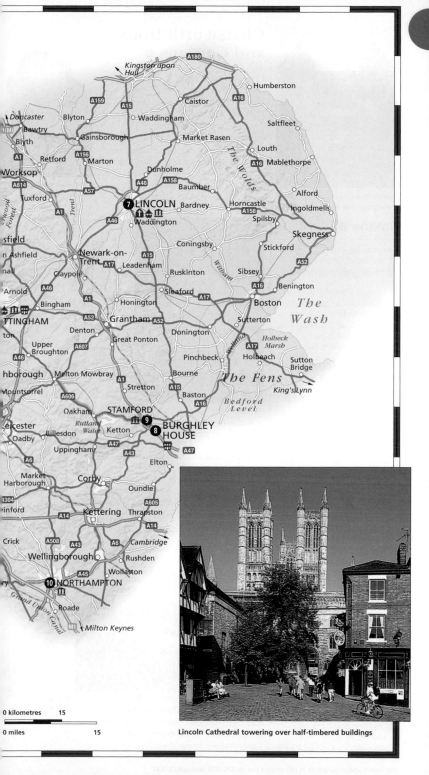

Lincoln Cathedral towering over half-timbered buildings

Buxton Opera House, a late 19th-century building restored in 1979

Buxton ❶

Derbyshire. 👥 20,000. 🚉 🚌
ℹ The Crescent (01298 25106).
🏪 Tue, Sat. www.highpeak.gov.uk

Buxton was developed as a
spa town by the 5th Duke of
Devonshire during the late
18th century. It has many fine
Neo-Classical buildings, including the **Devonshire Royal
Hospital** (1790), originally
stables, at the entrance to the
town. The **Crescent** was built
(1780–90) to rival Bath's
Royal Crescent (see p258).

At its southwest end, the
tourist information office is
housed in the former town
baths. Here, a spring where
water surges from the ground
at a rate of 7,000 litres (1,540
gallons) an hour can be seen.
Buxton water is bottled and
sold but there is a public fountain at **St Ann's Well**, opposite.

Steep gardens known as the
Slopes lead from the Crescent
to the small, award-winning
Museum and Art Gallery,
with geological and archaeological displays. Behind the
Crescent, overlooking the
Pavilion Gardens, is the striking 19th-century iron and
glass **Pavilion**, and the splen-
didly restored **Opera House**,
where a Music and Arts
Festival is held in summer.

🏛 **Buxton Museum and
Art Gallery**
Terrace Rd. **Tel** 01298 24658. ◯
Easter–Sep: Tue–Sun; Oct–Easter:
Tue–Sat. ● 25 Dec–2 Jan. ♿ 🚻
www.derbyshire.gov.uk

🏵 **Pavilion and Gardens**
St John's Rd. **Tel** 01298 23114.
◯ daily. ● 25 Dec. ♿ 🍴 🖾 🚻

Chatsworth House and Gardens ❷

Chatsworth is one of Britain's
most impressive stately homes.
Between 1687 and 1707, the 4th
Earl of Devonshire replaced the
old Tudor mansion with this
Baroque palace. The house has
beautiful gardens, landscaped in
the 1760s by Capability Brown
(see p26) and developed by the
head gardener, Joseph Paxton (see
pp56–7), in the mid-19th century.

First house built in 1552
by Bess of Hardwick

Summerhouse   Round ponds,
known as the
Spectacles

★ **Cascade**
*Water tumbles
down the steps of
the Cascade,
built in 1696 to
a French design.*

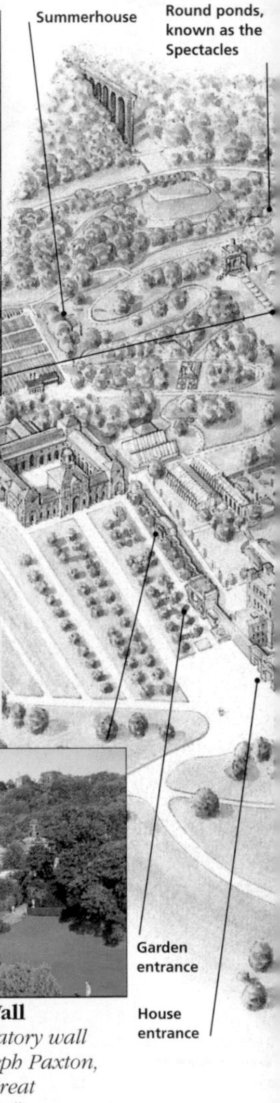

STAR SIGHTS

★ Cascade
★ Chapel

Paxton's "Conservative" Wall
*This wood-and-glass conservatory wall
was designed in 1848 by Joseph Paxton,
the creator of Chatsworth's Great
Conservatory (now demolished).*

Garden
entrance

House
entrance

VISITORS' CHECKLIST

Derbyshire. *Chesterfield, then bus.* ***Tel*** *01246 565300.* *mid-Mar–Dec: 11am–4:30pm (gardens: 11am–5pm) daily.* *gardens & some of house.* **www**.chatsworth.org

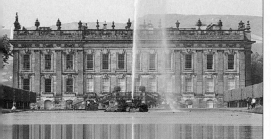

South front and canal pond with Emperor fountain

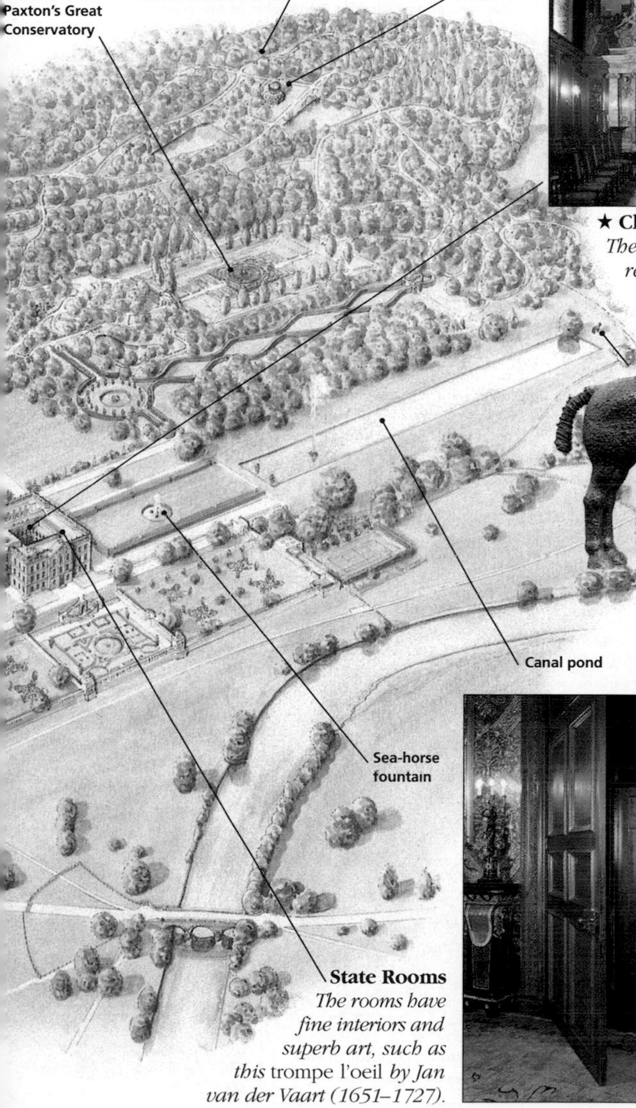

Maze: site of Paxton's Great Conservatory
Rhododendron Walk
Grotto
Canal pond
Sea-horse fountain

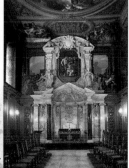

★ Chapel
The chapel (1693) is resplendent with art and marble.

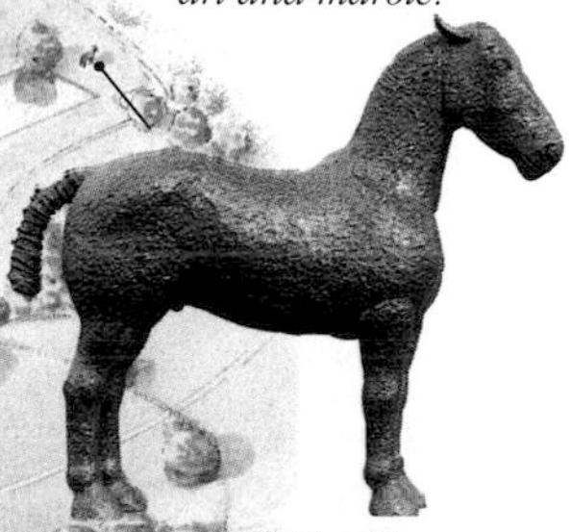

War Horse
This sculpture (1991) is by Elisabeth Frink.

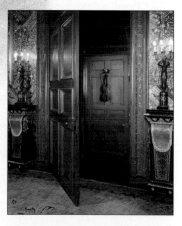

State Rooms
The rooms have fine interiors and superb art, such as this trompe l'oeil *by Jan van der Vaart (1651–1727).*

Matlock ❸

Derbyshire. 🏛 *23,000.* ≋
🛈 *Crown Square (01629 583388).*
www.visitderbyshire.co.uk

Matlock was developed as
a spa from the 1780s.
Interesting buildings include
the massive structure (1853) on
the hill above the town, built
as a hydrotherapy centre but
now council offices. On the
hill opposite is the mock-
Gothic **Riber Castle**.

From Matlock, the A6 winds
through the outstandingly
beautiful **Derwent Gorge** to
Matlock Bath. Here, cable
cars ascend to the **Heights of
Abraham** pleasure park,
with caves, nature trail and
extensive views. Lead-mining
is the subject of the **Peak
District Mining Museum**, and
visitors can inspect the old
Temple Mine nearby. **Sir
Richard Arkwright's Cromford
Mill** (1771), a world heritage
site and the first ever water-
powered cotton spinning mill,
lies at the southern end of the
gorge *(see p339)*.

🏛 **Heights of Abraham** On A6.
Tel *01629 582365.* ⬜ *Feb–Mar: Sat
& Sun (daily Feb half-term); Easter–
Oct: daily.* 🎫 🚻 *limited.* 🅿️ 🖼️
🏛 **Peak District Mining
Museum** The Pavilion, off A6. **Tel**
01629 583834. ⬜ *daily.* 🎫 🚻
🅿️ 🖼️ **www**.peakmines.co.uk
⛏️ **Temple Mine**
Temple Rd, off A6. **Tel** *01629
583834.* ⬜ *call for details.* 🎫
⛏️ **Cromford Mill**
Mill Lane, Cromford. **Tel** *01629
824297.* ⬜ *daily.* ⬛ *25 Dec.* 🎫
🚻 🍴 🖼️ **www**.cromfordmill.co.uk

Cable cars taking visitors to the Heights of Abraham

Tissington Trail ❹

See p337.

Peak District Tour ❺

See pp338–9.

Nottingham ❻

Nottinghamshire. 🏛 *269,000.*
≋ ✈ 🛈 *Smithy Row (0115
9155330).* 🖼️ *daily.* **www**.
experiencenottinghamshire.com

The name of Nottingham
often conjures up the
image of the evil Sheriff,
adversary of Robin Hood.
Nottingham Castle stands
on a rock riddled with
underground passages. The
castle houses a museum, with
displays on the city's history,
and what was Britain's first
municipal art gallery,
featuring works by Sir Stanley
Spencer (1891–1959) and

Dante Gabriel Rossetti
(1828–82). At the foot of the
castle, Britain's oldest tavern,
the **Trip to Jerusalem** (1189),
is still in business. Its name
may refer to the 12th- and
13th-century crusades, but
much of it is 17th-century.

There are several museums
near the castle, ranging from
the **Tales of Robin Hood**,
which tells the story of the
outlaw, to the **Museum of
Nottingham Life**, in which
you can go back in time and
experience life in Nottingham
over the last 300 years.

Environs: Stately homes
within a few miles of Nottingham include the Neo-
Classical **Kedleston Hall** *(see
pp28–9).* "Bess of Hardwick",
Countess of Shrewbury *(see
p334),* built the spectacular
Hardwick Hall *(see p302).*

🏰 **Nottingham Castle
and Museum**
Castle Rd. **Tel** *0115 9153700.*
⬜ *daily.* ⬛ *24–27 Dec, 1 Jan.* 🎫
🚻 🅿️ 🖼️
🏛 **Tales of Robin Hood**
30–38 Maid Marion Way. **Tel** *0115
9483284.* ⬜ *daily.* ⬛ *25 & 26
Dec.* 🎫 🚻 🅿️ 🖼️
🏛 **Museum of
Nottingham Life**
Castle Boulevard. **Tel** *0115
9153600.* ⬜ *daily.* ⬛ *24–26 Dec,
1 Jan.* 🎫 🖼️
🏯 **Kedleston Hall**
(NT) off A38. **Tel** *01332 842191.*
⬜ *Apr–Oct: Sat–Wed (pm).* 🎫
🚻 🍴 🖼️
🏯 **Hardwick Hall**
(NT) off A617. **Tel** *01246 850430.*
⬜ *Apr–Oct: Wed, Thu, Sat,
Sun & public hols.* 🎫 🚻 *limited.*
🍴 🖼️

ROBIN HOOD OF SHERWOOD FOREST

England's most colourful folk hero was a
legendary swordsman, whose adventures
are depicted in numerous films and
stories. He lived in Sherwood Forest,
near Nottingham, with a band of
"merry men", robbing the rich to
give to the poor. As part of an
ancient oral tradition, Robin Hood
figured mainly in ballads; the first
written records of his exploits date
from the 15th century. Today historians think that he was not one
person, but a composite of many
outlaws who refused to conform
to medieval feudal constraints.

**Victorian depiction of Friar
Tuck and Robin Hood**

Tissington Trail ❹

The full-length Tissington Trail runs for 13 miles (22 km), from the village of Ashbourne to Parsley Hay, where it meets the High Peak Trail. This is a short version, taking an easy route along a dismantled railway line around Tissington village and provid-ing good views of the beautiful White Peak countryside. The Derbyshire custom of well-dressing is thought to have originated in pre-Christian times. It was revived in the early 17th century, when the Tissington village wells were decorated in thanksgiving for deliverance from the plague, in the belief that the fresh water had had a medicinal effect. Well-dressing is still an important event in the Peakland calendar, and can be seen in other villages where the water supplies were prone to dry up.

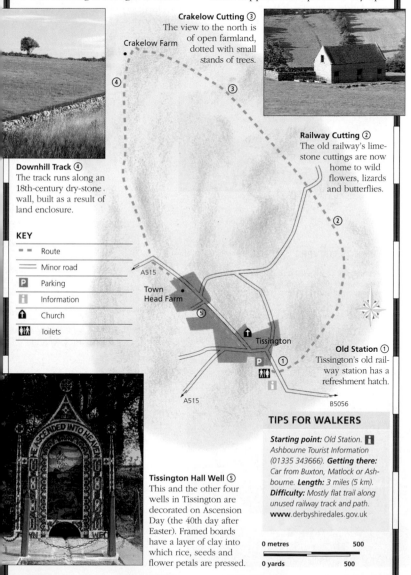

Crakelow Cutting ③
The view to the north is of open farmland, dotted with small stands of trees.

Crakelow Farm

④

③

Railway Cutting ②
The old railway's limestone cuttings are now home to wild flowers, lizards and butterflies.

②

Downhill Track ④
The track runs along an 18th-century dry-stone wall, built as a result of land enclosure.

KEY

- -	Route
===	Minor road
P	Parking
ℹ	Information
✝	Church
🚻	Toilets

A515

Town Head Farm

⑤

Tissington

P
🚻
ℹ

A515

①

B5056

Old Station ①
Tissington's old railway station has a refreshment hatch.

Tissington Hall Well ⑤
This and the other four wells in Tissington are decorated on Ascension Day (the 40th day after Easter). Framed boards have a layer of clay into which rice, seeds and flower petals are pressed.

TIPS FOR WALKERS

Starting point: Old Station. ℹ Ashbourne Tourist Information (01335 343666). **Getting there:** Car from Buxton, Matlock or Ashbourne. **Length:** 3 miles (5 km). **Difficulty:** Mostly flat trail along unused railway track and path. www.derbyshiredales.gov.uk

0 metres	500
0 yards	500

Peak District Tour ❺

Detail, Buxton Opera House

The Peak District's natural beauty and sheep-grazed crags contrast with the factories of nearby valley towns. Designated Britain's first National Park in 1951, the area has two distinct types of landscape. In the south are the gently rolling hills of the limestone White Peak. To the north, west and east are the wild, heather-clad moorlands of the Dark Peak peat bogs, superimposed on millstone grit.

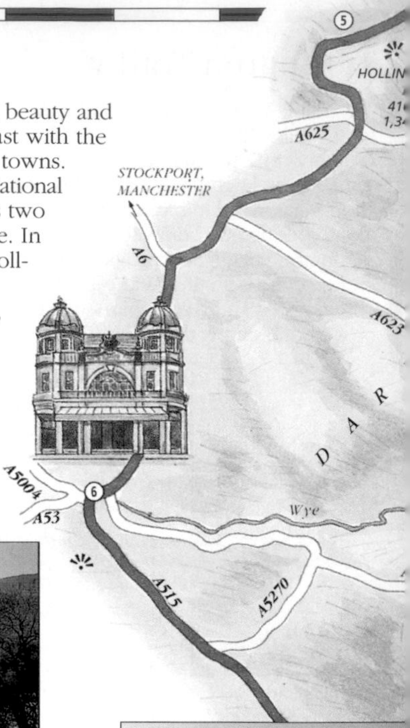

STOCKPORT, MANCHESTER

A625

A6

A623

A5004

A53

A515

A5270

Wye

Edale ⑤
The high plateau of scenic Edale mark the starting point of the 256 mile (412 km) Pennine Way footpath *(see p36)*.

TIPS FOR DRIVERS

Tour length: *40 miles (60 km).*
Stopping-off points: *There are refreshments at Crich Tramway Village and Arkwright's Mill in Cromford. Eyam has good old-fashioned tea shops. The Nag's Head in Edale is a charming Tudor inn. Buxton has many pubs and cafés. (See also pp684–5.)*

Buxton ⑥
This lovely spa town's opera house *(see p334)* is known as the "theatre in the hills" because of its magnificent setting.

Arbor Low ⑦
This stone circle, known as the "Stonehenge of the North", dates from around 2000 BC and consists of 46 recumbent stones enclosed by a ditch.

KEY

▬▬▬	Tour route
═══	Other roads
☀	Viewpoint

Dovedale ⑧
Popular Dovedale is one of the prettiest of the Peak District's river valleys, with its stepping stones, thickly wooded slopes and wind-sculpted rocks. Izaac Walton (1593–1683), author of *The Compleat Angler*, used to fish here.

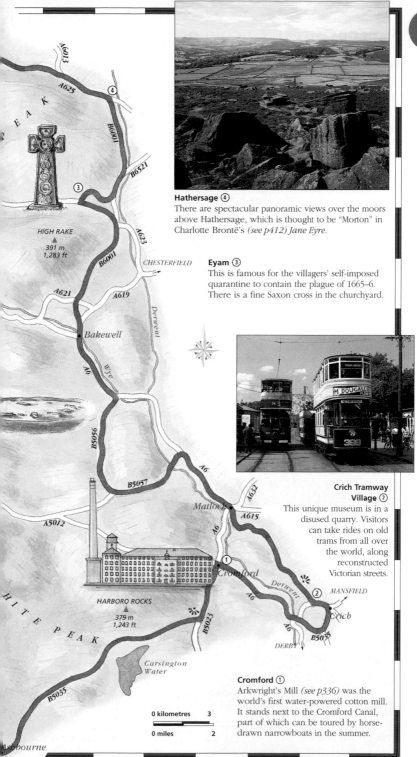

Hathersage ④

There are spectacular panoramic views over the moors above Hathersage, which is thought to be "Morton" in Charlotte Brontë's *(see p412) Jane Eyre*.

Eyam ③

This is famous for the villagers' self-imposed quarantine to contain the plague of 1665–6. There is a fine Saxon cross in the churchyard.

Crich Tramway Village ②

This unique museum is in a disused quarry. Visitors can take rides on old trams from all over the world, along reconstructed Victorian streets.

HIGH RAKE
▲
391 m
1,283 ft

CHESTERFIELD

Bakewell

Matlock

Cromford

Crich

MANSFIELD

DERBY

HARBORO ROCKS
▲
379 m
1,243 ft

WHITE PEAK

Carsington Water

Ashbourne

↓DERBY

0 kilometres 3

0 miles 2

Cromford ①

Arkwright's Mill *(see p336)* was the world's first water-powered cotton mill. It stands next to the Cromford Canal, part of which can be toured by horse-drawn narrowboats in the summer.

Street-by-Street: Lincoln ❼

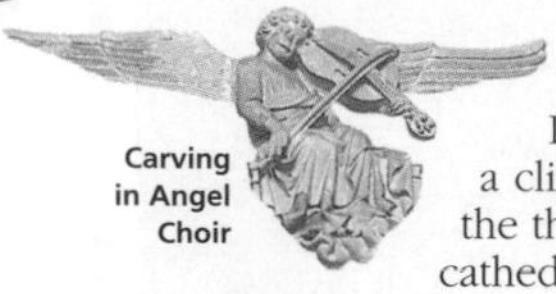

Carving in Angel Choir

Surrounded by the flat landscape of the Fens, Lincoln rises dramatically on a cliff above the River Witham, the three towers of its massive cathedral visible from afar. The Romans *(see pp44–5)* founded the first fortress here in AD 50. By the time of the Norman Conquest *(see p47)*, Lincoln was one of the most important cities in England (after London, Winchester and York). The city's wealth was due to its strategic importance for the export of wool from the Lincolnshire Wolds to Europe. Lincoln has managed to retain much of its historic character. Many remarkable medieval buildings have survived, most of which are along the aptly named Steep Hill, leading to the cathedral.

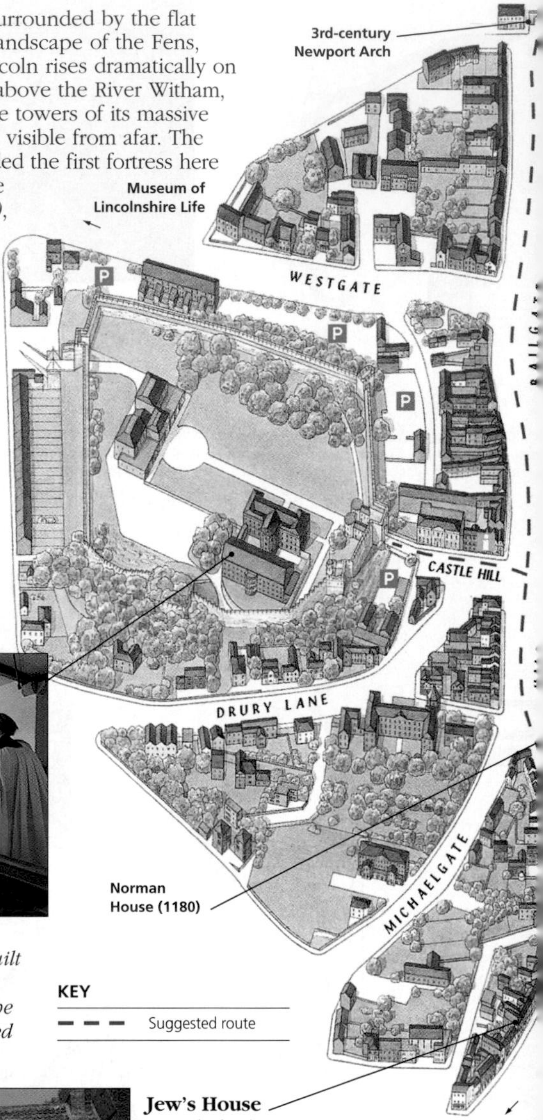

3rd-century Newport Arch
Museum of Lincolnshire Life
WESTGATE
P
CASTLE HILL
DRURY LANE
MICHAELGATE
Norman House (1180)
15th-century Stonebow Gate and bus and railway stations

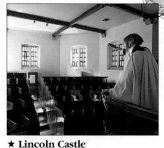

★ Lincoln Castle
The early Norman castle, rebuilt at intervals, acted as the city prison from 1787 to 1878. The chapel's coffin-like pews served to remind felons of their fate.

KEY

— — — Suggested route

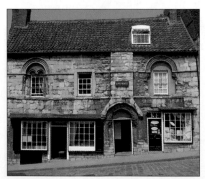

Jew's House
Lincoln had a large medieval Jewish community. This mid-12th-century stone house, one of the oldest of its kind, was owned by a Jewish merchant.

0 metres 100

0 yards 100

STAR SIGHTS

★ Lincoln Castle

★ Lincoln Cathedral

For hotels and restaurants in this region see pp578–580 and pp632–634

VISITORS' CHECKLIST

Lincoln. 👥 90,000. ✈ Humberside, 30 miles (48 km); E Midlands, 51 miles (82 km). 🚉 St Mary St. 🚌 Melville St. 🛈 Castle Hill (01522 873213), The Cornhill (01522 873256).
www.lincoln.gov.uk

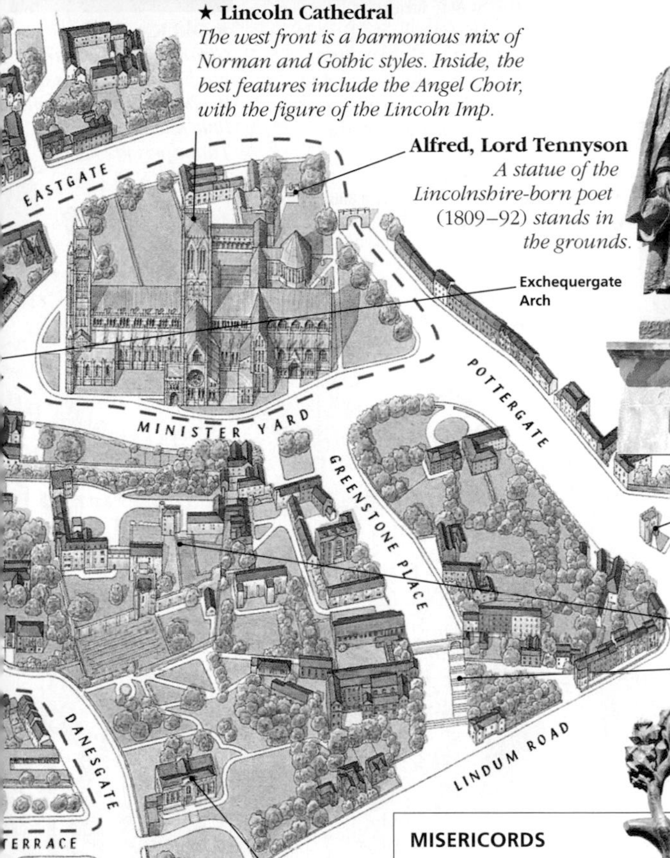

★ Lincoln Cathedral
The west front is a harmonious mix of Norman and Gothic styles. Inside, the best features include the Angel Choir, with the figure of the Lincoln Imp.

Alfred, Lord Tennyson
A statue of the Lincolnshire-born poet (1809–92) stands in the grounds.

EASTGATE

Exchequergate Arch

MINISTER YARD

GREENSTONE PLACE

POTTERGATE

The 14th-century Pottergate Arch

Victorian Arboretum

Ruins of Medieval Bishop's Palace

Greenstone Stairs

LINDUM ROAD

DANESGATE

TERRACE

Usher Art Gallery
This is packed with clocks, ceramics, and silver. There are paintings by Peter de Wint (1784–1849) and J M W Turner (see p91).

MISERICORDS
Misericords are ledges that project from the underside of the hinged seat of a choir stall, which provide support while standing.

St Francis of Assisi

Lincoln Cathedral's misericords in the early Perpendicular-style canopied choir stalls are some of the best in England. The wide variety of subjects includes parables, fables, myths, biblical scenes and irreverent images from daily life.

One of a pair of lions

Burghley House ⑧

Portrait of Sir Isaac Newton, Billiard Room

William Cecil, 1st Lord Burghley (1520–98) was Queen Elizabeth I's adviser and confidant for 40 years. He built the wonderfully dramatic Burghley House in 1555–87, probably designing it himself. The roof line bristles with stone pyramids, chimneys disguised as Classical columns and towers shaped like pepper pots. The busy skyline only resolves itself into a symmetrical pattern when viewed from the west, where a lime tree stands, one of many planted by Capability Brown *(see p26)* when the surrounding deer park was landscaped in 1760. Burghley's interior is lavishly decorated with Italian paintings of Greek gods enacting their dramas across the walls and ceiling.

★ Old Kitchen
Gleaming copper pans hang from the walls of the fan-vaulted kitchen, little altered since the Tudor period.

North Gate
Intricate examples of 19th-century wrought-iron work adorn the principal entrances.

The Billiard Room
has many fine portraits inset in oak panelling.

Cupolas were very fashionable details, inspired by European Renaissance architecture.

A chimney has been disguised as a Classical column.

Mullioned windows were added in 1683 when glass became less expensive.

The Gatehouse, with its side turrets, is a typical feature of the "prodigy" houses of the Tudor era *(see p302)*.

West Front
Featuring the Burghley crest, the West Front was finished in 1577 and formed the original main entrance.

STAR SIGHTS

★ Old Kitchen

★ Heaven Room

★ Hell Staircase

VISITORS' CHECKLIST

Off A1 SE of Stamford, Lincs. ***Tel*** *01780 752451.* *Stamford.* *Apr–Oct: 11am–4:30pm Sat–Thu.* *1 day Sep (horse trials).* **www**.burghley.co.uk

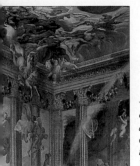

★ Heaven Room
Gods tumble from the sky, and satyrs and nymphs play on the walls and ceiling in this masterpiece by Antonio Verrio (1639–1707).

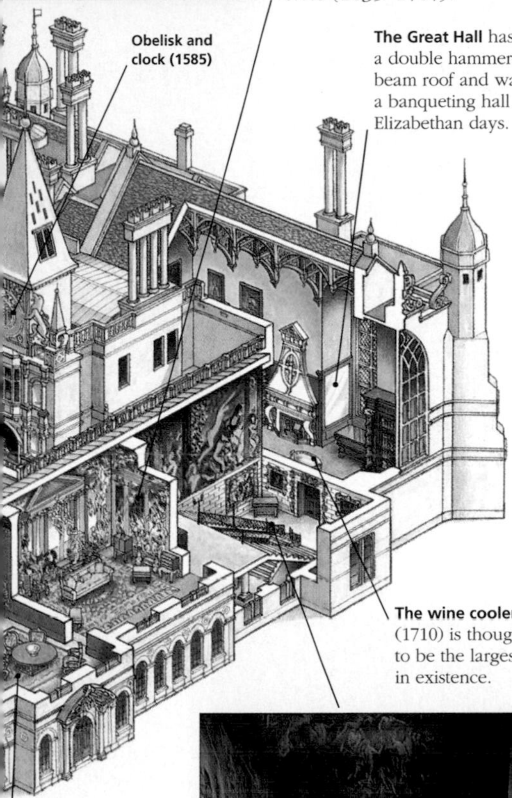

Obelisk and clock (1585)

The Great Hall has a double hammer-beam roof and was a banqueting hall in Elizabethan days.

The wine cooler (1710) is thought to be the largest in existence.

The Fourth George Room, one of a suite, is panelled in oak stained with ale.

★ Hell Staircase
Verrio painted the ceiling to show Hell as the mouth of a cat crammed with tormented sinners. The staircase, of local stone, was installed in 1786.

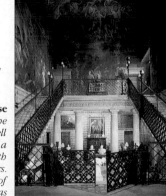

Stamford ⑨

Lincolnshire. *18,000.* *27 St Mary's St (01780 755611).* *Fri.* **www**.southkesteven.gov.uk

Stamford is a showpiece town, famous for its many churches and its Georgian townhouses. Stamford retains a medieval street plan, with a warren of winding streets and cobbled alleys.

The spires of the medieval churches (five survive of the original eleven) give Stamford the air of a miniature Oxford.

Barn Hill, leading up from All Saints Church, is the best place for a view of Stamford's Georgian architecture in all its variety. Below it is Broad Street, where the **Stamford Museum** covers the history of the town. By far the most popular exhibit is a waxwork of Britain's fattest man, Daniel Lambert, who was 336 kg (53 stone) and died while attending Stamford Races in 1809.

Stamford Museum
Broad St. ***Tel*** *01780 766317.* *Apr–Sep: daily (Sun: pm); Oct–Mar: Mon–Sat.* *limited.* **www**.lincolnshire.gov.uk/stamfordmuseum

Northampton ⑩

Northamptonshire. *187,000.* *The Guildhall, St Giles Sq (01604 838800).* *Mon–Sat (Thu: antiques).* **www**.northampton.gov.uk

This market town was once a centre for shoe-making, and the **Central Museum and Art Gallery** holds the world's largest collection of footwear. One of many fine old buildings is the Victorian Gothic **Guildhall**. Six miles west of the town is **Althorp House**, family home of Diana Princess of Wales. Visitors can tour the house, grounds, see an exhibition on Diana and her island resting place.

Central Museum and Art Gallery
Guildhall Rd. ***Tel*** *01604 238548.* *daily (Sun: pm).* *25, 26 Dec.*

Althorp House
Great Brington (off A428). ***Tel*** *01604 770107.* *Jul–Sep daily.* *31 Aug.* **www**.althorp.com

THE NORTH COUNTRY

The North Country at a Glance

Rugged coastlines, spectacular walks and climbs, magnificent stately homes and breathtaking cathedrals all have their place in the north of England, with its dramatic history of Roman rule, Saxon invasion, Viking attacks and border skirmishes. Reminders of the industrial revolution are found in towns such as Halifax, Liverpool and Manchester, and peace and inspiration in the dramatic scenery of the Lake District, with its awe-inspiring mountains and waters.

Hadrian's Wall (see pp422–3), *built around 120 to protect Roman Britain from the Picts to the north, cuts through rugged Northumberland National Park scenery.*

NORTHUMB
(see pp414–

Northumbe

Dur

The Lake District (see pp354–69) *is a combination of superb peaks, tumbling rivers and falls and shimmering lakes such as Wast Water.*

Cumbria

Yorkshire Dales National Park (see pp384–86) *creates a delightful environ-ment for walking and touring the farming landscape, scattered with attractive villages such as Thwaite, in Swaledale.*

Lancashire

LANCASHIRE AND THE LAKES (see pp354–379)

The Walker Art Gallery (see pp378–9) *in Liverpool is one of the jewels in the artistic crown of the north, with an internationally renowned collection ranging from Old Masters to modern art. Sculpture includes John Gibson's Tinted Venus (c.1851–6).*

Manchester

Liverpool

◁ **The 11th-century Alnwick Castle, Alnwick, Northumberland, from across the River Aln**

Durham Cathedral (see pp428–9), *a striking Norman structure with an innovative southern choir aisle and fine stained glass, has towered over the city of Durham since 995.*

Fountains Abbey (see pp390–91), *one of the finest religious buildings in the north, was founded in the 12th century by monks who desired simplicity and austerity. Later the abbey became extremely wealthy.*

Castle Howard (see pp398–9), *a triumph of Baroque architecture, offers many magnificent settings, including this Museum Room (1805–10), designed by CH Tatham.*

York (see pp404–409) *is a city of historical treasures, ranging from the medieval to Georgian. Its magnificent minster has a large collection of stained glass and the medieval city walls are well preserved. Other sights include churches, narrow alleyways and notable museums.*

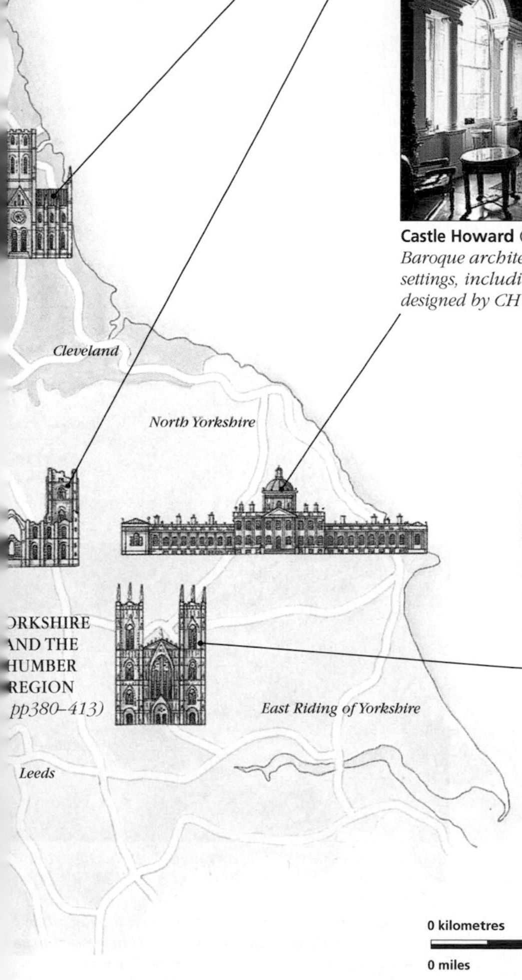

Cleveland

North Yorkshire

**ORKSHIRE
AND THE
HUMBER
REGION**
pp380–413)

East Riding of Yorkshire

Leeds

0 kilometres 25

0 miles 25

The Industrial Revolution in the North

The face of Northern England in the 19th century was dramatically altered by the development of the coal mining, textile and shipbuilding industries. Lancashire, Northumberland and the West Riding *(see p381)* of Yorkshire all experienced population growth and migration to cities. The hardships of urban life were partly relieved by the actions of several wealthy industrial philanthropists, but many people lived in extremely deprived conditions. Although most traditional industries have now declined sharply or disappeared as demand has moved elsewhere, a growing tourist industry has developed in many of the former industrial centres.

Back-to-backs *or colliers' rows, such as these houses at Easington, were provided by colliery owners from the 1800s onwards. They comprised two small rooms for cooking and sleeping, and an outside toilet.*

1815 Sir Humphrey Davy invented a safety oil lamp for miners. Light shone through a cylindrical gauze sheet which prevented the heat of the flame igniting methane gas in the mine. Thousands of miners benefited from this device.

Coal mining *was a family industry in the North of England with women and children working alongside the men.*

1750	1800
PRE-STEAM	STEAM AGE
1750	1800

1781 Leeds–Liverpool Canal opened. The building of canals facilitated the movement of raw materials and finished products, and aided the process of mechanization immeasurably.

1830 Live **and Manchester** ra opened, connecting tv the biggest cities ou London. Within a mont railway carried passer

Halifax's Piece Hall (see p413), *restored in 1976, is the most impressive surviving example of industrial architecture in northern England. It is the only complete 18th-century cloth market building in Yorkshire. Merchants sold measures of cloth known as "pieces" from rooms lining the cloisters inside.*

Hebden Bridge (see p412), *a typical West Riding textile mill town jammed into the narrow Calder Valley, typifies a pattern of workers' houses surrounding a central mill. The town benefited from its position when the Rochdale Canal (1804) and then the railway (1841) took advantage of this relatively low-level route over the Pennines.*

Saltaire (see p411) *was a model village built by the wealthy cloth merchant and mill-owner Sir Titus Salt (1803–76), for the benefit of his workers. Seen here in the 1870s, it included houses and facilities such as shops, gardens and sportsfields, with almshouses, a hospital, school and chapel. A disciplinarian, Salt banned alcohol and pubs from Saltaire.*

George Hudson *(1800–71) built the first railway station in York (see p408) in 1840–42. In the 1840s he owned more than a quarter of the railways in Britain and was known as the "railway king".*

1842 Coal Mines Act prevented women and children from working in harsh conditions in the mines.

Port Sunlight (see p379) *was founded by William Hesketh Lever (1851–1925) to provide housing for workers at his Sunlight soap factory. Between 1889 and 1914 he built 800 cottages. Amenities included a pool.*

Strikes to improve working conditions were common. Violence flared in July 1893 when colliery owners locked miners out of their pits and stopped their pay after the Miners' Federation resisted a 25 per cent wage cut. Over 300,000 men struggled without pay until November, when work resumed at the old rate.

1850	1900
FULL MECHANIZATION	
1850	1900

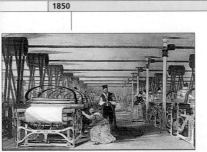

Power loom weaving *transformed the textile industry while creating unemployment among skilled hand loom weavers. By the 1850s, the West Riding had 30,000 power looms, used in cotton and woollen mills. Of 79,000 workers, over half were to be found in Bradford alone.*

Furness dry dock *was built in the 1890s when the shipbuilding industry moved north, in search of cheap labour and materials. Barrow-in-Furness, Glasgow (see pp516–19) and Tyne and Wear (see p424) were the new centres.*

Joseph Rowntree *(1836–1925) founded his chocolate factory in York in 1892, having formerly worked with George Cadbury. As Quakers, the Rowntrees believed in the social welfare of their workers (establishing a model village in 1904), and, with Terry's confectionary (1767), they made a vast contribution to York's prosperity. Today, Nestlé Rowntree is the world's largest chocolate factory and York is Britain's chocolate capital.*

North Country Abbeys

Northern England has some of the finest and best preserved religious houses in Europe. Centres of prayer, learning and power in the Middle Ages, the larger of these were designated abbeys and were governed by an abbot. Most were located in rural areas, considered appropriate for a spiritual and contemplative life. Viking raiders had destroyed many Anglo-Saxon religious houses in the 8th and 9th centuries *(see pp46–7)* and it was not until William the Conqueror founded the Benedictine Selby Abbey in 1069 that monastic life revived in the north. New orders, Augustinians in particular, arrived from the Continent and by 1500 Yorkshire had 83 monasteries.

Cistercian monk

Ruins of St Mary's Abbey today

The Liberty of St Mary was the name given to the land around the abbey, almost a city within a city. Here, the abbot had his own market, fair, prison and gallows – all exempt from the city authorities.

ST MARY'S ABBEY

Founded in York in 1086, this Benedictine abbey was one of the wealthiest in Britain. Its involvement in the wool trade in York and the granting of royal and papal privileges and land led to a relaxing of standards by the early 12th century. The abbot was even allowed to dress in the same style as a bishop, and was raised by the pope to the status of a "mitred abbot". As a result, 13 monks left in 1132, to found Fountains Abbey *(see pp390–91).*

Gatehouse and St Olave's church

Interval tower

Water tower

Hospitium or guest house

MONASTERIES AND LOCAL LIFE

As one of the wealthiest landowning sections of society, the monasteries played a vital role in the local economy. They provided employment, particularly in agriculture, and dominated the wool trade, England's largest export during the Middle Ages. By 1387 two thirds of all wool exported from England passed through St Mary's Abbey, the largest wool trader in York.

Cistercian monks tilling their land

WHERE TO SEE ABBEYS TODAY

Fountains Abbey *(see pp390–91)*, founded by Benedictine monks and later taken over by Cistercians, is the most famous of the numerous abbeys in the region. Rievaulx *(see p393)*, Byland *(see p392)* and Furness *(see p368)* were all founded by the Cistercians, and Furness became the second wealthiest Cistercian house in England after Fountains. Whitby Abbey *(see p396)*, sacked by the Vikings, was later rebuilt by the Benedictine order. Northumberland is famous for its early Anglo-Saxon monasteries, such as Ripon, Lastingham and Lindisfarne *(see pp418–19).*

Mount Grace Priory (see p394), *founded in 1398, is the best-preserved Carthusian house in England. The former individual gardens and cells of each monk are still clearly visible.*

THE DISSOLUTION OF THE MONASTERIES (1536–40)

By the early 16th century, the monasteries owned one-sixth of all English land and their annual income was four times that of the Crown. Henry VIII ordered the closure of all religious houses in 1536, acquiring their wealth in the process. His attempt at dissolution provoked a large uprising of Catholic northerners led by Robert Aske later that year. The rebellion failed and Aske and others were executed for conspiracy. The dissolution continued under Thomas Cromwell, who became known as "the hammer of the monks".

Thomas Cromwell (c.1485–1549)

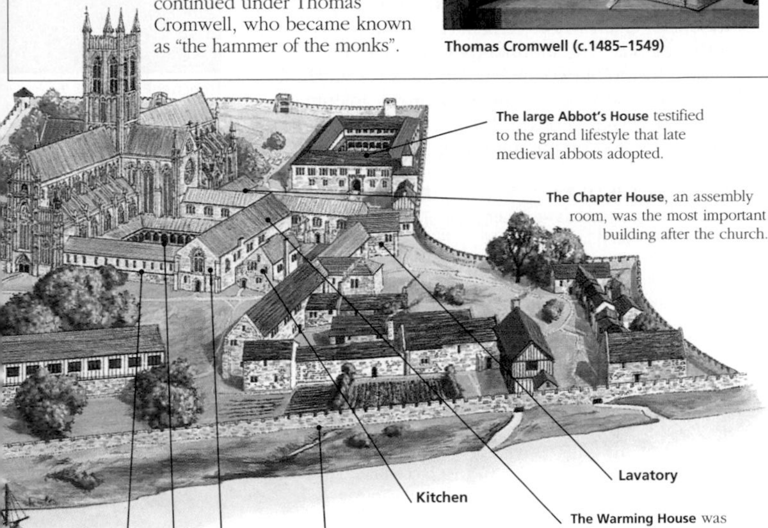

The large Abbot's House testified to the grand lifestyle that late medieval abbots adopted.

The Chapter House, an assembly room, was the most important building after the church.

Lavatory

Kitchen

The Warming House was the only room in the monastery, apart from the kitchen, which had a fire.

Refectory

The Abbey Wall had battlements added in 1318 to protect it against raids by Scottish armies.

Common parlour

Cloister

Kirkham Priory, an Augustinian foundation of the 1120s, enjoys a tranquil setting on the banks of the River Derwent, near Malton. The finest feature of the ruined site is the 13th-century gatehouse which leads into the priory complex.

...asby Abbey lies beside the River Swale, outside the pretty market town of Richmond. Among the ...mains of this Premonstratensian ...house, founded in 1155, are the ...-century refectory and sleeping ...rters and 14th-century gatehouse.

Kirkstall Abbey *was founded in 1152 by monks from Fountains Abbey. The well-preserved ruins of this Cistercian house near Leeds include the church, the late Norman chapter house and the abbot's lodging. This evening view was painted by Thomas Girtin (1775–1802).*

The Geology of the Lake District

Piece of Lake District slate

The Lake District contains some of England's most spectacular scenery. Concentrated in just 900 sq miles (231 sq km) are the highest peaks, deepest valleys and longest lakes in the country. Today's landscape has changed little since the end of the Ice Age 10,000 years ago, the last major event in Britain's geological history. But the glaciated hills which were revealed by the retreating ice were once part of a vast mountain-chain whose remains can also be found in North America. The mountains were first raised by the gradual fusion of two ancient landmasses which, for millions of years, formed a single continent. Eventually the continent broke into two, forming Europe and America, separated by the widening Atlantic Ocean.

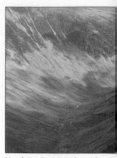

Honister Pass, with its distinctive U-shape, is an example of a glaciated valley, once completely filled with ice.

GEOLOGICAL HISTORY

The oldest rock formed as sediment under an ocean called Iapetus. Some 450 million years ago, Earth's internal movements made two continents collide, and the ocean disappear.

1 **The collision** buckled the former sea bed into a mountain range. Magma rose from Earth's mantle, altered the sediments and cooled into volcanic rock.

2 **In the Ice Age**, glaciers slowly excavated huge rock basins in the mountainsides, dragging debris to the valley floor. Frost sculpted the summits.

3 **The glaciers retreated** 10,000 years ago, their meltwaters forming lakes in valleys dammed by debris. As the climate improved, plants colonized the fells.

RADIATING LAKES

The diversity of lakeland scenery owes much to its geology: hard volcanic rocks in the central lakes give rise to rugged hills, while soft slates to the north produce a more rounded topography. The lakes form a radial pattern, spreading out from a central volcanic rock zone.

Scafell Pike is the highest peak in England. One of the three Scafell Pikes, its two neighbours are Broad Crag and Ill Crag.

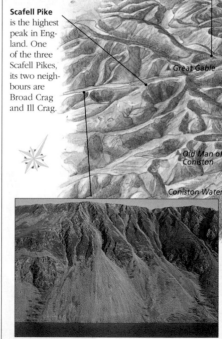

Great Gable

Old Man of Coniston

Coniston Water

Wast Water is the deepest of the lakes. Its southeastern cliffs are streaked with granite scree – the debris formed each year as rock shattered by the winter frost tumbles down during the spring thaw.

MAN ON THE MOUNTAIN

The sheltered valley floors with their benign climate and fertile soils are ideal for settlement. Farmhouses, dry-stone walls, pasture and sheep pens are an integral part of the landscape. Higher up, the absence of trees and bracken are the result of wind and a cooler climate. Old mine workings and tracks are the relics of once-flourishing industries.

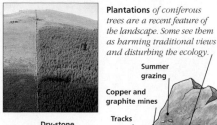

Plantations *of coniferous trees are a recent feature of the landscape. Some see them as harming traditional views and disturbing the ecology.*

Summer grazing

Copper and graphite mines

Tracks

Dry-stone walls *(see p305)*

400–500 m (130–170 ft)

300–400 m (100–130 ft)

Sheep pens for winter grazing

Slate *and other local stone has long been incorporated into buildings: slate roofs, stone walls, lintels and bridges.*

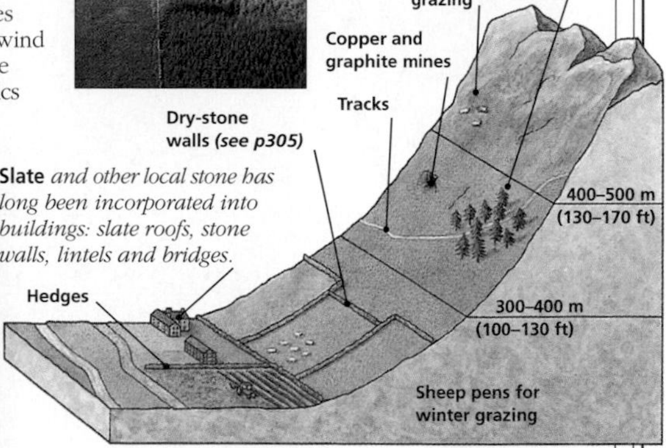

Hedges

Blencathra

Helvellyn | **Ullswater**

Place Fell

High Street

Windermere

t Water

vaite

Skiddaw *is composed of slate, formed when the muddy sediment of the ancient ocean floor was altered by extreme pressure.*

Striding Edge *is a long, twisting ridge which leads to the summit of Helvellyn. It was sharpened by the widening of the valleys on either side caused by the build up of glaciers.*

The Langdale Pikes *are remnants of the volcanic activity which once erupted in the area. They are made of hard igneous rocks, known as Borrowdale Volcanics. Unlike the Skiddaw Slates, they have not eroded smoothly, so they leave a craggy skyline.*

MERSEYSIDE
MARITIME
MUSEUM

LANCASHIRE AND THE LAKES

CUMBRIA · LANCASHIRE

The landscape painter John Constable (1776–1837) declared that the Lake District, now visited by 18 million people annually, had "the finest scenery that ever was". The Normans built many religious houses here, and William II created estates for English barons. Today, the National Trust is its most important landowner.

Within the 30 mile (45 km) radius of the Lake District lies an astonishing number of fells and lakes. Today, all looks peaceful, but from the Roman occupation to the Middle Ages, the northwest was a turbulent area, as successive kings and rulers fought over the territory. Historians can revel in the various Celtic monuments, Roman remains, stately homes and monastic ruins. Although the scenery is paramount, there are many outdoor activities as well as spectator sports, such as Cumbrian wrestling, and wildlife to observe.

Lancashire's portfolio of tourist attractions includes the fine county town of Lancaster, bright Blackpool with its autumn illuminations and fairground attractions, and the peaceful seaside beaches to the south. Inland, the most appealing regions are the Forest of Bowland, a sparse expanse of heathery grouse moor, and the picturesque Ribble Valley. Further south still are the industrial conurbations of Manchester and Merseyside, where the attractions are more urban.

There are many fine Victorian buildings in Manchester, where the industrial quarter of Castlefield has been revitalized. Liverpool, with its restored Albert Dock, is best known as the seaport city of the Beatles. It has a lively club scene and is increasingly used as a film location. Both cities have good art galleries and museums.

Jetty at Grasmere, one of the most popular regions of the Lake District

◁ Restored Albert Dock, lining the River Mersey in Liverpool

Exploring Lancashire and the Lakes

The Lake District's natural scenery outweighs any of its man-made attractions. Its natural features are the result of geological upheavals over millennia *(see pp352–3)*, and four of its peaks are more than 1,000 m (3,300 ft). Human influences have left their mark too: the main activities are quarrying, mining, farming and tourism.

The Lakes are most crowded in summer when activities include lake trips and hill-walking. The best bases are Keswick and Ambleside, while there are also good hotels on the shores of Windermere and Ullswater and in the Cartmel area.

Lancashire's Bowland Forest is an attractive place to explore on foot, with picturesque villages. Further south, Manchester and Liverpool have excellent museums and galleries.

Watersports on Derwentwater in the Northern Fells and Lakes area

GETTING AROUND

For many, the first glimpse of the Lake District is from the M6 near Shap Fell, but the A6 is a more dramatic route. You can reach Windermere by train, but you need to change at Oxenholme, on the mainline route from Euston to Carlisle. Penrith also has rail services and bus links into the Lakes. L'al Ratty, the miniature railway up Eskdale, and the Lakeside & Haverthwaite railway, which connects with the steamers on Windermere,

make for enjoyable outings. Regular buses link all the main centres where excursions are organized. One of the most enterprising is the Mountain Goat minibus, in Windermere and Keswick.

Lancaster, Liverpool and Manchester are on the main rail and bus routes and also have airports. For Blackpool, you need to change trains in Preston. Wherever you go in the area, one of the best means of getting around is on foot.

View over Crummock Water, north of Buttermere, one of the quieter Western Lakes

SIGHTS AT A GLANCE

KEY

▭	Motorway
▭	Major road
▭	Secondary road
▭	Minor road
▭	Scenic route
▭	Main railway
▭	Minor railway
△	Summit

0 kilometres   20

0 miles   10

SEE ALSO

• ***Where to Stay*** pp580–83

• ***Where to Eat*** pp634–7

Preserved docks and Liver Building, Liverpool

Carlisle ❶

Cumbria. 🏘 102,000. ✈ *mainly private.* 🚌 🚇 🛈 *The Old Town Hall, Green Market (01228 625600).* **www**.visitcumbria.com

Due to its proximity to the Scottish border, this city has long been a defensive site. Known as Luguvalium by the Romans, it was an outpost of Hadrian's Wall *(see pp422–3)*. Carlisle was sacked and pillaged repeatedly by the Danes, the Normans and border raiders, and suffered damage as a Royalist stronghold under Cromwell *(see p52)*.

Today, Carlisle is the capital of Cumbria. In its centre are the timber-framed Guildhall and market cross, and forti-fications still exist around its West Walls, drum-towered gates and its Norman **castle**. The castle tower has a small museum devoted to the King's Own Border Regi-ment. The cathedral dates from 1122 and features a decorative east window. Carlisle's **Tullie House Museum** recreates the city's past with sections on Roman history and Cumbrian wildlife. Nearby lie the evocative ruins of

Saxon iron sword in the Tullie House Museum

Façade of Hutton-in-the-Forest with medieval tower on the right

Lanercost Priory (c.1166) and the remains of the unique **Birdoswald Roman Fort**.

⛪ Carlisle Castle
(EH) Castle Way. **Tel** 01228 591922. ⭕ *daily.* 🅿 ♿ *limited.* 🎫 🛈

🏛 Tullie House Museum
Castle St. **Tel** 01228 534781. ⭕ *daily (Sun: pm).* 🅿 ♿ 🛈

♫ Lanercost Priory
(EH) Nr Brampton. **Tel** 016977 3030. ⭕ *Mar–Sep: daily, Oct: Thu–Mon.* 🎫 🅿 ♿ *limited.*

⛪ Birdoswald Roman Fort
(EH) Gilsland, Brampton. **Tel** 016977 47602. ⭕ *Mar–Nov: daily.* 🅿 ♿ *limited.* 🎫 🛈

Penrith ❷

Cumbria. 🏘 15,000. 🛈 *Robinson's School, Middlegate (01768 867466).* 🚌 *Tue, Sat, Sun.* **www**.visiteden.co.uk

Timewarp shopfronts on the market square and a 14th-century **castle** of sandstone are Penrith's main attractions.

There are some strange hog-back stones in St Andrew's churchyard, allegedly a giant's grave, and the 285 m (937 ft) Beacon provides stunning views of distant fells.

Environs: Just northeast of Penrith at Little Salkeld is a famous Bronze Age circle (with 66 tall stones) known as **Long Meg and her Daughters**. Six miles (9 km) northwest of Penrith lies **Hutton-in-the-Forest**. The oldest part of this house is the 13th-century tower. Inside is a magnificent Italianate staircase, a sumptuously panelled 17th-century Long Gallery, a delicately stuccoed Cupid Room dating from the 1740s, and several Victorian rooms. Outside, you can walk around the walled garden and topiary terraces, or explore the woods.

⛪ Penrith Castle (EH)
Ullswater Rd. ⭕ *daily.* ♿ *in grounds.*

🏯 Hutton-in-the-Forest
Off B5305. **Tel** 017684 84449. **House** ⭕ *Easter–Sep: Sun–Thu & public hols (pm).* **Grounds** ⭕ *Apr–Oct: Sun–Fri.* ⬤ *25 Dec.* 🅿 ♿ *limited.* 🛈 🛈

Dalemain ❸

Penrith, Cumbria. **Tel** 017684 86450. 🚌 🚇 *Penrith then taxi.* ⭕ *Mar–Oct: Sun–Thu.* 🅿 ♿ *limited.* 🎫 🛈 🛈 **www**.dalemain.com

A seemly Georgian façade gives this fine house near Ullswater the impression of architectural unity, but hides a much-altered medieval and Elizabethan structure with a maze of rambling passages. Public rooms include a superb Chinese drawing room with

---

TRADITIONAL CUMBRIAN SPORTS

Cumberland wrestling is one of the most interesting sports to watch in the summer months. The combatants, often clad in longjohns and embroidered velvet pants, clasp one another in an armlock and attempt to topple each other over. Technique and good balance outweigh physical force. Other traditional Lakeland sports include fell-racing, a gruelling test of speed and stamina up and down local peaks at ankle-breaking speed. Hound-trailing is also a popular sport in which specially bred hounds follow an aniseed trail over the hills. Sheep-dog trials, steam fairs, flower shows and gym-khanas take place in summer. The Egremont Crab Fair in September holds events such as greasy-pole climbing.

Cumberland wrestlers

Sheep resting at Glenridding, on the southwest shore of Ullswater

hand-painted wallpaper, and a panelled 18th-century drawing room. Several small museums occupy various outbuildings, and the gardens contain a fine collection of fragrant shrub roses and a huge silver fir.

Sumptuous Chinese drawing room at Dalemain

Ullswater **4**

Cumbria. 🚂 Penrith. 🚹 Main car park, Glenridding, Penrith (017684 82414). www.lake-district.gov.uk

Often considered the most beautiful of all Cumbria's lakes, Ullswater stretches from gentle farmland near Penrith to dramatic hills and crags at its southern end. The main western shore road can be very busy. In summer, two restored Victorian steamers ply

regularly from Pooley Bridge to Glenridding. One of the best walks crosses the eastern shore from Glenridding to Hallin Fell and the moorland of Martindale. The western side passes Gowbarrow, where Wordsworth's immortalized "host of golden daffodils" bloom in spring (see p366).

Keswick **5**

Cumbria. 🏘 5,000. 🚹 Moot Hall, Market Sq (017687 72645). www.keswick.org

Popular as a tourist venue since the advent of the railway in Victorian times, Keswick now has guest houses, a summer repertory theatre, outdoor equipment shops and a serious parking problem in high season. Its most striking central building is the **Moot Hall**, dating from 1813, now used as the tourist office. The town prospered on wool and leather until, in Tudor times, deposits of graphite were discovered. Mining then took over as the main industry and Keswick became an important centre for pencil manufacture. In World War II, hollow pencils were made to hide espionage maps on thin paper. The factory includes the **Pencil Museum** with

interesting audiovisual shows. Among the many fine exhibits at the **Keswick Museum and Art Gallery** are the original manuscripts of Lakeland writers, musical stones and many other curiosities.

To the east of the town lies the ancient stone circle of Castlerigg, thought to be older than Stonehenge.

🏛 **Pencil Museum**
Carding Mill Lane. **Tel** 017687 73626. ◯ daily. ● 25, 26 Dec, 1 Jan. 📷 ♿ 🚻 www.pencil.co.uk

🏛 **Keswick Museum and Art Gallery**
Fitz Park, Station Rd. **Tel** 017687 73263. ◯ call for details. 📷 ♿ 🚻

Outdoor equipment shop in Keswick

Northern Fells and Lakes ❻

The rare red squirrel, native to the area

Many visitors praise this northern area of the Lake District National Park for its scenery and geological interest *(see pp352–3)*. It is ideal walking country, and nearby Derwentwater, Thirlmere and Bassenthwaite provide endless scenic views, rambles and opportunities for watersports. Large areas surrounding the regional centre of Keswick *(see p359)* are accessible only on foot, particularly the huge mass of hills known as Back of Skiddaw – located between Skiddaw and Caldbeck – or the Helvellyn range, east of Thirlmere.

The Whinlatter Pass is an easy route from Keswick to the farmland of Lorton Vale. It gives good view of Bassenthwaite Lake and a glimpse of Grisedale Pike

Bassenthwaite is best viewed from the east shore; however accessibility is limited. Park is easier from the west s

Lorton Vale
The lush, green farmland south of Cockermouth creates a marked contrast with the more rugged mountain landscapes of the central Lake District. In the village of Low Lorton is the private manor house of Lorton Hall, dating from the 15th century.

Derwentwater
Surrounded by woodland slopes and fells, this attractive oval lake is dotted with tiny islands. One of these was inhabited by St Herbert, a disciple of St Cuthbert (see p419), who lived there as a hermit until 687. A boat from Keswick provides a lake excursion.

THE MAJOR PEAKS

The Lake District hills are the highest in England. Although they seem small by Alpine or world standards, the scale of the surrounding terrain makes them look extremely grand. Some of the most important peaks are shown on the following pages. Each peak is regarded as having its own personality. This section shows the Skiddaw fells, which are north of Keswick.

KEY

▬ From ① Blencathra to ② Cockermouth *(see opposite)*

▬ From ③ Grisedale Pike to ④ the Old Man of Coniston *(see pp362–3)*

▬ From ⑤ the Old Man of Coniston to ⑥ Windermere and Tarn Crag *(see pp364–5)*

— National Park boundary

Skiddaw
*At 931 m (3,054 ft) Skiddaw is England's
fourth highest peak. Its rounded shape
makes it a four- to five-hour walk for anyone reasonably fit and suitably equipped.*

Blencathra, also
known as Saddleback
because of its twin
peaks (868 m; 2,847 ft),
is a challenging climb,
especially in winter.

St John's in the Vale
*This valley contains Castle
Rock for climbers, and its
old legends were used by
Sir Walter Scott (see
p512) in* The Bridal
of Triermain. *Lakeland
poet John Richardson is
buried in the churchyard.*

Mosedale

BLENCATHRA OR
SADDLEBACK

868 m
2,847 ft

A66
PENRITH

River Glenderamackin

Glenderaterra beck

Legburthwaite

Thirlmere
was created
as a reservoir
to serve
Manchester
in 1879.

THIRLMERE

DERMERE

Castlerigg Stone Circle
*Described by Keats (see p123) as "a dismal
cirque of Druid stones upon a forlorn
moor", these ancient stones overlook
Skiddaw, Helvellyn and Crag Hill.*

KEY
ℹ️ Information
━ Major road
━ Minor road
⁂ Viewpoint

0 kilometres 5
0 miles 3

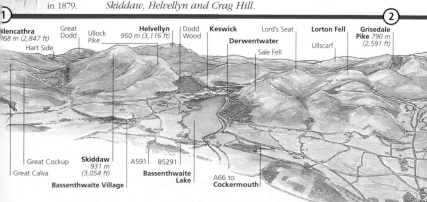

Blencathra
868 m (2,847 ft)
Hart Side
Great Dodd
Ullock Pike
Helvellyn 950 m (3,116 ft)
Dodd Wood
Keswick
Derwentwater
Lord's Seat
Sale Fell
Ullscarf
Lorton Fell
Grisedale Pike 790 m (2,591 ft)

Great Cockup
Great Calva
Skiddaw 931 m (3,054 ft)
Bassenthwaite Village
A591 B5291
Bassenthwaite Lake
A66 to **Cockermouth**

Crummock Water, one of the quieter "western lakes"

Cockermouth 𝟟

Cumbria. 🏠 *8,000.* 🚊
Workington. 🚌 **ℹ** *Town Hall,
Market St (01900 822634).*
www.western-lakedistrict.co.uk

Colourwashed terraces and
restored workers' cottages
beside the river are especially
attractive in the busy market
town of Cockermouth, which
dates from the 12th century.
The place not to miss is the
handsome **Wordsworth
House**, in the Main Street,
where the poet was born *(see
p366).* This fine Georgian

building still contains a few of
the family's possessions, and
is furnished in the style of the
late 18th century. Wordsworth
mentions the attractive
terraced garden, which overlooks the River Derwent, in
his *Prelude.* The local parish
church contains a Wordsworth
memorial window.

Cockermouth **castle** is partly
ruined but still inhabited and
closed to the public. The town
has small museums of printing,
toys and a mineral collection,
and an art gallery. The
Jennings Brewery invites
visitors for tours and tastings.

🏛 Wordsworth House
(NT) Main St. *Tel 01900 820884.* ☐
Mar–Oct: Mon–Sat. 🈺 *non-members.*
☐ **www**.wordsworthhouse.org.uk

🍺 Jennings Brewery
Castle Brewery. *Tel 0845 1297190.*
☐ *Mon–Sat (Jul, Aug: daily).* 🍺
☐ **www**.jenningsbrewery.co.uk

Newlands Valley 𝟠

Cumbria. 🚊 *Workington then bus.* 🚌
Cockermouth. **ℹ** *Town Hall, Market
St, Cockermouth (01900 822634);
Market Sq, Keswick (017687 72645).*
www.lake-district.gov.uk

From the gently wooded
shores of Derwentwater, the
Newlands Valley runs through
a scattering of farms towards
rugged heights of 335 m
(1,100 ft) at the top of the
pass, where steps lead
to the waterfall, Moss Force.
Grisedale Pike, Grasmoor
and Knott Rigg all provide
excellent fell walks. Local
mineral deposits of copper,
graphite, lead and even small
amounts of gold and silver
were extensively mined here
from Elizabethan times
onwards. **Little Town** was
used as a setting by Beatrix
Potter *(see p367)* in *The Tale
of Mrs Tiggywinkle.*

Kitchen, with an old range and tiled floor, at Wordsworth House

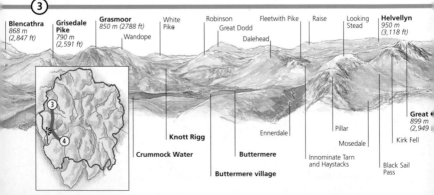

③

Blencathra
*868 m
(2,847 ft)*

**Grisedale
Pike**
*790 m
(2,591 ft)*

Grasmoor
850 m (2788 ft)

Wandope

White
Pike

Knott Rigg

Crummock Water

Robinson

Great Dodd

Dalehead

Fleetwith Pike

Ennerdale

Buttermere

Buttermere village

Raise

Pillar

Innominate Tarn
and Haystacks

Mosedale

Looking
Stead

Helvellyn
*950 m
(3,118 ft)*

Great ●
*899 m
(2,949*

Kirk Fell

Black Sail
Pass

Buttermere ❾

Cumbria. 🚆 *Penrith.* 🚌 *Cocker-mouth.* 🚌 *Penrith to Keswick; Keswick to Buttermere.* ℹ️ *Town Hall, Market St, Cockermouth (01900 822634).*

Interlinking with Crummock Water and Loweswater, Buttermere and its surroundings contain some of the most appealing countryside in the region. Often known as the "western lakes", the three are remote enough not to become too crowded. Buttermere is a jewel amid grand fells: High Stile, Red Pike and Haystacks. Here the ashes of the celebrated hill-walker and author of fell-walking books, A W Wainwright, are scattered.

The village of Buttermere, with its handful of houses and inns, is a popular starting point for walks round all three lakes. Loweswater is hardest to reach and therefore the quietest, surrounded by woods and hills. Nearby Scale Force is the highest waterfall in the Lake District, plunging 36 m (120 ft).

Verdant valley of Borrowdale, a favourite with artists

Borrowdale ❿

Cumbria. 🚆 *Workington.* 🚌 *Cockermouth.* ℹ️ *Town Hall, Market St, Cockermouth (01900 822634).*

This romantic valley, subject of a myriad sketches and watercolours before photography stole the scene, lies beside the densely wooded shores of Derwentwater

under towering crags. It is a popular trip from Keswick and a great variety of walks are possible along the valley.

The tiny hamlet of **Grange** is one of the prettiest spots, where the valley narrows dramatically to form the "Jaws of Borrowdale". Nearby Castle Crag has superb views.

From Grange you can complete the circuit of Derwentwater along the western shore, or move southwards to the more open farmland around Seatoller. As you head south by road, look out for a National Trust sign *(see p29)* to the **Bowder Stone**, a delicately poised block weighing nearly 2,000 tonnes, which may have fallen from the crags above or been deposited by a glacier millions of years ago.

Two attractive hamlets in Borrowdale are **Rosthwaite** and **Stonethwaite**. Also worth a detour, preferably on foot, is Watendlath village, off a side road near the famous beauty spot of **Ashness Bridge**.

WALKING IN THE LAKE DISTRICT

Typical Lake District stile over dry-stone wall

Two long-distance footpaths pass through the Lake District's most spectacular scenery. The 70 mile (110 km) Cumbrian Way runs from Carlisle to Ulverston via Keswick and Coniston. The western section of the Coast-to-Coast Walk *(see pp36–7)* passes through this area. There are hundreds of shorter walks along lake shores, nature trails or following more challenging uphill routes. Walkers should stick to paths to avoid erosion, and check weather conditions at National Park information centres.

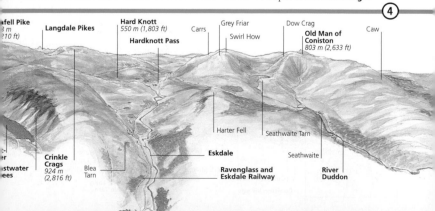

fell Pike	Langdale Pikes	Hard Knott 550 m (1,803 ft)	Carrs	Grey Friar	Dow Crag	Caw
8 m 10 ft)		Hardknott Pass		Swirl How	Old Man of Coniston 803 m (2,633 ft)	

Harter Fell   Seathwaite Tarn

Eskdale   Seathwaite

:-   Crinkle Crags 924 m (2,816 ft)   Blea Tarn   Ravenglass and Eskdale Railway   River Duddon

stwater ees

④

Convivial Wasdale Head Inn at Wasdale Head

Wastwater ⓫

Cumbria. ⊠ *Whitehaven.* ℹ *12 Main St, Egremont (01946 820693).*

A silent reflection of truly awesome surroundings, black, brooding **Wastwater** is a mysterious, evocative lake. The road from Nether Wasdale continues along its northwest side. Along its eastern flank loom walls of sheer scree over 600 m (2,000 ft) high. Beneath them the water looks inky black, whatever the weather, plunging an icy 80 m (260 ft) from the waterline to the bottom to form England's deepest lake. You can walk along the screes, but it is an uncomfortable and dangerous scramble. Boating on the lake is banned for conservation reasons, but fishing permits are available from the nearby National Trust camp site.

At **Wasdale Head** lies one of Britain's grandest views: the austere pyramid of **Great Gable**, centrepiece of a fine mountain composition, with

the huge forms of Scafell and **Scafell Pike**. The scenery is utterly unspoilt, and the only buildings lie at the far end of the lake: an inn and a tiny church commemorating fallen climbers. Here the road ends, and you must turn back or take to your feet, following signs for Black Sail Pass and Ennerdale, or walk up the grand fells ahead. Wasdale's irresistible backdrop was the inspiration of the first serious British mountaineers, who flocked here during the 19th century, insouciantly clad in tweed jackets, carrying little more than a length of rope slung over their shoulders.

Eskdale ⓬

Cumbria. ⊠ *Ravenglass then narrow-gauge railway to Eskdale (Easter–Oct: daily; Dec–Feb: phone to check).* ℹ *12 Main St, Egremont (01946 820693).* **www**.eskdale.info.co.uk

The pastoral delights of Eskdale are best encountered over the gruelling **Hardknott**

Pass, which is the most taxing drive in the Lake District, with steep gradients. You can pause at the 393-m (1,291-ft) summit to explore the Roman **Hardknott Fort** or enjoy the lovely view. As you descend into Eskdale, rhododendrons and pines flourish in a landscape of small hamlets, narrow lanes and gentle farmland. The main settlements below are the attractive village of Boot and coastal Ravenglass, both with old corn mills.

Just south of Ravenglass is the impressive **Muncaster Castle**, the richly furnished home of the Pennington family. Another way to enjoy the scenery is to take the miniature railway (La'l Ratty) from Ravenglass to Dalegarth.

⚓ **Muncaster Castle**
Ravenglass. **Tel** *01229 717614.*
Castle ◯ *mid-Feb–mid-Nov: Sun–Fri (pm) & public hols.*
Garden ◯ *daily.* 🏠 🍴 🅿 ♿ *ground floor and garden.* 🖼
www.muncaster.co.uk

Remains of the Roman Hardknott Fort, Eskdale

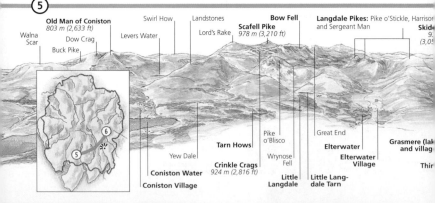

⑤

Walna Scar

Old Man of Coniston
803 m (2,633 ft)

Dow Crag
Buck Pike

Levers Water

Swirl How

Landstones

Lord's Rake

Scafell Pike
978 m (3,210 ft)

Bow Fell

Langdale Pikes: Pike o'Stickle, Harrison and Sergeant Man

Skid
9.
(3,05

⑥

⑤

Yew Dale

Pike o'Blisco

Tarn Hows

Coniston Water

Crinkle Crags
924 m (2,816 ft)

Wrynose Fell

Little Langdale

Great End

Elterwater

Little Lang-
dale Tarn

Elterwater Village

Grasmere (lak and villag

Thir

Coniston Village

Autumnal view of Seathwaite, in the Duddon Valley, a popular centre for walkers and climbers

Duddon Valley ⑬

Cumbria. 🚊 *Foxfield, Ulverston.*
🛈 *The Square, Broughton-in-Furness
(01229 716115; Easter–Oct only).*
www.lakelandgateway.info

Also known as Dunnerdale,
this picturesque tract of
countryside inspired 35 of
Wordsworth's sonnets *(see
p366)*. The prettiest stretch lies
between Ulpha and Cockley
Beck. In autumn the colours
of heather moors and a light
sprinkling of birch trees are
particularly beautiful. Stepping
stones and bridges span the
river at intervals, the most
charming being Birk's Bridge,
near Seathwaite. At the southern end of the valley, where

the River Duddon meets the
sea at Duddon Sands, is the
pretty village of Broughton-
in-Furness. Note the stone
slabs used for fish on market
day in the square.

Langdale ⑭

Cumbria. 🚊 *Windermere.* 🛈 *Market
Cross, Ambleside (015394 32582).*
www.lakelandgateway.info

Stretching from Skelwith
Bridge, where the Brathay
surges powerfully over waterfalls, to the summits of Great
Langdale is the two-pronged
Langdale Valley. Walkers and
climbers throng here to take
on **Pavey Ark, Pike o'Stickle,**

Crinkle Crags and **Bow Fell**.
The local mountain rescue
teams are the busiest in Britain.
   Great Langdale is the more
spectacular valley and it is
often crowded, but quieter
Little Langdale has many
attractions too. It is worth
completing the circuit back to
Ambleside via the southern
route, stopping at Blea Tarn.
Reedy **Elterwater** is a picturesque spot, once a site of the
gunpowder industry. Wrynose
Pass, west of Little Langdale,
climbs to 390 m (1,281 ft), a
warm-up for Hardknott Pass
further on. At its top is Three
Shires Stone, marking the
former boundary of the old
counties of Cumberland,
Westmorland and Lancashire.

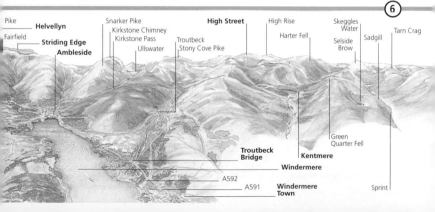

Rydal Water, one of the major attractions of the Lake District

Grasmere and Rydal ⑮

Cumbria. **Grasmere** 🏔 700.
Rydal 🏔 100. 🚃 Grasmere.
🛈 Redbank Rd, Grasmere (015394
35245). **www**.lake-district.gov.uk

The poet William Wordsworth lived in both these pretty villages on the shores of two sparkling lakes. Fairfield, Nab Scar and Loughrigg Fell rise steeply above their reedy shores and offer good opportunities for walking. Grasmere is now a sizable settlement and the famous Grasmere sports *(see p358)* attract large crowds every August.

The Wordsworth family is buried in St Oswald's Church, and crowds flock to the annual ceremony of strewing the church's earth floor with fresh rushes. Most visitors head for **Dove Cottage**, where the poet spent his most creative years. The museum in the barn behind includes such artefacts as the great man's socks. The Wordsworths moved to a larger house, **Rydal Mount**, in

Rydal in 1813 and lived here until 1850. The grounds have waterfalls and a summerhouse. Dora's Field nearby is a blaze of daffodils in spring and Fairfield Horseshoe offers an energetic, challenging walk.

🏛 **Dove Cottage and the Wordsworth Museum**
Off A591 nr Grasmere. **Tel** 015394
35544. ⬜ daily. ⬤ 24–26 Dec,
mid-Jan–mid-Feb. 🎫 🗐 🖥 🛈
www.wordsworth.org.uk

🏛 **Rydal Mount**
Rydal. **Tel** 015394 33002. ⬜ Mar–
Oct: daily; Nov–Feb: Wed–Mon. ⬤
Dec & Jan. 🎫 🔊 limited. 🛈

Ambleside ⑯

Cumbria. 🏔 3,400. 🚃 🛈 Central
Buildings, Market Cross (015394
32582). 🛒 Wed.
www.lakelandgateway.info

Ambleside has good road connections to all parts of the Lakes and is an attractive base, especially for walkers and climbers. Mainly Victorian in character, it has a good range of outdoor clothing, crafts and specialist food shops. An enterprising little cinema and a summer classical music festival add life in the evenings. Sights in town are small-scale: the remnants of the Roman fort of Galava, AD 79, Stock Ghyll Force waterfall and **Bridge House**, now a National Trust information centre.

Environs: Within easy reach are the wooded Rothay valley and **Touchstone Interiors** at Skelwith Bridge, with their contemporary design products. At nearby Troutbeck is the restored farmhouse of **Townend**, dating from 1626,

The tiny Bridge House over Stock Beck in Ambleside

WILLIAM WORDSWORTH (1770–1850)

Best known of the Romantic poets, Wordsworth was born in the Lake District and spent most of his life there. After school in Hawkshead and a period at Cambridge, a legacy enabled him to pursue his literary career. He settled at Dove Cottage with his sister Dorothy and in 1802 married an old school friend, Mary Hutchinson. They lived simply, walking, bringing up their children and receiving visits from poets such as Coleridge and de Quincey. Wordsworth's prose works include one of the earliest guidebooks to the Lake District.

BEATRIX POTTER AND THE LAKE DISTRICT

Although best known for her children's stories with characters such as Peter Rabbit and Jemima Puddleduck, which she also illustrated, Beatrix Potter (1866–1943) became a champion of conservation in the Lake District after moving there in 1906. She married William Heelis, devoted herself to farming, and was an expert on Herdwick sheep. To conserve her beloved countryside, she donated land to the National Trust.

Cover illustration of *Jemima Puddleduck* (1908)

whose interior gives an insight into Lakeland domestic life.

🏛 Touchstone Interiors
Skelwith Bridge. *Tel 015394 34002.*
⬜ *daily.* ⬤ *24–26 Dec.* 🔲 🔲 🔲

🏛 Townend
(NT) Troutbeck, Windermere. *Tel 015394 32628.* ⬜ *Apr–Oct: Wed–Sun, Sun & bank hol Mon; pm.* 🔲

Windermere ⑰

Cumbria. 🚋 *Windermere.* 🚌 *Victoria St.* 🅸 *Victoria St (015394 46499)* or *Glebe Rd, Bowness-on-Windermere (015394 42895).* **www**.lakelandgateway.info

At over 10 miles (16 km) long, this dramatic watery expanse is England's largest mere. Industrial magnates built mansions around its shores long before the railway arrived. Stately **Brockhole**, now a national park visitor centre, was one such grand estate. When the railway reached Windermere in 1847, it enabled crowds of workers to visit the area on day trips.

Today, a year-round car ferry service connects the lake's east and west shores (it runs between Ferry Nab and Ferry House), and summer steamers link Lakeside, Bowness and Ambleside on the north-south axis. Belle Isle, a wooded island on which a unique round house stands, is one of the lake's most attractive features, but landing is not permitted. **Fell Foot Park** is at the south end of the lake, and there are good walks on the northwest shore. A quite stunning viewpoint is Orrest Head 238 m (784 ft) northeast of Windermere town.

Environs: Bowness-on-Windermere, on the east shore, is a hugely popular centre. Many of its buildings display Victorian details, and St Martin's Church dates back to the 15th century. The **Windermere Steamboat Museum** has a collection of superbly restored craft, and one of these, *Swallow*, makes regular lake trips. The **World of Beatrix Potter** recreates her characters in an exhibition, and a film tells her life story.

Beatrix Potter wrote many of her books at **Hill Top**, the 17th-century farmhouse at Near Sawrey, northwest of Windermere. Hill Top is furnished with many of Potter's possessions, and left as it was in her lifetime. The **Beatrix Potter Gallery** in Hawkshead holds annual exhibitions of her manuscripts and illustrations.

🅸 Brockhole Visitor Centre
On A591. *Tel 015394 46601.*
⬜ *Apr–Oct: daily.* 🔲 🔲 🔲

♣ Fell Foot Park
(NT) Newby Bridge. *Tel 015395 31273.* ⬜ *daily.* 🔲 🔲

🏛 Windermere Steamboat Museum
Rayrigg Rd, Windermere. *Tel 015394 45565.* ⬜ *late Mar–Nov: daily.* 🔲
🔲 🔲 🔲 🔲

🏛 World of Beatrix Potter
The Old Laundry, Crag Brow. *Tel 015394 88444.* ⬜ *daily.* ⬤ *25 Dec, last three wks in Jan.* 🔲 🔲 🔲 🔲 *limited.* **www**.hop-skip-jump.com

🎪 Hill Top
(NT) Near Sawrey, Ambleside. *Tel 015394 36269.* ⬜ *Apr–Oct: Sat–Wed.* 🔲 🔲

🏛 Beatrix Potter Gallery
(NT) The Square, Hawkshead. *Tel 015394 36355.* ⬜ *Apr–Oct: Sat–Wed.* 🔲 🔲

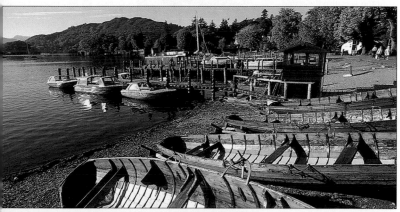

Boats moored along the shore at Ambleside, the north end of Windermere

Peaceful Coniston Water, the setting of Arthur Ransome's novel, *Swallows and Amazons* (1930)

Coniston Water ⑱

Cumbria. 🚆 *Windermere then bus.* 🚌 *Ambleside then bus.* ℹ️ *Coniston car park, Ruskin Ave (015394 41533).* **www**.coniston-net.com

For the finest view of this stretch of water just outside the Lake District, you need to climb. The 19th-century art critic, writer and philosopher John Ruskin, had a fine view from his house, **Brantwood**, where his paintings and memorabilia can be seen today. Contemporary art exhibitions and events take place throughout the year.

An enjoyable excursion is the summer lake trip from Coniston Pier on the National Trust steam yacht, *Gondola*, calling at Brantwood. Coniston was also the scene of Donald Campbell's fatal attempt on the world water speed record in 1967. The green slate village of Coniston, once a centre for copper-mining, now caters for local walkers.

Also interesting is the traffic-free village of **Hawkshead** to the northwest, with its quaint alleyways and timber-framed houses. To the south is the vast Grizedale Forest, dotted with woodland sculptures.

Just north of Coniston Water is the man-made **Tarn Hows**, a landscaped tarn surrounded by woods. There is a pleasant climb up the 803 m (2,635 ft) Old Man of Coniston.

🏛 Brantwood

Off B5285, nr Coniston. **Tel** *015394 41396.* 🕐 *mid-Mar–mid-Nov: daily; mid-Nov–mid-Mar: Wed–Sun.* 📷 🍴 🖥 📷 **www**.brantwood.org.uk

Kendal ⑲

Cumbria. 🏛 *26,000.* 🚆 ℹ️ *Town Hall, Highgate (01539 725758).* 🛒 *Wed & Sat.* **www**.kendaltown.org.uk

A busy market town, Kendal is the administrative centre of the region and the southern gateway to the Lake District. Built in grey limestone, it has an arts centre, the **Brewery**, and a central area which is best enjoyed on foot. **Abbot Hall**,

Kendal mint cake, the famous lake-land energy-booster for walkers

built in 1759, has paintings by Turner and Romney as well as Gillows furniture. In addition, the hall's stable block contains the **Museum of Lakeland Life**, with occasional lively workshops demonstrating local crafts and trades. There are dioramas of geology and wildlife in the **Museum of Natural History and Archaeology**. About 3 miles (5 km) south of the town is 14th-century

Sizergh Castle, with a fortified tower, carved fireplaces and a lovely garden.

🏛 Abbot Hall Art Gallery & Museum of Lakeland Life

Kendal. **Tel** *01539 722464.* 🕐 *mid-Jan–20 Dec: Mon–Sat.* 📷 ♿ *gallery.* 📷 *by arrangement.* 📷 📷 **www**.abbothall.org.uk

🏛 Kendal Museum of Natural History and Archaeology

Station Rd. **Tel** *01539 721374.* 🕐 *mid-Feb–24 Dec: Mon–Sat.* 📷 📷 **www**.kendalmuseum.org.uk

♣ Sizergh Castle

(NT) off A591 & A590. **Tel** *015395 60951.* 🕐 *Apr–Oct: Sun–Thu.* 📷 ♿ *ground floor & grounds.* 📷 📷

Furness Peninsula ⑳

Cumbria. 🚆 🚌 *Barrow-in-Furness.* ℹ️ *Forum 28, Duke St, Barrow-in-Furness (01229 894784).* **www**.barrowtourism.co.uk

Barrow-in-Furness *(see p349)* is the peninsula's main town. Its **Dock Museum**, built over a Victorian dock where ships were repaired, traces the history of Barrow using interactive computer displays.

Ruins of the red sandstone walls of **Furness Abbey** remain in the wooded Vale of Deadly Nightshade, with a small exhibition of monastic life. The historic town of Ulverston received its charter in 1280. **Ulverston Heritage**

Centre charts its development from market town to port. Stan Laurel, of Laurel and Hardy fame, was born here in 1890. His memorabilia **museum** has a cinema.

🏛 Dock Museum
North Rd, Barrow-in-Furness. *Tel 01229 894444.* ☐ *Easter–Oct: Tue–Sun; Nov–Easter: Wed–Sun (Sat, Sun: pm); public hols.* ♿ ☐ ☐ www.dockmuseum.org.uk

🏛 Furness Abbey
Vale of Deadly Nightshade. *Tel 01229 823420.* ☐ *Easter–Sep: daily; Oct–Easter: Thu–Mon.* ● *24–26 Dec, 1 Jan.* ☐ ▨ ♿ *limited.*

🏛 Ulverston Heritage Centre
Sir John Barrow Cottage. *Tel 01229 583811.* ☐ *Sat & Sun.* ● *25 & 26 Dec, 1 Jan.* ☐ ▨ ♿ *limited.*

🏛 Laurel and Hardy Museum
Upper Brook St, Ulverston. *Tel 01229 582292.* ☐ *daily.* ● *25 Dec; Jan.* ▨ ♿

Staircase at Holker Hall

Cartmel ㉑

Cumbria. 🏠 *700.* 🚉 *Main St, Grange-over-Sands (015395 34026).* www.grangetic@southlakeland.gov.uk

The highlight of this pretty village is its 12th-century **priory**, one of the finest Cumbrian churches. Little

remains of the original priory except the gatehouse in the village centre. The restored church has an attractive east window, a stone-carved 14th-century tomb, and beautiful misericords.

Cartmel also boasts a small racecourse. The village has given its name to its surroundings, a hilly district of green farmland with mixed woodland and limestone scars.

A major local attraction is **Holker Hall**, former residence of the Dukes of Devonshire. Inside are lavishly furnished rooms, with fine marble fireplaces, and a superb oak staircase. Outside are stunning gardens and a deer park.

🏰 Holker Hall
Cark-in-Cartmel. *Tel 015395 58328.* ☐ *Mar–Oct: Sun–Fri.* ▨ ♿ *limited.* 🎧 *by arrangement.* ☐ ☐ www.holker-hall.co.uk

Levens Hall ㉒

Nr Kendal, Cumbria. *Tel 015395 60321.* 🚌 *from Kendal or Lancaster.* ☐ *Apr–mid-Oct: Sun–Thu.* ☐ ▨ ♿ *gardens only.* ☐ www.levenshall.co.uk

The outstanding attraction of this Elizabethan mansion is its topiary, but the house itself has much to offer. Built around a 13th-century tower, it contains a fine collection of

Jacobean furniture and watercolours by Peter de Wint (1784–1849). Also of note are the ornate ceilings, Charles II dining chairs, the earliest example of English patchwork and the gilded hearts on the drainpipes.

The 18th-century Turret Clock has a single hand, a common design of the period.

Main entrance

The yew and box topiary was designed in 1694 by French horticulturist Guillaume Beaumont.

Over 300 years old, the garden's box-edged beds are filled with colourful herbaceous displays.

Box hedges were a common component of geometrically designed gardens of this period.

The complex topiary, shaped into cones, spirals and pyramids, is kept in shape by gardeners. Some specimens are 6 m (20 ft) high.

Morecambe Bay, looking northwest towards Barrow-in-Furness

Morecambe Bay ㉓

Lancs. 🚆 Morecambe. ⛴ Heysham
(to Isle of Man). ℹ️ Marine Rd. (01524
582808). www.lancaster.gov.uk

The best way to explore
Morecambe Bay is by train
from Ulverston to Arnside.
The track follows a series of
low viaducts across a huge
expanse of glistening tidal
flats where thousands of
wading birds feed and breed.
The bay is one of the most
important bird reservations in
the country. On the Cumbrian
side of the bay, retirement
homes have expanded the
sedate Victorian resort of
Grange-over-Sands, which
grew up after the arrival of
the railway in 1857. Nearby,
Hampsfield Fell and
Humphrey Head Point give
fine views along the bay.

Leighton Hall ㉔

Carnforth, Lancashire. **Tel** 01524 734
474. 🚌 to Yealand Conyers (from
Lancaster). ◯ May–Jul & Sep: 2–5pm
Tue–Fri & bank hols; Aug: noon–5pm
Sun, Tue–Fri & bank hols. 🎫 ♿
ground floor only. 📷 🖥 🅿️
www.leightonhall.co.uk

Leighton Hall's estate dates
back to the 13th century,
but most of the building is
19th-century, including its
Neo-Gothic façade. It is
owned by the Gillow family, of
the Lancastrian furniture business, whose products are
now prized antiques. Excellent pieces can be seen here,
including a ladies' work-box
inlaid with biblical scenes. In
the afternoon, weather
permitting, the hall's large
collection of birds of prey
display their aerial prowess.

Lancaster ㉕

Lancashire. 🏠 50,000. 🚆
🚌 ℹ️ Castle Hill (01524
32878). 🛒 Mon–Sat.
www.lancaster.gov.uk

This county town
of Lancashire is
tiny compared to
Liverpool or
Manchester
(now counties
in their own
right), but it
has a long history.
The Romans named it after
their camp over the River Lune.
Originally a defensive site, it
developed into a prosperous
port largely on the proceeds
of the slave trade. Today, its
university and cultural life still
thrive. The Norman **Lancaster
Castle** was expanded in the
14th and 16th centuries. It has
been a crown court and a
prison since the 13th century.
The Shire Hall is decorated
with 600 heraldic shields.
Some fragments from
Hadrian's Tower (which has a
collection of torture instruments) are 2,000 years old.

The nearby priory church
of **St Mary** is on Castle Hill.
Its main features include a
Saxon doorway and carved
14th-century choir stalls. There
is an outstanding museum of
furniture in the 17th-century
Judge's Lodgings, while the
Maritime Museum, in the
Georgian custom house
on St George's Quay,
contains displays on the
port's history. The **City
Museum**, based in the
old town hall, concen-
trates on the history
of Lancaster.

The splendid **Lune
Aqueduct** carries the
canal over the
River Lune on
five wide arches.
Other attractions
are found in
**Williamson
Park**, site of

Tawny eagle at
Leighton Hall

the 1907 Ashton Memorial.
This folly was built by the
local linoleum magnate and
politician, Lord Ashton.

CROSSING THE SANDS

Morecambe Bay sands are very dangerous. Travellers used to
cut across the bay at low tide to shorten the long trail around
the Kent estuary. Many perished as they were caught by
rising tides or quicksand, and sea fogs hid the paths. Locals
who knew the bay became guides, and today you can travel
with a guide from Kents Bank to Hest Bank near Arnside.

The High Sheriff of Lancaster Crossing Morecambe Sands (anon)

There are fine views from the top of this 67 m (220 ft) domed structure. Opposite is the tropical butterfly house and the pavilion café.

♣ Lancaster Castle
Castle Parade. **Tel** *01524 64998.* ☐ daily. ● mid-Dec–early Jan. ☐ only (limited when court is in session).
☐ www.lancastercastle.com

🏛 Judge's Lodgings
Church St. **Tel** *01524 32808.* ☐ Apr–Jun, Oct: daily (Sat, Sun: pm only); Jul–Sep: daily. ● Nov–Good Fri. 📷 🅿

🏛 Maritime Museum
Custom House, St George's Quay. **Tel** *01524 64637.* ☐ daily (Nov–Easter: pm). ● 24–26, 31 Dec, 1 Jan. 📷 ♿
☐ 🅿 www.nettingthebay.org.uk

🏛 City Museum
Market Sq. **Tel** *01524 64637.* ☐ Mon–Sat. ● 24 Dec–2 Jan. ♿ 🅿

♣ Williamson Park
Wyresdale Rd. **Tel** *01524 33318.* ☐ daily. 📷 ♿ limited. 🅿 🅿
www.williamsonpark.com

Ribble Valley ㉖

Lancashire. 🚉 *Clitheroe.* 🛈 *Market Place, Clitheroe (01200 425566).* 🗓 *Tue, Thu, Sat.*
www.ribblevalley.gov.uk

Clitheroe, a small market town with a hilltop castle, is a good centre for exploring the Ribble Valley's rivers and old villages, such as Slaidburn. Ribchester has a **Roman Museum**, and there is a ruined **Cistercian abbey** at Whalley. To the east is 560 m (1,830 ft) Pendle Hill, with a Bronze Age burial mound at its peak.

🏛 Roman Museum
Ribchester. **Tel** *01254 878261.* ☐ daily. 📷 ♿ 🅿 by arrangement. 🅿

♙ Whalley Abbey
Whalley. **Tel** *01254 828400.* ☐ daily. ● 24 Dec–2 Jan. 📷 ♿ 🅿 🅿
www.whalleyabbey.org

Blackpool ㉗

Lancashire. 🏙 *150,000.* ✈ 🚉 🚌
🛈 *Clifton St (01253 478222).*
www.visitblackpool.com

British holiday patterns have changed in the past few decades, and Blackpool is no longer the apogee of seaside entertainment, but it remains a

Coming from the Mill (1930) by L S Lowry *(See p375)*

unique experience. A wall of amusement arcades, piers, bingo halls and fast-food stalls stretch behind the sands. At night, entertainers strut their stuff under the bright lights. The town attracts thousands of visitors in September and October when the Illuminations trace the skeleton of the 158 m (518 ft) Blackpool Tower. Blackpool's resort life dates back to the 18th century, but it burst into prominence when the railway first arrived in 1840, bringing Lancastrian workers to their holiday resort.

Blackpool Tower, painted gold for its centenary in 1994

Salford Quays ㉘

Salford. 🚊 *Harbour City (from Manchester).* 🛈 *The Lowry, Pier 8 (0161 848 8601).* www.visitsalford.com

The Quays, to the west of Manchester city centre (15 minutes by tram), were once the terminal docks for the **Manchester Ship Canal**. However, after the docks closed in 1982, the area became sadly run down. Since the 1990s when a massive redevelopment plan was launched, all this has changed dramatically, with the creation of a world-class business, cultural and residential area of great architectural and regional significance. More people are now employed at the Quays than in its heyday as a major seaport.

There is a wealth of entertainment, leisure and cultural facilities on offer, including **The Lowry** *(see p375)*, the **Manchester United Museum** *(see p375)*, the **Imperial War Museum North** *(see p375)* and The Lowry Outlet Mall, as well as numerous bars, restaurants and shops. There are various water-based activities, with a specialized watersports centre on site, and ship-canal cruises for the more faint-hearted of visitors. The Quays was also a major venue for the Commonwealth Games in 2002, and has now established itself as host for the annual Triathlon World Cup.

Manchester 29

Sign for the John Rylands Library

Manchester dates back to Roman times, when in AD 79, Agricola set up a base called Mancunium. It rose to prominence in the late 18th century, when Richard Arkwright introduced cotton processing. By 1830, the first railway linked Manchester and Liverpool, and in 1894 the Manchester Ship Canal *(see p371)* opened, allowing cargo vessels inland. Civic buildings sprang up from the proceeds of cotton wealth, but these were in stark contrast to the slums of the mill-workers. Social discontent led writers, politicians and reformers to espouse liberal or radical causes.

The exploits of local football team Manchester United and the international success of bands such as The Smiths and The Stone Roses, gave Manchester a cachet of cool during the 1980s and 1990s. Devastation caused by an IRA car-bombing of the city centre in 1996 was seized as an opportunity to redevelop the main shopping areas. This regeneration has since spread to other areas of the city, notably the old dockside area of Salford Quays.

Urbis, an interactive attraction on life in cities

Exploring Manchester

Manchester is a fine, compact city with much to see in its central areas. The Victorian era of cotton wealth has gifted the city an imposing heritage of industrial architecture, much of which is providing sites for development. The former central railway station, for example, is now the **G-Mex Centre**, a huge exhibition and conference complex. Among other fine 19th-century buildings are the dramatic **John Rylands Library** on Deansgate, founded over 100 years ago by the widow of local cotton millionaire, and the 1856 Renaissance-styled **Free Trade Hall**, now the Radisson Edwardian hotel, which stands on the site of the Peterloo Massacre.

MANCHESTER CITY CENTRE

Free Trade Hall ①
G-Mex Centre ②
John Rylands Library ③
Manchester Art Gallery ⑦
Manchester Town Hall ④
Museum of Science and
   Industry in Manchester ⑧
Royal Exchange ⑤
Urbis ⑥

0 metres 250
0 yards 250

Key to Symbols *see back flap*

The Neo-Gothic Town Hall by Alfred Waterhouse

dedicated to the consort of Queen Victoria, which is similar in style but predates the one in London's Hyde Park.

🏛 Royal Exchange

St Ann's Square. **Tel** 0161 833 9833. ◯ Mon–Sat. ♿ ▣ 🛈 **www.royalexchange.co.uk**

Built in 1729, the Manchester Royal Exchange, as it was then known, was once claimed to be the "biggest room in the world". It was built as the main trading hall of the cotton industry and at the end of the 19th century it was reckoned that over 80 percent of world trade in cloth was controlled from these premises. During the Second World War the building was severely damaged by bombs. This coincided with the decline of the cotton trade in the United Kingdom and when the Exchange was rebuilt it was reduced to half its original size. The doors were finally closed to trading in 1968. A daring scheme saw the main hall converted into a theatre in the mid-1970s with the auditorium enclosed in a high-tech structure supported by the old building's

pillars; it nestles like a lunar module beneath the great dome. The rest of the Exchange building contains an arcade, shops and cafes.

🏛 Urbis

Cathedral Gdns. **Tel** 0161 605 8200. ◯ Tue–Sun & public hols. 🎫 for temporary exhibitions only. ♿ 🍴 ▣ 🛈 www.urbis.org.uk

The Urbis, opened in 2002, explores life around the world in different cities. It's housed in a striking ski slope-shaped glass building. The visit begins with a glass-elevator ride up the incline, then proceeds via an introductory film show down through three staggered floors of interactive exhibits.

The lower level houses temporary exhibitions on an urban theme, for which there is usually an admission fee. The interactive galleries, on levels two to four, explore the people, place and pulse of the modern city.

Across the plaza from Urbis is **Manchester Cathedral**, which largely dates from the 19th century but stands on a site that has been occupied by a church for over a millennium.

🏛 Manchester Town Hall

Albert Square. **Tel** 0161 234 5000. ◯ Mon–Fri. ♿

Manchester's majestic town hall was designed by Liverpool-born Alfred Waterhouse (1830–1905), an architect who would later find fame with his Natural History Museum in London. Waterhouse won the commission for the building in an architectural competition, his design finding favour for making best use of the awkward triangular site.

The building was completed in 1877 in an English Gothic style with its roots in the 13th century. Tours take place at 2pm every other Saturday but visitors can also explore the building on their own. Sign in inside the main entrance, where a statue of General Agricola, the Roman who founded Manchester in AD 79, looks down on passers-by. The highlight is the Great Hall adorned by 12 murals painted by Ford Maddox Brown, the celebrated Pre-Raphaelite painter.

Throughout the building the decoration includes numerous examples of cotton flowers and bees, the latter a symbol of Manchester's industriousness. In the square in front of the town hall is Manchester's **Albert Memorial**,

THE PETERLOO MASSACRE

In 1819, the working conditions of Manchester's factory workers were so bad that social tensions reached breaking point. On 16 August, 50,000 people assembled in St Peter's Field to protest at the oppressive Corn Laws. Initially peaceful, the mood darkened and the poorly trained mounted

troops panicked, charging the crowd with their sabres. Eleven were killed and many wounded. The incident was called Peterloo (the Battle of Waterloo had taken place in 1815). Reforms such as the Factory Act came in that year.

G Cruikshank's Peterloo Massacre cartoon

Museum of Science and Industry, set in old passenger railway buildings

🏛 Manchester Art Gallery

Mosley St & Princess St. **Tel** 0161 235 8888. ○ Tue–Sun. ● Mon (except Bank Holidays), 24–26, 31 Dec, 1 Jan, Good Fri. 🎨 & 🍽 🖵 🛈 www.manchestergalleries.org

The gallery reopened in summer 2002, doubling its display space after a £35 million makeover and a brand new extension by architect Sir Michael Hopkins. The original building was designed by Sir Charles Barry (1795–1860) in 1824, and contains an excellent collection of British art, notably Pre-Raphaelites such as Holman Hunt and Dante Gabriel Rossetti. Early Italian, Flemish and French Schools are also represented.

The gallery has a fine collection of decorative arts, from the Greeks to Picasso to contemporary craftworkers, in the Gallery of Craft & Design. There is also a changing programme of special exhibitions in two fantastic new galleries on the top floor. Most exhibitions are free and there is a programme of accompanying events for adults and families.

A new and lively space called the Clore Interactive Gallery offers a combination of real artworks and hands-on activities for children.

🏛 Museum of Science and Industry

Liverpool Rd. **Tel** 0161 832 2244. ○ daily. ● 24–26 Dec. & 🖵 🍽 🛈 www.msim.org.uk

One of the largest science museums in the world, the spirit of scientific enterprise and industrial might of Manchester's heyday is conveyed here. Among the best sections are the Power Hall, a collection of working steam engines, the Electricity Gallery, tracing the history of domestic power, and an exhibition on the Liverpool and Manchester Railway. A collection of planes that made flying history are displayed in the Air and Space Gallery.

🏛 Manchester Museum

Oxford Road. **Tel** 0161 275 2634, ○ daily. & 🍽 🖵 🛈 www.museum.man.ac.uk.

Part of Manchester University, this venerable museum (opened 1885) houses around six million items from all ages and all over the world, but it specializes in Egyptology and zoology. The collection of ancient Egyptian artefacts is one of the largest in the United Kingdom and numbers about 20,000 objects including monumental stone sculpture and a number of mummies, displayed together with their coffins and funerary

goods. There are also various sections that deal with funerary masks, tomb models and mummified animals. The zoological collections number over 600,000 objects, ranging from stuffed animals to a cast of one of the most complete skeletons of a T Rex dinosaur, which was added to the museum in November 2004.

The original museum building was designed by Alfred Water-house, the same architect responsible for the city's magnificent Town Hall *(see p373)*.

🏛 Whitworth Art Gallery

University of Manchester, Oxford Rd. **Tel** 0161 275 7450. ○ daily (Sun: pm). ● 24 Dec–2 Jan, Good Fri. & 🖵 🛈 www.whitworth.man.ac.uk

Jacob Epstein's Genesis, Whitworth Art Gallery

The Stockport-born machine tool manufacturer and engineer Sir Joseph Whitworth bequeathed money for this gallery, originally intended to be a museum of industrial art and design that would inspire the city's textile trade. Founded in 1889, it has been a part of the University of Manchester since 1958. The fine red-brick building is from the Edwardian period, while the modern interior dates from the 1960s.

The gallery houses a superb collection of drawings, sculpture, contemporary art, textiles and prints. Jacob Epstein's *Genesis* nude occupies the entrance, and there is an important collection of British watercolours by Turner *(see p91)*, Girtin and others. Look out for the Japanese woodcuts and the Collection of historic and modern wallpapers, built up from donations from wallpaper manufacturers, as well as through the gallery's active Collecting Policy.

There is a well-developed Education Department that organizes a full programme of activities for groups and individuals of all ages and abilities, for both formal and informal learning.

Lawrence Alma-Tadema, Etruscan Vase Painters, Manchester Art Gallery

Exterior of the Imperial War Museum North, designed by Daniel Libeskind to represent a globe shattered by conflict

⏛ Lowry Centre

Pier 8, Salford Quays. *Tel 0870 787 5788.* ⭘ *daily. Admission free, but donations requested.* ♿ 🍴 🖥 📷 **www**.thelowry.com.

On a prominent site beside the Manchester Ship Canal, the Lowry is a shimmering, silvery arts and entertainment complex that combines two theatres, a restaurant, terrace bars and cafes, art galleries and a shop.

The centre is named after celebrated reclusive artist Laurence Stephen Lowry (1887–1976), who was born locally and lived all his life in the Manchester area. A rent collector by day, in his leisure hours he painted cityscapes dominated by the smoking chimneys of industry beneath heavy soot filled skies.

However, he is most famous as a painter of "matchstick men", the term frequently applied to the crowds of slight and ghostly figures peopling his canvases. Some of Lowry's work is displayed in one of the galleries here; another hosts regularly changing temporary exhibitions. There is also a room where a 20-minute documentary "Meet Mr Lowry" is screened throughout the day.

The centre provides many facilities and activities for children, and is perfect for a family day out.

⏛ Imperial War Museum North

Trafford Wharf Road, Salford Quays. *Tel 0161 836 4000.* ⭘ *daily.* ⬤ *24– 26 Dec.* 🎫 ♿ 🍴 🖥 📷 **www**.iwm.org.uk.

This most striking piece of modern architecture comes courtesy of Daniel Libeskind, the architect nominated to design a replacement for New York's World Trade Centre. His Manchester building is a water-front collision of three great aluminium shards, representing a globe shattered by conflict. Inside, a vast, irregular space is used to display a small but well presented collection of military hardware and ephemera, with nine "silos" devoted to exhibits on people's experiences of war.

On the hour the lights are extinguished for an audio-visual display using the angled walls of the main hall.

As visitors leave they are invited to take the elevator up the 55-metre (180-ft) "Air Shard" for views over the city.

⏛ Manchester United Museum

Salford Quays. *Tel 0870 442 1994,* ⭘ *daily. Tours must be booked in advance.* 🎫 🖥 📷 🍴 **www**.manutd.com.

Premier League football (soccer) team Manchester United's ground Old Trafford also includes a purpose-built museum. In addition to the historic displays there is much interactive fun such as a chance to test your own penalty-taking skills.

The museum tour takes in the dressing rooms, the trophy room and the players' lounge and culminates in a walk down the tunnel tracing the route taken by players at every home game.

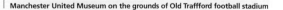

Manchester United Museum on the grounds of Old Traffford football stadium

Liverpool ⏱

Traces of settlement on Merseyside date back to the 1st century. In 1207 "Livpul", a fishing village, was granted a charter by King John. The population was only 1,000 in Stuart times, but during the 17th and 18th centuries Liverpool's westerly seaboard gave it a leading edge in the lucrative Caribbean slave trade. The first docks opened in 1715 and eventually stretched 7 miles (11 km) along the Mersey. Liverpool's first ocean steamer set out from here in 1840, and would-be emigrants to the New World poured into the city from Europe, including a flood of Irish refugees from the potato famine. Many settled permanently in Liverpool and a large, mixed community developed. Today, the port handles even greater volumes of cargoes than in the 1950s and 1960s, but container ships use Bootle docks. Despite economic and social problems, the irrepressible "Scouse" or Liverpudlian spirit re-emerged in the Swinging Sixties, when four local lads stormed the pop scene. Many people still visit Liverpool to pay homage to the Beatles, but the city is also known for its orchestra, the Liverpool Philharmonic, its sport (football and the Grand National steeplechase) and its universities.

Liver Bird on the Royal Liver Building

Victorian ironwork, restored and polished, at Albert Dock

Exploring Liverpool

Liverpool's waterfront by the Pier Head, guarded by the mythical Liver Birds (a pair of cormorants with seaweed in their beaks) on the **Royal Liver Building**, is one of the most easily recognized in Britain. Nearby are the famous ferry terminal across the River Mersey and the revitalized

LIVERPOOL CITY CENTRE

Beatles Story ⑥
Cavern Quarter ①
Merseyside Maritime
  Museum ⑧
Metropolitan Cathedral ⑤
Museum of Liverpool Life ⑨
Royal Liver Building ⑩

St George's Hall ④
Tate Liverpool ⑦
Town Hall ⑪
The Walker pp378–9 ③
World Museum Liverpool ②

0 metres 250
0 yards 250

Key to Symbols *see back flap*

docklands. Other attractions include top-class museums and fine galleries, such as the **Walker** *(see pp378–9)*. Its wealth of interesting architecture includes some fine Neo-Classical buildings in the city centre, such as the gargantuan **St George's Hall**, and two cathedrals.

Albert Dock

🛈 *0151 708 7334.* ◯ *daily.* ● *25 Dec, 1 Jan.* 🎫 *some attractions.* 🚶 www.albertdock.com

There are five warehouses surrounding Albert Dock, all designed by Jesse Hartley in 1846. The docks were closed by 1972. After a decade of dereliction, these Grade I listed buildings were restored in a development that includes museums, galleries, shops, restaurants, bars and businesses.

Albert Dock quay beside the River Mersey

🏛 Merseyside Maritime Museum

Albert Dock. *Tel 0151 478 4499.* ◯ *daily.* 🚶 *limited.* ▢ 🛈 www.liverpoolmuseums.org.uk

Devoted to the history of the Port of Liverpool, this large complex has good sections on shipbuilding and the Cunard and White Star liners as well as a Transatlantic Slavery gallery. The area on the Battle of the Atlantic in World War II includes models and charts. Another gallery deals with emigration to the New World. The **HM Customs and Excise National Museum** is also located here, and examines the history of the subject, including smuggling, as well as customs and excise today. Across the quayside is the rebuilt Piermaster's House and the Cooperage.

Ship's bell in the Maritime Museum

🏛 Museum of Liverpool Life

Pier Head, Albert Dock. *Tel 0151 478 4080.* ◯ *daily.* 🚶 🛈 www.liverpoolmuseums.org.uk

Many aspects of Liverpool culture converge here. Exhibits cover the history of Liverpool, its people and their contribution to international life. The *City Soldier's* gallery explores life in the King's Regiment in times of war and peace. Other interactive exhibits and accounts of daily life tell stories of sporting and political events since the 1800s.

Liverpool. 🏘 *450,000.* ✈ *7 miles (11 km) SE Liverpool.* 🚉 *Lime St.* 🚌 *Norton St.* ⛴ *from Pier Head to the Wirral, also sightseeing trips; to Isle of Man & N Ireland.* 🛈 *Whitechapel (09066 806886).* 🏪 *Sun (heritage market).* 📞 *0906 680 6886; Liverpool Show: May; Clipper Round the World Yacht Race: Jun; Beatles Week: Aug.* www.visitliverpool.com

🏛 Beatles Story

Britannia Vaults. *Tel 0151 709 1963.* ◯ *daily.* ● *25, 26 Dec.* 🎫 🚶 🛈 www.beatlesstory.com

In a walk-through exhibition, this museum records the history of The Beatles' meteoric rise to fame, from their first record, *Love Me Do,* through Beatlemania to their last live appearance together in 1969, and their eventual break-up. The hits that mesmerized a generation can be heard.

🏛 Tate Liverpool

Albert Dock. *Tel 0151 702 7400.* ◯ *Tue–Sun, public hols.* ● *Mon; Good Fri, 24–26 Dec, 1 Jan.* 🎫 *some exhibitions.* 🚶 🛒 *by arrangement.* ▢ 🛈 www.tate.org.uk/liverpool

Tate Liverpool has one of the best contemporary art collections outside London. Marked by bright blue and orange panels and arranged over three floors, the gallery was converted from an old warehouse by architect James Stirling. It opened in 1988 as Tate Britain's *(see p91)* first outstation.

THE BEATLES

Liverpool has produced many good bands and a host of singers, comedians and entertainers before and since the 1960s. But the Beatles – John Lennon, Paul McCartney, George Harrison and Ringo Starr – were the most sensational, and locations associated with the band, however tenuous, are revered as shrines in Liverpool. Bus and walking tours trace the hallowed ground of the Salvation Army home at *Strawberry Fields* and *Penny Lane* (both outside the city centre), as well as the boys' old homes. The most visited site is Mathew Street, near Moorfields Station, where the Cavern Club first throbbed to the Mersey Beat. The original site is now a shopping arcade, but the bricks have been used to create a replica. Nearby are statues of the Beatles and *Eleanor Rigby*.

Liverpool: The Walker

Italian dish
(c.1500)

Founded in 1873 by Sir Andrew Barclay Walker, a local brewer and Mayor of Liverpool, this gallery houses one of the finest art collections in the North. Paintings range from early Italian and Flemish works to Rubens, Rembrandt, Poussin, and French Impressionists such as Degas's *Woman Ironing* (c.1892–5). Among the strong collection of British artists from the 18th century onward are works by Millais and Turner and Gainsborough's *Countess of Sefton* (1769). There is 20th-century art by Hockney and Sickert, and the sculpture collection includes works by Henry Moore.

Seashells *(1874)*
Albert Moore painted female figures based on antique statues. Influenced by Whistler (see p519), he adopted subtle shading.

15

14

13

5

8

12

11

10

9

Ground floor

First flo

Interior at Paddington
(1951) Lucian Freud's friend Harry Diamond posed for six months for this picture, intended by the artist to "make the human being uncomfortable".

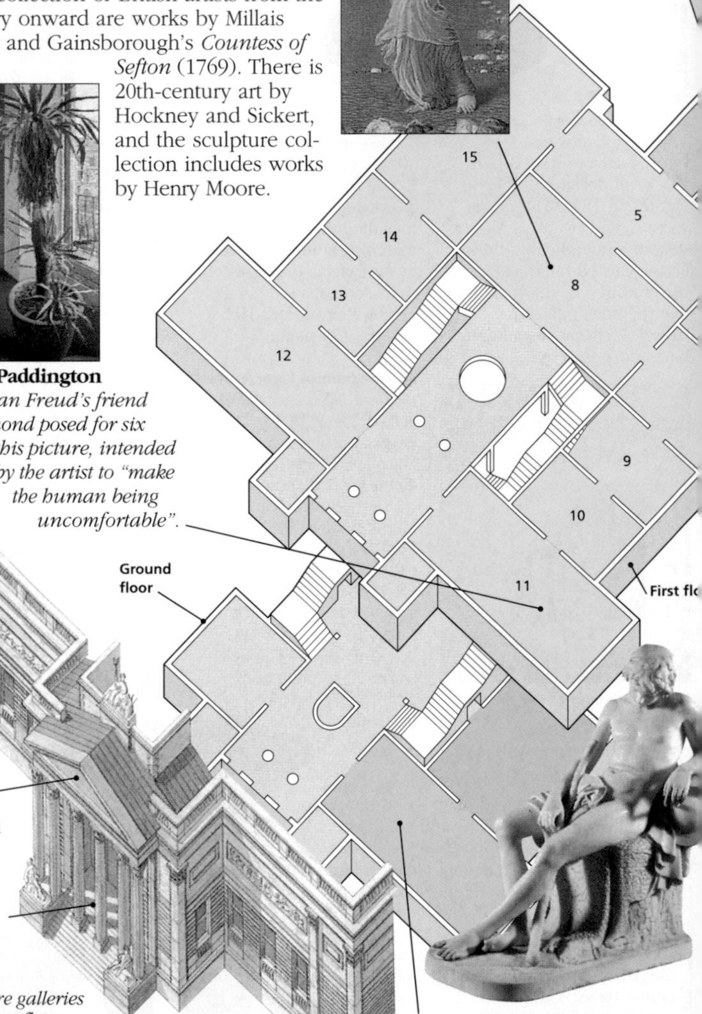

Façade was designed by H H Vale and Cornelius Sherlock.

Main entrance

GALLERY GUIDE

All the picture galleries are on the first floor.
Rooms 1–2 house medieval and Renaissance paintings; Rooms 3 and 4 have 17th-century Dutch, French, Italian and Spanish art. British 18th- and 19th-century works are in Rooms 5–9. Rooms 11–15 have 20th-century and contemporary British art, and Room 10 has Impressionists and Post-Impressionists.

The Sleeping Shepherd Boy
(c.1835) The great Neo-Classical sculptor of the mid-19th century, John Gibson (1790–1866), used traditional colours to give his statuary a smooth appearance.

The 7th-century Kingston Brooch in World Museum Liverpool

🏛 World Museum Liverpool

William Brown St. **Tel** 0151 478 4393. ⏰ 10am–5pm Mon–Sat, noon–5pm Sun. ⊘ 23–26 Dec, 1 Jan. ♿ 📷 www. worldmuseumliverpool.org.uk

Six floors of exhibits in this excellent museum include collections of Egyptian, Greek and Roman pieces, natural history, archaeology, space and time. Highlights include hands-on Exploration Zones, a planetarium, a Discovery Centre, an aquarium, a world cultures gallery and a Bug House.

🔒 Anglican Cathedral

St James' Mount. **Tel** 0151 709 6271. ⏰ daily. ♿ 📷 www.liverpoolcathedral.org.uk

Although Gothic in style, this building was only completed in 1978. The largest Anglican cathedral in the world is a fine red sandstone edifice designed by Sir Giles Gilbert Scott. The foundation stone was laid in 1904 by Edward VII but, dogged by two world wars, building work dragged on to modified designs.

🔒 Metropolitan Cathedral of Christ the King

Mount Pleasant. **Tel** 0151 709 9222. ⏰ daily. Donation. ♿ 📷 www.liverpoolmetrocathedral.org.uk

Liverpool's Roman Catholic cathedral rejected traditional forms in favour of a striking modern design. Early plans, drawn up by Pugin and later by Lutyens (see p29) in the 1930s, proved too expensive. The final version, brainchild of Sir Frederick Gibberd and built from 1962–7, is a circular building surmounted by a stylized crown of thorns 88 m (290 ft) high. It is irreverently known as "Paddy's Wigwam" by non-Catholics (a reference to Liverpool's large Irish population). Inside, the stained-glass lantern, designed by John Piper and Patrick Reyntiens, floods the circular nave with diffused blueish light. There is a fine bronze of Christ by Elisabeth Frink (1930–94).

Environs: A spectacular richly timbered building dating from 1490, **Speke Hall** lies 6 miles (10 km) east of Liverpool's centre, surrounded by lovely grounds. The oldest parts of the hall enclose a cobbled courtyard dominated by two yew trees, Adam and Eve.

Birkenhead on the Wirral peninsula has been linked to Liverpool by ferry for over 800 years. Now, road and rail tunnels supplement access. The Norman Priory is still in use on Sundays, and stately Hamilton Square was designed from 1825–44 by J Gillespie Graham, one of the architects of Edinburgh's New Town.

On the Wirral side is **Port Sunlight Village** (see p349), a Victorian garden village built by enlightened soap manufacturer William Hesketh Lever for his factory workers. He also founded the **Lady Lever Art Gallery** here for his collection of works of art, including Pre-Raphaelite paintings.

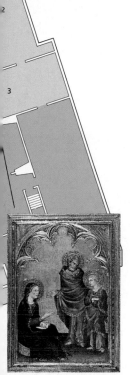

Christ Discovered in the Temple (1342)
Simone Martini's Holy Family conveys emotional tension through highly expressive body language.

KEY TO FLOORPLAN

- ☐ 13th–17th-century European
- ☐ 18th–19th-century British, Pre-Raphaelites and Victorian
- ☐ Impressionist/Post-Impressionist
- ☐ 20th-century and contemporary British
- ☐ Sculpture gallery
- ☐ Craft and design gallery
- ☐ Special exhibitions
- ☐ Non-exhibition space

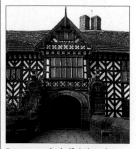

Entrance to the half-timbered manor house of Speke Hall

YORKSHIRE AND THE HUMBER REGION

NORTH YORKSHIRE · EAST RIDING OF YORKSHIRE

With the historic city of York at its heart, this is an area of picturesque moorland and valleys. To the north lie the Yorkshire Dales and the North York Moors; eastwards, a coastline of beaches; and southwards, a landscape of lush meadows.

Yorkshire was originally made up of three separate counties, formerly known as "Ridings". Today it covers over 5,000 sq miles (12,950 sq km). The northeast section has dramatic limestone scenery that was carved by glaciers in the Ice Age. Farming was the original livelihood, and the dry-stone walls weaving up precipitous scars and fells were used to divide the land. Imposed on this were the industries of the 19th century; blackened mill chimneys and crumbling viaducts are as much a part of the scenery as the grand houses of those who profited from them.

Close to the Humber, the landscape is very different, dominated historically by the now flagging fishing industry, and geographically by lush, sprawling meadows. Its coastline is exceptional, and further north are the attractions of wide, sandy beaches and bustling harbour towns. Yet it is the contrasting landscapes that make the area so appealing, ranging from the bleak moorland of the Brontë novels to the ragged cliff coast around Whitby, and the flat expanse of Sunk Island.

The city of York, where Roman and Viking relics exist side by side, is second only to London in the number of visitors that tread its streets. Indeed the historical centre of York is the region's foremost attraction. Those in search of a real taste of Yorkshire, however, should head for the countryside. In addition to excellent touring routes, a network of rewarding walking paths range from mellow ambles along the Cleveland Way to rocky scrambles over the Pennine Way at Pen-y-Ghent.

Lobster pots on the quayside at the picturesque fishing port of Whitby

◁ The peaceful valley of Rosedale, North York Moors

Exploring Yorkshire and the Humber Region

Yorkshire covers a wide area, once made up of three counties or "Ridings". Until the arrival of railways, mining and the wool industry in the 19th century, the county was a farming area. Dry-stone walls dividing fields still pepper the northern part of the county, alongside 19th-century mill chimneys and country houses. Among the many abbeys are Rievaulx and the magnificent Fountains. The medieval city of York is a major attraction, as are Yorkshire's beaches. The Humber region is characterized by the softer, rolling countryside of the Wolds, and its nature reserves attract enormous quantities of birds.

Rosedale village in the North York Moors

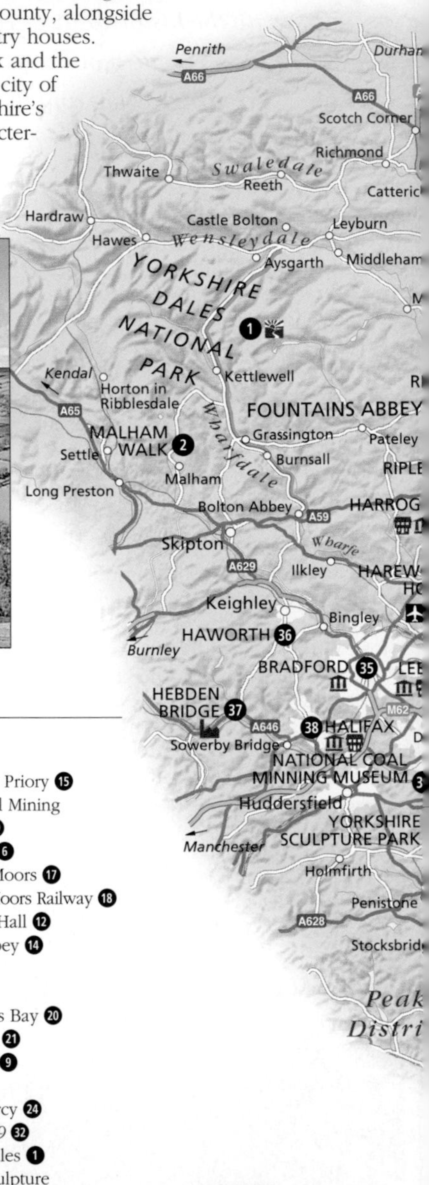

SIGHTS AT A GLANCE

Bempton and Flamborough
　Head **26**
Beverley **27**
Bradford **35**
Burton Agnes **25**
Burton Constable **28**
Byland Abbey **10**
Castle Howard pp398–9 **22**
Coxwold **11**
Eden Camp **23**
Fountains Abbey pp390–91 **7**
Grimsby **31**
Halifax **38**
Harewood House **33**
Harrogate **3**
Haworth **36**
Hebden Bridge **37**
Helmsley **13**
Holderness and Spurn
　Head **30**
Hutton-le-Hole **16**
Kingston upon Hull **29**
Knaresborough **4**

Leeds **34**
Magna **41**
Mount Grace Priory **15**
National Coal Mining
　Museum **39**
Newby Hall **6**
North York Moors **17**
North York Moors Railway **18**
Nunnington Hall **12**
Rievaulx Abbey **14**
Ripley **5**
Ripon **8**
Robin Hood's Bay **20**
Scarborough **21**
Sutton Bank **9**
Whitby **19**
Wharram Percy **24**
York pp404–9 **32**
Yorkshire Dales **1**
Yorkshire Sculpture
　Park **40**

Walks
Malham Walk **2**

SEE ALSO

• *Where to Stay* pp583–6

• *Where to Eat* pp637–40

For additional map symbols *see back flap*

Penrith
Durham
A66
A66
Scotch Corner
Richmond
Swaledale
Thwaite
Reeth
Catteric
Hardraw
Castle Bolton
Leyburn
Hawes
Wensleydale
Aysgarth
Middleham
YORKSHIRE
DALES
NATIONAL
PARK
Kettlewell
Kendal
Horton in
Ribblesdale
FOUNTAINS ABBEY
A65
MALHAM
WALK **2**
Grassington
Pateley
Settle
Burnsall
RIPLE
Malham
Wharfedale
Long Preston
Bolton Abbey
A59
HARROG
Skipton
Wharfe
A629
Ilkley
HAREW
Keighley
HC
Bingley
HAWORTH **36**
Burnley
BRADFORD **35**
LEE
HEBDEN
BRIDGE **37**
A646
HALIFAX **38**
Sowerby Bridge
M62
NATIONAL COAL
MINING MUSEUM **39**
Huddersfield
YORKSHIRE
Manchester
SCULPTURE PARK
Holmfirth
A628
Penistone
Stocksbrid
Peak
District

Section of Lendal Bridge (1863) crossing the Ouse in York

Guisborough
Hinderwell
Great Ayton
A171
Stokesley
A19
WHITBY **19**
A172
ROBIN HOOD'S BAY **20**
MOUNT GRACE PRIORY **15**
17
NORTH YORK MOORS
Goathland
Cleveland Hills
allerton
Rosedale Abbey
NORTH YORKSHIRE MOORS RAILWAY **18**
HUTTON-LE-HOLE **16**
Scalby
SCARBOROUGH **21**
LX ABBEY **14**
HELMSLEY **13**
Pickering
A170
9 A170
NUNNINGTON HALL **12**
Brompton
Filey
TTON **10** BANK
BYLAND ABBEY
Hovingham
Derwent
A64
Staxton
A165
11 COXWOLD
EDEN CAMP **23**
Malton
Rudston
BEMPTON **26**
Y HALL
CASTLE HOWARD **22**
Flamborough Head
oughbridge
WHARRAM PERCY **24**
Sledmere
Bridlington
BURTON AGNES **25**
A19 Haxby A64
Fridaythorpe
A166
Driffield
ESBOROUGH
Ouse
A59
Stamford Bridge
The Wolds
A614
Skipsea
YORK **32**
A1079 Pocklington
Hutton Cranswick
Hornsea
therby
Derwent
Leven
Tadcaster
Escrick
A165
Aberford
Riccall
Holme on Spalding Moor
Market Weighton
BEVERLEY **27**
BURTON CONSTABLE **28**
orth
Selby
A614
Cottingham
Roos
A63
M62
A63
KINGSTON UPON HULL **29**
astleford
Howden
Welton
HOLDERNESS & SPURN HEAD **30**
Withernsea
Aire
Snaith
Goole
Whitton
Humber
Barton-upon-Humber
Easington
M62
A19
M18
A15
Appleby
Ulceby
Immingham
Spurn Head
msworth
Askern
Thorne
Crowle
Scunthorpe
A180
GRIMSBY **31**
Cleethorpes
South Kirkby
M180
A18
Broughton
Brigg
Waltham
A635
nbwell
Doncaster
Belton
A16
ough
M18
A1(M)
Scotter
Caistor
Bawtry
Misterton
A15
Rotherham
Anston
M1
Nottingham

GETTING AROUND
The area is served by the A1, the M1, the M62 and the A59. Trains run to major cities such as York and Leeds, and there are train or coach (bus) links between many towns and hamlets. The Yorkshire Dales and North York Moors national parks are good for walkers, and cyclists can enjoy rides around York and the river Humber.

kilometres 15
miles 10

KEY

══	Motorway
▬	Major road
▬	Secondary road
══	Minor road
▬	Scenic route
▬	Main railway
▬	Minor railway

Yorkshire Dales ❶

The Yorkshire Dales is a farming landscape, formed from three principle dales, Swaledale, Wharfedale and Wensleydale, and a number of small ones, such as Deepdale. Glaciation in the Ice Age helped carve out these steep-sided valleys, and this scenery contrasts with the high moorlands. However, 12 centuries of settlement have altered the landscape in the form of cottages, castles and villages which create a delightful environment for walking. A national park since 1954, the area provides recreation while serving local community needs.

Monk's Wynd – one of Richmond's narrow, winding streets

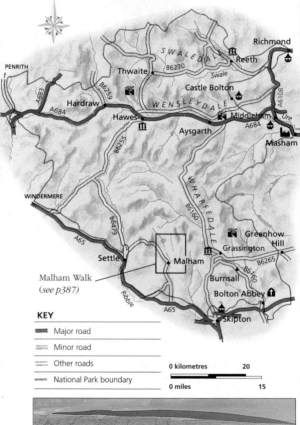

KEY

- ▬ Major road
- ▭ Minor road
- ▭ Other roads
- ▬ National Park boundary

Malham Walk (see p387)

0 kilometres 20

0 miles 15

Exploring Swaledale

Swaledale's prosperity was founded largely on wool, and it is famous for its herd of sheep that graze on the wild higher slopes in the harshest weather. The fast-moving river Swale that gives the northernmost dale its name travels from bleak moorland down magnificent waterfalls into the richly wooded lower slopes, passing through the village of Reeth and the town of Richmond.

♜ Richmond Castle

(EH) Tower Street. **Tel** 01748 822493. ☐ Oct–Apr: Thu–Mon; May–Sep: daily. 🎫 ♿ limited. 📷

Swaledale's main point of entry is the medieval market town of Richmond, which has the largest cobbled marketplace in England. Alan Rufus, the Norman 1st Earl of Richmond, began building the castle in 1071, and some of the masonry on the curtain walls probably dates from that time. It has a fine Norman keep, 30 m (100 ft) high with walls 3.3 m (11 ft) thick. An 11th-century arch leads into a courtyard containing Scolland's Hall (1080), one of England's oldest buildings.

Richmond's marketplace was once the castle's outer bailey. Its quaint, narrow streets gave rise to the song, *The Lass of Richmond Hill* (1787), written by Leonard McNally for his wife, Frances I'Anson, who was brought up in Hill House,

The green, rolling landscape of Deepdale, near Dent

on Richmond Hill. Turner *(see p91)* depicted the town many times. The Georgian Theatre (1788) is the only one of its age still surviving.

🏛 Swaledale Folk Museum
Reeth Green. *Tel* 01748 884118.
⭘ *Easter–Oct: daily.* 🖼 ⬛ 🚻
Reeth, a town that became known as the centre of the lead-mining industry and helped bring prosperity to the region, houses this museum in a former Methodist Sunday school (1830). Included in it are mining and wool-making artifacts (wool from the hardy Swaledale sheep was another mainstay of the economy) and brass band memorabilia.

🌾 Buttertubs
Near Thwaite, on the B6270 Hawes road, are a series of potholes that streams fall into. These became known as the Buttertubs when farmers going to market lowered their butter into the holes to keep it cool.

Buttertubs, near Thwaite

Exploring Wensleydale
The largest of the Yorkshire dales, Wensleydale is famous for its cheese and more recently for James Herriot's books and the television series, *All Creatures Great and Small.* It is easy walking country for anyone seeking an alternative to major moorland hikes.

🏛 Dales Countryside Museum
Station Yard, Hawes. *Tel* 01969 666210. ⭘ *daily.* ⬤ *24–26 Dec, 1 Jan.* 🖼 ♿ 🚻
In a former railway goods warehouse in Hawes, capital of Upper Wensleydale, is a

Barrels at the Theakston Brewery

fascinating museum, filled with items from life and industry in the 18th- and 19th-century Upper Dales. This includes cheese- and butter-making equipment. Wensleydale cheese was created by monks at nearby Jervaulx Abbey. There is also a rope-making works a short walk away.

Hawes itself is the highest market town in England, at 259 m (850 ft) above sea level. It is a thriving centre where thousands of sheep and cattle are auctioned each summer.

🌾 Hardraw Force
🖼 *at Green Dragon Inn, Hardraw.*
At the tiny village of Hardraw, nearby, is England's tallest single-drop waterfall, with no outcrops to interrupt its 29 m (96 ft) fall. It became famous in Victorian times when the daredevil Blondin walked across it on a tightrope. Today, you can walk right under this fine waterfall, against the rock face, and look through the stream without getting wet.

🌾 Aysgarth Waterfalls
ℹ *National Pk Centre (01969 663424)*
⭘ *Fri–Sun.*
An old packhorse bridge gives a clear view of the point at which the previously placid River Ure suddenly begins to plunge in foaming torrents over wide limestone shelves. Turner painted the impressive lower falls in 1817.

🏛 Theakston Brewery
Masham. *Tel* 01765 680000. ⭘ *daily.* ⬤ *23 Dec–early Jan.* 🖼 🖼 🚻 *www.*theakstons.co.uk
The pretty town of Masham is the home of Theakston brewery, creator of the potent ale Old Peculier. The history

of this local family brewery from its origin in 1827 is on display in the visitors' centre. Masham village itself has an attractive square once used for sheep fairs, surrounded by 17th- and 18th-century houses. There is a medieval church.

♣ Bolton Castle
Castle Bolton, nr Leyburn. *Tel* 01969 623981. ⭘ *daily.* ⬤ *23–25 Dec.* 🖼 ⬛ 🚻 *www.*boltoncastle.co.uk
Situated in the village of Castle Bolton, this castle was built in 1379 by the 1st Lord Scrope, Chancellor of England. It was used as a fortress from 1568 to 1569 when Mary, Queen of Scots *(see p511)* was held prisoner here by Elizabeth I *(see pp50–51).*

♣ Middleham Castle
(EH) Middleham, nr Leyburn. *Tel* 01969 623899. ⭘ *Apr–Sep: 10am–6pm daily; Oct–Mar: 10am–4pm Thu–Mon.* ⬤ *24–26 Dec, 1 Jan.* 🚻 🖼 ♿ *limited.*
Owned by Richard Neville, Earl of Warwick, it was built in 1170. The castle is better known as home to Richard III *(see p49)* when he was made Lord of the North. It was once one of the strongest fortresses in the north but became un-inhabited during the 15th century, when many of its stones were used for nearby buildings. The keep provides a fine view of the landscape.

Remains of Middleham Castle, once residence of Richard III

Extensive ruins of Bolton Priory, dating from 1154

Exploring Wharfedale

This dale is characterized by gritstone moorland, contrasting with quiet market towns along meandering sections of river. Many consider Grassington a central point for exploring Wharfedale, but the showpiece villages of Burnsall, overlooked by a 506 m (1,661 ft) fell, and Buckden, 701 m (2,302 ft), near Buckden Pike, also make excellent bases.

Nearby are the Three Peaks of Whernside, 736 m (2,416 ft), Ingleborough, 724 m (2,376 ft) and Pen-y-Ghent 694 m (2,278 ft). They are known for their potholes and tough terrain, but this does not deter keen walkers from attempting to climb them all in one day. If you sign in at the Pen-y-Ghent café at Horton-in-Ribblesdale, at the centre of the Three Peaks, and complete the 20 mile (32 km) course, reaching the summit of all three peaks in less than 12 hours, you can qualify for membership of the Three Peaks of Yorkshire Club.

R Burnsall

St Wilfrid's, Burnsall. *Tel* 01756 720331. ⬤ Apr–Oct: daily to dusk. ♿

Preserved in St Wilfrid's church graveyard are the original village stocks, gravestones from Viking times and a head-stone carved in memory of the Dawson family by sculptor Eric Gill (1882–1940). The village has a five-arched bridge and hosts Britain's oldest fell race every August.

🏛 Upper Wharfedale Museum

The Square, Grassington. ⬤ Mar–Oct: daily (pm). ♿ limited.

This folk museum is set in two 18th-century lead miners' cottages. Its exhibits illustrate the domestic and working history of the area, including farming and lead mining.

🔒 Bolton Priory

Bolton Abbey, Skipton. *Tel* 01756 718009. ⬤ daily. ♿

One of the most beautiful areas of Wharfedale is around the village of Bolton Abbey, set in an estate owned by the Dukes of Devonshire. While preserving its astounding beauty, its managers have incorporated over 30 miles (46 km) of foot-paths, many suitable for the disabled and young families.

The ruins of Bolton Priory, established by Augustinian canons in 1154 on the site of a Saxon manor, are extensive.

They include a church, chapter house, cloister and prior's lodging. These all demonstrate the wealth accumulated by the canons from the sale of wool from their flocks of sheep. The priory nave is still used as a parish church. Another attraction of the estate is the "Strid", a point where the River Wharfe surges spectacularly through a gorge, foaming yellow and gouging holes out of the rocks.

🦇 Stump Cross Caverns

Greenhow Hill, Pateley Bridge. *Tel* 01756 752780 or 01423 711282. ⬤ Apr–Oct: daily; Nov–Mar: Sat, Sun & public hols (call for details). 📷 📷 📷 www.stumpcrosscaverns.co.uk

These caves were formed over a period of half a million years: trickles of underground water formed intertwining passages and carved them into fantastic shapes and sizes. Sealed off in the last Ice Age, the caves were only discovered in the 1850s when lead miners sank a mine shaft into the caverns.

♦ Skipton Castle

High St. *Tel* 01756 792442. ⬤ daily (Sun: pm). ⬤ 25 Dec. 📷 📷 📷 www.skiptoncastle.co.uk

The market town of Skipton is still one of the largest auctioning and stockraising centres in the north. Its 11th-century castle was almost entirely rebuilt by Robert de Clifford in the 14th century. Beautiful Conduit Court was added by Henry, Lord Clifford, in Henry VIII's reign. The central yew tree was planted by Lady Anne Clifford in 1659 to mark restoration work to the castle after Civil War damage.

Conduit Court (1495) and yew tree at Skipton Castle

Malham Walk ❷

The Malham area, shaped by glacial erosion 10,000 years ago, has one of Great Britain's most dramatic limestone landscapes. The walk from Malham village can take over four hours if you pause to enjoy the viewpoints and take a detour to Gordale Scar. Those who are short of time tend to go only as far as Malham Cove. This vast natural amphitheatre, formed by a huge geological tear, is like a giant boot-heel mark in the landscape. Above lie the deep crevices of Malham Lings, where rare flora such as hart's-tongue flourishes. Unusual plants grow in the lime-rich Malham Tarn, said to have provided inspiration for Charles Kingsley's *The Water Babies* (1863). Coot and mallard visit the tarn in summer and tufted duck in winter.

Sandpiper at Malham Tarn

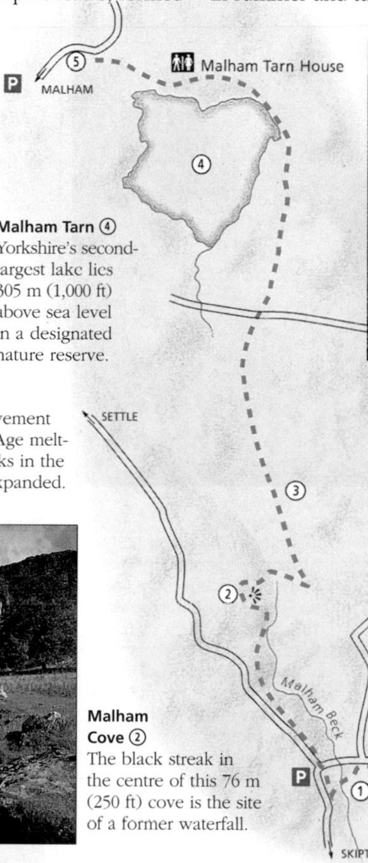

Where the path meets the road ⑤
From here, you can catch a bus back to Malham village.

🚻 Malham Tarn House

Ⓟ MALHAM

Malham Tarn ④
Yorkshire's second-largest lake lies 305 m (1,000 ft) above sea level in a designated nature reserve.

Malham Lings ③
This fine limestone pavement was formed when Ice Age meltwater seeped into cracks in the rock, then froze and expanded.

SETTLE

Gordale Scar ⑥
Guarded by steep limestone cliffs, this deep gorge was created by meltwater from Ice Age glaciers(

Malham Cove ②
The black streak in the centre of this 76 m (250 ft) cove is the site of a former waterfall.

Malham Beck

Ⓟ ① ℹ

Gordale Beck

SKIPTON

KEY

▪▪	Walk route
══	Minor road
�view	Viewpoint
Ⓟ	Parking
ℹ	Tourist information
🚻	Toilets

Malham ①
An attractive riverside village, it has an information centre with details of drives and walks.

TIPS FOR WALKERS

*Starting point: Malham. **Getting there:** Leave M65 at Junction 14 and take A56 to Skipton, then follow signs to Malham which is off A65. **Length:** 7 miles (11 km). **Difficulty:** Malham Cove is steep but the Tarn area is flatter.*
ℹ *01729 830363.*

0 kilometres   1

0 miles   ½

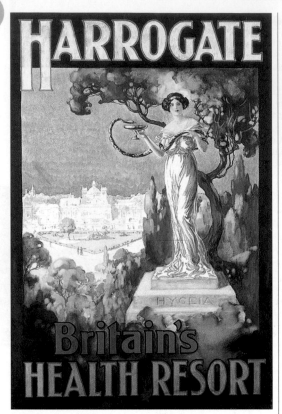

A 1920s poster advertising the spa town of Harrogate

Harrogate ❸

North Yorkshire. 🏠 *69,000.* 🚄 🚌
ℹ️ *The Royal Baths, Crescent Rd
(01423 537300).*
www.enjoyharrogate.com

Between 1880 and World
War I, Harrogate was the
north's leading spa town, with
nearly 90 medicinal springs.
It was ideal for aristocrats
who, after a tiring London
season, were able to stop for
a health cure before
journeying on to grouse-
shooting in Scotland.

Today, Harrogate's main
attractions are its spa town
atmosphere, fine architecture,
public gardens and its convenience as a centre for visiting
North Yorkshire and the Dales.

The naturally welling spa
waters may not currently be
in use, but you can still go
for a Turkish bath in one of
the country's most attractive
steam rooms. The entrance at
the side of the Royal Bath
Assembly Rooms (1897) is
unassuming, but once inside,
the century-old **Harrogate
Turkish Baths** are a visual
feast of tiled Victoriana.

The town's spa history is
recorded in the **Royal Pump
Room Museum**. At the turn
of the century, the waters
were thought to be rich in
iron early in the day. So,
between 7am and 9am the
1842 octagonal building
would have been filled with
rich and fashionable people
drinking glasses of water.
Poorer people could take
water from the pump outside.
Today you can sample the
waters and enjoy the
museum's exhibits, including
a Penny Farthing bicycle.

Harrogate is also known for
the rainbow-coloured flowerbeds in **The Stray**, a common
space to the south of the town
centre, and for the ornamental
Harlow Car Gardens, owned
by the Royal Horticultural
Society. Visitors can enjoy the
delicious cakes at **Betty's
Café Tea Rooms** (*see p628*).

🏛 **Harrogate Turkish Baths**
The Royal Baths, Crescent Rd.
Tel *01423 556746.* ⬜ **Men**: *Mon,
Wed & Fri:* (pm); *Sat.* **Women**: *Mon
(am); Tue & Thu:* (pm); *Fri (am); Sun.*
Mixed *(in bathing suits): Tue (am);
(couples only in bathing suits): Wed
& Fri (both eve); Sun (eve).* 🖼️

🏛 **Royal Pump Room
Museum**
Crown Pl. **Tel** *01423 556188.* ⬜
daily. ⬤ *24–26 Dec, 1 Jan.* 🖼️ ♿ ⬛

🏛 **Betty's Café Tea Rooms**
1 Parliament St. **Tel** *01423 502746.*
⬜ *daily.* ⬤ *25–26 Dec, 1 Jan.*
www.bettysandtaylors.co.uk

🌿 **Harlow Car Gardens**
Crag Lane. **Tel** *01423 565418.* ⬜
daily. 🖼️ ♿ 🍴 ⬛ **www.**rhs.org.uk

Knaresborough ❹

North Yorkshire. 🏠 *14,000.* 🚄
🚌 *from Harrogate.* ℹ️ *9 Castle
Courtyard, Market Place (01423
866886).* ⬤ *Wed.*

Perched precipitously above
the River Nidd is one
of England's oldest towns,
mentioned in the Domesday
Book of 1086 (*see p48*). Its
historic streets – which link the
church, John of Gaunt's ruined
castle, and the market place
with the river – are now lined
with fine 18th-century houses.

Nearby is **Mother Shipton's
Cave**, reputedly England's
oldest tourist attraction. It first
went on show in 1630 as the
birthplace of Ursula Sontheil,

**Mother Shipton's cave, with
objects encased in limestone**

The south front of Newby Hall

a famous local prophetess. Today, people can view the effect the well near her cave has on objects hung below the dripping surface. Almost any item, from umbrellas to soft toys, will become encased in limestone within a few weeks.

⛏ Mother Shipton's Cave
Prophesy House, High Bridge.
Tel 01423 864600. ◯ Easter–Oct: daily; Nov, Feb–Easter: Sat, Sun. ⬤ Dec, Jan. 🖼 🎫 🖵 🏠

Ripley ❺

North Yorkshire. 🏘 150. 🚌 from Harrogate or Ripon. ℹ 01423 537300. www.harrogate.gov.uk

Since the 1320s, when the first generation of the Ingilby family lived in an early incarnation of **Ripley Castle**, the village has been made up almost exclusively of castle employees. The influence of one 19th-century Ingilby had the most visual impact. In the 1820s, Sir William Amcotts Ingilby was so entranced by a village in Alsace Lorraine that he created a similar one in French Gothic style, complete with an *Hotel de Ville*. Present-day Ripley has a cobbled market square, and quaint cottages line the streets.

Ripley Castle, with its 15th-century gatehouse, was where Oliver Cromwell *(see p52)* stayed following the Battle of Marston Moor. The 28th generation of Ingilbys live here, and it is open for tours. The attractive grounds contain two lakes and a deer park, as well as more formal gardens.

♣ Ripley Castle
Ripley. **Tel** 01423 770152. ◯ Oct–Apr: Tue, Thu, Sat & Sun; Jun–Sep: daily. ⬤ 25 Dec. 🖼 ♿ 🎫 🖵 🏠

Newby Hall ❻

Nr Ripon, North Yorkshire.
Tel 01423 322583. ◯ Apr–Jun & Sep: Tue–Sun; Jul & Aug: daily.
🖼 ♿ 🍴 🏠
www.newbyhall.com

Newby Hall stands on land once occupied by the de Nubie family in the 13th century, and has been in the hands of the current family since 1748. The central part of the present house was built in the late 19th century in the style of Sir Christopher Wren.

Visitors will find 25 acres of gardens to explore. Laid out in a series of compartmented areas off a main axis, each garden is planted to come into flower during a different season. There is also a Woodland Discovery Walk, where contemporary sculpture is displayed.

For children, there is an adventure garden with activities and a miniature railway that runs through the gardens alongside the river Ure. River boat rides are also available. Each year a number of special events are staged, including Plant Fairs, a Historic Vehicle Rally and two Craft Fairs.

Fountains Abbey ❼

See pp390–91.

Ripon ❽

North Yorkshire. 🏘 14,000. 🚌 from Harrogate. ℹ Minster Rd (01765 604625). 📅 Thu.
www.riponcity.info

Ripon, a charming small city, is best known for the cathedral and "the watch", which has been announced since the Middle Ages by the Wakeman. In return for protecting Ripon citizens, he would charge an annual toll of two pence per household. Today, a man still blows a horn in the Market Square each evening at 9pm, and every Thursday a handbell is rung to open the market.

The **Cathedral of St Peter and St Wilfrid** is built above a 7th-century Saxon crypt. At less than 3 m (10 ft) high and just over 2 m (7 ft) wide, it is held to be the oldest complete crypt in England. The cathedral is known for its collection of misericords *(see p341)*, which include both pagan and Old Testament examples. The architectural historian Sir Nikolaus Pevsner (1902–83) considered the cathedral's West Front the finest in England.

Ripon's **Prison and Police Museum**, housed in the 1686 "House of Correction", looks at police history and the conditions in Victorian prisons.

🏛 Prison and Police Museum
St Marygate. **Tel** 01765 690799.
◯ Apr–Oct: daily. ⬤ Nov–Mar. 🖼 ♿ 🏠 www.riponmuseums.co.uk

Ripon's Wakeman, blowing his horn in the Market Square

Fountains Abbey ❼

Nestling in the wooded valley of the River Skell are the extensive sandstone ruins of Fountains Abbey and the outstanding water garden of Studley Royal. Fountains Abbey was founded by Benedictine monks in 1132 and taken over by Cistercians three years later. By the mid-12th century it had become the wealthiest abbey in Britain, though it fell into ruin during the Dissolution (*see p50*). In 1720, John Aislabie, the MP for Ripon and Chancellor of the Exchequer, developed the land and forest of the abbey ruins. He began work, continued by his son William, on the famous water garden, the statuary and Classical temples in the grounds. This makes a dramatic contrast to the simplicity of the abbey.

Fountains Hall
Built by Sir Stephen Proctor around 1611, with stones from the abbey ruins, its design is attributed to architect Robert Smythson. It included a great hall with a minstrels' gallery and an entrance flanked by Classical columns.

THE ABBEY

The abbey buildings were designed to reflect the Cistercians' desire for simplicity and austerity. The abbey frequently dispensed charity to the poor and the sick, as well as travellers.

The Chapel of Nine Altars *at the east end of the church was built from 1203 to 1247. It is ornate, compared to the rest of the abbey, with an 18-m (60-ft) high window complemented by another at the western end of the nave.*

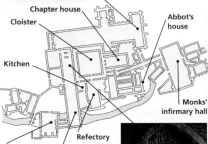

Chapter house
Cloister
Kitchen
Abbot's house
Monks' infirmary hall
Refectory
Lay brothers' infirmary
Lay brothers' refectory

Cellarium and dormitory undercroft, *with vaulting 90 m (300 ft) long, was used for storing fleeces which the abbey monks sold to Venetian and Florentine merchants.*

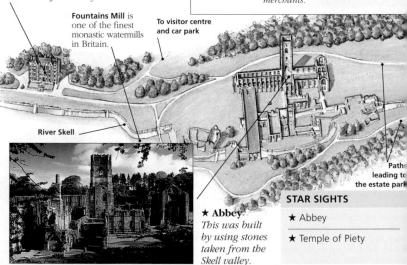

Fountains Mill is one of the finest monastic watermills in Britain.

To visitor centre and car park

River Skell

Path leading to the estate park

★ **Abbey**
This was built by using stones taken from the Skell valley.

STAR SIGHTS

★ Abbey

★ Temple of Piety

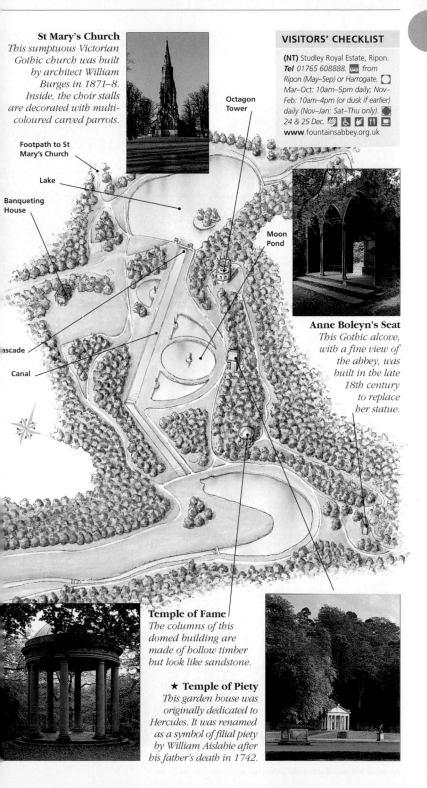

St Mary's Church
This sumptuous Victorian Gothic church was built by architect William Burges in 1871–8. Inside, the choir stalls are decorated with multi-coloured carved parrots.

Octagon Tower

Footpath to St Mary's Church

Lake

Banqueting House

Moon Pond

Cascade

Canal

VISITORS' CHECKLIST

(NT) Studley Royal Estate, Ripon. **Tel** 01765 608888. from Ripon (May–Sep) or Harrogate. Mar–Oct: 10am–5pm daily; Nov–Feb: 10am–4pm (or dusk if earlier) daily (Nov–Jan: Sat–Thu only). 24 & 25 Dec. www.fountainsabbey.org.uk

Anne Boleyn's Seat
This Gothic alcove, with a fine view of the abbey, was built in the late 18th century to replace her statue.

Temple of Fame
The columns of this domed building are made of hollow timber but look like sandstone.

★ **Temple of Piety**
This garden house was originally dedicated to Hercules. It was renamed as a symbol of filial piety by William Aislabie after his father's death in 1742.

The 19th-century white horse, seen on one of the walks around Sutton Bank

Sutton Bank **9**

North Yorkshire. *Thirsk.*
Sutton Bank (01845 597426).

Notorious among motorists
for its 1 in 4 gradient, which
climbs for about 107 m
(350 ft), Sutton Bank itself is
well known for its panoramic
views. On a clear day you can
see from the Vale of York to
the Peak District *(see pp338–9)*.
William and his sister Dorothy
Wordsworth stopped here to
admire the vista in 1802, on
their way to visit his future
wife, Mary Hutchinson, at

Brompton. Apart from Sutton
Bank, where you can walk
round the white horse, the area
is less wild than the coastal
side, and suitable for children.

Byland Abbey **10**

(EH) Coxwold, York. **Tel** *01347 868
614.* from York or Helmsley.
Thirsk. Apr–Jul & Sep: Thu–Mon;
Aug: daily. limited. **www.**
english-heritage.org.uk/yorkshire

This Cistercian monastery was
founded in 1177 by monks
from Furness Abbey in

Cumbria. It featured what was
then the largest Cistercian
church in Britain, 100 m (328
ft) long and 41 m (135 ft) wide
across the transepts. The layout of the monastery, including
cloisters and the west front of
the church, is still visible, as
is the green and yellow glazed
tile floor. Fine workmanship is
shown in carved stone details
and in the capitals, kept in
the small museum.

In 1322 the Battle of Byland
was fought nearby, and King
Edward II *(see p40)* narrowly
escaped capture when the
invading Scottish army learned
that he was dining with the
Abbot. In his hurry to escape,
the king had to leave many
treasures behind, which were
looted by the invading soldiers.

Coxwold **11**

North Yorkshire. *160.* *49
Market Place, Thirsk (01845 522755).*
www.herriotcountry.com

Situated just inside the
bounds of the North York
Moors National Park *(see
p395)*, this charming village
nestles at the foot of the
Howardian Hills. Its pretty
houses are built from local
stone, and the 15th-century
church has some fine Georgian

Shandy Hall, home of author Laurence Sterne, now a museum

box pews and an impressive octagonal tower. But Coxwold is best known as the home of the the author Laurence Sterne (1713–68), whose writings include *Tristram Shandy* and *A Sentimental Journey*.

Sterne moved here in 1760 as the church curate. He rented a rambling house that he named **Shandy Hall** after a Yorkshire expression meaning eccentric. Originally built as a timber-framed, open-halled house in the 15th century, it was modernized in the 17th century and Sterne later added a façade. His grave lies beside the porch at Coxwold's church.

Shandy Hall
Coxwold. *Tel 01347 868465.* ◯
May–Sep: Wed & Sun (pm). ◻ ◻
limited. **Gardens** ◯ *Sun–Fri.* ◻

Nunnington Hall ⓬

(NT) Nunnington, York. *Tel 01439 748283.* ☒ Malton, then bus or taxi. ◯ Mar–May, Sep–Oct: Wed–Sun (pm); Jun–Aug: Tue–Sun, public hols (pm). ◻ ◻ ◻ ground floor. ◻

Set in alluring surroundings, this 17th-century manor house is a combination of architectural styles, including features from the Elizabethan and Stuart periods. Both inside and outside, a notable architectural feature is the use of the broken pediment (the upper arch is left unjoined).

Nunnington Hall was a family home until 1952, when Mrs Ronald Fife donated it to the National Trust. A striking

The miniature Queen Anne drawing room at Nunnington Hall

feature is the panelling in the Oak Hall. Formerly painted, it extends over the three-arched screen to the Great Staircase. Nunnington's collection of 22 miniature furnished period rooms is popular with visitors.

A mid-16th-century tenant Dr Robert Huickes, physician to Henry VIII *(see p50–51)*, is best known for advising Elizabeth I that she should not, at the age of 32, consider having any children.

Helmsley ⓭

North Yorkshire. ⓰ *2,000.* ⛟ *from Malton or Scarborough.* ⓘ *Town Hall, Market Place (01439 770173).* ⛟ *Fri.* www.ryedale.gov.uk/tourism

This pretty market town is noted for its **castle**, now an imposing ruin. Built from 1186 to 1227, its main function and strength as a fortress is illustrated by the remaining keep, tower and curtain walls. The original D-shaped keep had one part blasted away in the Civil War *(see p52)*, but remains the

dominant feature. The castle was so impregnable that there were few attempts to force entry. However, in 1644, after holding out for a three-month seige against Sir Thomas Fairfax, the Parliamentary general, the castle was finally taken.

Helmsley church tower

Rievaulx Abbey ⓮

(EH) Nr Helmsley, North Yorkshire. *Tel 01439 798228.* ☒ Thirsk or Scarborough, then bus or taxi. ◯ Apr–Sep: daily; Oct–Mar: Thu–Mon. ● 24–26 Dec, 1 Jan. ◻ ◻ limited. ◻

Rievaulx is perhaps the finest abbey in the area, due to both its dramatic setting in the steep wooded valley of the River Rye and its extensive remains. It is surrounded by steep banks that form natural barriers from the outside world. Monks of the French Cistercian order from Clairvaux founded this, their first major monastery in Britain, in 1132. The main buildings were finished before 1200. The layout of the chapel, kitchens and infirmary give an idea of monastic life.

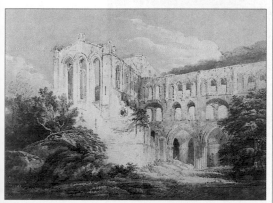
Rievaulx Abbey, painted by Thomas Girtin (1775–1802)

Mount Grace Priory ruins, with farm and mansion in foreground

Mount Grace Priory ⓯

(EH/NT) On A19, NE of Northallerton, North Yorks. *Tel 01609 883494.* ⇌ *Northallerton then bus.* ◯ *Apr–Sep: daily; Oct–Mar: Thu–Mon.* 🎫 ♿ *ground floor, shop & grounds.* 📷 **www**.english-heritage.org.uk/yorkshire

Founded by Thomas Holland, Duke of Surrey, and in use from 1398 until 1539, this is the best-preserved Carthusian or charterhouse monastery *(see pp350–51)* in England. The monks took a vow of silence and lived in solitary cells, each with his own garden and an angled hatch so that he would not even see the person serving his food. They only met at matins, vespers and feast-day services. Attempts at escape by those who could not endure the rigour of the rules were punished by imprisonment.

The ruins of the priory include the former prison, gatehouse and outer court, barns, guesthouses, cells and the church. The 14th-century church, the best-preserved section of the site, is particularly small, as it was only rarely used by the community. A cell has been reconstructed to give an impression of monastic life.

Hutton-le-Hole ⓰

North Yorkshire. 🚶 *400.* ⇌ *Malton then bus.* 🛈 *The Ropery, Pickering (01751 473791).* **www**.ryedale.gov.uk/tourism

This picturesque village is characterized by a spacious green, grazed by roaming sheep, and surrounded by houses, an inn and shops. Lengths of white wood, replacing stone bridges, span the moorland stream. Its cottages, some with date panels over the doors, are made from limestone, with red pantiled roofs. In the village centre is the excellent

Wheelwright's workshop at Ryedale Folk Museum

Ryedale Folk Museum, which records the lifestyle of an agricultural community using Romano-British artifacts and reconstructed buildings.

🏛 **Ryedale Folk Museum** Hutton-le-Hole. *Tel 01751 417367.* ◯ *late Jan–mid-Dec: daily.* 🎫 ♿ 📷

North York Moors ⓱

See p395.

North Yorkshire Moors Railway ⓲

Pickering & Grosmont, North Yorkshire. *Tel 01751 472508.* ◯ *Apr–Oct: daily; Nov–Mar: some weekends (call for details).* 🎫 ♿ 🖥 📷 **www**. northyorkshiremoorsrailway.com

Designed in 1831 by George Stephenson as a route along the North York Moors and links with the Esk Valley, Pickering and Whitby *(see p382)*, this railway is considered an engineering miracle. Due to budget constraints, Stephenson was not able to build a tunnel, so had to lay the route down the mile-long (1.5 km) incline between Beck Hole and Goathland. The area around Fen Bog had to be stabilized using timber, heather, brushwood and fleeces so that a causeway could be built over it. A horse was used to pull a coach along the track at 10 miles (16 km) per hour. After horsepower came steam, and for almost 130 years the railway linked Whitby to the rest of the country. In the early 1960s the line was closed but in 1967, a group of locals began a campaign to relaunch it, and in 1973 it was officially reopened. Today, the 18 mile (29 km) line runs from Pickering via Levisham, Newtondale Halt and Goathland before stopping at Grosmont, through the scenic heart of the North York Moors.

North York Moors ⑰

The area between Cleveland, the Vale of York and the Vale of Pickering is known as the North York Moors National Park. The landscape consists of bleak yet beautiful moors interspersed with lush green valleys. Agriculture is still the main source of income here as it has been for centuries, and until the advent of coal, the communities' local source of fuel was turf. In the 19th century, the geology of the area created extractive industries which included ironstone, lime, coal and building stone.

Mallyan Spout
A footpath leads to this waterfall from Goathland.

Farndale
During springtime, this area is famous for the beauty and profusion of its daffodils.

"Fat Betty" White Cross Crosses and standing stones are a feature of the Moors.

Goathland
A centre for forest and moorland walks, it has 19th-century houses and good accommodation.

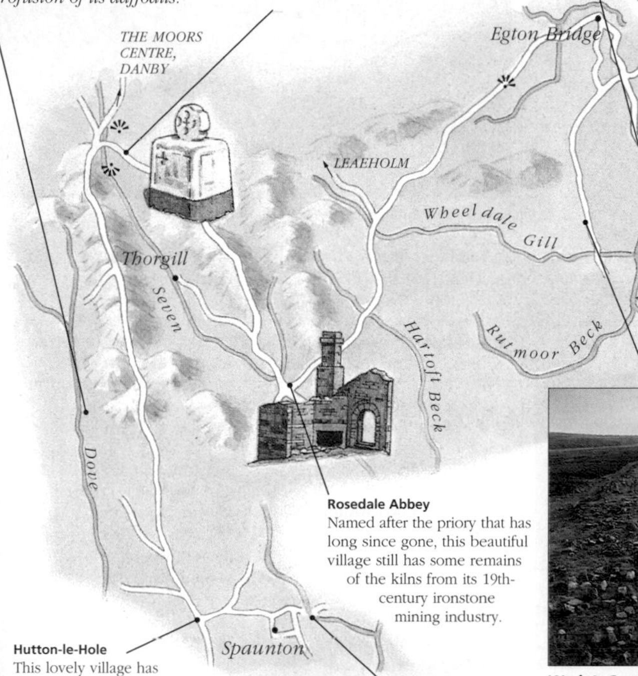

THE MOORS CENTRE, DANBY

Egton Bridge

LEAEHOLM

Wheeldale Gill

WHITBY

West Beck

Thorgill

Seven

Hartoft Beck

Rutmoor Beck

Blawarth Beck

Dove

Rosedale Abbey
Named after the priory that has long since gone, this beautiful village still has some remains of the kilns from its 19th-century ironstone mining industry.

Wade's Causeway
Often called the Roman Road, its origins and destination are unknown. Long considered Roman in date, this is now less certain, although it may date from towards the end of the Roman occupation.

Hutton-le-Hole
This lovely village has the excellent Ryedale Folk Museum.

Spaunton

VISITORS' CHECKLIST

North Yorkshire. 🚆 *Pickering.* 🚌 *Pickering (Easter–Oct).* **Moorsbus Tel** *01845 597000.* ℹ️ *Eastgate, Pickering (01751 473791); Moors Centre (01439 772737).* **www**.moors.uk.net

Lastingham
Lastingham's church, dating from 1078, has a Norman crypt with stone carving.

0 kilometres   2

0 miles   2

Whitby ⑲

Whitby's known history dates back to the 7th century, when a Saxon monastery was founded on the site of today's famous 13th-century abbey ruins. In the 18th and early 19th centuries it became an industrial port and shipbuilding town, as well as a whaling centre. In the Victorian era, the red-roofed cottages at the foot of the east cliff were filled with workshops crafting jet into jewellery and ornaments. Today, the tourist shops that have replaced them sell antique-crafted examples of the distinctive black gem.

Jet comb (c.1870)

VISITORS' CHECKLIST

North Yorkshire. 🗻 13,500. ✈ Teeside, 50 miles (80 km) NW Whitby. 🚂 Station Sq. 🚉 Langborne Rd (01723 383637). 🚌 Tue, Sat. 🎭 Whitby Festival: Jun; Angling Festival: Apr; Lifeboat Day: Jul or Aug; Folk Week: 17–23 Aug; Whitby Regatta: Aug. **www.** discoveryorkshirecoast.com

Exploring Whitby

Whitby is divided into two by the estuary of the River Esk. The Old Town, with its pretty cobbled streets and pastel-hued houses, huddles round the harbour. High above it is St Mary's Church with a wood interior reputedly fitted by ships' carpenters. The ruins of the 13th-century Whitby Abbey, nearby, are still used as a landmark by mariners. From them you get a fine view over the still-busy harbour, strewn with colourful nets. A pleasant place for a stroll, the harbour is overlooked by an imposing bronze clifftop statue of the explorer Captain James Cook (1728–79), who was apprenticed as a teenager to a Whitby shipping firm.

Lobster pots lining the quayside of Whitby's quaint harbour

Medieval arches above the nave of Whitby Abbey

🏚 Whitby Abbey

(EH) Abbey Lane. **Tel** 01947 603568. ☐ Apr–Sep: daily; Oct–Mar: Thu–Mon. 📷 ♿ 🚻
The monastery founded in 657 was sacked by Vikings in 870. In the 11th century it was rebuilt as a Benedictine Abbey. The ruins date mainly from the 13th century. A visitor centre has recently been added.

🔒 St Mary's Parish Church

East Cliff. **Tel** 01947 603421. ☐ daily.
Stuart and Georgian alterations to this Norman church have left a mixture of twisted wood columns and maze-like 18th-century box pews. The 1778 triple-decker pulpit has rather avant-garde decor – ear-trumpets used by a Victorian rector's deaf wife.

🏛 Captain Cook Memorial Museum

Grape Lane. **Tel** 01947 601900. ☐ Mar–Oct & Feb half-term: daily. 📷 🚻 **www.**cookmuseumwhitby.co.uk
The young James Cook slept in the attic of this 17th-century harbourside house when he was apprenticed nearby. The museum has displays of period furniture in the style described in the inventories of the house, and watercolours by artists who travelled on his voyages.

🏛 Whitby Museum and Pannett Art Gallery

Pannett Park. **Tel** 01947 602908. ☐ May–Sep: daily (Sun: pm); Oct–Apr: Tue–Sun (Sun: pm). ● Sun: am; 24 Dec–2 Jan. 📷 museum. ♿ limited. 🚻

The Pannett Park grounds, museum and gallery were a gift of Whitby solicitor, Robert Pannett (1834–1920), to house his art collection. Among the museum's treasures are objects illustrating local history, such as jet jewellery, and Captain Cook artifacts.
  A three-storey extension was completed at the Pannett Art Gallery in 2005, which houses a costume gallery and photography and map collections.

🔒 Caedmon's Cross

East Cliff.
On the path side of the abbey's clifftop graveyard is the cross of Caedmon, an illiterate labourer who worked at the abbey in the 7th century. He experienced a vision that inspired him to compose cantos of Anglo-Saxon religious verse, which are still sung today.

Cross of Caedmon (1898)

Robin Hood's Bay ㉒

North Yorkshire. 👥 *1,400.* 🚂 🚌 *Whitby.* ℹ️ *Langbourne Rd, Whitby (01947 602674).*
www.discoveryorkshirecoast.com

Legend has it that Robin Hood (*see p336*) kept his boats here in case he needed to make a quick getaway. The village has a history as a smugglers' haven, and many houses have ingenious hiding places for contraband. The cobbled main street is so steep that visitors need to leave their vehicles in the car park. In the village centre, attractive, narrow streets full of colour-washed stone cottages huddle around a quaint quay. There is a rocky beach with rock pools for children to play in. At low tide, the pleasant walk south to Boggle Hole takes 15 minutes, but you need to keep an eye on the tides.

Cobbled alley in the Bay Town area of Robin Hood's Bay

The fishing port and town of Scarborough nestling round the harbour

Scarborough ㉓

North Yorkshire. 👥 *54,000.* 🚂 🚌 ℹ️ *Pavilion House, Valley Bridge Rd (01723 383636).* 🛒 *Mon–Sat.*
www.discoveryorkshirecoast.com

The history of Scarborough as a resort can be traced back to 1626, when it became known as a spa. In the Industrial Revolution (*see pp348–9*) it was nicknamed "the Queen of the Watering Places", but the post-World War II trend for holidays abroad has meant fewer visitors. The town has two beaches; the South Bay amusement arcades contrast with the quieter North Bay.

Playwright Alan Ayckbourn premiers his work at the Stephen Joseph theatre, and Anne Brontë (*see p412*) is buried in St Mary's Church.

Bronze and Iron Age relics have been found on the site of **Scarborough Castle**, and **Wood End Museum** exhibits local geology and history. The **Rotunda** (1828–9) was one of Britain's first purpose-built museums. Works by local artist Atkinson Grimshaw (1836–93) hang in **Scarborough Art Gallery**. The **Sea-Life and Marine Sanctuary**'s baby seals are its main attraction.

🏰 **Scarborough Castle**
(EH) Castle Rd. **Tel** 01723 372451.
⏰ mid-Mar–Sep: daily; Oct–mid-Mar: Thu–Mon. 🔲 ♿ 🏛
🏛 **Wood End Museum**
The Crescent. **Tel** 01723 367326.
⏰ Jun–Sep: Tue–Sun; Oct–May: Wed, Sat, Sun & public hols. 🏛 🔲
🏛 **Rotunda Museum**
Vernon Rd. **Tel** 01723 374839.
⏰ Jun–Sep: Tue–Sun; Oct–May: Tue, Sat, Sun & public hols. ⬤ 25 & 26 Dec, 1 Jan. 🏛 🔲
🏛 **Scarborough Art Gallery**
The Crescent. **Tel** 01723 374753.
⏰ Jun–Sep: Tue–Sun; Oct–May: Thu, Fri, Sat & public hols. ⬤ 25 & 26 Dec, 1 Jan. 🏛 🔲 🔲
🐟 **Sea-Life and Marine Sanctuary**
Scalby Mills Rd. **Tel** 01723 376125.
⏰ daily. ⬤ 25 Dec. 🔲 ♿ 🔲 🏛
www.sealifeeurope.com

THE GROWING POPULARITY OF SWIMMING

During the 18th century, sea-bathing came to be regarded as a healthy pastime, and from 1735 onwards men and women, on separate stretches of the coast, could be taken out into the sea in bathing huts, or "machines". In the 18th century, bathing was segregated although nudity was permitted. The Victorians brought in fully clothed bathing, and 19th-century workers from Britain's industrial heartlands used the new steam trains to visit the coast for their holidays. At this time, British seaside resorts such as Blackpool (*see p371*) and Scarborough expanded to meet the new demand.

A Victorian bathing hut on wheels

Castle Howard ㉒

Pillar detail in the Great Hall, carved by Samuel Carpenter

Still owned and lived in by the Howard family, Castle Howard was created by Charles, 3rd Earl of Carlisle. In 1699, he commissioned Sir John Vanbrugh, a man of dramatic ideas but with no previous architectural experience, to design a palace for him. Vanbrugh's grand designs of 1699 were put into practice by architect Nicholas Hawksmoor *(see p28)* and the main body of the house was completed by 1712. The West Wing was built in 1753–9, using a design by Thomas Robinson, son-in-law of the 3rd Earl. Castle Howard was used as the location for the television version of Evelyn Waugh's novel *Brideshead Revisited* (1945).

Temple of the Four Winds
Vanbrugh's last work, designed in 1724, has a dome and four Ionic porticoes. Situated in the grounds at the end of the terrace, it is typical of an 18th-century "landscape building".

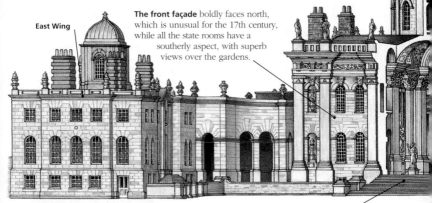

East Wing

The front façade boldly faces north, which is unusual for the 17th century, while all the state rooms have a southerly aspect, with superb views over the gardens.

North Front

★ Great Hall
Rising 20 m (66 ft), from its 515 sq m (5,500 sq ft) floor to the dome, the Great Hall has columns by Samuel Carpenter (1660–1713), wall paintings by Pellegrini and a circular gallery.

SIR JOHN VANBRUGH

Vanbrugh (1664–1726) trained as a soldier, but became better known as a playwright, architect and member of the Whig nobility. He collaborated with Hawksmoor over the design of Blenheim Palace, but his bold architectural vision, later greatly admired, was mocked by the establishment. He died while working on the garden buildings and grounds of Castle Howard.

Chapel Stained Glass
Admiral Edward Howard ...ered the chapel in 1870–75. ...e windows were designed by Edward Burne-Jones and ...ade by William Morris & Co.

VISITORS' CHECKLIST

A64 from York. *Tel* 01653 648 333. York then bus, or Malton then taxi. **House** mid-Feb–Oct: 11am–4pm daily. **Grounds** 10am–4:30pm daily. www.castlehoward.co.uk

Bust of the 7th Earl
J H Foley sculpted this portrait bust, which stands at the top of the Grand Staircase in the West Wing, in 1870.

★ Long Gallery
The Howard lineage is illustrated here by a large number of portraits, including works by Reynolds and Pannini.

West Wing

Tourist entrance

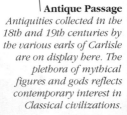

Antique Passage
Antiquities collected in the 18th and 19th centuries by the various earls of Carlisle are on display here. The plethora of mythical figures and gods reflects contemporary interest in Classical civilizations.

STAR SIGHTS

★ Great Hall

★ Long Gallery

Museum Room
Furniture here includes Regency chairs, Persian rugs and this 17th-century cabinet.

Eden Camp ㉓

Malton, North Yorkshire. *Tel 01653 697777.* ⚞ *Malton then taxi.* ○ *mid-Jan–late Dec: daily.* 🎫 📷 ♿ 🖥 www.edencamp.co.uk

This is an unusual, award-winning theme museum which pays tribute to the British people during World War II. Italian and German prisoners of war were kept at Eden Camp between 1939 and 1948. Today, some original huts built by Italian prisoners in 1942 are used as a museum, with period tableaux and a soundtrack. Each hut adopts a theme to take the visitor through civilian life in wartime, from Chamberlain's radio announcement of the outbreak of hostilities to the coming of peace. Visitors, including schoolchildren and nostalgic veterans, can see the Doodle-bug V-1 bomb which crashed outside the Officers' Mess, take tea in the canteen or experience a night in the Blitz. A tour can last for several hours.

British and American flags by the sign for Eden Camp

Wharram Percy ㉔

(EH) North Yorkshire. *Tel 01904 601 901.* ⚞ *Malton, then taxi.* ○ *daily.* www.english-heritage.org.uk

This is one of England's most important medieval village sites. Recent excavations have unearthed evidence of a 30-household community, with two manors, and the remains of a medieval church. There is also a millpond which has beautiful wild flowers in late spring. Wharram Percy is set in a pretty valley, signposted off the B1248 from Burdale, in the heart of the green, rolling Wolds. It is about 20 minutes' walk from the car park, and makes an ideal picnic stop.

Alabaster carving on the chimney-piece at Burton Agnes

Burton Agnes ㉕

On A614, nr Driffield, East Yorks. *Tel 01262 490324.* ⚞ *Driffield, then bus.* ○ *Apr–Oct: daily.* 📷 ♿ *limited.* 🖥 🎫 www.burton-agnes.com

Of all the grand houses in this area, Burton Agnes Hall is a firm favourite. This is partly because the attractive, red-brick Elizabethan mansion has such a homely atmosphere. One of the first portraits you see in the Small Hall is of Anne Griffith, whose father, Sir Henry, built the house. There is a monument to him in the local church.

Burton Agnes has remained in the hands of the original family and has changed little since it was built, between 1598 and 1610. You enter it by the turreted gatehouse, and the entrance hall has a fine Elizabethan alabaster chimney piece. The massive oak staircase is an impressive example of Elizabethan woodcarving.

In the library is a collection of Impressionist and Post-Impressionist art, pleasantly out of character with the rest of the house, including works by André Derain, Renoir and Augustus John. The extensive grounds include a purpose-built play area for children.

Bempton and Flamborough Head ㉖

East Yorkshire. 🏘 *4,300.* ⚞ *Bempton.* 🚢 *Bridlington.* ℹ *25 Prince St, Bridlington (01262 673474).* www.eastriding.gov.uk

Bempton, which consists of 5 miles (8 km) of steep chalk cliffs between Speeton and Flamborough Head, is the largest seabird-breeding colony in England, and is famous for its puffins. The ledges and fissures provide ideal nest-sites for more

Nesting gannet on the chalk cliffs at Bempton

than 100,000 pairs of birds. Today, eight different species, including skinny black shags and kittiwakes, thrive on the Grade 1 listed *(see p671)* Bempton cliffs. Bempton is the only mainland site for goose-sized gannets, well known for their dramatic fishing techniques. May, June and July are the best bird-watching months.

The spectacular cliffs are best seen from the north side of the Flamborough Head peninsula.

Beverley ㉗

East Riding of Yorkshire. 🔲 *30,000.*
ℹ️ *34 Butcher Row (01482 867430).*
🚆 *Sat.* www.visiteastyorkshire.com

The history of Beverley dates back to the 8th century, when Old Beverley served as a retreat for John, later Bishop of York, who was canonized for his healing powers. Over the centuries Beverley grew as a medieval sanctuary town. Like York, it is an attractive combination of both medieval and Georgian buildings.

The best way to enter Beverley is through the last of five medieval town gates, the castellated North Bar (rebuilt

1409–10). The bars were constructed so that market goods had to pass through them and a toll (levy) paid.

The skyline is dominated by the twin towers of the magnificent **minster**. This was co-founded in 937 by Athelstan, King of Wessex, in place of the church that John of Beverley had chosen as his final resting place in 721. The decorated nave is the earliest surviving building work which dates back to the early 1300s. It is particularly famous for its 16th-century choir stalls and 68 misericords *(see p341).*

The minster contains many early detailed stone carvings, including a set of four from about 1308 that illustrate figures with ailments such as toothache and lumbago. On the north side of the altar is the richly carved 14th-century Gothic Percy tomb, thought to be that of Lady Idoine Percy. Also on the north side is the Fridstol, or Peace Chair, said to date from 924-39, the time of Athelstan. Anyone who sat on it would be granted 30 days' sanctuary. Within the North Bar, **St Mary's Church** has a 13th-century chancel and houses Britain's largest number of medieval

Minstrel Pillar in St Mary's Church

The inspiration for Lewis Carroll's White Rabbit, St Mary's Church

stone carvings of musical instruments. The brightly painted 16th-century Minstrel Pillar is particularly notable. Painted on the panelled chancel ceiling are portraits of monarchs after 1445. On the richly sculpted doorway of St Michael's Chapel is the grinning pilgrim rabbit said to have inspired Lewis Carroll's White Rabbit in *Alice in Wonderland*.

There is a great day out to be had at **Beverley Races**, with various theme days throughout the season and excellent food and drink.

🔵 **Beverley Races**
York Rd. *Tel 01482 867488.*
⭕ *20 meetings Apr–Sep.* 📋
♿ 🍴
@ info@beverleyracecourse.co.uk

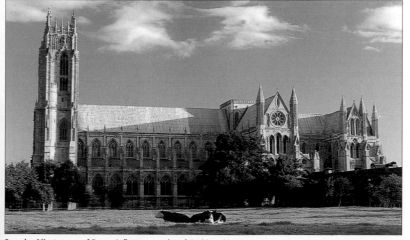

Beverley Minster, one of Europe's finest examples of Gothic architecture

Burton Constable 28

Nr Hull, East Yorkshire. *Tel 01964 562400.* 🚃 *Hull then taxi.* ⬜ *Easter– Oct: Sat–Thu.* 🏞 ♿ ▣ ▢ 🖬
www.burtonconstable.com

The Constable family have been leading landowners since the 13th century, and have lived at Burton Constable since work began on it in 1570. It is an Elizabethan house, altered in the 18th century by Thomas Lightholer, Thomas Atkinson and James Wyatt. Today, its 30 rooms include Georgian and Victorian interiors. It has a fine collection of Chippendale furniture and family portraits dating from the 16th century. Most of the collections of prints, textiles and drawings belong to Leeds City Art Galleries. The family still lives in the south wing.

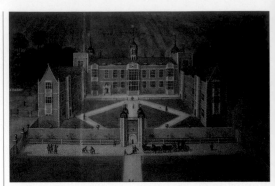
Painting of Burton Constable (c.1690) by an anonymous artist

The Princes' Dock in Kingston upon Hull's restored docks area

Kingston upon Hull 29

Kingston upon Hull. 🏛 *270,000.* 🚃 🚌 ⛴ 🚕 *Paragon St. (01482 223559).* 🏪 *Mon–Sat.*
www.hullcc.gov.uk

There is a lot more to Hull than the heritage of a thriving fishing industry. The restored town centre docks are attractive, and Hull's Old Town, laid out in medieval times, is all cobbled, winding streets and quaintly askew red-brick houses. You can follow the "Seven Seas" Fish Trail, a path of inlaid metal fishes on the city's pavements that illustrates the many different varieties that have been landed in Hull, from anchovy to shark.

In Victoria Square is the **Maritime Museum**. Built in 1871 as the offices of the Hull Dock Company, it traces the city's maritime history. Among its exhibits are an ornate whalebone and vertebrae bench and a display of complicated rope knots such as the Eye Splice and the Midshipman's Hitch.

An imposing Elizabethan building, **Hands on History**, explores Hull's story through a collection of some of its families' artifacts.

In the heart of the Old Town, the **William Wilberforce House** is one of the surviving examples of the High Street's brick merchants' dwellings. Its first-floor oak-panelled rooms date from the 17th century, but most of the house is dedicated to the Wilberforce family. The house will be reopening in 2007, following a £1.6 million refurbishment.

Nearby is the **Streetlife Transport Museum**, Hull's most popular and noisiest museum, loved by children. It features Britain's oldest tramcar. New to Hull, at the mouth of the River Hull, **The Deep** is the world's only submarium, in a stunning building and dramatic setting. With lots of exciting sea life and state-of-the-art technology, it is ideal for families.

🏛 **Maritime Museum**
Queen Victoria Sq. *Tel 01482 613903.* ⬜ *daily (Sun: pm).* ♿ 🖬
www.hullcc.gov.uk/museums

🏛 **Hands on History**
South Churchside. *Tel 01482 613902.* ⬜ *daily (Sun: pm).* ● *23–27 Dec, 1 Jan, Good Fri.* 🖬 ♿

WILLIAM WILBERFORCE (1758–1833)

William Wilberforce, born in Hull to a merchant family, was a natural orator. After studying Classics at Cambridge, he entered politics and in 1784 gave one of his first public addresses in York. The audience was captivated, and Wilberforce realized the potential of his powers of persuasion. From 1785 onwards, adopted by the Pitt government as spokesman for the abolition of slavery, he conducted a determined and conscientious campaign. But his speeches won him enemies, and in 1792, threats from a slave-importer meant that he needed a constant armed guard. In 1807 his bill to abolish the lucrative slave trade became law.

A 19th-century engraving of Wilberforce by J Jenkins

🏛 William Wilberforce Hse
High St, Hull. *Tel* 01482 613921.
⭘ *daily (Sun: pm).* 🅿 ⚿ *limited.*

🏛 Streetlife Transport Museum
High St, Hull. *Tel* 01482 613956.
⭘ *Mon–Sat, Sun pm.* ⚿ 🅿

💢 The Deep
Hull (via Citadel Way). *Tel* 01482 381000. ⭘ *daily.* ⚿ 📷 📹 🅿
🅿 www.thedeep.co.uk

Holderness and Spurn Head ㉚

East Riding of Yorkshire. 🚆 *Hull (Paragon St) then bus.* 🚌 *120 Newbegin, Hornsea (01964 536404).*

This curious flat area east of Hull, with straight roads and delicately waving fields of oats and barley, in many ways resembles Holland, except that its mills are derelict. Beaches stretch for 30 miles (46 km) along the coastline. The main resort towns are **Withernsea** and **Hornsea**.

The Holderness landscape only exists because of erosion higher up the coast. The sea continues to wash down tiny bits of rock which accumulate. Around 1560, this began to form a sandbank, and by 1669 it had became large enough to be colonized as Sonke Sand. The last bits of silting mud and debris joined the island to the mainland as recently as the 1830s. Today, you can drive through the eerie, lush wilderness of Sunk Island on the way east to Spurn Head. This is located at the tip of the Spurn Peninsula,

a 3.5 mile (6 km) spit of land that has also built up as the result of coastal erosion elsewhere. Flora, fauna and birdlife have been protected here by the Yorkshire Wildlife Trust since 1960. Walking here gives the eerie feeling that the land could be eroded from under your feet at any time. A surprise discovery at the end of Spurn Head is a tiny community of pilots and lifeboat crew, constantly on call to guide ships into Hull harbour, or help cope with disasters.

Fishing boat at Grimsby's National Fishing Heritage Centre

Grimsby ㉛

NE Lincs. 🏘 92,000. 🚆 🚌 🛈 42–43 Alexandra Rd, Cleethorpes (01472 323111). www.nelincs.gov.uk

Perched at the mouth of the River Humber, Grimsby was founded in the Middle Ages by a Danish fisherman

by the name of Grim, and rose to prominence in the 19th century as one of the world's largest fishing ports. Its first dock was opened in 1800 and, with the arrival of the railways, the town secured the means of transporting its catch all over the country. Even though the traditional fishing industry had declined by the 1970s, dock area redevelopment has ensured that Grimsby's unique heritage is retained.

This is best demonstrated by the award-winning **National Fishing Heritage Centre**, a museum that recreates the industry in its 1950s heyday, capturing the atmosphere of the period. Visitors sign on as crew members on a trawler and, by means of a variety of vivid interactive displays, travel from the back streets of Grimsby to the Arctic fishing grounds. On the way, they can experience the roll of the ship, the smell of the fish and the heat of the engine. The tour can be finished off with a guided viewing of the restored 1950s trawler, the *Ross Tiger*.

Other attractions in Grimsby include an International Jazz Festival every September, a restored Victorian shopping street called Abbeygate, a market, a wide selection of restaurants, and the nearby seaside resorts of Cleethorpes, Mablethorpe and Skegness.

🏛 National Fishing Heritage Centre
Heritage Sq, Alexandra Dock.
Tel 01472 323345. ⭘ *Easter–Oct: daily.* 📷 ⚿ 📹 🅿

Isolated lighthouse at Spurn Head, at the tip of Spurn Peninsula

Street-by-Street: York ❷

Monk Bar coat of arms

The city of York has retained so much of its medieval structure that walking into its centre is like entering a living museum. Many of the ancient timbered houses, perched on narrow, winding streets, such as the Shambles, are protected by a conservation order. Cars are banned from the centre, so there are always student bikes bouncing over cobbled streets. Its strategic position led to its development as a railway centre in the 19th century.

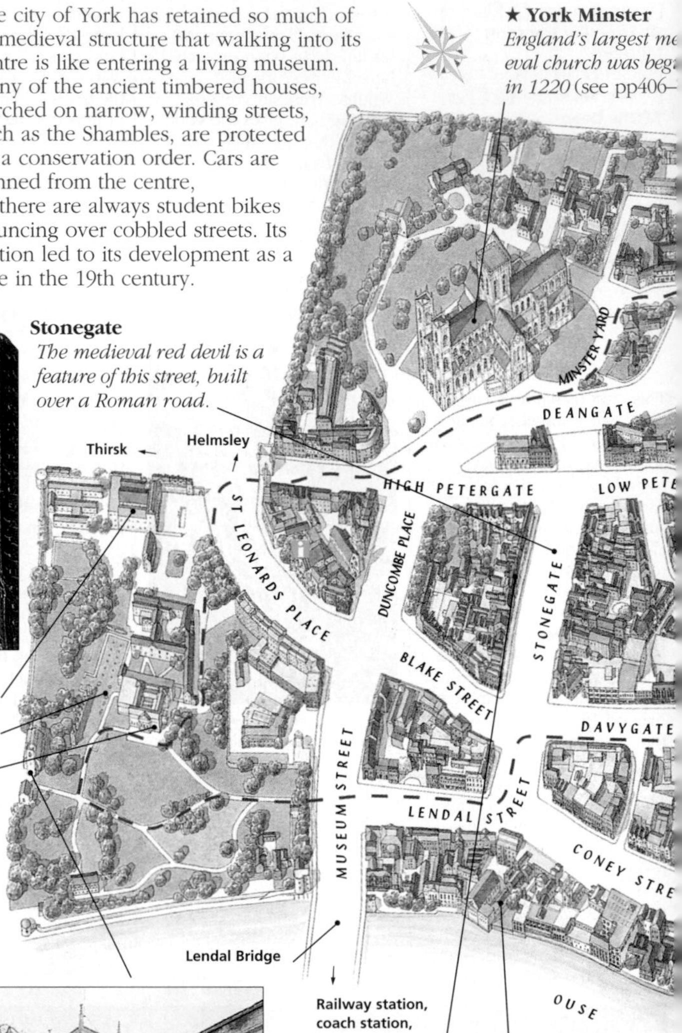

★ York Minster
*England's largest me[di]-
eval church was beg[un]
in 1220 (see pp406–*

Stonegate
*The medieval red devil is a
feature of this street, built
over a Roman road.*

Thirsk ←   Helmsley

ST LEONARDS PLACE

HIGH PETERGATE
LOW PETE[R]
DEANGATE
MINSTER YARD
DUNCOMBE PLACE
STONEGATE
BLAKE STREET
DAVYGATE
MUSEUM STREET
LENDAL STREET
CONEY STRE[ET]

**York City
Art Gallery**

St Mary's Abbey

**Yorkshire
Museum**
contains a fine
collection
of fossils,
discovered at
Whitby in the
19th century.

Lendal Bridge

Railway station,
coach station,
National Rail-
way Museum,
and Leeds

OUSE

**Ye Old Starre
Inne** is one of
the oldest
pubs in York.

St Olave's Church
*The 11th-century church, next to the gate-
house of St Mary's Abbey (see p350), was
founded by the Earl of Northumbria in
memory of St Olaf, King of Norway. To the
left is the Chapel of St Mary on the Walls.*

Guildhall
*This two-headed
medieval roof boss
is on the 15th-
century Guildhall,
situated beside the River Ouse and restored
after bomb damage during World War II.*

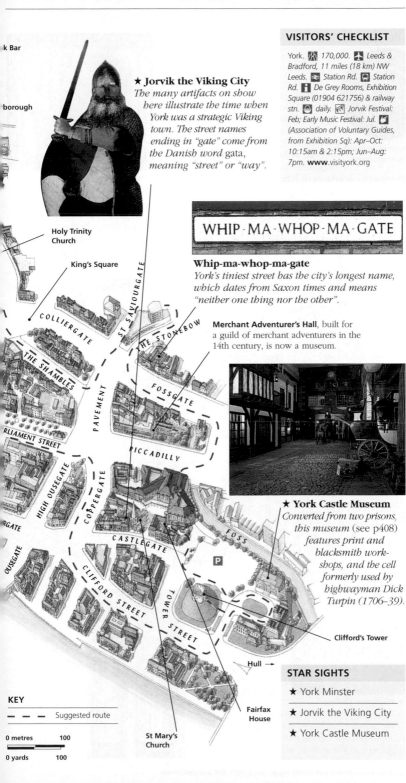

★ Jorvik the Viking City
The many artifacts on show here illustrate the time when York was a strategic Viking town. The street names ending in "gate" come from the Danish word gata, meaning "street" or "way".

k Bar

borough

Holy Trinity Church

King's Square

ST SAVIOURGATE

COLLIERGATE

THE STONEBOW

THE SHAMBLES

PARLIAMENT STREET

PAVEMENT

FOSSGATE

PICCADILLY

HIGH OUSEGATE

COPPERGATE

RGATE

OUSEGATE

CASTLEGATE

FOSS

CLIFFORD STREET

TOWER STREET

VISITORS' CHECKLIST

York. 170,000. Leeds & Bradford, 11 miles (18 km) NW Leeds. Station Rd. Station Rd. De Grey Rooms, Exhibition Square (01904 621756) & railway stn. daily. Jorvik Festival: Feb; Early Music Festival: Jul. (Association of Voluntary Guides, from Exhibition Sq): Apr–Oct: 10:15am & 2:15pm; Jun–Aug: 7pm. www.visityork.org

WHIP·MA·WHOP·MA·GATE

Whip-ma-whop-ma-gate
York's tiniest street has the city's longest name, which dates from Saxon times and means "neither one thing nor the other".

Merchant Adventurer's Hall, built for a guild of merchant adventurers in the 14th century, is now a museum.

★ York Castle Museum
Converted from two prisons, this museum (see p408) features print and blacksmith work-shops, and the cell formerly used by highwayman Dick Turpin (1706–39).

Clifford's Tower

Hull →

STAR SIGHTS

★ York Minster
★ Jorvik the Viking City
★ York Castle Museum

Fairfax House

St Mary's Church

KEY

– – –   Suggested route

0 metres   100
0 yards   100

York Minster

The largest Gothic cathedral north of the Alps, York Minster is 158 m (519 ft) long and 76 m (249 ft) wide across the transepts, and houses the largest collection of medieval stained glass in Britain *(see p409)*. The word "minster" usually means a church served by monks, but priests always served at York. The first minster began as a wooden chapel used to baptize King Edwin of Northumbria in 627. There have been several cathedrals on or near the site, including an 11th-century Norman structure. The present minster was begun in 1220 and completed 250 years later. In July 1984, the south transept roof was destroyed by fire. Restoration cost £2.25 million.

Central sunflower in rose window

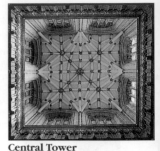

Central Tower
This lantern tower was reconstructed in 1420–65 (after partial collapse in 1407) from a design by the master stonemason William Colchester.

Great East Window *(p409)*

The Choir has a vaulted entrance with a 15th-century boss of the Assumption of the Virgin.

South transept entrance

The 16th-century rose window

★ Choir Screen
Sited between the choir and the nave, this 15th-century stone screen depicts kings of England from William I to Henry VI, and has a canopy of angels.

★ Chapter House
A Latin inscription near the entrance of the wooden-vaulted Chapter House (1260–85) reads: "As the rose is the flower of flowers, so this is the house of houses".

The Nave, begun 1291, was severe[ly] damaged by fire [in] 1840. Rebuildin[g] costs were heav[y] but it was re-open[ed] with a new peal [of] bells in 184[?]

VISITORS' CHECKLIST

Deangate, York. ***Tel** 01904 557216.* ◯ *Mon–Sat: 9am–5pm (from 9:30am Nov–Mar); Sun: noon–3:45pm. Opening times may change subject to major services.* ● *Good Fri, Easter Sun, 24 & 25 Dec.* *to Minster, Undercroft & the Tower.* *Mon–Sat: 7:30am, 7:45am, 12:30pm, 5:30pm (evensong); Sun: 8am, 10am, 11:30am, 4pm.* *main floors.*
www.yorkminster.org

The western towers, with their 15th-century decorative panelling and elaborate pinnacles, contrast with the simpler design of the north transept. The southwest tower is the minster belfry.

Great West Door
West Window

STAR SIGHTS

★ Chapter House

★ Choir Screen

Timbered interior of the Merchant Adventurers' Hall

Monk Bar

This is one of York's finest original medieval gates, situated at the end of Goodramgate. It is vaulted on three floors, and the portcullis still works. In the Middle Ages, the rooms above it were rented out, and it was a prison in the 16th century. Its decorative details include men holding stones ready to drop on intruders.

York City Art Gallery

Exhibition Sq. ***Tel** 01904 697979.* ◯ *daily.* ● *24–26 Dec, 1 Jan.*
www.york.art.museum

This Italianate building of 1879 holds a wide-ranging collection of paintings from western Europe dating from the early 14th century. There is also a collection of British and foreign studio pottery, including work by Bernard Leach, William Staite Murray and Shoji Hamada.

A 15th-century French portrait of St Anthony in York City Art Gallery

Clifford's Tower

(EH) Clifford's St. ***Tel** 01904 646940.* ◯ *daily.* ● *24–26 Dec, 1 Jan.*
www.english-heritage.org.uk

Sited on top of a mound that William the Conqueror built for his original wooden castle, destroyed by fire during anti-Jewish riots in 1190, Clifford's Tower dates from the 13th century. Built by Henry III, it was named after the de Clifford family, who were constables of the castle.

ARC

St Saviourgate. ***Tel** 01904 543403.* ◯ *daily (advisable to book in advance).* ● *24–25 Dec.*

Housed in a restored medieval church off the Shambles, this is a centre for exploring archaeology. Visitors become archaeological detectives and discover how archaeologists have pieced together clues from the past to unravel the history of the Viking age in York.

Merchant Adventurers' Hall

Fossgate. ***Tel** 01904 654818.* ◯ *Easter–Sep: daily; Oct–Easter: Mon–Sat.* ● *24 Dec–3 Jan.*
www.theyorkcompany.co.uk

Built by the York Merchants' Guild, which controlled the northern cloth trade in the 15th–17th centuries, this building has fine timberwork. The Great Hall is probably the best example of its kind in Europe. Among its paintings is an unattributed 17th-century copy of Van Dyck's portrait of Charles I's queen, Henrietta Maria. Below the Great Hall is the hospital, which was used by the guild until 1900, and a private chapel.

Exploring York

The appeal of York is its many layers of history. A medieval city constructed on top of a Roman one, it was first built in AD 71, when it became capital of the northern province and was known as Eboracum. It was here that Constantine the Great was made emperor in 306, and reorganized Britain into four provinces. A hundred years later, the Roman army had withdrawn. Eboracum was renamed Eoforwic, under the Saxons, and then became a Christian stronghold. The Danish street names are the reminder that it was a Viking centre from 867, and one of Europe's chief trading bases. Between 1100 and 1500 it was England's second city. The glory of York is the minster *(see pp406–7)*. The city also boasts 18 medieval churches, 3 mile long (4.8 km) medieval city walls, elegant Jacobean and Georgian architecture and fine museums.

The Middleham Jewel, Yorkshire Museum

🏛 York Castle Museum

The Eye of York. *Tel 01904 687687.*
◯ *daily.* ● *24–26 Dec.* ▨ ♿ *ground floor only.* ▢ 🖪
www.york.castle.museum
Housed in two 18th-century prisons, the museum has a fine folk collection, started by Dr John Kirk of the market town of Pickering. Opened in 1938, its period displays include a Jacobean dining room, a moorland cottage, and a 1950s front room. It also contains an exhibition on the traditions of birth, marriages and death in Britain from 1700 to 2000.

The most famous exhibits include the reconstructed Victorian street of Kirkgate, complete with shopfronts, and the Anglo Saxon York Helmet, discovered in 1982.

🛡 York Minster

See pp406–7.

🏛 Jorvik, The Viking City

Coppergate. *Tel 01904 643211.*
◯ *daily.* ● *25 Dec.* ▨ ♿ *ring first.*
🖥 www.vikingjorvik.com
This popular centre is built on the site of the original Viking settlement which archaeologists uncovered at Coppergate. It is most famous for recreating the smells of Viking York. A dynamic vision of 10th-century York combines with new technology to transform archaeological evidence and bring the hub of the Viking world to life.

🏛 Yorkshire Museum and St Mary's Abbey

Museum Gardens. *Tel 01904 551800.*
◯ *daily.* ▨ ♿ 🖪
Yorkshire Museum was in the news when it purchased the 15th-century Middleham Jewel for £2.5 million, one of the finest pieces of English Gothic jewellery found this century. Other exhibits include 2nd-century Roman mosaics and an Anglo-Saxon silver gilt bowl.

St Mary's Abbey *(see p350)* in the riverside grounds is where the medieval York Mystery Plays are set every few years.

Grand staircase and fine plaster ceiling at Fairfax House

♛ Fairfax House

Castlegate. *Tel 01904 655543.* ◯ *daily* *(Sun: pm, Fri: booked tour only 11am, 2pm).* ● *24, 26 & 31 Dec, 1 Jan.* ▨ 🖪 ♿ *limited.* 🖪
www.fairfaxhouse.co.uk
From 1755 to 1762 Viscount Fairfax built this fine Georgian town house for his daughter, Anne. The house was designed by John Carr *(see p28),* and restored in the 1980s. Between 1920 and 1965 it was a cinema and dancehall. Today, visitors can see the bedroom of Anne Fairfax (1725–93), and a fine collection of 18th-century furniture, porcelain and clocks.

🏛 National Railway Museum

Leeman Rd. *Tel 01904 621261.*
◯ *daily.* ● *24–26 Dec.* ♿ 🖪 🖪
www.nrm.org.uk
In what is the world's largest railway museum, nearly 200 years of history are explored using a variety of visual aids. Visitors can try wheel-tapping and shunting in the interactive gallery, or find out what made Stephenson's *Rocket* so successful. Exhibits include uniforms, rolling stock from 1797 onward and Queen Victoria's Royal Train carriage, as well as the very latest rail innovations.

Reproduction of Stephenson's Rocket (right) and 1830s first-class carriage in York's National Railway Museum

The Stained Glass of York Minster

York Minster houses the largest collection of medieval stained glass in Britain, some of it dating from the late 12th century. The glass was generally coloured during production, using metal oxides to produce the desired colour, then worked on by craftsmen on site. When a design had been produced, the glass was first cut, then trimmed to shape. Details

Window detail

were painted on, using iron oxide-based paint which was fused to the glass by firing in a kiln. Individual pieces were then leaded together to form the finished window.

Part of the fascination of the minster glass is its variety of subject matter. Some windows were paid for by lay donors who specified a particular subject, others reflect ecclesiastical patronage.

Miracle of St Nicholas *(late 12th century) was put in the nave over 100 years after it was made. It shows a Jew's conversion.*

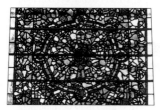

The Five Sisters *in the north transept are the largest examples of* grisaille *glass in Britain. This popular 13th-century technique involved creating fine patterning on clear glass and decorating it with black enamel.*

St John the Evangelist, *in part of the Great West Window (c.1338), is holding an eagle, itself an example of stickwork, where paint is scraped off to reveal clear glass.*

Noah's Ark *with its distinct boat-like shape is easily identified in the Great East Window.*

Edward III *is a fine example of the 14th-century "soft" style of painting, achieved by stippling the paint.*

The Great East Window *(1405–8), the size of a tennis court, is the largest area of medieval painted glass in the world. The Dean and Chapter paid master glazier John Thornton four shillings a week for this celebration of the Creation.*

Walter Skirlaw, *whose bishopric was revoked in favour of Richard Scrope, donated this window on its completion in 1408.*

Harewood House ㉝

Leeds. **Tel** 0113 2181010. ▐▐ *Leeds then bus.* ◯ *Feb– Nov: daily.* 🏷 ▐ 📷 *by arrangement.* 📷 📷
www.harewood.org

Designed by John Carr in 1759, Harewood House is the Yorkshire home of the Earl and Countess of Harewood.

The grand Palladian exterior is impressive, with interiors created by Robert Adam and an unrivalled collection of 18th-century furniture made specifically for Harewood by Yorkshire-born Thomas Chippendale (1711–79). There is a collection of paintings by Italian and English artists, including Reynolds and Gainsborough, and two watercolour rooms. The grounds by Capability Brown *(see p26)* include the **Harewood Bird Garden**, which has exotic species and a breeding programme of certain endangered varieties.

Bali starling, one of Harewood's rare birds

Leeds ㉞

Leeds. 🏛 750,000. ▐ ▐▐ ▐ ℹ *Leeds City Station (0113 2425242).* 📧 *Mon–Sat.* **www.**leeds.gov.uk

The third largest of Britain's provincial cities, Leeds was at its most prosperous during the Victorian period. The most impressive legacy from this era is a series of ornate, covered shopping arcades. Also of note is the **Town Hall**, designed by Cuthbert Brodrick and opened by Queen Victoria in 1858.

Today, although Leeds is primarily an industrial city, it also offers a thriving cultural scene. Productions at **The Grand** by Opera North, one of Britain's top operatic companies, are of a high quality (undergoing refurbishment in 2006).

The **City Art Gallery** has impressive collections of British 20th-century art and of Victorian paintings, including works by local artist Atkinson

Grimshaw (1836–93). Among the late 19th-century French art are works by Signac, Courbet and Sisley. The Henry Moore Institute, added in 1993, is devoted to the research, study and display of sculpture of all periods. It comprises a reading room, study centre, library and video gallery, as well as galleries and an archive of material on and by Moore and other sculptural pioneers.

The **Armley Mills Museum**, in a 19th-century woollen mill, explores the industrial heritage of Leeds. Filled with original equipment, recorded sounds and models in 19th-century workers' clothes, it traces the history of the ready-to-wear industry.

A striking waterfront development by the River Aire has attracted two museums. The **Royal Armouries Museum**, from the Tower of London, tells the story of arms and armour around the world in battle, sport, self-defence and fashion. The **Thackray Medical Museum**, the largest of its kind in Europe, is a fascinating interactive display of medical advances, from a re-created vision of Victorian slum life to modern-day medical challenges.

Leeds has two sights that are especially suitable for children. **Tropical World**

The County Arcade, one of Leeds' restored shopping arcades

features crystal pools, a rainforest house, butterflies and tropical fish. There is also a farm and a Rare Breeds centre in the grounds of the Tudor-Jacobean **Temple Newsam House**, which has major art and furniture collections including Chippendale pieces.

🏛 **City Art Gallery**
The Headrow. **Tel** 0113 2478248.
◯ *daily (Sun: pm).* 📷 ▐ 📧

🏛 **Armley Mills Museum**
Canal Rd, Armley. **Tel** 0113 2637861.
◯ *Tue–Sun (Sun: pm); public hols.*
● *25, 26 Dec, 1 Jan.* 🏷 ▐ 📷

🏛 **Royal Armouries**
Armouries Drive. **Tel** 0113 2201999.
◯ *daily.* ● *24, 25 Dec.* ▐ 📷 📷

🏛 **Thackray Medical Museum**
Beckett St. 📷 0113 2457084.
◯ *daily.* ● *24–26, 31 Dec, 1 Jan.*
🏷 ▐ 📷

♣ **Tropical World** Canal Gdns,
Princes Ave. **Tel** 0113 266 1850. ◯ *daily.* ● *25, 26 Dec.* 🏷 ▐ 📷 📷

🎪 **Temple Newsam House**
Off A63. **Tel** 0113 2645535. ◯ *Tue–Sun.* ● *25 & 26 Dec, Jan.* 🏷 📷 📷

Working loom at the Armley Mills Museum in Leeds

The Other Side (1990–93) by David Hockney at Bradford's 1853 Gallery in Saltaire

Bradford ㉟

Bradford. 492,000. City Hall, Centenary Square (01274 433678). Mon–Sat. www.visitbradford.com

In the 16th century, Bradford was a thriving market town, and the opening of its canal in 1774 boosted trade. By 1850, it was the world's capital for worsted (fabric made from closely twisted wool). Many of the city's well-preserved civic and industrial buildings date from this period, such as the Wool Exchange on Market Street. In the 1800s a number of German textile manufacturers settled in what is now called Little Germany. Their houses are characterized by decorative stone carvings that illustrated the wealth and standing of the occupants.

Daguerreotype camera by Giroux (1839)

The **National Museum of Photography, Film and Television**, founded in 1983, explores the technology and art of these media. There is a television section called TV Heaven, where visitors can ask to watch their favourite programme. They are also encouraged to see themselves read the news on TV. The giant IMAX screen uses the world's largest film format. Film subjects include journeys into space, the ocean and the natural world.

The **Colour Museum** traces dyeing and textile printing from ancient Egypt to the present day with an emphasis on hands-on elements. **Bradford Industrial Museum** is housed in an original spinning mill. As well as seeing and hearing all the mill machinery, you can ride on a horse-drawn tram.

Saltaire, a Victorian industrial village (*see p349*), is on the outskirts of the city. Built by Sir Titus Salt for his Salts Mill workers, it was completed in 1873. The **1853 Gallery** has the world's largest collection of works by David Hockney, born in Bradford.

National Museum of Photography, Film and Television
Pictureville. **Tel** 01274 202030. daily (school hols); Tue–Sun (school terms); public holidays. 24–26 Dec. www.nmpft.org.uk

Colour Museum
1 Providence St. **Tel** 01274 390955. Tue–Sat. 24 Dec–2 Jan. www.sdc.org.uk

Bradford Industrial Museum
Moorside Mills, Moorside Rd. **Tel** 01274 435900. Tue–Sat, Sun (pm), public hols. www.visitbradford.com/attractions

1853 Gallery
Salts Mill, Victoria Rd. **Tel** 01274 531 163. daily. 25 & 26 Dec. www.saltsmill.org.uk

BRADFORD'S INDIAN COMMUNITY

Immigrants from the Indian subcontinent originally came to Bradford in the 1950s to work in the mills, but with the decline of the textile industry many began small businesses. By the mid-1970s there were 1,400 such enterprises in the area. Almost one fifth were in the food sector, born out of simple cafés catering for mill-workers whose families were far away. As Indian food became more popular, these restaurants thrived, and today there are over 200 serving the highly spiced dishes of the Indian subcontinent.

Balti in a Bradford restaurant

Haworth Parsonage, home to the Brontë family, now a museum

Haworth 🗆

Bradford. 🗆 *5,000.* 🗆 *Keighley.*
🗆 *2–4 West Lane (01535 642329).*
www.visithaworth.com

The setting of Haworth, in
bleak Pennine moorland
dotted with farmsteads, has
changed little since it was
home to the Brontë family. The
village boomed in the 1840s,
when there were more than
1,200 hand-looms in operation,
but it is more famous today
for the Brontë connection.

You can visit the **Brontë
Parsonage Museum**, home
from 1820–61 to novelists
Charlotte, Emily and Anne,
their brother Branwell and
their father, the Revd Patrick
Brontë. Built in 1778–9, the
house remains decorated as it
was during the 1850s. Eleven
rooms, including the children's
study and Charlotte's room,
display letters, manuscripts,

furniture and personal objects.
The nostalgic Victorian
**Keighley and Worth Valley
Railway** runs through
Haworth. It stops at Oakworth
station, where parts of *The
Railway Children* were filmed.
At the end of the line is the
Railway Museum at Oxenhope.

**🏛 Brontë Parsonage
Museum**
Church St. **Tel** *01535 642323.*
🗆 *daily.* 🗆 *24–27 Dec; Jan.* 🗆 🗆
🗆 *limited.* **www**.bronte.org.uk

Charlotte Brontë's childhood story
book, for her sister, Anne

THE BRONTË SISTERS

Charlotte Brontë (1816–55)

During a harsh, motherless childhood, Charlotte, Emily and Anne
retreated into fictional worlds of
their own, writing poems and
stories. As adults, they had to work
as governesses, but still published
a poetry collection in 1846. Only
two copies were sold, but in the
following year Charlotte's *Jane Eyre*,
became a bestseller, arousing interest in Emily's *Wuthering Heights*
and Anne's *Agnes Grey*. After her

siblings' deaths in 1848–9, Charlotte published her last novel,
Villette, in 1852. She married the Revd Nicholls, her father's
curate, in 1854, but died shortly afterwards.

Hebden Bridge 🗆

Calderdale. 🗆 *12,500.* 🗆 🗆
New Rd (01422 843831). 🗆 *Thu.*
www.hebdenbridge.co.uk

Hebden Bridge is a delightful
South Pennines former mill
town, surrounded by steep
hills and former 19th-century
mills. The houses seem to
defy gravity as they cling to
the valley sides. Due to the
gradient, one house is made
from two bottom floors, and
the top two floors form
another unit. To separate
ownership of these "flying
freeholds", an Act of
Parliament was devised.

There is a superb view of
Hebden Bridge from nearby
Heptonstall, where the poet
Sylvia Plath (1932–63) is
buried. The village contains a
Wesleyan chapel (1764).

Halifax 🗆

Calderdale. 🗆 *88,000.* 🗆 🗆 🗆
Piece Hall (01422 368725). 🗆 *Thu–
Sat.* **www**.calderdale.gov.uk

Halifax's history has been
influenced by textiles since
the Middle Ages, but today's
visual reminders date mainly
from the 19th century. The
town inspired William Blake's
vision of "dark Satanic mills"
in his poem *Jerusalem* (1820).
The wool trade helped to
make the Pennines into
Britain's industrial backbone.

Until the mid-15th century
cloth production was modest,
but vital enough to contribute
towards the creation of the
13th-century Gibbet Law,
which stated that anyone
caught stealing cloth could be
executed. There is a replica of
the gibbet used for decapi-
tation at the bottom of Gibbet
Street. Many of Halifax's 18th-
and 19th-century buildings
owe their existence to wealthy
cloth traders. Sir Charles Barry
(1795–1860), architect of the
Houses of Parliament, was
commissioned by the Crossley
family to design the Town Hall.
They also paid for the land-
scaping of the People's Park
by the creator of the Crystal
Palace, Sir Joseph Paxton
(1801–65). Thomas Bradley's

Large Two Forms (1966–9) by Henry Moore in Bretton Country Park

18th-century **Piece Hall** was where wool merchants once sold their cloth, trading in one of the 315 "Merchants' Rooms". It has a massive Italianate courtyard, now beautifully restored. Today, Halifax's market takes place here.

Eureka! is a hands-on children's museum, with exhibits such as the Giant Mouth Machine. **Shibden Hall Museum** is a fine period house, parts of which date to the 15th century.

Environs: The nearby village of **Sowerby Bridge** was an important textile centre from the Middle Ages to the 1960s. Today visitors come to enjoy the scenic canals.

Eureka!
Discovery Rd. 01422 330069.
☐ daily. ● 24–26 Dec. www.eureka.org.uk

Shibden Hall Museum
Listers Rd. **Tel** 01422 352246.
☐ daily (Sun: pm). ● 24 Dec–2 Jan.

National Coal Mining Museum 39

Wakefield. **Tel** 01924 848806. ☒ Wakefield then bus. ☐ daily (last tour 3:15pm). Children under 5 not allowed underground. ● 24–26 Dec, 1 Jan. www.ncm.org.uk

Housed in the old Caphouse Colliery, this museum gives visitors the chance to go into a real mine shaft: warm clothing is advised. An underground tour takes you 137 m (450 ft) down, equipped with a hat

and a miner's lamp. You can enter some of the narrow seams and see exhibits such as life-size working models. Other displays depict mining from 1820 to the present day.

Yorkshire Sculpture Park 40

Wakefield. **Tel** 01924 830302.
☒ Wakefield then bus. ☐ daily.
● 24, 25, 29–31 Dec. www.ysp.co.uk

This is one of Europe's leading open-air galleries, situated in 200 ha (500 acres) of 18th-century parkland dotted with changing exhibitions of the work of Henry Moore, Anthony Caro, Eduardo Chillida, Barbara Hepworth, Antony Gormley and others. The indoor display spaces include the ambitious visitor centre, which leads on to the stunning new Underground Gallery exhibition space.

Magna 41

Rotherham. **Tel** 01709 720002.
☒ Rotherham Central or Sheffield then bus (No. 69). ☐ Jan: Tue–Sun, Feb–Dec: daily. ● 24–25 Dec. www.visitmagna.co.uk

A former steel works has been imaginatively converted into a huge science adventure centre, with an emphasis on interactive exhibits, noise and spectacle designed to appeal to 4–15-year-olds. In the Air, Fire, Water and Earth Pavilions visitors can get close to a tornado, operate real diggers or discover what it's like to detonate a rock face. There are also multimedia displays on the lives of steelworkers and on how a giant furnace operated, as well as a show that features robots with artificial intelligence that evolve and learn as they hunt each other down.

The Face of Steel display at Magna

NORTHUMBRIA

NORTHUMBERLAND · COUNTY DURHAM

Engand's northeast extremity is a tapestry of moorland, ruins, castles, cathedrals and huddled villages. With Northumberland National Park and Kielder Water reservoir to the north, a rugged eastern coastline, and the cities of Newcastle and Durham to the south, the area combines a dramatic history with abundant natural beauty.

The empty peaceful hills, elusive wildlife and panoramic vistas of Northumberland National Park belie the area's turbulent past. Warring Scots and English, skirmishing tribes, cattle drovers and whisky smugglers have all left traces on ancient routes through the Cheviot Hills. Slicing through the southern edge of the park is the famous reminder of the Romans' 400-year occupation of Britain, Hadrian's Wall, the northern boundary of their empire.

Conflict between Scots and English continued for 1,000 years after the Romans departed, and even after the 1603 union between the two crowns. A chain of massive crenellated medieval castles punctuates the coastline, while other forts that once defended the northern flank of England along the River Tweed lie mostly in ruins. Seventh-century Northumbria was the cradle of Christianity under St Aidan, but this was sharply countered by Viking violence from 793 onward, as the Scandinavian invaders raided the monasteries. But a reverence for Northumbrian saints is in the local psyche, and St Cuthbert and the Venerable Bede are both buried in Durham Cathedral. The influence of the Industrial Revolution, concentrated around the mouths of the rivers Tyne, Wear and Tees, made Newcastle upon Tyne the north's main centre for coal mining and ship-building. Today, the city is famous for its "industrial heritage" attractions and urban regeneration schemes.

Section of Hadrian's Wall, built by the Romans in about 120, looking east from Cawfields

◁ The towers of Durham Cathedral, rising above the River Wear

Exploring Northumbria

Historic sites are plentiful along Northumbria's coast. South of Berwick-upon-Tweed, a causeway leads to the ruined priory and castle on Lindisfarne, and there are major castles at Bamburgh, Alnwick and Warkworth. The hinterland is a region of wide open spaces, with wilderness in the Northumberland National Park, and fascinating Roman remains of Hadrian's Wall at Housesteads and elsewhere. The glorious city of Durham is dominated by its castle and cathedral, and Newcastle upon Tyne has a lively nightlife.

SIGHTS AT A GLANCE

Alnwick Castle **5**
Bamburgh **4**
Barnard Castle **17**
Beamish Open Air Museum **13**
Berwick-upon-Tweed **1**
Cheviot Hills **8**
Corbridge **10**
Durham pp428–9 **14**
Farne Islands **3**
Hadrian's Wall pp422–3 **11**
Hexham **9**
Kielder Water **7**
Lindisfarne **2**
Middleton-in-Teesdale **16**
Newcastle upon Tyne **12**
Warkworth Castle **6**

Walks and Tours
North Pennines Tour **15**

SEE ALSO

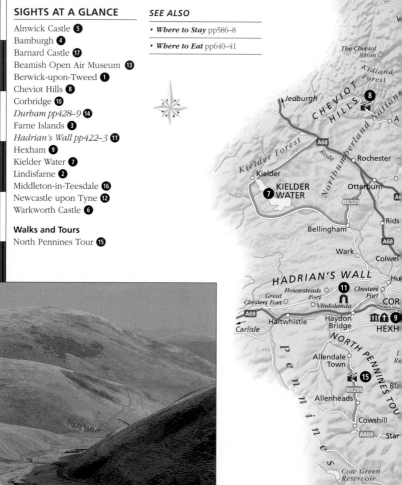

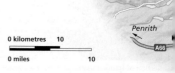

The wilderness of Upper Coquetdale in the sparsely populated Cheviot Hills

0 kilometres   10

0 miles   10

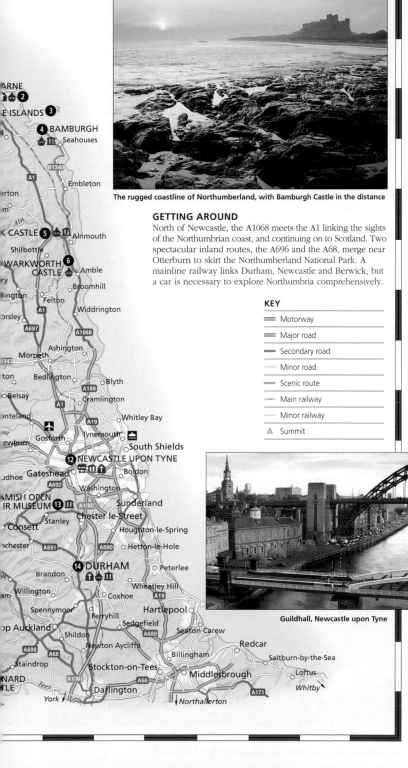

The rugged coastline of Northumberland, with Bamburgh Castle in the distance

GETTING AROUND

North of Newcastle, the A1068 meets the A1 linking the sights of the Northumbrian coast, and continuing on to Scotland. Two spectacular inland routes, the A696 and the A68, merge near Otterburn to skirt the Northumberland National Park. A mainline railway links Durham, Newcastle and Berwick, but a car is necessary to explore Northumbria comprehensively.

KEY

▬	Motorway
▬	Major road
▬	Secondary road
▬	Minor road
▬	Scenic route
—	Main railway
—	Minor railway
△	Summit

Guildhall, Newcastle upon Tyne

View over Berwick-upon-Tweed's three bridges

Berwick-upon-Tweed **❶**

Northumberland. 🏚 *13,000.*
🚉 ℹ️ *106 Mary Gate (01289 330733).* 🏛 *Wed, Sat.*
www.berwickonline.org.uk

Between the 12th and 15th centuries Berwick-upon-Tweed changed hands 14 times in the wars between the Scots and English. Its position, at the mouth of the river which divides the two nations, made the town strategically vital.

The English finally gained permanent control in 1482 and maintained Berwick as a fortified garrison. Ramparts dating from 1555, 1.5 miles (2.5 km) long and 7 m (23 ft) thick, offer superb views over the Tweed. Within the 18th-century barracks are the **King's Own Scottish Borderers Regimental Museum**, an **art gallery**, and **By Beat of Drum**, charting the history of British infantrymen.

🏛 King's Own Scottish Borderers Regimental Museum

The Barracks. **Tel** *01289 307426.*
⏰ *Easter–Oct: Mon–Sat;*
Nov–Easter: Wed–Sat. ⏺ *22 Dec–*
3 Jan, public hols. 📷 🔲

Lindisfarne **❷**

Northumberland. 🚌 *Berwick-upon-Tweed then bus.* ℹ️ *106 Mary Gate, Berwick-upon-Tweed (01289 330733).* **www**.lindisfarne.org.uk

Twice daily a long, narrow neck of land sinks under the North Sea tide for five hours, separating Lindisfarne, or Holy Island, from the coast. At low tide, visitors stream over the causeway to the island made famous by St Aidan, St Cuthbert and the Lindisfarne gospels. Nothing remains of the Celtic monks' monastery, finally abandoned in 875 after successive Viking attacks, but the magnificent arches of the 11th-century **Lindisfarne Priory** are still visible.

After 1540, stones from the priory were used to build **Lindisfarne Castle**, which was restored and made into a private home by Sir Edwin Lutyens *(see p29)* in 1903. It includes a walled garden by Gertrude Jekyll *(see p27)*.

♠ Lindisfarne Castle
(NT) Holy Island. **Tel** *01289 389244.*
⏰ *Mar–Oct & Feb half-term:*
Tue–Sun. Opening times depend on tide – phone to check. 📷

Farne Islands **❸**

(NT) Northumberland. 🚤 *from Sea-houses (Apr–Oct).* ℹ️ *106 Mary Gate, Berwick-upon-Tweed (01289 330733).*

There are between 15 and 28 Farne Islands off the coast from Bamburgh, some of them periodically covered by sea. Nature wardens and lighthouse keepers share them with seals, puffins and other seabirds. Boat tours depart from **Seahouses** harbour and can land on Staple and Inner Farne, site of St Cuthbert's 14th-century chapel, or Longstone, where Grace Darling's lighthouse is located.

Lindisfarne Castle (1540), the main landmark on the island of Lindisfarne

Celtic Christianity

The Irish monk St Aidan arrived in Northumbria in 635 from the island of Iona, off western Scotland, to evangelize the north of England. He founded the monastery on the island of Lindisfarne, and it became one of the most important centres for Christianity in England. This and other monastic communities thrived in Northumbria, becoming rich in scholarship, although the monks lived simply. It also emerged as a place of pilgrimage after miracles were reported at the shrine of St Cuthbert, Lindisfarne's most famous bishop. But the monks' pacifism made them defenceless against 9th-century Viking raids.

St Cuthbert on a sea voyage

St Aidan's Monastery *was added to over the centuries to become Lindisfarne Priory. This 8th-century relic with interlaced animal decorations is from a cross at the site.*

The Venerable Bede *(673–735), the most brilliant early medieval scholar, was a monk at the monastery of St Paul in Jarrow. He wrote The Ecclesiastical History of the English People in 731.*

St Aidan *(600–651), an Irish missionary, founded a monastery at Lindisfarne and became Bishop of Northumbria in 635. This 1960 sculpture of him, by Kathleen Parbury, is in Lindisfarne Priory grounds.*

St Cuthbert *(635–87) was the monk and miracle worker most revered of all. He lived as a hermit on Inner Farne (a chapel was built there in his memory) and later became Bishop of Lindisfarne.*

Lindisfarne Priory *was built by Benedictines in the 11th century, on the site of St Aidan's earlier monastery.*

THE LINDISFARNE GOSPELS

This book of richly illustrated portrayals of Gospel stories is one of the masterpieces of the "Northumbrian Renaissance" which left a permanent mark on Christian art and history-writing. The work was carried out by monks at Lindisfarne under the direction of Bishop Eadfrith, around 700. Monks managed to save the book and carried it with them when they fled from Lindisfarne in 875 after suffering repeated Viking raids. Other treasures were plundered.

Elaborately decorated initial to the *Gospel of St Matthew* (c.725)

Illustration of Grace Darling from the 1881 edition of *Sunday at Home*

Bamburgh ❹

Northumberland. 🏰 *1,100.* 🚂 *Berwick.* ℹ️ *Seahouses (01665 720884; Apr–Oct); 106 Mary Gate, Berwick-upon-Tweed (01289 330733).*

Due to Northumbria's history of hostility against the Scots, there are more strongholds and castles here than in any other part of England. Most were built from the 11th to the 15th centuries by local warlords, as was Bamburgh's red sandstone **castle**. Its coastal position had been fortified since prehistoric times, but the first major stronghold was built in 550 by a Saxon chieftain, Ida the Flamebearer.

In its heyday between 1095 and 1464, Bamburgh was the royal castle that was used by the Northumbrian kings for coronations. By the end of the Middle Ages it had fallen into obscurity, then in 1894 it was bought by Newcastle arms tycoon Lord Armstrong, who restored it. Works of art are exhibited in the cavernous Great Hall, and there are suits of armour and medieval artifacts in the basement.

Bamburgh's other main attraction is the tiny **Grace Darling Museum** which celebrates the bravery of the 23-year-old, who, in 1838, rowed through tempestuous seas with her father, the keeper of the Longstone lighthouse, to rescue nine people from the wrecked *Forfarshire* steamboat.

Carrara marble fireplace (1840) at Alnwick Castle

♨️ **Bamburgh Castle**
Bamburgh. **Tel** *01668 214515.*
⬜ *Mar–Nov: daily.* 🎫 ♿ 🖥️ 🏠
www.bamburghcastle.com

🏛️ **Grace Darling Museum**
Radcliffe Rd. ⬜ *Easter–Oct: daily.* ♿

Alnwick Castle ❺

Alnwick, Northumberland. **Tel** *01665 510777.* 🚂 🚌 *Alnmouth.* ⬜ *April–Oct: daily.* 🎫 ♿ *limited.* 🖥️ 🏠 **www**.alnwickcastle.com

Dominating the market town on the River Aln is another great fortress, Alnwick Castle. Described by the Victorians as the "Windsor of the north", it is the main seat of the Duke of Northumberland, whose family, the Percys, have lived here since 1309.

This border stronghold has survived many battles, but now peacefully dominates the pretty market town of Alnwick, overlooking landscape designed by Capability Brown. The stern medieval exterior belies the treasure house within, furnished in palatial Renaissance style with a collection of Meissen china and paintings by Titian, Van Dyck and Canaletto. The Postern Tower contains early British and Roman relics. The **Regimental Museum of Royal Northumberland Fusiliers** is in the Abbot's Tower. Other attractions are the Percy State coach, the dungeon and superb countryside views.

Warkworth Castle ❻

(EH) Warkworth, nr Amble. **Tel** *01665 711423.* ⬜ *Nov–Mar: Sat–Mon; Apr–Oct: daily.* 🌑 *24–26 Dec, 1 Jan.* 🏠 🎫 ♿ *limited.*

Warkworth Castle sits on a green hill overlooking the River Coquet. It was one of the Percy family homes. Shakespeare's *Henry IV* features the castle in the scenes between the Earl of Northumberland and his son, Harry Hotspur. Much of the present-day castle remains date from the 14th century. The unusual turreted, cross-shaped keep, also added in the 14th century, is a central feature of the castle tour.

Warkworth Castle reflected in the River Coquet

Kielder Water ❼

Yarrow Moor, Falstone, Hexham. **Tel** *0870 2403549.* ⬜ *daily.* ♿ **www**.kielder.org

One of the top attractions of Northumberland, Kielder Water lies close to the Scottish border, surrounded by spectacular scenery. With a perimeter of 27 miles (44 km), it is Europe's largest man-made lake, and offers facilities for sailing, windsurfing, canoeing, water-skiing and fishing. In summer, the cruiser *Osprey* departs from Leaplish on trips around the lake. The Kielder Water Exhibition, next to the Tower Knowe Visitor Centre, depicts the history of the valley from the Ice Age to the present day.

For hotels and restaurants in this region see pp586–588 and pp640–641

Cheviot Hills ⑧

These bare, lonely moors, smoothed into rounded humps by Ice Age glaciers, form a natural border with Scotland. Walkers and outdoor enthusiasts find a near-wilderness unmatched anywhere else in England.

This remotest extremity of the Northumberland National Park nevertheless has a long and vivid history. Roman legions, warring Scots and English border raiders, cattle drovers and whisky smugglers have all left traces along the ancient routes and tracks they carved out here.

The Cheviots' *isolated burns and streams are among the last habitats in England for the shy, elusive otter.*

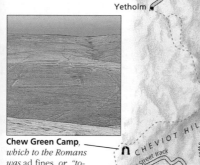

Chew Green Camp, *which to the Romans was* ad fines, *or, "towards the last place", has fine views from the remaining fortified earthworks.*

The Pennine Way *starts in Derbyshire and ends at Kirk Yetholm in Scotland. The final stage (shown here) goes past Byrness, crosses the Cheviots and traces the Scottish border.*

Uswayford Farm track

Uswayford Farm, *is perhaps the most remote farm in England, and one of the hardest to reach. It is set in deserted moorland.*

KEY

▬▬	A roads
▭▭	B roads
═══	Minor roads
- - -	Pennine Way
🔆	Viewpoint

0 kilometres 5

0 miles 5

Alwinton, *a tiny village built mainly from grey stone, is situated beside the River Coquet. It is an access point for many fine walks in the area, and the wild landscape is deserted except for sheep.*

Hexham ⑨

Northumberland. 🏠 14,000. 🚉
🅿 ℹ Wentworth Car Park
(01434 652220). 🛒 Tue.
www.hadrianswallcountry.org

The busy market town of Hexham was established in the 7th century, growing up around the church and monastery built by St Wilfrid, but the Vikings sacked and looted it in 876. In 1114, Augustinians began work on a priory and abbey on the original church ruins to create **Hexham Abbey**, which still towers over the market square. The Saxon crypt, built partly with stones from the former Roman fort at Corbridge, is all

Ancient stone carvings at Hexham Abbey

that remains of St Wilfrid's Church. The south transept has a 12th-century night stair: stone steps leading from the dormitory. In the chancel is the Frith Stool, a Saxon throne in the centre of a circle which protected fugitives.

Medieval streets, many with Georgian and Victorian shopfronts, spread out from the market square. The 15th-century Moot Hall was once a council chamber and the old gaol (jail) contains a **museum** of border history.

Hadrian's Wall ⑪

On the orders of Emperor Hadrian, work began in AD 120 on a 73 mile (117 km) wall to be erected across northern England, to mark and defend the northern limits of the British province and the northwest border of the Roman Empire. Troops were stationed at milecastles along the wall, and large turrets, later forts, were built at 5 mile (8 km) intervals. The wall, now the responsibility of English Heritage, was abandoned in 383 as the Empire crumbled, but much of it remains.

Location of Hadrian's Wall

Vindolanda *is the site of several forts. The first timber fort dated from AD 90 and a stone fort was not built until the 2nd century. The museum has a collection of Roman writing tablets providing details of food, clothes and work.*

Carvoran Fort is probably pre-Hadrianic. Little of the fort survives, but the Roman Army museum nearby covers the wall's history.

Great Chesters Fort was built facing east to guard Caw Gap, but there are few remains today. To the south and east of the fort are traces of a civil settlement and a bathhouse.

Housesteads Settlement includes the remains of terraced shops or taverns.

Cawfields, 2 miles (3 km) north of Haltwhistle, is the access point to one of the highest and most rugged sections of the wall. To the east, the remains of a milecastle sit on Whin Sill crag.

Emperor Hadrian *(76–138) came to Britain in 120 to order a stronger defence system. Coins were often cast to record emperors' visits, such as this bronze sestertius. Until 1971, the penny was abbreviated to d, short for denarius, a Roman coin.*

Hexham Abbey
Market Place. **Tel** 01434 602031.
☐ daily. ⛪ 🖥 🏛

🏛 Border History Museum
Old Gaol, nr Hallgate. **Tel** 01434 652349. ☐ Feb–Oct: daily; Nov: Mon, Tue, Sat. 🖼 ⛪ 🏛

Corbridge ❿

Northumberland. 🅿 4,000. 🚇
🅸 Hill St (01434 632815).

This quiet town conceals a few historic buildings constructed with stones from the Roman garrison town of nearby Corstopitum. Among these are the thickset Saxon tower of St Andrew's Church and the 14th-century fortified tower house built to protect the local clergyman. Excavations of Corstopitum, now known as **Corbridge Roman Site and Museum**, have exposed earlier forts, a well-preserved granary, temples, fountains and an aqueduct.

The parson's 14th-century fortified tower house at Corbridge

🏛 Corbridge Roman Site and Museum
(EH) Tel 01434 632349. ☐ Apr–Oct: daily; Nov–Mar: Wed–Sun. ● 24–26 Dec, 1 Jan. 🖼 ⛪ limited. 🖼 🏛 🏛

THE WALL COAST-TO-COAST

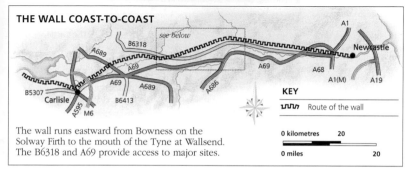

see below

A1

Newcastle

B6318   A69

A689   A69   A69   A686   A69   A68   A1(M)   A19

B5307   Carlisle   A595   M6   B6413   A689

KEY

〰〰 Route of the wall

0 kilometres   20
0 miles   20

The wall runs eastward from Bowness on the Solway Firth to the mouth of the Tyne at Wallsend. The B6318 and A69 provide access to major sites.

Carrawburgh Fort, a 500-man garrison, guarded the Newbrough Burn and North Tyndale approaches.

Limestone Corner Milecastle is sited at the northernmost part of the wall and has magnificent views of the Cheviot Hills (see p421).

Sewingshields Milecastle, *with magnificent views west to Housesteads, is one of the best places for walking. This reconstruction shows the layout of a Roman milecastle on the wall.*

Chesters Fort was a bridgehead over the North Tyne. In the museum are altars, sculptures and inscriptions.

Chesters Bridge crossed the Tyne. The original Hadrianic bridge was rebuilt in 207. The remains of this second bridge abutment can still be seen.

Housesteads Fort *is the best-preserved site on the wall, with fine views over the countryside. The excavated remains include the commanding officer's house and a Roman hospital.*

0 metres   500
0 yards   500

Newcastle upon Tyne ⑫

🏛 273,000. 🚆 🚢 🚇 🚤 ℹ
Railway station; 132 Granger St (0191 2778000). 🗓 *Sun.* **www.** visitnewcastlegateshead.com

Newcastle owes its name to its Norman **castle** which was founded in 1080 by Robert Curthose, the eldest son of William the Conqueror *(see p47).* The Romans had bridged the Tyne and built a fort on the site 1,000 years earlier. During the Middle Ages it was used as a base for English campaigns against the Scots. From the Middle Ages, the city flourished as a coal mining and exporting centre. It was known in the 19th century for engineering, steel production and later

as the world's foremost shipyard. The city's industrial base has recently declined, but "Geordies", as inhabitants of the city are known, have refocused their civic pride on the ultra-modern Metro Centre shopping mall at Gateshead, southwest of the city, and

Bridges crossing the Tyne at Newcastle

Newcastle United soccer team. The city's lively night scene includes clubs, pubs and ethnic restaurants. The visible trappings of its past are reflected in the magnificent **Tyne Bridge** and in **Earl Grey's Monument**, as well as the grand façades in the city centre thoroughfares, such as Grey Street. On the quayside there are some dramatic new features, notably **Baltic**, the contemporary art centre, **The Sage Gateshead**, the international centre for music, and the tilting **Gateshead Millennium Bridge**.

♠ The Castle
St Nicholas St. **Tel** 0191 232 7938. ⬜ *daily.* 🅿 📷
Curthose's original wooden "new castle" was rebuilt in stone in the 12th century. Only

Beamish, The North of England Open Air Museum ⑬

Tram symbol

This giant open air museum, spread over 120 ha (300 acres) of County Durham, recreates an authentic picture of family, working and community life in the northeast in the 19th and early 20th centuries.

It has a 1913 Town Street, colliery village with drift mine, working farm and railway station. A tramway serves the different parts of the museum, which carefully avoids romanticizing the past.

The station, which dates back to 1913, has a platform, a signal box, a wrought-iron footbridge and a goods yard.

Home Farm *recreates the atmosphere of an old-fashioned farm. Rare breeds of cattle and sheep, more common before the advent of mass breeding, can be seen.*

🚻 🖥
School

Miners' houses were tiny, oil-lit dwellings, backing onto vegetable gardens and owned by the colliery.

Chapel

the thickset, crenellated keep remains intact with two suites of royal apartments. A series of staircases spiral up to the renovated battlements, from which there are fine views over the city and the Tyne.

🏠 St Nicholas Cathedral
St Nicholas Sq. **Tel** 0191 2321939. ◯ daily. ⚐
This is one of Britain's tiniest cathedrals. There are remnants inside of the original 11th-century Norman church on which the present 14th- and 15th-century structure was founded. Its most striking feature is its ornate "lantern tower" – half tower, half spire – of which there are only three others in Britain.

🏛 Bessie Surtees' House
(EH) 41–44 Sandhill. **Tel** 0191 2691200. ◯ Mon–Fri. ⬤ 25 Dec–2 Jan, public hols. ⚐ limited. ▯
The story of beautiful, wealthy Bessie, who lived here before

Reredos of the Northumbrian saints in St Nicholas Cathedral

eloping with penniless John Scott, later Lord Chancellor of England, is the romantic tale behind these half-timbered 16th- and 17th-century houses. The window through which Bessie escaped now has a blue glass pane.

🏛 Tyne Bridge
Newcastle–Gateshead.
◯ daily. ⚐
Opened in 1928, this steel arch was the longest of its type in Britain with a span of 162 m (531 ft). Designed by Mott, Hay and Anderson, it soon became the city's most potent symbol.

🏛 Earl Grey's Monument
Grey St.
Benjamin Green created this memorial to the 2nd Earl Grey, Liberal Prime Minister from 1830 to 1834.

🏛 Baltic
The Centre for Contemporary Art Gateshead. **Tel** 0191 478 1810. ◯ daily. ▯ 🍴 ▭ www.balticmill.com
This former grain warehouse has been converted by architect Dominic Williams into a major new international centre for contemporary art, one of the biggest in Europe, with amazing views of Tyneside from its rooftop restaurant.

♿ ▭ *The Town has a sweet factory, newspaper office, solicitor, dentist and music teacher. There is also a pub.*

VISITORS' CHECKLIST

Beamish, Co. Durham. **Tel** 0191 370 4000. 🚆 🚌 Durham, then bus. ◯ Apr–Oct: 10am–5pm daily (last adm 3pm); Nov–Mar: High Street only 10am–4pm Tue–Thu, Sat & Sun. ▭ ▯ www.beamish.org.uk

The Co-op stocked everything a family needed at the turn of the century. A full range of foods available in 1913 is displayed.

Pockerley Manor

The 1825 Railway

Steam Winding Engine

Mahogany Drift mine, *a tunnel driven into coal seams near the surface, was here long before the museum and was worked from the 1850s to 1958. Visitors are given guided tours underground.*

Entrance
♿ ▯ ▭
🅿 /

Houses built by the London Lead Company in Middleton-in-Teesdale

Durham ⑭

See pp428–9.

North Pennines Tour ⑮

See p427.

Cotherstone cheese, a speciality of the Middleton-in-Teesdale area

Middleton-in-Teesdale ⑯

Co. Durham. 🏠 *1,100.* 🚆 *Darlington.* ℹ *10 Market Place (01833 641001).* **www**.visitteesdale.co.uk

Clinging to a hillside amid wild Pennine scenery on the River Tees is this old lead mining town. Many of its rows of grey stone cottages were built by the London Lead Company, a paternalistic, Quaker-run organization who influenced every corner of its employees' daily lives.

The company began mining in 1753, and soon it virtually owned the town. Workers were expected to observe strict temperance, send their children to Sunday school and conform to the many company maxims. Today, mining has all but ceased in Teesdale, with Middleton standing as a monument to the 18th-century idea of the "company town". The offices of the London Lead Company can still be seen, as well as Nonconformist chapels from the era and a memorial fountain made of iron.

The crumbly Cotherstone cow's milk cheese, a speciality of the surrounding dales, is available in the shops.

Barnard Castle ⑰

County Durham. 🏠 *5,000.* 🚆 *Darlington.* ℹ *Woodleigh, Flatts Rd (01833 690909).* 🗓 *Wed.* **www**.visitteesdale.co.uk

Barnard Castle, known in the area as "Barney", is a little town full of character, with old shopfronts and a cobbled market overlooked by the ruins of the Norman castle from which it takes its name. The original Barnard Castle was built around 1125– 40 by Bernard Balliol, ancestor of the founder of Balliol College, Oxford *(see p222)*. Later, the market town grew up around the fortification.

Today, Barnard Castle is known for the extraordinary French-style château to the east of the town, surrounded by acres of formal gardens. Started in 1860 by the local aristocrat John Bowes and his French wife Josephine, an artist and actress, it was never a private residence, but always intended as a museum and public monument. The château finally opened in 1892, by which time the couple were both dead. Nevertheless, the **Bowes Museum** stands as a monument to his wealth and her extravagance.

The museum houses a strong collection of Spanish art which includes El Greco's *The Tears of St Peter*, dating from the 1580s, and Goya's *Don Juan Meléndez Váldez*, painted in 1797. Clocks, porcelain, furniture, musical instruments, toys and tapestries are among its treasures, with a mechanical silver swan as a showpiece.

🏛 **Bowes Museum**
Barnard Castle. **Tel** *01833 690606.*
🔵 *daily.* 🔒 ♿ 🏪 *(summer).* ▣
📷 **www**.bowesmuseum.org.uk

The Bowes Museum, a French-style château near Barnard Castle

North Pennines Tour ⓯

Starting just to the south of Hadrian's Wall, this tour explores the South Tyne Valley, and Upper Weardale. It crosses one of England's wildest and most remote tracts of moorland, then heads north again. The high ground is mainly blanketed with heather, dotted with sheep or criss-crossed with dry-stone

Sheep grazing on the moors

walls, a feature of this region. Harriers and other birds hover above, and streams tumble into valleys of tightly huddled villages.

Celts, Romans and other settlers have left imprints on the North Pennines. The wealth of the area was based on lead mining and stone quarrying which has long co-existed with farming.

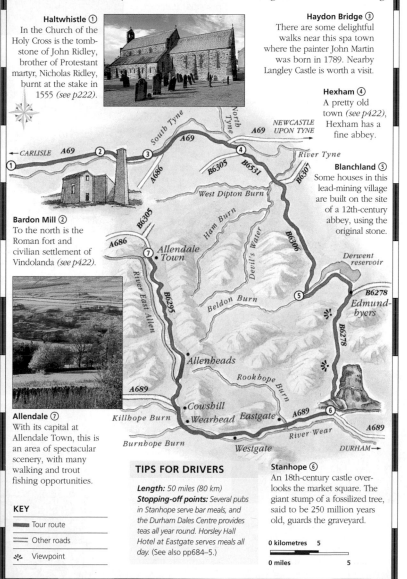

Haltwhistle ①
In the Church of the Holy Cross is the tombstone of John Ridley, brother of Protestant martyr, Nicholas Ridley, burnt at the stake in 1555 *(see p222)*.

Haydon Bridge ③
There are some delightful walks near this spa town where the painter John Martin was born in 1789. Nearby Langley Castle is worth a visit.

Hexham ④
A pretty old town *(see p422)*, Hexham has a fine abbey.

Blanchland ⑤
Some houses in this lead-mining village are built on the site of a 12th-century abbey, using the original stone.

Bardon Mill ②
To the north is the Roman fort and civilian settlement of Vindolanda *(see p422)*.

Allendale ⑦
With its capital at Allendale Town, this is an area of spectacular scenery, with many walking and trout fishing opportunities.

Stanhope ⑥
An 18th-century castle overlooks the market square. The giant stump of a fossilized tree, said to be 250 million years old, guards the graveyard.

KEY

▬▬	Tour route
═══	Other roads
❋	Viewpoint

TIPS FOR DRIVERS

Length: *50 miles (80 km)*
Stopping-off points: *Several pubs in Stanhope serve bar meals, and the Durham Dales Centre provides teas all year round. Horsley Hall Hotel at Eastgate serves meals all day. (See also pp684–5.)*

0 kilometres   5

0 miles   5

Durham ⑭

The city of Durham was built on Island Hill or "Dunholm" in 995. This rocky peninsula, which defies the course of the River Wear's route to the sea, was chosen as the last resting place for the remains of St Cuthbert. The relics of the Venerable Bede were brought to the site 27 years later, adding to its attraction for pilgrims. Durham Cathedral was treated by architects as an experiment for geometric patterning, while the Castle served as the Episcopal Palace until 1832, when Bishop William van Mildert gave it up and surrendered part of his income to found Britain's third university. The 23 ha (57 acre) peninsula has many footpaths, views and fine buildings.

Cathedral Sanctuary knocker

★ Cathedral
Built from 1093 to 1274, it is a striking Norman structure.

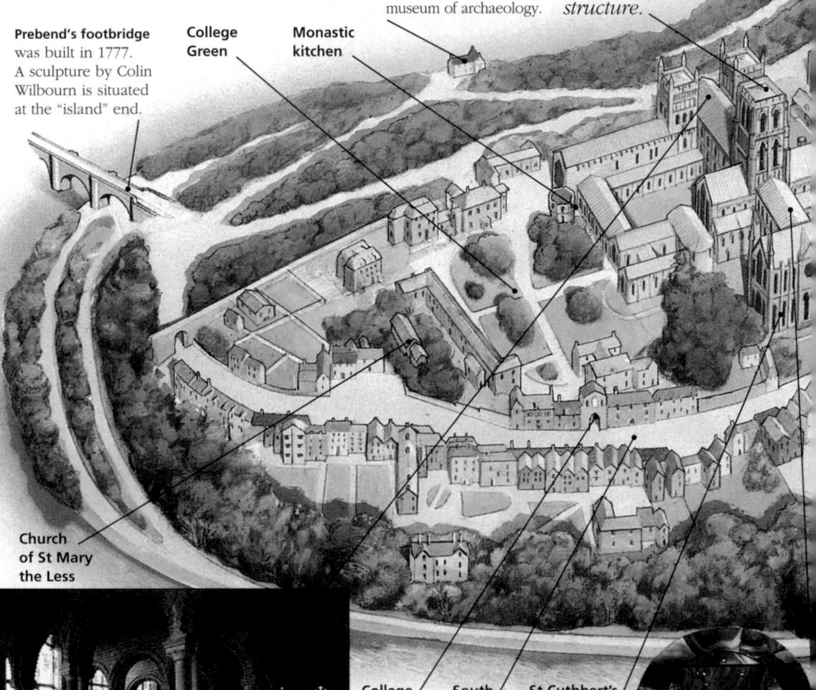

Old Fulling Mill, a largely 18th-century building, houses a museum of archaeology.

Prebend's footbridge was built in 1777. A sculpture by Colin Wilbourn is situated at the "island" end.

College Green

Monastic kitchen

Church of St Mary the Less

Galilee Chapel
Architects began work on the exotic Galilee Chapel in 1170, drawing inspiration from the Great Mosque of Cordoba in Andalusia. It was altered by Bishop Langley (d.1437) whose tomb is by the west door.

College gatehouse   **South Bailey**   **St Cuthbert's Tomb**

"Our Daily Bread" Window
This modern stained-glass window in the north nave aisle was donated in 1984 by a local department store.

STAR SIGHTS

★ Cathedral

★ Castle

For hotels and restaurants in this region see pp586–588 and pp640–641

★ Castle
Begun in 1072, the castle is a fine Norman fortress. The keep, sited on a mound, is now part of the university.

Town Hall (1851)

St Nicholas' Church (1857)

VISITORS' CHECKLIST

Co.Durham. 🚊 Station Approach. ℹ️ Millennium Pl (0191 384 3720). **Cathedral. Tel** 0191 386 4266. ⬜ 9:30am–6:15pm daily (to 5pm Sun). **www.**durhamcathedral. co.uk 🔒 **Castle. Tel** 0191 334 3800. ⬜ univ hols: daily; term: Mon, Wed, Sat (pm) 🔲 mandatory. **www.**durhamcastle.com

Tunstal's Chapel
Situated at the end of the Tunstal's Gallery, the castle chapel was built c.1542. Its fine woodwork includes this unicorn misericord (see p341).

University buildings were built by Bishop John Cosin in the 17th century.

Castle Gatehouse
Traces of Norman stonework can be seen in the outer arch, while the sturdy walls and upper floors are 18th century, rebuilt in a style dubbed "gothick" by detractors.

ch of St le Bow

ingsgate otbridge, uilt from –3, leads to North Bailey.

CATHEDRAL ARCHITECTURE

The vast dimensions of the 900-year-old columns, piers and vaults, and the inventive giant lozenge and chevron, trellis and dogtooth patterns carved into the stone columns, are the main innovative features of Durham Cathedral. It is believed that 11th- and 12th-century architects such as Bishop Ranulph Flambard tried to unify all parts of the structure. This can be seen in the south aisle of the nave below.

Ribbed vaults, *criss-crossing above the nave, are now common in church ceilings. One of the major achievements of Gothic architecture, they were first built at Durham.*

The lozenge *shape is a pattern from prehistoric carving, but never before seen in a cathedral.*

Chevron patterns *on some of the piers in the nave are evidence of Moorish influence.*

WALES

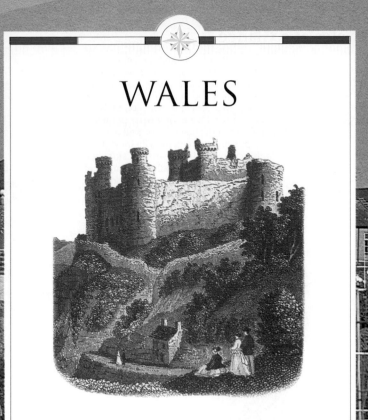

Wales at a Glance

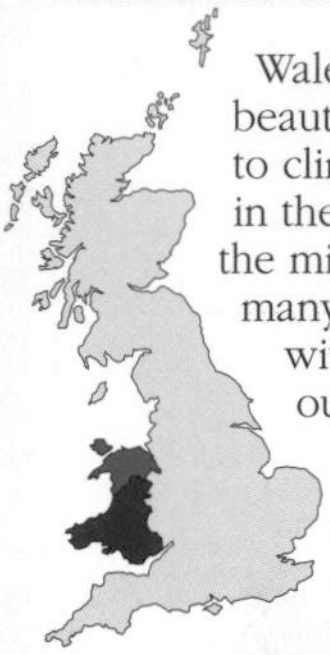

Wales is a country of outstanding natural beauty with varied landscapes. Visitors come to climb dramatic mountain peaks, go walking in the forests, fish in the broad rivers and enjoy the miles of unspoilt coastline. The country's many seaside resorts have long been popular with English holidaymakers. As well as outdoor pursuits there is the vibrancy of Welsh culture, with its strong Celtic roots, to be experienced. Finally there are many fine castles, ruined abbeys, mansions and cities full of magnificent architecture.

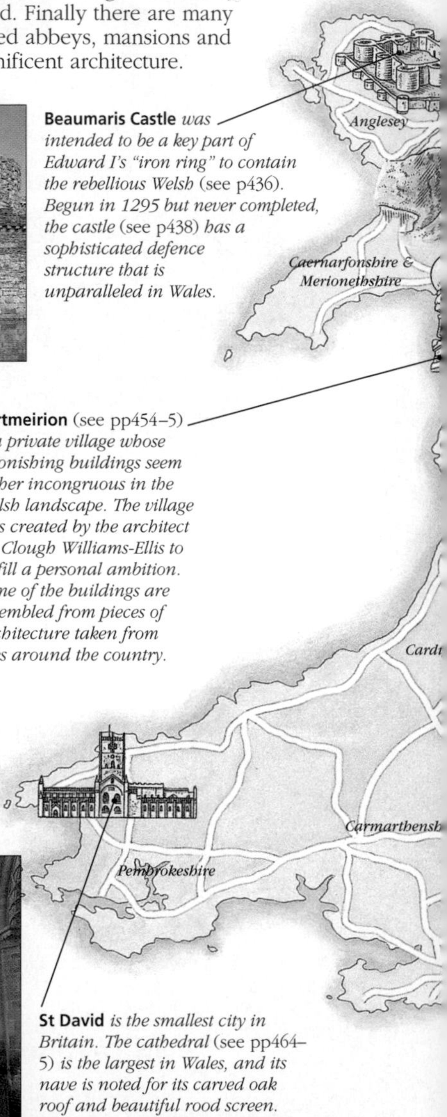

Beaumaris Castle *was intended to be a key part of Edward I's "iron ring" to contain the rebellious Welsh* (see p436). *Begun in 1295 but never completed, the castle* (see p438) *has a sophisticated defence structure that is unparalleled in Wales.*

Anglesey

Caernarfonshire & Merionethshire

Portmeirion (see pp454–5) *is a private village whose astonishing buildings seem rather incongruous in the Welsh landscape. The village was created by the architect Sir Clough Williams-Ellis to fulfill a personal ambition. Some of the buildings are assembled from pieces of architecture taken from sites around the country.*

Cardi

Carmarthensh

Pembrokeshire

St David *is the smallest city in Britain. The cathedral* (see pp464–5) *is the largest in Wales, and its nave is noted for its carved oak roof and beautiful rood screen. Next to the cathedral is the medieval Bishop's Palace, now a ruin.*

◁ **Caernarfon's colourful quayside marina**

Llanberis and Snowdon
(see p451) *is an area famous for dangerous, high peaks, long popular with climbers. Mount Snowdon's summit is most easily reached from Llanberis. Its Welsh name,* Yr Wyddfa Fawr, *means "great tomb" and it is the legendary burial place of a giant slain by King Arthur (see p285).*

Flintshire

conwy
olwyn

Denbighshire

NORTH WALES
(see pp440–55)

Wrexham

Conwy Castle *guards one of the best-preserved medieval fortified towns in Britain (see pp446–7). Built by Edward I, the castle was besieged and came close to surrender in 1294. It was taken by Owain Glyndŵr's supporters in 1401.*

Powys

SOUTH AND MID-WALES
(see pp456–75)

The Brecon Beacons *(see pp468–9) is a national park, a lovely area of mountains, forest and moorland in South Wales, which is a favourite with walkers and naturalists. Pen-y-Fan is one of the principal summits.*

Cardiff Castle's
(see pp472–3) Clock Tower is just one of many 19th-century additions by the eccentric but gifted architect William Burges. His flamboyant style still delights and amazes visitors.

Monmouthshire

iff, Swansea & Environs

0 kilometres   25

0 miles   25

A PORTRAIT OF WALES

L ong popular with British holidaymakers, the many charms of Wales are now becoming better known internationally. They include spectacular scenery and a vibrant culture specializing in male-voice choirs, poetry and a passionate love of team sports. Governed from Westminster since 1536, Wales has its own distinct Celtic identity and in 1999 finally gained partial devolution.

Much of the Welsh landmass is covered by the Cambrian Mountain range, which effectively acts as a barrier from England. Wales is warmed by the Gulf Stream and has a mild climate, with more rain than most of Britain. The land is unsuitable for arable farming, but sheep and cattle thrive; the drove roads, along which sheep used to be driven across the hills to England, are now popular walking trails. It is partly because of the rugged terrain that the Welsh have managed to maintain their separate identity and their ancient language.

One of Wales's splendid National Parks

Welsh is an expansive, musical language, spoken by only one-fifth of the 2.7 million inhabitants, but in parts of North Wales it is still the main language of conversation. There is an official bilingual policy: road signs are in Welsh and English, even in areas where Welsh is little spoken. Welsh place names intrigue visitors, being made up of native words that describe features of the landscape or ancient buildings. Examples include *Aber* (river mouth), *Afon* (river), *Fach* (little), *Llan* (church) *Llyn* (lake) and *Nant* (valley).

Wales was conquered by the Romans, but not by the Saxons. The land and the people therefore retained Celtic patterns of settlement and husbandry for six centuries before the Norman Conquest in 1066. This allowed time for the development of a distinctive Welsh nation whose homogeneity continues to this day.

The early Norman kings subjugated the Welsh by appointing "Marcher Lords" to control areas bordering England. A string of massive castles provides evidence of the turbulent years when Welsh insurrection was a constant threat. It was not until 1535 that Wales formally became part of Britain, and it would take nearly 500 years before the people of Wales regained partial autonomy.

Rugby: the popular Welsh sport

Religious non-conformism and radical politics are deeply rooted in Welsh consciousness. Saint David converted the country to Christianity in the 6th century. Methodism, chapel and teetotalism became firmly entrenched in

Mountain sheep: a familiar sight in rural Wales

A *gorsedd* (assembly) of bards at the eisteddfod

of music derives from the ancient bards: minstrels and poets, who may have been associated with the Druids. Bardic tales of quasi-historical figures and magic were part of the oral tradition of the Dark Ages. They were first written down in the 14th century as the *Mabinogion,* which has inspired Welsh poets up to the 20th century's Dylan Thomas. The male-voice choirs found in many towns, villages and factories, particularly in the industrial south, express the Welsh musical heritage. Choirs compete in eisteddfods: festivals that celebrate Welsh culture.

the Welsh psyche during the 19th century. Even today some pubs stay closed on Sundays (alcohol is not sold at all in the Llŷn Peninsula). A long-standing oral tradition in Wales has produced many outstanding public speakers, politicians and actors. Welsh labour leaders have played important roles in the British trade union movement and the development of socialism.

Welsh heritage is steeped in song, music, poetry and legend rather than handicrafts, although one notable exception is the carved Welsh lovespoon – a craft recently revived. The well-known Welsh love

Welsh lovespoon

In the 19th century, the opening of the South Wales coalfield in Mid-Glamorgan – for a time the biggest in the world – led to an industrial boom, with mass migration from the countryside to the iron and steelworks. This prosperity was not to last: apart from a brief respite in World War II, the coal industry has been in terminal decline for decades, causing severe economic hardship. Today tourism is being promoted in the hope that the wealth generated, by outdoor activities in particular, will be able to take "King Coal's" place.

Conwy's picturesque, medieval walled town, fronted by a colourful harbour

The History of Wales

St David, patron saint of Wales

Wales has been settled since prehistoric times, its history shaped by many factors, from invasion to industrialization. The Romans set up bases in the mountainous terrain, but it was effectively a separate Celtic nation when Offa's Dyke was built as the border with England in 770. Centuries of cross-border raids and military campaigns followed before England and Wales were formally united by the Act of Union in 1535. The rugged northwest, the former stronghold of the Welsh princes, remains the heartland of Welsh language and culture.

Owain Glyndwr, heroic leader of Welsh opposition to English rule

THE CELTIC NATION

Ornamental Iron Age bronze plaque from Anglesey

Wales was settled by waves of migrants in prehistoric times. By the Iron Age (see pp42–3), Celtic farmers had established hillforts and their religion, Druidism. From the 1st century AD until the legions withdrew around 400, the Romans built fortresses and roads, and mined lead, silver and gold. During the next 200 years, Wales was converted to Christianity by missionaries from Europe. St David (see pp464–5), the Welsh patron saint, is said to have turned the leek into a national symbol. He per-suaded soldiers to wear leeks in their hats to distinguish themselves from Saxons dur-ing a 6th-century skirmish.

The Saxons (see pp46–7) failed to conquer Wales, and in 770 the Saxon King Offa built a defensive earthwork along the unconquered ter-ritory (see p461). Beyond Offa's Dyke the people called themselves Y Cymry (fellow countrymen) and the land Cymru. The Saxons called the land "Wales" from the Old English wealas, meaning foreigners. It was divided into kingdoms of which the main ones were Gwynedd in the north, Powys in the centre and Dyfed in the south. There were strong trade, cultural and linguistic links between each.

MARCHER LORDS

The Norman invasion of 1066 (see p47) did not reach Wales, but the border territory ("the Marches") was given by William the Conqueror to three powerful barons based at Shrewsbury, Hereford and Chester. These Marcher Lords made many incursions into Wales and controlled most of the lowlands. But the Welsh

Edward I designating his son Prince of Wales in 1301

princes held the mountainous northwest and exploited English weaknesses. Under Llywelyn the Great (d.1240), North Wales was almost com-pletely independent; in 1267 his grandson, Llywelyn the Last, was acknowledged as Prince of Wales by Henry III.

In 1272 Edward I came to the English throne. He built fortresses and embarked on a military campaign to con-quer Wales. In 1283 Llywelyn was killed in a skirmish, a shattering blow for the Welsh. Edward introduced English law and proclaimed his son Prince of Wales (see p444).

OWAIN GLYNDWR'S REBELLION

Welsh resentment against the Marcher Lords led to rebellion. In 1400 Owain Glyndŵr (c.1350–1416), a descendant of the Welsh princes, laid waste to English-dominated towns and castles. Declaring himself Prince of Wales, he found Celtic allies in Scotland, Ireland, France and Northumbria. In 1404 Glyndŵr captured Harlech and Cardiff, and formed a parliament in Machynlleth (see p462). In 1408 the French made a truce with the English king, Henry IV. The rebellion then failed and Glyndŵr went into hiding until his death.

UNION WITH ENGLAND

Wales suffered greatly during the Wars of the Roses *(see p49)* as Yorkists and Lancastrians tried to gain control of the strategically important Welsh castles. The wars ended in 1485, and the Welshman Henry Tudor, born in Pembroke, became Henry VII. The Act of Union in 1535 and other laws abolished the Marcher Lordships, giving Wales parliamentary representation in London instead. English practices replaced inheritance customs and English became the language of the courts and administration. The Welsh language survived, partly helped by the church and by Dr William Morgan's translation of the Bible in 1588.

Vernacular Bible, which helped to keep the Welsh language alive

INDUSTRY AND RADICAL POLITICS

The industrialization of south and east Wales began with the development of open-cast coal mining near Wrexham and Merthyr Tydfil in the 1760s. Convenient ports and the arrival of the railways helped the process. By the second half of the 19th century open-cast mines had been superseded by deep pits in the Rhondda Valley.

Living and working conditions were poor for industrial and agricultural workers. A series of "Rebecca Riots" in

Miners from South Wales pictured in 1910

South Wales between 1839 and 1843, involving tenant farmers (dressed as women) protesting about tithes and rents, was forcibly suppressed. The Chartists, trade unions and the Liberal Party had much Welsh support.

The rise of Methodism *(see p279)* roughly paralleled the growth of industry: 80 per cent of the population was Methodist by 1851. The Welsh language persisted, despite attempts by the British government to discourage its use, which included punishing children caught speaking it.

WALES TODAY

In the 20th century the Welsh, for the first time, became a power in British politics. David Lloyd George, although not born in Wales, grew up there and was the first British Prime Minister to come from a Welsh family. Aneurin Bevan, a miner's son who became a Labour Cabinet Minister, helped create the National Health Service *(see p59)*.

Welsh nationalism continued to grow: in 1926 Plaid Cymru, the Welsh Nationalist Party, was formed. In 1955 Cardiff was recognized as the capital of Wales *(see p470)* and four years later the ancient symbol of the red dragon became the emblem on Wales' new flag. Plaid Cymru won two parliamentary seats at Westminster in 1974, and in a 1998 referendum the Welsh espoused limited home rule.

The Welsh language has declined: whereas half the population could speak it in 1901, the figure was down to 21 per cent 70 years later. The 1967 Welsh Language Act gave it protection by making Welsh compulsory in schools and the television channel S4C (Sianel 4 Cymru), formed in 1982, broadcasts many programmes in Welsh.

From the 1960s the steel and coal industries declined, creating mass unemployment. This has been only partly alleviated by the emergence of new, high-tech industries, and by the recent growth in tourism and higher education.

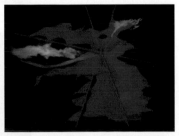

The logo of S4C, Wales's own television station

Castles of Wales

A French 15th-century painting of Conwy Castle

Wales is rich in romantic medieval castles. Soon after the Battle of Hastings, in 1066 *(see p47)*, the Normans turned their attentions to Wales. They built earth and timber fortifications, later replaced by stone castles, initiating a building programme that was pursued by the Welsh princes and invading forces. Construction reached its peak during the reign of Edward I *(see p436)*. As the need for security lessened in the later Middle Ages, some castles became stately homes.

The north gatehouse was planned to be 18 m (60 ft) high, providing lavish royal accommodation, but its top storey was never built.

The inner ward was lined with a hall, granary, kitchens and stables.

Rounded towers, with fewer blind spots than square ones, gave better protection.

Arrow slit

BEAUMARIS CASTLE

The last of Edward I's Welsh castles *(see p444)*, this perfectly symmetrical, concentric design was intended to combine impregnable defence with comfort. Invaders would face many obstacles before reaching the inner ward.

Moat

Curtain wall

WHERE TO SEE WELSH CASTLES

In addition to Beaumaris, in North Wales there are medieval forts at Caernarfon *(see p444)*, Conwy *(see p446)* and Harlech *(see p454)*. Edward I also built Denbigh, Flint (near Chester) and Rhuddlan (near Rhyll). In South and mid-Wales, Caerphilly (near Cardiff), Kidwelly (near Carmarthen) and Pembroke were built between the 11th and 13th centuries. Spectacular sites are occupied by Cilgerran (near Cardigan), Criccieth (near Porthmadog) and Carreg Cennen *(see p468)*. Chirk Castle, near Llangollen, is a good example of a fortress that has since become a stately home.

Caerphilly, *6 miles (10 km) north of Cardiff, is a huge castle with concentric stone and water defences that cover 12 ha (30 acres).*

Harlech Castle (see p454) *is noted for its massive gatehouse, twin towers and the fortified stairway to the sea. It was the headquarters of the Welsh resistance leader Owain Glyndŵr* (see p436) *from 1404–8.*

CASTELL-Y-BERE

This native Welsh castle at the foot of Cader Idris (see p440) was founded by Llywelyn the Great in 1221 (see p422), to secure internal borders rather than to resist the English.

Entrance

The D-shaped, elongated tower is a typical feature of Welsh castles.

The castle's construction follows the shape of the rock. The curtain walls are too low and insubstantial to be of much practical use.

Drawbridge

Chapel Tower has a beautiful medieval chapel.

The protected dock, on a channel that originally led to the sea, received supplies during sieges.

Inner wall, with an upper passage, was higher than the curtain wall to permit simultaneous firing.

Twin-towered gatehouse

EDWARD I AND MASTER JAMES OF ST GEORGE

In 1278 Edward I brought over from Savoy a master stonemason who became a great military architect, James of St George. Responsible for planning and building at least 12 of Edward's fine Welsh castles, James was paid well and liberally pensioned off, indicating the esteem in which he was held by the king.

Edward I (see p436) *was the warrior king whose castles played a key role in the subjugation of the Welsh people.*

A plan of Caernarfon Castle *illustrates how its position, on a promontory surrounded by water, has determined the building's shape and defence.*

Caernarfon Castle (see p444), *birthplace of the ill-fated Edward II (see p327), was intended to be the official royal residence in North Wales, and has palatial private apartments.*

Castell Coch *was restored in Neo-Gothic style by Lord Bute and William Burges (see p472). Mock-castles were built by many Victorian industrialists.*

Conwy Castle (see p447), *like many other castles, required forced labour on a massive scale for its construction.*

NORTH WALES

ABERCONWY & COLWYN · ANGLESEY · CAERNARFONSHIRE &
MERIONETHSHIRE · DENBIGHSHIRE · FLINTSHIRE · WREXHAM

*he North Wales landscape has a dramatic quality reflected in
its history. In prehistoric times, Anglesey was a stronghold of
the religious elite known as the Druids. Roman and Norman
invasions concentrated on the coast, leaving the mountains to the
Welsh. These wild areas are the centre of Welsh language and culture.*

Defence and conquest have been constant themes in Welsh history. North Wales was the scene of ferocious battles between the Welsh princes and Anglo-Norman monarchs determined to establish English rule. The string of formidable castles which still stand in North Wales are as much a testament to Welsh resistance as to the wealth and strength of the invaders. Several massive fortresses, including Beaumaris, Caernarfon and Harlech, almost surround the rugged high country of Snowdonia, an area that even today maintains an untamed quality.

Sheep and cattle farming are the basis of the rural economy here, though there are also large areas of forestry. Along the coast, tourism is a major activity. Llandudno, a purpose-built Victorian resort, popularized the sandy northern coastline in the 19th century. The area continues to attract large numbers of visitors, though major development is confined to the narrow coastal strip that lies between Prestatyn and Llandudno, leaving the island of Anglesey and the remote Llŷn Peninsula largely untouched.

The Llŷn Peninsula remains one of the strongholds of the Welsh language, along with rather isolated inland communities, such as Dolgellau and Bala.

No part of North Wales can truly be called industrial, though there are still remnants of the once-prosperous slate industry in Snowdonia, where the stark, grey quarries provide a striking contrast to the natural beauty of the surrounding mountains. At the foot of Snowdon (the highest mountain in Wales), the villages of Beddgelert, Betws-y-Coed and Llanberis are popular bases for walkers who come to enjoy the spectacular views and striking beauty of this remote region.

Caernarfon Castle, one of the forbidding fortresses built by Edward I

◁ The River Dee at Llangollen, still an area of unspoilt natural beauty

Exploring North Wales

The dominant feature of North Wales is Snowdon, the highest mountain in Wales. Snowdonia National Park extends dramatically from the Snowdon massif south beyond Dolgellau, with thickly wooded valleys, mountain lakes, moors and estuaries. To the east are the softer Clwydian Hills, and unspoilt coastlines can be enjoyed on Anglesey and the beautiful Llŷn Peninsula.

A lighthouse perched on the sea cliffs of Anglesey

KEY

▬▬▬	Major road
▬▬▬	Minor road
═══	Secondary road
▬▬▬	Scenic route
┅┅	Main railway
───	Minor railway
△	Summit

Cemaes   A5025   Amlwch
Carmel Head
Holyhead Bay
Llyn Alaw   A5111
Moelfre
Holyhead
Benllech
Holy Island
Anglesey
LLANDUDNO
Great Ormes Head
Gwalchmai   Pentraeth
BEAUMARIS **2**
CONWY
Rhosneigr   Langefni   A5025
Llanfairfechan
Penma
A5
Bangor
Aberffraw   A4080   Port Dinorwic
Bethesda
Dolgarroc
Newborough
Carnedd Llw 1064m
Lla
CAERNARFON **1**   A4086
Llanberis
Carnarfon Bay
LLANBERIS AND SNOWDON **10**
Capel Curig
Penygroes
Snowdon 1085m
BETW CO
Llanllyfni
BEDDGELERT **11**
A498
Dolwydd
A499
A470
A487
A498
BLAE FFES **9**
Llanaelhaearn
Tan-y-Bwlch
Ffestin
Nefyn   A4417
Porthmadog
Maentwrog
Tudweiliog
LLŶN PENINSULA
Pwllheli   Criccieth
PORTMEIRION **13**
Traw
12   Llanbedrog
Tremadog Bay
A470
Plas-yn-Rhiw   B4413   Abersoch
HARLECH **14**
Rhinog Fawr 720m
Aberdaron   Porth Neigwl
Llanbedr
Y Llethr 754m
Braich y Pwll
Cardigan Bay
A496
Snowdon National
Bardsey Island
Llanaber
DOLGELLAU **15**
Barmouth
Cader Idr 892m
Barmouth Bay
Fairbourne
A493
Llwyngwril
Abergynolwyn
A4
Tywyn
A493
Aberystwyth ↓
16 ABERDYFI

The peaks and moorland of Snowdonia

For additional map symbols see back flap

GETTING AROUND

The main route into North Wales from the northwest of England is the A55, a good dual carriageway which bypasses several places that used to be traffic bottlenecks, including Conwy. The other main route through the region is the A5 Shrewsbury to Holyhead road, which follows a trail through the mountains pioneered by the 19th-century engineer Thomas Telford *(see p447)*. Rail services run along the coast to Holyhead, connecting with ferries across the Irish Sea to Dublin and Dun Laoghaire. Scenic branch lines travel from Llandudno Junction to Blaenau Ffestiniog (via Betws-y-Coed) and along the southern Llŷn Peninsula.

SIGHTS AT A GLANCE

Aberdyfi **16**
Bala **7**
Beaumaris **2**
Beddgelert **11**
Betws-y-Coed **8**
Blaenau Ffestiniog **9**
Caernarfon **1**
Conwy pp446–7 **3**
Dolgellau **15**
Harlech **14**
Llanberis and Snowdon **10**
LLandudno **4**
LLangollen **6**
Llŷn Peninsula **12**
Portmeirion pp454–5 **13**
Ruthin **5**

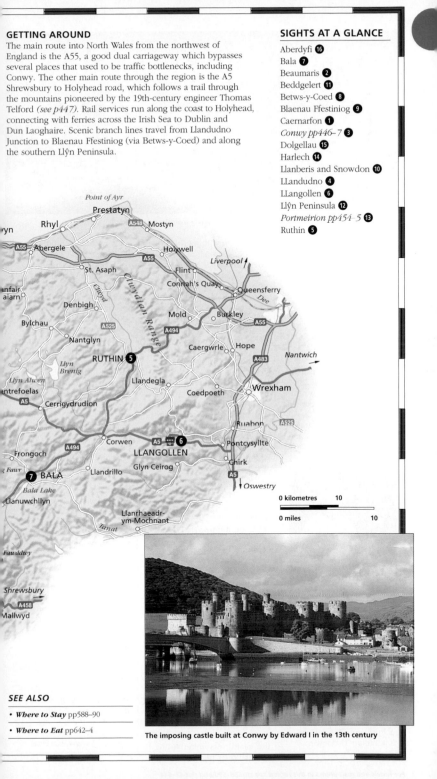

| 0 kilometres | 10 |
| 0 miles | 10 |

The imposing castle built at Conwy by Edward I in the 13th century

Caernarfon Castle, built by Edward I as a symbol of his power over the conquered Welsh

Caernarfon ❶

Caernarfonshire & Merionethshire (Gwynedd). 🏛 10,000. 🚂
ℹ Castle St (01286 672232). 🚌
Sat. www.gwynedd.gov.uk

One of the most famous castles in Wales looms over this busy town. Both were created after Edward I's defeat of the last native Welsh prince, Llywelyn ap Gruffydd (Llywelyn the Last) in 1283 (see p436). The town walls merge with modern streets that spread beyond the medieval centre to a market square.

Overlooking the town and its harbour, **Caernarfon Castle**

THE INVESTITURE

In 1301 the future Edward II became the first English Prince of Wales (see p436), a title since held by the British monarch's eldest son. In 1969 the investiture in Caernarfon Castle of Prince Charles (above) as Prince of Wales drew 500 million TV viewers.

(see p439), with its polygonal towers, was built as a seat of government for North Wales. Caernarfon was a thriving port in the 19th century, and during this period the castle ruins were restored by the architect Anthony Salvin. Displays in the castle include the Royal Welch Fusiliers Museum, and exhibitions tracing the history of the Princes of Wales and exploring the theme "Chieftains and Princes".

On the hill above the town are the ruins of **Segontium**, a Roman fort built in about AD 78. Local legend claims that the first Christian Emperor of Rome, Constantine the Great, was born here in 280.

♣ **Caernarfon Castle**
Y Maes. **Tel** 01286 677617. ☐ daily. 🎫 📷 call for details. ♿
www.cadw.wales.gov.uk

♫ **Segontium** Beddgelert Rd.
Tel 01286 676767. ☐ Tue–Sun (Sun: pm). ● 24, 26 Dec, 1 Jan. ♿ limited. ♿ www.segontium.org.uk

Beaumaris ❷

Anglesey (Gwynedd). 🏛 2,000. 🚌
ℹ Llanfair PG, Station Site, Holyhead Rd, Anglesey (01248 713177).
www.islandofchoice.com

Handsome Georgian and Victorian architecture gives Beaumaris the air of a resort on England's southern coast. The buildings reflect this sailing centre's past role as Anglesey's chief port, before the island was linked to the mainland by the road and

railway bridges built across the Menai Strait in the 19th century. This was the site of Edward I's last, and possibly greatest, **castle** (see p438), which was built to command this important ferrying point to the mainland of Wales.

Ye Olde Bull's Head inn, on Castle Street, was built in 1617. Its celebrated literary patrons have included Dr Samuel Johnson (1709–84) and Victorian novelist Charles Dickens (see p189).

The town's **Courthouse**, was built in 1614 and the recently restored 1829 **Gaol** preserves its soundproofed punishment room and a huge treadmill for prisoners. Two public hangings took place here. Richard Rowlands, the last victim, protested his innocence and cursed the church clock as he was led to the gallows, declaring that its four faces would never show the same times again. It failed to show consistent times until it had an overhaul in 1980.

Beaumaris's award-winning **Museum of Childhood** contains a collection of toys from the 19th and 20th centuries.

♣ **Beaumaris Castle**
Castle St. **Tel** 01248 810361. ☐ daily.
🎫 ♿ www.cadw.wales.gov.uk

🏛 **Courthouse** Castle. **Tel** 01248 810921. ☐ Apr–Sep: daily. 🎫 ♿ ♿

🏛 **Gaol**
Bunkers Hill. **Tel** 01248 810921. ☐ Apr–Sep: daily. 🎫 ♿ limited. ♿

🏛 **Museum of Childhood**
Castle St. **Tel** 01248 712498. ☐ 2 wks before Easter–Nov: daily (Sun: pm). 🎫 ♿ www.aboutbritain.com/ museumofchildhoodmemories.htm

ALICE IN WONDERLAND

The Gogarth Abbey Hotel, Llandudno, was the summer home of the Liddells. Their friend, Charles Dodgson (1832–98), would entertain young Alice Liddell with stories of characters such as the White Rabbit and the Mad Hatter. As Lewis Carroll, Dodgson wrote his magical tales in *Alice's Adventures in Wonderland* (1865) and *Through the Looking-Glass* (1871).

Arthur Rackham's illustration (1907) of *Alice in Wonderland*

🏛 **The Alice in Wonderland Centre**
Trinity Sq. **Tel** 01492 860082. ⬭
Easter–Oct: daily; Nov–Easter: Mon–Sat.
⬤ *1 Jan, 2 wks in Nov, 25–26 Dec.* 🆗
🆗 🖪 🖍 www.wonderland.co.uk

⛏ **Great Orme Copper Mines**
Off A55. **Tel** 01492 870447. ⬭
Feb–Oct: daily. 🆗 🆗 *limited.* ▢ ▯
www.greatormemines.info

Ruthin ➎

Denbighshire (Clwyd). 🏘 *5,000.*
🚌 🖍 *Craft Centre, Park Rd (01824 703992).* 🅿 *1st Tue of every month; Thu (indoor).*
www.borderlands.co.uk

Ruthin's long-standing prosperity as a market town is reflected in its fine half-timbered medieval buildings. These include the National Westminster and Barclays banks in St Peter's Square. The former was a 15th-century courthouse and prison, the latter the home of Thomas Exmewe, Lord Mayor of London in 1517–18. **Maen Huail** ("Huail's stone"), a boulder outside Barclays, is said to be where King Arthur *(see p285)* beheaded Huail, his rival in a love affair.

St Peter's Church, on the edge of St Peter's Square, was founded in 1310 and has a Tudor oak roof in the north aisle. Next to the Castle Hotel is the 17th-century pub **The Seven Eyes** (formerly the Myddleton Arms), whose seven unusual, Dutch-style, dormer windows are known locally as the "eyes of Ruthin".

Conwy ➌

See pp446–7.

Llandudno ➍

Gwynedd. 🏘 *19,000.* 🚋 🚐 🖍
1–2 Chapel St (01492 876413).
www.llandudno-tourism.co.uk

Llandudno's crescent-shaped bay

Llandudno retains much of the holiday spirit of the 19th century, when the new railways brought crowds to the coast. Its **pier**, more than 700 m (2,295 ft) long, and its canopied walkways recall the heyday of seaside holidays. The town is proud of its association with the author Lewis Carroll. **The Alice in Wonderland Centre** is a grotto decorated with life-sized scenes from his books.

Llandudno's cheerful seaside atmosphere owes much to a strong sense of its Victorian roots – unlike many British seaside towns, which embraced the flashing lights and funfairs of the 20th century. To take full advantage of its sweeping beach, Llandudno was laid out between its two headlands, Great Orme's Head and Little Orme's Head.

Great Orme's Head, now a Country Park and Nature Reserve, rises to 207 m (670 ft) and has a long history. In the Bronze Age copper was mined here; the **copper mines** and their excavations are open to the public. The **church** on the headland was built from timber in the 6th century by St Tudno, rebuilt in stone in the 13th century, restored in 1855 and is still in use. Local history and wildlife can be traced in an information centre on the summit.

There are two effortless ways to reach the summit: on the **Great Orme Tramway**, one of only three cable-hauled street tramways in the world (the others are in San Francisco and Lisbon), or by the **Llandudno Cable Car**. Both operate only in summer.

The "eyes of Ruthin", an unusual feature in Welsh architecture

Street-by-Street: Conwy ❸

Conwy is one of Britain's most underrated historic towns. Until the early 1990s it was famous as a traffic bottleneck, but thanks to a town bypass, its concentration of architectural riches – unparalleled in Wales – can now be appreciated. The castle dominates: a brooding, intimidating monument built by Edward I *(see p438)*. But Conwy is set apart from other medieval towns by its amazingly well-preserved town walls. Fortified with 21 towers and three gateways, the walls form an almost unbroken shield around the old town.

Smallest House
This fisherman's cottage on the quayside, just over 3 m (10 ft) high, is said to be the smallest house in Britain.

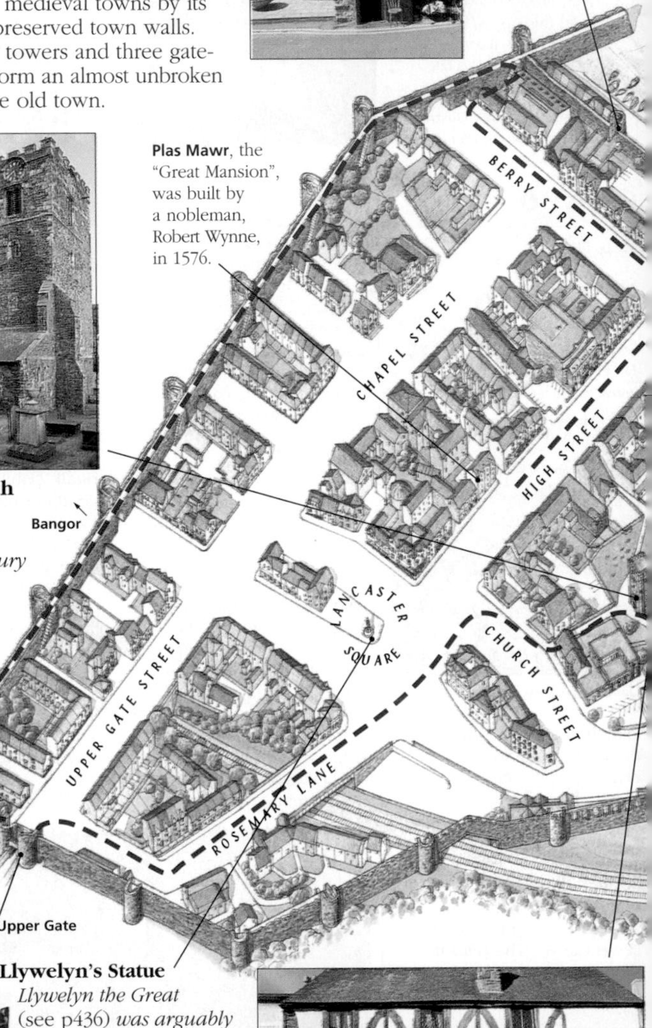

Plas Mawr, the "Great Mansion", was built by a nobleman, Robert Wynne, in 1576.

BERRY STREET

CHAPEL STREET

HIGH STREET

CHURCH STREET

LANCASTER SQUARE

ROSEMARY LANE

UPPER GATE STREET

Bangor

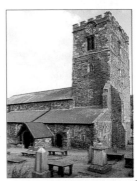

St Mary's Church
This medieval church, on the site of a 12th-century Cistercian abbey, is set in peaceful grounds.

Upper Gate

Llywelyn's Statue
Llywelyn the Great (see p436) was arguably Wales's most successful medieval leader.

Aberconwy House
This restored 14th-century house was once the home of a wealthy merchant.

THOMAS TELFORD

Thomas Telford (1757–1834) was the gifted Scottish engineer responsible for many of Britain's roads, bridges and canals. The Menai Bridge *(see p444)*, the Pontcysyllte Aqueduct *(see p450)* and Conwy Bridge are his outstanding works in Wales. Telford's graceful bridge at Conwy has aesthetic as well as practical qualities. Completed in 1826 across the mouth of the Conwy estuary, it was designed in a castellated style to blend with the castle. Before the bridge's construction the estuary could only be crossed by ferry.

VISITORS' CHECKLIST

Conwy. 🏰 8,000. 🚂 Conwy. ℹ 01492 592248. **Aberconwy House (NT). Tel** 01492 592246. ⬜ Wed–Mon. ⬛ Nov–Mar. 🏷 **Conwy Castle Tel** 01492 592358. ⬜ daily. 🏷 📷 **Smallest House Tel** 01492 593484. ⬜ Apr–Oct: daily. 🏷 **www**.gonorthwales.co.uk

★ Town Walls
These remarkably well-preserved medieval walls are 1,280 m (4,200 ft) long and over 9 m (30 ft) high.

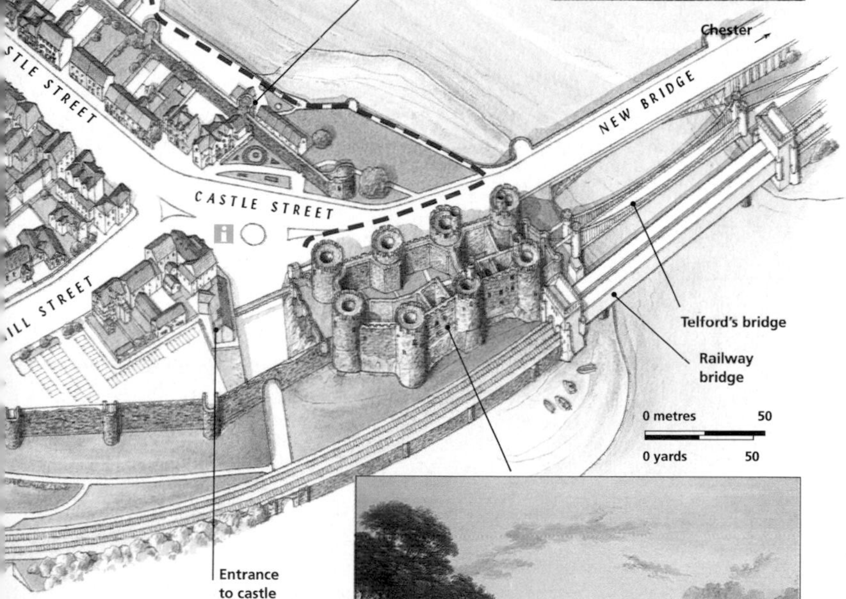

Chester

NEW BRIDGE

CASTLE STREET

CASTLE STREET

MILL STREET

ℹ

Telford's bridge

Railway bridge

| 0 metres | 50 |
| 0 yards | 50 |

Entrance to castle

KEY

– – – Suggested route

STAR SIGHTS

★ Town Walls

★ Conwy Castle

★ Conwy Castle
This atmospheric watercolour, Conwy Castle *(c.1770), is by the Nottingham artist Paul Sandby.*

Pontcysyllte Aqueduct, built in 1795–1805, carrying the Llangollen Canal

Llangollen 6

Denbighshire. 🚶 *5,000.* 🚌 🛈 *y Capel, Castle St (01978 860828).* ⛴ *Tue.* www.llangollen.org.uk

Best known for its annual Eisteddfod (festival), this pretty town sits on the River Dee, which is spanned by a 14th-century bridge. The town became notorious in the 18th century, when two eccentric Irishwomen, Lady Eleanor Butler and Sarah Ponsonby, the "Ladies of Llangollen", set up house together in the half-timbered **Plas Newydd**. Their unconventional dress and literary enthusiasms attracted such celebrities as the Duke of Wellington *(see p162)* and William Wordsworth *(see p366)*. The ruins of a 13th-century castle, **Castell Dinas Brân**, occupy the summit of a hill overlooking the house.

Environs: Boats on the **Llangollen Canal** sail from Wharf Hill in summer and cross the spectacular 300 m (1,000 ft) long Pontcysyllte Aqueduct, built by Thomas Telford *(see p447)*.

🏛 **Plas Newydd**
(NT) Hill St. **Tel** *01978 861314.* ☐ *Easter–Oct.* 🈹 🕭 *limited.* 🖳 🛈

Bala 7

Gwynedd. 🚶 *2,000.* 🚌 *from Llangollen.* 🛈 *Penllyn, Pensarn Rd (01678 521021).* www.visitsnowdonia.info

Bala Lake, Wales's largest natural lake, lies between the Aran and Arenig mountains at the fringes of Snowdonia National Park. It is popular for water-sports and boasts a unique fish called a *gwyniad*, which is related to the salmon.

The little grey-stone town of Bala is a Welsh-speaking community, its houses strung out along a single street at the eastern end of the lake. Thomas Charles (1755–1814), a Methodist church leader, once lived here. A plaque on his former home recalls Mary Jones who walked 28 miles (42 km) barefoot from Abergynolwyn to buy a Bible. This led to Charles establishing the Bible Society, providing cheap bibles to the working classes.

The narrow-gauge **Bala Lake Railway** follows the lake shore from Llanuwchllyn, 4 miles (6 km) southwest.

Betws-y-Coed 8

Conwy. 🚶 *600.* 🚆 🛈 *The Old Stables (01690 710426).* www.betws.org.uk

This village near the peaks of Snowdonia has been a hill-walking centre since the 19th century. To the west are

---

WORLD CULTURES IN LLANGOLLEN

Llangollen's International Eisteddfod *(see p63)* in the first half of July draws musicians, singers and dancers from around the world. First held in 1947 as a gesture of post-war international unity, it now attracts over 12,000 performers from nearly 50 countries to the six-day-long competition-cum-fair.

Choristers at the Eisteddfod, a popular Welsh festival

---

the **Swallow Falls**, where the River Llugwy flows through a wooded glen. The bizarre **Ty Hyll** ("Ugly House"), is a *tŷ unnos* ("one-night house"); traditionally, houses erected between dusk and dawn on common land were entitled to freehold rights, and the owner could enclose land as far as he could throw an axe from the door. To the east is **Waterloo Bridge**, built by Thomas Telford to celebrate the victory against Napoleon.

🏛 **Ty Hyll**
Capel Curig. **Tel** *01690 720287.* **House** ☐ *Easter–Sep: daily.* **Grounds** ☐ *Easter–Sep: daily; Oct–Easter: Mon–Fri.* 🈹 🕭 *limited.*

The ornate Waterloo Bridge, built in 1815 after the famous battle

◁ **The picturesque village of Beddgelert in Snowdonia National Park**

A view of the Snowdonia countryside from Llanberis Pass, the most popular route to Snowdon's peak

Blaenau Ffestiniog **9**

Gwynedd. 🏠 5,500. 🚇 ℹ️ Betws-y-Coed (01690 710426); Jun–Sep: 01766 830360. 🛒 Tue (Jun–Sep).

Blaenau Ffestiniog, once the slate capital of North Wales, sits among mountains riddled with quarries. The **Llechwedd Slate Caverns**, overlooking Blaenau, opened to visitors in the early 1970s, marking a new role for the declining industrial town. The electric Miners' Tramway takes passengers on a tour into the original caverns.

On the Deep Mine tour, visitors descend on Britain's steepest passenger incline railway to the underground chambers, while sound effects recreate the atmosphere of a working quarry. The dangers included landfalls and floods, as well as the more gradual threat of slate dust breathed into the lungs.

There are slate-splitting demonstrations on the surface, a quarryman's cottage and a re-creation of a Victorian village to illustrate the cramped and basic living conditions endured by workers between the 1880s and 1945.

The popular narrow-gauge **Ffestiniog Railway** *(see pp452–3)* runs from Blaenau to Porthmadog.

🏛 Llechwedd Slate Caverns
Off A470. **Tel** 01766 830306. ◯ daily. 🎟 ♿ except the Deep Mine. ▣ 🎁

Llanberis and Snowdon **10**

Gwynedd. 🏠 2,100. ℹ️ High St, Llanberis (01286 870765). **www**.gwynedd.gov.uk

Snowdon, which at 1,085 m (3,560 ft) is the highest peak in Wales, is the main focus of the vast Snowdonia National Park, whose scenery ranges from this rugged mountain country to moors and sandy beaches.

The easiest route to Snowdon's summit begins in Llanberis: the 5 mile (8 km) **Llanberis Track**. From Llanberis Pass, the Miners' Track (once used by copper miners) and the Pyg Track are alternative paths. Walkers should beware of sudden weather changes and dress accordingly. The narrow-gauge **Snowdon Mountain Railway**, which opened in 1896, is an easier option.

Llanberis was a major 19th-century slate town, with grey terraces hewn into the hills. Other attractions are the 13th-century shell of **Dolbadarn Castle**, and, above Lake Peris, the **Electric Mountain**, which has tours of Europe's biggest hydro-electric pumped storage station.

🏰 Dolbadarn Castle
Off A4086 nr Llanberis. **Tel** 01286 870765. ◯ daily.

ℹ️ Electric Mountain
Llanberis. **Tel** 01286 870636. ◯ Apr–Oct: daily; Feb & Mar, Nov & Dec: Wed–Sun. 🎟 ♿ ▣ 🎁 **www**.fhc.co.uk

---

BRITAIN'S CENTRE OF SLATE

Welsh slates provided roofing material for Britain's new towns in the 19th century. In 1898, the slate industry employed nearly 17,000 men, a quarter of whom worked at Blaenau Ffestiniog. Foreign competition and new materials later took their toll. Quarries such as Dinorwig in Llanberis and Llechwedd in Blaenau Ffestiniog now survive on the tourist trade.

The dying art of slate-splitting

The village of Beddgelert, set among the mountains of Snowdonia

Beddgelert ⓫

Gwynedd. 🏘 500. ℹ Canolfan-Hebog (01766 890615).
www.eryri-npa.gov.uk

Beddgelert enjoys a spectacular location in Snowdonia. The village sits on the confluence of the Glaslyn and Colwyn rivers at the approach to two mountain passes: the beautiful Nant Gwynant Pass, which leads to Snowdonia's highest reaches, and the Aberglaslyn Pass, a narrow wooded gorge which acts as a gateway to the sea.

Business was given a boost by Dafydd Pritchard, the landlord of the Royal Goat Hotel, who in the early 19th century adapted an old Welsh legend to associate it with Beddgelert. Llywelyn the Great *(see p436)* is said to have left his faithful hound Gelert to guard his infant son while he went hunting. He returned to find the cradle overturned and Gelert covered in blood. Thinking the dog had savaged his son, Llywellyn slaughtered Gelert, but then discovered the boy, unharmed, under the cradle. Nearby was the corpse of a wolf, which Gelert had killed to protect the child. To support the tale, Pritchard created **Gelert's Grave** *(bedd Gelert* in Welsh) by the River Glaslyn, a mound of stones a short walk south of the village.

Environs: There are many fine walks in the area: one leads south to the Aberglaslyn Pass and along a disused part of the Welsh Highland Railway. The **Sygun Copper Mine**, 1 mile (1.5 km) northeast of Beddgelert, offers self-guided tours of caverns recreating the life of Victorian miners.

🏔 Sygun Copper Mine
On A498. **Tel** *01766 890595 or 01766 510100.* ◯ *Mar–Nov: daily; Christmas hols & Feb.*
📷 ♿ *limited.* ▢ ▯
www.syguncoppermine.co.uk

Ffestiniog Railway

Railway crest

The Ffestiniog narrow-gauge railway takes a scenic 14 mile (22 km) route from Porthmadog Harbour to the mountains and the slate town of Blaenau Ffestiniog *(see p451)*. Designed to carry slate from the quarries to the quay, the railway replaced a horse-drawn tramway constructed in 1836, operating on a 60 cm (2 ft) gauge. After closure in 1946, it was reconstructed by volunteers and re-opened in sections from 1955–82.

Steam traction *trains were first used on the Ffestiniog Railway in 1863. There are some diesel engines but most trains on the route are still steam-hauled.*

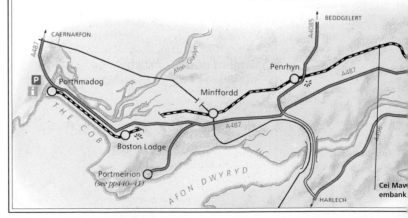

Llŷn Peninsula ⑫

Gwynedd. 🚲 🚌 *Pwllheli.*
🚢 *Aberdaron to Bardsey Island.*
ℹ️ *Min-y-don, Station Sq, Pwllheli
(01758 613000).*
www.nwt.co.uk

This 24mile (38km) finger of land points southwest from Snowdonia into the Irish Sea. Although it has popular beaches, notably at Pwllheli, Criccieth, Abersoch and Nefyn, the coast's overriding feature is its untamed beauty. Views are at their most dramatic in the far west and along the mountain-backed northern shores.

The windy headland of **Braich-y-Pwll**, to the west of Aberdaron, looks out towards Bardsey Island, the "Isle of 20,000 Saints". This became a place of pilgrimage in the 6th century, when a monastery was founded here. Some of the saints are said to be buried in the churchyard of the ruined 13th-century **St Mary's Abbey**. Close by is **Porth Oer**, a small bay also known as "Whistling Sands" (the sand is meant to squeak, or whistle, underfoot).

East of Aberdaron is the 4 mile (6.5 km) bay of **Porth Neigwl**, known in English as Hell's Mouth, the scene of many shipwrecks due to the bay's treacherous currents. Hidden in sheltered grounds above Porth Neigwl bay, 1 mile (1.5 km) northeast of Aberdaron, is **Plas-yn-Rhiw**, a small, medieval manor house with Tudor and Georgian additions and lovely gardens.

The former quarrying village and "ghost town" of **Llithfaen**, tucked away below the sheer cliffs of the mountainous north coast, is now a centre for Welsh language studies.

🏠 **Plas-yn-Rhiw**
(NT) off B4413. **Tel** 01758 780219.
◯ *Apr–mid-May: Thu–Mon; mid-May–Sep: Wed–Mon.* 🦽 ♿ *limited.*

Llithfaen village, now a language centre, on the Llyn Peninsula

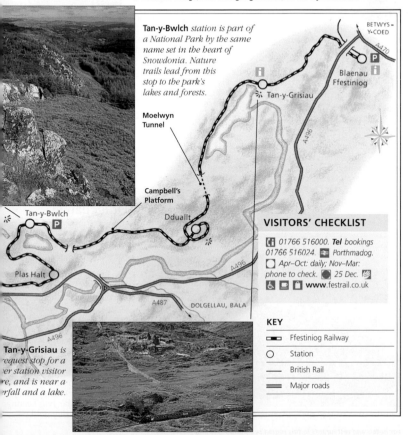

Tan-y-Bwlch station is part of a National Park by the same name set in the heart of Snowdonia. Nature trails lead from this stop to the park's lakes and forests.

Moelwyn Tunnel

Campbell's Platform

Tan-y-Bwlch 🅿️

Plas Halt

Dduallt

Tan-y-Grisiau

A496

A487

DOLGELLAU, BALA

BETWYS-Y-COED

A470

Blaenau Ffestiniog

A496

Tan-y-Grisiau *is a request stop for a power station visitor centre, and is near a waterfall and a lake.*

VISITORS' CHECKLIST

📞 *01766 516000.* **Tel** *bookings 01766 516024.* 🚲 *Porthmadog.*
◯ *Apr–Oct: daily; Nov–Mar: phone to check.* ● *25 Dec.* 🦽
♿ 🖥️ 🎁 **www**.festrail.co.uk

KEY

▄▄▄	Ffestiniog Railway
◯	Station
—	British Rail
══	Major roads

Portmeirion ⑬

Gwynedd. *Tel 01766 770000.*
🚉 *Minffordd.* ○ *daily.* ● *25 Dec.*
📷 ♿ *limited.* ✔ 🍴 ☐ 📷
www.portmeirion-village.com

This bizarre Italianate village on a private peninsula at the top of Cardigan Bay was created by Welsh architect Sir Clough Williams-Ellis (1883–1978). He fulfilled a childhood dream by building a village "to my own fancy on my own chosen site". About 50 buildings surround a central piazza, in styles from Oriental to Gothic. Visitors can stay at the luxurious hotel or in one of the charming village cottages. Portmeirion has been an atmospheric location for many films and television programmes, including the popular 1960s television series *The Prisoner*.

Sir Clough Williams-Ellis at Portmeirion

Hercules *is a life-size 19th-century copper statue near the Town Hall, where a 17th-century ceiling, rescued from a demolished mansion, depicts his legend.*

Fountain Cottage is where Noel Coward (1899–1973) wrote *Blithe Spirit.*

The *Amis Reunis* is a stone replica of a boat that sank in the bay

Swimming pool

The Portmeirion Hotel *has many exotic interiors: the furniture in the Jaipur Bar comes from Rajasthan, India.*

Harlech ⑭

Gwynedd. 🏚 *1,300.* 🚉 ℹ *High St (01766 780658).* 🛒 *Sun (summer).*
www.gwynedd.gov.uk

This small town with fine beaches is dominated by **Harlech Castle**, a medieval fortress *(see p438)* built by Edward I between 1283 and 1289. The castle sits on a precipitous crag, with superb views of Tremadog Bay and the Llŷn Peninsula to the west, and Snowdonia to the north. When the castle was built, the sea reached a fortified stairway cut into the cliff, so that supplies could arrive by ship, but now the sea has receded. A towering gatehouse protects the inner ward, enclosed by walls and four round towers.

Despite its defences, Harlech Castle fell to Owain Glyndŵr *(see p436)* in 1404, and served as his court until its recapture four years later. The song *Men of Harlech* is thought to have been inspired by the castle's heroic resistance during an eight-year siege in the Wars of the Roses *(see p49)*.

⚜ **Harlech Castle**
Castle Sq. *Tel 01766 780552.* ○ *daily.*
📷 📷 **www**.cadw.wales.gov.uk

Dolgellau ⑮

Gwynedd. 🏚 *2,650.* ℹ *Eldon Sq (01341 422888).* 🛒 *Fri (livestock).*
www.gwynedd.gov.uk

The dark local stone gives a stern, solid look to this market town, where the Welsh language and customs are still very strong. It lies in the long shadow of the 892 m (2,927 ft) mountain of Cader Idris where, according to legend, anyone who spends a night on its summit will awake a poet or a madman – or not at all.

Dolgellau was gripped by gold fever in the 19th century, when high-quality gold was

Harlech Castle's strategic site overlooking mountains and sea

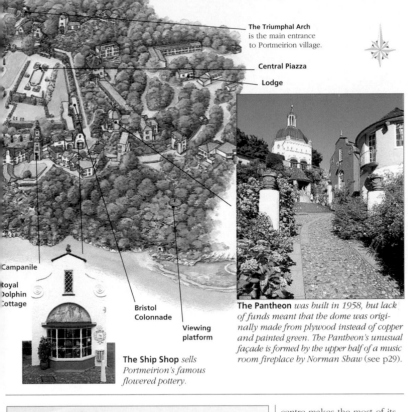

The Triumphal Arch is the main entrance to Portmeirion village.

Central Piazza

Lodge

Campanile

Royal Dolphin Cottage

Bristol Colonnade

Viewing platform

The Ship Shop sells Portmeirion's famous flowered pottery.

The Pantheon was built in 1958, but lack of funds meant that the dome was originally made from plywood instead of copper and painted green. The Pantheon's unusual façade is formed by the upper half of a music room fireplace by Norman Shaw (see p29).

Dolgellau's grey-stone buildings, dwarfed by the mountain scenery

discovered in the Mawddach Valley nearby. The deposits were not large enough to sustain an intensive mining industry for long. Nevertheless, up until 1999, small amounts were mined and crafted locally into fine jewellery.

Dolgellau is a good centre for walking, whether you wish to take gentle strolls through beautiful leafy countryside or strenuous hikes across extreme terrain with dramatic mountain views. The lovely **Cregennen lakes** are set high in the hills

above the thickly wooded **Mawddach Estuary** to the northwest; north are the harsh, bleak **Rhinog moors**, one of Wales's last true wildernesses.

Aberdyfi ⑯

Gwynedd. 🏘 900. ⊠ 🛈 Wharf Gardens (01654 767321). **www**.gwynedd.gov.uk

Perched on the mouth of the Dyfi Estuary, this little harbour resort and sailing

centre makes the most of its splendid but rather confined location, its houses occupying every yard of a narrow strip of land between mountain and sea. In the 19th century, local slate was exported from here, and between the 1830s and the 1860s about 100 ships were built in the port. *The Bells of Aberdovey*, a song by Charles Dibdin for his opera *Liberty Hall* (1785), tells the legend of Cantref-y-Gwaelod, thought to have been located here, which was protected from the sea by dykes. One stormy night, the sluice gates were left open by Prince Seithenyn, when he was drunk, and the land was lost beneath the waves. The submerged church bells are said to peal under the water to this day.

Neat Georgian houses by the sea, Aberdyfi

SOUTH AND MID-WALES

CARDIFF, SWANSEA & ENVIRONS · CARDIGANSHIRE
CARMARTHENSHIRE · MONMOUTHSHIRE · POWYS · PEMBROKESHIRE

*S*outh and mid-Wales are less homogeneous regions than North Wales. Most of the population lives in the southeast corner. To the west is Pembrokeshire, the loveliest stretch of Welsh coastline. To the north the industrial valleys give way to the wide hills of the Brecon Beacons and the rural heartlands of central Wales.

South Wales's coastal strip has been settled for many centuries. There are prehistoric sites in the Vale of Glamorgan and Pembrokeshire. The Romans established a major base at Caerleon, and the Normans built castles all the way from Chepstow to Pembroke. In the 18th and 19th centuries, coal mines and ironworks opened in the valleys of South Wales, attracting immigrants from all over Europe. Close communities developed here, focused on the coal trade, which turned Cardiff from a sleepy coastal town into the world's busiest coal-exporting port.

The declining coal industry has again changed the face of this area: slag heaps have become green hills, and the valley towns struggle to find alternative forms of employment. Coal mines such as Blaenafon's Big Pit are now tourist attractions; today, many of the tour guides taking visitors underground are ex-miners, who can offer a first-hand glimpse of the hard life found in mining communities before the pits closed.

The southern boundary of the Brecon Beacons National Park marks the beginning of rural Wales. With a population sparser than anywhere in England, this is an area of small country towns, hill-sheep farms, forestry plantations and spectacular man-made lakes.

The number of Welsh-speakers increases and the sense of Welsh culture becomes stronger as you travel further from the border with England, with the exception of an English enclave in south Pembrokeshire.

The changing face of the coal industry: former miners take visitors down the Big Pit in Blaenafon

◁ Magnificent coastal scenery near St David's, Pembrokeshire

Exploring South and Mid-Wales

Magnificent coastal scenery marks the Pembrokeshire Coast National Park and cliff-backed Gower Peninsula, while Cardigan Bay and Carmarthen Bay offer quieter beaches. Walkers can enjoy grassy uplands in the Brecon Beacons and gentler country in the leafy Wye Valley. Urban life is concentrated in the southeast of Wales, where old mining towns line the valleys north of Cardiff, the capital.

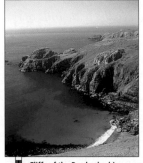

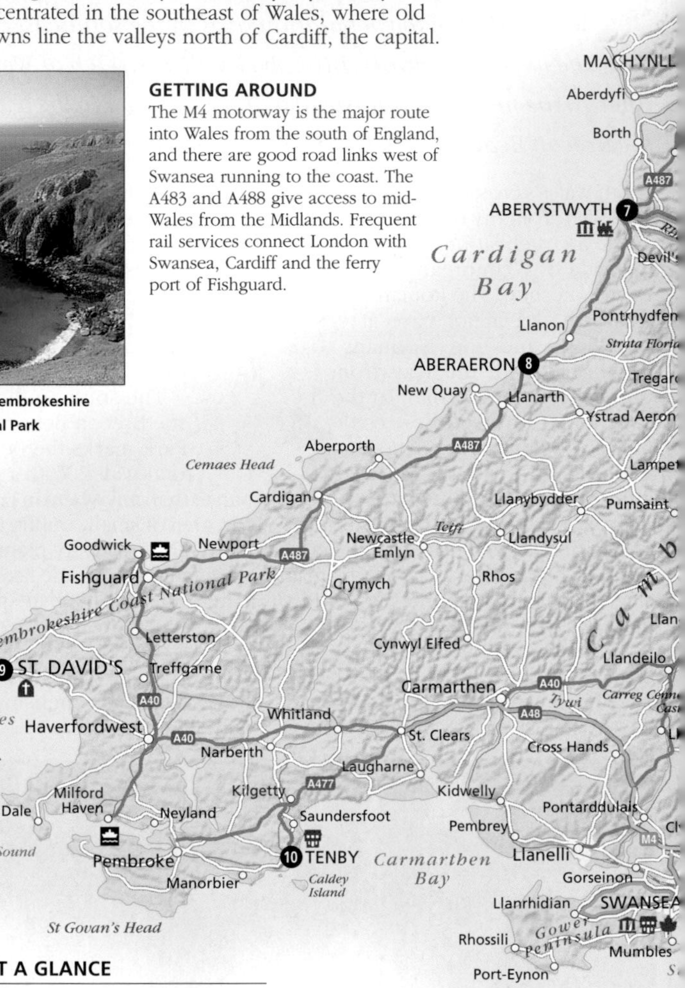

Cliffs of the Pembrokeshire Coast National Park

GETTING AROUND

The M4 motorway is the major route into Wales from the south of England, and there are good road links west of Swansea running to the coast. The A483 and A488 give access to mid-Wales from the Midlands. Frequent rail services connect London with Swansea, Cardiff and the ferry port of Fishguard.

MACHYNLL
Aberdyfi
Borth
A487
ABERYSTWYTH 7
Cardigan Bay
Devil's
Llanon
Pontrhydfen
Strata Floria
ABERAERON 8
New Quay
Llanarth
Tregar
Ystrad Aeron
Aberporth
A487
Cemaes Head
Lampet
Cardigan
Llanybydder
Pumsaint
Goodwick
Newport
A487
Newcastle Emlyn
Teifi
Llandysul
Fishguard
Pembrokeshire Coast National Park
Crymych
Rhos
Letterston
Cynwyl Elfed
Llan
Llandeilo
9 ST. DAVID'S
Treffgarne
Carmarthen
A40
Tywi
Carreg Cenn
A40
St. Brides Bay
Haverfordwest
Whitland
A48
A40
St. Clears
Narberth
Cross Hands
Skomer Island
Laugharne
A477
Milford Haven
Kilgetty
Kidwelly
Dale
Neyland
Saundersfoot
Pontarddulais
Pembrey
M4
Broad Sound
Pembroke
10 TENBY
Carmarthen Bay
Llanelli
Manorbier
Caldey Island
Gorseinon
Llanrhidian
SWANSEA
St Govan's Head
Rhossili
Gower Peninsula
Mumbles
Port-Eynon

SIGHTS AT A GLANCE

Aberaeron 8
Aberystwyth 7
Blaenafon 16
Brecon Beacons pp468–9 13
Caerleon 15
Cardiff pp470–71 14
Elan Valley 5
Hay-on-Wye 3
Knighton 2
Llandrindod Wells 4
Machynlleth 6
Monmouth 17
Powis Castle 1
St Davids pp464–5 9
Swansea and the Gower Peninsula 11
Tenby 10
Tintern Abbey 18

Walks and Tours

Wild Wales Tour 12

SEE ALSO

• ***Where to Stay*** pp590–93

• ***Where to Eat*** pp644–46

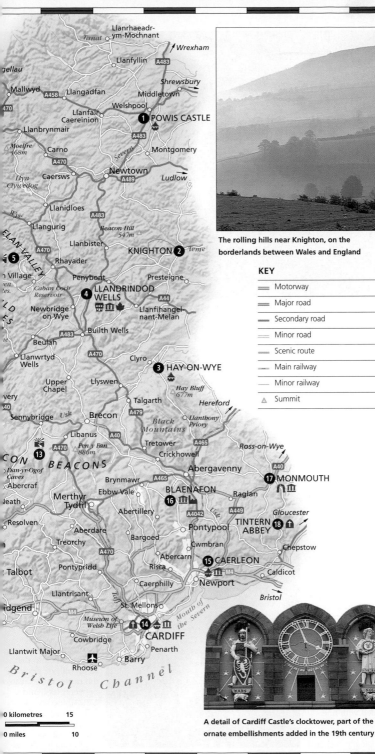

Llanrhaeadr-
ym-Mochnant
Tanat   Wrexham
Llanfyllin   A483
gellau   Shrewsbury
Mallwyd A458 Langadfan   Middletown
A470   Welshpool
Llanfair   1 POWIS CASTLE
Caereinion
Llanbrynmair   A483
Moelfre   Montgomery
_468m_   Carno
A470   _Severn_
Llyn   Caersws   Newtown
Clywedog   A489   _Ludlow_

Wye   Llanidloes
A483
Llangurig   _Beacon Hill_
_547m_
ELAN VALLEY   Llanbister   KNIGHTON 2 _Teme_
5   Rhayader
Village Penybont   Presteigne
Caban Coch
Reservoir   4 LLANDRINDOD
Newbridge   WELLS
on Wye   A44
Llanfihangel-
Builth Wells   nant-Melan

Beulah   A470
Llanwrtyd   Clyro
Wells   3 HAY-ON-WYE
Upper   Llyswen
Chapel   _Hay Bluff_
_677m_
very   _Hereford_
40   Talgarth
Sennybridge _Usk_   A479
Brecon   _Black_   _Llanthony_
Mountains   _Priory_
Libanus   A40   A465
13   _Pen y Fan_   _Ross-on-Wye_
A470 _886m_ Tretower
ON BEACONS Crickhowell   A40
Dan-yr-Ogof
Caves   Brynmawr   Abergavenny
Abercraf   A465
leath Merthyr Ebbw Vale BLAENAFON Raglan 17 MONMOUTH
Tydfil   16   A449
Resolven   Abertillery   _Gloucester_
Aberdare   A4042   TINTERN
Treorchy   Bargoed   Pontypool   18 ABBEY
A470   Cwmbran
Talbot Pontypridd Abercarn   Chepstow
Risca 15 CAERLEON
idgend Llantrisant Caerphilly   M4 Caldicot
St. Mellons   Newport
M4 _Museum of_   _Bristol_
Welsh Life 14
CARDIFF
Llantwit Major Cowbridge Penarth
Barry
Rhoose
Bristol   _Channel_

The rolling hills near Knighton, on the
borderlands between Wales and England

KEY

▬▬	Motorway
▬▬	Major road
▬▬	Secondary road
▬▬	Minor road
▬▬	Scenic route
▬▬	Main railway
▬▬	Minor railway
△	Summit

0 kilometres   15
0 miles   10

A detail of Cardiff Castle's clocktower, part of the
ornate embellishments added in the 19th century

Italianate terraces and formal gardens at Powis Castle, adding a Mediterranean air to the Welsh borderlands

Powis Castle ❶

(NT) Welshpool, Powys. 📷 *01938 551944.* 🚇 *Welshpool then bus.* ◐ *Apr–Jun & Sep–Oct: Thu–Mon; Jul–Aug: Wed–Mon & public hols.* 🏷 ⛰ *limited.* ◻ ◻ **www.**castlewales.com/powis

Powis Castle – the spelling is an archaic version of "Powys" – has outgrown its military roots. Despite its sham battlements and dominant site, 1 mile (1.6 km) to the southwest of the town of Welshpool, this red-stone building has served as a country mansion for centuries. It began life in the 13th century as a fortress, built by the princes of Powys to control the border with England.

The castle is entered through one of few surviving medieval features: a gateway, built in 1283 by Owain de la Pole. The gate is flanked by two towers.

The castle's lavish interiors soon banish all thoughts of war. A **Dining Room**, decorated with fine 17th-century panelling and family portraits, was originally designed as the castle's Great

Hall. The **Great Staircase**, added in the late 17th century and elaborately decorated with carved fruit and flowers, leads to the main apartments: an early 19th-century library, the panelled **Oak Drawing Room** and the Elizabethan **Long Gallery**, where ornate plasterwork on the fireplace and ceiling date from the 1590s. In the **Blue Drawing Room** there are three 18th-century Brussels tapestries.

The Herbert family bought the property in 1587 and were proud of their Royalist connections; the panelling in

The richly carved 17th-century Great Staircase

the **State Bedroom** bears the royal monogram. Powis Castle was defended for Charles I in the Civil War *(see pp52–3)*, but fell to Parliament in 1644. The 3rd Baron Powis, a supporter of James II, had to flee the country when William and Mary took the throne in 1688 *(see pp52–3)*.

The castle's **Clive Museum** has an exhibition concerning "Clive of India" (1725–74), the general and statesman who helped strengthen British control in India in the mid-18th century. The family's link with Powis Castle was established by the 2nd Lord Clive, who married into the Herbert family and became the Earl of Powis in 1804.

The gardens at Powis are among the best-known in Britain, with their series of elegant Italianate terraces, adorned with statues, niches, balustrades and hanging gardens, all stepped into the steep hillside beneath the castle walls. Created between 1688 and 1722, these are the only formal gardens of this period in Britain that are still kept in their original form *(see pp26–7)*.

Knighton ❷

Powys. ⚒ *3,500.* ⊟ ℹ️ *West St (01547 528753).* ⌂ *Thu.*
www.offasdyke.demon.co.uk

Knighton's Welsh name, Tref y Clawdd ("The Town on the Dyke"), reflects its status as the only original settlement on **Offa's Dyke**. In the 8th century, King Offa of Mercia (central and southern England) constructed a ditch and bank to mark out his territory, and to enable the enforcement of a Saxon law: "Neither shall a Welshman cross into English land without the appointed man from the other side, who should meet him at the bank and bring him back again without any offence being committed." Some of the best-preserved sections of the 6 m (20 ft) high earthwork lie in the hills around Knighton. The Offa's Dyke Footpath runs for 177 miles (285 km) along the border between England and Wales.

Knighton is set on a steep hill, sloping upwards from **St Edward's Church** (1877) with its medieval tower, to the summit, where a castle once stood. The main street leads via the market square, marked by a 19th-century clock tower, along **The Narrows**, a Tudor street with little shops. **The Old House** on Broad Street is a medieval "cruck" house (curved timbers form a frame to support the roof), with a hole in the ceiling instead of a chimney.

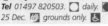

Knighton's clock

Hay-on-Wye ❸

Powys. ⚒ *1,300.* ℹ️ *Oxford Rd (01497 820144).* ⌂ *Thu.*
www.hay-on-wye.co.uk

Book-lovers from all over the world come to this quiet border town in the Black Mountains. Hay-on-Wye has over 30 second-hand book-shops stocking millions of titles, and in early summer hosts a prestigious Festival of Literature. The town's love affair with books began when a bookshop was opened in the 1960s by Richard Booth, who claims the (fictitious) title of King of Independent Hay and lives in **Hay Castle**, a 17th-century mansion in the grounds of the original 13th-century castle. Hay's oldest inn, the 16th-century **Three Tuns** on Bridge Street, is still functioning and has an attractive half-timbered façade.

Environs: Hay sits on the approach to the Black Mountains and is surrounded by rolling hills. To the south are the heights of Hay Bluff and the Vale of Ewyas, where the 12th-century ruins of **Llanthony Priory** *(see p469)* retain fine pointed arches.

♠ **Hay Castle**
Tel 01497 820503. ⬜ *daily.* ⬤ *25 Dec.* 🖼 *grounds only.* ♿

Llandrindod Wells ❹

Powys. ⚒ *5,000.* ⊟ ℹ️
Memorial Gardens (01597 822600). 🅰 *farmers' market last Thu of month; Fri.*
www.visitllandrindod.co.uk

Llandrindod is a perfect example of a Victorian town, with canopied streets, delicate wrought ironwork, gabled villas and ornamental

One of Hay-on-Wye's bookshops

parklands. This purpose-built spa town became Wales's premier inland resort of the 19th century. Its sulphur and magnesium spring waters were taken to treat skin complaints and a range of other ailments.

The town now makes every effort to preserve its Victorian character, with a lake and the well-tended **Rock Park Gardens**. The restored 19th-century **Pump Room** in Temple Gardens is where, during the last full week of August, residents don period costume and cars are banned from the town centre.

The **Radnorshire Museum** traces the town's past as one of a string of 19th-century Welsh spas which included Builth, Llangammarch and **Llanwrtyd** (now a pony trekking centre).

🏛 **Radnorshire Museum**
Memorial Gardens. *Tel 01597 824513.* ⬜ *Phone for opening times.* ⬤ *25 & 26 Dec, 1 Jan.*
🖼 ♿ **www**.powysmuseums.powys.gov.uk

Victorian architecture on Spa Road, Llandrindod Wells

Craig Goch, one of the original chain of Elan Valley reservoirs

Elan Valley ❺

Powys. ⭙ *Llandrindod.*
🛈 *Rhayader (01597 810898).*
www.elanvalley.org.uk

A string of spectacular
reservoirs, the first of the
country's man-made lakes,
has made this one of Wales's
most famous valleys. **Caban
Coch**, **Garreg Ddu**, **Pen-y-
Garreg** and **Craig Goch**, were
created between 1892 and
1903 to supply water to
Birmingham, 73 miles (117
km) away. They form a chain
of lakes about 9 miles (14 km)
long, holding 50 billion litres
(13 billion gallons) of water.
Victorian engineers selected
these high moorlands on the
Cambrian Mountains, for their
high annual rainfall of 1,780
mm (70 inches). The choice
created bitter controversy
and resentment: more than
100 people had to move from
the valley that was flooded in
order to create Caban Coch.

Unlike their more utilitarian
modern counterparts, these
dams were built during an era
when decoration was seen as
an integral part of any design.
Finished in dressed stone,
they have an air of grandeur
which is lacking in the huge
Claerwen reservoir, a stark
addition built during the early
1950s to double the lakes' cap-
acity. Contained by a 355 m
(1,165 ft) dam, it lies 4 miles
(6 km) along the B4518 that
runs through Elan Valley and
offers magnificent views.

The remote moorlands and
woodlands surrounding the
lakes are an important habitat

for wildlife; the red kite can
often be seen here. The **Elan
Valley Visitors' Centre**, beside
the Caban Coch dam,
describes the construction of
the lakes, as well as the
valley's own natural
history. **Elan Village**,
set beside the centre,
is an unusual ex-
ample of a model
workers' village, built
during the 1900s to
house the water-
works staff. Outside
the centre is a statue
of the poet Percy
Bysshe Shelley
(see p222), who
stayed in the valley at
the mansion of
Nantgwyllt in 1810
with his wife, Harriet. The
house now lies underneath
the waters of Caban Coch,
along with the rest of the old
village. Among the buildings
submerged were the village
school and a church.

The trail from Machynlleth to
Devil's Bridge, near Aberystwyth

Machynlleth ❻

Powys. 🏘 *2,200.* ⭙ 🛈 *Canolfan
Owain Glyndŵr (01654 702401).* 🖴
Wed. **www**.exploremidwales.com

Half-timbered buildings and
Georgian façades appear
among the grey-stone houses
in Machynlleth. It was here
that Owain Glyndŵr, Wales's
last native leader *(see p436)*,
held a parliament in 1404.
The restored **Parliament
House** has displays on his life
and a brass-rubbing centre.

The ornate **Clock Tower**,
in the middle of Maengwyn
Street, was erected in 1874 by
the Marquess of Londonderry
to mark the coming of age of
his heir, Lord Castlereagh.
The Marquess lived in **Plas
Machynlleth**, a 17th-century
house in parkland off the main
street, which is now
a centre of Celtic
heritage and culture.

Environs: In an old
slate quarry 2.5 miles
(4 km) to the north,
a "village of the
future" is run by the
**Centre for Alter-
native Technology**.
A water-balanced
cliff railway takes
summer visitors to
view low-energy
houses and organic
gardens, to see how to make
the best of Earth's resources.

Parliament House
sign, Machynlleth

🏛 **Parliament House**
Maengwyn St. **Tel** 01654 702827.
🔲 *Easter–Sep: Mon–Sat.* 🚻 🛈
🏛 **Centre for Alternative
Technology** On A487. **Tel** 01654
702400. 🔲 *daily.* ⬤ *early Jan.* 🈹
🈯 🚻 🍴 🛈 www.cat.org.uk

Aberystwyth ❼

Ceredigion. 🏘 *11,000.* ⭙ 🚉 🛈
Terrace Rd (01970 612125).
www.ceredigion.gov.uk

This seaside and university
town claims to be the
cultural capital of mid-Wales.
By the standards of this rural
area, "Aber" is a big place, its
population increased for
much of the year by students.

To Victorian travellers,
Aberystwyth was the "Biarritz

of Wales". There have been no great changes along the promenade, with its gabled hotels, since the 19th century. **Constitution Hill**, a steep outcrop at the northern end, can be scaled in summer on the electric **Cliff Railway**, built in 1896. At the top, in a *camera obscura*, a lens

Buskers on Aberystwyth's seafront

projects views of the town. The ruined **Aberystwyth Castle** (1277) is located south of the promenade. In the town centre, the **Ceredigion Museum**, set in a former music hall, traces the history of the town.

To the northeast of the town centre, **The National Library of Wales**, next to Aberystwyth University, has a valuable collection of ancient Welsh manuscripts.

SAVIN'S HOTEL

When the Cambrian Railway opened in 1864, businessman Thomas Savin put £80,000 into building a new hotel in Aberystwyth for package tourists. The scheme made him bankrupt, but the seafront building, complete with mock-Gothic tower, was bought by campaigners attempting to establish a Welsh university. The "college by the sea" opened in 1872, and is now the Theological College.

Mosaics on the college tower

Environs: During the summer the narrow-gauge Vale of Rheidol Railway runs 12 miles (19 km) to **Devil's Bridge**, where a dramatic series of waterfalls plunges through a wooded ravine and a steep trail leads to the valley floor.

🏛 **Ceredigion Museum**
Terrace Rd. **Tel** 01970 633088.
⬜ Mon–Sat. ⬛ 25 Dec–2 Jan,
Good Fri. 📷 ♿

Aberaeron ❽

Ceredigion. 🏠 *1,500.*
🚂 *Aberystwyth, then bus.* ❗ *The Quay (01545 570602).*
www.tourism.ceredigion.gov.uk

Aberaeron's harbour, lined with Georgian houses, became a trading port and shipbuilding centre in the early 19th century. Its orderly streets were laid out in pre-railway days, when the ports along Cardigan Bay enjoyed considerable wealth. The last boat was built here in 1994 and its harbour is now full of holiday sailors. The harbour can be crossed via a wooden footbridge.

On the quayside, the popular Honey Bee Ice Cream Parlour serves world-renowned ice creams to a loyal clientele. There is also a centre of local crafts in the town, Clos Pengarreg.

Rows of brightly painted Georgian houses lining the purpose-built harbour at Aberaeron

St Davids ❾

St David, the patron saint of Wales, founded a monastic settlement in this remote corner of southwest Wales in about 550, which became one of the most important Christian shrines. The present cathedral, built in the 12th century, and the Bishop's Palace, added a century later, are set in a grassy hollow below St Davids town, officially Britain's smallest city. The date of St David's death, 1 March, is commemorated throughout Wales.

Icon of Elijah, south transept

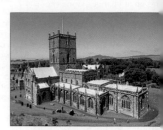

St Davids' Cathedral, the largest in Wales

The Private Chapel was a late 14th-century addition, built, like the rest of the palace, over a series of vaults.

★ Great Hall
The open arcade and decorated parapet were added by Bishop Gower (1328–47) to unify different sections of the palace.

Entrance

BISHOP'S PALACE
The bishop's residence, built between 1280 and 1350 and now in ruins, had lavish private apartments.

Palace latrines

Typical medieval window

Rose window

The Bishop's Hall, smaller than the Great Hall, may have been reserved for private use.

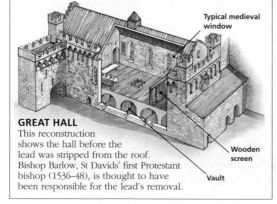

GREAT HALL
This reconstruction shows the hall before the lead was stripped from the roof. Bishop Barlow, St Davids' first Protestant bishop (1536–48), is thought to have been responsible for the lead's removal.

Wooden screen

Vault

STAR SIGHTS

★ Great Hall

★ Nave Ceiling

★ St Davids' Statue

★ **Nave Ceiling**
The roof of the nave is lowered and hidden by an early 16th-century oak ceiling. A beautiful 14th-century rood screen divides the nave from the choir.

VISITORS' CHECKLIST

Cathedral Close, St Davids.
Tel 01437 720199.
Haverfordwest then bus.
9am–6pm daily (Sun: pm).
www. stdavidscathedral.org.uk

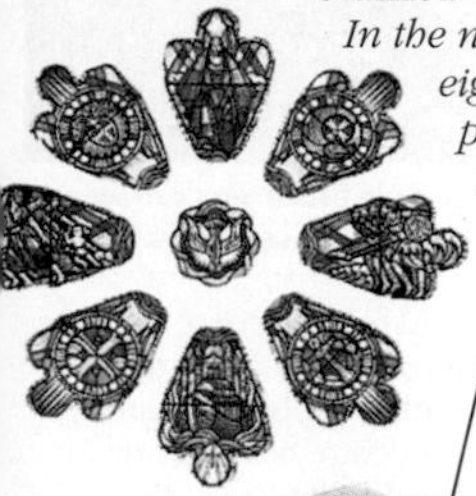

Stained-Glass Window
In the nave's west end, eight panels, produced in the 1950s, radiate from a central window showing the dove of peace.

CATHEDRAL

St David was one of the founders of the 6th-century monastic movement, so this was an important site of pilgrimage. Three visits here equalled one to Jerusalem.

St Mary's College Chapel

Bishop Vaughan's Chapel has a fine fan-vaulted early Tudor roof.

Entrance

Tower Lantern Ceiling
The medieval roof was decorated with episcopal insignia when restored in the 1870s by Sir George Gilbert Scott.

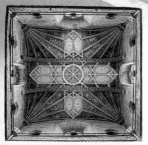

Sixteenth-Century Choir Stalls
The royal coat of arms on one of the carved choir stalls shows that the sovereign is a member of St Davids' Chapter. There are some interesting misericords (see p341) in these stalls.

★ **St Davids' Statue**
A statue of the saint is placed near the shrine. Thought to symbolize the Holy Spirit, a dove is said to have landed on David's shoulder as he spoke to a gathering of bishops.

Tenby ⑩

Pembrokeshire. 🏘 5,000. 🚉 🚌
🚢 ℹ The Croft (01834 842402).
www.tenbywales.co.uk

Tenby has successfully trodden the fine line between over-commercialization and popularity, refusing to submit its historic character to the garish excesses of some seaside towns. Georgian houses overlook its handsome harbour, which is backed by a well-preserved medieval clifftop town of narrow streets and passages. The old town was defended by a headland fortress, now ruined, flanked by two wide beaches and a ring of 13th-century walls. These survive to their full height in places, along with a fortified gateway, the **Five Arches**.

The three-storeyed **Tudor Merchant's House** is a 15th-century relic of Tenby's highly prosperous seafaring days, with original fireplaces and chimneys. There are regular boat trips from the harbour to **Caldey Island**, 3 miles (5 km) offshore, home of a perfume-making monastic community.

🏛 **Tudor Merchant's House**
(NT) Quay Hill. **Tel** 01834 842279.
⭕ Mar–Oct: Sun–Fri. ⬤ Nov–Mar.
📷 📷 for pre-booked parties.

A partly medieval restaurant next to the Tudor Merchant's House

Swansea and the Gower Peninsula ⑪

Swansea. 🏘 230,000. 🚉 🚌 🚢 ℹ
Plymouth St (01792 468321). 🚌 Mon–Sat. www.swansea.gov.uk

Swansea, Wales's second city, is set along a wide, curving bay. The city centre was rebuilt after heavy bombing in World War II but, despite the modern buildings, a traditional Welsh atmosphere prevails. This is particularly noticeable in the excellent food market, full of Welsh delicacies such as laverbread (see p606) and locally caught cockles.

The award-winning **Maritime Quarter** redevelopment has transformed the old docklands, and is worth a visit.

A statue of copper magnate John Henry Vivian (1779–1855) overlooks the marina. The Vivians, a leading Swansea

Swansea's most celebrated son, the poet Dylan Thomas

family, founded the **Glynn Vivian Art Gallery**, which has exquisite Swansea pottery and porcelain. Archaeology and Welsh history feature at the **Swansea Museum**, the oldest museum in Wales.

The life and work of local poet Dylan Thomas (1914–53) is celebrated in the recently opened **Dylan Thomas Centre**. A permanent exhibition, Man and Myth, includes the original drafts of his poems, letters and memorabilia. His statue overlooks the Maritime Quarter. Thomas spent his childhood in the city's suburbs. **Cwmdonkin Park** was the scene of an early poem, The Hunchback in the Park, and its water garden has a memorial stone quoting from his Fern Hill.

Swansea's austere **Guildhall** (1934) has a surprisingly rich interior. The huge panels, by Sir Frank Brangwyn (1867–1956), on the theme of the British Empire, were originally

Picturesque fishermen's cottages at the Mumbles seaside resort

painted for the House of Lords.

Swansea Bay leads to the **Mumbles**, a popular watersports centre at the gateway to the 19 mile long (30 km) Gower Peninsula, which in 1956 was the first part of Britain to be declared an Area of Outstanding Natural Beauty. A string of sheltered, south-facing bays leads to Oxwich and Port-Eynon beaches.

Rhossili's enormous beach leads to north Gower and a coastline of low-lying burrows, salt marshlands and cockle beds. The peninsula is littered with ancient sites such as **Parc Le Breose**, a prehistoric burial chamber.

Near Camarthen is the **National Botanic Garden of Wales**, with formal gardens centred on The Great Glasshouse which contains a Mediterranean ecosystem.

🏛 **Glynn Vivian Art Gallery**
Alexandra Rd. **Tel** 01792 516900.
⭕ Tue–Sun & public hols. ⬤
limited. 📷 by arrangement. 📷
www.glynnviviangallery.org

🏛 **Swansea Museum**
Victoria Rd. **Tel** 01792 653763.
⭕ Tue–Sun & public hols. ⬤ limited.
📷 www.swanseaheritage.net

🏛 **Dylan Thomas Centre**
Somerset Pl. **Tel** 01792 463980.
⭕ daily. ⬤ 📷 by arrangement.
🍴 📷 📷
www.dylanthomas.com

🏛 **Guildhall**
St Helen's Rd. **Tel** 01792 635489.
⭕ Mon–Fri. ⬤ public hols. ⬤

🌱 **National Botanic Garden of Wales** Middleton Hall,
Llanarthne. **Tel** 01558 668768. ⭕
daily. ⬤ 25 Dec. 📷 ⬤ 🍴 📷
📷 www.gardenofwales.org.uk

Wild Wales Tour ⑫

This tour weaves across the Cambrian Mountains' windswept moors, green hills and high, deserted plateaux. New roads have been laid to the massive Llyn Brianne Reservoir, north of Llandovery, and the old drover's road across to Tregaron has a tarmac surface. But the area is still essentially a "wild Wales" of hidden hamlets, isolated farmsteads, brooding highlands and traditional, quiet market towns.

Llanidloes ⑥
The town was a centre of religious and social unrest in the 17th and 18th centuries (see p437). There is a rare example of a free-standing Tudor market hall. The medieval church was restored in the late 19th century.

Devil's Bridge ④
This is a popular, romantic beauty spot with waterfalls, rocks, wooded glades and an ancient stone bridge – built by the Devil, according to legend.

Strata Florida ③
This famous ruined abbey was an important political, religious and educational centre during the Middle Ages.

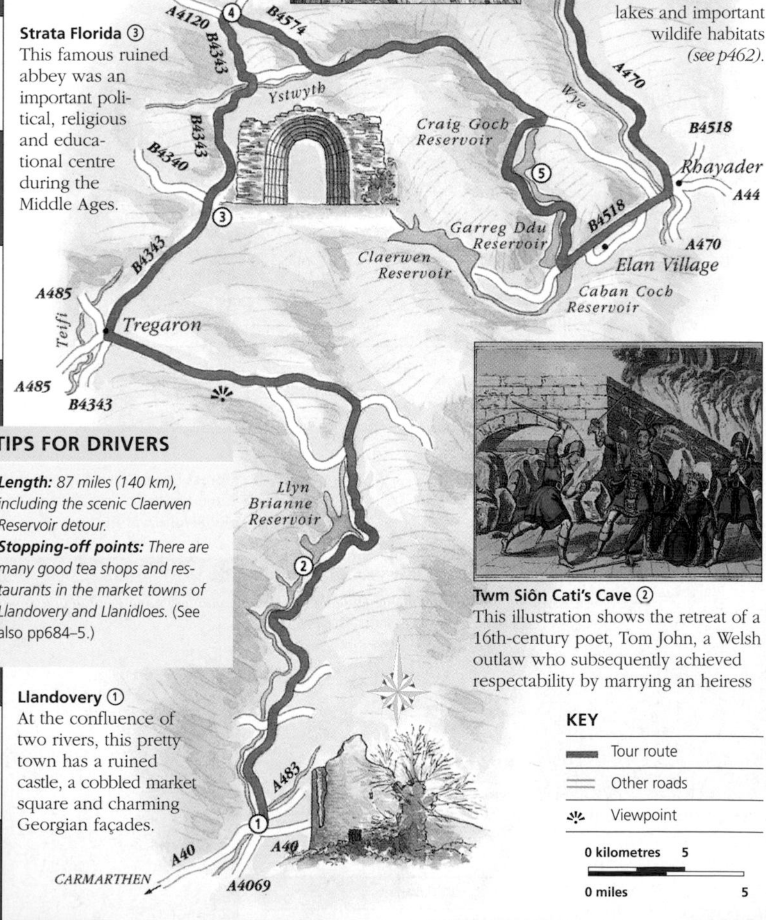

Elan Valley ⑤
This is an area of lakes and important wildlife habitats (see p462).

TIPS FOR DRIVERS

Length: 87 miles (140 km), including the scenic Claerwen Reservoir detour.
Stopping-off points: There are many good tea shops and restaurants in the market towns of Llandovery and Llanidloes. (See also pp684–5.)

Llandovery ①
At the confluence of two rivers, this pretty town has a ruined castle, a cobbled market square and charming Georgian façades.

Twm Siôn Cati's Cave ②
This illustration shows the retreat of a 16th-century poet, Tom John, a Welsh outlaw who subsequently achieved respectability by marrying an heiress

KEY

▬▬	Tour route
═══	Other roads
☼	Viewpoint

0 kilometres 5

0 miles 5

Brecon Beacons ⑬

Trekking in the Beacons

The Brecon Beacons National Park covers 520 sq miles (1,345 sq km) from the Wales–England border almost all the way to Swansea. There are four mountain ranges within the park: the Black Mountain (to the west), Fforest Fawr, the Brecon Beacons and the Black Mountains (to the east). Much of the area consists of high, open country with smooth, grassy slopes on a bedrock of red sandstone. The park's southern rim has limestone crags, wooded gorges, waterfalls and caves. Visitors can enjoy many outdoor pursuits, from fishing in the numerous reservoirs to pony trekking, caving and walking.

Llyn y Fan Fach
This remote, myth-laden glacial lake is a 4 mile (6.5 km) walk from Llanddeusant.

The Black Mountain, a largely unexplored wilderness of knife-edged ridges and high, empty moorland, fills the western corner of the National Park.

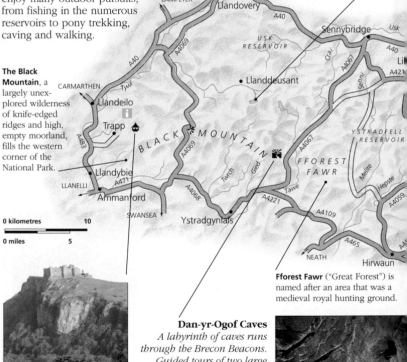

BUILTH WELLS
LAMPETER
Llandovery
A40
USK RESERVOIR
Sennybridge
Usk
A40
A421
Li
CARMARTHEN
Twyl
A40
A4067
Cray
Llanddeusant
A4067
Senni
YSTRADFELL RESERVOIR
Llandeilo
Trapp
B L A C K   M O U N T A I N
A4069
FFOREST FAWR
Melte
A4067
Twrch
Gledd
Hepste
A483
Llandybie
A471
A4069
Tawe
A4221
A4109
A4059
LLANELLI
Ammanford
A4068
Ystradgynlais
A465
SWANSEA
NEATH
Hirwaun
A4

0 kilometres   10
0 miles   5

Fforest Fawr ("Great Forest") is named after an area that was a medieval royal hunting ground.

Dan-yr-Ogof Caves
A labyrinth of caves runs through the Brecon Beacons. Guided tours of two large caves are offered here.

Carreg Cennen Castle
Spectacularly sited, the ruined medieval fortress of Carreg Cennen (see p438) stands on a sheer limestone cliff near the village of Trapp.

KEY

▬▬	A road
▭▭	B road
⁓⁓	Minor road
– –	Footpath
☆	Viewpoint

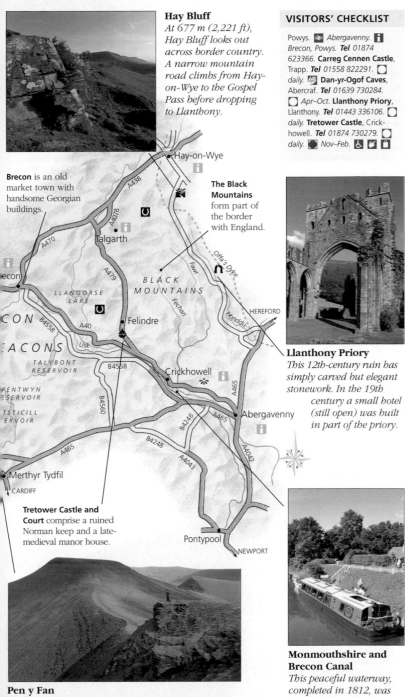

Hay Bluff

At 677 m (2,221 ft), Hay Bluff looks out across border country. A narrow mountain road climbs from Hay-on-Wye to the Gospel Pass before dropping to Llanthony.

VISITORS' CHECKLIST

Powys. ➤ Abergavenny. ℹ Brecon, Powys. **Tel** *01874 623366.* **Carreg Cennen Castle**, Trapp. **Tel** *01558 822291.* ◯ daily. 🏞 **Dan-yr-Ogof Caves**, Abercraf. **Tel** *01639 730284.* ◯ *Apr–Oct.* **Llanthony Priory**, Llanthony. **Tel** *01443 336106.* ◯ daily. **Tretower Castle**, Crickhowell. **Tel** *01874 730279.* ◯ daily. ● *Nov–Feb.* 🔋 📷 📱

Brecon is an old market town with handsome Georgian buildings.

The Black Mountains form part of the border with England.

Llanthony Priory

This 12th-century ruin has simply carved but elegant stonework. In the 19th century a small hotel (still open) was built in part of the priory.

Tretower Castle and Court comprise a ruined Norman keep and a late-medieval manor house.

Pen y Fan

At 886 m (2,907 ft), Pen y Fan is the highest point in South Wales. Its distinctive, flat-topped summit, once a Bronze Age burial ground (see pp42–3), can be reached by footpaths from Storey Arms on the A470.

Monmouthshire and Brecon Canal

This peaceful waterway, completed in 1812, was once used to transport raw materials between Brecon and Newport. It is now popular with leisure boats.

Cardiff

Cardiff was first occupied by the Romans, who built a fort here in AD 75 *(see pp44–5)*. Little is known of its subsequent history until Robert FitzHamon *(see p472)*, a knight in the service of William the Conqueror, was given land here in 1093. By the 13th century, the settlement was substantial enough to be granted a royal charter, but it remained a quiet country town until the 1830s when the Bute family, who inherited land in the area, began to develop it as a port. By 1913 this was the world's busiest coal-exporting port, profiting from rail links with the South Wales mines. Its wealth paid for grandiose architecture, while the docklands became a raucous boom-town. Cardiff was confirmed as the first Welsh capital in 1955, by which time demand for coal was falling and the docks were in decline. The city is now dedicated to commerce, tourism and administration, and is being transformed by urban renewal programmes.

Fireplace detail in the Banqueting Hall, Cardiff Castle *(see pp458–9)*

City Hall's dome, adorned with a dragon, the emblem of Wales

Exploring Cardiff

Cardiff is a city with two focal points. The centre, laid out with Victorian and Edwardian streets and gardens, is the first of these. There is a Neo-Gothic castle and Neo-Classical civic buildings, as well as indoor shopping malls and a 19th-century **covered market**. Canopied arcades, lined with shops, lead off the main streets, the oldest being the **Royal Arcade** of 1856. The **Millennium Stadium** (on the site of Cardiff Arms Park, the first home of Welsh rugby) opened in 1999 with the Rugby World Cup, and is open for tours every day.

To the south of the centre, the docklands are now being transformed into the second focal point by the creation of a marina and waterfront. A new Cardiff is taking shape, especially around the Inner Harbour area. The terracota **Pier Head Building** (1896) is a

reminder of the city's heyday, and stands in direct contrast to the striking modern architecture of the **Wales Millenium Centre**, home to the Welsh National Opera. Other attractions in the area are the **Welsh Assembly Government Debating Chamber** and **Techniquest**, a hands-on science museum.

The wooden **Norwegian Church** on Waterfront Park was first erected in 1868 for Norwegian sailors bringing wooden props for use in the coal pits of the South Wales valleys. Once surrounded by warehouses, it was taken apart and rebuilt during the dockland development. The

Cardiff Bay Visitor Centre, near the Pier Head Building, has displays on the various building projects that are uniting the civic centre with the maritime district.

♣ Cardiff Castle
See pp472–3.

⊞ City Hall and Civic Centre
Cathays Park. *Tel* 029-2087 1727.
◯ Mon–Fri. ● public hols. ⭦ ⧉
Cardiff's civic centre of Neo-Classical buildings in white Portland stone is set among parks and avenues around Alexandra Gardens. The City Hall (1905), one of its first buildings, is dominated by its 60 m (200 ft) dome and clock tower. Members of the public can visit the first-floor Marble Hall, which is furnished with Siena marble columns and statues of Welsh heroes, among them St David, Wales's patron saint *(see pp464–5)*. The Crown Building, at the northern end of the complex,

The entrance to the Wales Millenium Centre

now houses the Welsh Office, which is responsible for all Welsh government affairs.

🏛 National Museum Cardiff

Cathays Park. **Tel** 029-2039 7951. ⬤ Tue–Sun, public hols. ⬤ 24, 25 Dec & 1,2 Jan. ⬤ ⬤ by arrangement. ⬤ ⬤

www.museumwales.ac.uk

Opened in 1927, the museum occupies an impressive civic building with a colonnaded portico, guarded by a statue of David Lloyd George *(see p437)*. The art collection is among the finest in Europe with works on display by Renoir, Monet and Van Gogh.

🏛 Crafts in the Bay

The Flourish, Lloyd George Ave., Cardiff Bay. **Tel** 029-2048 4611. ⬤ daily. ⬤ ⬤

An extensive new crafts gallery, organized by the Makers' Guild in Wales, opened here in March 1996. The building now houses a wide variety of craft displays and demonstrations, including textile weaving and ceramic making.

As well as the permanent displays, there are frequently changing exhibitions on crafts-related themes. Visitors are free to browse around the centre or to book up for one of the workshops (www. makersguildinwales.org.uk).

Environs: Established during the 1940s at St Fagans, on the western edge of the city, the open-air **St Fagans National History Museum** was one of the first of its kind. Buildings from all over Wales, including workers' terraced cottages, farmhouses, a tollhouse, row of shops, chapel and old schoolhouse have been carefully reconstructed within the 40 ha (100 acre) parklands, along with a recreated Celtic village. There is also a Tudor mansion which can be visited,

Statue of Welsh politician David Lloyd George

boasting its own beautiful gardens in the grounds.

Llandaff Cathedral lies in a deep, grassy hollow beside the River Taf at Llandaff, 2 miles (3 km) northwest of the city centre. The cathedral was first a medieval building, occupying the site of a 6th-century monastic community.

Restored after suffering severe bomb damage during World War II, it was eventually reopened in 1957 with the addition of Sir Jacob Epstein's huge, stark statue, *Christus*, which is mounted on a concrete arch.

🏛 St Fagans National History Museum

St Fagans. **Tel** 029-2057 3500. ⬤ daily. ⬤ ⬤

www.museumwales.ac.uk

CARDIFF TOWN CENTRE

Cardiff Castle pp472–3 ③
City Hall & Civic Centre ②
Covered market ⑤
Crafts in the Bay ⑥
Millennium Stadium ④
National Museum of Wales ①
Techniquest Science Discovery Centre ⑦
Norwegian Church ⑨
Pier Head Building ⑧

0 metres 500
0 yards 500

Key to Symbols see back flap

Cardiff Castle

Cardiff Castle began life as a Roman fort, whose remains are separated from later work by a band of red stone. A keep was built within the Roman ruins in the 12th century. Over the following 700 years, the castle passed to several powerful families and eventually to John Stuart, son of the Earl of Bute, in 1776. His great-grandson, the 3rd Marquess of Bute, employed the "eccentric genius", architect William Burges, who created an ornate mansion between 1869 and 1881, rich in medieval images and romantic detail.

Arab Room
The gilded ceiling, with Islamic marble and lapis lazuli decorations, was built in 1881.

Animal Wall
A lion and other creatures guard the wall to the west of the castle. They were added between 1885 and 1930.

Herbert Tower

★ **Summer Smoking Room**
This was part of a complete bachelor suite in the Clock Tower, that also included a Winter Smoking Room.

Clock Tower

Main entrance to apartments

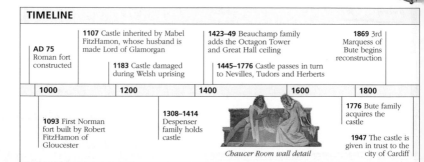

TIMELINE

AD 75 Roman fort constructed	**1107** Castle inherited by Mabel FitzHamon, whose husband is made Lord of Glamorgan	**1423–49** Beauchamp family adds the Octagon Tower and Great Hall ceiling		**1869** 3rd Marquess of Bute begins reconstruction
	1183 Castle damaged during Welsh uprising	**1445–1776** Castle passes in turn to Nevilles, Tudors and Herberts		
1000	**1200**	**1400**	**1600**	**1800**
1093 First Norman fort built by Robert FitzHamon of Gloucester	**1308–1414** Despenser family holds castle		**1776** Bute family acquires the castle	
		Chaucer Room wall detail	**1947** The castle is given in trust to the city of Cardiff	

VISITORS' CHECKLIST

Castle St, Cardiff. ***Tel** 029-2087 8100.* *Mar–Oct: 9:30am–6pm daily; Nov–Feb: 9:30am–4:30pm daily.*
www.cardiffcastle.com

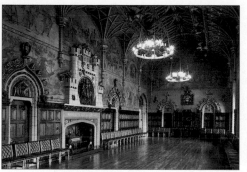

★ Banqueting Hall
The design and decoration of this room depicts the castle's history, making impressively ingenious use of the murals and castellated fireplace.

The Octagon Tower, also called the Beauchamp Tower, is the setting for Burges's Chaucer Room, decorated with themes from the *Canterbury Tales (see p186).*

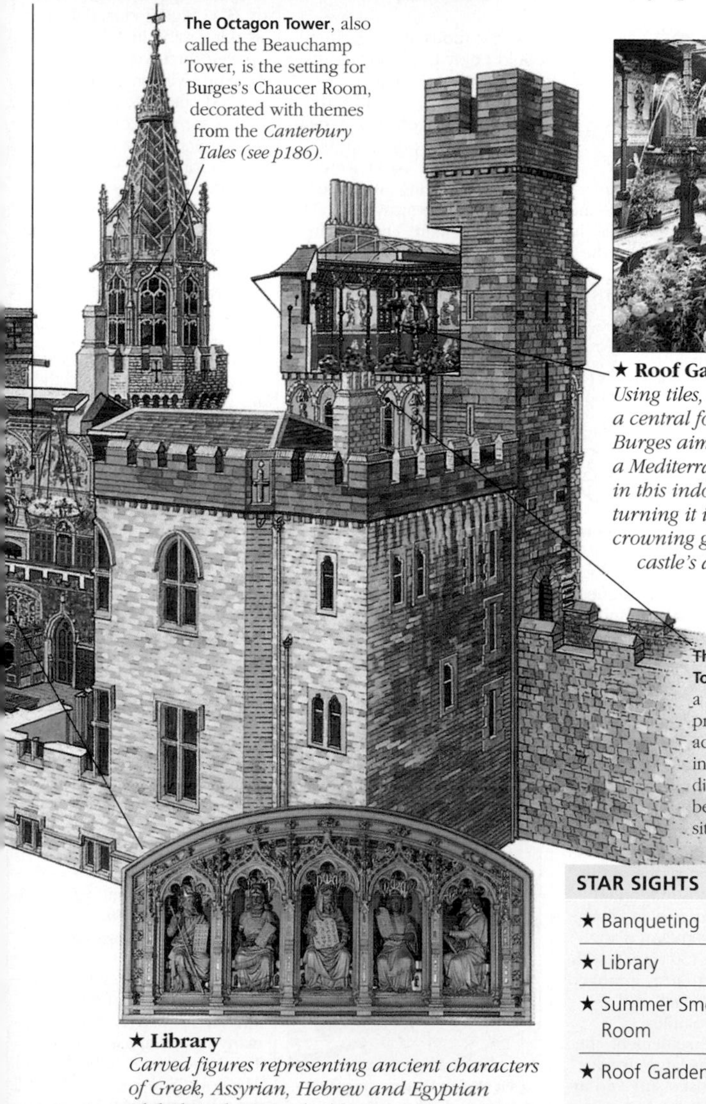

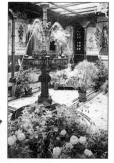

★ Roof Garden
Using tiles, shrubs and a central fountain, Burges aimed to create a Mediterranean feel in this indoor garden, turning it into the crowning glory of the castle's apartments.

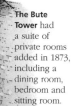

The Bute Tower had a suite of private rooms added in 1873, including a dining room, bedroom and sitting room.

★ Library
Carved figures representing ancient characters of Greek, Assyrian, Hebrew and Egyptian alphabets decorate the library's chimneypiece.

STAR SIGHTS

- ★ Banqueting Hall
- ★ Library
- ★ Summer Smoking Room
- ★ Roof Garden

Remains of Caerleon's amphitheatre, built in the 2nd century

Caerleon ⑮

Newport (Gwent). 🚹 11,000.
ℹ️ 5 High St (01633 422656).
www.caerleon.net

Together with York *(see pp404–5)* and Chester *(see pp310–11)*, Caerleon was one of only three fortress settlements in Britain built for the Romans' elite legionary troops. From AD 74 Caerleon *(Isca* to the Romans, after the River Usk, which flows beside the town) was home to the 2nd Augustan Legion, which had been sent to Wales to crush the native Silures tribe. The remains of their base now lie between the modern town and the river.

An altar at Caerleon's Legionary Museum

The excavations at Caerleon are of great social and military significance. The Romans built not just a fortress for their crack 5,500-strong infantry division but a complete town to service their needs, including a stone amphitheatre. Judging by the results of the excavation work carried out since the archaeologist Sir Mortimer Wheeler unearthed the amphitheatre in 1926, Caerleon is one of the largest and most important Roman military sites in Europe. The defences enclosed an area of 20 ha (50 acres), with 64 rows of barracks, arranged in pairs, a hospital, and a bath-house complex.

Outside the settlement, the amphitheatre's large stone foundations have survived in an excellent state of preserva-tion. Six thousand spectators could enjoy the blood sports and gladiators' combat.

More impressive still is the fortress baths complex, which opened to the public in the mid-1980s. The baths were designed to bring all the home comforts to an army posted to barbaric Britain. The Roman troops could take a dip in the open-air swimming pool, play sports in the exercise yard or covered hall, or enjoy a series of hot and cold baths.

Nearby are the foundations of the only Roman legionary barracks on view in Europe. The many excavated artifacts, including a collection of engraved gem-stones, are displayed at the **Roman Legionary Museum**.

🏛 **Roman Legionary Museum**
High St. **Tel** 01633 423134. ⬤ Mon–Sat, Sun (pm). ⬤ 24–26 Dec, 1 Jan. ⬤ 🔲 www.nmgw.ac.uk

Big Pit Mining Museum, reminder of a vanished industrial society

Blaenafon ⑯

Torfaen. 🚹 6,000. ℹ️ Blaenafon Ironworks, North St. **Tel** 01495 792615. **www**.blaenafontic.com

Commercial coal-mining has now all but ceased in the South Wales valleys – an area which only 100 years ago was gripped by the search for its "black gold". Though coal is no longer produced at **Big Pit** in Blaenafon, the **Mining Museum** provides a vivid reminder of this tough industry. The Big Pit closed as a working mine in 1980, and opened three years later as a museum. Visitors follow a marked-out route around the mine's surface workings to the miners' baths, the blacksmith's forge, the workshops and the engine house. There is also a replica of an underground gallery, where mining methods are explained. But the climax of any visit to Big Pit is beneath the ground. Kitted out with helmets, lamps and safety batteries, visitors descend by cage 90 m (300 ft) down the mineshaft and then are guided by ex-miners on a tour of the underground workings and pit ponies' stables.

Blaenafon also has remains of the iron-smelting industry. Across the valley from Big Pit stand the 18th-century smelting furnaces and workers' cottages that were once part of the **Blaenafon Ironworks**, and which are now a museum.

🏛 **Big Pit Mining Museum**
Blaenafon. **Tel** 01495 790311. ⬤ mid-Feb–Nov: daily; Dec & Jan: phone for details. ⬤ phone first. 🔲 🔲 🔲
🏛 **Blaenafon Ironworks**
North St. **Tel** 01495 792615.
⬤ mid-Mar–Oct: daily. 🔲 🔲 🔲

Monmouth ⑰

Monmouthshire (Gwent). 🚹 12,000.
🚍 ℹ️ Shire Hall (01600 713899).
🚩 Fri, Sat. **www**.visitwyevalley.com

This market town, which sits at the confluence of the Wye and Monnow rivers, has many historical associations. The 11th-century castle, behind Agincourt Square, is in ruins but the **Regimental Museum**,

Monnow Bridge in Monmouth, once a watchtower and jail

beside it, remains open to the public. The castle was the birthplace of Henry V *(see p49)* in 1387. Statues of Henry V (on the façade of Shire Hall) and Charles Stewart Rolls stand in the Square. Rolls, born at nearby Hendre, co-founded Rolls-Royce cars, and died in a flying accident in 1910.

Lord Horatio Nelson *(see p54)*, the famous admiral, visited Monmouth in 1802. An excellent collection of Nelson memorabilia, gathered by Lady Llangattock, mother of Charles Rolls, is displayed at the **Nelson Museum**.

Monmouth was the county town of the old Monmouthshire. The wealth of elegant Georgian buildings, including the elaborate **Shire Hall**, which dominates Agincourt Square, reflect its former status. The most famous architectural feature in Monmouth is **Monnow Bridge**, a narrow 13th-century gateway on its western approach, thought to be the only surviving fortified bridge gate in Britain.

For a lovely view over the town, climb the Kymin, a 256 m (840 ft) hill crowned by a **Naval Temple** built in 1801.

⋔ Monmouth Castle and Regimental Museum
The Castle. *Tel 01600 772175.* ◯ *Apr–Oct: daily (pm); Nov–Mar: Sat & Sun (pm).* ● *25 Dec.* ♿ www. monmouthcastlemuseum.org.uk

🏛 Nelson Museum
Priory St. *Tel 01600 710630.* ◯ *daily (Sun: pm).* ♿ 🅿

Tintern Abbey ⑱

Monmouthshire (Gwent). *Tel 01291 689251.* ▤ *Chepstow then bus.* ◯ *daily.* ● *24–26 Dec, 1 Jan.* 🅿 ⬚ ♿ www.cadw.wales.gov.uk

Ever since the 18th century, travellers have been enchanted by Tintern's setting in the steep and wooded Wye Valley and by the majestic ruins of its abbey. Poets were often inspired by the scene. Wordsworth's sonnet, *Lines composed a few miles above Tintern Abbey*, embodied his romantic view of landscape:

> *once again*
> *Do I behold these steep and*
> *lofty cliffs,*
> *That on a wild, secluded*
> *scene impress*
> *Thoughts of more deep*
> *seclusion*

The abbey was founded in 1131 by Cistercian monks, who cultivated the surrounding lands (now forest), and developed it as an influential religious centre. By the 14th century this was the richest abbey in Wales, but along with other monasteries it was dissolved in 1536. Its skeletal ruins are now roofless and exposed, the soaring arches and windows giving them a poignant grace and beauty.

Tintern Abbey in the Wye Valley, in the past a thriving centre of religion and learning, now a romantic ruin

SCOTLAND

Scotland at a Glance

Stretching from the rich farmlands of the Borders to a chain of isles only a few degrees south of the Arctic Circle, the Scottish landscape has a diversity without parallel in Britain. As you travel northwest from Edinburgh, the land becomes more mountainous and its archaeological treasures more numerous. In the far northwest, Scotland's earliest relics stand upon the oldest rock on Earth.

Western Isles

THE HIGHLANDS AND ISLANDS
(see pp524–49)

Skye (see pp534–5), *renowned for its dramatic scenery, has one of Scotland's most striking coastlines. On the east coast, a stream plunges over Kilt Rock, a cliff of hexagonal basalt columns named after its likeness to an item of Scottish national dress.*

Argyll and Bute

Clyde Valley

Ayrsh

The Trossachs (see pp494–5) *are a beautiful range of hills straddling the border between the Highlands and the Lowlands. At their heart, the forested slopes of Ben Venue rise above the still waters of Loch Achray.*

Culzean Castle (see pp522–3) *stands on a cliff's edge on the Firth of Clyde, amid an extensive country park. One of the jewels of the Lowlands, Culzean is a magnificent showcase of work by the Scottish-born architect, Robert Adam (see p28).*

◁ Loch Lomond, the Lowlands

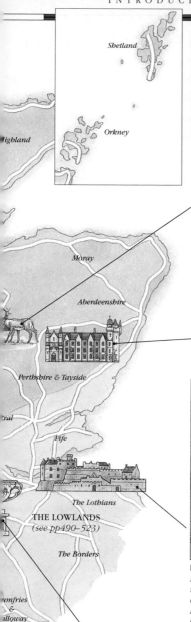

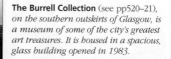

The Cairngorms (see pp544–45) *cover an area prized for its beauty and diversity of wildlife, though there are also many historical relics to be found, such as this early 18th-century arch at Carrbridge.*

Royal Deeside (see pp540–41) *in the Grampians has been associated with British royalty since Queen Victoria bought Balmoral Castle in 1852.*

Edinburgh (see pp504–11) *is the capital of Scotland. Between its medieval castle and the Palace of Holyroodhouse stretches the Royal Mile – a concentration of historic sights, ranging from the old Scottish Parliament buildings to the house of John Knox. Georgian terraces predominate in the New Town.*

The Burrell Collection (see pp520–21), *on the southern outskirts of Glasgow, is a museum of some of the city's greatest art treasures. It is housed in a spacious, glass building opened in 1983.*

Shetland

Orkney

Highland

Moray

Aberdeenshire

Perthshire & Tayside

ral

Fife

The Lothians

THE LOWLANDS
(see pp490–523)

The Borders

umfries
&
alloway

0 kilometres   50

0 miles   50

A PORTRAIT OF SCOTLAND

From the grassy hills of the Borders to the desolate Cuillin Ridge of Skye, the landscape of Scotland is breathtaking in its variety. Lonely glens, sparkling lochs and ever-changing skies give the land a challenging character, which is reflected in the qualities of the Scottish people. Tough and self-reliant, they have made some of Britain's finest soldiers, its boldest explorers and most astute industrialists.

The Scots are proud of their separate identity and their own systems of law and education and, in 1998, voted overwhelmingly for their own parliament. Many Scots welcomed this as a long-awaited reversal of the Act of Union that united the English and Scottish parliaments in 1707. But despite their national pride, they are not a homogeneous people, the main division is between traditionally Gaelic-speaking Highlanders, and the Lowlanders who spoke Scots, a form of Middle English which is now extinct. Today, though Gaelic survives (chiefly in the Western Isles), most people speak regional dialects or richly accented English. Many Scottish surnames derive from Gaelic: the prefix "mac" means "son of". A Norse heritage can be found in the far north, where Shetlanders welcome the annual return of the sun during the Viking fire festival, Up Helly Aa.

A hammer-thrower at the Braemar Games

In the 16th century, a suspicion of authority and dislike of excessive flamboyance attracted many Scots to the Presbyterian church with its absence of bishops and its stress on simple worship. The Presbyterian Church of Scotland was established in 1689, though a substantial Catholic minority remained which today predominates in the crofting (small-scale farming) communities of the Western Isles. Now sparsely populated, the Isles preserve a rural culture that once dominated the Highlands, a region that is the source of much that is distinctively Scottish. The clan system originated there, along with the tartans, the bagpipes and such unique sports as tossing the caber – a large tree trunk. Highland sports, along with traditional dances, are still performed at annual games *(see p64).*

Edinburgh bagpiper

Resourcefulness has always been a prominent Scottish virtue, and Scotland has produced a disproportionately high number of Britain's geniuses. James Watt designed the first effective steam engine to power the Industrial Revolution, while Adam Smith became the 18th century's most influential economist. In the 19th century, James Simpson discovered the anaesthetic qualities of

The Viking festival, Up Helly Aa, in Lerwick, Shetland

A traditional stone croft on the Isle of Lewis

With some of the harshest weather conditions in Europe it is perhaps less surprising that Scotland has bred numerous great explorers, the most famous being Robert Scott (of the Antarctic) and African missionary David Livingstone. There is also a strong intellectual and literary tradition, from the 18th-century philosopher David Hume, through novelists Sir Walter Scott and Robert Louis Stevenson, to the poetry of Robert Burns. Today Scotland hosts a variety of arts festivals, such as Edinburgh's.

chloroform, James Young developed the world's first oil refinery and Alexander Bell revolutionized communications by inventing the telephone. The 20th century saw one of the greatest advances in medicine with the discovery of penicillin by Alexander Fleming.

The Scots are also known for being shrewd businessmen, and have always been prominent in finance: both the Bank of England and the Royal Bank of France were founded by Scots, while Andrew Carnegie created one of 19th century-America's biggest business empires.

Detail of Edinburgh's Festival Fringe office

With a population density only one-fifth of England and Wales, Scotland has vast tracts of untenanted land which offer numerous outdoor pleasures. It is richly stocked with game, and the opening of the grouse season on 12 August is a highlight on the social calendar. Fishing and hill-walking are popular and in winter thousands flock to the Cairngorms and Glencoe for skiing. Though the weather may be harsher than elsewhere, the Scots will claim that the air is purer – and that enjoying rugged conditions is what distinguishes them from their soft southern neighbours.

The blue waters of Loch Achray in the heart of the Trossachs, north of Glasgow

The History of Scotland

Bonnie Prince Charlie, by G Dupré

Since the Roman invasion of Britain, Scotland's history has been characterized by its resistance to foreign domination. The Romans never conquered the area, and when the Scots extended their kingdom to its present boundary in 1018, a long era of conflict began with England. After many wars, the Scots finally accepted union with the "auld enemy": first with the union of crowns, and then with the Union of Parliament in 1707. In 1999 the inauguration of the Scottish Parliament was a dramatic change.

An elaborately carved Pictish stone at Aberlemno, Angus

EARLY HISTORY

There is much evidence in Scotland of important prehistoric population centres, particularly in the Western Isles, which were peopled mostly by Picts who originally came from the Continent. By the time Roman Governor Julius Agricola invaded in AD 81, there were at least 17 independent tribes, including the Britons in the southwest, for him to contend with.

The Romans reached north to the Forth and Clyde valleys, but the Highlands deterred them from going further. By 120, they had retreated to the line where the Emperor Hadrian had built his wall to keep the Picts at bay (not far from today's border). By 163 the Romans had retreated south for the last time. The Celtic influence began when

"Scots" arrived from Ireland in the 6th century, bringing the Gaelic language with them.

The Picts and Scots united under Kenneth McAlpin in 843, but the Britons remained separate until 1018, when they became part of the Scottish kingdom.

THE ENGLISH CLAIM

The Norman Kings regarded Scotland as part of their territory but seldom pursued the claim. William the Lion of Scotland recognized English sovereignty by the Treaty of Falaise (1174), though English control never spread to the northwest. In 1296 William Wallace, supported by the French (the start of the Auld Alliance, which lasted two

centuries), began the long war of independence. During this bitter conflict, Edward I seized the sacred Stone of Destiny from Scone *(see p498)*, and took it to Westminster Abbey. The war lasted for more than 100 years. Its great hero was Robert the Bruce, who defeated the English in 1314 at Bannockburn. The English held the upper hand after that, even though the Scots would not accept their rule.

John Kr statue Edinbu

THE ROAD TO UNION

The seeds of union between the crowns were sown in 1503 when James IV of Scotland married Margaret Tudor, daughter of Henry VII. When her brother, Henry VIII, came to the throne, James sought to assert independence but was defeated and killed at Flodden Field in 1513. His granddaughter, Mary, Queen of Scots *(see p511)*, married the French Dauphin in order to cement the Auld Alliance and gain assistance in her claim to

Bruce in Single Combat at Bannockburn (1906) by John Hassall

the throne of her English cousin, Elizabeth I. She had support from the Catholics wanting to see an end to Protestantism in England and Scotland. However, fiery preacher John Knox won support for the Protestants and established the Presbyterian Church in 1560. Mary's Catholicism led to the loss of her Scottish throne in 1568, and her subsequent flight to England, following defeat at Langside. Finally, after nearly 20 years of imprisonment she was executed for treason by Elizabeth in 1587.

The factories on Clydeside, once creators of the world's greatest ships

UNION AND REBELLION

On Elizabeth I's death in 1603, Mary's son, James VI of Scotland, succeeded to the English throne and became James I, king of both countries. Thus the crowns were united, though it was 100 years before the formal Union of Parliaments in 1707. During that time, religious differences within the country

Articles of Union between England and Scotland, 1707

reached boiling point. There were riots when the Catholic-influenced Charles I restored bishops to the Church of Scotland and authorized the printing of a new prayer book. This culminated in the signing, in Edinburgh in 1638, of the National Covenant, a document that condemned all Catholic doctrines. Though the Covenanters were suppressed, the Protestant William of Orange took over the English throne in 1688 and the crown passed out of Scottish hands.

In 1745, Bonnie Prince Charlie *(see p535)*, descended from the Stuart kings, tried to seize the throne from the Hanoverian George II. He marched far into England, but was driven back and defeated at Culloden field *(see p537)* in 1746.

INDUSTRIALIZATION AND SOCIAL CHANGE

In the late 18th and 19th centuries, technological progress transformed Scotland from a nation of crofters to an industrial powerhouse. In the notorious Highland Clearances *(see p531)*, from the 1780s on, landowners ejected tenants from their smallholdings and gave the land over to sheep and other livestock. The first ironworks was established in 1760 and was soon followed by coal mining, steel production and shipbuilding on the Clyde. Canals were cut, railways and bridges built.

A strong socialist movement developed as workers sought to improve their conditions. Keir Hardie, an Ayrshire coal miner, in 1892 became the first socialist elected to parliament, and in 1893 founded the Independent Labour Party. The most enduring symbol of this time is the spectacular Forth rail bridge *(see p502)*.

SCOTLAND TODAY

Although the status of the country appeared to have been settled in 1707, a strong nationalist sentiment remained and was heightened by the Depression of the 1920s and '30s which had severe effects on the heavily industrialized Clydeside. This was when the Scottish National Party formed, advocating self-rule. The Nationalists asserted themselves in 1950 by stealing the Stone of Scone from Westminister Abbey.

The discovery of North Sea oil in 1970 encouraged a nationalist revival and, in 1979, the Government promised to establish a separate assembly if 40 per cent of the Scottish electorate endorsed the plan in a referendum. This figure was finally surpassed in 1998, and the Scottish Parliament was duly inaugurated in 1999.

A North Sea oil rig, helping to provide prosperity in the 1970s

Clans and Tartans

The clan system, by which Highland society was divided into tribal groups led by autocratic chiefs, can be traced to the 12th century, when clans were already known to wear the chequered wool cloth later called tartan. All members of the clan bore the name of their chief, but not all were related by blood. Though they had noble codes of hospitality, the clansmen had to be warriors to protect their herds, as can be seen from their mottoes. After the Battle of Culloden *(see p537)*, all the clan lands were forfeited to the Crown, and the wearing of tartan was banned for nearly 100 years.

The Mackays, *also known as the Clan Morgan, won lasting renown during the Thirty Years War.*

The MacLeods *are of Norse heritage. The clan chief still lives in Dunvegan Castle, Skye (see p534).*

The MacDonalds *were the most powerful of all the clans, holding the title of Lords of the Isles.*

The Mackenzies *received much of the lands of Kintail (see p530) from David II in 1362.*

CLAN CHIEF

The chief was the clan's patriarch, judge and leader in war, commanding absolute loyalty from his clansmen who gave military service in return for his protection. The chief summoned his clan to do battle by sending a runner across his land bearing a burning cross.

Bonnet with eagle feathers, clan crest and plant badge.

Dirk

Sporran, or pouch, made of badger's skin.

Feileadh-mor, or "great plaid" (the early kilt), wrapped around waist and shoulder.

Basket-hilted sword

The Campbells *were a widely feared clan who fought the Jacobites in 1746 (see p537).*

The Black Watch, *raised in 1729 to keep peace in the Highlands, was one of the Highland regiments in which the wearing of tartan survived. After 1746, civilians were punished by exile for up to seven years for wearing tartan.*

The Sinclairs *came from France in the 11th century and became Earls of Caithness in 1455.*

The Frasers *came to Britain from France with William the Conqueror (see p47) in 1066.*

George IV, *dressed as a Highlander, visited Edinburgh in 1822, the year of the tartan revival. Many tartan "sets" (patterns) date from this time, as the original ones were lost.*

The Gordons *were famously good soldiers; the clan motto is "by courage, not by craft".*

The Stuarts *were Scotland's royal dynasty. Their motto was "no one harms me with impunity".*

CLAN TERRITORIES

The territories of 10 prominent clans are marked here with their clan crests. Dress tartans tend to be colourful, while hunting tartans are darker.

The Douglas *clan were prominent in Scottish history, though their origin is unknown.*

PLANT BADGES

Each clan had a plant associated with its territory. It was worn on the bonnet, especially on the day of battle.

Scots pine was worn by the MacGregors of Argyll.

Rowan berries were worn by the Clan Malcolm.

Ivy was worn by the Clan Gordon of Aberdeenshire.

Spear thistle, now a national symbol, was a Stuart badge.

Cotton grass was worn by the Clan Henderson.

HIGHLAND CLANS TODAY

Once the daily dress of the clansmen, the kilt is now largely reserved for formal occasions. The one-piece *feileadh-mor* has been replaced by the *feileadh-beag,* or "small plaid", made from approximately 7 m (23 ft) of material with a double apron fastened at the front with a silver pin. Though they exist now only in name, the clans are still a strong source of pride for Scots, and many still live in areas traditionally belonging to their clans. Many visitors to Britain can trace their Scots ancestry *(see p31)* to the Highlands.

Modern Highland formal dress

Evolution of the Scottish Castle

There are few more romantic sights in the British Isles than a Scottish castle on an island or at a lochside. These formidable retreats, often in remote settings, were essential all over the Highlands, where incursions and strife between the clans were common. From the earliest Pictish *brochs (see p43)* and Norman-influenced motte and bailey castles, the distinctively Scottish tower-house evolved, first appearing in the 14th century. By the mid-17th century fashion had become more important than defence, and there followed a period in which numerous huge Scottish palaces were built.

Detail of the Baroque façade, Drumlanrig

MOTTE AND BAILEY

These castles first appeared in the 12th century. They stood atop two adjacent mounds enclosed by a wall, or palisade, and defensive ditches. The higher mound, or motte, was the most strongly defended as it held the keep and chief's house. The lower bailey was where the people lived. Of these castles little more than earthworks remain today.

Duffus Castle, *(c.1150), was atypically made of stone rather than wood. Its fine defensive position dominates the surrounding flatlands north of Elgin.*

Keep, with chief's house, lookout and main defence

All that remains today of Duffus Castle, Morayshire

Bailey enclosing dwellings and storehouses

Motte of earth or rock, sometimes partially man-made

EARLY TOWER-HOUSE

Designed to deter local attacks rather than a major assault, the first tower-houses appeared in the 13th century, though their design lived on for 400 years. They were built initially on a rectangular plan, with a single tower divided into three or four floors. The walls were unadorned, with few windows. Defensive structures were on top, and extra space was made by building adjoining towers. Extensions were made as vertically as possible, to minimize the area open to attack.

Crenellated parapet for sentries

Featureless, straight walls with arrow slits for windows

Claypotts Castle (c.1570) with uniquely projecting garrets above its towers

Small, inconspicuous doorway

Braemar Castle (c.1630), a conglomeration of extended towers

Neidpath Castle, *standing upon a steep rocky crag above the River Tweed, is an L-shaped tower-house dating from the late 14th century. Once a stronghold for Charles II, its walls still bear damage from a siege conducted by Oliver Cromwell (see p52).*

LATER TOWER-HOUSE

Though the requirements of defence were being replaced by those of comfort, the style of the early tower-house remained popular. By the 17th century, wings for accommodation were being added around the original tower (often creating a courtyard). The battlements and turrets were kept more for decorative than defensive reasons.

Drum Castle *(see p541)*, a 13th-century keep with a mansion house extension from 1619

Priest's room with secret access

The original 15th-century tower-house

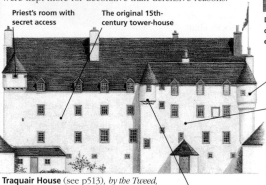

Round angle tower, containing stairway

A 16th-century horizontal extension

Traquair House (see p513), *by the Tweed, is reputedly the oldest continuously inhabited house in Scotland. The largely unadorned, roughcast exterior dates to the 16th century, when a series of extensions were built around the original 15th-century tower-house.*

Decorative, corbelled turret

Blair Castle *(see p543)*, incorporating a medieval tower

CLASSICAL PALACE

By the 18th century, the defensive imperative had passed and castles were built in the manner of country houses, rejecting the vertical tower-house in favour of a horizontal plan (though the building of imitation fortified buildings continued into the 19th century with the mock-Baronial trend). Outside influences came from all over Europe, including Renaissance and Gothic revivals, and echoes of French châteaux.

Dunrobin Castle (c.1840), Sutherland

Larger windows due to a lesser need for defence

Balustrades instead of battlements

Decorative cupola

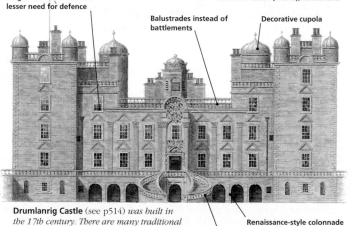

Drumlanrig Castle (see p514) *was built in the 17th century. There are many traditional Scots aspects as well as such Renaissance features as the decorated stairway and façade.*

Renaissance-style colonnade

Baroque horseshoe stairway

The Flavours of Scotland

At its best, Scottish food is full of the natural flavour of the countryside. Served with few sauces or spices, its meat is lean and tasty. Beef doesn't get better than Aberdeen Angus, the lamb is full flavoured, and the venison superb. Scottish salmon and trout are renowned, but there are also excellent mussels, lobster and crabs. Wheat does not grow here, so oatcakes and bannocks (flat, round loaves) replace bread. The Scots have a sweet tooth, not just for cakes and shortbread but also for toffee and butterscotch.

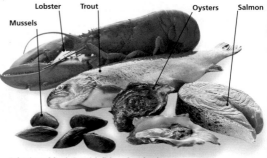

Smoked Salmon

Pedigree Aberdeen Angus cattle grazing the Scottish moors

THE LOWLANDS

The pasturelands of southern Scotland nourish dairy cattle and sheep, producing cheeses such as Bonnet, Bonchester and Galloway Cheddar. To accompany them are summer fruits such as loganberries, tayberries and strawberries that ripen in the Carse of Gowrie beside the River Tay. Oats, the principal cereal, appears in much Scottish cookery, from porridge to oatcakes. Pearl barley is also a staple, used in Scotch Broth (made with mutton and vegetables) or in a milk pudding. Oats are also used in the making of haggis, a round sausage of sheep or venison offal – the "chieftain o' the puddin' race", as the poet Robert Burns described it. It is often served with "neeps and tatties" (mashed swede and potato).

THE HIGHLANDS

From the Highlands comes wonderful game, including grouse, partridge, capercaillie (a large type of grouse) and deer. Fish are smoked around the coast, the west coast producing kippers, the east coast Finnan haddock, notably Arbroath Smokies. Smoked white fish is the main ingredient of Cullen Skink, a soup served on Burns' Night.

Lobster   Trout   Oysters   Salmon   Mussels

Selection of fresh Scottish fish and seafood

TRADITIONAL SCOTTISH FOOD

Kippers (oak-smoked herrings) are one way to start the day in Scotland, and porridge – traditionally served with salt rather than sugar – is another, although oatcakes or some other kind of griddled scone are usually present. A bowl of porridge would once last all week, just as one-pot Scotch broths bubbled in iron cauldrons over peat fires for days. Sometimes broths were made with kale or lentils, or they might contain an old boiling fowl and leeks, in which case they were known as cock-a-leekie. Any leftover meat went **Oats** into making stovies, a potato and onion hash. The evening meal in Scotland is traditionally "high tea" taken in the early evening which might start with smoked fish, cold meats and pies, followed by shortbread, fruit cake or drop scones, all washed down with cups of tea.

Haggis with neeps and tatties
This is the definitive Scottish dish, traditionally served on Burns' Night (25 January).

HOW WHISKY IS MADE

Traditionally made from just barley, yeast and stream water, Scottish whisky (from the Gaelic *usquebaugh*, or the "water of life") takes a little over three weeks to produce, though it must be given at least three years to mature. Maturation usually takes place in oak casks, often in barrels previously used for sherry. The art of blending was pioneered in Edinburgh in the 1860s.

Barley grass

1 Malting is the first stage. Barley grain is soaked in water and spread on the malting floor. With regular turning the grain germinates, producing a "green malt". Germination stimulates the production of enzymes which turn the starches into fermentable sugars.

2 Drying of the barley halts germination after 12 days of malting. This is done over a peat fire in a pagoda-shaped malt-kiln. The peat-smoke gives flavour to the malt and eventually to the mature whisky. The malt is gleaned of germinated roots and then milled.

3 Mashing of the ground malt, or "grist", occurs in a large vat, or "mash tun", which holds a vast quantity of hot water. The malt is soaked and begins to dissolve, producing a sugary solution called "wort", which is then extracted for fermentation.

4 Fermentation occurs when yeast is added to the cooled wort in wooden vats, or "washbacks". The mixture is stirred for hours as the yeast turns the sugar into alcohol, producing a clear liquid called "wash".

5 Distillation involves boiling the wash twice so that the alcohol vaporizes and condenses. In copper "pot stills", the wash is distilled – first in the "wash still", then in the "spirit still". Now purified, with an alcohol content of 57 per cent, the result is young whisky.

6 Maturation is the final process. The whisky mellows in oak casks for a legal minimum of three years. Premium brands give the whisky a 10- to 15-year maturation, though some are given up to 50 years.

Traditional drinking vessels, or *quaichs*, made of silver

Blended whiskies are made from a mixture of up to 50 different single malts.

Single malts vary according to regional differences in the peat and stream water used.

THE LOWLANDS

CLYDE VALLEY · CENTRAL SCOTLAND · FIFE · THE LOTHIANS
AYRSHIRE · DUMFRIES AND GALLOWAY · THE BORDERS

*S*outheast of the Highland boundary fault line lies a part of
Scotland very different in character from its northern neighbour.
If the Highlands embody the romance of Scotland, the Lowlands
have traditionally been her powerhouse. Lowlanders have always prospered in agriculture and, more recently, in industry and commerce.

Being the region of Scotland closest to the English border, the
Lowlands inevitably became
the crucible of Scottish history. For centuries after the
Romans built the Antonine
Wall *(see p44)* across the Forth–
Clyde isthmus, the area was
engulfed in conflict. The Borders
are scattered with the castles of
a territory in uneasy proximity
to rapacious neighbours, and
the ramparts of Stirling Castle
overlook no fewer than seven different battlefields fought over in the
cause of independence.

The ruins of medieval abbeys, such
as Melrose, also bear witness to the
dangers of living on the invasion route
from England, though the woollen
trade founded by their monks still
flourishes in Peebles and Hawick.

North of the Borders lies Edinburgh,
the cultural and administrative capital of Scotland. With its Georgian
squares dominated by a medieval castle, it is one of Europe's most elegant
cities. While the 18th and 19th centuries saw a great flowering of the
arts in Edinburgh, the city of
Glasgow became a merchant
city second only to London.
Fuelled by James Watt's development of the steam engine in
the 1840s, Glasgow became the cradle
of Scotland's Industrial Revolution,
which created a prosperous cotton
industry and launched the world's
greatest ships.

Both cities retain this dynamism
today: Edinburgh annually hosts the
world's largest arts festival, and
Glasgow is acclaimed as a model of
industrial renaissance.

A juggler performing at the annual arts extravaganza, the Edinburgh Festival

◁ Glamis Castle, 12 miles (19 km) north of Dundee, with its typically Scottish turreted exterior

Exploring the Lowlands

The Lowlands are traditionally all the land south of the fault line stretching northeast from Loch Lomond to Stonehaven. Confusingly, they include plenty of wild upland country. The region illustrates the diversity of Scotland's scenery. The wooded valleys and winding rivers of the borders give way to the stern hills of the Cheviots and Lammermuirs. Fishing villages cling to the rocky east coast, while the Clyde coast and its islands are dotted with holiday towns. Inland lies the Trossachs, a romantic area of mountain, loch and woodland east of Loch Lomond that is a magnet for walkers *(see pp36–7)* and well within reach of Glasgow.

Loch Katrine seen from the Trossachs

SEE ALSO

SIGHTS AT A GLANCE

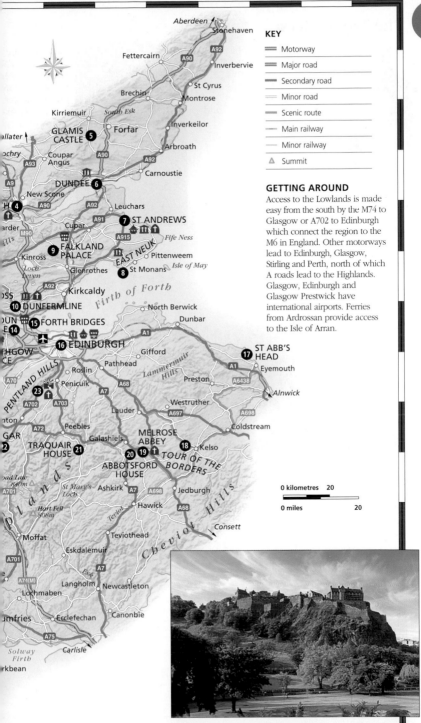

KEY

══ Motorway

▬ Major road

▬ Secondary road

═ Minor road

─ Scenic route

── Main railway

── Minor railway

△ Summit

GETTING AROUND

Access to the Lowlands is made easy from the south by the M74 to Glasgow or A702 to Edinburgh which connect the region to the M6 in England. Other motorways lead to Edinburgh, Glasgow, Stirling and Perth, north of which A roads lead to the Highlands. Glasgow, Edinburgh and Glasgow Prestwick have international airports. Ferries from Ardrossan provide access to the Isle of Arran.

Aberdeen
Stonehaven
Fettercairn
A90
Inverbervie
A92
St Cyrus
Brechin
Montrose
Kirriemuir
South Esk
Inverkeilor
allater
GLAMIS CASTLE ⑤
Forfar
ochry
Coupar Angus
A90
Arbroath
A93
A9
DUNDEE ⑥
New Scone
A90
Carnoustie
④
A92
Leuchars
arder
M90
Cupar
A91
⑦ ST ANDREWS
Kinross
⑨ FALKLAND PALACE
A915
Fife Ness
Loch Leven
Glenrothes
EAST NEUK
Pittenweem
⑧ St Monans
Isle of May
OSS
A92
Kirkcaldy
Firth of Forth
⑩ DUNFERMLINE
North Berwick
DUN ⑭ ⑮ FORTH BRIDGES
Dunbar
E
A1
⑯ EDINBURGH
Gifford
ST ABB'S HEAD ⑰
HGOW
Eyemouth
CE
Roslin
Pathhead
Lammermuir Hills
A1
A70
⑳ Penicuik
A68
Preston
A6438
PENTLAND HILLS
A702
A703
Westruther
Alnwick
nton
Lauder
A7
A697
A698
A72
Peebles
Galashiels
MELROSE ABBEY
Coldstream
GAR
⑱
TRAQUAIR HOUSE ㉑
⑳ ⑲
Kelso
②
ABBOTSFORD HOUSE
TOUR OF BORDERS
St Mary's Loch
Ashkirk
A7
A698
Jedburgh
ad Law
808m
A701
Hawick
A68
Hart Fell
808m
Teviot
Consett
Moffat
Cheviot Hills
Eskdalemuir
Esk
A7
A701
Langholm
Newcastleton
A74(M)
Lochmaben
Canonbie
imfries
Ecclefechan
A75
Carlisle
Solway Firth
rkbean

0 kilometres 20

0 miles 20

Edinburgh Castle viewed from Princes Street

The Trossachs ●

Combining the ruggedness of the Grampians with the pastoral tranquillity of the Borders, this beautiful region of craggy hills and sparkling lochs is the colourful meeting place of the Lowlands and Highlands. Home to a wide variety of wildlife, including the golden eagle, peregrine falcon, red deer and the wildcat, the Trossachs have inspired numerous writers,

Golden eagle

including Sir Walter Scott (*see p512*) who made the area the setting for several of his novels. It was the home of Scotland's folk hero, Rob Roy, who was so well known that, in his own lifetime, he was fictionalized in *The Highland Rogue* (1723), a novel attributed to Daniel Defoe.

Loch Katrine
The setting of S Walter Scott's L of the Lake (18 this freshwater loch can be ex plored on the Victorian steam SS Sir Walter Sc which cruises fr the Trossachs Pi

Loch Lomond
Britain's largest freshwater lake was immortalized in a ballad composed by a local Jacobite soldier, dying far from home. He laments that though he will return home before his companions who travel on the high road, he will be doing so on the low road (of death).

The West Highland Way
provides a good footpath through the area.

KEY

ℹ️	Tourist information
▬	A road
▭	B road
═	Minor road
‑ ‑	Footpath
☆	Viewpoint

0 kilometres   5

0 miles   5

Map labels: FORT WILLIAM • Inveruglas • LOCH ARKLET • Tarbet • BEN LOMOND 974 m 3,196 ft • Kinloc • BEN UIRD 596 m 1,955 ft • Luss • Balm • LOCH LOMOND • Balloch • GLASGOW • A82 • A811

Luss
With its exceptionally picturesque cottages, Luss is one of the prettiest villages in the Lowlands. Surrounded by grassy hills, it occupies one of the most scenic parts of Loch Lomond's western shore.

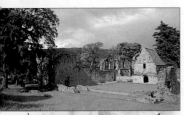

Inchmahome Priory
Mary, Queen of Scots (see p511) *was hidden in this island priory to escape the armies of Henry VIII* (see p512).

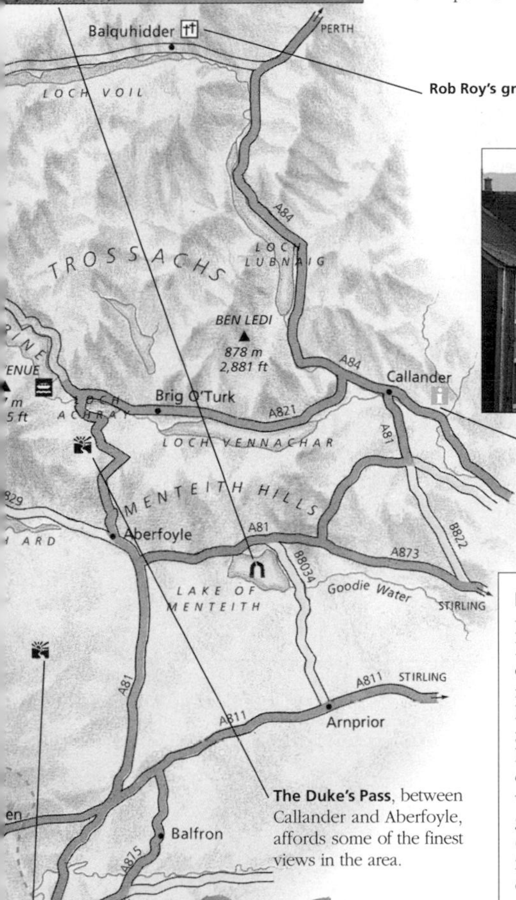

Balquhidder
PERTH
LOCH VOIL
Rob Roy's grave
TROSSACHS
LOCH LUBNAIG
A84
BEN LEDI
878 m
2,881 ft
Callander
Brig O'Turk
LOCH ACHRAY
A821
LOCH VENNACHAR
A81
MENTEITH HILLS
Aberfoyle
A81
B822
A873
LAKE OF MENTEITH
B8034
Goodie Water
STIRLING
A81
A811
STIRLING
Arnprior
A811
Balfron
A875
Killearn

The Duke's Pass, between Callander and Aberfoyle, affords some of the finest views in the area.

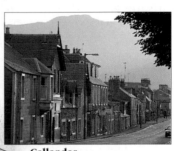

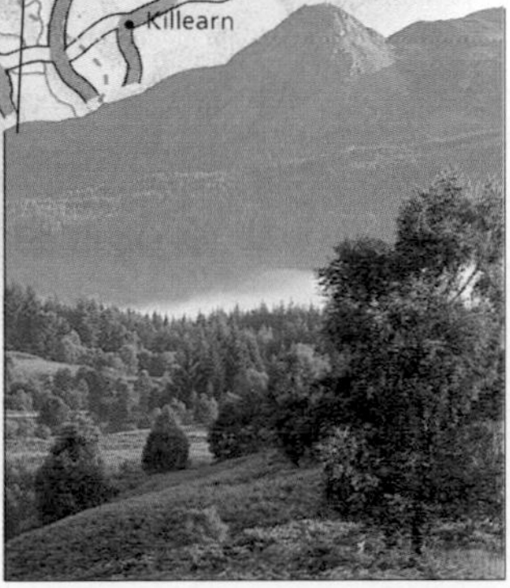

Queen Elizabeth Forest Park
There are woodland walks through this vast tract of countryside, home to black grouse and red deer, between Loch Lomond and Aberfoyle.

VISITORS' CHECKLIST

Stirling. *Stirling. Callander.* *Rob Roy & Trossachs Visitor Centre, Ancaster Sq, Callander (0870 7200628), Loch Lomond Aquarium Visitor Centre (01389 721500)* **www**.lochlomond aquarium.com. *daily.*
Inchmahome Priory, off A81, nr Aberfoyle; by ferry to Lake of Monteith. ***Tel*** *0870-7200628.* *Apr–Sep: daily. limited.*
SS *Sir Walter Scott*: *ring Visitor Centre (01877 376316).*

Callander
With its Rob Roy and Trossachs Visitor Centre, Callander is the most popular town from which to explore the Trossachs.

ROB ROY (1671–1734)

Robert MacGregor, known as Rob Roy (Red Robert) from the colour of his hair, grew up as a herdsman near Loch Arklet. After a series of harsh winters, he took to raiding richer Lowland properties to feed his clan, and was declared an outlaw by the Duke of Montrose who then burned his house to the ground. After this, Rob's Jacobite *(see p537)* sympathies became inflamed by his desire to avenge the crime. Plundering the duke's lands and repeatedly escaping from prison earned him a reputation similar to England's Robin Hood *(see p336)*. He was pardoned in 1725 and spent his last years freely in Balquhidder, where he is buried.

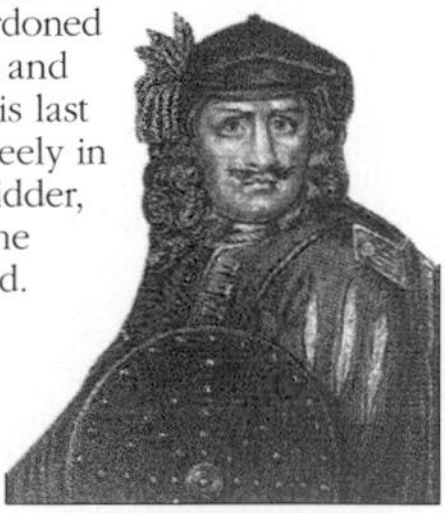

The 17th-century town house of the Dukes of Argyll, Stirling

Stirling ②

Stirling. 🏛 41,000. � ☐
🛈 41 Dunbarton Rd (0870 7200620).
www.visitscottishheartlands.com

Situated between the Ochil Hills and the Campsie Fells, Stirling grew up around its castle, historically one of Scotland's most important fortresses. Below the castle the Old Town is still protected by the original 16th-century walls, built to keep Mary Queen of Scots safe from Henry VIII. The medieval **Church of the Holy Rude**, on Castle Wynd, where the infant James VI was crowned in 1567, has one of Scotland's few surviving hammerbeam oak roofs. The ornate façade of **Mar's Wark** is all that remains of a grand palace which, though never completed, was commissioned in 1570 by the 1st Earl of Mar. It was destroyed by the Jacobites (see p537) in 1746. Opposite stands the beautiful 17th-century town house of the Dukes of Argyll.

Environs: Two miles (3 km) south, the **Bannockburn Heritage Centre** stands by the field where Robert the Bruce defeated the English (see p482). After the battle, he dismantled the castle so it would not fall back into English hands. A bronze equestrian statue commemorates the man who is an icon of Scottish independence.

🛈 **Bannockburn Heritage Centre**
(NTS) Glasgow Rd. **Tel** 01786 812664. ☐ Mar–Oct: 10am–5:30pm daily. ☐ 24 Dec–Feb. ♿ ♿

Stirling Castle

Rising high on a rocky crag, this magnificent castle, which dominated Scottish history for centuries, now remains one of the finest examples of Renaissance architecture in Scotland. Legend says that King Arthur (see p285) wrested the original castle from the Saxons, but there is no evidence of a castle before 1124. The present building dates from the 15th and 16th centuries and was last defended, against the Jacobites (see p537), in 1746. From 1881 to 1964 the castle was a depot for recruits into the Argyll and Sutherland Highlanders, though now it serves no military function.

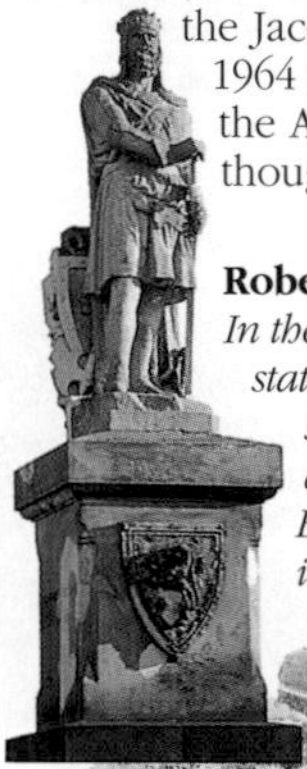

Gargoyle on castle wall

Robert the Bruce
In the esplanade, this modern statue shows Robert the Bruce sheathing his sword after the Battle of Bannockburn in 1314.

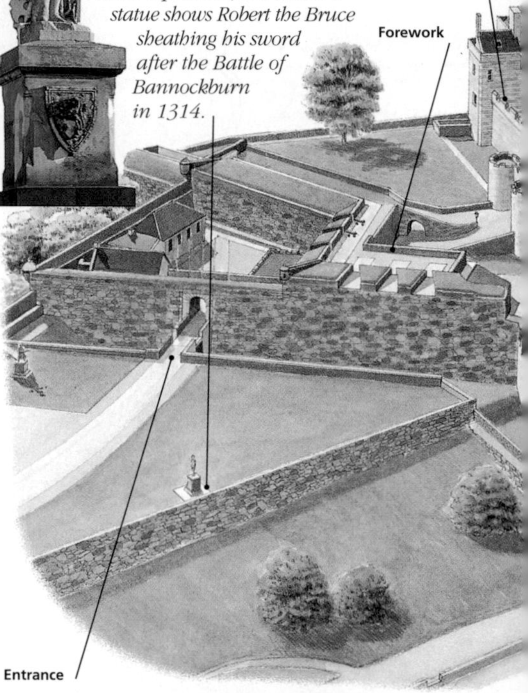

Prince's Tower

Forework

Entrance

Stirling Castle in the Time of the Stuarts, painted by Johannes Vorsterman (1643–99)

★ Palace
The otherwise sparse interiors of the royal apartments contain the Stirling Heads. These Renaissance roundels depict 38 figures, thought to be contemporary members of the royal court.

VISITORS' CHECKLIST

Castle Wynd, Stirling. ***Tel*** 01786 450000. *late Mar–late Sep: 9:30am–6pm daily; Oct–late Mar: 9:30am– 5pm daily (last adm: 45 mins before closing).* *25–26 Dec, 1–2 Jan.* except museum. *limited.* **www**.historic-scotland.gov.uk

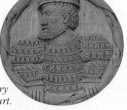

The King's Old Building houses the Regimental Museum of the Argyll and Sutherland Highlanders.

★ Chapel Royal
Seventeenth-century frescoes by Valentine Jenkins adorn the chapel, reconstructed in 1594.

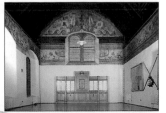

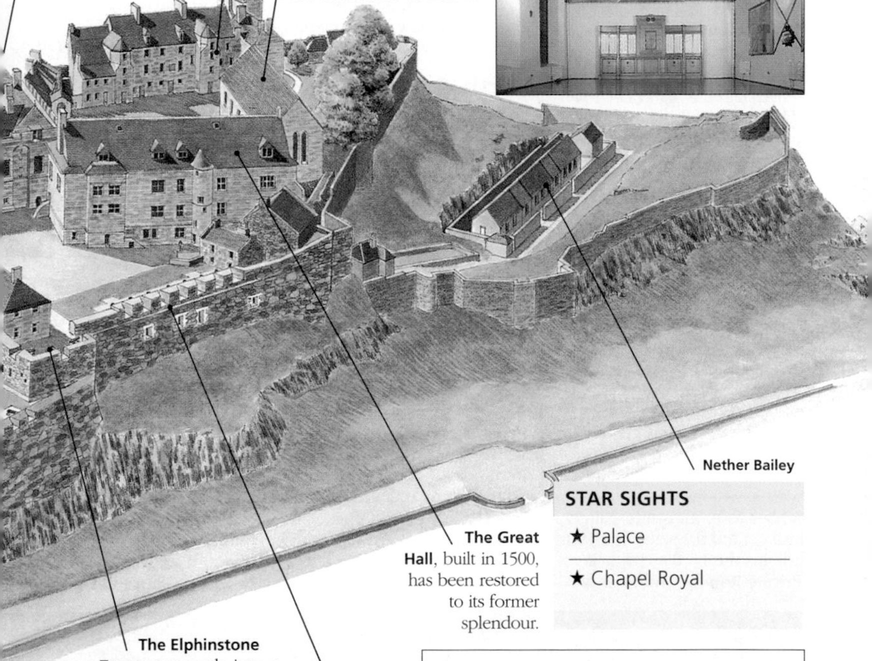

Nether Bailey

STAR SIGHTS

★ Palace

★ Chapel Royal

The Great Hall, built in 1500, has been restored to its former splendour.

The Elphinstone Tower was made into a gun platform in 1714.

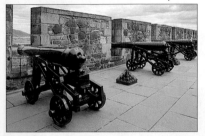

Grand Battery
Seven guns stand on this parapet, built in 1708 during a strengthening of defences following the revolution of 1688 (see p53).

STIRLING BATTLES

At the highest navigable point of the Forth and holding the pass to the Highlands, Stirling occupied a key position in Scotland's struggles for independence. Seven battlefields can be seen from the castle; the 67 m (220 ft) Wallace Monument at Abbey Craig recalls William Wallace's defeat of the English at Stirling Bridge in 1297, foreshadowing Bruce's victory in 1314 *(see p482)*.

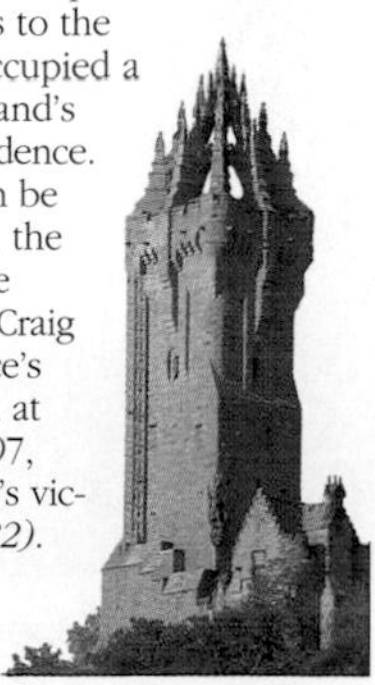

The Victorian Wallace Monument

Perth seen from the east across the Tay

Doune Castle ❸

Doune, Stirling. **Tel** *01786 841742.*
🚆 🚌 *Stirling then bus.* 🕐 *Apr–Sep: 9:30am–6:30pm daily; Oct–Mar: 9:30am–4:30pm daily; last entry 30 mins before close.* ⬤ *21 Dec–8 Jan.* 🖼 ♿ *limited.*
www.historic-scotland.gov.uk

Built as the residence of Robert, Duke of Albany, in the 14th century, **Doune Castle** was a Stuart stronghold until it fell into ruin in the 18th century. Now fully restored, it is one of the most complete castles of its time and offers a unique insight into the medieval royal household.

The Gatehouse, once a self-sufficient residence, leads through to the central court-yard from which the Great Hall can be entered. Complete with its reconstructed open-timber roof, minstrels' gallery and central fireplace, the Hall adjoins the Lord's Hall and Private Room. A number of private stairs and narrow passages reveal the ingenious ways the royal family tried to hide during times of danger.

Perth ❹

Perthshire. 🏘 *45,000.* 🚆 🚌
ℹ️ *West Mill St (01738 450600).*
www.perthshire.co.uk

Once the capital of medieval Scotland, Perth's rich heritage is reflected in many of its buildings. It was in the **Church of Saint John**, founded in 1126, that John Knox *(see p483)* delivered many of his fiery sermons. The Victor-ianized **Fair Maid's House**, on North Port, is one of the oldest houses in town (c.1600) and was the fictional home of the heroine of Sir Walter Scott's *(see p512) The Fair Maid of Perth* (1828).

In **Balhousie Castle**, the Museum of the Black Watch commemorates the first Highland regiment, while the **Perth Museum & Art Gallery** has displays on local industry and exhibitions of Scottish art.

Environs: Two miles (3 km) north of Perth, the Gothic mansion of **Scone Palace** stands on the site of an abbey destroyed in 1559. Between the 9th and 13th centuries, Scone guarded the sacred Stone of Destiny *(see pp482–3)*, now kept in Edinburgh Castle *(see pp506–7)*. Some of Mary, Queen of Scots' *(see p511)* embroideries are on display.

⛪ **Balhousie Castle**
RHQ Black Watch, Hay St. **Tel** *0131 310 8530.* 🕐 *Mon–Sat.*
www.theblackwatch.co.uk
🏛 **Perth Museum & Art Gallery**
78 George St. **Tel** *01738 632488.*
🕐 *10am–5pm Mon–Sat.* ♿
⛪ **Scone Palace**
A93 to Braemar. **Tel** *01738 840393.*
🕐 *daily (grounds close at 6pm).*
🖼 ♿ **www**.scone-palace.co.uk

Glamis Castle ❺

Forfar, Angus. **Tel** *01307 840393.*
🚆 🚌 *Dundee then bus.* 🕐 *mid-Mar–late Dec: 10am–6pm daily (last tour 4pm).* 🖼 📷
www.glamis-castle.co.uk

With the pinnacled fairytale outline of a Loire chateau, the imposing medieval tower-house of **Glamis Castle** began

Glamis Castle with statues of James VI (left) and Charles I (right)

as a royal hunting lodge in the 11th-century but underwent extensive reconstruction in the 17th century. It was the childhood home of Queen Elizabeth the Queen Mother, and her former bedroom can be seen with a youthful portrait by Henri de Laszlo (1878–1956).

Many rooms are open to the public, including Duncan's Hall, the oldest in the castle and Shakespeare's setting for the king's murder in *Macbeth*. Together, the rooms present an array of china, paintings, tapestries and furniture spanning five centuries. In the grounds stand a pair of wrought-iron gates made for the Queen Mother on her 80th birthday in 1980.

Dundee ❻

Dundee City. 🏠 *144,000.* ✈ ⇄
🚌 🛈 *21 Castle Street (01382 527527).* 🛒 *Tue, Fri–Sun; farmers' market 3rd Sat of month.*
www.angusanddundee.co.uk

Famous for its cake, marmalade and the DC Thomson publishing empire (creators of children's magazines *Beano* and *Dandy*), **Dundee** was also a major ship-building centre in the 18th and 19th centuries, a period which can be atmospherically recreated by a trip to the Victoria Docks.

HMS Unicorn, built in 1824, is the oldest British-built warship still afloat and is still fitted as it was on its last voyage. Berthed at Riverside is the royal research ship *Discovery*, built here in 1901 for Captain

View of St Andrews over the ruins of the cathedral

Scott's first voyage to the Antarctic. Housed in a Victorian Gothic building, the **McManus Galleries** provide a glimpse of Dundee's industrial heritage, as well as exhibitions on archaeology and Victorian art. The **Howff Burial Ground**, near City Square, has intriguing Victorian tombstones.

🏛 HMS *Unicorn*
Victoria Docks, City Quay.
Tel 01382 200900. ⬜
Apr–Oct: daily;
Nov–Mar: Sat & Sun,
pm only Wed–Fri. ⬤
late Dec–early Jan. 📷
♿ *limited.*
🏛 *Discovery*
Discovery Point.
Tel 01382 201245.
⬜ *daily (Sun pm).* 📷 ♿
www.rrsdiscovery.com
🏛 McManus Galleries
Albert Sq. *Tel 01382 432350.* ⬤
for redevelopment until late 2007. ♿
www.dundeecity.gov.uk

St Mary's College insignia, St Andrews University

St Andrews ❼

Fife. 🏠 *16,000.* 🚉 *Leuchars.*
🚌 *Dundee.* 🛈 *70 Market St (01334 472021).* **www**.standrews.co.uk

Scotland's oldest university town and one-time ecclesiastical capital, **St Andrews** is now a shrine to golfers from all over the world (*see below*). Its three main streets and numerous cobbled alleys, full of crooked housefronts, dignified university buildings and medieval churches, converge on the venerable ruins of the 12th-century **cathedral**. Once the largest in Scotland, the cathedral was later pillaged for stones to build the town. **St Andrew's Castle** was built for the bishops of the town in 1200. The dungeon can still be seen. The city's golf courses to the west are each open for a modest fee. The **British Golf Museum** tells how the city's Royal and Ancient Golf Club became the ruling arbiter of the game.

♟ St Andrew's Castle
The Scores. *Tel 01334 477196.*
⬜ *Apr–Sep: 9:30–6:30pm daily;*
Oct–Mar: 9:30–4:30pm daily. ⬤ *25 & 26 Dec, 1 & 2 Jan.* 📷 ♿
🏛 British Golf Museum
Bruce Embankment. *Tel 01334 460 046.* ⬜ *Mar–Oct: 9:30am–5:30pm Mon–Sat, 10am–5pm Sun; Nov–Mar: 10am-4pm Mon–Sun.* 📷 ♿

THE ANCIENT GAME OF GOLF

Scotland's national game was pioneered on the sandy links around St Andrews. The earliest record dates from 1457, when golf was banned by James II on the grounds that it was interfering with his subjects' archery practice. Mary, Queen of Scots (*see p511*) enjoyed the game and was berated in 1568 for playing straight after the murder of her husband Darnley.

Mary, Queen of Scots at St Andrews in 1563

The central courtyard of Falkland Palace, bordered by rose bushes

East Neuk ❽

Fife. ⬌ *Leuchars.* ▦ *Glenrothes & Leuchars.* ℹ *70 Market Street, St Andrews (01334 472021).*

A string of pretty fishing villages scatters the shoreline of the **East Neuk** (the eastern "corner") of Fife, stretching from Earlsferry to Fife Ness. Much of Scotland's medieval trade with Europe passed through these ports, a connection reflected in the Flemish-inspired crow-stepped gables of many of the cottages. Although the herring industry has declined and the area is now a peaceful holiday centre, the sea still dominates village life. Until the 1980s, fishing boats were built at St Monans, a charming town of narrow twisting streets, while Pittenweem is the base for the East Neuk fishing fleet.

The town is also known for **St Fillan's Cave**, the retreat of a 9th-century hermit whose relic was used to bless the army of Robert the Bruce *(see p482)* before the Battle of Bannockburn. A church stands among the cobbled lanes and colourful cottages of Crail; the stone by the church gate is said to have been hurled to the mainland from the Isle of May by the Devil.

Several 16th- to 19th-century buildings in the village of Anstruther contain the **Scottish Fisheries Museum** which tells the area's history with the aid of interiors, boats and displays on whaling. From the village you can also embark for the nature reserve on the **Isle of May** which teems with seabirds and grey seals. The statue of Alexander Selkirk in Lower Largo recalls the local boy whose adventures inspired Daniel Defoe's *Robinson Crusoe* (1719). Disagreeing with his captain, he was dumped on a desert island for four years.

🏛 **Scottish Fisheries Museum**
St Ayles, Harbourhead, Anstruther. **Tel** *01333 310628.* ⬭ *daily.* ⬤ *25 & 26 Dec, 1, 2 Jan.* 🈲 ♿
www.scotfishmuseum.org

THE PALACE KEEPER

Due to the size of the royal household and the necessity for the king to be itinerant, the office of Keeper was created by the medieval kings who required custodians to maintain and replenish the resources of their many palaces while they were away. Now redundant, it was a hereditary title and gave the custodian permanent and often luxurious lodgings.

James VI's bed in the Keeper's Bedroom, Falkland Palace

Falkland Palace ❾

(NTS) *Falkland, Fife.* **Tel** *01337 857397.* ⬌ 🚌 *Ladybank, Kirkcaldy, then bus.* ⬭ *Mar–Oct: 10am–5pm daily (Sun: pm).* 📷 🈲 ♿
www.nts.org.uk

This stunning Renaissance palace was designed as a hunting lodge of the Stuart kings. Although its construction was begun by James IV in 1500, most of the work was carried out by his son, James V *(see p510)*, in the 1530s. Under the influence of his two French wives he employed French workmen to redecorate the façade of the East Range with dormers, buttresses and medallions, and to build the beautifully proportioned South Range. The palace fell into ruin during the years of the Commonwealth *(see p52)* and was occupied briefly by Rob Roy *(see p495)* in 1715.

After buying the estates in 1887, the 3rd Marquess of Bute became the Palace Keeper and restored it. The richly panelled interiors are filled with superb furniture and portraits of the Stuart monarchs. The royal tennis court is the oldest in Britain.

Dunfermline ❿

Fife. 🏘 *55,000.* ⬌ 🚌 ℹ *1 High St (01383 720999).*
www.standrews.com/fife

Scotland's capital until 1603, Dunfermline is dominated by the ruins of the 12th-century abbey and palace which recall its royal past. In the 11th century, the town was the seat of King Malcolm III, who founded a priory on the present site of the **Abbey Church**. With its Norman nave and 19th-century choir, the church contains the tombs of 22 Scottish kings and queens, including Robert the Bruce *(see p482)*.

The ruins of King Malcolm's **palace** soar over the beautiful gardens of Pittencrieff Park. Dunfermline's most famous son, philanthropist Andrew Carnegie (1835–1919), had been forbidden entrance to the park as a boy. After making his fortune, he bought the entire Pittencrieff estate and gave it to the people of Dunfermline. He was born in the town, though moved to Pennsylvania in his teens. There he made a vast fortune in the iron and steel industry. The **Carnegie Birthplace Museum** is still furnished as it was when he lived there, and tells the story of his meteoric career.

🏛 **Carnegie Birthplace Museum**
Moodie St. **Tel** *01383 724302.* ◯
Apr–Oct: daily (Sun: pm). 🔲 🖼 ♿

The 12th-century Norman nave of Dunfermline Abbey Church

Culross ⓫

(NTS) *Fife.* 🚶 *450.* 🚆 *Dunfermline.* 🚌 *Dunfermline.* 🛈 *NTS, The Palace (01383 880359).* ◯ *Easter–Sep: Garden* ◯ *10am–dusk all year.* 🖼 ♿ *limited.* 🖼 🔲

An important religious centre in the 6th century, the town of Culross is said to have been the birthplace of St

Mungo in 514. Now a beautifully preserved 16th- and 17th-century village, Culross prospered in the 16th century with the growth of its coal and salt industries, most notably under Sir George Bruce. He took charge of the Culross colliery in 1575 and created a drainage system called the "Egyptian Wheel" which cleared a mile-long (1.5 km) mine beneath the River Forth.

During its subsequent decline Culross stood unchanged for over 150 years. The National Trust for Scotland began restoring the town in 1932 and now provides a guided tour, which starts at the **Visitors' Centre**.

Built in 1577, Bruce's **palace** has the crow-stepped gables, decorated windows and red pantiles typical of the period. The interior retains its original early 17th-century painted ceilings. Crossing the Square, past the **Oldest House**, dating from 1577, head for the **Town House** to the west. Behind it, a cobbled street known as the Back Causeway (with its raised section for nobility) leads to the turreted **Study**, built in 1610 as a house for the Bishop of Dunblane. The main room is open to visitors and should be seen for its original Norwegian ceiling. Continuing northwards to the ruined abbey, fine church and Abbey House, don't miss the Dutch-gabled **House with the Evil Eyes**.

The 16th-century palace of industrialist George Bruce, Culross

Linlithgow Palace ⓬

Linlithgow, West Lothian. **Tel** *01506 842896.* 🚆 🚌 ◯ *Apr–Sep: 9:30am–6:30pm daily; Oct–Mar: 9:30am–4:30pm daily.* ● *25, 26 Dec, 1, 2 Jan.* 🖼 ♿ *limited.* www.historic-scotland.gov.uk

On the edge of Linlithgow Loch stands the former royal palace of **Linlithgow**. Today's remains are mostly of the palace of James I in 1425. The scale of the building is demonstrated by the 28 m (94 ft) long Great Hall, with its huge fireplace and windows. Mary, Queen of Scots *(see p511)*, was born here in 1542.

Falkirk Wheel ⓭

Lime Rd, Falkirk. **Tel** *01324 619888; booking line: 08700 500208.* 🚆 *Falkirk.* ◯ *Apr–Oct:* **Boat trips** *9:30am–5pm daily.* **Visitor Centre** *daily. Nov–Feb: phone for times.* 🖼 *boat trip.* 🔲 🔲 www.thefalkirkwheel.co.uk

This impressive boat lift is the first ever to revolve, and the centrepiece of Scotland's ambitious canal regeneration scheme. Once important for commercial transport, the Union and the Forth and Clyde canals were blocked by several roads in the 1960s. Now the Falkirk Wheel gently swings boats between the two waterways creating an uninterrupted link between Glasgow and Edinburgh. Visitors can ride the wheel on boats that leave the visitor's centre every half hour.

The rotating Falkirk Wheel boat lift

Hopetoun House ⑭

West Lothian. **Tel** 0131 331 2451. 🚇
Dalmeny then taxi. 🕐 mid-Apr–late
Sep: 11am-5:30pm daily. 🖼 🏛 ♿
limited. 📷 for groups – book ahead.
💻 **www**.hopetounhouse.com

An extensive parkland by the
Firth of Forth, designed in
the style of Versailles, is the
setting for one of Scotland's
finest stately homes. The original house was built by
1707; it was later absorbed
into William Adam's grand
extension. The dignified,
horseshoe-shaped plan and
lavish interior plasterwork
represent Neo-Classical 18th-
century architecture at its
finest. The drawing rooms,
with their Rococo plasterwork
and highly ornate mantel-
pieces, are particularly
impressive. The Marquess of
Linlithgow, whose family still
occupies part of the house, is
a descendant of the 1st Earl
of Hopetoun, for whom the
house was built.

A wooden panel above the main
stair, depicting Hopetoun House

Forth Bridges ⑮

Edinburgh. 🚇 🚍 Dalmeny, Inver-
keithing. 🚏 Queensferry Lodge Hotel,
N Queensferry (01383 417759).

The small town of South
Queensferry is dominated
by the two great bridges that
span the mile (1.6 km) across
the River Forth to North
Queensferry. The spectacular
rail bridge, the first major steel-
built bridge in the world, was
opened in 1890 and remains

The shattered crags and cliffs of St Abb's Head

one of the greatest engineering achievements of the late
Victorian era. Its massive cantilevered sections are held
together by more than 6.5
million rivets, and the painted
area adds up to some 55 ha
(135 acres). The saying "it's
like painting the Forth Bridge"
has become a byword for
non-stop, repetitive endeav-
our. It also inspired *The Bridge*
(1986) by the writer Iain Banks.

The neighbouring road
bridge was the largest suspension bridge outside the USA
when it was opened in 1964,
a distinction now held by the
Humber Bridge in England.
The two bridges make an impressive contrast, best seen
from South Queensferry promenade. The town received its
name from the 11th-century
Queen Margaret *(see p507)*,
who used the ferry here on her
journeys between Edinburgh
and the royal palace at
Dunfermline *(see p501)*.

Edinburgh ⑯

See pp504–11.

St Abb's Head ⑰

(NTS) Scottish Borders. 🚍 *Berwick-
upon-Tweed.* 🚍 *from Edinburgh.*

The jagged cliffs of St Abb's
Head, rising 91 m (300 ft)
from the North Sea near the
southeastern tip of Scotland,
offer a spectacular view of
thousands of seabirds wheeling
and diving below. This 80 ha
(200 acre) nature reserve is an
important site for cliff-nesting
sea birds and becomes, during
the May to June breeding season, the home of more than
50,000 birds, including fulmars,
guillemots, kittiwakes and
puffins that throng the headland near the fishing village
of St Abbs. The village has one
of the few unspoiled working
harbours on Britain's east
coast. A clifftop trail begins at
the **Visitors' Centre**, where
displays include identification
boards and a touch table where
young visitors can get to grips
with wings and feathers.

🏛 **Visitors' Centre**
St Abb's Head. **Tel** 018907 71443.
🕐 Apr–Oct: 10am-5pm daily. 📷

The huge, cantilevered Forth Rail Bridge, seen from South Queensferry

A Tour of the Borders ⑱

Because of their proximity to England, the Scottish Borders are scattered with the ruins of many ancient buildings destroyed in the conflicts between the two nations. Most poignant of all are the Border abbeys, whose magnificent architecture bears witness to their former spiritual and political power. Founded during the 12th-century reign of David I, the abbeys were destroyed by Henry VIII *(see p512)*.

Kelso Abbey ②
The largest of the Border Abbeys, Kelso was once the most powerful ecclesiastical establishment in Scotland.

Melrose Abbey ⑥
Once one of the richest abbeys in Scotland, it is here that Robert the Bruce's heart is buried *(see p512)*.

Floors Castle ①
The largest inhabited castle in Scotland, it is the Duke of Roxburghe's ancestral home and was built in the 18th century by William Adam.

Scott's View ⑤
This was Sir Walter Scott's favourite view of the Borders. Out of habit his horse stopped here during Scott's funeral procession.

Dryburgh Abbey ④
Set on the banks of the Tweed, Dryburgh is considered the most evocative monastic ruin in Scotland. Sir Walter Scott is buried here.

KEY

▬▬▬	Tour route
═══	Other roads
☀	Viewpoint

TIPS FOR DRIVERS

Length: 32 miles (50 km).
Stopping-off points: There is a delightful walk northwards from Dryburgh Abbey to the footbridge over the River Tweed.

0 kilometres   5

0 miles   3

Jedburgh Abbey ③
Though established in 1138, fragments of 9th-century Celtic stonework survive from an earlier structure. A Visitors' Centre illustrates the lives of the Augustinian monks who once lived here.

Edinburgh ⑯

With its striking medieval and Georgian districts, overlooked by the extinct volcano of Arthur's Seat and, to the northeast, Calton Hill, Edinburgh is widely regarded as one of Europe's most handsome capitals. The city is famous for the arts (it was once known as "the Athens of the North"), a pre-eminence reflected in its hosting every year of Britain's largest arts extravaganza, the Edinburgh Festival *(see p509)*. Its museums and galleries display the riches of many cultures.

Royal Scots soldiers from the castle

Exploring Edinburgh

Edinburgh falls into two main sightseeing areas, divided by Princes Street, the city's most famous thoroughfare and commercial centre. The Old Town straddles the ridge between the castle and the Palace of Holyroodhouse, with most of the city's medieval history clustered in the alleys of the Grassmarket and Royal Mile areas. The New Town, to the north, evolved after 1767 when wealthy merchants expanded the city beyond its medieval walls. This district contains Britain's finest concentration of Georgian architecture.

🏛 National Gallery of Scotland

The Mound. *Tel* 0131 624 6200.
⭘ 10am–5pm Fri–Wed, 10am–7pm Thu (extended during the festival).
♿ 🅿 by appointment.
www.nationalgalleries.org

One of Scotland's finest art galleries, the National Gallery of Scotland is worth visiting for its 15th-to 19th-century British and European paintings alone,

though plenty more can be found to delight the art-lover. Highlights among the Scottish works include portraits by Allan Ramsay and Henry Raeburn, such as his *Reverend Robert Walker Skating on Duddingston Loch* (c.1800). The Early German collection includes Gerard David's almost comic-strip treatment of the *Three Legends of Saint Nicholas* (c.1500). Works by Raphael, Titian and Tintoretto accompany southern European paintings such as Velázquez's *An Old Woman Cooking Eggs* (1620) and the entire room devoted to *The Seven Sacraments* (c.1640) by Nicholas Poussin.

Raeburn's *Rev. Robert Walker Skating on Duddingston Loch*

The new £30-million Weston Link is an underground complex that connects the gallery with the Royal Scottish Academy. It contains a lecture theatre/cinema, shop, restaurant, café, and an IT and education room.

The doorway of the Georgian House, 7 Charlotte Square

🏨 Georgian House

(NTS) 7 Charlotte Sq. *Tel* 0131 226 3318. ⭘ Mar & Nov: 11am–3pm daily; Apr–Jun & Sep–Oct: 10am–5pm daily; Jul–Aug: 10am–7pm daily. (Last admission half an hour before closing.) ⬤ mid-Dec–mid-Jan. ♿ 🅿 limited.
www.nts.org.uk

In the heart of the New Town, Charlotte Square is a superb example of Georgian architecture, its north side, built in the 1790s, being a masterwork by the architect Robert Adam *(see pp28–9)*. The Georgian House at No. 7 has been furnished and repainted in its original 18th-century colours which provide a memorable introduction to the elegance of wealthy New Town life. In stark contrast, "below stairs" is the household staff's living quarters, demonstrating how Edinburgh's working class lived and worked.

The view from Duncan's Monument on Calton Hill, looking west towards the castle

🏛 Scottish National Gallery of Modern Art & Dean Gallery

Belford Rd. **Tel** 0131 624 6200. ⬚ 10am–5pm daily (Thu to 7pm). ♿
www.nationalgalleries.org

Situated in extensive grounds to the northwest of the city centre, a classical 19th-century school is home to this gallery. Most European and American 20th-century greats are represented here, from Vuillard and Picasso, to Magritte and Lichtenstein. Work by John Bellany can be found among the Scottish painters. Sculpture by Henry Moore is on display in the garden.

Medieval chessmen, Museum of Scotland

Lichtenstein's In the Car, National Gallery of Modern Art

🏛 Museum of Scotland

Chambers St. **Tel** 0131 247 4422. ⬚ 10am–5pm Mon–Sat (Tue to 8pm), noon–5pm Sun. ● 25 Dec. 🚻 ♿ 🎫 free. 🍴 www.nms.ac.uk

This purpose-built museum houses the Scottish Collections of the National Museums of Scotland. Exhibitions tell the story of Scotland, the land and its people, dating from its geological beginnings right up to the constitutionally exciting events of today.

Key exhibits include the famous medieval *Lewis Chessmen*; *Pictish Chains*, known as Scotland's earliest crown jewels, and the *Ellesmere* railway locomotive. There is also a new special exhibition gallery which houses fascinating temporary displays.

🏛 Scottish National Portrait Gallery

1 Queen St. **Tel** 0131 624 6200. ⬚ 10am–5pm daily (Thu to 7pm). ♿ 🎫 by appointment. www.nationalgalleries.org

The National Portrait Gallery provides a unique visual history of Scotland told through the portraits of those who shared it, from Robert the Bruce (see p482) to Queen Anne. Memorabilia from many reigns include Mary, Queen of Scots' (see p511) jewellery and a silver travelling canteen abandoned by Bonnie Prince Charlie (see p535) at Culloden (see p537). The upper gallery has portraits of famous Scots, including Robert Burns (see p515) by Alexander Nasmyth.

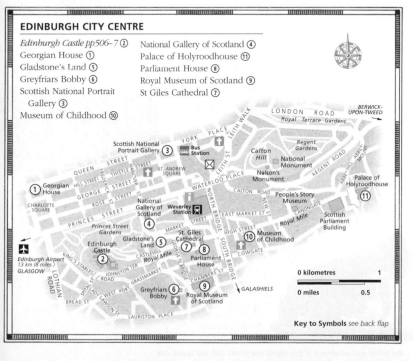

EDINBURGH CITY CENTRE

0 kilometres 1
0 miles 0.5

Key to Symbols see back flap

Edinburgh Castle

Beam support in the Great Hall

Standing upon the basalt core of an extinct volcano, Edinburgh Castle is an assemblage of buildings dating from the 12th to the 20th centuries, reflecting its changing role as fortress, royal palace, military garrison and state prison. Though there is evidence of Bronze Age occupation of the site, the original fortress was built by the 6th-century Northumbrian King Edwin, from whom the city takes its name. The castle was a favourite royal residence until the Union of Crowns *(see p483)* in 1603, after which the king resided in England. After the Union of Parliaments in 1707, the Scottish regalia were walled up in the Palace for over a hundred years. The castle is now the zealous possessor of the so-called Stone of Destiny, a relic of ancient Scottish kings which was seized by the English from Scone Palace, Perthshire and not returned until 1996.

Scottish Crown
On display in the palace, the Crown was restyled by James V of Scotland in 1540.

Military Prison

Governor's House
Complete with Flemish-style crow-stepped gables, this building was constructed for the governor in 1742. It can only be viewed from the outside only as it is still reserved for ceremonial use.

Old Back Parade

MONS MEG

Positioned outside St Margaret's Chapel, the siege gun (or *bombard*) Mons Meg was made in Belgium in 1449 for the Duke of Burgundy, who gave it to his nephew, James II of Scotland. It was used by James against the Douglas family in their stronghold of Threave Castle *(see p515)* in 1455, and later by James IV against Norham Castle in England. After exploding during a salute to the Duke of York in 1682, it was kept in the Tower of London until it was returned to Edinburgh in 1829, at Sir Walter Scott's request.

Vaults
This French graffiti, dating from 1780, recalls the many prisoners who were held in the vaults during the wars with France in the 18th and 19th centuries.

STAR SIGHTS
★ Great Hall
★ Royal Palace

Argyle Battery
*This fortified wall commands a spec-
tacular view to the north beyond the
city's Georgian district of New Town.*

★ Royal Palace
*Mary, Queen of
Scots (see p511)
gave birth to James
VI in this 15th-
century palace,
where the Scottish
regalia are on
display.*

Entrance

Royal
Mile
→

The Esplanade is the
location of the Military
Tattoo *(see p509).*

**The Half Moon
Battery** was built in the
1570s as a platform for
the artillery defending
the northeastern wing
of the castle.

St Margaret's Chapel
*This stained-glass
window depicts Malcolm
III's saintly queen, to
whom the chapel is
dedicated. Probably built
by her son, David I, in
the early 12th century,
the chapel is the castle's
oldest existing building.*

★ Great Hall
*With its restored open-timber
roof, the Hall dates from the
15th century and was the
meeting place of the Scottish
parliament until 1639.*

Exploring the Royal Mile: Castlehill to High Street

The Royal Mile is a stretch of four ancient streets (from Castlehill to Canongate) which formed the main thoroughfare of medieval Edinburgh, linking the castle to the Palace of Holyroodhouse. Confined by the city wall, the "Old Town" grew upwards, with some tenements climbing to 20 storeys. It is still possible, among the 66 alleys and closes off the main street, to sense the city's medieval past.

Eagle sign outside Gladstone's Land

Locator map

Gladstone's Land is a preserved 17th-century merchant's house.

Scotch Whisky Heritage Centre introduces visitors to Scotland's national drink.

The Camera Obscura contains an observatory from which to view the city.

← Edinburgh Castle   CASTLE HILL   LAWNMARKET

Lady Stair's House
This 17th-century house is now a museum of the lives and works of Burns, Scott (see p512) and Stevenson.

The "Hub" (c.1840) has the city's highest spire.

🏛 Gladstone's Land

(NTS) 477B Lawnmarket. **Tel** *0131 2265856.* ◯ *Easter–Jun & Sep–Oct: 10am–5pm daily; Jul–Aug: 10am–7pm daily.* **www.**nts.org.uk 🎫
This 17th-century merchant's house provides a window on

The bedroom of Gladstone's Land

life in a typical Old Town house before overcrowding drove the rich to the Georgian New Town. "Lands", as they were known, were tall, narrow buildings erected on small plots of land. The six-storey Gladstone's Land was named after Thomas Gledstanes, the merchant who built it in 1617. The house still has the original arcade booths on the street front and a painted ceiling with fine Scandinavian floral designs. Though extravagantly furnished, it also contains items which are a reminder of the less salubrious side of the old city, such as wooden overshoes which had to be worn in the dirty streets. A chest in the

beautiful Painted Chamber is said to have been given by a Dutch sea captain to a Scottish merchant who saved him from a shipwreck. A similar house, Morocco Land, can be found on Canongate *(see p511)*.

🏛 Parliament House

Parliament Sq, High St. **Tel** *0131 2252595.* ◯ *9am–4:30pm Mon–Fri.* ◯ *public hols.* ♿ *limited.*
This majestic, Italianate building was constructed in the 1630s for the Scottish parliament. Parliament House has been home to the Court of Session and the Supreme Court since the Union of Parliaments *(see p483)* in 1707. It is worth seeing, as much for the spectacle of its gowned and wigged advocates as for the stained-glass window in its Great Hall, commemorating the inauguration of the Court of Session by James V, in 1532.

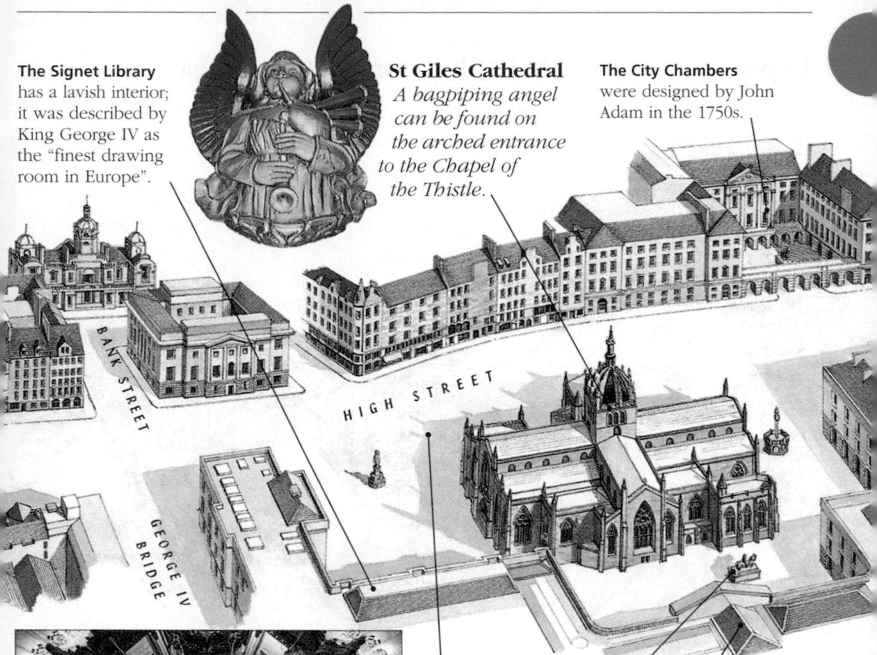

The Signet Library has a lavish interior; it was described by King George IV as the "finest drawing room in Europe".

St Giles Cathedral *A bagpiping angel can be found on the arched entrance to the Chapel of the Thistle.*

The City Chambers were designed by John Adam in the 1750s.

BANK STREET

HIGH STREET

GEORGE IV BRIDGE

Charles II Statue

The Heart of Midlothian is an arrangement of granite cobblestones on the former site of the city jail.

Parliament House was built in 1639. The Scottish parliament convened here from 1640 until 1707.

Rib-vaulting in the Thistle Chapel, St Giles Cathedral

⌂ St Giles Cathedral
Royal Mile. *Tel* 0131 2259442. ☐
May–Sep: 9am–7pm Mon–Fri, 9am–5pm Sat, 9am–1pm Sun; Oct–Apr: 9am–5pm Mon–Sat, 1–5pm Sun.
● 25 & 26 Dec, 1 Jan. ⌨ donation appreciated. ✉ www.stgiles.net
Properly known as the High Kirk (church) of Edinburgh, it is ironic that St Giles is popularly known as a cathedral. Though it was twice the seat of a bishop in the 17th century, it was from here that John Knox *(see p483)* directed the Scottish Reformation with its emphasis on individual worship freed from the authority of bishops. A tablet marks the place where Jenny Geddes, a stallholder from a local market, scored a victory for the Covenanters *(see p483)* by hurling her stool at a preacher reading from an English prayer book in 1637.

The Gothic exterior is dominated by a 15th-century tower.

Inside, the impressive Thistle Chapel can be seen, with its elaborate rib-vaulted roof and carved heraldic canopies. The chapel honours the knights, past and present, of the Order of the Thistle. The carved royal pew in the Preston Aisle is used by the Queen when she stays in Edinburgh.

EDINBURGH FESTIVAL

Every year, for three weeks in late summer *(see p63)*, Edinburgh hosts one of the world's most important arts festivals, with every available space (from theatres to street corners) overflowing with performers. It has been held in Edinburgh since 1947 and brings together the best in international contemporary theatre, music, dance and opera. The alternative Festival Fringe balances the classic productions with a host of innovative performances. The most popular event is the Edinburgh Tattoo, held on the Castle Esplanade – a spectacle of Scottish infantry battalions marching to pipe bands. The Edinburgh Book Festival is a key event in the August Festival Season and attracts big names like J.K. Rowling.

Street performer from the Edinburgh Festival Fringe

Exploring the Royal Mile: High Street to Canongate

The second section of the Royal Mile passes two monuments to the Reformation: John Knox's House and the Tron Kirk. The latter is named after a medieval *tron* (weighing beam) that stood nearby. The Canongate was once an independent district, owned by the canons of the Abbey of Holyrood, and sections of its south side have been restored. Beyond Morocco's Land, the road stretches for the final half-mile (800 m) to the Palace of Holyroodhouse.

THE PALACE OF HOLYROODHOUSE

EDINBURGH CASTLE

LOCATOR MAP

HIGH STREET

SOUTH BRIDGE STREET

The Mercat Cross marks the city centre. It was here that Bonnie Prince Charlie *(see p535)* was proclaimed king in 1745.

The Tron Kirk was built in 1630 for the Presbyterians who left St Giles Cathedral when it came under the Bishop of Edinburgh's control.

⬛ Museum of Childhood

42 High St. *Tel* 0131 529 4142. ⬤ 10am–5pm Mon–Sat (& Sun pm during Festival). ⬤ 25–27 Dec. ⬤ limited.

This lovely museum is not merely a toy collection but a magical insight into childhood, with all its joys and trials. Founded in 1955 by a city councillor, Patrick Murray (who claimed to enjoy eating children for breakfast), it was the first museum in the world to be devoted to the history and theme of childhood. The collection includes medicines, school books and prams as well as galleries full of old-fashioned toys. With its nickelodeon, antique slot machines

The entrance to the Palace of Holyroodhouse, seen from the west

and the general enthusiasm of visitors, this has been called the world's noisiest museum.

🏛 Palace of Holyroodhouse

East end of Royal Mile. *Tel* 0131 524 1120. ⬤ Apr–Oct: 9:30am–6pm; Nov–Mar: 9:30am–4:30pm daily. 🔳 ⬤ limited. **www**.royal.gov.uk

Now the Queen's official Scottish residence, the Palace of Holyroodhouse is named after the "rood", or cross, which King David I is said to have seen between the antlers of a stag he was hunting here in 1128. The present palace was built in 1529 to accommodate James V *(see p501)* and his French wife, Mary of Guise, though it was remodelled in

the 1670s for Charles II. The Royal Apartments (including the Throne Room and Royal Dining Room) are used for investiture and banquets whenever the Queen visits the palace, though they are otherwise open to the public. A chamber in the James V tower is associated with the unhappy reign of Mary, Queen of Scots. It was here, in 1566, that she saw the murder of her trusted Italian secretary, David Rizzio, by her jealous husband, Lord Darnley. She had married Darnley a year earlier in Holyroodhouse chapel.

Bonnie Prince Charlie held court here in 1745 in the Jacobite *(see p537)* rising.

An 1880 automaton of the Man on the Moon, Museum of Childhood

John Knox's House
Dating from 1490, the oldest house in the city was the home of John Knox (see p483) in the 1560s. It has recently undergone an extensive refurbishment.

Morocco Land is a reproduction of a 17th-century tenement house. It takes its name from the statue of a Moor which adorns the entrance.

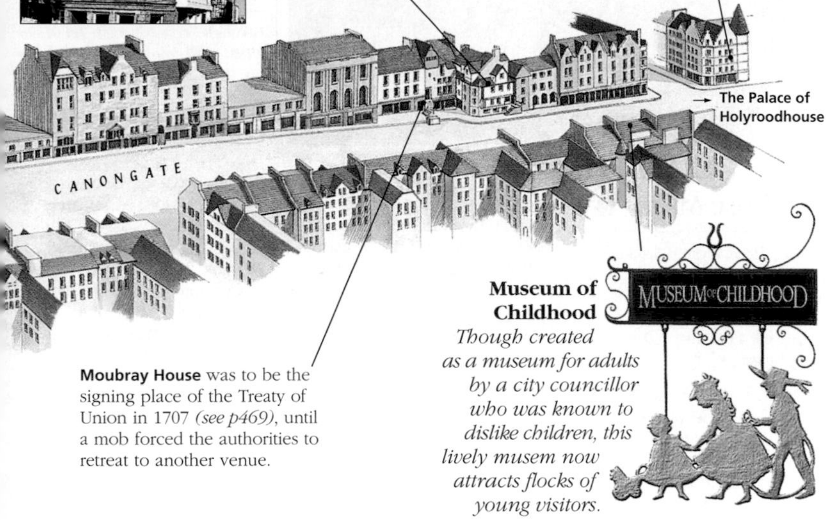

→ **The Palace of Holyroodhouse**

CANONGATE

Museum of Childhood
Though created as a museum for adults by a city councillor who was known to dislike children, this lively museum now attracts flocks of young visitors.

MUSEUM OF CHILDHOOD

Moubray House was to be the signing place of the Treaty of Union in 1707 (*see p469*), until a mob forced the authorities to retreat to another venue.

🏛 Royal Museum of Scotland
Chambers St. **Tel** 0131 247 4219.
⏲ 10am–5pm Mon–Sat, noon–5pm Sun. ⬤ 25 Dec. ▯ 🚻 ✉ 🎫 🍴
www.nms.ac.uk

The Royal Museum first opened its doors in 1866. The Main Hall features a fine collection of Asian sculptures, such as the Hindu Goddess Parvati, while European Art from 1200 to 1800 is on the first floor. On the second floor are rare scientific instruments, and geological specimens, and Eastern decorative arts are on the top floor. The most recent addition to the Royal Museum's ground floor is the new science and technology gallery, Connect,

Parvati, at the Royal Museum of Scotland

where Dolly the Sheep can be found. Geological specimens and Eastern decorative arts are on the top floor.

🐕 Greyfriars Bobby
On an old drinking fountain near the gateway to Greyfriars Church stands the statue of a little Skye terrier. This commemorates the dog who, for 14 years, guarded the grave of his master, John Gray, who died in 1858. The people of Edinburgh fed him until his death in 1872. He was also granted citizenship to prevent him being destroyed as a stray.

MARY, QUEEN OF SCOTS (1542–87)

Born only days before the death of her father, James V, the young Queen Mary spent her childhood in France, after escaping Henry VIII's invasion of Scotland (*see p512*). A devout Catholic, she married the French Dauphin, and made claims on the English throne. This alarmed Protestants throughout England and Scotland, and when she returned as a

widow to Holyroodhouse, aged 18, she was harangued for her faith by John Knox (*see p483*). In 1567 she was accused of murdering her second husband, Lord Darnley. Two months later, when she married the Earl of Bothwell (also implicated in the murder), rebellion ensued. She lost her crown and fled to England where she was held prisoner for 20 years, before being charged with treason and beheaded at Fotheringhay.

The ruins of Melrose Abbey, viewed from the southwest

Melrose Abbey ⓳

Abbey Street, Melrose, Scottish Borders. **Tel** 01896 822562. ◐ Oct–Mar: 9:30am–4:30pm daily; Apr–Sep: 9:30am–6:30pm daily. ● 25, 26 Dec, 1, 2 Jan. 🎫 ♿ limited.

The rose-pink ruins of one of the most beautiful of the border abbeys (see p503) bear testimony to the hazards of standing in the path of successive English invasions. Built by David I in 1136 for Cistercian monks from Yorkshire, and also to replace a 7th-century monastery, Melrose was repeatedly ransacked by English armies, notably in 1322 and 1385. The final blow, from which none of the abbeys

recovered, came in 1545 during Henry VIII's destructive Scottish policy known as the "Rough Wooing". This resulted from the failure of the Scots to ratify a marriage treaty between Henry VIII's son and the infant Mary, Queen of Scots (see p511). What remains of the abbey are the outlines of cloisters, the kitchen and other monastic buildings and the shell of the abbey church with its soaring east window and profusion of medieval carvings. The rich decorations of the south exterior wall include a gargoyle shaped like a pig playing the bagpipes.

An embalmed heart, found here in 1920, is probably that of Robert the Bruce (see p482), who had decreed that

his heart be taken on a crusade to the Holy Land. It was returned to Melrose after its bearer, Sir James Douglas (see p515), was killed in Spain.

Abbotsford House ⓴

Galashiels, Scottish Borders. **Tel** 01896 752043. 🚌 from Galashiels. ◐ late Mar–late Oct: 9:30am–5pm daily; Jun–Sep: daily (Sun: pm only). 🎫 ♿ limited. 📷 **www**.melrose. bordernet.co.uk/abbotsford

Few houses bear the stamp of their creator so intimately as Abbotsford House, the home of Sir Walter Scott for the last 20 years of his life. He bought a farm here in 1811, known as Clarteyhole ("dirty hole" in Scots), though he soon renamed it Abbotsford, after the monks of Melrose Abbey who used to cross the River Tweed nearby. He later demolished the house to make way for the turreted building we see today, funded by the sales of his novels.

Scott's library contains more than 9,000 rare books and his collections of historic relics reflect his passion for the heroic past. An extensive collection of arms and armour includes Rob Roy's broadsword (see p495). Stuart mementoes include a crucifix that belonged to Mary, Queen of Scots and a lock of Bonnie Prince Charlie's (see p535) hair. The small study in which he wrote his *Waverley* novels can be visited as can the room, overlooking the river, in which he died in 1832.

SIR WALTER SCOTT

Sir Walter Scott (1771–1832) was born in Edinburgh and trained as a lawyer. He is best remembered as a major champion and literary figure of Scotland, whose poems and novels (most famously his *Waverley* series) created enduring images of a heroic wilderness filled with the romance of the clans. His orchestration, in 1822, of the state visit of George IV to Edinburgh (see p485) was an extravaganza of Highland culture that helped re-establish tartan as the national dress of Scotland. He served as Clerk of the Court in Edinburgh's Parliament House (see p508) and for 30 years was Sheriff of Selkirk in the Scottish Borders, which he loved. He put the Trossachs (see pp494–5) firmly on the map with the publication of the *Lady of the Lake* (1810). His final years were spent writing to pay off a £114,000 debt following the failure of his publisher in 1827. He died with his debts paid, and was buried at Dryburgh Abbey (see p503).

The Great Hall at Abbotsford, adorned with arms and armour

Traquair House ㉑

Peebles, Scottish Borders. *Tel 01896 830 323.* from Peebles. Easter–May & Sep: noon–5:30pm; Jun–Aug: 10:30am–5pm; Oct: 11am–4pm; daily; Nov: noon–4pm Sat & Sun. limited. **www**.traquair.co.uk

As Scotland's oldest continuously inhabited house, Traquair has deep roots in Scottish religious and political history, stretching back over 900 years. Evolving from a fortified tower to a stout-walled 17th-century mansion *(see p487)*, the house was a Catholic Stuart stronghold for 500 years. Mary, Queen of Scots *(see p511)* was among the many monarchs to have stayed here and her bed is covered by a counter-pane which she made. Family letters and engraved Jacobite *(see p537)* drinking glasses are among relics recalling the period of the Highland rebellions.

Mary, Queen of Scots' crucifix, Traquair House

After a vow made by the 5th Earl, Traquair's Bear Gates (the "Steekit Yetts"), which closed after Bonnie Prince Charlie's *(see p535)* visit in 1745, will not reopen until a Stuart reascends the throne. A secret stairway leads to the Priest's Room which attests to the problems faced by Catholic families until Catholicism was legalized in 1829. Traquair House Ale is still produced in the 18th-century brewhouse.

Biggar ㉒

Clyde Valley. 2,000. High St (01899 221066).

This typical Lowland market town has a number of museums worth visiting. The **Gladstone Court Museum** boasts a reconstructed Victorian street complete with a milliner's, printer's and a village library, while the grimy days of the town's industrial past are recalled at the **Gasworks Museum**, with its collection of engines, gaslights and appliances. Established in 1839 and preserved in the 1970s, the Biggar Gasworks is the only remaining rural gasworks in Scotland.

m Gladstone Court Museum
Northback Rd. *Tel 01899 221050.* Apr–Oct: 11am–4:30pm Mon–Sat, 2–4:30pm Sun.
m Gasworks Museum
Gasworks Rd. *Tel 01899 221070.* Jun–Sep: 2–4:30pm daily.

Pentland Hills ㉓

The Lothians. Edinburgh, then bus. Regional Park Headquarters, Biggar Rd, Edinburgh (0131 4453383).

The Pentland Hills, stretching for 16 miles (26 km) southwest of Edinburgh, offer some of the best hill-walking country in the Lowlands. Leisurely walkers can saunter along the many signposted footpaths, while the more adventurous can take the chairlift at the Hillend dry ski slope to reach the higher ground leading to the 493 m (1,617 ft) hill of Allermuir. Even more ambitious is the classic scenic route along the ridge from Caerketton to West Kip.

To the east of the A703, in the lee of the Pentlands, stands the exquisite and ornate 15th-century **Rosslyn Chapel**. It was originally intended as a church, but after the death of its founder, William Sinclair, it was also used as a burial ground for his descendants. The delicately wreathed Apprentice Pillar recalls the legend of the apprentice carver who was killed by the master stone-mason in a fit of jealousy at his pupil's superior skill.

â Rosslyn Chapel
Roslin. *Tel 0131 4402159.* daily (Sun: pm only).

Details of the decorated vaulting in Rosslyn Chapel

The Classical 18th-century tenements of New Lanark on the banks of the Clyde

New Lanark ㉔

Clyde Valley. 🚶 185. 🚋 🚌 Lanark.
🛈 Horsemarket, Ladyacre Rd
(01555 661661). 🛍 Mon (Apr only).
www.newlanark.org

Situated by the falls of the River Clyde, the village of New Lanark was founded in 1785 by the industrial entrepreneur David Dale. Ideally located for the working of its water-driven mills, the village had become Britain's largest cotton producer by 1800. Dale and his successor, Robert Owen, were philanthropists whose reforms proved that commercial success need not undermine the wellbeing of the workforce. Now a museum, New Lanark is a window on to working life in the early 19th century. The **New Millennium Experience** provides a special-effects ride through time, from the life of a mill girl in 1820 to the 23rd century.

Environs: 15 miles (24 km) north, Blantyre has a memorial to the famous Scottish explorer David Livingstone.

🏛 **New Millennium Experience**
New Lanark Visitor Centre. **Tel** 01555 661345. ◯ 11am–5pm daily. 🎥 ⅃
🎫 groups only, by appt – book ahead.

DAVID LIVINGSTONE

Scotland's great missionary doctor and explorer was born in Blantyre where he began working life as a mill boy at the age of ten. Livingstone (1813–73) made three epic journeys across Africa, from 1840, promoting "commerce and Christianity". He became the first European to see Victoria Falls and died in 1873 while searching for the source of the Nile. He is buried in Westminster Abbey *(see pp92–3)*.

Glasgow ㉕

See pp516–21.

Sanquhar ㉖

Dumfries & Galloway. 🚶 2,500. 🚋
🚌 🛈 64 Whitesands, Dumfries
(01387 253862).

Now of chiefly historic interest, the town of **Sanquhar** was famous in the history of the Covenanters *(see p483)*. In the 1680s, two declarations opposing the rule of bishops were pinned to the Mercat Cross, the site of which is now marked by a granite obelisk. The first protest was led by a local teacher, Richard Cameron, whose followers became the Cameronian regiment. The Georgian **Tolbooth** was designed by William Adam *(see p548)* in 1735 and houses a local interest museum and tourist centre. The Post Office, opened in 1763, is the oldest in Britain, predating the mail coach service.

Drumlanrig Castle ㉗

Thornhill, Dumfries & Galloway. **Tel**
01848 331555. 🚋 🚌 Dumfries, then bus. ◯ **Grounds** Apr–Oct: 11am–5pm daily. **Castle** May–Jun: noon–4pm daily; Jul–Aug: 11am–4pm. 🎥 ⅃
🎫 www.buccleuch.com

Rising squarely from a grassy platform, the massive fortress-palace of **Drumlanrig** *(see p487)* was built from pink sandstone

The Baroque front steps and doorway of Drumlanrig Castle

between 1679 and 1691 on the site of a 15th-century Douglas stronghold. A formidable multi-turreted exterior contains a priceless collection of art treasures such as paintings by Holbein and Rembrandt, as well as such Jacobite relics as Bonnie Prince Charlie's camp kettle and sash. The emblem of a crowned and winged heart, shown throughout the castle, recalls Sir James, the "Black Douglas", who bore Robert the Bruce's *(see p482)* heart while on crusade. After being mortally wounded he threw the heart at his enemies with the words "forward brave heart!"

The sturdy island fortress of Threave Castle on the Dee

Threave Castle ㉘

Castle Douglas, Dumfries & Galloway. **Tel** 07711 223101. ⬤ Dumfries. ⬤ Apr–Sep: 9:30am–6:30pm daily (last boat leaves island 6pm). 📷

This menacing giant of a tower, a 14th-century Black Douglas *(see above)* stronghold standing on an island in the Dee, commands the most complete medieval riverside harbour in Scotland. Douglas's struggles against the early Stewart kings culminated in his surrender here after a two-month siege in 1455 – but only after James II had brought the cannon Mons Meg *(see p506)* to batter the castle. Threave was dismantled after Protestant Covenanters *(see p483)* defeated its Catholic defenders in 1640. Inside the tower, only the

shell of the kitchen, great hall and domestic levels remains. Over the 15th-century doorway is the "gallows knob", a reminder of when the owners are said to have boasted that it never lacked its noose. Access to the castle is by small boat.

Whithorn ㉙

Dumfries & Galloway. ⬤ 1,000. ⬤ Stranraer. ⬤ ⬤ Dashwood Sq, Newton Stewart (01671 402431). **www.**visitdumfriesandgalloway.co.uk

The earliest site of continuous Christian worship in Scotland, Whithorn (meaning white house) takes its name from the white chapel built here by St Ninian in 397. Though nothing remains of his chapel, a guided tour of the archaeological dig reveals evidence of Northumbrian, Viking and Scottish settlements ranging from the 5th to the 19th centuries. A visitors' centre, **The Whithorn Story**, provides information on the excavations and contains a collection of carved stones. One, dedicated to Latinus, dates to 450, making it Scotland's earliest Christian monument.

🏛 The Whithorn Story
The Whithorn Trust, 45–47 George St. **Tel** 01988 500508. ⬤ Apr–Oct: 10:30am–5pm daily. 📷 ⬤ ⬤ **www.**whithorn.com

Culzean Castle ㉚

See pp522–3.

Robert Burns surrounded by his creations, by an unknown artist

Burns Cottage ㉛

Burns National Heritage Park, Alloway, South Ayrshire. **Tel** 01292 443700. ⬤ Ayr, then bus. ⬤ Oct–Mar: 10am–5pm; Apr–Sep: 10am–5:30pm; daily. ⬤ 25 & 26 Dec, 1 & 2 Jan. 📷 ⬤ ⬤ **www.**burnsheritagepark.com

Robert Burns (1759–96), Scotland's favourite poet, was born and spent his first seven years in this small thatched cottage in Alloway. Built by his father, the cottage still contains much of its original furniture. There is also a small museum next door displaying many of Burns's manuscripts along with early editions of his works. Much of his poem *Tam o' Shanter* (1790) is set in Alloway, which commemorates him with a huge monument on the outskirts of the village.

Burns became a celebrity following the publication in 1786 of the Kilmarnock Edition of his poems. Scots everywhere gather to celebrate Burns Night *(see p65)* on his birthday, 25 January.

SCOTTISH TEXTILES

Weaving in the Scottish Borders goes back to the Middle Ages, when monks from Flanders established a thriving woollen trade with the Continent. Cotton became an important source of wealth in the Clyde Valley during the 19th century, when handloom weaving was overtaken by power-driven mills. The popular Paisley patterns were based on Indian designs.

A colourful pattern from Paisley

Glasgow ㉕

Though its Celtic name, *Glas cu*, means "dear green place", Glasgow is more often associated with its industrial past, and once enjoyed the title of Second City of the Empire (after London). Glasgow's architectural standing, as Scotland's finest Victorian city, reflects its era of prosperity, when ironworks, cotton mills and ship-building were fuelled by Lanarkshire coal.

The coat of arms of Glasgow city

The Science Centre sits on the Clyde's revitalized south bank, and Glasgow rivals Edinburgh *(see pp504–11)* in the arts, with galleries such as the Kelvingrove and the Burrell Collection *(see pp520–21).*

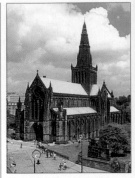

Glasgow's medieval cathedral viewed from the southwest

Exploring Glasgow

With some relics of its grimy industrial past and glossy new image, modern Glasgow is a city of contrasts. The deprived East End, with its busy week-end market, "the Barras", stands by the restored 18th-century Merchant City and Victorian George Square. The more affluent West End prospered in the 19th century as a retreat for wealthy merchants escaping the industrialized Clydeside, and it is here that Glasgow's chief galleries and museums can be found. South

Side, next to affluent Pollok-shields, is Pollok Country Park, site of the Burrell Collection. An underground network and good bus and rail links provide easy travel around the city.

🏛 Glasgow Cathedral

Cathedral Square. **Tel** 0141 5526891.
⬜ Apr–Sep: 9:30am–6pm Mon–Sat, 1–5pm Sun; Oct–Mar: 9:30am–4pm Mon–Sat, 1–4pm Sun. ♿
As one of the only cathedrals to escape destruction during the Scottish Reformation *(see pp482–3)* – by adapting itself to Protestant worship – this is

a rare example of an almost complete 13th-century church. It was built on the site of a chapel founded by the city's patron saint, St Mungo, a 6th-century bishop of Strathclyde. According to legend, Mungo placed the body of a holy man named Fergus on a cart yoked to two wild bulls, telling them to take it to the place ordained by God. In the "dear green place" at which the bulls stopped he built his church. Because of its sloping site, the cathedral is on two levels.

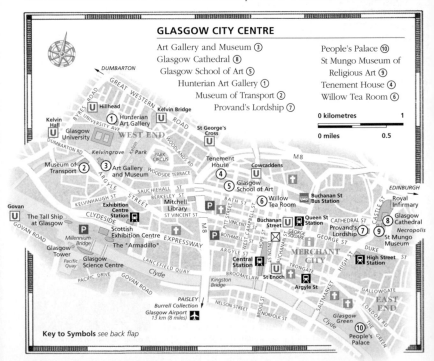

GLASGOW CITY CENTRE

Art Gallery and Museum ③
Glasgow Cathedral ⑧
Glasgow School of Art ⑤
Hunterian Art Gallery ①
Museum of Transport ②
Provand's Lordship ⑦

People's Palace ⑩
St Mungo Museum of Religious Art ⑨
Tenement House ④
Willow Tea Room ⑥

0 kilometres   1

0 miles   0.5

Key to Symbols *see back flap*

Dali's *Christ of St John of the Cross* at the
St Mungo Museum of Religious Life and Art

Situated in the cathedral precinct, this new museum is a world first. The main exhibition illustrates religious themes with superb artifacts, including a 19th-century dancing Shiva and an Islamic painting entitled the *Attributes of Divine Perfection* (1986) by Ahmed Moustafa. An exhibition on religion in Glasgow throws light on the life of the missionary David Livingstone *(see p514)*. Moved from the Kelvingrove Art Gallery and Museum *(see p519)*, Salvador Dali's powerful work *Christ of St John of the Cross* (1951) is now here. Outside you can visit Britain's only permanent Zen Buddhist garden.

The crypt contains the tomb of St Mungo, surrounded by an intricate forest of columns springing up to end in delicately carved rib-vaulting. The Blackadder Aisle, reputed to have been built over a cemetery blessed by St Ninian *(see p515)*, has a ceiling thick with decorative bosses.

🏛 St Mungo Museum of Religious Life and Art

2 Castle St. **Tel** *0141 5532557.*
⬤ *10am–5pm daily (11am Fri).* ♿
▢ *by appointment.* ▢ ▢

🛏 Tenement House

(NTS) 145 Buccleuch St.
Tel *0141 3330183.* ⬤ *Mar–Oct: 1–5pm daily.* 🖼 ▢ *by appointment.*
Less a museum than a time capsule, the Tenement House is an almost undisturbed record of life in a modest Glasgow flat in a tenement estate during the early 20th century. Glasgow owed much of its vitality and neighbourliness to tenement life, though many of these Victorian and Edwardian apartments were to earn a bad name for poverty

VISITORS' CHECKLIST

City of Glasgow. 🏙 *585,000.*
✈ 🚆 *Argyle St (Glasgow Central).* 🚌 *Buchanan St.*
ℹ *11 George Square (0141 2044400).* 🗓 *Sat, Sun.*
www.seeglasgow.com

**The preserved Edwardian kitchen
of the Tenement House**

and overcrowding, and many have now been pulled down. The Tenement House was first owned by Miss Agnes Toward who lived here from 1911 until 1965. It remained largely unaltered and, since Agnes threw very little away, it is now a treasure-trove of social history. The parlour, previously used only on formal occasions, has afternoon tea laid out on a white lace cloth. The kitchen, with its coal-fired range and box bed, is filled with the tools of a vanished era such as a goffering iron for crisping waffles, a washboard and a stone hot-water bottle.

Agnes's lavender water and medicines are still in the bathroom, as though she had stepped out for a minute 70 years ago, and forgotten to return home.

The Kelvingrove Art Gallery and the Glasgow University buildings, viewed from the south

Glasgow's medieval house, Provand's Lordship

⚜ Provand's Lordship

3 Castle St. **Tel** 0141 5528819.
◯ 10am–5pm Mon–Thu, Sat;
11am–5pm Fri & Sun.

Now a museum, Provand's Lordship was built as a canon's house in 1471, and is the city's oldest surviving house. Its low ceilings and austere wooden furnishings create a vivid impression of life in a wealthy 15th-century household. It is thought that Mary, Queen of

Mackintosh's interior of the Willow Tea Room

Scots (see p511) may have stayed here in 1566 when she made a visit to see her cousin and husband, Lord Darnley.

⚜ Willow Tea Room

217 Sauchiehall St (also 97 Buchanan St). **Tel** 0141 332 0521. ◯ 9am–5pm Mon–Sat, 11am–4:15pm Sun.
🔒 www.willow tearooms.co.uk

This is the sole survivor of a series of delightful tea rooms created by Charles Rennie Mackintosh in 1904 for the celebrated restaurateur Miss Kate Cranston. Everything from the high-backed chairs to the tables and cutlery was his design. In particular, the 1904 Room de Luxe sparkles with silver furniture and flamboyant leaded glass work. The No. 97 Buchanan Street branch opened in 1997, and recreates Cranston's original Ingram Street Tea Rooms.

🏛 Museum of Transport

1 Bunhouse Rd. **Tel** 0141 2872720.
◯ 10am–5pm Mon–Thu, Sat, 11am– 5pm Fri, Sun. 🔒 📁 📷
www.glasgowmuseums.com

Housed in Kelvin Hall, this imaginative museum conveys the optimism and vigour of the city's industrial heyday. Model ships and ranks of gleaming Scottish-built steam engines, cars and motorcycles recall the 19th and early 20th centuries, when Glasgow's supremacy in shipbuilding, trade and manufacturing made her the "second city" of the British Empire. Old Glasgow can be seen through fascinating footage of the town in the cinema and through a reconstruction of a 1938 street, with Art Deco shop fronts, a cinema and an Underground station.

The Museum of Transport's reconstructed 1938 street, with Underground station

♪ Glasgow Necropolis

Cathedral Sq. **Tel** 0141 2873961.
◯ daily. 🔒 ♿ limited.

Behind the cathedral, the reformer John Knox (see p483) surveys the city from his Doric pillar overlooking a Victorian cemetery. It is filled with crumbling monuments to the dead of Glasgow's wealthy merchant families.

CHARLES RENNIE MACKINTOSH

A Mackintosh floral design

Glasgow's most celebrated designer, Charles Rennie Mackintosh (1868–1928), entered Glasgow School of Art at 16. After his first big break with the Willow Tea Room, he became a leading figure in the Art Nouveau movement, developing a unique style that borrowed from Gothic and Scottish Baronial designs. He believed a building should be a fully integrated work of art, creating furniture and fittings that complemented the overall construction. Nowhere is this total design better seen than in the Glasgow School of Art, which he designed in 1896. Unrecognized in his lifetime, Mackintosh's work is now widely imitated. Its characteristic straight lines and flowing detail are the hallmark of early 20th-century Glasgow style, in all fields of design from textiles to architecture.

🏛 People's Palace
Glasgow Green. **Tel** 0141 2712951.
◯ 10am–5pm Mon–Thu & Sat,
11am–5pm Fri & Sun. ♿ ▢ ▢
www.glasgowmuseums.com

This Victorian sandstone structure was built in 1898 as a cultural museum for the people of Glasgow's East End. It houses everything from temperance tracts to trade-union banners, suffragette posters to comedian Billy Connolly's banana-shaped boots, providing a social history of the city from the 12th century. A conservatory at the back contains an exotic winter garden.

🏛 Glasgow School of Art
167 Renfrew St. **Tel** 0141 3534500.
◯ by appointment only. 📷
📷 ♿ limited. **www**.gsa.ac.uk

Widely considered to be Charles Rennie Mackintosh's greatest architectural work, the Glasgow School of Art was built between 1897 and 1909 to a design he submitted in a competition. It was built in two periods due to financial constraints. The later, western wing displays a softer design than the more severe eastern half, built only a few years earlier and compared by a contemporary critic to a prison.

A student guide takes you through the building to the Furniture Gallery, Board Room and the Library, the latter a masterpiece of spatial composition. Each room is an exercise in contrasts between height, light and shade with innovative details echoing the architectural themes of the structure. How much of the school can be viewed depends on curricular requirements at the time of visiting.

🏛 Hunterian Art Gallery
82 Hillhead St. **Tel** 0141 3305431.
◯ 9:30am–5pm Mon–Sat. ● 24
Dec–5 Jan & public hols. ▢ ♿
limited. **www**.hunterian.gla.ac.uk

Built to house a number of paintings bequeathed to Glasgow University by ex-student and physician Dr William Hunter (1718–83), the Hunterian Art Gallery contains Scotland's largest print collection and works by major European artists stretching back to the 16th century. A collection of work by Charles

George Henry's *Japanese Lady with a Fan* (1894), Art Gallery and Museum

Mackintosh is supplemented by a complete reconstruction of No. 6 Florentine Terrace, where he lived from 1906 to 1914. A major collection of 19th- and 20th-century Scottish art includes work by William McTaggart (1835–1910), but the gallery's most famous collection is of work by the painter James McNeill Whistler (1834–1903).

Whistler's *Sketch for Annabel Lee* (c.1869), Hunterian Art Gallery

🏛 Kelvingrove Art Gallery and Museum
Argyle St, Kelvingrove. **Tel** 0141 287
2699. ◯ 10am–5pm Mon–Thu &
Sat, 11am–5pm Fri & Sun.
www.glasgowmuseums.com

The imposing red sandstone building that is Kelvingrove is a striking Glasgow landmark – even though it was supposedly built the wrong way round – and the gallery and museum is the most visited in Scotland. Recently reopened in 2006, having undergone a major (£27.9 million) refurbishment, the gallery and museum will house and display 50 per cent more art and artefacts. The outstanding collection has paintings of inestimable value, including works by Botticelli, Giorgione (*The Adulteress Brought Before Christ*) and Rembrandt. Its impressive representation of 17th-century Dutch and 19th-century French art is augmented by the home-grown talent of the Glasgow Boys and the Scottish Colourists.

The Georgian Pollok House, viewed from the south

🏛 Pollok House

(NTS) 2060 Pollokshaws Rd. **Tel** *(0141) 616 6410.* ○ *10am–5pm daily.* ● *25, 26 Dec, 1, 2 Jan.* 🏷 *Apr–Oct only.* **www**.nts.org.uk

Pollok House is Glasgow's finest 18th-century domestic building and contains one of Britain's best collections of Spanish paintings. The Neo-Classical central block was finished in 1750, the sobriety of its exterior contrasting with the exuberant plasterwork within. The Maxwells have lived at Pollok since the mid-13th century, but the male line ended with Sir John Maxwell, who added the grand entrance hall in the 1890s and designed most of the terraced gardens and parkland beyond.

Hanging above the family silver, porcelain, hand-painted Chinese wallpaper and Jacobean glass, the Stirling Maxwell collection is strong on British and Dutch schools, including William Blake's *Sir Geoffrey Chaucer and the Nine and Twenty Pilgrims* (1745) and William Hogarth's portrait of James Thomson, who wrote the words to *Rule Britannia*.

Spanish 16th- to 19th-century art predominates: El Greco's *Lady in a Fur Wrap* (1541) hangs in the library, while the drawing room contains works by Francisco de Goya and Esteban Murillo. In 1966 Anne Maxwell Macdonald gave the house and 146 ha (361 acres) of parkland to the City of Glasgow. The park provides the site for the city's fascinating Burrell Collection.

Glasgow: The Burrell Collection

Given to the city in 1944 by Sir William Burrell (1861–1958), a wealthy shipping owner, this internationally acclaimed collection is the star of Glasgow's renaissance, with objects of major importance in numerous fields of interest. The building was purpose-built in 1983. In the sun, the stained glass blazes with colour, while the shaded tapestries seem a part of the surrounding woodland.

Figure of a Lohan
This sculpture of Buddha's disciple dates from the Ming Dynasty (1484).

Hutton Castle Drawing Room
This is a reconstruction of the Drawing Room at Burrell's own home – the 16th-century Hutton Castle, near Berwick-upon-Tweed. The Hall and Dining Room can also be seen nearby.

Bull's Head
Dating from the 7th century BC, this bronze head from Turkey was once part of a cauldron handle.

Hornby Portal
This detail shows the arch's heraldic display. The 14th-century portal comes from Hornby Castle in Yorkshire.

Main entrance

STAR EXHIBITS

★ Stained Glass

★ Tapestries

Rembrandt van Rijn
This self-portrait, signed and dated 1632, has pride of place among the Dutch paintings hanging in the 17th- and 18th-century room.

Mezzanine floor

VISITORS' CHECKLIST

2060 Pollokshaws Rd, Glasgow. **Tel** (0141) 287 2550. ⬛ Pollokshaws West. 🚌 45, 47, 48, 57 from Glasgow. ◯ 10am–5pm Mon–Thu, Sat, 11am–5pm Fri, Sun. 🍴
🔲 ⊘ 🎦 🔲 ♿ 🔲 🔲

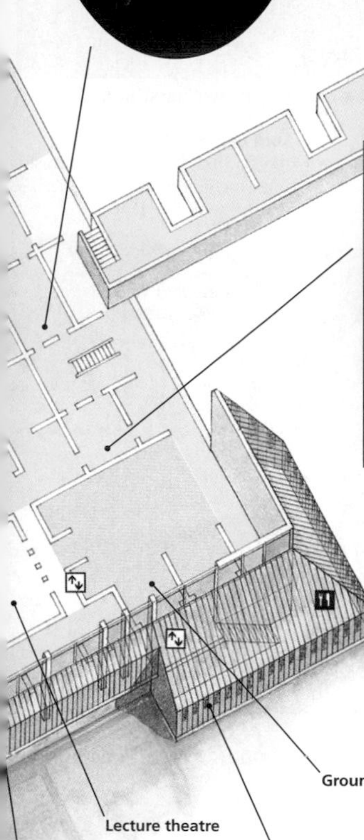

GALLERY GUIDE
Except for a mezzanine-floor display of paintings, the exhibitions are on the ground floor. Right of the entrance hall, rooms are devoted to tapestries, stained glass and sculpture, while ancient civilizations, Oriental art and the period galleries are ahead.

Matthijs Maris
This popular Dutch painter's ethereal style appealed to late 19th-century tastes. The Sisters (1875) is one of over 50 Maris works acquired by Burrell.

Ground floor

Lecture theatre

KEY TO FLOORPLAN

☐	Ancient civilizations
☐	Oriental art
☐	Medieval and post-medieval European art, stained glass and tapestries
☐	Period galleries
☐	Hutton Castle Rooms
☐	Paintings and drawings
☐	Temporary exhibition area

★ Stained Glass
This 15th-century Norwich School panel, depicting a youth snaring birds, is one of many secular themes illustrated in the stained-glass display.

★ Tapestries
Scenes from the Life of Christ and of the Virgin *(c.1450), a Swiss work in wool, is one of many tapestries on show.*

Culzean Castle ③

Robert Adam by George Willison

Standing on a cliff's edge in an extensive parkland estate, the 16th-century keep of Culzean (pronounced Cullayn), home of the Earls of Cassillis, was remodelled between 1777 and 1792 by the Neo-Classical architect Robert Adam *(see p28).* Restored in the 1970s, it is now a major showcase of his later work. The grounds became Scotland's first public country park in 1969 and, with farming flourishing alongside ornamental gardens, they reflect both the leisure and everyday activities of a great country estate.

View of Culzean Castle (c.1815), by Nasmyth

Lord Cassillis' Rooms contain typical mid-18th-century furnishings, including a gentleman's wardrobe of the 1740s.

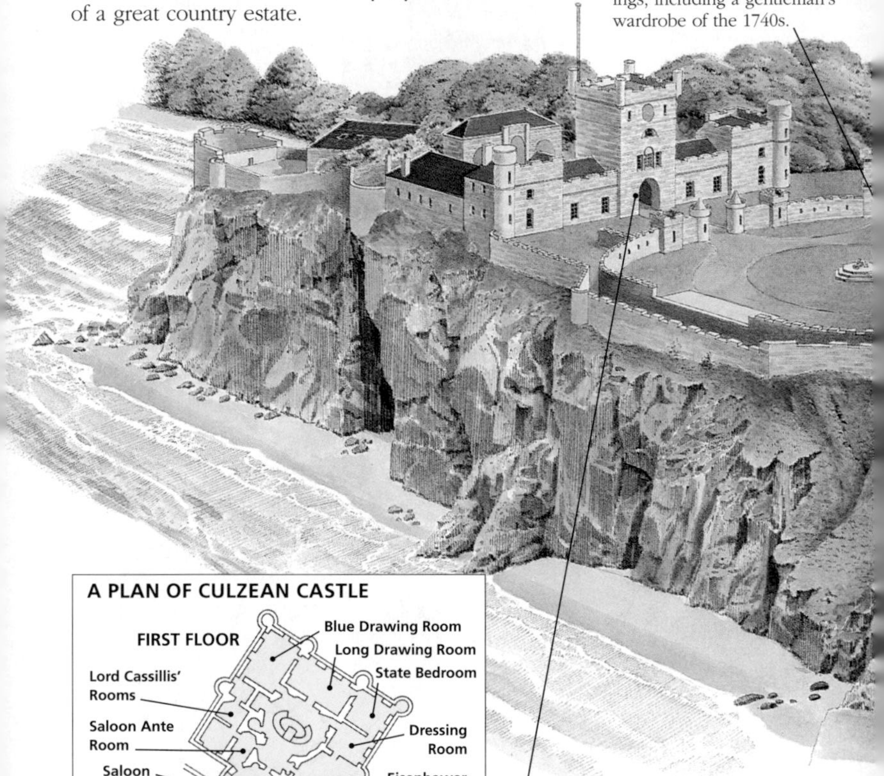

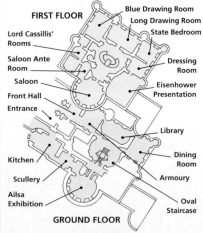

A PLAN OF CULZEAN CASTLE

FIRST FLOOR

Blue Drawing Room
Long Drawing Room
State Bedroom
Lord Cassillis' Rooms
Saloon Ante Room
Dressing Room
Saloon
Front Hall
Entrance
Eisenhower Presentation
Library
Kitchen
Dining Room
Scullery
Armoury
Ailsa Exhibition
Oval Staircase

GROUND FLOOR

The clock tower, fronted by the circular carriageway, was originally the coach house and stables. The clock was added in the 19th century, and today the buildings are used for residential and educational purposes and a shop.

STAR SIGHTS

★ Saloon

★ Oval Staircase

Armoury
Displayed on the walls is the world's most important collection of flintlock pistols, used by the British Army and Militia between the 1730s and 1830s.

VISITORS' CHECKLIST

(NTS) 4 miles (6 km) West of Maybole. **Tel** *0870 118 1945.*
🚆 *Ayr, then bus.* **Castle** ◯ *Apr–Oct: 10am–5pm daily (last adm: 4pm).* **Grounds** ◯ *dawn until dusk daily.* 🚻 ♿ 🎫 🍴
www.culzeanexperience.org

Fountain Court
This sunken garden is a good place to begin a tour of the grounds to the east.

The Eisenhower Presentation
honours the general who was given the top floor of Culzean in gratitude for his role in World War II.

Carriageway

★ Saloon
With its restored 18th-century colour scheme and Louis XVI chairs, this elegant saloon perches on the cliff's edge 46 m (150 ft) above the Firth of Clyde. The carpet is a copy of the one designed by Adam.

★ Oval Staircase
Illuminated by an overarching skylight, the staircase, with its Ionic and Corinthian pillars, is considered one of Adam's finest achievements.

THE HIGHLANDS AND ISLANDS

ABERDEENSHIRE · MORAY · ARGYLL & BUTE · PERTH & KINROSS
SHETLAND · ORKNEY · WESTERN ISLES · HIGHLANDS · ANGUS

M*ost of the stock images of Scottishness – clans and tartans, whisky and porridge, bagpipes and heather – originate in the Highlands and enrich the popular picture of Scotland as a whole. But for many centuries the Gaelic-speaking, cattle-raising Highlanders had little in common with their southern neighbours.*

Clues to the non-Celtic ancestors of the Highlanders lie scattered across the Highlands and Islands in the form of stone circles, brochs and cairns some over 5,000 years old. By the end of the 6th century, the Gaelic-speaking Celts had arrived from Ireland, along with St Columba who taught Christianity. Its fusion with Viking culture in the 8th and 9th centuries produced St Magnus Cathedral in the Orkney Isles.

For over 1,000 years, Celtic Highland society was founded on a clan system, built on family ties to create loyal groups dependent on a feudal chief.

However, the clans were systematically broken up by England after 1746, following the defeat of the Jacobite attempt on the British crown, led by Bonnie Prince Charlie *(see p521)*. A more romantic vision of the Highlands started in the early 19th century. Its creation was largely due to Sir Walter Scott, whose novels and poetry depicted the majesty and grandeur of a country previously considered merely poverty-stricken and barbaric. Another great popularizer was Queen Victoria, whose passion for Balmoral helped to establish the trend for acquiring Highland sporting estates. But behind the sentimentality lay harsh economic realities that drove generations of Highlanders to seek a new life overseas.

Today, over half the inhabitants of the Highlands and Islands still live in communities of less than 1,000. Oil and tourism have supplemented fishing and whisky as the main businesses and population figures are rising.

A wintry dawn over the Cairngorms, the home of Britain's only herd of reindeer

◁ The stunningly sited castle of Eilean Donan, Loch Duich in Glen Shiel

Exploring the Highlands and Islands

To the north and west of Stirling (the historic gateway to the Highlands) lie the magnificent mountains and glens, fretted coastlines and lonely isles that are the epitome of Scottish scenery. Inverness, the Highland capital, makes a good starting point for exploring Loch Ness and the Cairngorms, while Fort William holds the key to Ben Nevis. Inland from Aberdeen lie Royal Deeside and the Spey Valley whisky heartland. The romantic Hebrides can be reached by ferry from Oban or Ullapool.

0 kilometres 25

0 miles 25

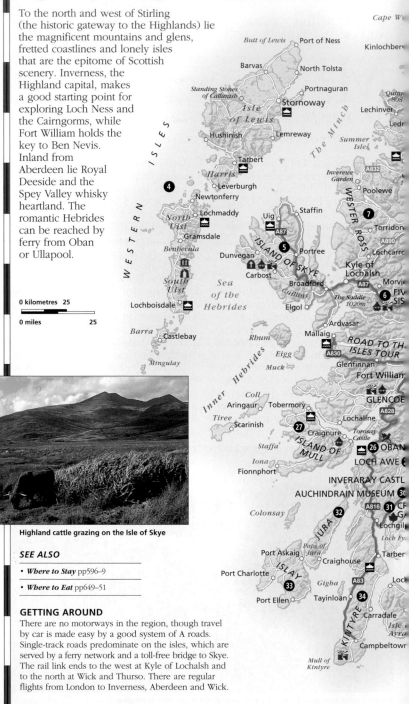

Highland cattle grazing on the Isle of Skye

SEE ALSO

- **Where to Stay** pp596–9

- **Where to Eat** pp649–51

GETTING AROUND

There are no motorways in the region, though travel by car is made easy by a good system of A roads. Single-track roads predominate on the isles, which are served by a ferry network and a toll-free bridge to Skye. The rail link ends to the west at Kyle of Lochalsh and to the north at Wick and Thurso. There are regular flights from London to Inverness, Aberdeen and Wick.

For additional map symbols *see back flap*

Thurso
JOHN O'GROATS 3
Strathy
Wick
A882
Achavanich
A99
Forsinard
Latheron
Morven 705m
Kildonan
Helmsdale
Lairg
A9
Brora
NORTH SEA
Dunrobin Castle
DORNOCH 8
Tain
Balintore
Lossiemouth
BLACK ISLE 10
Cromarty
ELGIN 16
A98
FORT GEORGE 14
A941
Keith
CAWDOR CASTLE 15
A96
CULLODEN 13
Huntly
A95
Rhynie
Grantown-on-Spey
LOCH NESS 11
Tomintoul
Newburgh
Aviemore
Cairn Gorm 1245m
Colnabaichin
ABERDEEN 17
Augustus
Ben Macdui 1309m
Drum Castle
A93
Kingussie
CAIRNGORMS 23
Ballater
Banchory
Mountains
Balmoral
ROYAL
Stonehaven
Braemar
DEESIDE TOUR 18
A90
A9
BLAIR CASTLE 22
A93
A92
KILLIECRANKIE WALK 21
PITLOCHRY 20
Dundee
Aberfeldy
DUNKELD 19
Killin
Perth
A85
Stirling
A84

Inset map (North Sea islands):

Yell, Unst, Fetlar
SHETLAND ISLANDS 1
Mainland
Whalsay
Lerwick
Foula
Mousa Broch
Sumburgh
NORTH SEA
Fair Isle
Westray, Sanday
Maes Howe
ORKNEY ISLANDS 2
Kirkwall
Stromness
Mainland
Hoy
JOHN O' GROATS 3

0 kilometres 50
0 miles 25

KEY

▬▬	Motorway
▬▬	Major road
▬	Secondary road
▬	Minor road
▬	Scenic route
—	Main railway
—	Minor railway
△	Summit

SIGHTS AT A GLANCE

Aberdeen ⑰
Auchindrain Museum ㉚
Black Isle ⑩
Blair Castle ㉒
Cairngorms pp544–5 ㉓
Cawdor Castle ⑮
Crarae Gardens ㉛
Culloden ⑬
Dornoch ⑧
Dunkeld ⑲
Elgin ⑯
Five Sisters ⑥
Fort George ⑭
Glencoe ㉔
Inveraray Castle ㉙
Inverness ⑫
Islay ㉝
John o'Groats ③

Jura ㉜
Kintyre ㉞
Loch Awe ㉘
Loch Ness ⑪
Mull ㉗
Oban ㉖
Orkney ②
Pitlochry ⑳
Shetland ①
Skye pp534–5 ⑤
Strathpeffer ⑨
Western Isles ④
Wester Ross ⑦

Walks and Tours

Killiecrankie Walk ㉑
Road to the Isles Tour ㉕
Royal Deeside Tour ⑱

Colour-washed houses at the harbour of Tobermory, Mull

Shetland ❶

Shetland. 22,000. from Aberdeen and Stromness on mainland Orkney. Lerwick (01595 693434). **www**.*visitshetland.com*

Lying six degrees south of the Arctic Circle, the rugged Shetland islands are Britain's most northerly region and were, with Orkney, part of the kingdom of Norway until 1469. In the main town of Lerwick, this Norse heritage is remembered during the ancient midwinter festival Up Helly Aa *(see p480)*, in which costumed revellers set fire to a replica Viking longship. Also in the town, the **Shetland Museum** tells the story of a people dependent on the sea, right up to modern times with the discovery of North Sea oil and gas in the 1970s.

One of Shetland's greatest treasures is the Iron Age tower, **Mousa Broch**, which can be visited on its isle by boat from Sandwick. There is more ancient history at Jarlshof where a museum explains the sprawling sea-front ruins which span 3,000 years.

A boat from Lerwick sails to the isle of Noss where grey seals bask beneath sandstone cliffs crowded with Shetland's seabirds – a spectacle best seen between May and June.

🏛 **Shetland Museum**
Hay's Dock, Lerwick. **Tel** *01595 694688. newly refurbished – call for opening times.*

Orkney ❷

Orkney. 19,800. from Gills Bay, Caithness; John o'Groats (May–Sep); Scrabster, Aberdeen. Broad St, Kirkwall (01856 872856). **www**.*visitorkney.com*

The fertile isles of Orkney are remarkable for the wealth of prehistoric monuments which place them among Europe's most treasured archaeological sites. In the town of Kirkwall, the sandstone **St Magnus Cathedral** stands amid a charming core of narrow streets. Its many interesting tombs include that of its 12th-century patron saint.

Nearby, the early 17th-century **Earl's Palace** is widely held to be one of Scotland's finest Renaissance buildings. To the west of Kirkwall lies Britain's most impressive chambered tomb, the cairn of **Maes Howe**. Dating from 2000 BC, the tomb has runic graffiti on its walls believed to have been left by Norsemen returning from the crusades in 1150.

Nearby, the great **Standing Stones of Stenness** may have been associated with Maes Howe rituals, though these still remain a mystery. Further west, on a bleak heath, stands the Bronze Age **Ring of Brodgar**.

Another archaeological treasure can be found in the Bay of Skail – the complete Stone Age village of **Skara Brae**. It was unearthed by a storm in 1850, after lying buried for 4,500 years. Further south, the

The Norman façade of the St Magnus Cathedral, Orkney

town of Stromness was a vital centre of Scotland's herring industry in the 18th century. Its story is told in the newly renovated local museum, while the **Pier Arts Centre** displays British and international art.

🏯 **Earl's Palace**
Palace Rd, Kirkwall. **Tel** *01856 871918. Apr–Sep: 9:30am–6:30pm daily. limited.* **www**.*historic-scotland.gov.uk*
🏛 **Pier Arts Centre**
Victoria St, Stromness. **Tel** *01856 850209. by mid 2007.*

John o'Groats ❸

Highland. 500. Wick John o'Groats to Burwick, Orkney (May–Sep). John o'Groats (01955 611373).

Some 876 miles (1,409 km) north from Land's End, Britain's most northeasterly mainland village faces Orkney, 8 miles (13 km) across the turbulent Pentland Firth. The village takes its name from a 15th-century Dutchman John de Groot, who, to avoid accusations of favouritism, is said to have built an octagonal house here with one door for each of his eight heirs. The spectacular cliffs and rock stacks of Duncansby Head lie a few miles further east.

Western Isles ❹

Western Scotland ends with this remote chain of islands, made of some of the oldest rock on Earth. Almost treeless landscapes are divided by countless waterways, the western, windward coasts edged by miles of white sandy beaches. For centuries, the eastern shores, composed largely of peat bogs, have provided the islanders with fuel. Man has been here for 6,000 years, living off the sea and the thin turf, though such monuments as an abandoned Norwegian whaling station on Harris attest to the difficulties in commercializing the islanders' traditional skills. Gaelic, part of an enduring culture, is widely spoken.

The Black House Museum, a traditional croft on Lewis

The monumental Standing Stones of Callanish in northern Lewis

Lewis and Harris

Western Isles. 🏠 22,000. ✈ Stornoway. ⛴ Uig (Skye), Ullapool, Kyle of Lochalsh. 🛈 Stornoway, Lewis (01851 703088).
www.visitthebrides.com
Black House Museum. *Tel* 01851 710395. ☐ daily. 🎫 ᗕ 🎥 🏠

Forming the largest landmass of the Western Isles, Lewis and Harris are a single island, though Gaelic dialects differ between the two areas. From **Stornoway**, with its bustling harbour and colourful house fronts, the ancient **Standing Stones of Callanish** are only 16 miles (26 km) to the west. Just off the road on the way to Callanish are the ruins of **Carloway Broch**, a Pictish *(see p482)* tower over 2,000 years old. The more recent past can be explored at Arnol's **Black House Museum** – a showcase of crofting life as it was until only 50 years ago.

South of the rolling peat moors of Lewis, a range of mountains marks the border with Harris, which one enters as one passes Aline Lodge at the head of Loch Seaforth. Only a little less spectacular than the "Munros" (peaks over 914 m; 3,000 ft) of the mainland and the Isle of Skye

(see pp534–5), the mountains of Harris are a paradise for the hillwalker and, from their summits on a clear day, the distant Isle of St Kilda can be seen 50 miles (80 km) to the west.

The ferry port of Tarbert stands on a slim isthmus separating North and South Harris. Some local weavers of the famous Harris Tweed still follow the old tradition of using plants to make their dyes.

From the port of Leverburgh, close to the southern tip of Harris, a ferry can be taken to the isle of North Uist, where a causeway has been built to Berneray.

The Uists, Benbecula and Barra

Western Isles. 🏠 7,200. ✈ Barra, Benbecula. ⛴ Uig (Skye), Ullapool, Oban. 🚗 🚆 Oban, Mallaig, Kyle of Lochalsh. 🛈 Lochmaddy, North Uist (01876 500321); Lochboisdale, South Uist (01878 700286); Castlebay, Barra (01871 810336).
www.visitthebrides.com

After the dramatic scenery of Harris, the lower-lying, largely waterlogged southern isles may seem an anticlimax, though they nurture secrets well worth discovering. Long, white, sandy beaches fringe the Atlantic coast, edged with one of Scotland's natural treasures: the lime-rich soil known as *machair*. During the summer months, the soil is covered with wild flowers.

From **Lochmaddy**, North Uist's main village, the A867 crosses 3 miles (5 km) of causeway to Benbecula, the isle from which Flora Mac-Donald smuggled Bonnie Prince Charlie *(see p535)* to Skye. Another causeway leads to South Uist, with its golden beaches renowned as a National Scenic Area. From Lochboisdale, a ferry sails to the tiny isle of Barra. The ferry docks in Castlebay, affording an unforgettable view of **Kisimul Castle**, the ancestral stronghold of the MacNeils of Barra.

The remote and sandy shores of South Uist

The western side of the Five Sisters of Kintail, seen from above Loch Duich

Skye ⑤

See pp534–5.

The Five Sisters ⑥

Skye & Lochalsh. 🚉 *Kyle of Lochalsh.* 🚌 *Glenshiel.* ℹ️ *Bayfield Road, Portree, Isle of Skye (01478 612137).* www.visithighlands.com

Dominating one of Scotland's most haunting regions, the awesome summits of the Five Sisters of Kintail rear into view at the northern end of Loch Cluanie as the A87 enters Glen Shiel. The **Visitor Centre** at Morvich offers ranger-led excursions in the summer. Further west, the road passes **Eilean Donan Castle**, connected by a bridge. A Jacobite (*see p537*) stronghold, it was destroyed in 1719 by English warships. In the 19th century it was restored and now contains Jacobite relics.

♣ **Eilean Donan Castle**
Off A87, nr Dornie. *Tel 01599 555202.* ☐ *Apr–Oct: 10am– 5:30pm daily.* 📷

Wester Ross ⑦

Ross & Cromarty. 🚉 *Achnasheen, Strathcarron.* ℹ️ *Visit Scotland (01445 712130).*

Leaving Loch Carron to the south, the A890 suddenly enters the northern Highlands and the great wilderness of Wester Ross. The Torridon Estate includes some of the oldest mountains on Earth (Torridonian rock is over 600 million years old), and is home to red deer, wild cats and wild goats. Peregrine falcons and golden eagles nest in the towering sandstone mass of Liathach, above the village of Torridon with its breathtaking views over Applecross to Skye. The **Torridon Countryside Centre** provides guided walks in season and essential information on the natural history of the region.

To the north, the A832 cuts through the Beinn Eighe National Nature Reserve in which remnants of the ancient Caledonian pine forest still stand on the banks and isles of Loch Maree.

Along the coast, exotic gardens thrive in the warming currents of the Gulf Stream, most impressive being **Inverewe Garden** created in 1862 by Osgood Mackenzie (1842–1922). May and June are the months to see the display of

Typical Torridonian mountian scenery in the Wester Ross

rhododendrons and azaleas; July and August for the herbaceous borders.

🏛 **Torridon Countryside Centre**
(NTS) *Torridon. Tel 01445 791368.* ☐ *Easter–Sep: 10am–6pm daily.* 📷 ♿ www.nts.org.uk

🌷 **Inverewe Garden**
(NTS) *off A832, nr Poolewe. Tel 01445 781200.* ☐ *daily.* 📷 ♿

Dornoch ⑧

Sutherland. 👥 *2,200.* 🚉 *Golspie, Tain.* ℹ️ *The Square, Dornoch (01862 810916).* www.visithighlands.com

With its first-class golf course and extensive sandy beaches, **Dornoch** is a popular holiday resort, though it has retained a peaceful atmosphere. Now the parish church, the medieval cathedral was all but destroyed in a clan dispute in 1570; it was finally restored in the 1920s for its 700th anniversary. A stone at the beach end of River Street marks the place where Janet Horne, the last woman to be tried in Scotland for witchcraft, was executed in 1722.

Environs: Twelve miles (19 km) northeast of Dornoch is the stately Victorianized pile of **Dunrobin Castle**, magnificently situated in a great park with formal gardens overlooking the sea. Since the 13th century, this has been the seat of the Earls of Sutherland.

Many of its rooms are open to visitors. A steam-powered fire engine is among the miscellany of objects on display.

South of Dornoch stands the town of **Tain**. Though patronized by medieval kings as a place of pilgrimage, it became an administrative centre of the Highland Clearances. All is explained in the heritage centre, **Tain Through Time**.

♦ **Dunrobin Castle**
Nr Golspie. *Tel* 01408 633177.
☐ Apr–Oct: daily (Sun pm only).
🖳 www.highlandescape.com

🏛 **Tain Through Time**
Tower St. *Tel* 01862 894089.
☐ Apr–Oct: Mon–Sat. 🖳 ♿ 📷
www.tainmuseum.org.uk

The serene cathedral precinct in the town of Dornoch

Strathpeffer ❾

Ross & Cromarty. 👥 1,400.
🚊 Dingwall, Inverness. 🚌 Inverness.
🛈 Visit Scotland (01463 731505;
Easter–Oct).

Standing 5 miles (8 km) from the Falls of Rogie and to the east of the Northwest Highlands, the popular town of Strathpeffer still has the refined charm for which it was well known in Victorian times, when it flourished as a spa and health resort. The grand hotels, individually designed buildings and gracious layout of Strathpeffer recall the days when royalty from all over Europe used to flock to the chalybeate- and sulphur-laden springs, which were believed to help in the cure of tuberculosis, and in the treatment of rheumatism.

The shores of the Black Isle in the Moray Firth

The Black Isle ❿

Ross & Cromarty. 🚊 🚌 Inverness.
🛈 Visit Scotland (01463 731505;
Easter–Oct).

Though the drilling platforms in the Cromarty Firth are reminders of how oil has changed the local economy, the peninsula of the Black Isle is still largely composed of farmland and fishing villages. The town of **Cromarty** was an important port in the 18th century, with thriving rope and lace industries. Many of its merchant houses still stand; the museum in the **Cromarty Courthouse** provides heritage tours of the town. The **Hugh Miller Museum** is a museum to the theologian and geologist Hugh Miller (1802–56), who was born in the cottage; adjacent is the superb, new

Miller House, which has exhibitions on three floors. **Fortrose** boasts a ruined 14th-century cathedral, while a stone on Chanonry Point commemorates the Brahan Seer, a 17th-century prophet burnt alive in a tar barrel by the Countess of Seaforth after he foresaw her husband's infidelity. For local archaeology, visit **Groam House Museum** in Rosemarkie.

🏛 **Cromarty Courthouse**
Church St, Cromarty. *Tel* 01381
600 418. ☐ daily. 🖳
🏚 **Hugh Miller Museum**
(NTS) Church St, Cromarty. *Tel* 01381
600245. ☐ Easter–Sep: daily; Oct:
Sun–Wed pm. 🖳 ♿ limited.
🏛 **Groam House Museum**
High St, Rosemarkie. *Tel* 01381 620
961. ☐ May–Sep: 10am–5pm daily
(Sun pm); Oct–Apr: Sat & Sun (pm).

THE HIGHLAND CLEARANCES

During the heyday of the clan system (see p484), tenants paid their clan chiefs rent for their land in the form of military service. However, with the decline of the clan system after the Battle of Culloden (see p537) and the coming of sheep from the borders, landowners were able to command a financial rent their tenants were unable to afford and the land was bought up by Lowland and English farmers. In what became known as "the year of the sheep" (1792), thousands of tenants were evicted to make way for sheep. Many emigrated to Australia, America and Canada. Ruins of their crofts can still be seen in Sutherland and Wester Ross.

The Last of the Clan
(1865) by Thomas Faed

Isle of Skye

Otter by the coast at Kylerhea

The largest of the Inner Hebrides, Skye can be reached by the bridge linking Kyle of Lochalsh and Kyleakin. A turbulent geological history has given the island some of Britain's most varied and dramatic scenery. From the rugged volcanic plateau of northern Skye to the ice-sculpted peaks of the Cuillins, the island is divided by numerous sea lochs, leaving the traveller never more than 8 km (5 miles) from the sea. Limestone grasslands predominate in the south, where the hillsides, home of sheep and cattle, are scattered with the ruins of crofts abandoned during the Clearances *(see p531)*. Historically, Skye is best known for its association with Bonnie Prince Charlie.

Skeabost has the ruins of a chapel which is associated with St Columba. Medieval tombstones can be found in the graveyard.

Grave of Flora MacDonald

WESTERN ISLES

LOCH SNIZORT

- Lusta

B886

A850

Milovaig

B884

Dunvegan

A863

Portnalong

B8009

Talisker   Carbost

0 kilometres   10
0 miles   5

The Talisker Distillery produces one of the best Highland malts, often described as "the lava of the Cuillins".

Dunvegan Castle
For over seven centuries, Dunvegan Castle has been the seat of the chiefs of the Clan Mac-Leod. It contains the Fairy Flag, a fabled piece of magical silk treasured for its protection.

Cuillins
Britain's finest mountain range is within walking distance of Sligachan, and in summer a boat sails from Elgol to the desolate inner sanctuary of Loch Coruisk. As he fled across the surrounding moorland, Bonnie Prince Charlie is said to have claimed: "even the Devil shall not follow me here!"

KEY

	Tourist information
	Major road
	Minor road
	Narrow lane
	Viewpoint

◁ **Dawn over the desolate tablelands of northern Skye, viewed from the Quiraing**

Quiraing

A series of landslides has exposed the roots of this volcanic plateau, revealing a fantastic terrain of spikes and towers. They are easily explored off the Uig to Staffin road.

Kilt Rock

The Storr

The erosion of this basalt plateau has created the Old Man of Storr, a monolith rising to 49 m (160 ft) by the Portree road.

Loch Coruisk

Luib has a beautiful thatched cottage, preserved as it was 100 years ago.

Portree

With its colourful harbour, Portree (meaning "port of the king") is Skye's metropolis. It received its name after a visit by James V in 1540.

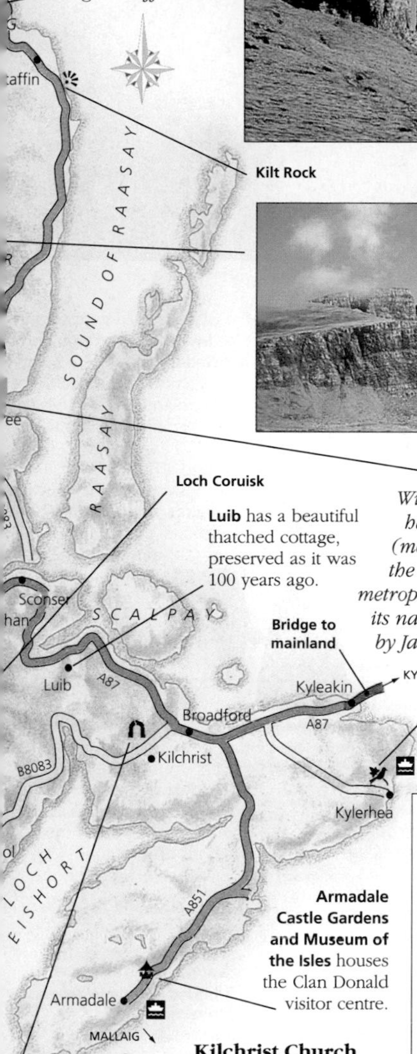

Bridge to mainland

KYLE OF LOCHALSH

Kyleakin

Broadford   A87

• Kilchrist

Kylerhea

Otters can be seen from the haven in Kylerhea.

Armadale Castle Gardens and Museum of the Isles houses the Clan Donald visitor centre.

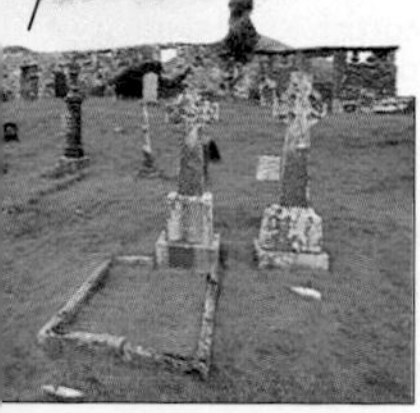

MALLAIG

Kilchrist Church

This ruined pre-Reformation church's last service was held in 1843. It once served Skye's most populated areas, though the surrounding moors are now deserted.

BONNIE PRINCE CHARLIE

The last of the Stuart claimants to the Crown, Charles Edward Stuart (1720–88), came to Scotland from France in 1745 to win the throne. After marching as far as Derby, his army was driven back to Culloden where it was defeated. Hounded for five months through the Highlands, he escaped to Skye, disguised as the maidservant of a woman called Flora MacDonald, from Uist. From the mainland, he sailed to France in September 1746, and died in Rome. Flora was buried in 1790 at Kilmuir, on Skye, wrapped in a sheet taken from the bed of the "bonnie" (handsome) prince.

The prince, disguised as a maidservant

The ruins of Urquhart Castle on the western shore of Loch Ness

Loch Ness ⓫

Inverness. ⇄ 🚆 *Inverness*. 🛈 *Castle Wynd, Inverness (01463 234353)*. **www**.loch-ness-scotland.com

At 24 miles (39 km) long, one mile (1.5 km) at its widest and up to 305 m (1,000 ft) deep, **Loch Ness** fills the northern half of the Great Glen fault from Fort William to Inverness. It is joined to lochs Oich and Lochy by the 22 mile (35 km) Caledonian

THE LOCH NESS MONSTER

First sighted by St Columba in the 6th century, "Nessie" has attracted increasing attention since ambiguous photographs were taken in the 1930s. Though serious investigation is often undermined by hoaxers, sonar techniques continue to yield enigmatic results: plesiosaurs, giant eels and too much whisky are the most popular explanations. Nessie appears to have a close relative in the waters of Loch Morar *(see p546)*.

Canal, designed by Thomas Telford *(see p447)*. On the western shore, the A82 passes the ruins of the 16th-century **Urquhart Castle**, which was blown up by government supporters in 1692 to prevent it falling into Jacobite hands. A short distance west, **Loch Ness 2000 Exhibition Centre** offers a wealth of audiovisual information.

♣ Urquhart Castle
Nr Drumnadrochit. *Tel 01456 450551.* ◻ *Easter–Sep: 9:30am–6:30pm; Oct–Easter: 9:30am–4:30pm; daily.* 🎞 🚻 🛍

🏛 Loch Ness 2000 Exhibition Centre
Drumnadrochit. *Tel 01456 450573.* ◻ *daily throughout the year with extended opening hours in peak season and shorter opening hours during the winter months.* 🎞 ♿ 🖥 🛍

Inverness ⓬

Highland. 🏘 60,000. ⇄ 🚆 🛈 *Castle Wynd (0845 2255121)*. **www**.visithighlands.com

As the Highland capital, Inverness makes an ideal base from which to explore the surrounding countryside. The Victorian castle dominates the town centre, the oldest buildings of which are found in nearby Church Street. Today

the castle is used as law courts. The **Inverness Museum and Art Gallery** provides a good introduction to the history of the Highlands with exhibits including a lock of Bonnie Prince Charlie's *(see p535)* hair and a fine collection of Inverness silver. The **Scottish Kiltmaker Visitor Centre** explores the history and tradition of Scottish kilts as well as workshops, while those in search of tartans and knitwear should visit the **James Pringle Weavers of Inverness**.

Kilt maker with royal Stuart tartan

Jacobite Cruises run a variety of year-round cruises along the Caledonian Canal and on to Loch Ness. The unfolding scenery makes this a most pleasant and tranquil way to spend a sunny afternoon.

🏛 Museum and Art Gallery
Castle Wynd. *Tel 01463 237114.* ◻ *9am–5pm Mon–Sat.* ♿ **www**.invernessmuseum.com

🛍 James Pringle Weavers of Inverness
Holm Woollen Mill, Dores Rd. *Tel 01463 223311.* ◻ *daily.* ♿

🏛 Scottish Kiltmaker Visitor Centre
Huntly St. *Tel 01463 222781.* ◻ *May–Sep: daily; Oct–Apr: Mon–Sat.* ● *25 Dec, 1 Jan.* 🎞

Jacobite Cruises
Glenurquhart Road. *Tel 01463 233999.* ◻ *daily.* 🎞 ♿ **www**.jacobite.co.uk

Culloden

(NTS) Inverness. ⭥ 🏛 *Inverness.*
www.nts.org.uk

A desolate stretch of moorland, Culloden looks much as it did on 16 April 1746, the date of the last battle to be fought on British soil *(see p483)*. Here the Jacobite cause, with Bonnie Prince Charlie's *(see p535)* leadership, finally perished under the onslaught of Hanoverian troops led by the Duke of Cumberland. All is explained in the excellent **NTS Visitor Centre**.

Environs: Signposted for a mile (1.5 km) or so east are the outstanding Neolithic burial sites, the **Clava Cairns**.

🛈 **NTS Visitor Centre**
On the B9006 east of Inverness.
Tel 01463 790607. ◯ Apr–Sep: daily. ● 24–26 Dec, Jan. 🗺 🚹

Fort George ⓮

Inverness. *Tel 01667 460232.*
⭥ 🏛 *Inverness, Nairn.* ◯ Apr–Sep: 9:30am–6pm daily (to 4:30pm Oct–Mar). ● 25 & 26 Dec. 🗺 🚹
🖥 www.historic-scotland.gov.uk

One of the finest works of European military architecture, Fort George stands on a windswept promontory jutting into the Moray Firth, ideally located to suppress the Highlanders. Completed in 1769, the fort was built after the Jacobite risings to discourage further rebellion in the Highlands and has remained a military garrison

THE JACOBITE MOVEMENT

The first Jacobites (mainly Catholic Highlanders) were the supporters of James II of England (James VII of Scotland) who was deposed by the "Glorious Revolution" of 1688 *(see p53)*. With the Protestant William of Orange on the throne, the Jacobites' desire to restore the Stuart monarchy led to the uprisings of 1715 and 1745. The first, in support of James VIII, the "Old Pretender", ended at the Battle of Sheriffmuir (1715). The failure of the second uprising, with the defeat at Culloden, saw the end of Jacobite hopes and led to the end of the clan system and the suppression of Highland culture for over a century *(see p485)*.

James II, by Samuel Cooper (1609–72)

The drawbridge on the eastern side of Cawdor Castle

ever since. The Fort houses the **Regimental Museum** of the Highlanders Regiment, and some of its barrack rooms reconstruct the conditions of the common soldiers stationed here more than 200 years ago. The **Grand Magazine** contains an outstanding collection of arms and military equipment. The battlements also make an excellent place from which to watch dolphins in the Moray Firth.

Cawdor Castle ⓯

On B9090 (off A96). *Tel 01667 404401.* ⭥ Nairn, then bus. 🚌 from Inverness. ◯ May–8 Oct: 10am–5:30pm daily. 🗺 🚹 gardens & ground floor only. 🍽
www.cawdorcastle.com

With its turreted central tower, moat and drawbridge, Cawdor Castle is one of the most romantic stately homes in the Highlands. Though the castle is famed for being the 11th-century home of Shakespeare's *(see p322)* Macbeth and the scene of his murder of King Duncan, it is not historically proven that either came here.

An ancient holly tree preserved in the vaults is said to be the one under which, in 1372, Thane William's donkey, laden with gold, stopped for a rest during its master's search for a place to build a fortress. According to legend, this was how the site for the castle was chosen. Now, after 600 years of continuous occupation (it is still the home of the Thanes of Cawdor) the house is a treasury of family history, containing a number of rare tapestries and portraits by the 18th-century painters Joshua Reynolds (1723–92) and George Romney (1734–1802). Furniture in the Pink Bedroom and Woodcock Room includes work by Chippendale and Sheraton. In the Old Kitchen, the huge Victorian cooking range stands as a shrine to below-stairs drudgery. The grounds provide nature trails and a nine-hole golf course.

A contemporary picture, *The Battle of Culloden* (1746), by D Campbell

Elgin ⑯

Moray. 🏛 *21,000.* ✈ 🚌
ℹ️ *17 High St, Moray (01343 542666).*

With its cobbled marketplace and crooked lanes, the popular holiday centre of Elgin still retains much of its medieval layout. The 13th-century **cathedral** ruins next to King Street are all that remain of one of Scotland's architectural triumphs, the design of its tiered windows reminiscent of the cathedral at St Andrews *(see p499).* Once known as the Lantern of the North, the cathedral was severely damaged in 1390 by the Wolf of Badenoch (the son of Robert II) in revenge for his excommunication by the Bishop of Moray. Even worse damage came in 1576 when the Regent Moray ordered the stripping of its lead roofing. Among its outstanding re-mains is a Pictish cross-slab in the nave, and a basin in a

Details of the central tower of Elgin Cathedral

corner where one of Elgin's benefactors, Andrew Anderson, was kept as a baby by his homeless mother. As well as local history, the **Elgin Museum** has anthropological, geological displays, while the **Moray Motor Museum** has over 40 vehicles.

🏛 **Elgin Museum**
1 High St. **Tel** *01343 543675.*
⏰ *Apr–Oct: Mon–Sat. Phone to check times.* 📷 ♿ *limited.* 📷
🏛 **Moray Motor Museum**
Bridge St, Bishopmill. **Tel** *01343 541120.* ⏰ *Easter–Oct: 11am–5pm daily.* 📷 ♿

Aberdeen ⑰

Scotland's third largest city and Europe's offshore oil capital, Aberdeen has prospered since the discovery of petroleum in the North Sea in 1970. The sea bed has now yielded over 100 oilfields. Widely known as the Granite City, its rugged outlines are softened by sump-tuous year-round floral displays in its public parks and gardens, the Duthie Park Winter Gardens being one of the largest indoor gardens in Europe. The picturesque village of Footdee, which sits at the end of the city's 2 mile (3 km) beach, has good views back to the busy harbour.

The spires of Aberdeen, rising behind the city harbour

Exploring Aberdeen
The city centre flanks the mile-long (1.5 km) Union Street ending to the east at the Mercat Cross. The cross stands in Castlegate, the one-time site of the city castle. From here the cobbled Shiprow winds southwest and passes Provost Ross's House *(see p540)* on its way to the harbour with its fish market. A bus can be taken a mile (1.5 km) north of the centre to Old Aberdeen which, with its medieval streets and wynds, has the peaceful character of a separate village. Driving is restricted in some streets.

🚏 **King's College**
College Bounds, Old Aberdeen. **Tel** *01224 272000.* **Chapel** ⏰ *Opening times vary – phone to check.* ♿
King's College was founded in 1495 as the city's first univer-sity. The inter-denominational chapel (the only part of the college open to the public), in the past consecutively Catholic and Protestant, has a lantern tower rebuilt after a storm in 1633. Stained-glass windows by Douglas Strachan add a contemporary touch to the interior which contains a 1540 pulpit, later carved with heads of Stuart monarchs.

🔒 **St Andrew's Cathedral**
King St. **Tel** *01224 640290.*
⏰ *May–Sep: 11am–4pm Tue–Fri.* ♿
📷 *by appointment.*
The Mother Church of the Episcopal Communion in America, St Andrew's has a memorial to Samuel Seabury, the first Episcopalian bishop in the United States, who was consecrated in Aberdeen in 1784. Coats of arms adorn the ceiling above the north and south aisles, contrasting col-ourfully with the white walls and pillars. They represent the American States and local Jacobite *(see p537)* families.

The elegant lantern tower of the chapel at King's College

For hotels and restaurants in this region see pp596–599 and pp649–651

PROVOST SKENE'S HOUSE

Guestrow. **Tel** *01224 641086.* ◯ *daily.* ● *25 & 26, 31 Dec–2 Jan.*
www.aagm.co.uk

Once the home of Sir George Skene, a 17th-century provost
(mayor) of Aberdeen, the house was built in 1545. Inside, period
rooms span 200 years of design. The Duke of Cumberland
stayed here before the Battle of Culloden *(see p537)*.

The 18th-century Parlour,
with its walnut harpsichord and
covered chairs by the fire, was
the informal room in which the
family would have tea.

The Regency Room typifies
early 19th-century elegance.
A harp dating from 1820 stands
by a Grecian-style sofa and a
French writing table.

The Painted Gallery has
one of Scotland's most important cycles of religious art. The
panels are early 17th century,
though the artist is unknown.

The 17th-century Great Hall
contains heavy oak dining
furniture. Provost Skene's
wood-carved coat of arms
hangs above the fireplace.

The Georgian Dining Room,
with its Classical design, was
the main formal room in the
16th century and still has its
original flagstone floor.

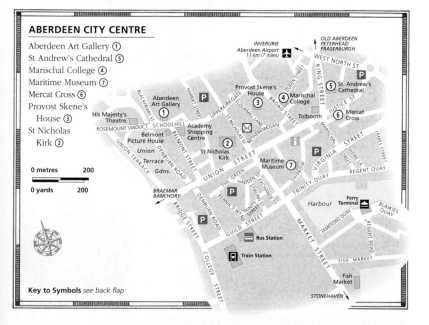

Entrance

ABERDEEN CITY CENTRE

Aberdeen Art Gallery ①
St Andrew's Cathedral ⑤
Marischal College ④
Maritime Museum ⑦
Mercat Cross ⑥
Provost Skene's House ③
St Nicholas Kirk ②

0 metres 200
0 yards 200

Key to Symbols see back flap

🏛 Art Gallery

Schoolhill. **Tel** *01224 523700.* ⬤
10am–5pm Mon–Sat, 2–5pm Sun. ⬤
25 Dec–2 Jan. ♿ www.aagm.co.uk

Housed in a Neo-Classical building, purpose-built in 1884, the Art Gallery has a wide range of exhibitions, with an emphasis on contemporary work. A fine collection of Aberdonian silver can be found among the decorative arts on the ground floor, and is the subject of a video presentation. A permanent collection of 18th–20th-century fine art features such names as Toulouse-Lautrec, Reynolds and Zoffany. Several of the works were bequeathed in 1900 by a local granite merchant, Alex Macdonald. He commissioned many of the paintings in the Macdonald

Aberdonian silver in the Art Gallery

Room, which displays 92 self-portraits by British artists. Occasional poetry-readings, music recitals and films are on offer.

🔒 St Nicholas Kirk

Union St. **Tel** *01224 643494.*
⬤ *May–Sep: noon–4pm daily;*
1–3pm Sat. ♿

Founded in the 12th century, St Nicholas is Scotland's largest parish church. Though the present structure dates from 1752, many relics of earlier times can be seen inside.

After being damaged during the Reformation, the interior was divided into two. A chapel in the East Church contains iron rings used to secure witches in the 17th century, while in the West Church there are some embroidered panels attributed to one Mary Jameson (1597–1644).

🏛 Maritime Museum

Shiprow. **Tel** *01224 337700.* ⬤
10am–5pm Mon–Sat, noon–3pm Sun.
♿ ▯ ▯

Overlooking the harbour is Provost Ross's House, which dates back to 1593 and is one of the oldest residential buildings in the town. This museum traces the history of Aberdeen's seafaring tradition. Exhibitions include ship-wrecks, rescues, shipbuilding and the oil installations off Scotland's east coast.

🔒 St Machar's Cathedral

The Chanonry. **Tel** *01224 485988.* ⬤
9am–5pm daily (10am–4pm winter). ♿

Dominating Old Aberdeen, the 15th-century edifice of St Machar's is the oldest granite building in the city. The stonework of one arch even dates as far back as the 14th century. The impressive nave now serves as a parish church and its magnificent oak ceiling is adorned with the coats of arms of 48 popes, emperors and princes of Christendom.

Royal Deeside Tour ⓲

Since Queen Victoria's purchase of the Balmoral estate in 1852, Deeside has been best known as the summer home of the British Royal Family, though it has been associated with royalty since the time of Robert the Bruce *(see p482)*. The route follows the Dee, formerly a prolific salmon river, through some magnificent Grampian scenery.

Muir of Dinnet Nature Reserve ④
An information centre on the A97 provides an excellent place from which to explore this beautiful mixed woodland area, formed by the retreating glaciers of the last Ice Age.

Balmoral ⑥
Bought by Queen Victoria for 30,000 guineas in 1852, after its owner choked to death on a fishbone, the castle was rebuilt in the Scottish Baronial style at Prince Albert's request.

Ballater ⑤
The old railway town of Ballater has royal warrants on many of its shop fronts. It grew as a 19th-century spa town, its waters reputedly providing a cure for tuberculosis.

Dunkeld ⑲

Perth & Kinross. 🏠 *2,500*. 🚂 *Birnam*.
🚌 ℹ️ *The Cross (01350 727688)*.
www.perthshire.co.uk

Situated by the River Tay,
this ancient and charming
village was all but destroyed
in the Battle of Dunkeld, a
Jacobite *(see p537)* defeat, in
1689. The **Little Houses** lining
Cathedral Street were the first
to be rebuilt, and are fine
examples of imaginative
restoration. The ruins of the
14th-century **cathedral** enjoy
an idyllic setting on shady
lawns beside the Tay, against
a backdrop of steep and
wooded hills. The choir is used
as the parish church and its
north wall contains a Leper's
Squint: a hole through which
lepers could see the altar
during mass. It was while on
holiday in the Dunkeld countryside that Beatrix Potter *(see
p367)* found the location for
her Peter Rabbit stories.

The ruins of Dunkeld Cathedral

Pitlochry ⑳

Perth & Kinross. 🏠 *2,900*. 🚂 🚌
ℹ️ *22 Atholl Rd (01796 472215)*.
www.perthshire.co.uk

Surrounded by the pine-
forested hills, Pitlochry
became famous after Queen
Victoria *(see p56)* described it
as one of the finest resorts in
Europe. In early summer,

salmon swim up the ladder
built into the Power Station
Dam, on their way to spawning
grounds upriver. The **Power
Station Visitor Centre** outlines
the hydro-electric scheme
which harnesses the waters
of the River Tummel. The
home of Bell's whisky, the
Blair Athol Distillery, gives
an insight into whisky making
(see p489) and is open for
tours. The **Festival Theatre**,
one of Scotland's most famous,
puts on a summer season when
the programme changes daily.

ℹ️ **Power Station Visitor
Centre** Pitlochry. *Tel 01796
473152*. ⬜ *Apr–Oct: 10am–5:30pm
Mon–Fri (Jul & Aug: daily)*. 🔖 ✓

🎭 **Festival Theatre**
Port-na-Craig. *Tel 01796 484626*.
⬜ *daily*. 🔖 ♿ ✓

🏭 **Blair Athol Distillery**
Perth Rd. *Tel 01796 482003*. ⬜
*Easter–Sep: Mon–Sat (& Sun pm Jun–
Sep); Oct–Mar: Mon–Fri*. ⬛ *22 Dec–
3 Jan*. 🔖 ♿ *limited*. ✓ 🅿️
www.discovering-distilleries.com

TIPS FOR DRIVERS

Length: *69 miles (111 km)*.
Stopping-off points: *Crathes
Castle café (May–Sep: daily);
Station Restaurant, Ballater (food
served all day). (See also pp684–5)*

Drum Castle ①
This impressive 13th-century keep
was granted by Robert the Bruce to
his standard bearer in 1323, in
gratitude for his services.

Banchory ③
Local lavender is a popular
attraction here. From the 18th-
century Brig o' Feugh, salmon
can be seen.

**Crathes Castle
and Gardens** ②
This is the family home of
the Burnetts, who were
made Royal Foresters of
Drum by Robert the Bruce.
Along with the title, he
gave Alexander Burnett
the ivory Horn of Leys
which is still on display.

PETERHEAD

A96

ABERDEEN

A93

• Peterculter

Crathes

Dee

B9077

STONEHAVEN

0 kilometres   5

0 miles   4

KEY

━━━ Tour route

═══ Other roads

☆ Viewpoint

Killiecrankie Walk ㉑

In an area famous for its scenery and historical connections, this circular walk offers typical Highland views. The route is fairly flat, though ringed by mountains, and follows the River Garry south to Loch Faskally, meandering through a wooded gorge, passing the Soldier's Leap and a Victorian viaduct. There are several ideal picnic spots along the way. Returning along the River Tummel, the walk crosses one of Queen Victoria's favourite Highland areas, before doubling back along the rivers to complete the circuit.

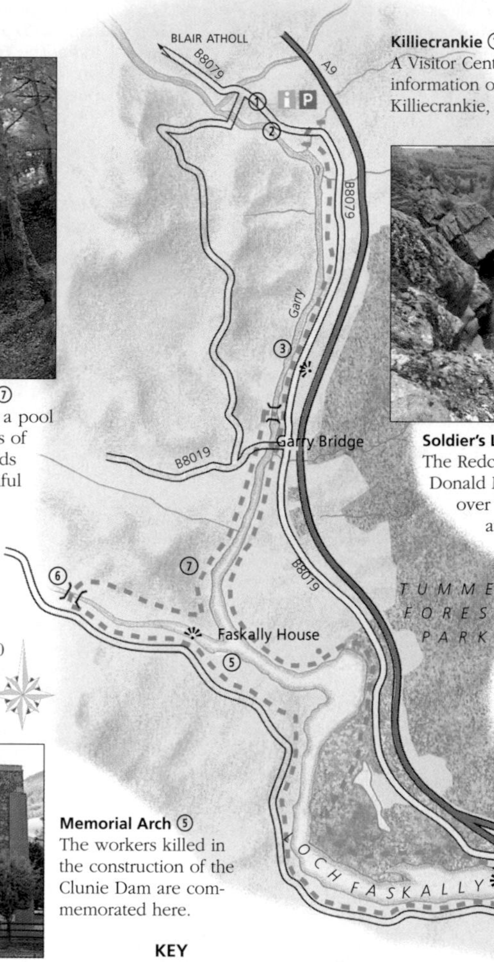

Killiecrankie ①
A Visitor Centre provides information on the Battle of Killiecrankie, fought in 1689.

Linn of Tummel ⑦
The path passes a pool beneath the Falls of Tummel and leads through a beautiful forest trail.

Coronation Bridge ⑥
Spanning the River Tummel, this footbridge was built in 1860 in honour of George IV.

Soldier's Leap ②
The Redcoat soldier Donald Macbean leapt over the river here to avoid capture by Jacobites during the 1689 battle.

Killiecrankie Pass ③
A 17th-century military road built by General Wade follows the gorge.

Memorial Arch ⑤
The workers killed in the construction of the Clunie Dam are commemorated here.

Clunie Foot Bridge ④
This bridge crosses the artificial Loch Faskally, created by the damming of the River Tummel for hydro-electric power in the 1950s.

KEY

- = = Route
- ▬ Major road
- ▭ B road
- ▭ Minor road
- ⚶ Viewpoint
- P Parking
- ℹ Visitor Centre

TIPS FOR WALKERS

Starting point: NTS Visitor Centre Killicrankie. **Tel** 01796 473233.
Getting there: Bus from Pitlochry or Aberfeldy.
Length: 10 miles (16 km).
Difficulty: Very easy.

0 kilometres   1

0 miles   0.5

Map labels: BLAIR ATHOLL, B8079, A9, Garry, Garry Bridge, B8019, TUMMEL FOREST PARK, Faskally House, LOCH FASKALLY, PITLOCHRY

The Three Sisters, Glencoe, in late autumn

Blair Castle ㉒

Blair Atholl, Perthshire. **Tel** 01796 481207. ⬛ Blair Atholl. ◯ Apr–Oct: 9:30am–4:30pm daily. 🏷 ♿ limited. **www**.blair-castle.co.uk

This rambling, turreted castle has been altered so often in its 700-year history that it provides a unique insight into the history of Highland aristo-cratic life. The 18th-century wing, with its draughty Victori-an passages hung with antlers, has a display containing the gloves and pipe of Bonnie Prince Charlie (see p535) who spent two days here gathering Jacobite (see p537) support. Family portraits cover 300 years and include paintings by such masters as Johann Zoffany and Sir Peter Lely. Sir Edwin Landseer's *Death of a Stag in Glen Tilt* (1850) was painted nearby.

In 1844 Queen Victoria vis-ited the castle and conferred on its owners, the Dukes of Atholl, the distinction of being allowed to maintain a private army. The Atholl Highlanders still flourish.

The Cairngorms ㉓

See pp544–5.

Glencoe ㉔

Highland. ⬛ Fort William. 🚌 Glencoe. ℹ Visit Scotland (01397 703781).

Renowned for its awesome scenery and savage history, Glencoe was compared by Dickens to "a burial ground of a race of giants". The precip-itous cliffs of Buachaille Etive Mor and the knife-edged ridge of Aonach Eagach (both over 900 m; 3,000 ft) present a formidable challenge even to experienced mountaineers.

Against a dark backdrop of craggy peaks and the tumb-ling River Coe, the Glen offers superb hill-walking in the summer. Stout footwear, waterproofs and attention to safety warnings are essential. Details of routes, ranging from the easy half-hour between the **NTS Visitor Centre** and Signal Rock (from which the signal was given to commence the massacre) to a stiff 6 mile (10 km) haul up the Devil's Staircase can be had from the Visitor Centre. Guided walks are offered in summer by the NTS Ranger service.

ℹ NTS Visitor Centre
Glencoe. **Tel** 01855 811307. ◯ daily. 🏷 ♿ limited.

THE MASSACRE OF GLENCOE

In 1692, the chief of the Glencoe MacDonalds was five days late in registering an oath of submission to William III, giving the government an excuse to root out a nest of Jacobite (p537) supporters. For ten days 130 soldiers, cap-tained by Robert Campbell, were hospitably entertained by the unsuspecting MacDonalds. At dawn on 13 February, in a terrible breach of trust, the soldiers fell on their hosts, killing some 38 MacDonalds. Many more died in their wintry mountain hideouts. The mas-sacre, unsurprisingly, became a political scandal, though there were to be no official reprimands for three years.

Detail of The Massacre of Glencoe by James Hamilton

The Cairngorms ㉒

Wild goat

Rising to a height of 1,309 m (4,296 ft), the Cairngorm mountains form the highest landmass in Britain. Cairn Gorm itself is the site of one of Britain's first ski centres. A weather station at the mountain's summit provides regular reports, essential in an area known for sudden changes of weather. Walkers should be sure to follow the mountain code without fail. The funicular railway that climbs Cairn Gorm affords superb views over the Spey Valley. Many estates in the valley have centres which introduce the visitor to Highland land use.

Strathspey Steam Railway
This track between Aviemore and Broomhill dates from 1863.

Aviemore, the commercial centre of the Cairngorms, provides buses to the ski area 13 km (9 miles) away.

INVERNESS
A 938 Carrbridge
B9153
Boat of Gar
Aviemore
Coylu
Beanaidh
A9 B9152 Spey LOCH AN EILEIN
Kincraig
LOCH INSH
Feshie
BRAERIA 1,295 m (4,248 f)
LOCH EINICH
Kingussie
NEWTONMORE
B970
PERTH
Tolvah

0 kilometres 5
0 miles 5

Kincraig Highland Wildlife Park
Driving through this park, the visitor can see bison alongside wolves and wild boar. All of these animals were once common in the Highlands.

The Cairngorms by Aviemore

Rothiemurchus Estate
Highland cattle can be seen among many other creatures at Rothiemurchus. A visitor centre provides guided walks and illustrates life on a Highland estate.

Loch Garten Nature Reserve

Ospreys now thrive in this reserve in Abernethy Forest, which was established in 1959 to protect the first pair seen in Britain for 50 years.

GRANTOWN-ON-SPEY

Broomhill

Nethy Bridge

A 95

B970

HITEN

The **Cairngorm Reindeer Centre** provides walks in the hills among Britain's only herd of reindeer.

Nethy

HIICH

P

CAIRN GORM
1,245 m
(4,084 ft)

Skiing
From the Coire Cas car park, a funicular railway can be taken to the restaurant at the summit. There are 28 ski runs in all.

BEN MACDHUI
1,309 m
(4,296 ft)

CAIRNGORM
MOUNTAINS

Ben MacDhui is Britain's second highest peak, after Ben Nevis.

KEY

🛈	Tourist information
▬▬	Major road
▭▭	Minor road
▭▭	Narrow lane
- -	Footpath
☀	Viewpoint

VISITORS' CHECKLIST

The Highlands. 🚆 🚍 *Aviemore.* 🛈 *Grampian Rd, Aviemore (0845-225 5121).* **Cairngorm Reindeer Centre**, *Loch Morlich.* **Tel** *01479 861228.* ☐ *daily.* 📷 **Kincraig Highland Wildlife Park. Tel** *01540 651270.* ☐ *daily (weather permitting).* **Rothiemurchus Visitor Centre**, *near Aviemore.* **Tel** *01479 812345.* ☐ *daily.* **Loch Garten Nature Reserve. Tel** *01479 821409.* ☐ *daily.* **Skiing Tel** *01479 861261.*

FLORA OF THE CAIRNGORMS

With mixed woodland at their base and the summits forming a sub-polar plateau, the Cairngorms present a huge variety of flora. Ancient Caledonian pines (once common in the area) survive in Abernethy Forest, while arctic flowers flourish in the heights.

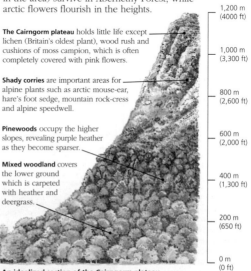

The Cairngorm plateau holds little life except lichen (Britain's oldest plant), wood rush and cushions of moss campion, which is often completely covered with pink flowers.

Shady corries are important areas for alpine plants such as arctic mouse-ear, hare's foot sedge, mountain rock-cress and alpine speedwell.

Pinewoods occupy the higher slopes, revealing purple heather as they become sparser.

Mixed woodland covers the lower ground which is carpeted with heather and deergrass.

1,200 m (4000 ft)
1,000 m (3,300 ft)
800 m (2,600 ft)
600 m (2,000 ft)
400 m (1,300 ft)
200 m (650 ft)
0 m (0 ft)

An idealized section of the Cairngorm plateau

Road to the Isles Tour ㉕

This scenic route goes past vast mountain-corridors, breathtaking beaches of white sand and tiny villages, to the town of Mallaig, one of the ferry ports for the isles of Skye, Rum and Eigg. As well as the stunning scenery, the area is steeped in Jacobite history *(see p537)*.

(see p537)

TIPS FOR DRIVERS

Tour length: 45 miles (72 km).
Stopping-off points: Glenfinnan NTS Visitors' Centre (01397 722 250) explains the Jacobite risings and serves refreshments; the Old Library Lodge, Arisaig, has good Scottish food. (See also pp684–5.)

Mallaig ⑦
The Road to the Isles ends at Mallaig, an active little fishing port with a very good harbour and one of the ferry links to Skye *(see pp534–5)*.

Morar ⑥
The road continues through Morar, an area renowned for its white sands, and Loch Morar, rumoured to be the home of a 12 m (40 ft) monster known as Morag.

Prince's Cairn ⑤
Crossing the Ardnish Peninsula to Loch Nan Uamh, a cairn marks the spot from which Bonnie Prince Charlie finally left Scotland for France in 1746.

Oban ㉖

Argyll & Bute. 8,500. Argyll Sq (01631 563122). www.oban.org.uk

Located on the Firth of Lorne and commanding a magnificent view of the Argyll coast, the bustling port of Oban is a popular destination for travellers on their way to Mull and the Western Isles *(see p529)*.

Dominating the skyline is McCaig's Tower, an unfinished Victorian imitation of the Colosseum in Rome. It is worth making the 10-minute climb from the town centre for the sea views alone. Attractions in the town include working centres for glass, pottery and whisky; the Oban distillery produces one of the country's finest malt whiskies *(see p489)*. The **Scottish Sealife Sanctuary** rescues injured and orphaned seals and has displays of underwater life. A busy harbour shelters car ferries going to Barra and South Uist, Mull, Tiree and Colonsay islands.

🏛 Scottish Sealife Sanctuary
Barcaldine. **Tel** 01631 720386. ○ daily. ● 25 Dec, 1 Jan. 🎟 🚻
🖥 www.sealsanctuary.co.uk

Mull ㉗

Argyll & Bute. 2,800. from Oban, Kilchoan, Lochaline. Main Street, Tobermory (01688 302182).

Most roads on this easily accessible Hebridean island follow the sharply indented rocky coastline, affording wonderful sea views. From Craignure, the Mull and West Highland Railway serves the baronial **Torosay Castle**. A pathway through its gardens is lined with statues, while inside, 19th-century furniture and paintings can be found. On a promontory to the east lies **Duart Castle**, home of the chief of Clan Maclean. Visitors can see the Banqueting Hall and State Rooms in the 13th-century keep. Its dungeons once held prisoners from a Spanish Armada galleon sunk by a Donald Maclean in 1588.

Looking out to sea across Tobermory Bay, Mull

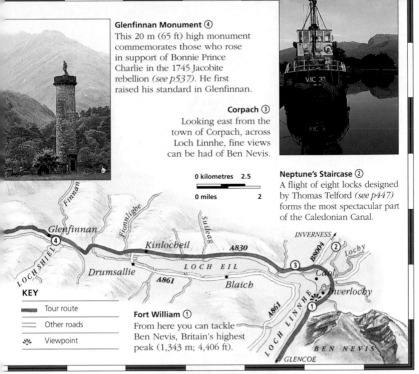

Glenfinnan Monument ④
This 20 m (65 ft) high monument commemorates those who rose in support of Bonnie Prince Charlie in the 1745 Jacobite rebellion *(see p537)*. He first raised his standard in Glenfinnan.

Corpach ③
Looking east from the town of Corpach, across Loch Linnhe, fine views can be had of Ben Nevis.

Neptune's Staircase ②
A flight of eight locks designed by Thomas Telford *(see p447)* forms the most spectacular part of the Caledonian Canal.

KEY

━━━ Tour route

═══ Other roads

⟋ Viewpoint

Fort William ①
From here you can tackle Ben Nevis, Britain's highest peak (1,343 m; 4,406 ft).

Environs: From Fionnphort, a ferry goes to **Iona**, where St Columba *(see p525)* began his mission in Scotland in 563. North of Iona, the Isle of Staffa should be visited for its magnificent **Fingal's Cave**.

⛪ **Torosay Castle**
Off A849, Nr Craignure. *Tel 01680 812421.* **Castle** ☐ *Easter–Oct: daily.* **Gardens** ☐ *Apr–Sep: 9am–7pm; Oct–Mar: dawn–dusk; daily.* 🖼 ♿ 🎫 *for groups.*

⛪ **Duart Castle**
Off A849, nr Craignure. *Tel 01680 812309.* ☐ *Apr–Oct: 10:30am–5:30pm daily.* 🖼

The ruins of Kilchurn Castle on the shore of Loch Awe

Loch Awe ㉘

Argyll & Bute. 🚤 🚉 *Dalmally.* 🛈 *Inveraray (01499 302063).*

One of the longest of Scotland's freshwater lochs, Loch Awe fills a 25 mile (40 km) glen in the southwestern Highlands. A short drive east of the village of Lochawe leads to the lochside remains of **Kilchurn Castle**, which was abandoned after being struck by lightning in the 18th century. Dwarfing the castle is the huge bulk of Ben Cruachan, whose summit can be reached by the narrow Pass of Brander, in which Robert the Bruce *(see p482)* fought the Clan MacDougal in 1308. From the A85, a tunnel leads to the cavernous Cruachan Power Station.

Near the village of Taynuilt the preserved Lorn Furnace at Bonawe is a reminder of the iron-smelting industry that caused the destruction of much of the area's woodland in the 18th and 19th centuries.

Marked prehistoric cairns are found off the A816 between Kilmartin and Dunadd. The latter boasts a 6th-century hill fort from which the Stone of Destiny *(see p482)* originated.

Inveraray Castle ㉙

Inveraray, Argyll & Bute. 🚃 Arrochar, then bus. **Tel** 01499 302203. ☐ Apr & May, Oct: 10am–5.45pm Sat–Thu (closed 1–2pm; Sun open from 1pm); Jun–Sep: 10am–5.45pm daily (Sun pm only); last adm 5pm. 🅿️ 🚻 limited. 📷 ▢ 🏠 **www**.inveraray-castle.com

This multi-turreted mock Gothic palace is the family home of the powerful Clan Campbell who have been the Dukes of Argyll since 1701. The castle was built in 1745 by architects Roger Morris and William Adam on the ruins of a 15th-century castle, and the conical towers added later, after a fire in 1877. Magnificent interiors, designed by Robert Mylne in the 1770s, form a backdrop to a huge collection of Oriental and European porcelain and Regency furniture and portraits by Ramsay, Gainsborough and Raeburn. The Armoury Hall features a display of weaponry collected by the Campbells to fight the Jacobites (see p537).

Auchindrain Museum ㉚

Inveraray, Argyll & Bute. **Tel** 01499 500235. 🚌 Inveraray, then bus. ☐ Apr–Sep: 10am–5pm daily. 🅿️ 🚻 limited. **www**.auchindrainmuseum.org.uk

The first open-air museum in Scotland, Auchindrain illuminates the working lives of the kind of farming community that was typical of the Highlands until the late 19th century. Originally a township of some 20 thatched buildings, the site was communally farmed by its tenants until the last one retired in 1962. Visitors can wander through the buildings,

The pinnacled, Gothic exterior of Inveraray Castle

many of which combine living space, kitchen and cattle shed under one roof. Some are furnished with box beds and old rush lamps. The homes of Auchindrain are a fascinating memorial to the time before the transition from of subsistence to commercial farming.

An old hay turner at the Auchindrain Museum

Crarae Gardens ㉛

Crarae, Argyll & Bute. **Tel** 01546 886614 or NTS (01852 200366). 🚌 Inveraray, then bus. ☐ 9:30am–sunset daily. **Visitor Centre** ☐ Easter–Sep 10am–5pm daily. 🅿️ 🚻 limited.

Considered the most beguiling of the gardens of the West Highlands, the **Crarae Gardens** were created in the 1920s by Lady Grace Campbell. She was the aunt of explorer Reginald Farrer, whose specimens from Tibet were the beginnings of a collection of exotic plants. The gardens are nourished by the warmth of the Gulf

Stream and the high rainfall. Although there are many unusual Himalayan rhododendrons flourishing here, the gardens are also home to exotic plants from various countries including Tasmania, New Zealand and the USA. Plant collectors still contribute to the gardens, which are best seen in spring and early summer against the blue waters of Loch Fyne.

Jura ㉜

Argyll & Bute. 🏠 200. 🚢 from Kennacraig to Islay, then Islay to Jura. ℹ️ Bowmore (01496 810254).

Barren, mountainous and overrun by red deer, the isle of Jura has only one road which connects the single village of Craighouse to the Islay ferry. Though walking is restricted during the stalking (deer hunting) season between August and October, the island offers superb hillwalking, especially on the slopes of the three main peaks, known as the Paps of Jura. The tallest of these is Beinn An Oir at 784 m (2571 ft). Beyond the northern tip of the isle are the notorious whirlpools of Corryvreckan. The novelist George Orwell (who came to the island to write his final novel, 1984) nearly lost his life here in 1946 when he fell into the water. A legend tells

Lagavulin distillery, producer of one Scotland's finest malts, on Islay

Mist crowning the Paps of Jura, seen at sunset across the Sound of Islay

of Prince Breackan who, to win the hand of a princess, tried to keep his boat anchored in the whirlpool for three days, held by ropes made of hemp, wool and maidens' hair. The Prince drowned when a single rope, containing the hair of a girl who had been untrue, finally broke.

Islay ③③

Argyll & Bute. 🦌 *3,500.* 🚢 *from Kennacraig.* 🛈 *The Square, Bowmore (0870 7200617).* **www**.isle-of-islay.com

The most southerly of the Western Isles, Islay (pronounced 'Eyeluh') is the home of respected Highland single malt whiskies Lagavulin and Laphroaig. Most of the island's distilleries produce heavily peated malts with a distinctive tang of the sea. The Georgian village of Bowmore has the island's oldest distillery and a circular church designed to minimize the Devil's possible lurking-places. The **Museum of Islay Life** in Port Charlotte contains fascinating information on social and natural history. Seven miles (11 km) east of Port Ellen stands the Kildalton Cross. A block of local green stone adorned with Old Testament scenes, it is one of the most impressive 8th-

century Celtic crosses in Britain. Worth a visit for its archaeological and historical interest is the medieval stronghold of the Lords of the Isles, **Finlaggan**. Islay's beaches support a variety of bird life, some of which can be observed at the RSPB reserve at Gruinart.

🏛 **Museum of Islay Life**
Port Charlotte. **Tel** *01496 850358.*
⬜ *Easter–Oct: 10am–5pm Mon–Sat, 2–5pm Sun.* 🎫 ♿

Kintyre ③④

Argyll & Bute. 🦌 *6,000.* ✈ *Oban.* 🚢 *Campbeltown.* 🛈 *MacKinnon House, The Pier, Campbeltown (01586 552056).* **www**.kintyre.org

A long, narrow peninsula stretching far south of Glasgow, Kintyre has superb views across to the islands of Gigha, Islay and Jura. The 9 mile (14 km) Crinan Canal,

opened in 1801, is a delightful inland waterway, its 15 locks bustling with pleasure craft in the summer. The town of Tarbert (meaning "isthmus" in Gaelic) takes its name from the neck on which it stands, which is narrow enough to drag a boat across between Loch Fyne and West Loch Tarbert. This feat was first achieved by the Viking King Magnus Barfud who, in 1198, was granted by treaty as much land as he could sail around. Travelling south past Campbeltown, the B842 ends at the headland known as the Mull of Kintyre, which was made famous when former Beatle Paul McCartney commercialized a traditional pipe tune of the same name. Westward lies the isle of Rathlin, where Robert the Bruce *(see p482)* learned patience in his struggles against the English by watching a spider weaving a web in a cave.

Fishing boats and yachts moored at Tarbert harbour, Kintyre

TRAVELLERS'
NEEDS

WHERE TO STAY

Hotel doorman, London

Whatever your budget or accommodation preferences, you should be able to find somewhere to suit you from the large choice given in the hotel listings section that follows *(see pp556–99)*. The listings include over 500 suggestions, ranging from palatial five-star establishments to humble guest-houses. The common factor in this selection is that they are all good of their kind, offering distinctive character or exceptional qualities of hospitality, facilities or value for money. Location is another prime consideration for inclusion. All the hotels and guesthouses listed make convenient touring bases for one or more of the destinations featured in this book, or have attractive or interesting settings enjoyable in their own right. On the next few pages we outline some of the types of accommodation available in Britain, along with various aspects of choosing, booking and payng for somewhere to stay.

COUNTRY-HOUSE HOTELS

The quintessentially British country-house hotel has proliferated in the last few decades. Many indifferent hotels try to claim the title with a cursory decorative makeover, but the genuine article stands head and shoulders above them. Individual examples vary widely, but the best country-house hotels are usually set in buildings of architectural or historic interest filled with antiques or high-quality traditional furnishings. They generally have extensive grounds, but are not always in deeply rural locations. Comfort, even luxury, is assured, along with good food and service – frequently with a high price tag. Many such hotels are still owned and personally managed by resident proprietors; others belong to groups or chains.

BOUTIQUE AND DESIGNER HOTELS

There is a new breed of sophisticated, contemporary hotel that has been making waves in Britain for some years now. These ultra-cool temples of style revel in innovative architecture, funky décor and hip high-tech gadgetry. Most exude an air of uncluttered minimalism, and some have outstanding restaurants. The best-known examples are perhaps in London (the Metropolitan, *p557*, for instance, or the Sanderson, *p558*), but they can be found elsewhere too, usually in city centres. Trendsetting, upmarket microchains like **Malmaison** or **Hotel du Vin** could perhaps be included in this category. Most of these hotels are expensive, but facilities, furnishings, service and privacy justify the cost.

Atholl Palace Hotel *(see p599)*

HOTEL GROUPS

New hotel groups have taken the place of many of the long-established names, providing reliably standardized accommodation at all price levels in most parts of Britain. The majority of chain hotels (operated by the same company under identical corporate branding) lie in accessible, convenient locations. Though lacking in much individuality, they are practical and efficiently run, and usually represent good value for money.

Budget chains offering no-frills, motel-lodge-style accommodation include **Ibis**, **Travelodge** and **Premier Travel Inn**; further up the scale are mid-market chains like **Holiday Inn** or **Novotel.** Chain-hotel rates generally don't include breakfast, but look out for inclusive leisure-

Buckland Manor *(see p576)*, Worcestershire

◁ **The 11th-century ruins of Corfe Castle, Dorset**

The Swan at Lavenham, Suffolk *(see p565)*, a converted coaching inn

break rates at pricier chains like **Moat House**.

Hotel consortiums – groups of similar but individually owned hotels which market themselves under the same umbrella – include **Best Western** and **Pride of Britain**. There's also **Wolsey Lodges**, a group of private houses, many beautifully furnished and often sited in buildings of notable architectural or historic interest.

INNS AND PUBS WITH ROOMS

The coaching inn is a familiar concept in Britain. Many of these fine old hostelries date from the 18th century, though some are even older, such as The George of Stamford *(see p580)*, and often provide reliable restaurants, traditional décor and a warm and friendly atmosphere.

Other types of pub or inn now offer accommodation and reputable food, and many have become much more welcoming to families. Britain's best inns are very comfortable and stylish and bear comparison with any good hotel. Some budget hotel chains, such as the already mentioned Premier Travel Inn, specialize in adding purpose-built accommodation blocks to existing branded dining pubs like Beefeater or Vintage Inns.

BED-AND-BREAKFASTS AND GUEST HOUSES

The B&B is probably the best-known and certainly the most widely used type of budget accommodation in Britain. These establishments are generally family-owned private homes or farmhouses. Accommodation and facilities tend to be simple (bedrooms may not have TV, telephones, or en-suite bathrooms, for instance), but the best can be quite sophisticated. Prices include breakfast (generally a traditional British fry-up, but other options are usually available as well).

Many B&Bs are reluctant to accept credit cards or travellers' cheques, or may charge a premium for doing so. It's advisable to have some alternative method of payment, preferably cash or, for British residents, a personal cheque backed by a cheque guarantee card. Any regional tourist office should be able to supply a list of local registered B&Bs on request, though they cannot make specific recommend-ations, and may charge a fee or a commission for making bookings on your behalf.

HOTEL GRADINGS

Recent but only partially successful attempts have been made to harmonize the confusing and often conflicting systems of accommodation classification used by the various tourist boards and motoring organizations, such as the AA and RAC. In England, hotel gradings are now based on a system of one to five stars awarded for facilities and service (the more stars, the more luxurious you can expect your hotel to be). Guesthouses and B&Bs are graded with one to five diamonds, a quality score which is based on various aspects of the accommo-dation, including cleanliness and hospitality. Special awards (gold and silver, ribbons, rosettes, eggcups, etc) are given for excellence in certain categories, such as an exceptional breakfast or a warm welcome. Scotland and Wales have their own quality-based gradings.

Hintlesham Hall, Suffolk *(see p564)*

PRICES AND BOOKINGS

Make sure you understand clearly what terms you are being offered when you book. Some hotels just quote room rates, others quote a B&B or half board (dinner, bed and breakfast) rate per person. Rates are generally inclusive of VAT and service but some top-range hotels make additional charges; most charge hefty single-person supplements.

Prices in London start at around £80 per night for a standard en-suite double room, including breakfast, but could be well over £200 (without breakfast) at the top end of the scale. Outside London, prices tend to be cheaper, starting from around £60 for an en-suite double

The folly of Doyden Castle, Cornwall, now a National Trust holiday cottage

The elegant hallway of the Gore Hotel in London (see p560)

with breakfast. Bed-and-breakfast accommodation outside London starts from around £35 per person per night (though prices vary seasonally and regionally). Farm guesthouses (which often include dinner) can be very good value, at around £30 for half board per person.

Most hotels request confirmation in writing and a deposit in advance (a credit card number will generally do). E-mail bookings are now commonplace, and some hotels have an on-line booking facility. Websites are usually updated more often than hotel brochures and tariffs. Business or chain hotels often give big discounts; contact central reservations as well as the hotel

itself to see which one will give you the best deal. Sometimes it is also possible to negotiate a discount during the low season.

Any hotel booking is a legally binding contract. If you don't show up, the full cost of your stay may be charged. Most hotels will refund your deposit if they are able to relet the room, but some will charge a penalty, depending how close to your stay you cancel. Most travel insurance policies cover cancellation charges for pre-booked UK hotel stays of more than two days, if you have a satisfactory reason.

Watch out for those hidden extras. Telephone charges from hotel rooms have a high mark-up, and rates quoted per unit do not always indicate too clearly how much time you get for your money. Consider using a lobby payphone instead.

Roadside signboard for bed-and-breakfast

Certain chains have a regrettable policy of charging meals or other extras to your credit card weeks after you have left the hotel; check your card statement carefully.

There is no need to tip staff unless they go out of their way to perform some very exceptional duty, such as booking theatre tickets or restaurants for you.

SELF CATERING

Self catering has many attractions, especially for families on a budget and with young children. Tourist boards give accommodation a one to five star rating for quality and facilities, much the same as for hotels. The range of places to let for holiday rentals is huge, from luxury apartments to log cabins or converted farm buildings. Character properties are available from conservation organizations such as the **Landmark Trust**, which restores buildings of historic or architectural interest and makes them available for short-term lets, or the **National Trust** (see p29), which has a number of holiday cottages on its estates. They tend to be very popular, so book well ahead.

Annually updated self-catering guides are a useful source of listings. Also try specialist agencies, tour operators and the small ads in newspapers. Tourist offices can supply up-to-date regional lists and can also offer a booking service.

Confirm what is included in the price (cleaning, electricity, etc.) and check whether any extra fees, deposits or insurance charges will be added to the bill.

CARAVANNING, CAMPING AND MOTOR HOMES

Most of Britain's campsites and caravan (trailer) parks open only for about six months of the year (typically from Easter to October), but you will need to make reservations in advance. Helpful organizations in Britain include the **Camping and Caravanning Club** and the Caravan Club, which publish lists of their member parks and operate their own grading systems.

Camping or caravanning pitches typically cost between £10 and £15 per night. The **Forestry Commission** operates a number of sites in scenic woodland locations throughout the UK.

Motor homes give greater freedom to explore at your own pace and a wider choice of places to stay – including most campsites and caravan parks. Some operators will let you pick up your vehicle directly from an airport or ferry terminal. The **Motor Caravanners' Club** produces a useful monthly magazine.

Campsite, Ogwen Valley, Snowdonia

DISABLED TRAVELLERS

All the UK's tourist boards now provide detailed information about disabled access in their accommodation and sight-seeing guides, and can send further information on request. National Accessible Scheme gradings are awarded to properties inspected and approved under the Tourism for All initiative for various categories of disability.

For more information on these gradings, or other advice on accommodation and travel for disabled visitors, contact **Holiday Care**. Another useful organization is **RADAR** (the Royal Association for Disability and Rehabilitation), which publishes a yearly *Holidays in the British Isles: A Guide for Disabled People*. The listings on pp556–99 indicate which hotels have wheelchair access, but you are strongly advised to check when booking that it matches your needs. The same is true of camping and caravan sites.

DIRECTORY

For more useful tips on all different types of accommodation, see **www.visitbritain.com**

HOTELS

Accor Hotels
(Ibis, Novotel)
Tel 020-8237 7474.
www.accorhotels.com

Best Western
Tel 08454 567050.
www.bestwestern.co.uk

Hilton International
Tel 0870 590 9090.
www.hilton.co.uk

Holiday Inn
Tel 01962 841414.
www.holiday-inn.co.uk

Hotel du Vin
Tel 01962 850676.
www.hotelduvin.com

Malmaison
Tel 08453 654247.
www.malmaison.com

Moathouse
www.moathousehotels.com
Tel 01708 730 522.

Premier Travel Inn
www.premiertravelinn.com

Pride of Britain
Tel 0870-609 3012.
www.prideofbritainhotels.com

Travelodge
www.travelodge.co.uk

Wolsey Lodges
Tel 01473 822058.
www.wolsey-lodges.co.uk

CARAVANNING, CAMPING AND MOTOR HOMES

Camping and Caravanning Club
Westwood Way, Coventry, West Midlands, CV4 8JH.
Tel 0247 669 4995.
www.campingandcaravanningclub.co.uk

Forestry Commission
231 Corstorphine Road, Edinburgh, EH12 7AT.
Tel 0131 334 0303.
www.forestry.gov.uk

Motor Caravanners' Club
Freepost, TK1292 Twickenham TW2 5BR.
Tel 020-8893 3883.
www.motorcaravanners.org.uk

SELF-CATERING

Landmark Trust
Shottesbrooke, Maidenhead, Berkshire SL6 3SW.
Tel 01628 825925.
www.landmarktrust.org.uk

National Trust
PO Box 39, Bromley, Kent BR1 3XL.
Tel 0870 458 4000.
www.nationaltrust.org.uk

National Trust for Scotland
Wemyss Hse, 28 Charlotte Square, Edinburgh EH2 4ET.
Tel 0131 243 9300.
www.nts.org.uk

Snowdonia Tourist Services
High Street, Porthmadog, Gwynedd LL49 9PG.
Tel 01766 513829.
www.sts-holidays.com

DISABLED TRAVELLERS

Holiday Care
7th flr, Sunley Hse, 4 Bedford Pk, Croydon CR0 2AP.
Tel 0845 124 9971.
www.holidaycare.org.uk

RADAR
Unit 12, City Forum, 250 City Road, London, EC1V 8AF.
Tel 020-7250 3222.
www.radar.org.uk

Choosing a Hotel

The hotels in this guide have been selected across
a wide price range for their excellent, facilities, good
value and location. Many also have a recommended
restaurant. The chart lists the hotels by region, starting
with London. For more details on restaurants see
pages 608–651.

PRICE CATEGORIES
For a standard double room per night,
inclusive of service charge and any
additional taxes such as VAT:

£ under £65
££ £65–£100
£££ £100–£150
££££ £150–£200
£££££ £200 plus

LONDON

WEST END AND WESTMINSTER Dover Hotel £££
42–44 Belgrave Rd, SW1 **Tel** *020 7821 9085* **Fax** *020 7834 6425* **Rooms** *34*　　　　**Map** *18 F2*

This well-maintained hotel is terrific value for money. It may not be luxurious once past the grand stucco façade,
but the decor is refreshingly modern and every room has satellite TV and pristine en suite shower and WC.
It's handy for Victoria Station and Pimlico's many pubs and cafés. **www.dover-hotel.co.uk**

WEST END AND WESTMINSTER Citadines Covent Garden/Holborn £££
94–99 High Holborn, WC1 **Tel** *020 7395 8800* **Fax** *0207 395 8799* **Rooms** *192*　　　　**Map** *11 C1*

This centrally located branch of the French apart'hotel chain offers pleasant, good-value accommodation for
up to four people. Studios or one-bedroom apartments have kitchenettes, dining tables, satellite TVs and hi-fis.
There are also handy business facilities and an on-site breakfast room. **www.citadines.com**

WEST END AND WESTMINSTER Elizabeth Hotel and Apartments £££
37 Eccleston Square, SW1 **Tel** *020 7828 6812* **Fax** *020 7828 6814* **Rooms** *37 & 5 apartments*　　　**Map** *18 E2*

The rates are surprisingly reasonable in this elegant town house hotel on a grand garden square, Winston Churchill
used to live a couple of doors down. Rooms are simple yet tastefully furnished and guests have access to the private
gardens and stately drawing room with newspapers, tea, coffee and biscuits. **www.elizabethhotel.com**

WEST END AND WESTMINSTER City Inn Westminster £££££
30 John Islip St, SW1 **Tel** *020 7630 1000* **Fax** *020 7233 7575* **Rooms** *460*　　　　**Map** *19 B2*

Around the corner from Tate Britain, City Inn is unpretentiously modern. Rooms have floor-to-ceiling windows,
some of which command Thames views, and luxuries such as robes, flatscreen TVs and DVD players. There's a
red cocktail lounge and café with outside tables. Enquire about cheap weekend deals. **www.cityinn.com**

WEST END AND WESTMINSTER Claridges £££££
Brook St, W1 **Tel** *020 7629 8860* **Fax** *020 7499 2210* **Rooms** *203*　　　　**Map** *10 E2*

Favoured by the European aristocracy in the 19th century, Empress Eugènie wintered here. Nowadays it attracts
show business *glitterati* and business clients alike. Rooms range from Victorian to contemporary by way of fabulous
Art Deco suites. Gordon Ramsay's fêted restaurant and a smart bar are further draws. **www.claridges.co.uk**

WEST END AND WESTMINSTER Covent Garden Hotel £££££
10 Monmouth St, WC2 **Tel** *020 7806 1000* **Fax** *020 7806 1100* **Rooms** *58*　　　　**Map** *11 B2*

This exquisite hotel's Covent Garden location is one reason why it's popular with thespians. Part of the Firmdale
chain, it is decorated in contemporary-English style with antiques and fresh fabrics. Brasserie Max is a popular
meeting spot and films are shown in the luxurious screening room at weekends. **www.firmdalehotels.com**

WEST END AND WESTMINSTER Metropolitan £££££
Old Park Lane, W1 **Tel** *020 7447 1047* **Fax** *020 7447 1147* **Rooms** *150*　　　　**Map** *10 D3*

The Metropolitan redefined the London luxury hotel when it opened in 1997 and its blond wood, pale fabrics and
large plate-glass windows still epitomise modern chic. With holistic spa treatments, a top Japanese restaurant
upstairs and entry to the exclusive Met Bar, you won't have to stray far. **www.metropolitan.co.uk**

WEST END AND WESTMINSTER One Aldwych £££££
1 Aldwych, WC2 **Tel** *020 7300 1000* **Fax** *020 7300 1001* **Rooms** *105*　　　　**Map** *11 C2*

A grand contemporary hotel in former Edwardian newspaper offices. Impressive details include original art and
tarazzo-stone bathrooms with heated floors and mini TVs. There's a spacious health club with a swimming pool,
several trendy restaurants and the buzzing, high-ceilinged Lobby Bar. **www.onealdwych.com**

WEST END AND WESTMINSTER Radisson Edwardian Hampshire £££££
31–36 Leicester Square, WC2 **Tel** *020 7839 9399* **Fax** *020 7930 8122* **Rooms** *124*　　　　**Map** *11 B2*

Colourful, cinema-lined Leicester Square is a good base if you want to make the most of London's nightlife, as it's
well placed for the theatre district, bars, clubs and restaurants. This luxurious Radisson has designer bedrooms with
Philippe Starck bathrooms and Bose sound systems in the suites. **www.radissonedwardian.com**

Key to Symbols *see back cover flap*

WEST END AND WESTMINSTER Ritz

150 Piccadilly, W1 **Tel** *020 7493 8181* **Fax** *020 7493 2687* **Rooms** *133*

Map *10 F3*

There are two staff for every room in this famous grand hotel on the edge of Green Park. You can even have your luggage unpacked for you. Rooms are in lavish Louis XVI style with antique furnishings and gold leaf, plus all mod cons. The Rivoli Bar has been restored to its Art Deco splendour. **www.theritzlondon.com**

WEST END AND WESTMINSTER Savoy

Strand, WC2 **Tel** *020 7836 4343* **Fax** *020 7240 6040* **Rooms** *263*

Map *11 C2*

This legendary hotel was an afterthought, Richard D'Oyly Carte capitalized on the success of his Savoy Theatre by providing a place to stay. The rest is history. Monet painted the Thames view from his window, Elton John flooded a bathroom and the dry martini was invented in the bar. There's a rooftop pool as well. **www.fairmont.com/savoy**

WEST END AND WESTMINSTER The Connaught

Carlos Place, W1 **Tel** *020 7499 7070* **Fax** *020 7495 3262* **Rooms** *92*

Map *10 E3*

The Connaught maintains its traditional charm while moving with the times. Facilities include butler service and a state-of-the-art gym. The interior feels less stuffy since many of the public rooms, including the Grill and the Connaught Bar, were restyled by renowned designer Nina Campbell. **www.maybourne.com**

WEST END AND WESTMINSTER The Dorchester

Park Lane, W1 **Tel** *020 7629 8888* **Fax** *020 7409 0114* **Rooms** *250*

Map *10 D3*

The epitome of the glamorous luxury hotel, with an outrageously lavish lobby and a star-studded history, the Dorchester has recently been revamped but maintains its tasteful floral bedrooms. The Art Deco-style marble baths are probably the deepest in London. For even more pampering, pop down to the fabulous Art Deco spa. **www.thedorchester.com**

SOUTH KENSINGTON AND HYDE PARK Edward Lear

28–30 Seymour St, W1 **Tel** *020 7402 5401* **Fax** *020 7706 3766* **Rooms** *31*

Map *9 C2*

This characterful small hotel is in the former home of Victorian poet and artist Edward Lear. Rooms are tidy and spacious with satellite TVs. Opt for en suite or shared facilities to keep the cost down. There's a computer with free Internet access and leather seating in the pleasant guests' lounge. **www.edlear.com**

SOUTH KENSINGTON AND HYDE PARK Knightsbridge Green Hotel

159 Knightsbridge, SW1 **Tel** *020 7584 6274* **Fax** *020 7225 1635* **Rooms** *28*

Map *9 C5*

A shopaholic's dream, this well-kept hotel is right on Knightsbridge and rates are reasonable for more spending power in Harrods and Harvey Nichols. The tidy, modern rooms are regularly upgraded and feature air conditioning and satellite TVs. There's also a small business centre on-site. **www.thekghotel.com**

SOUTH KENSINGTON AND HYDE PARK The Capital Hotel

22–24 Basil St, SW3 **Tel** *020 7589 5171* **Fax** *020 7225 0011* **Rooms** *49*

Map *9 C5*

Situated between Harrods and Harvey Nichols, this service-oriented hotel even offers personal shoppers and jogging partners. Its Michelin two-starred restaurant has been refurbished in 1940s-influenced style. Bedrooms feature king-size beds, designer fabrics and the latest technology. **www.capitalhotel.co.uk**

SOUTH KENSINGTON AND HYDE PARK The Franklin Hotel

28 Egerton Gardens, SW3 **Tel** *020 7584 5533* **Fax** *020 7584 5449* **Rooms** *47*

Map *17 B1*

Occupying four 19th-century town houses in a quiet Knightsbridge Street, the Franklin creates the pleasant illusion of staying with an aristocratic relation. Rooms are decorated with antiques and fine English fabrics. Best of all are the large, secluded gardens at the back, shared with well-heeled residents. **www.franklinhotel.co.uk**

SOUTH KENSINGTON AND HYDE PARK The Halkin

Halkin St, SW1 **Tel** *020 7333 1000* **Fax** *020 7333 1100* **Rooms** *41*

Map *10 D5*

Modern comforts meet Eastern serenity at this gracious luxury hotel. Warm wood, curving lines and creamy bed linen are accented by Southeast Asian art handpicked by the Singaporean owner. Be sure to have a meal at Nahm, it's the only Michelin-starred Thai restaurant outside Thailand. **www.halkin.como.bz**

REGENT'S PARK AND BLOOMSBURY Hotel Cavendish

75 Gower St, WC1 **Tel** *020 7636 9079* **Fax** *020 7580 3609* **Rooms** *31*

Map *3 A5*

This characterful B&B near London University has a fascinating history, DH Lawrence and the Beatles stayed here once. Rooms are simple yet comfortably furnished, and some have original fireplaces. Original artworks brighten up the breakfast room and there's a pretty garden as well. Shared facilities available. **www.hotelcavendish.com**

REGENT'S PARK AND BLOOMSBURY Crescent Hotel

49–50 Cartwright Gardens, WC1 **Tel** *020 7387 1515* **Fax** *020 7383 2054* **Rooms** *27*

Map *3 B4*

One of several hotels in this striking Regency Street, the Crescent has been run by the same family since the 1950s. Most of the well-kept bedrooms have en suite facilities. Soft drinks and snacks are served in the lounge, and guests can use the tennis courts in the private gardens. **www.crescenthoteloflondon.com**

REGENT'S PARK AND BLOOMSBURY 22 York Street

22–24 York St, W1 **Tel** *020 7224 2990* **Fax** *020 7224 1990* **Rooms** *20*

Map *1 C5*

This beautiful property is a cut above most B&Bs. Liz and Michael Callis ensure that rooms in these two immaculately preserved Georgian houses are spotless and stylishly furnished with antiques and French quilts. A gourmet continental breakfast is served in the rustic kitchen. Non-smoking. **www.22yorkstreet.co.uk**

REGENT'S PARK AND BLOOMSBURY Euston Square Hotel

152–156 North Gower St, NW1 **Tel** *020 7388 0099* **Fax** *020 7383 7165* **Rooms** *75*   **Map** *3 A4*

A chic stopover close to Euston Station. Rooms may be on the small side, but they are stylishly kitted out in dark wood and cream leather, with flatscreen TVs, a music library and tasteful tiled bathrooms. Complimentary papers and squashy sofas are on offer in the airy lounge and there's also a restaurant. **www.euston-square-hotel.com**

REGENT'S PARK AND BLOOMSBURY Durrants Hotel

George St, W1 **Tel** *020 7935 8131* **Fax** *020 7487 3510* **Rooms** *92*   **Map** *10 D1*

Established in 1790, Durrants occupies a row of terraced houses and its warren of creaky rooms is delightfully old fashioned. Decor is traditional, old prints and antiques, but TVs are hidden in cabinets and bathrooms are modern. The restaurant and bar are period pieces. Only a few rooms are air conditioned. **www.durrantshotel.co.uk**

REGENT'S PARK AND BLOOMSBURY The Langham

1C Portland Place, W1 **Tel** *020 7636 1000* **Fax** *020 7323 2340* **Rooms** *427*   **Map** *10 E1*

The Langham was London's first grand hotel when it opened in 1865 and still offers an ultra-luxurious experience behind its sprawling Victorian façade. Rooms achieve a tasteful middle ground between modern and traditional and there are extensive spa facilities including a swimming pool. Near Regent's Park. **www.langhamhotels.com**

REGENT'S PARK AND BLOOMSBURY Charlotte Street Hotel

15–17 Charlotte St, W1 **Tel** *020 7806 2000* **Fax** *020 7806 2002* **Rooms** *52*   **Map** *11 A1*

The ground floor bar is always buzzing with local workers as well as guests in this exquisitely designed hotel in a street full of restaurants. Reflecting the area's history, its decor nods to the Bloomsbury Set period with original artworks by Vanessa Bell and others. Weekend films in the screening room. **www.charlottestreethotel.com**

REGENT'S PARK AND BLOOMSBURY Sanderson

50 Berners St, W1 **Tel** *020 7300 1400* **Fax** *020 7300 1401* **Rooms** *150*   **Map** *10 F1*

The Sanderson's witty decor, red lips sofa and a framed portrait that seems to hang in mid-air is like a surreal stage set. Rooms have every comfort, and the Alain Ducasse Spoon restaurant and two sophisticated cocktail bars are destinations in their own right. The Agua spa offers holistic pampering. **www.morganshotelgroup.com**

REGENT'S PARK AND BLOOMSBURY Sherlock Holmes Hotel

108 Baker St, W1 **Tel** *020 7486 6161* **Fax** *020 7958 5211* **Rooms** *119*   **Map** *1 C5*

The name may suggest a tacky theme hotel, yet this is anything but that. You enter this Baker Street boutique hotel via its stylish bar. Contemporary rooms, many with wooden floors, are softened with tactile throws and cushions; there are thoughtful details such as European and US sockets. The gym has spa facilities. **www.sherlockholmes.com**

THE CITY AND SOUTHWARK Travel Inn London County Hall

Belvedere Rd, SE1 **Tel** *0870 238 3300* **Fax** *020 7902 1619* **Rooms** *313*   **Map** *12 D5*

This branch of the budget premier Travel Inn chain is housed in the massive former County Hall on the Thames. The more expensive Marriott, which shares the building, has all the river views, but it's a good-value option next to the London Eye, near Waterloo and the South Bank arts complex. Wireless Internet on-site. **www.premiertravelinn.com**

THE CITY AND SOUTHWARK The Zetter

86–88 Clerkenwell Rd, EC1 **Tel** *020 7324 4444* **Fax** *020 7324 4445* **Rooms** *59*   **Map** *4 F4*

In an area known for its loft apartments, this is a loft hotel in a 19th-century warehouse. Rooms have exposed brick, quirky 1970s furniture, old Penguin books, hot-water bottles and high-tech extras, while vending machines on each floor dispense necessities. Hip-Italian restaurant at street level. **www.thezetter.com**

THE CITY AND SOUTHWARK Novotel London City South

53–61 Southwark Bridge Rd, SE1 **Tel** *020 7089 0400* **Fax** *020 7089 0410* **Rooms** *182*   **Map** *13 A3*

Billed as a "New Generation" Novotel, the interior has an airy, minimalist feel. Rooms are equipped with extras such as wireless Internet, minibar and even a radio in the bathroom. The fitness centre has a sauna and steam room, and the location is convenient for the venues and galleries of the South Bank. **www.novotel.com**

THE CITY AND SOUTHWARK Great Eastern

40 Liverpool St, EC2 **Tel** *020 7618 5000* **Fax** *020 7618 5001* **Rooms** *267*   **Map** *13 C1*

This magnificent 19th-century railway hotel was given a makeover by design guru Terence Conran, juxtaposing dramatic modern elements with the original-Victorian features. Cutting-edge art is displayed throughout, bedrooms are furnished with Eames and Jacobson pieces and there are five fabulous eateries. **www.great-eastern-hotel.co.uk**

THE CITY AND SOUTHWARK Rookery

Peter's Lane, Cowcross St, EC1 **Tel** *020 7336 0931* **Fax** *020 7336 0932* **Rooms** *33*   **Map** *4 F5*

Occupying six-Georgian houses and shops (with faded butcher's and baker's signs still visible on some), this Dickensian hideaway retains many original features, such as flagstone floors in the hall and ceiling beams in some of the rooms. Decorated with antiques throughout, it also offers all the latest technology. **www.rookeryhotel.com**

FURTHER AFIELD Fulham Guest House

55 Wandsworth Bridge Rd, SW6 **Tel** *020 7731 1662* **Rooms** *5*

Sam and George Doubledee run this friendly B&B from their Victorian home on a wide tree-lined street in affluent Fulham. Rooms are simple and comfortable and shared facilities are clean and up-to-date. The laid-back atmosphere makes it a good choice for families; children are very welcome and toys are available. **www.fulhamguesthouse.com**

Key to Price Guide *see p556* **Key to Symbols** *see back cover flap*

FURTHER AFIELD Stylotel

160–162 Sussex Gardens, W2 **Tel** 020 7723 1026 **Fax** 020 7262 2983 **Rooms** 40   *Map 9 A2*

Offering some of the cheapest rates in central London, Stylotel is true to its name, although the high-tech style may not suit all tastes. Rooms have wooden floors, aluminium walls, light-box bedside tables and futuristic bathrooms. There's a groovy lounge with curved stainless steel bar and blue leather seats. **www.stylotel.com**

FURTHER AFIELD Hampstead Village Guesthouse

2 Kemplay Rd, NW3 **Tel** 020 7435 8679 **Fax** 020 7794 0254 **Rooms** 9

This Victorian home, in the picturesque village of Hampstead, is intriguingly cluttered with antiques and curios. Breakfast is served in the garden in summer, English weather permitting. Rooms are equipped with hot-water bottles and fridge. The rates are cheaper if you forego en suite facilities. Non-smoking. **www.hampsteadguesthouse.com**

FURTHER AFIELD Mayflower Hotel

26–28 Trebovir Rd, SW5 **Tel** 020 7370 0991 **Fax** 020 7370 0994 **Rooms** 48   *Map 16 D2*

This beautifully furnished, budget-boutique hotel is a cut above the rest. The spacious, contemporary rooms have wooden floors and Eastern elements such as elaborately carved beds and rich silks. Marble bathrooms, ceiling fans and CD players are luxurious perks. There are also 35 tasteful apartments nearby. **www.mayflower-group.co.uk**

FURTHER AFIELD Pavilion Hotel

34–36 Sussex Gardens, W2 **Tel** 020 7262 0905 **Fax** 020 7262 1324 **Rooms** 30   *Map 9 A1*

The Pavilion's understated brick exterior may not stand out in this hotel-lined strip, but inside it's a world away from boring B&Bs. The fabulously themed rooms, from the rich panelling and tartan of "Highland Fling" to the antique Chinese chests and silks of "Enter the Dragon" are favoured by rock stars. **www.pavilionhoteluk.com**

FURTHER AFIELD Rushmore

11 Trebovir Rd, SW5 **Tel** 020 7370 3839 **Fax** 020 7370 0274 **Rooms** 22   *Map 15 C2*

Like the nearby Mayflower, the Rushmore is proof that accommodation doesn't have to be expensive to be stylish. Each room in this Victorian townhouse has been designed in a different style; even the bathrooms have been customized to fit in with the mood. Breakfast is served in a chic conservatory. **www.rushmore-hotel.co.uk**

FURTHER AFIELD Swiss House

171 Old Brompton Rd, SW5 **Tel** 020 7373 2769 **Fax** 020 7373 4983 **Rooms** 15   *Map 16 E3*

This charming, small hotel is especially good for families. Rooms are pretty without being fussy. Well placed for South Kensington's museums, the Swiss House prides itself on its child-friendly attitude and the concierge can suggest activities and restaurants geared towards kids. **www.swisshousehotel.com**

FURTHER AFIELD Guesthouse West

163–165 Westbourne Grove, W11 **Tel** 020 7792 9800 **Fax** 020 7792 9797 **Rooms** 20   *Map 7 C2*

Formerly the Westbourne, Guesthouse West is a budget-conscious design hotel in an Edwardian house. Minimalist dark wood and beige rooms boast high-tech entertainment systems and Molton Brown toiletries. The hip restaurant has terrace tables and Westbourne Grove's bars and boutiques are on the doorstep. **www.guesthousewest.com**

FURTHER AFIELD Mornington

12 Lancaster Gate, W2 **Tel** 020 7262 7361 **Fax** 020 7706 1028 **Rooms** 66   *Map 8 F2*

This formerly Swedish-owned hotel is now part of the quality Best Western chain. Bedrooms in the grand Victorian building near Hyde Park maintain a light, airy Scandinavian feel and a buffet smorgasbord-style breakfast caters to the many Swedish clientele. Inquire about special rates. **www.bw-morningtonhotel.co.uk**

FURTHER AFIELD Tophams

28 Ebury St, SW1 **Tel** 020 7730 8147 **Fax** 020 7823 5966 **Rooms** 51   *Map 18 E1*

Changes have been afoot at this endearingly eccentric hotel comprising five adjoining houses in an affluent street near Victoria Station. Formerly run by the Topham family since 1937, it has recently been bought by a British chain and has been extensively refurbished. There is a pleasant bar and brasserie. **www.zolahotels.com**

FURTHER AFIELD Aster House

3 Sumner Place, SW7 **Tel** 020 7581 5888 **Fax** 020 7584 4925 **Rooms** 13   *Map 17 A2*

Three-time winner of the Tourist Board's best B&B award, this friendly hotel in a grand white stucco house has immaculate bedrooms in a typical English-floral style. A superior breakfast served in the palm-filled conservatory and a pretty garden complete with pond and resident ducks attracts guests. **www.asterhouse.com**

FURTHER AFIELD Colonnade

2 Warrington Crescent, W9 **Tel** 020 7286 1052 **Fax** 020 7286 1057 **Rooms** 43

Near the picturesque canals of Little Venice, this hotel in two Victorian mansions has been operating since the 1930s. Freud stayed here while his house was being redecorated, and JFK paid a visit in the 1960s. The interior is grand yet unintimidating and every luxurious room has a different feel. **www.theetoncollection.com**

FURTHER AFIELD The Lennox

34 Pembridge Gardens, W2 **Tel** 020 7229 9977 **Fax** 020 7727 4982 **Rooms** 20   *Map 7 C3*

This elegant, detached 19th-century town house is furnished in a classic, modern style, and is situated in a quiet, residential location, which is handy for Portobello Road. Amenities include 24-hour room service for drinks and snacks, a mini business centre, and bar. **www.thelennox.com**

FURTHER AFIELD Sydney House

9–11 Sydney St, SW3 **Tel** *020 7376 7711* **Fax** *020 7376 4233* **Rooms** *21*

£££££ **Map** *17 A2*

This small hotel, steps away from the chic shops of Brompton Cross, was given a contemporary revamp in 2003. Airy rooms are furnished with blond wood furniture, Frette linen, contemporary art and thoughtful features such as American wall sockets and water softeners in the ultra-modern bathrooms. **www.sydneyhousechelsea.com**

FURTHER AFIELD The Petersham

Nightingale Lane, Richmond, Surrey, TW10 **Tel** *020 8940 7471* **Fax** *020 8939 1098* **Rooms** *61*

£££££

This sprawling Victorian hotel perches on Richmond Hill overlooking the Thames. The elegant rooms are in keeping with the building's period grandeur, while integrating modern elements; some have spectacular views of the Thames. Unsurprisingly given its romantic location, it is popular for weddings. **www.petershamhotel.co.uk**

FURTHER AFIELD The Portobello Hotel

22 Stanley Gardens, W11 **Tel** *020 7727 2777* **Fax** *020 7792 9641* **Rooms** *24*

£££££ **Map** *7 B2*

This divinely decadent Notting Hill mansion has lured rock royalty for over 30 years with its hip location and extravagantly decorated rooms. Choose from such exotic retreats as the serene Japanese room with private grotto garden and the notorious "Round Bed Room", with its freestanding Victorian bath. **www.portobello-hotel.co.uk**

FURTHER AFIELD The Royal Park

3 Westbourne Terrace, W2 **Tel** *020 7479 6600* **Fax** *020 7479 6601* **Rooms** *48*

£££££ **Map** *8 F2*

This new town house hotel near Hyde Park has a discreet luxury, which has attracted celebrity guests. Classic, unfussy rooms are furnished with exquisite fabrics, original prints and stone-tiled bathrooms. All the usual gadgetry, plus free afternoon tea and evening champagne in the gracious drawing room. **www.theroyalpark.com**

FURTHER AFIELD Blakes Hotel

33 Roland Gardens, SW7 **Tel** *020 7370 6701* **Fax** *020 7373 0442* **Rooms** *45*

££££££ **Map** *16 F2*

Blakes is the original "boutique hotel", created by designer Anouska Hempel over two decades ago. Rooms range in style from baronial manor to opulent Oriental and contain pieces collected on her travels. The discreet residential location has made it a favourite celebrity hideaway. Only some suites are air conditioned. **www.blakeshotels.com**

FURTHER AFIELD The Gore

190 Queen's Gate, SW7 **Tel** *020 7584 6601* **Fax** *020 7589 8127* **Rooms** *49*

££££££ **Map** *8 F5*

The Gore has been in operation for more than 110 years and, while it has recently been refurbished, it preserves the atmosphere of a bygone age. Rooms feature four-poster beds, framed pictures, luxurious draperies and opulent fabrics. There's a panelled bar and casual bistro as well. **www.gorehotel.co.uk**

FURTHER AFIELD The Milestone Hotel

1 Kensington Court, W8 **Tel** *020 7917 1000* **Fax** *020 7917 1010* **Rooms** *57 & 6 apartments*

££££££ **Map** *8 E5*

This plush hotel opposite Kensington Palace features originally designed rooms, from the smart "Savile Row" to the Colonial-style "Safari Suite". Extras include gym and resistance pool, broadband Internet and Penhaligon's toiletries, 24-hour butler and use of the hotel Bentley. **www.milestonehotel.com**

THE DOWNS AND CHANNEL COAST

BATTLE Fox Hole Farm

Kane Hythe Rd, Battle, Sussex, TN33 9QU **Tel** *01424 772053* **Fax** *01424 772053* **Rooms** *3*

£

A delightful retreat with just three rooms to let. Originally an 18th-century woodcutter's cottage, this gem has heavily beamed ceilings, an inglenook fireplace and everything else that makes an English country dream home. There's a large shrub and flower-filled garden. Non-smoking.

BEAULIEU Master Builders House

Bucklers Hard, Beaulieu, Hampshire, SO42 7XB **Tel** *01590 616253* **Fax** *01590 616297* **Rooms** *25*

£££££

Marketed by Distinguished Hotels, the Master Builders House stands on the creek where the famed "Hearts of Oak" ships of the Royal Navy were once built. It is on Lord Montagu's estate, which puts the National Motor Museum within minutes while the glorious New Forest is also at the doorstep. Breakfast included. **www.themasterbuilders.co.uk**

BRIGHTON Premier Travel Inn

144 North St, Brighton, East Sussex, BN1 1RE **Tel** *0870 990 6340* **Fax** *0870 990 6341* **Rooms** *160*

£

Finding clean, comfortable and, above all, affordable accommodation in the centre of bustling Brighton is no easy task, or wasn't until the Premier Travel Inn value hotel chain came to the rescue with this perfectly sited location. The Lanes *(see p175)* and the Royal Pavilion are just steps away. **www.premiertravelinn.com**

BRIGHTON De Vere Grand Brighton

Kings Rd, Brighton, East Sussex, BN1 2FW **Tel** *01273 224300* **Fax** *01273 224321* **Rooms** *200*

££££

Brighton's only five-star hotel, this is arguably the nation's finest big seaside hotel. There's a hair and beauty salon, an indoor swimming and spa pool, sauna, solarium, steam bath and gymnasium. The hotel's nightclub, Midnight Blues, opens on Friday and Saturday. Includes breakfast. **www.grandbrighton.co.uk**

Key to Price Guide *see p556* **Key to Symbols** *see back cover flap*

BRIGHTON Hotel Du Vin Brighton ©©©

2–6 Ship St, Brighton, East Sussex, BN1 1AD **Tel** *01273 718588* **Fax** *01273 718599* **Rooms** *37*

Set in the Lanes conservation area, a stone's throw away from the seafront, this cutting-edge hotel and bistro is housed in a collection of eccentric, Gothic Revival and mock-Tudor buildings. All the bedrooms are elegantly decorated with Egyptian linen and handsprung mattresses. **www.hotelduvin.com**

BROCKENHURST Balmer Lawn ©©©

Lyndhurst Rd, Brockenhurst, Hampshire, SO42 7ZB **Tel** *01590 623116* **Fax** *01590 623864* **Rooms** *56*

Built in the 1880s as a hunting lodge in the New Forest, Balmer Lawn is now an oasis of comfort and good service. The in-house Beresford's Restaurant has two AA Rosettes for fine dining. Indoor and outdoor heated pools, health spa and tennis courts are among the leisure amenities. Breakfast is included. **www.balmerlawnhotel.com**

BROCKENHURST Rhinefield House ©©©©©

Rhinefield Rd, Brockenhurst, Hampshire, SO42 7QB **Tel** *01590 622922* **Fax** *01592 622800* **Rooms** *32*

Set in a New Forest clearing and surrounded by rhododendrons, Rhinefield is a magnificent 19th-century Jacobean Revival mansion, with Grindling Gibbons wood carvings and other priceless features. Star of the show is the Moorish-style Alhambra Room, now a gracious bar. Breakfast included. **www.handpicked.co.uk/rhinefieldhouse**

CANTERBURY The Falstaff ©©

8–10 St Dunstans St, Canterbury, Kent, CT2 8AF **Tel** *01227 462138* **Fax** *01227 463525* **Rooms** *47*

The Falstaff, at the heart of one of England's most historic cities, celebrated its 600th year in 2005. The one-time coaching inn has been extended into a recently-restored wood mill. All rooms are en suite, and have TV and hot drink facilities. It stands next to the imposing Westgate Tower. **www.swallowhotels.co.uk/falstaff**

CANTERBURY The County ©©©©

High St, Canterbury, Kent, CT1 2RX **Tel** *01227 766266* **Fax** *01227 451512* **Rooms** *74*

Located on the pedestrianized High Street in Canterbury, The County dates from the 16th century and has many original features. All the bedrooms, some furnished in Tudor or Georgian style, have satellite TV. Enjoy food and drinks at the Sully's Restaurant or Jacobs Brasserie. Breakfast included. **www.thecountyhotel-canterbury.co.uk**

DORKING Burford Bridge ©©©©

Box Hill, Dorking, Surrey, RH5 6BX **Tel** *0870 400 8283* **Fax** *01306 880386* **Rooms** *57*

Just outside the M25 circle and at the foot of the wooded South Downs, this hotel gives easy access to both London and the South Coast. Try a walk to the summit of Box Hill or visit Denbies winery, across the road, or the many antique shops in nearby Dorking. Then return to a true gourmet experience. **www.burfordbridgehotel.co.uk**

DOVER Wallett's Court Country Hotel & Spa ©©©

Westcliffe, Dover, Kent, CT15 6EW **Tel** *01304 852424* **Fax** *01304 853430* **Rooms** *17*

Relax in a Tudor-style room in the manor house, with fine sea views and an oak-beamed ceiling, or enjoy a room in one of the converted ancient barns that are stylishly furnished. The Spa, set in the grounds of Wallett's Court, has a Romanesque exercise pool, sauna and a mineral steam room. Breakfast included. **www.wallettscourt.com**

EAST GRINSTEAD Gravetye Manor ©©©©©

Vowels Lane, East Grinstead, West Sussex, RH1 94LJ **Tel** *01342 810567* **Fax** *01342 810080* **Rooms** *18*

Regarded by many as the establishment that set the country-house hotel movement in motion. A Relais et Châteaux affiliate, it has an oak-panelled Michelin-star restaurant. In 1884, William Robinson, one of England's great gardeners, laid out the wonderful shrubs and flowerbeds. Breakfast included. **www.gravetyemanor.co.uk**

EASTBOURNE The Grand Hotel ©©©©©

King Edwards Parade, Eastbourne, East Sussex, BN21 4EQ **Tel** *01323 412345* **Fax** *01323 412233* **Rooms** *152*

Appropriately named, the imposing Grand is one of Britain's classic seaside hotels. Owners Elite Hotels have lavishly refurbished the property to meet 21st-century five-star requirements. Ideal for touring Sussex or just taking the sea air with strolls down the prom. Prices include breakfast. **www.grandeastbourne.com**

FOLKESTONE Clifton Hotel ©©

Leas, Folkestone, Kent, CT20 2EB **Tel** *01303 851231* **Fax** *01303 223949* **Rooms** *80*

The Clifton is set amid the manicured lawns and well-tended gardens of the cliff-top Leas area in the heart of Folkestone. Built in 1864, this imposing Victorian edifice offers sweeping Channel views and is very close to the Le Shuttle Eurotunnel terminal and the ferry port of Dover. Breakfast included. **www.thecliftonhotel.com**

FOLKESTONE Quality Hotel Burlington ©©

Earls Avenue, Folkestone, Kent, CT20 2HR **Tel** *01303 255301* **Fax** *01303 251301* **Rooms** *66*

This Victorian boutique hotel, situated close to the beach, has extensive public rooms, including a choice of lounges, the Bay Tree restaurant and a large cocktail bar. Bedrooms are pleasantly decorated and equipped with modern facilities. Some rooms have sea views. **www.theburlingtonhotel.com**

FOREST ROW Ashdown Park ©©©©©

Wych Cross, Forest Row, East Sussex, RH18 5JR **Tel** *01342 824988* **Fax** *01342 826206* **Rooms** *106*

Set in 186 acres, in the heartland of Ashdown Forest and boasting its own golf course and country club, with a pool and spa. This Victorian Gothic stately home has been carefully restored and modernized. Splendid rooms and suites plus the award-winning Anderida restaurant make it a winner. Breakfast included. **www.ashdownpark.com**

GUILDFORD Angel Posting House & Livery
91 High St, Guildford, Surrey, GU1 3DP **Tel** *01483 564555* **Fax** *01483 533770* **Rooms** *21*

Jane Austen and Admiral Nelson have been guests at this town centre coaching inn that welcomed its first guests in 1500. Old-world charm and high standards of hospitality ensure popularity. The atmospheric salon has a minstrel gallery, a fireplace and a 1685 coaching clock. **www.angelpostinghouse.com**

LENHAM Chilston Park
Sandway, Lenham, Kent, ME17 2BE **Tel** *01622 859803* **Fax** *01622 858588* **Rooms** *53*

The M20 motorway is just minutes away but thankfully the traffic noises are out of earshot as you stroll in what was once Lord Chilston's estate. This is country-house style at its finest – overflowing with antiques and reeking of log fires. Offers conference rooms as well. The cuisine is of true gourmet standard. **www.handpicked.co.uk/chilstonpark**

LEWES Millers
134 High St, Lewes, East Sussex, BN7 1XS **Tel** *01273 475631* **Rooms** *3*

Behind a neat Georgian frontage in Lewes's charming conservation area stands a historic 16th-century timber-framed building, which once belonged to the first Duke of Newcastle. Two of the double letting rooms have magnificent four-poster beds. Book in advance. The town is renowned for its antiques shops. Non-smoking.

MIDHURST Spread Eagle Hotel & Health Spa
South St, Midhurst, West Sussex, GU29 9NH **Tel** *01730 816911* **Fax** *01730 815668* **Rooms** *39*

Built in 1430, it once hosted Queen Elizabeth I and still features vast fireplaces and impressive bread ovens. The restaurant spotlights head chef Gary Moreton-Jones's modern classic menu while bedrooms are elegant and spacious. The Aquila Health Spa has a beauty centre and a fully equipped gym. Includes full breakfast. **www.hshotels.co.uk**

NEW MILTON Chewton Glen
Christchurch Rd, New Milton, Hampshire, BH25 6QS **Tel** *01425 275341* **Fax** *01425 272310* **Rooms** *58*

The epitome of Edwardian elegance, Chewton Glen is renowned for its food and now also boasts a magnificent indoor pool and spa to add to a range of outdoor sports and leisure activities. The owners, Martin and Brigitte Skan, at the helm for 40 years, are always on hand to ensure warm, friendly service. **www.chewtonglen.com**

RINGWOOD Moortown Lodge
244 Christchurch Rd, Ringwood, Hampshire, BH24 3AS **Tel** *01425 471404* **Fax** *01425 476527* **Rooms** *7*

Acquired by new owners and fully refurbished in 2003, this unpretentious country inn at the gateway to the New Forest, offers all modern in-room amenities, including high-speed Internet via broadband. Guests have access to the adjacent David Lloyd club, with its gym and pool. A full English breakfast is included. **www.moortownlodge.co.uk**

ROYAL TUNBRIDGE WELLS Hotel Du Vin & Bistro
Crescent Rd, Tunbridge Wells, Kent, TN1 2LY **Tel** *01892 526455* **Fax** *01892 512044* **Rooms** *34*

Superb quality without unnecessary frills. Sensible prices and trendy service are the key to success for the small but steadily growing Vin & Bistro chain. This branch opened in 1997 and immediately became a favourite for its modern styles of accommodation and cuisine catered in a spacious historic building. **www.hotelduvin.com**

RYE Jeake's House
Mermaid St, Rye, East Sussex, TN31 7ET **Tel** *01797 222828* **Fax** *01797 222263* **Rooms** *11*

Creeper-clad Jeake's House is tucked away in Rye's atmospheric jumble of little cobbled streets. Guests are welcomed by the two resident cats and proprietors Jenny Hadfield and Richard Martin. There's an oak-beamed parlour and a book-lined bar, plus roaring fires on colder days. Breakfast included. **www.jeakeshouse.com**

SEAVIEW Seaview
High St, Seaview, Isle of Wight, PO34 5EX **Tel** *01983 612711* **Fax** *01983 613729* **Rooms** *19*

Once described as "the perfect seaside hotel", this is just the spot for an idyllic weekend. It's good for family holidays too. The kitchen has just been refurbished and the food is as deliciously inventive as ever. Crisp linen, maritime bric-à-brac and a warren of corridors and stairways all add to the romance. **www.seaviewhotel.co.uk**

SOUTHAMPTON Elizabeth House
42–44 The Avenue, Southampton, Hampshire, SO17 1XP **Tel** *023 8022 4327* **Fax** *023 8022 4327* **Rooms** *27*

Set in a quiet residential area, less than a mile from Southampton city centre, the Elizabeth House gives easy access to the new West Quay Shopping Centre and the cruise and ferry terminals. Southampton's attractions include ancient city walls while the New Forest and the Isle of Wight are nearby. Breakfast included. **www.elizabethhousehotel.com**

SOUTHSEA Seacrest
11/12 South Parade, Southsea, Hampshire, PO5 2JB **Tel** *023 9273 3192* **Fax** *023 9283 2523* **Rooms** *28*

Under the same ownership for 14 years, this hotel has been constantly improved and upgraded to give guests the best in comfort. A premier position on Southsea's seafront commands fine views across the Solent towards the Isle of Wight. All the rooms are individually designed. Includes breakfast. **www.seacresthotel.co.uk**

VENTNOR The Royal Hotel
Belgrave Rd, Ventnor, Isle of Wight, PO38 1JJ **Tel** *01983 852186* **Fax** *01983 855395* **Rooms** *55*

The Isle of Wight's largest premier hotel can be found in the elegant Victorian town of Ventnor. Gourmets can indulge in inspired cuisine in a palatial dining room replete with rich drapes, high ceilings and massive chandeliers. Explore the island or the staff can arrange a yacht charter. Breakfast included. **www.royalhoteliow.co.uk**

Key to Price Guide *see p556* **Key to Symbols** *see back cover flap*

WICKHAM Old House Hotel & Restaurant   ⓔⓔ

The Square, Wickham, Hampshire, PO17 5JG **Tel** *01329 833049* **Fax** *01329 833672* **Rooms** *15*

Conveniently located just off Junction 10 of the M27 South Coast motorway, this property is a good option·for those wishing to explore the Portsmouth, Southampton, Winchester triangle. Built in 1715 as a gentleman's town house, the building was converted into a hotel in 1970. Breakfast included. **www.oldhousehotel.co.uk**

WINCHESTER Lainston House ⓔⓔⓔⓔ

Sparsholt, Winchester, Hampshire, SO21 2LT **Tel** *01962 863588* **Fax** *01962 776672* **Rooms** *50*

One of England's most handsome hotels, Lainston House has country style yet is just minutes from the centre of Winchester. Behind that imposing Queen Anne red-brick frontage is a friendly welcome. There are 63 acres to wander in, a gourmet restaurant and you can always order a DVD from room service. **www.exclusivehotels.co.uk**

WORTHING The Beach Hotel ⓔⓔⓔ

Marine Parade, Worthing, Sussex, BN11 3QJ **Tel** *01903 234001* **Fax** *01903 234567* **Rooms** *79*

Lovingly restored by the Farnes family, The Beach is an Art Deco time warp, located right on Worthing's seafront promenade. Every period detail has been painstakingly renovated, but the amenities are now fully modern. Lifts serve all four floors and the hotel has its own car park. Inclusive of breakfast. **www.thebeachhotel.co.uk**

EAST ANGLIA

ALDEBURGH Wentworth ⓔⓔⓔ

Wentworth Rd, Aldeburgh, Suffolk, IP15 5BD **Tel** *01728 452312* **Fax** *01728 454343* **Rooms** *35*

Replete with antiques and log fires, the Wentworth Hotel has been run by succeeding generations of the Pritt family since 1920. All the bedrooms are well equipped with latest facilities, including satellite TV, and offer fine sea views. There are also three local golf courses. Includes breakfast. **www.wentworth-aldeburgh.com**

BUCKDEN Lion ⓔⓔ

High St, Buckden, Cambridgeshire, PE19 5XA **Tel** *01480 810313* **Fax** *01480 810070* **Rooms** *15*

Rescued from corporate ownership in 1982, this 15th-century, Grade II listed hotel is a classic country inn. It also has a resident ghost. Well-furnished bedrooms. The oak-panelled restaurant offers excellent wholesome food using the best of local produce. Breakfast is included. **www.lionhotel.co.uk**

BURNHAM MARKET The Hoste Arms ⓔ

The Green, Burnham Market, King's Lynn, Norfolk, PE31 8HD **Tel** *01328 738777* **Fax** *01328 730103* **Rooms** *36*

You can choose from the pretty main part of the inn, the Zulu wing with its modern styling and leather couches, or rooms in an old railway station, a five minutes walk away. Host Jeanne Whittome has stamped her personality on all of them. A great wine list. Rate includes breakfast. **www.hostearms.co.uk**

BURY ST EDMUNDS Angel Hotel ⓔⓔⓔ

Angel Hill, Bury St Edmunds, Suffolk, IP33 1LT **Tel** *01284 714000* **Fax** *01284 714001* **Rooms** *75*

The virginia creeper-clad Angel dominates Bury St Edmunds' largest square. Rooms are individually decorated with modern flair or classical grace. Its public areas have always been the place for the local elite to meet. These days they are joined by a global clientele drawn by the hotel's reputation for contemporary British fine dining. **www.theangel.co.uk**

BURY ST EDMUNDS Ounce House ⓔⓔ

Northgate St, Bury St Edmunds, Suffolk, IP33 1HP **Tel** *01284 761779* **Fax** *01284 768315* **Rooms** *3*

A merchant's house dating from 1870, this spacious family home stands at the top of one of the finest residential streets in Bury St Edmunds. Bedrooms have a chintzy, Victorian style and are equipped with all the modern facilities. A bar operates in the drawing room. Includes breakfast. **www.ouncehouse.co.uk**

CAMBRIDGE Cambridge Fourwentways ⓔ

A11/A1307 Fourwentways, Cambridgeshire, CB8 6AP **Tel** *08700 191 1519* **Fax** *01223 839479* **Rooms** *71*

Convenient for both the M11 and the A14, this branch of the nationwide budget hotel chain is ideally located close to the Imperial War Museum's aviation displays at Duxford as well as the equestrian museums and training gallops of Newmarket. A Little Chef eatery is on the same site. Offers good online deals. **www.travellodge.co.uk**

CAMBRIDGE Arundel House Hotel ⓔⓔⓔ

Chesterton Rd, Cambridge, Cambridgeshire, CB4 3AN **Tel** *01223 367701* **Fax** *01223 367721* **Rooms** *105*

This hotel, created from a terrace of late 19th-century Victorian houses, overlooks the River Cam and is a short walk across the park from the city centre. The historic façade and gracefully decorated rooms have been retained while providing all the latest amenities. Parking is available. Includes continental breakfast. **www.arundelhousehotels.co.uk**

CAMPSEA ASHE The Old Rectory ⓔⓔ

Campsea Ashe, Woodbridge, Suffolk, IP13 0PU **Tel** *01728 746524* **Rooms** *8*

All the delights of the Suffolk coastline are in easy reach – the music and culture of Snape Maltings, the Sutton Hoo Saxon burial ground and the towns of Woodbridge and Aldeburgh. An elegant Georgian house encircled by gardens, it's furnished in chic contemporary style. Includes breakfast. **www.theoldrectorysuffolk.com**

CLACTON-ON-SEA Chudleigh Hotel £

13 Agate Rd, Marine Parade West, Essex, CO15 1RA **Tel** *01255 425407* **Fax** *01255 470280* **Rooms** *10*

Near the pier, the promenade and Clacton's shopping area, the Chudleigh overlooks the resort's central gardens. It has been run by the same caring family for 41 years. This is classic English seaside hospitality at its best. Comfortable bedrooms providing all modern facilities including DVDs.

COGGESHALL The White Hart ££

Market End, Coggleshall, Essex, CO6 1NH **Tel** *01376 561654* **Fax** *01376 561789* **Rooms** *18*

Sleepy Coggleshall once boasted of having more inns and pubs per capita than any other town in the country. The atmospheric White Hart is one of the survivors, offering outstanding value for money in one of East Anglia's secret gems. All the rooms have en suite facilities. Full breakfast is included. **www.whitehart-coggeshall.com**

DEDHAM Maison Talbooth ££££

Stratford Rd, Dedham, Colchester, Essex, CO7 6HN **Tel** *01206 322367* **Fax** *01206 322752* **Rooms** *10*

The Milsom family are a legend in Constable country, taking hospitality to new levels of excellence. The essence of Victorian country-house grace and style, the hotel is just a few minutes from the riverside half-timbered Le Talbooth restaurant and the sister Milsom's hotel. **www.milsomhotels.com**

DUNWICH Ship Inn £

St James St, Dunwich, Suffolk, IP17 3DT **Tel** *01728 648219* **Fax** *01728 648675* **Rooms** *3*

Before it sank into the sea, medieval Dunwich was East Anglia's busiest port and had a population of 3,000. The 500-year old ship survived and offers simple rooms in an out-of-the-way location. The restaurant is renowned for simply prepared home food, including fish and chips. **www.shipinndunwich.co.uk**

ELY Lamb Hotel ££

2 Lynn Rd, Ely, Cambridgeshire, CB7 4EJ **Tel** *01353 663574* **Fax** *01353 662023* **Rooms** *31*

The Lamb makes no secret of its 15th-century coaching inn origins at the heart of the Fens *(see p196)*, close to the glorious cathedral. Oak panelling, arched picture-end windows, antique furnishings and candle-lit suppers – it's a haven of traditional values. Includes breakfast. **www.oldenglishinns.co.uk**

GREAT DUNMOW The Starr £££

Market Place, Gt Dunmow, Essex, CM6 1AX **Tel** *01371 874321* **Fax** *01371 876337* **Rooms** *8*

The Starr's elegant conservatory is just the place to enjoy the owners', Terry and Louise George, good food and fine wines before retiring to one of the eight comfortable bedrooms located in a cleverly converted stable block. One room has a four-poster and an impressive Victorian bathtub. Breakfast included. **www.the-starr.co.uk**

HARWICH The Pier Hotel & Restaurant ££

The Quay, Harwich, Essex, CO12 3HH **Tel** *01255 241212* **Fax** *01255 551922* **Rooms** *14*

Set close to where the Pilgrim Fathers set off on their epic voyage, The Pier overlooks neighbouring Felixstowe, the UK's busiest commercial port. Not surprisingly, there's an emphasis on fresh fish in the restaurant. The lovingly and individually furnished rooms are the latest in modern chic style. Includes continental breakfast. **www.milsonhotels.com**

HERTFORD The Ponsbourne Park Hotel £££

New Gate St Village, Hertford, Hertfordshire, SG13 8QZ **Tel** *01707 876191* **Fax** *01707 875190* **Rooms** *51*

Originally developed as a training centre and hotel, this stylish conversion of a one-time convent school offers modern minimalism within a gracious Victorian shell. Features include a nine-hole golf course, a heated outdoor pool and five all-weather tennis courts. Includes breakfast. **www.ponsbournepark.co.uk**

HINTLESHAM Hintlesham Hall ££££

George St, Hintlesham, Ipswich, Suffolk, IP8 3NS **Tel** *01473 652268* **Fax** *01473 652463* **Rooms** *33*

Hintlesham Hall has a long-standing reputation as one of England's most exquisite country-house hotels. There's a charming health club with indoor and outdoor heated pools and a year-round programme of special culinary events. You can even learn to cook here. Includes breakfast. **www.hintleshamhall.co.uk**

HUNTINGDON Old Bridge £££

1 High St, Huntingdon, Cambridgeshire, PE29 3TQ **Tel** *01480 424300* **Fax** *01480 411017* **Rooms** *24*

While the rooms are comfortable in this historic ivy-clad hostelry, the focus is very much on serious cuisine. A morning espresso, a light pasta lunch or a full dinner – they cater for it all with aplomb and gusto and will happily send a menu on request. Breakfast is included. Business centre is a plus. **www.huntsbridge.com**

IPSWICH Salt House Harbour £££

1 Neptune Quay, Ipswich, Suffolk, IP4 1AX **Tel** *01473 226789* **Fax** *01473 226927* **Rooms** *43*

Set right on the River Orwell, from which the writer George Orwell took his name. A substantial old seven-storey warehouse by Neptune Marina has been converted into a trendy loft-style hotel. Bedrooms are en suite with TVs, DVDs and Internet access. The food is equally good and they have an interesting wine list. **www.salthouseharbour.co.uk**

IPSWICH Swallow Belstead Brook Hotel £££

Belstead Rd, Ipswich, Suffolk, IP2 9HB **Tel** *01473 684241* **Fax** *01473 681249* **Rooms** *88*

Hidden away in secluded gardens on the outskirts of Ipswich, this hotel has an indoor pool, air-conditioned gym and sauna. Enjoy delicious cuisine in the elegant oak-panelled Manor restaurant. Originally a 16th-century hunting lodge, this is now a modern hotel, catering to business and leisure travellers. Includes breakfast. **www.swallowhotels.com**

Key to Price Guide *see p556* **Key to Symbols** *see back cover flap*

KINGS LYNN Hotel Elizabeth Dukes Head

Tuesday Market Place, Kings Lynn, Norfolk, P30 1JS **Tel** *01553 774996* **Fax** *01553 763556* **Rooms** *71*

The Duke's Head has pride of place on King Lynn's Market Square, where public executions took place until 1801. Modern-day guests can anticipate an altogether more attentive, friendly welcome, with such facilities as TV, conference suites and a private car park. **www.elizabethhotels.co.uk**

KINGS LYNN Knights Hill Hotel

South Wootton, Norfolk, PE30 3HQ **Tel** *01553 675566* **Fax** *01553 675568* **Rooms** *73*

Close to King's Lynn, the royal estate at Sandringham and the North Norfolk coast, Knights Hill is a restored farm complex in 11 acres of gardens. Style ranges from the relaxed elegance of Rising Lodge to the rustic charms of the Farmers Arms. The health and leisure centre provides a pool and exercise areas. **www.knightshill.co.uk**

LAVENHAM Lavenham Priory

Water St, Lavenham, Sudbury, Suffolk, C010 9RW **Tel** *01787 247404* **Fax** *01787 248472* **Rooms** *6*

At this 13th-century hotel you can have an-out-of-the-world experience at affordable prices, with exposed beams, polished floors and beds carved by a local craftsman. All the rooms are comfortably furnished with all the latest facilities, and they have a no smoking policy. Breakfast included in the price. **www.lavenhampriory.co.uk**

LAVENHAM Swan

High St, Lavenham, Sudbury, Suffolk, C010 9QA **Tel** *01787 247477* **Fax** *01787 248286* **Rooms** *49*

Luxuriate below a wealth of exposed beams in a wonderful bedroom named after a local village. Other comforts include rich fabrics, cotton sheets and feather pillows. Some rooms have four-poster beds. The heavily-beamed restaurant has fine food and an extensive wine list. The Garden Bar is much simpler. **www.theswanatlavenham.co.uk**

LOWESTOFT Premier Travel Inn

249 Yarmouth Rd, Lowestoft, Suffolk, NR32 4AA **Tel** *08701 977165* **Fax** *01502 581223* **Rooms** *60*

This coastal Suffolk budget hotel provides a low-cost base for visiting a rich kaleidoscope of castles, stately homes, formal gardens and historic fishing ports such as Lowestoft and Yarmouth. A nationwide brand, Premier Travel Inn provides quality and convenient location. Close to reasonably priced restaurants. **www.premiertravelinn.com**

LOWESTOFT Ivy House Country Hotel

Ivy Lane, Beccles Rd, Lowestoft, Suffolk, NR33 8HY **Tel** *01502 501353* **Fax** *01502 501539* **Rooms** *20*

Surrounded by countryside, Ivy House has huge gardens, with herbaceous borders and lily ponds. Rooms come with colour TV, tea and coffee making machines and en suite bathrooms. Also has conference rooms and the Crooked Barn restaurant is famous for its cuisine. Includes breakfast. **www.ivyhousecountryhotel.co.uk**

MALDON Five Lakes Resort

Colchester Rd, Tolleshunt Knights, Maldon, Essex, CM9 8HX **Tel** *01621 868888* **Fax** *01621 869696* **Rooms** *194*

Set in the country seclusion of Essex, the stylish Four Lakes Resort is close to the charming little town of Maldon *(see p209)*, where Danes and Saxons once fought. Besides the huge indoor pool and extensive spa and leisure facilities, the big attraction comes from two superbly landscaped 18-hole golf courses. **www.fivelakes.co.uk**

NEWMARKET Swallow Hotel

High St, Newmarket, Suffolk, CB8 8MB **Tel** *01638 664251* **Fax** *01638 666298* **Rooms** *46*

Newmarket is England's horse-racing capital and owners, trainers and jockeys are among the regulars at a hotel that is jam-packed with period features in bedrooms and public rooms alike. It's one of Newmarket High Street's prime buildings and has a pleasant courtyard for alfresco summer meals. **www.swallowhotels.com**

NORTH WALSHAM Beechwood

20 Cromer Rd, North Walsham, Norfolk, NR28 0HD **Tel** *01692 403231* **Fax** *01692 407284* **Rooms** *17*

In 2003 this establishment became the first two-star hotel ever to win the VisitBritain "Hotel of the Year". Rooms are styled with antique furniture, some with four-poster beds. The highlight of the hotel is chef Steven Norgate's speciality, the "Ten-Mile Dinner", with all ingredients sourced from within 10 miles. **www.beechwood-hotel.co.uk**

NORWICH Beeches Hotel & Victorian Gardens

2–6 Earlham Rd, Norwich, Norfolk, NR2 3DB **Tel** *01603 621167* **Fax** *01603 620151* **Rooms** *43*

Just a short stroll from the city centre, the Beeches offers peace and quiet, with spacious traditionally furnished rooms and the hidden delights of an amazing sunken garden. A crunchy gravel drive and sheltering trees give a country-house ambience. The included breakfast is substantial. **www.mjbhotels.com**

NORWICH The Old Rectory

103 Yarmouth Rd, Norwich, Norfolk, NR7 OHF **Tel** *01603 700772* **Fax** *01603 300772* **Rooms** *8*

The Old Rectory was built in 1754. The hotel overlooks the River Yare in a pleasant residential suburb that is now a conservation area. All the rooms are beautifully furnished, and chef James Perry has earned a good reputation for his daily changing fixed-price menus. The outdoor heated pool is a real treat. Includes breakfast. **www.oldrectorynorwich.com**

PETERBOROUGH Sleep Inn

Gt North Rd, Haddon, Cambridgeshire, PE7 3UQ **Tel** *01733 396850* **Fax** *01733 396869* **Rooms** *82*

Budget priced, yes, but Sleep Inn properties have consistently high standards of modern accommodation. A good night's sleep and you are ready to hit the famous A1 for the Midlands, Yorkshire and all points north into Scotland. It's just as good if you use it as a base for exploring the Fens. **www.choicehotelseurope.com**

PETERBOROUGH Marriott   ℰℰℰ

Peterborough Pk, Lynchwood, Cambridgeshire, PE2 6GB **Tel** *01733 371111* **Fax** *01733 236725* **Rooms** *167*

Though it features one of England's oldest cathedrals, Peterborough is a modern business city, a fact that keeps this thoroughly modern hotel busy. Don't be put off by the business park location, the hotel is pleasantly landscaped and has all the amenities you would expect from a Marriott. Includes breakfast. **www.marriott.co.uk**

SOUTHWOLD The Crown Hotel   ℰℰℰ

90 High St, Southwold, Suffolk, IP18 6DP **Tel** *01502 722275* **Fax** *01502 727263* **Rooms** *14*

Next to its sister Adnams hotel, the Swan, this traditional hotel with modern facilities stands at the heart of East Anglia's most gracious little seaside resort. The beach is just five minutes walk away. A venue for all four seasons, it's a wonderful retreat from big city pressures and has a delightful restaurant. Includes breakfast. **www.adnams.co.uk**

SOUTHWOLD The Swan Hotel   ℰℰℰℰ

Market Place, Southwold, Suffolk, IP18 6EG **Tel** *01502 722186* **Fax** *01502 724800* **Rooms** *42*

Paintings and photographs of local scenes make the Swan an evocative showcase for what is East Anglia's most delightful resort town. Being owned by Adnams, the town's brewers and wine importers, ensures the quality of beverages offered. Individualized rooms are part of the experience. Includes breakfast. **www.adnams.co.uk**

WOODBRIDGE Seckford Hall   ℰℰℰ

Woodbridge, Suffolk, IP13 6NU **Tel** *01394 385678* **Fax** *01394 380610* **Rooms** *32*

One of East Anglia's most successful country-house hotels, the Tudor façade features mullion windows and giant chimneys above a huge carved oak entrance door. The bedrooms have en suite facilities, and leisure activities include a pool, gym, beauty salon; and a golf club for a small fee. Includes breakfast. **www.seckford.co.uk**

THAMES VALLEY

AYLESBURY Hartwell House   ℰℰℰℰℰ

Oxford Rd, Aylesbury, Oxfordshire, HP17 8NL **Tel** *01296 747444* **Fax** *01296 747450* **Rooms** *52*

A member of the Pride of Britain consortium, this hotel was once the home of the exiled King of France. Relax in palatial reception rooms with decorative ceilings, antique furniture and fine paintings. Enjoy the gourmet restaurant, the luxurious spa or walk in the Lancelot "Capability" Brown designed grounds. **www.hartwell-house.com**

BEDFORD Woodlands Manor   ℰℰℰ

Green Lane, Clapham, Bedfordshire, MK41 6EP **Tel** *01234 363281* **Fax** *01234 272390* **Rooms** *32*

Gracious country living awaits at this secluded Grade II listed manor house, with comfortable, well-appointed bedrooms offering sweeping views across the lawns and gardens. Facilities include conference rooms, ample parking space and special offers on particular days. Includes breakfast. **www.signaturegroup.co.uk**

BICESTER Bignell Park Hotel   ℰℰ

Chesterton, Bicester, Oxfordshire, OX26 1UE **Tel** *01869 326550* **Fax** *01869 322729* **Rooms** *22*

Built in 1740 and set in two and a half well-tended acres, the picturesque Bignell Park Hotel offers outstanding views from its luxurious individually styled rooms. Modern cuisine tempts the taste buds and romantic suppers may be taken on the minstrel's gallery. Includes breakfast. **www.bignellparkhotel.co.uk**

BRACKNELL Coppid Beech Hotel   ℰℰℰ

John Nike Way, Bracknell, Berkshire, RG12 8TF **Tel** *01344 303333* **Fax** *01344 301200* **Rooms** *205*

A large modern hotel, this popular family and business venue has its own dry ski slope and ice rink. There's a conference room, an evening entertainment programme and the Waves Leisure health and fitness suite, which includes a children's pool. The restaurant has a good reputation. Includes breakfast. **www.coppidbeech.com**

BURFORD The Lamb Inn   ℰℰℰℰ

Sheep St, Burford, Oxfordshire, OX18 4LR **Tel** *01993 823155* **Fax** *01993 822228* **Rooms** *15*

Among the best in Burford, The Lamb Inn is a classic golden stone building with beamed ceilings. All the bedrooms are comfortably designed with en suite facilities. You can enjoy lunch or a traditional tea here but need to look elsewhere for dinner. Close to many local attractions. **www.lambinn-burford.co.uk**

CHARLBURY The Bell At Charlbury   ℰℰ

Church St, Charlbury, Oxfordshire, OX7 3PP **Tel** *01608 810278* **Fax** *01608 811447* **Rooms** *11*

Mellow golden Cotswold stone gives a handsome air to this convenient town-centre inn. Comfortable accommodation, fine food and drink and proximity to all the Cotswold attractions keep it eternally popular. Charlbury was once a centre for glove makers and Quakers. **www.bellhotel-charlbury.co.uk**

CHIPPERFIELD Two Brewers   ℰℰ

The Common, Chipperfield, Hertfordshire, WD4 9BS **Tel** *01923 265266* **Fax** *01923 261884* **Rooms** *20*

Set on the edge of the 115-acre common in the peaceful village of Chipperfield, the Two Brewers was once the training quarters for great boxers such as Jem Mace and Bob Fitzimmons. There's a stone-floored taproom and the food is of gastro-pub quality. Bedrooms are simply furnished. Includes breakfast. **www.twobrewers.com**

Key to Price Guide *see p556* **Key to Symbols** *see back cover flap*

GLOUCESTERSHIRE Lower Slaughter Manor

Lower Slaughter, nr Cheltenham, Gloucestershire, GL54 2HP **Tel** *01451 820456* **Fax** *01451 822150* **Rooms** *16*

Hidden in a deep fold of the Cotswold Hills, this is one of England's most charming secrets. The manor stands in its own private walled grounds, and splendid plaster ceilings, stone fireplaces and antiques add to the ambience. Superb cuisine and an impressive wine list. Includes breakfast. **www.lowerslaughter.co.uk**

GREAT TEW Falkland Arms

Great Tew, Chipping Norton, Oxfordshire, OX7 4DB **Tel** *01608 683653* **Fax** *01608 683656* **Rooms** *5*

Oak beams, a flagstone floor and an inglenook fireplace set the mood in a Cotswold premises that is part thatch-roofed. This local pub is famous for its drinks and also provides comfortable B&B accommodation. All the rooms have en suite facilities and a colour TV. **www.falklandarms.org.uk**

HARPENDEN Harpenden House

18 Southdown Rd, Harpenden, Hertfordshire, AL5 1PE **Tel** *01582 449955* **Fax** *01582 769858* **Rooms** *76*

Conveniently located close to the M1, Luton Airport and for travelling to London, Harpenden House is a well-integrated mix of modern and traditional, with a loyal following among the business community. The main four-storey building is a handsome Georgian edifice. Also has a cocktail bar. **www.corushotels.com/harpenden**

HENLEY-ON-THAMES Red Lion

Hart St, Henley-on-Thames, Oxfordshire, RG9 2AR **Tel** *01491 572161* **Fax** *01491 410039* **Rooms** *26*

Overlooking the Royal Regatta course on the Thames and next to the church where the singer Dusty Springfield is buried, the Red Lion is a charming redbrick riverside inn. The pleasant, individually decorated rooms, many of them with river views, offer en suite facilities, and also has a restaurant and a bar. **www.redlionhenley.co.uk**

LONG CRENDON Angel

47 Bicester Rd, Long Crendon, Buckinghamshire, HP18 9EE **Tel** *01844 208268* **Fax** *01844 202497* **Rooms** *3*

In a village 32 km (20 miles) from Oxford, the age-old Angel is renowned for its good food. A Pacific Rim influence pervades the kitchen's mouthwatering output. There are just three elegantly decorated letting rooms so personal attention is assured here. The Cotswolds are in easy reach, as is Milton Keynes. **www.angelrestaurant.co.uk**

MAIDENHEAD Elva Lodge Hotel

Castle Hill, Maidenhead, Berkshire, SL6 4AD **Tel** *01628 622948* **Fax** *01628 778954* **Rooms** *26*

A standard-style modern hotel close to the centre of Maidenhead, the Elva Lodge is convenient for touring Windsor Castle, Henley and the other attractions of the Thames Valley. Service is efficient and while the hotel is orientated to business travellers, families will also feel welcome. Includes breakfast. **www.elvalodgehotel.co.uk**

MARLOW Cliveden

Taplow, Buckinghamshire, SL6 0JF **Tel** *01628 668561* **Fax** *01628 661837* **Rooms** *38*

Built by the second Duke of Buckingham in 1666 and once the home of the fabulously wealthy Lord and Lady Astor, this palace above the Thames has welcomed royalty, film stars and writers. All the rooms are handsomely decorated, and they have indoor and outdoor pools and extensive leisure facilities. **www.clivedenhouse.co.uk**

MARLOW Danesfield House Hotel & Spa

Henley Rd, Marlow, Buckinghamshire, SL7 2EY **Tel** *01628 891010* **Fax** *01628 890408* **Rooms** *87*

Tucked away in the Chilterns, overlooking the Thames as it winds between Henley and Marlow, this gracious and much extended mansion sits in 65 acres of glorious gardens. The extensive state-of-the-art spa has a pool, gym and treatment rooms. Bedrooms are luxurious, and the restaurant classy. **www.danesfieldhouse.co.uk**

MARLOW McDonald Compleat Angler

Marlow Bridge, Marlow, Buckinghamshire, SL17 1RG **Tel** *0870 400 8100* **Fax** *01628 486388* **Rooms** *64*

This is one of England's most renowned historic hostelries. All the rooms are comfortably furnished with en suite facilities and have satellite TV, CD players, playstations and a minibar. Service standards are legendary. Its location overlooking Marlow Weir attracts guests. **www.compleatangler-hotel.co.uk**

MILTON Le Manoir Aux Quat' Saisons

Church Rd, Great Milton, Oxfordshire, OX44 7PD **Tel** *01844 278881* **Fax** *01844 278847* **Rooms** *32*

This is where French expat Raymond Le Blanc literally carved his reputation as one of Britain's most acclaimed gourmet chefs. As if the food was not enough, the building is a handsome manor, surrounded by herb gardens, while the bedrooms are a pretty mix of classic French and British style. **www.manoir.com**

MILTON KEYNES Innkeeper's Lodge

Burchard Cres., Milton Keynes, Buckinghamshire, MK41 0DS **Tel** *0870 243 0500* **Fax** *01908 340002* **Rooms** *50*

The new Inkeeper's Lodge chain already has 75 locations across the country, lifting the "pub with rooms" concept to a new level of consistency. The Milton Keynes location gives an easy-on-the-pocket base for trips to Woburn Abbey, the Cotswolds and the South Midlands. Includes breakfast. **www.innkeeperslodge.com**

MOULSFORD Beetle & Wedge

Ferry Lane, Moulsford on Thames, Oxfordshire, OX10 9JF **Tel** *01491 651381* **Fax** *01491 651376* **Rooms** *10*

A gorgeous Thames-side setting is the highlight of this ever-popular upscale hotel and its renowned restaurant, where it always pays to pre-book a table. The style is Anglo-French. Rooms are classic in decor, with river views and opulent bathrooms. **www.beetleandwedge.co.uk**

NEWBURY The Vineyard At Stockcross ⬚🍴♨️👥🅿️ £££££

Stockcross, Newbury, Berkshire, RG20 8JU **Tel** *01635 528770* **Fax** *01635 528398* **Rooms** *49*

Created as a labour of love by a wealthy entrepreneur, the Vineyard raises the bar when it comes to country-house style. Best rooms are in the original house but those in the modern wing are also outstanding for their contemporary look. Serves highly inventive British cuisine and has an amazing wine list. Includes breakfast. **www.the-vineyard.co.uk**

OXFORD Travel Lodge Oxford Peartree 🅿️

Woodstock Rd, Oxford, Oxfordshire, OX2 8JZ **Tel** *08700 850950* **Fax** *01865 513474* **Rooms** *150*

Travel Lodge has a number of their budget properties within easy striking distance of Oxford's fabled dreaming spires. This one sits on the northern section of the Ring Road, making it especially convenient for visitors travelling from the Midlands and North. All rooms are en suite and have TV and tea-making facilities. **www.travellodge.co.uk**

OXFORD Macdonald Randolph Hotel 🅿️🍴 £££

Beaumont St, Oxford, Oxfordshire, OX1 2LN **Tel** *0870 400 8200* **Fax** *01865 791678* **Rooms** *151*

The refined Randolph has starred in the TV series *Inspector Morse* and numerous movies, including *Shadowlands*. It's the veritable heart of Oxford, and a favourite with students' parents, American tourists and the business community. Rooms are tastefully decorated. Dining is in classical silver-service mode. **www.macdonaldhotels.co.uk**

OXFORD Old Bank 🅿️🍴📺 ££££

92–94 High St, Oxford, Oxfordshire, OX1 4BN **Tel** *01865 799599* **Fax** *01865 799598* **Rooms** *42*

As the name implies, this handsome stone building in the heart of this hallowed University City used to serve as a bank. Money still flows here as it is often fully booked – tribute to the sharp Armani styling of the rooms and the tempting new British cuisine. Conference room and beauty treatments are a plus. **www.oldbank-hotel.co.uk**

OXFORD The Old Parsonage Hotel 🍴👥 ££££

1 Banbury Rd, Oxford, Oxfordshire, OX2 6NN **Tel** *01865 310210* **Fax** *01865 311262* **Rooms** *30*

Walls of Cotswold stone screen the Old Parsonage from Oxford's passing hubbub, creating the pleasing illusion of a country retreat. The luxurious bedrooms are air conditioned and now have broadband Internet. Fresh Jersey lobsters are served in the restaurant from May through September. Includes breakfast. **www.oldparsonage-hotel.co.uk**

READING Premier Travel Inn 🍴👥 £

Goring Lane, Grazeley Green, Reading, Berkshire, RG7 1LS **Tel** *0870 990 6454* **Fax** *0870 990 6455* **Rooms** *32*

Premier Travel Inn is a brand name worth remembering if you are seeking quality budget accommodation in convenient locations. This one is set just south of Reading, with convenient access to the M4 corridor. Comfortably furnished rooms, with a few especially adapted for disabled guests. **www.premiertravelinn.com**

READING Millennium Madejski Hotel Reading 🅿️🍴♨️👥📺 £££

Madejski Stadium, Reading, Berkshire, RG2 0FL **Tel** *0118 925 3500* **Fax** *0118 925 3501* **Rooms** *140*

John Madejski made his fortune from *Auto Trader* magazines, then saved Reading Football Club from extinction and built them a new stadium of which this outstanding hotel is a part. His love of fine food explains the high quality of the fare offered here while the rooms are of an equally high standard. **www.millennium-hotels.com**

ST ALBANS Comfort 🅿️🍴 ££

Ryder House, Holywell Hill, St Albans, Hertfordshire, AL1 1HG **Tel** *01727 848849* **Fax** *01727 812210* **Rooms** *60*

One of America's biggest groups, Choice and their Comfort brand are now making their mark in the UK thanks to consistent quality and value prices. All the rooms are spacious, with big and firm beds. This hotel occupies a historic building in the centre of this hilltop town that was once a Roman stronghold. **www.choicehotels.com**

WINDSOR Sir Christopher Wren's House Hotel & Spa 🍴📺 £££££

Thames St, Windsor, Berkshire, SL4 1PX **Tel** *01753 861354* **Fax** *01753 860172* **Rooms** *90*

Stroll through the pedestrianized Thames Bridge from Eton College and on the right side is this handsome Georgian mansion. The riverside setting makes for a romantic dining experience while the spacious, individualized rooms brim with antiques. They also have a gym and a spa offering beauty treatments. **www.wrensgroup.com**

YATTENDON Royal Oak 🍴 £££

The Square, Yattendon, Thatcham, Berkshire, RG18 0UG **Tel** *01635 201325* **Fax** *01635 201926* **Rooms** *5*

A classic country pub in Berkshire, serving a pretty little village and tourists alike. The mood is smart, informal and the traditional food with a French twist is deservedly award winning. Now a member of the Corus hotels group. All rooms are individually decorated and en suite. Includes Breakfast. **www.royaloakyattendon.com**

WESSEX

BATH Villa Magdala 🍴 ££

Henrietta Rd, Bath, Somerset, BA2 6LX **Tel** *01225 466329* **Fax** *01225 483207* **Rooms** *18*

Roy and Lois Thwaites create a homey ambience at this Victorian mansion basking in a peaceful location overlooking lovely Henrietta Park. It's a five-minute flat walk to the Roman baths and city centre shops. This is one of the few local hotels to have on-site guest parking. **www.villamagdala.co.uk**

Key to Price Guide *see p556* **Key to Symbols** *see back cover flap*

BATH The Windsor Hotel

69 Gt Pulteney St, Bath, Somerset, BA2 4DL **Tel** *01225 422100* **Fax** *01225 422550* **Rooms** *14*

Set in an elegant Grade I protected Georgian terrace, just a short walk from Poultney Bridge and the heart of Bath, the rooms in this hotel are individually decorated. Facilities include 24-hour room service, a wonderful Japanese restaurant, conference rooms and broadband access. Includes breakfast. **www.bathwindsorhotel.com**

BATH Royal Crescent

16 Royal Crescent, Bath, Somerset, BA1 2LS **Tel** *01225 823333* **Fax** *01225 339401* **Rooms** *45*

Located at the centre of Bath's glorious semi-circle of Georgian grandiosity. The simple but imposing Bath stone façade is the first glimpse of one of Britain's great hotels. Rooms brim with antiques, beds are luxuriant, there's a spa and the restaurant is elegance personified. **www.royalcrescent.co.uk**

BLANDFORD FORUM Best Western Crown Hotel

West St, Blandford Forum, Dorset, DT11 7AJ **Tel** *01258 456626* **Fax** *01258 451084* **Rooms** *32*

A former coaching inn at the heart of a pretty market town, on the edge of Salisbury Plain, with strong military connections, including a fascinating tank museum nearby. Rooms are spacious and well equipped. Popular wood-panelled bar and restaurant and a small private bar for residents. Includes breakfast. **www.bestwestern.co.uk**

BOURNEMOUTH Miramar

East Overcliff Dr, Bournemouth, Dorset, BH1 3AL **Tel** *01202 556581* **Fax** *01202 291242* **Rooms** *43*

The Miramar occupies one of Bournemouth's most stunning vantage points, with views to the Isle of Wight and the Purbeck Hills. This attractive Edwardian mansion offers a wide range of rooms and suites. There are two restaurants as well as terraces with lawns sweeping down towards the sea. **www.miramar-bournemouth.com**

BOURNEMOUTH Arlington Hotel

Exeter Park Rd, Bournemouth, Dorset, BH2 5BD **Tel** *01202 552879* **Fax** *01202 298317* **Rooms** *28*

Situated in the town centre, the Arlington stands in its own beautiful grounds among scented pine trees. The well-equipped rooms are comfortable, and the hotel prides itself on friendly hospitality. The hotel's private gateways lead directly into the Bournemouth flower gardens, which are just a short walk from the beach. **www.arlingtonbournemouth.co.uk**

BOURNEMOUTH Bay View Court

35 East Overcliff Drive, Bournemouth, Dorset, BH1 3AH **Tel** *01202 294449* **Fax** *01202 292883* **Rooms** *70*

An East Cliff location gives lovely panoramic views across Bournemouth Bay. This comfortable family-run hotel serves international cuisine. A large heated indoor pool, spa bath, steam room, snooker, pool, darts and games machines are located in the popular Purbeck suite. There are relaxing lounges and sun terraces. **www.bayviewcourt.co.uk**

BRADFORD-ON-AVON Bradford Old Windmill

4 Masons Lane, Bradford-on-avon, Wiltshire, BA15 1QN **Tel** *01225 866842* **Fax** *01225 866648* **Rooms** *3*

And now for something completely different. Yes, it really is an old and extremely atmospheric stone windmill – and the round room has a circular bed. Evening meals are vegetarian but breakfast offers hearty fare for meat-eaters, vegetarians and vegans alike. Price includes breakfast. **www.bradfordoldwindmill.co.uk**

BRISTOL The Town & Country Lodge

Bridgewater Rd, Bristol, Somerset, BS13 8AG **Tel** *01275 392441* **Fax** *01275 393362* **Rooms** *36*

This modern hotel has easy access to the M4 and M5 motorways and to Temple Meads station, with its high-speed links to London and other cities. Providing friendly and efficient hospitality in a comfortable atmosphere, Town and Country Lodge is popular with the business community as well as leisure travellers. **www.tclodge.co.uk**

BRISTOL Westbourne

40–44 St Pauls Rd, Clifton, Bristol, Somerset, BS8 1LR **Tel** *0117 973 4214* **Fax** *0117 974 3552* **Rooms** *31*

The well-located Westbourne Hotel provides superb accommodation for business travellers and families alike, within easy reach of the city centre and all its attractions. The cuisine and levels of service are exemplary, though there are plenty of good restaurants within walking distance. Includes breakfast. **www.westbournehotel-bristol.co.uk**

BRISTOL The Brigstow

5–7 Welsh Back, Bristol, Somerset, BS1 4SP **Tel** *0117 929 1030* **Fax** *0117 929030* **Rooms** *116*

Occupying a prime city centre position at Welsh Back, on the banks of the River Avon, the Brigstow is at the heart of an historic but vigorously modern city. Facilities are first rate, including air conditioning and even a plasma screen in the bathroom. Also has a business centre well equipped with all the amenities. **www.brigstowhotel.co.uk**

CALNE Best Western Lansdowne Strand Hotel

The Strand, Calne, Wiltshire, SN11 0EH **Tel** *01249 812488* **Fax** *01249 815323* **Rooms** *26*

In the centre of the market town, this 16th-century former coaching inn still retains many period features. Individually decorated rooms vary in size. There are two bars; one offers a wide selection of ales and a cosy fire to sit by. An interesting menu and choice of wines is available in the brasserie-style restaurant. **www.lansdownestrand.co.uk**

CASTLE COMBE The Manor House Hotel & Golf Club

Castle Combe, Chippenham, Wiltshire, SN14 7HR **Tel** *01249 782206* **Fax** *01249 782159* **Rooms** *48*

A secluded valley position on its own golf course makes this a truly idyllic retreat within easy reach of both Bath and the Cotswolds. Accommodation is in a row of individual cottages and dining in the main Jacobean-styled house. They also have meeting and private dining rooms. Excellent cuisine. **www.exclusivehotels.co.uk**

CHIPPENHAM Angel Hotel

Market Place, Chippenham, Wiltshire, SN15 3HD **Tel** *01249 652615* **Fax** *01249 443210* **Rooms** *50*

Originally an 18th-century coaching inn, this is now a modern hotel offering 15 rooms of individual character and 35 executive suites. Popular with business guests due to its conference facilities and location, this is also a great place to come for a relaxing break, with its own leisure club, bar and restaurant. **www.angelhotelchippenham.co.uk**

CHIPPENHAM Stanton Manor Hotel

Stanton Saint Quinton, nr Chippenham, Wiltshire, SN14 6DQ **Tel** *01666 837552* **Fax** *01666 837022* **Rooms** *23*

Set in seven acres within a mile of the M4, the original classic Wiltshire stone house has been extended to create a traditional country hotel that offers spacious rooms and the acclaimed Gallery Restaurant. It is also well suited for business travellers. Special rates are available if bookings are done online. **www.stantonmanor.co.uk**

DORCHESTER Casterbridge

49 High East St, Dorset, DT1 1HU **Tel** *01305 264043* **Fax** *01305 260884* **Rooms** *15*

Here's a peaceful haven in a busy county town. Dorchester was the Casterbridge in Thomas Hardy's novel, *The Mayor of Casterbridge*, hence the name of this hotel. Ground floor rooms enjoy a patio and wheelchair access. Four-poster room available. Enjoy a generous breakfast in the dining room or the conservatory. **www.casterbridgehotel.co.uk**

DULVERTON Ashwick House

Dulverton, Somerset, TA22 9QD **Tel** *01398 323868* **Rooms** *6*

Ashwick House is a delightful little Edwardian country estate. Manicured lawns sweep down through the six-acre grounds to water gardens and the River Barle. The suites are baronial and in the grounds there's a sculpture trail featuring carved tree trunks. Dinner can be taken on the terrace. Includes breakfast. **www.ashwickhouse.co.uk**

EVERSHOT Summer Lodge

Evershot, Dorset, DT2 0JR **Tel** *01935 482000* **Fax** *01935 482040* **Rooms** *24*

Set in the picturesque village of Evershot, this Relais et Châteaux property has a spa as well as a large heated indoor swimming pool. Enjoy croquet, tennis or an alfresco afternoon tea. In the 2005 Tatler Awards, Summer Lodge was rated as having the best out-of-town restaurant. Includes breakfast. **www.summerlodgehotel.com**

EYPE'S Eype's Mouth Country Hotel

Eype, Bridport, Dorset, DT6 6AL **Tel** *01308 423300* **Fax** *01308 420033* **Rooms** *18*

With dramatic sea views and located just a few minutes walk to the beach, this hotel occupies a coveted position on the heritage coast, with immediate access to the much-lauded coastal path. Family-run, it exudes a welcoming and relaxed atmosphere, ensuring a pleasant and comfortable stay. Includes breakfast. **www.eypesmouthhotel.co.uk**

GILLINGHAM Stock Hill House Hotel & Restaurant

Stockhill, Dorset, SP8 5NR **Tel** *01747 823626* **Fax** *01747 825628* **Rooms** *9*

A beech-lined drive leads to the very definition of peace and seclusion. A member of Relais et Châteaux, this is one of the country's finest country-house hotels. Chef and patron Peter Hauser and his wife Nita have spent two decades refurbishing to exacting standards. Provides business facilities, and price includes dinner. **www.stockhillhouse.co.uk**

LACOCK The Sign of the Angel

6 Church St, Lacock, Wiltshire, SN15 2LB **Tel** *01249 730230* **Fax** *01249 730527* **Rooms** *10*

If you are looking for character, you've found it. Run by the Levis family since 1953, the hotel has low beams, log fires and squeaky floorboards. Luxuriously furnished bedrooms with TVs, tea and coffee making facilities and phone lines. Includes breakfast. Lacock is now owned by the National Trust. **www.lacock.co.uk**

LYME REGIS Hotel Alexandra

Pound St, Lyme Regis, Dorset, DT7 3HZ **Tel** *01297 442010* **Fax** *01297 443229* **Rooms** *26*

Lauded for its hospitality, comfort and good food, the Alexandra has sloping lawns and magnificent views of the Cobb. All the bedrooms are finely decorated with private bathrooms, TVs, hairdryers and all the standard facilities. Elegant dining room with first-class menu and wine list. **www.hotelalexandra.co.uk**

MALMESBURY The Old Bell

Abbey Row, Wiltshire, SN16 0BW **Tel** *01666 822344* **Fax** *01666 825145* **Rooms** *31*

Established in 1220 adjacent to historic Malmesbury Abbey, this is reputed to be Britain's oldest purpose-built hotel. Welcoming rooms and outstanding levels of service amid the ambience of a bygone age. Pretty terrace for outdoor dining in summer. Outstanding wine list. Includes breakfast. **www.oldbellhotel.com**

PORLOCK WEIR Andrews on the Weir

Porlock Weir, Minehead, Somerset, TA24 8PB **Tel** *01643 863300* **Fax** *01643 863311* **Rooms** *5*

Andrews on the Weir stands on one of Europe's most beautiful stretches of coast, where thick woods sweep down to the sea. Bedrooms are comfortably furnished and the inventively presented food is quite exquisite. It also has a beautiful garden and is close to nearby attractions. Breakfast included. **www.andrewsontheweir.co.uk**

SHEPTON MALLET Charlton House

Charlton Rd, Somerset, BA4 4PR **Tel** *01749 342008* **Fax** *01749 346362* **Rooms** *25*

Decorated with imagination, flair and a sense of theatre, this country-house hotel is set amid rolling hills just 18 miles (30 km) south of Bath. Relaxation comes easy in an ambience of informal splendour. The exotic and the traditional find harmony in the outstanding restaurant and the spa is special. Includes breakfast. **www.charltonhouse.com**

Key to Price Guide *see p556* **Key to Symbols** *see back cover flap*

STON EASTON Ston Easton Park ⓔⓔⓔⓔ

Ston Easton, nr Bath, Somerset, BA3 4DF **Tel** *01761 241631* **Fax** *01761 241377* **Rooms** *22*

An elegant Palladian mansion sited on a romantic estate offering upscale country life at its best. Wonderfully ornate ceilings, masses of antique furniture and priceless paintings make for a comfortable stay while the cuisine is truly sublime. Facilities include conference and business meeting rooms. Inclusive of breakfast. **www.stoneaston.co.uk**

SWINDON, WILTS Marsh Farm Hotel ⓔⓔ

Wooton Bassett, Swindon, Wiltshire, SN4 8ER **Tel** *01793 848044* **Fax** *01793 851 528* **Rooms** *50*

In three acres, surrounded by open countryside, this large Victorian farmhouse has been restored, converted and extended into a 50-bedroom luxury hotel located to the west of Swindon close to Junction 16 of the M4. Various kinds of meeting rooms are available with all sorts of mod cons. **www.marshfarmhotel.co.uk**

TAUNTON The Mount Somerset ⓔⓔⓔⓔ

Lower Henlade, Somerset, TA3 5NB **Tel** *01823 442500* **Fax** *01823 442900* **Rooms** *11*

Cradled by the Quantock and Blackdown Hills, the Regency-styled Mount is noted for the elegance and warmth of its greeting. Log fires, abundant scatter cushions and a superb sweeping staircase reek of the good life. Just the place for a calm, unhurried stay. Includes breakfast. **www.mountsomersethotel.co.uk**

WAREHAM The Priory ⓔⓔⓔⓔⓔ

Church Green, Wareham, Dorset, BH20 4ND **Tel** *01929 551666* **Fax** *01929 554519* **Rooms** *18*

Landscaped gardens fronting the River Frome, it offers fine views of the Purbeck Hills. Sumptuous yet relaxed in style, this 16th-century masterpiece has moorings for those arriving by boat. Furnished with antiques, all rooms are en suite, and you may stay in the main house or the hotel's houseboats. Includes breakfast. **www.theprioryhotel.co.uk**

WELLINGTON Bindon Country House ⓔⓔⓔ

Langford, Budville, Somerset, TA21 0RU **Tel** *01823 400070* **Fax** *01823 400071* **Rooms** *12*

Extravagantly decorated bedrooms and great food draw people back to this unusually styled and historic Somerset mansion with its extensive gardens, swimming pool, croquet lawn and bicycles. Opt for a four-poster bedroom. Exmoor is within striking distance. Includes breakfast. **www.bindon.com**

WELLS The Crown At Wells ⓔⓔ

Market Place, Wells, Somerset, BA5 2RP **Tel** *01749 673457* **Fax** *01749 679792* **Rooms** *15*

Set in the bustling market place at the centre of one of England's smallest cities, this attractive Grade II listed building is overlooked by the cathedral and the Bishops Palace, with its moat. All the bedrooms are comfortably furnished with en suite facilities, and Anton's Bistrot is well known for its excellent food. **www.crownatwells.co.uk**

WEYMOUTH Seaham ⓔ

3 Waterloo Place, Dorset, DT4 7NU **Tel** *01305 782010* **Rooms** *5*

The highest graded guesthouse in town, the Seaham is conveniently located close to the vibrant town centre and picturesque harbour. Recently refurbished, the bedrooms are warmly decorated and have en suite facilities. Breakfast included. Children are not welcome. **www.theseaham.co.uk**

WOOKEY HOLE Glencot House ⓔⓔⓔ

Glencot Lane, Wookey Hole, Somerset, BA5 1BH **Tel** *01749 677160* **Fax** *01749 670210* **Rooms** *13*

Glencot House is a Jacobean inspired late-Victorian mansion perfectly set in 18 acres of amazing gardens and parkland, facing the river. It also has its own cricket pitch. All the rooms are beautifully furnished and have four-poster beds. Also has an indoor pool, sauna and a library. Includes breakfast. **www.glencothouse.co.uk**

WOOLTON School House Hotel and Restaurant ⓔ

Hook St, Hook, Wiltshire, SN4 8EF **Tel** *01793 851198* **Fax** *01793 851025* **Rooms** *16*

Close to Swindon and at the gateway to the Cotswolds, this transformed Victorian school building is just minutes from Junction 16 on the M4. Car hire, station and airport transfers can be arranged. The restaurant has a Victorian beamed ceiling. Suitable for business travellers as well. Includes breakfast. **www.schoolhotel.com**

DEVON AND CORNWALL

BIGBURY-ON-SEA Burgh Island ⓔⓔⓔⓔ

Burgh Island, Bigbury-On-Sea, South Devon, TQ7 4BG **Tel** *01548 810514* **Fax** *01548 810243* **Rooms** *23*

This Art Deco treasure is where Agatha Christie did her famous disappearing act. Set 200 m (656 ft) off the South Devon coast, all the bedrooms are individually decorated with all the modern facilities. Call for the elevated four-wheel drive or stroll by the sea. Inclusive of breakfast and dinner. **www.burghisland.com**

BOSCASTLE The Old Rectory ⓔ

St Juliot, Boscastle, Cornwall, PL35 0BT **Tel** *01840 250225* **Rooms** *4*

Beautiful gardens surround the house where Thomas Hardy fell in love with Emma Lavinia Gifford, leading to some of his best poetry. A family home that has been renovated and decorated beautifully in period style. The breakfast is all-inclusive in this B&B close to the coast and the Eden Project. **www.stjuliot.com**

BOSCASTLE The Bottreaux Hotel & Restaurant

Boscastle, Cornwall, PL35 OBG **Tel** *01840 250231* **Fax** *01840 250170* **Rooms** *8*

Just five minutes stroll from Boscastle's Elizabethan harbour, this town house is at the heart of the busy one-time fishing village. Bedrooms and public areas have been refurbished to very high standards and guest amenities include a car park. Rooms are non-smoking. Quality restaurant with breakfast inclusive. **www.boscastlecornwall.co.uk**

BOTALLACK Botallack Manor

Botallack, St Just, Penzance, Cornwall, TR19 7QG **Tel** *01736 788525* **Rooms** *3*

This 300-year-old guesthouse, star of TV's *Poldark* dramas, is granite on the outside, soft and romantic within. All the bedrooms are beautifully furnished, centrally heated and well appointed with every modern facility. It's also close to abandoned tin mines and rugged cliffs. Open all year except Christmas. **www.botallackmanor.co.uk**

BUDE The Falcon Hotel

Breakwater Rd, Cornwall, EX23 8SD **Tel** *01288 352005* **Fax** *01288 356359* **Rooms** *30*

There's 200 years of tradition behind this much-expanded one-time coaching inn overlooking the Bude Canal. All the rooms are tastefully decorated and one is a four-poster bedroom with its own luxury spa bath. It also has a stylish restaurant. The Falcon Inn is reputed for its food. **www.falconhotel.com**

CHAGFORD Three Crowns Hotel

High St, Chagford, Devon, TQ13 8AJ **Tel** *01647 433444* **Fax** *01647 433117* **Rooms** *18*

This 13th-century stone-built inn evokes a long history with its mullion windows, massive oak beams, great open fireplace and four-poster rooms. It is at the heart of Dartmoor National Park and conveniently located close to the Eden Project and the Lost Gardens of Heligan. Breakfast is included. **www.chagford-accom.co.uk**

CHAGFORD Gidleigh Park

Gidleigh, Chagford, Devon, TQ13 8HH **Tel** *01647 432367* **Fax** *01647 432574* **Rooms** *15*

Gidleigh Park has long been established as one of the UK's finest country-house hotels. It carries the prestigious Relais et Châteaux branding with pride. The rooms are comfortably furnished with all the modern facilities. Enjoy walks on its gardens, then savour the cuisine that has won two Michelin stars for chef Michael Caines. **www.gidleigh.com**

CHILLATON Quither Mill

Quither Mill, Quither, Chillaton, Devon, PL19 OPZ **Tel** *01822 860160* **Fax** *01822 860160* **Rooms** *3*

Breakfast is included at this Devonshire delight, with its beamed ceilings, eight acres of gardens and outstanding views towards Dartmoor. All rooms are individually decorated. A member of the highly commended Wolsey consortium and a non-smoking house. Children under 12 are not welcome. **www.quithermill.co.uk**

EXETER Innkeeper's Lodge Exeter East

Clyst St George, Exeter, Devon, EX3 OQJ **Tel** *01392 876121* **Fax** *01392 872022* **Rooms** *21*

A fast-growing nationwide chain of modern budget hotels, Innkeeper's Lodge choose their sites well. This one is located just off the M5, making it a suitable jumping off point for forays into the deepest West Country. Deals include two nights for the price of one, while Continental breakfast is complimentary. **www.innkeeperslodge.com**

EXETER Barcelona

Magdalen St, Exeter, Devon, EX2 4HY **Tel** *01392 281000* **Fax** *01392 281001* **Rooms** *46*

This brilliantly converted former eye hospital gives the wink to inspired 1950s style with all the convenience of a modern hotel. The rooms are stylishly furnished with comforts such as satellite TV, video players and Internet. Business facilities are available, and Café Paradiso prepares Mediterranean cuisine. **www.aliashotels.com**

FALMOUTH Budock Vean Hotel On The River

Helford Passage, Mawnan Smith, Falmouth, Cornwall, TR11 5LG **Tel** *01326 250288* **Fax** *01326 250892* **Rooms** *57*

Warm and hospitable, this hotel is set in 65 acres of grounds that lead down to the Helford River. The bedrooms have all the latest facilities, and some have fine views of the gardens and the golf course. They also have a swimming pool, health spa, two tennis courts and a fine restaurant. Includes breakfast and dinner. **www.budockvean.co.uk**

FOWEY Marina Villa

17 The Esplanade, Fowey, Cornwall, PL23 1HY **Tel** *01726 833315* **Fax** *01726 832779* **Rooms** *18*

Stunning sea and river views on a wooded inlet of Cornwall's beautiful south coast. But the real delights wait inside, with stylish rooms and the acclaimed Waterside Restaurant – a destination in its own right. Star chef Chris Eden has returned from the London hotspots to mastermind the kitchen. **www.marinavillahotel.co.uk**

ISLES OF SCILLY Hell Bay

Bryher, Isles of Scilly, TR23 OPR **Tel** *01720 422947* **Fax** *01720 423004* **Rooms** *25*

New England and the Caribbean meet Cornwall's offshore islands. Lloyd Loom furnishing and Malabar fabrics are set against cool ocean blues and greens. Robert and Lucy Dorrien-Smith have filled this secluded haven of tranquility with the works of renowned artists. Breakfast and dinner inclusive. **www.hellbay.co.uk**

LANDEWEDNACK Landewednack House

Church Cove, Landewednack, The Lizard, Cornwall, TR12 7PQ **Tel** *01326 290909* **Fax** *01326 290192* **Rooms** *5*

This former rectory is today a quintessential country-house B&B. There is a secluded two-acre walled garden with sea views and a heated swimming pool to keep you on-site, though the surrounding countryside is delightful. Full breakfast is included in the price. **www.landewednackhouse.com**

Key to Price Guide *see p556* **Key to Symbols** *see back cover flap*

LYNMOUTH The Rising Sun

Harbourside, Lynmouth, Devon, EX35 6EG Tel 01598 753223 Fax 01598 753480 Rooms 16

Percy Bysshe Shelley honeymooned in this 14th-century thatched smugglers inn. It overlooks Lynmouth's picturesque harbour and the highest hogback cliffs in England. Oak panelling, wonky ceilings, beachstone walls and uneven floorboards – it's atmosphere all the way, with well-appointed rooms. **www.risingsunlynmouth.co.uk**

MEMBURY Lea Hill

Membury, Axminster, Devon, EX13 7AQ Tel 01404 881881 Rooms 2

Superb walks along the South West Coastal Path, now a World Heritage Site, await at the doorstep of this former hotel, now offering a mix of B&B and self-catering accommodations. Lea Hill also offers six fully furnished cottages and apartments. Rates include breakfast. **www.leahill.co.uk**

MORTEHOE Lundy House Hotel

Chapel Hill, Mortehoe, North Devon, EX34 7DZ Tel 01271 870372 Fax 01271 871001 Rooms 9

Wet suits and surfboards can be rented at nearby Woolacombe Beach or you can ramble over Exmoor. You might, though, prefer to simply relax while admiring the view over to the romantic offshore Lundy Island and watch the stunning sunsets before retiring to contemporary four-poster luxury. **www.lundyhousehotel.co.uk**

MOUSEHOLE Old Coast Guard Hotel

The Parade, Mousehole, Penzance, Cornwall, TR19 6PR Tel 01736 731222 Fax 01736 731720 Rooms 21

Razed in 1595 by raiders from the Spanish Armada, tiny Mousehole has survived as a classic Cornish fishing village. As the name implies, this friendly hotel, with all the mod-con facilities, overlooks the local maritime scene. Most rooms have sea views and several have balconies. Breakfast included. **www.oldcoastguardhotel.co.uk**

MULLION The Polurrian Hotel

Polurrian Hotel, Mullion, South Cornwall, TR12 7EN Tel 01326 240421 Fax 01326 240083 Rooms 39

Excellent service is still a hallmark here, but what guests always talk about most is the stunning cliff-top location, set in beautiful landscaped gardens and with glorious views across to St Michael's Mount. All rooms are en suite and most have sea views. **www.polurrianhotel.com**

NEWQUAY Barrowfield Hotel

Hill Grove Rd, Newquay, Cornwall, TR7 2QY Tel 01637 878878 Fax 01637 879490 Rooms 83

This family hotel offers honeymoon suites, four posters and suites with separate sleeping areas for children. Golf breaks are another speciality. The location overlooks Tolcarne and Lusty Glaze beaches and is a short and flat walk to Newquay's prime shopping area. **www.cranstar.co.uk**

NEWQUAY Sands

Watergate Rd, Porth, Newquay, Cornwall, TR7 3LX Tel 01637 872864 Fax 01637 876365 Rooms 100

Spacious rooms with separate sleeping space for children await at this North Cornwall family favourite. Close to the golden sand beaches and surf, this full-on holiday resort features the Ocean Breeze Spa's relaxing therapies plus four age-banded children's clubs. Rates include full breakfast. **www.sandsresort.co.uk**

NEWQUAY The Headland Hotel

Fistral Beach, Newquay, Cornwall, TR7 1EW Tel 01637 872211 Fax 01637 872212 Rooms 104

High Victorian Gothic architecture dominating the cliff above one of Newquay's finest beaches gives this four-star hotel an imposing setting. Inside it is a friendly, family-orientated place and they also run a nearby holiday park. The rooms are comfortably furnished, and many have sea view. Full breakfast is standard. **www.headlandhotel.co.uk**

OAK HAMPTON Lewtrenchard Manor

Lewdown, nr Oak Hampton, Devon, EX20 4PN Tel 01566 783222 Fax 01566 783332 Rooms 14

Barely touched by time, this Jacobean delight is built on the site of an even earlier manor. It is famed for its heavenly 17th-century gardens, and is also ideal for business travellers. All the rooms are individually styled and have modern facilities. Full breakfast is inclusive. **www.lewtrenchard.co.uk**

OTTERY ST MARY Tumbling Weir

Canaan Way, Ottery St Mary, nr Exeter, Devon, EX11 1AQ Tel 01404 812752 Fax 01404 812752 Rooms 10

A thatched hotel set in half-an-acre of beautiful gardens beside a millstream. Conveniently located close to the M5 and Exeter, this gem is a short drive from historic Exeter and the coast. Comfortable beds and new bathrooms, while the restaurant creates wonderful dishes from local produce. **www.tumblingweir-hotel.co.uk**

PADSTOW The Seafood Restaurant

Riverside, Padstow, Cornwall, PL28 8BY Tel 01841 532700 Fax 01841 532942 Rooms 14

Described as "a restaurant-with-rooms" rather than a hotel, this harbour-side gem is the perfect showcase for Rick Stein's renowned fish cookery. Rooms are simple and tasteful while romantics will enjoy watching the coming and going of the fishing fleet. Breakfast is included. **www.rickstein.com**

PENZANCE Summer House

Cornwall Terrace, Penzance, Cornwall, TR18 4HL Tel 01736 363744 Fax 01736 360959 Rooms 5

This charming Garde II listed Regency house has been converted into a delightfully intimate hotel and lies very close to the sea. Tropical walled garden, fresh-cut flowers, polished wooden floors and inventive Mediterranean inspired cuisine await. All the bedrooms are individually styled. Breakfast is inclusive. **www.summerhouse-cornwall.com**

PENZANCE Queens Hotel

Promenade, Penzance, TR18 4HG **Tel** *01736 362371* **Fax** *01736 350033* **Rooms** *70*

This family run hotel has a Victorian elegance and is situated right on the town's promenade, with sweeping views across Mount Bay to St Michael's Mount. Fresh local fish is a speciality in the dining room. Ideal for the Tate St Ives gallery. Offers yoga classes, a hair salon and is suited for business travellers as well. **www.queens-hotel.com**

PLYMOUTH Athenaeum Lodge

4 Athenaeum St, The Hoe, Plymouth, Devon, PL1 2RQ **Tel** *01752 665005* **Fax** *01752 665005* **Rooms** *9*

Conveniently set near Plymouth Hoe, with the Theatre Royal and the historic Barbican nearby, this Grade II listed Georgian building is also close to the Brittany Ferries terminal. If you have difficulty with stairs, a downstairs guest room is available. Wi-Fi internet access available. Breakfast is inclusive. **www.athenaeumlodge.com**

PLYMOUTH Novotel

Plymouth Road, Marsh Mills, Plymouth, Devon, PL6 8NH **Tel** *01752 221422* **Fax** *01752 223922* **Rooms** *100*

Marsh Mills is the gateway into Plymouth, with all the delights of Devon and Cornwall within easy reach. Each of the modern rooms features a large double and a single bed and up to two under 16s stay free on a B&B basis when sharing their parents' room. Also has a swimming pool and private parking space. **www.novotel.com**

ROCK St Enodoc

Rock, nr Wadebridge, Cornwall, PL27 6LA **Tel** *01208 863394* **Fax** *01208 863970* **Rooms** *20*

Overlooking the beautiful Camel Estuary, and a short drive from the foodie mecca of Padstow, the St Enodoc hotel offers a bright, comfortable feel, with original paintings adding wit and colour. Rooms have microwaves and fridges. They also have a children's playroom. Breakfast inclusive. **www.enodoc-hotel.co.uk**

ST BLAZEY Nanscawen Manor

Prideaux Rd, Luxulyan Valley, St Blazey, Cornwall, PL24 2SR **Tel** *01726 814488* **Rooms** *3*

Don't be misled by the valley address – this is a hilltop-sited gem with lawns sweeping down to breathtaking views – and you can enjoy these from the sizeable outdoor pool or the hot tubs. Keith and Martin Fiona add flair and a gracious welcome to a charming building with 14th-century roots. Breakfast is inclusive. **www.nanscawen.com**

ST HILARY Ennys

Trewhella Lane, St Hilary, Cornwall, TR20 9BZ **Tel** *01736 740262* **Fax** *01736 740055* **Rooms** *5*

An idyllic country hideaway whose private fields stretch down to the delightful River Hayle. Sheltered formal gardens frame a large heated swimming pool and tennis courts. The rooms are comfortably furnished. Ideal for Lands End, St Michael's Mount, the Eden Project and the Lizard peninsula. Rates include an outstanding breakfast. **www.ennys.co.uk**

ST IVES The Garrack Hotel

Burthallam Lane, St Ives, Cornwall, TR26 3AA **Tel** *01736 796199* **Fax** *01736 798955* **Rooms** *20*

Unusually for the busy little artists' haunt of St Ives, the Garrack has its own on-site car parking, as well as delightfully themed subtropical gardens. All rooms have private bathrooms and TV while some have jacuzzi or spa baths. Dine on seafood, meat and vegetarian specialities. Includes breakfast. **www.garrack.com**

ST MAWES Rising Sun

The Square, St Mawes, Truro, Cornwall, TR2 5DJ **Tel** *01326 270233* **Fax** *01326 270198* **Rooms** *8*

Rooms are bright and cheery in this hotel with all the modern comforts. The property fronts directly on to St Mawes' picturesque little harbour, with views of the Roseland Peninsula. Ann Long, the only woman master chef in the entire West Country presides over the Rising Sun's much-acclaimed restaurant. **www.risingsunstmawes.com**

ST MAWES Hotel Tresanton

St Mawes, Truro, Cornwall, TR2 5DR **Tel** *01326 270055* **Fax** *01326 270053* **Rooms** *29*

St Anthony's Lighthouse is a beacon for one of Cornwall's best-loved hotels, formerly a club for yachtsmen. Two years' of re-design and restoration saw Olga Polizzi create a casually elegant venue ideal for weddings and holidays alike. Facilities include a conference room and a variety of treatments. Breakfast is inclusive. **www.tresanton.com**

STOKE CANON Barton Cross Hotel & Restaurant

Huxham, Stoke Canon, Exeter, Devon, EX5 4EJ **Tel** *01392 841245* **Fax** *01392 841942* **Rooms** *9*

Set in lush Devon countryside, close to Exeter city and an hour from bustling Torbay, this traditional-style hotel also accesses a number of magnificent National Trust properties. Fishing and three excellent golf courses are nearby and you can relax in the welcoming timber-beamed lounge afterwards. Includes full breakfast. **www.bartonxhuxham.com**

TAVISTOCK The Bedford

1 Plymouth Road, Tavistock, Devon, PL19 8BB **Tel** *01822 613221* **Fax** *01822 618034* **Rooms** *30*

Formerly a Benedictine Abbey, this elegant hotel was once the residence of the Dukes of Bedford. The rooms are charming and tastefully furnished to a high standard. Situated in the historic market town of Tavistock, the Bedford makes an excellent base from which to explore the wild beauty of Dartmoor. **www.bedford-hotel.co.uk**

TEIGNMOUTH Thomas Luny House

Teign St, Teignmouth, Devon, TQ14 8EG **Tel** *01626 772976* **Rooms** *4*

Once frequented by the captains of Nelson's navy, this Georgian house is furnished with antiques and collectibles. Tea and home-made cake are offered to afternoon arrivals, which may be enjoyed in the secluded garden. All rooms are individually designed, and expect faultless hospitality. Includes breakfast. **www.thomas-luny-house.co.uk**

Key to Price Guide *see p556* **Key to Symbols** *see back cover flap*

TINTAGEL Willapark Manor
🛏🏃 ££

Bossiney, Tintagel, Cornwall, PL34 0BA **Tel** *01840 770782* **Fax** *01840 770782* **Rooms** *13*

Some 14 acres of well-tended gardens overlook the most dramatic of rocky cliffs from which a coastal path leads down to the secluded beach. Well-appointed rooms with all the usual amenities and excellent food keep guests coming back. Children and pets are welcome. **www.willapark.co.uk**

TORQUAY Palace Hotel
££££

Babbacombe Rd, Torquay, Devon, TQ1 3TG **Tel** *01803 200200* **Fax** *01803 299899* **Rooms** *141*

Overlooking St Anstey's Cove and featuring a nine-hole golf course, tennis courts and indoor and outdoor swimming pools, this uncrowned queen of the English Riviera stands in 26 acres of glorious gardens. Well placed for visiting Dartmoor. Additionals include conference facilities and tennis tutorials. **www.palacetorquay.co.uk**

WIDEGATE Coombe Farm
£

Widegate, Looe, Cornwall, PL13 1QN **Tel** *01503 240223* **Rooms** *3*

Spacious rooms offer fine views of the wooded valley and the sea, and horse riding and sea and lake fishing are among other attractions. The rooms are warmly decorated, and there are some self-contained cottages as well. Dartmoor, Bodmin Moor and the Cornish Coastal Path are all at hand. Breakfast included. **www.coombefarmhotel.co.uk**

THE HEART OF ENGLAND

BIBURY The Swan
££££

Bibury, Gloucestershire, GL7 5NW **Tel** *01285 740 695* **Fax** *01285 740 473* **Rooms** *18*

A picturesque hotel, set in a converted, 17th-century coaching inn in the Cotswolds. The rooms are luxurious with views over the peaceful River Coln and expansive hotel gardens. Some rooms have en suite jacuzzis. Also boasts an award-winning restaurant and a beauty spa – the Swan Sanctuary. **www.swanhotel.co.uk**

BIRMINGHAM Plough & Harrow
££

135 Hagley Rd, Edgbaston, Birmingham, B16 8LS **Tel** *0121 4544111* **Fax** *0121 4541868* **Rooms** *44*

Part of the Swallow hotel chain, this red brick, Victorian hotel is full of character. It is located near the Birmingham city centre and Edgbaston cricket ground, and is a reasonably priced choice for both business travellers and families. The amenities are mostly basic, but the rooms are spacious. Also has conference facilities. **www.swallowhotel.com**

BIRMINGHAM Hotel du Vin & Bistro
£££

Church St, Birmingham, B3 2NR **Tel** *0121 200 0600* **Fax** *0121 236 0889* **Rooms** *66*

Large, elegant hotel in a converted Victorian building in the city's trendy Jewellery Quarter. Many of the building's original features, including the sweeping staircase and granite pillars, have been retained. Features a well-reputed bistro restaurant and the popular Cellar Bar. Also has a beauty spa. **www.hotelduvin.com**

BIRMINGHAM Malmaison
£££

1 Wharfside St, Birmingham, B1 1RD **Tel** *0121 2465000* **Fax** *0121 2465002* **Rooms** *189*

A stylish, award-winning hotel in a former 1960s Royal Mail sorting office, Malmaison sits amidst designer stores and within walking distance of the city centre. The rooms are furnished in chic chocolate and cream, with moody lighting and CD libraries. Also has a spa with sauna, Jacuzzi and choice of treatments. **www.malmaison-birmingham.com**

BLACKWELL Blackwell Grange
£

Blackwell, Shipston-on-Stour, Warwickshire, CV36 4PF **Tel** *01608 682357* **Fax** *01608 682856* **Rooms** *4*

Small B&B in a 17th-century farmhouse, complete with low-beamed ceilings and stone-flagged floors, to the north of the Cotswolds. Offers two self-catering cottages; one for up to six persons and the other for two. A great spot for walking. Picnics are provided on request. Also functions as a working farm. **www.blackwellgrange.co.uk**

BLOCKLEY The Crown Inn
££

High St, Blockley, Moreton-In-Marsh, Gloucestershire, GL56 9EX **Tel** *01386 700245* **Fax** *01386 700247* **Rooms** *24*

A converted 14th-century coaching inn with wood-beamed ceilings, whitewashed walls and log fires. Has individually furnished rooms with fireplaces and four-poster beds. The restaurant boasts an impressive cellar and an extensive choice of Real Ales. The nearby countryside is great for walking and horse riding. **www.crown-hotel-blockley.co.uk**

BROAD CAMPDEN Malt House
£££

Broad Campden, Chipping Campden, Gloucestershire, GL55 6UU **Tel** *01386 840295* **Fax** *01386 841334* **Rooms** *7*

Elegant and well-located B&B, which prides itself on its personal touch. Each of the six bedrooms (and one garden suite) is individually decorated with antique furnishings, four-poster beds, fine china and freshly-cut flowers from its carefully-tended gardens. Offers a large breakfast with home-made bread and jams. **www.malt-house.co.uk**

BROADWAY Barn House
££

152 High St, Broadway, Worcestershire, WR12 7AJ **Tel** *01386 858633* **Rooms** *4*

Welcoming and informal B&B in a Grade II listed country house, with oak panelling, exposed beams and log fires. Has a heated indoor pool, as well as expansive gardens and paddocks. Offers large bedrooms, a library and walking maps of the area. Barn House is located in a quiet part of the picturesque High Street. **www.karenbrown.com**

BUCKLAND Buckland Manor

Buckland, Gloucestershire, WR12 7LY **Tel** *01386 852626* **Fax** *01386 853557* **Rooms** *14*

This 13th-century country-house hotel, near Broadway, features antiques-filled rooms and fine views over the grounds. Hosts croquet lawns, tennis courts, a heated pool and a private putting green. The award-winning restaurant serves seasonal fruit, vegetables and herbs from the nearby Vale of Evesham. **www.bucklandmanor.com**

CHELTENHAM Georgian House

77 Montpellier Terrace, Cheltenham, Gloucestershire, GL50 1XA **Tel** *01242 515577* **Fax** *01242 545929* **Rooms** *3*

Small, reasonably-priced B&B in a terraced Georgian house built in 1807. The rooms are large and have period fireplaces, wall hangings and furnishings; one of the rooms has a balcony overlooking the garden. Serves hearty breakfasts. Garage parking is available, but it is best to reserve in advance. **www.georgianhouse.net**

CHELTENHAM Hotel Kandinisky

Bayshill Rd, Montepellier, Cheltenham, Gloucestershire, GL50 3AS **Tel** *01242 527788* **Rooms** *48*

An eclectic hotel with contrasting Regency exterior, located in the heart of Cheltenham. The rooms are large and luxurious. Features a sunlit conservatory and a large lounge for guests, and has a contract with a local gym, just ten minutes away. Also has an Italian restaurant and a basement cocktail bar. **www.hotelkandinsky.com**

CHIPPING CAMPDEN Nineveh Farm

Campden Rd, Mickleton, Chipping Campden, Gloucestershire, GL55 6PS **Tel** *01386 438923* **Rooms** *29*

Cosy and welcoming B&B in a 200-year-old Cotswold farmhouse, within easy reach of Chipping Campden and Stratford-upon-Avon. Rooms are furnished with oak beams, flagstone floors and log fires, with views over the vast grounds. Provides ample parking space, and offers discounts for longer stays. **www.ninevehfarm.co.uk**

CHIPPING CAMPDEN Badgers Hall

High St, Chipping Campden, Gloucestershire, GL55 6HB **Tel** *01386 840839* **Rooms** *3*

This non-smoking B&B and traditional English tearoom offers a friendly and comfortable stay in the beautiful old Cotswolds market town of Chipping Campden. The bedrooms are large, with antique pine furnishings and wood-beamed ceilings. Serves plentiful breakfasts and authentic cream teas. **www.badgershall.com**

CHIPPING CAMPDEN Cotswold House

Chipping Campden, Gloucestershire, GL55 6AN **Tel** *01386 840330* **Fax** *01386 840310* **Rooms** *29*

Located in a Regency town house, this elegant property offers a luxurious, relaxing break in some of England's most beautiful countryside. The deluxe rooms have fireplaces, hot tubs, king-sized beds and state-of-the-art facilities. **www.cotswoldhouse.com**

EVESHAM Evesham Hotel

Coopers Lane, off Waterside, Evesham, Worcestershire, WR11 1DA **Tel** *01386 765566* **Rooms** *40*

Family-friendly and well-priced hotel, often ranked among the top ten places to stay in Britain. The rooms provide all modern amenities, but are decorated to befit the building's Georgian heritage; some rooms offer great views of the grounds. Has an indoor swimming pool. **www.eveshamhotel.com**

GLEWSTONE Glewstone Court

Near Ross-on-Wye, Herefordshire, HR9 6AW **Tel** *01989 770367* **Fax** *01989 770282* **Rooms** *8*

Ideally located in the Wye Valley Area of Outstanding Natural Beauty. This family-friendly hotel is well placed for walking, horse riding, canoeing and other outdoor activities. Rooms are luxurious with polished floors, open log fires and antique furnishings. The restaurant serves fresh seasonal fare. **www.glewstonecourt.com**

HEREFORD New Priory

Stretton Sugwas, Hereford, Herefordshire, HR4 7AR **Tel** *01432 760264* **Fax** *01432 761809* **Rooms** *7*

Small, but grand, family-run hotel in an 18th-century building, on the outskirts of Hereford. Rooms are large with antique furnishings, including luxurious four-poster beds. The surrounding countryside is stunning and well worth a visit. The restaurant serves local produce (reservations should be made in advance). **www.newprioryhotel.co.uk**

HEREFORD Pilgrim Hotel

Much Birch, Hereford, Herefordshire, HR2 8HJ **Tel** *01981 540742* **Fax** *01981 540620* **Rooms** *20*

Delightful three-star, country-house hotel, set amid a vast parkland in the Wye Valley just outside Hereford. The rooms are cosy, with views over the rolling mountains into Wales. Boasts a three-hole pitch and putt course, as well as an award-winning restaurant. Guests can also enjoy scenic walks through the Dore Valley. **www.pilgrimhotel.co.uk**

HEREFORD Castle House Hotel

Castle St, Hereford **Tel** *01432 356321* **Fax** *01432 365909* **Rooms** *15*

Set in the heart of historic Hereford, Castle House occupies a gracious Georgian town house. Its award-winning restaurant and quiet gardens with views over the old castle moat really make this a special place to stay. The rooms are elegantly furnished with fine antiques and all have modern amenities. **www.castlehse.co.uk**

ILMINGTON Howard Arms

Lower Green, Ilmington, nr Shipston-on-Stour, Warwickshire, CV36 4LT **Tel** *01608 682226* **Rooms** *3*

Traditional Cotswolds pub offering B&B accommodation on the village green. The rooms at this non-smoking hotel have a beamed ceiling and antique, country-style furnishings. Voted "UK Dining Pub of the Year 2005" by the Good Pub Guide for its fresh seasonal produce and an extensive selection of wine and cask ale. **www.howardarms.com**

Key to Price Guide *see p556* **Key to Symbols** *see back cover flap*

IRONBRIDGE Library House

11 Severn Bank, Ironbridge, Telford, Shropshire, TF8 7AN **Tel** *01952 432299* **Fax** *01952 433967* **Rooms** *4*

A distinguished guesthouse, housed in a restored Grade II listed building in the World Heritage Site of Ironbridge Gorge. This non-smoking hotel sits in a peaceful location among immaculately-tended gardens, and is a short distance from the Telford town centre. Each of the rooms has en suite facilities. **www.libraryhouse.com**

LEYSTERS Hills Farm

Leysters, Leominster, Herefordshire, HR 60HP **Tel** *01568 750205* **Rooms** *3*

A family-run farmhouse B&B, set amid working farmland in the heart of rural Herefordshire. The bedrooms have en suite facilities, and are located in converted barn houses. Offers a sitting room, as well as maps and touring guides of the area. **www.thehillsfarm.co.uk**

LITTLE MALVERN Holdfast Cottage

Little Malvern, nr Malvern, Worcestershire, WR13 6NA **Tel** *01684 310288* **Fax** *01684 311117* **Rooms** *8*

This country-house hotel is a delightful place to unwind. Boasts attractive woodland gardens and magnificent views of the Malvern Hills. The cosy, oak-beamed rooms have en suite facilities, and the intimate dining room serves home baked cuisine using herbs and vegetables grown in the grounds. **www.holdfast-cottage.co.uk**

MALVERN WELLS Cottage in the Wood

Holywell Rd, Malvern Wells, Worcestershire, WR14 4LG **Tel** *01684 575859* **Fax** *01684 560662* **Rooms** *31*

An award-winning hotel, renowned for its unique location high on the Malvern Hills, and for one of the best views in England – panoramas extend as far as the Cotswolds and the spires of Cheltenham. This family-run hotel comprises three buildings shielded within vast woodlands. **www.cottageinthewood.co.uk**

NORTON Hundred House

Bridgnorth Rd (A442), Norton, nr Shifnal, Shropshire, TF11 9EE **Tel** *01952 730353* **Fax** *01952 730355* **Rooms** *10*

Each room in this friendly, acclaimed hotel offers something a little bit different: one has a four-poster bed and period furniture; another has a velvet covered swing; and another has patchwork drapes and fragrant bed sheets. The pub serves everything from pigs' trotter soup to smoked salmon from Loch Fyne. **www.hundredhouse.co.uk**

PAINSWICK The Painswick Hotel & Old Rectory Restaurant

Kemps Lane, Painswick, Gloucestershire, England, GL6 6YB **Tel** *01452 812160* **Fax** *01452 814059* **Rooms** *19*

Oft-considered Britain's best country-house hotel, this former rectory sits in the heart of the Cotswold Hills. The rooms are decorated with stylish period furniture and some contemporary designs, luxury fabrics and open fires. The award-winning restaurant offers classic British dishes and an extensive wine list. **www.painswickhotel.com**

PRESTBURY White House Manor

Prestbury, Cheshire, SK10 4HP **Tel** *01625 829376* **Fax** *01625 828627* **Rooms** *11*

Popular manor house, located within easy reach of Manchester. The rooms are luxurious and individually furnished with antiques, collectibles and rich fabrics. All the rooms offer basic amenities such as central heating and TV, as well as a range of tea, coffee and alcoholic beverages. Also hosts an acclaimed restaurant. **www.thewhitehouse.uk.com**

SHREWSBURY Albright Hussey Manor Hotel & Restaurant

Shrewsbury, Shropshire, SY4 3AF **Tel** *01939 290523/290571* **Fax** *01939 291143* **Rooms** *26*

Converted moated manor house with splendid views over the Shropshire countryside. All the rooms offer en suite facilties, and boast an atmospheric blend of historic oak panelling, open fireplaces, Tudor beams and modern ameni-ties. Six of the rooms feature original four-poster beds, spa baths and antique furnishings. **www.albrighthussey.co.uk**

STAFFORD The Swan

46 Greengate St, Stafford, ST16 2JA **Tel** *01785 258142* **Fax** *01785 223372* **Rooms** *31*

The Swan, a former 16th-century coaching inn, benefits from a central town location. Lovingly restored, many of the rooms have original features including stone fireplaces and exposed beams. There are amenities for business and leisure travellers as well as a brasserie and coffee shop. **www.theswanstafford.co.uk**

STRATFORD-UPON-AVON Victoria Spa Lodge

Bishopton Lane, Bishopton, Stratford-upon-Avon, Warwickickshire, CV37 9QY **Tel** *01789 267985* **Rooms** *7*

Built in 1837, this non-smoking Victorian spa hotel was visited by Queen Victoria, hence its name and the appearance of her coat of arms in the hotel gables. The bedrooms face forward onto the hotel grounds; some overlook Stratford-upon-Avon's canal. Serves a generous breakfast, and has a helpful staff. **www.stratford-uopn-avon.co.uk/victoriaspa**

STRATFORD-UPON-AVON Willow Corner

Armscote, Stratford-upon-Avon, Warwickshire, CV37 8DE **Tel** *01608 682391* **Rooms** *3*

Small, luxury B&B in a beautiful, 300-year-old thatched cottage, a short drive from Stratford-upon-Avon. The rates include a full English breakfast with home-made bread and jams, served beside the magnificent inglenook fireplace in the main lounge. **www.willowcorner.co.uk**

STRATFORD-UPON-AVON The Old Manor House

Halford, Stratford-upon-Avon, Warwickshire, CV36 5BT **Tel** *01789 740264* **Fax** *01789 740609* **Rooms** *3*

Friendly B&B in a Grade II listed, part-Tudor manor house, overlooking vast parklands. The rooms have oak-beamed ceilings, modern furnishings and fine views over the surrounding Warwickshire countryside. Also has a tennis court. The price includes a hearty breakfast, but dinner is only by arrangement. **www.oldmanor-halford.co.uk**

SUTTON COLDFIELD New Hall   🍴🛏🖼   ££££

Walmley Rd, Sutton Coldfield, West Midlands, B76 1QX **Tel** *0121 3782442* **Fax** *0121 3111745* **Rooms** *60*

The oldest, inhabited moated house in England, this Grade 1 listed building is set in 26 acres (10.5 ha) of peaceful grounds. The rooms have oak-panelling, four-poster beds and stained-glass windows. Also features a croquet lawn, putting green, tennis court, nine-hole golf course and beauty spa. **www.newhalluk.com**

TEWKESBURY Abbey Antiques   🖼   £

62 Church St, Tewkesbury, Gloucestershire, GL20 5RZ **Tel** *01684 298145* **Rooms** *3*

This small B&B in a Grade II listed Georgian town house showcases an excellent selection of antiques. The hotel lies a short walk from Tewkesbury's main sights, including the Norman Abbey and the ancient water meadows of the Avon and Severn Rivers. Serves up plenty of sightseeing advice along with a hearty breakfast. Also has a self-catering unit.

TRUMPET The Verzon   🍴🛏⛺   ££

Hereford Rd, Trumpet, Nr Ledbury, HR8 2PZ **Tel** *01531 670381* **Fax** *01531 670830* **Rooms** *8*

The Verzon is a stylish boutique hotel situated 2 miles (3 km) from the historic market town of Ledbury. All rooms have been recently refurbished and have walk-in showers. The Mulbery bar and brasserie offer informal dining. Stunning views of the Malvern Hills can be appreciated from the deck terrace. **www.theverzon.co.uk**

WILMCOTE Pear Tree Cottage   🖼   £

7 Church Rd, Wilmcote, Stratford upon Avon, CV37 9UX **Tel** *01789 205889* **Fax** *01789 262862* **Rooms** *3*

Perfectly located for exploring Shakespeare Country, this cosy B&B is just a short walk from Mary Arden's House – the home of Shakespeare's mother. Offers rooms as well as self-catering apartments. Guests are free to make use of the owners' comfortable lounge. **www.peartreecot.co.uk**

WINCHCOMBE Wesley House   🍴   ££££

High St, Winchcombe, Gloucestershire, GL54 5LJ **Tel** *01242 602366* **Fax** *01242 609046* **Rooms** *5*

Historic, half-timbered restaurant-with-rooms. The rooms overlook the North Cotswolds, and are small, but cosy. The Almsbury room has a private terrace and the best view, and the Preacher's room once gave shelter to the founder of the Methodist Church, John Wesley. **www.wesleyhouse.co.uk**

EAST MIDLANDS

BABWORTH The Barns Country Guesthouse   £

Morton Farm, Babworth, Retford, Nottinghamshire, DN22 8HA **Tel** *01777 706336* **Rooms** *6*

Non-smoking B&B in the heart of Robin Hood Country. Offers peaceful rooms in a converted, 18th-century farmhouse, near the busy market town of Retford. Vine-covered exterior walls, original oak beams and country furniture all add to the rural charm. Serves a hearty breakfast. **www.thebarns.co.uk**

BARNBY MOOR Ye Olde Bell Hotel   🍴⛺   ££

Barnby Moor, Retford, Nottinghamshire, DN22 8QS **Tel** *01777 705121* **Fax** *01777 860424* **Rooms** *51*

Set in expansive, tranquil grounds on the edge of Sherwood Forest, this converted coaching inn is one of Nottinghamshire's most characterful hotels. The rooms are decorated with oak panelling, log fires and leaded windows, and the restaurant serves award-winning cuisine. **www.swallowhotels.com**

BASLOW Hotel Cavendish   🍴   ££££

Baslow, Derbyshire, DE45 1SP **Tel** *01246 582311* **Fax** *01246 582312* **Rooms** *24*

This beautiful property is located on the Chatsworth Estate, at the heart of the Peak District National Park. Most of the furnishings – an elegant blend of antiques and modern art – come from Chatsworth House itself. The hotel is within reach of the spa town of Buxton. **www.cavendish-hotel.net**

BIGGIN-BY-HARTINGDON Biggin Hall   🍴   ££

Biggin-by-Hartington, Buxton, Derbyshire, SK17 0DH **Tel** *01298 84451* **Fax** *01298 84681* **Rooms** *19*

A peaceful, 17th-century country-house hotel, in the Peak District National Park. This Grade II listed building is set amid typical Derbyshire landscape, with heather-clad moorlands and deep wooded valleys. Offers spacious rooms, furnished with four-poster beds and open fires, as well as self-contained apartments. **www.bigginhall.co.uk**

EAST BARKWITH Bodkin Lodge   🖼   £

Torrington Lane, E Barkwith, Market Rasen, Lincolnshire, LN8 5RY **Tel & Fax** *01673 858249* **Rooms** *2*

This welcoming B&B, located on a working farm, is a popular stopping-off point for walkers – a nature trail departs from the door – and racing fans, who can visit the Cadwell Park Racing Circuit nearby. Hosts spacious rooms, and serves a generous breakfast, with Lincolnshire sausages.

GLOSSOP Wind in the Willows   🍴   £££

Glossop, Derbyshire, SK13 7PT **Tel** *01457 868001* **Fax** *01457 853354* **Rooms** *12*

Early Victorian country house with great views of the Peak District National Park. Boasts delightful oak-panelled rooms with antique furnishings and modern facilities. The popular restaurant serves traditional English fare in its period dining room. A nine-hole golf course adjoins the hotel. **www.windinthewillows.co.uk**

Key to Price Guide *see p556* **Key to Symbols** *see back cover flap*

HOPE Underleigh House ££

Off Edale Rd, Hope, Derbyshire, S33 6RF **Tel** *01433 621372* **Fax** *01433 621324* **Rooms** *6*

This small B&B is located in prime walking area, and offers panoramic views over the surrounding Peak District. Set in a converted cottage and barn, it provides comfortable, spacious rooms, and a generous breakfast in its stone-flagged dining room. The staff is friendly and helpful. **www.underleighhouse.co.uk**

LANGAR Langar Hall £££

Langar, Nottinghamshire, NG13 9HG **Tel** *01949 860559* **Fax** *01949 861045* **Rooms** *12*

This stately country-house hotel is popular for weddings and other celebrations. The elegant rooms are split between the main house and the chalet next to the croquet lawn. The restaurant serves simple English cuisine, including Stilton from Colston Bassett and fruits from the Belvoir fruit farm. **www.langarhall.com**

LINCOLN Bail House ££

34 Bailgate, Lincoln, Lincolnshire, LN1 3AP **Tel** *01522 520883* **Fax** *01522 521829* **Rooms** *10*

A 14th-century B&B, just a short walk from the town's castle and cathedral. The rooms have oak-beamed ceilings and a mix of period and modern furnishings. There is a patio for sunbathing in the summer, an outdoor pool and a large gravel car park. Also offers self-catering accommodation. **www.bailhouse.co.uk**

LINCOLN Branston Hall ££

Branston, Lincoln, Lincolnshire, LN4 1PD **Tel** *01522 793305* **Fax** *01522 790734* **Rooms** *48*

Elegant country-house hotel, set amid an expansive stretch of wooded parkland and lakes. The award-winning, lakeside restaurant has oak-panelled walls and fantastic views over the hotel grounds. Also has an indoor heated pool, jacuzzi, sauna and gym. **www.branstonhall.com**

LINCOLN Stragglethorpe Hall ££

Lincoln, Lincolnshire, LN5 0QZ **Tel** *01400 272308* **Fax** *01400 273816* **Rooms** *3*

Small, hospitable B&B in a Grade II listed building. The hotel has a wedding license for performing civil marriages, and is popular among couples for its four-poster honeymoon suite. Also organizes several classical performances in its formal gardens. Offers elegant rooms, and dinner is available on request. **www.stragglethorpe.com**

LOUTH The Priory ££

149 Eastgate, Louth, Lincolnshire, LN11 9AJ **Tel** *01507 602930* **Fax** *01507 609767* **Rooms** *10*

This newly-refurbished, Grade II listed building boasts beautiful gardens, a stunning wood-panelled bar, a Gothic function room (generally used for weddings) and a communal lounge for playing cards. The rooms are modern, but in line with the building's original architecture. **www.theprioryhotel.com**

MATLOCK BATH Hodgkinson's Hotel & Restaurant ££

150 S Parade, Matlock Bath, Derbyshire, DE4 3NR **Tel** *01629 582170* **Fax** *01629 584891* **Rooms** *7*

This stylish hotel dates back to the Georgian spa era, and is housed in a Grade II listed building. Offers carefully-renovated, luxurious rooms, furnished with original antiques and four-poster beds. The elegant restaurant serves delicious Italian cuisine. **www.hodgkinsons-hotel.co.uk**

MATLOCK BATH Whitworth Park Hotel ££

Dale Rd N, Matlock, Derbyshire, DE4 2FT **Tel** *01629 733111* **Fax** *01629 735222* **Rooms** *5*

An intimate hotel in a recently-renovated, Victorian building. The rooms in this non-smoking, Grade II listed property have oak-panelled walls and period furnishings. Advance reservations are recommended for the restaurant, which opens daily for lunch and dinner. **www.whitworthparkhotel.co.uk**

NOTTINGHAM Greenwood Lodge £

Third Ave, Sherwood Rise, Nottingham, NG7 6JH **Tel** *01159 621206* **Fax** *01159 621206* **Rooms** *6*

A small guesthouse, just a short distance from the city centre. The hotel is set in a charming courtyard garden, and offers non-smoking rooms, decorated with four-poster beds and exquisite antique furnishings. Children below the age of 12 are not allowed. **www.greenwoodlodgecityguesthouse.co.uk**

NOTTINGHAM Lace Market £££

29–31 High Pavement, The Lace Market, Nottingham, NG1 1HE **Tel** *0115 8523232* **Tel** *0115 8523223* **Rooms** *42*

This trendy hotel is home to a brasserie, gastropub and a cocktail bar. The luxurious rooms are equipped with modern facilities, and offer great views over St Mary's Church and the Galleries of Justice. Serves a variety of good food and drink, and provides free access to the nearby Holme's Place health club. **www.lacemarkethotel.co.uk**

NOTTINGHAM Restaurant Sat Bains £££

Restaurant Sat Bains, Old Lenton Lane, Nottingham, NG7 2SA **Tel** *0115 9866566* **Fax** *0115 9860343* **Rooms** *8*

Highly regarded and popular restaurant-with-rooms, in a peaceful riverside location. The rooms feature Molton Brown toiletries, freshly-brewed coffee and Egyptian cotton linen. Also boasts a cooking school, and offers a selection of holiday-package deals. **www.restaurantsatbains.net**

OAKHAM The Old Wisteria Hotel & Restaurant ££

4 Catmose St, Oakham, Rutland, Leicestershire, LE15 6HW **Tel** *01572 722844* **Fax** *01572 724473* **Rooms** *25*

Some sections of this welcoming country-house hotel date back to 1604. This former Georgian hunting lodge offers small, but elegant rooms, all equipped with en suite facilities. Also presents splendid views over Rutland Water. The restaurant serves traditional local cuisine. **www.wisteriahotel.co.uk**

OAKHAM Hambleton Hall
£££££

Oakham, Rutland, Leicestershire, LE15 8TH **Tel** *01572 756991* **Fax** *01572 724721* **Rooms** *15*

Part of the Relais & Chateaux network of hotels, this sophisticated country-house hotel has a stunning lakeside setting. The spacious rooms are decorated with comfortable furnishings and rich fabrics, and the gourmet restaurant offers a fine wine list. Also has a heated outdoor pool and tennis courts. **www.hambletonhall.com**

SARACENS HEAD Pipwell Manor
£

Washway Rd, Saracens Head, Holbeach, Spalding, Lincolnshire, PE12 8AL **Tel & Fax** *01406 423119* **Rooms** *4*

This stylish B&B, set in the heart of Lincolnshire, is the perfect destination for nature lovers and bird-watchers hoping to explore the Fens. A former outpost of Pipwell Abbey, the manor retains much of its original 1700s character, but for a few modern additions, such as the miniature railway around the large gardens. **www.smoothhound.co.uk/hotels**

STAMFORD George of Stamford
£££

71 St Martins, Stamford, Lincolnshire, PE9 2LB, **Tel** *01780 750750* **Fax** *01780 750701* **Rooms** *47*

Historic coaching inn with magnificent oak-panelled walls. The rooms are comfortable and spacious, equipped with en suite facilities and modern amenities. The well-reputed restaurant serves mouthwatering cuisine, which includes traditional English fare. Also has a business centre. **www.georgehotelofstamford.com**

WORKSOP Charnwood Hotel
££

Sheffield Rd, Blyth, Worksop, Nottinghamshire, S81 8HF **Tel** *01909 591610* **Fax** *01909 591429* **Rooms** *32*

A modern hotel, set in vast gardens, and well placed for exploring the countryside. Has large bedrooms and a reasonably-priced lounge bar. Popular with business travellers for its meeting facilities and conference equipment. The restaurant serves typical English specialities. **www.charnwood-hotel.com**

LANCASHIRE AND THE LAKES

AMBLESIDE Wateredge Inn
££

Waterhead Bay, Ambleside, Cumbria, LA22 OEP **Tel** *015394 323 32* **Fax** *015394 318 78* **Rooms** *21*

Delightful inn set in two adjoining 17th-century fishermen's cottages, near Lake Windermere. The colourfully decorated rooms have en suite facilities; many offer great views of the lake. Well-placed for exploring the scenic countryside and other local attractions. Includes breakfast. **www.wateredgeinn.co.uk**

AMBLESIDE Drunken Duck
£££

Barngates, Ambleside, Cumbria, LA22 ONG **Tel** *015394 363 47* **Fax** *015394 367 81* **Rooms** *16*

This lively dining-pub-with-rooms has been welcoming travellers for more than 400 years. Wood fires, oak floors and ales brewed on site add to the appeal. Offers breathtaking views of Lake Windermere. The rooms are stylish; ask for the Garden Room with its open-beamed ceiling. Room rate includes breakfast. **www.drunkenduckinn.co.uk**

BASSENTHWAITE Pheasant
££

Bassenthwaite Lake, Cockermouth, Cumbria, CA13 9YE **Tel** *01768 7762 34* **Fax** *01768 760 02* **Rooms** *14*

Where other inns have been ruthlessly stylized, this well-loved hostelry retains its traditional and tranquil ambience. Built 500 years ago as a farmhouse, it became an alehouse in 1778. Has bright and cheery bedrooms; some have en suite facilities. The snug bar is highly popular. Also has a spacious lounge. **www.the-pheasant.co.uk**

BLACKBURN Northcote Manor
£££

Northcote Rd, Blackburn, Lancashire, BB6 8BE **Tel** *01254 240 555* **Fax** *01254 246 568* **Rooms** *14*

A luxurious restaurant-with-rooms, housed in an elegant manor amid lovely gardens. This comfortable house is renowned for its warmth and friendly welcome, as well as superb cuisine. Offers individually decorated rooms, with modern amenities, a traditional English breakfast and complimentary newspaper. **www.northcotemanor.com**

BLACKPOOL Raffles
£

73–77 Hornby Rd, Blackpool, Lancashire, FY1 4QJ **Tel** *01253 294 713* **Fax** *01253 294 240* **Rooms** *19*

Flower-decked, white-and-blue painted B&B close to the famous Blackpool Tower. A decided notch above the usual seaside offering, it offers a warm welcome along with bright and stylish rooms. A great place for afternoon tea; the evening meals are generous. Includes breakfast. **www.raffleshotelblackpool.co.uk**

BLACKPOOL Hotel Sheraton
££

54–62 Queens Promenade, Blackpool, Lancashire, FY2 9RP **Tel** *01253 352 723* **Fax** *01253 595 499* **Rooms** *104*

Features an entertainment programme every night of the week, as well as several attractions for kids. The public areas and well-appointed bedrooms are exceptionally spacious, and the service standards high. Also has a large indoor pool. Includes breakfast. **www.hotelsheraton.co.uk**

BLACKPOOL The Imperial
£££

N Promenade, Blackpool, Lancashire, FY1 2HB **Tel** *01253 623 971* **Fax** *01253 751 784* **Rooms** *181*

Part of the Paramount Group, this opulent hotel recently underwent a £1 million refurbishment. Ideally located, it presents spectacular views over the beach and the sea, and is only minutes from the local attractions. Rooms and suites are elegantly furnished. Also has a sauna, steam room and spa. **www.paramount-hotels.co.uk**

Key to Price Guide *see p556* **Key to Symbols** *see back cover flap*

BOLTON The Last Drop Village Hotel

Bromley Cross, Bolton, Lancashire, BL7 9PZ **Tel** *01204 591 131* **Fax** *01204 304 122* **Rooms** *128*

One of a kind, this charming retreat is a re-creation of a typical North Country moorland village. Features arts and crafts shops and a range of eating options. Rooms are modern and well equipped. The glorious Pennine Hills are close by, and it's a short drive into bustling Manchester. **www.macdonaldhotels.co.uk/lastdropvillage**

BOWNESS-ON-WINDERMERE Lindeth Fell Country House Hotel
Lyth Valley Rd, Bowness-On-Windermere, Cumbria, LA23 3JP **Tel** *01539 443 286* **Fax** *01539 447 455* **Rooms** *14*

Relaxing country-house hotel, located in the beautiful hills above Lake Windermere. The decor is fresh and stylish, with original works of art adorning the walls. Has spacious, attractively furnished rooms, equipped with modern amenities. Includes breakfast. **www.lindethfell.co.uk**

BOWNESS-ON-WINDERMERE Linthwaite House
Crook Rd, Bowness-On-Windermere, Cumbria, LA23 3JA **Tel** *015394 88 600* **Fax** *015394 88 601* **Rooms** *27*

A fine country house, located on a sublime hilltop setting, overlooking the beautiful waters of Lake Windermere. The recently refurbished rooms are elegantly decorated, with modern conveniences and great views. This romantic retreat is an ideal venue for a wedding or honeymoon. **www.linthwaite.com**

BUTTERMERE Wood House

Buttermere, Cockermouth, Cumbria, CA13 9XA **Tel** *017687 702 08* **Fax** *017687 702 41* **Rooms** *3*

Magnificent views across the Lake District fells. The rooms personify simple elegance, furnished with lovely antiques. However, the greatest appeal of this tiny hideaway is the owner's home-baked bread. Also has a delightful stone cottage that can be rented on a weekly basis. **www.wdhse.co.uk**

CARLISLE Number Thirty-One
31 Howard Place, Carlisle, Cumbria, CA1 1HR **Tel** *01228 597 080* **Fax** *01228 597 080* **Rooms** *3*

A stylish Victorian town house in a quiet residential area, yet just a short distance from the city centre. The decor is bold and full of panache. Offers evening meals, provided they are pre-ordered as only fresh ingredients are used. Charming rooms, equipped with modern conveniences. **www.number31.freeservers.com**

CARTMEL FELL Lightwood
Cartmel Fell, Grange-Over-Sands, Cumbria, LA11 6NP **Tel** *015395 314 54* **Fax** *015395 314 54* **Rooms** *4*

This family-run guesthouse stands amid landscaped and natural gardens. It nestles high in the fells, but is still close to Windermere's shores. Oak beams and inglenook fireplaces are combined with modern home features. The rooms are spacious and comfortable. Breakfast is included. **www.lightwoodguesthouse.com**

CHIPPING The Gibbon Hotel
Chipping, Forest of Bowland, Preston, Lancashire, PR3 2TQ **Tel** *01995 614 56* **Fax** *01995 612 77* **Rooms** *29*

Stone-built, luxury hotel located in the Forest of Bowland – designated as an Area of Outstanding Natural Beauty. Offers fine dining, expansive gardens and tastefully decorated rooms. A profusion of country pursuits such as walks, cycling and bird-watching are available. Includes breakfast. **www.gibbon-bridge.co.uk**

CHORLEY Park Hallhotel
Charnock Richard, Chorley, Preston, Lancashire, PR7 5LP **Tel** *01257 455 000* **Fax** *01257 451 838* **Rooms** *140*

Contemporary hotel set beside a peaceful lake, and owned by the operators of the Camelot theme park next door. The spacious rooms have amenities such as modem points and a Sony PlayStation keypad. Entertainment includes a cabaret, nightclub and a medieval banquet hall. **www.parkhall-hotel.co.uk**

COCKERMOUTH The Trout

Crown St, Cockermouth, Cumbria, CA13 OEJ **Tel** *01900 823 591* **Fax** *01900 827 514* **Rooms** *43*

An appropriate name for a comfortable, if a little impersonal hotel that stands by the fast-moving River Derwent in the northern reaches of Lake District. Just a short walk into delightful Cockermouth – if you can tear yourself away from the hotel's lovely gardens. Room rates include breakfast. **www.trouthotel.co.uk**

GRANGE-INN-BORROWDALE Borrowdale Gates
Grange-Inn-Borrowdale, Keswick, Cumbria, CA12 5UQ **Tel** *01768 777 204* **Fax** *01768 777 254* **Rooms** *29*

In a wooded valley close to the shores of Derwentwater, "The Queen of the English Lakes". This relaxing hotel is a sensible base for walking, climbing and touring this scenic region. The ever-changing colours of the seasons add to the charm of this smart and well-managed hotel. **www.borrowdale-gates.com**

GRASSMERE Howfoot Lodge
Town End, Grassmere, Cumbria, LA22 9SQ **Tel** *015394 353 66* **Fax** *015394 352 68* **Rooms** *6*

This Victorian guesthouse is owned by the Wordsworth Trust. It stands in landscaped gardens and is furnished with period antiques in keeping with the house. Has pleasant and cheerful rooms. An excellent place for outdoor activities such as walks and bicycling. **www.howfoot.co.uk**

HAWKSHEAD Queens Head Hotel
Main St, Hawkshead, Cumbria, LA22 ONS **Tel** *015394 362 71* **Fax** *015394 367 22* **Rooms** *14*

At the heart of one of the prettiest Lakeland villages. Low, exposed oak-beamed ceilings, flagstone floors and a profusion of memorabilia create a relaxed and informal ambience. Offers comfortable rooms; some with four-poster beds. Also has family rooms. Food is prepared using fresh local produce. **www.queensheadhotel.co.uk**

KENDAL Riverside Hotel Kendal
££

Stramongate Gate, Beezon Rd, Kendal, Cumbria, LA9 4BZ **Tel** *015397 348 61* **Fax** *015397 348 63* **Rooms** *47*

This charming hotel is housed in an imposing and highly photogenic building, built in 1625. The recently refurbished rooms are tastefully decorated, with en suite facilities and other modern amenities; most offer striking views of the river. Well placed for exploring the various attractions the Lake District has to offer. **www.riversidekendal.co.uk**

KESWICK The Grange
££

Manor Brow, Keswick, Cumbria, CA12 4BA **Tel** *017687 72500* **Fax** *017687 72500* **Rooms** *10*

The only five-diamond establishment in the Keswick area, this small hotel now operates as a B&B. However, it has retained the hotel-style facilities, which have brought guests back time and again. The scenic views of England's highest mountains are breathtaking, the hospitality faultless. **www.grangekeswick.com**

LANCASTER Lancaster House
£££

Green Lane, Ellel, Lancaster, LA1 4GJ **Tel** *01524 844 822* **Fax** *01524 844 766* **Rooms** *99*

Savour the good things in life in this modern and elegant hotel, with its gourmet restaurant, intimate bar and balconied lounge. A recent £3.2 million development scheme has added new, well-appointed suites, with modern conveniences, as well as a spa and hot tubs in its leisure club. **www.elhmail.co.uk**

LIVERPOOL Premier Lodge
£

E Britannia Building, Albert Dock, Liverpool, L3 4AD **Tel** *0870 990 6432* **Fax** *0870 990 6433* **Rooms** *200*

A budget hotel maybe, but with spacious rooms featuring superb six-feet wide beds. The location is outstanding too – amid the restored warehouses of the Albert Dock. Nearby attractions include a Beatles museum, national gallery outpost, restaurants, bars and the mighty River Mersey. **www.premierlodge.com**

LYTHAM ST ANNES Lindum Hotel
££

63-67 S Promenade, Lytham St Annes, Lancashire, FY8 1LZ **Tel** *01253 721 534* **Fax** *01253 721 364* **Rooms** *78*

A delightful, family-run hotel, located within easy walking distance of the city centre. This seaside retreat has attractively decorated rooms, equipped with modern facilities; most rooms have great views and a sauna and jacuzzi. Serves fresh local produce. Sunday lunch is a much-anticipated affair. Room rates include breakfast. **www.lindumhotel.co.uk**

MANCHESTER Campanile
£

55 Ordsall Lane, Salford, Lancashire, M5 4RS **Tel** *0161 833 1845* **Fax** *0161 833 1847* **Rooms** *104*

Part of the Campanile chain of hotels. Although pitched at the budget end of the market, this hotel offers pleasant rooms with nice little touches such as tea and coffee makers, big beds and well-equipped bathrooms. The in-house restaurant offers good value French country-style food. **www.campanile.com**

MANCHESTER Malmaison
£££

Piccadilly, Manchester, Lancashire, M1 3AQ **Tel** *0161 278 1000* **Fax** *0161 278 1002* **Rooms** *167*

Stylish hotel housed in a converted, 19th-century building, located in the centre of town. Close to the Piccadilly train station, several shops and other downtown attractions. Offers contemporary rooms, decorated in bright, bold colours. Also has a bistro-style restaurant and a spa. **www.malmaison.com**

MANCHESTER The Victoria & Albert Hotel
£££

Water St, Manchester, Lancashire, M3 4JQ **Tel** *0161 8321188* **Fax** *0161 834 2484* **Rooms** *148*

Now part of the Marriott Group, this grand hotel occupies a converted, industrial building, on the banks of River Irwell. Architectural features such as bare brick and wrought iron add appropriate ambience. Within walking distance of several local attractions. Rooms are comfortable and modern. **www.marriotthotels.com**

MANCHESTER The Midland Hotel
££££

Peter St, Manchester, Lancashire, M60 2DS **Tel** *0161 236 3333* **Fax** *0161 932 4100* **Rooms** *303*

This imposing, red sandstone hotel has been one of Manchester's most familiar landmarks since it opened in 1903. Elegance, luxury and high standards of service, accommodation and cuisine are on offer. Also has an indoor pool and a spa. Breakfast is included in the room rates. **www.qhotels.co.uk**

MANCHESTER The Lowry
£££££

50 Dearmans Place, Chapel Wharf, Salford, Greater Manchester, M3 5LH **Tel** *0161 827 4000* **Rooms** *165*

This ultra-modern, ultra-chic riverside hotel is a member of the prestigious Leading Hotels of the World consortium. Frequented by celebrities, fashion icons, pop stars and sports personalities. Rooms are modern and elegant, while the restaurant purveys modernistic British cuisine. **www.roccofortehotels.com**

MELLOR Millstone
££

3 Church Lane, Mellor, Blackburn, Lancashire, BB2 7JR **Tel** *01254 813 333* **Fax** *01254 812 628* **Rooms** *23*

A former coaching inn that retains its original charm, while adding modern amenities. One of the highest-rated, two-star hotels in the country, it offers neat, practical bedrooms. A good base for those interested in exploring the countryside. Room rates include breakfast. **www.shirehotels.co.uk**

OLD TRAFFORD Old Trafford Lodge
£

Lancashire County Cricket Club, Old Trafford, Manchester, Lancashire, M16 OPX **Tel** *0161 874 3333* **Rooms** *68*

Built next to the cricket ground and just minutes from Manchester United's ground and the huge Old Trafford shopping centre. This modern hotel offers comfortable rooms, with en suite facilities and modern conveniences. A short drive from the city centre. Includes breakfast. **www.lccc.co.uk**

Key to Price Guide *see p556* **Key to Symbols** *see back cover flap*

PENRITH North Lakes Hotel & Spa £££

*Ullswater Rd, Penrith, Cumbria, CA11 8QT **Tel** 01768 868 111 **Fax** 01768 868 291 **Rooms** 84*

The use of local stone, natural wood and open log fires create a genuine "away from it all" mood at this delightful family resort. Features a children's activity programme, massive indoor pool and a spa. This contemporary hotel is a Shire Hotels property. Breakfast included in the room rate. **www.northlakeshotel.com**

PRESTON Hotel Ibis £

*Garstang Rd, Broughton, Preston, Lancashire, PR3 5JE **Tel** 01772 861 800 **Fax** 01772 861 900 **Rooms** 82*

Part of the French Accor group's mid-market brand, this smart hotel guarantees consistent quality. The rooms are bright and family-friendly, furnished with modern amenities. The culinary offer here is French, bistro style. Well placed for exploring the Pennines and the Lakes. **www.ibishotel.com**

SAWREY Sawrey Hotel £

*Far Sawrey, Ambleside, Cumbria, LA22 OLQ **Tel** 015394 434 25 **Fax** 015394 434 25 **Rooms** 17*

Set in the conservation area for Beatrix Potter's Hilltop Farm, this charming property has a homely atmosphere. The bedrooms are spacious and tastefully furnished; most of them offer stunning views of the surroundings. Attractions such as Estwaite Water and Grizedale Forest are located nearby. Includes breakfast.

SELSIDE Low Jock Scar £

*Selside, Kendal, Cumbria, LA8 9LE **Tel** 01539 823 259 **Fax** 01539 823 259 **Rooms** 4*

A secluded, but easily accessible guesthouse. Features relaxing gardens, appetizing meals, cosy guest rooms and generous breakfasts. Located north of Kendal, the hotel is an ideal springboard for the southern Lakes. Encourages outdoor pursuits such as walks, cycling and sailing.

ULLSWATER Sharrow Bay £££££

*Ullswater, Penrith, Cumbria, CA10 1LZ **Tel** 017684 863 01 **Fax** 017684 863 49 **Rooms** 24*

An exquisite country-house hotel, located in a magnificent lakeside setting. Renowned for its excellent cuisine, stylish decor and perfect service. The rooms are appropriately luxurious, and the view from the dining room is claimed as one of England's most beautiful. Dinner is included in the room rate. **www.sharrowbay.co.uk**

ULVERSTON Bay Horse £££

*Canal Foot, Ulverston, Cumbria, LA12 9EL **Tel** 01229 583 972 **Fax** 01229 580 502 **Rooms** 9*

This 18th-century, half-timbered hostelry is situated at the edge of the Leven Estuary. Offers individually decorated, en suite rooms; some with French windows that present striking views of the sea. Ideal for bird-watchers. Warm and welcoming ambience. Includes breakfast. **www.thebayhorsehotel.co.uk**

WHITEWELL Inn At Whitewell £££

*Whitewell, Forest of Bowland, Lancashire, BB7 3AT **Tel** 01200 448 222 **Fax** 01200 448 298 **Rooms** 23*

Old-fashioned, yet sophisticated riverside inn. This welcoming and friendly retreat shares its premises with an art gallery and a wine merchant. Parts of the building date to the early 1300s. The rooms are stylishly spectacular. Serves delicious food and wines. A memorable experience.

WINDERMERE Holbeck Ghyll ££££

*Holbeck Lane, Windermere, Cumbria, LA23 1LU **Tel** 015394 323 75 **Fax** 015394 347 43 **Rooms** 21*

An oasis of calm, perfect for relaxing on the terrace and soaking up fantastic views across Lake Windermere to the rugged fells beyond. Food is mouthwateringly good, and the plush armchairs and open fire of the lounge encourage an indulgent way of life. Also has a spa and sauna. **www.holbeckghyll.com**

WINDERMERE Gilpin Lodge £££££

*Crook Rd, Windermere, Cumbria, LA23 3NE **Tel** 015394 888 18 **Fax** 015394 880 58 **Rooms** 20*

Several acres of gardens, woods and moorland provide a glorious setting for this long-established country-house hotel. The roaring log fires, fine wines and superb food add to the feeling of utter contentment. Rooms are spacious and beautifully furnished. Includes breakfast. **www.gilpinlodge.com**

YORKSHIRE AND THE HUMBER REGION

AMPLEFORTH Shallowdale House ££

*Ampleforth, nr York, North Yorkshire, YO62 4DY **Tel** 01439 788 325 **Fax** 01439 788 885 **Rooms** 3*

Refined guesthouse, just 32 km (20 miles) from York and on the southern edge of the North York Moors National Park. This small retreat was built in the 1960s, and overlooks an exquisite landscape of unspoilt Yorkshire countryside. The rooms are simple, yet stylish. Includes breakfast. **www.shallowdalehouse.co.uk**

BARNSLEY Brooklands Hotel £££

*Barnsley Rd, Dodsworth, Barnsley, South Yorkshire, S75 3JT **Tel** 01226 299 571 **Fax** 01226 249 465 **Rooms** 77*

This recently opened four-star hotel features well-appointed rooms, blending traditional elegance with modern conveniences. Includes executive suites and some rooms with four-poster beds. Holds a license for conducting civil wedding ceremonies. Also has nine conference rooms. **www.brooklandshotel.com**

BEVERLEY Tickton Grange Hotel

Main St, Tickton, Beverley, East Yorkshire, HU17 9SH **Tel** *01964 543 666* **Fax** *01964 542 556* **Rooms** *17*

A charming Georgian country-house hotel, set amid lovely, landscaped grounds. Offers tastfully decorated, en suite bedrooms, with thoughtful touches adding to the charm. The tranquil setting is ideal for both weddings and conferences. Serves mouthwatering desserts. **www.ticktongrange.co.uk**

BRADFORD Beeties

7 Victoria Rd, Bradford, West Yorkshire, BD18 3LA **Tel** *01274 581 718* **Fax** *01274 581 718* **Rooms** *5*

This acclaimed restaurant-with-rooms is housed in a Grade II listed building. The rooms are bright and cheerful, with modern amenities. Has a tapas and wine bar. Serves hearty English fare and an excellent selection of wines. Also plays host to weddings, receptions and other celebrations. **www.beeties.co.uk**

EAST WITTON Blue Lion

E Witton, Leyburn, North Yorkshire, DL8 4SN **Tel** *01969 624 273* **Fax** *01969 624 189* **Rooms** *15*

A classy, 18th-century coaching inn, set amid beautiful surroundings. Offers simple, but comfortable rooms, with modern conveniences. Also caters for weddings, conferences and other events. The hotel is located just a short distance from many attractions, including Jervaulx Abbey. **www.thebluelion.co.uk**

FLAMBOROUGH Manor House

Flamborough, Bridlington, East Yorkshire, YO15 1PD **Tel** *01262 850 943* **Fax** *01262 850 943* **Rooms** *2*

An elegant Georgian country house in a Grade II listed building. Offers just two rooms, both decorated in a traditional style, yet with modern amenities. Ideal for those looking for an intimate and quiet retreat. The surrounding countryside is a favourite among walkers and bird-watchers. **www.flamboroughmanor.co.uk**

GRASSINGTON Ashfield

Summersfold, Grassington, North Yorkshire, BD23 5AE **Tel** *01756 752 584* **Fax** *07092 376562* **Rooms** *8*

This peaceful, 17-century hotel, located near Summersfold's cobbled square, has a warm and welcoming ambience. Has elegantly furnished rooms with modern conveniences. Well-placed to explore the beauty of the surrounding Yorkshire Dales. Activities such as fishing, sailing and horse riding are available. **www.ashfieldhouse.co.uk**

HALIFAX Holdsworth House

Holdsworth Rd, Holmfield, Halifax, West Yorkshire, HX2 9TG **Tel** *01422 240 024* **Fax** *01422 245 174* **Rooms** *25*

Grand, 17th-century Jacobean manor, just a short distance from Halifax. Has individually decorated rooms and suites, with modern amenities; some with four-poster beds. The expansive gardens are ideal for hosting weddings. Also offers conference facilities. **www.holdsworthhouse.co.uk**

HARROGATE Balmoral

Franklin Mount, Harrogate, North Yorkshire, HG1 5EJ **Tel** *01423 508208* **Fax** *01423 530652* **Rooms** *23*

A mock-Tudor frontage makes this luxurious hotel easy to spot. Offers tastefully furnished rooms, as well as well-equipped business facilities. The decor here is a perfect mix of traditional and contemporary. Boasts an award-winning restaurant. Room rate includes breakfast. **www.balmoralhotel.co.uk**

HAWORTH Old White Lion Hotel

Main St, Haworth, Keighley, West Yorkshire, BD22 8DU **Tel** *01535 642 313* **Fax** *01535 646 222* **Rooms** *14*

A 300-year-old, family-run coaching inn, set at the top of the cobbled main street in Haworth, a Yorkshire town redolent with memories of the Brontë sisters. The parsonage and the museum are a few steps away, and the Keighley & Wortley steam railway stops nearby. Offers comfortable rooms. **www.oldwhitelionhotel.com**

HELMSLEY Feversham Arms

1–8 High St, Helmsley, North Yorkshire, YO62 5AG **Tel** *01439 770766* **Fax** *01439 770346* **Rooms** *20*

This comfortable, refurbished coaching inn has been around for more than 150 years. Located next to the parish church, the hotel offers pleasant rooms. The cuisine here is impeccable, yet unpretentious. Also has tennis courts and a heated swimming pool. Includes breakfast. **www.fevershamarmshotel.com**

HOVINGHAM Worsley Arms

Main St, Hovingham, Yorkshire, YO62 4LA **Tel** *01653 628 234* **Fax** *01653 628 130* **Rooms** *19*

Built in the 1840s as a spa hotel, this exquisite and timeless country house features open log fires and stylish furnishings. The informal and relaxing environment, in the depths of the Yorkshire countryside, is perfect for a stress-relieving break. Room rate includes breakfast. **www.worsleyarms.com**

HUDDERSFIELD Swallow Huddersfield Hotel

33-47 Kirkgate, Huddersfield, West Yorkshire, HD1 1QT **Tel** *01484 512111* **Fax** *01484 421552* **Rooms** *39*

A member of the nationwide Swallow Hotels group, this town-centre hotel offers comfortable accommodation with en suite facilities, tea and coffee makers and a free car park. Within the complex they also have the Rosemary Lane Bistro, a traditional pub and Johnny's nightclub. **www.huddersfieldhotel.com**

KIRKBYMOORSIDE George & Dragon Hotel

17 Market Place, Kirkbymoorside, North Yorkshire, YO62 6AA **Tel** *01751 433 334* **Fax** *01751 432 933* **Rooms** *19*

A charming hotel housed in a building composed of three adjoining establishments – a 17th-century inn, a rectory and a cornmill. Offers spacious, elegantly furnished rooms; some with four-poster beds. All have modern amenities. Close to several sightseeing attractions. Serves real ale. **www.georgeanddragon.net**

Key to Price Guide *see p556* **Key to Symbols** *see back cover flap*

LEEDS Bewley's Hotel Leeds

City Walk, Sweet St, Leeds, West Yorkshire, LS11 9AT **Tel** *0113 234 2340* **Fax** *0113 234 2349* **Rooms** *334*

Recently opened, this is Leeds' largest hotel. Conveniently situated in the heart of the city's commercial and shopping district, it offers great value for money. The rooms are large and stylishly furnished, with Internet access, TVs, en suite facilities and more. The city station is just a ten-minute walk away. **www.bewleyshotels.com**

LEEDS Haley's Hotel & Restaurant

Shire Oak Rd, Headingley, Leeds, West Yorkshire, LS6 2DE **Tel** *0113 278 4446* **Fax** *0113 275 3342* **Rooms** *27*

Located in a leafy suburb, just a short distance from the city centre. The bedrooms are individually furnished with style and flair, and equipped with many modern conveniences. The cuisine is inventive and well presented by people who really care. Room rate includes breakfast. **www.haleys.co.uk**

LEEDS Malmaison Leeds

1 Swine Gate, Leeds, West Yorkshire, LS1 4AG **Tel** *0113 398 1000* **Fax** *0113 398 1002* **Rooms** *100*

Conceived ten years ago as a chic brasserie and bar with themed rooms, this stylish hotel has grown into a chain with its finger on the pulse of contemporary style hospitality. Situated in the centre of town, it is an easy walk from all local attractions. Offers striking views of the town's skyline. **www.malmaison.com**

LEEDS 42 The Calls

42 The Call, Leeds, West Yorkshire, LS2 &EW **Tel** *0113 244 0099* **Fax** *0113 234 4100* **Rooms** *41*

A refreshingly different town-house hotel that manages to be trendy without becoming a cliché. This converted cornmill, set beside River Nidd, features beamed ceilings, original mill mechanisms, modern handmade beds and a collection of original works of art. Offers luxurious rooms. **www.42thecalls.co.uk**

PICKERING White Swan

Market Place, Pickering, North Yorkshire, Y018 7AA **Tel** *01751 472 288* **Fax** *01751 475 554* **Rooms** *21*

Set in the picturesque Vale of Pickering, at the foot of the North Yorks Moors, this delightful country-house inn is priced affordably. Offers pleasant rooms that are plain, yet practical. Also has conference facilities. The restaurant serves highly-appreciated food. **www.white-swan.co.uk**

REETH Arkleside

Reeth, nr Richmond, North Yorkshire, DL11 6SG **Tel** *01748 884 200* **Fax** *01748 884 200* **Rooms** *8*

Set in a quaint village amid breathtaking scenery of the Yorkshire Dales. The ambience at this small guesthouse is warm and welcoming. Has smart and comfortable bedrooms. Perfect getaway for those interested in an intimate retreat. Also a favourite with walkers. **www.arklesidehotel.co.uk**

RICHMOND King's Head

Market Place, Richmond, North Yorkshire, DL10 4HS **Tel** *01748 850 220* **Fax** *01748 850 635* **Rooms** *30*

Close to King Henry VIII's favourite castle and overlooking the fast-flowing River Swale. The rooms at this hotel are individually styled and tastefully furnished. Local attractions such as the Georgian Theate Royal and three museums are also nearby. Boasts an acclaimed bar, and serves afternoon tea in the lounge. **www.kingsheadrichmond.co.uk**

ROYDHOUSE Three Acres Inn

Roydhouse, Shelley, West Yorkshire, HD8 8LR **Tel** *01484 602 606* **Fax** *01484 608 411* **Rooms** *20*

A rambling old millstone building with lots of character. The rooms are simple, yet comfortably furnished; many offer views of the open moorland. Has independent cottages as well, each with its own garden. Also hosts a traditional shop with pickles, spices and preserves. Ample car parking space. Room rate includes breakfast. **www.3acres.com**

SCARBOROUGH Interludes

32 Princess St, Scarbourough, North Yorkshire, YO11 1QR **Tel** *01723 360 513* **Fax** *01723 368 597* **Rooms** *5*

A refined guesthouse in a lively seaside town. Housed in a Grade II listed building, this hotel offers non-smoking, pleasant rooms; most with en suite facilities and sea views. Guests can avail of special theatre packages organized by the owners. Parking space is scarce during peak season. **www.interludeshotel.co.uk**

SETTLE The Plough Inn At Wigglesworth

Wigglesworth, nr Settle, Skipton, North Yorkshire, BD23 4RJ **Tel** *01729 840 243* **Fax** *01729 840 638* **Rooms** *9*

This charming, 17th-century inn has spectacular views of Pen-y-Ghent and Ingleborough, two of the renowned Three Peaks. The en suite rooms are simply decorated in bright, cheerful colours. Famous for good food and real ale. Ideally placed for exploring the surrounding countryside. **www.ploughinn.info**

THORNTON WATLASS The Buck Inn

Thornton Watlass, Ripon, North Yorkshire, HG4 4AH **Tel** *01677 422 461* **Fax** *01 677 422 447* **Rooms** *7*

An archetypal village hostelry with real ale, quality home-cooked food and comfortable bedrooms. The pub wall marks the boundary of the village cricket green. At the rear is a large and secluded garden with a children's play area. Located a short distance from the bustling A1 trunk road. **www.buckwatlass.co.uk**

WHITBY White Horse & Griffin

Church St, Whitby, North Yorkshire, YO22 4BH **Tel** *01947 604 857* **Fax** *01947 604 857* **Rooms** *10*

Quaint old inn set at the core of Whitby, home to the famous explorer Captain Cook and the fictional Count Dracula. Offers tastefully refurbished rooms, and serves delicious fresh fish and other seafood. Also has two, self-catering cottages. Close to the ruins of Whitby Abbey and its 119 steps. **www.whitehorseandgriffin.co.uk**

YARM Judges Country House Hotel

Kirklevington Hall, Yarm, Cleveland, North Yorkshire, TS15 9LW **Tel** *01642 789 000* **Fax** *01642 782 878* **Rooms** *21*

A luxury hotel housed in Kirklevington Hall, a glorious country mansion. The bedrooms and suites are stylishly decorated, with modern amenities such as jacuzzis, CD players, hairdryers, complimentary newspapers and more. Showcases several antiques and works of art as well. **www.judgeshotel.co.uk**

YORK Beechwood Close

19 Shipton Rd, Cliffton, York, Yorkshire, YO30 5RE **Tel** *01904 658 378* **Fax** *01904 647 124* **Rooms** *14*

A relaxing and welcoming hotel set amid scenic surroundings. Traditionally decorated bedrooms are comfortable and well-equipped. Hosts a restaurant, with splendid views of the secluded garden, and a friendly and well-stocked bar. **www.beechwood-close.co.uk**

YORK The Royal York

Station Rd, York, Yorkshire, YO24 2AA **Tel** *01904 653 681* **Fax** *01904 623 503* **Rooms** *165*

Part of the Principal Hotels chain, this magnificent Victorian retreat is set in vast, landscaped gardens. Offers en suite, luxury rooms, with all modern amenities; has two, specially designed rooms for the disabled as well. Also has a conference centre. Just a few steps from the centre of town. **www.principal-hotels.com**

YORK Middlethorpe Hall

Bishopthorpe Rd, York, Yorkshire, YO23 2GB **Tel** *01904 641 241* **Fax** *01904 620 176* **Rooms** *29*

One of the selective Historic House Hotels chain and, arguably, its finest. Set on 20 acres of outstanding gardens and parkland, this country-house hotel is filled with antiques and works of art. Built in 1699, it offers elegant accommodation in the main house and the adjacent mews cottages. **www.middlethorpe.com**

NORTHUMBRIA

ALNMOUTH The Schooner Hotel

Northumberland St, Alnmouth, Alnwick, Northumberland, NE66 2RS **Tel** *01665 830216* **Fax** *01665 830287* **Rooms** *32*

Comfort with character is the theme at this historic, 17th-century inn. Famous guests include Charles Dickens, John Wesley, Douglas Bader and King George III, but it is a certain Parson Smyth who is said to haunt the place. Offers comfortable, pleasant rooms and a welcoming ambience.

BAMBURGH Victoria Hotel

Front St, Bamburgh, Northumberland, NE69 7BP **Tel** *01668 214431* **Fax** *01688 214404* **Rooms** *30*

Set in the heart of Bamburgh, this 19th-century hotel has cheery rooms, decorated with period furniture and antiques. Romantic candle-lit suppers can be enjoyed in the glass-domed restaurant. Close at hand is Bamburgh's magnificent castle. Also offers facilities for weddings and conferences. **www.victoriahotel.net**

BELFORD Blue Bell Hotel

Market Place, Belford, Northumberland, NE70 7NE **Tel** *01668 213 543* **Fax** *01668 213 787* **Rooms** *17*

Virginia creeper covers the entire frontage of this 17th-century coaching inn. Recently refurbished on a lavish scale, this popular, family-run hotel has expansive gardens and a traditional restaurant. The rooms are comfortably furnished, and are equipped with modern amenities. **www.bluebellhotel.com**

BELFORD Waren House Hotel

Waren Mill, Belford, Northumberland, NE70 7EE **Tel** *01668 214581* **Fax** *01668 214484* **Rooms** *13*

This small hotel enjoys outstanding views of the Cheviot Hills from its six acres of mature woodlands and formal gardens. Features individually decorated rooms and suites. Its location next to Budle Bay, a bird life sanctuary, makes it a favourite with bird-watchers. Includes breakfast. **www.warenhousehotel.co.uk**

BERWICK-UPON-TWEED Number One Sallyport

Off Bridge St, Berwick-Upon-Tweed, Northumberland, TD15 1EZ **Tel** *01289 308827* **Fax** *01289 308827* **Rooms** *5*

This delightful 17th-century inn, set in a Grade II listed building, was voted the "Top B&B in England" for 2005 by *The Sunday Times*. The rooms are spacious and comfortable, furnished with white cotton linen and en suite facilities. This contemporary, yet traditional retreat serves an excellent breakfast. **www.1sallyport-bedandbreakfast.com**

CHESTER-LE-STREET Lumley Castle

Chester-le-St, Durham, DH3 4NX **Tel** *0191 389 1111* **Fax** *0191 387 1437* **Rooms** *59*

A genuine medieval castle, complete with battlements and arrow slits, that has been imaginatively converted into a luxurious hotel. The en suite rooms are elegantly decorated; some with antiques and four-poster beds. A perfect choice for a romantic break. Located a short distance from Durham and Newcastle. **www.lumleycastle.com**

CROOKHAM Coach House

Crookham, Cornhill-on-Tweed, Northumberland, TD12 4TD **Tel** *01890 820 293* **Fax** *01890 820284* **Rooms** *10*

Welcoming guesthouse set in a complex of renovated farm buildings that include a 1680s cottage and an old-smithy, all surrounding a sun-trap courtyard. Situated close to the Borders, it offers excellent home cooking and comfortable rooms, and has a reputation for maintaining high, award-winning standards. **www.coachhousecrookham.com**

Key to Price Guide *see p556* **Key to Symbols** *see back cover flap*

DURHAM Durham Marriott Hotel Royal County ⓔⓔⓔ
*Old Elvet, Durham, County Durham, DH1 3JN **Tel** 0191 386 6821 **Fax** 0191 386 0704 **Rooms** 150*

Well-placed in a historic city, dominated by a massive cathedral and castle. This large hotel offers spacious, tastefully furnished rooms, equipped with modern conveniences. Local attractions such as Beamish North Country Museum are within easy walking distance. **www.marriott.com**

DURHAM Whitworth Hall Country Park Hotel ⓔⓔⓔ
*Near Spennymoor, Durham, County Durham, DL16 7OX **Tel** 01388 811 772 **Fax** 01388 818 669 **Rooms** 120*

A Grade II listed building set amid several acres of lovely gardens. Offers stately en suite rooms; some with great views. The deer grazing in the surrounding grounds enhance the hotel's tranquil and relaxing ambience. An idyllic location for weddings. Also provides conference facilities. **www.whitworthhall.co.uk**

HALTWHISTLE Centre Of Britain ⓔ
*Main St, Haltwhistle, Northumberland, NE49 0BH **Tel** 01434 322 422 **Fax** 01434 322655 **Rooms** 12*

Part of the 15th-century Pele Tower, this building served as a manor house, post office, coaching inn and more before it was converted into a hotel. The original architectural features have been retained and tastefully combined with modern touches. Has simple rooms. Includes breakfast. **www.centre-of-britain.org.uk**

HEXHAM De Vere Slaley Hall ⓔⓔ
*Slaley, Hexham, Northumberland, NE47 0BX **Tel** 01434 673350 **Fax** 01474 673962 **Rooms** 139*

The northern flagship of the De Vere chain of hotels. This grand, Edwardian resort features two championship golf courses and other outdoor activities such as fishing, archery and even hot-air ballooning. Offers large, luxurious en suite rooms; some with jacuzzis. Conference facilities are also available. **www.devereonline.com**

HEXHAM The County Hotel & Restaurant ⓔⓔ
*Priestpopple, Hexham, Northumberland, NE46 1PS **Tel & Fax** 01434 603601 **Rooms** 7*

Housed in a listed building, that originally was a terrace of three houses, the County is a firm favourite with lovely soft furnishings, warm hearths and relaxed Northumbrian surroundings. Expect genuine hospitality and breathtaking scenery; Hadrian's Wall is close by. The restaurant uses all local produce. **www.thecountyhexham.co.uk**

MIDDLETON-IN-TEESDALE The Teesdale Hotel ⓔ
*Market Place, Middleton-in-Teesdale, County Durham, DL12 0QG **Tel** 01833 640264 **Fax** 01883 640651 **Rooms** 14*

This 17th-century, former coaching inn is located in the centre of the village. The rooms have recently been refurbished but are sympathetic to the original style of the inn; all offer en suite facilities. The vast moorland and scenic surroundings provide a relaxing break. Enjoy good home cooking and fine wines. Includes breakfast. **www.teesdalehotel.com**

MORPETH Linden Hall ⓔⓔⓔ
*Longhorsley, Morpeth, Northumberland, NE65 8XF **Tel** 01670 500000 **Fax** 01670 500001 **Rooms** 50*

Several hundred acres of woods and parkland, including an award-winning 18-hole golf course, frame this magnificent Georgian mansion. Boasts a health, leisure and fitness spa, a traditional pub and a much acclaimed restaurant. Includes breakfast. Has well-appointed and stylish rooms. **www.lindenhall.co.uk**

NEWCASTLE Caledonian ⓔⓔ
*Osborne Rd, Jesmond, Newcastle, Northumberland, NE2 2AT **Tel** 0191 281 7881 **Fax** 0191 281 6241 **Rooms** 89*

Situated in the popular town of Jesmond, this unassuming hotel is just a five-minute drive from Newcastle upon Tyne's busy city centre. All the key local attractions are within easy reach. The rooms are pleasant and tastefully decorated, well-equipped with modern amenities. A good base for exploring the countryside. **www.peelhotel.com**

NEWCASTLE UPON TYNE Malmasion Newcastle ⓔⓔⓔⓔ
*104 Quayside, Newcastle Upon Tyne, NE1 3DX **Tel** 0191 245 5000 **Fax** 0191 245 4545 **Rooms** 120*

Sophisticated warehouse conversion on the quayside, adjacent to the Millennium Bridge and opposite the outstanding Baltic arts centre. Part of the Malmaison chain of boutique hotels, which is renowned for its finger-on-the-pulse modern style, with much use of primary colours. **www.malmaison.com**

ROMALDKIRK Rose & Crown ⓔⓔⓔ
*Romaldkirk, Barnard Castle, County Durham, DL12 9EB **Tel** 01833 650213 **Fax** 01833 650828 **Rooms** 12*

Picture postcard England at its best. The village green makes a charming backdrop for this delightful little inn. Inside, it is smart, yet reassuringly traditional. Serves home-made soup and delicious food. The rooms are small, but cosy. Ideal for an intimate getaway. **www.rose-and-crown.co.uk**

SEAHOUSES Olde Ship ⓔⓔ
*7–9 Main St, Seahouses, Northumberland, NE68 7RD **Tel** 01665 720200 **Fax** 01665 721383 **Rooms** 18*

Defiantly traditional in the face of several commercially motivated pub makeovers, this charming inn sits above the tiny Northumbrian fishing village of Seahouses. It's a veritable museum of the sea, with maritime artefacts from fishing vessels and lifeboats. The rooms are attractive, and the menu features fresh fish and seafood. **www.seahouses.co.uk**

STANNERSBURN Pheasant ⓔⓔ
*Stannersburn, Kielder Water, Northumberland, NE48 1DD **Tel** 01434 240382 **Fax** 01434 240382 **Rooms** 8*

An ivy-covered inn near Kielder Water, the largest man-made lake in Europe. A friendly and warm place, full of character, offering spacious en suite rooms, many with countryside views. Food is freshly prepared, using local produce. Located close to Newcastle and Edinburgh. **www.thepheasantinn.com**

TILLMOUTH PARK Tillmouth Park Country House Hotel

Cornhill-On-Tweed, Northumberland, TD12 4UU **Tel** *01890 882255* **Fax** *01890 882540* **Rooms** *14*

Hunting, shooting, fishing and golf are all on the menu at this elegant venue. Serves contemporary British cuisine in an award-winning dining room. Organizes chauffeured limousine pick ups from Edinburgh and Newcastle airports, as well as from Berwick station. Includes breakfast. **www.tillmouthpark.co.uk**

WALLSEND Hadrian Lodge Hotel

Hadrian Rd, Wallsend, Newcastle, NE28 6HH **Tel** *0191 262 7733* **Fax** *0191 263 0714* **Rooms** *25*

Located at the eastern limit of Hadrian's Wall, hence this hotel's name. Offers simple, yet comfortable rooms, and the room rates include breakfast. A sensible and economical base for a visit to the Newcastle city centre, which is placed just a ten-minute drive away, or for a cross-country walk along the Roman wall. **www.hadrianlodgehotel.co.uk**

NORTH WALES

ABERDYFI Penhelig Arms

Aberdyfi, Gwynedd, LL35 0LT **Tel** *01654 767215* **Fax** *01654 767690* **Rooms** *14*

This whitewashed, seafront hotel is spread over three buildings – Penhelig House, Bodhelig and The Cottage. Offers lavish, contemporary rooms and suites, well-equipped with modern amenities. Most rooms boast splendid views of the sea. Serves tasty cuisine, and features an extensive wine list. **www.penheligarms.com**

ABERDYFI Trefiddian Hotel

Gwynedd, LL35 0SB **Tel** *01654 767213* **Fax** *01654 767777* **Rooms** *59*

A four-star, family-run hotel, located to the south of Snowdonia National Park, and overlooking Cardigan Bay. Has an indoor heated pool, a tennis court, a play area for children and a nine-hole putting green; an 18-hole golf course lies next door. Offers comfortable rooms with en suite facilities. **www.trefwales.com**

ABERSOCH Porth Tocyn Country Hotel

Abersoch, Pwllheli, Gwynedd, LL53 7BU **Tel** *01758 713303* **Fax** *01758 713538* **Rooms** *17*

Country-house hotel renowned for its fine cuisine. Boasts a fine panorama across Cardigan Bay. The cosy rooms are furnished with antiques; the rooms on the ground floor are suitable for disabled travellers (call in advance). Also hosts a children's play area, equipped with a TV, as well as Nintendo, video and board games. **www.porth-tocyn-hotel.co.uk**

BEAUMARIS Ye Olde Bull's Head Inn

Castle St, Beaumaris, Isle of Anglesey, LL58 8AP **Tel** *01248 810329* **Fax** *01248 811294* **Rooms** *13*

This charming inn on the Isle of Anglesey occupies a Grade II listed building dating back to the 15th century. The rooms combine modern facilities with ancient oak-beamed ceilings and antique furniture and fittings. Hosts an award-winning restaurant and a traditional freehouse bar that serves real ale. **www.bullsheadinn.co.uk**

BEDDGELERT Sygun Fawr Country House

Beddgelert, Gwynedd, LL55 4NE **Tel** *01766 890258* **Rooms** *11*

Set in a truly rural setting, this four-star, country-house hotel sits amid a vast expanse of mountains and gardens. The rooms at this former, 17th-century manor feature exposed stone work, oak beams and inglenook fireplaces. The dining room, located in the oldest part of the building, has antique furniture. **www.sygunfawr.co.uk**

BETWS-Y-COED Craig-y-Dderwen Riverside Hotel

Betws-y-Coed, Snowdonia National Park, North Wales, LL24 0AS **Tel** *01690 710293* **Fax** *01690 710362* **Rooms** *16*

Country-house hotel, set amid 16 acres of gardens in the heart of Snowdonia National Park. Boasts tastefully furnished rooms, with four-poster beds, log fires and modern amenities; a specially equipped room is available for disabled guests. This tranquil retreat also has a play area for children and free parking. **www.snowdoniahotel.com**

BODELWYDDAN Bodelwyddan Castle Hotel

Bodelwyddan, Rhyl, Denbighshire, N Wales, LL18 5YA **Tel** *01745 585088* **Fax** *01705 585089* **Rooms** *184*

Large luxury hotel, housed in a Grade II listed castle. Features many modern facilities, including a heated indoor swimming pool and a sauna and steam room. Activities such as tennis, croquet and archery are also on offer in the magnificent grounds. Has stylish rooms with four-poster beds and patios. Specialises in short break stays. **www.warnerbreaks.co.uk**

CAPEL GARMON Tan-y-Foel Country House

Near Betws-y-Coed, Llanrwst, Conwy, LL26 0RE **Tel** *01690 710507* **Fax** *01690 710681* **Rooms** *6*

This quiet and luxurious, family-run hotel is located within striking distance of Conwy Valley and Snowdonia. The rooms in this 17th-century, Welsh stone building are non-smoking and beautifully crafted to fuse traditional and modern styles. Activities such as hiking, horse riding and bird-watching are available nearby. **www.tyfhotel.co.uk**

COLWYN BAY Bryn Holcombe Hotel

9 Grosvenor Rd, Colwyn Bay, Conwy, LL29 7YF **Tel** *01492 530423* **Rooms** *6*

A peaceful, two-star hotel, well-placed for exploring Snowdonia National Park. Also a short drive from the World Heritage Site of Conwy Castle, the medieval walled town of Conwy, the Great Orme nature reserve and miles of sandy beaches. The price of the rooms includes a traditional Welsh breakfast.

Key to Price Guide *see p556* **Key to Symbols** *see back cover flap*

COLWYN BAY Rathlin Country House ££

48 Kings Rd, Colwyn Bay, Conwy, LL29 7YH **Tel** *01492 532173* **Fax** *0871 6619887* **Rooms** *3*

Small, luxury B&B in a beautiful conservation area, just minutes from Colwyn Bay. The rooms at this non-smoking retreat have en suite facilities; one even has a jacuzzi. The cosy dining room features an inglenook fireplace, oak panelling and oak parquet flooring. Also has a sauna. Serves a traditional Welsh breakfast. **www.rathlincountryhouse.co.uk**

CRICCIETH Mynydd Ednyfed Country House Hotel ££

Caernarfon Rd, Criccieth, Gwynedd, LL52 0PH **Tel** *01766 523269* **Fax** *01766 522929* **Rooms** *9*

Secluded, 400-year-old, country-house hotel. Small, intimate rooms overlook expansive gardens, woods, an orchard and a paddock. Offers striking views of Tremadog Bay and Criccieth Castle as well. This family-run, Welsh retreat is licensed to conduct civil marriage ceremonies too. Tennis courts and a holistic therapy room are available. **www.criccieth.net**

GANLLWYD Plas Dolmelynllyn Country Hotel ££

Ganllwyd, Dolgellau, Gwynedd, LL40 2HP **Tel** *01341 440273* **Fax** *01341 440640* **Rooms** *9*

Spacious National Trust country-house hotel, ideally placed for sports enthusiasts. Outdoor pursuits such as walking, mountain biking, horse riding, fishing, golf and water sports are all available nearby. Those looking for a peaceful and relaxing break will enjoy the vast, undisturbed gardens, as well as the waterfalls and woods. **www.dolly-hotel.co.uk**

HARLECH Gwrach Ynys £

Harlech, Talsamau, Gwynedd, LL47 6TS **Tel** *01766 780742* **Fax** *01766 781199* **Rooms** *7*

Secluded, non-smoking B&B, overlooking Snowdonia National Park. The rooms are cosy and modern, and the ground floor has two lounges. This Edwardian country house is located within reach of Harlech Castle, Royal St David's Golf Club, the Morfa Harlech Nature Reserve and the beach. **www.gwrachynys.co.uk**

LLANABER Llwyndu Farmhouse ££

Llanaber, Barmouth, Gwynedd, LL42 1RR **Tel** *01341 280144* **Rooms** *7*

Historic farmhouse set in a Grade II listed building, overlooking Cardigan Bay. This early 17th-century hotel has been renovated to provide en suite accommodation, and features oak-beamed ceilings, inglenook fireplaces and a stone spiral staircase, as well as many antiques and curios. **www.llwyndu-farmhouse.co.uk**

LLANBERIS Plas Coch £

High St, Llanberis, Gwynned, LL55 4HB **Tel** *01286 872122* **Fax** *01286 872648* **Rooms** *8*

Welcoming guesthouse at the foot of Snowdon. Offers modern B&B accommodation in a spacious Victorian house, built around 1865. All rooms are en suite. This family-friendly hotel is located a short distance from Snowdon Mountain Railway, Llanberis Lake Railway and Padarn Country Park.

LLANDRILLO Tyddyn Llan £££

Near Corwen, Denbighshire, LL21 0ST **Tel** *01490 440264* **Fax** *01490 440414* **Rooms** *12*

Award-winning restaurant-with-rooms occupying an elegant Georgian house, and located in the Vale of Edeyrnion. Rooms are spacious and tastefully furnished, with en suite facilties; most rooms have great views. Sports activities such as fishing, golf, sailing, horse riding and walking are all within easy reach. **www.tyddynllan.co.uk**

LLANDUDNO St Tudno Hotel & Restaurant £££

The Promenade, Llandudno, Conwy, LL30 2LP **Tel** *01492 874411* **Fax** *01492 860407* **Rooms** *18*

Luxurious hotel with a highly acclaimed restaurant. Occupies a Victorian seafront terrace with great views over the town's promenade, gardens and beach, and the nearby Great Orme headland. The lavish rooms and suites are individually decorated, with modern facilities. Also has spacious lounges. **www.st-tudno.co.uk**

LLANDUDNO The Imperial £££

The Promenade, Llandudno, Conwy, LL30 1AP **Tel** *01492 877466* **Fax** *01492 878043* **Rooms** *98*

This stylish, contemporary hotel is located on Llandudno's main promenade, and offers splendid views of the bay. The rooms are elegantly decorated, with several modern conveniences. The restaurant boasts fine views over the sea and some great local cuisine. Also provides conference facilities. **www.theimperial.co.uk**

LLANDUDNO Bodysgallen Hall ££££

Llandudno, Conwy, LL30 1RS **Tel** *01492 584466* **Fax** *01492 582519* **Rooms** *35*

Impressive, historic country-house hotel, set amid an expansive wooded parkland. Features a fabulous 17th-century rockery and walled garden. The luxurious rooms offer stunning views over Conwy Castle and the mountains of Snowdonia. Hosts an award-winning restaurant. **www.bodysgallen.com**

LLANGOLLEN The Wild Pheasant Hotel ££

Berwyn Road, Llangollen, Clwyd, LL20 8AD **Tel** *01978 860629* **Fax** *01978 861837* **Rooms** *46*

Charming hotel in a renovated 19th-century inn, the Wild Pheasant sits picturesquely in the beautiful surroundings of the Vale of Llangollen. Everything can be catered for here, from health and beauty spa retreats to gourmet breaks and even whitewater rafting, laser clay pigeon shooting and off-road driving. **www.wildpheasanthotel.co.uk**

PENMAENPOOL Penmaenuchaf Hall £££

Dogellau, Gwynedd, LL40 1YB **Tel** *01341 422129* **Fax** *01341 422787* **Rooms** *14*

Relaxing country-house retreat situated in Snowdonia National Park. The tastefully decorated rooms have wonderful views over the surrounding mountains. Outdoor pursuits such as mountain biking, fishing, walking, golf and horse riding are available nearby. The up-market restaurant serves modern British food. **www.penhall.co.uk**

PORTMEIRION Portmeirion ££££

Portmeirion, Gwynedd, LL48 6ET **Tel** *01766 770000* **Fax** *01766 771331* **Rooms** *68*

This village-like complex, built initially by Clough Williams-Ellis as a private peninsula, is now a holiday retreat with a popular hotel, self-catering cottage, shops and restaurants. The lavish rooms and suites are furnished in a contemporary style, and are well-equipped with modern facilities. **www.portmeirion-village.com**

RUTHIN Ruthin Castle Hotel £££

Ruthin, Denbighshire, LL15 2NU **Tel** *01824 702664* **Fax** *01824 705978* **Rooms** *62*

This luxurious, converted, 13th-century castle occupies a part of the former Crown Estate. The castle sits amid an ancient walled dry moat, with acres of landscaped gardens and parkland alongside the pretty River Clywd. Offers fine dining, a beauty spa and private fishing. Golf course located nearby. **www.ruthincastle.co.uk**

TALSARNAU Maes-y-Neuadd ££££

Talsarnau, Harlech, Gwynedd, LL47 6YA **Tel** *01766 780200* **Fax** *01766 780211* **Rooms** *15*

Charming, 14th-century manor house, beautifully placed at the base of Snowdonia National Park. Houses lavish, well-equipped rooms. The award-winning restaurant is noted for Wales's lamb, fish and farmhouse cheese, while the intimate bar features an ancient inglenook fireplace and period curios. **www.neuadd.com**

SOUTH AND MID-WALES

ABERGAVENNY Clytha Arms ££

Clytha, nr Abergavenny, Monmouthshire, NP7 9BW **Tel** *01873 840206* **Fax** *01873 840206* **Rooms** *3*

Small, welcoming hotel-restaurant just outside the market town of Abergavenny with an award-winning pub for its real ale. Well placed for exploring the Brecon Beacons and the Sugar Loaf Mountain. The rooms are homely and cheerful, with views over the large grounds. Fishing trips can be arranged on request. **www.clytha-arms.com**

ABERYSTWYTH Conrah Country House £££

Chancery, Aberystwyth, Ceredigion, SY23 4DF **Tel** *01970 617941* **Fax** *01970 624546* **Rooms** *17*

Stunning country-house with vast woodland grounds and gardens. Located on the outskirts of town, this traditional hotel features a croquet lawn and many footpaths leading down to the coast. The rooms are relaxing, but luxurious, with oak-beamed ceilings and panoramic views. Serves British cuisine with a French twist. **www.conrah.co.uk**

AMMANFORD Glynhir Estate £

Glynhir Rd, Llandybie, Carmarthenshire, SA18 2TD **Tel** *01269 850438* **Fax** *01269 851275* **Rooms** *4*

This secluded B&B is housed in a stylish mansion, on an 18th-century Huguenot estate, located at the foothills of the Black Mountains. It features a cascading waterfall and lovely gardens. Has comfortable rooms and self-catering cottages. Offers courses in painting, photography, quilting and sculpture. **www.theglynhirestate.com**

BRECON Cantre Selyf ££

5 Lion St, Brecon, Powys, LD3 7AU **Tel** *01874 622904* **Fax** *01874 622315* **Rooms** *3*

Small, historic B&B in a 17th-century town house. This non-smoking hotel is situated in Brecon's town centre. The rooms are cosy with beamed ceilings, Georgian fireplaces and cast-iron beds. Ask for a room overlooking the large walled garden and the Norman Town Wall that encloses it. **www.cantreselyf.co.uk**

BRECON Castle of Brecon ££

The Castle Square, Brecon, Powys, LD3 9DB **Tel** *01874 624611* **Fax** *01874 623737* **Rooms** *43*

A former 18th-century coaching inn, this outstanding family-run hotel occupies the remains of Brecon castle. The rooms are spacious, with en suite facilities; the south-facing rooms have breathtaking views over Brecon Beacons National Park. Ideally located for walking and horse riding. **www.breconcastle.co.uk**

BROAD HAVEN Druidstone ££

Broad Haven, Haverfordwest, Pembrokeshire, SA62 3NE **Tel** *01437 781221* **Fax** *01437 781133* **Rooms** *11*

Perched high above the sandy beach of Druidstone Haven, this seaside hotel offers splendid views. Accommodation here is split between en suite rooms in the main house and five, individually decorated cottages. Dining room, sitting room and cellar bar overlook the sea. Children and pets are welcome. **www.druidstone.co.uk**

CARDIFF The Big Sleep Hotel £

Bute Terrace, Cardiff, CF10 2FE **Tel** *02920 636363* **Fax** *02920 636364* **Rooms** *81*

A stylish hotel at affordable prices, housed in a converted 1960s office block. The interior is self-consciously retro, but the rooms are contemporary and comfortable, with en suite amenities. Offers stunning views as far as the Severn Bridge. Highly popular with both business and leisure travellers. **www.thebigsleephotel.com**

CARDIFF The Park Inn  £££

Circle Way E, Llanedeyrn, Cardiff, CF23 9XF **Tel** *02920 589988* **Fax** *02920 549092* **Rooms** *132*

Friendly hotel located just a ten-minute drive from the city centre. A popular choice for business travellers thanks to its conference facilities, but also ideal for exploring the nearby attractions, including Cardiff Bay, Cardiff Castle and Millennium Stadium. Also has a heated indoor swimming pool, spa and sauna. **www.parkinn.com**

Key to Price Guide *see p556* **Key to Symbols** *see back cover flap*

CARDIFF St David's Hotel & Spa

Havannah St, Cardiff, CF10 5SD **Tel** *02920 454045* **Fax** *02920 313075* **Rooms** *132*

Overlooking Cardiff's trendy waterfront bay, this five-star hotel and spa is one of Wales's most luxurious hotels. Offers plush rooms and state-of-the-art leisure amenities. Each room has a private, deck-style balcony with views across the bay. Tailormade spa packages are available, as are conference facilities. **www.thestdavidshotel.com**

CHEPSTOW Marriott St Pierre Hotel and Country Club

St Pierre Park, Chepstow, Monmouthshire, NP16 6YA **Tel** *0870 4007224* **Fax** *0870 629 975* **Rooms** *148*

Luxury hotel in a converted, 14th-century manor, set amid 400 acres of parkland. The lavish rooms retain the building's original features, while offering all modern facilities. Ask for a room overlooking the ornamental lake. Hosts business centres, two golf courses and a beauty salon. **www.marriotthotels.co.uk**

CRICKHOWELL The Bear Hotel

Crickhowell, Powys, NP8 1BW **Tel** *01873 810408* **Fax** *01873 811696* **Rooms** *36*

Charismatic, timbered hotel in the centre of the old market town of Crickhowell, A popular stopping off point for tourists and locals alike. This former coaching inn dates back to 1432, and has retained its cobbled forecourt and inner courtyard. Offers colourful, cheerful rooms and a much-liked low-beamed bar. **www.bearhotel.co.uk**

CRICKHOWELL Gliffaes Country House

Crickhowell, Powys, NP8 1RH **Tel** *01874 730371* **Fax** *01874 730463* **Rooms** *22*

Welcoming, Victorian country-house, set on expansive gardens and grouse-filled woodland. This scenic retreat is located just outside Crickhowell, on the road to Brecon Beacons National Park. It's proximity to River Usk makes it a popular destination for fly fishing enthusiasts. **www.gliffaeshotel.com**

EGLWYSFACH Ynyshir Hall

Eglwysfach, Machynlleth, Powys, SY20 8TA **Tel** *01654 781209/781268* **Fax** *01654 781366* **Rooms** *9*

Nestled in secluded, picturesque countryside above the Dovey estuary, this 16th-century house was once owned by Queen Victoria. Its nearness to one of Britain's finest wildfowl reserves makes it a favourite with bird-watchers. The non-smoking rooms are tastefully decorated with antique furnishings. **www.ynyshir-hall.co.uk**

HAVERFORDWEST The Wolfe Inn

Wolfscastle, Haverfordwest, Pembrokeshire, SA62 5LS **Tel** *01437 741662* **Fax** *01437 741676* **Rooms** *5*

Historic, stone-built coaching inn in the small village of Wolfscastle, just a ten-minute drive from Haverfordwest. Offers comfortable rooms, carefully furnished to match the original oak-beamed ceilings. Also has an award-winning brasserie. Children and pets are welcome. Cosy log fires in winter.

LAKE VYRNWY Lake Vyrnwy

Llanwyddyn, nr Welshpool, Powys, SY10 0LY **Tel** *01691 870692* **Fax** *01691 870259* **Rooms** *38*

Converted Victorian fishing lodge on the massive Vyrnwy Estate. Boasts fabulous views over mountains, untamed moorland, forests and, of course, Lake Vyrnwy itself. Has elegant rooms; some with luxuries such as jacuzzis, four-poster beds and balconies. Most rooms have lakeside views. **www.lakevyrnwy.com**

LAMPETER Falcondale Mansion Hotel

Falcondale Drive, Lampeter, Ceredigion, SA48 7RX **Tel** *01570 422910* **Fax** *01570 423559* **Rooms** *20*

Part of the Best Western chain of hotels, this Victorian mansion is set within a vast parkland, a short drive from the market town of Lampeter. The en suite rooms have four-poster beds and small balconies overlooking the well-tended gardens. The award-winning restaurant serves Welsh cuisine. **www.falcondalehotel.com**

LAMPHEY Lamphey Court Hotel & Spa

Lamphey, Pembrokeshire, SA71 5NT **Tel** *01646 672273* **Fax** *01646 672480* **Rooms** *38*

Magnificent Georgian mansion on the edge of Pembrokeshire National Park. This Best Western hotel boasts luxurious rooms, some fine views and modern amenities. Hosts a leisure spa with an indoor heated pool and jacuzzi, as well as floodlit tennis courts. Offers conference facilities. **www.lampheycourt.co.uk**

LLANDEILO Maerdy Cottages

Dan-y-Cefn, Llandeilo, Carmarthenshire, SA19 7BD **Tel** *01550 777448* **Fax** *01550 777067* **Rooms** *6*

Charming, self-catering stone cottages offering B&B rates on request. Set in one of Wales's most picturesque valleys, this 14th-century farmstead is an ideal intimate retreat. Rooms feature exposed brick work, oak panelling and period furniture. Wheelchair accessible cottages also available. **www.accommodation.uk.net/maerdycottages.htm**

LLANIGON Old Post Office

Llanigon, Hay-on-Wye, Powys, HR3 5QA **Tel** *01497 820008* **Rooms** *3*

Small, but charming, 17th-century B&B on the edge of Brecon Beacons, just outside Hay-on-Wye. The non-smoking rooms are located beneath wood-beamed ceilings at the top of a winding oak staircase. Serves a vegetarian breakfast. **www.oldpost-office.co.uk**

LLANTHONY Llanthony Priory

Llanthony, Abergavenny, Monmouthshire, NP7 7NN **Tel** *01873 890487* **Fax** *01873 890844* **Rooms** *5*

Stunning, retreat-style B&B in a 12th-century Augustinian priory on the edge of the Black Mountains. The rooms, housed in former abbey cells, are simple, with minimal furnishings. The low ceilings add to their character and charm. Perfectly located for exploring the scenic countryside. **www.llanthonypriory.supanet.com**

LLYSWEN Llangoed Hall

Llyswen, Brecon, Powys, LD3 0YP **Tel** *01874 754 525* **Fax** *01874 754 545* **Rooms** *23*

Luxury hotel housed in a stunning Edwardian country house in the middle of Wye Valley. Features a carved timber staircase, oak doors and antique furnishings in the rooms; works of art by renowned artists such as Whistler and Augustus John adorn the walls. Organizes fishing, rock climbing and other outdoor pursuits on request. **www.llangoedhall.com**

MILEBROOK Milebrook House

Knighton, Powys, LD7 1LT **Tel** *01547 528632* **Fax** *01547 520509* **Rooms** *10*

A converted, stone-built Georgian house, located on the border of England and Wales. This small hotel is perfectly placed for exploring Offa's Dyke, the man-made earthwork that marks the border. The comfortable rooms and restaurant overlook some fabulous countryside. Also has a croquet lawn. **www.milebrookhouse.co.uk**

MONMOUTH The Crown at Whitebrook

Near Monmouth, Monmouthshire, NP25 4TX **Tel** *01600 860254* **Fax** *01600 860607* **Rooms** *8*

This acclaimed restaurant-with-rooms sits in large gardens, in a tiny village on the edge of the Wye Valley Area of Outstanding Natural Beauty. The rooms at this 17th-century eatery are luxurious and beautifully decorated, but it is the gourmet cuisine that draws most visitors. **www.crownatwhitebrook.co.uk**

NEWPORT Cnapan Country House Hotel

East St, Newport, SA42 0SY **Tel** *01239 820575* **Fax** *01239 820878* **Rooms** *5*

A charming and intimate country house with a cheerful and welcoming ambience. Offers spacious rooms, carefully decorated with traditional oak Welsh furnishings. Serves excellent Welsh cuisine. The service is efficient and the hotel is ideally located to explore the countryside. **www.cnapan.co.uk**

PENALLY Penally Abbey Country House Hotel

Penally, Pembrokeshire, SA70 7PY **Tel** *01834 843033* **Fax** *01834 844714* **Rooms** *17*

Neo-Gothic architectural flourishes give this country house considerable character. Set amid expansive gardens and woodlands, this vine-covered hotel has peaceful rooms, with views over Tenby golf course and Carmarthen Bay. The elegant dining room features seasonal produce and an extensive wine list. **www.penally-abbey.com**

PEN-Y-CAE Craig-y-Nos Castle

Brecon Rd, Pen-y-cae, Powys, SA9 1GL **Tel** *01639 731167* **Fax** *01639 731077* **Rooms** *26*

Located in the Brecon Beacons, this impressive castle offers a not-to-be-missed glimpse into Wales's feudal history. Houses en suite rooms; some with great views of the gardens. This popular wedding venue once belonged to the renowned opera singer, Adelina Patti. Ideal for walkers and bird-watchers. **www.craigynoscastle.co.uk**

PORTHKERRY Egerton Grey

Porthkerry, Barry, South Glamorgan, CF62 3BZ **Tel** *01446 711666* **Fax** *01446 711690* **Rooms** *10*

Refined Victorian country-house hotel boasting a vast collection of antiques. The rooms are furnished with a wealth of period furnishings, original brasswork, open fireplaces, ornate mouldings and oak panelling – even the food in the restaurant is served on antique china. The huge grounds include a croquet lawn. **www.egertongrey.co.uk**

REYNOLDSTON Fairyhill

Reynoldston, Gower, Swansea, SA3 1BS **Tel** *01792 390139* **Fax** *01792 391358* **Rooms** *8*

Secluded country house set amid vast, mature woodlands on the Gower Peninsula Area of Outstanding Natural Beauty. Hosts luxurious rooms and an award-winning restaurant that serves a fusion of Welsh and European cuisine. Therapy treatments such as massages, reflexology and reiki are available on request. **www.fairyhill.net**

SPITTAL Lower Haythog Farm

Spittal, Haverfordwest, Pembrokeshire, SA62 5QL **Tel** *01437 731279* **Fax** *01437 731279* **Rooms** *6*

Converted, 14th-century farmhouse, set on several acres of working farmland. This reasonably priced hotel offers a luxurious experience. The en suite rooms are comfortably furnished and retain their cottage-like feel. Also has two, self-catering cottages. Serves home-cooked food, using the farm's produce. **www.lowerhaythogfarm.co.uk**

ST DAVID'S Lochmeyler Farm Guest House

Pen-y-Cwm, near Solva, St David's, Pembrokeshire, SA62 6LL **Tel** *01348 837724* **Rooms** *15*

This quiet guesthouse, on a huge working dairy farm, is a popular stopping off point on the Pembrokeshire Long Distance Coast Path. The accommodation is split between the main 16th-century farmhouse, the cottages and the barn. The rooms are tastefully furnished and equipped with modern amenities. **www.lochmeyler.co.uk**

ST DAVID'S The Old Cross Hotel

Cross Sq, St David's, Pembrokeshire, SA62 6SP **Tel** *01437 720387* **Fax** *01437 720394* **Rooms** *16*

This friendly and comfortable hotel is situated in the centre of the town, just a short walk from the famous cathedral. Bedrooms are spacious and have a good range of facilities. Public areas include comfortable lounges, a popular bar and an airy restaurant where good wholesome food is offered. **www.oldcrosshotel.co.uk**

SWANSEA Windsor Lodge

Mount Pleasant, Swansea, SA1 6EG **Tel** *01792 642158* **Fax** *01792 648996* **Rooms** *19*

Small hotel and restaurant in a 200-year-old, Grade II listed building. This two-star lodge, near the city centre, provides a reasonably priced break. The rooms are modern and comfortable, and the acclaimed restaurant draws both locals and travellers by serving British food with a French twist. **www.windsor-lodge.co.uk**

Key to Price Guide *see p556* **Key to Symbols** *see back cover flap*

TENBY Fourcroft Hotel

North Beach, Tenby, Pembrokeshire, SA70 8AP **Tel** *01834 842886* **Fax** *01834 842888* **Rooms** *40*

This charming hotel offers striking views of Tenby's sheltered North Beach and the fishing harbour. Boasts secluded trails leading down to the beach. The rooms are simple, yet comfortably furnished, with most modern amenities. The restaurant serves local produce with an emphasis on fresh seafood. **www.fourcroft-hotel.co.uk**

TENBY Heywood Lodge Country House Hotel

Heywood Lane, Tenby, Pembrokeshire, SA70 8BN **Tel** *01834 842684* **Fax** *01834 843976* **Rooms** *12*

Beautiful Victorian house that's a luxury four-star hotel. Offers elegant, en suite rooms with traditional furniture; some have four-poster beds. This country house hotel features a conservatory and king size, hydra spa baths. Welcomes pets. **www.heywoodlodge.com**

THE MUMBLES Carlton Mumbles

654–656 Mumbles Rd, Mumbles, Swansea, SA3 4EA **Tel** *01792 360450* **Fax** *01792 360450* **Rooms** *20*

Friendly and affordable B&B located in the hometown of the famous poet, Dylan Thomas. The rooms are plain, but comfortably furnished; some with great views over Swansea Bay. Water-skiing, sailing and powerboating facilities are available nearby, as are a number of golf courses. **www.carltonmumbles.co.uk**

THE MUMBLES Hillcrest House

1 Higher Lane, Mumbles, Swansea, SA3 4NS **Tel** *01792 363700* **Rooms** *6*

Small hotel with comfortable, themed bedrooms, such as Autumnal Canada, Country Garden England, Fresh Scotland and Traditional Wales. This quaint retreat prides itself on its personal touch. Serves an elaborate British breakfast. Guests can try any of the many restaurants nearby for lunch and dinner. **www.hillcresthousehotel.com**

TINTERN Parva Farmhouse

Tintern, Chepstow, Gwent, NP16 6SQ **Tel** *01291 689411/689511* **Fax** *01291 689557* **Rooms** *9*

Farmhouse and restaurant on the banks of River Wye. This welcoming stone house is well placed for exploring Tintern Abbey and its surrounding countryside. The rooms offer great views over the river; some have four-poster beds. Boasts an award-winning inglenook restaurant with a 4 m (14 ft) high beamed fireplace. **www.hoteltintern.co.uk**

THE LOWLANDS

AUCHTERARDER The Gleneagles Hotel

A9, Auchterarder, Perthshire, PH3 1NF **Tel** *0800 3893737* **Fax** *01764 662134* **Rooms** *266*

World-renowned château-style resort hotel with high standards of service, cuisine, and amenities. Boasts championship golf courses and state-of-the-art spa and leisure facilities. Well equipped to accommodate the most demanding of guests. Popular with both business travellers and families. **www.gleneagles.com**

AYR The Ivy House

2 Alloway, Ayr, Ayrshire, KA7 4NL **Tel** *01292 442336* **Fax** *01292 445572* **Rooms** *5*

Located near the famous Robbie Burns Cottage, this attractive hotel offers individually furnished, comfortable rooms, with modern amenities. Serves delicious food. This is an ideal place to explore the surrounding Ayrshire countryside. Within easy distance of Culzean Castle. **www.theivyhouse.uk.com**

BALQUHIDDER Monachyle Mhor

Balquhidder, Lochearnhead, Perthshire, FK19 8PQ **Tel** *01877 384622* **Fax** *01877 384305* **Rooms** *11*

A beautiful, family-run hotel situated in the heart of Highland Perthshire, near the picturesque shores of Loch Voil. Offers luxury rooms and suites, some with log fires, as well as self-catering cottages. Service is outstanding. Also has an award-winning restaurant. **www.monachylemhor.com**

BLAIRGOWRIE Kinloch House

By Blairgowrie, Perthshire, PH10 6SG **Tel** *01250 884237* **Fax** *01250 884333* **Rooms** *18*

This family-run, country-house hotel is set in a particularly scenic locale at the end of a remote lochside glen road. Has an especially warm and welcoming atmosphere. The rooms and suites are comfortable and well equipped with modern facilities. Hosts a sauna and spa, and serves good food. **www.kinlochhouse.com**

CALLANDER Leny House

Leny Estate, Callander, Perthshire, FK17 8HA **Tel** *01877 331078* **Rooms** *4*

This delightful B&B is a great base for exploring the Trossachs. Originally from the 16th-century, it retains many original features and Victorian finishes. Luxurious and stylish inside, it offers rooms and self-catering lodges and cottages. Ideally located for outdoor activities such as golf, cycling, fishing and water sports. **www.lenyestate.com**

CLINTMAINS Clint Lodge

Clinthill, St Boswells, Melrose, Roxburghshire, TD6 0DZ **Tel** *01835 822027* **Fax** *01835 822656* **Rooms** *5*

A traditional country-guesthouse and B&B, run by hospitable hosts. The hotel has great views of the Tweed, and its location close to Melrose Abbey makes it ideal for exploring the surrounding countryside. The rooms are tastefully decorated, with en suite facilities and modern amenities. Serves an excellent breakfast. **www.clintlodge.co.uk**

CUPAR Peat Inn

£££££

Peat Inn, by Cupar, Fife, KY15 5H **Tel** *01334 840206* **Fax** *01334 840530* **Rooms** *8*

Relaxed and informal restaurant-with-rooms. Boasts luxury suites, elegantly decorated with plush furnishings. The renowned restaurant serves mouthwatering dishes and an extensive selection of wines. Located just a short distance from St Andrews and other sightseeing attractions. **www.thepeatinn.co.uk**

DOLLAR Castle Campbell

££

11 Bridge St, Dollar, Clackmannanshire, FK14 7DE **Tel** *01259 742519* **Fax** *01259 743742* **Rooms** *9*

A simple, but dignified Georgian building, set in the town centre. Has non-smoking, spacious rooms, with en suite facilities and modern conveniences such as colour TVs, tea and coffee makers and telephones. A good base for enjoying some of the excellent walks in the surrounding countryside. **www.castle-campbell.co.uk**

EDINBURGH 7 Danube Street

£££

7 Danube St, Edinburgh, EH4 1NN **Tel** *0131 332 2755* **Fax** *0131 343 3648* **Rooms** *3*

A delightful B&B, housed in a Georgian town house, in a quiet, but central part of Edinburgh. The comfortable, non-smoking rooms have attached bathrooms, and provide modern amenities such as computer points and a personal key and entrance. Within easy reach of many attractions and eateries. **www.aboutedinburgh.com/danube.html**

EDINBURGH The Bonham

££££

35 Drumsheugh Gardens, Edinburgh, EH3 7RN **Tel** *0131 274 7400* **Fax** *0131 2266080* **Rooms** *48*

Ultra-smart town house, boasting a rich interior with a perfect blend of many original features and some contemporary touches, including modern works of art and furniture. The oak-panelled restaurant is popular and the cooking is skilled. Offers opulent and well-equipped rooms. **www.thebonham.com**

EDINBURGH The Scotsman

££££

20 N Bridge, Edinburgh, EH1 1YT **Tel** *0131 556 5565* **Fax** *0131 652 3652* **Rooms** *69*

This stylish hotel is housed in the converted former offices of *The Scotsman* newspaper, and offers great views of the city. The luxurious rooms and suites are decorated with authentic Scottish estate tweeds, and feature amenities such as DVD and CD players, TVS, Internet access, coffee makers and more. **www.thescotsmanhotel.co.uk**

EDINBURGH The Balmoral

£££££

1 Princes St, Edinburgh, EH2 2EQ **Tel** *0131 556 2414* **Fax** *0131 557 3747* **Rooms** *188*

Boasting the best known address in Edinburgh, The Balmoral is favoured by those who are accustomed to the very best in life. This elegant hotel has luxurious, tastefully furnished suites and rooms, with Internet access, fax machines, TVs, and more. Also offers conference facilities, a spa and excellent eateries. **www.thebalmoralhotel.com**

EDNAM Edenwater House

££

Ednam, Kelso, Roxburghshire, TD5 7QL **Tel** *01573 224070* **Fax** *01573 226615* **Rooms** *4*

A quiet, family-run traditional guesthouse located on the edge of the village. This stone building is comfortably furnished, and offers lovely views of the surrounding Cheviot Hills. The delicious home-cooked meals are accompanied by a particularly interesting wine list. **www.edenwaterhouse.co.uk**

GLASGOW Tulip Inn

£

80 Ballater St, Glasgow, G5 0TW **Tel** *0141 429 4233* **Fax** *0141 429 4244* **Rooms** *114*

This city-centre budget hotel offers modern, spacious and well-equipped rooms with facilities such as satellite TV, walk-in shower rooms and trouser presses. Families are well catered for here, and children under 16 stay for free. Full-Scottish breakfast is served in the trendy hotel bistro. **www.tulipinnglasgow.co.uk**

GLASGOW One Devonshire Gardens

££££

One Devonshire Gardens, Glasgow, G12 OUX **Tel** *0141 339 2001* **Fax** *0131 337 1663* **Rooms** *35*

A beautiful town house, located in the city's trendy and leafy West End. The rooms have been glamorously furnished and opulently decorated, and the food in the restaurant is extremely refined. Well equipped with a high standard of service to match – a place for a serious treat. **www.onedevonshiregardens.com**

GLASGOW Radisson SAS

££££

301 Argyle St, Glasgow, G2 8DL **Tel** *0141 204 3333* **Fax** *0141 204 3344* **Rooms** *250*

This contemporary, award-winning hotel is mainly recognized for its innovative design. Hosts lavishly furnished rooms, suites and an apartment, well-equipped with many innovative features. Also has conference rooms, a popular bar and a good restaurant. A definite choice for those who appreciate modern surroundings. **www.radisson.com**

GLASGOW Langs

££££

2 Port Dundas Place, Glasgow, G2 3LD **Tel** *0141 333 1500* **Fax** *0141 333 1500* **Rooms** *100*

A glamorous, style-conscious boutique hotel with two trendy restaurants, beauty salon, spa and leisure amenities. The bedrooms are comfortably minimalist. An excellent location for those who enjoy shopping. Also offers meeting and conference facilties. **www.langshotels.co.uk**

GLENROTHES Balbirnie

££££

Balbirnie Park, Markinch, Glenrothes, Fife, KY7 6NE **Tel** *01592 610066* **Fax** *01592 610529* **Rooms** *30*

This elegant Georgian mansion evokes an air of tastefully restrained hedonism. The hotel is family run and has been frequently recognised for its quality of service and dining. The ambience is luxurious and proves popular with corporate and leisure customers. Has opulent and comfortable rooms. **www.balbirnie.co.uk**

Key to Price Guide *see p556* **Key to Symbols** *see back cover flap*

GULLANE Golf Inn

Main St, Gullane, East Lothian, EH31 2AB **Tel** *01620 843259* **Fax** *01620 842066* **Rooms** *14*

An intimate inn, set in a lovely village in East Lothian – a short drive from Edinburgh – which makes it popular for day trips. Decorated with pine furnishings and crisp colour schemes. The accommodation here is comfortable, but not too expensive, and the appetizing meals are of excellent value. **www.golfinngullane.com**

GULLANE Greywalls

Muirfield, Gullane, East Lothian, EH31 2EG **Tel** *01620 842144* **Fax** *01620 842241* **Rooms** *23*

This beautiful Lutyens house overlooks the famous golf course and, despite its name, is built of warm golden coloured stone. Offers well-equipped, lavish rooms, elegant dining and a superb standard of service. The surrounding gardens are gorgeous. A wonderful treat to stay here. Closes Oct–Mar. **www.greywalls.co.uk**

HEITON Roxburghe

Heiton, Kelso, Roxburghshire, TD5 8JZ **Tel** *01573 450331* **Fax** *01573 450611* **Rooms** *22*

Grand, Jacobean-style house, set in acres of beautiful estate grounds. The house is luxuriously appointed in traditional style, with comfortable rooms. This hotel is a perfect base to enjoy the scenic Borders. Offers a range of outdoor activities such as golf, fishing, mountain biking, walks and more. **www.roxburghe.net**

INVERSNAID Inversnaid Lodge

Inversnaid, Aberfoyle, Stirlingshire, FK8 3TU **Tel** *01877 386254* **Rooms** *9*

This photogenic, lodge-style accommodation on the eastern shores of Loch Lomond is mainly geared towards photographers. Has simple, cottage-style bedrooms, and offers straightforward cooking. Good value for money. Makes an ideal setting for exploring the surrounding countryside. **www.inversnaidphoto.com**

JEDBURGH Hundalee House

Hundalee, Jedburgh, Roxburghshire, TD8 6PA **Tel** *01835 863011* **Fax** *01835 863011* **Rooms** *5*

Stylish B&B in a refined, Georgian-style property, which has been tastefully maintained. The classic interior, a welcoming ambience and good home cooking offers excellent value to its guests. This part of the Borders is perfectly placed for experiencing the scenic environs. **www.accommodation-scotland.org**

KIRKCUDBRIGHT Gladstone House

48 High St, Kirkcudbright, Kirkcudbrightshire, DG6 4JX **Tel** *01577 331734* **Fax** *01577 331734* **Rooms** *3*

Charming and popular B&B in an attractive town house, set back from the Solway waterfront. The interior is light and airy, and the hosts are welcoming and hospitable. Offers a good standard of accommodation, and serves delicious Scottish breakfasts.

LINLITHGOW Champany Inn

Champany, Linlithgow, West Lothian, EH49 7LU **Tel** *01506 834532* **Fax** *01506 834302* **Rooms** *16*

Stylish restaurant-with-rooms. Has spacious bedrooms, with en suite facilities, tasteful and elegant furnishings, bow windows with tartan curtains, and modern amenities. Serves an excellent Scottish breakfast. Located close to several sightseeing attractions and golf courses. **www.champany.com**

MELROSE The Townhouse Hotel

Market Square, Melrose, Roxburghshire, TD6 9PQ **Tel** *01896 822645* **Fax** *01896 823474* **Rooms** *11*

A smart hotel, decorated in a sensitive, yet modern style. The owners have a long-standing reputation as welcoming hosts. The chic brasserie serves tasty contemporary cooking. A good place from which to explore this delightful corner of the Borders. **www.thetownhousemelrose.co.uk**

MELROSE Burts Hotel

Market Square, Melrose, Roxburghshire, TD6 9PL **Tel** *01896 822285* **Fax** *01896 822870* **Rooms** *20*

Family-run, traditional hotel, carefully maintained over the years. Has a well-earned reputation, both locally and abroad. The restaurant and bar serve superb local produce in convivial surroundings. Offers a warm welcome and good service. Situated close to several golf courses. **www.burtshotel.co.uk**

ST ANDREWS St Andrews Bay Hotel

St Andrews Bay, St Andrews, Fife, KY16 8PN **Tel** *01334 837000* **Fax** *01334 471555* **Rooms** *209*

Just a short distance from St Andrews, this resort hotel is self contained and has just about everything one could look for – wonderful views, excellent facilities, a high standard of accommodation and good service. Also boasts a conference centre, two world-class golf courses and a relaxing spa. **www.standrewsbay.com**

ST ANDREWS Old Course Hotel

Old Station Rd, St Andrews, Fife, KY16 9SP **Tel** *01334 474371* **Fax** *01334 475234* **Rooms** *144*

Situated just on the edge of the town, this hotel boasts splendid views of Old Course – the legendary sea-side links. Features luxurious interiors and exemplary amenities. The luxurious rooms and suites are decorated in a contemporary style. Also has specially designed rooms for disabled guests and wonderful spa facilities. **www.oldcoursehotel.co.uk**

ST BOSWELLS Buccleuch Arms

The Green, St Boswells, Dumfriesshire, TD6 OEW **Tel** *01835 822243* **Fax** *01835 823965* **Rooms** *19*

A 16th-century coaching inn, which remains a popular meeting place for visitors to the area and an ideal spot to explore the countryside. The accommodation is comfortable and unpretentious, and the service is friendly and relaxed. The restaurant and bar serve good food. **www.buccleucharmshotel.co.uk**

ST BOSWELLS Dryburgh Abbey Hotel

St Boswells, Melrose, Dumfriesshire, TD6 ORQ **Tel** *01835 822261* **Fax** *01835 823945* **Rooms** *38*

An imposing, red sandstone baronial mansion, located in a picturesque setting on the edge of River Tweed. The ruined abbey adjacent to the building adds to the character of the setting. Offers large rooms, and is a popular destination for weddings, conferences and other celebrations. **www.dryburgh.co.uk**

ST FILLANS Four Seasons

St Fillans, Perthshire, PH6 2NF **Tel** *01764 685333* **Fax** *01764 685444* **Rooms** *12*

Set in particularly stunning countryside, with a waterfront location, this small hotel has comfortable rooms, with en suite facilities and striking views of Loch Earn. Also hosts six, self-catering log cabin chalets for those who want to enjoy a more intimate stay. This cosy retreat is ideal for a romantic getaway. **www.thefourseasonshotel.co.uk**

TIGHABRUAICH The Royal Hotel

Shore Rd, Tighnabruaich, Argyll, PA21 2BE **Tel** *01700 811239* **Fax** *01700 811300* **Rooms** *11*

Fine, family-run hotel, set on the picturesque shore. Offers comfortable and spacious accommodation. Dining here can be on a formal or informal basis, and the quality of food and ingredients is extremely high. The service is efficient and friendly. **www.royalhotel.org.uk**

TROON Highgrove House Hotel

Old Loans Rd, Troon, Ayrshire, KA7 7HL **Tel** *01292 312511* **Rooms** *9*

An intimate and stylish hotel, designed by a sea captain in the 1920s, with fantastic views over the Firth of Clyde to the Isle of Arran and beyond. A popular place with golfers and for weddings, it's a haven to relax, enjoy good food and convenient for many Ayrshire attractions. **www.costley-hotels.co.uk**

TROON Lochgreen House

Monktonhill Rd, Troon, Ayrshire, KA10 7EN **Tel** *01292 313343* **Fax** *01292 318661* **Rooms** *44*

Elegant, antiques-filled Edwardian hotel. The bedrooms are large and luxurious, as are the public rooms. The restaurant is modern, but baronial in style, and the cooking is superb. Also has well-maintained grounds. A delightful place to stay. **www.costleyhotels.co.uk**

TURNBERRY The Westin Turnberry Resort

Turnberry, Ayrshire, KA26 9LT **Tel** *01655 331000* **Fax** *01655 331706* **Rooms** *219*

One of the trendiest places to stay in Scotland. Boasts championship golf courses, a spa, and conference facilities. The well-appointed, en suite rooms are elegantly furnished, with modern amenities. Also has rooms with facilities for disabled guests. Allows pets. The restaurant serves excellent food. **http://turnberry.co.uk/**

YARROW Tibbie Shiels Inn

St Mary's Loch, Selkirk, Selkirkshire, TD7 5LH **Tel** *01750 42231* **Fax** *01750 42302* **Rooms** *5*

Once a hostelry favoured by Sir Walter Scott, this 18th-century inn remains a popular place to eat and stay while in the area. Many original features of this B&B have been retained. Has simply furnished, clean rooms, as well as camping facilities. Offers good food, warm service and a genuine welcome. **www.tibbieshielsinn.com**

THE HIGHLANDS AND ISLANDS

ABERDEEN Ardoe House Hotel

S Deeside Rd, Aberdeen, Aberdeenshire, AB12 5YP **Tel** *0870 1942104* **Fax** *01224 861283* **Rooms** *109*

Located 5 km (3 miles) from the city centre, this is one of Aberdeen's best hotels. The rooms at this luxurious retreat are lavish and tastefully decorated. The suites have four-poster beds. All rooms offer striking views of the countryside. Also has amenities such as a jacuzzi, tennis courts and beauty salons. **www.ardoehouse.com**

ABERDEEN Udny Arms

Main St, Newburgh, Aberdeenshire, AB41 6BL **Tel** *01358 789444* **Fax** *01358 789012* **Rooms** *26*

A comfortable, traditional hotel. The bright, cheerful bedrooms have attached bathrooms, and are decorated with antique furnishings and several modern conveniences. The public rooms are relaxing and welcoming. Located close to three championship golf courses. Also offers facilities for biking and archery. **www.udny.co.uk**

ABERDEEN Marcliffe at Pitfodels

N Deeside Rd, Pitfodels, Aberdeenshire, AB15 9YA **Tel** *01224 861000* **Fax** *01224 868860* **Rooms** *39*

Situated on the outskirts of the city, this up-market hotel has beautiful interiors and a warm and welcoming ambience. The stylish bedrooms offer en suite facilities and many other modern amenities. The conservatory restaurant is bright and airy, and the menus feature Aberdonian quality produce. **www.marcliffe.com**

ABERFOYLE Farleyer Restaurant and Rooms

Aberfeldy, Perthshire, PH15 2JE **Tel** *01887 820332* **Fax** *01887 829879* **Rooms** *6*

This restaurant-with-rooms is housed in an attractive country house, in beautiful countryside on the outskirts of Aberfeldy. Serves appetizing food in relaxed and modern surroundings. The rooms are well appointed, with many thoughtful extras to complete that special experience. **www.farleyer.com**

Key to Price Guide *see p556* **Key to Symbols** *see back cover flap*

ACHILTIBUIE Summer Isles

*Achiltibuie, Ross-shire, IV26 2YG **Tel** 01854 622282 **Rooms** 13*

A remote and picturesque setting overlooking the Summer Isles makes this charmingly low-key place an idyllic retreat. The hotel interior is sophisticated, and houses lovely, well-appointed bedrooms. The restaurant serves food made with locally-grown ingredients. Check opening timings. **www.summerisleshotel.co.uk**

ARISAIG Old Library Lodge

*Road to the Isles, Arisaig, Perthshire, PH39 4NH **Tel** 01687 450651 **Fax** 01687 450219 **Rooms** 6*

Modest and well-run restaurant-with-rooms, set on the Road to the Isles. Housed in a 200-year-old former stable, the hotel offers great views and comfortably furnished rooms. Dining here is a rich culinary experience, with five choices at each course – all beautifully prepared. **www.oldlibrary.co.uk**

AULDEARN Boath House

*Auldearn, by Nairn, Inverness-shire, IV12 5TE **Tel** 01667 454896 **Fax** 01667 455469 **Rooms** 6*

Known as a "jewel in the Highland crown", this gorgeous mansion is a must-see attraction. The rooms are elegantly furnished with antiques, works of art and modern amenities; all offer excellent views of the estate and the gardens. Also hosts a beauty salon and spa, and serves award-winning cuisine. **www.boath-house.com**

BALLATER Balgonie Country House

*Braemar Place, Ballater, Royal Deeside, Aberdeenshire, AB35 5NQ **Tel & Fax** 013397 55482 **Rooms** 9*

Welcoming and experienced hosts play an important role in the success of this secluded hotel. The interior is chic, and the rooms are decorated in a blend of traditional and contemporary styles; most overlook the golf course. Activities such as walks, biking and fishing are available. A good place to unwind. **www.balgonie-hotel.co.uk**

BALLATER Darroch Learg

*Braemar Rd, Ballater, Royal Deeside, Aberdeenshire, AB35 5UX **Tel** 013397 55443 **Fax** 013397 55252 **Rooms** 17*

Set on a hill in Ballater, amid attractive gardens, this charming Victorian hotel offers splendid views of Lochnagar. The accommodation is comfortable, and the cooking is highly skilled, using the best local produce. A superb wine list completes the experience. **www.darrochlearg.co.uk**

BEAULY Lovat Arms Hotel

*Beauly, Inverness-shire, IV4 7BS **Tel** 01463 782313 **Fax** 01463 782862 **Rooms** 22*

This family-run, traditional hotel is more than 200 years old. Has two popular restaurants and a bar. The rooms are en suite, equipped with modern amenities such as TVs, modem outlets, coffee makers and more. Plenty of golfing and fishing opportunities nearby. Good Scottish fare served by friendly staff. **www.lovatarms.com**

CLACHAN SEIL Willowburn

*Clachan Seil, by Oban, Argyll, PA34 4TJ **Tel** 01852 300276 **Fax** 01852 300597 **Rooms** 7*

Located just over Clachan Bridge, this delightful, family-run hotel is housed in a whitewashed cottage. Offers magnificent views of the surrounding countryside. The decor here is simple, and rooms are well equipped. Serves good food, made with locally sourced produce and freshly grown vegetables. **www.willowburn.co.uk**

CRINAN Crinan Hotel

*Crinan, by Lochgilphead, Argyll, PA31 8SR **Tel** 01546 830261 **Fax** 01546 830292 **Rooms** 20*

A popular base from where to enjoy the panoramic views over Loch Fyne and Jura Sound. The distinctive whitewashed building accommodates a bar and restaurant, where seafood is a speciality. The bedrooms are simply, but tastefully decorated. A friendly and bustling place. **www.crinanhotel.com**

DUNKELD The Pend

*5 Brae St, Dunkeld, Perthshire, PH8 0BA **Tel** 01350 727586 **Fax** 01350 727173 **Rooms** 3*

High-quality accommodation in a quiet, Georgian town house, located just off High Street. The interiors are furnished with many antiques and period pieces. Welcomimg hosts offer the best of Scottish hospitality, and serve imaginative and superbly-prepared dishes. **www.thepend.com**

DUNKELD Kinnaird

*Kinnaird Estate, by Dunkeld, Perthshire, PH8 0LB **Tel** 01796 482440 **Fax** 01796 482289 **Rooms** 9*

Charming country-house accommodation on an enormous Tayside sporting estate. The setting is tranquil and the amenities are extensive. Features elegantly furnished rooms, with en suite facilities. Provides self-catering cottages as well. Also has tennis courts and a croquet lawn. **www.kinnairdestate.com**

ERISKA Isle of Eriska Hotel

*Ledaig, by Oban, Argyll, PA37 1SD **Tel** 01631 720371 **Fax** 01631 720531 **Rooms** 17*

Family-run country estate, located on an island. Houses individually decorated rooms, as well as private cottages; all equipped with modern amenities. This luxurious, romantic hideaway offers several leisure facilities and elaborate dinners. Tranquil and peaceful surroundings. **www.eriskahotel.co.uk**

FORRES Cluny Bank Hotel

*69 St Leonard's Rd, Forres, Inverness-shire, IV36 1DW **Tel** 01309 674304 **Fax** 01309 671400 **Rooms** 10*

This historic, family-run hotel is located in the quiet residential part of Forres, and retains many of its original features. The bedrooms are comfortable and tastefully decorated, while the public rooms are welcoming and airy. The friendly staff can help arrange outdoor pursuits such as golfing, fishing, cycling and more. **www.clunybankhotel.co.uk**

FORT WILLIAM Ashburn House ££

4 Achintore Rd, Fort William, Perthshire, PH33 6RQ Tel 01397 706000 Fax 01397 702024 Rooms 7

This traditional, Highland B&B overlooking Loch Linnhe, extends a typical Scottish welcome. The bedrooms of this Victorian house are attractively decorated and well equipped to ensure a comfortable stay. Located a short walking distance from the town centre. Offers hearty breakfasts. **www.highland5star.co.uk**

FORT WILLIAM The Grange ££

Grange Rd, Fort William, Perthshire, PH33 6JF Tel 01397 705516 Fax 01397 701595 Rooms 4

This historic B&B has been skilfully and lovingly restored. Enjoys lovely views across Loch Linnhe, and is run by welcoming hosts. The interior is beautifully decorated with great attention to detail, and the rooms are individually furnished with antique beds and lavish bathrooms. Serves a generous breakfast. **www.thegrange-scotland.co.uk**

GLENLIVET Minmore House 🍴 ££

Glenlivet, Banffshire, Aberdeenshire, AB37 9DB Tel 01807 590378 Fax 01807 590472 Rooms 9

An elegant country house, set in the grand surroundings of the Glenlivet Estate – formerly the home of the distillery's founder. Offers elegant rooms, furnished with modern conveniences. Serves appetizing meals, made with fresh produce and presented with care. **www.minmorehousehotel.com**

INVERNESS Millwood House ££

36 Old Mill Rd, Inverness, Inverness-shire, IV2 3HR Tel 01463 237254 Fax 0870 429806 Rooms 3

This luxurious and welcoming B&B is located in a private home, set in beautiful, country-style gardens. The rooms are tastefully decorated and well equipped. Offers great views of the scenic environs, and serves elaborate breakfasts. Situated a few minutes walk from the city centre. **www.millwoodhouse.co.uk**

INVERNESS Glenmoriston Town House 🍴 £££

20 Ness Bank, Inverness, Inverness-shire, IV2 4SF Tel 01463 223777 Fax 01463 712378 Rooms 30

A traditional town-house hotel that has been tastefully and luxuriously upgraded. The hotel overlooks the River Ness and is only minutes from the town centre. The rooms are furnished in a contemporary style, with modern amenities. Boasts an award-winning French restaurant. **www.glenmoriston.com**

ISLE OF HARRIS Leachin House 🍴 ££

Tarbert, Isle of Harris, Outer Hebrides, HS3 3AH Tel 01859 502157 Fax 01859 502157 Rooms 3

A Victorian stone building, originally the home of the father of Harris Tweed – Norman McLeod. The rooms are non-smoking and have en suite facilities, as well as amenities such as TVs and central heating. A delightful place to stay and experience this particular corner of the Hebrides.

ISLE OF IONA Argyll Hotel 🍴 🧍 ££

Isle of Iona, Agryll and Bute, PA76 6SJ Tel 01681 700334 Fax 01681 700510 Rooms 16

A relaxing retreat with views over the Sound of Iona. This traditional hotel has a comfortable and welcoming ambience, enhanced by log fires. The bright, cheerful rooms are simply decorated and furnished with modern facilities. Also boasts a sunny conservatory, and serves good food. **www.argyllhoteliona.co.uk**

ISLE OF LEWIS Galson Farm £

S Galson, Isle of Lewis, Outer Hebrides, HS2 0SH Tel 01851 850492 Fax 01851 850492 Rooms 4

Charming, 18th-century farmhouse on the west coast of Lewis. Offers simple, homely accommodation. This working farm is set in a beautiful location, with striking views of the surroundings. Serves good home cooking with interesting vegetarian options. Bunkhouse accommodation also available. **www.galsonfarm.freeserve.co.uk**

ISLE OF MULL Druimard Country House 🍴 ££

Dervaig, Isle of Mull, Argyll, PA75 6QW Tel 01688 400345 Fax 01688 400345 Rooms 7

Welcoming and cosy Victorian hotel, set in a quiet Glenside setting. This stone building hosts Mull's Little Theatre in its grounds. The rooms are tastefully decorated and furnished with modern amenities. Offers simple, but tasty home cooking. **www.druimard.co.uk**

ISLE OF SKYE Duisdale 🍴 ££

Sleat, Isle Ornsay, Isle of Skye, Inverness-shire, IV43 8QW Tel 01471 833202 Fax 01471 833404 Rooms 17

Friendly Victorian house set on a hill, with magnificent views of the Sound of Sleat. This small hotel has been flamboyantly decorated and has lots of character. The rooms are spacious and comfortably furnished. Also offers delicious food and lovely gardens. **www.duisdale.com**

ISLE OF SKYE Three Chimneys 🍴 £££££

Colbost, Dunvegan, Isle of Skye, Inverness-shire, IV55 8ZT Tel 01470 511 258 Fax 01470 511358 Rooms 6

Arguably the finest restaurant-with-rooms in Scotland, this intimate hotel is recognized for the excellence of its cooking and hospitality of the owners. Features modern and luxurious accommodation. The retreat's spectacular location makes for a memorable visit. **www.threechimneys.co.uk**

KILLIECRANKIE Killiecrankie Hotel 🍴 ££

Killiecrankie, by Pitlochry, Perthshire, PH16 5LE Tel 01796 473220 Fax 01796 472451 Rooms 10

A relaxing and informal hotel, set by the scenic wooded cliffs of the Killiecrankie Pass – a Royal Society for the Protection of Birds reserve. The decor is stylish and bright, and the accommodation is comfortable and spacious. Known for serving good food; light meals are also available. **www.killiecrankiehotel.co.uk**

Key to Price Guide *see p556* **Key to Symbols** *see back cover flap*

KINGUSSIE The Cross ₤₤₤

Tweed Mill Brae, Ardbroilach Rd, Kingussie, Perthshire, PH21 1LB **Tel** *01540 661166* **Fax** *01540 661080* **Rooms** *8*

Highly acclaimed restaurant-with-rooms, located in a converted tweed mill near the Cairngorms. The smartly refurbished and attractively decorated interior is light and bright. An ideal base for those interested in exploring this area. Good food, excellent wine list and caring hosts. **www.thecross.co.uk**

KIRRIEMUIR Lochside Lodge and Roundhouse Restaurant ₤₤

Bridgend of Lintrathen, by Kirriemuir, Forfarshire, DD8 5JJ **Tel** *01575 560340* **Fax** *01575 560251* **Rooms** *6*

A beautifully converted farm steading, set in a scenic location. This family-run hotel is known for the superb skills of the chef. The bedrooms are well appointed and comfortable, and feature hayloft windows and original coomed ceilings. Dogs are welcome. Many golf courses nearby. **www.lochsidelodge.com**

LOCHINVER The Albannach ₤₤₤₤₤

Lochinver, Sutherland, Inverness-shire, IV27 4LP **Tel** *01571 844407* **Fax** *01571 844285* **Rooms** *5*

Set on a hill on the outskirts of Lochinver, this small hotel is a Mecca for those who enjoy the finer things in life. Offers great views of the countryside. The cooking here is quite superb, making innovative use of fresh, locally sourced produce. Welcoming and hospitable owners. **www.thealbannach.co.uk**

LOCHRANZA Apple Lodge ₤₤

Lochranza, Isle of Arran, Bute, KA27 8HJ **Tel** *01770 830229* **Fax** *01770 830229* **Rooms** *4*

This charming guesthouse is an excellent base for exploring the sights of Arran. Close to the Kintyre ferry with fine views over the nearby castle. Bedrooms are prettily floral; several located in a self-contained cottage annexe. Serves good home cooking.

MUIR OF ORD The Dower House ₤₤

Highfield, Muir of Ord, Inverness-shire, IV6 7XN **Tel** *01463 870090* **Fax** *01463 870090* **Rooms** *4*

This attractive, 18th-century hotel is one of the best-kept secrets in the Highlands. Offers tastefully decorated, pleasant rooms, equipped with modern amenities. The restaurant is renowned for its appetizing home-cooked meals, which emphasize the versatility of good local produce. **www.thedowerhouse.co.uk**

OBAN Lerags House ₤₤₤

Lerags, by Oban, Argyll, PA34 4SE **Tel** *01631 563381* **Rooms** *6*

Located on the outskirts of Oban, this lovely country house is run by caring and welcoming hosts. Has clean, simply furnished bedrooms, with modern facilities. Provides a self-catering cottage as well. Serves tasty food, made from fresh local produce. Scenic surroundings. Price includes dinner, bed and breakfast. **www.leragshouse.com**

ORKNEY ISLANDS Foveran ₤₤

St Ola, Kirkwall, Orkney, KW15 1SF **Tel** *01856 872389* **Fax** *01856 876430* **Rooms** *8*

A fine, family-run hotel, with splendid views over Scapa Flow. The hotel has been tastefully refurbished to a high standard, and the staff gives a true taste of Orcadian hospitality. A wonderful base for exploring these magical islands. Offers superb cooking and pleasant accommodation. **www.foveranhotel.co.uk**

PITLOCHRY Atholl Palace ₤₤₤₤

Pitlochry, Perthshire, PH16 5LY **Tel** *01796 472400* **Fax** *01796 473036* **Rooms** *108*

This grandiose hotel is an excellent example of Scottish baronial architecture. The accommodation is on a large scale with spacious bedrooms and public areas. Features a wide range of leisure and spa facilities, as well as varying dining options to suit all tastes. **www.athollpalace.com**

PLOCKTON Plockton Hotel ₤₤

Harbour St, Plockton, Ross-shire, IV52 8TN **Tel** *01599 544274* **Fax** *01599 544475* **Rooms** *14*

A comfortable and tastefully furnished hotel, set across the waterfront, with breathtaking views of the countryside. The bedrooms are stylishly simple, with en suite facilities; many overlooking the loch and the mountains. Serves good food, using fresh local produce. **www.plocktonhotel.co.uk**

STRONTIAN Kilcamb Lodge ₤₤₤

Strontian, Argyll, PH36 4HY **Tel** *01967 402257* **Fax** *01967 402041* **Rooms** *12*

This elegant country house is located on the quiet Ardnamurchan peninsula. A lovely place to relax and enjoy the striking views over a winding sea loch. Welcoming hosts, excellent food and intimate ambience complete the experience. **www.kilcamblodge.co.uk**

TORLUNDY Inverlochy Castle ₤₤₤₤₤

Torlundy, Fort William, Perthshire, PH33 6SN **Tel** *01397 702177* **Fax** *01397 702953* **Rooms** *17*

A grand, luxurious castle, set amid beautiful grounds, on the outskirts of Fort William. The interior is decorated in a traditional, classic style. Offers high standards of food, accommodation and service. Dining here is a memorable experience. Fishing, tennis and croquet facilities are also available. **www.inverlochycastlehotel.com**

ULLAPOOL Tanglewood House ₤₤

Ullapool, Ross-shire, IV26 2TB **Tel** *01854 612059* **Rooms** *3*

This modern, highly individual house commands panoramic vistas of Loch Broom from its huge picture windows. The hotel is tastefully furnished and extremely comfortable. The hostess is a highly accomplished cook, who serves imaginative and innovative cuisine. **www.tanglewoodhouse.co.uk**

WHERE TO EAT

Hakkasan in central London
(see p610)

British food need strike no terrors to the visiting gourmet's heart; the UK's restaurant scene has moved far from its once dismal reputation. This is partly due to an influx of foreign chefs and cooking styles; you can now sample a wide range of cuisine throughout Britain, with the greatest choice in London and the other major cities. Home-grown restaurateurs have risen to the challenge of redeeming British food too, and the indigenous cooking (once thought to consist only of fish and chips, overcooked vegetables, meat pies and lumpy custard) has improved out of all recognition in the last decade. You can now also eat very well in Britain whatever your budget – and at most times of day in the towns. Much less elaborate, but well-prepared, affordable food is making a mark in all types of restaurants and cafés throughout the country; more modern approaches combine fresh produce and dietary common sense with influences from around the world. The restaurant listings *(see pp608–651)* feature some of the very best places as well as those with a steady track record.

WHAT'S ON THE MENU?

The choice seems endless in large cities, particularly London. Cuisines from all over the world are represented, as well as their infinite variations – Thai and Tex-Mex, Turkish and Tuscan, Tandoori, Bhel Poori and Balti. There are many more unusual styles of cooking such as Hungarian, Polish, Caribbean and Pacific Rim. French and Italian restaurants are still highly regarded, offering everything from pastries and espresso coffee to the highest standards of *haute cuisine*. Outside the major cities the food scene is more limited, but most towns will have at least a couple of Italian, Indian and Chinese restaurants. The vague term "modern-international cuisine" adopted by many restaurants disguises a diverse rag-bag of styles. The spectrum ranges from French to Asian recipes, loosely characterized by the imaginative use of fresh, high-quality ingredients, which are cooked simply with imaginative seasonings.

Nostalgic yearnings for British food have produced a revival of hearty traditional dishes such as steak and kidney pie and treacle pudding *(see p607)*, though "Modern British" cooking adopts a lighter, more innovative approach to old-fashioned stodge. The distinctions between this and Modern International food are starting to blur, which is mostly a change for the better as young chefs apply Oriental and Mediterranean flavours to home-grown ingredients.

BREAKFAST

It used to be said that the best way to enjoy British food was to eat breakfast three times a day. Traditional British breakfast starts with cereal and milk followed by bacon, eggs and tomato, perhaps with fried black pudding *(see p606)* in the North and Scotland. It is finished off with toast and marmalade washed down with tea. Or you can just have black coffee and fruit juice, with a croissant or two (known as Continental breakfast in hotels). The price of breakfast is often included in hotel tariffs in Britain.

LUNCH

Many restaurants offer light lunches at fixed prices, sometimes of only two courses. The most popular lunchtime foods are sandwiches, salads, baked potatoes with fillings and ploughman's lunches *(see p606)*, the latter found mainly in pubs. A traditional Sunday lunch of roast chicken, lamb or beef is served in some pubs and restaurants.

Gay Hussar, London, a top Hungarian restaurant *(see p610)*

AFTERNOON TEA

No visitor should miss the experience of a proper English afternoon tea, which rivals breakfast as the most enjoyable meal of the day *(see p606)*. Some of the most palatial teas are offered by country-house and top London hotels such as the Ritz or Browns. The area that is best known for its classic "cream teas" is the West Country; these always include scones, spread with clotted cream, butter and jam. Wales, Scotland, Yorkshire and the Lake District also offer tasty teas with regional variations; in the North Country a slice of apple pie or fruit cake is served hot with a piece of North Yorkshire Wensleydale cheese on top.

An afternoon tea including sandwiches, cakes and scones

DINNER

At dinner time, the grander restaurants and hotels offer elaborately staged meals, sometimes billed as five or six courses (though one may be simply a sorbet, or coffee with *petits fours*). Dessert is often followed by cheese and biscuits (crackers). Confusingly, in the North of England and Scotland "lunch" can be called "dinner" and "dinner" may be called "tea".

Generally, you can choose to take your dinner before 6pm or after 9pm only in larger towns, where there is a broad choice of ethnic restaurants, bars and all-day brasseries, which often have long opening hours.

Leith Docks in Edinburgh, a centre of good pubs, bars and restaurants

PLACES TO EAT

Eating venues are extremely varied, with brasseries, bistros, wine bars, tearooms, *tapas* bars and theatre cafés now competing with the more conventional cafés and restaurants. Many pubs also now serve excellent bar food at often reasonable prices *(see p652–5)*.

BRASSERIES, BISTROS AND CAFES

French-style café-brasseries are now popular in Britain. Sometimes they stay open all day, serving coffee, snacks and fairly simple dishes along with a selection of beers and wines. Alcoholic drinks, however, may only be available at certain times of day. The atmosphere is usually young and urbane, with decor to match. Drinks such as imported bottled beers, exotic spirits or cocktails may be fairly expensive.

The café at Tate St Ives, Cornwall *(see p628)*

Wine bars are similar to brasseries, but with a better selection of wines, which may include English varieties *(see p160)*. Some bars have a good range of ciders and real ales as well *(see p604)*. Bistros are another French import, serving full meals at lunch and dinner time with less formality and more moderate prices than you would expect at a restaurant. You should expect to pay anything from £12 to £30 for a standard three-course meal in a bistro.

RESTAURANTS-WITH-ROOMS AND HOTELS

Restaurants-with-rooms are a new breed of small establishments with only a handful of bedrooms and usually excellent food. They tend to be expensive and are usually in a rural location.

Many hotel restaurants happily serve non-residents. They tend to be expensive, but the best can be unparalleled. Hotels serving a high standard of food are also included on pages 556–99.

RESTAURANT ETIQUETTE

As a rule of thumb, the more expensive the restaurant, the more formal the dress code – though few restaurants nowadays will expect men to wear a shirt and tie. If you are not sure, ring first.

A total smoking ban in public places will have been implemented throughout most of the UK by summer 2007.

Raymond Blanc's Le Manoir Aux Quat'Saisons *(see p622)*, one of Britain's most acclaimed restaurants-with-rooms

ALCOHOL

Britain's laws concerning the sale of alcohol, the "licensing laws", were once among the most restrictive in Europe. Now they are much more relaxed, with some restaurants operating extended opening hours, especially at weekends. Some establishments, however, may only serve alcohol at set times with food. Some unlicensed restaurants operate a "Bring Your Own" policy. A corkage fee is often charged.

VEGETARIAN FOOD

Britain is ahead of many of its European counterparts in providing vegetarian alternatives to meat dishes. A few places in this section serve only vegetarian meals, but most also cater for carnivores. Vegetarians who want a wider choice should seek out South Indian, Chinese and other ethnic restaurants which have a tradition of vegetarian cuisine.

FAST FOOD

Fast food usually costs well under £10. Apart from the numerous individually owned fish and chip shops, there are many of the usual fast food chains in Britain, as well as some more up market options such as Pizza Express and Yo

Sushi. Sandwich bars are very popular, and are often good value; some also have seating. Budget cafés, nicknamed "greasy spoons", serve simple, inexpensive food, often in the form of endless variations of the breakfast fry-up *(see p606)*.

Blackfriars restaurant *(see p641)*

BOOKING AHEAD

It is always safer to book a table first before making a special journey to a restaurant; city restaurants can be very busy and some of the more renowned establishments can be fully booked a month in advance. If you cannot keep a reservation, you should ring up and cancel. A lot of restaurants operate on knife-edge profit margins, and customers not turning up can threaten their livelihood.

CHECKING THE BILL

All restaurants are required by law to display their current prices outside the door. These amounts include Value Added Tax (VAT), currently at 17.5 per cent. Service and cover charges (if any) are also specified. So you should have a rough idea of what a meal may cost beforehand.

Wine is always pricey in Britain, and extras like coffee or bottled water can be disproportionately expensive.

Service charges (usually between 10 per cent and 15 per cent) are sometimes automatically added to your bill. If you feel that the service has been poor, you are entitled to subtract this service charge. If no service charge has been added, you are expected to add 10 to 15 per cent to the bill, but it is your decision.

Some restaurants may leave the "total" box of credit card slips blank, hoping customers will add something extra to the service charge. Another growing trend is for smart restaurants to boost their sagging profit margins with a "cover charge" for flowers, bread and butter, etc. Live entertainment may also be costed. The majority of restaurants accept credit cards, or UK cheques with a guarantee card, but traditional pubs and cafés will often expect cash.

MEALTIMES

Breakfast is a moveable feast. It may be as early as 6:30am in a city business hotel (most hoteliers will make special arrangements if you have a plane to catch or some other reason for checking out early) or as late as 10:30am in relaxed country house establishments. Few hoteliers relish cooking bacon and eggs that late, however, and some insist you are up and about by 9:00 sharp if you want anything to eat. But you can find breakfast all day long in some urban restaurants. The American concept of Sunday "brunch" (a leisurely halfway house between breakfast and lunch) is becoming increasingly popular in some hotels, restaurants and cafés.

Lunch in pubs and restaurants is usually served between noon and 2:30pm. Try to arrive in time to order the main course before 1:30pm, or you may find choice restricted and service peremptory. Most tourist areas have plenty of cafés, fast-food diners and coffee bars where you can have a snack at any time of day. During peak hours there may be a minimum charge.

If you are lucky enough to be in one of the places where you can get a traditional afternoon tea, it is usually served between 3pm and 5pm.

Dinner is usually served from 6pm until 10pm; some places, especially ethnic restaurants, stay open later. In guest houses or small hotels, dinner may be served at a specific time (sometimes uncomfortably early).

CHILDREN

The continental norm of dining out *en famille* is steadily becoming more acceptable in Britain, and visiting a restaurant may no longer entail endless searches for a babysitter. Many places welcome junior diners, and some actively encourage

Langan's Brassserie, a popular choice for Anglo-French cuisine *(see p610)*

families, at least during the day or early evening. Formal restaurants sometimes cultivate a more adult ambience at dinner time, and some impose age limits. If you want to take young children to a restaurant, check when you book. Italian, Spanish, Indian, fast-food restaurants and ice-cream parlours nearly always welcome children, and sometimes provide special menus or high chairs for them. Even traditional English pubs, which were once a strictly adult preserve, are now relaxing their rules to accommodate families and may even provide special rooms or play areas.

The places that welcome and cater for children are indicated in both the pubs guide *(see pp652–55)* and the restaurant listings.

Ice-cream parlour sign

DISABLED ACCESS

As in most walks of life, restaurant facilities in Britain could be better for disabled visitors, but things are gradually improving. Modern premises usually take account of mobility problems, but it's always best to check first if you have special needs.

PICNICS

Eating outside is becoming more popular in Britain, though it is more likely that you will find tables outside pubs in the form of a beer garden, than outside restaurants. One inexpensive option is to make up your own picnic; most towns have good delicatessens and bakeries where you can collect provisions, and in Britain you do not usually have to worry about shops closing at mid-day as they often do on the Continent.

Look out for street markets to pick up fresh fruit and local cheeses at bargain prices. Department stores like Marks & Spencer and supermarkets such as Sainsbury's and Tesco often sell an excellent range of pre-packed sandwiches and snacks; large towns usually have several sandwich bars to choose from. Your hotel or guest house may also be able to provide a packed lunch. Ask for it the night before.

An option for a chillier day is a hot takeaway meal; fish and chips with salt and vinegar all wrapped in paper is not only a British cliché but a national institution.

Eating alfresco at Grasmere in the Lake District

The Traditional British Pub

Beer label c.1900

Every country has its bars, but Britain is famous for its pubs or "public houses". Ale was brewed in England in Roman times – mostly at home – and by the Middle Ages there were inns and taverns which brewed their own. The 18th century was the heyday of the coaching inn as stage coaches brought more custom. In the 19th century came railway taverns for travellers and "gin palaces" for the new industrial workers. Today, pubs come in all styles and sizes and many cater to families, serving food as well as drink *(see pp652–55)*.

Early 19th-century coaching inn – also a social centre and post office

THE VICTORIAN PUB

A century ago, many pubs in towns and cities had smart interiors, to contrast with the poor housing of their clients.

Pint glasses (containing just over half a litre) are used for beer.

The Red Lion pub name is derived from Scottish heraldry *(see p26)*.

Elaborately etched glass is a feature of many Victorian interiors.

Pub games, *such as cribbage, bar billiards, pool and dominoes are part of British pub culture. Here some regular customers are competing against a rival pub's darts team.*

Beer gardens *outside pubs are a favourite venue for family summer treats.*

Old-fashioned cash register contributes to the period atmosphere of the bar.

Pewter tankards, seldom used by drinkers today, add a traditional touch.

WHAT TO DRINK

Draught bitter is the most traditional British beer. Brewed from malted barley, hops, yeast and water, and usually matured in a wooden cask, it varies from region to region. In the north of England the sweeter mild ale is popular, and lagers served in bottles or on tap are also widely drunk. Stout, made from black malt, is another variation.

Beer pump

Draught bitter is drunk at cellar temperature.

Draught lager is a light-coloured, carbonated beer.

Guinness is a thick, creamy Irish stout.

Pavement tables, crowded with city drinkers during the summer months

A village pub, offering a waterside view and serving drinks in the garden

Bottles of spirits, as well as the popular port and sherry, are ranged behind the bar.

Glass lamps imitate the Victorian style.

Wine, once rarely found in pubs, is now increasingly popular.

A deep-toned mahogany bar forms part of the traditional setting.

Draught beer, served from pumps or taps, comes from national and local brewers.

Optics dispense spirits in precise measures.

Mild may be served by the pint or in a half-pint tankard (as above).

Top cocktails are gin-and-tonic (right) and Pimm's.

PUB SIGNS

Early medieval inns used vines or evergreens as signs – the symbol of Bacchus, the Roman god of wine. Soon pubs acquired names that signalled support for monarchs or noblemen, or celebrated victories in battle. As many customers could not read, pub signs had vivid images.

The George *may derive from one of the six English kings of that name, or, as here, from England's patron saint.*

The Bat and Ball *celebrates cricket, and may be sited near a village green where the game can be played.*

The Green Man *is a woodland spirit from pagan mythology, possibly the basis for the legend of Robin Hood (see p336).*

The Magna Carta *sign commemorates and illustrates the "great charter" signed by King John in 1215 (see p48).*

The Bird in Hand *refers to the ancient country sport of falconry, traditionally practised by noblemen.*

The Flavours of Britain

A rich agriculture that provides meat and dairy products such as well as fruit, vegetables and cereals, gives the British table a broad scope. Traditional dishes – cooked breakfasts, roast beef, fish and chips – are famous, but there is much more on offer, varying from region to region. Many towns give their names to produce and dishes. Seasonal choices include game and seafood, while other produce can be seen at the increasingly popular farmers' markets. Britons still have a penchant for pies and puddings, and most regions have cakes and buns they can call their own. Scotland has its own distinctive cuisine *(see p488)*.

Asparagus

Local fresh beetroot on sale at a greengrocer's shop

CENTRAL AND SOUTHERN ENGLAND

All tastes are catered for in the metropolis, and the surrounding countryside has long been given over to its demands. The flat lands of East Anglia provide vege-tables and root crops; the South Downs have been shorn by sheep; geese have

made Nottingham famous; and the county of Kent is known as "the Garden of England" for its glorious orchards and its fields of soft fruits. From around the coast come Dover sole, Whitstable oysters (popular since Roman times) and the Cockney favourites, cockles and whelks. The game season runs from November to February, and pheasant is often on the menu.

WEST OF ENGLAND

The warmest part of England is renowned for its classic cream teas, the key ingredient provided by its dairy herds. In Cornwall, pasties have long been a staple. Once eaten by tin miners and filled with meat at one end and jam the other, to give two courses in one, they are now generally made with meat and veg-

Cornish Yarg   **Cider-washed Celtic Promise**   **Dorstone goats'-milk cheese**   **Cropwell Bishop Stilton**

Montgomery Cheddar

Ewes'-milk Wigmore

Selection of fine, farm-produced British cheeses

TRADITIONAL BRITISH FOOD

Though many traditional dishes, such as Lancashire hotpot, beef Wellington and even fish and chips, can be harder to hunt down than tapas, pizza or chicken tikka masala, other reliable regulars remain. Among them are shepherd's pie (minced lamb with mashed potatoes), steak and kidney pie (beef and kidney in gravy baked in a pastry crust), or game pie and "bangers and mash" (sausages with mash potatoes and onion gravy). For pudding there is a variety of trifles, pies, tarts and crumbles, often eaten with custard, as well as a lighter summer pudding of seasonal fruit. A "full English breakfast" is a fry-up of sausages, eggs, bacon, tomatoes, mushrooms and bread, perhaps with black pudding or laverbread. Lunchtime snacks include a "Ploughman's lunch" of cheese and pickles with a "doorstep" of bread.

Dover sole *This is the most tasty flatfish, best served simply grilled with lemon, spinach and new potatoes.*

Display of British breads at a local farmers' market

etables. The clear waters around the peninsula offer up such seafood as sardines, mackerel and crab in abundance, and many of the region's best restaurants specialize in fish. Bath gives its name to special biscuits and buns.

NORTH OF ENGLAND

Cumberland sausage, Lancashire hotpot, Goosnargh duck and Yorkshire pudding – the names tell you exactly where the food on your plate originated. These are the staples, but restaurants these days are creating new dishes from old, such as trout with black (blood) pudding, and even being adventurous with "mushy" peas. Bradford, with its large Asian community, is the best place to eat Indian food.

WALES

The green grass of Wales is appreciated by sheep, who turn into fabulous lamb that is simply roasted and eaten with mint sauce – a favourite all over Britain. The grass is

A Cornish fishmonger displays a locally caught red mullet

good for dairy products, too, including white, crumbly Caerphilly. Cheese is the principal ingredient of Welsh rarebit (pronounced rabbit), made with cheese grilled on toast and occasionally augmented with beer. Look out for prize-winning Welsh Black beef – prime fillets are often accompanied by horseradish sauce. The Irish Sea provides plenty of fish, but there is also freshwater trout and salmon. A curiosity of the South Wales seashore is laver, a kind of sea spinach, which is mixed with oatmeal and fried in small cakes called *bara lawr*, or laverbread, to be served with sausage and bacon for breakfast.

BRITISH CHEESES

Caerphilly Fresh, white, mild cheese from Wales.

Cheshire Crumbly, silky and full-bodied cheese.

Cheddar Often imitated, never bettered; the best comes from the West Country.

Double Gloucester Mellow flavoured, smooth and creamy.

Sage Derby Flavoured with green veins of sage.

Stilton The king of British cheeses, a strong, blue-veined cheese with a creamy texture. Popular at Christmas.

Wensleydale Young, moist and flaky-textured, with a mild, slightly sweet flavour.

Cornish mackerel *The ideal partner for this rich fish is a piquant sauce make of English gooseberries.*

Roast beef *Horseradish sauce is a traditional accompaniment, as are crisp Yorkshire puddings made of batter.*

Welsh lamb with leeks *The leek is the national vegetable of Wales, and perfectly complements roast lamb.*

Choosing a Restaurant

The restaurants in this guide have been selected across a wide range of price categories for their good value, exceptional food and interesting location. This chart lists the restaurants by region, starting with London. It also highlights some of the factors that may influence your choice. For pub listings, see pages 652–657.

PRICE CATEGORIES
Include a three-course meal for one, half a bottle of house wine, and all unavoidable extra charges such as cover, service, VAT:
£ under £20
££ £20–£35
£££ £35–£45
££££ £45–£ 55
£££££ over £55

LONDON

WEST END AND WESTMINSTER Bam-Bou   ££

1 Percy St, W1T 1DB **Tel** *020 7323 9130*   **Map** 11 A1

A nice bar upstairs lures you in for a few drinks before you descend to the restaurant proper. Seated at a low table with just candlelight playing off dark wood, you feel a million miles from London. This is not your average Vietnamese restaurant. The food is excellent and the atmosphere relaxed and warm.

WEST END AND WESTMINSTER Belgo Centraal   🔥♿   ££

50 Earlham St, WC2H 9HP **Tel** *0207 813 2233*   **Map** 11 B2

Nice and handy for Neal Street, Belgo Centraal remains popular every night. The cool young staff whip up a great variety of mussels dishes, from *moules marinières* to more exotic creations featuring Belgium's famous beers. Meat-eaters are also catered for. Eat at the long refectory tables and enjoy the fun.

WEST END AND WESTMINSTER Bigun's Ribs   🔥   ££

2 Warwick Way, SW1V 1RU **Tel** *020 7834 7350*   **Map** 18 F2

A typical American restaurant, Bigun's Ribs is known to serve generous proportions of food at rock-bottom prices. A little too noisy for romantic dining, it's ideal for a hearty meal. Though ribs are the main attraction, dishes such as rack of lamb are also really good value for money. The service is brisk and ambience bustling.

WEST END AND WESTMINSTER Busaba Eathai   🔥   ££

106–110 Wardour St, W1F 0TR **Tel** *020 7255 8686*   **Map** 11 A2

The immense popularity of Busaba Eathai rests on its reasonably priced Thai food and efficient service. Get there early, as the queue here can be of legendary proportions after 8pm. However, be prepared to share a table whatever time you arrive. Food is good – try Thai calamari and the rose apple curry.

WEST END AND WESTMINSTER Café Med   🔥   ££

57 & 59 Endell St, WC2H 9AJ **Tel** *020 7240 8085*   **Map** 11 C2

Great salads, family-sized pizzas and warm, friendly staff all contribute to a winning formula at Café Med. Always great value and very popular, this restaurant is also preferred by lone diners. The downstairs Moroccan-themed lounge is a cool retreat from the hustle and bustle of Covent Garden.

WEST END AND WESTMINSTER Vasco & Piero's Pavilion   ££

15 Poland St, W1F 8QE **Tel** *020 7437 8774*   **Map** 11 A2

Of Umbrian heritage, the owner of this restaurant ensures that chickpeas and lentils feature frequently on the largely Italian menu which changes twice daily. The pasta is made in-house, with the finest quality ingredients. The truffles, particularly, make the place worth a visit. In season, black and white truffles are imported from Umbria.

WEST END AND WESTMINSTER Atrium   🔥♿🍷   £££

4 Millbank, SW1P 3JA **Tel** *020 7233 0032*   **Map** 19 B1

As the name suggests, bright and modern Atrium has a vast glass-covered space. The well-priced menu wonderfully mixes and matches ingredients to largely good effect. For starters, try salted cod and white bean soup with leeks and truffle oil, while paprika smoked monkfish tail with anchovies makes an excellent main course.

WEST END AND WESTMINSTER Beotys   ♿   £££

79 Saint Martins Lane, WC2N 4AA **Tel** *020 7836 8768*   **Map** 11 B2

Reputedly the best Greek restaurant in London, Beotys is a perfect place to sample all that Greek cuisine has to offer. Authentic Greek favourites are available, including a bewildering yet tasty variety of meze (small portioned dishes). Ever pulsating with a lively crowd, the atmosphere is very friendly. Closed on Sundays.

WEST END AND WESTMINSTER Bertorelli   🔥🍷♿   £££

44A Floral St, WC2E 9DA **Tel** *020 7836 3969*   **Map** 11 C2

An Italian institution in Covent Garden, Bertorelli's Roman empire now extends further afield. This is the flagship, though, not the one you may have seen in the film *Sliding Doors*. Freshly prepared and flavourful home cooking is served in a friendly ambience. Sensible prices are an extra bonus. Closed Sundays.

Key to Symbols *see back cover flap*

WEST END AND WESTMINSTER Café Pacifico
5 Langley St, WC2H 9JA **Tel** *020 7379 7728* **Map** *11 B2*

Café Pacifico is frequented by the young and young-at-heart. Mexican live music and a buzzy atmosphere promise a lively night, though those looking for a romantic dinner might want to stay away. A few cocktails followed by some filling and reasonably priced food will send you singing out into the street.

WEST END AND WESTMINSTER Christopher's American Grill
18 Wellington St, WC2E 7DD **Tel** *020 7240 4222* **Map** *11 C2*

Rather more formal than you might expect from an American restaurant, but then this is a superior establishment. There are plenty of American favourites to choose from, including delicious ham hocks, large steaks and excellent lobsters. Good value and unpretentious.

WEST END AND WESTMINSTER ECapital
8 Gerrard St, W1D 5PJ **Tel** *020 7434 3838* **Map** *11 A2*

ECapital's pink interior could be a little garish for some, but the food more than makes up for it. Shanghai-style cooking is a speciality and the menu offers a distinct Shanghai meal that's unique to the locality. The "cubed belly of pork in the poet's style" is particularly good. Service is unusually unhurried and the set menus can be a bargain.

WEST END AND WESTMINSTER L'Escargot Marco Pierre White
48 Greek St, W1D 4EF **Tel** *020 7437 6828* **Map** *11 A1*

Another Soho institution, this restaurant is now run by Marco Pierre White, a legendary chef. Expect high standards but be surprised by the very reasonable prices. In the Picasso Room you can look at some of the master's works while eating artistically crafted fine food. Try the parfait of foi gras *en gelée* with toasted Poilane. Closed on Sundays.

WEST END AND WESTMINSTER Loch Fyne
2–4 Catherine St, WC2B 5JS **Tel** *020 7240 4999* **Map** *11 C2*

At Loch Fyne, a seafood restaurant, the fish and shellfish are brought in fresh from Scotland. The wine list is suitably chosen to match the crustaceans and other edible sea creatures on offer. Portions are generous whether you choose a platter of oysters or a large plate of poached smoked haddock.

WEST END AND WESTMINSTER Mango Tree
46 Grosvenor Place, SW1X 7AW **Tel** *020 7823 1888* **Map** *10 E5*

Just opposite the back gate of Buckingham Palace, Mango Tree was created from the remains of the Enron building. Taking Thai cuisine to a new level, the menu performs fresh twists, as the chefs here create remarkable tastes and effects. The service and decor are impeccable. Not cheap, but worth a trip.

WEST END AND WESTMINSTER Palm Court Brasserie
39 King St, WC2E 8JS **Tel** *020 7395 5803* **Map** *11 C2*

A good location and a sophisticated interior make Palm Court Brasserie a firm favourite with the locals. Mediterranean flavours are well infused with the southern sunshine. Sharing platters are good fun and great value, while a roast rump of lamb is quite filling. Like most restaurants in this area, there are special pre-theatre deals.

WEST END AND WESTMINSTER Porter's English Restaurant
17 Henrietta St, WC2E 8QH **Tel** *020 7836 6466* **Map** *11 C2*

A great place for proper fish and chips, Porter's is known for serving for hearty British "grub" with tasty pie dishes such as steak and Guinness, haddock and salmon or prawn. Desserts are equally large and not for those on a diet. Prices are good for the location. Cheerful staff.

WEST END AND WESTMINSTER Rock Garden
4–6 The Piazza, WC2E 8HB **Tel** *020 7257 8613* **Map** *11 C2*

Contrary to its name, this is not a tacky themed restaurant. The Rock Garden serves Modern European cuisine with a wide variety of meat, fish and vegetarian dishes. It is ideal for children and has a good pre-theatre menu. The location is one of the best in Covent Garden, especially in summer.

WEST END AND WESTMINSTER Signor Zilli
41 Dean St, W1D 4PY **Tel** *020 7734 3924* **Map** *11 A2*

The owner of this eponymous restaurant is often in attendance, adding a special touch to the place. The Italian food is first rate, if sometimes unadventurous, and the atmosphere is always inviting. The prices are a little steep, but worth it for the large, hearty portions. Closed on Sundays.

WEST END AND WESTMINSTER Sofra
36 Tavistock St, WC2E 7PB **Tel** *020 7240 3773* **Map** *11 C2*

A reputed London institution, Sofra has been serving superior Turkish food for many years. The speciality is the healthy option involving a variety of little dishes to share. Bread and olives come free throughout the meal, while dips such as hummous and *tzatziki* always taste fresh and clean.

WEST END AND WESTMINSTER Thai Metro
38 Charlotte St, W1T 2NL **Tel** *020 7436 4201* **Map** *3 A5*

Thai Metro offers top-notch Thai cuisine at affordable prices. The green curry is a must-try, but be warned about the chillies. The zingy flavours that characterize Thai food are all here in abundance. If the weather is warm, you can enjoy your food in the fresh air. Service is brisk, which may not be ideal for a relaxed meal.

WEST END AND WESTMINSTER The Gaucho Grill

€€€

125–126 Chancery Lane, WC2A 1PU **Tel** *020 7242 7727*   **Map** *12 E1*

There are a few of branches of the Gaucho around London and they remain of consistent value. The star attraction is still its delicious steak. A large wine list helps wash down an enormous meal and the cocktails are good too. Ideal for a pleasant, no-frills dining, it's a well-priced place in a reasonably expensive area.

WEST END AND WESTMINSTER Tiger Green Brasserie

€€€

Half Moon St, W1J 7BN **Tel** *020 7629 7522*   **Map** *10 E4*

Located in the recently refurbished Hilton London Green Park hotel, this restaurant welcomes all with an arresting menu. The classic combination of contemporary and modern design with an eclectic mix of traditional English and Mediterranean cuisine is well worth the experience. They also have a wide range of cocktails to choose from.

WEST END AND WESTMINSTER Elena's L'Etoile

€€€€

30 Charlotte St, W1T 2NA **Tel** *020 7636 7189*   **Map** *11 A1*

This long-standing local eatery is extremely busy at lunchtime, with advertizing media people from surrounding ad agencies and TV companies. The time-tested menu delivers classic French bistro food under the gaze of celebrity pictures that cover the walls. It's not cheap but guarantees quality and that indefinable extra – real atmosphere.

WEST END AND WESTMINSTER Gay Hussar

€€€€

2 Greek St, W1D 4NB **Tel** *020 7437 0973*   **Map** *11 A1*

Once the place of choice for old journalists to meet and gossip and enjoy second-rate food that reminded them of their private schools. Now, however, it provides a proper insight into Eastern European cuisine, wines and spirits albeit at quite a high price.

WEST END AND WESTMINSTER Green's Restaurant & Oyster Bar

€€€€

36 Duke St, SW1Y 6DF **Tel** *020 7930 4566*   **Map** *10 F3*

With wonderful old-world ambience and an extensive champagne list, this is a great establishment. Excellent lobster salads, first-class chips and, of course, a nice choice of oysters, most of them down from Scotland that very day. Those who don't fancy fish can try Green's steak tartare. Closed on Sundays from May to September.

WEST END AND WESTMINSTER Just St James

€€€€

12 St James St, SW1A 1ER **Tel** *020 7976 2222*   **Map** *10 F4*

With plush surroundings, as befits a restaurant in St James, this impressive place was built from a former Edwardian banking hall. The high-class cooking constantly surprises with its far-reaching, but not overambitious, choices. Strong British favourites such as calves' liver and bacon sit alongside steak and chips and dishes of more global provenance.

WEST END AND WESTMINSTER Langan's Brasserie

€€€€

Stratton St, W1J 8LB **Tel** *020 7491 8822*   **Map** *10 F3*

The original and perhaps still the best in this chain of restaurants, Langan's faithfully adheres to the style of its late eponymous owner. Service is discreetly attentive and the staff are friendly. Try and get a table downstairs where they serve soufflé with anchovy sauce. Try the house speciality, Langan's bangers and mash with white onion sauce.

WEST END AND WESTMINSTER Little Italy

€€€€

21 Frith St, W1D 4RN **Tel** *020 7734 4737*   **Map** *11 A2*

As the name suggests, this tiny restaurant re-creates Italy in its delicious home cooking. It's a busy and vibrant place with a late licence until 4am. The large variety of pasta dishes is a safe bet. The main courses are good too. You might miss the unassuming doorway so back up and look again, it's there. Some live music and dancing most nights.

WEST END AND WESTMINSTER Origin

€€€€

24 Endell St, WC2H 9RD **Tel** *020 7170 9200*   **Map** *11 C2*

Fashionable Origin serves beautifully crafted dishes in pleasant surroundings. The team behind the highly-acclaimed Thyme restaurant, which transferred from South London to Covent Garden, has transformed its operation into a sophisticated affair. With excellent service, it delivers an award-winning Modern European Cuisine.

WEST END AND WESTMINSTER Hakkasan

€€€€€

8 Hanway Place, W1T 1HF **Tel** *020 7927 7000*   **Map** *11 A1*

A very expensive Chinese restaurant, Hakkasan has maintained a consistently high turnover. The decor is superbly stylish and the food even more so. No windows mean you can't peer in to check it out before entering. Though busy and a bit smoky, it's a great choice for gourmets who can afford it. Don't miss the dim sums.

WEST END AND WESTMINSTER L'Oranger

€€€€€

5 St James St, SW1A 1EF **Tel** *020 7839 3774*   **Map** *10 F4*

A very formal French restaurant in the heart of London, L'Oranger exudes classic opulence. The decor is heavy with timeless quality and the traditionally cooked dishes are classy in their presentation. Tables are beautifully laid with expensive linen, high-quality glasses and plates. The regularly changing menu features Provençal dishes.

WEST END AND WESTMINSTER Umu

€€€€€

14–16 Bruton Place, W1J 6L **Tel** *020 7499 8881*   **Map** *10 E3*

Seriously expensive but extremely stylish, Umu has a futuristic front door that will make you gasp. The beautiful interior, friendly service by great staff are impressive too. With a remarkable sake list, this is one of the few places in London where you can find genuine Japanese *kaiseki*. There's also a good, though expensive, tasting menu.

Key to Price Guide *see p608* **Key to Symbols** *see back cover flap*

WEST END AND WESTMINSTER Wilton's

55 Jermyn St, SW1Y 6LX **Tel** *020 7629 9955*   **Map** *11 A3*

A landmark institution, there has been a Wilton's in London since 1742. A quintessential expensive club-dining experience. Morecambe Bay potted shrimps, grilled Dover sole, Scottish lobster thermidor and West Mersey Oysters are the main attractions here, but you will also want to bask in the atmosphere and in the attentive and well-mannered service.

SOUTH KENSINGTON AND HYDE PARK Angie's

381 Harrow Rd, W9 3NA **Tel** *020 8962 8761*   **Map** *1 B1*

Angie's has a modern, light interior and offers a collection of dishes from the different regions of Africa and the Carribean, with specials such as Whole Guineafowl and grilled, spiced rabbit. Friday nights are busy as are the family-orientated Sunday buffets. Closed 25–26 Dec, 1 Jan.

SOUTH KENSINGTON AND HYDE PARK La Maja

43-45 Porchester Road, W2 5DP **Tel** *020 7792 5885*   **Map** *8 D1*

Loads of lovely tapas, as well as generous main courses, keep locals coming back for more. La Maja really feels authentic in an unforced way and the variety of dishes is mouthwatering. A great range of robust Riojas compliment the food, which is hearty and garlicky and just perfect for accompanying lively conversation.

SOUTH KENSINGTON AND HYDE PARK One

1 Kensington High St, W8 5NP **Tel** *020 7937 0393*   **Map** *8 E5*

Persian/Greek food par excellence with perfect kebabs grilled to smoky brilliance. Tasty, moist pieces of marinated lamb and/or chicken over saffron-scented, buttery rice. Friendly staff are happy to advise on choice of dishes and to stop you from over-ordering, as you may be tempted to do so. Good value, too.

SOUTH KENSINGTON AND HYDE PARK Aphrodite Taverna

15 Hereford Rd, W2 4AB **Tel** *020 7229 2206*   **Map** *8 D2*

Small and unpretentious, this little tavern tries hard and succeeds. Halloumi, *kleftiko*, moussaka, baklava and all the Greek delicacies are well cooked, and their stuffed vine leaves aren't bathed in brine. Though not home-made, they are carefully prepared. Aphrodite excels at starters and is popular with guests from nearby hotels.

SOUTH KENSINGTON AND HYDE PARK Bugis Street Brasserie

The Millennium Gloucester Hotel, Ashburn Place, SW7 4LH **Tel** *020 7331 6211*   **Map** *16 E2*

Though called a brasserie, this place doesn't offer French cuisine. Expat Singapore natives regard it as the best in London for their kind of food. Dishes are robust, extremely tasty and come in gigantic portions. Plus, for the area, it's not very expensive. For starters, the salt and pepper squid is exceptional.

SOUTH KENSINGTON AND HYDE PARK Racine

239 Brompton Rd, SW3 2EP **Tel** *020 7584 4477*   **Map** *17 B1*

Racine sets out to showcase French cuisine and succeeds very well. Genuine French food, French waiters and great atmosphere all combine to keep locals coming back for more. The venison, when in season, is excellent and the menu changes regularly. The service is good.

SOUTH KENSINGTON AND HYDE PARK Saigon Mekong Restaurant

48 Queensway, W2 3RY **Tel** *020 7229 9111*   **Map** *8 E3*

While Thai food has taken off in the capital, it's hard to find real Vietnamese cuisine that isn't a disgrace. This widely-known Vietnamese eatery is considered authentic by regulars. It can hold its head up and point to zingy flavours in well-balanced dishes served by charming staff who are happy to help and advise.

SOUTH KENSINGTON AND HYDE PARK Whits

21 Abingdon Road, W8 6AH **Tel** *020 7938 1122*   **Map** *15 C1*

A neighbourhood restaurant on a side lane off busy High Street Kensington. Because of its position it does not attract the masses. Try the whole roasted sea bass with rocket and artichoke salad. Other mains include pork with crackling or Elwy lamb. Food is consistently good and very seasonal, but always very affordable.

SOUTH KENSINGTON AND HYDE PARK Amaya

15 Halkin Arcade, off Motcomb Street, SW1 8JT **Tel** *020 7823 1166*   **Map** *10 D5*

A very distinguished Indian restaurant, Amaya is spacious, stylish and with the kitchen on honest display. Specializing in grills, it has three stations – tandoori, sigra and tawa – in action all evening. The range of meats and vegetables is brilliant and the presentation and service faultless. Though it is expensive, it's worth dining here.

SOUTH KENSINGTON AND HYDE PARK L'Étranger

36 Gloucester Rd, SW7 4QT **Tel** *020 7584 1118*   **Map** *16 E1*

L'Étranger is a gem of a place serving extremely good French-Asian fusion food in very stylish surroundings. People rave about the black cod with miso and with good reason. Every dish on the menu is delectable and there's a massive wine list that has been created with passion and love. You can dance in the club downstairs.

SOUTH KENSINGTON AND HYDE PARK Nahm

The Halkin, 5 Halkin St, SW1X 7DJ **Tel** *020 7333 1234*   **Map** *10 D5*

This remarkable Thai restaurant has a Michelin star so you can arrive with high expectations. The set menu doesn't disappoint. A recommended appetizer is *ma hor* (minced prawns and chicken simmered in palm sugar with deep fried shallots, garlic and peanuts, served on pineapple and mandarin orange). Not cheap but worth the price.

SOUTH KENSINGTON AND HYDE PARK Pasha

*1 Gloucester Rd, SW7 4PP **Tel** 020 7589 7969*   **Map** 16 E1

North Africans love lamb, and here it comes at its best in a spicy tagine with loads of couscous to mop the lovely juices. The tables are rather tiny and it can be tricky keeping all your dishes from tumbling to the floor. Breads and *mezza* are delicious. Look out for occasional live music and belly dancers.

SOUTH KENSINGTON AND HYDE PARK Tom Aikens

*43 Elystan St, SW3 3NT **Tel** 020 7584 2003*   **Map** 17 B2

Chef Aikens is the twinkliest star in the cooking firmament with other chefs praising his cooking no end. That said, some people find the cuisine a touch rich but everyone loves the experience. Dishes are lovingly constructed and beautifully plated with flavours finely balanced with a watchmaker's care. Very popular so book ahead.

SOUTH KENSINGTON AND HYDE PARK Zafferano

*5 Lowndes St, SW1X 9EY **Tel** 0871 223 8114*   **Map** 18 D1

Zafferano has long been recognized as one of the capital's premier Italian restaurants. It's a discreet place, where the emphasis is firmly on the food. Dishes such as risotto with white wine truffle and char-grilled lamb with aubergine (eggplant) allow the quality of the ingredients to shine through.

SOUTH KENSINGTON AND HYDE PARK 1880 at The Bentley

*27–33 Harrington Gardens, SW7 4JX **Tel** 020 7244 5555*   **Map** 16 F2

This restaurant is very expensive, but you won't get much better in London with seven-, eight- and nine-course "grazing menus". There is an opulent interior and attentive staff. They enjoy your gastronomic journey with you and the sommelier is a joy. Specialities include seared foie gras, coulis of green apple and confit duck neck.

SOUTH KENSINGTON AND HYDE PARK Foliage

*Mandarin Oriental Hyde Park, 66 Knightsbridge, SW1X 7LA **Tel** 020 7235 2000*   **Map** 9 C5

Foliage is a fantastic restaurant, which seems able to serve the most remarkable food at very reasonable prices. Even the spectacular views of Hyde Park will not distract you from the menu. The three-course set meal includes little tasters in between and the service is faultless. A real jewel.

SOUTH KENSINGTON AND HYDE PARK Mju

*Millennium Knightsbridge, 17 Sloane Street, SW1X 9NU **Tel** 020 7201 6330*   **Map** 17 C1

The food is a bit hard to categorize at Mju but the restaurant isn't. In this location you expect style and you get it. The best way to appreciate the food is to go for the multicourse tasting menu. Each small dish is assembled with a smart precision. Try oysters with ginger and mirin as well as sea urchin and *foie gras* custard served in a shot glass!

SOUTH KENSINGTON AND HYDE PARK Zuma

*5 Raphael St, SW7 1DL **Tel** 0207584 1010*   **Map** 9 C5

Zuma is a very fashionable restaurant, right opposite Harrods. Celebrities can be spotted here but they come for the great food just like everyone else. Great sashimi, *nigiri*, sushi and tempura with fancy service and fancy prices. It's definitely an experience, but be prepared to dig deep into your pocket.

REGENTS PARK AND BLOOMSBURY Defune

*34 George St, W1U 7DP **Tel** 020 7935 8311*   **Map** 10 D1

Top-class sushi at a high price, but well worth it. A charming minimalist decor is matched by an atmosphere that some find austere but is really just a cool appreciation of the food. This is a decent place and the service is superb. When you're eating raw fish you expect the highest standards and you pay for them.

REGENT'S PARK AND BLOOMSBURY Ishtar

*10–12 Crawford St, W1U 6AZ **Tel** 020 7224 2446*   **Map** 1 C5

Modern Turkish, so no exotic dancers and no photos of the Istanbul landmarks, either. You can dine on two levels, including under some romantic cellar arches and the dishes are familiar but updated. Go for grilled sea bass with potatoes and saffron sauce or some well-marinated kebabs. Leave room for some pastries too.

REGENT'S PARK AND BLOOMSBURY Caffe Caldesi

*118 Marylebone Lane, W1U 2NE **Tel** 020 7935 1144*   **Map** 10 D1

This airy Italian restaurant offers classic dishes and a very reasonable wine list, with a slightly more formal dining space upstairs. Tuck into a big Tuscan breakfast or sit down to a traditional home-cooked dinner. Try the fresh ravioli stuffed with beetroot and ricotta with sage and butter sauce. There is also a patisserie, a delicatessen and a bar.

REGENT'S PARK AND BLOOMSBURY Garangers Restaurant Bar

*114–115 Crawford St, W1H 2JQ **Tel** 020 7935 8447*   **Map** 1 C5

Though regulars rave over the chocolate desserts, the whole restaurant deserves wider praise. A cool and well-designed interior is well served by jolly, upbeat staff. Try warm octopus salad with sautéed squid and Charlotte potato or the chef's creation of the day. The downstairs bar is good for a drink or dance.

REGENT'S PARK AND BLOOMSBURY Michael Moore

*19 Blandford St, W1U 3DH **Tel** 002 7224 1989*   **Map** 10 D1

This perennially popular restaurant mixes excellent food with a genuinely friendly ambience. Michael Moore (no relation to the American film-maker) is there virtually every night and tours the tables for a chat. A very accomplished chef, he changes his delightful menu regularly and keeps his regulars flocking back for more of Moore.

Key to Price Guide *see p608* **Key to Symbols** *see back cover flap*

THE CITY AND SOUTHWARK Fusebox

€

12 Stoney St, SE1 9AD **Tel** *020 7407 9888*

Map *13 B4*

Fusebox is not so much a restaurant as a good place to eat when exploring Borough Market. Asian is the main food style with dishes such as tea-smoked salmon and aubergine (eggplant) with oyster mushrooms. There's a great selection of hot and cold things to try and the price is right too.

THE CITY AND SOUTHWARK Tito's

€

4–6 London Bridge **Tel** *020 7407 7787*

Map *8 D4*

Tito's is a Peruvian restaurant that serves up plentiful portions at great prices. Typical Peruvian staples such as seafood, fish soups, fried yucca and rice are on the menu. The ceviche and king prawn chupe are recommended as are the Pisco-based cocktails.

THE CITY AND SOUTHWARK El Vergel

€€

8 Lant St, SE1 1QR **Tel** *020 7357 0057*

Map *13 A5*

Perhaps the only restaurant in town for Chilean food and it does it well. Home-cooked *empanadas*, and *pastel de choclo* are very popular. A small place and not really styled for fine dining, it has a very friendly atmosphere and portions can be huge. Rather charming and very Chilean.

THE CITY AND SOUTHWARK Haz

€€

9 Cutler St, E1 7DJ **Tel** *020 7929 7923*

Map *14 D1*

Lively, fun and a little posh too, this is a true touch of Turkey in the city. Go for a mixed *meze* starter. They just keep coming and they're all delicious. Go for the well-marinated meat dishes and kebabs and mop up the juice with the lovely flat bread. The office workers throng into Haz at lunchtime so get here before noon.

THE CITY AND SOUTHWARK Mar I Terra

€€

14 Gambia St, Waterloo, SE1 0XH **Tel** *020 7928 7628*

Map *12 F4*

Described as a little gem by its fans, this local Spanish restaurant has also been steadily building custom. The quality of the ingredients is one of its secrets as is its location off the main drag. This means the diners are discerning gourmets who have come for the food and the cheerful atmosphere.

THE CITY AND SOUTHWARK Silka

€€

6–8 Southwark St, London Bridge, SE1 1RQ **Tel** *020 7378 6161*

Map *13 B4*

Ayurvedic food is a speciality here, which is essentially food balanced for body and soul, and is particularly good for vegetarians. Of course, there are also all the usual Indian dishes too. There is some reluctance on the staff's part to write down your order so do check that what arrives is actually what you asked for.

THE CITY AND SOUTHWARK The Don

€€

The Courtyard, 20 St Swithin's Lane, EC4N 8AD **Tel** *020 7626 2606*

Map *13 B2*

This used to be a wine warehouse so it's no surprise that it has an excellent winelist. It also has very attentive staff, who go out of their way to be helpful. A good sommelier and a range of interesting and unique dishes make this a very popular restaurant indeed and reservations are pretty much obligatory.

THE CITY AND SOUTHWARK Baltic

€€€

74 Blackfriars Rd, SE1 8HA **Tel** *020 7928 1111*

Map *12 F4*

Located inside a former coach house with exciting high ceilings, Baltic exudes charm. The eastern European influence is noticeable in Baltic's crayfish in vodka. There's a massive range of vodkas and the food constantly surprises with dishes such as beef and venison meatballs. The kitchen is on show and there's often live jazz.

THE CITY AND SOUTHWARK Bengal Cuisine

€€€

12 Brick Lane, E1 6RF **Tel** *020 7377 8405*

Map *6 E5*

Just about every building in Brick Lane is an Indian restaurant, but the quality varies. Bengal Cuisine is certainly a lot more modern than most of them. The food is very good value and the cook goes easy on the chilli to suit the Western palate. Staff are happy to advise on dishes if asked. There's a good Sunday buffet as well.

THE CITY AND SOUTHWARK The Chancery

€€€

9 Cursitor St, EC4A 1LL **Tel** *020 7831 4000*

Map *12 E1*

This little gem is a stylish new-wave restaurant tucked away down a side street. The well-cooked food is adventurous, modern and very reasonably priced. Try the ham hock and piccalilli with foie gras and green beans or the potage of baby monkfish and oysters with summer truffle shavings.

THE CITY AND SOUTHWARK County Hall

€€€

London Marriott County Hall, Queens Walk, SE1 7PB **Tel** *020 7902 8000*

Map *11 C5*

A great view of the Thames is just one reason to dine here, close to the Houses of Parliament. Prices are reasonable for the location and the cooking assured if not terribly inventive. That said, the food never fails to do a good job with dishes such as slow-cooked pork with a chorizo and pea risotto and enjoyable smoked duck.

THE CITY AND SOUTHWARK East is East

€€€

230 Commercial Rd, E1 2NB **Tel** *020 7702 7222*

Map *16 E1*

A very decent Indian restaurant that doesn't serve all the Bangladeshi dishes like some do. Of course, you are spoiled for choice in this part of London for "Indian" food, but this restaurant gets top marks every time for its authentic cuisine and friendly service. It's also reasonably priced, which is always a bonus.

THE CITY AND SOUTHWARK Georgetown Restaurant

10 London Bridge St, SE1 9SG **Tel** *020 7357 7359* **Map** *13 B4*

The colonial setting and ambience at Georgetown Restaurant is enhanced by the Singapore Sling cocktails. The menu features a variety of Asian dishes including dim sums, curries with chicken and prawn dumplings as well as the outstanding lamb curry with beans. Look out for special deals.

THE CITY AND SOUTHWARK Kennington Tandoori

313 Kennington Rd, SE11 4QE **Tel** *020 7735 9247* **Map** *20 E3*

One of the best Indian curry houses in London, Kennington Tandoori offers reliable food in calm oasis. Its proximity to Westminster means that many curry-loving MPs can be found debating policy over a chicken *jalfrezi*. Besides classic dishes, there are some unique innovations such as their own Nilgiri *murgh*.

THE CITY AND SOUTHWARK Ming Court

54–56 Ludgate Hill, EC4M 7HX **Tel** *020 7248 4303* **Map** *12 F2*

Just into the city, Ming Court is close to China in quality and style. Though slightly more expensive than comparable places in China Town, it is ahead of them in decor and ambience. Peking duck scores highly here. The staff are welcoming and the service good.

THE CITY AND SOUTHWARK Moro

34–36 Exmouth Market, EC1R 4QE **Tel** *020 7833 8336* **Map** *4 E4*

Moro is well known for its Spanish-Moroccan cuisine and serves up consistently good food to regulars. Courgette (zucchini) and mint tortilla is an example of light, flavoursome food and there are some very good breads. Buy ingredients next door and take their famous cookbook home with you.

THE CITY AND SOUTHWARK Noto

2–3 Bassishaw Highwalk, EC2V 5DS **Tel** *020 7256 9433* **Map** *13 B1*

Local Londoners and visiting Japanese recognize Noto as authentic and great value. Fresh sushi is the main attraction, while there's also a fine selection of curries as well as good sashimi, crispy tempura and well-priced teriyaki. However, the place is small and, as usual with Japanese restaurants, home to a lot of smokers.

THE CITY AND SOUTHWARK Ozu

County Hall, Riverside Building, Westminster Bridge Rd, SE1 7PB **Tel** *020 7928 7766* **Map** *11 C5*

At Ozu, the French owner's classic taste in Japanese food has been inspired by Japanese director Yasujiru Ozu. There is exquisite attention to detail here. Relaxed ambience, a big flat screen used for projecting movies and the 1940s- and 50s-style decor are worth it. A perfect place to enjoy the French-Japanese dishes with a glass of wine.

THE CITY AND SOUTHWARK Rajasthan

49 Monument St, Monument, EC3R 8BU **Tel** *020 7626 1920* **Map** *13 C3*

A newly-built Indian restaurant, Rajasthan is bright and airy, with fresh flowers on show and not a Bengal tiger or Taj Mahal in sight. The staff are happy to help you avoid the usual curry cliché dishes, but are equally happy to give you chicken tikka masala if that's what you require. Or try something extra special such as a whole poussin.

THE CITY AND SOUTHWARK Tentazioni

2 Mill St, SE1 2BD **Tel** *020 7237 1100* **Map** *14 E5*

Although a bit more expensive than the average Italian eatery, Tentazioni matches the price with its very high standards. Excellent food is on offer and the five-course tasting menu is a delight, especially at the very reasonable price. A busy and friendly restaurant that's well worth making the walk from Tower Bridge.

THE CITY AND SOUTHWARK The Lobster Pot

3 Kennington Lane, SE11 4RG **Tel** *020 7582 5556* **Map** *20 F2*

A remarkable little restaurant in an unprepossessing location. The French owners set out to recreate Brittany (even down to seagull soundtracks) and succeed brilliantly. The eight-course "surprise" menu is fantastic and the fish is always superbly fresh. Do book in advance, as it's not very big.

THE CITY AND SOUTHWARK Abacus

24 Cornhill, EC3V 3ND **Tel** *020 7337 6767* **Map** *13 B2*

Hidden away in a basement near Bank Station, Abacus is a true jewel and expects you to pay accordingly. Meals are punctuated by small *amuse-bouches*, tiny, tasty creations from the chef many of which are so delicious they could be courses on their own. There's a seasonal menu and superior levels of service and presentation. A real treat.

THE CITY AND SOUTHWARK The Spitz

109 Commercial St, E1 6BG **Tel** *020 7392 9032* **Map** *6 D5*

The Spitz is a friendly place, with live background music setting the ideal tone. The location near Spitalfields Market attracts a mixed crowd. Food is diverse and imaginative: goat's cheese with pecans on a salad is a speciality. The live jazz is only on Fridays and Saturdays.

FURTHER AFIELD Brown's Kew

3–5 Kew Green, Richmond, TW9 3AA **Tel** *020 8948 4838*

From its first beginning in Brighton, the Brown's empire has spread out. The main draw is its solid British cooking. Sitting amid dark wooden café chairs and palms and whirling fans, you get quite a Colonial feel. A lovely part of town deserves a pretty restaurant like this. Al fresco dining is possible in the summer.

Key to Price Guide *see p608* **Key to Symbols** *see back cover flap*

FURTHER AFIELD Babalou

The Crypt, St Matthew's Church, Brixton Hill, SW2 **Tel** *020 7738 3366*

With Brixton still trying to live up to its hype and outgrow its past, Babalou fits in perfectly. A new bar-restaurant-club, it offers a global fusion of good organic cooking and a host of dishes to suit the eclectic multiracial area. It's in a basement, but in summer you can comfortably sit outside and chill out.

FURTHER AFIELD Karma

44 Blythe Rd, W14 0HA **Tel** *020 7602 9333*

A modern Indian restaurant, Karma takes you on a culinary journey of the Indian sub-continent, exploring the many regional styles of cooking that India has to offer. The chef Dilwar Khan's signature dishes are classic Goan recipes, Chicken Vindaloo and Lamb Xacuti. The restaurant's wine list has been specially created to complement the cuisine.

FURTHER AFIELD Lomo

222 Fulham Rd, SW10 9NB **Tel** *020 7349 8848*   **Map** *16 F4*

Described by its patrons as a bit of Barcelona in London, Lomo has giant TV screens showing Spanish football, while the exuberant crowd tucks into delicious tapas, sherry and Riojas. There are always new dishes on the menu as well as ones that are firm favourites. Perfect for a meal for two or a large group, the ambience is ever upbeat.

FURTHER AFIELD Randall & Aubin

329–331 Fulham Rd, SW10 9QL **Tel** *020 7823 3515*   **Map** *16 F4*

There is some meat on the menu; however, this restaurant is definitely geared towards fish and seafood fanatics. Oysters, scallops and whole brick-red lobsters are just a few dishes served at big tables or in small, intimate booths. A nice venue for a night out

FURTHER AFIELD The Lane Restaurant

12–20 Osborn St, E1 6TE **Tel** *020 7456 1067*   **Map** *14 E1*

Located at the south end of famous Brick Lane, but not an Indian restaurant. It's actually a rather cool and trendy place doing a variety of dishes at very reasonable prices. The cocktail bar area is nice too. It's in an up-and-coming area, so you may find yourself surrounded by young people with cool clothes and a disposable income.

FURTHER AFIELD Safir

116 Heath St, NW3 1DR **Tel** *020 7431 9888*

This popular Moroccan restaurant, with its green and yellow tented room, is especially good at weekends, that's if you like it busy; for a calmer experience go earlier in the week. Recommended is the tagine of lamb with prunes or couscous with caramelised onions and sultanas. Safir's success lies in the food's simplicity.

FURTHER AFIELD The Spread Eagle

1–2 Stockwell St, SE10 9JN **Tel** *020 8853 2333*

Fiercely championed by locals, this place radiates confidence with its innovative French cuisine. Small, intimate booths to dine in and a real, roaring fire in winter all conspire to make you want to stay long after the coffee has been cleared away. The food is rich and satisfying and the whole experience is equal to the West End and at half the price.

FURTHER AFIELD Borscht nTears

46 Beauchamp Place, SW3 1NX **Tel** *020 7584 9911*   **Map** *17 B1*

This place has been here since before the Berlin Wall came down, doing its very best bit for Anglo-Russian relations. The vodka flows pretty freely and the tables can become dance floors. The food is traditional and delicious, if occasionally a bit heavy. You'll have a fun night, even if you cannot remember anything afterwards!

FURTHER AFIELD Mezedepolio

14–15 Hoxton Market, N1 6HG **Tel** *020 7739 8212*   **Map** *5 C3*

Join the crowd at Mezedepolio and choose from a massive selection of Greek dishes. The home-style cooking is unique, and many of the dishes on the menu have never been seen in the country before. They're all very tempting but be warned to keep an eye on the prices. The Real Greek wine bar serves Greek wines as well.

FURTHER AFIELD Nirvana

430 Kings Rd, SW10 0LJ **Tel** *020 7352 7771*   **Map** *17 F4*

With a rather concealed entrance, Nirvana is quite likely to be missed, but still achieves high standards in a basement room. It's a family affair and it shows in the casual and unstressed way the team deal with a lot of people in quite a small space. Stir-fried baby squid with chilli and ginger is a speciality. Local celebrities can be spotted dining here.

FURTHER AFIELD North Pole

131 Greenwich High Rd, SE10 8JA **Tel** *020 8853 3020*

A little Greenwich gem, North Pole is comfortably warm with a nice bar downstairs and a fire in the grate upstairs. A small piano tinkles away in the background. Food is of a very high standard. It has a Michelin rating but the prices don't reflect this too badly. Traditional Sunday roasts of beef or chicken are available with all the trimmings.

FURTHER AFIELD The Belvedere

Holland House, Abbotsbury Road, W8 6LU **Tel** *020 7602 1238*   **Map** *7 B5*

Tucked away in leafy Holland Park, the Belvedere has a perfect location. The opulence of the main room doesn't get reflected in the bill. Instead, a brilliant variety of dishes is effortlessly combined with a very fair price. "Gastro-pub" type food means hearty and heartening meals that comfort the senses while tickling the palate.

FURTHER AFIELD The Pelican   ♿   ⓔⓔⓔ

45 All Saints Rd, W11 1HE   **Tel** *020 7727 6126*   **Map** *7 B1*

Usually jammed full with a funky hip crowd, Pelican is rather genteelly tattered around the edges. The menu is full of British-type staples, including cod and chips. Specialities include roasted beef and suckling pig as well as other meaty delights. Interestingly, it features the first Marine Conservation Society-approved menu.

FURTHER AFIELD Thyme   ♿🍷   ⓔⓔⓔ

1–3 Station Crescent, Westcombe Park, SE3 7EQ   **Tel** *020 8293 9183*

Small, intimate and minimalistic, Thyme has remained an all-time favourite neighbourhood restaurant. Serving great meals at reasonable prices, it has an edge over other eating choices in Greenwich. It's especially popular with tourists, though locals are also fans.

FURTHER AFIELD Yas   ♿   ⓔⓔⓔ

7 Hammersmith Rd, Kensington Olympia, W14 8XJ   **Tel** *020 7603 9148*   **Map** *15 A1*

Persian food means plenty of meat on the main course, although vegetarians can fill up on a great variety of dips. At Yas, the bread is baked on the premises. Open well past midnight, this remarkable place begins to get busy at a rather late hour. On a warm night, sit outside and watch the world go by.

FURTHER AFIELD Base   ♿🍷   ⓔⓔⓔⓔ

3A Downshire Hill, 71 Hampstead High St, NW3 1NR   **Tel** *020 7431 2224*

During the day, Base is a bistro serving breakfast, coffee, pastries and snacks. In the evening it becomes a fine dining Mediterranean fusion restaurant, offering sumptuous food with an emphasis on fresh ingredients. The menu changes regularly and is complemented by an extensive wine list.

FURTHER AFIELD Cibo   ♿🍷   ⓔⓔⓔⓔ

3 Russell Gardens, W14 8EZ   **Tel** *020 7371 6271*   **Map** *7 A5*

Cibo has been around long enough to become a dependable local institution. Its clever mix of tried and trusted northern Italian favourites, combined with more adventurous dishes, never fails to satisfy its young crowd. There's plenty of bread and olives to savour while waiting at the table. The wine list matches the restaurant's high quality.

FURTHER AFIELD Le Vacherin   ♿🍷♿   ⓔⓔⓔⓔ

76–77 South Parade, W4 5LF   **Tel** *020 8742 2121*

Le Vacherin is a chef-patron restaurant in deepest Chiswick, a lovely area of London. Here they have re-created a charming Parisian bistro, serving top-notch food in a nice unpretentious way to a loyal local clientele. Sunday brunch is particularly popular. October to March they serve the speciality cheese, le Vacherin, baked with black truffles, almonds and white wine.

FURTHER AFIELD Gordon Ramsay At 68 Royal Hospital Road   ♿♿🍷♿   ⓔⓔⓔⓔⓔ

68 Royal Hospital Rd, SW3 4HP   **Tel** *020 7352 4441*   **Map** *17 C4*

Awarded with three Michelin stars, this restaurant strives for perfection and the effort reflects in everything from place settings to service. For an astonishing average of £100 per person, it is reputedly the best restaurant in London as well as all of England. As a souvenir of London, meal memories here will last a lifetime.

FURTHER AFIELD The River Café   ♿♿🍷♿   ⓔⓔⓔⓔⓔ

Thames Wharf, Rainville Rd, Hammersmith, W6 9HA   **Tel** *020 7386 4200*

The michelin-starred River Café is a well-established favourite among Londoners and tourists alike. With outstanding service, beautifully prepared rustic Italian dishes such as buffalo ricotta and turbot, and an excellent wine list, it's well worth the price. Floor-to-ceiling windows offer lovely views of the gardens and river beyond.

THE DOWNS AND CHANNEL COAST

ARUNDEL Amberley Castle   ♿🍷   ⓔⓔⓔⓔⓔ

Amberley, nr Arundel, West Sussex, BN18 9LT   **Tel** *01798 831992*

Nestled in some wonderfully imposing 18-m (60-ft) walls with a 12th-century portcullis, this fine restaurant offers a seasonally adjusted menu of local treats. Afternoon tea is served Mon–Thu. Its popularity as a wedding venue makes it necessary to book ahead.

ASHFORD The Manor Restaurant   🍷   ⓔⓔⓔⓔ

Eastwell Park, Boughton Lees, Ashford, Kent, TN25 4HR   **Tel** *01233 213000*

Set against a backdrop of the North Downs, Eastwell Manor has a formal, wood-panelled dining room called the Manor Restaurant. Modern English cuisine, with the odd Gallic flourish, is served here. The Brasserie, also on the premises, is ideal for afternoon tea and savouries out on the terrace.

BRIGHTON Café Paradiso   ♿🎵   ⓔⓔⓔ

Brighton Marina, Brighton, East Sussex, BN2 5WA   **Tel** *01273 679799*

A sleek Brighton favourite overlooking the Marina, Café Paradiso lays stress on mod-Med flavours and seafood delicacies. Wood-burning ovens take pride of place in the busy kitchen, which also serves up a decent selection of pastas. The well-stocked and busy cocktail bar adds to the chic buzz. Children's menu available.

Key to Price Guide *see p608*   **Key to Symbols** *see back cover flap*

BRIGHTON China Garden Ⓧ♿ ⒺⒺⒺ
88–91 Preston St, Brighton, East Sussex, BN1 2HG **Tel** *01273 325124*

A well-regarded and well-established Brightonian Chinese institution, China Garden benefits from a recent face-lift: the swish new decor has the feel of a 1930s ocean liner. The balanced menu waves the flag for Cantonese seafood and other more meatier options. Veggies get a good deal too.

BRIGHTON Hotel du Vin ⓍⓅ ⒺⒺⒺ
Ship St, Brighton, East Sussex, BN1 1AD **Tel** *01273 718588*

Part of the reliable, cheerful Hotel du Vin mini-chain, this natty bistro is tucked away in the Lanes. The menu opts for gamey Euro dishes that steer clear of frills. Vegetarians are also catered for. Some choice selections from the extensive wine list are on offer.

BRIGHTON La Fourchette Ⓟ ⒺⒺⒺ
105 Western Rd, Brighton, East Sussex, BN1 2AA **Tel** *01273 722556*

Lauded as one of Brighton's best restaurants, this handsome bistro is a relaxed showcase for confident regional Gallic comfort classics. The odd Moroccan twist spices up proceedings. An excellent wine list to match, while the choice of desserts will test the strongest resolve.

BRIGHTON Seven Dials Ⓧ♿Ⓟ ⒺⒺⒺ
1, Buckingham Place, Seven Dials, Brighton, East Sussex, BN1 3TD **Tel** *01273 885555*

A bustling eatery much beloved by Brighton's Sunday supplement set, Seven Dials is housed in a converted bank. The menu makes good use of Sussex farmland and local organic produce. Private dining is provided in the downstairs Vault, while a summer terrace offers the perfect spot for al fresco people-watching

BRIGHTON One Paston Place ♿Ⓟ ⒺⒺⒺⒺ
1 Paston Place, Brighton, East Sussex, BN2 1HA **Tel** *01273 606933*

Seasonal British ingredients benefit from an Italian approach that matches flavours perfectly, courtesy of an Anglophile Neapolitan chef with classic French training at this popular, smart restaurant. Good, unfussy fare is served in the recently refurbished dining room. Children aged over seven are welcome.

BROCKENHURST Simply Poussin Ⓧ♿Ⓟ⚘ ⒺⒺⒺ
The Courtyard, Brookley Road, Brockenhurst, Hampshire, SO42 7RB **Tel** *01590 623063*

This brasserie is hidden away in a village mews that enjoys a more informal air than its hugely popular sister restaurant nearby. The quality of food is equally good. The two-course daily set menu is great value and the predominantly New World wine list is extensive. Closed Sundays and Mondays.

CANTERBURY The Goods Shed ⒺⒺⒺ
Station Road West, Canterbury, Kent, CT2 8AN **Tel** *01227 459153*

At this farmers' market diner-cum-café, there's a simple blackboard menu offering well-constructed treats. The simple home cooking uses the best of the day's produce from the myriad stalls. As it is increasingly popular with local foodies, seating is at quite a premium during peak times. Closed Mondays; lunch only Sundays.

CHICHESTER Comme Ça ⓍⓅ⚘ ⒺⒺⒺⒺ
67 Broyle Rd, Chichester, West Sussex, PO19 6BD **Tel** *01243 788724*

Just around the corner from Chichester's historic centre, Comme Ça is a busy centrepiece for full-blooded Normandy cooking genially served in a comfortably rustic ambience. Outside dining is available on the terrace during the summer months, while the Garden Room is a popular spot for private functions.

EAST CHILTINGTON The Jolly Sportsman Ⓧ♿Ⓟ⚘ ⒺⒺⒺⒺ
Chapel Lane, East Chiltington, East Sussex, BN7 3BA **Tel** *01273 890400*

This acclaimed gastropub is a relaxed rural retreat, famed for its free-range chicken and duck, with enjoyable Euro stylings elsewhere on a surprisingly refined menu. Contemporary art adorns the walls, while the shaded terrace has a distinctly Moroccan feel. Microbrewery on the premises.

EAST GRINSTEAD Gravetye Manor Ⓟ ⒺⒺⒺⒺⒺ
Nr East Grinstead, West Sussex, RH19 4LJ **Tel** *01342 810567*

Michelin-starred Gravetye Manor is an oak-panelled country house with a sophisticated air. Its refined ambience complements the stately Anglo-French menu enriched with vegetables freshly picked from its celebrated gardens. The long and winding wine list includes over 600 bins. Children aged over seven are welcome.

EAST LAVANT Royal Oak Ⓧ♿Ⓟ ⒺⒺⒺ
Pook Lane, East Lavant, West Sussex, PO18 0AX **Tel** *01243 527434*

Once the local watering hole in an off-the-beaten-track Downland village close to Goodwood, the Royal Oak is now a highly reputed gastro pub and still maintains its original 200-year-old charm. On the menu you'll find high-class renditions of pub classics plus specials with a more modern accent

EMSWORTH 36 on the Quay Ⓟ ⒺⒺⒺⒺⒺ
47 South St, Emsworth, Hampshire, PO10 7EG **Tel** *01243 375592*

Located in a fishing village overlooking the bay, this bright and affable dining room focuses largely on fish. In addition, plenty of landlubber local produce feature on the menu. The "Little Big" tasting menu allows diners to enjoy a little bit of everything. Overnight accommodation available.

EVERSLEY New Mill Restaurant €€€€

New Mill Rd, Eversley, Hampshire, RG27 0RA **Tel** *0118 973 2277*

Rural honey pot perched on the banks of River Blackwater and the Millpond. The main restaurant is home to à la carte lighter fare, while the grill room, basing itself on the rural gastropub template, is the place for belt-loosening, comfort classics. There's an award-winning wine list.

FAVERSHAM Read's Restaurant with Rooms   €€€€€

Macknade Manor, Canterbury Rd, Faversham, Kent, ME13 8XE **Tel** *01795 535344*

Traditional Georgian manor house with self-styled "restaurant-with-rooms", Read's is set in its own wooded grounds. The kitchen produces a delicious range of seasonal, Med-influenced fare. Plenty of vegetables, fresh from its own walled garden, are accompanied by locally caught game and fish.

HASLEMERE Auberge de France   €€€€€

Lythe Hill Hotel and Spa, Petworth Rd, Haslemere, Surrey, GU27 3BQ **Tel** *01428 651251*

Auberge de France, the oak-panelled dining room at Lythe Hill Hotel, dates from the 14th century. The extensive menu covers a range of Gallic gastro points. Antiques and candlelight add to the cosy Tudor feel, while the windows overlook a nearby lake and parkland. Private dining rooms available.

HAYWARDS HEATH Jeremy's at Borde Hill   €€€€

Borde Hill Gardens, Balcombe Rd, Haywards Heath, West Sussex, RH16 1XP **Tel** *01444 441102*

Overlooking a walled Victorian garden, this family-run restaurant cooks up Euro staples, with strong Spanish and French accents. Local artwork on the walls and friendly service add to the pleasingly relaxed air. The outdoor dining on the terrace is a perfect spot for Sunday lunch.

HYTHE BAY Hythe Bay Fish Restaurant   €€€

Marine Parade, Hythe Bay, Kent, CT21 6AW **Tel** *01303 267024*

This beachfront charmer conjures up a whole range of innovative recipes with the local catch. The Whitstable oysters are a house speciality. Vegetarian dishes are on offer too. The well-established Sunday buffets draw a buzzy, family crowd, as does the sunny terrace, weather permitting. Beach picnics available.

JEVINGTON The Hungry Monk   €€€€

Jevington, nr Polegate, East Sussex, BN26 5QF **Tel** *01323 482178*

Local game and fish jostle for position and are given a Gallic twist on the enjoyable menu on offer at this 14th-century flint cottage. A one-time monastic retreat, complete with log fireplaces, candlelight and assorted antiques, the Hungry Monk is at its finest when the nights are drawing in.

LENHAM Chilston Park Marble Hall Restaurant   €€€€

Sandway, Lenham, nr Maidstone, Kent, ME17 2BE **Tel** *01622 859803*

Housed in a dapper country pile, this Francophile restaurant sits pretty in what used to be the entrance hall, complete with sparkling chandeliers and formal family portraits. Well-stocked cellar straddles old and new worlds, while a post-meal brandy in the Drawing Room is a fine way to round off the evening.

NEWBURY Dew Pond €€€€

Old Burghclere, Newbury, Berkshire, RG20 9LH **Tel** *01635 278408*

A cosy country-house restaurant on the edge of Watership Down, Dew Pond specializes in Scottish beef. Closer to home, Hampshire cheeses and local game also feature on the menu. Oak beams and outside decking add to the allure. Watch out for a series of monthly gastro evenings featuring five-course dinners.

PORTSMOUTH The American Bar   €€€

58 White Hart Rd, Portsmouth, Hampshire, PO1 2JA **Tel** *023 9281 1585*

The name is slightly misleading, as the American Bar is more a seafood restaurant than a bar. There's much to enjoy in this affable place overlooking the fish market. Certainly not ideal if you are just having drinks, though you can get yourself a passable martini here. For mains, try the spiced goat's cheese and marinated beetroot salad.

RIPLEY Drakes   €€€€

The Clock House, High Street, Ripley, Surrey, GU23 6AQ **Tel** *01483 224777*

A fine Queen Anne town house with variegated brickwork and a very attractive garden, Drakes is becoming an increasingly popular destination for London foodies. Well-crafted modern French favourites are created by a confident young chef, whose impressive CV includes stints with über-chefs Marco Pierre White and Nico Landenis.

RYE Landgate Bistro €€€

5–6 Landgate, Rye, Sussex, TN31 7LH **Tel** *01797 222829*

Rye is famed for its agreeably uncomplicated modern Brit bistro fare that has a growing army of fans. Its fishcakes and other clever tricks with seafood are much celebrated. Gloucester Old Spot pork with a sage and apple sauce is one of many pinstriped comfort classics on offer. Closed Mondays and Sundays.

SEAVIEW Priory Bay Hotel €€€€

Priory Drive, Seaview, Isle of Wight, PO34 5BU **Tel** *01983 613146*

Dating back to the medieval times, this hotel has a pair of hotel dining rooms set on the bay itself, with their own private beach. The Island Room specializes in seafood and light mod-Med flavours that come with a good and healthy zing. The Winter Brasserie is usually preferred by the less calorie-conscious.

Key to Price Guide *see p608* **Key to Symbols** *see back cover flap*

STOCKBRIDGE The Greyhound

*31 High St, Stockbridge, Hampshire, SO20 6EY **Tel** 01264 810833*

Superior gastropub with a Channel-hopping menu, the Greyhound makes plentiful use of produce from the nearby New Forest and the River Test, which runs through the grounds. On the menu, meat options outweigh the fish-based dishes. Though the place can get loud, there's much to recommend here.

TUNBRIDGE WELLS Thackeray's

*85 London Rd, Tunbridge Wells, Kent, TN1 1EA **Tel** 01892 511921*

Thackeray's offers agreeable modern French flavours in a Grade II-listed building, once home to the eponymous novelist. The warm, chatty atmosphere draws a contended clientele, both local and from further afield. Cocktails are served beforehand in the Gold Room, and a post-meal Scotch in the gold leaf-lined Throne Room.

WHITSTABLE Wheelers Oyster Bar

*8 High St, Whitstable, Kent, CT5 1BQ **Tel** 01227 273311*

Justly celebrated shellfish emporium that closes at 9pm, Wheelers Oyster Bar is the oldest fish and shellfish establishment in Britain. It doesn't have a licence so bring your own wine to the Oyster Parlour, tucked behind the main seafood bar, or nip over to the pebble beach for an impromptu picnic on the sands. Closed Wednesdays.

WHITSTABLE Whitstable Oyster Fish Company

*Horsebridge, Whitstable, Kent, CT5 1BU **Tel** 01227 276856*

This is an extremely popular seafood restaurant based in an old Naval warehouse overlooking the North Sea. There's a busy open kitchen with skilled staff getting to grips with fish freshly caught by the company's own band of fishermen. The nautically-themed decor is enthusiastic but stops short of going too overboard.

WICKHAM The Old House Hotel Restaurant

*The Square, Wickham, Hampshire, PO17 5JG **Tel** 01329 833049*

Converted from an old Georgian house, this hotel dining room is an atmospheric spot to enjoy some interesting European dishes. Fish is a house speciality. The room is a cosy affair, with all exposed old oak beams and some wonderful original 17th-century fittings.

WILMINGTON Crossways Hotel

*Wilmington, nr Polegate, East Sussex, BN26 5SG **Tel** 01323 482455*

A short stroll from the famed Long Man of Wilmington, the Crossways is a great spot for those visiting Glyndebourne. Its classic-Brit-with-global-frills cooking wins over patrons. Though the slightly chintzy dining room may not impress the style-conscious, it's well worth the experience.

EAST ANGLIA

ALDEBURGH 152 Aldeburgh

*152 High St, Aldeburgh, Suffolk, IP15 5AX **Tel** 01728 454594*

A leisurely pebble's throw from the beach, chic little 152 Aldeburgh serves up modern European cooking with a bias towards flavours from south of the Alps. Open for breakfast, lunch and dinner, the restaurant benefits from a well-travelled kitchen and the bountiful fresh produce on its doorstep.

ALDEBURGH Regatta Restaurant and Wine Bar

*171-173 High St, Aldeburgh, Suffolk, IP15 5AN **Tel** 01728 452011*

Favoured spot for seasonal asparagus, this cheery, family-run restaurant waves the flag for Suffolk's acclaimed regional produce. Specialities include good fish from the beach and game from the surrounding estates in winter. A worthy addition to Aldeburgh's burgeoning foodie scene.

ALDEBURGH The Lighthouse

*77 High St, Aldeburgh, Suffolk, IP15 5AU **Tel** 01728 453377*

The Lighthouse is a breezy, busy bistro that specializes in fishy flavours, courtesy of deck-fresh produce from the Suffolk coast. The lunch and dinner menus change daily, while there are also good fixed-price options. The summer terrace is a local favourite, weather permitting.

BURY ST EDMUNDS Maison Bleue

*31 Churchgate St, Bury St Edmunds, Suffolk, IP33 1RG **Tel** 01284 760623*

Maison Bleue specializes in Gallic fish, though the daily-changing menu does include a special "butcher's corner" for the meat-lovers. The smart dining room is well served by a kitchen that conjures up interesting, yet simple, fare using the best of the local catch. The nautical-themed bar is decorated with paintings of the sea.

CAMBRIDGE Riverside Brasserie

*The Cambridge Garden House Hotel, Granta Place, Mill Lane, Cambridge, Cambridgeshire, CB2 1RT **Tel** 01223 259988*

Perched on the side of the River Cam, this brasserie is beautifully set in its own secluded gardens. Lighter, French-influenced fare makes it a popular drop-in for the city's ladies-who-lunch, though evening visits are delightful too. A brisk stroll away from Cambridge's historic centre.

CAMBRIDGE Graffiti at Hotel Felix

Whitehouse Lane, Huntingdon Rd, Cambridge, Cambridgeshire, CL3 0LX **Tel** *01223 277973*

Overlooking landscaped gardens, this handsome hotel dining room is set in a converted Victorian mansion. The menu features a selection of mod-Med dishes as well as a choice of game. Despite being just a short distance away from the bustle of Cambridge city centre, the place is quite peaceful.

CAMBRIDGE Restaurant 22

22 Chesterton Rd, Cambridge, Cambridgeshire, CB4 3AX **Tel** *01223 351880*

Small but perfectly formed, Restaurant 22 is set in a smart Victorian town house that serves British and French favourites, with the odd Asian twist added for extra interest. The decent wine list is predominantly French, but does travel further afield to good effect.

CAMBRIDGE Venue

4th Floor, Cambridge Arts Theatre, 6 St Edwards Passage, Cambridge, Cambridgeshire, CB2 3PJ **Tel** *01223 367333*

Artful modern Mediterranean creations attract local culture vultures to Venue, one of the city centre's best restaurants. The rooftop canteen is suprisingly airy and light, with live music a regular feature on Friday and Saturday nights. It's an increasingly popular venue for wedding receptions, so booking is advised.

CAMBRIDGE Midsummer House

Midsummer Common, Cambridge, Cambridgeshire, CB4 1HA **Tel** *01223 369299*

On the banks of the River Cam, Midsummer House is a plush restaurant that boasts an array of awards. The elegant ambience is well-served by a kitchen with a heavy French accent. A recent face-lift adds to the charm, with a slate floor and warm shades giving a distinctly Mediterranean feel to proceedings.

CLAVERING The Cricketers

Whyken Rd, Clavering, nr Saffron Walden, Cambridgeshire, CB11 4QT **Tel** *01799 550442*

This rural retreat has become a popular destination for London foodies. The extra allure is provided by the fact that this is actually TV chef Jamie Oliver's family home. Menus change seasonally, with the robust cooking treading that well-worn path between the UK and Italy.

COLCHESTER The Warehouse Brasserie

The Old Chapel, Chapel St North, Colchester, Essex, CO2 7AT **Tel** *01206 765656*

One of the better dining options in the area, the Warehouse Brasserie is set in the heart of Colchester. A decent collection of British comfort food classics is served to an appreciative mix of diners in a relaxed, friendly atmosphere. The attentive service here makes for a pleasant dining experience.

CROMER Bolton's Bistro

The Cliftonville Hotel, Seafront, Cromer, Norfolk, NR27 9AS **Tel** *01263 512543*

There's a really traditional feel to this seafront bistro affair with its daily-changing blackboard menu displaying prepared-to-order fresh fish specialities, including some fine seasonal Cromer crab and lobster. Red meat-eaters and vegetarians get their share of goodies too, while the ice cream has a local fan club.

FRESSINGFIELD EYE The Fox and Goose Inn

Church Rd, Fressingfield Eye, Suffolk, IP21 5PB **Tel** *01379 586247*

Once a poorhouse, the Fox and Goose Inn has been a local favourite since the mid-1800s. Over the years, the restaurant has maintained its good standards, and perfected its interpretation of regional specialities, with a pro-European touch added occasionally. Closed Mondays.

HARWICH The Harbourside Restaurant

The Pier Hotel and Restaurant, The Quay, Harwich, Essex, CO12 3HH **Tel** *01255 241212*

Living up to its name, the Pier has a nautical setting, complete with fishing boats moored at the front door and the Stour and Orwell estuaries stretching out to the horizon. Seafood understandably tends to get most of the attention here but there's also a range of meat dishes featured on the menu.

HOLKHAM The Victoria at Holkham

Holkham Estate, nr Wells-Next-The-Sea, Norfolk, NR23 1RG **Tel** *01328 713230*

A stroll from the windswept sands of Holkham Beach, this neat hotel diner serves local shellfish, organic delicacies and wild game. Crab and mussels are the house specialities. On-site microbrewery produces plenty of quaffable delights to wash it all down with. Barbeques in the summer months.

HOLT Morston Hall

Holt, nr Blakeney, Norfolk, NR25 7AA **Tel** *01263 741041*

Increasingly popular honeypot for happy-go-lucky locals and yachting types from nearby Morston Quay, Morston Hall is an inviting, relaxed place. The five-course daily-changing menu features superior cooking with French foundations. Afternoon tea is served daily by the open fire.

HORRINGER Fredericks at The Ickworth

Horringer, nr Bury St Edmunds, Suffolk, IP29 5QE **Tel** *01284 735350*

Set in one of the wings of a very stately country pile, Frederick's is the centrepiece of a sleek hotel. A range of ambitious modern European cooking is on offer for a well-heeled clientele. The smooth service comes with a cheery geniality. The ambience is warm and relaxing.

Key to Price Guide *see p608* **Key to Symbols** *see back cover flap*

HUNTINGDON The Terrace

The Old Bridge, 1 High St, Huntingdon, Cambridgeshire, PE29 3TQ **Tel** *01480 424300*

With light, airy decor, the Terrace is known for its well-regarded food with a global reach but local starting points. All the food, including bread, is made on the premises and served in a cheery, informal ambience. There's a good-value set lunch menu on offer, while the excellent wine list is worth exploring.

HUNTINGDON The Pheasant

Keyston, Huntingdon, Cambridgeshire, PE18 0RE **Tel** *01832 710241*

This thatched inn, with oaked-beam dining room, is home to some heartening Anglo-French fare. The secret of its outstanding cooking lies in the successful blending of classical French techniques with the pick of local game. The well-considered wine list includes a wide by-the-glass choice.

IPSWICH Il Punto

Neptune Quay, Ipswich, Suffolk, IP4 1AX **Tel** *01473 289748*

A former Belgian gunboat dating from the 1800s, Il Punto now serves as a floating brasserie with a distinctly Gallic outlook. The interior makes good use of its original fittings, while there's plenty of outside deck dining to be enjoyed when waters are calmer. No lunch served on Saturdays.

MELBOURN Sheene Mill

Station Rd, Melbourn, Cambridgeshire, SG8 6DX **Tel** *01763 261393*

The cosy interior and chatty, informal air belie the meticulous kitchen at this restored rural mill. Proudly waving the flag for British cuisine, albeit with plenty of influences from sunnier climes, the cooking here is of a very high quality. The vegetables and herbs are all from the garden on the premises.

NORWICH Tatlers

21 Tombland, Norwich, Norfolk, NR3 1RF **Tel** *01603 766670*

A long-standing brasserie, Tatler's is situated in the heart of town, just around the corner from the cathedral. The staff dispense modern British fare to an appreciative mix of diners in an informal atmosphere. The seasonal menu uses local ingredients and includes decent vegetarian options. Closed Sundays.

NORWICH Adlard's

79 Upper St Giles, Norwich, NR2 1AB **Tel** *01603 633522*

This highly rated restaurant has a Michelin star and offers a menu of fresh, seasonal food best described as British with French undertones. Elegant and modern in style, the restaurant has a welcoming, friendly and unpretentious atmosphere. Relaxation sets the scene, so that the superb food can be appreciated. Closed Sun.

OULTON BROAD The Crooked Barn Restaurant

Ivy House Country Hotel, Ivy Lane, Oulton Broad, Suffolk, NR33 8HY **Tel** *01502 501353*

An 18th-century thatched barn, Crooked Barn Restaurant is ideal for candlelit dining in a light and spacious room. The excellent cooking, which uses local free-range and organic produce, is predominantly British. The odd garnish from further afield is also added to good effect, with touches from southern Europe, as well as Down Under.

STANTON The Leaping Hare Restaurant

Wyken Hall, Stanton, Bury St Edmunds, Suffolk, IP31 2DW **Tel** *01359 250287*

This well-known restaurant stands in a converted 18th-century barn. The attractive dining room is set on the edge of a country estate, nestled among woods, vineyards and perfect gardens. An appealing rustic menu featuring Suffolk fare matches the ambience. The excellent wine list includes wines produced from the Wyken vineyard.

WELLS-NEXT-THE-SEA The Crown Hotel

The Buttlands, Wells-Next-The-Sea, NR23 1EX **Tel** *01328 710209*

Restored from a 16th-century coaching inn, the Crown serves decent British fare with a few interesting Pacific Rim touches. The kitchen enjoys the best of fresh produce caught in the picturesque harbour town on the Norfolk coast. Lighter bites, served on a black slate, are available in the bar, with an open fire and old oak beams.

WERRINGTON The Cherry House Restaurant

125 Church St, Werrington, Cambridgeshire, PE4 6QF **Tel** *01733 571721*

In a relaxed, rural setting, this smart Francophile eatery has earned a good reputation for quality. The chef's elaborate, confident cooking uses the best of local ingredients and a wealth of experience gained from stints in some of London's more celebrated hotel kitchens. There's an excellent, if slightly short, wine list. Closed Mondays.

WOODBRIDGE Crown & Castle

Orford, Woodbridge, Suffolk, IP12 2LJ **Tel** *01394 450205*

Sitting in the shadows of a Norman castle, this relaxed, elegant hotel dining room plays to its strengths: a quintessentially English menu for such a perfect English setting. The recently refurbished private dining room is home to a large round table, and suitable for small dinner parties.

WYMONDHAM Number 24 Restaurant

24 Middleton St, Wymondham, Norfolk, NR18 0AD **Tel** *01953 607750*

Located in a charming Grade II listed building, this restaurant has a seasonal menu featuring contemporary English cuisine. The dishes are usually spiced up with plenty of Thai-fused trimmings. The Sunday lunch, however, tends to follow a more traditional route. Closed Sunday evenings and all day Monday.

THAMES VALLEY

BRAY-ON-THAMES The Fat Duck
High St, Bray, Berkshire, SL6 2AQ **Tel** *01628 580333*

One of the most exquisite restaurants in the region, Fat Duck is located in a 15th-century listed building. The exterior gives way to clean, modernist decor, where diners undergo a once-in-a-lifetime experience. Multiple, double-figure courses include such culinary inventions as snail porridge and egg and bacon ice cream.

BUCKINGHAM Prego Restaurant and Wine Bar
4 High St, Buckingham, Buckinghamshire, MK18 1NT **Tel** *01280 821205*

This friendly family restaurant exudes sunny Mediterranean ambience. Well located on Buckingham high street, it specializes in authentic Italian home cooking including fine pizza and pasta dishes. Friday and Tuesday evenings are even more upbeat with a range of music from guitarists to violinists. Booking essential.

DINTON La Chouette
Westlington Green, Dinton, Buckinghamshire, HP17 8UW **Tel** *01296 747422*

Forget calories and fat content as you enter this Belgian restaurant situated on the village green. The fabulously rich menu caters to the indulgent food-lover. Dishes are modern European blended with a little Belgian stodge. Perfect place for jazz-loving beer connoisseurs, but watch out for low beams as you walk away from the bar.

EASINGTON The Mole and Chicken
Easington, nr Long Crendon, Buckinghamshire, HP189EY **Tel** *01844 208387*

Well-heeled diners come from afar to this former 19th-century village store for views of the Buckinghamshire and Oxfordshire countryside. The adventurous cooking features daily fish and vegetarian specials. There's a good wine list with bottles to suit all. While it's open-plan and snug inside, visitors flock to the garden in summer. Book in advance.

GODSTOW The Trout Inn
195 Godstow Rd, Lower Wolvercote, Oxford, Oxfordshire, OX2 8PN **Tel** *01865 302071*

Built in 1133 and steeped in history, the Trout Inn was where Lewis Carroll dreamt up *Alice in Wonderland*, and Colin Dexter, the creator of Inspector Morse, regularly sunk a pint. On the banks of Oxford Canal, punters enjoy passing boats and feed the fish, ducks swans and peacocks as they tuck into traditional pub grub.

GREAT MILTON Le Manoir aux Quat' Saisons
Church Rd, Great Milton, Oxford, Oxfordshire, OX44 7PD **Tel** *01844 278881*

Acclaimed as an art gallery for the taste buds, this restaurant has a two-acre kitchen garden producing the vegetables and herbs used in their imaginatively crafted dishes. The new season milk-fed lamb is one of the specialities. Lovingly prepared picnic hampers sustain explorations around the surrounding countryside.

GREAT MISSENDEN La Petite Auberge
107 High St, Great Missenden, Buckinghamshire, HP16 0BB **Tel** *01494 865370*

Set in the idyllically quiet Chiltern village, La Petite Auberge is a quaint French restaurant run by a self-effacing French couple. Though the decor is modest and traditional, the impeccable authentic French cuisine more than makes up for it. The restaurant has a loyal following of locals and travellers.

HADDENHAM The Green Dragon
8 Churchway, Haddenham, Buckinghamshire, HP178AA **Tel** *01844 291403*

Set amidst picturesque Buckinghamshire countryside, the 350-year-old Green Dragon has two spacious dining rooms. The main draw here is the fresh local produce. The day's catch from Devon is sautéed to create succulent dishes, just as local honey makes the perfect glaze for the duck. The food is worth its price.

KINTBURY The Dundas Arms
53 Station Rd, Kintbury, Berkshire, RG17 9UT **Tel** *01488 658263*

Nestled on the banks of the River Kennet and Kennet and Avon Canal, the Dundas Arms is a late 18th-century restaurant-pub. Local produce is imaginatively whipped up into creative dishes and served amid simple but effective decor. The beer and wine selections are handsome, beefed up by local Butts and West Berkshire brews.

MAIDENHEAD The Waterside Inn
The Waterside Inn, Ferry Rd, Bray, Berkshire, SL6 2AT **Tel** *01628 620691*

The crown in chef entrepreneur Michel Roux's restaurant empire, this formal establishment offers French dining at its very finest. Enjoy roasted Challandais duck with lemon, while the Thames refracts beautifully throughout this riverside gem. Finish up with indulgent digestifs in one of the summerhouses or by the roasting fire.

MOULSFORD Beetle and Wedge
Moulsford-on-Thames, Oxfordshire, OX10 9JF **Tel** *01491 651381*

Beetle and Wedge is encircled by beautiful gardens running alongside the river immortalized in Kenneth Grahame's *The Wind in the Willows*. The relaxed Boathouse Restaurant is not to be missed during long evenings when dishes are grilled to perfection. Inside, the dining room is used exclusively for private parties. Booking ahead is a must.

Key to Price Guide *see p608* **Key to Symbols** *see back cover flap*

OXFORD Al-Shami
25 Walton Crescent, Oxford, Oxfordshire, OX1 2JG **Tel** *01865 310066*

For those who have never explored Lebanese cuisine, Al-Shami is worth a try. Going beyond the typical vine leaves, the menu is spectacular, with prices to suit everyone's budget. Highlights are the *mohammara bil-jawz* (mixed crushed nuts, red capsicum, olive oil and spices) and charcoal grill selection. Don't miss the Lebanese wines.

OXFORD Browns
5–11 Woodstock Rd, Oxford, Oxfordshire, OX2 6HA **Tel** *01865 511995*

A branch of the booming brasserie chain, Browns is a firm favourite with business folk and weekend lunchers. The menu has recently been polished with more contemporary dishes, such as asparagus and wild mushroom risotto, to complement snacks and salads, sandwiches and steaks. Pretty seating spills out onto the pavement in summer.

OXFORD Cherwell Boathouse
Bardwell Rd, Oxford, Oxfordshire, OX2 6SR **Tel** *01865 552746*

With a riverfront location at a punting station, Cherwell Boathouse is a favourite with wine buffs and romancers. Simple, but flawless, modern European cooking is enhanced by a well-priced and famously good wine selection. Try the honed-to-perfection goat's cheese or adventurous dishes such as pan-fried pollock.

OXON Sir Charles Napier
Sprigg's Alley, nr Chinnor, Oxon, Oxfordshire, OX39 4BX **Tel** *01494 483011*

A favourite with showbiz types seeking retreat, this isolated pub-restaurant in the Chiltern hills is not easily accessed, but the stunning views make it more than worth it. The British menu is slightly pricey, but features some rare dishes. Try the pigeon breast with lentils or guinea fowl and chestnuts. Remarkable garden sculptures and paintings.

PENN STREET VILLAGE Hit or Miss Inn
Penn St Village, Penn St, Amersham, Buckinghamshire, HP7 0PX **Tel** *01494 713109*

Voted Chiltern's best pub, Hit or Miss is a gastro-pub in the most traditional sense. Its location, opposite a cricket club, makes it a favourite destination for locals or walkers strolling from Penn Wood. The menu is vast, covering everything from crayfish to a reasonable set Sunday roast. Watch out for special Morris dancing and jazz events.

POTTERS BAR Paparazzi
1 Barnet Rd, Potters Bar, Hertfordshire, EN6 2QX **Tel** *01707 662623*

Paparazzi lives up to its name: national football teams, minor celebrities and anyone who wants to be seen comes to dine here. The menu is simple and Italian, with plenty of well-priced options. Although there is no formal entertainment, watch out if it's your birthday, as you're likely to be serenaded by the whole restaurant.

READING Pepe Sale
3 Queens Walk, Reading, Berkshire, RG1 7QF **Tel** *0118 959 7700*

A Sardinian-Italian restaurant, Pepe Sale is a stone's throw from busy Broad Street and local Hexagon Theatre. The menu offers Mediterranean specialities such as wild boar for the adventurous diner, plus dishes both traditional and unorthodox. Rustic yet minimalist decor, warm ambience and a decent wine list add to the appeal.

READING London Street Brasserie
2–4 London St, Reading, Berkshire, RG1 4SE **Tel** *01189 505036*

Reading prides itself on being an antidote to generic, conveyor-belt eateries. Waiting staff wear black, but are allowed to express individuality in no set uniform. The menu mixes British, French and Mediterranean cuisine, yet manages to avoid becoming confusing, while the contemporary decor makes this brasserie a romantic dining destination.

READING L'Ortolan
Church Lane, Shinfield, Reading, Berkshire, RG2 9BY **Tel** *01189 888500*

One of the best restaurants in the country, this British and French eatery is an absolute pleasure. Its lovely setting in luxurious gardens is complemented by the terrace and conservatory. Wine-tasting evenings emphasize their focus on fine drinking as well as dining. Set lunches and menus are tasty and affordable.

REED The Cabinet at Reed
The Cabinet, High St, Reed, nr Royston, Hertfordshire, SG8 8AH **Tel** *01763 848366*

Boasting a unique blend of English, French and transatlantic fare, the Cabinet is a rising star in the quiet Hertfordshire countryside. It is housed in a 16th-century building, with a pleasant decor comprising beamed ceilings and leather chairs. Outside, it is stunning with a large al fresco dining area and a wood-burning rotisserie.

SPEEN The Old Plow Bistro & Restaurant
Flowers Bottom Lane, Speen, Buckinghamshire, HP27 0PZ **Tel** *01494 488300*

A 17th-century building set in the heart of the Chiltern countryside, Old Plow is famed for a very high quality of modern eclectic cuisine. Specialities are French dishes with wonderful sauces, and seafood which arrives direct from the Devon coast. Friendly service to match the excellent standards of this bistro-restaurant.

STREATLEY The Swan at Streatley
Streatley-on-Thames, Berkshire, RG8 9HR **Tel** *01491 878800*

The restaurant at this efficient business and leisure hotel serves carefully prepared dishes with the best local produce. The star attraction on the menu is the roast breast of Gressingham duck with citrus fruits. Adjourn from the Riverside Terrace to the Drawing Room Bar for a coffee or liqueur for the full dining experience.

THURLEIGH The Jackal
3 High St, Thurleigh, Bedfordshire, MK44 2DB **Tel** *01234 771293*

Recently taken over and revitalized, this pub-restaurant offers outstanding and award-winning bistro-style food. With a huge outdoor garden and an inviting interior filled with sofas and easy chairs, it's the perfect place to spend an evening or lunch time. The home-made sticky toffee pudding is fast becoming famous across the district.

WINDSOR Al Fassia
27 St Leonards Rd, Windsor, Berkshire, SL4 3BP **Tel** *01753 855370*

Shining out among the traditional Windsor restaurants, Al Fassia serves a host of North African delights. The caring concern of a family-run business is matched with a strictly professional attention to detail. The fluffy, melt-in-the-mouth couscous is well worth a try. Some specialities must be ordered a couple of days ahead.

WINDSOR Amalfi
9 Datchet Rd, Windsor, Berkshire, SL4 1QB **Tel** *01753 855576*

With views across to Windsor Castle, this long-established, cosy little Italian restaurant serves all the usual favourites, as well as a variety of continental and vegetarian dishes. Starters come in very generous portions, and the fish dishes are highly recommended. Friendly service and a relaxed atmosphere make this place a favourite among locals.

WOBURN Paris House
Woburn Park, Woburn, Bedfordshire, MK17 9QP **Tel** *01525 290692*

A mock-Tudor building set in the grounds of Woburn Abbey, Paris House is a fancy, but friendly, restaurant serving contemporary French cuisine. Varied menus range from gastronomic to special occasions (such as *Phantom of the Opera* evenings) to fine à la carte choices. Don't miss the wonderfully dripping hot raspberry soufflé.

WOBURN SANDS Spooners
61 High St, Woburn Sands, Milton Keynes, Buckinghamshire, MK17 8QY **Tel** *01908 584385*

Converted from a derelict Victorian building in the mid-1980s by the Spooners, this lovely restaurant lies in the heart of Woburn Sands. A friendly atmosphere prevails, with regular events such as race days during Ascot and lunch-time bargains. Look out for classical and romantic guitar entertainment. Never miss the tasty steaks.

WOODSTOCK The Feathers Hotel
Market St, Woodstock, Oxfordshire, OX20 1SX **Tel** *01993 812291*

Situated next to historic landmarks such as Blenheim Palace and the Oxford University's "dreaming spires", the Feathers successfully combines modern cuisine with traditional dishes. Originally seven separate 17th-century houses, the building has a cosy and charismatic interior, with roasting log fires and interesting antique furniture.

WESSEX

AVEBURY The Circle Restaurant
High St, Avebury, Marlborough, Wiltshire, SN8 1RF **Tel** *01672 539514*

Vegetarians and wholefood fans rave about this counter-service restaurant beside the ancient stone circle. Using local products, they serve up wonderful home-made soups and organic teas – all at an extremely reasonable price. It's a perfect place to allow the wonder of Avebury stone circle to properly sink in, along with their nutritious flapjacks.

BATH Hole in the Wall
16 George St, Bath, Somerset, BA1 2EN **Tel** *01225 425242*

With probably the best menu in Bath, this vaulted restaurant has been refurbished to bring sleek minimalism to dazzling period features. The old-fashioned service and subdued atmosphere merely adds to its glamour. The contemporary British cuisine, with a French flair, is superb. Don't miss the buttered cabbage.

BATH Moon and Sixpence
6A Broad St, Bath, Somerset, BA1 5LJ **Tel** *01225 460962*

A well-kept secret, Moon and Sixpence is a favourite with locals and discerning visitors. Slightly hidden up a cobbled path, it offers quiet dining right in the bustling city centre. The reasonably priced food is loosely termed modern-international. Particularly pleasant in summer when table service is provided in the downstairs conservatory.

BATH The Bath Priory
Weston Road, Bath, Somerset, BA1 2XT **Tel** *01225 331922*

Not the original Priory, this top-notch establishment stands in a vast 19th-century Bath property, surrounded by four acres of award-winning gardens. While the views are gasp-worthy, the food, too, is not far behind. French and English Michelin-star cuisine includes the glorious sautéed escalope of salmon in lobster sauce.

BEAMINSTER Bridge House Hotel
Prout Bridge, Beaminster, Dorset, DT8 3AY **Tel** *01308 862200*

A few minutes from the Dorset coast, amongst beautiful countryside that inspired most of Thomas Hardy's writings, this ancient clergy makes a jewel of a refreshment break. Raw ingredients are transformed here into dishes that change daily, but are likely to include fresh scallops or their speciality, organic pork medallions.

Key to Price Guide *see p608* **Key to Symbols** *see back cover flap*

BISHOPSTON The Barn Restaurant

The Annexe Courtyard, Seymour Rd, Bishopston, Bristol, BS7 9EQ **Tel** *0117 904 9996*

Steeped in history, this inviting family-run establishment is housed in a 17th-century converted barn. While the interior exudes period charm, traditional English dishes are presented in a stylish contemporary way. The ingredients, too, are served with a culinary twist, such as special apple cider sauce.

BOURNEMOUTH Chez Fred

10 Seamoor Rd, Westbourne, Bournemouth, Dorset, BH4 9AN **Tel** *01202 761023*

The only place to eat fish and chips by the seaside, Chez Fred is famous for its interpretation of the national delicacy as well as mouthwatering puddings. Quintessentially British, the setting of this family-run eatery is welcoming and the atmosphere children-friendly and lively, with competitions to win extra portions of chips.

BRADFORD-ON-AVON Woolley Grange

Woolley Green, Bradford-on-Avon, Wiltshire, BA15 1TX **Tel** *01225 864705*

This intriguing 17th-century Jacobean manor house, built of Bath stone, is beautifully surrounded by 14 acres of leafy grounds. The extensive menu features everything from children's food to fine international cuisine. A casual, cosy atmosphere prevails in the dining room decorated with Oriental rugs and antiques.

BRISTOL Howards Restaurant

1a Avon Crescent, Hotwells, Bristol, BS1 6XQ **Tel** *0117 926 2921*

Beautifully set in a Georgian waterside building, Howards offers an extensive, modern French menu with a well-considered accompanying wine list, all at very reasonable prices. The main dining room has delightful views over the harbour below. Staff are famously polite and attentive.

BRISTOL Riverstation

The Grove, Bristol, BS1 4RB **Tel** *0117 914 4434*

Formerly a harbourside police station left in decline, Riverstation has fully exploited its potential to become one of the city's top restaurants offering modern European cuisine. Of its two floors, the dock floor has a bar and kitchen which is busy and buzzing all day long. The other floor is a light and airy restaurant.

BRISTOL Lords

43 Corn St, Bristol, BS1 1HT **Tel** *0117 926 2658*

Excellent service and setting, this restaurant trips slightly with its steep prices. However, the small menu belies the fact that everything is freshly prepared, and made with special care. The unusual location in a former bank vault adds to the experience, making it ideal for a special dining occasion.

COLERNE Lucknam Park

Colerne, Chippenham, Wiltshire, SN14 8AZ **Tel** *01225 742777*

Situated in a splendid country manor with hotel, spa and equestrian facilities, the restaurant is a suitably posh addition. The menu includes specialities such as smoked haddock fishcakes with beetroot tartare and organic leaves. It's steeped heavily in tradition, so men must wear a jacket and tie and women must dress to impress.

LACOCK Sign of the Angel

Church St, Lacock, Wiltshire, SN15 2LB **Tel** *01249 730230*

The only sheep that this converted 15th-century wool merchant's house comes across now, is in the form of delicious roast lamb. The ambience is that of a quaint village restaurant, with log fires, oak panelling, low beams and squeaky floorboards, all teeming with history and character. The friendly, informal staff serve stellar steak and kidney pie.

MAIDEN NEWTON Le Petit Canard

Dorchester Road, Maiden Newton, Dorchester, DT2 0BE **Tel** *01300 320536*

The owners recently took over this charming, candlelit place, with the desire to express their culinary creativity. Their success reflects in the deliciously unique dishes such as the paprika-rubbed pork fillet finished with cream, on a bed of linguine. The service impeccable and the cottage environment endearing.

POOLE Storm Fish Restaurant

16 High Street, Poole, Dorset, BH15 1BP **Tel** *01202 674970*

With a rustic interior and a cosy, intimate atmosphere, Storm is perfect for a romantic dinner. Owner Pete Miles is a fisherman by day and chef by night, serving up the freshest produce in what is reputedly Poole's finest seafood restaurant. Desserts are home-made and the "Piggies' Platter" allows those with a sweet tooth to mix and match.

POOLE Museum Inn

Farnham, nr Blandford Forum, Dorset, DT11 8DE **Tel** *01725 516261*

With a timber-panelled dining room, a huge inglenook fireplace, flagstoned floors and wooden tables, this classic English pub-restaurant is lovingly called "the shed". Clientele may include the hunting jet set. The weekly menu is reasonable and perfectly executed.

SALISBURY Café Med

68 Castle St, Salisbury, Wiltshire, SP1 3TS **Tel** *01722 328402*

Renowned for its essential wine list, this lively restaurant-cum-wine bar has a simple but effective menu featuring satisfying dishes such as grilled salmon. The service is efficient and funky, with an emphasis on ensuring you enjoy your night. Early bird specials are available.

SANDBANKS La Roche
The Haven, Banks Rd, Sandbanks, Dorset, BH13 7QL **Tel** *01202 707333*

Perched at the very tip of the exclusive Sandbanks peninsula with breathtaking views across the bay, this glass-fronted dining room provides a stylish backdrop for a showcase of local fish and seafood. Luxurious ingredients and modern flavours are expertly coordinated without over-indulgence. Popular, so book early.

STON EASTON Cedar Tree
Ston Easton Park Hotel, Ston Easton, nr Bath, Somerset, BA3 4DF **Tel** *01761 241631*

Overlooking the River Nor and Ston Easton Park's beautiful gardens, this Georgian restaurant harks back to a bygone era. The food, however, is modern British, with Mediterranean influences, made with fresh local produce. Open to both residential and non-residential hotel guests.

STURMINSTER NEWTON Plumber Manor
Sturminster Newton, Dorset, DT10 2AF **Tel** *01258 472507*

In the middle of Thomas Hardy's "Vale of Little Dairies" and in the centre of a triangle of charming country towns, this family-run country house and restaurant is an idyllic stopping point. Portraits adorn the walls and friendly Labradors greet guests as they come to enjoy fine food, particularly fish as well as delightful desserts.

SWANAGE Cauldron Bistro
5 High St, Swanage, Dorset, BH19 2LN **Tel** *01929 422671*

Quality ingredients fresh from the sea have long been the secret to the success of this town-centre restaurant close to the quay, with French posters adding to the classic bistro atmosphere. Firm, juicy scallops are heavenly, whether served with lemon, garlic and balsamic or as a classic *coquilles* St Jacques. Invigorate the palate with the ginger ice cream.

TAUNTON Castle Hotel
Castle Green, Taunton, Somerset, TA1 1NF **Tel** *01823 272671*

Once a Norman fortress, this friendly hotel has been welcoming travellers since the 12th century, and has been run by the same family for the last half-century. While the antiquated interior is preserved, the food is the main focus in the restaurant. Celebrating British beef, the steamed oxtail pudding is superb.

WARMINSTER The Mulberry Restaurant
Bishopstrow House, Warminster, Wiltshire, BA12 9HH **Tel** *01985 212312*

Named after a tree in Bishopstrow House's beautiful grounds, golden-yellow Mulberry Restaurant is gracious with a Georgian feel. It may look old and rambling but its clientele is young. Enjoy light lunches and dinners overlooking acres of land and opt for the set meals. Outstanding value and good-quality food.

WEST BAY Riverside
West Bay, Bridport, Dorset, DT6 4EZ **Tel** *01308 422011*

This restaurant boasts wonderful service, superb food and a festive atmosphere indoors. Its position as one of the best fish restaurants in the Southwest is quite an achievement, since most coastal places serve seafood. The langoustines with mayonnaise or char-grilled mackerel with chips are heavenly.

WEST BEXINGTON Manor Hotel
Beach Rd, West Bexington, Dorchester, Dorset, DT2 9DF **Tel** *01308 897616 or 897785*

Just when you think you've taken one coastal path too far, you'll hit upon this gorgeous old stone inn. The restaurant serves a range of delicious dishes, while the daily-changing menu features local produce and seafood. The Cellar Bar offers a selection of wines from around the world. Walk off the burn later with a jaunt to Chesil beach.

YEOVIL Little Barwick House
Little Barwick House, Barwick, Yeovil, Somerset, BA22 9TD **Tel** *01935 423902*

Located right on the Devon and Somerset border, this idyllic family-run hotel is a great place to stop for food while touring each county's gorgeous scenery. The decor is elegantly minimalistic, to let you focus on the fine British food, such as the celebrated roast guinea fowl with wild mushroom risotto. Children over five years welcome.

DEVON AND CORNWALL

AVONWICK Avon Inn
Avonwick South Brent, Devon, TQ10 9NB **Tel** *01364 73475*

On the banks of the Avon, this dining pub is a perfect respite during a river walk. English and French food is prepared with a Continental twist. Specialities include risotto of scallops, prawns and mussels or John Dory in a champagne sauce with baby vegetables. Enjoy with fine wines or real ales. Friendly pub quiz on Mondays.

BARNSTAPLE The Restaurant at Broomhill
Broomhill Art Hotel, Muddiford Rd, Barnstaple, Devon, EX31 4EX **Tel** *01271 850262*

Part of an intriguing sculpture garden art gallery and hotel, this restaurant provides a four-course gourmet lunch that can last the entire afternoon, and even push on late into the evening. Food is cheap and top quality, and they make a strong effort to use local and organic produce. Impromptu jazz concerts create a convivial ambience.

Key to Price Guide *see p608* **Key to Symbols** *see back cover flap*

BARNSTAPLE Lynwood House

*Bishops Tawton Rd, Barnstaple, Devon, EX32 9EF **Tel** 01271 343695*

Formerly a Victorian gentleman's residence, this top-class fish and seafood restaurant has retained its classic elegance. The Roberts family use local organic products in their superb cooking. Don't miss the famed pot of Lynwood seafood. Well-sourced wines are served in their classy glassware, the finest Dartington Crystal.

BIGBURY Oyster Shack

*Milburn Orchard Farm, Stakes Hill, Bigbury, Devon, TQ7 4BE **Tel** 01548 810876*

The name suggests that Oyster Shack is little more than a shack with a tarpaulin, but the front remains secondary to the unmissable food served here. The main draw is the ultra-fresh seafood: local mussels and oysters, pan-fried sardines, potted shrimp, shell-on prawns or whatever the catch of the day might be. Booking is essential.

CHAGFORD 22 Mill Street

*22 Mill St, Chagford, Devon, TQ13 8AW **Tel** 01647 432244*

Nestled behind a cream-and-green shop front, this modern European restaurant lies on a street of attractive old town houses. The atmosphere is unusually relaxing, welcoming and unintimidating. Attention to detail, clear flavours and attractive presentation make the place worth its slightly high prices. Savour the wide-ranging wine list too.

CHAGFORD Gidleigh Park

*Gidleigh Park, Chagford Devon, TQ13 8HH **Tel** 01647 432367*

Officially one of the best restaurants this country has to offer, Gidleigh Park has won several awards and accolades. The attention to detail is what sets it apart. Menus change according to the season, but expect fine quality whatever the month. The wine choice is also among the nation's best. Perfect for special occasions.

DARTINGTON Cott Inn

*Dartington, Totnes, Devon, TQ9 6HE **Tel** 01803 863777*

Charming Cott Inn is a 14th-century restaurant-with-rooms with all the antiquated extras: exposed beams, open fireplace, horse brasses, soft lights. The restaurant has cosy cushioned pews, wall lanterns and a very reasonable menu, while the bar is ideal for the occasional a sing-along and to watch Friday night morris dancers.

DARTMOUTH The New Angel

*2 South Embankment, Dartmouth, Devon, TQ6 9BH **Tel** 01803 839425*

Formerly called Carved Angel, this restaurant takes its new name from its present Michelin-starred owner. Unlike formal, old-fashioned dining rooms, it welcomes the entire family, except dogs, in an unpretentious environment. No fixed-price menus, just individually priced dishes. Get there early for 8.30am coffee, croissants and cooked breakfast.

DODDISCOMBSLEIGH The Nobody Inn

*Doddiscombsleigh, nr Exeter, Devon, EX6 7PS **Tel** 01647 252394*

A 16th-century country inn set in the rolling Devon countryside, Nobody Inn was renamed after an unfortunate incident with a deceased landlord. Enjoy the traditional interior and fresh local produce as well as its imaginative wine and whisky list, comprehensive selection of local cheeses and creative cooking. Unspoilt old-world charm.

EXETER Thai Orchid

*5 Cathedral Yard, Exeter, Devon, EX1 1HJ **Tel** 01392 214215*

Very friendly and welcoming service greets you as soon as you step inside this pleasing Oriental establishment. Authentic Thai cuisine is on offer in the 16th-century building, where the stone-masons who built Exeter's glorious cathedral originally boarded. Fresh orchids on each table are a thoughtful finishing touch.

KINGSBRIDGE Buckland-Tout-Saints Hotel

*Goveton, Kingsbridge, Devon, TQ7 2DS **Tel** 01548 853055*

Set in a wonderful 1690 Grade II listed residence in the middle of lush woodland countryside, Buckland-Tout-Saints is a magnificent manor house from Queen Anne's time, with plenty of character. Winner of a double AA Rosette Award, the restaurant serves British cuisine with Gallic skill and finesse. Don't miss the luxury wines.

LEWDOWN Lewtrenchard Manor

*Lewdown, Okehampton, Devon, EX20 4PN **Tel** 01566 783222*

Mentioned in the *Domesday Book* of 1086, this impressive manor was once a popular hangout of knights. Even today, diners are treated to generous helpings of well-cooked, wholesome modern English food. An excellently stocked cellar features modestly-priced bottles from every region in the world.

LIFTON The Arundell Arms Hotel

*Fore St, Lifton, Devon, PL16 0AA **Tel** 01566 784666*

The Arundell Arms serves as an escape from the hustle and bustle. The lovely surrounding countryside provides activities such as fishing, riding, walking and golf. The restaurant serves fixed-price menus featuring local game and fish, created by two of Britain's official master chefs. Bar snacks are also available for lunch or dinner.

LYNMOUTH The Rising Sun

*Harbourside, Lynmouth, Devon, EX35 6EG **Tel** 01598 753223*

Percy Bysshe Shelley stayed at this 14th-century thatched smugglers' inn that overlooks a picturesque harbour and Lynmouth Bay. Lobster literally lands at their door, as well as local Exmoor game and salmon fished from the River Lyn. There are also plenty of other offerings served in the romantic candlelit, oak-panelled dining room.

MARLDON Church House Inn

Village Rd, Marldon, Devon, TQ3 1SL **Tel** *01803 558279*

Located in the centre of the village, delightful Church House Inn is as old as the 15th-century church beside it. The restaurant, renowned for its traditional menu with a Mediterranean twist, serves as the centre of the local community. A perfect slice of quintessential countryside life comes with a full-bodied pint.

MOUSEHOLE Old Coastguard Hotel

Mousehole, Penzance, Cornwall, TR19 6PR **Tel** *01736 731222*

As the name suggests, this restaurant-hotel is right on the tip of the coast, with some absolutely beautiful views from the rooms and restaurant. The menu is modern and dishes are made to perfection. Don't miss the kippers and poached egg for breakfast. The "Real Fishy Feast", with sea bass and roasted tomatoes, is outstanding.

PADSTOW The Seafood Restaurant

Riverside, Padstow, Cornwall, PL28 8BY **Tel** *01841 532700*

Much more special than its matter-of-fact name, this fish and shellfish restaurant has been around since 1975. Just across the quay from the lobster boats and trawlers, it procures much of the fish literally straight off the boats. Expertly cooked by the chef, Rick Stein, seafood is fresh and succulent.

PENZANCE Bay Restaurant

Britons Hill, Penzance, Cornwall, TR18 3AE **Tel** *01736 366890*

This stylish two AA Rosette restaurant has an outdoor deck that opens out in summer for magnificent views across Mount's Bay and over the rooftops to Penzance Harbour. Generous and creative European cuisine is served by knowledgeable staff. Local fish, vegetables and herbs are complemented by excellent Cornish wine.

PENZANCE Harris's

46 New St, Penzance, Cornwall, TR18 2LZ **Tel** *01736 364408*

Run by the Harris family for over 30 years, this small restaurant wins acclaim for freshly made dishes served with local produce and fish from nearby Newlyn market. There are excellent-value fixed-price menus for both lunch and dinner, where you can choose one, two or three courses. The crab Florentine comes highly recommended.

POLPERRO Kitchen

The Coombes, Polperro, Cornwall, PL13 2RQ **Tel** *01503 272780*

This delightful little restaurant serves mainly home-made food. Bread is baked daily and ice cream is made nearby. Delicious fish is garnered from Cornish day boats, with the exception of the odd exotic dish. The atmosphere is cosy, and while service is unobtrusive during the meal, diners can often go into the kitchen for a chat and tour afterwards.

PORT ISAAC Slipway Hotel and Seafood Restaurant

The Habour Front, Port Isaac, Cornwall, PL29 3RH **Tel** *01208 880264*

Recently taken over by new owners, this quaint fish restaurant offers a perfect sample of Cornish fishy fare in season. Though there's no live music inside, diners can hear the tuneful noise of fisherman singing in the forecourt, or else a local live band. Reasonably-priced and consistently good, with a 40-plus wine list to boot.

SALCOMBE Winking Prawn

Waterfront Brasserie and Garden, North Sands, Salcombe, Devon, **Tel** *01548 842326*

In a thickly wooded valley, this little place appears beside an empty beach. There's an evening barbecue of steak and king prawns that can be taken outside on fine days. When it rains, the restaurant offers bowls of soup and *fruits de mer*. The floor is so covered in sand you could build a castle on it. A holiday treat.

ST IVES Tate Café and Restaurant

Porthmeor Beach, St Ives, Cornwall, TR26 1TG **Tel** *01736 796226*

Enjoy the views over the old town of St Ives and Porthmeor Beach from this art-gallery brasserie while tucking into wholefood dishes made from produce created by Cornish growers and suppliers where possible. They stock and sell premium Cornish goods, ranging from cheese to fish, potatoes to ice cream and cider to wine.

ST IVES Alba

Old Lifeboat House, Wharf Rd, St Ives, Cornwall, TR26 1LF **Tel** *01736 797222*

With spectacular views of the bay, mesmerizing Alba is housed in the old lifeboat building. Equally breathtaking is the double AA Rosette cuisine, predominantly seafood, all sourced locally. The accompanying wine list is as impressive. The restaurant is split between two floors.

ST MAWES Hotel Tresanton

27 Lower Castle Rd, St Mawes, Cornwall, TR2 5DR **Tel** *01326 270055*

Situated at the edge of the unspoiled village of St Mawes, the Tresanton was created in the 1940s as a yachtsmen's club. Its unique interior comprises old houses on different levels. The lovely restaurant has pretty views of the sea, looking towards St Anthony's Lighthouse. The food is exquisite and benefits from the local seafood easily available.

SUMMERCOURT Viner's

Carvynick, Summercourt, Cornwall, TR8 5AF **Tel** *01872 510544*

A former pub, this bar and restaurant is run by Kevin Viner, the first-ever chef in Cornwall to win a Michelin star. The interior has been tranformed with flair. Moving from his former fine dining, the owner-chef strives to keep the dishes simple. The emphasis is on the stand-alone strength of first-rate local fish and shellfish, Cornish lamb and beef.

Key to Price Guide *see p608* **Key to Symbols** *see back cover flap*

TAVISTOCK The Horn of Plenty
Gulworthy, Tavistock, Devon, PL19 8JD **Tel** *01822 832528*

With stunning views over the tranquil Tamar Valley near Tavistock in Devon, this inviting country-house hotel is set in five acres of immaculate gardens and wild orchards. The award-winning restaurant excels itself under the baton of its executive head chef, TV chef Peter Gorton. The menu is kept current and the food maintains the highest quality.

TOTNES Willow
87 High St, Totnes, Devon, TQ9 5PB **Tel** *01803 862605*

Willow holds the crown in the area for vegetarian cuisine, offering low-priced wholesome dishes and an organic wine list amid cheerful decor with a pretty courtyard at the back. The staff are helpful, and welcoming towards children. Wednesdays are Curry Nights and music sessions on Fridays are regularly jammed, so it's worth booking ahead of time.

TORQUAY Mulberry House
1 Scarborough Rd, Torquay, Devon, TQ2 5UJ **Tel** *01803 213639*

A calm and soothing atmosphere exudes at this restaurant-with-rooms. The menu changes frequently and all dishes are home-made to complement local seasonal produce. The bread and cakes are remarkable. Note that on weeknights dinner is served only to residential customers.

TREBURLEY Springer Spaniel
Treburley, nr Launceston, Cornwall, PL15 9NS **Tel** *01579 370424*

Picturesque, award-winning Springer Spaniel is a country-food pub, set in an attractive 18th-century beamed building. The staff are friendly and laid-back, and an easy-going ambience prevails throughout. The menu changes frequently, reflecting the owner's desire to use local produce including home-grown vegetables and salads.

VIRGINSTOW Percy's
Coombeshead Estate, Virginstow, Devon, EX21 5EA **Tel** *01409 211236*

Award-winning dishes burst with colour and flavour at this restaurant and hotel. The kitchen, supervised by one of Devon's top female chefs, Tina Bricknell-Webb, creates consistently good contemporary country cuisine, with a wine selection to match. The comfortable lounges are perfect to enjoy an after-dinner drink.

THE HEART OF ENGLAND

ANSLOW The Burnt Gate
59 Hopley Rd, Anslow, Burton upon Trent, Staffordshire, DE13 9PY **Tel** *01283 563664*

Friendly pub and restaurant with a homely decor featuring dark wood beams and an open coal fire. This award-winning eatery serves traditional dishes made with fresh, local produce, and is well known for steak, gammon, poultry, seasonal game and a variety of seafood. Also has dedicated menus for vegetarians and coeliacs.

BIRMINGHAM Le Petit Blanc
9 Brindleyplace, Birmingham, B1 2HS **Tel** *0121 633 7333*

Part of the chain of restaurants run by acclaimed chef Raymond Blanc. This stylish restaurant prides itself on its warm welcome and quality French cuisine. The menu features innovative dishes such as parfait of chicken liver with red onion marmalade, and whole lemon sole meuniere.

BIRMINGHAM Titash Balti Restaurant
2278 Coventry Rd, Birmingham, B26 3JR **Tel** *0121 722 2080*

A must-try speciality here is Balti, a spicy, aromatic dish that was originally introduced by the city's large Kashmiri Pakistani community, and is cooked in a wok-like pot. This winner of "Curry Chef of the Year" has recently been refurbished. An à la carte menu offers delicious food and dishes are accompanied by naan bread.

BIRMINGHAM La Toque d'Or
27 Warstone Lane, Hockley, Birmingham, B18 6JQ **Tel** *0121 233 3655*

Elegant dining in a tiny alleyway in Birmingham's Jewellery Quarter. The Parisian-style cuisine is based on the vision of AA Rosette-winning chef, Didier Philipot. Food is traditionally French, but with a British twist, using ham from Cumbria, scallops from the Isle of Skye and organic eggs from the Cotswolds. Advance reservations are advised.

BIRMINGHAM Jessica's
1 Montague Rd, Edgbaston, Birmingham, B16 9HN **Tel** *0121 455 0999*

This recently opened restaurant has already won many awards, including the "Metro Restaurant of the Year 2005". Presents modern British fare with a distinctly French influence. Some of the specialities here include sea bass with apple purée, ravioli of pigs trotters, poached chicken with *gambas* and roast duck. The desserts are also good.

CHELTENHAM Le Champignon Sauvage
24–26 Suffolk Rd, Cheltenham, Gloucestershire, GL50 2AQ **Tel** *01242 573449*

Renowned French restaurant and winner of several awards. The interior is lovingly decorated in cream, with modern art on the walls and large, comfortable chairs for an informal dining experience. The seasonal menu has a strong emphasis on local ingredients. Eel tortellini, Wiltshire pork and pigeon breast are some of the favourites here.

CHELTENHAM Le Petit Blanc

The Queen's Hotel, The Promenade, Cheltenham, Gloucestershire, GL50 1NN **Tel** *01242 266800*

Fine dining under the helm of award-winning chef Raymond Blanc. Set in an elegant Georgian building, this modern, vibrant brasserie as well known for its cocktail bar as it is for its rich, French food. The kids menu offers a mix of haute cuisine and popular favourites such as gratinèed macaroni cheese and home-made French fries.

CHELTENHAM Off the Square

8 The Courtyard, Montpellier St, Cheltenham, Gloucestershire, GL50 1SR **Tel** *01242 227757*

A neat, non-smoking restaurant with a cream-and-blue decor and an al fresco terrace. The friendly waiters serve large, tasty dishes from a menu that features new, imaginative combinations every two months. The popular dessert menu offers a hot liquid chocolate pudding with home-made banana ice cream. A good choice for vegetarians.

CHIPPENHAM Bybrook Restaurant

Manor House Hotel and Golf Club, Castle Combe, nr Bath, Wiltshire, SN14 7HR **Tel** *01249 782206*

Outstanding food in a breathtaking setting in the Manor House hotel on the southern edge of the Cotswolds. Named after the Bybrook River that runs beside the hotel, this restaurant uses fresh produce from the house's kitchen garden and orchards. Stained-glass windows offer views over the Italian garden and the adjacent golf course.

COVENTRY Ryton Organic Gardens

Ryton Organic Gardens, nr Wolston, Coventry, Warwickshire, CV8 3LG **Tel** *0247 630 7142*

Organic restaurant run by a registered organic association. The menu features home-made dishes cooked to order, using organically grown produce from the gardens. Vegan and vegetarian meals also feature on the menu, which changes periodically.

GLOUCESTER The Fountain Inn

Westgate Street, Gloucester, Gloucestershire, GL1 2NW **Tel** *01452 522562*

With a pretty patio and delightful flower garden, this place is great for al fresco dining in the summer. Everyone is catered for, with a good mixture of mediterrannean dishes, seafood and traditional pub fare. The Sunday menu is particularly tempting.

HEREFORD La Rive at Castle House

Castle St, Hereford, Herefordshire, HR1 2NW **Tel** *01432 356321*

Award-winning restaurant in the Castle House hotel. The seasonal menu here draws on fresh meat and produce delivered daily from the hotel's farm nearby. Try the Hereford prime beef or the Gloucester Old Spot pork, and finish with a vanilla crème brûlée with cinnamon roast pear. Also hosts a cocktail bar for a pre-meal apéritif.

INGLESHAM Inglesham Forge Restaurant

Inglesham, Highworth, Swindon, Wiltshire, SN6 7QY **Tel** *01367 252298*

Welcoming restaurant set in a 15th-century forge. The decor is old fashioned, with wood-beamed ceilings. Serves a tasty range of Mediterranean cuisine. The specials vary from season to season, but can include anything from escargot Bourguignonne to breast of duck with morello cherries.

LEAMINGTON SPA Newbold Bar & Brasserie

18 Newbold St, Leamington Spa, Warwickshire, CV32 4HN **Tel** *01926 424667*

Atmospheric setting and friendly service make this restaurant a favourite with the pre-theatre crowd. Occupies two floors of an airy, old Georgian building near the centre of town. The à la carte menu on the upper floor serves a wide variety of mouthwatering international cuisine, while the long bar downstairs serves bar snacks.

LITTLE BEDWYN The Harrow at Little Bedwyn

Little Bedwyn, Marlborough, Wiltshire, SN8 3JP **Tel** *01672 870871*

Rated by the *Wine Spectator* as having one of the finest restaurant wine lists in the world. This non-smoking eatery is primarily known for its extensive collection of Australian premium wines, and diners can opt for the "tasting menu with Aussie wines" meal. Also serves an à la carte menu.

LUDLOW Ego Café Bar

Quality Square, Ludlow, Shropshire, SY8 1AR **Tel** *01584 878000*

Stylish bistro in a renovated bakery, with bright furnishings and art-covered walls. Features a small, but delicious British menu, a bustling outdoor patio and live jazz on most weekends. The cuisine draws on local produce, and ranges from guinea fowl and venison steak to roasted organic red pepper and *Dolcelatte pithivier* (a French pastry).

LUDLOW The Clive Restaurant with Rooms

Bromfield, Ludlow, Shropshire, SY8 2JR **Tel** *01584 856565*

This converted farmhouse, with 15 bedrooms, has been decorated to emphasize many of the building's original features, including whitewashed walls and wood-beamed ceilings. The seasonal menu serves high-quality British fare, using produce from the surrounding countryside. The atmosphere is warm and informal.

LUDLOW Hibiscus

17 Corve St, Ludlow, Shropshire, SY8 1DA **Tel** *01584 872325*

An award-winning culinary giant, occupying an old 17th-century building in the heart of Ludlow. Serves modern French cuisine at high but fair prices. The head chef, Claude Bosi, has built a reputation for presenting inventive dishes, including his famous *foie gras* ice cream. The small dining room ensures personal service.

Key to Price Guide *see p608* **Key to Symbols** *see back cover flap*

PAXFORD The Churchill Arms

Paxford, Chipping Campden, Gloucestershire, GL55 6XH **Tel** *01386 594000*

Restaurant with four rooms on a B&B basis, set in a small, working Cotswolds village. Offers an appetizing menu of local produce to accompany the popular real ales from local breweries. The menu is constantly updated, but dishes such as grilled fish, pot-roast partridge and poached chicken are regular favourites.

SALT Holly Bush Inn

Salt, nr Stafford, Staffordshire, ST18 0BX **Tel** *01889 508234*

This picturesque country inn with a large beer garden is one of England's oldest pubs. Serves award-winning food. Dishes range from green shelled mussels to home-made steak and kidney pudding, and from pan-fried Cornish brie to slow cooked lamb and barley stew. Ideal for a family stop-off point.

STOW-ON-THE-WOLD The King's Arms

Market Square, Stow-on-the-Wold, Gloucestershire, GL54 1AF **Tel** *01451 830364*

A charming, 500-year-old coaching inn, which can trace its history back to 1645, when King Charles I was reported to have stayed here. The menu focuses on fresh local ingredients, including trout, Gloucester Old Spot pork and British cheeses. Has two dining areas, with log fires. Also offers accommodation on a B&B basis.

STRATFORD-UPON-AVON Marlowe's Restaurant

18 High St, Stratford-upon-Avon, Warwickshire, CV37 6AU **Tel** *01789 204999*

Two restaurants housed in an Elizabethan town house, in the heart of Stratford. Serves both as a silver-service formal restaurant, perfect for business clients and posh events, and as a more informal and lower priced bistro with patio dining. Autographed pictures of visiting glitterati such as Vanessa Redgrave and Sir Alec Guinness line the bar.

SWINDON Pear Tree Restaurant

Church End, Purton, Swindon, Wiltshire, SN5 4ED **Tel** *01793 772100*

AA Rosette-winning restaurant in an elegant Cotswold stone hotel on the outskirts of Purton. Has 17 luxury bedrooms and a small conservatory dining room with great views over the Marlborough Downs. Menu offers modern English cooking, including seasonal asparagus, roasted guinea fowl and delicious chocolate desserts.

TETBURY The Trouble House Inn

Cirencester Rd, Tetbury, Gloucestershire, GL8 8SG **Tel** *01666 502206*

Excellent local food in a stunning historical setting. Offers everything from the local ale to a fabulous three-course meal. Specials such as Gloucester Old Spot sausages with creamy mashed potato and onion gravy are a clear favourite. Features an atmospheric dining room with polished wooden floors, black beams and ancient fireplaces.

TITLEY The Stagg Inn & Restaurant

Titley, Kington, Herefordshire, HR5 3RL **Tel** *01544 230221*

Small hotel and restaurant overlooking the beautiful Welsh Marshes. A well-reputed wine list accompanies its classic menu of regional English fare. Diners have a choice of eating in the bar, the non-smoking dining room or the garden. The produce, which includes organic rare breed pork and home-cured bacon, is sourced from local shops.

ULLINGSWICK Three Crowns Inn

Ullingswick, nr Hereford, Herefordshire, HR1 3JQ **Tel** *01432 820279*

An unassuming gastro pub, with one of the best-priced menus in the area. Serves simple British favourites, even dishes such as black pudding, with a Mediterranean flavour. Fish and other seafood make a good showing, as does traditional Welsh fare, especially the borderland cheeses.

WINCHCOMBE 5 North Street

5 North St, Winchcombe, Gloucestershire, GL54 5LH **Tel** *01242 604566*

Small, Michelin-starred restaurant, set in a picturesque village. The cosy interior features heavy wood beams, and has a cottage-like feel. Presents a tasty menu of traditional English fare with a French twist. Serves pork, crackling, stuffed cabbage and cider *jus*, as well as brill braised in red wine with bubble and squeak.

WINCHCOMBE Wesley House

Wesley House, High St, Winchcombe, Gloucestershire, GL54 5LJ **Tel** *01242 602366*

Hotel and restaurant in the old Cotswolds town of Winchcombe. The food here is simple, with an emphasis on seasonal local ingredients. Specialities to look out for include braised lamb shank and roasted duck breast. Keep some space for the delicious home-made desserts, such as the outstanding amaretti crème brûlée.

WISTANSTOW The Plough Inn

Wistanstow, Craven Arms, Shropshire, SY7 8DG **Tel** *01588 673251*

Timeless village pub with a warm and welcoming ambience. The inn may look unexceptional from outside, but the menu makes it well worth the visit. A great choice for family Sunday lunches. Home-made chutneys and sauces all add to the charm. Fabulous real ale is provided by the brewery located next door.

WORCESTER King Charles House

29 New St, Worcester, Worcestershire, WR1 2DP **Tel** *01905 22449*

Historic restaurant serving international cuisine. The decor is stylish, and features fine lace tablecloths, crystal glasses and an elegant ambience. It was from here that King Charles II escaped Cromwell's forces after his defeat in the Battle of Worcester in 1651. The restaurant itself is situated above a dungeon.

EAST MIDLANDS

BASLOW Fischer's
Baslow Hall, Calver Rd, Baslow, Derbyshire, DE45 1RR **Tel** *01246 583259*

An award-winning restaurant, located in a popular country-house hotel on the edge of the Chatsworth estate. The Michelin-starred menu serves dishes made using the local produce; some from Chatsworth's farm shop. Venison, wild hare and spring lamb provide the seasonal highlights.

BAKEWELL Renaissance
Bath St, Bakewell, Derbyshire, DE45 1BX **Tel** *01629 812687*

An attractively converted barn houses this relaxed restaurant serving traditional French cuisine made from fresh local produce. Light starters such as blue cheese soufflé with leek casserole prepare the appetite for the rich and hearty main courses to follow. If there's room, try one of the original and beautifully presented desserts.

BECKINGHAM Black Swan
Hillside, Beckingham, Lincolnshire, LN5 0RQ **Tel** *01636 626474*

Fabulous country inn serving French and modern English cuisine. This friendly and welcoming restaurant has been winning awards for the past 20 years. Dishes are made from locally sourced produce. Favourites such as Colston Bassett Stilton make its mark on the three-course table d'hote menu. Patio dining available in summer.

BIRCH VALE The Waltzing Weasel Inn
New Mills Rd, Birch Vale, High Peak, Derbyshire, SK22 1BT **Tel** *01663 743402*

This highly acclaimed restaurant is located at the bottom of Kinder Scout, and is very popular with Ramblers, a UK-based walking association. Special gastronomic evenings are arranged through the week, such as the seasonal lobster nights. Also hosts eight, panoramic en suite bedrooms.

BUCKMINSTER The Tollemache Arms
Main St, Buckminster, Lincolnshire, NG33 5SA **Tel** *01476 860007*

Country pub with restaurant and accommodation, the Tollemache Arms sits in a prime location near the market towns of Oakham, Melton Mowbray and Grantham. The smart restaurant serves a beautifully presented blend of modern and classic cuisine, such as "Grilled sea bass with basil mash and baby chorizo sausages".

CAUNTON Caunton Beck
Main St, Caunton, Newark, Nottinghamshire, NG23 6AB **Tel** *01636 636793*

Lovingly run gastro-pub in a delightfully restored 16th-century ale house. The family friendly restaurant has a welcoming ambience, and a modern European menu that is served at any time of the day. Also features a large and popular outdoor terrace in the summer.

CHESTERFIELD Buckinghams
85–87 Newbold Rd, Newbold, Chesterfield, Derbyshire, S41 7PU **Tel** *01246 201041*

Hotel and unusual restaurant, with just one table that seats up to eight diners. The chef consults with the guests before the meal, and provides a unique, "surprise" seasonal menu depending on their requirements and wishes. The setting is cosy, and the decor elegant. The hotel also offers cooking courses.

CLIPSHAM Olive Branch
Main St, Clipsham, Oakham, Rutland, LE15 7SH **Tel** *01780 410355*

A country pub, housed in three adjacent cottages that were joined in 1890 and later renovated. This delightful eatery has a reputation for fine dining and won a Michelin star in 2002. In addition to a wide range of delicious regional dishes, the gastro-pub also offers sloe gin and damson vodka. The decor is traditional, with antique furnishings.

COLSTON BASSETT Martins Arms Inn
School Lane, Colston Bassett, Nottingham, Nottinghamshire, NG12 3FD **Tel** *0194981361*

Well-reputed for its game and fish, not to mention the Stilton produced in the village of Colston Bassett itself. Provides a great stopping-off point in the agricultural haven of the Vale of Belvoir. The food is modern European making the most of local ingredients. A welcoming fire and comfortable sofas add to the informal ambience.

DAVENTRY Fawsley Hall
Fawsley, Daventry, Northamptonshire , NN11 3BA **Tel** *01327 892000*

Magnificent Tudor country-house hotel with a panoramic restaurant. Offers some of the best desserts in the country. The dark chocolate tart and banana ice cream warrants a visit in itself. The main courses, which include dishes such as rabbit with langoustine and bass stuffed with crab, all add to the richness. The menu changes regularly.

FOTHERINGHAY The Falcon
Fotheringhay, Northamptonshire, PE8 5HZ **Tel** *01832 226254*

Welcoming inn known as much for its selective wine list as it is for its real ales. International menu featuring pub fare as it should be served. Whole roast sea bass, char-grilled pave of lamb and sirloin steak with thyme *salmoriglio* (an Italian sauce) are some of the notable options. Log fires and eclectic decoration add to the effect.

Key to Price Guide *see p608* **Key to Symbols** *see back cover flap*

LEICESTER Sayonara Thali ⓔ

*49 Belgrave Rd, Leicester, Leicestershire, LE4 6AR **Tel** 0116266 5888*

Popular South Indian restaurant on Leicester's Golden Mile, so-called for its gold jewellery shops. Serves thali food – curry dishes served on a large metal plate along with chapatis and deep fried bread made with plain flour. Delicious milk drinks flavoured with pistachio and cardamom are also available.

LEICESTER Entropy ⓔⓔ

*3 Dover St, Leicester, Leicestershire, LE1 6PW **Tel** 0116 254 8530*

Modern cuisine in a contemporary setting. Serves an updated version of classical French fare. Terrine of chicken and leek is offered along with Puy lentils; pigeon *pot au feu* with tarragon ravioli; and *foie gras* sauce fillet of local beef with sautéed ratte potatoes. Closed on Sunday.

LEICESTER Stones ⓔⓔ

*29 Millstone Lane, Leicester, Leicestershire, LE1 5JN **Tel** 0116 291 0004*

Elegant restaurant in a converted factory; the menus here present an eclectic range of international cuisine. Char-grilled Leon chorizo picante with buffalo mozzarella sits happily with breast of Barbary duck and strawberry hollandaise or seared salmon with ratatouille spaghetti. Also serves chicken tikkas, Thai chicken and seafood risotto.

LEICESTER The Case ⓔⓔⓔⓔ

*4–6 Hotel St, St Martins, Leicester, Leicestershire, LE1 5AW **Tel** 0116 251 7675*

A modern European menu with an English twist. This trendy restaurant has built a reputation for innovative and imaginative cuisine. Specials include roast duck breast in soy, honey and walnut oil, char-grilled beef fillet on potato rosti, and Cajun spiced monkfish on bubble and squeak. Features wine-tasting evenings.

LINCOLN Jews House ⓔⓔ

*15 The Strait, Lincoln, Lincolnshire, LN2 1JD **Tel** 01522 524851*

Reputedly Lincoln's oldest building, this l2th-century, Jewish merchant's house is also the town's most famous restaurant. Located beside the town's cathedral, the venue is small, cosy and exclusive; advance booking is recommended. A well-stocked wine cellar accompanies a menu featuring a mix of British and French cuisines.

LINCOLN Lea Gate Inn ⓔⓔ

*Leagate Rd, Coningsby, Lincolnshire, LN4 4RS **Tel** 01526 342370*

Built in the mid-16th century, this former fen guide house is now a friendly pub with rooms. Many of its period features, including beam ceilings and inglenook fireplaces, have been retained. Offers traditional specialities such as steak and kidney pie and Lincolnshire sausages with mash. Also has a children's playground.

MATLOCK Red House ⓔⓔⓔ

*Old Rd, Darley Dale, Matlock, Derbyshire, DE4 2ER **Tel** 01629 734854*

Country-house hotel with just ten bedrooms. This small restaurant is well reputed in Derbyshire for its panoramic dining room and home-made cuisine. Locally sourced ingredients create such dishes as baked duck with red cabbage and fillet of venison with red wine *jus*. The dress code is smart casual.

MELTON MOWBRAY The Gringling Gibbons ⓔⓔⓔ

*Stapleford Park, nr Melton Mowbray, Leicestershire, LE14 2EF **Tel** 01572 787015*

A highly-renowned restaurant, set in a tranquil country hotel and spa. The menu is traditionally English with an emphasis on fish, including seared turbot with braised baby fennel and roast John Dory with smoked eel. Also offers a children's menu. Smart casual attire is requested in the restaurant.

MELTON MOWBRAY The Tollemache Arms ⓔⓔⓔⓔ

*48 Main St, Buckminster, nr Melton Mowbray, NG33 5SA **Tel** 01476 860007*

Country gastro-pub with rooms. This non-smoking inn is a modern, friendly dining venue, located on the outskirts of town. The menu is traditional, made with fresh local produce. Features specialities such as pan-fried pigeon breast with onion marmalade and calves' liver with sauté potatoes and tomato fondue. The desserts are also worth trying.

NEWHAVEN Carriages Italian Restaurant ⓔⓔⓔ

*Newhaven, nr Hartingdon, Buxton, Derbyshire, SK17 0DU **Tel** 01298 84528*

Heartwarming Italian welcome followed by an appetizing variety of traditional Sicilian cuisine and fresh seafood. The decor features two railway carriages bedecked with velvet armchairs and period style table lamps. Favourites include *saltimbocca alla Romana* (veal medallions) and *filetto al Dolcelatte* (fillet steaks with blue cheeses and port).

NEWTON-LINFORD Gibson's Grey Lady ⓔⓔⓔ

*Sharpley Hill, Newtown Linford, Leicestershire, LE6 0AH **Tel** 01530 243558*

Scenic restaurant set in a quaint thatched cottage. This charming eatery prides itself on using the freshest ingredients for preparing its dishes. House specialities include steak, braised shank of lamb and grilled Dover sole. Also features a delightful selection of home-made chocolate desserts. An idyllic, relaxing spot.

NORTH KILWORTH Wordsworth Restaurant ⓔⓔⓔ

*Lutterworth Rd, N Kilworth, Leicestershire, LE17 6JE **Tel** 01858 880058*

This elegant restaurant is located in the Kilworth House Hotel, and provides an attractive setting for an evening meal. The classy interior features glittering chandeliers, a domed ceiling and stained-glass windows. Treats such as sweetbread salad with grape compote and white gazpacho with pepper jelly are on offer.

NORTHAMPTON The New French Partridge

Horton, Northampton, Northamptonshire, NN7 2AP **Tel** *01604 870033*

Stylish country dining in an acclaimed restaurant-with-rooms. Offers an innovative array of classic dishes. Braised belly of pork comes with sautéed artichoke hearts and ginger liqueur, while red mullet is accompanied by scallop and salmon roulade, mussel and saffron broth, and poached crayfish.

NOTTINGHAM French Living

27 King St, Nottingham, Nottinghamshire, NG1 2AY **Tel** *0115 958 5885*

Presenting an authentic taste of France in Nottingham, this delightful restaurant draws its set, seasonal menus from the best French produce. Look out for crisp, fruity desserts in summer and hot vegetable soups in winter. The red-brick cellar and scent of freshly-brewed coffee all add to the effect.

NOTTINGHAM Hart's

1 Standard Court, Park Row, Nottingham, Nottinghamshire,, NG1 6GN **Tel** *0115 9110666*

Impressive hotel and restaurant, well known for its fantastic British cooking. Food is sourced locally, but given an international twist, which produces such dishes as honey-glazed Gressingham duck breast with pak choi. Fabulous desserts include white chocolate parfait with mixed berries and espresso parfait with amaretto sabayon.

NOTTINGHAM Ye Olde Trip to Jerusalem

Brewhouse Yard, Nottingham, Nottinghamshire, NG1 6AD **Tel** *0115 947 3171*

With ancient cellar rooms and engravings on the walls, the atmosphere of Britain's oldest pub doesn't disappoint. The food is typical pub fare with a strong local influence. Ploughman's salad and chicken tikka masala make an appearance, as does Stilton and vegetable crumble and rump steak.

NOTTINGHAM World Service

Newdigate House, Castlegate, Nottingham, Nottinghamshire, NG1 6AF **Tel** *0115 847 5587*

An award-winning restaurant, this eatery has fast gained a reputation for serving outstanding local produce with an Eastern twist. Organic salmon comes with beetroot and orange salsa, while fried monkfish tail is accompanied with a curry sauce. The bar provides the perfect setting for a pre-meal drink.

PLUMTREE Perkins

Old Railway Station, Plumtree, Nottingham, Nottinghamshire, NG12 5NA **Tel** *0115 937 3695*

Friendly restaurant and bar, occupying a converted, late 19th-century village station. The main restaurant extends into a conservatory and garden patio. The seasonal menu changes every four weeks, and features everything from leek and rosemary soup to local Clipston fillet steak.

STAMFORD The Meadows

1–2 Castle St, Stamford, Lincolnshire, PE9 2RA **Tel** *01780 762739*

Stylish restaurant occupying an elegant 17th-century, stone building in Stamford's medieval town centre. The terrace seating overlooks Wellend River, home to weeping willows, oak trees and varied wildfowl and bird life. The menu features traditional English fare, such as rack of lamb and haunch of venison. Ideal for nature lovers.

STONY STRATFORD The Moghul Palace

7 St Paul's Court, High St, Stony Stratford, Buckinghamshire, MK11 1LJ **Tel** *01908 566577*

Outlandish Indian restaurant in a converted chapel. The building's original 200-year-old panelling and a copy of the Michelangelo fresco, *The Creation* from the Sistine Chapel, have been retained as part of the decor. Dining here has a slightly surreal feel as a result, but the modern food and friendly service add to the fun. Good vegetarian choice.

WINTERINGHAM Winteringham Fields

Winteringham, Lincolnshire, DN15 9PF **Tel** *01724 733096*

Gastronomic hotspot in a rambling old 16th-century manor house hotel, beautifully set in a peaceful country village. With five AA rosettes and a Michelin star, the award-winning menu doesn't disappoint. Try the seven-course surprise menu for the region's and season's best cuisine. A wide variety of seafood, poultry, game and delicious desserts.

LANCASHIRE AND THE LAKES

AMBLESIDE Drunken Duck Inn

Barngates, Ambleside, Cumbria, LA22 0NG **Tel** *015394 36347*

Oak beams and open log fires create a traditional setting in this 400-year-old inn. Serves imaginative dishes in a relaxed and informal atmosphere. The varied menu features specialities such as smoked haddock and pan-fried monkfish with sautéed baby leeks. Guests can also sample the delicious home-brewed beers.

AMBLESIDE Rothay Manor Hotel and Restaurant

Rothay Bridge, Ambleside, Cumbria, LA22 0EH **Tel** *01539 433605*

Renowned for its afternoon teas, this comfortable, family-run hotel and restaurant offers outstanding service. The smoked salmon and breast of guinea fowl served with wild mushrooms, asparagus and champagne and cream sauce are among the tempting dishes offered.

Key to Price Guide *see p608* **Key to Symbols** *see back cover flap*

AMBLESIDE The Samling

*Ambleside Rd, Ambleside, Cumbria, LA23 1LR **Tel** 015394 31922*

This delightful, award-winning restaurant offers dining in unashamed comfort. Line-caught sea bass, hand-dived scallops and succulent Herdwick lamb are some of the dishes on the gourmet menu. The well-stocked cellar holds choice wines from across the world, plus some fine old whiskies.

APPLETHWAITE Underscar Manor

*Underscar Manor, Applethwaite, Cumbria, CA12 4PH **Tel** 01768 775000*

A Victorian country house built in the Italianate style, set amid several acres of woodland and formal gardens. Serves a variety of inspirational dishes, which, in season, include venison, pheasant and fish from Scottish waters. Patrons can dine à la carte or opt for the six course "menu surprise". Children below the age of 12 are not allowed.

BLACKPOOL September Brasserie

*15 Queen St, Blackpool, Lancashire, FY1 1NL **Tel** 01253 623282*

Enjoy food, simply cooked, but with a twist, from an eclectic menu that reflects the changing seasons and uses organic produce wherever possible. The same care extends to the collection of wines, which highlights a different country or region each month. The venue is popular with theatre-goers, and advance booking is recommended.

CARLISLE Number 10

*10 Eden Mount, Stanwix, Carlisle, Cumbria, CA3 9LY **Tel** 01228 524183*

Friendly service and excellent cooking are the hallmarks of this delightful little restaurant. Locally sourced fish, beef, lamb, vegetables and cheese are the main features on the menu. Specialities such as roast smoked salmon and watercress tart are available. Many interesting vegetarian options are on offer as well.

CARTMEL Uplands

*Haggs Lane, Cartmel, Cumbria, LA11 6HD **Tel** 01539 536248*

A family-run hotel and restaurant, which enjoys several repeat customers. Serves modern British cooking in the relaxed and comfortable setting of an Edwardian gentleman's residence. The four-course set dinner provides options at each course, and includes a tureen of home-made soup served with delicious bread, hot from the oven.

CARTMEL L'Enclume Restaurant with Rooms

*Cavendish St, Cartmel, Cumbria, LA11 6PZ **Tel** 015395 36362*

Dining at this former village smithy is nothing short of a culinary adventure; a definite stop for discerning foodies. Award-winning chef Simon Rogan's bold and creative style explores unusual ingredients such as myrrh and ancient herbs. Choose from the à la carte menu or try one of the taste-and-texture menus offering 20 mini-taster courses.

COCKERMOUTH Quince and Medlar

*11–13 Castlegate, Cockermouth, Cumbria, CA13 9EU **Tel** 01900 823579*

A historic, Georgian building near Cockermouth Castle is home to this family-run, vegetarian restaurant. The stylish surroundings enhance the intimate candlelit dinners. For 17 years, this non-smoking eatery has been serving imaginative dishes, exploiting modern vegetarian cuisine to the full and drawing inspiration from around the world.

GRASMERE White Moss House

*White Moss House, Rydal Water, Grasmere, Cumbria, LA22 9SE **Tel** 01539 435295*

Family-run hotel and restaurant, set in a house once owned by renowned poet William Wordsworth. The five-course set dinner includes tasty soups, subtly flavoured with home-grown herbs, and local delicacies such as Lakeland char and Herdwick lamb. A favourite to finish is the traditional hot plum duff pudding.

KENDAL Bridge House Restaurant

*Bridge St, Kendal, Cumbria, LA9 7DD **Tel** 01539 738855*

Photographs of old Kendal decorate the walls of this fine historic house, where the small dining rooms create an intimate setting. Chef Roger Pergl-Wilson exploits the flavours of local specialities such as Flookburgh shrimps, Lancashire blue cheese and Lunesdale duck to create exciting and tasty dishes.

LANGHO Northcote Manor

*Northcote Rd, Langho, Blackburn, Lancashire, BB6 8BE **Tel** 01254 240555*

Set within the refined luxury of a 19th-century country house, the emphasis in this award-winning restaurant is on superlative cooking. Chef Nigel Haworth's inventiveness focuses on seasonal regional produce, creating some unique twists to local dishes. Black pudding and pink trout served with mustard and nettle sauce is a signature dish.

LIVERPOOL The Side Door

*29A Hope St, Liverpool, Merseyside, L1 9BQ **Tel** 0151 707 7888*

Located midway between the city's two cathedrals, this friendly restaurant offers imaginative modern British and European cooking, often with a Thai influence, but biased towards local cuisine. Expect to be guided through the carefully selected wine list, which features many unusual varieties from both the old and new world.

LIVERPOOL Simply Heathcotes

*25 The Strand, Beetham Plaza, Liverpool, Merseyside, L2 0XL **Tel** 0151 236 3536*

Overlooking the waterfront in the heart of the city, this lively, modern restaurant turns everyday food into a feast. There is something for everyone, from a light snack to a full evening dinner. Traditional dishes such as home-made black puddings and bread-and-butter pudding are popular, or visit on a gourmet evening for something special.

LIVERPOOL 60 Hope Street

60 Hope St, Liverpool, Merseyside, L1 9BZ **Tel** *0151 707 6060*

Ideal for a casual meal, the Café Bar in the basement serves a range of light meals, from sandwiches and salads to more substantial dishes. For a formal setting, choose the restaurant, which offers modern European cuisine within relaxed and unpretentious surroundings. The wine selection complements the food.

LONGRIDGE Thyme

1–3 Inglewhite Rd, Longridge, Preston, Lancashire, PR3 3JR **Tel** *01772 786888*

Chef Alex Coward has built a fine reputation for this lively town-centre restaurant with his easy-going, yet ambitious cooking. From snack lunches to special occasion dinners, his award-winning cuisine draws on local ingredients to produce favourites such as Barry Pugh's suckling pig served with black pudding, mashed potato and red wine jus.

LONGRIDGE The Longridge Restaurant

104–106 Higher Rd, Longridge, Preston, Lancashire, PR3 3SY **Tel** *01772 784969*

Opened in 1990 and awarded a Michelin star, this is acclaimed chef Paul Heathcote's flagship restaurant. Traditional local dishes such as black pudding and bread-and-butter pudding appear beside more flamboyant creations based on Goosnargh chicken and duck. The reasonably priced, two-course lunch is of great value.

MANCHESTER Restaurant Bar & Grill

14 John Dalton St, Manchester, Lancashire, M2 6JR **Tel** *0161 839 1999*

This vibrant, modern restaurant, close to many of Manchester's major venues, is a popular city-centre meeting place, both at lunch time and in the evening. Asian influences colour the à la carte menu with dishes such as Malay spiced chicken or crispy duck on Chinese greens.

MANCHESTER Yang Sing

34 Princess St, Manchester, Lancashire, M1 4JY **Tel** *0161 236 2200*

A highly acclaimed Chinese restaurant, and a culinary experience not to be missed. Expert waiters guide you through the extensive, 400 dish menu to create an individual banquet that perfectly suits your taste. Features a good range of Chinese beers.

MANCHESTER Le Mont

Le Mont at Urbis, Levels 5 & 6, Cathedral Gardens, Manchester, Lancashire, M3 4BG **Tel** *0161 605 8282*

From its lofty location above Urbis, this stylish restaurant treats diners to a spectacular panorama of the Manchester skyline. Serves excellent modern French cuisine, which has an unexpected Manchester flavour. Features fresh regional produce that includes seafood, poultry and game.

MANCHESTER The Moss Nook Restaurant

Ringway Rd, Manchester, Lancashire, M22 5WA **Tel** *0161 437 4778*

Everything on the menu is a speciality at this fine restaurant, located close to Manchester Airport. However, the pan-fried scallops and crispy roast duckling are particularly recommended. A pianist provides accompaniment on Thursday evening, and if the weather is good, the garden terrace offers a delightfully relaxed setting for a meal.

MELMERBY Village Bakery

Melmerby, Penrith, Cumbria, CA10 1HE **Tel** *01768 881811*

The smell of fresh bread and home baking greet guests as they enter one of the country's first totally organic restaurants. Even the wines, beers and ciders are organic. Noted for its warm and unfussy service, the eatery offers hearty breakfasts, wholesome lunches (with hot and cold selections), as well as tasty treats through the day.

SALFORD The River Restaurant

Lowry Hotel, 50 Dearman's Place, Salford, Lancashire, M3 5LH **Tel** *0161 827 4003*

Overlooking River Irwell, this stylish restaurant features a contemporary, yet classical decor. Offers modern European food with an English influence. Steaks are a speciality here, and guests might like to try fillet of beef with potato rosti and Madeira *jus*. A popular dessert is the *assiette*, a large plate of different chocolate desserts.

SAWLEY The Spread Eagle

The Spread Eagle, Sawley, nr Clitheroe, Lancashire, BB7 4NH **Tel** *01200 441202*

Built over the ruins of an old abbey, this restaurant offers a scenic, riverbank setting. One of the specialities is braised neck of lamb, slow cooked with layers of buttered potatoes, onions and black pudding – a great interpretation of the traditional Lancashire hot-pot. The select wine and champagne list is supported by over 50 malt whiskies.

SAWREY Ees Wyke Country House

Ees Wyke Country House, nr Sawrey, Cumbria, LA22 0JZ **Tel** *015394 36393*

Formerly the holiday home of Beatrix Potter and close to Hill Top, this charming restaurant is set in one of the most beautiful parts of the Lake District. The five-course set dinner is served in a small and intimate dining room. The menu changes daily and only local produce is used. Eight rooms are available for accommodation.

SILVERDALE Wolf House Gallery

Lindeth Rd, Silverdale, Lancashire, LA5 0TX **Tel** *01524 701405*

Set within a discerning arts and crafts gallery, in lovely limestone countryside overlooking Morecambe Bay, this friendly café, which is open during the day, has home-made soups, tasty snacks and a tempting range of home baking. On Friday and Saturday evenings, it offers an unusual venue for fine dining, but bring your own wine.

Key to Price Guide *see p608* **Key to Symbols** *see back cover flap*

TROUTBECK Queens Head

Queen's Head, Troutbeck, Windermere, Cumbria, LA23 1PW **Tel** *01539 432174*

Flag floors, oak beams and an Elizabethan four-poster bar are some of the timeless features of this 17th-century inn. The atmosphere is homely, and the food traditional. Try the roast loin of venison with redcurrant and red wine *jus*. While there is a good choice of wines, it is a great place to taste local ales such as Coniston Bluebird and Jennings.

ULLSWATER Sharrow Bay Country House Hotel

Lake Ullswater, Penrith, Cumbria, CA10 2LZ **Tel** *01768 486301*

Traditional country house, superbly located in its vast grounds beside idyllic Ullswater. Sample Michelin-starred cuisine from a six-course menu that has evolved over time, but where time-honoured favourites such as Stilton, onion and spinach soufflé or fillet of salmon with lemon and martini sauce make regular appearances.

ULVERSTON The Bay Horse Hotel

The Bay Horse Hotel, Canal Foot, Ulverston, Cumbria, LA12 9EL **Tel** *01229 583972*

An 18th-century inn, once serving coaches crossing the Morecambe Bay sands. This comfortable, family-run hotel and restaurant on the banks of Leven enjoys outstanding views of both the Cumbrian and Lancashire fells. The menu is equally superb and draws on fresh local ingredients such as shrimps, wild salmon and salt marsh lamb.

WATERMILLOCK Macdonald Leeming House

Leeming House, Watermillock, Ullswater, nr Penrith, Cumbria, CA11 0JJ **Tel** *01768 486622*

Beautifully positioned above the shores of Ullswater, this splendid early 19th-century country house, set within extensive grounds, retains the charm of its past. The elegance of its setting is matched by the simple perfection of the dishes, whether it be an informal lunch in the conservatory or full evening dinner in the Regency Restaurant.

WATERMILLOCK The Rampsbeck Country House Hotel

Watermillock, Ullswater, Cumbria, CA11 0LP **Tel** *01768 486442*

Fantastic views and fine dining are some of the highlights of this 18th-century country house, located on the shores of Ullswater, in one of the most picturesque corners of the Lake District. Imaginative dishes, using regional delicacies such as wild salmon, rabbit, Cumbrian ham and local lamb, are served in stylish surroundings.

WHITEWELL Inn at Whitewell

Whitewell, Forest of Bowland, Clitheroe, Lancashire, BB7 3AT **Tel** *01200 448222*

Dating back to the 15th century, this remote inn originally provided a welcome rest to travellers passing through the wilds of the Trough of Bowland, on their way to Lancaster. The stunning location is matched by the cooking of chef Jamie Cadman, whose contemporary style of British cooking incorporates many seasonal local specialities.

WINDERMERE Miller Howe

Rayrigg Rd, Windermere, Cumbria, LA23 1EY **Tel** *01539 442536*

A delightful restaurant that serves fine gourmet food in striking surroundings. Try the chef's set evening menu, which includes recommendations from the extensive wine list, or replace any course with the à la carte alternatives. Also offers a range of imaginative vegetarian options.

WINDERMERE Holbeck Ghyll Country House Hotel

Holbeck Lane, Windermere, Cumbria, LA23 1LU **Tel** *01539 432375*

Set in a 19th-century hunting lodge, this intimate, Michelin-star restaurant has fantastic views across Lake Windermere. Serves tasty English cuisine, which reflects just a hint of France. The set dinner offers a tempting range of choices at each course, such as scallops or langoustine followed by beef, pigeon or venison, with a rich port-based sauce.

WINSTER Low Sizergh Barn

Alison Park, Low Sizergh Farm, Sizergh, Kendal, Cumbria, LA8 8AE **Tel** *01539 560426*

Organic milk, cheese and eggs from the family-run farm are among the ingredients used in this unique tea room. Open throughout the day for snacks, lunch and tea. Part of a craft and farm produce shop, in a converted Westmorland slate barn, this eatery overlooks the milking parlour. Watch the cows being brought in for afternoon milking.

WRIGHTINGTON BAR The Mulberry Tree

9 Wood Lane, Wrightington Bar, Standish, Wigan, Lancashire, WN6 9SE **Tel** *01257 451400*

Just five years old, the restaurant of this former local pub has already earned an enviable reputation for imaginative cuisine. French influences add an unexpected twist to typically English dishes. Try the entrée of black pudding topped with a poached egg and hollandaise sauce, followed by roast loin of cod on a saffron and spring pea risotto.

YORKSHIRE AND THE HUMBER REGION

ASENBY Crab and Lobster

Crab Manor, Dishforth Rd, Asenby, Thirsk, North Yorkshire, YO7 3QL **Tel** *01845 577286*

Step back into time at this charming seafood eatery, decorated with antiques and artifacts. The chef's signature dish is lobster Thermidor, but the fish-and-chips is equally good. Lamb and chicken dishes are also featured on the menu. Located in the quiet countryside of the Vale of York and not far from Ripon. Jazz music on Sunday evenings.

BOLTON ABBEY Devonshire Arms Brasserie £££

The Devonshire Arms Country House Hotel, Bolton Abbey, Skipton, North Yorkshire, BD23 6AJ **Tel** *01756 710710*

Fringing the Yorkshire Dales and close to Bolton Priory, this characterful coaching inn has been in the family of the Duke and Duchess of Devonshire since 1753. The setting here is informal and relaxed, and the cuisine is a blend of modern British and French. Most of the dishes are available as either starters or main courses.

BOROUGHBRIDGE thediningroom £££

20 St James Square, Boroughbridge, North Yorkshire, YO51 9AR **Tel** *01423 326426*

Overlooking the Georgian square of a small market town, this cosy and friendly eating place is highly popular with the locals. Fish features prominently on the menu, which offers dishes best described as modern English. Everything is home-made and locally sourced where possible, and there is a good selection of wines and champagne.

BURNSALL The Devonshire Fell Hotel and Bistro £££

Burnsall, Skipton, North Yorkshire, BD23 6BT **Tel** *01756 729000*

Originally a club for 19th-century gentlemen mill owners, this hotel and restaurant is situated on a hillside, and offers spectacular views over Wharfedale. Recently refurbished, the hotel's interior is striking as well. A bright and colourful bar leads to an inviting dining room. The menu is simple, but innovative, with seafood, poultry and game.

EAST WITTON The Blue Lion £££

E Witton, nr Leyburn, North Yorkshire, DL8 4SN **Tel** *01969 624273*

Former coaching inn full of character, on the edge of the Yorkshire Dales and not far from Jervaulx Abbey. The home-prepared food, available both in the bar and restaurant, ranges from traditional hearty dishes, such as steak and kidney pudding, to more exotic creations reflecting Asian influences. Extensive wine list and hand-drawn beers.

ELLAND La Cachette ££

31 Huddersfield Rd, Elland, West Yorkshire, HX5 9AW **Tel** *01422 378833*

A busy and highly popular brasserie-style restaurant serving modern British food in a Mediterranean ambience. Fish features prominently on the menu, and there is a good choice of daily specials as well. The light, two-course lunch is of great value and the three-course dinner includes a half bottle of wine.

FERRENSBY The General Tarleton Inn £££

Boroughbridge Rd, Ferrensby, nr Knaresborough, North Yorkshire, HG5 0PZ **Tel** *01423 340284*

Named after a British general in the American War of Independence, this former, 18th-century coaching inn is renowned for its excellent fish dishes such as royal scallops or lung fish wrapped in Parma ham. Although the wine list is extensive, real ale fans can opt for a pint of Black Sheep or Timothy Taylor's, two of the best beers in the area.

HALIFAX Design House ££

Dean Clough (Gate 5), Halifax, West Yorkshire, HX3 5AX **Tel** *01422 383242*

A stylishly modern restaurant set within a former mill, which has found a new lease of life as the Dean Clough Arts and Business Complex. There is a distinct Mediterranean feel to the place. Tapas and lighter meals are popular during the day. The three-course set menu is of excellent value, while in the evening, there is full à la carte.

HAROME The Star Inn ££££

Harome, nr Helmsley, North Yorkshire, YO62 5JE **Tel** *01439 770397*

This attractive, 14th-century thatched inn exudes rustic charm, with original cow byres and a dormitory formerly used by travelling monks. The intimate, award-winning restaurant serves traditional British fare, and is justifiably popular. Advance reservations are recommended. The same menu is served in the bar.

HARROGATE Drum and Monkey ££

5 Montpellier Gardens, Harrogate, North Yorkshire, HG1 2TF **Tel** *01423 502650*

Elegant, but unpretentious, the old world ambience of this superb fish and seafood restaurant reflects the traditional character of the famous spa town of Harrogate. Dine in either the bar or the restaurant above. Dishes such as queen scallops with cheese and garlic butter, fisherman's pie and the shellfish platter are popular choices.

HAWORTH Weaver's ££

15–17 W Lane, Haworth, West Yorkshire, BD22 8DU **Tel** *01535 643822*

This long-established restaurant is set within three 17th-century weaver's cottages that once incorporated a café frequented by the Brontës. Flagged floors, bric-à-brac, low lighting and intimate alcoves in the dining room add to the atmosphere. Northern regional cooking is the hallmark, a popular choice being the Whitby fisherman's pie.

HETTON Angel Inn ££££

Hetton, Skipton, North Yorkshire, BD23 6LT **Tel** *01756 730263*

About 500 years old, this traditional inn once served cattle drovers. Wooden beams, nooks and crannies and log fires re-create the atmosphere of a bygone era. Dine in either the elegant restaurant or the more informal bar-brasserie. The separate menus offer a range of interesting dishes, including a choice of vegetarian and gluten-free options.

HUSTHWAITE The Roasted Pepper ££

Low St, Husthwaite, North Yorkshire, YO61 4QA **Tel** *01347 868007*

This former village pub has been transformed into a contemporary Mediterranean-style restaurant and tapas bar. Features an outside terrace, perfect for al fresco dining on sunny days or balmy evenings. There is an exciting à la carte menu or, for more informal meals, choose from the speciality sandwiches and salad bowls or the tapas.

Key to Price Guide *see p608* **Key to Symbols** *see back cover flap*

ILKLEY Box Tree

*35–37 Church St, Ilkley, West Yorkshire, LS29 9DR **Tel** 01943 608484*

Enjoy fine dining in the luxurious setting of one of Ilkley's oldest buildings. Awarded a Michelin star, the cuisine is modern French and draws upon the best of local and regional produce. The menu changes constantly, but dishes such as the hand-dived scallops served with white truffle oil are highly recommended.

LEEDS The Calls Grill

*36–38 The Calls, Calls Landing, Leeds, West Yorkshire, LS2 7EW **Tel** 0113 245 3870*

This former warehouse, overlooking River Aire, features girders, exposed brick and modern art on the walls – all creating a relaxed and unpretentious setting. The restaurant is renowned for steaks, brought to table on a sizzling skillet. Seafood dishes, such as a skewer of mixed fish, are also popular.

LEEDS Anthony's Restaurant

*19 Boar Lane, Leeds, West Yorkshire, LS1 6EA **Tel** 0113 245 5922*

Close to the station, passers-by would be surprised to find a restaurant of such gastronomic ambition among the everyday shops and bars. Complex constructions and compelling flavour juxtapositions are what to expect: duck neck, for instance, is filled with foie gras, accompanied by a deep-fried duck egg, some potato, a sharp dressing and a scattering of purple cress.

OSMOTHERLEY Golden Lion

*6 W End, Osmotherley, North Yorkshire, DL6 3AA **Tel** 01609 883526*

Traditional country pub in a picturesque village of 17th-century stone cottages. Serves as a starting point for the Lyke Wake Walk, and is close to Mount Grace Priory. Very popular with hill walkers, the pub offers well cooked, wholesome food using fresh local produce. The steak and kidney pie and tasty casseroles are firm favourites.

RAMSGILL IN NIDDERDALE The Yorke Arms

*Ramsgill-in-Nidderdale, Pateley Bridge, nr Harrogate, North Yorkshire, HG3 5RL **Tel** 01423 755243*

Acclaimed chef Frances Atkins is one of only four female chefs in the country to gain the coveted Michelin star. Her creative dishes in the modern British style are superb, using seasonal meats, fish and game in unusual combinations. Discreet service in the relaxing ambience of this 17th-century shooting lodge makes dining here a real pleasure.

RIDGEWAY The Old Vicarage

*Ridgeway Moor, Ridgeway Village, Sheffield, South Yorkshire, S12 3XW **Tel** 0114 247 5814*

Michelin-starred restaurant set within a Victorian vicarage. Welcoming winter log fires and an attractive garden terrace for apéritifs on balmy evenings are some of the attractions here. Produce from the kitchen garden and seasonal delicacies, often combined with unexpected ingredients, are at the heart of the inventive dishes on offer.

RIPLEY The Boar's Head Hotel

*Ripley, Harrogate, North Yorkshire, HG3 3AY **Tel** 01423 771888*

A former coaching inn beside the castle, in the heart of a charming estate village. The menus are nothing short of inspirational, whether you dine in the elegant restaurant or the more casual and informal setting of the bistro. Seasonal fish, meat and game feature prominently on the menu.

SHEFFIELD Baldwins Omega

*Brincliffe Hill, Psalter Lane, Sheffield, S11 9DF **Tel** 0114 255 1818*

This restaurant, family owned for the past 25 years, offers simple lunches through to a real banqueting experience. A reputation for fine cuisine has been built on excellent food combined with impeccable service. Menus offer both traditional and modern English styles.

SHEFFIELD Greenhead House

*84 Burncross Rd, Chapeltown, Sheffield, South Yorkshire, S35 1SF **Tel** 0114 246 9004*

Set within a 17th-century house to the north of Sheffield. Features a delightful walled garden, a comfortable lounge warmed by open fires and an intimate dining room that creates a distinctively homely feel. The husband and wife team offer carefully prepared dishes in an all-inclusive meal, supported by a comprehensive selection of wines.

SOWERBY BRIDGE The Millbank

*Mill Bank Rd, Mill Bank, Sowerby Bridge, West Yorkshire, HX6 3DY **Tel** 01422 825588*

This country pub lies in a small Pennine village, not far from the bustling towns of Halifax and Hebden Bridge. Bare floors and chunky furniture create a contemporary feel, while the garden offers a splendid view along the valley. Serves traditional food with a modern twist. An unusual feature of the bar is its gin list.

STOKESLEY Chapter's

*27 High St, Stokesley, Middlesborough, North Yorkshire, TS9 5AD **Tel** 01642 711888*

Set in a recently refurbished and characterful Grade II listed building, this stylish eatery overlooks Stokesley's market square, below the northern escarpment of the Cleveland Hills. Dine in the gourmet restaurant or the more casual brasserie bar. Serves a variety of seafood, game and poultry dishes.

SUTTON ON THE FOREST The Rose and Crown Inn

*Main St, Sutton-on-the-Forest, North Yorkshire, YO61 1DP **Tel** 01347 811333*

Informal dining in this village inn restaurant, which specializes in fish dishes presented in a classic brasserie style. Surrounded by pleasant gardens and set in the rural heart of Yorkshire, it is well placed between the attractive centres of Helmsley and York, and surrounded by a wealth of stately homes and abbeys.

WATH-IN-NIDDERDALE The Sportsman's Arms
Wath-in-Nidderdale, Pateley Bridge, Harrogate, North Yorkshire, HG3 5PP **Tel** *01423 711306*

Set within an old farmhouse and converted barn, this characterful inn emanates the charm of a former age. The food, served in a comfortable room, is cooked with a French influence, and includes fresh, seasonal fish and seafood brought from Whitby. Steaks, lamb, duck and guinea fowl also appear on the menu.

WHITBY Magpie Café
14 Pier Rd, Whitby, North Yorkshire, YO21 3PU **Tel** *01947 602058*

Looking out across the historic port towards St Mary's Church and the abbey, this distinctive black-and-white, former merchant's house became a café in the 1930s. Specialities revolve around seafood and fish-and-chips, of which there are some eight different varieties. However, there is also a wide selection of other dishes too.

YORK Melton's Too
25 Walmgate, York, North Yorkshire, YO1 9TX **Tel** *01904 629222*

Located in a former saddler's, this open plan bistro retains many original features, but has a distinctively modern feel. While losing nothing of the original Melton's dedication to good cooking, this place has a more informal appeal; an ideal venue whether you want just a light bite or a full dinner. The bar has a good range of speciality beers.

YORK The Blue Bicycle Restaurant
34 Fossgate, York, North Yorkshire, YO1 9TA **Tel** *01904 673990*

Seafood and modern European dishes are the specialities at this atmospheric restaurant. Situated beside River Foss, in a building that housed a 19th-century brothel, it still retains some of the original booths in the cellar. A guitarist provides an added attraction on Saturday evenings.

NORTHUMBRIA

AYCLIFFE The County
13 The Green, Aycliffe, Darlington, County Durham, DL5 6LX **Tel** *01325 312273*

Overlooking Aycliffe village green, the County is a historic building with a contemporary interior. The relaxed setting extends to the menu, you can combine dishes to get exactly what you want. The food is simply cooked and focuses on traditional and modern British cuisine. The wines are from the New World and there's a good range of real ales.

CARTERWAY HEADS The Manor House Inn
Carterway Heads, Shotley Bridge, Northumberland, DH8 9LX **Tel** *01207 255268*

Located in isolation, this 18th-century inn has stunning views across the open moors. Dine in a quiet, relaxed atmosphere, either in the restaurant or more informally at the bar, which is popular with walkers and cyclists. The home-made food is good and a small shop sells some of the chutneys, jams and ready meals on the menu.

CORBRIDGE The Angel of Corbridge
1 Main St, Corbridge, Northumberland, NE45 5LA **Tel** *01434 632119*

Known for its discerning shops, Corbridge is an attractive stop-over. The Angel, a former coaching inn and one of the oldest buildings in town, prides itself on good food and excellent service. Traditional dishes, often with an unusual tweak, appear on the constantly changing menu and are served in both the bar and dining room.

DURHAM Bistro 21
Aykley Heads House, Aykley Heads, Durham, County Durham, DH1 5TS **Tel** *0191 384 4354*

Set within an early 18th-century building, originally a farmhouse, this popular bistro retains a distinct bucolic feel and, in summer, tables appear in the courtyard for al fresco dining. The cuisine is modern British with overtones of the Mediterranean and there's an ever-changing list of special dishes exploiting seasonal fresh produce.

GATESHEAD Eslington Villa Hotel
8 Station Rd, Low Fell, Gateshead, Tyne and Wear, NE9 6DR **Tel** *0191 487 6017*

This stunning 19th-century house combines the charm of an earlier age with modern creativity and offers dining in the comfortable restaurant or the less formal setting of the conservatory. The award-winning kitchen team are passionate about food and conceive eclectic menus featuring the best in contemporary and original cuisine.

GATESHEAD McCoys Rooftop Restaurant
BALTIC Centre for Contemporary Arts, South Shore Road, Gateshead, Tyne and Wear, NE8 3BA **Tel** *0191 440 4949*

Innovative development has transformed the quayside warehouses of the former Baltic Flour Mill into a vibrant centre for contemporary art. Above it all is McCoys Rooftop Restaurant, offering guests a spectacular view across the city skyline. The cuisine is equally impressive and modern in style, served in the best traditions of fine dining.

GREAT WHITTINGTON Queens Head Inn
Great Whittington, Corbridge, Tynedale, Newcastle upon Tyne, Tyne and Wear, NE19 2HP **Tel** *01434 672267*

A welcoming early 17th-century village coaching inn not far from Hadrian's Wall. The very comfortable restaurant serves a bistro-style menu of freshly prepared tempting dishes featuring local meat, game and fish from the coast. There's a well-devised wine list and extensive range of malt whiskies as well as several fine ales at the bar.

Key to Price Guide *see p608* **Key to Symbols** *see back cover flap*

HAYDON BRIDGE General Havelock Inn ££

9 Ratcliffe Rd, Haydon Bridge, Hexham, Northumberland, NE47 6ER **Tel** *01434 684376*

Named after a famous general who helped put down the Indian Mutiny, this former roadside inn enjoys a delightful setting beside the river. Ingredients are sourced locally as much as possible, the dishes reflecting whatever is in season. One of the chef's signature dishes is Cullen Skink, a rich broth based around smoked haddock.

HEXHAM Valley Connection 301 ££

Market Place, Hexham, Northumberland, NE46 3NX **Tel** *01434 601234*

This Bangladeshi restaurant enjoys a pretty location off the main street beside Hexham Abbey. Unique dishes include Mr Daraz's very own *bhuna gosht* (stir-fired lamb) and *bongo po curry*, created around king prawns from the Bay of Bengal. The winner is *shat kora*, flavoured with a variety of lemon found in the valley of Sylhet in Bangladesh.

HUTTON MAGNA The Oak Tree Inn £££

Hutton Magna, Durham, County Durham, DL11 7HH **Tel** *01833 627371*

Unassuming Oak Tree Inn is local favourite and a real gem. The chef at this restaurant hails from the Savoy, bringing imaginative fine cuisine to the informality of an 18th-century village pub. A warm salad of crispy pork belly with black pudding precedes royal sea bream with wild mushroom and asparagus noodles. Booking is essential.

MATFEN Matfen Hall Country House Hotel £££

Matfen, Northumberland, NE20 0RH **Tel** *01661 886500*

This beautifully restored 19th-century country mansion, set within its own extensive grounds, offers a dining experience to remember. Both the library and smaller print room provide a truly atmospheric candlelit setting for an intimate meal. The food is superb and the service is discreet, but attentive.

NEWCASTLE Blackfriars Restaurant ££

Friars St, Newcastle upon Tyne, Tyne and Wear, NE1 4XN **Tel** *0191 261 5945*

Housed within a medieval Dominican monks' refectory, this restaurant is perhaps the oldest dining room still in use in the country. The atmospheric courtyard lends itself to al fresco dining in summer. The style of cooking is modern British using locally sourced and organic produce. AA rosette awarded.

NEWCASTLE Charley's Bar-Bistro ££

2–6 Shakespeare St, Newcastle upon Tyne, Tyne and Wear, NE1 6AQ **Tel** *0191 261 8177*

This basement, built as a bank vault, provides an unusual venue for a meal. The unpretentious decor, however, lends a comfortable and welcoming complexion to the setting. The dishes are often cosmopolitan and might include mixed shellfish served with a saffron risotto or Aberdeen-Angus *au poivre* with fondant potatoes and mushroom *jus*.

NEWCASTLE Fisherman's Lodge £££££

Jesmond Dene, Jesmond, Newcastle upon Tyne, Tyne and Wear, NE7 7BQ **Tel** *0191 281 3281*

Close to the city centre, but lying in the secluded wooded valley of Jesmond Dene, Fisherman's Lodge has earned an outstanding reputation for its fine dining. Seafood dishes are the particular speciality, but local meat and game also feature prominently on the menu. Exotic deserts and a carefully selected cheese board round off the meal.

PONTELAND Café Lowrey £££

33–35 The Broadway, Darras Hall Estate, Tyne and Wear, NE20 9PW **Tel** *01661 820357*

Recently renamed when the chef took over ownership, Café Lowrey offers bistro-style dining with a distinct French influence to the food. The service is friendly and the atmosphere relaxed, though there's generally a lively buzz to the place at the weekend. However, go mid-week when there's usually a quiet corner to be had.

REDWORTH Paramount Redworth Hall Hotel £££

Redworth, Bishop Auckland, Darlington, County Durham, DL5 6NL **Tel** *01388 770600*

Built in 1693 as a private house, Redworth Hall retains many of its original features and stands in 25 acres of beautifully kept grounds. The elegant 1744 dining room, named after the year in which it was added, offers fine dining in luxurious surroundings. For a less formal meal, opt for the conservatory overlooking the gardens.

ROMALDKIRK The Rose and Crown Inn £££

Romaldkirk, Barnard Castle, County Durham, DL12 9EB **Tel** *01833 650213*

This traditional stone-built coaching inn dates from the 18th century and stands on the green beside the church in the heart of a North Yorkshire village. Dine in style in the oak-panelled restaurant at tables bedecked in crisp white linen or choose the more rustic setting of the brasserie, perhaps selecting only one or two courses as you please.

TYNEMOUTH Sidney's Restaurant ££

3–5 Percy Park Rd, Tynemouth, Tyne and Wear, NE30 4LZ **Tel** *0191 257 8500*

A vibrant modern decor and constantly changing artwork set the scene for this bustling place. The kitchen team use the best fresh produce, meticulously creating an interesting variety of modern dishes, often European, but with underlying themes from across the globe. A variety of creative fish and vegetarian options give balance to the menu.

YARM Chadwick's £££

104B Yarm High St, Yarm, Stockton-on-Tees, County Durham, TS15 9AU **Tel** *01642 788558*

The attractive town of Yarm, surrounded by the snaking River Tees, is home to this bustling restaurant on the high street. The distinctly continental lunch offers lighter meals and snacks including pizzas and pasta. The evening menu is more formal, with a good range of specials and some interesting creations. Great service by the enthusiastic staff.

NORTH WALES

ABERDOVEY Penhelig Arms £££££
Aberdyfi, Gwynedd, LL35 0LT **Tel** *01654 767215*

Friendly restaurant with panoramic views, the Penhelig Arms has an award-winning wine list to accompany its fresh brasserie-like cuisine. The set menu begins with a glass of champagne with different wines (by the glass) recommended for each of the à la carte choices. Locally-reared meats make a good showing on the menu.

ABERSOCH Porth Tocyn Country Hotel £££££
Abersoch, Gwynedd, LL53 7BU **Tel** *01758 713303*

Panoramic hotel restaurant Porth Tocyn has appeared in good food guides for over 40 years. There's a choice between a four- and two-course evening menu. Ask for a table at the "picture window" for the best views over the peninsula. Tables in the garden for informal lunchtime dining.

BARMOUTH The Bistro ££
Church St, Barmouth, Gwynedd, LL42 1EW **Tel** *01341 281009*

Small restaurant recommended by *Les Routiers*, the Bistro uses locally-produced ingredients to create its award-winning range of seasonal dishes. The menu lays stress on the Welsh lamb and beef, but there's also a good choice of fish and excellent vegetarian choices. Booking is advised.

BEAUMARIS Ye Olde Bull's Head Inn £££££
Castle St, Beaumaris, Isle of Anglesey, LL58 8AP **Tel** *01248 810329*

Locally known as "the Bull", this restaurant-with-rooms is based in the centre of town. An ancient coaching inn, built in 1472, the building provides an elegant setting for the main restaurant in its oldest part. There's also a less formal brasserie and a popular bar.

CAERNARFON The Prince's Brasserie ££
The Prince of Wales Hotel, Bangor St, Caernarfon, Gwynedd, LL55 1AR **Tel** *01286 673367*

Restaurant in Caernarfon's Prince of Wales Hotel, The Prince's Brasserie provides a good range of home-cooked meals. The steaks are renowned, and equally good are the vegetable dishes. You can get anything from home-made paté (with peach and pineapple chutney) to liver and bacon casserole.

CAERNARFON Plas Dinas Country House Hotel & Restaurant £££
Bontnewydd, Caernarfon, Gwynedd, LL54 7YF **Tel** *01286 830214*

Elegant restaurant in a welcoming country-house hotel, Plas Dinas enjoys one of the most ambitious menus in the area. Where else can you order stuffed avocado mousse with a cucumber salsa, followed by fillet of prime Welsh beef on a slice of black pudding? A popular venue for wedding receptions.

CAPEL COCH Tre-Ysgawen Hall £££
Capel Coch, Llangefni, Isle of Anglesey, LL77 7UR **Tel** *01248 750750*

Hotel and spa with seasonal menu and excellent accompanying wine list, Tre-Ysgawen Hall has a delicious evening menu. The chef provides vegetarian and low-calorie fare on request. Residents have use of a gym and a golf course, available to help burn off the calories. There's also an atmospheric bar.

COLWYN BAY Stars Café Bar & Restaurant ££
124 Abergele Road, Colwyn Bay, Conwy, LL29 7PS **Tel** *01492 531555*

A café-bar-style restaurant in the heart of Colwyn Bay, Stars Café serves modern European fare. The locally-sourced produce is put to effective use, and breakfast, light lunch and full evening meals are served. A range of desserts are available. Good for families.

DOLGARROG The Lord Newborough ££
Dolgarrog, Conwy, LL32 8JX **Tel** *01492 660549*

Recently renovated and under a new ownership, the Lord Newborough prides itself on its simple, but tasty cuisine and friendly dining atmosphere. Using the best of Snowdonia's ingredients, the menu features Welsh lamb shank, Conwy Valley steak pie, Welsh potato bake (with leeks) and a delicious cheese board.

DOLGELLAU Bwyty Dylanwad Da £££
2 Ffos-y-felin, Dolgellau, Gwynedd, LL40 1BS **Tel** *01341 422870*

Small friendly café-restaurant with a long and impressive reputation, Bwyty Dylanwad Da also offers one of the best cappuccinos in town. Menu features traditional dishes such as faggot with spiced apple sauce, Welsh beef steak and Welsh honey and almond ice cream.

EWLOE Fountains Restaurant £££
St David's Park Hotel, Ewloe, nr Chester, Flintshire, CH5 3YB **Tel** *01244 520800*

Elegant Fountains is an award-winning restaurant in a four-star hotel on the Welsh border. It offers a delicious seasonal menu, an informal carvery perfect for family dining, and a tasty range of bar snacks. The classy surroundings create an ideal ambience to enjoy the superb food accompanied by an exceptional choice of wines.

Key to Price Guide *see p608* **Key to Symbols** *see back cover flap*

HARLECH Castle Cottage

Y Llech, Harlech, Gwynedd, LL46 2YL Tel 01766 780479

The award-winning restaurant at the Castle Cottage is a popular destination for locals and visitors alike. The seasonal menu features locally-caught lobster, sea bass and black bream, and there is also venison from the Brecon Beacons National Park. Recently voted one of the top 100 restaurants in Wales.

LLANBERIS The Gwynedd Hotel & Restaurant

Llanberis, Snowdonia, Gwynedd, LL55 4SU Tel 01286 870203

Fabulously situated at the foot of Mount Snowdon, this restaurant prides itself on the varied menu of local and seasonal cuisine. The owners, Mark and Dita Bartlett, pay meticulous attention to every detail. Dinner and lunch come complete with sightseeing information.

LLANDRILLO Tyddyn Llan

Llandrillo, nr Corwen, Denbighshire, LL21 0ST Tel 01490 440264

The rural location of this restaurant-with-rooms makes it the perfect stopping-off point after a hearty walk in the countryside. Set in a small elegant Georgian house, it is famed for the award-wining cuisine by owner Brian Webb. The imaginative menu, featuring local lamb and beef, justifies its reputation as one of Wales's finest restaurants.

LLANGOLLEN Greenbank Hotel and Restaurant

Victoria Square, Llangollen, Denbighshire, LL20 8EU Tel 01978 861835

Informal restaurant in a heritage building, Green Bank is a preferred family destination. Children can enjoy fish fingers with baked beans, while their parents dine on venison sausage with parsnip, carrot and potato mash or pan-fried steak on black pudding, paté and Brie.

LLANSANFFRAID GLAN CONWY Old Rectory Country House Restaurant

Llansanffraid Glan Conwy, nr Conwy, LL28 5LF Tel 01492 580611

Small hotel and restaurant, the Old Rectory has fantastic views over a nearby Royal Society for the Protection of Birds reserve. The restaurant offers outstanding seasonal cuisine under Master Chef Wendy Vaughan. Locally-caught turbot, bass, brill and Conwy salmon share a menu with Welsh mountain lamb, sausages and game.

NORTHOP Stables Bar Restaurant

Soughton Hall, Northop, Flintshire, CH7 6AB Tel 01352 840811

Part of the luxurious Soughton Hall Hotel, Stables Bar Restaurant offers a truly atmospheric setting with open fires, cobbled floors and timber-roofs. The menu features modern British cuisine. Evening dinner is served in the hayloft and the accompanying wine is chosen from the extensive restaurant cellars.

PENMAENPOOL Penmaenuchaf Hall

Penmaenpool, Dolgellau, Gwynedd, LL40 1YB Tel 01341 422129

The reputation of Penmaenuchaf Hall rests on its award winning cuisine. Modern British cooking, thoughtfully kept simple and light, is served in the elegant dining room with fine linen, silver cutlery and crystal wine glasses. Welsh beef and lamb make a good showing. A Celtic cheese board is also available.

PORTMEIRION Hotel Portmeirion

Off A487, Portmeirion, Gwynedd, LL48 6ET Tel 01766 770228

Designed by Clough Williams-Ellis in 1931, the formal hotel dining room has fabulous views overlooking the estuary. The modern Welsh menu uses the best of local Welsh produce. Castell Deudraeth Bar & Grill, another restaurant on the premises, specializes in fresh seafood, while the Town Hall Restaurant serves well-cooked meals and snacks.

PWLLHELI Plas Bodegroes

Nefyn Rd, Pwllheli, Gwynedd, LL53 5TH Tel 01758 612363

One of Wales's most well-known restaurants, Michelin-starred Plas Bodegroes may be pricey, but it's more than worth the expense. Locally-reared meat, fish and freshly-caught game make for a great menu, but the desserts are the main draw. Try the heart-shaped cinnamon biscuit of rhubarb and apple with elderflower custard.

RHOS-ON-SEA Forte's Restaurant

Penrhyn Avenue, Rhos-on-Sea, Conwy, LL28 4NH Tel 01492 544662

With contemporary decor, Forte's is a perfect lunch venue for families exploring Rhos-on-Sea. It doubles as an ice cream parlour with a delicious range of sundaes, all made with the house ice cream. The restaurant closes at 5:30pm, except during July and August when it remains open in the evening. Breathtaking views of the harbour.

RHYDLYDAN Y Giler Arms

Rhydlydan, nr Betws-y-Coed, Conwy, LL24 0LL Tel 01690 770612

Friendly country pub and hotel with its own fishing lake, the Giler Arms serves a flavourful seasonal menu in its atmospheric bar-restaurant. There's a good range of local ales, including Batham's traditional draught beers. Enjoys stunning views of the lake.

TALSARNAU Maes-y-Neuadd

Talsarnau, Gwynedd, LL47 6YA Tel 01766 780200

Housed in a scenic country house hotel, the restaurant at Maes-y-Neuadd serves an innovative four-course menu. Fresh meats and cheese come from local farms, fish from Cardigan Bay, and fresh vegetables and strawberries from the hotel garden. The courses in the set menus are carefully crafted to maintain harmony.

TAL-Y-BONT Ysgethin Inn

Tal-y-bont, nr Barmouth, Gwynedd, LL43 2AN **Tel** *01341 247578*

Informal family pub in a converted mill house on the banks of the River Ysgethin, the small dining room of this inn serves a mix of simple bar snacks, classic roasts and house specials, such as Ysgethin steak pie. There's an extensive children's menu. Riverside patio and children's adventure playground.

TREMEIRCHION Starters Restaurant

Ffynnon Beuno, Tremeirchion, St Asaph, Denbighshire, LL17 0UE **Tel** *01745 710475*

Cosy restaurant in Ffynnon Beuno Country House Hotel, Starters overlooks a sprawling open garden, including a 6th-century enclosed pool and a prehistoric cave thought to have been inhabited more than 30,000 years ago. It is so called because there are only starters and sweets served here.

SOUTH AND MID-WALES

BRECON Felin Fach Griffin

Felin Fach, Brecon, Powys, LD3 0UB **Tel** *01874 620111*

Award-winning pub with rooms midway between Brecon and Hay-on-Wye, the Felin Fach Griffin has been acclaimed as exceptional by critics. A delicious lunch and supper menu of traditional Welsh cuisine is on offer. Starters include squab pigeon, while mains range from fresh salted cod to Welsh rack of lamb. Great local cheese board.

BRIDGEND Elliot Restaurant

Coed-y-Mwstwr Hotel, Coychurch, Bridgend, CF35 6AF **Tel** *01656 860621*

In a country-house hotel, Coed-y-Mwstwr ("whispering trees"), Elliot Restaurant provides fabulous views over the picturesque Vale of Glamorgan. Daily table d'hôte menu includes Welsh lamb with celeriac dauphinois, medallions of beef with sautéed sweetbreads and venison fillet with wild mushrooms. There's also a family Sunday lunch menu.

BUILTH WELLS The Drawing Room

Twixt Cwmbach and Newbridge-on-Wye, Builth Wells, Powys, LD2 3RT **Tel** *01982 552493*

Five-star restaurant-with-rooms in the heart of Wales, the Drawing Room occupies an elegant Georgian country residence. Its location in the plush Wye Valley provides plenty of delicious seasonal ingredients, including prime Welsh black beef and lamb from local farms.

BUILTH WELLS Tudor Restaurant

Caer Beris Manor Hotel and Restaurant, Builth Wells, Powys, LD2 3NP **Tel** *01982 552601*

Popular restaurant in picturesque Caer Beris Manor Hotel, the Tudor uses the finest local produce to create its award-winning four-course menu. Dishes are seasonal, but Welsh lamb and Welsh black beef always make a good showing. The impressive wine list features over 150 bottles.

CARDIFF The Greendown Inn

Drope Rd, St Georges-Super-Ely, Cardiff, Vale of Glamorgan, CF5 6EP **Tel** *01446 760310*

Friendly inn in a pleasant country setting, the Greendown Inn is just a short drive from the bustling city of Cardiff. The menu showcases simple but well-prepared dishes, and the home-made beef pie is a continual favourite. Well priced for the decent quality of the cuisine.

CARDIFF The Armless Dragon

97 Wyeverne Road, Cathays, Cardiff, CF24 4BG **Tel** *029 2038 2357*

At the Armless Dragon, one of Cardiff's most popular dining venues, contemporary Welsh cuisine is served in a smart, but laid-back setting, The menu is arranged by theme, using local produce from Wales, such as chicken from Monmouthshire, ham from Carmarthen, spider crab from Pembrokeshire and lamb from Brecon.

CARDIFF Benedicto's

4 Windsor Place, Cardiff, CF10 3BX **Tel** *029 2037 1130*

Well-reputed restaurant with an elegant dining room, Benedicto's is best known for its tasty menu of "treasures from the sea". Choose from mixed fish *brodetto* (a selection of fish with saffron and light tomato sauce), *pauppiettes* of sole (stuffed with crab, flavoured with ginger set on a prawn sauce) or fresh lobster.

CARDIFF New House Country Hotel

Thornhill, Cardiff, CF14 9UA **Tel** *029 2052 0280*

The panoramic restaurant at this country-house hotel on the outskirts of Cardiff, is known to blend international flavours with the best local produce from the Vale of Glamorgan. Traditional Sunday lunch menu offers discounts for children. Ask for a table on the patio if you don't want to feel that you are dining at a hotel.

CRICKHOWELL Nantyffin Cider Mill

Brecon Road, Crickhowell, Powys, NP8 1SG **Tel** *01873 810775*

Pretty country restaurant in a converted mill at the base of the Black Mountains, the Nantyffin remains popular with locals and tourists alike. Dining is split between the bar and the white-washed main restaurant. Dishes are a mix of the local (Glanusk pheasant) and the international (parsnip, carrot and cauliflower korma).

Key to Price Guide *see p608* **Key to Symbols** *see back cover flap*

FISHGUARD Diners' Circle

*Tregynon, Gwaun Valley, nr Fishguard, Pembrokeshire, SA659TU **Tel** 01239 820531*

A 14th-century farmhouse restaurant, Diner's Circle has been steadily building itself a reputation since it first opened 25 years ago. All food is made on the premises by the owner, with an emphasis on beef and lamb reared on the nearby land. Only members can book to eat here, but one-night membership is available and well worth it.

HAY-ON-WYE Old Black Lion

*Lion St, Hay-on-Wye, Via Hereford, HR3 5AD **Tel** 01497 820841*

Colourful restaurant in a 17th-century inn, the Old Black Lion is consistently rated one of the UK's top 100 inns. Dating back to the 1300s, the dining room comes complete with exposed timber beams. Menus feature British produce, including seafood from Cornwall and seasonal vegetables and herbs from the hotel's gardens.

HAY-ON-WYE Three Cocks Hotel & Restaurant

*Three Cocks, nr Hay-on-Wye, Brecon, Powys, LD3 0SL **Tel** 01497 847215*

Listed hotel-restaurant on the main Hereford to Brecon road, the Three Cocks serves tasty home-made dishes using the best of local cuisine. The dining room is quiet, but inviting, with stone fireplaces, comfortable chairs and great views over the hotel garden. Booking recommended.

LLANWRTYD WELLS The Lasswade Country House Hotel & Restaurant

*Station Rd, Llanwrtyd Wells, Powys, LD5 4RW **Tel** 01591 610515*

The Lasswade, an Edwardian country-house hotel, is renowned for its fresh and locally sourced, mostly organic, produce. This AA rosette restaurant won the "True Taste of Wales" award, and the Welsh black beef is a speciality. Booking is recommended.

LLANWRTYD WELLS Carlton House

*Llanwrtyd Wells, Powys, LD5 4RA **Tel** 01591 610248*

Restaurant-with-rooms, the Carlton extends a warm welcome and an award-winning menu that uses the best locally-sourced ingredients. The 19th-century dining room has original wood panelling. All-inclusive gourmet breakfasts are on offer and the fantastic desserts include home-made sorbets, lime posset and Welsh cheeses.

MONMOUTH The Stone Mill

*Rockfield, Monmouth, Monmouthshire, NP25 5SW **Tel** 01600 716273*

On the outskirts of the Forest of Dean, picturesque Stone Mill occupies a converted 16th-century barn with oak beams and vaulted ceiling offset by modern furnishings. The menu features the best of British cuisine, including rock oysters from Ireland, dressed crab from Cornwall, English asparagus (in season) and goat's cheese from Wales.

MONMOUTH Bob's

*7 Church St, Monmouth, Monmouthshire, NP25 3BX **Tel** 01600 712600*

Informal restaurant-with-rooms on Monmouth's main shopping street, Bob's serves a mix of traditional Welsh fare, such as black pudding on a bed of mash, with innovative international choices that include baked figs in Parma ham with chilli. The light lunch menu is perfect for a break from shopping.

PEMBROKE George Wheeler Restaurant

*Old Kings Arms Hotel, Main St, Pembroke, Pembrokeshire, SA71 4JS **Tel** 01646 683611*

Award-winning restaurant in Pembrokeshire's oldest hotel, George Wheeler showcases the best of Wales's local produce, especially fish, sourced daily from Milford Haven. Traditional dishes, such as hot Welsh cockles with laver bread and bacon, sit neatly alongside more modern fare, such as the ever-popular king prawns with garlic butter.

SKENFRITH The Bell at Skenfrith

*Skenfrith, Monmouthshire, NP7 8UH **Tel** 01600 750235*

Renovated 17th-century coaching inn with guestrooms, the Bell is well worth the short drive out of Monmouth. The restaurant menu here ties in with the farmer's market at nearby Abergavenny. Welsh beef, lamb and wild mushrooms popularly feature on the menu.

SOLVA The Old Pharmacy

*5 Main St, Solva, Pembrokeshire, SA62 6UU **Tel** 01437 720005*

Formerly a chemist shop, this quaint little restaurant in the harbour village of Lower Solva specializes in local fish and seafood. The menu's star attraction is the bouillabaisse with freshly baked olive oil bread. The Solva lobster and crab, and Welsh organic beef and lamb are good too. There's a charming riverside patio. Children's menu available.

ST DAVIDS Morgan's Restaurant

*20 Nun St, St Davids, Pembrokeshire, SA62 6NT **Tel** 01437 720508*

Since it re-opened in April 2004, Morgan's Brasserie has gone from strength to strength. The menu is well priced with some innovative combinations, including monkfish medallions with mushrooms and laver bread sauce, and rack of lamb with Welsh honey and stem ginger. Save some room for the home-made desserts.

ST DAVIDS Warpool Court Hotel

*St Davids, Pembrokeshire, SA62 6BN **Tel** 01437 720300*

Hotel-restaurant with enviable views over St Davids peninsula, the Warpool Court boasts a delicious menu of modern British fare. Roast venison saddle comes with venison faggot and cassis *jus*, while the roast corn-fed chicken breast is laid on a bed of Parmesan, chorizo and spinach risotto.

SWANSEA Claudes

93 Newton Rd, Mumbles, Swansea, SA3 4BN **Tel** *01792 366006*

Elegant restaurant with a welcoming ambience, Claudes serves quality cuisine with a reasonable price tag. The eclectic menus offer everything from Welsh black beef to meatballs in a tomato sauce. Booking recommended. Traditional roasts, served on Sundays, include Yorkshire puddings.

SWANSEA Patrick's with Rooms

638 Mumbles Rd, Mumbles, Swansea, SA3 4EA **Tel** *01792 360199*

Fantastic restaurant-with-rooms overlooking the Mumbles, Patrick's caters for everyone: it also has a menu in Braille. The food is delicious with an accompanying wine list. Many of the ingredients used are sourced from the nearby countryside and sea, such as the tasty Gower mussels with leek and laver bread and St Iystydd cheese gratin.

SWANSEA Morgans Restaurant

Somerset Place, Swansea, West Glamorgan, SA1 1RR **Tel** *01792 484848*

Morgans is Swansea's only five-star hotel and it has a fantastic menu to match. The main restaurant serves an elegant range of European dishes with an emphasis on locally-grown produce. Try the melon with Carmarthan ham and noisettes of Welsh lamb with Mediterranean vegetables. You can also visit the less expensive Café Bar.

TALYBONT-ON-USK Usk Inn

Talybont-on-Usk, Brecon, Powys, LD3 7JE **Tel** *01874 676251*

Fabulous country pub with rooms in the heart of the Brecon Beacons National Park, Usk Inn sources its ingredients daily from all over Wales: fresh milk and cheese from Brecon, vegetables from Merthyr, meat from Bwlch. The menu caters for everything from bar snacks to three-course table d'hôte.

USK Three Salmons Hotel

Bridge St, Usk, Monmouthshire, NP15 1RY **Tel** *01291 672133*

Restaurant in a beautifully timbered 17th-century coaching inn, Three Salmons Hotel, in the market town of Usk, serves a carefully crafted menu of fresh, local fare with an Italian twist. The carpaccio of beef and baked salmon with pistachio and Parmesan crust, gives a flavour of what is on offer; however, the menu changes regularly.

WHITEBROOK Crown at Whitebrook

Whitebrook, nr Monmouth, Monmouthshire, NP25 4TX **Tel** *01600 860254*

Elegant restaurant in a charming hotel just outside of Monmouth, Crown at Whitebrook dates back to 1670. Head chef James Sommerin uses local ingredients but classic French training to create a mouthwatering menu, which mixes game with local beef, lamb and fish.

WOLFSCASTLE Wolfscastle Country Hotel

Wolfscastle, Haverfordwest, Pembrokeshire, SA62 5LZ **Tel** *01437 741225*

One of Wales's grandest country-house hotel-restaurants, the Wolfscastle occupies a panoramic old riverside vicarage near to Haverfordwest and Fishguard. The menu is, unsurprisingly, big on fish with salmon, monkfish and halibut making a good showing next to Welsh beef, lamb and duck. Gourmet breaks available.

THE LOWLANDS

ANSTRUTHER The Cellar

24 E Green, Anstruther, Fife, KY10 3AA **Tel** *01333 310378*

Housed in one of Fife's oldest buildings, this cosy, reasonably priced restaurant has lots of character. Award-winning chef Peter Jukes serves excellent seafood cuisine, with fish, crabs, lobsters and scallops playing a prominent role. Uses fresh local produce. Ideal for those looking for an intimate, romantic meal.

AYR Fouters Bistro

2A Academy St, Ayr, Ayrshire, KA7 1HS **Tel** *01292 261391*

A popular, lively bistro in a vaulted basement, located in the town centre, just off the main street. The ambience is warm and welcoming, and the menu offers classical French cuisine, making good use of local Scottish produce. The dishes are skilfully prepared and served in an accomplished, yet informal style.

CUPAR Ostlers Close

25 Bonnygate, Cupar, Fife, KY15 4BU **Tel** *01334 655574*

A cosy, comfortable restaurant serving traditional Scottish cuisine. The menu features a variety of seafood, as well as poultry and seasonal game. Uses fresh local produce. The wild mushrooms are highly recommended. Open for dinner from Tuesday to Saturday; lunch is offered only on Saturday.

DIRLETON The Open Arms

Main St, Dirleton, East Lothian, EH39 5EG **Tel** *01620 850241*

Situated on the edge of the village green, overlooking the 13th-century Dirleton Castle, this popular, family-owned country hotel has a well deserved reputation for good food. Guests can choose between the elegant, formal restaurant or the bright, informal brasserie. The convivial surroundings add to the charm.

Key to Price Guide *see p608* **Key to Symbols** *see back cover flap*

EDINBURGH Susie's Diner

51–53 W Nicolson St, Edinburgh, EH8 9DB **Tel** *0131 667 8729*

A well-established vegetarian café, centrally located near Edinburgh University. The food at this self-service diner has a Mexican and Middle Eastern theme, with an extensive repertoire of dishes that include enchiladas, moussaka and large salads. Follows a "bring your own booze" policy. Relaxed and welcoming atmosphere.

EDINBURGH Daniel's Bistro

88 Commercial St, Leith, Edinburgh, EH3 6SF **Tel** *0131 553 5933*

Located in the city centre, this stylish restaurant serves modern French (Alsacian-style) fare, with a Scottish influence. The ambience is light and airy, and the cooking is of good value and excellent quality. An award-winning bistro with friendly service.

EDINBURGH Hendersons

94 Hanover St, Edinburgh, EH2 1DR **Tel** *0131 225 2131*

Established for more than 40 years, this vegetarian restaurant is an Edinburgh institution. The family-run eatery is open all day, and serves a wide variety of snacks and complete meals. Favourites include chunky vegetable soup, baked lasagne and spring rolls. Also offers gluten-free and dairy-free specialities.

EDINBURGH Indigo Yard

7 Charlotte Lane, Edinburgh, EH2 4QZ **Tel** *0131 220 5603*

Situated in the centre of the city's West End, this highly acclaimed café-restaurant is a popular meeting venue as well. Open all day for coffee, snacks, lunch and dinner, and offers a wide variety of dishes, designed to suit all tastes. The ambience is contemporary, the servings are generous and the service friendly and efficient.

EDINBURGH Waterfront Wine Bar

1c Dock Place, Edinburgh, EH6 6LU **Tel** *0131 554 7427*

One of the best original Leith bar-restaurants, located on the water's edge, and offering a cosy place to relax. Friendly, knowledgeable staff and contemporary dishes ensure a good experience all round. Seafood plays a large part on the menu. The café is extremely popular and usually packed with locals and visitors to the area.

EDINBURGH Le Café St Honore

34 N W Thistle St Lane, Edinburgh, EH2 1EA **Tel** *0131 226 2211*

Located close to the main shopping streets, but in a quiet lane, this traditional French restaurant with a typical Parisian-style interior, is a favourite of many. All produce is of the finest quality, the dishes are imaginative and skilfully cooked and the staff are friendly and helpful.

EDINBURGH The Vintners Rooms Restaurant and Bar

The Vaults, 87 Giles St, Leith, Edinburgh, EH6 6BZ **Tel** *0131 554 6767*

This unusual candlelit restaurant is housed in a wine warehouse, and is one of Leith's more established eateries. Offers imaginative, contemporary Scottish menus. Guests can opt for a light lunch in the wine bar or a complete meal in the restaurant – the standard of food, service and atmosphere is admirable in both.

EDINBURGH Atrium and Blue Bar Café

10 Cambridge St, Edinburgh, EH1 2ED **Tel** *0131 228 8882*

Two restaurants run by consummate professionals. The more formal Atrium is open for lunch and dinner, and offers a fine, contemporary dining experience, while the informal Blue Bar Café is open all day for snacks, coffee, drinks, lunch and dinner. The cuisine is modern British with a Mediterranean twist. Superb quality in both places.

EDINBURGH Restaurant Martin Wishart

54 The Shore, Edinburgh, EH6 6RA **Tel** *0131 553 3577*

Possibly the finest dining experience in all of Scotland. Chef Martin Wishart's creative and innovative cuisine is in great demand by lovers of fine food, and justifiably so. Serves modern French fare, using the best produce available. The service is excellent, the ambience welcoming and the experience truly memorable.

EDINBURGH The Balmoral

The Balmoral Hotel, 1 Princes St, Edinburgh, EH2 2EQ **Tel** *0131 557 6727*

This classy and up-market restaurant is located in The Balmoral Hotel, and has its own entrance on Princes Street. Acclaimed chef Jeff Bland is renowned for his skill, imagination and passion for fine Scottish cuisine. The service at this Michelin-starred and multiple award-winning dining venue is also exceptional.

ELIE Sangster's

51 High St, Elie, Fife, KY9 1BZ **Tel** *01333 331001*

Located in a popular, coastal East Neuk village, this small, fine restaurant is run by one of Scotland's most recognized and skilled chefs, Bruce Sangster. Specialities include twice baked cheese soufflé, slow cooked noisette of lamb and delicious desserts. Closed on Monday, as well as for dinner on Sunday and for lunch on Tuesday and Saturday.

GLASGOW Firebird

1321 Argyle St, nr Museum of Transport, Glasgow **Tel** *0141 334 0594*

A popular bar-restaurant hang-out for drinks and an informal evening meal. All produce is of the freshest and highest quality, and the pizzas are among the best in Glasgow. It can get quite noisy at the weekends; if you like it quieter go during the week instead.

GLASGOW City Merchant

97 Candleriggs, Glasgow, G1 1NP **Tel** *0141 553 1577*

A warm and welcoming, family-run restaurant located in Glasgow's Merchant City. This bustling venue serves excellent seafood cuisine with a Scottish influence and uses the best local produce. The ambience is informal and rustic. Can accommodate more than 120 guests. Offers good value for money.

GLASGOW The Buttery

652 Argyle St, Glasgow, G3 8UF **Tel** *0141 221 8188*

Although located in a less than salubrious part of the city centre, this is one place that is well worth seeking out. This attractive pub has been converted into an elegant dining room, but retains elements of its past. Serves hearty Scottish fare, made from the freshest local produce. Also offers a wide selection of desserts and cheeses.

GLASGOW Brian Maule at Chardon d'Or

176 W Regent St, Glasgow, G2 4RL **Tel** *0141 248 3801*

One of the finest restaurants in the city. Highly acclaimed chef Brian Maule provides an innovative menu of French cuisine, using locally sourced Scottish ingredients. Serves a variety of fish, poultry and game. The stylish, yet unpretentious, ambience and the friendly and efficient staff complete the experience.

GLASGOW Gamba

225A W George St, Glasgow, G2 2ND **Tel** *0141 572 0899*

Popular, seafood restaurant, recognized for its high quality, varied cuisine. The food is meticulously prepared, using fresh seasonal produce such as fish, lobsters and oysters, and beautifully presented. The interior of this city centre eatery is modern, stylish and comfortable, while the ambience is cosy.

GLASGOW Stravaigin

28 Gibson St, Hillhead, Glasgow, G212 8NX **Tel** *0141 334 2665*

Well placed in the popular Gibson Street, in the Glasgow University neighbourhood. Features a popular café-bar and a highly successful restaurant. Serves award-winning pub fare: the best of Scottish produce flavoured with the world's sauces, herbs and spices.

GLASGOW Ubiquitous Chip

12 Ashton Lane, Glasgow, G12 8SJ **Tel** *0141 334 5007*

A Glasgow West-End institution, this prestigious restaurant serves traditional Scottish cuisine, made with fresh local ingredients, and has been a home of culinary excellence for over 30 years. Great atmosphere and a friendly staff make this a notable place.

GULLANE La Potinière

Main St, Gullane, East Lothian, EH31 2AA **Tel** *01620 843214*

Superior restaurant situated in a pretty East Lothian village. The menu changes from season to season, and offers well-prepared food, using fresh local produce. Boasts a caring and hospitable staff, as well as a private parking facility. The restaurant is closed on Monday and Tuesday.

KIPPFORD The Anchor Hotel

Main St, Kippford, Dalbeattie, Kirkudbrightshire, DG5 4LN **Tel** *01556 620205*

This seaside hotel and pub is situated on the waterfront in the pretty village of Kippford, with great views of the coastal activity. The friendly bar serves appetizing pub food, using seasonal, locally sourced produce. A popular spot to enjoy real ale and a filling meal. The hotel is comfortable and of good value.

LARGS Nardinis

The Esplanade, Largs, KA30 8NF, Ayrshire, **Tel** *01475 689313*

A splendid Art Deco interior sets the scene of this seafront lounge café. This well-known Scottish institution is definitely worth a visit if in the area. Breakfasts, cakes and Italian and British dishes are served all day. A perfect place to relax, sit back and read the paper. Extremely popular with both locals and tourists.

LINLITHGOW Champany Inn

Champany, nr Linlithgow, West Lothian, EH49 7LU **Tel** *01506 834532*

Located on the outskirts of Linlithgow, not far from Edinburgh, this charming restaurant has a well-earned reputation for offering some of the best steaks in Scotland. Diners can choose from strip loin, rib eye, fillet and porterhouse; all cooked to perfection. Must-try specialities include delicious Loch Gruinart oysters and succulent hot smoked salmon.

MOFFAT Well View Hotel

Ballplay Rd, Moffat, Dumfriesshire, DG10 9JH **Tel** *01683 220184*

An intimate hotel situated in a quiet residential street, a few minutes walk from the main street. Modern French cooking with some Scottish elements, using the best local produce available, is served in the dining room of this family-run establishment. Presents a peaceful atmosphere and comfortable surroundings.

PORTPATRICK Knockinaam Lodge

Off A77, nr Portpatrick, Dumfries and Galloway, DG9 9AD **Tel** *01776 810471*

This attractive country house has an idyllic location overlooking the sea, and even boasts its own small private beach. Comfort and pampering are top priority at this beautiful and stylish lodge. The dining room serves international cuisine, with modern Scottish influences. A welcoming ambience adds to the charm.

Key to Price Guide *see p608* **Key to Symbols** *see back cover flap*

ST ANDREWS The Peat Inn ⓔⓔⓔ
On B940, Cupar, nr St Andrews, Fife, KY15 5LH **Tel** *01334 840206*

Highly accomplished modern cooking, using regional produce and seasonal vegetables, has established this smart hotel-restaurant as one of the best in Britain. The innovative cuisine is prepared by renowned chef David Wilson, whose passion for good Scottish fare is evident in his creations. Lunch is particularly good value.

ST ANDREWS The Seafood Restaurant ⓔⓔⓔⓔ
Bruce Embankment, St Andrews, Fife, KY16 9AS **Tel** *01334 479475*

Located in an enviable seafront location, this superb restaurant offers a memorable dining experience, along with striking views of the coastline. The menu features a variety of seafood, which is carefully prepared and beautifully presented. The ambience at this stylish eatery is warm and cosy.

ST MONANS The Seafood Restaurant ⓔⓔⓔ
16 W End, St Monans, Fife, KY10 2BX **Tel** *01333 730327*

An excellent place to enjoy the very best of local seafood. Set in a stunning water's edge location, this fine, modern restaurant is attractively and elegantly fitted out. Serves a wide range of fresh, seasonal fish and seafood, including prawns, crabs, scallops and more. The food is meticulously prepared, and the staff friendly and attentive.

SOUTH QUEENSFERRY Orocco Pier ⓔⓔ
17 High St, S Queensferry, Edinburgh, EH30 9PP **Tel** *0131 331 1298*

Situated on the main street in South Queensferry, a short distance from Edinburgh city centre. Open all day for light snacks, coffees and meals, this elegant restaurant is a great place to enjoy the splendid views of the Forth estuary and its bridges. Fish and seafood play a prominent role in the menu.

TROON Highgrove House Hotel ⓔⓔ
Old Loans Rd, Troon, Ayrshire, KA7 7HL **Tel** *01292 312511*

Perched high on Dundonald Hill, this hotel-restaurant occupies a retired sea captain's house, and enjoys magnificent views over the Firth of Clyde and the Mull of Kintyre. The atmosphere is comfortable and welcoming. Serves informal meals from a varied menu, featuring some old favourites and newer innovations.

THE HIGHLANDS AND ISLANDS

ABERDEEN The Udny Arms ⓔⓔ
Main St, Newburgh, Nr Aberdeen, Aberdeenshire, AB41 6BL **Tel** *01358 789444*

A family-run village hotel with bistro and pub that's cosy, full of character, and serves up honest, wholesome and award-winning food. The locals rate this place very highly, not least because it is great value for money. Staff are friendly and efficient.

ABERDEEN The Silver Darling ⓔⓔⓔⓔ
Pocra Quay, Footdee, N Pier, Aberdeen, Aberdeenshire, AB11 5DQ **Tel** *01224 576229*

A superb seafood bistro restaurant located on the north side of Aberdeen harbour. This well-established venue is one of the best places to enjoy the daily catch, which has been carefully cooked and presented. Try and sit by the window if you can to make the most of the splendid coastline views.

ALEXANDRIA Georgian Room at Cameron House Hotel ⓔⓔⓔⓔ
Off A82, Loch Lomond, Alexandria, West Dunbartonshire, G83 8QZ **Tel** *01389 755565*

A formal dining room at a luxurious country house, situated on the tranquil shores of Loch Lomond and set amid beautiful grounds. This elegant and stylish restaurant has won several awards, and offers exquisitely prepared meals in comfortable surroundings. The staff are well trained and friendly. An experience of a lifetime.

AUCHMITHIE But 'n' Ben ⓔ
Off A92, 1 Auchmithie, nr Arbroath, Angus, DD11 5SQ **Tel** *01241 877223*

Housed in twin cottages in a working fishing village. The restaurant is open for lunch, dinner and the traditional high tea. Menus naturally feature the day's catch and offer superb value for money. This small eatery is somewhat of a local institution and worth taking the trouble to find. Welcoming ambience.

AUCHTERARDER Andrew Fairlie @ Gleneagles ⓔⓔⓔⓔⓔ
Gleneagles Hotel, Auchterarder, Perthshire, PH3 1NF **Tel** *01764 694267*

One of the finest dining experiences in Scotland. This elegant restaurant is set within the luxurious Gleneagles Hotel. The highly acclaimed chef presents imaginative French cuisine with a Scottish flavour. The must-try specialities include smoked lobster, roast Anjou squab with black truffle gnocchi and delicious hot chocolate biscuit dessert.

BALLATER Darroch Learg ⓔⓔⓔ
Braemar Rd, Ballater, Royal Deeside, AB35 AUX **Tel** *013397 55443*

A great restaurant, with a well-deserved reputation for excellence, set within a Victorian shooting lodge. The modern British cuisine is particularly outstanding, as the best local produce is used to create imaginative and flavoursome dishes. The setting of this award-winning venue is relaxed, and the adjacent conservatory adds to the charm.

BLAIRGOWRIE The Loft Restaurant
£££

Golf Course Rd, Blair Atholl by Pitlochry, Perthshire, PH18 5TE **Tel** *01796 481377*

An elegant venue with old-worldly beams and stone walls where guests can choose to dine in the more formal restaurant or enjoy a casual meal at the bistro. Both places offer skilfully prepared food using fresh local ingredients and a varying menu of seafood, poultry and game.

BUCKIE The Old Monastery
£££

Drybridge, by Buckie, Morayshire, AB56 5JB **Tel** *01542 832660*

A well-established restaurant, with a good local following. Situated in a converted church, this atmospheric venue is a great place to enjoy appetizing dishes made with superb regional produce. The food is well prepared and served in relaxed and comfortable surroundings. The service is hospitable and welcoming.

CAIRNDOW Loch Fyne Oyster Bar
£££

Clachan, Cairndow, Argyll, PA26 8BL **Tel** *01499 600236*

Highly renowned restaurant offering an impressive array of fish and seafood. The menu features an excellent selection of both hot and cold meals, including delicious oysters, mussels, two veggie options and a lobster platter. Also offers steaks, lamb, and chicken dishes, as well as vegetarian choices.

CARNOUSTIE 11 Park Avenue
££

11 Park Ave, Carnoustie, Angus, DD7 7JA **Tel** *01241 853336*

One of Scotland's little gems, this stylish restaurant has a warm and welcoming interior, which provides the setting for a lovely eating experience. Chef Stephen Henderson offers a creative menu, with dishes that have been prepared with the freshest regional ingredients.

COLBOST BY DUNVEGAN Three Chimneys
£££££

Colbost, Dunvegan, Isle of Skye, Inverness-shire, IV55 8ZT **Tel** *01470 511258*

Situated a short distance from Dunvegan, on the western shores of the loch. Once a stone-built crofter's cottage, this award-winning restaurant offers seafood and game, lovingly prepared with fresh local produce. The ambience is peaceful and relaxed, and the service friendly. One of the "not to miss" places in Scotland.

DRYMEN The Pottery
£

The Square, Drymen, Argyll, G63 0BJ **Tel** *01360 660458*

Delightful restaurant and coffee shop, located in the square of the pretty little village of Drymen. Offers good, home-cooked food all day and delicious afternoon teas and lunches – all prepared fresh. Boasts a charming terrace. A popular stopping point for locals as well as tourists exploring the area.

DUFFTOWN A Taste of Speyside
£££

10 Balvenie St, Dufftown, Moray, AB55 4AB **Tel** *01340 820860*

Set amid the mountains and glens of the Spey Valley, this restaurant has been offering an enjoyable culinary experience to customers for many years. The food here is wholesome and simply prepared, showing a strong commitment to quality local produce such as fish, poultry and game.

DUNKELD Kinnaird Estate
££££

Kinnaird Estate, off B898, nr Dunkeld, Perthshire, PH8 0LB **Tel** *01796 482440*

This stylish restaurant, located in an estate hotel, produces food of great originality. Lunch is more affordable and worth trying. The property is beautifully maintained, with a range of accommodation available. The surroundings are elegant and welcoming, and the staff professional and friendly. An excellent experience.

FORT WILLIAM Crannog Seafood Restaurant
££

The Waterfront, Fort William, Perthshire, PH33 7PT **Tel** *01397 705589*

Nothing can detract from the simple pleasure of eating exquisitely fresh seafood while overlooking a panoramic loch view. The helpings at this restaurant are generous, the atmosphere is warm and relaxing and the service quite efficient.

INVERNESS Culloden House
£££££

Culloden, Inverness, Inverness-shire, IV2 7BZ **Tel** *01463 790461*

A historic building with loads of character, set in lovely grounds, close to the Culloden Visitor Centre. Offers Scottish country house-style food, with sauces, jellies, sorbets and mousses interspersing a wide variety of hearty and appetizing meat, game and fish dishes. Accommodation is also available.

KILBERRY Kilberry Inn
££

Kilberry, by Tarbert, Loch Fyne, Argyll, PA29 6YD **Tel** *01880 770223*

This former post office is now run as a pub in a quiet coastal village. Serves traditional Scottish pub food at its best, with a constantly changing menu. However, a good selection of old favourites is also featured so not to disappoint the regular customers. Has a warm and cosy atmosphere.

KILLIECRANKIE Killiecrankie Hotel
£££

Off A9, nr Pitlochry, Perthshire, PH16 5LG **Tel** *01796 473220*

Attractive, well-appointed hotel, which has the feel of a village inn. The food served here is hearty and wholesome, with some unusual, yet innovative twists. The excellent bar meals supplement the fine, dinnertime fare, both of which are served in cosy and inviting surroundings. The staff are friendly and hospitable.

Key to Price Guide *see p608* **Key to Symbols** *see back cover flap*

KINCRAIG The Boathouse Restaurant ££

Loch Insh, Kincraig, Inverness-shire, PH21 1NU **Tel** *01540 651272*

Charming log-cabin restaurant overlooking Loch Insh. Features a traditional Scottish menu with local fish, haggis and steak, and serves tea, coffee, snacks and home-baked dishes throughout the day. Offers a special menu for children, and encourages outdoor meals on the balcony in summer. Also has a gift shop and a bar.

KIRRIEMUIR Lochside Lodge ££

Bridgend of Lintrathen, by Kirriemuir, Angus, DD8 5JJ **Tel** *01575 560340*

Situated deep in the countryside, this tastefully converted restaurant was once a farm steading. Located near the loch, this cosy lodge is a welcoming place to enjoy some of the best cooking in the area. The menu features well balanced and simply prepared meals, and the use of local produce is imaginative and highly successful.

KYLESKU The Kylesku Hotel ££

On A894 by Lairg, Sutherland, IV27 4HW **Tel** *01971 502231*

Lochs and mountains provide a magnificent backdrop to this hotel, which is located on the quayside. The bar and restaurant menus are extensive, and feature an array of local dishes. However, the speciality here is the freshly caught fish. The tranquil surroundings create an excellent setting in which to unwind and relax.

OBAN Wide Mouthed Frog £

Dunstaffnage Bay, by Oban, Argyll, PA37 1PX **Tel** *01631 567005*

Situated between the villages of Connel and Oban, this restaurant is a popular meeting place, particularly with the sailing fraternity. Good food and convivial surroundings make this a deservedly bustling venue. The menus feature local produce and the food is well cooked and presented. Accommodation also available.

OBAN Ee'usk £££

N Pier, Oban, Argyll, PA34 5QD **Tel** *01631 565666*

A recent addition to the eating scene in Oban, this stylish restaurant is located in a great waterside setting, and has something for everyone. Serves mouthwatering seafood, using fresh catches of the day. A must-visit for those who enjoy fish. A favoured choice of many, this eatery also offers great views of the coastline.

OBAN The Knipoch Hotel £££

On A816, nr Oban, Argyll, PA34 4QT **Tel** *01852 316251*

Situated on the outskirts of Oban, this traditional country hotel has been a popular stopping place for many years. The bar meals here are excellent, while the dinners range from three to five courses. In addition, the huge array of vegetables and flamboyant puddings are as eyecatching as they are tasty.

PERTH Let's Eat ££

77–79 Kinnoull St, Perth, Perthshire, PH1 5EZ **Tel** *01738 643377*

Local ingredients and skilled and passionate owners play a prominent role in this restaurant's success. Offers relaxing and comfortable surroundings, innovative menus and skilled cooking. Fish, game, beef and lamb are the mainstay of the delicious meals, and are usually accompanied by fresh vegetables and creative sauces.

PERTH 63 Tay Street £££

63 Tay St, Perth, Perthshire, PH2 8NN **Tel** *01738 441451*

Run by a husband and wife team, this central Perth restaurant has been justifiably recognized for the quality and style of food it offers. The cooking is superb, and the service friendly and professional. The menus feature the best regional produce available, which is used to create imaginative, flavoursome and thoroughly enjoyable dishes.

PLOCKTON Off the Rails ££

The Station, Plockton, Ross-shire, IV52 8YX **Tel** *01599 544423*

A tastefully converted restaurant-café, occupying a former, 19th-century railway station. Offers a varied menu with seafood, steaks, game and even a selection of international dishes. Dine inside with the warmth of the cosy log fires or enjoy a meal on the platform tables outside. The hot seafood platter and Scottish lamb cutlets are favourites here.

PORT APPIN The Airds Hotel £££££

Port Appin, Argyll, PA38 4DF **Tel** *01631 730236*

This hotel-restaurant is set on a fine waterfront location in Appin, and has a cheerful and comfortable interior. Offers a well balanced Michelin-star menu, with a variety of seafood, poultry and game, and uses fresh local produce to prepare appetizing dishes. The service is excellent, and the ambience warm and inviting.

ST MARGARET'S HOPE The Creel £££

Front Rd, St Margaret's Hope, Orkney, KW17 2SL **Tel** *01856 831311*

A front-runner for one of the best places to eat in Orkney. The dishes are emphatically Orcadian in style, with a commitment to the wonderful, locally sourced seafood – which features frequently on the menu – as well as beef and seaweed fed lamb. The service is friendly and helpful. Also offers accommodation.

ULLAPOOL The Ceilidh Place ££

14 W Argyle St, Ullapool, Sutherland, IV26 2TY **Tel** *01854 612103*

An interesting building, with a great atmosphere. Situated in an award-winning hotel with its own bookshop, rooms and bar, this restaurant serves superbly skilled and imaginative dishes, which are unashamedly local and of the highest quality. Meals incorporate fish, meat, poultry, vegetables and fruits – all prepared simply, yet excellently.

British Pubs

No tour of Britain could be complete without some exploration of its public houses. These are a great social institution, descendants of centuries of hostelries, ale houses and stagecoach halts. Some have colourful histories or fascinating contents, and occupy a central role in the community, staging quiz games and folk dancing. Many of those listed below are lovely buildings, or have attractive settings. Most serve a variety of beers, spirits and wine by the glass.

A "free house" is independent and will stock several leading regional beers, but most pubs are "tied" – this means that they are owned by a brewery and only stock that brewery's selection.

Many pubs offer additional attractions such as live music and beer gardens with picnic tables. Traditional pub food is often served at lunchtime, and increasingly, in the evenings as well. Traditional pub games take many forms, including cribbage, shove ha'penny, skittles, dominoes and darts.

LONDON

Bloomsbury: *Lamb*
94 Lamb's Conduit St, WC1.
Tel 020 7405 0713. **Map** 3 C5
Unspoilt Victorian pub with lovely cut-glass "snob screens" and theatrical photographs. Small courtyard at the rear. 🍴 📶 🚹 🏃

City: *Black Friar*
174 Queen Victoria St, EC4.
Tel 020 7236 7474. **Map** 12 F2
Eccentric inside and out, with intriguing Art Nouveau decor. Attentive service. 🍴 🚹

City: *Ye Olde Cheshire Cheese*
Wine Office Court, Fleet St EC4.
Tel 020 7353 6170. **Map** 12 E1
Authentic 17th-century inn that evokes shades of Dickens's London. Its stark glory is best enjoyed in front of the open fires. 🍴 🚹

Hammersmith: *Dove*
19 Upper Mall, W6.
Tel 020 8748 5405.
One of west London's most attractive riverside pubs – you can watch rowing crews from the terrace. 🍴 📶

Hampstead: *Spaniards Inn*
Spaniards Lane, NW3.
Tel 020 8731 6571.
Famous Hampstead landmark dating from the 18th century, once part of a tollgate. 🍴 📶 🚹

Kensington: *Windsor Castle*
114 Campden Hill Rd, W8.
Tel 020 7243 9551. **Map** 7 C4
A civilized Georgian inn with oak furnishings and open fires. The walled garden attracts well-heeled crowds in summer. Hearty English food. 🍴 📶 🏃

Southwark: *George Inn*
77 Borough High St, SE1.
Tel 020 7407 2056. **Map** 13 B4
Quaint coaching inn with unique galleried courtyard. Rooms ramble upstairs and downstairs, and the overspill sits outside. Morris dancers may be seen performing here at times *(see p120)*. 🍴 📶 🚹 ⚓

THE DOWNS AND CHANNEL COAST

Alciston: *Rose Cottage Inn*
Alciston nr Polegate.
Tel 01323 8703774.
In a creeper-covered cottage, this rural Sussex pub is decorated in classic rustic style, with beamed ceilings and open fireplaces. The local ales and busy kitchen add to its warmth. 🍴 📶 🚹

Brighton: *Market Inn*
Market St, BN1 1HH.
Tel 01273 329483.
Once home to the Prince of Wales's chimney sweep, this is now something of a Brighton institution, spilling out onto The Lanes in the summer months.

Ditchling: *The Bull Hotel*
2 High St, BN6 8SY.
Tel 01273 843147.
Housed in a 14th-century building, the main bar is large, rambling and pleasantly traditional with characterful old wooden floorboards, beams and furniture, and a blazing fire. 🍴 🎵 📶 🚹

Faversham: *White Horse Inn*
The Street, Boughton.
Tel 01227 751343.
Chaucer gave this place a passing mention in *The Canterbury Tales*. Among hop gardens and orchards, this genial country pub resounds with echoes from the past. Thirteen en suite bedrooms. 🍴 🚹 📶

Goodwood: *Star and Garter*
East Dean, nr Goodwood.
Tel 01243 811318.
Recently refurbished, this lovely 18th-century inn is nestled at the foot of the South Downs. Local ales and cider are served straight from barrels. A good selection of wines. Enjoy the mild Sussex summer on the patio. 🍴 📶 🚹

Isle of Wight:
The Wight Mouse Inn
Newport Rd, Chale.
Tel 01983 730431.
This pub draws in a good bunch of locals, especially those you enjoy the real ale. 🚹

Lewes: *Six Bells Inn*
Chiddingly, nr Lewes.
Tel 01435 812495.
Once a stopover for stagecoaches, this cosy drop-in now does a fine job of reviving weary ramblers and thirsty locals. Supposedly haunted by a grey cat and one Sara French, hanged in 1852 after serving her husband a pie seasoned with arsenic. 🍴 🎵 🚹 🏃

Romsey: *The Star Inn*
East Tytherley, nr Romsey.
Tel 01794 340225.
Popular watering hole on the edge of the New Forest. So quintessentially English, it even overlooks the village cricket pitch. The Rivers Test and Dunn are nearby. Overnight accommodation available. 🍴 📶 🚹 ♿

Rye: *The Mermaid*
Mermaid St. *Tel 01797 223065.*
Dating from 1136, this is one of the country's oldest inns. Situated on a cobbled street and constructed from old ship timbers, The Mermaid is an evocative slice of England's nautical history. 🍴 📶 🚹

Walliswood: *The Scarlett Arms*
Walliswood Green Rd.
Tel 01306 627243.
Handsome inn with flagstone bar, wooden benches and a grand inglenook fireplace. The staff make the experience all the more congenial. 🍴 📶 🚹 🏃

Key to Symbols *see back cover flap*

EAST ANGLIA

Cambridge: *The Boathouse*
14 Chesterton Rd. **Tel** 01223 460905.
This recently-renovated riverside
pub boasts a natty nautical theme
and exceedingly comfortable
armchairs. The beer garden is
always warm and toasty, courtesy
of heaters, allowing you to watch
the river flow all year around.

Itteringham:
The Walpole Arms
The Common. **Tel** 01263 587258.
Oak-beamed inn that has been
serving locally brewed ales since
the 1700s. The restaurant is also
highly regarded.

Kings Lynn: *The Lord Nelson*
Walsingham Rd, Burnham Thorpe.
Tel 01328 738321.
This watering hole was once one
of Lord Nelson's favourite haunts.
Kick back on any of the old high-
backed benches, and wait for the
attentive staff to take your order.
Private functions are held in the
handsome, flagstoned Victory Bar.

Norfolk: *Red Lion*
Wells Rd, Stiffkey. **Tel** 01328 830552.
The oldest parts of the simple
bars have a few beams, aged
flooring tiles or bare boards, and
big open fires. A back gravel
terrace has seats and tables for
enjoying the bar food on a sunny
day, and some pleasant walks are
nearby. Real ale and 30 malt
whiskies are available.

Walden: *Queen's Head Inn*
High St, Littlebury, Saffron Walden.
Tel 01799 522251.
Attractive coaching inn with a
relaxed, family ambience. Stocks a
decent selection of ales and has a
heady wine list. En suite rooms.

Norwich: *The Fat Cat*
49 W End St. **Tel** 01603 624364.
Rightly famed for its extensive real
ale selection, The Fat Cat is full of
attractions, starting with the well-
stocked bar and the lively local
clientele.

Ringstead: *The Gin Trap Inn*
6 High St. **Tel** 01485 525264.
Close to the Norfolk coastline and
just on the edge of the Ringstead
Downs nature reserve, this classic
country pub features hand-pumped
real ales and cosy log fires. The
restaurant has quite a devoted
following. Overnight accommodation available.

Southwold: *The Crown Hotel*
High St. **Tel** 01502 722186.
The pub remains the star of this
newly converted hotel, though the
chic restaurant is becoming a firm
local favourite. Excellent selection
of wines at the bar.

Stowmarket:
The Buxhall Crown
Mill Rd, Buxhall. **Tel** 01449 736521.
Four local real ales take pride of
place in this old village pub that
also does a roaring trade in home-
cooked food, with locally sourced
ingredients. Good list of wine by
the glass adds to its considerable
appeal.

Suffolk:
The Six Bells at Bardwell
Bardwell, Bury St Edmunds.
Tel 01359 250820.
This village green charmer, dating
from the 1500s, offers superb food
and peaceful accommodation.

THAMES VALLEY

Aylesbury: *The King's Head*
Kings Head Passage, Market Sq,
Buckinghamshire. **Tel** 01296 718812.
A small oasis in the heart of a
pretty market town, this airy pub
has excellent service and a courtyard perfect for whiling away long
summer afternoons.

Barley: *The Fox and Hounds*
Hertfordshire. **Tel** 01763 848459.
Despite the recent ban on hunting,
this traditional pub retains its large
sign of a fox being chased by
hounds. Excellent ales and eats.

Bedford: *The Park*
98 Kimbolton Rd, Bedfordshire.
Tel 01234 409305.
Recently refurbished, this warm
and friendly pub has traditional
features such as oak beams and
old fireplaces. Good, wholesome
food on offer.

Bicester: *The Hundred Acres*
Hart Place, Oxfordshire.
Tel 01869 329981.
A homely pub serving food and
open late on weekends. Welcomes
children until 8pm.

Chipping Norton:
The Falkland Arms
Great Tew, Chipping Norton,
Oxfordshire. **Tel** 01608 683653.
Award-winning cask ales and a
wonderful atmosphere. You can try

beer tasters before you buy at this
traditional gem of a place.

Faringdon: *The Trout*
Tadpole Bridge, Buckland Marsh, nr
Faringdon. **Tel** 01367 870382.
Always busy and bustling, this
17th-century pub boasts a riverfront garden where customers can
savour local dishes.

Luton: *The Bricklayers Arms*
High Town Rd, Bedfordshire.
Tel 01582 611017.
A friendly pub with ice-cold beers
and plenty of quiz machines. Order
whatever's on the left-hand pump,
since its contents are changed
constantly.

Newbury: *The Monument*
Northbrook St, Berkshire.
Tel 01635 41964.
The busiest pub around, there are
different events every night of the
week, from free Playstation and
live jazz to jugglers, belly dancers
and hypnotists.

Oxford: *The White Horse*
52 Broad St. **Tel** 01865 728318.
This cosy pub has loads of
character, with pictures of old
sports stars on the walls and a
great range of beers.

Watton-at-Stone: *The Bull*
113 High St, Herts. **Tel** 01920 831032.
Sit around the large, open-hearth
fire at this 14th-century inn, or
venture out to the picturesque
garden.

WESSEX

Abbotsbury: *Ilchester Arms*
Market St, Dorset. **Tel** 01305 871243.
A prominent landmark in this
quaint village, the 18th-century
stone Grade II listed inn features a
deluxe conservatory.

Bath: *The Bell*
103 Walcot St, Bath, Avon.
Tel 01225 460426.
Splendid little pub, with billiards,
live music and organic beers.
Soak in the friendly atmosphere
while tucking into tasty sandwiches
and cold plates.

Bridport: *Shave Cross Inn*
Shave Cross, Marshwood Vale,
Dorset. **Tel** 01308 868358.
Award-winning inn with fine
ales as well as English, Caribbean
and international food.

Pensford: *Carpenter's Arms*
Stanton Wick, nr Pensford, Somerset.
Tel 01761 490202.
Overlooking the lovely Chew
Valley, this twinkling pub is set
among a row of small miners
houses. With an excellent menu
and a comprehensive wine list, it
is one of the most welcoming
places around. 🍴 📷 🚶

Salisbury: *Haunch of Venison*
1 Minster St, Salisbury, Wiltshire.
Tel 01722 411313.
The severed, mummified hand of
an 18th-century card player is on
display (along with more pleasant
antiques) at this 650-year-old pub.
The restaurant is a must-visit for a
good meal. Keep an eye out for
the resident ghost. 🍴 🚶

Salisbury:
The New Inn and Old House
41/47 New St, Wiltshire.
Tel 01722 327679.
Salisbury's only non-smoking pub,
the low-beamed ceilings and
intimate interior lighting are offset
by views of the cathedral spire
opposite. The menu is broad and
vegetarian-friendly. 🍴 📷 ⛵ 🚶

DEVON AND CORNWALL

Dawlish: *The Mount Pleasant*
Mount Pleasant Rd, Dawlish Warren,
Devon. *Tel 01626 863151.*
This pub is renowned for its views
over Exmouth from the dining
area. Drinkers visit once and
become loyal customers for years.
The warm ambience makes a
winning combination with super
value for money. 🍴 📷 🚶 ✒

Exeter: *The Bridge*
Bridge Hill, Topsham, Devon.
Tel 01392 873862.
With its pink exterior, you can't
miss this riverside pub. Its several
separate rooms with fireplaces are
truly snug in winter, while the
garden is gorgeous on sunny days.
A pub with no bar, they serve
drinks through a hatch in the
corridor. 🍴 📷 🎵 🚶

Falmouth: *Pandora Inn*
Restronguet Creek, Mylor Bridge, nr
Falmouth, Cornwall.
Tel 01326 372678.
Medieval pub with a thatched
roof by the waterside. Full of cosy
corners, low wooden ceilings, panelled walls and a variety of maritime
memorabilia. 🍴 📷 ♿ 🎵 🚶 ✒

Knowstone: *Masons Arms Inn*
Devon. *Tel 01398 341231.*
An atmospheric Grade II listed
cottage that is full of character.

The decor includes farm tools
and a bread-oven fireplace.
Delicious restaurant food and
friendly hosts. 🍴 📷 🚶

Lynton: *Fox and Goose*
Parracombe, Barnstaple.
Tel 01598 763239.
A friendly and welcoming pub
with very good food and beer.
The log fire, plank ceiling and
assorted mounted antlers and
horns give a proper Exmoor feel
to the place. Serves real ale and
local cider. 🍴 📷

Newton Abbot: *Two Mile Oak*
Totnes Rd, Abbotskerswell.
Tel 01803 812411.
An old coaching inn with a beamed
lounge and an alcove just for two.
A mix of wooden tables and chairs,
and a fine winter log fire. 🍴 📷

Penzance: *The Pirate Inn*
Alverton Rd, Alverton, Cornwall.
Tel 01736 366094.
Recommended by the local youth
hostel, this is a friendly stop for a
beer and sandwich. Visitors often
invest in the souvenir T-shirts sold
here. 🍴 📷 🚶

Porthleven: *Harbour Inn*
Commercial Rd, Cornwall.
Tel 01326 573876.
Watch the sun go down and sip a
top-quality pint as you sit by
Porthleven's harbour. Recently
refurbished, this pub retains its
original character, the modern
sofas and coffee tables notwith-
standing. 🍴 📷 🚶

Saltash: *The Cecil Arms*
St Stephens, Cornwall.
Tel 01752 843408.
A pub with its own dedicated community, it serves wonderful ales and
food. The bartenders are exceedingly friendly. Children welcome
until 8.30pm. 🍴 📷 ♿ 🚶

Tiverton: *The White Ball Inn*
Bridge St, Devon. *Tel 01884 251525.*
Although the decor is slightly
generic, there is an unusual visible
well with a glass top. Vertigo
sufferers should not look down.
🍴 📷 🚶

THE HEART OF ENGLAND

Alderminster: *The Bell*
Warwickshire. *Tel 01789 450414.*
Smart 18th-century coach inn just
6.4 km (4 miles) out of Stratford-
upon-Avon, The Bell also boasts a
high-class restaurant. Great views
over Stour Valley from the garden
and conservatory. Rooms on a bed
and breakfast basis. 🚶 🍴 ♿ 📷

Armscote: *Fox & Goose*
Warwickshire. *Tel 01608 682293.*
This atmospheric bar-restaurant
(and B&B) is perfect for a light
supper or relaxing drink. Sit in the
vast lawns during summer. The
bar has an open fire in winter.
🍴 📷 🚶

Ashleworth: *Queen's Arms*
The Village, Gloucestershire.
Tel 01452 700395.
Sixteenth-century inn with a
noticeable Victorian makeover, this
pub features wood-beamed
ceilings and antique furnishings.
The fantastic kitchen serves traditional pub food as well as more
international flavours. 🍴 📷 🚶

Bickley Moss:
Cholmondeley Arms
Malpas, Cheshire. *Tel 01829 720300.*
The menu in this family-friendly
pub includes the very best of
traditional local cuisine. Children
will adore the desserts – baked
syrup sponge, black cherry
Pavlova, bakewell tart, ice creams
and sorbets. Accommodation is
also available. 🍴 📷 🚶

Bretforton: *Fleece Inn*
Near Evesham. *Tel 01386 831173.*
This real ale pub with its half-
timbered façade is also a National
Trust property. Beautifully located
in the Vale of Evesham. Rooms
available. Parking in village square.
🍴 📷 🎵 🚶 ⛵

Farnborough:
Inn at Farnborough
Near Banbury. *Tel 01295 690615.*
Classy inn in a Grade II listed free
house from the 1700s, this inn
serves delicious local cuisine,
including sumptuous organic
steak burgers. Large garden and
conservatory. 🍴 📷 🎵 🚶 🎣 ♿

Shrewsbury: *Armoury*
Welsh Bridge, Victoria Quay.
Tel 01743 340525.
This converted 18th-century
warehouse, with views over the
river, is a popular open-plan
venue. Go early if you want to
enjoy a leisurely sit-down
meal. Children are welcome
till 7pm. 🍴 🚶

Welford-on-Avon:
The Bell Inn
Nr Stratford-upon-Avon,
Warwickshire. *Tel 01789 750353.*
This lovely 17th-century country
pub serves wonderful real ale and
traditional bar food. The Bell Inn
lies just a short distance southwest
of Stratford-upon-Avon. Recently
renovated, there is a delightful
seating area in the garden.
🍴 📷 🚶

Wenlock Edge:
Wenlock Edge Inn
Hilltop, nr Much Wenlock, Shropshire.
Tel 01746 785678.
This award-winning pub is
especially popular with walkers –
there is a comprehensive selection
of maps and guidebooks on stand-
by. A fairly homely affair, Wenlock
Edge Inn serves good bar food
and ales. Three rooms on a bed
and breakfast basis. 🍴 🛏 🚶

EAST MIDLANDS

Alderwasley: *The Bear Inn*
Belper, Derbyshire. *Tel 01629 822585.*
Friendly country pub with real
olde-worlde charm, The Bear Inn
serves a good range of real ales
and delicious cuisine. Popular with
locals and visitors alike.
🍴 🛏 🚭 🚶

Birchover: *Druid Inn*
Main St, nr Matlock Derbyshire.
Tel 01629 650302.
In the lovely village of Birchover,
the old but recently revamped
Druid Inn has an excellent local
menu. Legend has it that the
nearby Row Tor rocks were once a
place of Druid rituals.
🍴 🛏 🚶 🚭

Gedney Dyke: *Chequers*
Main St, Gedney Dyke, Lincolnshire.
Tel 01406 362666.
In the quiet village of Gedney
Dyke, this award-wining Fenland
dining pub offers two menu
choices; simple bar snacks or more
elaborate restaurant fare. Whatever
your choice, you can be assured of
the high quality of the impressive
range of ales and wines.
🍴 🛏 🚭 ♿ 🚶

Glooston:
Old Barn Inn & Restaurant
St Andrews Lane, Market Harborough,
Leicestershire. *Tel 01858 545215.*
A renovated 16th-century coaching
inn in a tiny village, the Old Barn
Inn is more than just a friendly
pub with rooms. The menu here is
extensive and reasonably priced
for the high quality of the cuisine.
🍴 🛏 🚶 🚭

Grimsthorpe: *Black Horse*
Grimsthorpe Bourne, Lincolnshire.
Tel 01778 591247.
Nestled just below Grimsthorpe
Castle, this early 18th-century
inn has been renovated into a
high-class pub-eaterie. Lovers
of the outdoors will enjoy the
rambling grounds and lakeside
nature trail. Return to enjoy the
cosy atmosphere of the bar
and spend the night in one of the
six charmingly old-fashioned
rooms. 🍴 🛏 🚶

Hathersage: *Plough Inn*
Leadmill Bridge, Hope Valley,
Derbyshire. *Tel 01433 650319.*
In an idyllic location on the
banks of River Derwent, this
16th-century inn on nine acres of
private parklands offers the perfect
summer stop off. Fabulous food,
great views and five en suite
rooms. 🍴 🛏 🚶 🚭

Lyddington: *Old White Hart*
51 Main St, Rutland.
Tel 01572 821 703.
Charming country inn with an
award-winning à la carte menu.
The Old White Hart has lovingly
retained the oak-beamed ceilings,
exposed brick walls and open
fires of the renovated 17th-century
stone building. 🍴 🛏 🚶 🚭

Stamford:
The George of Stamford
71 St Martins, Lincolnshire.
Tel 01780 750750.
One of England's most famous
coaching inns, the George's bar,
restaurant and rooms are all rich
in history. Other than the award-
winning restaurant menu, there
are also more informal pub food
choices served in the ivy-covered
courtyard and in the York Bar.
🍴 🛏 ♿ 🎵 🚶

LANCASHIRE AND THE LAKES

Ambleside: *The Britannia Inn*
Elterwater, Cumbria.
Tel 015394 37210.
This traditional inn began life
as a farmhouse and cobbler's.
Standing on the village green and
surrounded by stunning scenery,
it is a delightful place to unwind
in after a day's walk.
🍴 🛏 🚶 🚭

Clitheroe: *The Shireburn Arms*
Hurst Green, Lancashire.
Tel 01254 826518.
Located in a picturesque village,
this characterful 17th-century inn
was one of author JRR Tolkien's
favourite haunts. The Shireburn
Arms takes its name from the
family who built Stonyhurst
College and nearby almshouses.
🍴 🛏 🚭 🚶

Downham: *Assheton Arms*
Downham, Lancashire.
Tel 01200 441227.
Previously known as The George
and Dragon, this pub was renamed
following the elevation of the
local squire, Ralph Assheton, to
Lord Clitheroe. Facing the old
church in a pretty village of stone
cottages, it has even been featured
in films and television series.
🍴 🚭 🚶

Hawkshead:
Queen's Head Hotel
Main St, Cumbria.
Tel 01539 436271.
Situated at the heart of one of the
prettiest Lake District villages.
The superb food ranges from
simple sandwiches at the bar to
full meals at the restaurant. William
Wordsworth was schooled in this
village. 🍴 🛏 🚭 🚶 🚶

Hawkshead: *Tower Bank Arms*
Near Sawrey, Hawkshead, Cumbria.
Tel 01539 436334.
Standing in a tiny picturesque
village, this 17th-century inn is
very close to Hill Top, where the
legendary children's book author
Beatrix Potter once lived. It even
features in one of her well-known
stories, *The Tale of Jemima
Puddle-Duck.* 🍴 🛏 🚶 🚭

Liverpool: *Ship and Mitre*
133 Dale St, Merseyside.
Tel 0151 236 0859.
Close to the city centre, this
traditional and down-to-earth pub
has a reputation for serving a
wide range of real ales along with
tasty nibbles at the bar. 🍴 🚶

Lonsdale: *Snooty Fox Tavern*
Main St, Kirkby Lonsdale, Cumbria.
Tel 01524 271308.
A listed Jacobean coaching inn in
the centre of the town, the Snooty
Fox lies in the picturesque Lune
Valley. Its rambling bars and
cobbled courtyard exude a quaint
charm. 🍴 🛏 🚭 ♿ 🚶 🚶

Manchester: *Lass o' Gowrie*
36 Charles St, Chorlton-cum-
Medlock. *Tel 0161 273 6932.*
Famous for its cask ales, this lively
pub lies close to the BBC studios
and is popular with students. The
menu offers a good range of
freshly-cooked food. 🍴 🚭 🚶 🚶

YORKSHIRE AND HUMBERSIDE

Askrigg: *Kings Arms*
Market Place, N Yorks.
Tel 01969 650817.
Fans of James Herriot's *All
Creatures Great and Small* will
recognize this as "The Drover's
Arms". There is a broad menu of
appetizing food and five real ales
on tap in the bar. 🍴 🛏 🚭 🚶 🚶

Byland Abbey: *Abbey Inn*
Byland Abbey, N Yorks.
Tel 01347 868204.
This charming inn, opposite the
evocative ruins of a 12th-century
abbey, serves excellent meals in
the restaurant. Filling sandwiches
for bar lunches. 🍴 🛏 🚭 🚶

Driffield: *Wellington Inn*
19 The Green, Lund, Driffield, E Yorks.
Tel 01377 217294.
Just north of the minster town
of Beverley, this attractive pub
overlooks a charming village
green. Its fine food and friendly
service have won it an enviable
reputation. 🍴 🏠 👤 ♿

Flamborough: *The Seabirds*
Tower St, Flamborough, E Yorks.
Tel 01262 850242.
Near the bird sanctuary *(see
pp400–401)* on the chalk cliffs of
Flamborough Head, this pub is
popular with both locals and
walkers. The specialities on the
menu revolve around fish, but a
range of other dishes is on offer
too. 🍴 🏠 ♿ 👤

Lancaster:
The Game Cock Inn
The Green Austwick, via Lancaster,
N Yorks. *Tel* 01542 512226.
Close to the Yorkshire "Three
Peaks", this 17th-century coaching
inn is the focal point of the tiny
village. The award-winning food
is home-cooked by a French chef,
and the menus offer a range of
options – everything from a simple
snack to an elaborate dinner.
🍴 🏠 ♿ 👤

Leyburn: *The Blue Lion*
E Witton, Leyburn, N Yorks.
Tel 01969 624273.
An 18th-century coaching and
drover's inn within a charming
Wensleydale village, it retains
many original features. Open
fires warm the rooms in winter.
The food is traditional, but often
with an unusual twist.
🍴 🏠 ♿ 👤 👤

Skipton: *The Red Lion Hotel*
By the Bridge, Burnsall, N Yorks. *Tel*
01756 720204.
Before the bridge was built across
the Wharfe at Burnsall, this
16th-century inn used to operate
a ferry across the river. Today, it
has a reputation for fine food;
its generous range of real ales at
the bar is also widely appreciated.
🍴 🏠 ♿ ♿ 👤

NORTHUMBRIA

Barnard: *The Morritt Arms Hotel*
Greta Bridge, Barnard Castle, Co
Durham. *Tel* 01833 627232.
Located between Carlisle and
London, this 17th-century stone
farmhouse eventually became a
coaching inn. Dickens stayed here
in 1839 while writing *Nicholas
Nickleby*. A wall sports a mural by
local artist John Gilroy, depicting
Dingley Dell from *The Pickwick
Papers*. 🍴 🏠 ♿ ♿ 👤 👤

Consett: *Lord Crewe Arms*
Blanchland, nr Consett, Co Durham.
Tel 01434 675251.
Built in 1160 as the abbot's house,
this delightful hotel faces an
unusual, enclosed cobbled square
at the heart of a very pretty
village. Dine in the formal
restaurant or opt for the more
casual style and menu at the bar.
🍴 🏠 ♿ 👤 👤

Cornhill on Tweed: *Black Bull*
Etal Village, Northumb.
Tel 01890 820200.
Close to the Norman castle in this
attractive estate village, the award-
winning Black Bull is famous as the
only thatched pub in Northumberland. Ingredients for the home-
cooked food are sourced locally
wherever possible and the menu
always includes tasty vegetarian
options. 🍴 🏠 ♿ ♿ 👤 👤

Craster: *Jolly Fisherman*
Off B1339 nr Alnwick, Northumb.
Tel 01665 576461.
Unassuming local pub with lovely
sea views. Home-made crab soup
and seafood are specialties.
🍴 🏠 ♿ 👤 👤

Hedley on the Hill:
The Feathers Inn
Northumb. *Tel* 01661 843607.
This family-run pub is popular
with foodies, and serves cuisine
that has a distinct Greek influence.
There is always a good selection
of vegetarian dishes too and at
least four guest ales on tap at
the bar. 🍴 🏠 ♿ 👤 👤

Hexham: *Dipton Mill Inn*
Dipton Mill Rd, Northumb.
Tel 01434 606577.
Originally an 18th-century mill,
this family-run pub lies beside
Dipton Burn in a wooded valley.
The characterful bar stocks a range
of locally brewed beers and serves
home-made food. 🍴 🏠 ♿ 👤 👤

Kielder Water:
The Pheasant Inn
Stannersburn, Falstone, Northumb.
Tel 01434 240382.
This 17th-century farmhouse has
functioned as a pub for the last
250 years. Popular with visitors to
Kielder Water and the surrounding
forest. Meals are served at the bar,
with the dining room opening for
Sunday lunch and evening dinner.
🍴 🏠 ♿ ♿ 👤 👤

Newton: *Cook and Barker Inn*
Newton on the Moor, Northumberland.
Tel 01665 575234.
Once a forge, the inn got its name
from its first proprietors, a Captain
Cook who married a Miss Barker.
Dine à la carte in the restaurant,

where the original fireplace and
well remain. Hearty pub meals are
available at the bar. Accommodation
available. 🍴 🏠 ♿ ♿ 👤

Seahouses: *The Olde Ship Hotel*
Northumb. *Tel* 01665 720200.
Situated above the tiny fishing
harbour with a view across Farne
Islands. Pleasant beer garden.
Interesting nautical memorabilia
decorate the bars. 🍴 🏠 ♿ ♿ 👤

NORTH WALES

Capel Curig: *Bryn Tyrch Hotel*
Conwy. *Tel* 01690 720223.
Pretty country inn in the heart of
Snowdonia National Park, this is a
popular stop-off point for walkers
and climbers. Traditional Welsh
cuisine. Great views of Mt Snowdon
from the bar. 🍴 🏠 ♿ 👤 👤

Denbigh: *Hope & Anchor*
94 Vale St, Denbighshire.
Tel 01745 815115.
Small, traditional village pub with
a bustling beer garden in the centre
of Denbigh. Darts competitions and
weekly quizzes are also hosted.
Rooms on a bed and breakfast
basis. 🍴 🏠 👤 👤

Ganllwyd: *Tyn-y-groes*
Dolgellau, Gwynedd.
Tel 01341 440275.
Picturesque 16th-century inn in the
heart of the Snowdonia National
Park, Tyn-y-groes hotel and pub
offers a friendly base for walking,
mountain biking and fishing in the
park. 🍴 🏠 ♿ 👤 👤

Glanwydden: *Queen's Head*
Llandudno. *Tel* 01492 546570.
This bustling village pub has a
reputed bar menu. Tables at the
Queen's Head fill quickly so it is
wise to arrive early. Great range
of real ales. No smoking in the
dining room. 🍴 🏠 👤

Maentwrog: *Grapes Hotel*
Blaenau Ffestiniog, Gwynedd.
Tel 01766 590365.
Said to be haunted, this Grade II
listed coaching inn serves fine ales
and home-made cuisine in a
stunning setting. Pitch pine pews,
exposed stone walls and a roaring
fire in winter all add to the effect.
🍴 🏠 ♿ 👤 👤

Mold: *Glasfryn*
Raikes Lane, Sychdyn, Mold.
Tel 01352 750500.
Pretty village pub known for its
theatre-going clientele (Theatre
Clywd is just next door), Glasfryn
is a converted farmhouse pub with
a warm welcome. Award-winning
menu and wine list. 🍴 🏠 ♿ 👤

Nant Gwynant: *Pen-y-Gwryd*
Gwynedd. *Tel 01286 870211.*
Hotel with a bustling pub in
the shadow of Mt Snowdon. It is
here that the 1953 Everest team
holed up here while training for
the ultimate ascent. Popular with
walkers for its prime location, it
also serves great food and drink.

Overton Bridge:
Cross Foxes Inn
Erbistock, Wrexham, Clwyd.
Tel 01978 780380.
Fabulous food in a fabulous
setting, Cross Foxes Inn, on the
banks of the River Dee, is a very
welcoming 18th-century coaching
inn with a distinctive dining room.
Good choice of real ales.

SOUTH AND MID-WALES

Aberaeron: *Harbourmaster*
Pen Cei, Ceredigion.
Tel 01545 570755.
Fabulous hotel-pub overlooking
the town's picturesque harbour.
This blue-washed building serves
tasty seafood such as Cardigan
Bay crab and lobster, Aberaeron
mackerel and several other such
freshly-caught delicacies in its
warm little bar and restaurant.

Aberystwyth: *Halfway Inn*
Devils Bridge Rd, Pisgah.
Tel 01970 880631.
Halfway between Aberystwyth and
Devil's Bridge (hence the name),
this large inn has steadily built a
strong reputation for its fine food
and fabulous real ale. Designated
restaurant area away from the bar.

East Aberthaw: *Blue Anchor*
Barry, S Glamorgan.
Tel 01446 750329.
This recently refurbished, thatched
pub in the seaside town of Barry
is just 16 km (10 miles) from
Cardiff, Blue Anchor has a friendly
little bar as well as an elegant
restaurant serving superior cuisine.
Estuary walks nearby.

Hay-on-Wye: *The Pandy Inn*
Dorstone, Herefordshire.
Tel 01981 550273.
A picturesque pub with rooms just
over the border in Herefordshire,
The Pandy Inn boasts a long and
illustrious history. Supposedly the
oldest pub in the county, it played
host to Oliver Cromwell during
the 17th-century Civil War. The
restaurant seats 50 and serves
wholesome, filling and tasty food.

Pembroke Ferry: *Ferry Inn*
Pembroke Dock.
Tel 01646 682947.
This early 17th-century inn
serves delicious seafood in a
prime location overlooking the
harbour. Ferry Inn has an
extensive waterfront terrace,
which is a perfect setting for
languid summer dining. Check
out the specials board for fish
caught fresh that day.

Penallt: *Boat Inn*
Lone Lane. *Tel 01600 712615.*
With a stunning location on the
banks of River Wye, the beer
garden of Boat Inn is a great
place to relax with a chilled
drink on a warm summer's day.
Bar food is available. Access is via
a footbridge.

Pontyclun:
High Corner House
The Square, Llanharan.
Tel 01443 238056.
Old inn from the early 1700s
with three luxury rooms, High
Corner House serves traditional,
hearty pub food in its jazzed-up
restaurant. It is conveniently
located between Cardiff and the
Swansea coast.

Tintern: *Cherry Tree Inn*
Raglan Rd, Monmouthshire.
Tel 01291 689292.
Fabulously placed in the heart
of the Wye Valley, the Cherry
Tree Inn has been recommended
in the CAMRA real ale guide for
over 30 years, such is the quality
of its choice. The menu doesn't
disappoint either, and features an
array of mouthwatering dishes.

Usk: *Nag's Head*
Twyn Sq. *Tel 01291 672820.*
Atmospheric village pub with
an extensive menu that is very
reasonably priced for the size
of the portions. The warmly
welcoming establishment places
an emphasis on the home-made
food, but there is also a bustling
bar area.

THE LOWLANDS

Edinburgh:
Café Royal Circle Bar
West Register St.
Refurbished in Victorian style,
this pub features tiled portraits
of Scottish worthies and ornate
chandeliers. Sink back into one
of the comfortable leather
chairs for a drink before making
your way to the oyster bar and
restaurant.

Elie: *Ship Inn*
The Harbour, Fife.
Atmospheric quayside pub with
nautical decor and attractive
views. Summer barbecues.

Glasgow: *Horseshoe*
17–19 Drury St.
Busy Victorian pub with a long
bar and plenty of period features.
Good value bar snacks. Karaoke
in the evenings.

Isle of Whithorn:
Steam Packet
Isle of Whithorn, Dumfries &
Galloway.
Superb setting on a lovely harbour.
Pleasant eating areas and a good
selection of real ales. Boat trips
from the harbour.

THE HIGHLANDS AND ISLANDS

Applecross: *Applecross Inn*
Shore St, Wester Ross, Highland.
Spectacularly located beyond
Britain's highest mountain pass,
this pub overlooks the Isle of Skye.
Local seafood is served, and there
is music some evenings.

Dundee: *Fishermans Tavern*
10–16 Fort St, Broughty Ferry, Tayside.
Choose between award-winning
real ales and the extensive
selection of malts, or savour a little
of both. Good seafront and views
of the Tay Rail Bridge. Rooms
available.

Isle of Skye:
Tigh Osda Eilean Larmain
Off A851, Isle Ornsay, Isle of Skye.
Welcoming hotel bar. Lots of
malts and good bar food.
Gorgeous setting.

Loch Lomond: *Oak Tree Inn*
Balmaha, (E side).
Traditional stone inn with a
well-stocked bar, restaurant and
B&B. Sit by the roaring fires in
winter and snack on the tasty
bar food that is served all day.

Portsoy: *The Shore Inn*
The Old Harbour, Banffshire.
A 300-year-old seafaring inn
nestled in a picturesque harbour.
Traditional cask ale and a real
open fire.

Ullapool: *Ferry Boat*
Shore St, Highland.
Good whiskies, bar lunches and
fine views over the harbour.
Coal fires and big windows
overlooking the loch.

SHOPPING IN BRITAIN

While the West End of London (see pp148–51) is undeniably the most exciting place to shop in Britain, many of the regional towns and cities offer nearly as wide a range of goods. Moreover, regional shopping can be less stressful, less expensive, and remarkably varied, with craft studios, farm shops, street markets and factory

Vivienne Westwood's designer label

outlets adding to the enjoyment of bargain-hunting. Britain is famous for its country clothing: wool, waxed cotton and tweed are all popular, along with classic prints such as Liberty or Laura Ashley and tartan. Other particularly British goods include antiques, floral soaps and scents, porcelain, glass and local crafts.

Antiques stall at Bermondsey Market

SHOPPING HOURS

In general, shops in Britain open during the week from 9am or 10am, and close after 5pm or 6pm. Hours on Saturdays may be shorter. Many town centre shops open on Sundays. Some stores open late for one evening a week – Thursday in London's West End – while village shops may close at lunch-time, or for one afternoon each week. Market days vary from town to town.

HOW TO PAY

Most large shops all over the UK accept well-known credit cards such as Access and VISA. Charge cards such as American Express or Diners Club are acceptable in some places, but markets and some small shops do not take credit cards. Traveller's cheques can be used in larger stores, though exchange rates for non-sterling cheques may be poor. Take your passport with you for

identification. Few places accept cheques drawn on foreign banks. Cash is still the most popular way to pay for small purchases.

RIGHTS AND REFUNDS

If something you buy is defective, you are entitled to a refund, provided you have kept your receipt as proof of purchase and return the goods in the same condition as when you bought them, preferably in the same packaging. This may not always apply to sale goods clearly marked as seconds, imperfect, or shop-soiled. Inspect these carefully before you buy. You do not have to accept a credit note in place of a cash refund.

ANNUAL SALES

Sales take place during January, and in June and July, when nearly every shop cuts prices to get rid of old stock. But you may find special offers at any time of the year. Some

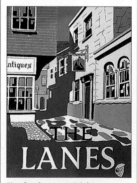

Sign for the Lanes, Brighton *(see p175)*

shops begin winter sales just before Christmas. Department stores and fashion houses have some excellent bargains for keen shoppers; one of the most prestigious sales is at Harrods *(see p97),* where queues form long before opening time.

VAT AND TAX-FREE SHOPPING

Value added tax (VAT) is charged on most goods and services sold in Britain – exceptions are food, books and children's clothes. It is usually included in the advertised price. Visitors from outside the European Union who stay less than three months may claim this tax back. Take your passport with you when you go shopping. You must complete a form in the shop when you buy goods and give a copy to the customs authorities when you leave the country. You may have to show your goods as proof of purchase. If you arrange to have goods shipped from the store, VAT should be deducted before you pay.

OUT-OF-TOWN SHOPPING CENTRES

These large complexes, built in the style of North American malls, are rapidly increasing around Britain. The advantages of car access and cheap parking are undeniable, and most centres are accessible by public transport too. The centres usually feature popular high street stores, with facilities such as cafés, crèches, restaurants and cinemas.

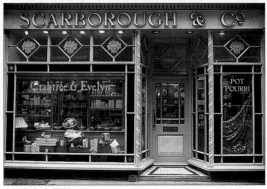

A traditional shop front in Stonegate, York *(see p404)*

DEPARTMENT STORES

A few big department stores, such as Harrods, are only found in London, but others have provincial branches. John Lewis, for example, has shops in 22 locations. It sells a huge range of fabrics, clothing and household items, combining quality service with good value. Marks & Spencer, with branches in most major towns and cities in Britain, is famed for its good-value clothing and pre-prepared food. Debenhams and British Home Stores (BhS) are other well-known general stores with inexpensive clothing and home furnishings. Habitat is a reputable supplier of modern furniture. The sizes of all these stores, and the range of stock they carry, differs from region to region.

Local Teesdale cheeses

CLOTHES SHOPS

Once again, London has the widest range, from *haute couture* to cheap and cheerful items ready-made. Shopping for clothing in the regions, however, can often be less tiring. Many towns popular with tourists – Oxford, Bath and York for instance – have independently owned clothes shops where you are likely to receive a more personal service. Or you could try one of the chain stores in any high street such as Principles or Next for smart, reasonably priced clothes, and Top Shop, Oasis and Miss Selfridge for younger and cheaper fashions.

SUPERMARKETS AND FOODSHOPS

Supermarkets are a good way to shop for food. The range and quality of items is usually excellent. Several large chains compete for market share and as a result prices are generally lower than in smaller shops. Sainsbury, Tesco, Asda, Safeway and Waitrose are some of the national names. The smaller town-centre shops such as bakeries, green-grocers or farm shops, may give you a more interesting choice of regional produce, and a more personal service.

SOUVENIR, GIFT AND MUSEUM SHOPS

Buying presents is a must for most travellers. Most reputable, large stores can arrange freight of high-value

The Mustard Shop *(see p201),* **Norwich**

items. If you want to buy things you can carry back in your suitcase, the choice is wide. You can buy attractive, well-made, portable craft items all over the country, especially in areas tourists are likely to visit. For slightly more unusual presents, have a look in museum shops and the gifts available in National Trust *(see p29)* and English Heritage *(see p671)* properties.

SECONDHAND AND ANTIQUE SHOPS

Britain's long history means there are many interesting artifacts to be found. A visit to any of Britain's stately homes will reveal a passion for antiques. Most towns have an antique or bric-a-brac (miscellaneous second-hand items) shop or two. Look for auctions – tourist information centres *(see pp668–9)* can help you to locate them. You may like to visit a jumble or car boot sale in the hope of picking up a bargain.

Book stall, Hay-on-Wye, Wales *(see p461)*

MARKETS

Large towns and cities usually have a central covered market which operates most weekdays, selling everything from fresh produce to pots and pans. The information under each town entry in this guide lists market days. Many towns hold weekly markets in the main square. While you browse among the stalls, look out for local fresh produce and the jams and cakes of the Women's Institute stalls.

ENTERTAINMENT IN BRITAIN

Punch and
Judy show

London is without a doubt the entertainment capital of Britain *(see pp152–5)*, with a whole wealth of shows, films and concerts to choose from, but many regional theatres, opera houses and concert halls also have varied programmes. Edinburgh, Manchester, Leeds Birmingham, and Bristol in particular have a lot to offer and there are a number of summer arts festivals around the country such as those at Bath and Aldeburgh *(see pp62–3)*. Ticket prices vary but are usually cheaper outside the capital and when booked in advance.

SOURCES OF INFORMATION

In London, check the listings magazines, such as *Time Out,* or the *Evening Standard,* London's evening newspaper. All of the high-brow newspapers *(see p672)* provide comprehensive arts reviews and listings of the cultural events and shows throughout the country. Local newspapers, libraries, or tourist offices *(see p669)* can supply details of regional events. Specialist magazines such as *NME* give up-to-date news of the pop music scene and are available from any newsagent.

THEATRES

Britain has an enduring theatrical tradition dating back to Shakespeare *(see pp324–5)* and beyond. All over the country, amateurs and professionals tread the boards in auditoriums, pubs, clubs and village halls. Production and performance standards are generally high, and British actors have an international reputation. London is the place to enjoy theatre at its most varied and glamorous *(see p152)*. The West End alone has more than 50 theatres *(see p153)* ranging from elaborate Edwardian, to Modernist-style buildings such as the National Theatre on the South Bank.

In Stratford-upon-Avon, the Royal Shakespeare Company presents a year-round programme of Shakespeare, as well as avant-garde and experimental plays. Bristol also has a long dramatic tradition, the Theatre Royal *(see p256)* is the oldest working theatre in Britain. Some of the best productions outside the capital can be found at the West Yorkshire Playhouse in Leeds, the Royal Exchange in Manchester *(see p372)* and the Traverse in Edinburgh. Open-air theatre ranges from the free street entertainment found in many city centres, to student performances on the grounds of university colleges, or a production at Cornwall's clifftop amphitheatre, the Minack Theatre *(see p276)*. Every fourth year, York also stages a series of open-air medieval mystery plays called the York Cycle. Perhaps the liveliest theatrical tradition in Britain is the Edinburgh Festival *(see p509)*. Ticket availability varies from show to show. For a midweek matinee, you may be able to buy a ticket at the door, but for the more popular West End shows tickets may have to be booked weeks or months in advance. You can book through agencies and some travel agents, and most hotels will organize tickets for you. Booking fees are often charged. Beware of tickets offered by touts *(see p67)* – these may be counterfeit. There are no age restrictions in Britain's theatres.

Street
entertainer

MUSIC

A diverse musical repertoire can be found in a variety of venues. Church choral music is a national tradition and many churches and cathedrals host concerts. London, Manchester, Birmingham, Liverpool, Bristol and Bournemouth all have their own excellent orchestras.

Rock, jazz, folk and country-and-western concerts are staged periodically in pubs, clubs and sometimes outdoors. Wales has a strong musical tradition which is evident in many of its pubs; northern England is known for its booming brass and silver bands; and Scotland has its famous bag-pipers *(see p480)*.

The Buxton Opera House, the Midlands

The multiplex Warner West End cinema, Leicester Square, London

CINEMAS

The latest films can be seen in any large town. Check the local papers or the tourist office to find out what is on.

Cinemas are having a revival, with luxurious multi-screen cinemas taking over from the local, single-screen cinemas. In larger cities a more diverse range of films is often on offer including foreign-language productions. These tend to be shown at arts or repertory cinemas. Mainstream English-speaking films are usually shown by the big chains. Age limits apply to certain films. Young children are allowed to see any feature film which is graded with a U (universal) or PG (parental guidance) certificate. Cinema prices vary widely; some are cheaper at off-peak times, such as Mondays or afternoons. For new releases it is advisable to book in advance.

CLUBS

Most cities have some sort of club scene, though London has the most famous venues (see p155). These may feature live music, discos, or DJ or dance performances. Some insist on dress codes or members only, and most have doormen, or "bouncers". Apart from the major cities, Brighton and Bristol have lively clubs.

DANCE

This covers a multitude of activities: everything from classical ballet and acid-house parties to traditional English Morris dancing or the Scottish Highland fling, which you may come upon in pubs and villages around the country.

Dance halls are rarer than they were, but ballroom dancing is alive and well. Other dance events you may find are ceilidhs (pronounced kay-lee), which is Celtic dancing and music; May Balls often held at universities (invitation only); dinner or tea dances and square dancing.

Birmingham is home to the Birmingham Royal Ballet and is the best place to see performances outside London. Avant-garde contemporary dance is also performed.

GAY

Most large communities will have some gay meeting places, mostly bars and clubs. You can find out about them from publications such as the free *Pink Paper* or *Gay Times* on sale in some newsagents, and in gay bars and clubs. London's gay life is centred around Soho (see p80) with its many European-style cafés and bars. Outside London, the most active gay scenes are in Manchester and Brighton. Gay Pride is the largest free outdoor festival in Europe.

Three revellers, Gay Pride Festival

CHILDREN

London offers children a positive goldmine of fun, excitement and adventure, though it can be expensive. From the traditional sights to something more unusual such as a discovery centre, London has a wide range of activities, many interactive, to interest children of all ages. The weekly magazine *Time Out* has details of children's events.

Outside London, activities for children range from nature trails to fun fairs. Your local tourist office or the local library will have information on things to do with children.

Pirate Ship, Chessington World of Adventures, Surrey

THEME PARKS

Theme parks in Britain are enjoyed by children of all ages. Alton Towers has conventional rides plus a motor museum. Chessington World of Adventures is a huge complex south of London. Based on a zoo, it includes nine themed areas, such as Calamity Canyon and Circus World. Legoland, the latest park, opened in March 1996. Thorpe Park is a large watery theme park full of model buildings and a peaceful pet farm.

Alton Towers
Alton, Staffordshire.
Tel 0870 444 4455.
www.altontowers.com

Chessington World of Adventures
Leatherhead Rd, Chessington, Surrey.
Tel 0870 9990045.
www.chessington.co.uk

Legoland
Winkfield Rd, Windsor, Berkshire.
Tel 08705 040404.
www.lego.com

Thorpe Park
Staines Rd, Chertsey, Surrey.
Tel 08704 444466.
www.thorpepark.co.uk

SPECIALIST HOLIDAYS AND OUTDOOR ACTIVITIES

Cycling on the Gower Peninsular, Wales

Britain offers a wide variety of special interest holidays and courses, where you can learn a new sport or skill, practise an activity you enjoy, or simply have fun and meet people. If you prefer less structured activities, there are numerous options to choose from, such as walking in Britain's national parks, pony trekking in Wales, surfing in Cornwall or skiing in Scotland. There are also several spectator sports for those who like to watch rather than participate, including Premier League football, test match cricket and historic horse races.

Arvon Foundation writing week at Totleigh Barton in Devon

SPECIAL INTEREST HOLIDAYS

There are a number of special interest holidays and residential courses available in Great Britain. One advantage of this type of vacation is that you can attend a course alone, and yet have plenty of congenial company – most people are delighted to meet others who share their interests. Whatever your passion, you are likely to come across a holiday package that suits your needs.

Centres such as **Wye Valley Art Centre** in Gloucestershire and **West Dean College**, West Sussex, offer engaging, residential courses in arts and crafts. These can range from familiar activities such as drawing and painting to more esoteric subjects such as mosaic art and glass engraving. Those interested in writing can enroll at the **Arvon Foundation**, which organizes week-long courses in fiction, poetry, songwriting and TV drama at four rural retreats in Devon,

Shropshire, West Yorkshire and Invernesshire. The **Ashburton Cookery School** in Devon and **Cookery at the Grange** in Somerset offer fun cookery courses with lots of hands-on involvement. Non-carnivores might try the Vegetarian Society's **Cordon Vert School** in Cheshire, which has innovative cookery courses catering to chefs at all levels – from complete beginners to talented amateurs.

Companies such as **Astral Travels**, **Inscape Tours** and the **Back-Roads Touring Company** provide a variety of themed holidays. History lovers can opt for a tour of King Arthur's Country or Shakespeare's England. Other tours designed for motor enthusiasts, garden lovers or fans of rock and roll are also available.

The prices of such holidays include expert guidance, transport, entry fees to attractions and accommodation, which could be anything from a farmhouse to a medieval castle.

WALKING

Walking is a popular activity in Britain and a network of long-distance footpaths and shorter routes criss-crosses the country (see pp36–7). It is also an excellent way to experience the spectacular variety of the British landscape, either by yourself or with a group. An advantage is that most routes are away from major tourist sites and often pass through picturesque villages that are off the beaten track.

The **Ramblers' Association** is Britain's main walking body, and its website provides useful information on most routes and walking areas. It also publishes a range of books, including *Walk Britain*, which lists many good walks as well as suitable hotels, bed and breakfasts and hostels along the way.

There is no shortage of companies providing guided and self-guided holidays for walkers. The cost of these holiday packages should cover

Walking on Holyhead Mountain near South Stack Anglesey, Wales

accommodation, transport and detailed route guides. The Ramblers' own **Countrywide Holidays** offers guided group walks through some of the country's most splendid landscapes. **Sherpa Expeditions** has a variety of self-led walks. Pick a challenging 15-day coast-to-coast walk, or a more leisurely ramble along South Downs Way. Individual companies will advise you on the level of fitness required and the type of clothing and footwear that will be needed.

If you are planning to walk on your own, especially in remote areas, remember that it is essential to not only be well equipped, but to also leave details of your route with someone.

Mountain biking in Yorkshire

CYCLING

The country's tranquil lanes, bridleways and designated tracks are perfect for cyclists who want to explore the back roads of Britain. Depending on your level of fitness, you may opt for demanding routes through mountainous areas such as the magnificent West Highland Way in Scotland *(see p494)*. Those who would like to take it easy can enjoy a relaxed tour along Devon's lanes and take the opportunity to stop off for a sinfully rich cream tea.

Country Lanes offers a good variety of guided holidays in small groups around the west of England. The price includes an experienced leader, high quality bicycle equipment, accommodation, meals and

entry to attractions along the way. **Compass Holidays** and **Wheely Wonderful Cycling** concentrate on self-led tours, with routes throughout the country. They also provide bicycles, accommodation, detailed route maps, (including details of pubs, cafés and places of interest along the way) and appropriate luggage transport. Such self-guided bicycling holidays are ideal for families or groups of friends.

If you wish to organize your own cycling holiday, you may contact the **Cyclists' Touring Club**, which is Britain's main recreational cycling body, and **Sustrans**, the organization that formed the National Cycle Network. Both can provide a wealth of information about cycling in the country, including advice on matters such as bringing a bike into Britain, taking your bike on the train and the rules of the road. *Cycling in the UK*, the official guide book for the National Cycle Network, has route details and maps for many of the best rides, and also offers tips on how to hire a bike and what to do along the way.

HORSE RIDING AND PONY TREKKING

There are good riding centres in most parts of Britain, but certain areas are especially suitable for this invigorating activity. The best of these locations include the New Forest *(see p168)*, the South Downs *(see p181)*, the Yorkshire Dales National Park *(see pp384–6)* and the Brecon Beacons on the border between Wales and England *(see pp468–9)*.

Pony trekking holidays are also becoming very popular, and generally include basic training, a guide, meals and accommodation. These vacations are perfect for novice riders and children since the ponies are very well-trained and rarely proceed above a canter. The **British Horse Society** has all the information on where to ride as well as a list of approved riding schools that offer training. You can also consult the **Horseweb-UK** website for information on riding centres

Horse riding on a country bridleway *(see p37)*

that offer trekking holidays. National park information offices can also provide details of the many equestrian centres that organize riding holidays in or around national parks.

GOLF

Over a quarter of Britain's 2000-odd golf clubs are in Scotland, which is unsurprising given that the ancient game was invented here. The first formal club was established in Edinburgh in 1744.

Today, the best known clubs are Carnoustie and St Andrews in Scotland, Royal St George's in England and Celtic Manor in Wales. These high-profile clubs only admit players above a certain handicap. Most other clubs, however, are more relaxed and welcome visitors.

Green fees vary greatly, as do the facilities offered by various clubs. Some clubs may ask to see a valid handicap certificate before they allow a player on the course. Failing that, a letter of introduction from a home club may be sufficient.

Specialist operators such as **Golf Vacations UK** and **Great Golf Holidays** can smooth the way to the first hole considerably by booking golf packages. They will organize travel and accommodation, reserve tee times and pay the green fees. They will also help you get temporary membership of a club if required.

If you wish to go it alone, the **Golf Club of Great Britain** can provide information on where to play. They also have an affiliated website for non-residents of the UK.

SURFING

The best areas for surfing are in the West Country and South Wales. Tuition is available at many resorts, and equipment can be hired.

The Cornwall-based **British Surfing Association** runs its own surf school with professional coaching catering to a range of abilities, from novices to advanced competition surfers. Other companies that offer good surfing courses include **Surf South West** in Devon and the **Welsh Surfing Federation Surf School** in South Wales.

Sailing in Cardigan Bay, Welsh coast

BOATING AND SAILING

The British are extremely enthusiastic about boating and sailing. The network of rivers, lakes and canals ensures an abundance of boating sites. Many excellent choices are available – the Isle of Wight and the south coast are full of pleasure crafts. Several inland areas such as the Lake District (see pp354–69) are among the most widely favoured. Canal cruising is also very popular (see p689) and the Norfolk Broads (see p198) provide one of the best inland boating experiences. Check with the **Broads Authority** for details.

Many sailing courses are available. The **Royal Yachting Association** can provide lists of approved courses and training centres around Britain. One of the most trusted is Dorset's **Weymouth & Portland National Sailing Academy**, which has a range of courses to suit all ages and levels of ability. The **Falmouth School**

of **Sailing** in Cornwall is a privately owned sailing and powerboat school, which conducts lessons in the enclosed, safe waters of the Fal Estuary. Courses include basic "taster sessions", one-to-one tuition for adults and children, as well as group lessons.

SKIING

Facilities for skiing are limited in the UK, especially since the weather is rather unreliable. However, skiing enthusiasts can head for Scotland, which has a range of challenging slopes. **Ski Scotland**, the official ski site of the Scottish Tourist Board, has information about ski packages, accommodation, up-to-date weather conditions and details of the main ski areas, including the Cairngorms and the Nevis Range. **Snowsport Scotland**, the governing body for all Scottish snowsports, provides information on other snow-based activities such as Nordic skiing and snowboarding.

FISHING

Fishing, both on the sea and in rivers, is one of Britain's most popular participation sports. Regulations, however, are strict and can be rather complicated. It is advisable to check for details about rod licences, close seasons and other restrictions at tourist offices, tackle shops or with the **National Federation of Anglers** in Nottingham.

The best game fishing (trout and salmon) is in the West Country, the Northeast, Wales and Scotland. Also, there are several websites with links to specialist operators who arrange fishing holidays.

Solitary sea fisherman, England's southeast coast

SPECTATOR SPORTS

Football (soccer) is a passion for a large section of the population. The English Premier League is run by the **Football Association** and is home to some of the world's top clubs, including **Manchester United** (see p375), **Arsenal FC** and **Chelsea FC**. The domestic football season runs from August to May. Tickets for Premier League games can be expensive and difficult to obtain, but it is worth attempting to get hold of returned or unsold tickets directly from the clubs.

The main tennis event of the year is Wimbledon, which is held at the **All England Lawn Tennis Club (AELTC)** in London. This two-week event takes place in the last week of June and the first week of July. The tournament sparks off a period of tennis fever in England, especially when British players such as Tim Henman progress in the competition. Most tickets for Centre Court are allocated by a public ballot. Check the official website of the AELTC for details on how to procure tickets. Around 6,000 tickets are available on the day of play (payment by cash only), except for the final four days of the tournament.

Rugby Football is administered by the **Rugby Football Union** and also has a good following. Games are played in cities such as Edinburgh, London and Cardiff.

Cricket, the English national game, is played from April to September. Tickets for country matches are relatively cheap. International test matches are played on historic grounds such as **Surrey County Cricket Club's** ground at the Oval in London, and the **Yorkshire County Cricket Club** situated at Headingley in Leeds.

Both steeplechasing and flat-racing are very popular, and betting is big business. The Grand National is the best known steeplechase and runs at **Aintree Racecourse** in early April. The main meeting is **Royal Ascot**, which takes place in Berkshire towards the end of June.

DIRECTORY

SPECIAL INTEREST HOLIDAYS

Arvon Foundation
42A Buckingham Palace Rd, London SW1.
Tel 020-7931 7611.

Ashburton Cookery School
Hare's Lane Cottage 76 E St, Ashburton TQ13.
Tel 01364 652784.

Astral Travels
72 New Bond St, Mayfair, London W1S.
Tel 0870 225 5303.

Back-Roads Touring Company
14A New Broadway, London W5.
Tel 020-8566 5312.

Cookery at the Grange
The Grange, Whatley, Frome, Somerset BA11.
Tel 01373 836579.

Cordon Vert School
The Vegetarian Society, Parkdale, Dunham Rd, Altrincham, Cheshire WA14.
Tel 0161 925 2000.

Inscape Tours
1 Farley Lane, Stonesfield, Oxfordshire OX29.
Tel 01993 891726.

West Dean College
West Dean, Chichester, W Sussex PO18.
Tel 01243 811301.

Wye Valley Art Centre
The Coach Hse, Mork, St Briavel's, Lydney, Gloucestershire GL15.
Tel 01594 530214.

WALKING

Countrywide Holidays
Box 43, Welwyn Garden City AL8.
Tel 01707 386800.

Ramblers' Association
2nd Floor Camelford Hse, 87–90 Albert Embankment, London SE1.
Tel 020-7339 8500.
www.ramblers.org.uk

Sherpa Expeditions
131A Heston Rd, Hounslow TW5.
Tel 020-8577 2717.

CYCLING

Compass Holidays
Cheltenham Spa Railway Station, Queens Rd, Cheltenham, Gloucestershire GL51.
Tel 01242 250642.

Country Lanes
Brokenhurst New Forest.
Tel 01590 622627.

Cyclists' Touring Club
69 Meadrow, Godalming, Surrey GU7.
Tel 0870 8730060.

Sustrans
National Cycle Network Centre, 2 Cathedral Sq, College Green, Bristol BS1.
Tel 0845 1130065.

Wheely Wonderful Cycling
Petchfield Farm, Elton, Ludlow, Shropshire SY8.
Tel 01568 770755.

HORSE RIDING AND PONY TREKKING

British Horse Society
Stoneleigh Deer Park, Kenilworth, Warwickshire CV8. *Tel 01926 707700.*
www.bhs.org.uk

Horseweb-UK
www.horseweb.org.uk

GOLF

Golf Club of Great Britain
3 Sage Yard, Douglas Rd, Surbiton, Surrey KT6.
Tel 020-8390 3113.
www.golfclubgb.co.uk

Golf Vacations UK
Tel 01228 527136.
www.golfvacationsuk.com

Great Golf Holidays
2nd Floor, Central Hse, 4–6 Crantock St, Newquay, Cornwall TR7.
Tel 01637 859965.

SURFING

British Surfing Association
The International Surfing Centre, Fistral Beach, Newquay, Cornwall TR7.
Tel 01637 876474.

Surf South West
PO Box 39, Croyde, N Devon EX33.
Tel 01271 890400.

Welsh Surfing Federation Surf School
The Barn, The Croft, Llangennith, Swansea SA3. *Tel 01792 386426.*

BOATING AND SAILING

Broads Authority
18 Colegate, Norwich, Norfolk NR3.
Tel 01603 610734.

Falmouth School of Sailing
Grove Place, Falmouth, Cornwall TR11.
Tel 01326 211311.

Royal Yachting Association
RYA Hse, Ensign Way, Hamble, Southampton, Hampshire SO31.
Tel 0845 345 0400.

Weymouth & Portland National Sailing Academy
Osprey Quay, Portland, Dorset DT5.
Tel 01305 866000.

SKIING

Ski Scotland
www.ski.visitscotland.com

Snowsport Scotland
Hillend, Biggar Rd, Midlothian EH10.
Tel 0131 445 4151.

FISHING

Fishing Net
www.fishingnet.com

Fishing UK
www.fishing.co.uk

National Federation of Anglers
National Water Sports Centre, Adbolton Lane, Holme Pierrepont, Nottingham NG12.
Tel 0115 981 3535.

SPECTATOR SPORTS

Aintree Racecourse
Ormskirk Rd, Aintree, Liverpool L9.
Tel 0151 523 2600.

All England Lawn Tennis Club (AELTC)
Church Rd, Wimbledon, London SW19.
Tel 020-8946 2244.
www.wimbledon.org

Arsenal FC
Arsenal Stadium, Avenell Rd, Highbury, London N5.
Tel 020-7704 4040.

Chelsea FC
Stamford Bridge, Fulham Rd, London SW6.
Tel 0870 300 2322.

Football Association
16 Lancaster Gate, London W2.
Tel 020-7262 4542.

Manchester United
Sir Matt Busby Way, Old Trafford, Manchester M16.
Tel 0161 868 8000.

Royal Ascot
Ascot Racecourse, Ascot, Berkshire SL5.
Tel 0870 7271234.

Rugby Football Union
Rugby Rd, Twickenham, Middlesex TW1.
Tel 020-8831 6527.

Surrey County Cricket Club
The Brit Oval, Kennington, London SE11.
Tel 020-7582 7764.

Yorkshire County Cricket Club
Headingley Cricket Ground, Leeds LS6.
Tel 0871 222 0994.

SURVIVAL
GUIDE

PRACTICAL INFORMATION

Millions annually seek out what the British often take for granted – the country's ancient history, colourful pageantry, and spectacularly varied countryside. The range of facilities on offer to visitors in Britain has expanded and improved considerably over the last few years. To enjoy Britain fully it is best to know something about the nuts and bolts of British life: when to visit, how to get around, where to find information and what to do if things go wrong. Whether

A mounted sentry, London

or not you find Britain an expensive country will depend a lot on the exchange rate between the pound and your own currency. Prices vary within Britain; regional differences in some items are very noticeable. London, not surprisingly, is the most expensive. The knock-on effect extends to most of southern England, Britain's most affluent region. Entertainment, food, hotels, transport and consumer items in shops are generally cheaper in other parts of the country.

Weymouth beach, Dorset, on a busy public holiday weekend

WHEN TO VISIT

Britain's temperate maritime climate does not produce many temperature extremes (see p68). There are many fine days but it is impossible to predict rain or shine reliably in any season. Weather patterns shift constantly, and the climate can differ widely in places only a short distance apart. The southeast is generally drier than elsewhere. But wherever you are going be sure to pack a mix of warm and cool clothes and an umbrella. Always get an up-to-date weather forecast before you set off on foot to remote mountain areas or moorland. Walkers can be surprised by the weather, and the Mountain Rescue services are often called out due to

A sign for the Mountain Rescue

unexpectedly severe conditions. Weather reports are given on television and radio, in newspapers, or by phone services (see p685).

Britain's towns and cities are all-year destinations, but many attractions open only between Easter and October. Some hotels are crammed at Christmas and New Year. The main family holiday months, July and August, and public holidays (see p65) are always busy. Spring and autumn offer a compromise between some good weather and a relative lack of crowds. The information at the beginning of each attraction listed in this guide gives opening days.

INSURANCE

It is sensible to take out travel insurance to cover cancellation or curtailment of your holiday, theft or loss of money and possessions, and the cost of any medical treatment (see p674). It is better to arrange this in advance, although you can organize it once on your trip if necessary. If your country has a reciprocal medical arrangement with Britain (for example Australia, New Zealand and the EU), you can obtain free treatment under the National Health Service, but there are a number of forms to fill in. Certain benefits covered by medical insurance will not be included. North American and

Canadian health plans or student identity cards may give you some protection against costs, but check the small print. If you want to drive a car in Britain, it is illegal to drive without third-party insurance and it is advisable to take out fully comprehensive insurance.

ADVANCE BOOKING

Out of season, you should have few problems booking accommodation or transport at short notice, but in the high season, if you have set your heart on a popular West End show, luxury hotel, well-known restaurant, or specific flight or tour, always try to book ahead. Contact **VisitBritain** in your country, or a travel agent for advice and general information.

TOURIST INFORMATION

Tourist information is available in many towns and public places, including airports, main rail and coach stations and at some places of historical interest. These bureaux will be able to help you on almost anything in their area. Look out for the tourist information symbol, which can indicate anything from a large and busy central

The most common English tourist information sign

◁ Fishing boats in Scarborough port, North Yorkshire

office to a simple kiosk or even an information board in a parking area.

Free leaflets are generally offered but a charge may be made for more detailed maps and booklets. Most tourist offices can suggest guided walks, places of interest and nearly all will reserve accommodation for you on request. During the busy holiday periods it is worth asking about the *Book-a-bed-ahead* scheme to places you intend to visit. Tourist office addresses and phone numbers are listed wherever possible in this guide. **VisitBritain**'s monthly magazine *In Britain*, available from tourist offices, contains articles about worthwhile places to visit and also includes a useful events diary.

VisitBritain's magazine

DISABLED TRAVELLERS

The facilities on offer for disabled visitors to Britain are steadily improving: recently designed or newly renovated buildings and public spaces now offer lifts and ramps for wheelchair access (information given in the headings for each entry in this book); specially designed toilets; grab rails, and for the hearing impaired, earphones. Given advance notice, British Rail *(see p686)*, ferry or bus

staff will help any disabled passengers. Ask a travel agent about the Disabled Persons Railcard, which entitles you to discounted rail fares. Many banks, theatres and museums can now provide aids for the visually or hearing impaired. Specialist tour operators, such as **Holiday Care Service**, cater for the physically handicapped visitor. If renting a car, Hertz offers hand-controlled vehicles for hire without any extra cost *(see p685)*. For permission to use any of the disabled parking spaces, you need to display a special sign in your car. For more general information contact **RADAR** or **Mobility International**.

One of the best series for disabled travellers is *Access* by Pauline Hephaistos, published by Survey Projects. You could also try *Holidays in the British Isles: a Guide for Disabled People* (RADAR), and *The World Wheelchair Traveller* by Ann Tyrrell and Susan Abbott (AA).

RADAR *Tel* 020-7250 3222.
www.radar.org.uk

Mobility International
North America *Tel* 541 343 1284.
www.miusa.org

Holiday Care Service
Tel 08451 249971.
www.holidaycare.org.uk

Lorna Doone Cottage and National Trust Information Centre, Somerset

A visit to HMS Victory (p169)

TRAVELLING WITH CHILDREN

Britain is not the easiest or most welcoming place for young children, but things are slowly changing.

Peak holiday times – Easter, July and August – and school holidays have most to offer in the way of entertainment for children. Many places have something child-centred going on at Christmas too, particularly pantomimes. Discounts for children, or family tickets, are now widely available for travel, theatre shows and other entertainments.

Choose accommodation that welcomes children, or opt for self-catering solutions with hard-wearing furnishings and room in which to run around. Many hotels now provide baby-sitting or baby-listening services, and may offer reductions or free accommodation for very young children (see pp552–99).

Restaurants are becoming less child-phobic than they used to be and many now provide highchairs and special child menus (see pp600–651). Italian eateries are often the most friendly and informal, but even the British pub, once resolutely child-free, is now relenting with beer gardens and family rooms. Under-18s are not permitted near the bars and must not buy or consume alcohol. The annual publication *Family Welcome* (HarperCollins) is available from newsagents and lists those places where children are made welcome.

PUBLIC TOILETS

Although many older-style supervised public toilets still exist, these have largely been replaced by the modern free-standing, coin-operated "Superloos". Young children should never use these toilets on their own.

STUDENT TRAVELLERS

Full-time students who have an International Student Identity Card (ISIC), are often entitled to discounts on things like travel, sports facilities and entrance fees. North American students can also get medical cover but it may be very basic (see p674). If you don't have an ISIC, they are available from **STA Travel**, or the **National Union of Students**.

An **International Youth Hostel Federation** card enables you to stay in Britain's hundreds of youth hostels. Inexpensive accommodation is also available (out of term) at many of the university halls of residence – such as the **University of London** – a good way of staying in city centres on a tight budget. If

Great British Heritage Pass

you are exploring the wilder regions of Britain, sleeping quarters can be found in camping barns (dormitory-style bunkhouses) which, though spartan, cost very little. For information on working in Britain, contact **BUNAC**.

BUSINESS HOURS

Many businesses and shops are closed on Sundays, though trading is now legal. Monday to Friday hours are generally 9 or 10am to 5 or 5:30pm, but shop hours can vary, with late shopping one evening a week, and lunch-time or even half-day closing – usually a Wednesday.

Museums in London often open late one day a week, but those outside the capital may have more inflexible hours, sometimes closing during the morning, or for one day a week – often on Mondays.

On public holidays, known as bank holidays in Britain, banks, offices, most shops, restaurants and attractions will generally close.

ADMISSION CHARGES

These vary widely from a nominal 50p to over £10 for the popular attractions, although many of the major national museums are now free. Museums now combine entertainment with education, and are livelier than ever before. Alongside this move, however, there is sometimes a rise in admission charges. But reductions are often available for groups, senior citizens, children or students (proof of identity will be required). Visitors from overseas may buy a

The privately owned, admission-charging, Hever Castle (see p189)

A Cotswold church, one of hundreds of parish churches open to the public free of charge

Great British Heritage Pass, which gives access to over 600 sights, available from VisitBritain offices abroad and, in the UK, from the Britain Visitor Centre in London's Lower Regent Street and some ports of entry and Tourist Information Centres (*see p669*). A few local authority museums and art galleries are free, but donations are always welcome. Other sights are in private hands, run either as a commercial venture or on a charitable basis. Stately homes open to the public may still belong to the gentry who have lived there for centuries; a charge is made to defray the enormous costs of upkeep. Many of these beautiful houses have added safari parks or garden centres to encourage and attract more visitors, such as Woburn Abbey (*see p230*).

Britain's thousands of small parish churches are among the country's greatest architectural treasures. None of the churches charge an entrance fee, although some, sadly, are locked because of vandalism. Increasingly, many of the great cathedrals expect a donation from visitors.

Information leaflets, National Trust

ENGLISH HERITAGE AND THE NATIONAL TRUST

Many of Britain's historic buildings, parks, gardens, and vast tracts of countryside and coastline are cared for by **English Heritage** (EH), the **National Trust** (NT) or the **National Trust for Scotland** (NTS). This guide identifies EH, NT and NTS properties at the beginning of each entry. Entrance fees are often high, so if you wish to visit several stately homes it may be worth taking out annual membership, which allows free access thereafter to any of their properties (remember many are closed in winter). Many of the NT's properties are "listed": buildings or sites that are recognized as having special architectural or historical interest and therefore protected from alterations and demolition.

ENGLISH HERITAGE

The sign and symbol of
English Heritage

DIRECTORY

BUNAC
16 Bowling Green Lane, London EC1R 0QH. *Tel* 020-7251 3472.
www.bunac.org

English Heritage (EH)
PO Box 569, Swindon SN2 2YP.
Tel 0870 333 1181.
www.english-heritage.org.uk

International Youth Hostel Federation
Tel 01707 324170.
www.hihostels.com

National Trust (NT)
PO Box 39, Bromley, Kent, BR1 3XL. *Tel* 0870-458 4000.
www.nationaltrust.org.uk

National Trust for Scotland (NTS)
28 Charlotte Sq,
Edinburgh EH2 4ET.
Tel 0131 243 9300.
www.nts.org.uk

National Union of Students
Tel 0871 221 8221.
www.nusonline.co.uk

STA Travel
Priory Hse, 6 Wrights Lane,
London W8 6TA.
Tel 08701 630026.
www.statravel.co.uk

University of London
Malet St, London WC1.
Tel 020-7862 8000.
www.housing.lon.ac.uk

USEFUL PUBLICATIONS

Both the regional and national tourist boards produce comprehensive lists of local attractions and registered accommodation. For route planning, excellent, clear, large-format motoring atlases are produced by the RAC and AA *(see p685)*. For rural exploration, *Ordnance Survey* maps are ideal.

MEDIA

British national newspapers fall into two categories: quality papers, such as *The Times, The Telegraph* or *The Guardian*; and those heavy on gossip, such as *The Sun* or *The Daily Mirror*.

The weekend newspapers are more expensive than dailies but are packed with supplements of all kinds, including sections on the arts, motoring, entertainment, travel, listings and reviews.

Specialist periodicals are available from newsagents on just about every topic from hamster-keeping to hi-fi. For a more in-depth analysis of current events buy *The Economist, New Statesman & Society* or *The Spectator*, while *Private Eye* cocks a satirical snook at public figures. There are a few foreign magazines and newspapers available in large towns, often at main railway stations, but mostly in London. One of the most popular is the *International Herald Tribune*, which is available on the day of issue.

Television is undergoing an upheaval in Britain as satellite, cable and Freeview become increasingly popular. Still

Some of Britain's national newspapers

A local newsagent and sub-post office at Arisaig, Scotland

more influential, however, is the state-run BBC (British Broadcasting Corporation), which operates eight channels and maintains its reputation for producing some of the best television in the world without commercial breaks. The BBC's commercial rivals include ITV, Channel Four and Channel 5, the first tending toward popular soap operas and game-shows, Channel Four catering for trendy and minority tastes (art films, offbeat chat shows, game-shows and documentaries), and the last relying on US imports and TV movies. There are also regional variations.

The BBC has a number of radio stations, ranging from pop music (Radio One) to the middlebrow Radio Four. There are many local commercial radio stations.

Full TV and radio schedules are listed in daily newspapers and several listings magazines; one of the best is the *Radio Times*, a weekly publication found in most newsagents.

SMOKING

A total smoking ban in all public spaces has already been implemented in Scotland; Northern Ireland is due to follow suit in April 2007 and England in the summer of 2007. The Welsh Assembly has the right to decide whether to implement a ban and has twice approved it in principle.

WORKING RESTRICTIONS

Residents of the EU can work in Britain with no permit, while Commonwealth citizens under the age of 27 may work part-time for up to two years in the UK. North American students can get a blue card through their university, which enables them to work for up to six months – get this before arrival in Britain. BUNAC *(see p671)* is a student club which will organize exchange schemes for students to work abroad.

ELECTRICITY

The voltage in Britain is 220/240 AC, 50 Hz. Electrical plugs have three square pins and take fuses of 3, 5 and 13 amps. Visitors will need an adaptor for North American or continental appliances which have been bought from home, such as portable computers, hairdriers and tape recorders. Most hotels will have two-pronged European-style sockets for shavers only.

Standard British three-pin plug

Clock, the Royal Observatory, Greenwich *(see p133)*

TIME

Britain is on Greenwich Mean Time (GMT) during the winter months, five hours ahead of Eastern Standard Time and ten hours behind Sydney. From the middle of March to October, the clocks go forward one hour to British Summer Time (equivalent to Central European Time). To check the correct time, you can dial 123 to contact the Speaking Clock service.

CUSTOMS AND IMMIGRATION

A valid passport is needed to enter Britain. Visitors from the European Union (EU), the United States, Canada, New Zealand and Australia do not require visas to enter the country. Nor are inoculations or vaccinations necessary. When you arrive at any British air or seaport you will find separate queues at immigration control – one for European Union nationals, and several others for everyone else. As a result of Britain's membership of the European Union, anyone who arrives in

Highland malt

Britain from a member country can pass through a blue channel – but random checks are still being made to detect entry of any prohibited goods, particularly drugs, indecent material and weapons. Never, under any circumstances, carry luggage or parcels through customs for someone else.

Travellers entering from outside the EU still have to pass through customs channels. Go through the green channel if you have nothing to declare over the customs allowances for overseas visitors, and the red channel if you have goods to declare. If you are unsure of importation restrictions go through the red channel.

For EU members there is no limit to the amount of excise goods (such as tobacco or alcohol) that can be brought into the UK (except from certain new Member States), provided these are carried by you and

Green and red customs channels at Heathrow airport (see p682)

are for your own use. No live animals may be imported without a permit as Britain is free of rabies. Any animals found will be impounded and may be destroyed. Non-EU residents can obtain a VAT refund on goods bought in Britain *(see p658)*.

HM Customs and Excise
Thomas Paine House, Angel Square, Torrens St, London EC1. *Tel 020-7865 3000; advice line 0845 0109000. Contact for information regarding import or export restrictions.* **www**.hmce.gov.uk

The mosque in Regent's Park (see p105), London

RELIGIOUS ORGANIZATIONS

Baptist
London Baptist Assn, 235 Shaftesbury Ave., London WC2. *Tel 020-7692 5592.* **www**.londonbaptist.org.uk

Buddhist
Buddhist Society, 58 Eccleston Sq, London SW1. *Tel 020-7834 5858.* **www**.thebuddhistsociety.org

Church of England
Great Smith St, London SW1. *Tel 020-7898 1000.* **www**.cofe.anglican.org

Evangelical Alliance
Whitefield Hse, 186 Kennington Park Rd, London SE11. *Tel 020-7207 2100.* **www**.eauk.org

Jewish
Liberal Jewish Synagogue, 28 St John's Wood Rd, London NW8. *Tel 020-7286 5181.* **www**.ljs.org

United Synagogue (Orthodox), Adler House, 735 High Rd, North Finchley, London, N12. *Tel 020-8343 8989.* **www**.unitedsynagogue.org.uk

Moslem
Islamic Cultural Centre, 146 Park Rd, London NW8. *Tel 020-7724 3363.* **www**.iccuk.org

Quakers
Friends Hse, 173–177 Euston Rd, London NW1. *Tel 020-7663 1000.* **www**.quaker.org.uk

Roman Catholic
Westminster Cathedral, Victoria St, London SW1. *Tel 020-7798 9055.* **www**.westminstercathedral.org.uk

EMBASSIES AND CONSULATES

Australian High Commission
Australia Hse, the Strand, London WC2. *Tel 020-7379 4334.* **www**.australia.org.uk

Canadian High Commission
Canada Hse, Trafalgar Sq, London SW1. *Tel 020-7258 6600.* **www**.canada.gc.ca

New Zealand High Commission
New Zealand Hse, 80 Haymarket, London SW1. *Tel 020-7930 8422.* **www**.nzembassy.com

United States Embassy
24 Grosvenor Sq, London W1. *Tel 020-7499 9000.* **www**.usembassy.org.uk

CONVERSION CHART

Britain is officially metricated in line with the rest of Europe, but imperial measures are still in common usage, including road distances (measured in miles). Imperial pints and gallons are 20 per cent larger than US measures.

Imperial to metric
1 inch = 2.5 centimetres
1 foot = 30 centimetres
1 mile = 1.6 kilometres
1 ounce = 28 grams
1 pound = 454 grams
1 pint = 0.6 litres
1 gallon = 4.6 litres

Metric to imperial
1 millimetre = 0.04 inch
1 centimetre = 0.4 inch
1 metre = 3 feet 3 inches
1 kilometre = 0.6 mile
1 gram = 0.04 ounce
1 kilogram = 2.2 pounds

Personal Security and Health

Britain is a densely populated country which, like any other, has its share of social problems. However, it is very unlikely that you will come across any violence. If you do encounter difficulties, never hesitate to contact the police for help. Britain's National Health Service can be relied upon for both emergency and routine treatment. However, you may have to pay if your country has no reciprocal arrangement with Britain.

HOSPITALS AND MEDICAL TREATMENT

All visitors to Britain are strongly advised to take out medical insurance against the cost of any emergency hospital care, repatriation and specialists' fees, especially for those visitors from outside the European Union (EU). Emergency medical treatment in a British National Health Service (NHS) casualty ward is free, but any kind of additional medical care could prove very expensive.

Residents of the European Union and nationals of some other Commonwealth and European countries are entitled to free medical treatment under the NHS, though the process is bureaucratic. Before travelling, you should obtain a form confirming that your country of origin has adequate reciprocal health arrangements with Britain. But some treatments are not covered and repatriation is not included, so medical insurance is preferable.

If you need to see a dentist while staying in Britain, you will have to pay. The cost varies, depending on your entitlement to NHS treatment, and whether you can find an NHS dentist to treat you. Emergency dental treatment is available in some hospitals, but if you would prefer a private dentist, try looking in the *Yellow Pages (see p676).*

PHARMACISTS

You can buy a wide range of proprietary medicines without prescription from chemists in Britain. Boots is the best-known and largest supplier, with branches in most towns. Many medicines, however, are only available with a doctor's prescription, which you must take to a chemist or pharmacist. If you are likely to need drugs, either bring your own or get your doctor to write out the generic (as opposed to the brand) name of the drug. If you are entitled to an NHS prescription, you will be charged a standard rate; without this you will be charged the full cost of the drug. Do ask for a receipt for any insurance claim. Some pharmacies are open until midnight; for emergencies contact the local hospital. Doctors' surgeries are normally open mornings and early evenings. You can call NHS Direct 24-hour helpline (0845 4647), or go to a hospital casualty department any time. In an emergency, dial 999 for an ambulance.

Pharmacy sign

CRIME

Britain is not a dangerous place for visitors, and it is most unlikely that your stay will be blighted by crime. Practical advice to help you avoid loss or injury is given below. Due to past terrorist attacks, there are occasional security alerts, especially on the Underground, but these are mainly false alarms often due to people accidentally leaving a bag or parcel lying around. Always co-operate with the authorities if your bag has to be searched or if you are asked to evacuate a building.

SUITABLE PRECAUTIONS

Take good care of your belongings at all times. Make sure your possessions are adequately insured before you arrive. Never leave them unattended in public places.

Keep your valuables well concealed (particularly mobile phones), especially in crowds. In all public places, keep handbags on your lap, not on the floor. It is always advisable not to carry too much cash or jewellery with you; leave it in your hotel safe instead. Pickpockets love crowded places like markets, busy shops and all modes of transport during rush-hour.

Female police constable   **Traffic police officer**   **Male police constable**

If you are travelling alone at night try to avoid deserted and poorly lit buildings and places such as back streets and car parks. By far the safest way of carrying large amounts of cash around is in traveller's cheques *(see p679)*.

Begging is an increasingly common sight in many British cities, and foreign visitors are frequent targets for hard-luck stories. Requests for money are usually polite; but any abuse should be reported to the police immediately.

WOMEN TRAVELLING ALONE

It is not unusual in Great Britain for women to travel unaccompanied, or visit a bar or restaurant with a group of female friends. Nor is it especially dangerous, but caution is advisable in deserted places, especially after dark. Try to avoid using public transport when there is just one other passenger or a group of young men. Summon a licensed taxi *(see p690)* rather than walk through a lonely area at night, especially if you do not know the district very well.

Legally, you cannot carry any offensive weapons around with you in Britain, even for self-defence. This includes knives, coshes, guns or tear-gas; however, personal alarm systems are allowed.

EMERGENCY SERVICES

The sight of a traditional British bobby patrolling the streets in a tall hat is now less common than the police patrol car, sometimes with wailing sirens and flashing lights. But the old-fashioned police constable does still exist, particularly in rural areas and in crowded city centres, and continues to be courteous, approachable and helpful.

Unlike in many countries, the police force in Great Britain do not carry guns. If you are lost, the advice to

Police car

Ambulance

Fire engine

ask a policeman or woman still applies. Traffic wardens may also be able to help you with directions.

In a crisis, dial 999 to get the police, fire and ambulance services which are on call 24-hours a day. Calls are free from any public or private phone, but they should only be made in real emergencies. Along the coastal areas of Great Britain this number will also put you in touch with Britain's voluntary coastguard rescue service, the Royal National Lifeboat Institute.

Royal National Lifeboat Institute logo

LOST PROPERTY

If you are unlucky enough to lose anything or have anything stolen, go straight to the nearest police station and make a report of your loss. If you plan to make a claim on your insurance for any theft, you will need a written report from the local police. All of the main bus or rail stations have lost property offices. Don't leave your valuables on display in your room: hotels usually disclaim all responsibility for valuables not kept in their safe.

Communications

Modern BT phone box

With continuously improving telecommunication systems and the spread of e-mail, staying in contact and making plans while travelling has never been easier. The telephone system in Britain is efficient and inexpensive. Charges depend on when, where and for how long you talk. The cheapest time to call is between 6pm and 8am Monday to Friday, and throughout the weekend. Local calls made on public payphones, however, are charged at a fixed rate per minute.

PAYPHONES

You can pay for a payphone using coins or a card. Payphones accept 10p, 20p, 50p and £1 pieces, while newer phones also accept £2 coins. The minimum cost of a call is 20p. If you expect a call to be short, use 10p or 20p pieces, as payphones only return unused coins. You may find a phone card more convenient than coins. BT (formerly British Telecom) has now stopped issuing its own prepaid phone cards,

but other phone companies' cards are available from newsagents and post offices. If you use a credit card, be warned that it carries a minimum charge and your phone calls will be charged at a higher rate.

TELEPHONE DIRECTORIES

Directories, such as *Yellow Pages* and *Thomson Local*, list local businesses and services. They can be found at local Post Office branches, libraries and often at your hotel.

DIRECTORY

A number of telephone services exist to help you find or reach a specific phone number. You will be charged more for enquiries if calling from a mobile phone.

Emergency Calls
Tel 999. Police, Fire, Ambulance, Coastguard, Mountain and Cave Rescue.

BT Directory Enquiries
Tel 118 500 (charge applies).

International Directory Enquiries
Tel 118 505 (charge applies).

International Operator
Tel 155 (freephone).

Operator Assistance
Tel 100.

Overseas Calls
Tel 00 followed by country code: Australia (61), Canada (1), Ireland (353), New Zealand (64), South Africa (27), United States (1).

Yellow Pages
Tel 118 247. Provides numbers for specific kinds of shops or services in any area.

USING A CARD AND COIN PHONE

1 Lift the receiver and wait for the dial tone.

2 Insert your phone card into the slot or deposit any of the following coins: 10p, 20p, 50p, £1, £2. The minimum amount is 20p.

3 Dial the number and wait to be connected.

4 The display indicates how much credit you have left. A rapid bleeping noise means your money has run out. Deposit more coins or insert another phone card.

5 If you want to make another call and you have money left in credit, do not replace the receiver, press the follow-on-call button.

6 When you have finished speaking, replace the receiver and retrieve your card or collect your change. Only wholly unused coins are refunded.

£1   50p   20p   10p

ACCESSING THE INTERNET

Most cities and towns now have some form of public access to computers and the Internet, including payphones in the street. Free Internet access is often available at main library branches, although you may have to book a time slot. Hotels are increasingly including Internet facilities as part of their service. Internet cafés usually charge by the minute for computer use. Charges tend to build up quickly, especially when including the cost of printed pages. Internet access is generally very cheap and is most reasonable during off-peak times.

24-hour Internet access at the Europe-wide chain EasyEverything

Sending a Letter

Red and gold Post Office logo

Besides main post office branches that offer all the mail services available, there are many Post Office branches in newsagents, grocery stores and general information centres, particularly in more isolated areas. In many villages the Post Office outlet is also the only shop. Post Office branches are usually open from 9am to 5:30pm Monday to Friday, and until 12:30pm on Saturday. Post boxes – in all shapes and sizes but always red – are found throughout cities, towns and villages.

A Cotswold Post Office outlet

POSTAL SERVICES

Stamps can be bought at many outlets, including supermarkets and petrol stations. Hotels often have post boxes at their reception. When writing to a British address always include the postcode, which can be obtained from either the **Royal Mail** enquiry line or website.

All air letters are 1st class

2nd-class stamp   1st-class stamp

Books of twelve 1st- and 2nd-class stamps

Letters and postcards can be sent either first or second class within the UK. First-class service is more expensive but quicker, with most letters reaching their destination the following day (except Sunday); second-class mail takes a day or two longer.

Royal Mail
Tel 0845 7740740.
www.royalmail.com

POSTE RESTANTE

Large urban Post Office branches have a *poste restante* service where letters can be sent for collection. To use the service be sure to print the surname (last name) clearly so it will be filed correctly. Send it to P*oste Restante* followed by the address of the Post Office branch. To collect your post you will have to show your passport or other form of identification. Post is kept for one month. London's main Post Office branch is in William IV Street, WC2. The American Express office at 30–31 Haymarket, London SW1 has a *poste restante* for customers.

POST BOXES

These may be either freestanding "pillar boxes" or wall safes, both painted bright red. Some pillar boxes have separate slots, one for overseas and first-class mail, another for second-class mail. Collections are usually made several times a day during weekdays (less often on Saturdays and Sundays); the last collection time is marked on the box.

A rural mailbox, embedded in a stone wall

MAILING ABROAD

Air letters go by Royal Mail's airmail service anywhere in the world; the cost depends on the destination. On average, it takes 3 days for them to reach cities in Europe, and 4 to 6 days for destinations elsewhere. Sending post by surface mail may be economical, but it can take up to 8 weeks for it to reach its destination. Royal Mail offers an express airmail service called **Airsure**. Available from all Post Office branches, mail goes on the first available flight to the country of destination. **Parcelforce Worldwide** offers courier-style services to most destinations and is comparable in price to **Crossflight**, **DHL**, **Expressair** or **UPS**.

Pillar box

Airsure (Royal Mail)
Tel 08457 740740.
www.royalmail.com

Crossflight
Tel 0870 224 1122.
www.crossflight.co.uk

DHL
Tel 08701 100300. **www.**dhl.co.uk

Expressair
Tel 020-8897 3336.
www.expressair.co.uk

Parcelforce Worldwide
Tel 08708 501150.
www.parcelforce.com

UPS
Tel 08457 877877. **www.**ups.com

Banking and Local Currency

Visitors to Britain usually find that the high-street banks offer them the best rates of exchange. However, if you do find yourself having to use one of the hundreds of privately owned bureaux de change that are found at nearly every major airport, rail station and tourist area, care should be taken to check the commission and minimum charges before completing any transaction. Traveller's cheques are by far the safest method of bringing currency to Britain with you.

Lloyds Bank with bureau de change facilities

BUREAUX DE CHANGE

Small private bureaux de change may be more con-veniently located and open when banks are closed. But rates of exchange can vary considerably and commission charges can be high, so it may be worth looking around.

The reputable firms such as **Exchange International**, **Travelex**, **American Express** and **Chequepoint** usually offer good exchange facilities and have branches throughout Britain.

British Banks
All these high-street banks have branches in most of Britain's towns and cities. Most will also offer exchange facilities, but proof of identity may be required.

BANKS

Banks generally offer the best rates of exchange for visitors, though commissions may vary considerably.

Every large town and city in Britain will have a branch of at least one of these five high-street clearing banks – **Barclays**, **Lloyds TSB**, **HSBC**, **National Westminster**, and the **Royal Bank of Scotland**.

Many banks have an ATM (cash dispenser) from which you can obtain money with a credit card and your personal identification number (PIN); arrange this before you leave home. Some of the most modern machines have easy-to-read computerized instruc-tions in several languages. American Express cards may be used at all ATM cash machines. Once again you will need a PIN number to access your personal account. There is a 2 per cent handling charge for each transaction that you make.

If you run out of funds, another way to get money is to contact your own bank

and ask them to wire the cash to the nearest British bank. You can also ask branches of Travelex or American Express to do this for you. North American visitors can get cash dispatched through **Western Union** to a bank or post office. Take along your passport to claim the money.

Banking hours vary, but the minimum opening times are 10am to 3:30pm, Monday to Friday. Many will stay open longer, especially in cities, and some open Saturday mornings. All banks close on Public Holidays *(see p65)*.

CREDIT CARDS

Credit and store cards are widely accepted throughout Britain, and you will definitely need a credit card in order to rent a car and usually for hotel bookings. But many smaller shops, markets, guesthouses and cafés may not accept them, so it is always wise to check in advance. Cards that are accepted are usually displayed on the windows of the establishment. The main card used throughout Britain is Visa, but other credit cards include Diners Club, American Express, Access and Mastercard.

You can get cash advances with a credit card (up to your credit limit) at any bank and ATM cash machine displaying the appropriate card sign. You will be charged the credit card company's interest rate for obtaining cash, which will appear on your statement with the amount advanced when you return home.

Barclays Bank logo

HSBC Bank logo

National Westminster logo

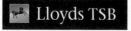

Lloyds TSB Bank logo

Royal Bank of Scotland logo

Exchange International
Tel 020-7630 1107.

Travelex
Tel 07333 18901.

American Express
Tel 020-7834 5555.
www.americanexpress.co.uk

Chequepoint
Tel 020-7373 0111.
www.chequepoint.com

Western Union
Tel 0800 833 833.
www.westernunion.com

CURRENCY AND TRAVELLER'S CHEQUES

Britain's currency is the pound sterling (£), which is divided into 100 pence (p). There are no exchange controls in Britain, so you may bring in and take out as much cash as you like. Scotland has its own notes, which, though legal tender throughout Britain, are not always accepted in England and Wales. Traveller's cheques are the safest alternative to carrying large amounts of cash.

A Scottish one pound (£1) bank note

Always keep the receipts from your traveller's cheques separately from the cheques themselves because it makes it easier to obtain a refund if your cheques are lost or stolen. Some high-street banks issue traveller's cheques free of commission to their account holders, but the normal rate is about 1 per cent. When changing money ask for some smaller notes, as these are easier to use.

Bank Notes

English notes are produced in denominations of £5, £10, £20, and £50. Always get small denominations as some shops may refuse the larger notes.

£50 note

£20 note

£10 note

£5 note

Coinage

Coins currently in use are £2, £1, 50p, 20p, 10p, 5p, 2p and 1p (shown here at actual sizes).

2 pounds (£2)

1 pound (£1)

50 pence (50p)

20 pence (20p)

10 pence (10p)

5 pence (5p)

2 pence (2p)

1 penny (1p)

TRAVEL INFORMATION

As it is an international gateway for air and sea traffic, travelling to Britain poses few problems. By air, travellers have a very large choice of carriers serving North America, Australasia and Europe. Coach (bus) travel is a cheap, albeit rather slow, form of transport from Europe, while travelling by train has been transformed thanks to the Channel Tunnel – less than three hours from Paris to London on

British Airways passenger jet

Eurostar. Travelling within Britain itself is fairly easy. There is an extensive network of roads to all parts of the country and hiring a car is often the best way of travelling around. The rail network is efficient and the network to the smaller towns, especially around London, is good. Travelling by coach is the cheapest option; the coach network serves most areas but can be slow. If time is short, air travel is possible but can be expensive.

Passenger concourse, Waterloo Station, London

TRAVELLING AROUND BRITAIN

Choosing the best way to travel around Britain depends very much on where and when you want to go, although the quickest and most convenient methods are generally the most expensive.

Distances between any two points within mainland Britain are relatively small (at least by American or Australian standards) so air travel usually makes sense only between the extremes, such as London to Edinburgh. For shorter journeys, the time spent getting to and from airports often outweighs any savings in actual travelling time. Rail services are the best alternative if you want to visit Britain's major cities, though fares, especially at peak times, can be quite expensive. If you plan to do much travelling within Britain, a rail pass can be very good value. You can buy a pass before you arrive in the UK as several schemes cater for overseas visitors *(see p686).*

Coach (bus) networks cover a wide number of UK destinations, and are cheaper than trains, but take longer and may be less comfortable *(see p688).* Taxis are available at all main coach or rail stations to take you to your hotel; without a car you will avoid the stress of driving in city centres.

If you plan a more flexible touring holiday, hiring a car is more feasible than relying on public transport. Car rental can be arranged at major airports, large railway stations and city centre outlets *(see p685).* To get the best deals, book from abroad. Small local firms often undercut the large operators in price, but may not be as reliable or convenient.

For detailed exploration of smaller areas such as Britain's National Parks or popular

regions like the Lake District *(see pp354–69)* you may prefer more leisurely transportation offered by bike, horse or narrowboat. Sometimes there are picturesque local options like a rowing-boat ferry, such as the one between Southwold and Walberswick on the Blyth Estuary *(see p202).* There are also larger car ferries which travel to Britain's islands.

Rowing-boat ferry on the River Blyth, Southwold, Suffolk

CHANNEL TUNNEL

This historic landlink between France and Britain opened for business in late 1994 and closed one of the "missing links" in the European transport system. The sleek new rolling-stock is high-tech and very comfortable, producing an experience more akin to air travel than rail. Passengers on buses and cars get onto a freight train run by **Eurotunnel** which takes 35 minutes to travel between Calais and Folkestone.

EURO TUNNEL

Eurotunnel logo

For those travelling by rail there are about 40 scheduled passenger-only **Eurostar** services, operated by the French, Belgian and British. They run direct services between Brussels, Lille, Paris, Frethun, Calais and London/Ashford. There are two passenger tunnels – and one service tunnel – which lie 25–45 m (82–147 ft) below the sea bed. All the tunnels are made of concrete and iron, and are 50 km (31 miles) long.

Arriving by Sea, Rail and Coach

If you are travelling from Europe by foot, car, coach (bus) or rail you will have to cross the English Channel or North Sea either by ferry or the Channel Tunnel. Ferry services operate from a huge number of ports on the European mainland and have good link-ups with international coaches, with services from most European cities to Britain. The Channel Tunnel has meant there is now a non-stop rail link between Europe and Britain. Prices between the ferries and the tunnel services remain competitive.

A Eurostar train, which takes less than 3 hours from Paris to London

Ferry arriving at Dover

FERRY SERVICES FROM EUROPE

A complex network of ferry services operate to over a dozen British ports, with around 20 car and passenger ferry services that travel regularly across the Channel and North Sea routes from many ports in northern and southern Europe *(see pp14–19)*.

Because of the number of areas they reach, ferries can be convenient and economical for those travelling in cars or on foot, depending on your destination. Fares vary greatly according to the season, time of travel and duration of stay. The shortest crossings are not always the cheapest: you pay for the speed of the journey.

CROSSING TIMES

Crossing times vary from just over an hour on the shortest routes to a full 24 hours on services from Spain and Scandinavia. If you take an overnight sailing, you may have to pay extra for sleeping accommodation, but it is often worth booking a cabin on the longer trips to avoid feeling exhausted when you arrive. Fast **Seacat** (catamaran) services between Calais and Dover, Ostend and Dover, and Dieppe and Newhaven are run by **Hoverspeed**. These are the fastest routes across the Channel, taking just under an hour, and catamarans can carry vehicles. The crossings lack the dip and sway of a conventional ship, and so may be less painful for poor sailors.

SEAPORT BUREAUCRACY

Those visitors from outside the European Union should allow plenty of time for immigration control and customs clearance at British seaports *(see p673)*. You are not allowed to bring pets into Britain because of rabies.

INTERNATIONAL COACH TRAVEL

Although coach (bus) travel is comparably cheaper than other methods of travel, it is not the most comfortable way of travelling across Europe. But if you have a lot of spare time and want to stop off en route it can be convenient. Once you have paid for your ticket you will not have to pay again to use the ferry or the Channel Tunnel.

INTERNATIONAL RAIL TRAVEL

With the advent of the Channel Tunnel, there is now access to Britain via **Eurostar** and **Eurotunnel** from the French and Belgian high-speed rail networks. Rail travel can be an efficient, comfortable and fast way of travelling across Europe to Britain – in France and Belgium, trains reach speeds of up to 186 mph (300 kmph). The cost is comparable to flying, although it is much more convenient.

DIRECTORY

FERRIES, RAIL AND COACH TRAVEL

Brittany Ferries
Tel 0870 366 5333.
www.brittanyferries.co.uk

European Rail Travel
Tel 08705 848 848 (for info).
www.raileurope.co.uk

Eurostar
Tel 08705 186186 (for foot & rail passengers).
www.eurostar.com

Eurotunnel/Le Shuttle
Tel 08705 353535 (for cars & coach travel).
www.eurotunnel.com

Hoverspeed/Seacat
Tel 0870 240 8070.
www.hoverspeed.com

International Coach Travel
Tel 020-7730 3466.

P&O Ferries
Tel 08705 202020.
www.poferries.com

Arriving by Air

Britain has about 130 licensed airports but only a handful of these are equipped for long-haul traffic. The largest is London's Heathrow, the world's busiest international airport and one of Europe's central routing points for international air travel. It is served by most of the world's leading airlines with direct flights from nearly all the major cities. The other major international airports include Gatwick, Stansted, Manchester, Glasgow, Newcastle, Birmingham and Edinburgh. Smaller airports such as London City, Bristol, Norwich and Cardiff have daily flights to European destinations.

Platform sign for express railway service to London

A British Airways 747 jet at Heathrow Airport

BRITISH AIRPORTS

The majority of Britain's largest and best known airports are run by the British Airports Authority – the rest are owned by a local authority or are in private hands. All BAA airports offer up-to-date facilities, including 24-hour banking, shops, cafés, hotels and restaurants. Security is strict at all British airports and it is important never to leave baggage unattended.

If you are starting your visit in London, flights to Gatwick, Heathrow or Stansted are equally convenient. But if you plan to visit northern England, there are an increasing number of flights going to Birmingham,

Newcastle and Manchester, while for Scotland you can fly to Glasgow or Edinburgh.

Heathrow has four terminals and some others have two. Before you fly, check with the airport from which terminal your flight leaves.

During severe weather conditions in the winter months, your flight may be diverted to another airport. If this happens, the airline will organize transportation back to your original destination.

British Airways has flights to nearly all the world's important destinations. Other British international airlines include **Virgin Atlantic**, with routes to the USA and the Far East, and **British Midland**,

which flies to Western Europe.

The main American airlines offering scheduled services to Britain include **Delta**, **US Air** and **American Airlines**. From Canada, the main carrier is **Air Canada**. From Australasia, the national carriers **Qantas** and **Air New Zealand** vie with many Far Eastern rivals.

Britain imposes an airport tax on all departing passengers – currently £10 for domestic and EC routes, and £20 for non-EC and long-haul flights.

TRANSPORT FROM THE AIRPORT

Britain's international airports lie some way from city centres, but transport to

Arrival terminal at Heathrow Airport

AIRPORT	ℹ INFORMATION	DISTANCE TO CITY CENTRE	TAXI FARE TO CITY CENTRE	PUBLIC TRANSPORT TO CITY CENTRE
Heathrow	08700 000123	14 miles (23 km)	£40–45	Rail: 15 min Tube: 45 min
Gatwick	08700 002468	28 miles (45 km)	£75	Rail: 30 min Bus: 70 min
Stansted	08700 000303	37 miles (60 km)	£80	Rail: 45 min Bus: 75 min
Manchester	0161 4893000	10 miles (16 km)	£15–16	Rail: 15 min Bus: 30 min
Birmingham	0870 733 5511	8 miles (13 km)	£12–15	Bus: 30 min
Newcastle	0870 122 1488	5 miles (8 km)	£10–12	Metro: 20 min Bus: 20 min
Glasgow	0870 040 0008	8 miles (13 km)	£12–15	Bus: 20 min
Edinburgh	0870 040 0007	8 miles (13 km)	£17–18	Bus: 25 min

and from them is efficient. Every airport has taxis and these are the most convenient form of door-to-door travel, but they are also expensive and can be slow if there is traffic congestion – very likely if you travel in the rush hour *(see p684)*. This can also be a problem with taking a coach or bus, although they are a lot cheaper than taxis.

Heathrow and Newcastle are both linked to the centre of the city by the Underground *(see p691)*. These are efficient, quick and cheap. Manchester, Stansted, Gatwick and Heathrow *(see p686)* have regular express trains which are not too expensive and are a reliable method for travelling into the heart of the city.

National Express Coaches *(see p688)* provide direct connections from major airports to many British destinations. They have a regular service between Gatwick and Heathrow.

CHOOSING A TICKET

Finding the right flight at the right price can be difficult. Promotional fares do come up and it is always worth checking with the airlines direct. Cheap deals are often available from package operators and are advertised in newspapers and travel magazines. Students and under 26s, senior citizens and regular or business travellers may be able to obtain a discount through student travel agencies. Children and babies also travel at cheaper rates.

The bar at the popular Posthouse Heathrow hotel

AIR FARES

Fares to Britain are usually seasonal, the highest being from June to September. The best deals are available from November to April, excluding the Christmas period – if you want to travel then, be sure to book well in advance.

APEX (Advance Purchase Excursion) fares are often the best value, though they must be booked up to a month ahead, and are subject to restrictions. Charter flights offer even cheaper seats, but are not usually flexible.

If you choose a discount fare, always buy from a reputable operator, and do not part with cash until you have seen your ticket and ensured your seat has been confirmed.

Packages may be worth considering, even if you enjoy independent travel, as sometimes car rental or rail travel is included. This can be cheaper than arranging it yourself when you have arrived in Britain.

TRAVELLING WITHIN BRITAIN BY AIR

Britain's size means that internal air travel only makes sense over longish distances, where it can save a great deal of time – for example, London to Scotland, or to one of the many offshore islands. Air fares can be expensive, but if you book well ahead, fares can be up to three times cheaper than if you just turn up at the airport – although you are still always guaranteed a seat. The British Airways shuttle flights that operate between London and cities such as Glasgow, Edinburgh and Manchester are extremely popular with business travellers. At peak times of the day, flights leave every hour, while at other times there is usually a flight every two hours. Bad weather can cause delays or diversions during the winter months. Even on domestic flights, security is stringent, and you should never leave your bags unattended.

DIRECTORY

AIRLINE NUMBERS

Air Canada
Tel 08705 247226.

Air New Zealand
Tel 0800 028 4149.

American Airlines
Tel 08457 789789.

British Airways
Tel 0845 779 9977.

British Midland
Tel 0870 607 0555.

Continental Airlines
Tel 0800 776464.

Delta Airlines
Tel 0800 414767.

Qantas
Tel 0845 774 7767.

US Airways
Tel 08456 003300.

Virgin Atlantic
Tel 01293 747747.

Award-winning exterior of Stansted Airport

Travelling Around by Car

The most startling difference for most foreign motorists is that in Britain you drive on the left, with corresponding adjustments at roundabouts and junctions. Distances are measured in miles. Once you adapt, rural Britain is an enjoyable place to drive, though traffic density in towns and at busy holiday times can cause long delays – public holiday weekends near the south coast can be particularly horrendous. An extensive network of toll-free motorways and trunk roads has now cut travelling time to most parts of the country.

WHAT YOU NEED

To drive in Britain you need a current driving licence with an international driving permit if required. In any vehicle you drive you must carry proof of ownership or a rental agreement, plus any insurance documents.

ROADS IN BRITAIN

Peak rush-hour traffic can last from 8–9:30am and 5–6:30pm on weekdays in the cities; at these times traffic can grind to a halt. In the country a good touring map is essential; the AA or RAC motoring atlases are fairly straightforward to use. For exploration of more rural areas, the Ordnance Survey series is the best. On

A motorway sign in miles

all road maps B roads are secondary roads and A roads, often dual carriageways (two lanes in each direction), are main routes. B routes are often less congested and more

The A30 dual carriageway going through Cornwall

enjoyable to use. Rural areas are crisscrossed by a web of tiny lanes. Motorways are marked with M followed by their identifying number.

ROAD SIGNS

Signs are now generally standardized in line with Europe. Directional signs are colour-coded: blue for motorways, green for major routes and white for minor routes. Signposting in Britain is not consistent and city suburbs can be confusing. Brown signs indicate places of interest. Advisory or warning signs are usually triangles in red and white, with easy to understand pictograms. Watch for electronic notices on motorways that warn of road works, accidents or patches of fog. Level crossings, found at rail lines, often have automatic barriers. If the lights are flashing red it means a train is coming and you must stop. The *UK Highway Code Manual* – available from most bookshops – is an up-to-date guide to all the current British driving regulations and traffic signs.

RULES OF THE ROAD

Speed limits are 30–40 mph (50–65 kmph) in built-up areas and 70 mph (110 kmph) on motorways or dual carriageways – look out for speed signs on other roads. It is compulsory to wear seat-belts in Britain. Drink-driving penalties are severe – see the *UK Highway Code Manual* for legal limits.

No stopping	**Speed limit applies**
No entry	**No right-turn allowed**
Railway level crossing	**Give way to all vehicles**
One-way traffic	**Gradient of a road**

PARKING

This is the bane of the British motorist's life. Parking meters operate during working hours (usually 8am–6:30pm Mon–Sat); keep a supply of coins for them. Some cities have "park and ride" schemes, where you can take a bus from an out-of-city car park into the centre. Other towns have parking schemes where you buy a card at the tourist office or newsagents, fill in your parking times and display the card. Avoid double yellow lines at all times; single lines sometimes mean you can park in the evenings and at weekends, but check carefully. Traffic wardens will not hesitate to ticket, clamp or tow your car away. If in any doubt, find a car park (*see pp690–91*). Outside urban areas and popular tourist zones, parking is easier. Look out for signs with a blue P, indicating parking spaces. Never leave any valuables or luggage in your car: thefts are common, especially in cities.

Sign for a car park

PETROL

North American visitors may find fuel (gas) very expensive in Britain. Large supermarkets often have the cheapest petrol; look out for branches of Tesco or Sainsbury with petrol stations. Motorway service areas are generally more expensive. Petrol is sold in three grades: diesel, LRP (lead replacement petrol) and unleaded. Most modern cars in Britain use unleaded petrol – any vehicle you hire will probably do so. Unleaded and diesel are cheaper than LRP. Most petrol stations in Britain are self-service but instructions at pumps are easy to follow.

BREAKDOWN SERVICES

Britain's major motoring organizations, the **AA** (Automobile Association) and the **RAC** (Royal Auto-mobile Club), provide a comprehensive 24-hour breakdown service for members, as well as many other motoring services. Both offer reciprocal assistance for members of overseas motoring organizations – before arrival check with your own group to see if you are covered. You can contact the AA or RAC from the roadside SOS phones found on motor-ways. **Green Flag** is the other major rescue service in Britain, which can some-times be quicker and cheaper since it makes greater use of local garages.

Most car hire agencies have their own cover, and their charges include membership of either the AA, the RAC or Green Flag while you are driving. Be sure to ask the rental company for the service's emergency number.

Even if you are not a member of an affiliated organization you can still call out a rescue service, although it will be expensive. Always follow the advice given on your insurance policy or rental agreement. If you have an accident that involves injury or another vehicle, call the police as soon as possible *(see p675)*.

A small rural petrol station in Goathland, North Yorkshire

CAR HIRE

Hiring a car in Britain can be expensive. One of the most competitive national companies is **Autos Abroad**, but small local firms may undercut even these rates. Many companies prefer you to leave a credit card number; otherwise you may have to part with a substantial cash deposit. You need your driving licence and a passport when you hire. Most companies will not hire to novice drivers, and set age limits (usually 21–74). Automatic cars are now generally available for hire. If you are touring Britain for three weeks or more, you may find a leasing arrange-ment cheaper than hiring. Remember to add VAT and insurance costs when you check hire rates.

HITCHHIKING

Hitchhiking is a common practice in Britain, and you are likely to thumb a long-distance lift if you stand near a busy exit road junction. In rural or walking areas like the Lake District, tired hikers may well be offered a lift. It is illegal to hitch on motorways or their approach roads. As anywhere, there is a risk in hitchhiking alone, especially for a woman. Lift-sharing is now a common practice. The small-ads magazine *Loot* (sold in newsagents in London, Manchester and Bristol) has a large section for lift-seekers.

DIRECTORY

BREAKDOWN

AA
Tel 0800 887 766.

Green Flag
Tel 0800 400 600.

RAC
Tel 0800 828 282.

CAR HIRE

Autos Abroad
Tel 0870 066 7788.
www.autosabroad.com

Avis
Tel 0870 010 0287.
www.avis.co.uk

Budget
Tel 0800 181 181.
www.budget.com

Europcar
Tel 0870 607 5000.
www.europcar.co.uk

Hertz
Tel 08708 448 844.
www.hertz.co.uk

National Car Rentals
Tel 08705 365 365.
www.nationalcar.co.uk

GENERAL INFORMATION

AA Road Watch
Tel 09003 401 100.

AA Disabled Line
Tel 0800 262 050.

Emergency Calls
Tel 999.

Weathercall
Tel 08706 004 242.

Travelling Around by Rail

Britain has a privatized rail network which covers the whole of the country. It is divided into regional sections which serve over 2,500 stations throughout Britain. The system is generally efficient and reliable. Parts of the network are occasionally closed for repairs, mostly at weekends, so check before travelling. Journeys across the country, rather than out of London, may involve a number of changes as most lines radiate from London, which has seven major terminals. There is a rail link with Continental Europe on Eurostar, from Waterloo Station in London and Ashford in Kent *(see p680)*.

Mainline train speeding through countryside

TICKETS

Large travel agents and all railway stations sell rail tickets. First-class tickets cost about one-third more than standard fares, and generally return fares are cheaper than two singles.

Allow plenty of time to buy your ticket and always ask about any special offers or reduced fares. There are four types of discounted fares for adults. Apex tickets are available in limited numbers on some long-distance routes and have to be booked at least a week in advance. SuperApex fares have to be purchased 14 days in advance and again are available in limited numbers on a few mainline services. Savers can be used at weekends and on most weekday trains outside rush hours. Finally, Supersavers cannot be used on Fridays, or any peak-hour service to, from or through London.

Ticket offices in rural areas may close at weekends, but small branch lines have a conductor on board who sells tickets. Otherwise buy a ticket beforehand as inspectors can levy on-the-spot fines if you do not have a valid ticket. Many stations have automatic ticket machines.

RAIL PASSES

If you plan to do much train travelling around Britain, buy a rail pass. These can be bought from many agents abroad, such as **Rail Europe** or **CIE Tours International**. An All Line Rail Rover gives adults unlimited travel throughout England, Scotland and Wales for 7 or 14 days. Children under 16 travel half price, or a Family Rail Card is available. It can be used for up to four adults and four children. Discounts are also available for 16- to 25-year-olds or full-time students attending a UK educational establishment with a Young Person's Rail Card. For those over the age of 60, the Senior Rail Card entitles you to a one-third price discount on most fares. There are special passes for London transport and a pass that covers London, Oxford, Canterbury and Brighton. Children of 5–15 years pay half fare; the under-5s travel free. Family tickets are also available. Disabled travellers qualify for many discounts. Keep a passport-sized photo handy for buying passes. If you have a pass, make sure you always show it when you buy a ticket.

GENERAL TIPS

Britain's fastest and most comfortable trains are those on the mainline routes. These are very popular services and get booked up quickly. It is always advisable to reserve your seat in advance, especially if you want to travel at peak times such as Friday evenings. Mainline trains have dining cars, air-conditioning and are fast, travelling to Edinburgh from London, for example, in just over four hours.

For those arriving at Heathrow Airport and travelling into London *(see pp682–3)*, an alternative to the Underground *(see p691)* is the Heathrow Express, the fast train to Paddington Station (www.heathrow express.com or 0845 600 1515). Trains run every 15 minutes from 5am until around midnight, and take 15 minutes (8 minutes more to and from Terminal 4).

Rail terminal, Liverpool Street Station

Porters are rare on British stations, although trolleys are often available for passengers to help themselves. If you are disabled and need help, call to book assistance at least 24 hours before your journey. A yellow line above a train window indicates a first class compartment. You cannot use these without paying the full fare, even if the train is full. Check which section of the train to join as they sometimes split through the journey and proceed to different destinations. Trains stop for only a minute at each station, so be ready to get on and off. Some stations are a little way from town centres, but are well signposted and nearly always on a bus route. Sunday trains and public holiday services are often a lot slower than normal.

SCENIC TRAIN RIDES

As motor transport made many rural railways redundant in the mid-20th century, picturesque sections of track, as well as many old steam engines, were rescued and restored to working order by enthusiasts. These services are often privately run: the local tourist office, railway station ticket office or travel agents will provide you with information. Most of the lines are short – around 20 miles (32 km) – but cover some of the prettiest parts of the country and are one of the best ways to enjoy its spectacular scenery. Lines include: the Ffestiniog Railway *(see pp452–3)* in North Wales; the North York

Moors Railway *(see p394)*; the Strathspey Steam Railway in the Cairngorm Mountains of the Scottish Highlands *(see p544)* and the La'l Ratty Railway in Cumbria *(see p364)*.

A reconditioned steam train, North Yorkshire

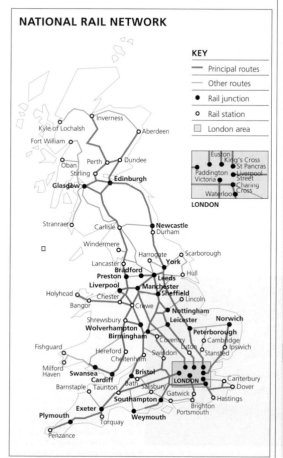

NATIONAL RAIL NETWORK

KEY

— Principal routes
— Other routes
● Rail junction
○ Rail station
□ London area

LONDON

Euston
King's Cross
St Pancras
Paddington
Victoria
Liverpool Street
Charing Cross
Waterloo

Inverness
Kyle of Lochalsh
Fort William
Aberdeen
Oban
Perth
Dundee
Stirling
Glasgow
Edinburgh
Stranraer
Carlisle
Newcastle
Durham
Windermere
Scarborough
Harrogate
Lancaster
York
Bradford
Hull
Preston
Leeds
Liverpool
Manchester
Holyhead
Chester
Sheffield
Lincoln
Bangor
Crewe
Nottingham
Shrewsbury
Leicester
Norwich
Wolverhampton
Birmingham
Peterborough
Coventry
Cambridge
Hereford
Luton
Ipswich
Cheltenham
Swindon
Stansted
Fishguard
Milford Haven
Swansea
Bristol
LONDON
Cardiff
Bath
Salisbury
Canterbury
Barnstaple
Taunton
Dover
Southampton
Gatwick
Hastings
Exeter
Brighton
Portsmouth
Plymouth
Weymouth
Torquay
Penzance

DIRECTORY

UK RAIL NUMBERS

Disabled Travel
Tel 0845 744 3366 (call 24 hrs before journey to book help).

Great North Eastern Railways
Tel 08457 225225 (bookings).

Great Western Trains
Tel 08457 000125 (bookings).

Lost Property
Tel 020-7387 8699 (Euston) or contact train company.

Midland Mainline
Tel 08457 221125 (bookings).

National Rail Enquiries Timetables
Tel 08457 484950.
www.nationalrail.co.uk

Rail Europe
Tel 0870 837 1371 (London).
www.raileurope.co.uk

Virgin Trains
Tel 08457 222333 (bookings).

OVERSEAS RAIL NUMBERS

CIE Tours International
Tel (201) 292-3438 or (212) 319 0561 (United States); (800) 243 8687 (Canada).

Rail Europe
Tel (914) 682-2999 (United States); (800) 848-7245 (Canada).

Travelling around by Coach

In Britain, coaches refer to the long-distance express buses and those used for sightseeing excursions. What the British refer to as buses, however, covers those vehicles that operate on regular routes with scheduled stops around or between villages, towns and cities. Many coach services duplicate rail routes, but are generally cheaper. Journey times, however, are longer and much less predictable on crowded roads. Modern coaches are comfortable, sometimes with refreshments and toilets on board. Some city to city routes, especially at weekends, are so popular that it is a good idea to buy a reserved journey ticket, which guarantees you a seat.

A coach tour, the Royal Mile, Edinburgh

NATIONAL COACH NETWORK

There are a lot of regional coach companies, but by far the largest British coach operator is **National Express** with a nationwide network of over 1,200 destinations *(see pp16–19)*. On the more popular routes – particularly on Friday evenings – it is best to book ahead.

Discounts are available for full-time students or anyone under 25. Anyone aged 50 or over can also qualify for a discount coach card, saving up to 30 per cent on many fares. Britexpass cards lasting 30 days and Tourist Trail Passes are also available for those planning to cover many destinations in a limited period. You can buy these from most coach travel agents in North America – via **British Travel Associates** – or while in the UK, at the major international airports, **Victoria Coach Station** and most large travel agents. The

Oxford Tube runs between Oxford and London, and is a frequent, wheelchair-friendly coach service. **Scottish Citylink** is a major operator running regular services between London, the North and Scotland. Some services run direct from Heathrow, Gatwick and Stansted airports. Allow plenty of time to buy your ticket before boarding. Luggage is stowed in the vehicle hold.

British Travel Associates
Tel 800 327 6097 (in North America).

National Express
Tel 08705 808080.
www.nationalexpress.com

Oxford Tube
Tel 01865 772250. **www**.
stagecoachbus.com/oxfordshire

Scottish Citylink
Tel 08705 505050.
www.citylink.co.uk

Victoria Coach Station
Tel 020-7730 3466.
www.tfl.gov.uk/vcs

COACH TOURS

Dozens of coach tours are available in the UK, for all interests, age groups and destinations. Some include a tour guide. They may last anything from a couple of hours to two weeks or more, touring coast or countryside and visiting places of interest. Some are highly structured, organizing every last photo opportunity or cup of tea; others leave you to sightsee or shop at your own pace. You can opt for a prearranged route, or commission your own itinerary for a group.

Coach tours are popular, but may leave you feeling somewhat herded. Groups always travel at the pace of their slowest member, which can mean a lot of waiting. But at the same time all the stress of organizing a similar trip for yourself is taken away. Some coach operators will pick up passengers from their hotels and then drop them back.

Any large town will have a selection of coach companies. Check the local *Yellow Pages (see p676)*, or ask your hotel or the local tourist office. You can also book coach trips direct from overseas through a specialist travel agent.

Seaside resorts and tourist sites are destinations for many day trips, especially in high season. In some of the more popular rural areas, such as the Lake District, special small buses operate for ease of movement. You can book

A National Express coach

these in advance, or just turn up before the coach leaves, although the tour is likely to be fully booked, especially in high season. The local tourist information point or travel agent will be able to tell you where these trips leave from, the cost and may even sell you tickets. It is customary to tip the guide after your tour.

REGIONAL BUSES

Regional bus services are run by a large number of companies, some private and some operated by local authorities. Less economic services to remote rural areas tend to be sporadic and expensive, with some buses running just once a week and many isolated villages having no service at all. Only a few rural buses are equipped for wheelchairs.

As a general rule, you can assume that the further you get from a city, the fewer the buses and the more expensive the fare. It is therefore unwise to rely on local buses for transport, and if you want to see a lot of the country, renting a car is a better option. But if you do have the time, local buses can be a pleasant and often sociable way of travelling around Britain's lovely countryside.

Most buses run with just one operator – the driver. All drivers prefer you to have the correct fare, so always have a selection of low denomination coins handy. Some routes do not operate on Sundays and public holidays, and those that do are much reduced.

Always check your routes, schedules and fares at the local tourist office or bus station before you depart on a bus. This will prevent your being stranded somewhere with no return transport.

The Postbus provides transport in remote parts of the Highlands

Travelling Britain's Coasts and Waterways

Britain has thousands of miles of inland waterways and hundreds of islands scattered along its coastline. Cruising along a canal in the beautiful Midlands countryside or travelling on one of the small local ferries to a remote Scottish island are both wonderful experiences. Canal boats can be hired and scores of ferries run between Britain's offshore islands.

A barge on the Welsh Backs, Bristol, Avon

CANALS

As industrial production grew in the 18th century, it became vital to find a cheap and effective way of transporting heavy loads. Canals fulfilled this need and a huge network was built, linking most industrial areas in the north and sea ports.

The arrival of the railways and their immediate success for freight made most canals redundant, but there are still some 3,200 km (2,000 miles) left, most in the old industrial heartland of the Midlands.

Today these canals lure the travellers who are content to cruise on old-fashioned, slow narrowboats, taking their time to enjoy the views and the canalside inns, originally built to satisfy the bargees' thirsts and to supply stabling for the barge horses. These canal holidays can be very relaxing if you have the time.

If you wish to hire a narrowboat, you can book with a specialist travel firm or contact **British Waterways**.

British Waterways
Tel 01923 201120 (head office).
www.britishwaterways.co.uk

LOCAL FERRIES

Britain's local ferries can offer anything from a ten-minute river journey to a seven-hour sea cruise.

Many of Scotland's ferries are operated by **Caledonian MacBrayne**. They sail to lots of different destinations, such as the Isle of Skye to the Kyle of Lochalsh, or the five-hour journey from Oban to Lochboisdale in the Western Isles. They offer a variety of different ticket types, from unlimited rover tickets for a specific period of time, to island-hop passes or all-inclusive coach tour and ferry tickets. Not all the island ferries take cars.

A car ferry travelling from Oban to Lochboisdale

River ferries make an interesting alternative to the more usual forms of transport. The ferry across the Mersey, between the cities of Liverpool and Birkenhead, is still used by many commuters. London's river trips, such as the one that runs from Westminster to Tower Bridge *(see p75)*, offer a different perspective on the city and make a change from tubes, buses and cars. Local tourist information centres can give you information about ferries in their area.

Caledonian MacBrayne
Tel 01475 650100.
www.calmac.co.uk

Travelling within Cities

Urban public transport in Britain is efficient and can be fun – children love London's double-decker buses. Fares are good value, bearing in mind that you avoid the expense and difficulty of parking a car. Most of the larger cities have good bus services. London, Newcastle and Glasgow also have an underground system, while Manchester and Blackpool have trams. Taxis are available at every railway station and at ranks near hotels and city centres. The best way to see many cities is on foot, but whatever transport you choose, try to avoid the rush hours from 8am to 9:30am, and 4:30pm to 6:30pm.

Local buses travelling along Princes Street, Edinburgh

LOCAL BUSES

The deregulation of bus services has led to a complex system with many buses often duplicating services on the busiest routes. On most buses you pay the driver as you enter. They will not always accept notes so keep a selection of coins handy. Credit cards and cheques are not accepted. The fare depends on the distance you travel. If you are exploring a city by bus, a daily pass is a good idea. Many of the larger cities have daily or weekly passes that can be used on all public transport in that city; these can often be bought from newsagents. Check with the tourist office for schedules and fares. All-night services are only available in major cities, from about 11pm until early morning. You cannot use a day pass on these.

A London double-decker bus

In London night buses are prefixed with the letter N and all of them pass through Trafalgar Square.

Be on your guard when travelling home alone late at night, when there may be few other passengers aboard.

Bus designs have become more innovative in the last few years. The old "big red bus" with a conductor still exists in London, but has been joined by a plethora of modern vehicles of all shapes, colours and sizes, with automatic doors and comfortable interiors. Many are small single-deckers, able to weave in and out of traffic more easily.

Many cities have bus lanes, intended to bypass car traffic jams during the rush hours. These can be effective but your journey could still take a long time. Schedules are hard to keep to, so regard timetables as advisory.

At some stops, called request stops, the driver will not halt unless you signal that you want to get on or off. If you want to board, raise your arm as the bus approaches the stop; if you want to get off, ring the bell once before your stop.

Destinations are shown on the front of buses. If you are not sure which stop you need, ask the driver or conductor to alert you and stay on the lower deck. Always keep your ticket until the end of the journey in case an inspector boards, who can impose an on-the-spot fine if you are without a valid ticket. Stops can often be quite a long distance apart.

DRIVING IN CITIES

Driving in city centres is being increasingly discouraged, most notably in London with the introduction of the congestion charge in spring 2003. If you drive or park within the congestion zone covering central London from Monday to Friday, 7am to 6:30pm, you will need to pay a £5 fee before 10pm that day at a newsagent, petrol station or Post Office. Not paying the charge will lead to a large fine. Go to www.cclondon.com for more information. Other cities are considering similar steps to keep drivers out of the centres.

A traditional parking meter

Parking in city centres is also strictly controlled to prevent congestion *(see p684)*.

An illegally parked car immobilized by a wheel clamp

TAXIS

In large towns there are plenty of taxis to be found at taxi ranks and train stations. Some operate by radio so you have to phone. The local *Yellow Pages (see p676)*, pubs, restaurants and hotels will all have a list of taxi numbers. Prices are usually controlled. Always ask the price before you start your journey if there is no taxi meter. If you are not sure of the correct fare ask the local tourist information point.

Licensed taxi drivers undergo strict tests and all licensed cabs must carry a "For Hire" sign, which is lit up whenever they are free. Care is needed if you use unlicensed minicabs – some may be mechanically unsound or even uninsured. Do not accept an unbooked minicab ride in the street. The famous London black cabs are almost as much of an institution as the big red bus. These are the safest cabs to use in London as all the drivers are licensed. They also know where they are going. Even these are changing, however, and you will see cabs of many colours, many covered with advertising. The newer cab designs are equipped to carry wheelchairs. If a cab stops for you in London, it must by law take you anywhere within a radius of 6 miles (10 km) so long as it is within the Metropolitan Police District. This includes most of London and Heathrow Airport.

All licensed cabs have meters that start ticking as soon as the driver accepts your custom. The fare will increase minute by minute or for each 311 m (1,020 ft) travelled. Surcharges are added for each piece of luggage, each extra passenger or unsocial hours. Most drivers expect a tip of between 10 and 15 per cent of the fare. If you have a complaint, note the serial number found in the back of the cab.

One of London's black cabs

GUIDED BUS TOURS

In most major tourist cities, sightseeing bus tours are available. Weather permitting, a good way to see the cities is from a traditional open-topped double-decker bus. Private tours can be arranged with many companies. Contact the tourist information centre.

TRAMS

After a long absence (apart from a few nostalgic remnants in Blackpool), trams are making a comeback in clean, energy efficient and more modern guises. One of the best tram schemes in Britain is Manchester's Metrolink.

LONDON UNDERGROUND

The Underground in London, known as the tube, is one of the largest systems of its kind in the world. It has over 270 stations, each of which are marked with the London Underground logo. The tube can get very overcrowded during the rush hour. The only other cities with an underground system are Glasgow and Newcastle, but both are small. London tube trains run every day, except Christmas Day, from about 5:30am until just after midnight. Fewer trains run on Sundays.

The 11 tube lines are colour-coded and maps called *Journey Planners* are posted at every station, while maps of the central section are displayed in each train. Most tube journeys between central destinations in London can be completed with only one or two changes of train. Smoking is not permitted on the Underground.

Newcastle's tube system is limited to the city centre but Glasgow's skirts around the centre. Both are clean and efficient, running the same hours as London's.

BAKER STREET

A London Underground sign outside a station

A tram along Blackpool's famous promenade

WALKING IN CITIES

Once you get used to traffic on the left, Britain's cities can be safely and enjoyably explored on foot.

There are two types of pedestrian crossing: striped zebra crossings and push-button crossings at traffic lights. At a zebra crossing traffic should stop for you, but at push-button crossings cars will not stop until the lights change in your favour. Look for instructions written on the road; these will tell you from which direction you can expect the traffic to come. More and more cities and towns are creating traffic-free zones in the city centre for pedestrians.

CYCLING

Cycling is a popular pastime in Britain. Even in the smallest town there is often somewhere you can hire bikes. Whether you cycle in towns or the countryside, a helmet is recommended. Cyclists may not use motorways or their approach roads, nor can they ride on pavements, footpaths or pedestrianized zones. Many city roads have cycle lanes and their own traffic lights. You can take a bike on most trains (phone to check). Never leave your bike unlocked.

Cycling under the Bridge of Sighs, Oxford

General Index

Acknowledgments

Dorling Kindersley would like to thank the following people whose contributions and assistance have made the preparation of this book possible.

MAIN CONTRIBUTOR
Michael Leapman was born in London in 1938 and has been a professional journalist since he was 20. He has worked for most British national newspapers and now writes about travel and other subjects for several publications, among them *The Independent, Independent on Sunday, The Economist* and *Country Life*. He has written 11 books, including the award-winning *Companion Guide to New York* (1983, revised 1995) and *Eyewitness Travel Guide to London*. In 1989 he edited the widely praised *Book of London*.

ADDITIONAL CONTRIBUTORS
Paul Cleves, James Henderson, Lucy Juckes, John Lax, Marcus Ramshaw.

ADDITIONAL ILLUSTRATIONS
Christian Hook, Gilly Newman, Paul Weston.

DESIGN AND EDITORIAL
MANAGING EDITOR Georgina Matthews
SENIOR ART EDITOR Sally Ann Hibbard
DEPUTY EDITORIAL DIRECTOR Douglas Amrine
DEPUTY ART DIRECTOR Gaye Allen
PRODUCTION David Proffit
PICTURE RESEARCH Ellen Root
DTP DESIGNER Ingrid Vienings
MAP CO-ORDINATORS Michael Ellis, David Pugh
RESEARCHER Pippa Leahy
Eliza Armstrong, Sam Atkinson, Moerida Belton, Josie Barnard, Hilary Bird, Louise Boulton, Julie Bowles, Roger Bullen, Deborah Clapson, Elspeth Collier, Gary Cross, Cooling Brown Partnership, Guy Dimond, Nicola Erdpresser, Danny Farnham, Joy Fitzsimmons, Fay Franklin, Ed Freeman, Charlie Hawkings, Martin Hendry, Andrew Heritage, Annette Jacobs, Gail Jones, Steve Knowlden, Nic Kynaston, Esther Labi, Kathryn Lane, Pippa Leahy, James Mills Hicks, Rebecca Milner, Kate Molan, Elaine Monaghan, Mary Ormandy, Marianne Petrou, Chez Picthall, Clare Pierotti, Andrea Powell, Mark Rawley, Jake Reimann, Carolyn Ryden, David Roberts, Mary Scott, Alison Stace, Hugh Thompson, Simon Tuite.

ADDITIONAL PHOTOGRAPHY
Max Alexander, Peter Anderson, Apex Photo Agency: Simon Burt, Stephen Bere, Deni Bown, June Buck, Michael Dent, Philip Dowell, Mike Dunning, Chris Dyer, Andrew Einsiedel, Philip Enticknap, Jane Ewart, DK Studio/Steve Gorton, Frank Greenaway, Alison Harris, Stephen Hayward, John Heseltine, Ed Ironside, Dave King, Neil Mersh, Robert O'Dea, Ian O'Leary, Stephen Oliver, Vincent Oliver, Roger Phillips, Kim Sayer, Karl Shone, Chris Stevens, Jim Stevenson, Clive Streeter, Harry Taylor, Conrad Van Dyk, David Ward, Mathew Ward, Alan Williams, Stephen Wooster, Nick Wright, Colin Yeates.

PHOTOGRAPHIC AND ARTWORK REFERENCE
Christopher Woodward of the Building of Bath Museum, Franz Karl Freiherr von Linden, Gendall Designs, NRSC Air Photo Group, The Oxford Mail and Times, and Mark and Jane Rees.

PHOTOGRAPHY PERMISSIONS
DORLING KINDERSLEY would like to thank the following for their assistance and kind permission to photograph at their establishments: Banqueting House (Crown copyright by kind permission of Historic Royal Palaces); Cabinet War Rooms; Paul Highnam at English Heritage; Dean and Chapter Exeter Cathedral; Gatwick Airport Ltd; Heathrow Airport Ltd; Thomas Woods at Historic Scotland; Provost and Scholars Kings College; Cambridge; London Transport Museum; Madame Tussaud's; National Museums and Galleries of Wales (Museum of Welsh Life); Diana Lanham and Gayle Mault at the National Trust; Peter Reekie and Isla Roberts at the National Trust for Scotland; Provost Skene House; Saint Bartholmew the Great; Saint James's Church;

London St Paul's Cathedral; Masters and Wardens of the Worshipful Company of Skinners; Provost and Chapter of Southwark Cathdcral; HM Tower of London; Dean and Chapter of Westminster; Dean and Chapter of Worcetser Cathedral and all the other churches, museums, hotels, restaurants, shops, galleries and sights too numerous to thank individually.

PICTURE CREDITS
t = top; tl = top left; tlc = top left centre; tc = top centre; tr = top right; cla = centre left above; ca = centre above; cra = centre right above; cl = centre left; c = centre; cr = centre right; clb = centre left below; cb = centre below; crb = centre right below; bl = bottom left; b = bottom; bc = bottom centre; bcl = bottom centre left; br = bottom right; d = detail.

Works of art have been reproduced with the permission of the following copyright holders: © ADAGP, Paris and DACS, London 1995: 171t; © Alan Bowness, Hepworth Estate 277bl; © Patrick Heron 1995 all rights reserved DACS: 240cb; © D Hockney: 1970–1 91tr, 1990–3 411t; © Estate of Stanley Spencer 1995 all rights reserved DACS 235t; © Angela Verren-Taunt 1995 all rights reserved DACS: 277br.

The work of Henry Moore, *Large Two Forms*, 1966, illustrated on page 413b *Recumbent Figure* 1938 illustrated on page 91c has been reproduced by permission of the Henry Moore Foundation.

The publisher would like to thank the following individuals, companies and picture libraries for permission to reproduce their photographs:

ABBOT HALL ART GALLERY AND MUSEUM, Kendal: 370b(d); ABERDEEN ART GALLERIES 540t; ABERDEEN AND GRAMPIAN TOURIST BOARD 479ca; ACTION PLUS: 67t; 480t; 434c; David Davies 67cr; Peter Tarry 66cla, 67bl; Printed by kind permission of MOHAMED AL FAYED: 97t; ALAMY IMAGES: Peter Adams Photography 11tr; Gina Calvi 373tl; Bertrand Collet 488cl; Nick Higham 375b; gkphotography 607 tl; Angus Palmer 217b; Edward Parker 11br; The Photolibrary Wales 607c, 662tc, 662b; Seb Rogers 663cl; Neil Setchfield 606cl; AMERICAN MUSEUM, Bath: 261tl; ANCIENT ART AND ARCHITECTURE COLLECTION: 42cb, 44ca, 44clb, 45ca, 45clb, 46bl, 46br, 48crb, 51ca, 232tl, 235br, 439t; THE ARCHIVE & BUSINESS RECORDS CENTRE, University of Glasgow: 483t; T & R ANNAN AND SONS: 516b(d); ASHMOLEAN MUSEUM, OXFORD: 47t. BARNABY'S PICTURE LIBRARY: 60tr; BEAMISH OPEN AIR MUSEUM: 424c; 415b, 425ca, 425cb, 425b; BLACKFRIARS CAFE BAR, NEWCASTLE: Andy Hook 602c; BRIDGEMAN ART LIBRARY, LONDON AND NEW YORK: Agnew and Sons, London 323t; Museum of Antiquities, Newcastle upon Tyne 44tl; Apsley House, The Wellington Museum, London 30tl; Bibliotheque Nationale, Paris *Neville Book of Hours* 322t(d); Birgmingham City Museums and Gallery 319t; Bonham's, London, *Portrait of Lord Nelson with Santa Cruz Beyond*, Lemeul Francis Abbot 54cb(d); Bradford Art Galleries and Museums 49clb; City of Bristol Museums and Art Galleries 256c; British Library, London, *Pictures and Arms of English Kings and Knights* 4t(d), 39t(d), *The Kings of England from Brutus to Henry* 26bl(d), Stowe manuscript 40tl(d), *Liber Legum Antiquorum Regum* 46t(d), *Calendar Anglo-Saxon Miscellany* 46–7t(d), 46–7c(d), 46–7b(d), *Decrees of Kings of Anglo-Saxon and Norman England* 47clb, 49bl(d), *Portrait of Chaucer*, Thomas Occleve 49br(d), *Portrait of Shakespeare*, Droeshurt 51bl(d), *Historia Anglorum* 40bl(d), 236tl(d), *Chronicle of Peter of Langtoft* 285b(d), *Lives and Miracles of St Cuthbert* 419tl(d), 419cl(d), 419cr(d), *Lindisfarne Gospels* 419br(d), *Commendatio Lamentabilis intransitu Edward IV* 436b(d), *Histoire du Roy d'Angleterre Richard II* 438t(d), 537b; Christies, London 445t; Claydon House, Bucks, *Florence Nightingale*, Sir William Blake Richmond 162t; Department of Environment, London 48tr; City of Edinburgh Museums and Galleries, *Chief of Scottish Clan*, Eugene Deveria 484bl(d); Fitzwilliam Museum, University of Cambridge, *George IV as Prince Regent*, Richard Cosway 179cb, 212bl, *Flemish Book of Hours*

Willemsznik 53bl(d), *Bubbler's Melody* 54br(d), *Triumph of Steam and Electricity*, The Illustrated London News 57t(d), *Great Exhibition, The transept from Dickenson's Comprehensive Pictures* 56–7, *A Balloon View of London as seen from Hampstead* 105c(d); Harrogate Museum and Art Gallery, North Yorkshire 388t; Holburne Museum and Crafts Study Centre, Bath 53t; Imperial War Museum, *London Field Marshall Montgomery*, J Worsley 31cbr(d); Kedleston Hall, Derbyshire 28br; King Street Galleries, London, *Bonnie Prince Charlie*, G Dupré 482tl; Lambeth Palace Library, London, *St Alban's Chronicle* 49t; Lever Brothers Ltd, Cheshire 349cra; Lincolnshire County Council, Usher Gallery, Lincoln, *Portrait of Mrs Fitzherbert after Richard Cosway* 179b; London Library, *The Barge Tower from Ackermann's World in minature*, F Scoberl 55t; Manchester Art Gallery, UK, *Etruscan Vase Painters* 1871, Sir Lawrence Alma-Tadema 374b; Manchester City Art Galleries 373b; David Messum Gallery, London 447b; National Army Museum, London, *Bunker's Hill*, R Simkin 54ca; National Gallery, London, *Mrs Siddons the Actress*, Thomas Gainsborough 54t(d), 163ca; National Museet, Copenhagen 46ca; Phillips, the International Fine Art Auctioneers, *James I*, John the Elder Decritz 52b(d); Private Collections: 8–9, 30ca(d), 604tl, 48–9, 55cla, 55bl, 56clb, Vanity Fair 57br, 163t, *Ellesmere Manuscript* 188b(d), *Armada: map of the Spanish and British Fleets*, Robert Adam 298t, 396t, 422b; Royal Geographical Society, London 163cb(d); Royal Holloway & Bedford New College, the *Princes Edward and Richard in the Tower*, Sir John Everett Millais 121b; Smith Art Gallery and Museum, Stirling 496b; Tate Gallery, London: 56crb, 237t; Thyssen-Bornemisza Collection, Lugo Casta, *King Henry VIII*, Hans Holbein the Younger 50b(d); Victoria and Albert Museum, London 28t(d), 56b, 97c, 204t, 351cr, 393b, *Miniature of Mary Queen of Scots*, by a follower of Francois Clouet 511br, 537t(d); Walker Art Gallery, Liverpool 378c; Westminster Abbey, London, *Henry VII Tomb effigy*, Pietro Torrigiano 30br(d), 40bc(d); The Trustees of the Weston Park Foundation, *Portrait of Richard III*, Italian School 49cla(d); Christopher Wood Gallery, London, *High Life Below Stairs*, Charles Hunt 29c(d); reproduced with permission of the BRITISH AIRWAYS: Adrian Meredith Photography 680t; BFI LONDON IMAX CINEMA WATERLOO: Richard Holttum 153c; BRITISH LIBRARY BOARD: *Cotton Faustina BVII folio 85* 49cb, 109cl; © THE BRITISH MUSEUM: 42cr, 43cb, 73tl, 85c, 103, 106–7 all except 107t and 107bl; © THE BRONTE SOCIETY: 412 all; BT PAYPHONES: 660tl, 660bla; BURTON CONSTABLE FOUNDATION: Dr David Connell 350t.

CADOGEN MANAGEMENT: 84b; CADW – Welsh Historic Monuments (Crown Copyright), 474t; CAMERA PRESS: Cecil Beaton 92bl; CARDIFF CITY COUNCIL: 472tr, 473t, 473c; FKB CARLSON: 605bcl; CASTLE HOWARD ESTATE LTD: 399tl; COLIN DE CHAIRE: 197c; TRUSTEES OF THE CHATSWORTH SETTLEMENT: 334b, 335b; MUSEUM OF CHILDHOOD, Edinburgh: 510b; BRUCE COLEMAN LTD: 35br; Stephen Bond 294b; Jane Burton 35cra; Mark N. Boulton 35cl; Patrick Clement 34clb; Peter Evans 544tl; Paul van Gaalen 250tl; Sir Jeremy Grayson 35bl; Harald Lange 34bc; Gordon Langsbury 545t; George McCarthy 34t, 35bl, 242b, 285br; Paul Meitz 528clb; Dr. Eckart Pott 34bl, 528t; Hans Reinhard 34cb, 35tc, 294t, 494tl; Dr Frieder Sauer 534t; N Schwiatz 35clb; Kim Taylor 35tl, 528cra; Konrad Wothe 528ca; COLLECTIONS: Liz Stares 30tr, Yuri Lewinski 373tl; CORBIS: Bruce Burkhardt 295c; Ashley Cooper 12tr; Tim Graham 3br, 95bl; John Heseltine 111br; Angelo Hornak 117tc, Bill Ross 688tr; Sygma/Sandro Vannini 11bl; JOE CORNISH: 403b; DOUG CORRANCE: 485b; JOHN CROOK: 171b; EASYEVERYTHING: James Hamilton 676br; 1805 CLUB: 31t; 1853 GALLERY, Bradford 411t; EMPICS LTD: Nigel French 66bl; Tony Marshall 66tl, 66c; ENGLISH HERITAGE: 126b, 208c, 208b, 209b, 248–9b, 263b, 350br, 351b, 394t, 419tr, 419c; Avebury Museum 42ca; Devizes Museum 42br, drawing by Frank Gardiner 423br; Salisbury Museum 42t, 43bl; Skyscan Balloon Photography 43t, 262b; 394t; 423bl; ENGLISH LIFE PUBLICATIONS LTD, Derby: 342tl, 342tr, 343t, 343b; ET ARCHIVE: 41tl, 41cr, 52cb, 53clb, 58crb, 162b; Bodleian Library, Oxford 48crb; British Library, London 48tl, 48ca; Devizes Museum 42cl, 43b,

262c; Garrick Club 436tl(d); Imperial War Museum, London 58clb(d), 59br; Labour Party Archives 60br; London Museum 43cla; Magdalene College 50ca; National Maritime Museum, London 39b; Stoke Museum Staffordshire Polytechnic 41bc, 52tl; Victoria & Albert Museum, London 50t(d); MARY EVANS PICTURE LIBRARY: 9 inset, 604tr, 40br, 41tl, 41cl, 41bl, 41br, 44bl, 44br, 46cb, 47cla, 51t, 51cb, 51br, 53crb, 54bl, 55br, 56tl, 58ca, 59ca, 59clb, 59crb, 79cb, 104t,105t, 157 inset, 162cb, 163b, 187c, 189c, 195b, 206c, 222bl, 228tl, 231c, 231bl, 231br, 234bl, 239 inset, 278t, 295 inset, 336b, 349t, 349cla, 420t, 447tl, 482b, 499b, 512bl, 514b, 515t, 535b, 667 inset. CHRIS FAIRCLOUGH: 295b, 352b, 688b; FALKIRK WHEEL: 507b; PAUL FELIX: 234c; FFOTOGRAFF © Charles Aithie: 435t; FISHBOURNE ROMAN VILLA: 45t; LOUIS FLOOD: 484br; FOREIGN AND BRITISH BIBLE SOCIETY: Cambridge University Library 435c; FOTOMAS INDEX: 105cra. GARDEN PICTURE LIBRARY: J S Sira 27crt; John Glover 27rb; Steven Wooster 26–27t; GLASGOW MUSEUMS: Burrell Collection 521ca, 520–1 all except 520tl; Art Gallery & Museum, Kelvingrove 519t, 531b, 543b(d); Saint Mungo Museum of Religious Life and Art 517tl; Museum of Transport 518cr; JOHN GLOVER: 62cr, 160cb, 205b; THE GORE HOTEL, London: 554c.

SONIA HALLIDAY AND LAURA LUSHINGTON ARCHIVE: 409t; ROBERT HARDING PICTURE LIBRARY: 182t, 548t; Jan Baldwin 287b; M H Black 288t; Teresa Black 675cb; Nigel Blythe 680ca; L Bond 337b; Michael Botham 36br; C Bowman 661c; Nelly Boyd 374tl; Lesley Burridge 304tr; Martyn F Chillman 305bc; Philip Craven 103t, 200b, 324b; Nigel Francis 219b, 683b; Robert Francis 66–7; Paul Freestone 226b; Sylvain Gradadom 295tl; Brian Harrison 529b; Van der Hars 538t; Michael Jenner 45b, 529c; Norma Joseph 65b; Christopher Nicholson 253t; B O'Connor 37ca; Jenny Pate 161bc; Rainbird Collection 47crb; Roy Rainsford 37b, 168t, 298b, 338cr, 368t, 386t, 475b; Walter Rawling 25t; Hugh Routledge 2–3; Peter Scholey 299t; Michael Short 305br; James Strachen 384b; Julia K Thorne 486bl; Adina Tovy 61tl, 486br; Andy Williams 179t, 234br, 346c, 432t, 524; Adam Woolfitt 24t, 24c, 44tr, 45crb, 260b, 272, 287ca, 305bl, 439bl, 468tl, 544tr; HAREWOOD HOUSE: 410c; PAUL HARRIS: 36t, 62cl, 301bl(d), 338b, 367b, 666–7, 663tr; HARROGATE INTERNATIONAL CENTRE: 389b; HAYWARD GALLERY: Richard Haughton 273tl; HEATHROW AIRPORT LTD: 673b; Crown copyright is reproduced with the permission of the Controller of HMSO: 73br, 118bl, 118br, 119tl; CATHEDRAL CHURCH OF THE BLESSED VIRGIN MARY AND ST ETHELBERT in HEREFORD: 316b; HERTFORDSHIRE COUNTY COUNCIL: Bob Norris 58–9; JOHN HESELTINE: 76t, 102, 107t, 108, 250tr, 250c, 469tl; HISTORIC ROYAL PALACES (Crown Copyright): 173, 235 all; HISTORIC SCOTLAND (Crown Copyright): 497c, 506tr, 506c, 5-7bl; PETER HOLLINGS: 348bl; NEIL HOLMES: 258b(d), 260c, 286t, 371b, 429tl, 429tr, 451b, 691t; ANGELO HORNAK LIBRARY: 406tl, 406bl, 406br, 409br; Reproduced by permission of the CLERK OF RECORDS, HOUSE OF LORDS: 483c; DAVID MARTIN HUGHES: 156–7, 164; HULTON-DEUTSCH COLLECTION: 26c, 26tr, 31cl, 31cr, 53cla, 54c, 56c, 57cb, 58tl 58tr, 58b, 59t, 60ca, 60bl, 162ca, 169c, 233b, 300t, 348c, 349crb, 350bl, 377b, 397b, 398br, 437t, 495b, 522tl, 536b; HUNTERIAN ART GALLERY: 519b; HUTCHISON LIBRARY: Catherine Blacky 604cb; Bernard Gerad 481t; HUTTON IN THE FOREST: Lady Inglewood 358t.

THE IMAGE BANK, London: Derek Berwin 552t; David Gould 357b; Romilly Lockyer 604bl; Colin Molyneux 469bl; Trevor Wood 286b; Simon Wilkinson 180b; Terry Williams 112tc; IMAGES COLOUR LIBRARY: 34cla, 43c, 221b, 234t, 249t, 250bl, 251b, 336t, 338cl, 339t, 352c, 686t, 686b; Horizon/Robert Estall 438c; Landscape Only 37cb, 248, 365, 439br; IMPERIAL WAR MUSEUM NORTH: 375t; IRONBRIDGE MUSEUM: 317b. JARROLD PUBLISHERS: 212br, 229t(d), 304bl; MICHAEL JENNER: 304tl, 340b, 528b; JORVIK VIKING CENTRE, York: 405t. FRANK LANE PICTURE AGENCY: 400b(d); W Broadhurst 254b; Michael Callan 242crb; ANDREW LAWSON: 27c, 27cb, 244br, 245tl, 245tr, 245br; LANGAN'S BRASSERIE: 603t; LEEDS CASTLE ENTERPRISES: 165b; LEIGHTON HOUSE, Royal Borough of Kensington: 122br; published by kind permission DEAN and CHAPTER of LINCOLN 340t, 341cb, 341bl; LINCOLNSHIRE COUNTY COUNCIL: USHER GALLERY, Lincoln: c 1820 by William Ilbery 341bl; LLANGOLEN INTERNATIONAL MUSICAL EISTEDDFOD 450c; LONDON AMBULANCE SERVICE: 675ca; LONDON AQUARIUM: 3c; LONDON FILM FESTIVAL: 62t; LONDON TRANSPORT MUSEUM: 84t; LONGLEAT HOUSE: 266t; THE LOWRY

MALDOM MILLENIUM TRUST: 209t; MANSELL COLLECTION, London: 31clb, 40tr, 52ca, 55cb, 261tr, 323bl, 349dlb, 402b; NICK MEERS: 22t, 238–9; METROPOLITAN POLICE SERVICE: 675t; ARCHIE MILES: 240ca; SIMON MILES: 352tr; MINACK THEATRE: Murray King 276b; MIRROR SYNDICATION INTERNATIONAL: 74b, 87b, 112; BTA/Julian Nieman 604ca; MUSEUM OF LONDON: 44crb, 113t; NATIONAL EXPRESS LTD: 688bl; NATIONAL FISHING HERITAGE CENTRE, Grimsby: 403t; NATIONAL GALLERY, London: 73tr, 82–3 all; NATIONAL GALLERY OF SCOTLAND: The Reverend Walker Skating on Duddington Loch, Sir Henry Raeburn 504c(d); NATIONAL LIBRARY OF WALES: 436tr, 439c(d), 467b; NATIONAL MUSEUM OF FILM AND TELEVISION, Bradford: 411c; Board of Trustees of the NATIONAL MUSEUMS AND GALLERIES ON MERSEYSIDE: Liverpool Museum 379t; Maritime Museum 377t; Walker Art Gallery 346b, 378tl, 378tr, 378b, 379c; NATIONAL MUSEUMS OF SCOTLAND: 505t, 511bl; NATIONAL MUSEUM OF WALES: 436c; By courtesy of the NATIONAL PORTRAIT GALLERY, London: First Earl of Essex, Hans Peter Holbein 351t(d); NATIONAL TRAMWAY MUSEUM, Crich: 339c; NATIONAL TRUST PHOTOGRAPHIC LIBRARY: Bess of Hardwick (Elizabeth, Countess of Shrewsbury), Anon 334tl(d); Mathew Antrobus 302br, 390cl, 391bl; Oliver Benn 29br, 278c, 293bl, 390b; John Bethell 279c, 279bl, 279br, 303t; Nick Carter 255b; Joe Cornish 456; Prudence Cumming 267c; Martin Dohrn 50crb; Andreas Von Einsiedel 29bl, 302cb, 303ca; Roy Fox 271t; Geoffry Frosh 289t; Jerry Harpur 244t, 244bl; Derek Harris 244clb, 267t; Nadia MacKenzie 28cl; Nick Meers 266b, 267b, 320b, 669b; Rob Motheson 292t; Cressida Pemberton Piggot 554t; Ian Shaw 460t; Richard Surman 303br, 362b; Rupert Truman 303br, 379; Andy Tryner 302bl; Charlie Waite 391t; Jeremy Whitaker 303bc, 393t, 460b; Mike Williams 302ca, 391c; George Wright 244crb, 292c; NATIONAL TRUST FOR SCOTLAND: 478b, 500b, 501c, 508b, 522tr, 523tl, 523tr, 523br; Glyn Satterley 523tr; Lindsey Robertson 523bl; NATIONAL WATERWAYS MUSEUM at Gloucester: 301bc, 301br; NHPA: Martin Garwood 395ca; Daniel Heuclin 282la; NATURE PHOTOGRAPHERS: Andrew Cleave 242cla; E A James 35cla, 360t; Hugh Miles 421t; Owen Newman 35ca; William Paton 528crb; Paul Sterry 34crb, 34br, 35cb, 35crb, 234c, 255t, 387t, 528cla; Roger Tidman 197b; NETWORK PHOTOGRAPHERS: Laurie Sparham 480b; NEW SHAKESPEARE THEATRE CO: 153t; NORFOLK MUSEUMS SERVICE: Norwich Castle Museum 201b; OXFORD SCIENTIFIC FILMS: Okapia 282lb; 'PA' NEWS PHOTO LIBRARY: John Stillwell 61cr. PALACE THEATRE ARCHIVE: 152c; PHOTOS HORTICULTURAL: 161tlc, 161ca, 161cb, 161crb, 244ca, 245c; PICTURES: 680t; PLANET EARTH PICTURES: David Phillips 27crca; POPPERFOTO: 31br, 59bl, 60clb, 60crb, 61bl, 86tl, 160tr, 203t, 284cl, 444b; AFP/ Eric Feferber 61br; SG Forester 67br; PORT MERION LTD: 454tl; THE POST OFFICE: 677tl, 689bl; PRESS ASSOCIATION: Martin Keene 62b; PUBLIC RECORD OFFICE (Crown Copyright): 48b.

ROB REICHENFELD: 174t, 175c, 175b, 300b, 658b, 663t; REX FEATURES LTD: 31ca, 41tr, 60tl, 61bc, 236c, 237br; Barry Beattie 259cl; Peter Brooke 31bc, 678br; Nils Jorgensen 30c, 661t, 684c; Eileen Kleinman 661br; Hazel Murray 61tr; Tess, Renn-Burrill Productions 269b; Brian Rasic 63t; Nick Rogers 61tc; Tim Rooke 64cr, 66tr; Sipa/Chesnot 31bl; Today 25c; Richard Young 60tl; REX FEATURES: Jonathon Player 294cla; tTHE RITZ, London: 81t; ROYAL ACADEMY OF ARTS, London: 84ca; ROYAL COLLECTION © 1995 Her Majesty Queen Elizabeth II: The Family of Henry VIII, Anon 38(d), 85c, 86tr, 86bl, 87t, 236tr, 237tl(d), 237tr, 237bl, George IV, in full Highland dress, Sir David Wilkie 85t; David Cripps 87c; John Freeman 88br; ROYAL COLLEGE OF MUSIC, London: 96c; ROYAL PAVILION, ART GALLERY AND MUSEUMS, Brighton: 178c, 178bl, 178br, 179cl, 179cr; ROYAL BOTANIC GARDENS, Kew:74ca; ROYAL SHAKESPEARE

THEATRE COMPANY: Donald Cooper 327c(d). ST. ALBAN'S MUSEUMS: Verulamium Museum 232b; ST. PAULS CATHEDRAL: Sampson Lloyd 114tr, 114cl, 114clb; SARTAJ BALTI HOUSE: Clare Carnegie 411b; SCOTTISH NATIONAL GALLERY OF MODERN ART: Roy Lichtenstein In the Car 507c; SCOTTISH NATIONAL PORTRAIT GALLERY: on loan from the collection of the Earl of Roseberry, Execution of Charles I, Unknown Artist 52–3; S4C (Channel 4 Wales): 437b; SIDMOUTH FOLK FESTIVAL: Derek Brooks 289b; SKYSCAN BALLOON PHOTO-GRAPHY: 262t; JOHN SNOCKEN: 27cr, 27ra; SOUTHBANK PRESS OFFICE: 154t; SPORTING PICTURES: 66cra, 66bc, 66br, 67cl, 358b; STILL MOVING PICTURES: Doug Corrance 548b; Wade Cooper 483b; Derek Laird 482c; Robert Lees 65t; STB 544br, 545c, Paisley Museum 515b; Paul Tomkins 529tr; SJ Whitehorn 495t; DAVID TARN: 389tl; TONY STONE IMAGES: 604–5, 550–1; Rex A.Butcher 81c; Richard Elliott 64b; Rob Talbot 353ca; David Woodfall 440; © TATE BRITAIN: 73bl, 91all, ; © TATE MODERN: Scrapheap Services (1985) Michael Landy, video and mixed media, presented by the patrons of New Art through the Tate Gallery Foundation 1997 121tr; Death from Death Hope Life Fear (d) 1984 © Gilbert and George 121cl; Soft Drain Pipe – Blue (Cool) Version, 1967 © Claes Oldenburg 121cr; © TATE ST. IVES: 277cr, 277clb, 277br; ROB TALBOT: 353cb; TRANSPORT FOR LONDON: 378cl; TUILLE HOUSE MUSEUM, Carlisle: 358c; URBIS: 372c; courtesy of the Board of Trustees of the VICTORIA AND ALBERT MUSUEM, London: 72b, 98–99.

CHARLIE WAITE: 549t; © WALES TOURIST BOARD: 433c, 434b, 438–9, 468br, 469tr, 469br; Roger Vitos 468tl, 468bl; THE WALLACE COLLECTION, London: 104cb; DAVID WARD: 525b, 543t; FREDERICK WARNE & CO: 367t(d); Courtesy of the Trustees of THE WEDGWOOD MUSEUM, Barlaston, Staffordshire, England: 311h; WEST MIDLANDS POLICE: 674bl, 674hr, 675tc; DEAN AND CHAPTER OF WESTMINSTER: 93bl; Tony Middleton 92bc; JEREMY WHITAKER: 228tr, 228c, 229b; WHITBREAD PLC: 604bl; WHITWORTH ART GALLERY, University of Manchester: courtesy of Granada Television Arts Foundation 374c; CHRISTOPHER WILSON: 404bl; WILTON HOUSE TRUST: 265b; WINCHESTER CATHEDRAL: 171t; WOBURN ABBEY – by kind permission of the Marquess of Tavistock and Trustees of the Bedford Estate: 50–1, 230t; TIMOTHY WOODCOCK PHOTOLIBRARY: 5b; Photo © WOODMAN-STERNE, Watford, UK: Jeremy Marks 114t, 115t. YORK CASTLE MUSEUM: 405cb; YORK CITY ART GALLERY: 407bl; DEAN & CHAPTER YORK MINSTER: 409cla, 409ca, 409cl; Peter Gibson 409cra, 409cr, 409cl; Jim Korshaw 406tr; Reproduced couresty of the YORKSHIRE MUSEUM: 408c; YORKSHIRE SCULP-TURE PARK: Jerry Hardman Jones 413t. ZEFA: 64t, 154b, 263t, 269t, 486c, 659t, 682c, 684bl; Bob Croxford 63cr; Weir 197t.

Front Endpaper: All special photography except ROBERT HARDING PICTURE LIBRARY/Andy Williams tl, Adam Woolfitt bl; DAVID MARTIN HUGHES brl; NATIONAL TRUST PHOTOGRAPHIC LIBRARY/Joe Cornish clc; TONY STONE IMAGES/David Woodfall cl. Back Endpaper: All special photography except JOHN HESELTINE tl, br.

JACKET
Front - A1 PIX: Superbild main image; DK IMAGES: Stephen Oliver bl. Back - GETTY IMAGES: Stone/David H. Endersbee clb; ROBERT HARDING PICTURE LIBRARY: Hugh Routledge bl; Andy Williams tl; SUPERSTOCK: Digital Vision/Allan Baxter cla. Spine - A1 PIX: Superbild t; DK IMAGES: Kim Sayer b.

All other images © Dorling Kindersley. For further information see www.DKimages.com

Central London

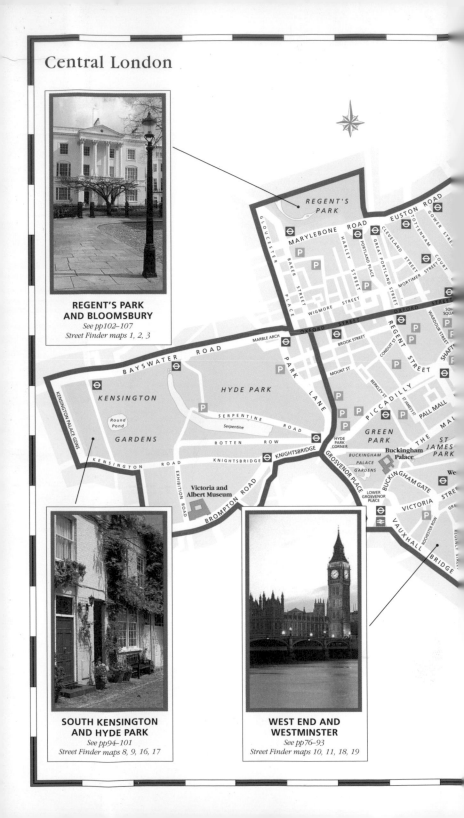

REGENT'S PARK AND BLOOMSBURY
See pp102–107
Street Finder maps 1, 2, 3

REGENT'S PARK

GLOUCESTER PLACE

MARYLEBONE ROAD

EUSTON ROAD

HARLEY STREET

BAKER STREET

PORTLAND PLACE

GREAT PORTLAND STREET

CLEVELAND STREET

TOTTENHAM COURT ROAD

GOWER STREET

MORTIMER STREET

WIGMORE STREET

OXFORD STREET

WARDOUR STREET

SHAFT

SO
SQUA

MARBLE ARCH

BAYSWATER ROAD

BROOK STREET

REGENT STREET

CONDUIT ST

KENSINGTON PALACE GDNS

KENSINGTON

HYDE PARK

PARK LANE

MOUNT ST

BERKELEY ST

PICCADILLY

ST JAMES'S ST

PALL MALL

Round Pond

GARDENS

SERPENTINE ROAD

Serpentine

GREEN PARK

THE MALL

ST JAMES PARK

KENSINGTON ROAD

ROTTEN ROW

HYDE PARK CORNER

Buckingham Palace

KNIGHTSBRIDGE

KNIGHTSBRIDGE

BUCKINGHAM PALACE GARDENS

EXHIBITION ROAD

Victoria and Albert Museum

BROMPTON ROAD

GROSVENOR PLACE

LOWER GROSVENOR PLACE

BUCKINGHAM GATE

We

VICTORIA STREET

GRE

VAUXHALL BRIDGE

ROCHESTER ROW

REGENCY STREET

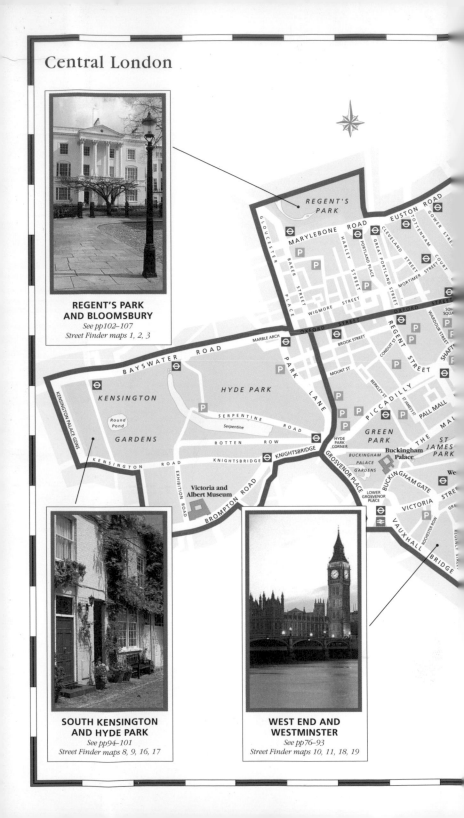

SOUTH KENSINGTON AND HYDE PARK
See pp94–101
Street Finder maps 8, 9, 16, 17

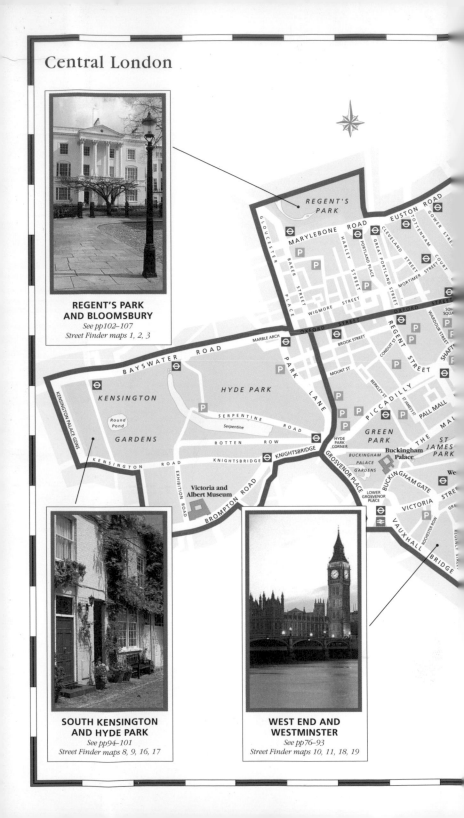

WEST END AND WESTMINSTER
See pp76–93
Street Finder maps 10, 11, 18, 19